THE MEDIEVAL AND REFORMATION CHURCH

CONTRIBUTORS

Volume 1

Karl Baus • Hans-Georg Beck • Eugen Ewig • Josef Andreas Jungmann • Friedrich Kempf • Hermann Josef Vogt

Volume 2

Quintín Aldea Vaquero • Hans-Georg Beck • Johannes Beckmann • Louis Cognet • Patrick J. Corish • Karl August Fink • Josef Glazik • Erwin Iserloh • Hubert Jedin • Oskar Köhler • Wolfgang Müller • Heribert Raab • Burkhart Schneider • Bernhard Stasiewski • Hans Wolter

Volume 3

Gabriel Adriányi • Quentín Aldea Vaquero • Roger Aubert • Günter Bandmann • Jakob Baumgartner • Johannes Beckmann • Mario Bendiscioli • Pierre Blet • Johannes Bots • Patrick J. Corish • Viktor Dammertz • Jacques Gadille • Erwin Gatz • Erwin Iserloh • Hubert Jedin • Oskar Köhler • Rudolph Lill • Georg May • Joseph Metzler • Luigi Mezzardi • Franco Molinari • Konrad Repgen • Leo Scheffczyk • Michael Schmolke • Antonio da Silva • Bernhard Stasiewski • André Tihon • Norbert Trippen • Robert Trisco • Ludwig Volk • Wilhelm Weber • Erika Weinzierl • Paul-Ludwig Weinacht • Félix Zubillaga

Translators

Peter W. Becker (Books 7, 8, and portions of 5) • Anselm Biggs (Books 2, 3, 4, 10, and portions of 5) • Gunther J. Holst (Book 6) • Margit Resch (Book 9)

THE MEDIEVAL AND REFORMATION CHURCH

An Abridgment of HISTORY OF THE CHURCH Volumes 4 to 6

Edited by Hubert Jedin

English Translation edited by John Dolan
Abridged by D. Larrimore Holland

CROSSROAD • NEW YORK

1993

The Crossroad Publishing Company
370 Lexington Avenue, New York, NY 10017

The complete *History of the Church* is a translation of the *Handbuch der Kirchengeschichte,* edited by Hubert Jedin, published by Verlag Herder, KG, Freiburg im Breisgau.

Printed in the United States of America

Library of Congress Cataloging-in-Publication Data

The Medieval and Reformation church : an abridgment of History of the church, volumes 4 to 6 / edited by Hubert Jedin ; abridged by D. Larrimore Holland.
p. cm. — (History of the church ; v. 2)
Contents: Bk. 4. From the high Middle Ages to the eve of the Reformation — Bk. 5. Reformation and Counter-Reformation — Bk. 6. The church in the age of Absolutism and Enlightenment.
ISBN 0-8245-1254-5
1. Europe—Church history—Middle Ages, 600–1500. 2. Catholic Church—History—16th century. 3. Catholic Church—History—17th century. 4. Catholic Church—History—18th century. I. Jedin, Hubert, 1900– . II. Holland, David Larrimore. III. Series: Handbuch der Kirchengeschichte. English (Crossroad (New York, N.Y. : Firm : 1992)) ; v. 2.
BR141.H35132 1992 vol. 2
[BX1068]
270 s—dc20
[270.5] 93-29474
CIP

Contents

Book Four/Part Two
The Late Middle Ages

Section One
The Popes at Avignon

Section Two
The Western Schism and the Councils

BOOK FIVE
REFORMATION AND COUNTER REFORMATION

Book Five/Part One
The Protestant Reformation

Section One
Martin Luther and the Coming of the Reformation (1517–1525)

Section Two
The Struggle over the Concept of Christian Freedom

Book Five/Part Two
Catholic Reform and Counter Reformation

Section Three
Religious Forces and Intellectual Content of the Catholic Renewal

BOOK SIX
THE CHURCH IN THE AGE OF ABSOLUTISM AND ENLIGHTENMENT

Book Six/Part One
The Leadership Position of France

Section One
Ecclesiastical Life in France

Section Two
The Papacy in the Period of French Hegemony

Book Four

FROM THE HIGH MIDDLE AGES TO THE EVE OF THE REFORMATION

Translated by Anselm Briggs

Part One

The High Middle Ages

Section One

The Post-Gregorian Epoch (1124–53)

Hans Wolter

CHAPTER 1

Honorius II, the Schism of 1130, and the Second Lateran Council

The Concordat of Worms (1122) and its ratification by the Church at the First Lateran Council (1123), which put an end to the Investiture Controversy in Germany and Italy also, meant for Christendom the beginning of an age of peaceful growth. Now the forces of reform, as represented by the new orders, were able to develop everywhere. The relationship of the Roman Church to the Empire and to the Western Kings was under the aegis of a trusting cooperation. However, an exception was constituted by the growing area of Norman rule in South Italy that was subject to the vigorous policies of Count Roger II. Its northward expansion could not but be a source of constant anxiety for the Curia. And yet the Normans had also been, since their enfeoffment by the Pope in 1059, a support for the Roman Church when the imperial pressure from the north jeopardized the autonomy of the *Patrimonium.*

The external peace which, as has just been mentioned, the Church had won was, to be sure, affected by a severe crisis within the Roman Church's leadership, which occurred in the Schism of 1130–38 and for the settlement of which the decision of the whole of Christendom had to be invoked.

The new Pope, Honorius II (1124–30), confirmed Cardinal Chancellor Aimeric in his office and thus facilitated his further rise. Of the ten cardinals created in this pontificate, seven strengthened the chancellor's group, as would appear in 1130.

A few months after the accession of Honorius II to the papal throne the Emperor Henry V died in Germany (23 May 1125). The election of his successor in the presence of the papal legate, Cardinal Gerard of Santa Croce, and under the authoritative guidance of the electoral assembly by Archbishop Adalbert of Mainz ended in favor of the Duke of Saxony, Lothar of Supplinburg. The princes passed over Frederick of Hohenstaufen, Duke of Swabia, who as nephew of the dead

Emperor would have had the expectation of the crown by hereditary right. The new King Lothar (1125–37) announced his election to the Pope and even asked its confirmation.

More instructive for the inner Church policies of the pontificate were the proceedings in regard to Cluny and Montecassino. Abbot Pons de Melgueil, who had succeeded Abbot Hugh at Cluny in 1109 and up to the time of the Concordat of Worms had been one of the prelates most favored by the Curia, had gone to Jerusalem *via* Rome in 1122. In any event the Pope allowed a new election at Cluny. The monks chose Hugh of Marcigny and, after his early death, Peter the Venerable. The return of Pons from Jerusalem was followed at Cluny by a violent struggle over the abbacy. Honorius II cited the rivals before his tribunal at Rome. Abbot Pons was condemned and died the same year, 1126, in papal custody. At Montecassino, Honorius II forced the Cardinal Abbot Oderisius to resign the abbatial office. Here too the *gravamina* of the bishops against the powerful abbey seem to have been taken seriously. A further change in the Curia's ecclesiastical policy became clear in the growing number of privileges for the canons regular. But because of their recognition of episcopal jurisdiction the Cistercians and the Premonstratensians were in their first years spared from having to oppose this new direction at the Curia. The papacy had to make it its business to gain everywhere the energetic collaboration of the episcopate for the religious reform of the West.

At Rome this change, simultaneously involving the disappearing of a generation in the College of Cardinals, led to strains, which became worse toward the close of Honorius' pontificate because of the interference of the competing noble factions, the Frangipani, who favored the trend represented by the Cardinal Chancellor Aimeric, and the Pierleoni, supporters of the Old Gregorians. The fateful year 1130 released these tensions, not for peace but for a schism of the type that the Church had been spared since the dark days of the feudalized papacy up to 1046. The Schism of 1130 was not imposed on the Church from without but originated within the Church's own bosom. What at first seemed to be a purely Roman confrontation between two claimants to the papacy was quickly cited before the forum of the Universal Church and there decided.

When Pope Honorius II fell gravely ill at the beginning of 1130, Cardinal Aimeric, probably recalling the tumultuous election of 1124, proceeded to make preparations which should facilitate a free and canonical election. The dying pontiff was conveyed to the monastery of San Gregorio all'Aventino, which was protected by the strongholds of the Frangipani. The College of Cardinals selected from its three orders representatives who would constitute an electoral commission of eight. On this group, following the death and burial of the Pope, would devolve the election of a successor. Five members of this commission belonged to Aimeric's faction; only three came from the ranks of the Old Gregorians. The church of Sant'Andrea was to be the place of the election, and the fortresses of the Frangipani were to be turned over to the College of Cardinals for the time of the election.

Actually, these arrangements were not adhered to. Honorius died during the night of 13–14 February and was buried with the utmost haste in a temporary grave. The commission was unable to meet in full strength, for two of its members, Cardinals Peter Pierleoni and Jonathan, were absent. But at daybreak, with the assent of his friends and despite the protest of Cardinal Peter of Pisa, Aimeric acclaimed as Pope the Cardinal Deacon Gregory of Sant'Angelo. Invested with the red mantle of his predecessor, Innocent II (1130–43) was enthroned at the Lateran.

When during the morning of 14 February people in Rome learned what had happened during the night, Cardinal Peter Pierleoni convoked the other cardinals, the majority of the college, at San Marco, protested against the uncanonical method of the election, and invited the gathering for its part to provide Honorius II with a successor. He himself designated as a candidate the Cardinal Bishop Peter of Porto, who, however, refused to be considered and in turn nominated Peter Pierleoni. The latter was unanimously elected by the cardinals present and acclaimed by the clergy and people who were at hand. Anacletus II (1130–38) was conducted to Saint Peter's for his enthronement. And so Rome had elected two Popes on one day. Both were likewise consecrated on the same day, 23 February: Innocent II by the Cardinal Bishop of Ostia in Aimeric's titular church, Santa Maria Nuova; Anacletus II by the Cardinal Bishop Peter of Porto in the Lateran.

Both rivals were Romans. Innocent II belonged to the Papareschi of Trastevere, Anacletus II to the powerful Pierleoni. The Pierleoni were of Jewish origin — hence Anacletus is known as "the Pope from the ghetto" — but they had been Christians since the days of Leo IX. They had rendered great services to the Popes up to Calixtus II inclusively and were closely bound to the Old Gregorians. Cardinal Peter, who had studied at Paris and had become a monk at Cluny, had been created a cardinal by Paschal II and had risen steadily in influence. Without any doubt he was intellectually outstanding, energetic and quick at making decisions, and, thanks to his experience at the Curia and on important legatine missions in England and France, he was also conversant with the government of the Church, and the adversary and match of the Cardinal Chancellor Aimeric. Beside Anacletus, Innocent was pale and middling. People praised his pleasing devotion and his blameless conduct. He too was experienced as a legate: he had taken part in the negotiations preceding the Concordat of Worms and together with Cardinal Pierleoni he had carried out a legatine mission in France. Neither election had taken place canonically. There was no court of arbitration to which appeal could be made. And so there remained only one way, if neither rival could impose himself in Rome by excluding the other or getting him to resign: an appeal to the Universal Church, on gaining whose recognition both claimants now concentrated all their energies. Innocent II had to leave Rome, for the Frangipani abandoned him and did homage to Anacletus II. Innocent was a canon regular and hence, together with Aimeric, he was friendly toward the influential circles of the new orders. Anacletus expected to have on his side Cluny, the most powerful monastic order of the West, to which he himself belonged. But the majority decision of the Church favored Innocent, especially since Cluny under Peter the Venerable let itself be ranged against Anacletus.

Innocent first wooed France, where Bernard of Clairvaux came out for him. Not all of France followed, it is true; England too, which initially hesitated, could eventually be brought over to Innocent by Bernard's influence on King Henry I, but Scotland, both King and clergy, held to Anacletus. Spain and Portugal acknowledged Innocent. While the crusader states and their Latin Patriarchs finally adhered to Innocent, the Greek Patriarch of Constantinople appears to have recognized Anacletus.

Especially important became the stand of the German Church and of King Lothar. Both claimants announced their election to the King and invited him to Rome. But it was only at the Diet of Würzburg in October 1130 that Lothar acceded to the majority decision of the bishops and prelates and recognized Innocent, whom he met in person in March 1131 at the Diet of Liège; here he promised the requested journey to Rome. In Germany Innocent's cause had been especially seconded by Norbert of Magdeburg and Conrad of Salzburg.

Anacletus could rely on Rome, Milan, and South Italy, in particular on Roger II, for whom he confirmed the royal title that the Count of Sicily had just assumed. The connection with the Normans allowed Anacletus to continue to act as Pope from Rome until his death on 25 January 1138. On his first expedition, in 1133, King Lothar did, it is true, gain at least the Lateran basilica, where on 4 June Innocent crowned him Emperor, but, once the Germans had again left Rome, Innocent could not maintain himself and in September he went to Pisa. There in 1135 he held a synod, which was well attended from beyond the Alps; Anacletus and Roger of Sicily were excommunicated.

When, finally, thanks to the efforts of Bernard of Clairvaux, Milan was gained for Innocent, the route was open for a second journey to Italy by the Emperor (1136–37). This time also Rome could not be taken, and the campaign against Roger II ended indecisively. Lothar died on 4 December 1137, *en route* back to Germany, without having seen the end of the schism. Meanwhile, the Innocentians had undertaken negotiations with Roger. The outcome was that both rivals sent embassies to present the claims and rights of their respective principals before the King as arbiter at Salerno in November 1137, but they were unable to bring him to a definitive stand.

Success in these debates was achieved only by Bernard of Clairvaux, who contrived to get Cardinal Peter of Pisa, hitherto one of the most loyal adherents of Anacletus, to submit to Innocent.

Only the death of Anacletus II ended the schism. His electors and the Pierleoni now recognized Innocent II, who had thus finally won the long and arduous fight for the assent of all of Christendom. The virtually unanimous consent of the old and the new orders, the confidence of the great congregations of canons regular, the recognition accorded by the leading princes of the West and their episcopates, had especially contributed to this success. The dynamic propaganda, fully displayed in these years, of the great Abbot of Clairvaux, who effectively supported the exertions of Innocent II in all aspects, above all in regard to Italy, must not be passed over in silence.

Innocent II summoned a general synod to meet at Rome in the Lateran in April 1139. Now following the model of Lateran I (1123), which had liquidated the confusion resulting from the Investiture Controversy, all problems growing out of the Schism of 1130 were to be settled. Like Lateran I, Lateran II obtained recognition as an ecumenical council only much later. In attendance were more than one hundred bishops, some of them from the crusader states. At the opening of the Council Innocent spoke on the unity of the Church, the mutilation of which he branded as a sin against the Holy Spirit. He refused to recognize any legitimacy in the pontificate of Anacletus II, since it had not obtained the assent of the Church, and so the synod declared that all acts, decisions, ordinations, and consecrations performed by Anacletus and his adherents were null and void. These adherents, including even Peter of Pisa, for whom Bernard had interceded, lost all offices and dignities. Bishop Godfrey of Chartres was made legate in France and Aquitaine to enforce these decisions. At the Council Innocent canonized Sturmi of Fulda at the request of the German episcopate. The synod's thirty decrees again comprised the reform program of the last decades and repeated the canons of Lateran I and of the Synods of Clermont (1130), Reims (1131), and Pisa (1135), but the sanctions were made more severe.

With its renewed rejection of lay investiture and of every sort of simony, with its tightening of religious and clerical discipline, with its concern for family and social morality, including its stress on the Peace of God, with its measures against simony and heresy, this Council has been called the "Epilogue of the Gregorian Age."

CHAPTER 2

The Reform Orders of the Twelfth Century and Bernard of Clairvaux

Though in some respects the papacy contributed to the founding of new orders, fundamentally involved was a religious movement coming from below, the heroic striving of monks, canons, and laymen to realize the spirit of the Gospel and of the primitive Church in the most austere poverty, in solitude, or as wandering preachers. The fact that not a few new foundations were again satisfied with the mitigated manner of life of the older Benedictinism did not necessarily imply decadence, for the Benedictines were still at a respectable level. Some of their monasteries even displayed an openness to the new ideas, as did even Cluny, whose congregation achieved its widest extent under the important Abbot Peter the Venerable (1122–56). Just the same, the future belonged to those new communities of monks and canons, who preserved more purely the ideal of the *vita evangelica* and slowly established it institutionally. Their amazingly rapid diffusion throughout the entire West, the deeply appealing seriousness of their lives, and to an extent their pastoral and missionary efforts enabled these orders to rank with the most important historical factors of this period. They profoundly re-shaped Christian piety, including that of the people, and in their copious literature are to be heard many *motifs* that remained vital long after this age. They were the bridges leading from the Gregorian reform to the epoch of the mendicant orders.

Hence, the development to be related here reflected a great part of the course taken by the reform in the post-Gregorian period.

The Cistercians

No other community can give so clear an idea of the reform energies operating within the sphere of monasticism as the Cistercian Order. The beginnings and the first and decisive decades are, unfortunately, obscure. To be regarded as established are: the founding of Cîteaux by Robert of Molesme in 1098; Robert's return to his former monastery; the government of Cîteaux by Abbot Alberic and, after his death, probably in 1109, by Stephen Harding (1109–34). Born at Sherborne in England, Stephen had studied at Paris, was acquainted with Rome, and had become a monk at Molesme under Robert. The ideas of the founding generation are adequately known to us: concerned with strict poverty and a life in an isolated and poor locality. The monks of Cîteaux sought nothing different from what many other communities originating at that time were looking for. They were able to found La Ferté, the first daughter house, in 1113, not far from Cluny. Then, in quick succession, came Pontigny in 1114 and Clairvaux and Morimond in 1115. With La Ferté they constituted the group of so-called "primary abbeys," from which all Cistercian monasteries derived their origin. In 1119 the order counted ten houses, and at the death of Stephen Harding in 1134 — he had resigned his abbacy in 1130 — the number was eighty.

This rapid growth presented Stephen Harding and the other Cistercian abbots with the question of how unity was to be preserved in so many foundations. From the bull of confirmation issued in 1119 by Calixtus II it appears that a first outline of an organization had been laid before the Pope, but we do not know its details. Undoubtedly it involved the matrix of the so-called *Carta Caritatis.* Its original form must now be regarded as lost.

The Cistercians sought to observe the Rule of Saint Benedict in its original purity. To avoid the charge of novelty they emphasized this return to the old, to the sources. But in fact the new observance did not in all respects adhere to the letter of the Rule. *Oblati* were no longer accepted, the institute of *conversi,* or lay brothers, was elaborated, and the limiting of the abbatial authority by the constitution was new.

New also was the annual general chapter, attendance at which was obligatory on all abbots. Presided over by the Abbot of Cîteaux, it possessed and exercised full power over the order — legislative, executive, and judicial — but left to the abbeys complete financial and administrative autonomy. Annual visitation provided supervision, even in regard to the instructions of the general chapter. Within each filiation group it was taken care of by the mother abbey. The visitation of Cîteaux pertained to the four "primary abbeys."

In contradistinction to the predominantly personal organization of the Order of Cluny, with its dependence of priors and, to a degree, of abbots on the Abbot of Cluny, the Cistercians succeeded in establishing their order on an objectively co-operative basis. Individual abbeys, autonomous in themselves, associated according to filiation groups, and corporately united in the general chapter attended by all abbots — these constitutional principles gave rise to an order in which both the rights of the individual monastery and the interests of the entire order were assured.

While, also contrary to the Cluniac and older Benedictine ideal, there was desired until the mid-century a subordination to local episcopal jurisdiction, there then appeared papal exemption, so that, under the Pope, the general chapter became the highest court of appeal in the order. The abbeys promised one another mutual economic help, the preservation of a uniform discipline, and the cultivation of a simplified liturgy, whose externals — church buildings, vestments, vessels, chant — were to be kept as unpretentious as possible.

Since the order wanted to keep itself free from the feudal ties prevailing in the Cluniac system, it declined benefices and reintroduced manual labor. The white habit, the strict seclusion from the world by means of settlement in deserted areas, the austerity of the life in food, dwelling, and clothing, and the simplicity of the liturgy gave the order a great reputation as something new in the monastic world. The observance of the Benedictine rule enabled it to remain interiorly a part of this world.

The dynamism of Cistercian expansion was determined up to the mid-century by the personality of Saint Bernard of Clairvaux. When he died in 1153, there were already 350 abbeys, and he alone had founded sixty-six of them.

Cîteaux made particular use of this new institution of lay brothers, which had long before been introduced into other communities. As elsewhere, the Cistercian lay brothers made the monastic renunciations, without thereby becoming monks in the strict sense; they had neither an active nor a passive vote in their community. They shared in the choral liturgy only on Sundays and holy days. With few exceptions they came from the ordinary folk. Their dedication to work gave the order a high economic prosperity in the twelfth century and was especially irreplaceable in the foundations penetrating the eastern frontier area with the clearings that had to be created there. The *conversi* lived in the abbey and on the granges more or less remotely surrounding it. Tensions with the real monastic community were not lacking and from the middle of the century there were revolts, boycotts, and even murderous attacks on abbots and superiors.

The new order contributed powerfully to the development of the spiritual life in the Church. Important French Cistercians, in addition to Saint Bernard, were William of Saint-Thierry (d. 1148), Guerric of Igny (d. 1157), and Isaac of Stella (d. 1169), and in the thirteenth century Adam of Perseigne (d. 1221) and Hélinand of Froidmont (d. 1235). In England the outstanding name is that of Aelred of Rievaulx (d. 1167); in Germany, that of the historian, Otto of Freising (d. 1158). The literary history of the twelfth century extols not only the order's historiographers but also its poets. Troubadours made their appearance.

The Popes utilized the services of the order in the most varied ways, Bernard's career becoming the model here too. The wide and very thickly woven network of houses, with their regular intercommunications, especially in their general chapters, constituted an excellent medium of active and passive communication. The order was very soon represented in the College of Cardinals, and Pope Eugene III was a Cistercian. The preaching of the crusade was often committed to the order; here too Bernard's famed preaching of the Second Crusade supplied the inspiration. In the course of the Curia's centralization of the ecclesiastical juridical system, many Cistercian abbots were assigned tasks as judges delegate. An eventual result of this recourse to the order by the Curia was a wealth of privileges, despite Bernard's warning against this very thing.

And so criticism was not absent; it came not only from the Cistercians' own ranks but also from without. Well known is the polemic between Cluny and Cîteaux, represented respectively by Peter the Venerable and Bernard of Clairvaux.

The Canons Regular

Only after the conclusion of the Investiture Controversy could the institute of canons regular develop freely. From the pontificate of Urban II it was already clear that it would have a great future. For the greater the number of reform-minded bishops became in the course of the Gregorian reform, the more urgent became the task of introducing the reform among clergy and people. The bishops themselves had to try to solve the problem in their dioceses, but of course they needed numerous helpers. Because of their cloister-centered lives, the Benedictines and other monastic communities were not too frequently considered for this work, and, besides, the relations between the episcopate and at least the older type of Benedictines were compromised by the monks' efforts to obtain exemption. And so it was understandable that the bishops should turn to the canons regular. Here at first there were no difficulties about exemption. The reform of the higher clergy was assured for the future by the canons regular, and these could directly take part in the care of souls.

The importance of the canons regular movement was early grasped by the papacy and effectively fostered, above all from the time of Urban II. The number of votes of canons regular in the College of Cardinals grew, and, except for Celestine II and Eugene III, all the Popes from Honorius II to Hadrian IV were canons regular. They were thereby clearly distinguished from the five Benedictine Popes of the Gregorian reform, from Gregory VII to Gelasius II, because, significantly, Anacletus II, whose elevation in 1130 produced a schism, had been a monk of Cluny and accordingly could be regarded as the exponent of the old and now outdated tradition.

Together with the Popes, many bishops now also favored the canons regular.

The Premonstratensians

Its origin was at first greatly influenced by the founder, especially after Norbert had become Archbishop of Magdeburg in 1126. In the same year he obtained from Honorius II the solemn confirmation of his order. He turned over the government of Prémontré to his disciple, Hugh of Fosses, in 1128. Norbert's friendship with Bernard of Clairvaux may explain the extensive dependence on the Cistercian *Carta Caritatis* that is to be noted in the oldest known statutes of the order, dating from about 1140. The result was that under Hugh of Fosses the desire to engage in the care of souls, otherwise a special characteristic of canons regular, was restricted and the *vita contemplativa* was more strongly emphasized. The organization knew the general chapter and a uniform direction, as in the case of Cîteaux, but the system of filiation was not adopted. Instead the order was divided into "circaries," or provinces, each headed by a *circator,* later called vicar general. The Abbot of Prémontré ranked as the Abbot General, and the three Abbots of Saint-Martin de Laon, Floreffe, and Cuissy were assigned to him as advisers.

The order experienced its strongest expansion in Germany, Bohemia, Belgium, and France; it was almost as widespread in England and Spain, but in other countries it was much less.

Like the Cistercians, the canons regular also displayed a vigorous and special spirituality. Leadership here belonged to the school of Saint-Victor de Paris in France and to the Brothers of Reichersberg in Germany. Augustine, John the Evangelist, Paul, and Gregory the Great were held in particular veneration. Devotion to the Passion and to the Sacred Heart and a mysticism of the Cross were congenial to them.

Emphasis upon the parochial care of souls especially by the Premonstratensians, who were themselves often nobles, meant a rise in the social level of the ministry in the lesser churches and at the same time the opening up of an important reservoir of recruits. Since the Premonstratensians, like the Cistercians, participated in the work of colonization and evangelization of the eastern territories, the parochial care of souls could only have contributed to the permanent effects of their exertions.

Bernard of Clairvaux

The most powerful ecclesiastical personality during the decades between 1120 and 1150 came from the Cistercian reform. With Norbert of Xanten and the Chancellor Aimeric he was one of the leaders of the late Gregorian reform and so stamped his features on his age that it has often been called the Age of Saint Bernard.

In April 1112 Bernard began his novitiate in newly founded Cîteaux under Stephen Harding. He completed it in 1113 when Cîteaux founded its first daughter abbey, La Ferté. Bernard's friend, Hugh of Mâcon, became Abbot of the second daughter abbey, Pontigny, founded in 1114. Finally, in 1115 Bernard himself was entrusted with the founding of Clairvaux.

Clairvaux was founded in the diocese of Langres, 116 kilometers northwest of Cîteaux. Bernard received the abbatial blessing from William of Champeaux, Bishop of Châlons-sur-Marne, who became the most effectual patron of the young monastery.

Although Bernard was often ill and bedridden, we know of much traveling. Clairvaux was able to think of making foundations as early as 1118. In place of the Abbot, who was so often away, the community was governed by the prior. In 1138 he was elected Bishop of Langres. Bernard was able to end the opposition to this. Hence for Clairvaux was assured the favor of the local Ordinary, while the good will of the territorial lord, Theobald of Champagne, was secured through Bernard's mediation between Theobald, the Bishops of Langres, and the Dukes of Burgundy. Clairvaux grew rapidly because of permanent foundations made by Bernard's kin and the great nobles friendly to him.

The spiritual authority of its Abbot likewise grew amazingly fast and spread far, first of all in the order itself, where he was one of the signers of Cîteaux's first organizational charter, the *Carta Caritatis.*

He was closely bound with the founder of Prémontré and likewise with Peter the Venerable of Cluny. But the second of these friendships had to weather serious problems, for Bernard criticized the manner of life of the great Burgundian abbey and its congregation. It was to the credit of the Abbot of Cluny that he not only did not break off relations with Bernard but even allowed Bernard to influence him in reforming his congregation. Something similar occurred in the circles of canonical reform, where Bernard advocated transformation from chapters of secular canons to those of canons regular.

How powerful the authority of the Abbot of Clairvaux had become by 1130 appeared when he decided for Innocent II at the Synod of Étampes. Through his active role in liquidating the Schism of 1130–38 in France and Italy, through his constantly growing correspondence with the leading personalities of Western Christendom, through his ever more frequently requested and obtained intervention in ecclesiastical crises, Bernard gradually became "le personnage le plus en vue de l'Europe," as he has been termed, the adviser of the great in Church and state. His friends and relatives soon occupied the most influential positions in the Church.

Bernard was closely connected with the Roman Curia because of his friendship with the Chancellor Aimeric. His letters to Honorius II, Innocent II, and Eugene III show the Abbot's intimate relations with the reform movement of canons regular that was favored under these Popes, especially by Aimeric. Bernard was always the friend and adviser of the congregations. This was true also of the founder of Saint-Victor, William of Champeaux, and of the great theologians at Paris, Hugh and Richard. To the Curia such a man, who had gained so powerful a prestige, not only in his own order, but in the Cluniac, the Premonstratensian, and the Carthusian orders, among the canons regular, and even in the world of hermits, must have seemed almost irreplaceable.

The preparations for the Second Crusade furnished further proof of this. Bernard had long been familiar with the world of the crusade. In 1128, at the Council of Troyes, he had collaborated on the constitution of the Knights Templars, whose first grand master was related to him, and in *De laude novae militiae* he had sketched a spiritual program for the order. He corresponded with Queen Mélisende of Jerusalem. When, after the fall of Edessa in 1144, King Louis VII of France decided to provide the requested armed assistance and asked Pope Eugene III to send crusade preachers, Bernard received the commission to preach the cross in France. He did so for the first time at Vézelay on 31 March 1146.

"The last of the Fathers," as Bernard has been called, left a bulky *corpus* of letters, sermons, and treatises, masterpieces of spiritual literature. Most of the treatises deal with questions of monastic spirituality, such as the *Degrees of Humility and Pride* (1124), the defense of the Cistercian ideal of life in comparison with that of Cluny (1125), several works on the love of God (1128–36), the explanation of *Precept and Dispensation* (before 1144), the *Praise of the New Knighthood* (before 1130), and the treatise on *Grace and Free Will* (before 1128). In 1135 Bernard began his chief work, the *Sermones super Canticum Canticorum,* of which he managed to finish eighty-six by the time of his death. The work of his old age,

De consideratione in five books, was written for Pope Eugene III. Finally, he also composed the biography of his friend Malachy, Archbishop of Armagh in Ireland.

Despite the variety of literary form Bernard was basically concerned with only one thing: like the Fathers, he sought to present to his environment the teachings of Scripture, in whose world of ideas he himself lived and whose language he managed to appropriate because of an identification of spirit. So long as he was alive and, even more, after his death there proceeded from him a far-reaching and enduring influence on the life of the entire Church.

His experience was, demonstrably, a mystical experience of the nearness of God, from which there poured out upon Bernard the wisdom of the final knowledge of God. Its most important presupposition, he taught, was humility, which had to inform all spiritual exertions. From it begins the ascent to God and it conditions all further stages, because it is basically the attitude of Christ: "habes commendatam a Deo humilitatem in Christo." This ascent is a constant growing in love, an incessant search for union with the triune God, which Bernard has described, as though in his last will, in the final sermons on the Canticle, as a union of the spirit with the Word who is God.

CHAPTER 3

The Papacy and the Western Kings in the Age of Saint Bernard

The peace brought to the Empire by the Concordat of Worms in 1122 had been preceded in the other countries of Christendom by similar agreements between the Church and the secular authority — in England in 1106–7 and in France at the same time but without any formal treaty. Following the intensive disputation of the Investiture Controversy views were to some extent theoretically clarified and even in agreement as to the function of kings and other secular powers within the Church, regarded as the Church of clerics and monks, of bishops and abbots, and of the Roman Pontiff. Protection and in particular cases even extensive defense with means suited to the secular power were meant: preservation of the order which was a legal order embracing the whole of Christendom in all its members and classes by means of a readily offered, or at least not refused, support of the ecclesiastical judgment through sanctions extending beyond purely spiritual measures and intervening in the civil sphere. Saint Bernard himself, in his letters to the Emperor Lothar and King Conrad III, discovered a formula for this, to be understood entirely in a Gregorian sense.

But in reality, even if one were to follow a stricter interpretation of Bernard's concept, bishops and Popes in their relations with Emperors, kings, and princes had to submit to the law of the politically possible. In the age of the unambiguous power of the reform spirit, which, represented by the orders of Cîteaux and Prémontré and the other congregations of canons regular, carried the day in the entire Church, and hence in the entire political field, in the crisis of the Schism of 1130–38, this law lay often in the hands of the clergy.

The Empire

The age of Saint Bernard corresponds in German history to the reigns of the Emperor Lothar (1125–37) and King Conrad III (1138–52). Both reigns were under the influence of the prevailing reform spirit and the aegis of peace with the papacy. By his decision for Innocent II, Lothar had made it clear that he was in agreement with this new tendency in the Church. In his two journeys to Italy, in 1133 and 1136–37, he complied with the desires of the Holy See, even if, especially in 1137, friction was not absent. Episcopal elections in Germany were free. Lothar renounced any royal interference in ecclesiastical disputes, even though, because of the constitution of the Empire, they touched upon the crown's interests.

At this period the activity of the papal legates was devoted no longer preferably to political but rather to expressly ecclesiastical questions and revealed an intimate co-operation of the German episcopate with the Curia. They convoked and directed provincial synods, adjusted disputes among bishops, confirmed elections and consecrated bishops, visited dioceses and regulated questions of Church discipline, and transmitted papal privileges. Year after year there came at least one legate, and sometimes three or more acted at the same time. The powerful Rhenish archbishops were reprimanded, many disputes pertaining to the jurisdiction of the metropolitan were immediately sent to the Holy See, the number of exemptions increased, many bishops went to Rome to be consecrated. The election of Conrad III at Koblenz on 7 March 1138 was determined by Archbishop Adalbero of Trier.

France

A map of twelfth-century France shows the royal *demesne*, where alone the King really ruled, as a strikingly small enclave in comparison with the entire Kingdom, hemmed in by the lands of the powerful Counts of Blois-Champagne. Flanders, Normandy, Brittany, Anjou, Poitou, Aquitaine (or Guienne), Gascony, Toulouse, Auvergne, and Ducal Burgundy — the great vassals of the crown — evaded the royal influence.

In 1137 Louis VI was succeeded by his son, Louis VII (1137–80). No Western prince was so much under the influence of the Church and the papacy as was this King, who, however, as husband of Eleanor of Aquitaine until 1152, sought at least for a time to extend the royal authority. Goaded by the Queen, he began to pursue a personal policy in various episcopal elections that was in opposition to the

Roman views. But the alliance of Count Theobald IV of Champagne, arranged by Bernard of Clairvaux, with the episcopate and the Curia forced him to yield. This appears in the matrimonial case of Raoul of Vermandois, who, having married a niece of Theobald's, had repudiated her for a sister of Queen Eleanor. A papal legate declared the second marriage invalid, excommunicated Raoul and Petronilla, and laid an interdict on Vermandois. Urged by Eleanor, Louis declared war on Theobald, who took his niece's part. Thirteen hundred persons perished in the flames of Vitry in 1144. Bernard arranged peace between the King and Theobald; Louis abandoned Raoul and decided to submit to Rome. During Louis' absence on the Second Crusade Suger looked after the royal interests. Not the crown but the French Church, especially the new orders and the canons regular, must be regarded as the leading influences in public life.

Anarchy in England

Following the peaceful settlement of the Investiture Controversy in 1107, King Henry I contrived until his death in 1135 to control the English Church with the firm hand characteristic of his father, William the Conqueror. While one cannot speak of an English territorial Church, still both in England and in Normandy it was customary that the participation of the bishops in councils beyond the King's territory depended upon his express permission. Without the same express permission no legate of the Pope might enter his lands. By a benevolent attitude to the monasteries Henry had assured himself a favorable judgment in ecclesiastical historiography, but the Church was certainly not free as this was understood by the Gregorians. Still, it was to her advantage that the peace in a Kingdom which was vigorously governed and, in contrast to the other West European countries, was united could only be of service in the development of ecclesiastical life.

The situation changed in the long period of the struggle over the throne between Henry's daughter Matilda, widow of the Emperor Henry V and wife of Count Geoffrey of Anjou, and Stephen of Blois, grandson of the Conqueror through his daughter Adele. A new era of political calm did not begin again until the accession of Henry II in 1154.

During the confusion of King Stephen's reign (1135–54) the Holy See guarded its authority by the conferring *permanenter* of legatine powers on the Archbishops of Canterbury. Thanks to the struggle over the succession to the throne, the episcopate was at last able to secure its freedom and to make extensive use against the crown of that right which Henry I had conceded to it: to appeal to Rome in doubtful cases.

At the same time there occurred an influx of recruits for the Cistercians and the canons regular, which had been prepared under Henry I but only now became a mighty stream. Fifty-seven abbeys were founded by 1153, if the monasteries of the Congregation of Savigny are counted.

The Iberian Peninsula

In the Iberian peninsula the difficult course of the *Reconquista* was scarcely the most favorable climate for a calm development of ecclesiastical life. Through their ecclesiastical activity the papal legates enhanced the total European influence of the Curia in the course of the centralization of the Roman administration and jurisdiction. During the Schism of 1130 Archbishop Diego Gelmírez of Compostela was decisive in supporting Innocent II. Of great importance was the withdrawal by Afonso Henriques, Count of Portugal, from his vassalage to Castile. He in 1143 declared his land to be a fief of the papacy and took the oath of fealty in the presence of the Cardinal Legate Guido. With the aid of the crusaders of 1147 he almost managed to free the country from Muslim domination. The final confirmation of his royal title, came only under Alexander III.

Christian Expansion Eastward

Otto, Bishop of Bamberg, set out upon his so-called first missionary journey (1124–25) to Pomerania on behalf of Poland with the result that Christianity was definitely assured in Pomerania.

Association with German eastward colonization decisively favored the missionary work. At the same time as Otto of Bamberg, Archbishop Adalbero of Hamburg-Bremen began a mission.

The service of the *Imperium* and the *Regna* to the Church in these decades of the age of Saint Bernard are seen in the rapid and unequivocal decision for Innocent II, in the freedom conceded to the Church after the Investiture Controversy, especially in the matter of episcopal elections, abbatial elections, and the relations of the higher clergy to the Roman Curia, and in the legal protection which kings and princes accorded to cathedrals, abbeys, and collegiate churches.

In France the close relationship of the crown with the bishops in the great principalities was the only way by which the crown could exercise its influence beyond the limits of the *demesne.* Accordingly, it was cultivated there as a relationship of mutual service. It is well known how intimately Louis VI was bound to the Church, which assisted him and his son in the direction of the Kingdom. Tensions, even with Bernard of Clairvaux, were not wanting, but the overall view showed the kingship in France in a productive cooperation with the Church of the Kingdom and with the Roman Church as the representative of Christendom. The same can be said of Germany and, with certain restrictions, of England and the Iberian peninsula. Italy, on the other hand, remained an agitated land of variety, with the constantly changing relations of the Curia to the Normans and its unstable connections with the North Italian communes and revolutionary Rome, which at the close of this period became a difficult problem in curial policy.

CHAPTER 4

Elaboration of the Curia and Criticism of Church and Papacy

The Gregorian reform had involved changes in the structure of the Roman ecclesiastical administration that were not completed before the middle of the twelfth century. But now the main lines of what people began to call the Curia were clearly discernible: court, household, and meeting all in one, as in the Germanic royal model, the pattern for the Roman development. Proper, that is, Roman traditional elements were added in the course of the renewal of the idea of Rome, reminiscences of the reorganization of Senate and courts by Diocletian. At the same time this Curia had a rapid expansion in size.

On the occasion of the double election of 1130, there being no tribunal above the two claimants which could have decided between them authoritatively or by arbitration, it was left to the Church as a whole, to Christendom itself, to give the final judgment. The Church did so in recognizing Innocent II by a great majority. For the first time Christendom had acted as a unity, as the *corpus mysticum Christi,* to use the term that persons began to apply to it in the early twelfth century. Christendom had, of course, been assisted in arriving at this knowledge of its unity by the crusade experience, which made Christians of many countries acquainted with one another; the sufferings endured in common for it and the common use of spiritual and physical energies attested one goal to be striven for by all in the same way. At the same time the crusade had impressively brought into prominence the head of the *corpus mysticum,* Pope Urban II, organizer and, in his legates, leader of the expedition.

The new Curia served the constantly increasing functions of the papacy in the social, political, and ecclesiastical spheres; from them the Curia received the impulse to further development. The change from the Roman urban clergy and administration to an instrument of government that could be used for all of Christendom was, it is true, already essentially complete at the beginning of this period. The College of Cardinals had taken shape, and the total numbers grew.

The charters now make known, in the signatures of the cardinals, how the college as an advisory body assisted the Pope in the government of the Church. The chiefs of the earlier offices of *arcarius* (treasurer), *saccellarius* (paymaster), *nomenculator* (care of the poor), *protoscriniarius* (archives), *bibliothecarius* (chancery), and the two *primicerii* of the *schola notariorum* (correspondence) and the *schola defensorum* (legal matters) — the so-called *iudices de clero* or *iudices palatini* — retained only judicial functions as the College of Seven. In their places appeared the Pope's *camerlengo* (for finances) and chancellor (for correspondence). Just as at royal courts, so there were also at the Curia the *dapifer* or seneschal, the *pincerna* (cup-bearer), the marshal. And, like the northern courts, the Curia too was often itinerant. The broad outlines of a papal *capella* were also discernible, apparently in imitation of the Frankish court chapel. While at first its members were still called *subdiaconi sanctae Romanae ecclesiae* and *subdiaconi domini nostri papae,* soon they were *subdiaconi et capellani* and in the thirteenth century merely *capellani.* A nucleus of this new structure was the *schola notariorum,* or *notarii palatini.* Under the chancellor, who united in himself the functions of the earlier *scriniarius* and of the *primicerius notariorum,* this college took charge of the Pope's correspondence. Other groups took over the tradition of the earlier seven palatine subdeacons (liturgy), of the regionary subdeacons (social service), of the subdeacons of the *schola cantorum.* Now, as each occasion demanded, missions were also probably required of all of them in addition to their liturgical and administrative duties. They accompanied legates on their journeys. They constituted a college at the Lateran, where they lived and worked in common and were provided for by the papal kitchen. Each obtained a benefice to provide for his proper support, but, unlike the cardinals, they were not attached to titular churches. In so far as they received judicial functions as *advocati* or *auditores,* they could participate in the consistory, which in these decades replaced the earlier Roman Lenten synods and, as a regular meeting of the cardinals under the presidency of the Pope, considered and settled *causae maiores.* The overall direction of the college of subdeacons or chaplains was in the hands of the *camerlengo.* Hence the chancellor, who headed only one group of them, was subordinate to him. Probably for this reason in the thirteenth century a vice-chancellor conducted the real business in place of the chancellor, who was a cardinal. In the late twelfth century the College of Cardinals obtained its own *camerlengo* for its own financial administration, which was separating itself from that of the papacy.

This imposing structure grew steadily. Especially from the pontificate of Innocent II the number of processes at the Roman Curia increased rapidly, over and above *causae maiores* in the strict sense. The enhanced prestige of the Pope in the whole of Christendom, the canon law that was gaining ground everywhere, the intensified drive for exemption on the part of monasteries and particular churches — all contributed to this. To the papal Curia belonged not only ecclesiastics but also, as earlier, lay persons, most of them from the great Roman families. The College of Cardinals and the *capella,* both of them together with the Pope constituting the Curia, displayed in the twelfth century, even in the lower echelons, a personnel that was remarkably international and no longer merely Roman.

If for some time fault had been found with the situation at Rome — during the Investiture Controversy this had, of course, been intensified by polemics — but the blame was quite often levelled rather at the Romans as such, now the reform papacy itself had to learn, from the representatives of the most important factors in this reform, how hard it was for a demand to improve the life and promote the sanctification of the people to maintain itself in this Church "of sinners and saints" if it was raised by sinners rather than by saints. But if now the reform itself or at least some of its results encounter harsh judgments from irreproachable spokesmen, persons pay attention.

This criticism was represented not by Arnold of Brescia, the canon regular inclining to spiritual radicalism, but by Saint Bernard, by John of Salisbury and his "common sense" with its orientation to humanistic moderation, and by Gerhoh of Reichersberg with his testimonials and treatises dedicated to Eugene III and Hadrian IV. Whereas Arnold demanded that the Pope and the bishops renounce property and dominion in order to keep themselves free for the care of souls exclusively, for the others the solution lay in the human. They required the right use of institutions which were not found to be blameworthy in themselves and seem not to have taken any offense at the feudalism which had established itself since 1059 in increasing measure in the life of the Roman Church. They apparently saw in them those *elementa mundi* which the Church makes use of, which indeed she must assimilate in order to remain true to her inner law as a representation of the mystery of the Incarnation. Arnold's radicalism, on the other hand, moved, with its spiritualism, entirely on that line whose beginnings were to be found in the poverty movement of the turn of the century — the *pauperes Christi,* the *vita apostolica* — and from which heretical extremes often enough developed and not first with Arnold.

Bernard of Clairvaux possessed a high regard for the authority of the Pope and the bishops in the Church of Christ. For that very reason he urgently warned against any misuse of this authority and combatted tendencies at the Curia, for example that of becoming too liberal with privileges of exemption, which would restrict episcopal freedom and authority, as a perversion of the traditional order established by God himself. Even the system of appeals was an abomination to him, not in itself but its excess, its practical operation. He made himself the spokesman of the grievances of all the churches: abbots were withdrawn from the bishops, bishops from the archbishops, archbishops from the patriarchs. To his way of thinking appeals mainly served to circumvent the local courts, which, however, possessed a more exact knowledge of the place and the case and had often already given a judgment in accord with equity and law. In the highest court of all was sought a pardon or an advantage, and in this way episcopal authority was gravely injured. To the complaints Gerhoh of Reichersberg added the bitter remark that "apparently these appeals were not unwelcome to the Romans": "Gravatur iam ecce universa terra, fastum et avariciam Romanorum non sustinens." One detects the real concern, and at the same time the tactful tendency, to attribute the guilt, not to the Pope, not even to the Curia, but only to those of its personnel who were Romans.

CHAPTER 5

The Second Crusade and the Wars in Spain and the Slavic East

The papacy, the Curia, and the West saw themselves faced around the middle of the century with a new task, which called upon all their resources: the peril of the crusader states. The Pope decided to summon a crusade, while Hugh proceeded to France and Germany. On 1 December 1145 a bull was sent to King Louis VII of France, inviting him and all the princes and faithful of the Kingdom to aid the East.

He did not appeal to King Conrad III of Germany, because he needed his help in Rome and against King Roger II of Sicily, and of course not to Roger, whose untrustworthiness and self-willed policy were sources of fear.

A first appeal by Louis VII from Bourges at Christmas of 1145 had little effect. The King thereupon asked the support of Bernard of Clairvaux, who was willing to comply. In 1146 Bernard began his amazingly effective crusade preaching. The Pope went to France in 1147 and at first Bernard had to reassure him in regard to the extension of the recruiting for the crusade to Germany.

Under the leadership of the two Kings, the German army at the end of May and the French army at the end of June took the land route to the East. Since Louis had come by the same route that the Germans had already traveled, and for this reason had not been suitably provisioned and dealt with, because of excesses by the Germans, relations between the two crusading armies were permeated with bitterness and suspicion even in Constantinople. Both were likewise not kindly disposed to Byzantium. The beginning gave little to hope for.

Louis VII was accompanied by his wife, Eleanor of Aquitaine. Conrad III joined the Byzantine Emperor Manuel in a common policy against Roger II of Sicily, and Conrad's sister-in-law, married Manuel. Manuel urged haste, for the crusaders were a heavy burden on the city. Louis VII was also amicably received and had no scruples about delivering possible conquests to the Byzantines as their own property. He had all his barons swear the same sort of oath.

When at the beginning of November the French army reached Nicaea, Conrad had lost almost all of his army and all his camp provisions in the battle of Dorylaeum on 25 October. The remnant joined the French army. They went on together as far as Ephesus, where Conrad fell sick and was invited to Constantinople by Manuel. He there recovered and in March 1148 was able to continue on to Palestine with his entourage on Byzantine ships. Acre was reached in mid-April. The French army, which had melted away to less than half its original strength through severe losses, made Antioch in the late spring of 1148. Here occurred the well known serious matrimonial crisis between Louis and Eleanor, provoked by the Queen's intimacy with Prince Raymond of Antioch. The King compelled her to proceed with him and the army to Jerusalem; they entered the city in May and were cordially received by Queen Mélisende. Never had Jerusalem seen so brilliant a gathering of knights and ladies.

A great council was arranged for 24 June at Acre, with King Baldwin III, the Patriarch Fulcher, the Archbishops of Caesarea and Nazareth, and the grand masters of the Templars and the Hospitallers acting as hosts. It was decided to unite all the forces for an attack on Damascus. Correct as the project was from the point of view of strategy — for with Damascus a wedge would have been driven between Egyptian-African and North Syrian-Eastern Islam — it was nevertheless a political blunder, for at that moment it was of great importance to the Burid Kingdom of Damascus to maintain friendship with the Franks against the common enemy, Nur-ed-Din. But now Damascus too was driven into the Caliph's camp. The city was besieged in vain, the Western lords departed and the legend of the invincibility of the Western knights was destroyed. A new confidence awoke in the world of Islam.

No enterprise of the Middle Ages began with more brilliant expectations.

Planned by the Pope, proclaimed and fired by the golden eloquence of Saint Bernard, and led by the two chief powers of the West, the crusade had promised so much for the glory and safety of Christendom. But when it came to a shameful end with the difficult retreat from Damascus, it had done nothing but push relations between the West and Byzantium almost to the breaking point, sow distrust and suspicion between the newly arrived crusaders and the Franks who were living in the East, divide the Western princes, bring the Muslims closer together, and irreparably damage the military reputation of the Franks. A new epoch began in Syria, for now the Christians had been forced to the defensive. In the West itself the reports of the returned soldiers spread a deep distrust of the Franks of the Holy Land, resident in the crusader states, by whom they felt they had been left in the lurch. The failure of the Second Crusade had an effect on the intellectual and religious life of Latin Christendom in that the crusade idea lost its luster. Persons no longer wanted to aid the Franks in Palestine. The indignation was even directed against the Pope and Saint Bernard, who had summoned to the expedition. The esteem of the Abbot of Clairvaux declined, at least in Germany. He wrote his *apologia* in the introductory chapter to Book II of *De Consideratione,* taking himself seriously to task. In it a deep psychological need becomes apparent, betraying something that the saint was able to establish even in his own entourage: that this misfortune caused men to entertain doubts of faith.

The Wend crusade, to which Bernard had given his assent at the Diet of Frankfurt in March 1147 and to which he had issued a summons, was also a failure. An inner contradiction became visible here, together with an ambiguity as to goals and planning. For some of the Slavs whom it was desired to subjugate proved to be good Christians, and hence a war against them could not be termed a crusade. Or if the Slavs who were subdued were and intended to remain pagans, it appeared senseless to destroy them and devastate their land, from which persons aspired to derive profit under their own rule. This contradicted Bernard's express instructions for the crusade. He had called for "extermination or conversion of the heathens" and had forbidden a concluding of peace or of a treaty so long as the people were still pagans. The princes did not adhere to Bernard's directions.

An enduring success was granted only to the taking of Lisbon and to the completion, thereby made possible, of the new Kingdom of Portugal. In this way the right wing of the campaign against Islam, comprising the entire Mediterranean, was consolidated. Roger II was able to establish himself in the center sector at Tripoli, first in 1143 and then definitively in 1146. Meanwhile, the left wing, the crusader states, was in increasing difficulty.

CHAPTER 6

Monastic Humanism

The twelfth century was an age of social restratification, of urban development, and of the communal movement. The horizon of the West was extended by the drive eastward in colonization and crusade, and contacts with the intellectual world of Islam became more frequent. Young clerics began to move restlessly from school to school, that is, from one celebrated teacher to another, apparently oblivious of any diocesan, or territorial boundaries. Until the mid-century monastic humanism, predominant from time immemorial, still maintained its primacy in the field of intellectual disputation and of literary creativity, despite the versatility of the new clerical personnel. This fact must be connected with the preeminence which the new orders of Cîteaux and Prémontré, that is, the reformed Benedictine and the reformed canonical life, occupied in the second phase of ecclesiastical reform.

In this period, when the enthusiasm of the beginnings was still operative in both orders, a sociological law procured for them not only the pious but also the intellectually most active forces. While the growth of the cathedral schools and of the schools of the unreformed chapters continued, the intellectual and literary achievement of Cluny, Cîteaux, and the congregations of canons regular maintained its lead, and especially among the last named group a public teaching activity was often to be found, as at Saint-Victor de Paris.

The cultivation of the *artes liberales* still dominated the entire educational process of the West but it was gradually restricted at the cathedral schools. In these began a sort of withering in the direction of pure utility aiming at rapid preparation for a real specialization in theology, law, and medicine.

But in the abbeys and in the chapters of canons regular, as earlier, the *artes liberales* were seen as the best way to a deeper understanding of Scripture and to a full mastery of the patristic and ecclesiastical tradition. In addition, this "humanistic" pursuit of grammar, rhetoric, and dialectic suggested a fostering of those literary forms which were used with predilection by the representatives of monastic humanism: the *sermo* the dialogue, the letter, the *florilegia,* the biography, and in fact all forms of historical writing in general.

Since this linguistically elegant dress served for the most part to express concepts of a deepened religious feeling, of mystical theology, of reform austerity, of enhanced claims in the area of the challenged freedom of the Church, the works of the monastic humanism of this epoch acquired greater importance as literary, journalistic, and theological achievements.

Cluny was represented especially by Abbot Peter the Venerable (d. 1156), in whom the reform of the famed monastic congregation found a protagonist in the spirit of the new orders. His apologetic treatises — *Ad-versus Iudaeos* and *Adversus sectam Saracenorum* — and the projected translation of the Koran and of other Arabic writings display the candor of the supreme superior responsible for a monastic union that was spread over many lands. This union involved, especially in the southern monasteries, numerous contacts with the non-Christian world which had to be intellectually assimilated.

The writing of history, alongside the letter an especially characteristic literary form of humanism, was, as earlier, cultivated within the Benedictine world, even outside the Cluniac union.

What was more important for monastic humanism was life, not knowledge and doctrine, as was the case with the teachers in the urban schools. And so Bernard of Clairvaux took his place among historians with his *Vita Malachiae,* and William of Saint-Thierry became the biographer of his still living friend, Bernard of Clairvaux. Among Cistercians mention must be made of Aelred of Rievaulx (d. 1167), whose literary work has come again into esteem through modern research.

First place among the canons regular was occupied in France by Hugh of Saint-Victor (d. 1141) and in Germany by Gerhoh of Reichersberg (d. 1169). Hugh's surpassing theological preeminence was undisputed. The encyclopedic breadth of his creativity justifies his being included in the humanism here under consideration, even though his teaching activity and the systematization of his theological works assign him also to early scholasticism. But with him too the exegetical-theological proposition revolves around a scene from salvation history. His creativity served the spiritual life, the reform of souls. Hugh and his entire Victorine school — Richard (d. 1173), Achard (d. 1171), Godfrey (d. ca. 1195) — combined their emphatically biblical theology with a rich spiritual experience.

Gerhoh of Reichersberg came from the school of Rupert of Deutz, from whom he took the salvation-history orientation of his theology. His typological interpretation of time, his exegesis related to the present, his historical-critical method, to the extent that it can be so called, set him apart from the nascent scholastic method. He may be regarded not only as a conservative theologian but as a representative of humanism, even though he was not a monk; for the canons regular, because of their strict poverty and their claustral mode of life, were very close to the monastic style — "pene eiusdem propositi," as Urban II put it. And both types of reform orders were equally aloof from rising scholasticism.

Chapter 7

The New Theology: Abelard, Peter Lombard, Gratian

Parallel with monastic humanism there developed in the twelfth century a new theology in the world of the cathedral and chapter schools. In contradistinction to the abbeys, where theological knowledge appeared as oriented to the religious life itself, to prayer, meditation, and mystical union with God, the new theology sought to throw light on the mysteries of the faith, transmitted in Scripture and the patristic tradition, to acquire a systematic total view of the truths of faith by means of intensive rational reflection. It thereby corresponded to an urgent need of the time, in which economic, social, and political changes were forming a type of man different from that known to previous centuries. The great pilgrimages of the eleventh century and the crusades of the twelfth, the colonization getting under way on the Germanic-Slavonic frontier areas, the numerically not very important but still considerable interchange of men and institutions such as was connected with the founding of Norman states in England, South Italy, and the Levant — all this meant that in the ever expanding awareness of Western Christendom, above all through the upsetting contact with non-Christians, the vital questions of the traditional *milieu* of faith were put more critically and more anxiously.

The new theology cannot be understood only from the mentality of its first proponents, as though here men less inclined to contemplation or scholars specially equipped for reasoning accounted for a new method of gaining insights into the faith. Far more importantly, it was entirely in accord with a more comprehensive new intellectual need, which made itself known in the questions of students and in the problems of journalism, as, for example, in the Investiture Controversy. The continuity of intellectual development precludes any surprise that the initial steps of the new theology were associated with the names of monks, that Anselm of Bec and Canterbury ranks as the father of scholasticism, that Anselm of Laon came from his school, that Abelard in turn was a student of the younger Anselm. Nor is it without symbolic significance that Abelard lived as a monk of Saint-Denis and as Abbot of Saint-Gildas and died under the protection of Cluny, in Cluny's priory of Saint-Marcel near Chalon-sur-Saône.

Later this new theology was given the name "scholasticism" and attributed as "early scholasticism" to the twelfth and as "high scholasticism" to the thirteenth century. It was called the "theology of the school," because it was at home in the urban schools from which the universities were to develop at the turn of the twelfth to the thirteenth century and because its leading teachers founded schools which were concerned to cultivate the theological specialization of their founders. Thus one speaks of the school of Anselm of Laon, of the school of Abelard, of the school of Gilbert de la Porrée, of the school of Saint-Victor, of the schools of Orléans, Chartres, Paris, Bologna. These numerous schools emerged almost simultaneously. The earliest appeared in the eleventh century — that of Bec with its two great teachers, Lanfranc and Anselm of Canterbury. Since the school of Bec does not fall within the scope of this presentation, the closely related school of Laon may be considered first.

Anselm of Laon (ca. 1050–1117) and his brother Raoul, both of them pupils of Anselm of Canterbury, taught at the cathedral school of Laon. Research has rediscovered many works of the "sentence" *genre* from their sphere of influence; works have come down anonymously. Since students came to Laon, just as they did to Bec, from great distances, including even the Slavic lands, the manuscripts of the school of Laon, scattered over the entire West, testify to a radiation over all of *christianitas latina.* New in the collections of sentences of the school of Laon was the manner in which the lecture notes of the *magistri* themselves were now set beside the patristic texts; in the further course of the development these notes acquired such great authority that the patristic texts were treated rather in the framework of the *theologoumena* of the teachers. Likewise discernible were the beginnings of the famous form of the *quaestio,* the classical method of teaching and of dealing with problems in scholastic theology.

Together with Anselm of Laon there is always simultaneously mentioned William of Champeaux (1068–1122), like Abelard a pupil of Roscelin of Compiègne. William taught at the cathedral school of Paris until a dispute with Abelard in 1108 induced him to withdraw to the left bank of the Seine. He settled down at the chapel of Saint-Victor, where soon arose the canonical institute of which he was the founder. Like many another celebrated teacher of these decades, he was made a Bishop, receiving the see of Châlons-sur-Marne in 1113, and as the friend and patron of the young Abbot of Clairvaux he could later enjoy a better publicity than that which overtook Anselm of Laon. His *Sententiae vel quaestiones,* which are not merely concerned with topics such as the problem of universals, but, bearing an Augustinian stamp, treat in an original manner especially questions of moral theology, were able to produce long-range effects through his pupils, above all in Germany. Even Bernard of Clairvaux found William's outlook congenial.

Of greater significance than the founder of Saint-Victor for the new theology was the young community's greatest teacher, Hugh (d. 1141). He probably came from Germany, for he received his first formation at Sankt Pankraz in Hamersleben, together with his introduction to the ideals of the canons regular; by his entry into the chapter of Saint-Victor de Paris between 1115 and 1120 he definitely adopted these ideals as his own. An encyclopedic mind, an esteemed teacher, an author on a broad range of subjects, Hugh, especially with his systematically organized theological works, in particular *De sacramentis christianae fidei,* his scriptural commentaries, and the *Summa sententiarum,* which originated in his school exerted a decisive influence on the century's history of theology, even on Peter Lombard, who often followed him. In addition to the surpassing influence of the Latin patristic theology, above all that of Saint Augustine the thought of pseudo-Dionysius also carried weight with Hugh, as his commentary on the *Hierarchia coelestis* shows. Through Richard of Saint-Victor Hugh acted as a stimulus on mediaeval mysticism down to Gerson and Dionysius the Carthusian.

Together with Hugh, Abelard was celebrated by contemporary historians as one of the two *luminaria* who lectured on theology in France before audiences from the entire West. Abelard stands beside Anselm of Canterbury as the real founder of scholastic theology — not of its doctrines but of its scientific method. The very name "theology" probably came from him; previously the expressions *divina pagina* and *sacra doctrina* had been used. Through Abelard the *ratio,* schooled in dialectics, moved up beside the *auctoritas patrum,* and with him especially began the speculative penetration of the individual truths of the traditional faith, hitherto arranged in a superficial classification according to points of view.

Born at Pallet near Nantes in 1079, Abelard emerged into the light of the history of theology with his criticism of Anselm of Laon and William of Champeaux. Under the cloud of his twofold condemnation at Soissons in 1121 and at Sens in 1141, his reputation was long tarnished, despite his writings and despite praise from contemporaries, by the overpowering fame of his opponent, Saint Bernard, especially since his relationship to Héloise was of more interest to a later age than was his significance within the new theological movement of the twelfth century.

With Abelard and his school the climax is reached between patristic and scholastic theology. Especially in method, but also in content, as, for example, by stressing the essential position of the theology of the Sacraments in the total structure of the scientific study of the faith, they caused an advance which was capable of assuring the future of theology as a science, even though it was William of Auxerre (d. 1231) who first expressly posed and discussed the problem of "theology as a science."

The theology of Gilbert de la Porrée was subjected to ecclesiastical judgment at almost the same time as Abelard's was. And like him, Gilbert, who died as Bishop of Poitiers in 1154, was one of those powerful figures who founded the schools. In him speculative theology was first discernible and active in a sense proper to scholasticism. If Abelard became the dialectician of theology, Gilbert became its metaphysician. Gilbert, who came from the circle of disciples surrounding Anselm of Laon, was equally under obligation to the school of Chartres. His dialectical method, already successfully resorted to by Abelard, his *Liber sex principiorum,* which established itself as a textbook, and his theological concepts made an impact through his school into the thirteenth century.

The school of Chartres, where Gilbert taught, fostered by virtue of its Platonism a Christian humanism of encyclopedic scope, but also sought, with the aid of all secular sciences, to arrive at a deeper understanding of revelation. It belonged to the new theology, which was represented and enriched by all the great schools of the time. The fame of schools of Chartres was only diminished in the second half of the twelfth century by the growing repute of the schools of Paris.

In Paris, where Hugh of Saint-Victor had taught until 1141, originated the most famous theological work of the century: the *Four Books Sentences* of Peter Lombard. First appeared the *Summa Sententiarum,* which the theological movements of Abelard and Hugh of Saint-Victor met and united. As a brief, precise, and systematically composed treatise on all of theology, it found an extraordinarily intensive use.

With Peter Lombard (d. 1160) and his chief work, the course development of the new theology reached its culmination, in so far it called for classification, for a codification, so to speak, and for an orderly synthesis of the traditional doctrine, now theologically assimilated. Theology emerged from the spell of the biblical and patristic tradition and the unique *auctoritas* into the pungent atmosphere of the critical reason and was now opening the gate to the great *summae* of high scholasticism.

Peter Lombard, who came to Paris between 1135 and 1139, was hospitably received at Saint-Victor. In Paris he may have listened to Abelard, and he certainly knew his works. During a stay at the Curia (1148–50) he became acquainted with the theological work of John Damascene in the translation of Burgundio of Pisa. At the Council of Reims in 1148 he belonged to the group of theologians hostile to Gilbert de la Porrée. His *Four Books of Sentences* were probably completed in 1157.

It is surprising that the author of this celebrated work, differing from his more famous contemporaries was hardly named by contemporary chroniclers and historians. It may be assumed that his teaching activity did not arouse an equally lively echo. The first book of the *Sentences* treats of God and the Trinity; the second, of creation, the angels, the six days, original sin, and grace; the third, of the

Incarnation, virtues, sins, the commandments; the fourth, of the sacraments and the last things. The work displays none of the genius of Anselm, the originality of Hugh of Saint-Victor, the keenly speculative clear-sightedness of Abelard. It adopted Abelard's method but not his *theologoumena.* Because of the lucid arrangement, the rich and well ordered fulness of its texts, and the *via media* of its theological propositions, it managed, not without first having been exposed to some criticism, to establish itself universally as a textbook for theological instruction in the West and maintained itself unchallenged until the sixteenth century. It was then replaced by the *Summa theologica* of Saint Thomas Aquinas.

Before the Lombard had composed his *Sentences,* the Camaldolese Gratian compiled at Bologna his *Decretum:* the *Concordia discordantium canonum.* Finished immediately after the Second Lateran Council (1139), it appeared in the context of the new theology, for it too was characterized by a process of systematization and synthesis. With it was born the new science of canon law, which met on equal terms the new science of theology of the French schools. Like the latter, Gratian sought to master the alleged contradictions of the assembled *auctoritates* by the light of reason. He discussed, critically but with an eye to harmonization, the value of passages in the texts and drew compelling conclusions. The *Decretum* did not know a real system in the sense of the classical canon law, but rather a line of thought that was logically planned and developed.

Gratian sought to resolve disagreement among the canons. This had become a burning problem the moment that the reform papacy had established itself, Christendom had become more keenly aware of its unity than earlier, and a universally accepted juridical order appropriate to it and taking precedence over particular customs and privileges seemed to be required. Since the authority of the papacy itself seemed not yet sufficiently effective everywhere, reason, or the dialectical method, came to its aid and with the new science of the decretists created a serviceable instrument.

The *Decretum* meant a substantial beginning, but for the moment only a beginning, for Gratian's wise rules of distinctions were by no means handled consistently, even by him. But, alongside the *lacunae,* defects, and inconsistencies of the *Decretum,* contemporaries saw especially its excellences: it contained everything essential in the numerous previous collections and took the place of a library. Reason reached useful conclusions and pointed out important groups of problems. The *Decretum,* assembling all texts of the Church's first millennium in an intelligible and ordered whole, fulfilled a double function: certainty was imparted and questions still open were indicated.

The new sciences, closely related through their sources, continued in this intimacy in the next stages of their development, especially since some of their topics, such as the sacraments, overlapped. What was new in both was the dialectical method, by virtue of which a structured order could be introduced into the apparently formless mass of traditional texts and an impetus was to be expected for the further elucidation of the context of the teachings of faith, morals, and law. Thus Peter Lombard drew from Ivo of Chartres and from Gratian's *Decretum,* and he may have observed Gratian's work coming into being at Bologna. He accepted some of his own work, but at the same time he energetically rectified certain conclusions of the *Decretum.*

Section Two

The Threats to the Freedom of the Church (1153–98)

Hans Wolter

CHAPTER 8

The Popes, the Emperor Frederick I, and the Third Lateran Council

Eugene III died at Tivoli on 8 July 1153, and a whole epoch drew to a close. In this Pope from the Cistercian Order in its spectacular development, the reform papacy produced its last representative. A long succession of monks and canons regular had for a whole century guided the destinies of the Roman Church, which more and more represented the Universal Church. The heirs to the successes of this century were very clearly distinguished from their predecessors. They were a new generation, stamped by the new theology and the new science of canon law, by the mentality of a cooler rationalism and a more soberly realistic political planning. The Church and the *Patrimonium Petri,* in which, as before, they saw the decisive guarantor of the freedom of the Universal Church, they intended to govern with as much centralization as possible.

Bernard of Clairvaux died on 20 August 1153, almost at the same time as Eugene III. Seldom has a new generation made its appearance in world history so unmistakably as at this moment. Henry II began his reign in England officially on 19 December 1154, though he had been designated as King after the death of Stephen's son Eustace on 17 August 1153. Roger II of Sicily died at Palermo on 26 February 1154.

A change occurred also on the German royal throne. Eugene III lived to see the death of Conrad III on 15 February 1152; Eugene had given his approval of the election of Frederick I Barbarossa on 4 March 1152; it had actually not been sought, and Frederick had merely sent an announcement. The negotiations then ensuing between Frederick and the Curia occurred toward the close of Eugene's pontificate and terminated in the novel bilateral Treaty of Constance of 23 March 1153, which stipulated a strictly mutual cooperation between King and Pope.

Hadrian IV

Hadrian IV (1154–59), who inaugurated the new age, also came from the ranks of the canons regular — he had been provost of the famed chapter of Saint-Ruf d'Avignon —, but he guided it into paths different from those hitherto trodden. His activity was determined not by the *consideratio* called for by Bernard, the commitment of the Supreme Shepherd, derived from the depth of spiritual meditation, but rather by the awareness of the fulness of power bestowed by God, the dispassionately cool eye for the politically attainable and for the juridical claim. Ever more to the fore moved the chancellor, Roland Bandinelli, pupil of Abelard and jurist, who, by reason of his intellectual background, could not but arouse mistrust in such men of the old school as Gerhoh of Reichersberg.

Nicholas Breakspear, thus far the only Pope of English origin, had been a fellow-student and friend of John of Salisbury and, presumably, a pupil of Abelard and of Gilbert de la Porrée at Paris, as were John and Roland Bandinelli. After entering the chapter of the canons regular of Saint-Ruf d'Avignon, he rose to the position of provost. He left there, not entirely peacefully, when Eugene III made him Cardinal Bishop of Albano in 1149. His community had complained to Rome of his excessive strictness. In 1152 he was in Norway as papal legate. He there convoked and directed a large council, established the archiepiscopal see of Nidaros (Trondheim), and sought to regulate the ecclesiastical situation in the spirit of the reform movement. In the spring of 1153 he presumably went to Sweden and convoked a council to Linköping. He managed to introduce Peter's Pence in both Norway and Sweden, but in the latter kingdom he did not succeed in erecting an ecclesiastical province as he had probably planned.

Immediately after his election Hadrian IV displayed great firmness in Rome. By laying an interdict on the city shortly before Easter of 1155 he induced the Senate to expel Arnold of Brescia and his adherents. In January 1155 he had renewed with Frederick I the Treaty of Constance on behalf of himself and his successors. This step was of great importance for the Pope, since William I of Sicily, Roger II's successor, had meanwhile occupied Benevento and was beginning incursions into the Roman *campagna.* Hadrian excommunicated him.

At Sutri on 8 June 1155 occurred the first meeting of the Pope with Frederick, who was *en route* to Rome for his imperial coronation. An offer by the Romans to confer the imperial crown at the Capitol, against a payment of 5,000 pounds of gold, was rejected by Frederick, who pointed out that the *Imperium* had long since passed to the Germans. On the day of the imperial coronation, 18 June 1155, Frederick had to put down in blood a rising of the Romans. Arnold of Brescia, whose extradition Frederick had achieved, was executed on the orders of the prefect of the city. Without having aided the Pope in his quarrel with the Normans, as provided by the Treaty of Constance, the Emperor, at the request of the German princes, returned home in the late summer. He had not brought Rome back under the Pope's control, though he had turned over Tivoli, which had placed itself under the Emperor's authority, to the Pope, reserving the rights of the Empire. There was no agreement on the key ideas of the Treaty of Constance, *honor imperii* and *honor Sancti Petri* (or *papatus*), nor in regard to the Normans and their Kingdom.

In his disappointment over Frederick's premature return to Germany, Hadrian IV gave to his policy that turn which Frederick had aimed to prevent by the Treaty of Constance. In 1156 he concluded the Peace of Benevento with King William I of Sicily. In it William's royal title, which had at first been denied him, was recognized, as was his legitimate authority over Capua, Apulia, Calabria, and Sicily. Extensive rights over the Church in his territories were conceded to him, substantially as a renewal of the privilege granted to Count Roger I for Sicily by Urban II. For his part, William acknowledged the feudal suzerainty of Saint Peter and obliged himself to a considerable annual *census* of 1,000 gold pieces to the Pope for South Italy. Naples, Salerno, Amalfi, and Marsia were awarded to William as a hereditary possession. Thanks to the peace with the Normans the Pope was able, with the assistance of the prudent and energetic Cardinal *Camerlengo* Boso, to consolidate papal authority in the various *terrae Sancti Petri,* and even his return to Rome became possible in November 1156.

In order to apprise the Emperor of the Peace of Benevento the Pope then dispatched two legates, the Cardinal Chancellor Roland Bandinelli, and Bernard, Cardinal Priest of San Clemente. They were also to concern themselves with the case of the imprisoned Archbishop Eskil of Lund. While *en route* from Rome to the north, this prelate had been arrested in Imperial Burgundy and imprisoned in the expectation that he would be ransomed at a high price. Eskil, to whom Hadrian, when legate in the north, had brought the pallium and whom, when Pope, he had constituted Primate of Sweden and Legate of the North, was regarded as an enemy of the Empire, because, in his new dignities, he was in opposition to the Nordic ambitions of Hamburg-Bremen, which were supported by Frederick. These were based on old papal privileges and through them Frederick intended to assure his influence in Scandinavia. At the Diet of Besançon in October 1157 occurred the well known incident, brought on by an expression in Hadrian's letter to the Emperor, which was translated, perhaps deliberately, by Rainald of Dassel, Frederick's chancellor since 1156, as "fief." In the letter, with reference to the *beneficium* of the imperial coronation, already conferred, still further *maiora beneficia* were held out to the Emperor by the Pope, if the former should be accommodating in regard to Rome's concerns, for example, the liberation of the Archbishop of Lund and the projected visitation of the German Church by the legates. Alleging the excitement of his magnates, the Emperor sent the legates back empty-handed, but not without having thereby seriously compromised his relations with the Curia by misunderstandings and tensions.

In the manifestoes sent out by the imperial chancery concerning the events at Besançon, the "Empire consciousness" in the circle around Frederick I for the first time found expression as a program. The independence of the imperial office from the Roman Church was proclaimed: the Emperor, it was maintained, owes his crown only to the grace of God and the free choice of the princes. An appeal by the Pope to the German episcopate obtained an unexpected reply: a corroboration of the imperial view and the request that Hadrian IV would appease the Emperor by another, milder letter, for the good of the Church and of the Empire. In June 1158 the Pope had such a letter delivered to the Emperor at Augsburg by two legates. In this he stated that the term *beneficium* in the letter read at Besançon should have been translated not as "fief" but as "benefit," while the use of *conferre* in regard to the imperial crown did not mean "to confer" but "to impose." The Emperor accepted this explanation, especially since the legates were able to assure him that the Pope would continue to be concerned for the *honor imperii* and to maintain the rights of the Empire.

Just as Hadrian IV renewed his feudal relationship to the Normans and appealed to the *Constitutum Constantini* in regard to Sicily, so, according to John of Salisbury, whom he used as middleman, did he also dispose of Ireland by virtue of his authority over the western islands, investing Henry II of England with the rule of Ireland by sending him an emerald ring.

Meanwhile the Emperor, having entrusted the defense of the Empire's interests on its eastern frontiers to new princely families in order to be free to devote himself entirely to the Italian problem, preceded southward again. At the Diet of Roncaglia near Piacenza in November 1158 he again enforced the old imperial rights in the Kingdom of Lombardy, as he had had them verified by the Four Doctors of Bologna and the representatives of twenty-eight cities — that is, the crown *regalia,* which had not been claimed for decades. Milan, which had submitted on 7 September 1158, had already surrendered them. If implemented, the Roncaglia decrees would have meant, not only the restoration of the old royal authority and a loss by the cities of their freedom and autonomy, but also an excessive increase in the economic and political power of the crown. Hence Milan, Brescia, and Piacenza undertook negotiations with Hadrian IV for an alliance against the Emperor, who was now beginning to apply the Roncaglia decrees also in Tuscany and even in the north of the *Patrimonium Petri.* Hadrian allowed him a respite of forty days within which to annul these measures; otherwise he would be compelled to excommunicate the Emperor. But before the interval had expired the Pope died at Anagni on 1 September 1159.

Shortly before his death Hadrian had had his interpretation of *honor Sancti Petri* expounded to the Emperor: the Pope's authority was unrestricted over Rome and the entire *Patrimonium Petri,* where Frederick intended to occupy a position like that of Charles the Great or Otto the Great; the Roncaglia decrees were not to be applied to the Italian bishops; and the Treaty of Constance was to be renewed, especially since the Treaty of Benevento had in no way offended against the letter and the spirit of Constance. Hadrian had naturally rejected an arbitration court, suggested by the Emperor, which would discuss and clarify the opposing views of the two powers.

Hadrian's corpse was transported to Rome and interred in Saint Peter's. He had contrived to consolidate his rule in the *Patrimonium* by means of a consistent continuation of the exemption policy of his predecessors, but in the case of abbeys and chapters reserving the rights of the bishops. He had further developed the actual government of the Universal Church by the Roman Curia. In Ireland, Scotland, and Spain he had renewed the ecclesiastical bonds and brought them more firmly into connection with Rome. By means of Peter's Pence he had caused the unity of Christendom and the relationship of individual Christians, and not merely of princes and prelates, with the See of Peter to become more vivid in the awareness of the faithful. He had quite intentionally defended the jurisdictional primacy of the Roman Church, especially against Byzantium, and had been able to exercise it, despite manifold difficulties. Finally, toward the close of his pontificate he had sought, by means of an understanding between the Emperor Manuel and William I of Sicily in 1158, to erect a dam against Frederick I's Italian policy, which was preparing systematically to advance from Lombardy *via* Tuscany to the south. And just before the Pope's death the Emperor's moderate advisors had all died in 1158.

Alexander III

The double papal election of 7 September 1159 took place under the influence of the methodically pursued Italian policy of the Emperor Frederick I. The frontiers of the *Patrimonium* had already been violated, contact had been made with circles in Rome, and Otto of Wittelsbach lingered in the city during the election. The majority of the Sacred College, at least two-thirds, decided on the chancellor, Cardinal Roland Bandinelli; a minority, favorably disposed to the Emperor, preferred Cardinal Octavian of Monticello (Tivoli). Bandinelli styled himself Alexander III (1159–81), while his rival took the name Victor IV (1159–64).

Once again a judgment by the Universal Church had to decide, since there was no institutional organ qualified to clarify such cases by arbitration. If the double election of 1130 had been determined by inner ecclesiastical motives, the existence in the College of Cardinals of opposing views of the tasks and methods of Church reform, this time clearly political considerations predominated. The developments of the next years made clear that more deeply grounded basic concepts were dialectically encountered in this double election and its consequences and pressed for a settlement in severe struggles that shook the Church. As Frederick's idea of the function of the imperial office in the Christian world was largely shaped by the revived Roman law as modified by Justinian and Christianity, so did the pontificate of Alexander III seem to be determined by a canon law, developing consistently and establishing itself in practice, which was entirely able to make methodical use of Roman juristic categories. At issue was the settlement of the question: which principle of order should have the primacy in the Christian world, *auctoritas sacrata pontificum* or *regalis potestas?*

When Victor IV died at Lucca on 20 April 1164, Rainald of Dassel, without awaiting a word from the Emperor, hastened to procure the election of Cardinal Guido of Crema, who became Paschal III (1164–68).

Frederick exploited the long drawn out peace negotiations to acquire by diplomacy what his arms had denied him. In the preliminary treaty of Anagni, in the negotiations for which representatives of the Lombard League had not been consulted, he was able to conclude a separate agreement with the Pope, which was to serve as the basis for the definitive discussions by all qualified parties. This preliminary treaty stipulated that Frederick should recognize Alexander as the lawful Pope, hand over to him the *regalia* of the *Patrimonium,* restore the confiscated properties, and renounce the Mathildine lands in Tuscany. It was agreed that the Lombards, the Normans, and the Byzantines should be included in the general peace. The Pope would release Frederick from excommunication and recognize him as Emperor and his son Henry as King of the Romans. All ecclesiastical decisions made by Frederick and his bishops during the schism were to retain their validity.

The Emperor, having been absolved from excommunication, entered Venice on 24 July. The Pope awaited him before San Marco. Frederick prostrated himself, but Alexander lifted him up, gave him the kiss of peace, and blessed him, while the Germans present sang the "Te Deum." The next day the Pope celebrated Mass in San Marco and preached in the Emperor's presence. Before and afterward Frederick performed the honorary service he had once objected to at Sutri. On 1 August in the episcopal palace the Emperor took an oath to abide by the peace and the armistice. Then a cardinal proceeded to Rovigo to obtain corresponding assurances from the Empress and King Henry, both of whom had been included in the Peace of Venice.

Thus was the schism ended. All of Christendom breathed a sigh of relief. While the peace did not bring a decision in principle in regard to the relations between *Imperium* and papacy, and the Emperor came out of it practically unimpeded, still Alexander may be regarded as the winner, even though he too, in order definitely to end the schism, renounced any clarification of the disputed ideologies. He had to be less concerned with that than with the peace, which at the moment contributed more for the welfare of the Universal Church than did a formal but revocable word from the Emperor.

The Third Lateran Council

A general council had been agreed upon both in the preliminary treaty of Anagni of October-November 1176 and in the Peace of Venice of 21 July 1177. Both treaties say in identical terms:

> The Lord Pope, together with the cardinals, bishops, and other devout men [abbots], who take part, will excommunicate at the council soon to be summoned, all who seek to break this peace. The same thing will then be done at the general council.

The council first mentioned took place in San Marco at Venice on 14 August. The Emperor occupied a throne beside the Pope, who pronounced excommunication on all who should violate the peace or armistice and did not present themselves for penance within forty days. At the same time Alexander renewed the excommunication of all who still adhered to the schism. When the torches were cast on the ground and extinguished, the Emperor, with the rest, cried aloud: "Fiat, fiat."

Archbishop Christian of Mainz conducted the Pope back to the *Patrimonium*. Alexander received a delegation of Romans at Anagni and was able to entrust to Christian's care the conditions for the return to Rome. The city's autonomy, a result of the revolution of 1143, was maintained, but the senators had to take an oath of fealty to the Pope, restore the *regalia*, and guarantee the safety of the Pope and of the pilgrims. *Via* Tusculum Alexander at length reentered his city on

12 March 1178. He had not hurried. The Romans were apparently enthusiastic, but Alexander had no confidence in them. He soon returned to Tusculum.

The Emperor had already made his way back to Germany in September 1177 and held aloof from the stipulated general council. The Curia's preparations for it began with the return to the *Patrimonium*. In the autumn of 1178 several legates visited the European states in order to invite bishops and abbots to the council, which was to meet in the Lateran. The overall political situation was not unfavorable. Louis VII and Henry II had concluded peace at Nonancourt on 25 September 1177, shortly after the peace between Emperor and Pope. Baldwin IV was still reigning in Jerusalem, and seven bishops and a delegation of Templars and Hospitallers were *en route* to Rome. Sicily authorized its prelates to attend the council, while Henry II granted permission to the Irish and to six English bishops.

The Pope opened the council on 5 March 1179. The inaugural address was delivered by the Bishop of Assisi, Magister Rufinus, one of the leading canonists of the age. Present were some 300 bishops from Italy, Germany, and Burgundy, from France, Spain, England and Ireland, from Sicily and the crusader states, even from Denmark and Hungary. Among them was John of Salisbury, now Bishop of Chartres. From Germany had come the Bishops of Mainz, Bamberg, Augsburg, Constance, Worms, Speyer, Chur, Salzburg, Regensburg, Passau, Trier, Metz, Liège, Zeitz, Meissen, Brandenburg, Hamburg-Bremen, and Schwerin — an impressive witness to the peace. Cologne, Magdeburg, and the Westphalian sees were not represented because the troubles between the Emperor and Henry the Lion kept them at home. Nectarius of Casula arrived as envoy of the Byzantine Church. Also present was a group of Waldensians from Lyons. If note is taken also of the uncounted abbots, priors, scholars, and attendants of bishops, it was an impressive gathering, a real representation of the Universal Church, before which, in his opening discourse Rufinus of Assisi developed the principles underlying the primacy of the Roman Church and extolled the personality and work of Alexander III.

Unfortunately, no real conciliar acts have been preserved. The formulation, the lucid and carefully chosen language of the extant decrees, is thought, probably correctly, to betray the hand of the jurist Pope. The diversity of their contents reflects the aim of evaluating the great events and decisions of the pontificate and having them ratified by the Universal Church. The measures agreed to in Anagni and Venice for the liquidation of the schism were confirmed. Canon 1, which regulated the papal election, was important and of permanent validity. Clearly inspired by the experience of 1159, it demanded a two-thirds majority for validity. At the same time the distinction insisted on in 1059 between bishops and non-bishops in the College of Cardinals was tacitly set aside and the election was restricted to the College exclusively, for neither the rest of the clergy nor the people was mentioned. Canons 3 and 8 became the bases on which was developed the right of devolution: if a benefice was not filled within six months, the right to fill it passed to the concurrent or next highest tribunal.

Decrees still had to be issued against simony and on celibacy (canons 7, 10, 15). Thus a century had not been long enough for correcting abuses, nor, as is well known, would the succeeding centuries suffice. Canon 18 promised exemption from fees for instruction, and Canon 25 forbade usury and traffic in war materials with infidels. Canons 24 and 25 regulated social relations of Christians with Jews or

Muslims. The last canon dealt with heresy — the prelude to the trying episode now beginning, which was to find its climax in the Albigensian wars of later pontificates. Canon 27 was in effect the charter of the crusade against heretics: the privileges hitherto intended for crusaders, the indulgences, the papal privileges accorded to them and their possessions were from now on granted to those who made themselves available for the armed struggle against heresy.

Alexander received the Waldensians who were present sympathetically and graciously, and praised their voluntary poverty, but he did not grant them permission to preach. The competent bishops were to decide this question. But the very first attempt at Lyons failed, since the Archbishop rejected the request and thus drove the Waldensians into opposition.

Like the case of the Waldensians, still other problems occupied the Council without being mentioned in the canons: for example, the reconciliation of schismatic bishops. The Council's measures in regard to the papal election, the right of devolution, the prosecution of heretics, and the care of lepers were of permanent validity.

CHAPTER 9

Thomas Becket and Henry II of England

In the Angevin Kingdom of England a confrontation between King Henry II and the Primate Thomas Becket, Archbishop of Canterbury, ran its course between 1162 and 1170. In many ways intertwined with the eighteen-year struggle between Alexander III and Frederick I, in certain of its moments of crisis it cannot be fully understood apart from that contest. The English struggle concerned the threat to that liberty of the Church that had been firmly established since the confusion of 1135–52 over the succession to Henry I. Especially at issue were episcopal elections, communication with Rome, and ecclesiastical courts. Because of its dramatic *dénouement* and the powerfully drawn personalities who figured in it, this struggle occupied the field of vision of contemporary observers even more than did the turning-points of the schism.

On the one side was a saint, who was likewise a man of brilliant intellect, a skillful diplomat, a reliable administrator, and a socially sensitive prelate, rising from the new social strata of an urban and mercantile self-consciousness, formed in the schools of the new theology and of the just then developing science of canon law, representative of all that was striving to establish itself in the world and in the Church.

On the other side was a still young King, the husband of the most important and best known lady of the epoch, Eleanor, former wife of the French King. Of a none too praiseworthy repute because of the Second Crusade, she had brought Aquitaine along when she married the future English monarch. Henry II (1154–89) was a son of the Empress Matilda, widow of Henry V, by her second marriage with Count Geoffrey of Anjou. Immediately after his accession to the throne in 1154 he had begun to restore the rights and claims of the crown which had been usurped during the anarchy. Among these was control of the English bishoprics and abbeys because of their importance in the feudal social and political constitution of the Kingdom. His guiding idea was to recover the position occupied by Henry I in Church and state, if not to win back the authority once exercised by William the Conqueror.

From 1155 Henry II had at his side as chancellor the archdeacon of Canterbury, Thomas Becket. Born in London in 1108, Thomas had been educated by Robert of Merton, then in France by Robert of Melun, a pupil of Abelard, and at Bologna. Archbishop Theobald had made him archdeacon when that position became vacant by the election of Roger de Pont-l'Évêque as Archbishop of York. Theobald died on 18 April 1161, whereupon Henry saw to it that his chancellor Thomas was chosen Metropolitan and Primate of the English Church in a canonically proper election on 27 May 1162.

The Archbishop

As chancellor Thomas Becket had been a friend of the King. But he had carefully represented the interests of the Church and had exerted himself with Henry in favor of Alexander III. But from his consecration Thomas seemed to be another man. Prayer, study, and spiritual discussions with his cultured and reform-minded clerics filled his days. He resigned the chancellorship and sent the seals back to the King at the end of 1162. People praised his grand-scale hospitality and his solicitude for the poor. He also practiced strict mortifications, the forms of which were in some cases discovered only after his death, such as the wearing of a hairshirt and self-flagellation. The Archbishop took his new position seriously and wanted to be only priest, bishop, pastor, theologian. Neither contemporaries nor later research has been unanimous in judging his career; to some it seemed to be a mere change of role, to others a genuine *conversio.*

The King, appealing to the customary law and to precedents in the common law, intended to restore the crown's authority in the English Church, to limit ecclesiastical jurisdiction and keep it in check and probably to subordinate it eventually to the royal justice and to keep royal control over appeals to the Curia.

The Archbishop, on the contrary, did not hesitate to stand up for rights and liberties of the Church hitherto acquired or won under King Stephen and to afford greater scope for the canon law that had been entering England since the appearance of Gratian's *Decretum* around 1140. But just as the reviving canon law was of great significance for the Archbishop, so too did the reviving Roman law play a great role for the King, following the example of the Emperor Frederick I, even though outwardly there was mention only of the restoration of the customs of the Kingdom. A confrontation was inevitable and it had to be all the sharper and more dramatic since both men, King and Archbishop, regarded themselves as representatives of the good and valid law, and both, for the sake of the highest goals, were prepared to make use of high intelligence, diplomatic skill, a will that expressed itself vigorously and even tempestuously, and at the same time all the intellectual, material, and personal helps which state or Church put at their disposal.

The Constitutions of Clarendon

Immediately after entering upon his office, Thomas asked for and obtained the pallium from Alexander III, who was staying at Montpellier. Along with his suffragans he was able to take part, with the King's permission, in the Council of Tours in 1163, which again strengthened Alexander's case and deepened in Thomas the awareness that the interests of the Roman Church and of the Church of Canterbury were identical. To be sure, the Council of Tours made clear the irreconcilable opposition between Canterbury and York in the question of the primacy in England. Archbishop Roger was to remain on the King's side to the last, an opponent of Thomas Becket.

The conflict with the crown began with measures of the King which limited ecclesiastical jurisdiction over clerics. At a council at Westminster on 1 October 1163 Henry complained of the increase in the number of crimes committed by clerics and the leniency of the spiritual courts. In February 1162 he had had the old customary law, again enforced for Normandy. Something analogous was to have happened at Westminster but the attempt was shattered on the united opposition of the episcopate under the leadership of the Archbishop of Canterbury.

Henry II summoned the royal council to meet at the end of January 1164 at Clarendon, and here the bishops were to express themselves on the renewal of the English customary law from the time of Henry I. After long discussions Thomas was able finally to induce the episcopate to agree, and he himself gave his consent orally. But when the King intended to have the written codification of the customs signed and sealed by the bishops, Thomas was alone in his refusal. For he was able tacitly to allow or dissimulate much in practice, just as the Curia was accustomed to do, but not to approve by signature and seal measures which clearly violated the prevailing canon law.

The sixteen articles of the Constitutions of Clarendon, different as were the particular points treated, aimed as a whole at nullifying the growing independence of the English Church from the crown. The feudal dependence of the episcopate was emphasized, episcopal elections were to take place under royal control, bishops-elect were to take the oath of fealty before being consecrated, bishops' rights of disposal of Church property were restricted, they were bound by the same services to the crown as were the secular vassals. Ecclesiastical courts had to accommodate themselves to the judicial procedures of the secular courts and their competence was considerably restricted, while that of the secular courts was extended to matters of debt, perjury, disputes over benefices, questions of patronage, and the criminal and civil cases of clerics. Bishops' power of excommunication were curtailed in regard to the crown's tenants-in-chief and members of the royal household and of the courts. Every appeal from English courts to the

Curia was subject to the King's examination and consent, as were also journeys by bishops to the Curia or to councils. None of this was new in regard to details, but here it was juridically formulated for the first time and made a law with the written assent of the episcopate.

Appealing to the canonical principles expressed in Gratian's *Decretum,* Thomas Becket protested this diminution of ecclesiastical jurisdiction and of episcopal liberties. In the Constitutions of Clarendon he feared a complete feudalization of the English Church, which was exposed to the danger of gradually losing both of its essential privileges —*privilegium fori* and *privilegium canonis,* — of being excluded from the jurisdictional sphere of the Universal Church, and of experiencing a lessening of its ties with its faith and its head.

Disenchanted with his chancellor, who as Archbishop first gave up the chancellorship and then rejected the King's policy of a restoration of the royal authority, Henry in October 1164 cited him before the council at Northampton on the basis of Article 9 of the Constitutions of Clarendon. The Archbishop did not accept the judgment but appealed to the Pope and thereby placed himself and his church under the protection of the Holy See. The episcopate held itself aloof. Protected by the people, who had long been grateful for the social welfare provided by the chancellor and Archbishop, Thomas left the royal castle of Northampton. The devotion of the canons regular of Sempringham enabled him to flee to the coast during the night following the judgment and then to France, where he was to spend six years.

Exile and Reconciliation

The fleeing Primate of England obtained a place of refuge from King Louis VII. Then at Sens he explained his case to Pope Alexander III and the cardinals and read to them the Constitutions of Clarendon; the Pope condemned nearly two-thirds of the articles: numbers 1, 3, 4, 5, 8, 9, 10, 12, 15. The Pope also absolved him from the oral promise he had earlier made to observe them. He refused the Archbishop's offer to resign his office, confirmed him in it, and at the same time recognized the primatial status of Canterbury.

Thomas took up residence in the Cistercian abbey of Pontigny near Auxerre, not far from Sens. He stayed there from the end of November 1164 to November 1166. Wearing the Cistercian habit, he devoted himself to prayer and to the study of theology and canon law. Meanwhile Henry II confiscated the ecclesiastical property of Canterbury and expelled from the Kingdom the Archbishop's family and the clerics who remained loyal to him, together with their relatives. Efforts at mediation came to nothing, even when undertaken by the Empress Matilda, the Pope, and King Louis VII (at Easter 1166). Before returning to Italy Alexander III solemnly annulled the judgment of Northampton.

Since in 1165–66 there occurred a *rapprochement* on Henry's part to the imperial policy of Frederick I and at Würzburg in 1165 English envoys signed the proclamation of intransigence in regard to Alexander, it was not to be expected that the Angevin would give in. The English episcopate, it is true, declined for its part to honor these signatures, but the King was satisfied with the pressure on Alexander that was made possible by his friendship with Frederick. He demanded that the Pope either depose Thomas or assign him another see. In spite of several compromises with the English King that depended on trivial circumstances, Alexander in the end upheld the Archbishop, confirmed him as Primate on 5–8 April 1166, and on 24 April 1166 even named him legate in England, a post he had refused to Roger of York, despite the King's intervention. But in order to accommodate Henry, he made Roger legate in Scotland and removed the province of York from the territory subject to the legate in England.

At Vézelay on Pentecost 1166, Thomas as legate solemnly excommunicated the King's councillors and officials, but not Henry himself. He thereby laid claim to a right which was denied him by the Constitutions of Clarendon. Henry's answer was to bring pressure to bear on the general chapter of the Cistercians, threatening to expel all members of the order from England if Thomas continued to obtain hospitality at Pontigny. The Archbishop left Pontigny and spent the remaining years of exile with the Benedictines of Sainte-Colombe de Sens. There followed the most varied negotiations, conducted by papal legates especially designated for this purpose, with Henry II; in these were at times reflected the complexities of Alexander's political situation *vis-à-vis* the threatening enterprises of Frederick I.

From the beginning of 1170 Henry completely isolated England from the continent and especially from the Curia. The Constitutions of Clarendon were strictly enforced. The coronation of Henry the Younger was prepared. In defiance of the prohibition obtained from the Pope by Thomas, the Archbishop of York crowned the Prince on 14 June at Saint Peter's, Westminster. It was an intentional affront by the King in the face of repeated prohibitions by the Pope, just recently renewed, and of the rights of the ancient metropolitan see of Canterbury. Henry, who now had to fear that Thomas would make use of his right to lay an interdict on England or other parts of the Angevin realm proceeded to the continent for a personal discussion with the Archbishop, at Fréteval-en-Dunois in the Orléanais on 22 July 1170. He assured the Primate peace, safety, the return of the church and the property of Canterbury, as these last were at the time of the rupture; he promised the restoration of all the rights of the primatial see and a repetition of the coronation by Thomas. They parted, seemingly reconciled. But the King had not given sureties, and the fulfilling of the various promises seemed almost hopeless, especially since the bishops from the time of the coronation were risking everything to prevent a reinstatement of the Archbishop. Before his return to England Thomas had himself provided by the Pope with the widest powers, but he excommunicated the bishops even before setting out on his journey, for he had to reckon with the possible confiscation of his papers by the officials when he landed.

His return to Canterbury in December 1170 was a profound satisfaction for the Archbishop, especially as it was celebrated by the people as a triumph. Only complications proceeded from the King and the bishops. The bishops appealed to the Pope against their excommunication and declined to make an oath of obedience to their Metropolitan and Primate. The Archbishop was forbidden to visit the young King at Winchester and was commanded to stay within the limits of his own bishopric and to keep silent about personal insults offered by royal officials and attendants. Furthermore, the excommunicated prelates proceeded at once to Henry II in Normandy. Irritated by the excommunication of these bishops, which he had not anticipated, Henry impetuously expressed his mind: "Isn't there anyone to deliver me from this hateful priest?"

Murder in the Cathedral

Four knights of the King's entourage, with a few armed men, forced their way into the episcopal residence, always open to guests and the poor, on the afternoon of 29 December 1170. They found the Archbishop in conversation with his clerics and began a long dispute with him, blaming him for having excommunicated members of the royal court without previous consultation with the King. At the hour of Vespers the Archbishop's attendants urged him to go to the cathedral, where the monks were just assembling. The Archbishop refused to have the gates barricaded behind him. The knights had departed to get their weapons. After the Archbishop and his retinue had reached the north transept, where a huge pillar upheld a gallery and there stood an altar dedicated to Saint Benedict, the knights sought to drive the prelate and his entourage out of the church. His back to the pillar, Thomas replied to the demand that he absolve the bishops from censure: "I can absolve them only when they have made satisfaction." "Then," said the four, "receive the death you deserve." "I am ready to die for my God, if thereby liberty and peace are restored to the Church." They then killed him amid the glow of torches. The assassins plundered his residence and departed late that night. Only then did the monks and clerics venture forth to bury the remains of the martyr in a marble coffin in the crypt before the altar of Saint John the Baptist and Saint Augustine, Apostle of the English. The blood was carefully collected.

The Sequel to the Martyrdom

Christendom very quickly learned of what had happened at Canterbury, and everywhere people were shocked. Responsibility for the murder was assigned to the English King, the Archbishop of York, and Gilbert Foliot, Bishop of London. On 25 January 1171 the Archbishop of Sens, as papal legate, laid an interdict on the continental lands of Henry II. The King, personally shaken by the consequences of his angry words, sent to Rome a delegation which was able to prevent the laying of an interdict on England but could not stop the Pope from excommunicating on Holy Thursday all who had contributed directly or indirectly to the murder. Alexander confirmed the sentence issued by the Archbishop of Sens and punished Henry with a personal interdict; only legates who should be expressly named would be able to release him from it. The King set out on his expedition to Ireland; he was able to conquer part of the island and was hailed as King by its subkings.

Meanwhile, negotiations were taking place with the Curia in regard to the reparation to be made by the King because of Thomas' murder. He had had the expedition to Ireland declared to be a crusade, an undertaking which would subject the Irish Church to the Holy See. After his return in the spring of 1172 he met the papal legates in Normandy. On 21 May Henry and the accused bishops purged themselves with an oath that they had neither commanded nor desired the death of the Archbishop of Canterbury. Henry further swore that he would hold 200 knights in readiness for a year for the defense of the Holy Land, that at Christmas of 1172 he would take the cross for three years and personally set out on the crusade the following summer, and that in any event he would keep himself at the disposal of the Pope. If a journey to Jerusalem should be impossible, he would carry out his vow in Spain against the Muslims. He would permit appeals to Rome in cases before ecclesiastical courts. He would disavow customs hurtful to the Church as these had been enforced under his authority. He would restore to the Church of Canterbury all its property. And finally he would receive in peace all clerics and lay persons who had remained loyal to Thomas and give back their possessions.

After Henry and his son had sworn to these promises he was absolved and reconciled with the Church. The promises of Avranches were confirmed by Alexander III in a bull of 2 September and ratified on 27 September by Henry at Saint-André. The Constitutions of Clarendon were not disavowed in their entirety, but appeals to Rome were allowed, and this was of the greatest importance. For the papal decretals that were issued for England from now on in great numbers laid the basis of an English canon law within the framework of the development in the Universal Church.

The grave of the murdered Archbishop very soon became the goal of the greatest pilgrimage movement of the High and the Late Middle Ages. Alexander III solemnly canonized Thomas Becket on 21 February 1173. King Henry himself made a pilgrimage to Canterbury in July 1174 and again did penance for his share in the saint's death. At his wish the Pope sent Hugh Pierleoni to England as Cardinal-Legate. He was not only able to arrange the filling of the many vacant sees but also reached a compromise with the King in regard to the disputed ecclesiastical jurisdiction. Only questions concerning clerics' fiefs and violations of the forest laws by clerics were for the future to be handled by a secular judge. The total result of the long conflict should not be estimated as meager. The Archbishop did not die in vain.

Chapter 10

The Heritage of Alexander III

The Peace of Venice was only a truce, made possible by a compromise. The German Church remained in the hands of the Emperor, who continued to exploit the *ius spolii* and placed the *regalia* at the service of the Empire. Alexander's legates let matters take their course. The Pope himself mediated between Frederick and the Lombard League. The League disintegrated, and such recent enemies as Milan and Alessandria allied with the Emperor. Alexander loyally observed the stipulations of the peace until his death, but he left behind as open questions the unclarified juridical and political situation of the Mathildine lands, the validity of the schismatic ordinations in Germany and Italy, and the relations of the Holy See with the Roman commune. In flight from rebellious Viterbo, he died at Cività Castellana. Nevertheless, his heritage did not consist merely of unsolved difficulties. Thanks to the tenacious struggle at the time of the schism and his consistently pursued government of the Universal Church, despite his always disputed legitimacy, it also meant the establishment of the prestige of Roman legal decisions in Christendom and the recognition of the Roman See as the supreme judge and legislator. At the same time the competence of this highest jurisdiction had been enlarged, and appeals from all countries to the Holy See had increased.

The Cardinal Bishop Ubaldo Allucingoli of Ostia was elected Alexander's successor on 1 September 1181 and styled himself Lucius III (1181–85). An old and prudent Cistercian, as a friend of Bernard of Clairvaux he was identified with the reform ideas of that saint's age. In November 1181 he arrived in Rome, where a college of twenty-five senators had control of the government. He was received cooly and remained only five months. A conflict erupted in regard to Tusculum, which the Romans wanted either to subjugate to their own rule or to destroy. Lucius appealed for aid to Archbishop Christian of Mainz, who was always close at hand. But in September 1183 he lost this helper, who ever since the Peace of Venice had loyally looked after the interests of the papacy in the *Patrimonium* and against the Roman commune. The warrior prelate succumbed to a fever before Tusculum. The Curia moved northward, for a meeting with the Emperor Frederick I had been arranged in Verona.

The Emperor had made peace with the Lombards at Constance in 1183 and, since it was important to him to settle with Alexander's successor the questions left open at Venice, he showed himself to be accommodating. Lucius III waited at Verona from 22 July 1184. The Emperor did not arrive until the end of September, after having spent some time at Milan, his new ally. The Pope profited by the presence of Heraclius, Patriarch of Jerusalem, and of the grand masters of the military orders, who, as envoys of King Baldwin IV, candidly expounded the situation of the Holy Land, to urge a crusade on the Emperor. Frederick assured him that the preparations would get under way by Christmas of that year. A uniform procedure by *regnum* and *sacerdotium* was also planned at Verona for the struggle against heretical movements, which were spreading ever more powerfully and becoming more threatening. In the decretal "Ad abolendam" of 4 November 1184 was found the classical formula, according to which the Church was to institute proceedings against heretics and, if the occasion arose, to condemn them, leaving or recommending the carrying out of the judgment and of the penalty to the secular arm. An imperial edict, whose text is not extant, corresponded to the papal decree. This papal-imperial decision has been called the charter of the Inquisition.

Following the Emperor's departure from Verona the discussions between the two courts continued. But Lucius III died on 25 November 1185, without having reached any final decisions. On the very same day the cardinals elected Archbishop Uberto Crivelli of Milan, an avowed opponent of the Emperor, thereby making clear how little they agreed with Frederick's new course. He called himself Urban III (1185–87), and as Pope did not resign his archbishopric in order not to allow the *regalia* to accrue to the Empire during a vacancy. The Pope kept aloof from the Hohenstaufen-Hauteville marriage at Milan, and Henry was crowned King of Italy by the Patriarch of Aquileia. There is no doubt that this was intended as an affront to the Pope, who reacted by consecrating the anti-imperial Folmar for the see of Trier on 1 June 1186. A break between Pope and Emperor seemed inevitable. Frederick ordered his son to occupy the *Patrimonium* and so to isolate the Pope and Curia at Verona as to prevent any contact with the Church. At the Diet of Gelnhausen in November 1186 the Emperor also succeeded in paralyzing the opposition around Philip of Cologne and of isolating the Archbishop. The German episcopate was again united behind the throne.

The brief pontificate of Gregory VIII (21 October–17 December 1187) was entirely preoccupied with preparations for the crusade. As Cardinal Chancellor, Albert de Morra had founded a congregation of canons regular of an austere observance in his native city of Benevento, and, like his predecessor Lucius III, he belonged to the group representing the Bernardine reform. In accord with its leading idea, he intended to work for a renewal of the Curia, but his early death saved him from failure and disappointment. Just the same, he had been able at least to put an end to Urban III's intransigent policy toward the Empire.

In view of the organizing of the crusade, then getting under way, the election of the new Pope could fall only on a conciliatory personality, in view of the fact that the Emperor Frederick himself was to be the most important leader. The Cardinal Bishop Paul Scolari, who became Clement III (1187–91), was a Roman by birth and related to several influential families of the Eternal City. He contrived to find a compromise between the Curia and the city, while a definitive peace with the Empire was also achieved. The Trier dispute was ended when the two rivals, Folmar and Rudolf, were discarded to make way for the Imperial Chancellor John.

Clement had to negotiate for quite some time with the Romans before the treaty of 31 May 1188 could be signed. With a considerable financial output and the loss of rights the Curia purchased a peace which still remained precarious and could be assured only by unending new payments.

In the Treaty of Strasbourg of April 1189 the Empire restored the *Patrimonium* to the Pope, reserving the *honor imperii,* and in return Clement held out the prospect of the imperial crown for King Henry. Again the Mathildine lands remained in the hands of the Emperor, who, however, dispensed with an express recognition of his proprietorship. In order to prepare for and carry out the crusade Clement put up with all the disadvantages of these treaties.

William II of Sicily died childless on 18 November 1189. His legitimate heir was Queen Constance, wife of Frederick's son Henry, who had just assumed the regency of the Empire for the absent Emperor.

Shortly before his death William had taken the vassal's oath to the Pope for Sicily. Would Henry, soon to succeed his father as ruler of the *Sacrum Imperium,* be prepared to do the same? The Sicilian magnates proclaimed as King a bastard cousin of William, Count Tancred of Lecce. The Archbishop of Palermo crowned him with Clement's consent.

Henry was determined to take possession of his wife's entire inheritance. Through the mediation of the Archbishop of Mainz he was reconciled with Henry the Lion at Fulda in July 1190 and, a companied by the Duke of Saxony, set out for Italy. But the news of his father's death in Asia Minor produced a delay and it was only in January 1191 that he entered Lombardy. Meanwhile, the presence in Messina of the Kings of France and England, who had set up winter quarters there *en route* to Palestine, so strengthened Tancred's position that in April he crossed to Apulia and began to conquer this part of the Norman Kingdom also in order to be armed for his confrontation with Henry.

Clement III died at the end of March 1191, and his successor could not avoid the fateful decisions following from the proximity of Henry, who was on his way to Rome for the imperial crown and was already at Anguillara. The aged Cardinal Hyacinth Bobone, an eighty-five-year-old curial prelate, who had belonged to the College of Cardinals for forty-seven years, was elected; he assumed the name of Celestine III (1191–98). A pupil of Abelard's, he had been critical of Bernard of Clairvaux. He had been the Curia's successful diplomat in embassies of reconciliation, notably that to Frederick I for settling the misunderstandings of Besançon and that to Henry II after the murder of Thomas Becket, and he had remained loyal to Alexander III during the schism. And so, despite his advanced age, he seemed to be the right man for a conciliatory policy toward the harsh new ruler of the Empire, who was consistently pursuing his father's Italian projects.

After some initial hesitations Celestine III gave Henry VI the imperial crown on Easter Sunday, 14 April 1191. He advised him not to continue southward, where the attempt to overthrow Tancred foundered before Naples, while Salerno even delivered the Empress Constance as a prisoner to Tancred. At the end of 1191 Henry had to return to Germany empty-handed. Celestine decided to recognize Tancred. He invested him with the Kingdom of Sicily and in June 1192 concluded with him the Concordat of Gravina, that was favorable to the Curia.

Back in Germany, the Emperor Henry was asked for a decision in the disputed election to the see of Liège. He rejected both claimants and in January 1192 gave the bishopric to Lothar of Hochstaden. Albert of Brabant, the choice of the majority of the chapter, proceeded to the Curia, and Celestine III confirmed his election. Since Albert was prevented from setting foot in the diocese of Liège, he had himself consecrated by the Archbishop of Reims and placed himself under his protection. At Reims he was assassinated by *ministeriales* of Liège. The blame was universally attributed to the Emperor, who took an oath of purgation but let off the assassins with a reprimand. Hence, suspicion was not allayed and the Rhenish episcopate united with some of the secular princes in opposition to the Emperor. Contact was also established with England, Sicily, and the Curia. Henry had himself been allied with King Philip II of France since the fall of 1191; they had met at Milan, when the French King was returning from the crusade. The Emperor's critical situation was corrected when Duke Leopold V of Austria delivered to him the English King, whom he had taken prisoner near Vienna. Richard, who thus had to pay dearly for his tactlessness in Syria, could purchase his freedom only by promising a huge ransom and agreeing to accept England as a fief of the Empire. And the episcopal and princely opposition in the Rhineland lost its decisive support.

The vast amount of money by which Richard obtained his liberty now enabled the Emperor to resume the conquest of Sicily. Tancred had died on 20 February 1194, and his wife Sibyl had assumed the regency for her minor-aged son,

William III; hence no serious opposition was to be expected. Henry set out from Trifels for Italy in May 1194 and as early as Christmas of the same year he could be crowned King at Palermo.

Contact with the Curia had been interrupted since the recognition of Tancred and the confirmation of Albert of Brabant as Bishop of Liège by Celestine III. In an effort to renew it, Henry VI offered to launch a well organized crusade. At the Curia it was clearly perceived that this crusade would at the same time further the Emperor's far-reaching Mediterranean projects of empire. Leo of Armenia and Amauri of Cyprus had already received their crowns as vassals of the Emperor. Hence Celestine was hesitant to enter into Henry's plan, though to reject it entirely was, of course, outside the realm of the possible. He had the crusade preached in England, Bohemia, Denmark, Poland, and Spain, thereby in a sense involving all of Christendom and eliminating the political thorn from the Emperor's crusade.

Henry's negotiations with the Curia also included his plan to have the Empire now recognized as an hereditary monarchy. He had offered the German princes extensive privileges, especially the heritability of the great fiefs, and he may have proposed to the Curia that the Empire as a whole be held as a fief of the Holy See. Protracted negotiations enabled Celestine to evade any decision on so tricky a question. Meanwhile there broke out in Sicily serious disturbances, which the Emperor succeeded in harshly suppressing in the summer of 1197. But on 6 August, before he was able to join his crusade, he fell mortally ill. During his sickness he is said to have drawn up his last will. According to this document, Sicily was to be acknowledged as a fief of the Roman Church, and Constance and Frederick were to take the oath of vassalage to the Pope. If the dynasty should become extinct, the Kingdom should escheat to the Pope.

The Emperor died at Messina on 26 September 1197 and was buried in the cathedral of Palermo. A few months later, on 8 January 1198, Celestine III followed him to the grave.

In particular Celestine's "inner pontificate" merits notice. The Pope, all along an administrator rather than a politician or one endowed with charisms, possessed an outstanding coworker in Cardinal Cencio Savelli, who, thanks to the influence of the future Celestine III, had been made *camerlengo* of the Roman Church under Clement III. Under Celestine the *camerlengo's* office increased in importance, since no chancellor was appointed. To introduce order into the Church's finances, which had suffered greatly ever since the schism and the uneasy pontificates that followed, Cencio drew up a comprehensive property register of the Roman Church, such as had been long before introduced in cities, monasteries, and principalities. This *Liber censuum* became an official survey and record of all spiritual institutions — sees, abbeys, chapters — and secular lordships that were dependent on the Roman Church and owed *census* to her. It was finished in 1192 and was of amazing, though not of complete, accuracy — out of 682 actually existing dependents Cencio was able to include all but 154. Moreover, the Cardinal *Camerlengo* succeeded not only in ordering the Curia's finances but also in actually increasing them.

As in previous pontificates, legal cases streamed from all of Christendom to Rome under Celestine III, especially since he solemnly declared that anyone who felt that he was threatened by others could and should seek justice at Rome.

Thus Celestine made the Curia the central office for all final legal decisions in the Church, placed the written law ahead of customary law, made his judgments up-to-date, and especially exercised control over their execution. More than previously, the papal jurisdiction was exercised by judges delegate, so that the Curia's routine became less burdensome and the way was made ready for central legislation. Chancery and *Camera* obtained their stable organization, and the importance of the College of Cardinals and its share in the government of the Universal Church grew.

CHAPTER 11

The Third Crusade

The Third Lateran Council, in contrast to the other general synods of the twelfth and thirteenth centuries, referred only indirectly to Christendom's responsibility for the crusade. Six bishops and two abbots from the crusader states had taken part in it, but not even Archbishop William of Tyre, the most distinguished among them, intimates that the Council concerned itself in any detail with the situation of the Kingdom of Jerusalem. William, chancellor of the leprous King Baldwin IV (1174–85), knew only too well the crisis produced by the energetic advance of Saladin (1171 to 1193). Propagandizing in Sicily, France, and England was not neglected. Alexander III's successors, likewise with an eye on the crusade, sought a comprehensive policy of peace in the West: between Curia and Empire, between Curia and Rome, and between kings and princes, above all between England and France. Louis VII of France had died in 1180, and his successor, Philip II, had begun his energetic reign.

But only the catastrophe of the battle of Hattin in Galilee and Saladin's capture of and entry into Jerusalem in 1187 were of a nature to shock the West so violently that the emotional presuppositions for a general European crusade were again present. The papacy once more undertook the duty of preaching the crusade but declined the actual leadership of the expedition, which was to lie in the hands of three monarchs: the Emperor and the Kings of England and France.

The Cistercian Cardinal Henry of Albano, who was accompanied by Archbishop Josias of Tyre, set to work with special zeal. He contrived to bring about the English-French armistice of Gisors of 21 January 1188, on which occasion both Kings took the cross under pressure from public opinion. At Cologne he succeeded in reconciling Archbishop Philip with the Emperor Frederick I. At the "Diet of Jesus Christ" at Mainz on Laetare Sunday, where the legate and Godfrey I of Helfenstein, Bishop of Würzburg, preached, the Emperor, his oldest son and namesake, who was Duke of Swabia, and numerous princes took the cross. The expedition was to set out in the spring of 1189, and the liberation of the Holy Sepulchre was to crown the Emperor's life work. A crusade tax, the Saladin Tithe, was raised for the first time in France and England. Scotland contributed nothing, for King William the Lion was unable to persuade his thrifty barons. The German expedition was financed by the participants. Clement III demanded a money contribution from members of the higher clergy, but the amount was not specified. This measure foreshadowed a development which in the next century led to the financing of crusades almost entirely by means of taxation of ecclesiastical incomes.

Crusade preaching was supplemented by literary propaganda, notably the crusade song in both courtly and popular form. The parish clergy even recruited with the aid of vivid pictures representing scenes from the Holy Land and the struggle with the Muslims in order to stimulate participation by the illiterate.

The German expedition got under way at Regensburg on 11 May 1189. It unquestionably supplied the mightiest fighting force and was praised by contemporaries for its good discipline and its careful preparation. Meanwhile, King William II of Sicily had dispatched the first assistance, thereby helping to save the cities of Tyre and Tripolis, but he died on 18 November 1189. English crusaders, in advance of the royal expedition, and Flemings and Danes went by sea. While the Emperor Frederick was moving through Hungary and the Balkans, the English and the French enterprises had bogged down because of the recent renewal of the struggle between the two Kings; it ended only two days before Henry II's death with a peace that was deeply humiliating to the English King, since his sons Richard and John were aligned with his French opponent. The Emperor Frederick wintered in the vicinity of Constantinople. The march across the interior made slow progress. After the Cilician foothills had finally been crossed and Cilician Armenia had been reached, the Emperor met his death in the river Saleph on 10 June 1190. Saladin could rightly see in this tragedy his own salvation. The dead Emperor's son, Duke Frederick of Swabia, was unable to hold the army together. A part of it returned home, others went on by ship; he led the remnant to Antioch, where on 21 June 1190 he fell sick and died. The Emperor's remains were interred at Antioch.

King Richard I Lionheart of England assumed his father's obligation to the crusade. The English and French hosts met at Vézelay on 4 July 1190 and decided to go to Syria by sea. The armies wintered on Sicily at Messina, where an English crusade fleet had turned up. *En route* to the Holy Land, King Richard managed to conquer the island of Cyprus, to which the political center of gravity of the crusader states was later to be transferred.

First of all, the English-French expedition on 13 July 1191 relieved Acre, which had been besieged for two years. Dissension then broke out among the crusaders, for the Kings, who had become enemies during the winter on Sicily, took sides in the quarrel over the succession to the throne of Jerusalem: Richard supported Guy of Lusignan; Philip, Conrad of Montferrat. But when the King of France chose to regard his crusade vow as having been fulfilled with the fall of Acre and returned home *via* Rome, where he had himself expressly absolved *ad cautelam* by Celestine III, Richard was able to assume the direction of the expedition against Saladin. Jerusalem could not be recovered, but Richard's brilliant victories near Jaffa and in the battle of Arsuf obtained for the Franks at least a military breathing-space, especially since Saladin died in 1193 and left a disintegrating state. The armistice of 2 September 1192 marked the end of the Third Crusade. Saladin assured pilgrims free access to Jerusalem and a corresponding protection, but the Holy Sepulchre remained for the time being in Muslim hands.

Only a narrow coastal strip from Beirut to Ascalon could be saved and even its political existence depended on the good pleasure of the mighty Islamic realm. Furthermore it could be maintained only in the most intimate contact with the Latin West. Hence from now on the leading monarchs of Christendom at the moment wore also the crown of Jerusalem.

The severe losses of the Third Crusade and the meager results disillusioned Christendom, even if to a lesser degree than had the Second Crusade. Before the end of the century the diminished Kingdom of Jerusalem obtained further help from the West in the crusade of the Emperor Henry VI, which must be viewed in the context of his Mediterranean policy. The Kings of Cyprus and Armenia were accepted as vassals of the Empire. The Emperor could not lead the crusade in person, for he died in September 1197. His chancellor, Bishop Conrad of Hildesheim, and Archbishop Conrad of Mainz, who had been named papal legate, came with a large army from the Rhineland and the Hohenstaufen lands. Individual groups arrived in Syria from August 1197 on. It was possible to take Sidon and Beirut and to preserve the coast, but the death of the Emperor and the anarchy ensuing in Germany with the double election prematurely ended the undertaking. Before the crusaders departed, what had been a German hospital brotherhood was organized in Acre on 5 March 1198 as a military religious order, which, as the Order of the Teutonic Knights, was to face an important future, but not in the Holy Land.

Crusade Piety

A glance at a century of military operations under the sign of the cross presents the question of whether and how these events formed and developed the devotional outlook of Christians. The history of piety in the twelfth century not only encounters that enrichment which was occasioned by an intensification and further development of monastic spirituality in the new orders. There also opened up to it entirely new fields of devout deportment, of generous self-sacrifice, even of mystical experience.

It participated in the tendencies common to all proponents of the ecclesiastical reform movement and arose out of a longing for a *vita apostolica* and a desire to belong to the *pauperes Christi.* But its forms were determined by the fact of crusading, the great epoch of which belonged preeminently, though not entirely, to the age of Saint Bernard. The fact that the appeals to the crusades were so overwhelmingly successful among all classes of the Christian population and the religious motive predominated in the determination to take the cross can hardly be otherwise explained than by the awakening and strengthening of a pious frame of mind, in which the elements of religious insights and decisions became effective.

There had long been pilgrimages to Compostela, Rome, and Jerusalem, motivated by penance, devotion, and vow. What was new was the armed pilgrimage, conditioned by the notion in the Latin West of the now more deeply Christianized class of knighthood. The unique origin of religious orders whose members by vocation bore arms testifies to this. Their beginnings lay also in the hospital idea, which knew its richest and most spontaneous development parallel to the crusades, in the whole of Christendom, first of all in the twelfth century. Characteristic features of this preparedness for hospital work recur among the hermits, who also belong to the many-sided picture of the piety of this epoch. The binding force that united such individual tendencies, at first glance incompatible even if not entirely contradictory, was a lively devotion to Christ, of an orientation different from what it had been earlier. The preaching and the pastoral contact of monks, canons, bishops, and diocesan clerics, stamped by a greater familiarity with Holy Scripture, especially the New Testament, began to complete the change from the Lord King Christ to Jesus of Nazareth, wandering, suffering, humanly close, redeeming, and not holding sway, in the characteristic attitude to piety. This had awakened in the laity the demand for the *vita apostolica,* that is, for personal nearness to Christ, who showed them the way to salvation, made it possible, and had already lived it directly as exemplar. All catechetical instruction was based from the twelfth century on the fundamental theological schema of the *via salutis.* Crusade piety appears as a characteristic form of the Christian's seeking after salvation, which he found in a threefold union: a union with God in obedient service — "God wills it" — with Christ in a suffering, dying, and triumphing imitation — for Christ and with him — with the Holy Spirit in the enthusiasm of the reorientation, esteemed as a newly experienced Pentecost.

It was above all the way of penance and prayer that led to this three-fold union with God. Penance belonged to the central themes of crusade preaching and crusade piety, just as it was also predominant in the basically soteriological schema of popular catechesis. Ennobled by the idea of the imitation of Christ, the penitential desire freed itself from the sphere of a striving directed solely to one's own salvation, all the more as the crusader was filled with an awareness of doing penance as the representative of those who remained at home. For crusading as such was a duty imposed, of itself, on all of Christendom. Corresponding to this was the attitude of the homeland, which supported the *expeditio sacra* by means of alms, money and other real contributions, intercessory prayer, fasting, and freely undertaken penitential works, and thereby participated in it. This self-sanctification, viewed as participation in the *via salutis* of crusading, united all of Christendom in a common pious undertaking and made crusade piety stand out as the first uniform type of Christian lay spirituality in Church history.

A fruit of this crusade piety was the military religious orders, which at the same time realized a predominant motive of the piety of the age in hospital service. People saw in the sick the *pauperes Christi* saw the Lord in them, served him by serving them. The grand master of the Hospitallers described himself as *servus pauperum Christi.* The late twelfth century saw a whole group of lay associations for the service of the sick. In this context came also the building movement, *la croisade monumentale,* which arose from the spirit of the new piety. Proceeding from Chartres, it spread through Normandy and a great part of France. In it too the idea of penance was the central motive. The pilgrims assembled their vehicles at the building site, as though it were a spiritual camp, and regarded themselves as an "army of the Lord."

Out of a movement in many ways turbulent, determined by eschatological fear but at the same time driven by an honoring of Christ and a love of God that were deepened by the Gospel and elevated to enthusiastic surrender, a movement which especially affected the masses of Latin Christendom, there proceeded a form of popular piety which extended throughout the period of the crusades themselves and far beyond it and became the root of many forms of devotion of the following epoch.

CHAPTER 12

Scholasticism, Canon Law, and the Universities

Early Scholasticism

Of the various works of the "sentence" type, which in the first half of the twelfth century constituted the special character of theological endeavor, especially outside the realm of monastic education, the work of Peter Lombard at Paris was outstanding. With its recourse to the dialectical method that had reached its important maturity in Abelard, it was almost as though it were the last word, the ultimate norm of these expositions of theological scholarship. In it Augustine was regarded as the principal witness of theological tradition. Basically conservative, it was a systematic and clearly and precisely organized summary of all the chief truths of the Christian faith that had been hitherto discussed by theologians. To every question it brought the relevant patristic citations and reliable solutions. In a relatively long period of reception, which ended with the celebrated text of the Fourth Lateran Council in 1215, Peter's work became the first and for centuries the leading theological textbook. His opponents, John of Cornwall and Gerhoh of Reichersberg, especially rejected his Christological theses or, like Joachim of Fiore, his formulation of the theology of the Trinity. More effective as journalism was the powerful indictment by the prior of Saint-Victor, Walter, who in *Contra quatuor labyrinthos Franciae* came out against dialectical theology at the Third Lateran Council of 1179, but the reputation of the theologians whom he attacked, Peter Lombard, Gilbert de la Porrée, Peter of Poitiers, and Peter Abelard, could not be impaired with contemporaries.

Dependent on Peter Lombard, there appeared up to 1200 still other collections of sentences and questions, theological *summae,* based on early excerpts from his work, and *abbreviationes,* as they were produced in this form also at Bologna by the *Decretum* of Gratian. In many copies of *The Sentences* of Peter Lombard, as produced by enterprising groups of copyists for school use, are marginal glosses, which were later compiled, as occasion offered, into complete and separately published commentaries.

Leader among the glossators of Peter Lombard, his successors in the teaching office, was *magister* Peter Comestor, with his *Historia scholastica,* gloss on the Gospels, and treatise on the Sacraments. In the last mentioned work he first introduced the concept of *transsubstantiatio,* later adopted by the Fourth Lateran Council.

Following Peter Comestor another pupil of Peter Lombard assumed the post of master of *The Sentences* as theological *magister* at Paris. This was Peter of Poitiers (1130–1205). As chancellor he was to exercise a deciding influence on the genesis of the university. His *Five Books of Sentences* appeared around 1170; more than a mere commentary on the Lombard, they became a theological compendium of a special character.

Outside the circle of pupils of Peter Lombard there worked at Paris around 1170 Peter Cantor (d. 1197), who left abundant writings on many aspects of theology; based on an intensive study of Scripture, they were above all oriented to moral theology. Educated in theology at the cathedral school of Reims, probably under *magister* Alberic, and familiarized by him with the thought of Anselm of Laon, Peter became a canon of Notre-Dame de Paris and in 1178 obtained the capitular post of chanter, from which he got his nickname. His works pertain to dogmatic and moral theology, to the theological encyclopedia, and especially to exegesis. His chief work is his *Summa de sacramentis et animae consiliis.* From canon law he received important suggestions as to form and content. Most widely circulated seems to have been his *Verbum abbreviatum,* with important remarks on the method of theological research. A mine of information in regard to cultural history, it became the important source for the condition of the clergy at Paris and at the same time, thanks to his familiarity with the authors of antiquity, a late witness of the Renaissance of the twelfth century.

As pupils of Peter Cantor were the Benedictine Liebhard of Prüfening, Guy of Orchelles, and especially the Englishmen, Richard of Leicester, who take us into the thirteenth century, and Stephen Langton (d. 1228), Cardinal and from 1206 Archbishop of Canterbury, who was one of the most celebrated theologians of his age.

Besides the theologians of the Lombard circle, scholars of the entourage of Gilbert de la Porrée also taught and wrote, such as the Archdeacon Ivo of Chartres and John Beleth. Outstanding among them was Alain de Lille (1120–1202), Cistercian, teacher at Paris, and later active in the Albigensian mission. With his *Regulae de sacra theologia* he wrote a much used theological compendium, a series of theses, which, established by argumentation as occasion called for, were an innovation in form alongside the previously preferred *quaestiones.* The *Distinctiones dictionum theologicalium* were a sort of theological lexicon, which collected and explained biblical expressions and especially the current theological terminology. Alain's voluminous literary work also includes poetry, treatises on penance, sermons, the much commented *Summa de arte praedicatoria,* and the *Liber poenitentialis.*

To the school of Gilbert de la Porrée also belonged Eudes (d. 1171), Abbot of the Cistercian monastery of Ourscamp from 1167 to 1170 and before that a teacher of theology at Paris. A shrewd dialectician, he opposed Peter Lombard in fundamental questions of theology, Christology, and the doctrine of the Sacraments. Through his influence on Simon of Tournai (d. 1201) his theology found a far-reaching response. Various collections of *quaestiones* from the group of his hearers prove that he founded a school. Simon of Tournai's chief work, the *Institutiones in Sacram Paginam* (1170/75), so far unpublished, displays Abelard's stock of ideas; new in Simon were the *disputationes,* which took their place beside the hitherto customary *lectiones, quaestiones,* and theses. Through him Aristotle obtained entry into theological speculation.

Early Canon Law

Whereas *The Sentences* of Peter Lombard were able only gradually and not without opposition to establish themselves in the world of higher education, the *Decretum Gratiani* succeeded very quickly and almost without effort in becoming at Bologna the basic text of the new science of canon law. Alongside the legists, who concentrated from the time of Irnerius and his four great pupils on the Roman law of late antiquity, stood the decretists, who dealt in detail, according to the scholastic method, with the *Decretum* and its content in lectures and treatises. As was true *of The Sentences* at Paris, so too here the *Decretum* obtained interlinear glosses, the textual exegesis was condensed in *summae,* legal *quaestiones* were treated, legal rules were drawn up, and in this way the practical application of the sources was taught. Complete, detailed expositions of the entire text, the so-called *apparatus,* later appeared, based on the glosses and *summae.* In addition to the decretists of Bologna, there were canonists in France also, above all in Normandy.

Gratian's best known pupil, Paucapalea, to whom is attributed the subdividing of Part I and Part III of the *Decretum* into *distinctiones,* began with a *summa* (1145–48). Without any doubt the "greatest of the decretists" was Huguccio of Pisa, termination and climax of the school of Bologna. His *summa* was finished in 1188–90 and he died in 1210 as Bishop of Ferrara. As a matter of fact, most of the teachers of law at Bologna became bishops, while some, such as Bandinelli, Albert de Morra, and, above all, Lothar di Segni became Popes. Others rose to be cardinals, such as Laborans and Gratian (d. 1197), namesake of the author of the *Decretum.* The age of the jurist Popes and jurist bishops had begun.

The French *summae* of the *Decretum* have all come down anonymously. They are often distinguished from their Italian counterparts by their arbitrary division of the content and their method. The French school (Paris and Normandy) and the wide diffusion of its manuscripts prove the rapid and general reception of the *Decretum* and its adaptations in all of Western Christendom. Under Alexander III the *Decretum* even came into use at the Curia.

The *Decretum* itself did not acquire any strictly legal force, but the copious literature on it, the intensive work of comparing and clarifying the law that it achieved, and its diffusion by the leading schools to all centers of ecclesiastical life laid the groundwork for the legislative accomplishment of the papal leadership, which from the time of Alexander III and especially of Innocent III showed itself as ever more universal in activity and as determining the whole ecclesiastical order.

The Rise of the Universities

The two new sciences here described, that of theoretical and practical theology and that of canon law, by the force of their attraction on students from all parts of Western Christendom and by the constantly more intensively developing cooperation of teachers and their students, especially though not exclusively at Bologna and Paris, laid the foundation for an institution whose proper history belongs to the thirteenth century, but whose beginnings occurred in the twelfth: the universities, or *studia generalia,* of the West.

In the wake of the general changes in the social, economic, and political structure, the educational system of the West also experienced a significant transformation in the twelfth century. Whereas previously clerics, monks, and lay persons had received a humanist and theological training at abbey, cathedral, or chapter schools, but, apart from a few exceptions, only the requirements of the current personnel of the monastery, chapter, or bishopric were envisaged, the picture quickly changed in the course of the twelfth century.

If for the moment the cathedral and chapter schools were predominant in the cities, there were already in places like Salerno, Montpellier, and Bologna schools that were not really ecclesiastical institutions. At Paris from the beginning of the century there was an increase in the number of teachers who still instructed their students on ecclesiastical premises but neither they nor their students were included in the personnel of the cathedral or the collegiate chapter. Such groups grew especially at Paris, but also elsewhere. The number of teachers rose in proportion as a rapidly growing movement of wandering scholars set in, a movement that can hardly be reckoned in numbers but was in accord with the general intellectual restlessness. It started in all parts of Christendom but moved especially westward to Paris and southward to Bologna.

It was as yet not the schools themselves as institutions which exerted the power of attraction but the names of teachers who had become renowned, such as Anselm at Laon and William of Champeaux and especially Abelard at Paris. The cities themselves expanded and offered greater possibilities as residences of teachers and students. In the second half of the century there emerged centers which were no longer dependent on the renown of an outstanding teacher but where the schools; themselves became permanent institutions; the teachers changed and whole groups of teachers gathered. The *scholasticus canonicus* or chancellor of the cathedral chapter of Notre-Dame — and this was also true of other cathedral and collegiate chapters — could give the teachers the authorization to teach; it had to be asked from him. Every qualified aspirant, so Alexander III had had the Third Lateran Council declare, was to obtain it.

Accordingly, the institutional nucleus of the University of Paris was present here. The chancellor retained supervision of the teachers, who even in the twelfth century, in accord with the tendency of the age, began to unite as a gild — *societas* or, later, *universitas.* The admission of new members usually took place in such a way that the *magister* introduced through the ceremony of *inceptio,* or commencement, his pupil who had completed his study. The twofold element of an official licensing by the chancellor and an academic cooptation thus remains to be noted.

Only later were there also formed the unions of the students, upon which in the course of time was to devolve the control of the university as a whole. These called themselves *universitates,* while the teachers became a *collegium.* The *magistri* retained the important right of judging the scholarly qualification of those who wished to be coopted to their *collegium* in the *conventus,* which corresponded to the Paris *inceptio,* but in all else the gilds of students retained the primacy.

Apart from a few generally observed imperial and papal decrees which were issued in the twelfth century with regard to studies, the royal and ecclesiastical, the communal and imperial privileges for particular universities began only from 1200. Until then there were found, especially at Paris, Bologna, Montpellier, Salerno, and Oxford, those communities of teachers and students out of which in the thirteenth century developed the universities, endowed especially by the papacy with specific rights. Hence they appeared as a spontaneous growth, not as an institution planned and set up by the highest authorities. Their beginnings belong to the twelfth century and its intellectual outburst, in which there became manifest not so much an interest directed to vocational training but rather the desire for a knowledge of the truth, for a knowledge transcending the needs of daily life. Of course, the general rapid development of urban culture and the increased connections among nations in the wake of the crusades contributed something to this. The early history of the universities as properly defined institutions belongs however to the thirteenth century.

CHAPTER 13

Heresy and the Beginnings of the Inquisition

The epoch of the Gregorian reform had known radical preachers under the auspices of the *vita apostolica.* Their anti-ecclesiastical and anti-sacramental tendencies had found some response among the lower classes.

The most important of the radicals of this period (after 1135) was Arnold of Brescia (d. 1155), pupil of Abelard and canon regular, who carried the reform ideas of his age to the ultimate consequences, called for an itinerant Church of apostolic poverty, and demanded contempt of the world and humility in priests and bishops. Arnold met defeat not only because his requirements were so extreme but also because of his imprudent attempt to lay the ground for them by political means. Frederick I had him arrested and turned him over to the Roman authorities, who made short work of him. His followers scattered. Common to them all was the fact that their preaching was not really a reaction against the Church reform but rather an exaggeration of the reform into the heretical and the radical.

Heresy first became a mass movement, no longer dependent on the presence of one or the other demagogic preacher, with the appearance of the Cathari from 1140. As a mass movement they belonged to this century of the crusades, of penitential journeys for the building of churches in northern France, of the communal movement everywhere, in the Midi and North Italy, on the Rhine and in Flanders, and in all regions with a rapidly developing urban organization.

It was probably merchants and crusaders who first brought back Bogomile ideas from the East. From Bulgaria Bogomiles had migrated to Byzantium; then, persecuted and expelled by the government of the Emperor Manuel Comnenus (1143–80), they had moved to the West. The Cathari, a name known from 1163, held as doctrine a dualism of Manichaean allure in the twofold direction of an absolute and a moderate form. The good God as creator of spirits and the evil God as creator of the visible world represented orders which were intermingled by the activity of Satan. The activity of Saint Michael and of Christ, who defeated the demon and thereby redeemed souls from Satan's dominion, dualistic, existing in division, would restore the old order. This was absolute Catharism. The moderate form knew only a creator God, whose order was disturbed by the revolt of Satan, who seduced the angels and inserted them as souls into the bodies of men. They were released from this prison of the flesh by Christ, who is not the Son of God but an angel who seemed to become man in Mary. This Christ lived, suffered, and died in an apparent body. At his baptism in the Jordan the Spirit dwelt in him and remained there until Christ's glorification. He then descended upon the Apostles. He communicated himself to believers through baptism; with the Cathari this was not a baptism of water, but an exorcism, a contact with the text of the Gospels, and an imposition of hands — the *consolamentum.* It imparted righteousness to the *perfecti,* the *élite* of leaders, while the simple *credentes* could be freed of their sins from time to time by the *apparellamentum,* a sort of penance. Death freed the angels for paradise, but it seems that a type of transmigration of souls was not excluded. The demons and the damned were to be annihilated at the end of the world, and there was no bodily resurrection. Thus God's victory was seen as all-embracing. The Trinity was denied, the Incarnation was rejected, and many early heresies, such as Gnosticism, Monarchianism, Docetism, and Manichaeism, were revived.

Perhaps even the heretics who were brought to trial at Liège in 1144 and then left for final judgment by Pope Lucius II were the first representatives of this new but soon increasingly threatening movement, for in the trial a regular hierarchy of hearers, believers, priests, and prelates was discovered among them. Similarly, Cathari bishops were active in Champagne and at Albi; they were able quietly to organize a growing membership. They cropped up in the neighborhood of the monastery of Steinfeld in the archbishopric of Cologne; the Premonstratensian provost Eberwin corresponded on their behalf with Bernard of Clairvaux, who replied in Sermons 65 and 66 on the Canticle of Canticles. After a three-day religious discussion with the Catholics, the Cathari were burned by the people, despite the resistance of the clergy. They had already gained many clerics and monks of Cologne and had their elect, believers, apostles, *continentes,* and missionaries; it was asserted that they all lived under a supreme authority, a sort of Pope of Heretics. Bernard's advice was to instruct, to warn, and finally to excommunicate heretics. If the canonical penalties did not suffice, the secular power should be asked to proceed against heretics, following advice given long before by Augustine.

From 1165 Catharism spread in North Italy, in the cities of Lombardy and Tuscany. Around 1162 it had even appeared in England. It was able to open schools at Cologne.

Independently of the Cathari, there appeared in southern France a lay movement which had been founded as a community of penance and poverty by the Lyons merchant, Peter Waldo, around 1175. He had had the New Testament and several books of the Old Testament translated into Provençal and, after having provided for his wife and daughters, gave away his property. Then he turned to itinerant preaching and soon attracted numerous followers from all classes of society. In groups of two they preached apostolic poverty and the imitation of Christ on the streets and squares, in houses and churches. At the Third Lateran Council Alexander III praised Peter Waldo's call for poverty but forbade doctrinal preaching and allowed preaching on moral subjects only under the supervision of the clergy. When this consent of hierarchy and parish clergy was not obtained, Waldo and his followers declared their independence and then began to preach against the sins of ecclesiastics. They incurred excommunication at the Synod of Verona in 1184. At first they had repudiated and attacked the Cathari, but from 1184 they came under their influence. They now began to reject the Church's teaching authority and to denounce hierarchy, tradition, Sacraments, and the veneration of saints, images, and relics. They rejected indulgences, oaths, tithes, military service, and the death penalty. Their strict moral conduct, oriented to the Gospel, gained them an increasing number of adherents. They too were divided into two classes: the perfect, who were preachers, supervisors, and pastors, and the believers, who were friends, promoters, sympathizers and ordinary followers. On his own authority Waldo ordained bishops, priests, and deacons. The spread of the Waldensians in the twelfth century was connected especially with the Poor Lombards in North Italy, where they became more radical in their anticlerical outlook than they had been in the Midi.

Densely populated Flanders, flourishing commercially and industrially, became a center of settlement for heresy. Its missionaries were active in the Rhine valley and along the Danube and everywhere else in Christendom, becoming a flood that threatened the Universal Church. How was the Church to react?

The people in northern France and the Rhineland killed heretics, whereas the hierarchical Church for the most part correctly instituted proceedings against them. Nevertheless, among both people and Church officials a keen instinct indicated that the movement was foreign to the faith and to the Church.

The situation was different in the Midi. Here the people remained indifferent and uninterested when they did not join in considerable numbers a movement that knew no sins, denied hell, and promised easy redemption by means of a *consolamentum* on the deathbed. In his correspondence with Archbishop Henry of Reims and King Louis VIII Alexander III had already outlined the main features of a systematic intervention against heresy, and these were put into fixed form at the Council of Tours. A definite change of methods was thereby announced. Instead of waiting for accusations to be made before officials by the people or the clergy, now the officials were themselves to proceed *ex officio* against heretics. The Inquisition was thereby sketched in principle.

In this way Alexander III, a former professor of canon law, made the teaching of Bologna the teaching of the whole Church. It called for active intervention in view of the danger to the purity of the Church's faith and the unity of her organization. It held that bishops and priests had the duty to inquire into the life and activities of heretics, to obtain information on the existence and type of their gatherings, and to proceed against them with canonical penalties. It seems certain that this last point refers to a search for heretics and the institution of a process.

Later, postponing a crusade to the Holy Land, Alexander III, under pressure from a report by Abbot Henry of Clairvaux, sought to bring about an ecclesiastical and military action in the Midi against the Cathari. Clergy, magistrates, and all orthodox citizens were invited to point out heretics. Those pointed out were excommunicated and imprisoned, their property was confiscated, their castles were destroyed; the penalties inflicted had already been envisaged by the Council of Tours. When the Cardinal returned to Italy, an actual Inquisition tribunal had met for three months in the County of Toulouse. The activity of the embassy of 1178 was reflected in the legislation of the Third Lateran Council of 1179. Canon 27 described the religious situation in Gascony and Languedoc, admonished the princes to carry out the Church's instructions, and finally called for a crusade in the areas infected by heresy. The same indulgences were announced as for the crusade to the Holy Land. The leadership of the army was to pertain to the bishops. During the Council Alexander made Abbot Henry Cardinal Bishop of Albano and dispatched him as legate to the Midi to inaugurate the crusade. In Canon 27 there was no mention of what was the specific characteristic of the Inquisition procedure: the seeking out of heretics, the *ex officio* denunciation by the ecclesiastical authorities, and the instituting of the process. On the other hand, the cooperation of the secular and ecclesiastical powers in the effort to suppress heresy by means proper to them respectively was clearly and emphatically demanded. The legate's crusade brought only meager and no enduring results.

In his decisions Alexander III was taking as his point of departure principles already found in Gratian and the decretists. Gratian saw in heresy a serious assault on the dogmatic and social structure of the Church and an attack on the public welfare — the *bonum commune* of both Church and state. In the common defense against such an attack the secular power seems to have been subordinated to the spiritual power of direction and to have been the executor of its judgments. Gratian likewise mentioned the war against heresy as a crusade. The heretic was equated with the infidel, and war against him was meritorious, a holy war. A Christian who fell while participating in it died a martyr. The view that "malos ad bonum cogendos," was defended. Through the war on heresy the death penalty was clearly suggested for the convicted heretic.

Similarly, Rufinus in his *Summa Decretorum* defended the opinion: "Armis etiam haeretici compellendi sunt." While Huguccio, like his predecessors, commented on the *Decretum* with reference to Roman law, he nevertheless added one remark that his great pupil, Pope Innocent III, was to take up: that heresy was to be regarded as *maiestas laesa.* All the decretists stressed that persons should proceed against heretics not "zelo ultionis, sed amore correctionis." The holy war against them, and hence the death penalty, continued to be considered as the *ultima ratio,* but they were systematically pondered and classified into an emerging penal law for heresy.

After the Peace of Venice in 1177 and its confirmation at Verona in 1184, these beginnings received a first legislative formulation in the decretal "Ad abolendam" of Lucius III, issued 4 November 1184. In it, first of all, a number of heretical groups were condemned *nominatim* by Pope and Emperor: Cathari, Patari, Humiliati, Poor Men of Lyons (Waldensians), Arnoldists, and others. Then the bishops were instructed to take penal action; but apparently it was as yet an accusing procedure rather than one of inquiring. The decretal "Vergentis in senium," issued for Viterbo by Innocent III on 25 March 1199, first carried the development further by describing heresy as "crimen laesae maiestatis." Thereby the Roman and the Germanic lines of legal transmission converged and set up the presuppositions for the creation of the Inquisition, which was completed in the thirteenth century.

It is plain that the Church clearly saw the threatening danger of an invasion by disintegrating forces into her organism and armed herself so as to meet it vigorously. This she did by inner reforms, by a crusade under her leadership, by an increasing juridical clarification of the possibilities of the penal process against heretics, by stepping up her legislation. The pontificate of Innocent III would bring into prominence the grand-scale counterattack.

CHAPTER 14

Lay Movements of the Twelfth Century, Christian Knighthood, Pastoral Care, Popular Piety, and Mystical Theology

From the beginning of the twelfth century the layman became much more prominent than before, alongside the cleric, in the life of the Church. This was a product of the crusades and especially of the vigorously developing urban culture. In Western society the city community, organized in patriciate and crafts, appeared as a new element which clearly acted not entirely in opposition to the structure — made up of nobility and peasantry — of the feudal and agrarian organization, but was integrated with it above all in Italy and even in Germany, by means of the families of ministerial rank. To the constantly growing international relations among armies, merchants, and scholars was added the migration of peasants to the cities.

The great response which the preaching of itinerant clerics had found around the turn of the eleventh century showed itself not only in the crowds of listeners who gathered but also in the not inconsiderable groups that attached themselves to the preachers when they moved on and, as occasion offered, settled down as colonies of ascetics. It is, therefore, not surprising that among the laity there was a desire to undertake the proclaiming of the teaching of Christ as a fulfilling of the *vita apostolica* that had been preached to them and was being practiced by them in poverty and common life. It was not enough for them to proclaim by example; they now wanted "to preach to the whole world" by word also. Out of the private profession of the faith emerged the public profession in the form of preaching. Heretical movements felt this impulse, and it is not to be wondered that, in addition to clerics, lay persons especially had a chance to speak in them.

Lay activity in the ecclesiastical sphere was seen in this century especially in the cities where, within the unity constituted by an association, the various professions of merchants and artisans joined in fraternities, gilds, corporations, and lodges; these, both in their purpose and even in their statutes, made clear the tendency toward a religious and ecclesiastical expression of aim. This was probably most evident among the hospital associations, in which brothers and sisters united for the exercise of charity to the sick and the aged. They were lay persons who did not thereby intend to found a new order and did not assume any such monastic obligations as vows. The Gospel itself became for them, as later for Saint Francis, the rule of life.

In the new schools also lay persons appeared among the teachers of medicine, law, and the liberal arts as well as among the students. In this way the laity gained something they had hitherto lacked for the most part: the possibility of expressing their concerns orally and especially in writing. The school and the city naturally aroused in lay persons especially the taste for freedom, and so one can understand why the new canon law sought, among other things, to determine more clearly the frontiers between laity and clergy.

At first the distinction was stressed, and then also the subordination of the laity to the clergy. The rights of the laity in the Church appeared, in their crudest expression, as concessions made by the clergy. The layman could have possessions, but only as much as he needed for his support. He could marry, go to court, make offerings, and tithe. Lay persons had a right to ask from the clergy the spiritual aid envisaged in the order of salvation as organized by the Church. In case of necessity they could baptize and confess one another. It had now been made clearer that the contracting parties administered the Sacrament of matrimony to each other. But the laity had no share in the *ministerium verbi,* which remained reserved to the clergy. Innocent III would merely allow them to criticize the clergy to the bishop in the event of a neglect of this *ministerium.* At the same time there was also now developing the institute of the guardianship of churches, whereby the laity acquired a very important share of the responsibility for the administration of Church property and the care of ecclesiastical building, and real estate.

In the eliminating of the law of the proprietary church there appeared in Gratian the initial steps in the development of the right of patronage, whereby an important right of lay persons in the Church was defined. But on the other hand they were ousted from ecclesiastical electoral bodies, from chapters, and from the sphere of ecclesiastical notaries, and above all they were now forbidden in principle to take the clergy to court — they were not permitted to denounce them nor to testify against them, to say nothing of judging them. On the whole, of course, the laity retained an important secular function in the service of the Church: the protecting of religion, especially by the Emperor and the kings as *defensores ecclesiae,* and the protecting of the moral order by the secular administration of justice to the extent that the clergy were not exempt from it by the *privilegium fori.* The position of the King or of the Emperor continued to be ambivalent for in the twelfth century the quasi-sacred status of rulers, despite the Investiture Controversy and the enduring tension between the powers, was still asserted, and hence kings should still not be reckoned merely as laymen.

This becomes clear if one looks into the Christian values of knighthood, which appeared in sharp outline in this century, and its estimation by the clergy.

Western knighthood, the chief representative of the crusade movement, opened itself in a special degree to the tendency toward a sacralization of the states of life and of calling.

In every country knighthood had its special characteristics and hence it was many-sided in its social appearance. But the values produced by the common experience of the crusade saw in the knight the fighter for God, *miles christianus,* in whom piety and the urge to do great deeds merged.

In his treatise *De laude novae militiae* Bernard of Clairvaux describes the religious outlook, even if one bears in mind the restriction that his expressions apply first of all and especially to the Templars. The Christian knight is subject to Christ as the Lord of hosts, the cross is his banner, death is his witness to the faith (*martyrium*) and his prize (certain beatitude). In this way the earlier, and not strictly ecclesiastical and Christian, demands of knightly morality — loyalty and service — were sanctified, just as weapons and standards were blessed and the ceremony of knighting became the consecration of the knight. God's fighter protected the Church and her goods, fought against the heathen, shielded the weak, widows, and orphans, and unselfishly established God's order on earth. That the reality did not fully correspond to this ideal and not all knights felt themselves obliged by it cannot detract from the fact that in the majority, and especially in the military orders, it acted as a determining motive. Since it found an echo in all of Christendom in its theological refinement at the hands of Bernard of Clairvaux and John of Salisbury, it may be regarded as a type of lay religious culture characteristic of the twelfth century, its probably most impressive form with the most enduring historical impact.

A powerful sympathy on the part of the world of women has been identified in the lay movement in regard to the itinerant preachers at the beginning of the century. Accordingly, one must ask what role woman played in the lay participation thus far intimated in the religious and ecclesiastical life of the twelfth century.

Woman began to play a more active role in the social life of this century, above all in the Midi, where the troubadours recognized her central position. A person such as Eleanor of Aquitaine, whose career was able to exert a powerful influence over almost the whole century, can be proposed as a model. The praise of woman dominated lyric poetry among both the French and Catalan troubadours and the German minnesingers. In regard also to woman's delight in education on speaks for many in the career of Héloise, pupil, wife, and intimate of Peter Abelard.

Within the family and the kindred a great share of responsibility devolved upon the woman if she was of a correspondingly strong character.

The lively tendency to forms of cultivated piety led numberless women of this century to the monasteries of the Premonstratensians and later to the Cistercian nuns. When these were no longer in a position to take care of them, groups of virgins and widows united for a common life near hospitals and leprosaria; from them arose the movement of the Beguines, which experienced its first and strongest growth in the thirteenth century. And the recluse type, in which women followed an eremitical life in cells according to monastic tradition, often in several cells adjoining under a superioress, experienced a flowering in the twelfth century and also contributed to the beginnings of the Beguine movement.

Care of Souls, Popular Devotion, and Mysticism

The laity's more intensive participation in ecclesiastical life did not have its origin only in changes in the social structure in the twelfth century. Rather it can be surmised that the care of souls was attended to in these changes in a more responsible manner than has commonly been admitted. The Christian people received religious instruction, were made receptive to the sacramental life, and through the cult of the saints and the pilgrimage had a manifold connection with the totality of the Church's piety.

Religious instruction began in the family. Hildebert of Lavardin impressively explained the duty of parents carefully to provide this initial proclamation as a participation in the teaching office of the Church. This instruction was taken up and carried further in the church building by means of worship and preaching. An abundant sermon literature also from this century attests the uninterrupted tradition. Even learned theologians naturally preached to the laity in the vernacular. In twelfth-century England Anglo-Saxon was still used in preaching. For the most part they were homilies or catechetical sermons. Only to persons at the universities were questions of any real theological depth addressed. A special type of popular preaching, which was very widespread and effective, must be mentioned: crusade preaching, the organizing of which got under way and developed its basic forms in this century. Organized according to dioceses, entrusted there to the most celebrated preachers, and carried out not merely in churches but also in public squares, on bridges, and at crossroads, it aimed at as widespread and all-embracing a proclamation as possible. Because it had as its point of departure a uniform theme, through it the piety of the people in all parts of Christendom came to know a definite form, which, together with Saint Bernard's turning to the suffering Lord, can be characterized as a movement from a Christ-piety to a Jesus-piety.

The sacramental life of the people grew to the extent that private auricular confession even included the recommendation of confession to lay persons. Theology was as yet unable to arrive at any completely clear rejection of the sacramental character of such confession. Especially in battles and combats, if no priest was available, was this form of confession of sins suggested (Jas. 5:16). Communion, on the other hand, became more rare. It was restricted to the great feasts and to a part of the rite of reconciliation, in which the parties received the broken Host. It was likewise received on solemn occasions, such as a knighting and a wedding. Baptism, formerly specified for Easter and Pentecost, now had to be conferred soon after birth, if possible on the same day. Now, as earlier, reception into a religious community, the *professio ad succurrendum,* continued to be for the nobles the method of preparation for death that was in keeping with their social position.

The cult of the saints developed remarkably in the twelfth century, and the royal saints became especially prominent. Of particular interest are the political canonizations of Charles the Great in 1164, Edward the Confessor in 1161, Olav II Haraldson of Norway, and Knut of Denmark in 1100–1101; veneration of the Archbishop of Canterbury, Thomas Becket, assassinated in 1170 and canonized in 1173, marks the climax. Together with Jerusalem, Rome, and Compostela, Canterbury became one of the most important European places of pilgrimage, followed by Vézelay with the alleged grave of Saint Mary Magdalen. Since in the change from the very liberally granted commutations to the indulgence, the practice of which spread powerfully in the twelfth century and even before the end of the century knew of the "plenary indulgence," the pilgrimage, especially the crusade, was recommended as an appropriate penitential work. Above all, pilgrimages of shrines of the Blessed Virgin sprang up everywhere, probably as a consequence of the outspoken Marian devotion of the new orders. Even more strongly than in regard to Marian devotion, Saint Bernard's influence is seen in the turning of popular piety to the mysteries of the Redeemer's life and death.

Mystical Theology

At the beginning of the century Anselm of Canterbury inaugurated the series of theologians of mysticism, which reached its climax in Bernard of Clairvaux, William of Saint-Thierry, and Aelred of Rievaulx, and was cultivated in the school of Saint-Victor, especially by Richard. Mystical theology was especially at home in the new orders, but monks and canons regular were definitely not the only ones to unite theological speculation with a certain degree of experienced love.

The Church is still living on this spiritual wealth of the twelfth century. Without any doubt the most important contribution to the mystical theology of the twelfth century was made by the great Cistercians in France and England especially since their works soon became the most significant elements in the theological libraries of the West. The systematic theology of the next decades was also promoted by them in essential questions.

Section Three

The Byzantine Church in the Epoch of the Crusades

Hans Georg-Beck

CHAPTER 15

The Byzantine Church from 1054 to 1203

While the date 1054 has quite firmly established itself in historiography as that of the definitive separation of the Byzantine Church from Rome, it was, however, only slowly fixed as such in the awareness of contemporaries and of the next generation. In any event, little was at first changed in the relations of the two Churches, for such relations had lost all cordiality long before 1054. The faithful on both sides and even a large part of the clergy did not at first take note of this date.

Of course, the dissatisfaction existing between the heads of the two Churches could hardly be concealed, and even on the political plane there long prevailed an attitude of more than annoyance. The fault here lay with the Normans. Persons at Constantinople may have been able to understand that the Popes had to make an arrangement with these intruders, but they could only regard it as an act of hostility when in 1059, Pope Nicholas II invested Robert Guiscard with territories which were former Byzantine lands and in fact were still partly under Byzantine rule. Thereby the sworn enemy of the Byzantine holdings in South Italy received the Pope's blessing on his further attacks.

Nevertheless, after the severe defeat administered by the Seljuk Turks to the imperial forces at Manzikert in 1071, the same year in which Bari, the last Byzantine bulwark in Italy, fell to the Normans, the Byzantine Emperor had to swallow his pride and seek peace with the Normans and the Popes in order to assure his rear in the West for the sake of the struggle in the East. Pope Gregory VII was all the more ready for such an understanding, since his own relations with the Normans were none too good. At the same time he was preoccupied with ambitious plans for a crusade, for which he could not dispense with Byzantine cooperation. Not the least significant element in these plans was the hope that in the course of such an expedition the papal claim to the primacy would be accepted at Constantinople and the separation of the Churches would be ended.

In view of the Norman threat to cross over to Greece, there was nothing left for the Emperor Michael VII (1071–78) except to go along with the papal plans. He seems to have made Gregory an offer of ecclesiastical and political negotiations, which induced the Pope to support the Emperor's offer of a marriage alliance to Robert Guiscard. From December 1074 people even had to reckon with the likelihood that Gregory VII would go to Constantinople in person.

The Pope's plans quickly came to nothing, but Byzantium had gained a reprieve. Nicephorus III Botaneiates (1078–81), annulled the marriage treaty. Robert now prepared for war, and the Pope excommunicated the Emperor in what was the first formal break between the Curia and the Emperor in centuries. This was a serious mistake. But not even from these events were any conclusions drawn which would merit the label of a formal schism. The next years provide noteworthy proofs of this.

The successor of Nicephorus III, Alexius I Comnenus (1081–1118), was also excommunicated by Gregory VII and from 1081 to 1085 the Normans sought to make their way to Constantinople *via* the Balkan peninsula. But Gregory died and Alexius was victorious over the Normans. The prudent Urban II lifted the censure and extended peace-feelers to Byzantium. Apparently he would have been satisfied with a mention in the Byzantine liturgy, that is, if his name were included in the diptychs. His inquiry, therefore, had to do with why this had thus far been neglected and why the churches of the Latin rite in Constantinople had been closed. The Emperor caused an investigation into these complaints to be made in the *patriarchium* with the aim of determining whether a document on the separation of the two Churches could be found in the archives. The search was a failure, according to the report of the ecclesiastical authorities. In other words, it seems that the Patriarch and his synod regarded the exchange of anathemas between the Patriarch Michael Caerularius and Cardinal Humbert as a personal matter between the two prelates, without consequences for the two Churches. The difficulty, it was said, lay in disciplinary differences between the two Churches, but these could be adjusted. The failure to mention Urban in the diptychs was connected with his not having sent notice of his elevation by means of the traditional synodical. Not all of the Latin churches had been closed, but only those of the Normans, because of the acts of war. The Patriarch suggested that the Pope should send on his synodical, to which a profession of faith was customarily attached; then the inscription in the diptychs would follow and a discussion of the disciplinary differences could get under way. The plan was not carried out.

These events occurred in 1089. It is significant that, despite this failure, relations between Urban and Alexius in no way cooled, but instead the Emperor apparently obtained from the Pope at that time the prospect of military aid. There was agreement, not on the basis of strict law or of dogma, but on the more useful basis of *oikonomia,* of mutual *laissez-faire.* And this was the basis for the common preparation of the First Crusade. And precisely this crusade had the duty and would have possessed the ability to bring the two parts of Christendom together in common distress and hope. That the Pope and the Emperor planned and prepared together can no longer be doubted.

But the enterprise slipped not only out of Urban's hands but also out of those of Alexius, and what would have been able to lead to peace actually produced a deepening of the schism. What was decisive in this respect was not, as has been claimed, the discrepancy of the fundamental idea — that the Byzantines were expecting auxiliary troops for their struggle against the Seljuks, while the crusaders had set as their immediate goal the capture of Jerusalem, which even for Urban II had been only a long-range goal and for Alexius was of little importance in view of the state of his diplomatic relations with the Fatimids. The trouble lay rather with the formalities. It is true that Alexius continued to assure, by means of a flexible system of feudal forms, his claims to sovereignty over the territories to be conquered as far as a bit south of Antioch, but the fact that the vanguard of the crusade possessed more enthusiasm than a sense of order or a talent for organization, and indeed that whole crusade armies took the land route going north to south through the Balkan peninsula, which was not prepared for them, led to ever more irksome tests of nerves. And if Alexius finally had to send home the vanguard, which had been routed by the Turks precisely because of its lack of discipline, the *perfidia Graecorum* was there alleged as the excuse for this misfortune.

The papal legate, Adhémar of Le Puy, had been able time and again to adjust the tensions that arose between the Byzantine escort and the crusade army, acting from the notion of a Universal Church that was not torn by schism. Thus it was at first taken for granted by the crusaders that the liberated Orthodox Patriarch of Antioch should be recognized as the only Bishop of that city. But when the legate died, Bohemond of Tarentum, the old enemy of the Byzantines, was able openly to promote his own policy, which amounted to a withholding of Antioch from the Byzantine Emperor. Finally, Bohemond even succeeded in gaining the new Pope, Paschal II, for his idea of the *perfidia Graecorum,* and the papal legate Bruno, who accompanied Bohemond to France in 1104, received the commission to preach the holy war against Byzantium. This was both a turning point and a catastrophe. The reply of the Byzantine hierarchy was not slow in coming, the theological opposition hardened, and Latin bishops, who, passing through Constantinople, entered into theological dispute, ran into a resistance that became less and less possible to overcome.

If, despite everything, the age of the Comneni was an uninterrupted series of attempts to reach an adjustment on the religious plane with the Holy See and hence with the West, these efforts almost always proceeded from the Emperors. They liked to surround themselves even with Western theological advisors. The Emperors sought contacts everywhere, and when they could no longer break the resistance of their own hierarchy, they still reduced it for the time being to silence. To put it simply, the Emperors had to handle the successive waves of the crusade. Under all circumstances they had to prevent their own capital from becoming the goal of an attack. And they had to avoid aggravating the danger which Paschal II had opened up; hence they could not afford to have the reproach of being schismatics hurled at them by the crusaders in addition to that of being untrustworthy.

And so from the time of the Comneni the policy of union became an element in a policy of self-preservation and eventually a diplomatic weapon which persons used without paying any too much attention to its essentially religious concept.

Without a doubt the closest affinity to the Western mentality was displayed by the Emperor Manuel I Comnenus (1143–80). His intensive and far-reaching political plans led finally to a special type of union endeavor. His ambition aimed at the reconquest of Byzantine Italy. His first military successes were soon followed by a serious setback: the defeat of the Byzantine troops at Brindisi by the Normans in 1156. But the Emperor did not abandon his plans and he even tried to turn the struggle between Pope Alexander III and the Emperor Frederick Barbarossa to his own advantage. In 1166 or 1167 he laid before the Pope a plan that was as grandiose as it was unrealistic: the Pope should crown him Universal Roman Emperor. In return Manuel promised the Pope protection and aid against Barbarossa and also an offer of union, reported by the Roman informant in the following terms: "ut sub una divinae legis observantia et uno ecclesiae capite uterque clerus et populus latinus videlicet et graecus, perpetua firmitate subsisteret." The Pope did not reject the plans *a limine* but sent an embassy to Constantinople, probably to drag out the negotiations. Why the plans then failed completely cannot be determined.

With the death of Manuel I the opposition solidified in regard to Latin and especially Venetian influence in the Empire; economic and national viewpoints probably played a stronger role than religious. The point of departure for a union became ever worse, and a crusade against Byzantium itself became more and more likely. Whatever the reasons why, the Fourth Crusade finally moved directly against Constantinople; the sources in any event make it clear that, for the ordinary participants in the crusade, this turn of the expedition could be sufficiently justified by the schism of the Greeks. And so the catastrophe of 1204.

CHAPTER 16

The Byzantine Church from 1203 to 1282

The Fourth Crusade brought the most important parts of he Byzantine Empire, including Constantinople, its capital, into the hands of "the Latins." This victory, destined to reveal itself as, in the words of Steven Runciman, "an act of gigantic political folly," produced no enduring advantages either for the crusade idea as such or for the security of the Frankish East, while for the notion of the reunion of the separated halves of Christendom it proved to be one of the worst hindrances. Pope Innocent III at first vacillated between indignation over the "abomination of desolation" which the crusaders had perpetrated on a Christian territory and a scarcely restrained satisfaction that this Empire, which had sought to pass itself off as Christian without being actually willing to acknowledge the papal primacy, had finally been brought low. Satisfaction clearly gained the upper hand and gave birth in the Pope to a legal concept, which in this trained lawyer can be explained only in the light of that gratification and which can appropriately be reduced to the dangerous phrase, *cuius regio, eius religio.* In any event, the papal instructions for the legate contained the unmistakable sentence: "... translato ergo imperio necessarium, ut ritus sacerdotii transferatur, quatenus Ephraim reversus ad Iudam in azymis sinceritatis et veritatis expurgato fermento veteri epuletur...."

National and cultural differences have always been charged with responsibility for the divergent disciplines of the two Churches. But these differences only now became decisive, when the self-esteem of the Byzantines was pierced to the heart. The Greek resistance has consolidated on the frontiers of the new Latin Empire, and there arose political structures, all of which aspired to the succession to the old Byzantine Empire: Trebizond, Nicaea, and Epirus. Their rivalries prevented a unified action against the Latin Empire and delayed the recovery of Constantinople and restoration in the former geographical extension.

Little as most of the conquerors and papal agents were aware of this dangerous situation, they were equally unmindful of the ancient religious unity of the Balkan peninsula. When the Bulgarian Tsar Kalojan then made contact with the Latin conquerors of Constantinople, he could not fail to note that the Emperor Baldwin, the haughty successor of the Byzantine *autokrator,* made completely unrealistic territorial claims on Bulgarian Thrace and Macedonia. Under the circumstances it was not difficult for the Bulgars' old coreligionists in Orthodoxy, the Greeks, to gain the Tsar to their side. In Easter week of 1205, hardly a year after the fall of Constantinople, Kalojan inflicted on the crusaders a severe defeat at Adrianople, which cost the Emperor Baldwin his liberty and plunged the young Empire into the greatest difficulties. Baldwin's brother, Henry of Flanders, who now mounted the throne (1206 to 1216), drew from this occurrence the not unimportant conclusion that he should deal more indulgently with the sensitivities of the Greeks of his Empire than his predecessor did, and so he conducted even religious discussions not so much in the spirit of the far-away Pope as with that discretion which political expediency forced on him.

And finally it must be emphasized that the papal legates who came to Constantinople with projects of union found there no fully legitimate partners for a dialogue. The last Patriarch of the Byzantine Empire, John Kamateros, had fled at the arrival of the crusaders and could not be induced to return to Constantinople. He died in 1206 in voluntary exile. This was the opportunity of Byzantine monachism, which could now pose as the spokesman of Orthodoxy without being further obstructed by the Patriarch and his attitude, always powerfully determined by political considerations. This hour of monachism remained decisive: for the future the ultimately determining word in all these questions very frequently was not that of the hierarchy. Cardinal Benedict of Santa Susanna arrived in Constantinople at the end of 1205 or early in 1206 as papal emissary. At first he organized gatherings of the Byzantine clergy. But then, apparently in the understanding that the monks counted for more than did the diocesan clergy of the capital, he arranged a meeting of the monks, seem to have been prepared to a certain degree to acknowledge the Emperor Henry as their sovereign but not to recognize the Pope's primacy of jurisdiction or to yield in dogmatic questions.

The Greeks applied, not to the legate, but to the Emperor Henry for permission to elect a Patriarch. Henry seems not to have been unwilling but he still had to require a certain recognition of the Pope. Two drafts of letters to Pope Innocent III were drawn up by the Orthodox, in the second of which at least an acclamation after the liturgy was conceded to the Pope. It is doubtful that either of these letters was really dispatched. A favorable opportunity was lost, for now the clergy of Constantinople contacted Theodore Lascaris, Emperor of Nicaea, and in Nicaea there took place the election of an Orthodox Patriarch, who was recognized also in Orthodox Constantinople. A further and portentous step in the consolidation of Orthodoxy had thereby been taken.

Now they no longer lodged their complaints with the Emperor Henry but with Theodore Lascaris. And so there was an exchange of intermediaries with Nicaea. Theodore Lascaris was not averse to the negotiations, for the mere *de facto* recognition of his sovereign dignity by the papal legate was again at the expense of the Latin Empire. And that is all it was. After the dead pledge, Constantinople showed itself in every discussion with Nicaea as the greatest obstacle, for the recovery of the ancient capital was for the Greek Emperor, admittedly or not, a *conditio sine qua non,* while for the Pope this Latin Empire, that was unable both to survive and to die, constituted an irritating burden. In any event people at Nicaea could now believe with reason that the city would soon fall to the Greek Emperor like a ripe fruit. Hence, in the confrontations in the eastern Mediterranean, union soon played merely the role of a political attendant circumstance, to be manipulated according to the situation of the respective opponents.

Authentically ecclesiastical disputes played only a slight role; enthusiasm for the crusade had long ago cooled off and a cavalier system of coalitions and countercoalitions with the single aim of one's own advantage became more widespread. Religious policy in the principalities of the Latin Empire was determined less by papal directives than by the advantage of the dukes and counts who had acquired sovereignty and property.

In general there prevailed in the entire territory of the Empire the rule that every Greek bishop who had made the oath of obedience to the Pope could continue in office — and a group of bishops had made it. The others for the most part resigned voluntarily or sought to govern their flocks from some safer place. For the monasteries it was probably enough if they paid taxes to the new bishops, and the lower clergy on the whole very likely got off with this tangible gesture. Of course, there were so many Latin clerics in the train of the conquerors who coveted the ecclesiastical property of Orthodoxy that we must allow for a large-scale bestowal of Greek benefices and a general impoverishment of the remaining Greek higher and lower clergy. Neither Church — neither Latin nor Greek — turned out to be the victor.

On 25 July 1261 Constantinople fell to the Greek Emperor. A nightmare was over, a dream fulfilled. But it soon became clear that the situation was something less than rosy, for Michael VIII (1259–82) was a usurper, and the opposition, especially that of the average and lower clergy, made serious difficulties for him in the name of the dethroned Lascarids. Trebizond remained outside the restored Empire, and the "Great Comneni" there could bring themselves to show no more than marks of respect to the Emperor at Constantinople. Epirus likewise escaped more and more from Byzantine sovereignty. At most the reconquest was successful in the Peloponnesus. Worst of all for Michael was the fact that the Latin West, which had at first looked on calmly as Constantinople and the shrinking Latin Empire became ever weaker until they fell an easy prey for the Greeks, now suddenly remembered the deserted Empire again and exerted itself, from the most varied reasons to retrieve the booty from the Greeks. Above all, the Hohenstaufen Manfred pursued this aim, unmindful of the alliance between Frederick II and John III Vatatzes. A power basis which included South Italy and the Greek lands across the Adriatic seemed to him to be important for his own ambitious plans, which were intended to lead to the imperial throne. And if Genoa was prepared to side with Michael VIII, this automatically meant the dangerous hostility of Venice. And Charles of Anjou, successor of the Hohenstaufen in South Italy, assumed all the hereditary claims of Manfred and, through a skillful policy, added new ones.

For Michael VIII there was only one possible, but difficult, ally: the Pope, who, in the ceaseless conflict with the Hohenstaufen, would, in the circumstances, be pleased with a Greek confederate. While in Charles of Anjou the papacy had found the right man to free it from the Hohenstaufen, at the same time it had to dread that there might be no limit to the aggrandizement of this new lord of South Italy. Naturally, an alliance with the papacy meant union, and so Michael VIII was quickly aware of the necessity of concluding one. The point of departure may have been political, but the Emperor took his duty seriously and pursued it honestly and persistently. The difficulties never lay in his good will but always in the circumstances. The monastic world, hostile to union, was, as always, conscious of its own importance, while the hierarchy, in order not to lose the people, had to yield time and again to the monks and at most could go along with the Emperor's plans only from afar and in a diplomatically zigzag course. Despite what the Pope believed to the contrary, the Byzantine Emperor was no longer in a position to impose on his people union in matters of faith by his mere authority.

The greatest difficulty in regard to Rome came from the question of priorities. The Byzantine Emperor was at first mostly interested in the papacy's diplomatic and military help and argued that this would best prepare the way for union. But Pope Urban IV flatly rejected this arrangement and demanded ecclesiastical submission as the first step. With Clement IV, Michael tried the promise of having all controverted points discussed at a general council, but again without success. Even his offer to take part in the crusade of Louis IX of France did not dissuade the Pope from his primary requirement of ecclesiastical submission.

The situation changed only with the pontificate of Gregory X (1271–76). Whatever judgment may be rendered on this Pope, in his Eastern policy he possessed something of the greatness, the restraint, and the clarity of the Pope of the First Crusade, Urban II. Above all, he had an unfailing sympathy for the difficult situation of his Byzantine partner in dialogue, and, even if he found himself unable to yield in matters of principle, still the style of his policy was entirely in the spirit of *oikonomia.* It was Gregory himself who acted *motu proprio* to renew the contact with Michael VIII. It was important that the Pope offered discussions at a general council but was at the same time prepared to enter at once upon political negotiations. Furthermore, he declared that he would be satisfied if at first only a part of the Byzantine episcopate would recognize the union; a universal personal taking of the oath to the union need take place only after the full realization of a *rapprochement* at a time to be determined by the Pope. What he first regarded as necessary was not an oath but a mere promise to acknowledge the Roman faith and the papal primacy after the conclusion of peace in the secular sphere. "Agnoscere desideramus" was the formula which he proposed as his minimal demand. Thereby was created a model case of a *modus procedendi* which is virtually unique in Church history.

Michael now had to work to gain at least a minority of the hierarchy for the union but he actually tried to obtain a majority. A first inventory among the higher clergy did not yield half a dozen partisans of the Emperor. The Patriarch even let himself be induced to swear not to assent to union. He seems later to have regretted this oath but regarded himself as bound by it. Just the same, he made it clear that he did not wish to stand in the way of union.

More serious was the fact the *chartophylax* John Beccus, the most learned theologian of the day, was unwilling to support the Emperor's efforts. Since he expressed himself only too frankly, he was imprisoned; but he was allowed a small theological library that he made use of to examine his theological views. This measure produced its effect. In prison Beccus read the works of a Byzantine theologian who died just around this time (1272), Nicephorus Blemmydes by name. While vacillating in regard to ecclesiastical politics, Nicephorus in his theological writings occasionally achieved an approach to the Latin position in the question of the procession of the Holy Spirit, in which *a filio* and *per filium* were equivalent, an approach of the greatest importance. And it was this very Blemmydes to whom Beccus would later appeal. Be that as it may, he left his prison to become the skillful and theologically unbeatable champion of union, to whose writings it is due that for the future a small but important party of *Latinophrones* could no longer be disregarded in Byzantine intellectual history. The archdeacon Constantine Meliteniotes, already a staunch advocate of union, now became the closest collaborator of Beccus. The archdeacon George Metochites was the third member of the group. In the higher civil hierarchy Michael VIII found a champion of his ideas in the esteemed historian George Acropolites, who, while he lacked theological depth, made his own the Christian idea of union as such. In addition there was doubtless a whole group of clerics and lay persons who intended to follow the Emperor's lead, some out of conviction, others out of indifference or opportunism. Finally, in February 1274, the imposing number of forty-four bishops, together with the higher clergy of Hagia Sophia, dispatched to the Pope a letter which recognized his primacy — "primum et summum pontificem esse et nominari" — and expressed their preparedness for union. At the same time the Emperor signed with purple ink the profession of faith that had been sent to him from Rome.

The Byzantine delegation, consisting of the former Patriarch Germanus III, the Metropolitan Theophanes of Nicaea, and the grand logothete George Acropolites, set sail on 11 March 1274 and entered Lyons on 24 June. The Emperor's profession of faith, which they brought, contained the dogmatic formulas of the Latin Church, including the *Filioque*. However, the Emperor asked the Pope to avoid any altering of the Creed in regard to the Greeks and to guarantee their rites. The solemn act of union was proclaimed on 29 June. The question of the addition to the Creed and of rites was presumably arranged, orally but successfully, between the Pope and the Greek delegates.

Shortly afterward the Patriarch Joseph resigned at Constantinople and on 16 January 1275 a union liturgy was solemnly celebrated in the imperial palace church. In May 1275 the Byzantine Church received, in the person of the *chartophylax* John Beccus, a new Patriarch in the spirit of the reunion of the Churches. But on 10 January 1276 death overtook Pope Gregory X, whose personality was so very necessary for the continuance of the reconciliation of the Greek Church.

Hostility to the Greeks once more gained the upper hand at the Curia. The agreement was preparing to collapse. Despite all the increased demands of the next Popes, despite all the multiplied formalities and demands for oaths, Michael VIII long continued to be the classical politician of unconditional fulfillment, even though Rome gave him none of the promised aid in the sphere of foreign policy. The resistance of the ecclesiastical opposition at Constantinople became ever harder. A rather vague recognition of the primacy, of the right to appeal to Rome, and of the commemoration of the Pope in the liturgy was all that could be obtained from a majority. But now the Popes were concerned not merely for these points but also for the express addition of the *Filioque* in the Creed, which thus afforded the opponents of union the satisfaction of arguing about a papal or imperial breach of faith.

The fateful development reached its climax with Pope Martin IV, who not only made no objection to an alliance of Charles of Anjou, Philip de Courtenay, and Venice for the reconquest of Constantinople, but removed any last religious scruples when, without any plausible reason, he excommunicated the Emperor Michael VIII on 18 November 1281, and on 26 March 1282, under pain of excommunication and interdict, forbade Catholics to have any contact with Michael or to send him any war material.

CHAPTER 17

The Inner Life of the Byzantine Church in the Age of the Crusades

Whereas in the preceding periods the Byzantine Imperial Church made its importance felt, collectively in synods or in assemblies with the Emperor, only occasionally and for the rest remained curiously amorphous as a population group and particular estate becoming distinctive only in individual personalities, from the middle of the eleventh century a profound change revealed itself. A new *esprit de corps* pervaded the clergy and even made itself noticeable in the constitutional life of the Empire. The causes were varied. The manner in which, for example, the Patriarch Michael Caerularius prevailed *vis-à-vis* the imperial power was certainly due to his own high-handed personality and not to the traditions of his office. Even though he finally failed, dying in 1058 after the Emperor had had him deported, the very action taken against him betrayed his importance. The hierarchy first appeared on the political stage as a compact group under this Patriarch on the occasion of the usurpation of the throne by the Emperor Isaac I Comnenus in 1057. The decisive electoral gathering which enabled Isaac to seize the capital now included not merely the earlier electoral elements — Senate, people, and representatives of the army, — but also the clergy, and it was the Patriarch who presided. And the initiative in the constitutional acclamation of Isaac was taken by a cleric, the Patriarch of Antioch. What had taken place somewhat tumultuously in 1057 was still so impressed on the memory in 1078 that it could be repeated almost as though required by protocol: Senate, people, and synod cooperated harmoniously on a footing of equality to pave the way for the candidate, Nicephorus III Botaneiates. And throughout the twelfth century, whenever the succession to the throne was not assured, and of course only then, the Emperors always sought to induce not only the Senate, army, and people, but also the synod of the clergy, with or without the Patriarch, to join in the formal acclamation.

When the "synod" is mentioned, it is the so-called "permanent synod," *synodos endemousa,* that is usually meant. It consisted of the highest dignitaries of the patriarchal see in deacon's orders and of all archbishops and bishops of the Empire who happened to be staying in the capital. Under the presidency of the Patriarch they regularly discussed and decided the business of the Church. The constantly increasing exemptions of bishoprics from metropolitan authority, which led the creation of ever more "autocephalous" archbishoprics, the pernicious bent of Byzantine provincial prelates for going to the capital as often as possible and staying there as long as possible, and finally the ever growing number of prelates fleeing before the Seljuk occupation of Asia Minor to Constantinople, where they lived on some sort of income, must have caused the number of persons entitled to take part in this synod to grow remarkably at the close of the eleventh century and the beginning of the twelfth. It was only natural that many of these unoccupied fugitive bishops should zealously throw themselves into the political bustle of the capital, which offered them a new and hitherto unknown field of activity, and that, as permanent guests of an institution which was only as such regarded as permanent, they should foster the constructing of a self-conscious *esprit de corps* — even if it was only because of the dissensions that soon appeared within the group. These last were promoted not least of all by the so-called *exokatakoiloi,* that is, the five (later six) highest deacons of Hagia Sophia, who not infrequently combined with the newly elected archbishops against the Patriarch and the representatives of the old, classical metropolitan sees in the synod.

The weapon of these higher clerics of Hagia Sophia was not least of all the canon law. The first director of the law faculty, which of course served especially the constitutional law and the formation of the secular officials, was John Xiphilinus, who soon became Patriarch (1064–75) and as such gave new stimulation to the canon law. The special cultivation of this branch of law then found its home above all with the Patriarch's *chartophylax,* who had meanwhile developed from librarian and archivist to being a sort of vicar general of the Patriarch, precisely because of his knowledge of law. Two belonged to the higher clergy of Hagia Sophia, and the greatest among them, Balsamon, was *chartophylax* before he was promoted to the see of Antioch. There began a scholastic and casuistic reflection on the canonical sources which constituted a counterpoint to the civil law and laid the foundation for a confrontation of state and Church which the early Byzantine epoch had not known in this form. Even the greatest of these canonists, Theodore Balsamon, did not develop in this regard any harsh antithesis to imperial law, and he followed no consistent line in the distribution of powers. But he introduced a manner of investigation which, despite all assurances of the Emperor's privileges in the Church, tended to see in these privileges a concession by the Church rather than a divine right.

The number of clerics at Hagia Sophia and the other great churches in Constantinople in all probability exceeded that at any cathedral in the West. Whether they sought to kill time or to increase their incomes, in any event they provided a great part of the higher instruction in the capital. It is not correct to speak of a reform of the study of theology by the Emperor Alexius I — there was no real study of theology as a discipline of higher education in Constantinople — since the imperial decree of 1107, which called for the installing of various *didaskaloi,* referred not to the teaching profession but to preaching and catechesis. Nevertheless, it can be established for the twelfth century that classical studies flourished under the care of the clergy of Constantinople, but it cannot be determined whether or not this was in any way connected with the decree. The dogmatic controversies that filled this whole period show also that the pursuit of theology was not unfamiliar to these clerics.

Here too must be sought the starting point in the reorganization of the so-called university at the middle of the eleventh century. Alongside the teaching of law stood the teaching of philosophy in which the effort to continue the traditional instruction in the direction of a platonizing, "liberal" philosophy is unmistakable. This trend, which must not be condemned as a movement toward mere verbiage, was halted by a keen logician, John Italus, with a marked interest in the question of universals, which probably went back to his early education in the spirit of the new scholasticism in his Italian homeland. Something of Abelard's *Sic et Non* can be detected in his method of philosophizing. Conflict with the Orthodox Church, which perceived a danger to the truths of revelation in his free philosophical investigation, did not fail to materialize. Proceedings, not unmixed with politics, were instituted against him. To some extent his pupils remained loyal to him, and they were probably not molested for some time. Going beyond his teacher, Eustratius measured his dialectical skill on questions of Christology, but without neglecting the fundamental study of the new age, the writings of Aristotle. But this led to the reappearance of the problem of nominalism, and even the Emperor's protection was unable to save him from, ecclesiastical condemnation in 1117. From the purely Christological viewpoint the exertions of Eustratius can be explained thus: he aspired to lead back to a tolerable degree the theses propounded with an ever decreasing prudence by a conventional and not carefully pondered "neo-Chalcedonianism."

Despite his condemnation the Christological quarrels were not settled, and it was always basically the same problem, even though with variations, that occupied minds. Furthermore, the result of theological encounter with persons from the Latin West, who were stopping in Constantinople or settled there permanently and did not dispute only the *Filioque,* became evident.

A first controversy was concerned with this question: From what point of view can Christ be at the same time the one who offered and the one who accepted the Sacrifice of the Cross. Soterichus Parteugenes, a candidate for the patriarchal see of Antioch, became entangled in distinctions which gained for him the reproach that he was confusing the unity of person with the duality of natures in Christ, and in 1157 he was disqualified for any ecclesiastical dignity. Implicated in his case were even a couple of bishops, in particular the one who brought on the confrontation, Nicephorus Basilakes, one of the *didaskaloi* of the patriarchal see, but of course they got off scot-free. Soon afterward the controversy blazed forth under new auspices: Christ's saying that "the Father is greater than I." A certain Demetrius of Lampe had returned from a diplomatic tour of the West with the relevant information and introduced the dispute into the Byzantine theological world, but we have no exact knowledge of his own position. The question was treated in a whole series of synods, and in 1166 the theological caprices of the Emperor Manuel I Comnenus finally forced a decision. It lacked precision and Hugh Eteriano termed it a sheer scandal, but at Reichersberg people were of the opinion that in it Gerhoh's theses would find support. A final echo of these controversies, called by J. Gouillard "les déviations des didascales," was heard in the theses of a monk, Michael (Myron) Sikidites, who is said to be identical with Michael Glykas. In these was broached the question of the corruptibility of Christ's body and blood in the Eucharist. Synods in 1199 and 1200 basically avoided these theses and reverted to positions which no one questioned.

The monastic life of the time still suffered from the evil consequences of the charistikariate. In the reign of Alexius I there proceeded from the pen of the resigned Patriarch of Antioch, John Oxeites, one of the most important reform writings against this institution. Among the best known monastic founders of the age was Christodulus, who, after a number of attempts, finally in 1088 obtained the island of Patmos, where he established the celebrated monastery of Saint John, bestowing on it complete exemption from any supervision by state or Church. He also gave it a rule, in which he laid down his own strict principles. In the capital in 1136 the Emperor John II Comnenus founded the monastery of the Pantokrator, whose charitable institutions — an infirmary and a home for the aged — were among the most ambitious of any in the Middle Ages, at least according to the tenor of the foundation charter, but they were not directly administered by the monastery. The other monastic foundations of the period also betray the trend to an association between themselves and charitable institutions. At the same time they appear to force the principle of "autodispotism" and to guarantee independence on all sides. The first Serbian foundation on Mount Athos belongs to the close of the twelfth century. This was Chilandarion, which Saint Savas, together with his father, the retired Kral Stephen Nemanja, made the center of "Serbianism" in the monastic republic.

In spite of many new foundations and of a steady increase of monastery property, which was accompanied by a constant granting of privileges, the moral situation of monasticism left much to be desired. Conditions on Athos again and again called for intervention by Emperors and Patriarchs. The complaints of the Metropolitan Eustathius of Thessalonica cast special shame on the status of monastic culture. Above all he deplored that the recruits in the monasteries came for the most part from persons who were interested only in a guaranteed livelihood. He was especially irritated by the turning from the contemplative ideal to a strong economic activity and to the complete neglect of all intellectual interests, which even led to the squandering of the treasures of the monastic libraries. It is worthy of note that to a certain degree Eustathius excluded the monasteries of the capital. Since these monasteries were supported chiefly by pensions for the individual monks, they were probably not obliged to take up the economic reconstruction of their means of subsistence as were those houses which had been jeopardized by the charistikariate.

While the preceding period was the great age of hagiography, characterized by the work of Simeon Metaphrastes, there now began in the great contemporary homiliaries the "codification" of the homiletic tradition. In the first place stood John Xiphilinus, nephew of the Patriarch Xiphilinus; making copious use of Chrysostom he compiled the standard homiliary. The Patriarch John IX Agapetus (1111–34), following the work of Xiphilinus, compiled what is today called the "Patriarchate homiliary."

In short, the time seemed full of most promising beginnings. How they would have developed if the Fourth Crusade had not been diverted can, of course, not be determined. The twelfth century was a period when the West was drawing closer than ever before to the Byzantine East, here and there provoking dangerously, elsewhere ready for symbiosis. The incipient economic "sell out" to the Italian maritime cities, forced by the needs of foreign policy, could not but nourish the animosity felt in many circles for all that was Western, and it is here that the reason is to be sought why Byzantine resistance was especially stiff in the spheres of theology and Church unity. This was no longer, it is true, a resistance which drew its strength from an absolute feeling of superiority. Men like Hugh Eteriano gave Byzantium an idea of the theological potentiality of the West, and hence in Byzantine theological circles of the century a not insignificant nervousness was apparent. To be regarded not as a cause but as concomitants, the to some extent painful confrontations on the "déviations des didascales" were a reason why the distrust of whatever was regarded as "scholasticism" became stronger rather than weaker. But in this way official Byzantium permanently excluded itself from the great Western progress in scientific theology. Elsewhere, however, for example in the world of mysticism and of monastic spirituality, this Byzantine century did not dispose of those leading minds who in concentration on this field would have been able to build a counterweight equal to scholasticism, such as Hesychasm and Palamism formed in the late Byzantine period. And if the twelfth century made available to Byzantium for the first time a real encounter with the freer Western ecclesiastical organization, the political presuppositions were lacking for deducing sound consequences for its own ecclesiastical system. The presuppositions were not present until a generation later. Then persons would take up the experiences of the twelfth century but without having enough time left.

Section Four

The Papacy at the Height of its Power (1198–1216)

Hans Wolter

The period known as the High Middle Ages was without any doubt dominated by the personality of the Pope whose pontificate joined the twelfth and thirteenth centuries together. In it there matured those energies in theology and canon law which had begun to unfold in the twelfth century. At the same time the main features of the thirteenth-century development appeared in the ecclesiastical decisions of this reign. Rarely has a Pope found in his contemporaries so unanimously favorable a judgment as did Innocent III. Most of the problems pertaining to the basic stock of the intellectual life of Church History in the High Middle Ages found under Innocent a settlement which seemed to approach a real solution. He sought to bring the relationship of *regnum* and *sacerdotium,* even in its special form of tension between the papacy and the imperial office, to a practical and a theoretical solution. The Church's commission to foster the sanctification of the world through the proclaiming of the Gospel and the administration of the Sacraments obtained in Innocent an extraordinarily talented pontiff, who made this commission the program of his reign. The demand for poverty, made energetically and angrily on the Church of the poor Saviour by the saints, the laity, the heretics of the twelfth century, did not die away unheard by this Pope. If the irresistible march of canon law presented the Church with a danger, with the institutionalizing of what must properly be filled by the charism of love, namely, the religious life of Christendom, then Innocent sought not unsuccessfully to find the balance between law and love. Between theology as a science and the mystical knowledge of God in the imitation of Christ there was developing a tension which threatened to lead to a diastase, perhaps even to an alienation of the two. Here too Innocent could intervene as mediator. It was his great merit to see the reform needs of the Church in their full compass and in his constant exertions for them to be in accord with the justified concern of criticism, including that of heretics; at the same time he thereby made the most positive contribution to overcoming this dangerous threat to the unity and the truth of Christendom.

The presupposition for these exertions was not merely a claim, but a really exercised authority over Christendom, the possession of a real *dominium orbis christiani,* with which was joined the possibility of enforcing a planning, adjusting, and clarifying will as far as the frontiers of Christendom. Hence, the motto of this unique pontificate of the High Middle Ages can be concisely stated by saying that it sought to realize a "spiritual *dominium mundi.*"

CHAPTER 18

Personality and Program of Innocent III

The Cardinal Deacon Lothar dei Conti di Segni was not yet thirty-eight years old when, on the day of the death of his predecessor. Celestine III, 8 January 1198, in the Septizonium of Septimius Severus, whose ruins had been turned into a stronghold by the Frangipani, he received a majority of votes in the first balloting and all of them in the second. Accepting the election he styled himself Innocent III.

He was born at the end of 1160 or the beginning of 1161. His family's early move to Rome enabled him to obtain his first education there. It was later entrusted to Peter Ismael, probably in the monastery of Sant'Andrea, and was then completed with his philosophical and theological studies at Paris, which lasted till 1187.

Among his teachers at Paris was Peter de Corbeil, whom he was later to appoint as Bishop of Cambrai and eventually as Archbishop of Sens. His fellow-students included Stephen Langton and Robert de Courçon, both of whom he later promoted to the cardinalate, and Eudes de Sully, who, as Bishop of Paris, was eventually his man of confidence in France. At the Fourth Lateran Council he set up a monument to the school of Paris under the auspices of the Master of the Sentences through the mention of the Lombard in a context that gave him the highest praise. Occasional remarks in sermons and letters indicate how much Paris meant to him, even though later he did not show the same confidence in the dialectical method which he had clearly entertained during his studies. In 1187 he left Paris in order to pursue law at Bologna, especially under the most celebrated of the decretists, Huguccio of Pisa. Innocent later made him Bishop of Ferrara.

In November of the year when he transferred to Bologna Lothar received the subdiaconate from Pope Gregory VIII. In 1189 his maternal uncle, Clement III, brought him into the College of Cardinals, bestowing on him the deaconry of Santi Sergio e Bacco, which Clement had himself formerly administered. Lothar's activity at the Curia, more in matters of ecclesiastical jurisdiction than in political questions of any great moment, allowed him time for literary works on ascetical and moral, dogmatic, and canonical topics. Best known and much read until the sixteenth century was his *De miseria humane conditionis,* which sketches a picture of man under the shadow of sin. A corresponding treatise on the dignity of man in the light of grace, which was to round out the work by supplementing and completing it, was not finished. As Pope, he revised his *De missarum mysteriis* and the *De quadripartita specie nuptiarum.*

Innocent III postponed his episcopal consecration and coronation till the feast of Saint Peter's Chair, 22 February, a date that naturally suggested itself because of its symbolic importance.

Innocent III took up his office in the consciousness of a divine summons, and from it apparently derived that much admired sureness of decision and the essentially invariable consistency of his administration — qualities that endured to the end. His superb theological formation enabled him in almost every one of his innumerable letters and decretals to stamp with fundamentally theological explanations a word of instruction which revealed him as the herald of conservative ecclesiastical doctrine. To this was added his command of canon law whose methods he so dominated both in his proceedings and his decisions and was able to carry out so masterfully that in his hand the papal judicial practice was regarded by many experts as a higher school of their discipline. Furthermore, he possessed, perhaps from his mother's Roman family, a sophistication in politics and its ways, especially the instinct for the possible, the famed "snap judgment," which "in every situation caused [him] to desire only the possible, but all of it." Innocent

> was born to rule. Fate had bestowed on him all the gifts for this purpose: an inexhaustible wealth of invention, the most skilful handling of men, an unrivalled combining of tenacity of will with flexibility in execution, the boldest energy in endeavor and the most sober calculation of the means, the vision of a genius for what was great, and painstaking diligence in details. (Haller)

From his years at Paris and Bologna — and at Bologna because of Huguccio especially — he possessed a clearly reasoned notion, which would be a decisive factor in his pontificate, of the fulness of the authority pertaining to him as Pope, of its relationship to the power of secular rulers, above all to that of the Emperor, in whom authority as King in Germany, Burgundy, and Italy differed from the function and power which were his as ruler of the *Sacrum Imperium Romanum.*

To speak of a program of government in the strict sense would be as much a mistake in regard to the accession of Innocent III as at any other change of pontificate. But from the decrees and letters of the first months one can form a sketch of the most important problems which, even in a survey of the entire pontificate, must be regarded as the Pope's chief concerns: order in the Papal State, its protection *vis-à-vis* the threats of expansion from south and north, intensification of the crusade idea and promotion of the project of a crusade, overcoming of the progressively stronger and more dangerous heretical movements, and, finally, what lay at the basis of all the rest and took precedence over them, the reform of the Church in head and members. No one of these four concerns nor all of them together was new. They somehow made their presence known as a program, and as an effort to do justice to the program, in all the pontificates of the twelfth century and determined the legislation of the three Lateran Councils. Innocent III again took up the themes of the Gregorian reform and sought to realize them on a lasting basis.

Celibacy was always, or perhaps even again, a remote and only defectively realized ideal in the Latin West. Simony had by no means been eradicated but again and again emerged in various forms on the lowest and the highest plane. The freedom of the lesser churches, of the bishoprics, and even of the papacy itself remained, as before, either a postulate or at most a precarious achievement. In the monastic world the Cistercian *élan,* which more than anything else had distinguished the twelfth century, was in danger of dying out; had not Alexander III already sent letters of admonition to the general chapter? The canons regular and the Premonstratensians also stood in urgent need of new impulses. The Pope may have entertained little hope that the comfortable peace of the Benedictines could be aroused to life again. Nevertheless, his letters betray a lively awareness of his expecting substantial help from the cooperation of the orders precisely for his work of renewal in the Church. In many respects Innocent III suffered especially from the political and human strife within Latin Christendom, the ceaseless quarrelling of kings and princes, and the interminable feuds of barons and knights, of cities and communes. Internal peace, not only for its own sake, but also for the sake of the external tasks on the frontiers of Christendom became one of his central concerns.

From the outset and, without interruption, to the end of his pontificate, Innocent III carried out his *officium pastorale* in the consciousness of possessing the full authority necessary for it. This corresponded to the comprehensive extent of the office, which was to bear responsibility first for the Roman Church and its property, the *Patrimonium Petri,* and then for all of Christendom. The *plenitudo potestatis* was understood by Innocent, just as it had been taught by his mentor Huguccio, as a *plenitudo potestatis ecclesiasticae,* not as a fullness embracing all spiritual and secular power whatever. It must be regarded as a defining of what is today termed the primacy of jurisdiction of the Bishop of Rome. An overlapping of this power on to the sphere of secular law was not excluded in Innocent's mind, but it happened only in a subsidiary way, when, in accord with the current theory of emergency, cases were referred to the Pope's decision in which the secular stages of appeal had broken down; for example, in a case of strife between kings, when no superior judge, deciding with authority, could be called upon. Emperor and kings received their power, as Innocent recognized, directly from God, just as the papacy did. The kingship claimed by Innocent himself as a secular dominion referred to the royal possessions of the Roman Church in Central Italy, the *Patrimonium Petri,* where he considered himself as a King among kings, and not, following the Carolingian model, as the autonomous ruler of a territory. Perhaps the claim to possess not only spiritual but also secular power referred to the coercive power of the Church intervening even in secular legal relationships, to papal intervention, by means of instructions, *ratione peccati.*

Innocent had his idea concisely formulated at the Fourth Lateran Council:

> Just as we do not want the laity to usurp the rights of clerics, similarly we must see to it that clerics do not claim the rights of the laity. And so we forbid all clerics to extend their privileges to the prejudice of secular authority, under the pretext of the liberty of the Church. On the contrary, they should be content with the written law and the previously approved customs, so that what is Caesar's will be rendered to Caesar and what is God's to God, in accord with the objectively right order which is proper to each. (Constitutio 42)

In addition to the separation of powers, Innocent stressed the higher unity of Christendom and the consequent rights of the Holy See, and he likewise intended to maintain his own rights relevant to the Empire, which in his view did not affect the principle that the imperial authority was derived directly from God. Kings, princes and magistrates within the frontiers of Christendom were to the Pope not merely bearers of an independent power of jurisdiction but at the same time outstanding members of the mystical body of the Church. As such, not only as private persons but precisely as officials, they were subject to the pastoral care of the Roman Bishop. Only thus can one interpret the official statements of emperors and kings when in their correspondence with the Pope they spoke of obedience, devotion, and readiness to carry out the mandates of the Holy See. Innocent himself defined the limits of his full authority, which lay fixed on the one hand in the *ius divinum,* on the other hand in the conscience of the individual. By its very nature as *potestas ecclesiastica* it was clearly distinct from the *potestas saecularis.* Canon law still indicates that any clearer delimitation of boundaries is not always possible in practice. The decision as to whether a matter pertained to the sphere of divine or of human law, in which the Pope possessed the power of dispensing, was left by Innocent to tradition and in practice to deliberation by a council.

> Under Innocent III the Pope's position in the Church did not become something basically different. But he gave to the doctrine of the primacy a strict formulation and systematic justification and deeply impressed on the consciousness of the Western Church the Roman Bishop's position as the ordinary holder of all ecclesiastical power. (H. Tillman)

Chapter 19

The Spiritual Monarch as Arbiter Mundi

The order of Christendom — *pax et iustitia* — was entrusted to two powers, the spiritual power, which belonged in its fulness to the Pope, and the secular power, which was shared by a number of bearers: kings, princes, magistrates. Among these secular authorities, the imperial dignity was, in accord with tradition, confided to the German King. To the imperial office, because of its function as *advocatus* of the Roman Church, pertained a certain universality that had never been precisely defined. The intimate interrelationship of the spiritual and the secular in the whole of Christendom in the High Middle Ages thus caused the Pope, whose plenitude of spiritual power was undisputed, to appear as its real monarch. The real power of the Emperor, on the other hand, never went beyond the bounds of those areas over which he reigned as King: Germany, Burgundy, Lombardy. Since, moreover, the spiritual power, because of the interrelationship just mentioned, maintained also in the secular areas claims which were partly of public law or of a political nature, there belonged to the monarchy of its holder an enhanced importance, which was asserted in many ways, if not always successfully, during the pontificate of Innocent III, thanks both to his statesmanlike personality and also to the total political situation at the turn of the century, which was favorable to him. Innocent always acted ultimately from motives deriving from his all-embracing and universal responsibility for the welfare of all of Christendom: for *pax et iustitia.* He aspired to promote this *mundus christianus* and its peace as arbiter, able, it is true, to dispose of only a limited and by no means always effective coercive power, but also in possession of the moral power of his universally acknowledged primacy as the Vicar of Christ. Whoever confessed Christ — and this included kings, princes, and magistrates — was for that very reason subject, in respect to his thinking and acting as a Christian, to that directing authority of the Vicar of Christ which Innocent made use of with amazing assurance and in countless cases everywhere throughout Christendom.

The Papal State

The freedom of the Roman Church, her Curia, and her Bishop was a presupposition for an effective exercise of this directing authority. In accord with current notions, the guarantee of this freedom was the possession and revenues of the *Patrimonium Petri,* that territorial complex whose real frontiers were always in dispute and whose constitutional structure, also involved in constant change, was at that time tending toward complete feudalization. And so Innocent began his pontificate by establishing peace and order in the *Patrimonium* and in those states that had long been vassals of the Holy See.

The *Patrimonium,* which Innocent aimed to rule with the forms of a strictly secular royal authority, had to be again subjugated because of the confusion produced under Henry VI. The Romans were victorious, thanks to the Pope's support, in their quarrel with Viterbo, but Innocent also contrived to bind Viterbo to himself. Basing himself on the titles of donation and privileges compiled by Cencio in the *Liber censuum,* Innocent then began his so-called policy of recovery, which, not without resistance, brought again under the papacy's control the Duchy of Spoleto and the Marches of Ancona. But what was recovered lay like a bar, from sea to sea, between the Kingdom of Sicily to the south and North Italy, disputed between the cities and the imperial power. In this territory Innocent regarded himself as the sovereign lord, not even subject to the feudal suzerainty of the Emperor.

The Vassal States

In accord with the arrangements made by the Emperor Henry VI in his last will, the Empress Constance, as regent, received the Kingdom of Sicily in fief from the Pope in her own name and that of the young King Frederick. For her part she disposed by her own last will that, following her death, which occurred on 28 November 1198, the Pope should assume the regency and the wardship of Frederick, who had been crowned on 17 May 1198. Innocent carried out this office for ten years. He first of all obtained from the crown, in a concordat at the end of 1198, the renunciation of the state's ecclesiastical supremacy. Innocent obtained the ratification of this separation by the imperial authority. The moment that the Emperor Otto IV moved to conquer the Kingdom of Sicily he was excommunicated by Innocent on 18 November 1210, and the sentence was solemnly published on 21 March 1211. Finally, Frederick II, whom Innocent declared the champion of the Church against the excommunicated Emperor, repeated in the Golden Bull of Eger on 12 July 1213 a promise given earlier to leave Sicily independent. To the end of his life, accordingly, Innocent was able to maintain the order that he sought in Sicily. And even after King Frederick had been declared of age on 26 December

1208, the Pope contrived in every single case to prevent him from restoring the ecclesiastical regime of his forebears.

Nevertheless, the ten-years' regency meant for Innocent a heavy financial and political burden, implicated as he was in unending struggles with the great vassals of the crown. Despite everything, at the end of the regency Innocent could hand over to Frederick only a seriously disorganized Kingdom. This attempt at real rule, even though it was made for and in the name of another, was basically a failure.

In the Christian lands Innocent often and not without success called for a like cooperation of the territorial episcopate in his effort to assure the peace and order of Christendom.

The Empire

Central in more than one sense in the Pope's thoughts, plans, and decisions throughout his pontificate was his concern for the *Imperium* and for the theoretical and practical relations between the papacy and the imperial office. The Empire became vacant on the death of Henry VI in 1197. The sequel was the double election of 1198: of Philip of Swabia on 8 March and of Otto of Brunswick on 9 July. A decision could, as always, be reached only by a clear preponderance of power on the part of one of the rivals, that is, by an appeal to arms. While Innocent was apprised of the elections he was not asked to give a decision as arbiter. In regard to the imperial crown the Pope reserved the freedom to bestow it on the one whom he would regard as the "more suited." With this crown was involved the duty of aiding the Roman Church, and so the Pope felt it was up to him to determine which claimant could best fulfill this task. When both men applied to Rome for the imperial crown, Innocent at first postponed a decision. Plenipotentiaries of both Kings went to Rome, where an understanding was reached: Otto's retirement was agreed upon and Philip's recognition as King and Emperor-elect was decided. But Philip's assassination at Bamberg on 21 June 1208 by the Count Palatine Otto of Wittelsbach eventually led to the general recognition of Otto of Brunswick in Germany, and this was ratified by his unanimous election at Frankfurt on 11 November.

Otto IV received the imperial crown from Innocent III on 4 October 1209. But then, contrary to the Pope's expectations and his own earlier assurances, Otto launched an attack on the Kingdom of Sicily. The moment that the Emperor violated the Sicilian frontier, on 18 November 1210, Innocent excommunicated him; the sentence was renewed in stronger terms on the following Holy Thursday and all persons were released from oaths they had taken to the Emperor. In September of the same year, 1211, Innocent obtained the election at Nürnberg of Frederick of Sicily as King of Germany. When the latter arrived in Germany in the autumn of 1212, there ensued an unending defection of the German princes from the Emperor Otto. The decision taken at Nürnberg was confirmed by a new election at Frankfurt in December 1212, and then Frederick was crowned at Mainz. The decision between him and the Emperor Otto was made at the battle of Bouvines on 27 July 1214, in which Otto, who had taken the field on behalf of the English, was defeated by the French. This was, at the same time, the end of the contest over the German throne, for now even the princes of the lower Rhineland accepted King Frederick II.

In the Golden Bull of Eger, on 12 July 1213, Frederick promised the Pope all that Otto IV had promised at Speyer in 1209: recognition of the recovery of papal territory in Central Italy, abandonment of the *ius spolii* and the *regalia* in regard to the spiritual princes, renunciation of intervention and participation in elections of abbots and bishops, allowing of appeals to the Curia, and, finally, aid in the struggle against heresy. The Golden Bull created imperial law, legalized the Pope's territorial policy in regard to the Papal State, and replaced the Concordat of Worms by a new regulation that was far more favorable for the Church. Frederick's position as King of Germany was confirmed by the Lateran Council of 1215.

Without the Pope's knowledge Frederick had taken the cross at his second coronation at Aachen on 23 July 1215. Shortly before his death Innocent obtained from Frederick the promise that, after receiving the imperial crown, he would turn over the Kingdom of Sicily to his son Henry, who had already been crowned. In this connection Frederick again acknowledged the feudal suzerainty of the Roman Church over Sicily.

England

England had played an important role in the contest over the German throne, both because of King Richard I's active involvement in the candidacy of his nephew, Otto of Brunswick, and because of the later association of King John with Otto in his struggle against Frederick II, who was supported by Philip II of France.

After Richard's death on 6 April 1199, war broke out again, since Philip II was promoting the succession of John's nephew, Prince Arthur, to the Angevin fiefs in France. In the Peace of Le Goulet (May 1200) John had to bind himself not to support Otto of Brunswick. Innocent annulled this article of the treaty and admonished the English King to give effective aid to his nephew. War between John and Philip was resumed in 1202, despite the Pope's threats, and ended with the conquest of Normandy and most of John's other French fiefs by Philip Augustus.

Conflict erupted over the succession to Archbishop Hubert Walter of Canterbury, who died in July 1205. In December 1206 Innocent had some of the monks who were then in Rome elect a candidate of his own, the English curial Cardinal Stephen Langton. Though King John angrily rejected Langton, the Pope consecrated him in June 1207 and invested him with the pallium despite the absence of the royal approval. He intended to force his admission to Canterbury by threat of interdict. In March 1208 the Pope actually laid on England an interdict that was in general carefully observed. The King expelled the Canterbury monks, confiscated the property and revenues of clerics and bishops who obeyed the interdict, and left sees and abbeys which became vacant unfilled. Negotiations for a settlement broke down and King John was excommunicated in January 1209.

The King ruthlessly continued his oppressive policy in regard to the Church, and the resumed negotiations collapsed in the summer of 1211. Complaints by the banished bishops induced the Pope at the end of February 1213 to absolve the

King's subjects from their oaths. No actual deposition of the King, however, was pronounced, even though Innocent had threatened it, but the Pope declared the war of Philip II of France against John a crusade. Since Philip strenuously pushed forward his preparations, while John was not sure of the support of his barons, the English King accepted the papal conditions of peace on 13 May 1213 to recognize Archbishop Langton, to permit the return of the fugitive bishops, to restore all the confiscated Church property. Two days later on his own initiative, he placed the Kingdom under the protection of the Holy See as a papal fief, promising 700 pounds sterling for England and 300 for Ireland as an annual *census*. This payment, in addition to which the customary Peter's Pence continued to be paid, was not definitely abolished until 1366.

Innocent thereupon deprived the French undertaking against England of its character as a crusade and forbade any attack on England, which was now under his protection. The ordering of the ecclesiastical situation lay in the hands of the papal agent Pandulf and Cardinal Nicholas of Tusculum. In the war with France, recently begun by John himself, which resulted in the battle of Bouvines, the Cardinal Legate Robert de Courçon was able, despite the French victory, to arrange a five-years' armistice on the basis of the *status quo* (18 September 1214). In the war against the rebel barons, who on 15 June 1215 compelled John to issue the *Magna carta libertatum*, which restricted the crown's feudal and sovereign rights, Innocent stood by the King, who had, moreover, taken the cross on 4 March 1215 in order to assure himself even more of the Church's protection. On 24 August 1215 Innocent declared *Magna carta* null and void. But this judgment was disregarded in England, even by Archbishop Langton, who was thereupon suspended.

In Rome Langton strove in vain for the lifting of his suspension, and the Pope forbade his return to England. At the Fourth Lateran Council Innocent renewed the excommunication of the rebel barons, laid an interdict on London, and rebuked the French King for supporting the rebels. These had offered the English throne to the French Crown Prince Louis, whose wife was a niece of John's. Even though the Cardinal Legate Gualo again forbade an attack on England at the assembly of Melun, Louis landed in England on 21 May 1216. He was excommunicated by Gualo and the areas already occupied fell under interdict. While the letters in which Innocent asked the French bishops for their part to publish these sentences were *en route*, the Pope died on 16 July. John Lackland followed him to the grave on 19 October. The Cardinal Legate was able to have John's underage son, Henry III, crowned and to induce the barons to take the oath of loyalty to him on 11 November. Louis was obliged to abandon the English enterprise, and the Cardinal Legate arranged the Peace of Kingston on 12 September 1217. Louis left England, and Henry III obtained general recognition. The unusual course of events in England, culminating in what was at least an external success on the part of Innocent III, shows the Pope in almost every phase of the dramatic succession of events not merely as the tenacious "master of politics" but also at the same time as guided by the religious concerns and motives of his pontificate: freedom of the Church, the crusade, and peace among nations.

France

The Curia and the papacy had long been bound to France by especially active and cordial relations. But the Church's "eldest daughter" was also her most demanding. After a long resistance King John had conceded the freedom of the Church in England; the Empress Constance had promulgated the renunciation of interference by the crown in the Sicilian Kingdom; and the contest over the throne had produced the same result in Germany. But in France the Church continued to be strictly dependent on the crown.

King Philip II Augustus (1180–1223) of France was one of the most self-willed princes who ever resisted the measures of Innocent III. He abandoned his second wife, Ingeborg of Denmark, the day following their marriage in 1193 and sought to obtain an annulment, thereby beginning a matrimonial case which clouded his relations with Innocent throughout that Pope's pontificate. Occasionally the King found himself compelled to make a seeming submission, as, for example, on the occasion of the interdict which was laid on the royal *demesne* on 13 January 1200, even though the Pope could not count on the loyalty of all the bishops there. The Pope tried several times to mediate in the ceaseless strife with England. But when Philip undertook measures against John on the basis of feudal law — the war ended with the conquest of Normandy in May-June 1204 — he resisted an intervention by the Pope and at the assembly of Mantes on 22 August 1203 made the celebrated declaration that, according to feudal law, he was not bound in what pertained to his relations with his vassals to heed the admonitions of the Holy See. The Pope then expressly confirmed this. But within the royal *demesne* itself Philip was not at all willing to let the Church be governed by the Pope; he regarded himself as her master first of all and only then the Pope. Innocent's consistently affable language in his correspondence with this King, his great gentleness *vis-à-vis* the French crown, is amazing in view of the fact that in his scandalous marriage case Philip did not retreat, he did not submit to the Pope's will, and the final settlement proceeded from his free decision, based on political motives, in April 1213. The King defended his clergy against the claims of the princes and the demands of the communes, but he insisted on their subordination to the crown and the services corresponding to this. He seldom interfered in elections, but the clergy remained subject to the royal tribunal. Philip Augustus intended to be, and was, master of the Church in France, and Innocent tolerated the situation.

Scandinavia, Poland, and the Balkan Peninsula

While in Sweden Innocent III supported the legitimate King, or at least the one he regarded as legitimate, against a real, or alleged usurper, in Norway he decided against the claims of King Sverre and aided the opposition to him in the country. Whether he acted rightly can no longer be decided. He commanded King Knut VI of Denmark and King Sverker II Carlsson of Sweden — "per apostolica scripta mandamus" — to support the Baglar party, which was friendly to the Church, in order to assure the protection of the churches, the freedom of the clergy, and the care of the poor. The generally opposed Birkebein Sverre, however, did not yield, despite excommunication and interdict, and it was only under his successor, Haakon IV, that an agreement, based on the arrangement of 1152, was reached.

In Denmark Innocent found a sympathetic collaborator in the clever, energetic, and powerful Archbishop Absalom of Lund, the founder of Copenhagen, until the latter's death in 1201. Primate of Denmark and Sweden from 1177, Absalom was one of the strongest personalities in Scandinavian ecclesiastical history.

Like Absalom in the north, in Poland the Primate, Archbishop Henry Kietlicz of Gniezno (1199–1219), a friend of the Pope from his school days in Paris, worked in close union with the Holy See. Through him Innocent deprived the refractory Vladislas III of authority by excommunicating him in 1206. In 1210 the Pope even achieved the recognition of Poland's feudal dependence on the Roman Church, already prepared for earlier.

Besides the Bulgarians, already mentioned, Innocent was approached in 1198 by King Vulk of Dalmatia and Vulk's brother, the Great Zupan Stephen of Serbia. He declared that he was prepared to regulate ecclesiastical conditions in Dalmatia by erecting a separate province. The tension existing between Hungary and Serbia-Dalmatia and between Hungary and the Ruthenians of Volhynia, in addition to the political changes in Greece from the time of the Fourth Crusade, rendered impossible a continuation of the Pope's policy.

CHAPTER 20

The Fourth Crusade and the Latin Empire

Concern for the East dominated the entire pontificate of Innocent III. In the Pope were united a number of goals, the legacy of the Gregorian ideas: reunion of the Greek and Latin Churches, safety of the holy places, recovery of lost areas of the crusader states, peace among Western princes and within their respective dominions, both as a prerequisite for participation in the crusade and as a value in its own right, the *bonum pacis,* that is, as the optimum essential condition of an orderly ecclesiastical life. Furthermore, the Kingdom of Jerusalem was a vassal state of the Holy See, which was therefore obliged to aid it actively. In the Empire there was no Emperor and the contest for the throne monopolized all the resources of the princes. The Kings of France and England were in conflict over the succession to Richard Lionheart. The Kingdom of Sicily had been turned over by the Empress Constance to the Pope as regent and guardian of her son, Frederick. So the year 1200 appeared favorable for the arranging of a crusade as a repetition of that of Urban II a century before.

The preparations began with a letter from the Pope to the Emperor Alexius III

Angelus on behalf of reunion. Fulk of Neuilly preached the crusade in France, Abbot Martin of Pairis in Germany. Not the Kings but the barons and manorial lords were gained for the cause.

Egypt, as the most vulnerable part of the Ayubite Empire, had been selected as the immediate goal of the crusade. But at a meeting between Montferrat and Philip of Swabia, which was attended also by the latter's brother-in-law, Alexius, it was discussed whether the expedition could not intervene *en route* to place Alexius on the Byzantine imperial throne. Meanwhile, Geoffrey de Villehardouin had concluded a treaty with Venice in regard to the means of transportation. In return for 85,000 silver marks of Cologne the Republic of Venice agreed to supply ships and provisions for one year from 28 June 1202 for 4,500 knights and their horses, 9,000 squires, and 20,000 infantry; in addition, fifty galleys were promised as convoy on condition that one-half of all conquests was awarded to Venice. When the army gathered at Venice in June 1202, the money agreed upon was not forthcoming, and so the expedition was at Venice's mercy.

The crusading army, which did not put to sea until 8 November, had first of all to recover Zara from Hungary for the Republic — an enterprise that Innocent had formally forbidden. Then it also had to winter there. Venice or, rather, the Doge Henry Dandolo, was excommunicated. Philip of Swabia now made known that responsibility for the crusaders' debt to Venice would be accepted if the expedition were to make for Constantinople and enthrone Alexius; furthermore, the crusade to the Holy Land would then be provisioned and supplied with a military force of 10,000 men. Despite some hesitations and a papal warning the majority of the crusaders allowed themselves to be gained for this project.

Accompanied by the young Prince Alexius, the fleet appeared before Constantinople on 24 June 1203. While the usurper, Alexius III, fled, the officials he had deserted brought his blinded predecessor and brother, Isaac II, out of prison and reinstated him on the throne, thinking that they had thus deprived the Venetians and the leaders of the crusade, who had come to restore the deposed Emperor, of the essential motive for conquering the city. And in fact it sufficed to have Alexius crowned as co-Emperor in Hagia Sophia on 1 August 1203. His government had first bound itself to pay the Venetians the promised money, but this was impossible. Then it obliged itself to work for the recognition of Rome by the Greek Church, but the clergy and people protested. The presence of the crusaders in the city and its environs aggravated the situation.

In February 1204 a palace revolution gave the imperial throne to a new usurper, Alexius V Mourtzouphlos. Then in April the crusaders took the city, which was given over to a three-days' sack. The plundering and bloodshed reduced the vast and beautiful city to a heap of rubble. "Even the Muslims," wrote Nicetas Choniates, "would have been more merciful." The Latin leaders, together with the Venetians, chose as Emperor, not Montferrat, but the weaker Count Baldwin IX of Flanders; he was supposed to become suzerain of all the conquered territory except for the areas assigned to the Doge of Venice, such as the three-eighths of Constantinople, administered by a Venetian *podestà.* Since a Frank had become Emperor, then, according to the arrangement, a Venetian had to become Patriarch; Thomas Morosini thus obtained that office. A constitution, the *Assises of Romania,* made the Emperor the chairman of an hereditary House of Lords. Almost all the European provinces of the Byzantine Empire were conquered and divided among several hundred crusade barons. In the remnant of the Byzantine dominions beyond the straits Greek successor states were set up at Trebizond and Nicaea, and some of Epirus was preserved. The recovery was planned and carried out from Nicaea.

Following a first report from the new Emperor Baldwin, Innocent III gave his assent to what was happening at Constantinople, but more exact information evoked energetic protests and threats from the Pope, who was deeply shocked by the sack of Constantinople and who, as a statesman, had a presentiment of unhappy results. But meanwhile his legate had dispensed all the crusaders from continuing to the Holy Land if they would oblige themselves to support for two years the new Latin Empire, which was called Romania. If, nevertheless, the Pope had hoped that the happenings at Constantinople would result in reunion with the Greek Church, the negotiations were unsuccessful, especially as the tactlessness of the Cardinal Legate Pelagius was not an appropriate means of effecting reconciliation. The city's fate and the misguided policy of the Latin hierarchy deepened the breach instead of helping to close it. The policy of imposing Latinization on Greece was a fatal mistake.

And so the ill-advised enterprise that was the Fourth Crusade turned out to be an immense folly and brought the Holy Land itself no aid but instead a further burden in so far as, from now on, many crusaders preferred to assist Romania in Greece instead of keeping alive the collapsing rule of the Franks in Palestine. With the Byzantine Empire, a powerful bulwark against the advancing Turks had been almost ruined. Something that could not be erased from memory had been allowed to take place and a great hatred had been born, which was to envenom the relations of the Christian East and the Christian West for generations to come.

However, indirect help had been provided the Holy Land by the fall of Byzantium. The frightened Sultan concluded a ten-years' armistice with the Kingdom of Jerusalem. In 1210 John de Brienne married Mary, the heiress of King Amauri, and on this occasion received from both the French King and Pope Innocent the sum of 40,000 silver pounds. In 1212 he was able to have the armistice extended for five more years. Mary died giving birth to Yolande in 1212, and John, who acted as regent, married Stephanie of Armenia in 1214.

The Pope sought to mediate at Antioch between Bohemond IV and his nephew, Raymond Ruben. Bohemond remembered that Antioch was formally a fief of Byzantium, but his nephew's part was vigorously taken by King Leo of Armenia, who then entered into personal negotiations with the Pope. The long drawn out contest was left for settlement by the Patriarch of Jerusalem, since Innocent became weary of it, above all when Bohemond rejected his intervention as unjustified on the ground that a question of pure feudal law was at stake. Despite these and many other difficulties in the Christian remnant in Syria-Palestine, Innocent continued to exert himself to realize a new crusade, without being discouraged by the catastrophe of that of 1203–4.

That the mood of the West could still be directed to one was probably made evident to him by the singular story of the French and German Children's Crusade of 1212. Many youngsters from Lower Lotharingia and the Rhineland, from ten to eighteen years of age, made their way south. They aspired to recover the Holy Land, unarmed and penniless. Nicholas of Cologne had gone as far as Rome with what was left of his band, but Innocent sent them home. The French groups under Stephen of Cloeys reached Marseilles and were then taken on board ships by merchants; some of them perished in a storm, the others were sold into slavery in Egypt and North Africa.

Pope Innocent finally utilized the Fourth Lateran Council as a new means of arousing interest in the crusade.

CHAPTER 21

Reform and the Struggle against Heresy

Like the crusade, the will for reform also dominated the thought and activity of Innocent III. This care embraced the whole Christian world. Thus, in the first year of his pontificate, Innocent wrote to Iceland to admonish the episcopate and the clergy that "certain things are to be extirpated with particular effectiveness so that thorns and thistles may not suffocate the seed of the Gospel.

Canonical obedience was enjoined; prelates were urged to an exemplary life in order to facilitate such obedience on the part of their subjects; murder, arson, incontinence were mentioned as common crimes; contact with the excommunicated Norwegian usurper Sverre was denounced; the bishops were advised to display courage in rebuking, "for a shepherd who is unwilling to rebuke those who do wrong leads them to death by his silence."

Concern for the maintaining of the purity of ecclesiastical morals and discipline recurs like a leitmotif in many letters, admonishing the episcopate and religious superiors, individuals and groups, princes and magistrates. The crusades had evoked new needs and introduced an oriental and Byzantine luxury into the West. The courtly love of the troubadours had begun to exercise a destructive influence on family and marriage morality. The amendment of prostitutes and the arranging of marriages for them was clearly a problem. Usury was eating into the economic and social structure like a cancer and had to be resisted. The clergy were greatly exposed to the general moral decay. Their avarice, especially among the lower clergy, who saw the worst example in the higher ranks, compromised the care of souls. Celibacy was scarcely observed any more among both the higher and the lower clergy, and the hankering after luxury and a comfortable life persisted in showing itself in their ranks. Divine worship was carelessly celebrated, the care of souls was neglected. The secularization of the higher clergy increased, and monasteries, such as those belonging to the orders of Cluny, Cîteaux, Grandmont, and Prémontré, were in need of reform.

Innocent III inaugurated reform with himself and with the Curia. The centralization of ecclesiastical administration and legislation had in the course of the twelfth century reached a degree which began to involve an intolerable burden for the Curia. Innocent sought to restore the balance between episcopal administration and final recourse to the Holy See, and so he insisted on limiting or abolishing improper appeals to Rome. In cases that were clear, any appeal to Rome was forbidden — "omni appellatione remota" — and all appeals were curtailed. Metropolitans were admonished of their duty of visitation. If there appears here a certain tendency toward decentralization of the administrative power, Innocent, very keenly mindful of his *plenitudo potestatis,* still reserved *causae maiores* to himself: the rearrangement of diocesan boundaries and jurisdiction in Spain, France, Hungary, and Germany, where he detached Prague from the province of Mainz and created the autonomous province of Prague; the rendering of decisions in disputed episcopal elections; and the confirmation of elections. Only the Pope was qualified to approve a transfer from one see to another, only he could remove a bishop from office. Hence the episcopate was closely bound to the Holy See, but in their dioceses the bishops' freedom of action was guaranteed.

Together with administrative reform the moral renewal of the Church was Innocent's weightiest concern: he simplified the living standard of the Curia, sought to revive propriety and honesty at the Curia, established an exact tariff of fees, and forbade the acceptance of bribes. In the episcopate he was interested in the choosing of candidates of such quality that a morally sound generation could arise, and hence candidates who were too young, too little educated, or of an evil reputation were rejected. Innocent stressed bishops' duty of making the *visitatio ad limina* every four years in order to report on the state of their dioceses. In the event that the frequently inculcated duty of visitation was fulfilled, a report was not difficult to obtain. In admonishing negligent bishops, Innocent often resorted to fraternal reproof, given by a neighboring bishop. In regard to erring prelates or those who had been accused in Rome, Innocent took action prudently. He first sought to clarify the actual state of affairs, either directly interrogating the person concerned or having an inquiry made. He then proceeded sternly against those really found guilty. His basic principle was expressed thus: the bishop is for the Church, not the Church for the bishop. Especially in regard to the lower clergy he demanded of the bishops a firm hand and a stubborn enforcing of law and precept. Violation of celibacy, a secularized mode of life in dress and appearance, avarice, forgery, pluralism, simoniacal practices — such were some of the offenses that had to be reprimanded and eliminated in the lower clergy. The bishop was to remember to convoke diocesan synods again; the metropolitan was to hold provincial synod.

In the lay world, Innocent made himself the defender of the indissolubility of marriage and stressed that the *consensus de praesenti* established the matrimonial bond. His procedure in regard to royal marriage cases in France, Aragón, Bohemia, and Castile proved that he made no distinction between high and low and for the sake of the sanctity of marriage put up with political difficulties and losses. He took a stand against usury and supported the bishops' measures against this widespread evil.

He wanted to lead monasteries, monks, and canons back to fidelity to their rule and their particular constitutions in order here also to pave the way for reform. The road to this reform of monasteries was indicated by means of excellent canons at the Council of Paris in 1212 under the presidency of the papal legate, Cardinal Robert de Courçon. Poverty, enclosure, stability, hospitality, a fair paternal administration on the part of the superiors, and obedience were again demanded and enjoined. Innocent encouraged the founding of new orders, as, for example, the Hospitallers of the Holy Spirit, was confirmed by Innocent in 1213. For it he founded the Hospital of the Holy Spirit at Rome. He likewise encouraged John of Matha, who established the Order of the Most Holy Trinity for the ransom and exchange of captives. This society was completely in accord with the age of the crusades. He then confirmed its rule on 17 December 1198. The growing danger from heresy, above all in France, even induced the Pope to call upon the Cistercian order to undertake preaching even outside the monastery.

The reform of the Church was the more necessary since the critical forces, which were competing in the breakdown of ecclesiastical morality and were driven even to doubt the Church herself, managed to appeal to ever wider circles in the Church and win them for themselves. Various groups had already been specified and condemned by one of Innocent's predecessors. The Cathari especially became the real danger to the unity of the Church's faith around the turn of the century. Apart from the Balkan Bogomiles, they were found mainly in Lombardy, Tuscany, the Marches of Ancona, Romagna, and even in the *Patrimonium.* A particularly close and well organized social class caused alarm in the Midi, especially in the County of Toulouse and the neighboring areas. In the cities, above all Albi, which thus contributed to them the name "Albigensians," and even in the country they often enjoyed the protection of magistrates and lords. The parochial clergy were often sympathetic with the ideas of the Cathari because of daily contact with them, and hence all the decisive forces — hierarchy, religious, parish clergy, and secular powers — appeared to have broken down. Thus Innocent III, appealed to by an apprehensive minority in the district, was moved to intervene.

Innocent exerted himself in an all-embracing manner everywhere in Christendom for an energetic attack on heresy, with recourse to all the spiritual and secular means that were at his disposal. In the countries beyond the Alps, such as Bosnia, in Aragón, and in Italy, and above all in the Midi his efforts were clearly to be seen. He began with admonitions to the bishops to make themselves conversant with the increasing danger from heretical movements and to take action against them. He gave the proper example in person in the districts and cities of the *Patrimonium.* This is the background of the later celebrated decretal "Vergentis in senium," of 25 March 1199, in which for the first time heresy was equated with the *crimen laesae maiestatis* of Roman Law. But he modified the strictness of the law, which judged, condemned, and punished, by expanding the Roman Law's *misericordia,* which allowed the descendants of the condemned their lives but not the confiscated family property, by restoring their possessions to these in the event of a sincere conversion. In the fight against heresy the Church saw herself dependent on a close collaboration of the spiritual and secular powers. But in the event that princes and cities, especially in Italy and the Midi, were either too indolent for such collaboration or were opposed to it, there was still a final, radical means: the crusade against heretics.

At first Innocent commissioned members of the Cistercian Order to proceed against heretics, as his legates to the bishops and princes, as his theologians to the heretics themselves.

The behavior of the Cistercians — from 1204 they were Abbot Arnaud-Amaury of Cîteaux and two monks of Fontfroide, Rudolph and Peter of Castelnau — evoked criticism from Saint Dominic Guzmán, who in 1206 sought out the Pope at Rome with practical proposals and, furnished by him with corresponding instructions and mandates, returned to the Midi. They represented the view, long shared by the Pope too, that it was necessary to make use of those means which the heretics themselves successfully employed in their cause: preaching and, especially on the part of the preachers, a simple mode of life.

Meanwhile, the Pope himself was proceeding with disciplinary measures against the careless episcopate, which he succeeded in almost entirely renewing in the course of the years up to the Fourth Lateran Council. He then took action also against Raymond VI, Count of Toulouse, the most important prince in the French Midi, whom he excommunicated in 1207 because of his neutral attitude toward the heretics. When Peter of Castelnau was assassinated on 14 January 1208, the whole situation became aggravated to such an intolerable degree that the Pope felt constrained to have recourse to the ultimate means at his disposal, the crusade. Innocent had made it clear to the princes from the start of his pontificate that their fight against heresy was a crusade. He now turned to King Philip II Augustus of France, feudal suzerain of the Count of Toulouse, and requested military intervention. Innocent promised him support and for this purpose declared that the war was a crusade. He arranged crusade preaching in order to encourage enlistment and promised a plenary indulgence to the participants and the protection of the law for their possessions and their families. The King was permitted to collect a tenth and a twentieth of the annual income of ecclesiastical benefices. Nevertheless, Philip, whom the Pope had already approached for help several times since 1204, declined to participate in person because of his strained relations with England.

Nevertheless, the preaching of the crusade was so successful that Raymond VI in 1209 sought to immobilize the impending campaign by a spectacular reconciliation with the Church, agreeing to put himself, as a crusader, at the head of the approaching contingents. He intended to use the expedition especially to suppress a vassal who opposed him, Raymond-Roger, Viscount of Béziers and Carcassonne. Leadership of the expedition was formally vested, it is true, in the legates, but they needed the services of an expert for military strategy and tactics, and so they accepted Raymond VI's offer. Béziers was taken on 21 July 1209. The massacre of 7,000 women, children, and old persons in the church of La Madeleine and the burning of the cathedral became ineffaceable memories of the harshness of these struggles. Carcassonne fell on 8 August 1209, and the Viscount Raymond-Roger was captured and imprisoned. His fiefs were acquired by Simon de Montfort, Earl of Leicester, who, following the renewal of the excommunication of the Count of Toulouse at the Synod of Avignon on 6 September 1209, also received the leadership of the crusade.

Raymond went to Rome to justify himself. The Pope dealt kindly with him and had his case reexamined by a legatine court in the Midi, which ratified the sentence of Avignon. Once again Innocent tried to save the Count. But at a synod held at

Montpellier on 22 January 1211, Raymond's excommunication was renewed, and finally, on 15 April 1211, the sentence was ratified by the Pope. Apparently the legates had collaborated with Simon de Montfort, who now turned the crusade against Toulouse itself. Simon was eventually able to conquer the entire county, except for the city of Toulouse itself and Montauban. In the statutes of Pamiers, of 1 December 1212, the freedom of the Church was guaranteed and a reorganization of the entire district was regulated. Nothing was said of the heretics.

The King of Aragón perished at Muret on 12 September 1213, while aiding his brother-in-law to defend Toulouse. Finally the cities of Toulouse and Montauban also fell into Simon's hands. Innocent, frequently misled by his legates and probably too accommodating toward Simon de Montfort, sent the Cardinal Legate Peter of Benevento to neutralize Simon's victory and again make the war a real struggle against heretics. The Fourth Lateran Council was to wind up the affair.

One of the religious colloquies with which it was hoped to gain converts at the beginning of the efforts to win the Cathari achieved a notable success. It took place at Pamiers in September 1207, and ended with a judgment in favor of the Catholics, rendered by the arbiter.

As a consequence of this colloquy, a group of Waldensians, or Poor Men of Lyons, returned to the Church under the leadership of Durandus of Huesca. Innocent III received them sympathetically and had them swear to the same profession of faith which he had already required of the converted Poor Men of Milan. As Catholics, the Poor Men spread in Languedoc, Lombardy, and Aragón under the protection of the Pope, who often had to defend them against the distrust of the bishops. Around Milan they encountered groups of similarly converted heretics, the Poor Catholics, who, likewise supported by the Pope's sensible and tactful instructions, could live undisturbed according to their prudent ideal of perfection.

Innocent wanted to win back the heretics, not to exterminate them. In his decretals he did not call for their death. Far from being made stricter, this legislation was toned down by the stress on the principle of mercy in regard to the posterity of those condemned.

Chapter 22

The Fourth Lateran Council

The crusade was one of the determining motives for the summoning of the Synod. The occurrence of 1204 could not be regarded by anyone as a fulfilling of the program of the pontificate: the Holy Sepulchre had not yet been liberated. Together with the call for the West to make ready for a new crusade, there now went out an invitation to take part in a general council, which was to provide the publicizing, organizational, and legal basis for the expedition.

Over and above this, Innocent planned the Council as a summarizing of his previous reform activity, which, expressed in carefully prepared and systematically pondered legislation and ratified by the Council, could prove that it was capable of supplying constructive impulses for the future. Both the experiences of his own administrative, legislative, and disciplinary action over the years and those of all the bishops and prelates who had been invited were to contribute to the establishing of a model of renewal which should be suited for and obligatory on the Universal Church. And that is why the invitation went out so early — 19 April 1213 — and so urgently.

The whole Church was asked to meet in Rome on 1 November 1215: clergy and laity, bishops and princes, monasteries and chapters, the orders and cities of Christendom. All were to be there, either in person or, in the case of the corporate bodies — chapters, orders, cities, — by proxy.

For the bishops in particular, participation in the Council was a canonical duty, from which they were dispensed only in the event of demonstrable necessity. In each province one or the other suffragan could remain at home because of necessary pastoral work. The time before the date of convocation was to be utilized not only for zealous promoting of the crusade but also for amassing all the *gravamina,* for the settling of which the Council was summoned.

The bull of convocation, *Vineam Domini Sabaoth,* clearly outlined the Council's program. It would deal with the welfare of all of Christendom; vices were to be uprooted, virtues planted, abuses eliminated, morals renewed; heresies were to be suppressed, the faith to be strengthened; and peace was to be assured so that Christian princes and peoples could hasten to the assistance of the Holy Land. A new development was his emphatic request that cathedral and collegiate chapters should send proxies, for the Council was to deal with questions that especially concerned these bodies. Kings, princes, and city magistrates were invited especially because of the crusade, in regard to which the Pope stressed that he retained the responsibility for the organization and goals of the expedition.

More than 400 bishops from eighty provinces and over 800 abbots and superiors of chapters took part in this greatest medieval Council. The Eastern Church, to be sure, was represented, apart from the Primate of the Maronites, only by the Latin episcopate of Greece and the crusader states.

Innocent III could rightly assume that this unique representation of the West was a ratification of his efforts over many years to bring the papal primacy to effective recognition as far as the outermost frontiers of Christendom.

The Council completed its work in the three solemn sessions of 11, 20, and 30 November, and hence it lasted one month. Before and between the solemn sessions proceeded discussions and deliberations and even decisions on many pending disputes.

At the opening of the Council Innocent III delivered a sermon on the text: "I have greatly desired to eat this passover with you before I suffer" (Luke 22:15). Reform of the Church and the crusade were stressed as the Council's chief topics. Immediately afterward the Patriarch of Jerusalem commented on the help requested for the Holy Land, while Bishop Thedisius of Agde reported on the proceedings against the Albigensians. Following tumultuous discussions in the second solemn session the decision on the imperial schism went to Frederick II, but it was not proclaimed by the Pope until the last solemn session, when he confirmed Frederick's election at Frankfurt and definitively abandoned Otto IV.

This session was begun with a solemn profession of faith (canon 1), the rejection of heresy (canon 2), and the unanimous acceptance of the decrees. A general peace was proclaimed, the crusade was summoned, and the decisions already given were published. The *Te Deum* and the papal blessing with a relic of the true cross closed the Council.

The union with the Eastern Church, which Innocent believed had been achieved by the establishing of the Latin Empire, was indirectly ratified by canons 4 and 5. The constitution *Ad liberandam* (canon 71) contained the planning of the crusade. First came the assessment of a general three-years' crusade tax, then the commission to the bishops to preach the expedition and induce the princes to agree to a four-years' armistice. There followed the laying of an embargo on commerce in war materials and the prohibition of any commerce at all with Islamic states for the next four years. No particular military enterprise, not even the continuation of the *Reconquista* in Portugal, was to interfere with the collective effort. The departure was set for 1 June 1217, and for this purpose everyone was to assemble at Brindisi in South Italy or at Messina in Sicily; hence Venice was excluded. No previous crusade had been planned in so practical a manner or sketched on so broad a basis.

The other conciliar constitutions had to do with the purity of the faith and the renewal of ecclesiastical discipline. The introductory profession of faith (canon 1) repeated, almost *verbatim,* the formula which in 1210 Bernard Primus had had to swear to on behalf of himself and his adherents, the Poor Men of Lombardy; but added to it were some elements from the profession taken by Durandus of Huesca. Much space was occupied by the doctrine of the Eucharist and of the official priesthood, and into this was inserted the term *transsubstantiatio,* coined by the early scholastics. Also contained in this profession was the orthodox doctrine of baptism, penance, and matrimony. And canon 3 condemned all heresies and formulated measures against them, especially stressing the collaboration of the spiritual and temporal powers for their suppression. Canon 3 included nothing new; it was merely a statement of the procedure that had developed in the Midi. The episcopal Inquisition, already introduced and in operation, was now declared obligatory for the whole Church.

In analyzing the Council's legislation reference has been made to the preparatory work, and especially to the third of the celebrated five collections of decretals which preceded Gregory IX's *Liber Extra.* Commissioned by the Pope, *Magister* Peter of Benevento had assembled them in 1209, and Innocent sent them to Bologna for use in academic instruction. The entire experience of his long pontificate was incorporated into the conciliar decrees, which in many respects took up and further developed the synodal decisions of the twelfth century.

The guide-lines of the conciliar legislation affected clergy, religious, and laity, and the Church's administration and law. The responsibility of the episcopate was often stressed, especially in regard to synods, visitations, preaching, the education of priests, and the conferring of benefices. The law on ecclesiastical elections obtained its definitive regulation, whereby the role of the chapters was strengthened. Some decrees gave detailed demands in the matter of the moral discipline of the clergy. These conciliar desires for improvement applied also to monks. The institution of general chapters was recommended to them. The duty of reform and visitation of non-exempt monasteries was made incumbent on the bishops and specifically insisted upon.

The imposition on all Christians of the obligation of annual confession which included a stricter inculcation of the seal, and of Easter communion are among the best known regulations of the Council.

Opposing the swelling flood of appeals to Rome, the Council referred energetically to the normal juridical procedure and added clarifications on ecclesiastical processes. The important forty-second canon supplied a clear distinction of ecclesiastical and secular courts. And ecclesiastical courts were warned against extending their competence at the cost of the proper secular authorities.

In its nineteenth canon the Third Lateran Council had already demanded the immunity of the clergy in the cities from taxation, but it had urged them to make voluntary contributions in time of need to the burdens of their city. This was now confirmed in canon 46 but a previous consultation of the ecclesiastical authorities was made a necessary condition. Measures taken by excommunicated urban officials were declared null and void in this context.

In regard to matrimony, the Council limited the impediments of consanguinity and affinity, renewed the prohibition of clandestine marriages, and introduced the obligation of the banns.

Canon 62 attacked abuses in the cult of relics and decreed that new relics could be exposed for veneration only with the express consent of the Holy See. Other decrees sought to put a stop to simony, which was still practiced, and attacked the clerical vice of avarice. The concluding decrees took cognizance of the practice of usury by Jews and prescribed for them a special dress. This regulation and the declaration of the Jews' second-class citizenship were not innovations of the Council. They are understandable in the climate of preparation for the crusade. Racial grounds were not the determining causes of them; rather they were probably intended to prevent Christians from having social contacts with Jews because of a lack of knowledge of the difference of religion. Muslims in Christian lands were subject to similar prescriptions.

While the Council's political decisions were not of lasting importance and soon appeared out of date because of events, its legislation persisted because it was taken into the general law of the Church.

CHAPTER 23

The Mendicant Orders

Throughout his pontificate Innocent III had exerted himself for a renewal of the monastic life in the Church. Not only had the Benedictine abbeys fallen, economically and religiously, into a threatening crisis, but even the reform orders of the twelfth century, Cistercians and canons regular, seemed to have succumbed to a similar loss of spiritual substance. The Pope appealed to the orders themselves, commissioned the episcopate to undertake visitations, and had his legates investigate and try to deal with emergencies. At the same time Innocent encouraged new foundations, such as the Hospitallers of Guy of Montpellier and the order established by John of Matha for the exchange of captives between Islam and the Christian nations. Furthermore, the Teutonic Knights obtained papal confirmation on 19 February 1199.

Above all, however, Innocent sought prudently to devote to the service of the Church the gift for founding communities that was manifesting itself in many areas of France and Italy in the poverty movement of his age, notably among heretical groups. He succeeded to a degree in winning back the Humiliati of Lombardy; likewise, parts of the Waldensian movement were reincorporated into the unity of the Church under Durandus of Huesca in Spain.

To this total context belong the beginnings of the two great mendicant orders, foundations which in the course of the thirteenth century were the models for other religious foundations. It should cause no surprise that both had their origin where the most dangerous centers of the crisis were found, in the Midi and Central Italy. However, contact with heresy was far more decisive for Saint Dominic than was a grasp of the corresponding phenomena in the environment of his Umbrian homeland for Saint Francis.

On the one hand they attested the uninterrupted *élan* of the movement for apostolic poverty. On the other, they demonstrated the interdependence of ecclesiastical and heretical forms within this impulse toward the realization of the *vita apostolica.*

The Dominicans

The very title "Order of Preachers" indicates the origin and aim of the Dominican friars. Dominic Guzmán, born around 1170 at Caleruega in Old Castile, had, as superior of the cathedral chapter of canons regular of Osma, accompanied his Bishop, Diego, on journeys to Denmark and Rome. Both men, apostolic in spirit and theologically well grounded, had become acquainted in the Midi with the Cathari movement, so full of peril for the Church. At first, it is true, at Rome in 1206 they asked Pope Innocent III for permission to undertake missionary work among the Cumans in Hungary, but he directed their attention to the more urgent tasks in the Midi. Diego of Osma returned home in 1207 and died there the same year. Dominic, joined by a few companions, at first took charge of the house established at Prouille by Diego for converted women, who not only continued there the common life of pious poverty which they had already followed among the Cathari, but also interested themselves thereafter in the education of girls. This tactic of taking over from the enemy his own instrument, so to speak, of grasping his own spiritual concerns and making them one's own, and, like him, of proclaiming *verbo et exemplo* the Lord's glad tidings, became the unique characteristic of the Dominican institute. Prouille had to serve also as the temporary lodging of the itinerant preachers, Dominic and his companions, until they could establish a house of their own near Saint-Romain at Toulouse. The Bishop appointed them as diocesan preachers but this did not measure up to the original *élan* of Saint Dominic, and so the Bishop and the preachers sought to obtain at Rome confirmation and encouragement of the incipient religious community from the Pope. Out of regard for canon 13 of the Fourth Lateran Council, just concluded, Innocent got them to accept the Augustinian rule and then gave the brotherhood the requested confirmation. However, official confirmation came only from Honorius III in bulls of 22 December 1216 and 21 January 1217. The first general chapter of the new order, held in Bologna at Pentecost 1220, drew up a constitution.

Dominic died at Bologna on 6 August 1221. Following the first papal confirmation he had sent friars from Toulouse to Paris and Spain, thereby demonstrating his intention of now having his diocesan missionaries become preachers for the Universal Church. In the last years of his life he was tireless in his journeys from country to country in order everywhere to provide for the rapidly spreading order, which was soon in a position to found houses in Italy, Germany, and England, to acquire experience, to represent the needs of the home as well as of the foreign mission, to acclimatize the order at the universities, especially at Paris and Bologna. This last was of particular importance for Dominic. From his very first encounter with the Cathari of the Midi it had been clear to him that a solid theological formation was essential for preaching, not only for apologetics but for catechesis within the Catholic fold. The lay preacher movement, which so often ended up in heretical side-roads, had, of course, made known the need of the word of God among the faithful, but, as unsupervised proclamation, it had at the same time shown only too vividly the necessity of a clear grasp of dogmatic and moral theology in the preacher. The declared intention of pursuing a theological approach in the renewal of the preaching of Christian doctrine gained for Saint Dominic from the very start many companions from the university circles.

The constitution stressed the poverty of both the individual and the community. It adopted traditional elements from the congregations of canons regular, and was oriented also to the monastic life. New, however, was the requirement of living on alms; fixed revenues and landed property were rejected. The church building was to be as unpretentious as among the early Cistercians. The first houses were founded in university cities and in episcopal and commercial cities. Here were found the hoped for fields for attracting recruits, for the care of souls, for study, and also for livelihood. Here were held the annual general chapters, by turns in all countries where the friars settled. The general chapter, apparently derived from the Cistercian model, which Innocent III had made of obligation for the other orders also at the Fourth Lateran Council in canon 12, was the supreme legislative authority in the order and elected the master general, whom it could also depose. The provincial superiors were likewise elected by the provincial chapters;

in regard to them the master general had only the right of confirmation. From 1228 there were provinces in Spain, Provence, France, Lombardy, Rome, Germany, England, Hungary, the Holy Land, Greece, Poland, and Scandinavia. To the general chapter and the provincial chapters pertained the function of supervising the superiors elected by them. Hence there existed a unique and, as was to appear, a very effective combination of monarchical and democratic elements in the overall construction of the organization.

The central role of preaching in the order's program caused the legislative authority to demand for every house a lecturer in theology and a director of studies, to establish in every province a *studium generale,* and finally to have the best recruits formed at Saint-Jacques in Paris. The strict subordination to the Pope — the master general resided in Rome — and to the national episcopates was to serve the work of preaching and assured to the founding generations a far-reaching support by the local bishops and to preaching a secure place within the Church. Their strict mode of life, their poverty, fasting, abstinence, and personal penance gained for the Friars Preachers the notice of the faithful and a steadily growing number of vocations, above all in the university circles and the upper middle class.

Dominic clearly stamped his order with the traits of his own character. He lived according to "the rule of the Apostles" and was a "man of the Gospel in the footsteps of his Redeemer," as Gregory IX said in 1234 in the bull of canonization. He wanted not only to realize this evangelical outlook in his own life but also, as a "man of the Church," to establish institutionally in her the forms of the apostolic life. He knew the canon law and accepted the Pope's universal directing authority. For Dominic the Gospel and the hierarchical Church belonged together.

Under the energetic leadership of his first successors, Jordan of Saxony (1222–37), Raymond of Peñaforte (1238–40), John the German (1241–52), Humbert of Romans (1254–63), the order experienced a rapid and astounding rise. At the end of the thirteenth century there were 557 convents in eighteen provinces and the number of members amounted to about 15,000. Under Humbert of Romans the constitution acquired its definitive form, a framework for the further legislative development of the order, which did not need to be changed until 1924.

While at first the friars carried on a missionary apostolate among the people in a close collaboration with the bishops and the parochial clergy, from 1240 on the convents themselves appeared as pastoral centers, with preaching, administration of the Sacraments, the confraternity system, and so forth. The Popes, notably Gregory IX and Innocent IV, lavished rich privileges on the order, drew many of their advisers from it and made use especially of Dominicans in constructing the Inquisition.

Service on the tribunal of the Inquisition did not exclude discussions in controversial theology or preaching; on the contrary, it fostered theological scholarship. The new order's special achievement lay in this field of education, university, and theological literature. The convents at Paris, Orléans, Bologna, Cologne, and Oxford especially lodged the leading theologians of the century. Dominican missionary ardor found fields in Prussia, the Holy Land, Spain, and North Africa. In Greece it was directed, in accord with the mind of the Popes, to the problem of reunion with the Orthodox Church. Missions to the Cumans and Mongols are to be noted.

The Second Order of Saint Dominic, originating at Prouille and at San Sisto in Rome, became the model for other establishments of communities of women. The constitutions of San Sisto were, alongside the rule of the Cistercian nuns, decisive for the Order of the "Penitents of Saint Mary Magdalene," which spread quickly, especially in Germany.

The Third Order of Brothers and Sisters of Penance of Saint Dominic grew out of a lay brotherhood of the *Militia Christi.*

The Franciscans

Fed by similar sources and running its course before the same historical background, but obtaining its inspiration from an even more powerfully charismatic personality, the poverty and preaching movement of the Friars Minor of Saint Francis made its appearance at the same time as did that of the Friars Preachers.

Francis of Assisi, born around 1181–82, was the son of a well-to-do cloth merchant, Peter Bernardone, and of Pica, daughter of a respected French family. Baptized John, he was called "Francesco" by his father. He was of a sensitive nature, of more than average intelligence, endowed with intuition, gifted musically, open, and generous. He obtained the ordinary education of the day in the city school of Assisi. A rather long captivity due to the war between Assisi and Perugia in 1202 and a subsequent illness brought about a profound change in his religious development, the stages of which cannot easily be pinpointed. It was marked by an experience of the majesty of God the Father, by an awakening concern for the deterioration of the Church, concretely realized by the rebuilding of decayed chapels, and by the distress of the poor and the sick, especially the lepers, in the environs of wealthy Assisi. Conflict with his father in 1206–7 ended with his being disinherited. Francis placed himself as a poor man under the protection of the Bishop. To his devotion to poverty was added the desire for the apostolate, aroused by reading Matthew 10:5–16, the account of the mission of the twelve Apostles. The imitating of the Lord — poor, preaching, aiding — became the life program of Saint Francis.

Companions joined him from Assisi; they went in twos through the cities and countryside, preaching the good news. The bishops' reserve in regard to a movement so similar to the heretical lay preaching could be overcome only by papal approval. Francis, who had already visited Rome as a pilgrim in 1206, was able to obtain a verbal confirmation of his first rule from Innocent III through the good offices of the Bishop of Assisi, who was in residence there, and of Cardinal John Colonna. It is not extant and was probably only a brief collection of scriptural passages. The Pope took the friars under the jurisdiction of the Church by giving them the tonsure, and Francis himself was ordained a deacon. The brothers called themselves Friars Minor and lived part of the time at the Portiuncula, where Clare of Assisi, foundress of the Second Order, or Poor Clares, also turned up with her sister Agnes in 1212. The movement was everywhere well received and the number of friars grew rapidly. Francis, who also envisaged the preaching of the word to non-Christians, left for the East in 1212 but got only as far as Dalmatia. He wanted to go to North Africa but fell sick in Spain around 1213–15, and finally joined the Fifth Crusade in 1219. He contrived to preach in person before the Sultan al-Kamil, who was not converted, it is true, but allowed Francis to preach in his lands. The latter went to Palestine before returning to Italy, probably in the fall of 1220.

There awaited him the need to give an organization to his now very large brotherhood, but, quite unlike Saint Dominic, he lacked all planning and organizational ability. The *Regula bullata* of 1223, became the real fundamental law of the new order. Cardinal Ugolino of Ostia had played a decisive role in drawing it up. It was incorporated in its entirety into Honorius III's bull of confirmation of 29 November 1223. The home and foreign mission was mentioned as the order's chief goal, and the poverty of the individual and of the communities, including a strict prohibition of accepting money, was sternly demanded. The Chapter of Mats sent out friars to all countries of Europe.

Francis himself had already turned over the direction of the friars to one of his first companions, Peter Catanii, had asked the Pope to give the order a Cardinal Protector, and had obtained one in Ugolino of Ostia. While the *regula non bullata* knew nothing of a Cardinal Protector, the *regula bullata* required one. Hence the institution must have been projected between 1221 and 1223. Peter Catanii died on 10 March 1221 and was succeeded by Elias of Cortona. In the same year Francis founded the Third Order, a community of lay persons, even married, who sought to realize the Franciscan ideal of life outside a religious order.

After his return from the East, Francis had dissolved the house of studies which had been founded at Bologna. The Cardinal Protector intervened for its restoration and Francis yielded, even naming its first lecturer, Anthony of Padua. The necessity of theological studies for a fruitful preaching apostolate could not have remained unknown to him, above all as more and more priests were joining the order. The beginnings proper to a trend of the apostolic lay movement seemed to have been left behind.

Francis stayed at Greccio until April 1224 and at Pentecost took part in the general chapter at which the *regula bullata* was promulgated. Then, with a few companions he withdrew to Monte Alverno for a life of prayer, penance, and contemplation, and there on 14 September 1224 he received the stigmata. Much sickness plagued his poor body. In particular he had contracted a serious malady of the eyes in the East. He had it treated, but in vain, at Rieti on the suggestion of Cardinal Ugolino and at Siena at the command of Brother Elias. From February 1226 he stayed at Assisi, where he was the Bishop's guest. He was unable to take part in the Pentecost Chapter of 1226; instead, in August of that year he wrote his "testament," which again inculcated the strictest poverty and, above all, obedience to the Roman Church. Before his death on 3 October 1226 he was able to make peace between the Bishop and the municipal council of Assisi and to complete his celebrated "Canticle of the Sun." He died in a hut near the Portiuncula and was buried in the church of San Giorgio. Pope Gregory IX, the former Cardinal Ugolino, canonized him less than two years later, on 29 July 1228.

The figure of the *Poverello* interested his own and later ages much more than did that of Dominic, who withdrew far more decidedly behind his work. Whereas the Dominican Order was already an institution when Dominic died, the Franciscan remained even after 1226 still a sort of movement. Francis was just not an organizer, but, according to Dante, "he rose on the world like a sun." He was a mystic, poet, singer, man of prayer, but no canonist, theologian, or controversialist. Nor was he a fool, as has been supposed, but an intelligent, shrewd, and deeply religious man, who knew his limitations and hence so early desired the cooperation of the Curia. The Cardinal Protector was not forced on him; he himself asked for this "gubernator, protector et corrector." At the same time he fulfilled the function of representing the order at the Curia and to the hierarchy and of smoothing its path in the Church. Such a notion hardly reveals in Francis any ignorance of the world. And the sources display much evidence of a good knowledge of men in the seraphic saint, even if this did not amount to genius.

It was only then that those trends which determined the destiny of the order after 1226 began to show themselves more clearly. The zealots for poverty defended the literal observance of the rule, appealing especially to the testament of the saint. In response to inquiries Gregory IX in 1230 declared that the testament possessed no legal standing. From this trend were later to spring the Spirituals.

Especially during his time as minister general (1232–39), Elias of Cortona advocated assimilation to other orders, as the model of the Dominican Order permanently gained influence in the course of the years, for example, in the assurance of the organization through the position of the minister general and in the order's turning to the cultivation of scholarship.

The middle party was represented by Anthony of Padua, Bonaventure, John Pecham, and others, who, while maintaining the original ideals so far as possible, demanded and carried through an accommodation to changing conditions of the time. The tensions among these tendencies were at first not very severe and did not become aggravated until after 1250, to develop into a serious crisis for the entire order at the beginning of the fourteenth century.

Until then the Friars Minor had been able to spread everywhere in the Church — to Ireland, Scotland, Scandinavia, Syria, the Holy Land — so that by 1300 they must be reckoned as having from 30,000 to 40,000 members. Due to the close ties which Francis, like Dominic, maintained from the start with the Roman Curia, the order's influence was from the beginning geared to the Universal Church. Freedom of movement, contrary to the *stabilitas loci* hitherto cultivated by the old orders, enabled all the chief convents to have an international composition. A lively exchange from country to country, in all offices of the order and for all sorts of missions, remained characteristic. The Franciscan school, especially at Oxford and Paris, was soon able to serve theological scholarship on an equal footing with the Dominican.

Naturally, the Friars Minor displayed their chief influence in the ministry of the word (popular and crusade preaching) and of the Sacraments (confession) and in fostering popular devotions centering on the Lord's Incarnation and Passion. They preached in cities, soon in their own churches, and, like Francis, in the country as itinerant preachers.

Following both the example and the desire of Saint Francis, the Friars Minor could especially take part as pioneers in the work of evangelizing pagans. As Francis, preaching before the Sultan, aspired to prepare a change from the crusade as military offensive and defense of Christian positions to a Way of the Cross as a peaceful concern for the faith of non-Christian peoples, so too the Friars Minor went as preachers to North Africa, Syria, and Palestine to the Muslims, and, under a papal mandate, to the Mongols.

For the Holy See they, like the Dominicans, meant an important assistance in Church reform, in the struggle against heresy, and in politics, such as the undertaking of embassies and interventions on behalf of peace.

Other Mendicant Orders

The two orders just discussed set the pattern for other foundations in the course of the century. In 1247 Innocent IV included the Carmelites among the mendicant orders. Simon Stock became their first general (1247–65). But their origins go back to the twelfth century, to a hermit colony, which the crusader, Berthold of Calabria (d. 1195), had instituted on Mount Carmel in 1185. When, hard pressed by Islam, they emigrated to Cyprus, Sicily, France, and England and from 1238 reorganized themselves as cenobites, it was natural to give them a constitution corresponding to that of the mendicant orders.

The Order of Hermits of Saint Augustine likewise developed out of eremitical groups.

In 1233 there appeared at Florence the Order of Servants of the Blessed Virgin Mary, or Servites. It too originated in a lay brotherhood of merchants and urban patricians. It adopted the Augustinian rule in 1240 and in 1255 was confirmed by Alexander IV, but it did not rank as a mendicant order until Martin V declared it one in 1424. They devoted themselves especially to the care of the sick.

Summary

The mendicant orders decisively stamped the ecclesiastical and religious life of the thirteenth century, certainly more powerfully than did the reform orders of the twelfth century in their day. On the one hand, by virtue of the centralization of their organization, which was tempered by the relative autonomy of the several provinces, and, on the other hand, by the freedom of movement of their personnel on the international plane, and, especially in the case of the Friars Minor, their broad pastoral contacts with all strata of society, above all in the cities, they presented the papacy with incomparable resources for the government of the Church — many bishops and cardinals and even Popes came from their ranks as early as the thirteenth century — for the renewal of popular piety, especially through the influence of the three types of orders which they had created, and for the growth of theological scholarship, whose most important representatives at all universities were soon Dominicans and Franciscans, from Alexander of Hales to Bonaventure and Duns Scotus, from Hugh of Saint-Cher to Albert the Great and Thomas Aquinas. They accomplished very much, especially the Friars Preachers, in the struggle against heresy through the Inquisition and in the repeated efforts to reunite the Eastern and Western Churches. The first phase of the history of the world mission was determined by them. Ecclesiastical literature was enriched by them, with, to some extent, immortal works in all fields: homiletics, catechesis, apologetics, philosophy, theology, historiography, exegesis, liturgy, poetry.

While it is true that their integration into university life and the pastoral ministry was not achieved without friction, especially at Paris between 1250 and 1260, still the main difficulties could be surmounted, at least in principle, by papal intervention. The human shadows could in this first century of their history be steadily eclipsed by the uncontested brilliance of their accomplishments.

Chapter 24

The Medieval Western Hospital

In the early Middle Ages it was the canons and monks who had received the poor and the sick, the pilgrim and the traveler into their houses and cared for them. In these *hospites* was to be seen and served Christ himself, according to the prescriptions of rule and constitution. Alongside the *opus Dei* in worship, work, and self-sanctification — the *vita contemplativa* — the service of guests and the infirm had, it is true, only a secondary significance and was scarcely anywhere regarded as a central preoccupation of religious communities.

A change occurred in the age of the Gregorian reform, when there began a more active participation by the laity in the public life of the Church. Prominent among the motives of the *vita apostolica* was the example of Christ as healer and helper: the *pauperes Christi* wanted to become poor in order to succor others in their necessities. At the same time the crusades produced homelessness, sickness, physical disability, and poverty wherever they played a role, at home and abroad. *Caritas* in the hitherto familiar form was in no position to provide ample assistance in such massive need, and so new forms had to be found for dealing effectively with it.

One such form was the renewed hospital service in West and East under the auspices of chapters and monasteries, above all in cities and along pilgrimage routes. The source of this renewal in the West was, among other factors, the Augustinian rule followed by the canons regular, including the cathedral chapters. Especially among the Premonstratensians it produced a vigorous impact on hospital work.

In the cities were formed hospital confraternities of men and women, at first in already available hospitals and usually connected with a chapter or monastery. However, there soon appeared a tendency to become autonomous, and this was facilitated by the expansion or transfer of the hospital. The confraternities were frequently inclined to adopt a monastic organization, and from such confraternity hospitals there developed foundations of Augustinian canons or independent monasteries of nuns.

Alongside this process in the thirteenth century, whereby confraternities became religious orders, in the cities there occurred also the so-called "communalization" of the confraternity hospital, in the case of both civic foundations and already existing religious houses. Hospital service thereby became all the more urgent, when transformation into a religious order caused it to be neglected.

From the twelfth century hospitals directed by confraternities were encountered in all countries of the West in a relatively ample distribution that was favored by the urban development then getting under way. They were even established wherever cities appeared in the colonial and missionary area beyond the Elbe. The climax of the new foundations was achieved by the middle of the thirteenth century.

The Military Hospital Orders

The Hospitallers and the Templars were treated above. Far clearer is the hospital origin of the Teutonic Knights, who proceeded from the hospital erected by citizens of Bremen and Lübeck during the siege of Acre in 1189–90. Even more impressive are the beginnings of the Order of Lazarus from a leprosary at Jerusalem in 1120. This hospital association likewise followed the Augustinian rule, but it did not become a military order, on the model of the others, until the thirteenth century. Since in the course of time these institutes devoted themselves especially to military service, their original hospital apostolate yielded often enough to military and economic preoccupations without, however, being entirely given up.

In their very title the Hospitallers maintained a constant connection with their original aim, and after their transformation into a military order their principal house at Jerusalem remained for a while dedicated to the care of the infirm and the poor. Their rapidly appearing houses in the West served rather for the military and economic maintenance of their warfare in the East than for the direction and growth of hospitals. Thus, for example, only a few hospitals can be discovered among their numerous German houses, but these were busy as hospices. While the competition of the Teutonic Order in the thirteenth century may be attributed in Germany to the lack of hospitals among the Hospitallers, the fact remains that the claims of the East on the homeland demanded a pooling of all available financial means with the result that there were far-reaching restrictions on the strictly charitable apostolate.

The Teutonic Order, even after its removal to the West, always maintained the care of the infirm. In fact, its first decades, up to 1230 when it assumed its fateful task in Prussia, stood expressly under the auspices of hospital work in regard to gifts, undertakings, and foundations. Care of the sick was an essential element in its constitution. This ordered that a permanent hospital should be established at the principal house, but elsewhere only if the grand master and the chapter should so decide. It knew those *hospitalia oblata,* which marked the path of its advance into Germany, and subjected them to the local commandant. Houses without hospitals might be erected as such only with the special permission of the grand master. As a matter of fact, in Germany and later in its own principality the Teutonic Order accomplished far more in the sphere of public assistance than did the other military hospital orders.

Of these others, the Order of Lazarus was able to establish itself in Europe only later, after its expulsion from Syria in 1253, especially in France, where the grand master settled at Boigny near Orléans, in England, Scotland, Italy, Switzerland, Hungary, and Germany. It continued faithful to its origin in so far as it devoted itself above all to the care of lepers. In 1266 Clement IV granted it a monopoly of this apostolate, which, however, could not really be maintained in view of the wide spread of this disease.

The Non-Military Hospital Orders

At the close of the eleventh century there appeared in the Midi the Hospital Order of Saint Anthony at the church of La Motte-des-Bois at Saint-Didier. As early as 1247 the members had bound themselves to the Augustinian rule and adopted the organization of the Augustinian canons regular. From the beginning of the thirteenth century they spread everywhere, especially in lands of Romance speech but also in Germany: Upper Swabia, Hesse, Alsace, Mecklenburg. Their contribution, however, to strictly hospital work was relatively meager — they had hospitals at Strasbourg, Basel, and Memmingen. Elsewhere the infirm were attended to in the houses of the order itself or by visits. On the other hand, their almsgiving was famous and made the Antonians very popular.

The Hospital Order of the Holy Spirit, which also originated in the Midi, at Montpellier, made a more significant contribution to the care of the sick. In 1198 Innocent III confirmed the order, which then had ten daughter houses and had its center in Rome at the Hospital of Santo Spirito *in Sassia.* Its rule made the service of the poor and the infirm its first duty. Most of its houses were in Italy and France, though it had ten houses in Germany, especially South Germany, in the thirteenth century.

The Order of Bearers of the Cross with the red star, which had grown out of a hospital association at Prague, spread in Bohemia and the adjacent countries around the middle of the thirteenth century. Like many other hospital orders, it followed the Augustinian rule. Its members made foundations also in Silesia and Poland. In the fourteenth century the apostolate to the infirm often flagged among them, as among the other hospital orders.

Finally, mention should be made here of the Order of the Brothers of the Holy Sepulchre at Jerusalem, to be distinguished from the Military Order of the Holy Sepulchre.

The Municipal Hospital

The Western urban middle class, powerfully growing and aspiring to autonomy especially in the thirteenth century, made important contributions to the development of the hospital system.

The old ecclesiastical institutes proved to be inadequate *vis-à-vis* the constantly increasing city population. Consequently, the bourgeoisie itself assumed the duty of public assistance, for which it possessed amply growing means. The allotment of such means naturally implied the claim to share in or entirely to assume the direction or control of the hospital system. Thereby the bourgeoisie came into competition with the Church. However, the communalization, now beginning, of the hospital system did not involve anything such as secularization. Alongside the ever stronger pervading, in the first half of the thirteenth century, of the ecclesiastical hospitals conducted by confraternities or by religious institutes by municipal organs in the form of supervisors, there often appeared new municipal foundations. In these the connection with the Church and her apostolate to the sick was always maintained. The municipality assumed the secular administration and direction, the Church retained the spiritual care under the bishop's supervision.

This development got under way first of all in Italy, the Low Countries, and to a degree in France. It took place in Germany especially in the thirteenth century, though it was not completed before the fourteenth century.

In general, after the mid-century lay bourgeois emerged as supervisors (*procuratores*) and administrators of hospital property, especially where such institutions originated from purely municipal means. Such superintendencies possessed the future, not only in regard to hospitals but in the case of all other ecclesiastical institutes and even churches.

Section Five

The Contest for the Leadership of the West (1216–74)

Hans Wolter

Chapter 25

The Papacy's Victory over Frederick II

For a brief moment in world history the papacy in Innocent III had acted as the leading power responsible for order in Western Christendom; the Fourth Lateran Council could be regarded as the visible sign of this domination. With Innocent's death on 16 July 1216, the grand-scale experiment did not at once collapse, but in Frederick II the Holy See found an ever more demanding competitor, in Italy if not in the Latin West. Frederick, whose tenure of the German throne had been ratified by the Council, had not yet been crowned Emperor. Besides, at the eleventh hour, on 1 July 1216, he had promised the Pope to turn over to his son Henry, who had already been crowned King in 1212 at Innocent's bidding, the Kingdom of Sicily, whose political separation from the Empire he had guaranteed. It was now incumbent on the successors of the great Innocent to continue and bring to completion what he had achieved in this question as well as in the other policies he had formulated: crusade, reform, and fight against heresy.

Honorius III (1216–27), was the first one to be called upon to continue and complete Innocent's work. The crusade planned and called for at the Fourth Lateran Council was an overriding task of his pontificate. To assure it he let the election of Frederick's son Henry as King of the Romans at Frankfurt in April 1220 go unchallenged and crowned Frederick Emperor in Saint Peter's on 23 November 1220. The Emperor again took the cross from the hand of Ugolino of Ostia and promised to set out on the expedition in 1221. But the settlement of the affairs of the Kingdom of Sicily, which the Emperor now turned to, probably with a view to creating an assured point of departure for the crusade, claimed more time than the brief period that had been set. Hence Honorius consented to numerous postponements, until the Treaty of San Germano in July 1225 definitely set the term for the summer of 1227. The Emperor agreed under oath that he would regard himself as excommunicated if this date were further postponed.

Meanwhile, the crusade planned by the Fourth Lateran Council had frittered away its strength in isolated operations and ended with failure in the defeat at Mansurah, for peace could be bought from Malik al-Kamil only with the evacuation of Egypt and the surrender of Damietta, the single gain in these operations. It is true that the Emperor had sent aid under Duke Louis of Bavaria and Hermann of Salza, but his intervention was fruitless.

Concern for the crusade also induced Honorius III to mediate between France and England. King John, dying on 19 October 1216, had left England to his minor son, Henry III, under the guidance of the Cardinal Legate Gualo, and the country was afflicted by the invading army of the heir to the French throne, Louis. Louis' defeat led to the Peace of Kingston on 12 September 1217.

Honorius had especially to continue the struggle against heresy, which had in no sense been ended by the measures of the Fourth Lateran Council but rather was spreading further, energetically and in the most varied forms. The Albigensian War flared up again. Only Louis VIII, who had already intervened as heir to the throne, promised effective aid. In 1226 he conquered the Midi, except for Toulouse. The episcopate threw in its lot with the King, as did also the nobility. The Cathari among the common folk fled to the mountains, to Lombardy, and even to Aragón. The ending of the Albigensian War with the Peace of Paris of 12 April 1229 meant for France an extension of the power of the crown, but for the Church it in no way implied the definite overcoming of heresy in the Midi.

When Honorius III died on 18 March 1227, the preparations for the Emperor's crusade were in full swing. Gregory IX (1227–41), cousin of Innocent III and friend of Saint Francis, was, in contrast to his gentle predecessor, a high-spirited, obstinate, and energetically active personality. He took up in their true sense the program of the Innocentian ideas. His pontificate was to present the first phase of the Curia's fight against Frederick II's aspirations for hegemony. The raising of the curtain came with the first excommunication of the Emperor. When in August 1227, on the date set by the Treaty of San Germano, a large crusade army, which had however been weakened by epidemics, set to sea, the Emperor became ill and returned to Pozzuoli for treatment; he had the fleet sail on without him. His excuses were not accepted by Gregory; in fact, the Pope declared on 29 September 1227 that the penalty of excommunication, as stipulated by the Treaty of San Germano, had been incurred.

Nevertheless, Frederick held to his crusade. He replied to the Pope's accusing manifesto in a circular of 6 December 1227, which calmly and objectively denied Gregory's charges and declared that the Emperor would start on the crusade in May 1228. And even when on 23 March 1228, Gregory renewed the censure, this did not stop Frederick from carrying out his declaration. He left Brindisi for the voyage to the East on 28 June 1228, with forty galleys. On Cyprus he renewed the feudal sovereignty of the Empire over the island as established by the Emperor Henry VI, and on 7 September he reached Acre. After long negotiations he was able on 18 February 1229 to conclude a treaty with the Sultan al-Kamil, who had meanwhile conquered Jerusalem. By the terms of the agreement the Holy City, except for the mosque of Omar, was relinquished to the Christians, as were also

Bethlehem, Nazareth, and a strip of coast from Jaffa to Acre with the pilgrim routes to Jerusalem and Nazareth. The treaty was to be in force for ten years and envisaged a mutual assistance by the contracting parties.

In Jerusalem Frederick, without any ecclesiastical solemnity, placed on his own head the crown of the Kingdom of Jerusalem. He had dispensed with any sacred rite because he was still under excommunication and was in need of an understanding with Gregory IX.

For the Pope, by no means satisfied with a renewal of the Emperor's excommunication, had had recourse to further measures. He sought to have an antiking set up in Germany, released Frederick's subjects in the Kingdom of Sicily from their oaths of loyalty, and, when Frederick's vicar in Tuscany and the Marches of Ancona, Rainald of Urslingen Duke of Spoleto, attacked the *Patrimonium Petri,* excommunicated the latter and hastened to take military countermeasures. Papal mercenaries drove out Rainald; others occupied large parts of the Kingdom of Sicily.

Having returned on 10 June 1229, the Emperor was able without too much difficulty to save the situation, but without violating the frontiers of the *Patrimonium Petri.* He succeeded in entering into negotiations with Gregory IX. In July 1230 they ended in the Treaty of San Germano. Frederick was absolved from censure on 28 August, and a meeting with Gregory IX at Anagni on 1 September sealed the reconciliation of the two universal powers. The Lombard question continued to be excluded. Frederick's extensive concessions in the Sicilian Kingdom, in addition to the Pope's military defeat and fruitless exertions in Germany, provided Gregory with the presuppositions for the Emperor's absolution. For the Emperor himself his release from the ban was an important preliminary to the realizing of his total political aspirations, which amounted basically to a unification of Italy under his rule. In this regard at least the neutrality of the Church was necessary; in any event her opposition could only mean an extremely serious hindrance.

The Peace of San Germano-Ceprano endured for almost nine years. During this period the two powers aided each other in various ways and simultaneously both found time to carry out the constructive aspect of their own administrative programs in their respective spheres. Nevertheless, they always regarded each other with suspicion, for the tension continued, despite all protestations of peace.

Frederick was successful in consolidating the basis of his power: the Sicilian Kingdom. In September 1231 he published the *Liber Augustalis,* containing his Constitutions of Melfi. This grand-scale legislative work amalgamated the older constitutional and administrative law and the financial legislation of Norman origin with his own decree. Then he consistently completed the construction of the Kingdom into a tightly organized bureaucratic state, in which only his will counted and all law proceeded from him.

In the Peace of San Germano he had exempted the Sicilian clergy from the jurisdiction of the state, freed them from general taxes, and even renounced the royal right of assent to episcopal elections — all of this obviously in opposition to the building up of a centralized state. Here, always ready, lay the centers of conflict between Emperor and Pope, for the actual exercise of Frederick's absolutist notion of the state could hardly allow so far-reaching an exemption of most important elements — there were 140 sees in the Kingdom — from his authority.

Together with the reorganization of the Sicilian Kingdom Frederick again took up the question of North Italy, the restoration of the imperial authority in Lombardy. He ordered an imperial diet to meet at Ravenna in November 1231; the cities resisted, whereupon Frederick laid them under the ban of the Empire. With the aid of the Pope, who excommunicated the rebel King Henry in Germany for having even joined the Lombards against his father, Frederick managed to put down the revolt in the north in 1235. From Germany the Emperor announced his campaign against the Lombards, though he knew that Gregory was seeking by diplomatic means to prevent such a war of the Empire against the cities.

In September 1236 Frederick was able to extend the area of his rule in the eastern part of North Italy. In the summer of 1237, he proceeded with new recruits from Augsburg through the Brenner Pass. The final negotiations between representatives of the Pope, the Emperor, and the cities had failed. At Cortenuova on 27 November Frederick defeated a Lombard army as it was returning home from Brescia. The victory appeared to secure for him domination in North Italy, but his success was ruined by his demand, made especially on Milan, for unconditional surrender. Milan, in alliance with Alessandria, Brescia, Piacenza, Bologna, and Faenza, continued the struggle. The Emperor besieged Brescia in vain for three months, until 9 October 1238. On this occasion he had managed to reinforce his German, Sicilian, and Muslim contingents with mercenaries from England, France, Castile, Burgundy, Hungary, Greece, and Egypt. The Emperor's increasing power, the fact that in October 1238 he arranged the marriage of his son Enzio to the heiress of a great part of Sardinia without consulting the Pope, who regarded himself as suzerain of the island, and that he thus seemed to be striving to assume control even in Rome in order to make it, as far as possible, the real or at least the theoretical center of a renewed Empire — all this contributed to strengthen the opposition to Frederick in the Curia, above all by the Pope. He dispatched as legate to Lombardy Gregory of Montelongo, who brought together the anti-imperialist cities. The Pope was successful in allying Venice and Genoa and in again establishing his own authority in Rome.

When Frederick, in a decree of February 1239 against the Empire's rebels, as he termed them, issued a summons to a total war against the Lombards and to a social and economic boycott, binding all subjects of the Empire, Gregory IX decided on 20 and 24 March to renew the Emperor's excommunication. Without mentioning the Lombards he justified this step especially by referring to Frederick's ecclesiastical policy in the Sicilian Kingdom, which was contrary to the promises of the treaty of 1230, and to his efforts to establish his rule in Rome.

With this decision began the final struggle of the Curia against the Emperor and his dynasty. Frederick answered Gregory's Measures with the occupation of the *Patrimonium* and the encirclement of Rome. For his part, Gregory decided to appeal to Christendom and summoned a council to meet in Rome at Easter of 1241. But Frederick countered by arresting most of the non-Italian participants, who were traveling in a Genoese fleet, after a sea-battle near Montecristo, on 4 May 1241.

At the beginning of August the Emperor drew near to Rome, but his intended attack on the city did not take place, for the Pope died on 21 August 1241. Frederick returned to the Sicilian Kingdom to await the outcome of the new election.

By virtue of the official journalism of the immediately preceding years, which had striven to bring the struggle before the forum of Christendom by solemn manifestoes issued by both Pope and Emperor, the conflict between the papacy and the imperial office seemed to have been elevated to the plane of a confrontation in fundamentals. Nevertheless, Frederick had constantly stressed that there was question, not of a conflict with the Church, but with the personality of the Pope, whereas Gregory, for his part, did not attack the role of the *Imperium* in its function as universal *defensor* and *protector* of the Roman Church, but rather rejected the present holder of the office, who, instead of being a defender, attacked the Church, instead of being an orthodox Emperor, lived under the suspicion of heresy without clearing himself.

In its predominant motives the language of the manifestoes, indicated that on both sides persons were prepared to take up the decisive principles that lay behind questions of personality, principles affecting the relationship between the secular and the spiritual powers in their claim to the leadership of the West.

The cardinals refused to proceed to a new election until the Emperor had released the two of their number whom he was holding prisoner since the battle of Montecristo. On 25 June 1243 the Genoese Cardinal Sinibaldo Fieschi was unanimously elected Pope Innocent IV (1243–54).

Frederick hailed the election, believing that in Innocent IV a representative of the peace party in the Sacred College had been elevated. But he soon had to realize that "no Pope [could] be a Ghibelline." Innocent IV, an outstanding jurist and, as a diplomat, entirely in sympathy with his native city, shrewd, objective, tenacious, and far-sighted, took up the legacy of Gregory IX, which included not only the conflict with the Emperor but also the threat to the West from the expansion of the Mongols, concern for the disintegrating Latin Empire, and the repressing of heresy. He was determined to harmonize them with one another, including the crusade. The settlement of the conflict with Frederick presented itself as the most urgent problem. The Emperor himself initiated the negotiations, which, with interruptions, were protracted for years. They almost brought about peace in Holy Week of 1244, when Frederick's envoys solemnly swore to the stipulations of a provisional treaty. The Emperor was to be released from excommunication and in return evacuate the Papal State, perform ecclesiastical penance, give the imprisoned prelates their freedom and compensation, and assure immunity to the Church's adherents. Once again the Lombard question was left unsolved, and the mistrust between Emperor and Pope was not eliminated. In fact, both sides attempted to improve their positions. The Treaty of Rome was not ratified. Instead, Innocent decided on the decisive step of leaving Italy and convoking outside Frederick's sphere of power, even though on imperial territory, the council intended by Gregory IX but obstructed by the Emperor, in order to lay the conflict before the forum of Christendom and bring it to a binding solution.

On 28 June 1244 the Pope sailed to Genoa in a Genoese fleet that was already at hand. He fell ill and stayed there several months; then in the late autumn he crossed the Alps and at the beginning of December took up residence at Lyons with the canons regular of Saint-Just. Without his being able to anticipate it, he was to rule the Church from Lyons until the Emperor's death six years later.

How very much this step implied liberation can be inferred from the accelerated activity of the papal chancery, the lively visits to the Curia, the abundance of far-reaching decisions which occurred almost immediately after the arrival at Lyons and led in the most varied sectors of Church life to new starts and new ways of life. This showed, as would also be the case later at Avignon, that Rome could not for a long time be regarded basically as the centrally located residence of the Popes, not to speak of the continuing difficulties which the city's local politics caused — hardly the climate suited for a peaceful government.

The First Council of Lyons (1245)

Innocent IV announced on 27 December 1244 that he would convoke a general council, which was to meet at Lyons on 24 June 1245. The invitations were sent out from 3 January 1245 to the episcopate, to cathedral chapters and abbots, to princes and cities. The matters to be treated were reform ("status debitus ecclesiae romanae"), the crusade, aid to Constantinople, measures against the Mongols, and finally the conflict with the Emperor ("de negotio, quod inter ecclesiam et principem vertitur"). Since, besides the Mongols, also "other despisers of the faith and persecutors of the Christian people" were mentioned, it may be surmised that the reference was to heretics. In addition to the conflict with the Emperor, these were the classical conciliar themes of the Middle Ages.

The Emperor, the Pope wrote, had been called upon by him in his sermon of 27 December to come to the Council, not as a participant, as were the other kings and princes, but as a defendant ("citavimus"), who was to justify himself ("responsurus") there to the Pope and the others.

When the reports of the severe setbacks in the Holy Land — the taking of Jerusalem by the Khwarazmian Turks and the defeat of the knights at Gaza and Ascalon — reached Italy around the end of the year through the Patriarch of Antioch, and the Emperor in a circular appealed to the Christian princes for help, there simultaneously began the final peace negotiations between Emperor and Pope, in which the Patriarch was involved. It is true that on Holy Thursday Innocent renewed Frederick's excommunication, probably because of pressure from the Archbishops of Mainz and Cologne, who kept aloof from the Emperor in Germany. Still, we possess a letter of 6 May 1245, in which the Pope declared his readiness to lift the censure if Frederick would really take his promises seriously. But simultaneous encroachments of the imperial troops in the *Patrimonium* and the Emperor's clumsy diplomatic maneuvers in England, where the Pope's request for financial help was to be thwarted, brought to nothing these attempts of the eleventh hour.

And so the Council assembled with its program unchanged. Attendance by the bishops of lands ruled by Frederick was naturally meager. Altogether there were present 150 bishops and, in addition, abbots, the generals of the new orders, deputies of invited chapters, of cities, and of princes.

Between 26 June and 17 July 1245, there were four sessions of the Council, which of course continued its work between sessions in discussions, consistories, and committee meetings. On 28 June, in the first of the three principal sessions, which took place in the cathedral of Lyons, Innocent IV delivered the introductory address, outlining the program: the decay of ecclesiastical discipline among clergy and laity ("status debitus ecclesiae"), the distress of the Holy Land because of the arrogance of the Muslims, the Greek Schism as reflected in the problem of the Latin Empire, the Mongol problem, and finally the persecution of the Church by the Emperor Frederick II.

At all the sessions the Emperor's case was pleaded especially by the Grand Justiciar, Thaddeus of Suessa, who exerted some influence on the assembly in his discourses. In addition, Frederick was championed by the Patriarch of Aquileia and the English envoys.

And so there was handed down in the final session the decision which the Pope had previously discussed thoroughly with the prelates individually and which was approved by most of them without any objection. He had the decisions of the Council read: issued in the form of juridical decrees and constitutions, they addressed themselves to the various problems considered, as laws, instructions, admonitions, and proclamations. The Council promoted reform by its clarification of juridical, especially procedural, problems, its tightening of administrative controls, chiefly in regard to an improvement of monastic economic management, and its more precise definition of the powers of papal legates. It tried to meet the Mongol peril by its call for intensive measures of defense. Ecclesiastical taxes were prescribed for the safety of the Latin Empire, while in regard to the crusade the decrees of Lateran IV were renewed, but, significantly, no concrete planning was attempted. Then, before Innocent could have the bull of deposition read, Thaddeus of Suessa lodged a formal appeal against it to the next Pope and to an authentic general council. Innocent calmly defended the universality of the Council of Lyons, to which, he said, all in Christendom who were qualified had been invited; he also noted that Frederick himself was the reason why certain regional episcopates had been unable to attend.

The Council's final act was the reading of the bull of deposition and its confirmation by the assembly. Because of the four crimes of perjury, breach of peace, sacrilege in imprisoning prelates, and suspicion of heresy, Frederick II was deposed as Roman Emperor, King of Germany, and King of Sicily; he was stripped of all honors and dignities, his subjects were released from their oaths of loyalty, and the German princes were invited to proceed to a new election. The Pope, with the advice of the cardinals, intended himself to decide the future of the Sicilian Kingdom.

The session ended with the *Te Deum.* Incidentally, Frederick's excommunication had purposely not been renewed, and so there was here involved what was until now the single case of an implementation of statement 13 of Gregory VII's *Dictatus Papae.*

The First Council of Lyons was a turning point. Despite harsh words the Emperor did not cease, even after the Council, his efforts for peace with the Curia. But the sentence of Lyons intensified the breach between him and the Pope. The struggle for hegemony in Italy and the reaction of the Curia, which feared for its ecclesiastical independence, had now become a struggle over the continuance or non-continuance of the imperial office in the House of Hohenstaufen and at the same time over the validity of the Hohenstaufen concept of the Empire. The Pope mobilized all of his strength in Germany, Italy, and the Sicilian Kingdom in order to enforce the sentence of Lyons. Henry III of England, who was Frederick's brother-in-law, and Louis IX of France maintained a strict neutrality. The Pope contrived to win back Hungary, which had expected help from the Emperor against the Mongols. As had already been clear at the Council, Spain was entirely on the Pope's side, even though Ferdinand III of Castile remained neutral.

But the Emperor made his presence felt everywhere by means of envoys, letters, threats, demands. The journalism of 1239–42 was resumed but its tenor had changed. The question now was whether the Pope had a right to depose the Emperor. Innocent IV maintained that he did, pointing to the authority whereby he constituted the Emperor. The Pope "makes" the Emperor, he said, and hence in a given case he can again deprive him of office and dignity.

The Emperor likewise argued from principle, while coming forward with a reform plan, which relegated the Church, and in her the Pope, to properly spiritual functions, to the apostolic ideal of the Primitive Church, with its subordination to the divinely established authority of kings. Frederick's letter of February 1246 was, of course, not intended as a plan for a reform actually to be carried out but as an element in a journalistic confrontation. It found an echo in a manifesto of French barons of November 1246, which even led to a league of the barons against the Clergy.

In Germany Innocent managed powerfully to arrange the fronts in his own favor, thanks to a consistent personal policy on a high level. In the Kingdom of Sicily he had a crusade preached against Frederick. But the struggle could not be decided until Frederick's death on 13 December 1250. Innocent returned to Italy in order to oppose first Conrad IV, who died on 21 May 1254, before the Pope's death, and then Manfred. But Manfred continued to cause anxiety for the papacy until his death at Benevento in 1266. When on 29 October 1268 Conradin was executed at Naples, the male line of the Hohenstaufen Dynasty was extinguished. Italy did not lay eyes on another Emperor in the thirteenth century.

Chapter 26

The Veering of the Papacy to France and the Angevin Domination in Italy

After the deposition of Frederick II at the Council of Lyons, Innocent IV had left the succession to the Hohenstaufen in the Empire to the qualified electors, but he had reserved the new order in the Kingdom of Sicily to himself and the cardinals. The "Sicilian question" was greatly to embarrass the Curia's policy until the end of the century. There were two possibilities for solving it: The Roman Church could either undertake the administration of the Kingdom or enfeoff a new dynasty with it. At first Innocent seemed to be inclined to assume the direct rule. As a matter of fact, the Curia's financial, military, and personnel resources quickly proved to be too weak, and so the second possibility had to be seriously considered.

After the death on 21 May 1254 of Conrad IV, the Pope felt he was in a position to incorporate Sicily into the Papal State, and hence he broke off the negotiations with England. The envisaged conquest of Sicily under the leadership of the papal nephew, Fieschi, failed. Its collapse was the last message given to Innocent IV, who died at Naples on 7 December 1254. The Hohenstaufen policy was quickly taken up and continued by Manfred, independently and successfully. Without having any support in Germany, Manfred sought to realize in their fulness the Italian plans of his imperial father.

Because of this turn of events, Alexander IV, who had succeeded Innocent IV on 12 December 1254, resumed the negotiations with England. He excommunicated Manfred on 25 March 1255, and on 9 April enfeoffed Edmund with Sicily. When Henry III was unable to meet the high financial and military commitment he had contracted, Alexander cancelled the agreement in 1258, but he had no alternative solution ready. In the same year Manfred had himself crowned King at Palermo on 10 August. His influence grew steadily in Spoleto, the Marches of Ancola, and Romagna. Even at Rome the Ghibellines contrived in the spring of 1261, at the very time when Richard of Cornwall was elected Senator, to secure this dignity for Manfred also.

Alexander IV died on 25 May 1261. For three months the conclave sweated over the succession, which was finally bestowed on an outsider, the Patriarch of Jerusalem, James Pantaléon, a Frenchman from Troyes in Champagne. He had taken part in the Council of Lyons as Archdeacon of Liège; then, in the service of the Curia he had got to know North and East Germany and Poland on extensive legatine journeys. An energetic, shrewd, and diplomatically patient ruler, Urban IV (1261–64), being a Frenchman, was not compromised by the problems of Italy and hence he was freer. He was determined to solve the Sicilian question in order to free his hands for the problems of the whole Church. Under him was completed the papacy's veering to France.

He first succeeded in again strengthening papal influence in North and Central Italy to the detriment of Manfred. He abandoned the English candidacy and asked Louis IX to permit one of his sons to accept enfeoffment with Sicily. The French King refused, referring to Edmund's rights and to the claims of Conradin of Hohenstaufen. Hence Urban turned to Charles of Anjou. The treaty with England was formally annulled, the consent of Louis IX was won, and on 17 June 1263 a treaty was drawn up which sketched in broad outline the Curia's ideas about the envisaged solution of the Sicilian question. South Italy and the island of Sicily were to remain united, and Charles of Anjou would be enfeoffed with the Kingdom in return for a single payment of 50,000 marks sterling. A yearly census of 10,000 ounces of gold was anticipated. The freedom of the Church in the Kingdom was to be assured, and Charles promised the Curia military aid. He had to oblige himself to reject any offer of the German or the imperial crown, and there was to be no question of his ruling the imperial provinces in Italy or the Papal State. Other stipulations explained the aid which the Curia expected from Charles, who was to take possession of his fief within one year. When Manfred, in view of the now clear candidacy of the Angevin, seriously harassed the Pope, Charles was easily able to have the draft of the treaty modified in his favor. Even before it was signed Charles had violated its stipulations by accepting election as Senator of Rome. Nevertheless, Urban confirmed the election, which made it obvious that there would be other complications. Before the Pope died on 2 October 1264, the Curia's treaty with Charles of Anjou had been signed. The Angevin domination had been established, not only in the Sicilian Kingdom, but, as events were to prove, also in Italy.

The long vacancy of the Holy See, which lasted until 5 February 1265, facilitated the assuming of power by the new lord of Sicily. He prepared for this by underpinning it with a long series of alliances which he concluded with North Italian rulers and cities. Such a procedure hardly corresponded to the spirit of the treaty he had just signed with the Roman Church. But the new Pope, Clement IV (1265–68), less vigorous than his predecessor, had also, as a Frenchman, close personal ties with the House of Anjou. On 28 June 1265 he solemnly invested the new King of Sicily at Rome. Thanks to his good offices, Charles was able to make contacts with Tuscan bankers, who granted him extensive credit against a thirty-years' tithe on the French Church. In this way Tuscany became involved in the new Sicilian policy: Charles opened up his new Kingdom to economic exploitation. The confrontation with Manfred led to the decisive battle of Benevento, where on 26 February 1266, the last Hohenstaufen ruler of Sicily lost both Kingdom and life. The route into the Kingdom was now open for its new master.

But Conradin of Hohenstaufen, Duke of Swabia and King of Jerusalem, was still alive and he claimed the succession in Sicily. After Manfred's death a diet at Augsburg in October 1266 decided on an Italian expedition by the youthful Conradin. All who were unhappy with the papacy's award to Anjou had turned to him: the Hohenstaufen faction in Sicily, the opposition in the Papal State, and the Ghibellines of Tuscany under Pisa's leadership. *Condottieri* of every sort joined him, including two *Infantes* of Spain, Henry and Frederick, brothers of King Alfonso X of Castile, who had himself been elected King of the Romans in 1257.

Papal objections had thus far prevented Conradin's election as King. Clement IV now tried to stop Conradin's expedition. He threatened excommunication and interdict, in April 1267 appointed Charles *paciarius generalis* to safeguard disinterestedly the rights of all during the vacancy of the Empire, permitted the Angevin to hold power for six years as *podestà* in Florence and other cities of Tuscany, and in the cathedral of Verona on 18 November 1267 declared that Conradin had incurred excommunication for having disregarded the prohibition of coming to Italy; if he advanced farther, he would be deprived of the Kingdom of Jerusalem. On Holy Thursday, 5 April 1268, Clement formally deposed him from the throne of Jerusalem, had a crusade preached against him and, finally, on 17 April, named Charles imperial vicar in Tuscany. But meanwhile Conradin moved from Verona via Pavia, Pisa, and Siena to Rome, where on 24 July 1268 he was elected Senator. When he set out to conquer the Sicilian Kingdom he lost the decisive battle of Tagliacozzo on 23 August. He was overtaken in flight. Charles put him on trial and had him beheaded at Naples on 29 October 1268. Exactly one month later Clement IV died at Viterbo.

Charles of Anjou, now unchallenged master of the Kingdom of Sicily, in possession of Tuscany, and influential in Lombardy, prepared to gain all of Italy as heir of the Hohenstaufen. Persons had already heard of his intention of supporting the powerless Emperor Baldwin I in reconquering Byzantium, whereupon Jerusalem was to be liberated. A comprehensive imperialist scheme unfolded itself.

For almost three years — from 29 November 1268 to 1 September 1271 — the Holy See remained vacant. Charles of Anjou utilized this time to suppress opposition in his Kingdom, to arrange the affairs of Tuscany as its master, to hold in check his Ghibelline opponents in North Italy. At Rome he was elected Senator for life. Hence in 1270 he seemed to rule all of Italy. The papacy saw him as its assistant, but now he had risen to become master. Innocent IV's mighty exertions had been apparently in vain.

For twenty years after its victory over the Hohenstaufen the Curia had been so seriously hampered by its concern for the succession to Sicily and by the unrest in the other parts of Italy that important tasks in the East and in the government of the Universal Church had been neglected. In 1261 Constantinople was lost, as far as the West was concerned. In the Empire the double election of 1257 had inaugurated the dark age of the Interregnum. A religious and moral deterioration in many strata of Christian society made itself felt. The territorial prince's authority over the Church was everywhere consolidated. Reform was needed and persons looked for a man who could master the confusion of the age and restore order.

CHAPTER 27

Pope Gregory X and the Second Council of Lyons

The election of Tedaldo Visconti on 1 September 1271 ended the longest vacancy of the Holy See in the thirteenth century. Archdeacon of Liège, he was crowned at Rome on 26 March. As early as 13 April invitations went out for a general council, which once again was to meet in Lyons. Reform of the Church, union with the Greeks, and aid for the Holy Land were to be the principal themes of the gathering. They were also the essential concerns of the program laid down for his pontificate by Gregory X (1271–76).

The leitmotif was the liberation of the Holy Places, and peace with Byzantium was regarded as its prerequisite. The renewal of ecclesiastical life in Western Christendom was likewise to serve this end. The schemes of Charles of Anjou with regard to Byzantium had to be stopped. While still in Syria Gregory X had initiated negotiations with the Emperor Michael VIII Palaeologus. To protect himself against the threat from Charles of Anjou, the Emperor was ready for far-reaching concessions, even for the recognition of the Roman Primacy. However, his clergy and people made it clear to the Emperor that he would find no support among them for his policy, and the Patriarch Joseph abdicated.

In Italy, Gregory, while allowing Charles of Anjou to continue as Roman Senator and as imperial vicar in Tuscany, avoided giving any appearance that the papacy was dependent on Charles. He aimed at an energetic effort to settle the strife between Guelfs and Ghibellines, which was tearing all of Italy to pieces. The principal factor in settling this difficult complex of problems was to be the election of a new Emperor. By means of a friendly cooperation with him, the Pope intended to try to restore peace to Italy.

As candidates there came forward King Ottakar II of Bohemia, King Philip III of France, Duke Henry of Bavaria, Conradin's uncle and heir, and the Duke's brother, the Count Palatine Louis, himself one of the Electors. However, agreement was eventually reached in the Landgrave of Alsace, Rudolf of Habsburg, who was elected at Frankfurt on 1 October 1273 and crowned at Aachen on 24 October.

The Electors informed the Pope of Rudolf's election and coronation and asked that he be given the imperial crown. Rudolf sent an embassy to Rome to convey his respects and assured the Pope of his readiness to take the cross. Gregory cordially accepted the messages from Germany but postponed a decision until the Council.

The preparations for the Council were aided by testimonials on the state of the Church, which the Pope requested from everywhere. Of the extant replies the most useful were those of Bishop Bruno of Olomouc and of the former general of the Dominicans, Humbert of Romans. They sketched a gloomy picture of the religious condition of both clergy and people. Bruno's reform proposal amounted to a strengthening of episcopal authority, notably *vis-à-vis* the richly privileged mendicant orders. Humbert demanded especially a reform of the Curia.

The Council met in Lyons on 7 May 1274. Almost 300 bishops, sixty abbots, generals of orders, and prelates, and leading theologians attended, but Thomas Aquinas had died *en route.* King James I of Aragón was the only prince to accept the invitation in person; the others were represented by envoys.

Of the three principal topics, the most important, Church reform, for which the best preliminary work had been done, seems to have been the least discussed. The union with the Greeks was realized because the Emperor had already previously declared for it in principle. For the crusade there was at hand Michael VIII's promise to participate in it if the West would first make a lasting peace with him, a condition aimed at frustrating the projects of Charles of Anjou and Baldwin II. With the envoys of the Khan of Persia was made a treaty which provided for a common front against Islam. The Kings of France, England, Aragón, and Sicily agreed in principle to take part in the crusade. At the conciliar consistory of 6 June 1274, the Chancellor Otto swore, on behalf of King Rudolf, to maintain the privileges and promises made to the Roman Church by Otto IV and Frederick II; included was the renunciation of the Sicilian Kingdom. Rudolf's recognition by the Pope was given on 26 September.

In agreement with the cardinals at Lyons the Pope appointed 23 May of the following year for the imperial coronation, but the date was soon put off until 1 November 1275. In October 1275 the Pope and King Rudolf met at Lausanne, where Rudolf in person made the promises already sworn to by his chancellor; he also intended, if necessary, to preserve and defend the Kingdom of Sicily for the

Church, but not to assume the government himself, as this is usually understood. Now 2 February 1276 was agreed upon as the date of the imperial coronation and then Rudolf, together with the princes present and 500 knights, took the cross. But this date also could not be kept, for Gregory X died at Arezzo on 10 January 1276.

The Council met from 7 May to 17 July, longer than any of its predecessors. The proxies of the chapters were dismissed after the second session, 18 May. The Byzantine embassy arrived a month late. The discussions between the Pope and the cardinals relative to the rules of the conclave were protracted, and the meetings with the representatives of Alfonso of Castile and of Rudolf of Habsburg claimed much time. On 4 July the Pope received the sixteen envoys of the Mongol Khan Abaga. The publication of the conciliar decrees was distributed among several sessions, and so the impression is created that the Council worked intensively. Among the results of the Council, in addition to the union with the Greeks, which is reflected in the *professio fidei,* were the preparations for the crusade. Provision was made for a tithe on all ecclesiastical incomes over a period of six years. Princes and kings had promised to take part, and Michael Palaeologus also seemed ready to cooperate under certain conditions. More detailed plans were not outlined, nor was a date appointed. The Pope's early death was a severe blow to the enterprise.

The Council's decrees continued the legislative work of 1215 and 1245. First place among them belongs to the constitution *Ubi periculum,* which made new rules for the papal election. Frequently revised, it is still in force today. The cardinals were not to wait more than ten days from the Pope's death for the arrival of the absent. The election was to occur in the place where the Pope died. The cardinals were to stay together, cut off from all contact with the outside world, until they had completed the election. The longer the election took, the more scanty should their provisions become. In addition, the constitution deprived the cardinals of all revenues during the vacancy. Such stern conditions explain the resistance of those affected. For the constitution was annulled by Gregory's successors and only put back into effect by Celestine V. It was included in the *Liber Sextus* by Boniface VIII and from then on was an element of the canon law that is still valid.

The other decrees attacked abuses, as these were specified in the various testimonials. The constitution *Religionum diversitatem* repeated the prohibition made in 1215 of founding new orders and congregations and suppressed all establishments made since that time without the consent of the Holy See; the others were subjected to severe restrictions. This constitution was to have a great impact on the further development of relations between the regular and the diocesan clergy.

Finally, usury was again reprobated, the penal law was made more precise, and decrees were issued for the course of trials; these last were directed especially against excessive prolonging. In his closing address Gregory X charged the bishops especially to tackle the reform of the parochial care of souls; they should so reform themselves and, by a careful personal policy, their estate, that the anticipated overcoming of the decay of Church life, complained of and described on all sides, might now begin and its permanence might be assured. It is the tragedy of Gregory X that the union with the Greeks was not lasting, the crusade did not take place, and the sought for reform was not realized.

CHAPTER 28

Heresy and the Inquisition in the Thirteenth Century

Waldensians, Humiliati, Cathari — a legacy of the late twelfth century — were not regained to the unity of the Church, despite Innocent III's policy of conciliation and the measures of the Fourth Lateran Council. On the contrary, they again spread throughout Europe, apart from England. The Cathari continued to be in congenial surroundings especially in Languedoc and to a lesser degree in Lombardy. Related to them were the Albanenses on Lake Garda under John di Luglio. The Garatenses and Bagnolenses were regarded as moderate dualists. Groups of Cathari were formed around Vicenza and in Tuscany. Mutually hostile, they nevertheless occasionally closed ranks on the outbreak of persecution. Cathari were encountered also in Catalonia, Aragón, and Castile. They were often organized into churches: three in Languedoc, six in Italy, others in the Balkan peninsula and the Near East and in France, Germany, and Spain. The Cathari often formulated their doctrine during the crusades against them and in the conflict with the Inquisition. They published Latin writings. Little of this is extant; for the most part it is known from quotations in Catholic literature. The *Liber de duobus principiis,* written after 1240, contains a Cathar ritual in Latin; corresponding to it is a ritual drawn up in Provençal around 1280. These works could not have contributed any new impulse to the Cathar movement itself. Following the wars in the Midi they could maintain themselves only as harmless sectaries. The last proceedings against them took place around 1300 in the Midi and North Italy.

The Waldensians, who have maintained themselves until the present, were more tenacious. As the "Poor Lombards" they began to play a role of their own in North Italy and distinguished themselves from the French "Poor Men of Lyons." They were connected with the Humiliati, flatly rejected the notion of Sacraments, and aspired to live, not by begging, but in communities of workers. They also refused any control of their beliefs by the French Waldensians. In Germany they made their appearance as *Runcarii,* apparently so called from John of Ronco, the first leader of the "Poor Lombards." The German Waldensians maintained a rather slight contact with the Lombard brethren and bishops and sent them money. In Lombardy, France, and Spain they were liquidated by the Inquisition. But Waldensian communities survived in Calabria and Apulia and in the Alpine valleys of Piedmont and Savoy.

Alongside Cathari and Waldensians there everywhere emerged in the thirteenth century, at first in isolation, then in variously increasing numbers, heresies of another sort, which did not, however, organize themselves as sects. Their basic sources included theological and philosophical speculations of learned circles, while spiritualistic tendencies, above all among the women, became apparent.

Joachim's doctrine of the Three Ages — the Old Testament as the Age of the Father, the New Testament as the Age of the Son, and an epoch of a monastically colored spirituality as the Age of the Holy Spirit — influenced also a Parisian heretical circle of disciples of Amaury of Bene, who was first condemned in 1210. They regarded the Holy Spirit as incarnate in themselves, and a pantheistic ontology, as propounded by Amaury, became among them a fanaticism which found a response among both lay men and women. At the University of Paris a line of so-called Averroists led from David of Dinant to Siger of Brabant and others. They understood their Aristotle as a concept of being which was independent of the faith and theology, as a truth apart from theological truth — the "double truth." Averroism continued to be influential among lay scholars, jurists and physicians, though it was repeatedly forbidden and the Inquisition proceeded energetically against its proponents, among others Siger of Brabant.

Analogous notions, similar to those represented by the disciples of Amaury and by David of Dinant, appeared also in Ortlieb of Strasbourg, who intended to obey only the Holy Spirit revealing himself to him most intimately. Ortlieb's followers in Germany did not believe in creation, taught the eternity of the world with the Averroists, and denied the resurrection and the last judgment. They held that whoever did not join them in Noah's Ark was lost. They understood the sacraments and the articles of faith in a mystical sense and the Gospels in a moral sense, but not literally or sacramentally in the sense of tradition. Like the Waldensians and the Cathari, they rejected oaths and every form of lying and killing, but they permitted marriage and called for asceticism, in particular fasting and penance. They did not organize a sect. They were everywhere and nowhere. As the opportunity arose, they were arrested, interrogated, and punished. Soon after 1270 Albert the Great wrote at Cologne an opinion on about one hundred statements of heretics in Swabian Ries near Nördlingen, which, as the *Compilatio de novo spiritu,* was included in the collection of the so-called Passau Anonymous and was there supplemented by a list of errors of this "heresy of the new Spirit."

The Beghard-Beguine movement of the thirteenth century was also early infected by heretical elements, which, however, were not seen to be dangerous until the fourteenth century. Because of the wide distribution and varied organization of the Beguines, these elements could not be localized and at first seemed to be merely enthusiastic admixtures in the fabric of what was in itself a pious and orthodox organization. Still so far as the Church was concerned, these groups had to be kept under surveillance, because they quickly settled especially in the great cities, but these centers were located in those regions where heresy was at home by predilection: Byzantium, the Danube districts, the valleys of the Rhine, Meuse, Rhone and Saone, and Loire, Champagne, Flanders, North Italy, Provence, Languedoc, and Aragón.

The papal reaction against these heretical movements that were spreading everywhere proved to be ineffective. The secular arm was called upon for help in France, Spain, Italy, and the Empire, and warlike methods were employed under the guise of a crusade. But then the papacy developed an institution whose origins go back to the twelfth century but which first obtained its organization in the second quarter of the thirteenth century: the Inquisition. At Verona in 1184 Lucius III, in the presence of the Emperor Frederick I, took up a decision rendered by Alexander III at the Council of Tours in 1163 and made it universally binding in his bull "Ad abolendam," which was later included in the decretals of Gregory IX. According, to this, the bishop, as the ordinary judge in questions of heresy, was to search out heretics in biennial visitations of his diocese in order to prosecute them on his own authority, without waiting for a formal accusation. Thus, inquisition proceedings were to replace accusation proceedings. Here were the beginnings of the

Inquisition. In his bull "Vergentis in senium" of 1199 Innocent III had confirmed these directives of 1184 and their strict sanctions, declared the offense of heresy to be *crimen maiestatis* a concept of Roman law, and regulated the penalties there provided, stressing, it is true, that the Church may not disregard her obligation to exercise mercy. The Fourth Lateran Council made these rules law for the Universal Church, emphasized the lawfulness of investigations from parish to parish, demanded that processes be initiated *ex officio,* without awaiting charges, and required the confiscation of the goods and the relinquishing, not the surrendering, of the condemned to the secular power for punishment, but with the *animadversio debita.* In this way the procedure of the Inquisition was essentially determined.

Honorius III proceeded further. He first intensified the Albigensian Crusade, for which the heir to the French throne made himself available. As King Louis VIII, the latter brought it to a close to the great advantage of the crown. In April 1226 Louis issued an ordinance of significance for the development of the Inquisition: that every heretic condemned by the episcopal court was to be forthwith punished through the *animadversio debita,* while the penalty of infamy was to be the lot of followers and abettors. The bishop was thus the judge of heretics, and the canonical formula, *animadversio debita,* of Verona in 1184 became an element of French royal law. This ordinance of 1226 can be regarded as the model of all later legislation.

As in France, so also in Aragón Honorius III gained the help asked from the crown. King James I forbade his vassals to receive heretics and commanded them to refuse any aid to them and their friends. But the essential support of the papal action against heresy was to be the Emperor. At his coronation Frederick II issued some laws, concerning which it has been possible to establish that they were formulated by the Curia. Among them was an edict against heretics.

Heretics condemned by the Church were exiled and they and their heirs suffered confiscation of property. Persons suspected of heresy incurred, as provided by the Fourth Lateran Council, infamy, excommunication, and, in the case of the obstinate, the same penalties as heretics. City authorities were obliged under oath to expel them. If lords were involved, their land and possessions were liable to seizure, reserving the rights of the respective overlord. With this edict the canons of the Fourth Lateran Council became the law of the Empire. Frederick II sent the edict to Bologna to be inscribed in the University's register and proclaimed as the norm of instruction. A year later Honorius III did the same. In 1224 Frederick II introduced the penalty of burning. In a reply of March 1224 to an inquiry from Archbishop Albert of Magdeburg, who was acting as imperial legate in Romagna, occurs the following:

> Anyone who has been convicted of heresy by the bishop of his diocese must immediately, on the bishop's demand, be arrested by the secular judicial authority and delivered up to the pyre. Should the judges mercifully spare his life, he must at least suffer the loss of his tongue, by which the Catholic faith has been assailed.

In Italy, however, Frederick II called for recourse to the pyre, whereas the Curia hesitated to do so. Still, the imperial constitution of 1224 appeared neither in the

Compilatio quinta nor in Gregory IX's collection of decretals. Hence the papacy did not adopt it officially, though it tacitly tolerated its implementation.

Honorius III, acting as arbiter between Lombard League and Emperor, commanded the envoys of the cities to adopt both the papal conciliar decrees and the imperial constitutions against heresy into their municipal legislation.

The Lombard cities complied in their peace proclamation of 26 March 1227. Included in the recommended imperial constitutions was certainly that of 1224, which provided death by fire for condemned heretics.

Gregory IX energetically pursued the policy of his predecessor, who had made the canons of the Fourth Lateran Council respected in France, Spain, and the Empire but had abandoned the restrictions favoring mercy as laid down by Innocent III.

Since he made the Lombards' peace formula a guiding principle and imposed it upon all cities, through him the Church officially recognized death at the stake as a penalty. Hesitant and negligent bishops in Lombardy were ordered by Gregory to procure the aid of preachers who could edify the people by word and example. Gregory now expressly gave the task of inquisitor to religious.

On 12 April 1229 there was concluded at Paris between King Louis IX and Count Raymond VII of Toulouse a peace which is to be regarded as the definitive end of the Albigensian wars. The royal ordinance of 1229, which dealt with the procedure against heretics in connection with the peace treaty, repeated the order of 1226. The collaboration of ecclesiastical and secular authorities in discovering and punishing heretics was now officially recognized and confirmed by Louis IX in 1229.

Since the Emperor was thereafter often obstructed by his quarrel with the Curia, the policy with regard to heretics in France became of special importance for the further development of legislation on heresy and hence of the Inquisition. The Council of Toulouse in the year of the Peace of 1229 played a great role in this, since there for the first time the assembling of a permanent law court was decreed, a permanent college of judges with delegated episcopal authority, whose task consisted solely in seeking out heretics and bringing them before the court. About twenty of the Council's forty-five articles were concerned with the question of heretics.

Following the Peace of Paris and the Council of Toulouse the Cathari and other heretics went underground and open resistance ceased.

Gregory IX carried further the Curia's legislation on heretics. In January 1231 he accepted Frederick II's constitution of 1224, including the punishment by fire, into his register and in February 1231 incorporated it into his own constitution "Excommunicamus," so that from then on *animadversio debita* became synonymous with the penalty of death at the stake. Public and private discussions of faith among the laity were forbidden, and ecclesiastical burial was denied to those put to death. Immurement, or life-imprisonment for penitent heretics, prohibition of any appeal to other tribunals, denial of any legal assistance for the accused, and finally social ostracism of the descendants of the condemned — to the second generation they lost the ability to hold any ecclesiastical offices — were among the fundamental components of this legislation. Gregory also had the Roman Senate's decision in cases of the condemnation of relapsed heretics included in his register immediately after his constitution of February 1231, so that, together with his own and the imperial enactment of 1224, it constituted in a sense one *corpus*. It gave the secular arm a delay of eight days for the carrying out of the *animadversio debita*, ordered the destruction of the immovable property, assigned one-third of the goods to those making the denunciation, and expelled from the city all followers of the condemned, confiscating one-third of their possessions also.

With the 1231 edicts of Gregory IX the basic legislation for the procedure of the Inquisition was complete. All the essential elements can be identified in it: infamy, loss of civil and political rights, banishment, deprivation of feudal holdings, and *animadversio debita* as death at the stake, so far as the series of penalties was concerned. The Pope also made universally binding the wearing of the cross by the condemned, the secrecy of trials and the withholding of the names of witnesses, the prohibition of lodging an appeal and of asking legal assistance from lawyers. The duty of maintaining prisoners was defined, and the exhuming of the remains of heretics who had gone undetected in their lifetime was ordered. The episcopal judges and those from the diocesan clergy thereby obtained their manual of penal procedure and penal law for the future. From now on there was question of its use and of the activation of Inquisition tribunals everywhere in the Church.

In addition to the episcopal Inquisition, such as it had been decided upon, though, of course, to a great extent ineffectively, at Verona in 1184, Gregory IX now appointed papal inquisitors with the permanent duty of seeking out heretics systematically, of bringing them to trial, of condemning them if they were unable to free themselves of suspicion, and of relinquishing then to the secular power for burning.

From 1232 on Gregory IX, and later his successors, turned over the Inquisition to the new orders, especially to the Dominicans. Textbooks and manuals for inquisitors appeared, in which were to be found fundamental, even if often one-sided and polemical explanations of heresy and the harsh methods for combatting it. But this systematically organized Inquisition, becoming everywhere effective, was unable completely to eradicate heresy. Still, because of it a keener defensive struggle was possible in the event of any deviation from the faith of the Church.

The episcopal and the legatine Inquisition and that administered by religious were intended by the Pope to co-operate in principle, even though there were shifts of emphasis according to the various territories. Under Innocent IV occurred the completion of the Inquisition as an institution of canon law. In this connection he frequently modified the procedure, whose original severity had evoked opposition. In the struggle against Frederick II he had to be concerned about a rapid and thorough settlement of the many disturbances in the Midi, about a reconciliation with Count Raymond VII of Toulouse, and about the co-operation of the German bishops. He was able to arrange a harmonious collaboration of crown and papacy in France, and in Spain and Germany the episcopates were prepared to support the Inquisition. After the Emperor's death in 1250, Innocent IV was able to establish the Inquisition as a permanent institution in Italy. All earlier papal and imperial enactments were combined in the bull "Ad exstirpanda" of 15 May 1252. The introduction of torture in the process was new. But the Pope's actual policy brought many modifications and amnesty for all who were reconciled to the Church within a year. All this was, one might say, a return to the merciful firmness of Innocent III.

The establishing of the Inquisition and its activity, the collaboration of ecclesiastical and secular power in the fight against heresy, the harshness of the procedure, and the cruelty of the penalties — none of this can be understood apart from the assumptions of the social order in the High Middle Ages. The bond unifying them was the faith, which heresy threatened to destroy. With all the means provided by its ecclesiastical and secular powers Christendom waged a war to maintain itself against this threat. Perhaps a real Christian self-understanding was obscure in some circles.

CHAPTER 29

The Missionary Work of the Church in the Twelfth and Thirteenth Centuries

The epoch of the elaboration of legal structures and of religious renewal, of theological scholarship and of mystical emotion, could not neglect a task so central to the very being of the Church as was that of announcing salvation to all peoples. This was all the more urgent as the crusade movement constantly brought new peoples into view on the frontiers of Christendom, from the Muslims to the Mongols. In addition, there took place from Scandinavia to Central Germany a constant encounter with the still pagan world of the Elbe Slavs, the Baltic Sea area, and Finland. While efforts had begun there as early as the ninth and tenth centuries to press eastward, with the exception of Poland in 966, no North Slavic people could be incorporated into Christendom until the twelfth and thirteenth centuries.

Missionary work among these peoples was influenced by the idea then current of a *dilatatio imperii christiani* and continued necessarily to be characterized by the intimate interrelationship of political and religious motives that marked the contemporary self-awareness of the Church. The mission of the sword and the mission of the word were inextricably combined; conquest, constructing of an ecclesiastical organization, and a comprehensive pastoral activity on the part of monastery and parish succeeded one another. Protection by the state remained essential both for beginning and for continuing any Christianization. The results were due chiefly to the reform orders of the twelfth century — Cistercians, Premonstratensians, and canons regular — and to the mendicant orders of the thirteenth century. As regards secular powers, the initiative passed from the Emperor to the princes of the marches and the northern kings and, especially in the Baltic area, to the military orders, in particular to the Teutonic Knights in Prussia.

The resumption of Christian evangelization in the twelfth century began in

Pomerania, which King Boleslas III of Poland conquered in 1122. He asked assistance from Bishop Otto of Bamberg.

Not much later than in Pomerania an effort was made from Hamburg-Bremen to convert the Slavs beyond the Elbe.

The Augustinian canon, Meinhard of Segeberg, was active in Livonia from 1180. He resided at Üxküll on the Dvina as a suffragan of Bremen. A pagan reaction put an end to this start until Albert of Buxhövden, consecrated Bishop of the Livs in 1199, organized a crusade, which was successful under his leadership. In 1201 Albert founded Riga, which became his episcopal city. He founded the Military Order of the Knights of the Sword, *Fratres militiae Christi,* with whose help he subjugated Estonia, and other areas. In 1255 Alexander IV made Riga an archbishopric, the first metropolitan being Albert Suerbeer, former Archbishop of Armagh. Bishop Albert's dominion — it has been said that he intended to found an ecclesiastical state — was divided through the intervention of the Curia. The Bishop, the Knights of the Sword, and the city of Riga each obtained one-third. Albert had declared Livonia to be the "property of the Mother of God" and had thereby in principle subjected it to the Church. Even after the division of power this idea remained the unifying bond among Bishop, city, and knights.

Farther north the intervention of the Danes had continued the Church's missionary work among the Esths since 1170.

Christian influence had made itself felt in Finland in the eleventh century but it required Swedish crusades, in 1157 under King Eric IX Jedvardson and in 1239 and 1295, to subjugate the country. The Dominicans played a substantial role in the Christianization of Finland, and the see even adopted their liturgy.

The first attempts at the evangelization of the pagan Prussians between the Vistula and the Memel were ordered by Boleslas I of Poland toward the end of the tenth century. But it was due to the initiative of Innocent III that the work was seriously continued. The struggle to subjugate the Prussians lasted from 1230 to 1283. German peasants, especially Westphalians, were invited into the country, and the mendicant orders, again the Dominicans in particular, took charge of the pastoral work. The Papal Legate William of Modena erected sees in 1243 at Chelmno, Pomesania, Ermeland, and Samland. At first they were combined into one Archbishopric of Prussia, but when Riga was made a metropolitan see in 1255 they were incorporated into that province. The Lithuanians remained unconquered and for the time being unconverted, even though Prince Mindaugas received baptism in 1250 and obtained the royal title from Innocent IV. In 1260 he apostatized. Not until toward the end of the thirteenth century was the strength of the Teutonic Order's state so secure that the grand master could in 1309 transfer his residence from Venice to the Marienburg.

The missions among the Slavs and in the Baltic area remained closely tied to conquest and domination; here the crusade developed from a means of defense into an instrument of forcible expansion. The situation was different in the eastern Mediterranean and on the African Coast. Only in the Spanish *Reconquista* can analogous developments be surmised, even if a quite different social and historical context must be considered: that of Christian communities on Islamic territory.

The crusader states in Syria and Palestine, it is true, had non-Christian populations under their rule, but apart from a few indications in the twelfth century, there was very little eagerness to preach the Gospel to them. Pastoral activity, to the extent that it was taken seriously, was directed to the Christian population, which, extraordinarily mixed, — Latins and Greeks, French and Italians, long resident families and pilgrims, — resisted any systematic care.

Serious reflection to the effect that the warlike contacts with Islam, though they might have been pursued with the noblest defensive aims, could not free the West from the responsibility of seeking to preach Christianity even in Islamic territory first occurred in the thirteenth century. Well known are the attitude of Saint Francis of Assisi and his discussion from Damietta in 1219 with the Sultan al-Kamil, which at least obtained for him personally the freedom to preach. From now on, especially in the new orders, it was seen ever more clearly that, wherever the crusade made it possible, there was a duty to activate an evangelization. As is well known, this effort nowhere led to real successes when it had to face Islam, whose attitude was one of fundamental rejection and obstruction. Toward the end of the century the bases of the problem of the mission to Islam were grappled with by the Franciscan tertiary, Raymond Lull (d. 1316). With him the holy war clearly retired in favor of an intellectual campaign to win unbelievers.

Like the Franciscans, the Dominicans also sought to promote the mission to Islam.

The actual results of such missionary activity were, it is true, meager. The scanty reports are frequently limited to individual conversions and to work among Arabs and Muslims in lands under Christian rule. In North Africa there were only occasional contacts, for there, with the assent of the princes, the strictly pastoral activity served the Christians.

As early as the pontificate of Gregory IX the Curia was aware of the danger from the Mongols, who had already invaded Eastern Europe. The Mongol storm fell upon Poland and Hungary in 1240 to 1241. The German defeat at Liegnitz in Silesia in 1241 appeared to present the worst threat, but actually it was the turning point, for the death of the Great Khan Ogdai in 1242 caused the Mongols to evacuate Central Europe, though they remained in Russia.

It was known in the West that in Asia there had long been living Persian Nestorians, who had penetrated as far as India and China. The Curia could learn from previous reports that the Mongols, belonging to none of the known world religions, practiced an extensive toleration toward them, including that of the Christian Nestorians.

And so on several occasions Innocent IV and King Louis IX of France sent Franciscans and Dominicans to the Mongols. Probably there was no question of missionary activity; inquiries and contacts were envisaged. The mission in the sense of a preaching of the faith was first taken up by the Franciscan John of Montecorvino, who from 1294 to 1328 worked at Cambalu (Beijing) among Nestorians and Buddhists with a group of confrères. The end of the Mongol domination in China and the assumption of power by the Ming Dynasty in 1368 destroyed the Beijing mission.

Missionary zeal was kept aglow among the Dominicans, especially by the master general Humbert of Romans (1254–63). Toward the close of the thirteenth century the Order established the *Societas fratrum peregrinantium propter Chris-*

tum, which was active particularly in the lands around the Black Sea and in Asia Minor.

In general it can be established in regard to the Church's missionary endeavor in this period that, in connection with the political opening up of the Baltic countries for the West, Christianity was also able to take root there. The encounter with Islam continued, because it was for the most part of a military and political nature, to be without particular impact because of its exclusion of any religious propaganda, if one disregards the catechetical efforts in the reconquered parts of Spain. The advance in the countries under Mongol rule was merely casual, except for the Franciscan mission in Beijing.

CHAPTER 30

Canon Law and the Constitution of the Church in the Thirteenth Century

Since the appearance of Gratian's *Decretum* around 1140 the scientific study of canon law had developed at Bologna and Paris and later also at Montpellier, Oxford, and Salamanca. Applying the scholastic method, the decretists had prepared the material in glosses, *quaestiones,* treatises, and *summae* for use in academic instruction and the courts. The collaboration of theory and practice gave rise to what Gabriel Le Bras calls the "new law." The legislative activity of the papacy in the decretals and of councils in constitutions contributed the most to this development. These new decisions became especially numerous from the pontificate of Alexander III. Collections were made, at first privately, then with papal authorization. More than eighty such collections have been discovered; the best known are the five great compilations made between 1191 and 1226. Two of them were officially approved: the *Compilatio tertia* of Peter of Benevento by Innocent III in 1209 and the *Compilatio quinta,* perhaps of Tancred, by Honorius III in 1220; they were sent to the courts and schools for their use. Gregory IX decided to unify the decretal legislation of the last century; it was published by the Pope on 5 September 1234. Thus Gregory IX's *Liber Extra* (*Liber decretalium extra decretum vagantium*) became the first "official, authentic, uniform, universal, and exclusive" law book of the Church. Pope Boniface VIII published this *Liber Sextus* on 3 March 1298; Gregory IX's *Liber Extra* retained its legal force. These two codifications of the thirteenth century stimulated and provided the models for the legislation of kings and princes that was now everywhere in process.

The methods employed in systematic instruction in canon law were similar to those developed at the theological faculties, above all that of Paris. In addition to the lecture (*lectio, praelectio, lectura*), *disputatio* was also practiced. In it the *quaestiones* already treated in the lecture were discussed again between teachers and students, mostly in an analytical and exegetical manner. As in theology, the works of the glossators — collections of glosses, later apparatus — became important. Eventually there appeared the great *summae,* real commentaries, intended as texts and manuals for practice. Among them the *summae* of apparatus had special prestige.

The Golden Age of the decretalists began with the promulgation of the *Liber Extra* in 1234 and included the career of the celebrated John Andreae (1270–1348). Hence it lasted a century and was at the same time the expression of the most vigorous period of the constructing and consolidating of the ecclesiastical organization of the High Middle Ages and of the acceptance by the West of the canon law as the universally valid and effective legal order of Christendom.

The canonists did not develop a comprehensive theory of the Church as legislator; rather, they presupposed this, so to speak, and in their lectures, disputations, and commentaries were more concerned with the thousand particular problems that resulted from the ceaseless alteration of structures. Theology also knew no real treatise on the Church but understood quite well that the legislative Church of the jurists was to be identified with the Church experienced in faith, which, as the *corpus Christi mysticum,* to use an expression of Aquinas, constituted the proper ontological basis for all ways of life in Christendom that became visible in the law. The historical development led to this that the hierarchical order of divine institution gained preeminence in the thought and action of the High Middle Ages, while the concept of the Church as the "people of God on earth," which was engaged in its journey to God, retired to the background. And so there was sketched a picture of the constitution of the Church in this period which was determined by one of the stable institutional elements in her.

The great epoch of classical canon law was at the same time the epoch of the papacy as the authoritative guide of the destinies of Christendom, from Innocent III to Boniface VIII. Neither before nor after was the papacy able to raise its claim so effectively, thanks precisely to the successful activity of canon lawyers and their students in the various offices — the papacy itself, the Curia, bishoprics, abbeys, and chapters — which converted theory into practice, to act and to lead as the universally acknowledged teacher, judge, and guide of *christianitas.*

The fundamental lines of the ecclesiastical organization did not change in the thirteenth century. The distinction between the power of orders and the power of jurisdiction in the one *potestas ecclesiastica* was worked out more clearly, again chiefly by Aquinas. The legislative power was exercised more firmly and more consciously, especially by the Pope. In the case of the Pope it found its limits in the divine law, both positively revealed and naturally known, but it could be developed beyond the conciliar law of earlier centuries. The Pope's sovereignty *vis-à-vis* the Council remained undisputed so long as he did not fall into heresy, which meant that he ceased to be Pope. He summoned general synods, directed them and promulgated their decisions as his decrees. There was no longer any question of an essential co-operation of the laity, such as the Emperor.

The papal right to legislate included the right to bestow privileges and grant dispensations from papal and universal as well as from particular law. Celestine II

(1143–44) had introduced the legal reservation *salva Sedis Apostolicae auctoritate*. To be sure, in the case of unrestrained exercise of the right to dispense there lay grave dangers for the security of the legal structures, but for the time being these did not seem to be threatening.

All clerical and non-clerical members of Christendom were subject to the supreme judicial authority. There had developed, in particular since the time of Alexander III (1159–81), the institution of delegated jurisdiction. Judges delegate undertook especially the investigation of disputed cases but occasionally also received authority to render decisions. Certain legal and penal cases were reserved exclusively to the Pope.

The Pope's supreme administrative rights were completed. To them belonged the right of supervision for the Universal Church. The canonization of saints was reserved to the Holy See from Alexander III and definitively by a regulation of Gregory IX. The system of ecclesiastical indulgences was concentrated in the Curia and restricted in regard to bishops. The Pope also had a leading role in the educational system of the age through the founding of universities and the conferring of privileges on them. The most important division of administration was that dealing with the filling of offices, in which there began a development leading to the Pope's universal right to fill all ecclesiastical benefices. At first specific classes were reserved. A vigorous opposition, which flared up because of the practice of Innocent IV during his struggle with the Hohenstaufen, was overcome. The Curia more and more made its own appointments, bestowed expectatives to benefices that were yet to be vacated, developed a right of devolution, and received postulation from everywhere. This universal competence of the Pope in the disposing of all offices and benefices in the Church was, however, not fixed in law until later.

The papal election law, first regulated under Nicholas II in 1059, was modified in the sense that now the election was declared to be the exclusive prerogative of all the cardinals. If unanimity could not be achieved, a two-thirds majority was to suffice. There was no mention of any assent or participation by Emperor or by clergy and people of Rome. And the election did not have to take place in Rome. The one elected could exercise the papal right; as soon as he had accepted the election. While all clerics had a passive vote, still, with few exceptions, only cardinals were elected. At the Second Council of Lyons in 1274 the law was extended to include the rules for the conclave. The two-thirds majority and the conclave were maintained with a few modifications and proved their worth in the succeeding centuries.

To the general councils, convoked and held under papal control, were invited, in addition to the cardinals, the metropolitans, bishops, abbots, and the deans of cathedral and collegiate chapters. Only cardinals and bishops had a deliberative vote; all others were competent in an advisory function only, which pertained also to princes and representatives of cities who were present. There was no strict regulation for councils but it became the practice that statements of principle were heard and decrees were promulgated in a few solemn sessions; they were prepared in consistories and in committee consultations that took place between sessions. The final decision in regard to conciliar decrees lay with the Pope, who was under no obligation to accept them. Councils which were summoned by legates in connection with their function could also be regarded as papal synods.

In its canon 6 the Fourth Lateran Council had ordered the annual meeting of provincial councils, which especially saw to the promulgating and implementing of the decrees of ecumenical synods and at the same time served, as earlier, for the further growth of particular law proper to their area.

The papal registers of the thirteenth century reveal the constant contacts between the Holy See and the Western episcopate. These were due, not only to the increasing prestige of the papacy, the completing of a universally valid canon law, and the regular meeting of general synods, but also to the emancipation of the bishops from control by the princes. It is true that the legal and spiritual concentration of ecclesiastical power in the Pope's hands restricted the position of the bishops, but it could not but be important to the Pope that he should strengthen the position of the bishop within each diocese. As successor of the Apostles, the bishop retained unchallenged, even in the epoch of the canon law, the autonomous right to act within his bishopric as chief priest, judge, and ruler of his people. The erecting, dividing, or suppressing of a see had become a papal prerogative, which extended also to an ecclesiastical province, but within the boundaries of this diocese the bishop governed according to his own decrees, but, of course, in conformity with the requirements of the general canon law.

As metropolitans archbishops had the right to confirm the election of their suffragans and to consecrate them. They had to summon and direct them at provincial synods, to be held annually. Their right of visitation was undisputed, but Innocent IV decreed in 1246 that they were not allowed to exercise it until they had visited their own dioceses. Furthermore, a visitation of the whole province required the consent of the *comprovinciales.* In cases of failure of duty, jurisdiction devolved on the metropolitan, whose court was also that of second instance in orderly judicial procedure. The metropolitan possessed no direct power of jurisdiction over the subjects of his suffragans. He was supposed to request the pallium in person from the Pope, who occasionally granted it to simple bishops.

Many bishops were bound to the Pope in law by their oath of obedience. The growing papal legislative activity, especially the right to dispense, could not but limit the bishop's rights within his diocese. The custom of regularly calling on the Pope and reporting to him became of obligation from Gregory IX as the *visitatio liminum.* If impeded, bishops could perform it by means of accredited proxies.

In the course of the consolidation and completion of the judicial and administrative system larger dioceses were divided into districts which were directed by archdeacons. Possessing ordinary jurisdiction, though the development varied by countries, the archdeacon conducted the annual visitations and supervised the discipline of the clergy, their manner of life, financial administration, and performance of duty. Several times a year the clergy met for the archidiaconal chapters. Even parts of the episcopal judicial authority were handed over to the archdeacon. There gradually occurred among the bishops a reaction against this institution that threatened their autonomy. The episcopal rights of reservation were more firmly stressed, such as nomination of rural deans, visitation of monasteries, jurisdiction in the external forum and in the forum of conscience in serious offenses of clerics and laity, jurisdiction over religious, in disputes over property, and in marriage cases. Bishops appointed an *officialis* for the judicial system and a vicar general for administration as their personal official representatives, thereby reducing the competence of the archdeacon. The period of the decline of the archdeacon's office began with the end of the thirteenth century.

Rural deaneries, which comprised several parishes, were in part subdivisions of archdeaconries, in part subject immediately to the bishop. The dean, also called archpriest, had to intervene in various ways between bishop and parishes, make known episcopal regulations, visit his deanery, and supervise the discipline of the clergy. Like the archdeacon, he convoked meetings of the clergy of the deanery several times a year. In the gild-conscious thirteenth century the parochial clergy also organized into rural chapters. The number of parishes grew because of the dividing up of cities. Even parochial associations of persons — gilds, confraternities, national groups, especially in Eastern Europe and the crusader states — were temporarily established, but only the territorial organization of parishes endured. Their erection lay with the bishop. The care of souls — administration of the Sacraments, preaching, ministry to the sick, burial — was incumbent on the pastor, who, as the prelate over his church, possessed also a power of jurisdiction to a certain extent.

The pastor obtained his post through appointment by the bishop or the one enjoying the *ius patronatus,* and not infrequently also by election by the congregation. All three elements might co-operate. Assistants were necessary in larger parishes and known as *capellani, viceplebani, socii in divinis.* In the thirteenth century they were appointed by the pastor, who could even call them from another diocese. Apart from the parish, other chaplains served in a particular pastoral capacity as court chaplains, chaplains in the castles of nobles, in hospitals, and in subsidiary churches.

In this organization of the Church the clergy occupied a position superior to that of the laity, constituted a special *ordo,* and regarded themselves as an *élite.* Besides special duties they also had special rights and, thanks to the subdivision of Church property into an enormous number of benefices, were quite secure economically.

Associations of clerics, grouped around the various functionaries, did not fit in the strict sense into the hierarchical order of pastors, bishops, metropolitans, and Pope. They extended from the College of Cardinals downward, through cathedral chapters and deanery chapters, to the gilds of vicars that would later be organized in the large urban churches. Reference must now be made to the significantly growing power of the cathedral chapters at this period. An outgrowth of the *presbyterium,* the cathedral chapter already had a long history. In the High Middle Ages it perfected its legal structure and influence and became an integral element in the diocesan organization. Naturally, in the 800 dioceses of Christendom its concrete forms displayed much variety, but the decretal law sketched a common plan for all of them. The cathedral chapter consisted of canons, who were responsible for the liturgy, canonical hours and Mass, in the cathedral and service in the episcopal administration. They elected the bishop. Thanks to the Roman law, received since the twelfth century, they became a corporation, a legal person. As such they had rights of ownership and of property, could enter into contracts, could be represented in court. Their common property increased considerably. Their chapters were presided over by their elected dean. They had a seal of their own and regarded themselves as constituting, alongside the bishop, an autonomous legal structure, with their own statutes and proper jurisdiction over the capitulars.

Direction belonged to a provost or, more commonly, to the dean. Elected by the chapter, he had to belong to it and be a priest. To him pertained pastoral authority over all the cathedral clergy. He had his own seal, and occasionally his income exceeded that of the bishop. There were also a chanter, a *camerarius,* a treasurer, and in the large chapters the subdean and subchanter substituted for the dean and chanter. When absent, capitulars had to appoint vicars for the choir service. Thus the rights of the cathedral chapter grew, especially since the administration of the bishopric, *sede vacante,* fell to it. An indication of its enhanced importance was its right to be represented at the provincial synod and, through its dean, to be invited to general councils. The amazingly extensive correspondence between the Holy See and the cathedral chapters in the twelfth and thirteenth centuries shows the consistently increasing importance of these corporations, which was even occasionally displayed in their exemption from the bishop and direct subordination to the Holy See. At this period the cathedral chapter became a real power in the Church and in civil society.

The laity, the mass of the Christian people, were apparently taken less into consideration in ecclesiastical legislation than the privileged class that was the clergy, and finally canon law came to look like a clerical law. However, this law often regulated the relations of the layman to the clergy; many of its decrees referred to all Christians, not exclusively to the clergy. One of the five books of the decretals had to do with matrimonial law. And, in addition to the written law, the customary law, valid in very many areas, also served the laity. In the thirteenth century, which in many aspects of social life experienced a rapid upsurge of new, educated, wealthy, and politically active strata among the urban bourgeoisie, the ecclesiastical self-awareness of the laity also increased. It not infrequently revealed itself in opposition to the clergy.

Still, despite the great separation from the clergy, who reserved to themselves the *magisterium* in the Church and extended their jurisdiction over the laity to purely secular spheres, the rights of the laity were real and could grow. Lay persons administered the Sacraments of baptism and matrimony; lay confession continued to be controverted. In regard to the clergy the laity had a positive right to pastoral care in all its forms: Sacraments, preaching, burial. They were especially active in the administration of Church property, above all in the cities. In the replacing of the proprietary church right by the *ius patronatus,* from the time of Gratian, the laity retained a determining influence on personnel policy in the Church. The contemporary tendency to form associations led to many such groups of lay persons, the confraternities, with a well developed religious orientation — direction of hospitals, defence of the faith, piety — and a gradually growing autonomy.

Despite many a dispute and much tension between clergy and laity the basic feature of the age was the peaceful co-operation and common exertions for the spiritual, economic, and social welfare of *christianitas* into which all were equally incorporated by baptism and which intended for all the same goal of sanctification and perfection.

Section Six

The Crisis of the Papacy and of the Church (1274–1303)

Hans Wolter

CHAPTER 31

The Papacy Subject to Angevin Influence

Gregory X died on 10 January 1276, too soon to be able to continue with the energy proper to him the things the Second Council of Lyons had initiated and the program of his pontificate. But since the French Martin IV (1281 to 1285) turned the helm completely around and placed himself unreservedly at the service of the interests of Anjou, even to the extent of terminating the reunion of the Churches that had been agreed upon at Lyons, this final phase of the Church's development in the thirteenth century was under the sign of dependence on Anjou and France.

Innocent V, formerly Peter of Tarentaise, was French, even though born within the frontiers of the Empire, a scholar, and, as the first Dominican to ascend the papal throne, a proof of the importance which the Order of Preachers had achieved in the Church. He confirmed Charles of Anjou in his functions as Senator of Rome and Imperial Vicar in Tuscany and thereby seemed to indicate a return of curial policy to the line abandoned by Gregory X. The election of Nicholas III meant a return to the policy of Gregory X. As a Cardinal, it is true, he had supported the invitation of the Angevin into the Hohenstaufen Kingdom of Sicily, but when he perceived in King Charles' struggle for power a threat to the freedom of the Papal State he conformed himself to Gregory X's resistance. Like the latter he intended to find in a collaboration with Rudolf of Habsburg, King of Germany, a counterweight to Anjou and to weaken Charles' position in Italy itself. Negotiations with the German King secured Romagna as a part of the Papal State, while Rudolf on 14 February 1279 renounced the imperial interests in that province. A series of charters of the German princes, requested and granted, supported this important decision. King Rudolf was again promised the imperial crown. With Romagna the Papal State definitively rounded out its frontiers, as they were to be maintained until 1860.

Thus began the papal *signoria* over Rome; the one or two Senators were only the deputies of the Pope, who at his election also assumed the dignity of Senator of Rome.

In Lombardy and Tuscany, where Charles of Anjou had been able to consolidate his position, Nicholas likewise sought to check his influence.

In the interests of an agreement between Charles of Anjou, leader of the Italian Guelfs, and Rudolf of Habsburg, presumptive leader of the Italian Ghibellines, Nicholas worked for the realization of a project: Rudolf's daughter Clementia was to marry Charles Martel, grandson of Charles of Anjou, and to receive the Kingdom of Arles as her dowry. In 1280 Rudolf actually enfeoffed Charles of Anjou with the Counties of Provence and Forcalquier, and in March 1281 Clementia was handed over to Charles' envoys at Orvieto.

Simon de Brie was elected Pope as Martin IV on 22 February 1281, after a six-months' vacancy and a conclave that was powerfully influenced by pressure from Charles of Anjou. He not only abandoned the policy of his predecessor but was prepared to make the most far-reaching concessions to the Angevin. This most French of all the thirteenth-century Popes had risen in the service of the French crown, as a Cardinal had played a substantial role in the transfer of power in Italy to Charles of Anjou, and as Pope was to be a willing tool in the hand of the King of Sicily. He placed himself wholly at the service of the Guelfs and their leader, believing that he was thereby serving the interests of the French Kings. Far from concealing his antipathy toward Germany and the Ghibellines, he availed himself of every opportunity to show it.

Charles of Anjou took no part in these confrontations for he was again preoccupied with his far-reaching plans in regard to the East. When Martin IV in 1281 excommunicated the Byzantine Emperor Michael VIII Palaeologus and thus undid the reunion accomplished by the Second Council of Lyons, he was serving the Eastern policy of the King of Sicily. While the union had been proclaimed at Constantinople in April 1277, the Greek bishops had been unwilling to take the personal oath of loyalty required by Gregory X and had refused to insert the *Filioque* in the Creed, as agreed.

In 1281, after the signing of the treaty which bound Venice to him, Charles appeared to be on the point of reestablishing the Latin Empire of Constantinople.

The Sicilian Vespers of Easter Monday, 30 March 1282, wrecked all these plans. This revolt of Sicily brought the island under the rule of the King of Aragón, restricting Charles of Anjou to the mainland, thereafter usually known as the Kingdom of Naples. But Pope Martin upheld Charles. He and his immediate successors did all they could, though in vain, to procure for the Angevins their rights. In reality the revolt delivered the papacy from the peril presented by Angevin imperialism, which was thereafter able to gain influence only during the brief pontificate of Celestine V. Boniface VIII would get rid of it entirely.

Steven Runciman has now definitively presented the history of the Sicilian Vespers. The absolute rule, exercised by Frenchmen for the absent King, had pushed the Sicilians into a revolt in which Aragón, aiming to establish an extensive domination in the western Mediterranean, came to their aid.

The Sicilian revolt was directed against Charles of Anjou, not against the papacy, to which the rebel government, representing a communal union of the most important cities of the island, offered itself in vassalage. Martin IV rejected the offer, called upon the island to submit to Charles, and promised the King his assistance in recovering it. Neither the proposal of a modified constitution nor the intercession of the Pope was successful, and so Charles had no alternative to winning back the island by force. Meanwhile, the Sicilians had proffered the crown to King Peter of Aragón. He sailed with his fleet and on 1 September 1282 had himself crowned at Palermo. Charles of Anjou raised the blockade of Messina because he was afraid of being cut off from Naples by the Aragonese fleet. He thereby abandoned this part of his Kingdom forever. In prolonged guerilla fighting Peter of Aragón tried to conquer Calabria, but he was excommunicated by Martin IV, who threatened, in the event of disobedience, to deprive him of his Kingdom of Aragón. His depositions was proclaimed by the Pope on 21 March 1283, and the Kingdom was offered by Martin to the King of France, Philip III, for his younger son, Charles of Valois.

When Charles of Anjou died in January 1285, his son and heir, the Prince of Salerno, Charles the Lame, was being held prisoner by the Sicilian Aragonese, who had twice thwarted his attempts to reconquer the island. Calabria was in their hands and revolt was threatening in the rest of the Kingdom around Naples. Charles died a thoroughly beaten man. He had designated as heir his twelve-year-old grandson, Charles Martel. He governed the Kingdom of Naples, by papal mandate, together with the Papal Legate Gerard of Parma, until 1285, when Charles II returned from captivity. Pope Martin died on 28 March 1285, three months after his friend, leaving to his successor the irksome legacy of the Sicilian question. The Roman James Savelli, who styled himself Honorius IV (1285 to 1287), was elected on 2 April in order to free the Curia from the Angevin connection. He abandoned the warlike policy of his predecessor in Romagna, pacified the Ghibellines, and received the submission of their leader, Guy of Montefeltro, to whom he granted Asti as his residence.

King Philip III of France had accepted Martin IV's proposal that he take possession of Aragón, of which the Pope had solemnly deprived Peter III, for his son, Charles of Valois. A real crusade was made ready in France for this purpose. The crusade itself was a disaster. Philip III died at Perpignan and his son, Philip the Fair, declined to continue the enterprise. The captive Charles II the Lame was prepared to renounce Sicily to obtain his freedom. The event that contributed most to solve the Sicilian question, however, was the death of Peter III of Aragón on 10 November 1285. He named his oldest son, Alfonso, as his successor in Aragón; his second son, James, in Sicily. The Pope had ratified this agreement, but he would not consent to the lifting of the censure. Neither did he accept the treaty whereby Charles the Lame had obtained his freedom by renouncing Sicily and the Calabrian archbishopric of Reggio. Meanwhile, the two regents were governing the remnant of the Kingdom around Naples.

With Nicholas IV (1288–92), who was elected on 22 February 1288, after a rather long vacancy, a Franciscan for the first time succeeded to the papal throne. Under him the Sicilian question continued without a solution and in 1291 Acre, the last Christian outpost in the Holy Land, fell. On 25 July 1287 Charles II the Lame had acquired his freedom again and at Rieti on 29 May 1289 Nicholas crowned him King of Sicily, Calabria, and Apulia. The excommunication of Alfonso of Aragón was lifted when, in a treaty with Charles II and with Philip IV of France, he bound himself not to assist his brother James in Sicily. But Alfonso died on 18 June 1291, thus opening up the whole situation again. For now James was King of both Aragón and Sicily; he appointed his brother Frederick as governor of the island. The Aragonese forced James to accept the Treaty of Figueras with Charles II in December 1293; according to it Sicily was to be returned to the Pope, who could dispose of it only by agreement with Aragón. Frederick was to be compensated elsewhere for the loss of Sicily. The Pope promised to lift James' excommunication and to annul the grant of Aragón to Charles of Valois. It was left to Celestine V to ratify this treaty.

Chapter 32

Christian Fanaticism in the Thirteenth Century

The Cathari and Waldensians were defeated by the Church's determined defensive. The crusade, the mendicants' preaching, and the Inquisition had finally overcome this extremely dangerous crisis, even if only by long stages that were marked by losses. In addition to organized heresy with its doctrinal and sectarian opposition to the institutional Roman Church, there also emerged certain movements that advocated devotional practices not in accord with accepted norms. They were resident in those ranks of the mendicants, especially of the Franciscans, that were most responsive to the people, and in the quasi-religious associations among the laity, the Beghards and the Beguines. The basic source of these tendencies was, as it had been from time immemorial, the awareness that one must make one's own the requirements of the *vita apostolica* in order really to take seriously the imitation of Christ. However, the fanatical element of the movement lay rather in its view and purpose not to limit this strict standard only to those charismatically endowed but to prescribe it for all of Christendom. Wherever this standard was lightly esteemed, there was an apostasy from Christianity which had to be condemned and repelled.

And so the demand was often heard that the legal and institutional Church must be left behind, if not superseded, by an *ecclesia spiritualis,* which would be radically serious about the requirements of the Gospel, especially the Sermon on the Mount. In this demand were encountered the most varied intellectual traditions, among which one of the more recent became especially influential: the apocalyptic theology of history of Joachim, founder and Abbot of San Giovanni at Fiore (d. 1202). According to this tradition, the Age of the Father, the Old Testament, of the carnal man of marriage, was followed by the Age of the Son, the New Testament, of the carnal minded man, especially of clerics, and this was now to be replaced by the Age of the Holy Spirit, the Eternal Gospel, of the spiritual and pneumatic man, who would find the proper form of his existence in monachism. While this idea lacked any anti-hierarchical tone in Joachim, now views were to be propounded which, carried to their ultimate conclusion, aimed at an invisible Church, without hierarchy, Sacraments, and external worship, and in which the spirit of poverty, of peace, and of a spiritual understanding of Scripture was to prevail. The year 1260 was calculated as the time between the Age of the Son and the arrival of that of the Holy Spirit. Joachimite ideas were found especially in broad circles of the Friars Minor, where they were connected with the disputes over the interpretation of the ideal of poverty proper to the order. In 1257 John of Parma resigned, but, because of his integrity and the esteem in which he was held in all circles in the Church and the order, he was allowed to name his successor: Saint Bonaventure. The wide circulation of Joachimite ideas, of which, moreover, traces can be found even in Bonaventure's writings, was thereafter promoted also by popular prophecies which appeared in these decades. Even outside the Franciscan Order, they succeeded in fostering in various strata and groups of people an overenthusiasm in religious notions and expectations, they also increased the general disquiet with regard to an official Church that was involved in the power struggles of the time, they incited criticism of her riches, her clerical leadership, her unconcern *vis-à-vis* the spiritual needs of the people.

In the closing decades of the century the Franciscan "Spirituals" became the important spokesmen of the tendency. The beginnings of the Spiritual movement went back to the generation of Saint Francis. At first it had to do with the consistent realization of the founder's concept of poverty, of his rule, and his testament. But Gregory IX's bull "Quo elongati" of 1230 had denied the testament any legal binding force and had directed the order's development in a more moderate line, which Brother Elias also championed at that time. The stricter disciples of the founder retired, frequently into hermitages, hostile to learning, living for contemplation. avoiding the pastoral apostolate.

Almost reconciled under John of Parma but less pleased with Bonaventure's compromise statutes of 1260 at Narbonne, their fears for the purity of the order's poverty increased when it was rumored that the Second Council of Lyons intended to do it still greater damage than the previous papal privileges had already done. And so now groups were formed in Provence, where Hugh of Digne (d. 1255) was regarded as their "father," in the Marches of Ancona, and in Tuscany. From now on they often succumbed to the pressure of the majority in the order, known as the Conventuals. The latter had to be concerned for a uniform interpretation of the ideal of poverty that could be shared by all member of the order. But instead of guaranteeing to the dissidents their own special corporate rights, they took disciplinary measures against them, sought to distribute them among remote houses, and sent them to far-off mission areas.

The Spiritual movement remained for the most part limited to the order and acted only incidentally on public opinion in the Church. The situation was different with regard to the Apostolics of Gerard Segarelli of Parma, who were constituted from a penitential brotherhood in the Joachimite year 1260. From it proceeded the first flagellant processions, which, full of apocalyptic expectations, carried the summons to penance through city and country. These persons demanded a return to the poverty ideal of the primitive Church and united to this a loud criticism of the wealthy Church of the present, which was acting like a state. Leadership was assumed by Fra Dolcino of Novara, who addressed the faithful in circulars. He proclaimed that the Age of the Spirit had dawned and condemned the Church of the clergy, in which he included even the mendicant friars, because through their possessions they belonged to the carnal Church. Dolcino rejected any subjection to rules that opposed the freedom of the Spirit and demanded apostolic poverty from all. The final age of the world, he said, had begun and people had to hasten it, so to speak, by their actions and contribute to its realization. Dolcino was able to win thousands of adherents. Pursued by the Inquisition, many withdrew into the mountains of northern Lombardy to await the appearance of the Emperor of Peace and of the Angel Pope, from whom they expected help. Against them was organized a crusade, which at Novara in March 1307 brought the movement to a bloody end. One hundred and forty Apostolics were captured and executed along with Fra Dolcino.

From all these trends of fanatical extremism other groups were to develop in the following century, such as the Fraticelli and the adherents of Michael of Cesena.

Subjected together with the Spirituals of the Midi to ecclesiastical disciplinary measures were also the Beguines, who could be regarded as secular followers of the left-wing Franciscans. The Beguines were able to look back to a longer history, not at first affected by the impulse to fanaticism, a history beginning early in the thirteenth century.

There were associations of devout women, virgins and widows, who wished to lead a community life without the vows of religion and established themselves especially in cities. The houses of canonesses were reserved to the nobility, as were also many convents of Benedictine nuns. The reform orders of the twelfth century had at first allowed for the ascetical aspirations of many women by means of their double monasteries, such as Fontevrault and Prémontré. But Prémontré had abandoned the double monastery around 1140 and let the nuns become independent. Cistercian nuns did not appear until late in the twelfth century, because of the aloofness in principle which Cîteaux maintained in regard to the pastoral care of women religious, but then foundations occurred rapidly and everywhere. But whatever the different orders permitted in convents of nuns, it was insufficient by far to take care of the constantly growing number of women who asked for a life according to a religious rule and a common ascetical existence. This female movement, based on economic and religious and mystical motives, almost spontaneously created a form for itself in the Beguine system, whose origins must be sought in the institute of recluses of earlier epochs.

The first communities came into being in Flanders and Brabant, under Lambert the Stammerer at Liège (ca. 1175), at Mont-Cornillon, at Huy (ca. 1182), where Blessed Ivetta was friendly with them, at Willamsbroux near Nivelles (ca. 1192) under the influence of Blessed Mary of Oignies, at Nivelles (ca. 1207) together with Blessed Ida. These women, like the Cistercian nuns, belonged to the sphere of crusade piety. Thereafter they spread fast and in some cases constituted very large communities. They were in France and Germany, especially on the lower Rhine and in Bavaria, and in almost the whole of Europe. They lived partly by begging, partly by manual labour, and in the course of time on the income from their growing property. Settled, so to speak, between the religious house and the world, they lived under the control of the bishop according to an organization which he had given them or as it had been outlined in the foundation statutes. Varying from the very small house to settlements analogous to cities, the Beguine houses found acceptance in almost all the cities of the countries just mentioned. Without vows, they obliged themselves to daily spiritual exercises, to fasting, and to regular reception of the Sacraments. The uniform gray dress distinguished them from the middle-class women. The government was in the hands of a mistress with her council, while discipline was supervised in a weekly chapter of faults. Procurators or *provisores* often took charge of the economic administration.

The communities of Beguines were often entrusted to the pastoral care of the mendicant orders in Germany and France. If they had their own churches, these orders supplied the rector, if no special chaplain was appointed.

Wherever the pastoral care of Beguines was able thus to move in the proper paths, the institute of Beguines remained free of the suspicion of fanaticism. Nevertheless, after the mid-century the shadows of such a suspicion began to gather around them. The reason for this was probably that at this very time the term Beguine was applied generally to all women and men who devoted themselves to the life of piety outside a type of religious community and gave themselves a special gray dress, as, for example, the Brothers of the New Spirit, male and female recluses, Spirituals who were refugees from their monasteries, and begging and preaching laymen. Since these persons were correctly suspected of fanaticism, through them the very name Beguine acquired a pejorative sound.

CHAPTER 33

The Flowering of Scholasticism and of the Western Universities

The classical period of mediaeval intellectual culture reached its perfection in the thirteenth century. Three factors especially contributed to its construction. The first of these was the making available and the reception of the entire *corpus* of Aristotle by translation, commentary, and assimilation into Christian philosophy and theology. This took place in confrontation with Arab commentators, Jewish thinkers, and, after 1260, Greek commentators, notably Proclus. The second was the rapidly progressing development of the universities in this century, in particular at Paris, Oxford, and Bologna. Finally, there was the decisive contribution of the mendicant orders, whose members, from the middle of the century, played an outstanding role at Paris and Oxford in the growth of scholarship.

Educational centers of European stature had been formed in the twelfth century, above all at Chartres, Paris, Reims, Laon, Bologna, Salerno, and Toledo. Some of them, however, later lost their importance, as the chief interest of both teachers and students was concentrated on Paris, Oxford, and Bologna. At Paris, Bologna, and Oxford the structures developed that determined the notion of the university of the High Middle Ages.

They were related to and similar to the co-operative organizations formed in the great cities to take care of the social and economic tasks of a population that was constantly undergoing an increasing differentiation of function. City and papal statutes in the course of the thirteenth century regulated the organization of Bologna, where various conflicts between city and student-body had frequently led to emigrations. From 1224 the Holy See managed to establish its control of the university, for which it remained characteristic that the students and not the professors were constituted as gilds. The organization, originally determined by lay persons, was altered by the Holy See in the sense that all, professors and students, clerics and laymen, were strictly subordinated to the jurisdiction of the local bishop, who appointed an archdeacon as chancellor. From 1245 the *universitates* of students could also be incorporated into the city organism. There were now two of them: the Italian or cismontane and the foreign or ultramontane. Each elected its own rector, before whom was made the important oath of obedience, the formality incorporating the student into the *universitas.* Their autonomy was guaranteed by the Holy See.

At Paris the situation developed differently from that at Bologna. Professors and students combined in opposition to the citizens and the local bishop; in 1200 they were exempted by King Philip II Augustus from secular jurisdiction and between 1212 and 1222 also from that of the bishop. The Curia, which, through the Cardinal Legate Robert de Courçon, gave a statute "universis magistris et scolaribus Parisiensibus" in 1215, maintained its supervision of the "university," as the institution was called for the first time in 1219. The University of Paris was complete in its essential characteristics by 1222. Four faculties were to be distinguished: theology, medicine, the liberal arts, the *Decretum,* that is, canon law. In addition, the university was divided into four nations. The Dominicans settled near the university from 1217, the Franciscans from 1219; in 1224–26 they were more closely linked to it. By means of the bull "Parens Scientiarum" of 13 April 1231, Gregory IX managed to restore peace and conferred new privileges on the university. During this crisis the position of the theologians belonging to religious orders could be consolidated, so that after 1231 three of the twelve theological chairs were occupied by religious, the cathedral chapter of Notre Dame provided three others, and the remaining six continued to be reserved to diocesan clerics.

Innocent IV confirmed the so-called "foundation bull" issued by Gregory IX in 1231 and in 1245–46 gave the university its own seal and hence full legal existence. The favor and protection of the French Kings enabled it to develop freely.

Beside Paris, preeminent in theology, and Bologna, which maintained its leadership in law, other universities which received papal privileges in the thirteenth century could play only a far less active role.

The University of Oxford developed in England as the third outstanding higher educational center alongside Paris and Bologna. Out of the numerous religious houses and particular schools there had arisen there toward the close of the twelfth century an important center of instruction, where just at that time Aristotelianism was establishing itself. The incipient university was subjected to the Bishop of Lincoln, who was to direct it through a chancellor, consistently selected from the ranks of the professors of theology. Under the chancellor the university was able slowly to develop its autonomy. The emigration from Paris in 1229–31 brought to the young university a considerable growth, at the invitation of King Henry III. When Robert Grosseteste, who had himself been chancellor, became Bishop of Lincoln in 1235, he further elaborated the chancellor's position. In contradistinction to Paris, at Oxford the chancellor became a member of the university corporation. Oxford received its statutes from Grosseteste in 1252–53.

Differing again from Paris, the mendicant orders, above all the Franciscans, had no difficulty in entering the Oxford theological faculty, where they soon occupied a leading position. The number of nations at Oxford, apart from the English, was restricted to two: the Scots or *Boreales* and the Irish or *Hibernenses.*

Cambridge, which had branched off from Oxford in 1209, likewise profited by the Paris exodus of 1229–31. King Henry III especially favored Cambridge.

Common to all the universities mentioned was a basic structure which recalled their origins in the cathedral schools. First of all there was the chancellor; at Bologna he was a decretist, at Paris and Oxford a theologian, but with authority and possibilities of influence that differed from one place to another. The nations under the direction of elected rectors gained extensive autonomy. At Bologna they even received the oath which was the binding element in all the gilds. At Paris the members of the arts faculty, thanks to their numerical superiority, assumed leadership in the nations. The nations were led by procurators, who in turn decided on the rector; he held office for three months. In 1245 he was head of the university council which included all the masters, had the right to make its own statutes, and in cases of conflict could appoint arbiters. From the mid-century on the head of the arts faculty was rector of the entire university.The statutes of the arts faculty, regulating the course of instruction and of studies, became a model for all the faculties at all the contemporary universities, except for the faculty of theology, which had its own special regulations. The intellectual connection of the arts with theology was maintained by the circumstance that almost all the theologians had first taught in the arts faculty, which developed in the course of the century into a real faculty of philosophy because literary culture was less and less emphasized and, except at Oxford, the *quadrivium* was also neglected. Since it was less under the magisterial control of the Holy See than were the theologians, it was able, alongside this stronghold of orthodoxy, to exert for the future a decided influence or the development of philosophical movements in the West.

Life at the universities, for which Paris and the Parisian style were always standard, was lived in an ecclesiastical environment, since almost every student was a cleric. And, except at Bologna, the professors had to belong to the clergy. Among masters and students were formed communities that lived together, and, because the students were attached to a specific teacher, there was also a sort of common life within the framework of the *universitas magistrorum et scholarium.*

Instruction was to be imparted basically free of charge, at least in the faculties of the arts and theology. Payment was demanded in the faculties of law and medicine. But gradually it became the custom that fees were required; this can be demonstrated in regard to examination fees, for example. Ecclesiastical benefices were assigned to the masters for their support. Students also, particularly the foreigners, found a similar means of support later.

Financial need and lack of space prevailed, especially at the large university centers, where the numbers were in the thousands the lack of room applied both to lodgings and to places of instruction. In so far as students did not live in private houses or with teachers they were accommodated in hospitals, which were enlarged for this purpose. But there soon appeared, especially for the poor students, foundations where they could be lodged and take their meals. The religious houses included boarding facilities for foreign students, even if they did not belong to the order; their organization served as a model for the rapidly growing number of burses or colleges. Thus in 1257 Robert de Sorbon founded his college, later to become so famous; it was intended for diocesan clerics, who entered it as masters of arts in order to study theology. Such houses were rarer at Bologna, but at Oxford the development was similar to that at Paris. Balliol College was founded at Oxford in 1263, Merton in 1264.

In the thirteenth century, as the monastic schools and those of the canons declined, the universities became the centers of predilection for philosophical and theological scholarship, for scientific medicine, and for the pursuit of both laws. The lively interchange among the faculties was one of the causes of the investigation, becoming more intensive and more methodical from generation to generation, of theoretical as well as of more practical sciences. Exercising an impact in the field of philosophy and, influenced and stimulated by it, of theology in this thirteenth century was the imparting of a stock of ideas, in the center of which stood the complete *corpus* of Aristotle.

Toledo and Naples were of particular importance in this regard, since both of them lay at the intersection of Christian and Arabic civilization and the Aristotelian legacy was passed on to Western scholarship by means of Arabic and Jewish channels. Authoritative Arabic and Jewish works were translated into Latin at Toledo, which had returned to Christian hands in 1085. But no creative ideas are to be found among these men.

Translation and the pursuit of philosophy likewise characterized the new (1224) University of Naples. Arabs, Jews, and Latins worked together there in harmony. Peter of Ireland commented on Aristotle and Porphyry. Michael the Scot, coming from Spain, became court astrologer in 1220 and as the director of a whole team of co-workers translated the writings of Averroes into Latin. People were still translating here from Arabic and Greek into Latin as late as the time of Manfred (from 1254). At the University of the Roman Curia, founded by Innocent IV, Thomas Aquinas, who lectured there from 1259 to 1265 and from 1267 to 1268, met the great translator of Aristotle, his fellow Dominican, William of Moerbeeke. At Oxford the work of translating was fostered by the chancellor, Robert Grosseteste, who himself knew Greek.

The result of this activity was an almost limitless output of literary works from hitherto inaccessible sources. They included writings of Arabic and Jewish philosophers, who had become acquainted with Aristotle, especially the *Organon,* through the agency of Syrians. In addition, there was a group of for the most part Neoplatonist commentaries on Aristotle. The Arabs also made use of other Syriac translations: of Theophrastus, Galen, Hippocrates, Euclid, Archimedes. This Aristotelian and Neoplatonic stock of ideas and its literary transmission were independently assimilated by the Arab philosophers. Only the most important names can be mentioned here: Alfarabi (d. 950) and Ibn Sina (Avicenna, d. 1037). More Aristotelian than Avicenna was Ibn Rushd (Averroes, d. 1198) of Córdoba. To these must be added the Jewish philosophers, who had already been influenced by the Arabs and made use of an Aristotle infected by Neoplatonism: Solomon Ibn Gebirol (Avencebrol or Avicebron, d. 1070), with his *Fons vitae,* which advocated a pantheistic emanationism, and Moses Maimonides (d. 1204), whom Aquinas highly esteemed and who was dependent on Alfarabi and Avicenna. Like Averroes, these Jewish philosophers lived in Spain. Hence the translators' school at Toledo was so important for their transmission.

But Aristotle came to the Western universities also in direct translations from the Greek. If persons had thus far learned to study an Aristotle who was for the most part understood in a Neoplatonic refraction through the Syriac, Arabic, and Jewish translations, now the genuine Aristotle became known: his hitherto lacking logical treatises — thus far only the so-called Old Logic was known — his entire metaphysics, ethics, politics, and natural philosophy. And early commentators on Aristotle also found translators.

The scholastic reception of Aristotle has its own history, which of course can be sketched here only in its essential factors. It took place at Oxford with less difficulty than at the University of Paris, where as early as 1210 a provincial council, meeting in Paris, forbade the reading of Aristotle's writings on natural philosophy and their commentaries. The prohibition was repeated in 1215 and extended to the metaphysics, when the legate, Robert de Courçon, gave the university its basic statute. The traditional study of Aristotle was not affected. For the Aristotle handed down by the Arabs and Jews was, in fact, of a Neoplatonic coloring. Aristotle was not forbidden at Toulouse, and there, as at Oxford, persons were thereafter preoccupied with the new Aristotle. At Paris, on the other hand, the prohibitions were renewed in 1231 and 1245 and they were mentioned as late as 1263. But they were apparently quickly forgotten, for the reception proceeded apace. Gregory IX had already modified his prohibitions when he entrusted to a commission of theologians the examination of the natural philosophy. Even if this did not meet, people understood the envisaged adjustment as an ecclesiastical permission for the study, especially since only the official, not the private use of Aristotle had been forbidden.

In the Paris arts faculty, in any event, persons were keenly interested in the new ideas, whereas in theology this tendency began to make itself felt only around the middle of the century with Albert the Great. At Paris, for the time being, only the *Organon* and the *Ethics* of Aristotle were commented and lectured on, while at Oxford this activity extended also to his natural philosophy and *Metaphysics.* Peter of Spain (before 1246) died as Pope John XXI in 1277; his *Summulae logicales* became the most popular manual of logic at the Western universities. His *Liber de anima* combined Aristotelian with elements recalling Augustine and Avicenna.

Robert Grosseteste translated and commented on Aristotle's *Ethics* at Oxford, while from 1245 the Franciscan Roger Bacon was working on the controverted *libri naturales.* In an effort to overtake Oxford, William of Auvergne, Bishop of Paris, allowed their study at Paris after the death of Gregory IX. Boethius, Avicenna, and Averroes were also esteemed as authorities in philosophy. After 1250 there appeared in the arts faculty the so-called Latin Averroism, a heterodox Aristotelian, under Siger of Brabant. Theologians of all camps strenuously opposed it.

The new philosophy put itself at the service of theology, but without supplanting the Augustinian tradition. At first it was used in an eclectic manner and in the event of conflict the primacy of theology was unreservedly guaranteed. Albert the Great and Thomas Aquinas were the first to rethink Aristotle and to use, very critically of course, the Arabic and Jewish commentaries.

The theology of the early thirteenth century was divided into the conservative wing of the school of Peter Lombard, represented by Peter of Poitiers, lecturing till 1205, Stephen Langton till 1206, Robert de Courçon till 1210, Peter of Capua till 1219, the chancellor Prévotin of Cremona till 1210, and Thomas Gallus of Saint-Victor till 1218, and the progressive wing of the school of Gilbert de la Porrée, represented by Simon of Tournai till 1203, the chancellor Philip till 1236, William of Auxerre till 1228, and William of Auvergne till 1228, when he became Bishop of Paris, dying in 1249. Their extensive writings included scriptural commentaries of an increasingly systematic character and commentaries on *The Sentence.* The *Summa universae theologiae* of the Franciscan Alexander of Hales constituted one climax of this production of theological *summae.* In addition innumerable smaller works of a liturgical, homiletic, and pastoral character, sermons and sermon collections, were composed. Apologetically oriented was the *Summa contra haereticos* of Prévotin (between 1184 and 1210), while controversial theology gave rise to the *Summa contra Catharos et Waldenses* of Moneta of Cremona (d. 1260) and the *Summa de Catharis et Leonists* of Rainer Sacconi (d. 1262).

This wealth of academic and literary production proved the growing importance of the University of Paris, which, by virtue of the activity, shortly to begin, of scholars from the mendicant orders, was to be led to the classic peak of achievement. These scholars succeeded in realizing the long sought synthesis of theology with the new philosophy of the century.

The first phase of the Franciscans' work was that of Alexander of Hales and the beginning of the Franciscan school with his pupils. A development of its own must be ascribed to Oxford. These beginnings were carried further under Bonaventure. John Duns Scotus himself (ca. 1270–1308) stood on the threshold of the new age.

The older Dominican school began with Roland of Cremona (d. 1259) and the well known exegete, Cardinal Hugh of Saint-Cher. To it belonged Peter of Tarentaise (d. 1276 as Pope Innocent V). These scholars still followed the paths of a doctrine that was determined by Augustinianism. The Aristotelian orientation was established by Albertus Magnus (ca. 1193–1280). In a comprehensive Aristotelian encyclopedia, which also cited pseudo-Aristotelian works, he laid the ground for a Christian Aristotelianism. Albert obtained the scholastic title of *doctor universalis,* because not only was his knowledge of the sources universal but his scholarship was able to master all fields of philosophy, natural science, and theology. And his influence in the academic world became universal. He commented on all the books of Aristotle, on *The Sentences* of Peter Lombard, on the *De divinis nominibus* of pseudo-Dionysius. His *Summa theologiae* remained unfinished; more famous became the *Summa de creaturis,* which included, among other things, a systematic ethics, a doctrine of the Sacraments, and an eschatology. Many lesser works discussed dogmatic questions of Mariology, the Eucharist, and much else.

Thomas Aquinas (1225–74) ranks as the chief representative of classical scholasticism. He was Albert's pupil at Paris, and followed him to Cologne, where he studied from 1248 to 1252. He himself taught at Paris from 1252 to 1259, then at the University of the Roman Curia from 1259 to 1268, at Paris again from 1268 to 1272, and finally at Naples from 1272 to 1274. He died, *en route* to the Second Council of Lyons, at the Cistercian abbey of Fossanuova near Naples, on 7 March 1274.

His vast literary output can be arranged under six headings. First are the philosophical commentaries on Aristotle's most important works and on the *Liber de causis.* With these he was able to improve on the inadequate commentaries on Aristotle by Averroes and by Albertus Magnus. The second category includes scriptural commentaries on many books of the Old and the New Testaments. His *Catena Aurea* was a collection of patristic texts on the four Gospels, probably intended as a handbook for preachers. Next come theological commentaries on the works of Boethius (*De Trinitate, De hebdomadibus*), pseudo-Dionysius (*De divinis nominibus*), and Peter Lombard (*Liber sententiarum*). The *Scriptum super sententiis* was reckoned among the great works of theological synthesis. The fourth class consists of works of theological synthesis. The *Summa contra gentiles* was begun at Paris in 1258. There followed the great and uncompleted *Summa theologica;* Thomas spent seven years on it, and Reginald of Priverno finished it by adding material from the *Scriptum super sententiis.* To his friend and pupil Reginald Thomas, dedicated the likewise incomplete *Compendium theologiae.* Next come the notes for academic disputations, the *Quaestiones disputatae* and *Quaestiones quodlibetales.* These provide a mirror of the ideas and controversies of the age. Finally, there are the lesser works, for the most part occasional pieces of the most varied content. Some deal with philosophical questions, such as *De ente et essentia, De aeternitate mundi, De unitate intellectus, De substantiis separatis;* some with theology, including *De articulis fidei et Ecclesiae sacramentis, De regimine Iudaeorum;* some are apologetic: *De rationibus fidei contra Saracenos, Graecos et Armenos* and *Contra errores Graecorum;* and defense of the position of the mendicant orders at the university: *Contra impugnantes Dei cultum, De perfectione vitae spiritualis,* and so forth. Finally, there are works of a devotional, liturgical, canonical, and homiletic content, the most important being the office for the feast of Corpus Christi and the *Expositio de Ave Maria.*

Thomas Aquinas possessed an exhaustive knowledge of the patristic tradition. His exegesis, however, was hindered by his unfamiliarity with Hebrew and Greek. For all his critical method he was, like his contemporaries, tied to the theological acquaintance with the sacred text that the patristic writers and the early scholastics had cultivated, because of the deficiency of his historical horizon, of his knowledge of the auxiliary sciences, and of a technically perfect philology. His definitive achievement lay in the field of speculative theology and of the unique intellectual accomplishment whereby he placed the philosophy of Aristotle's genius at the service of revealed doctrine and of its conceptual presentation.

The point of departure in the method of his speculative theology was, it is true, challenged as early as three years after his death, when Bishop Stephen Tempier of Paris included twenty-one texts from Thomas' works among the 219 condemned propositions of 1277; he thereby rejected the rationalism and naturalism of heterodox Aristotelianism, then a threat at the university. The canonization of Thomas by John XXII in 1323 effaced this shadow from the Church.

The tendency in thought that was really attacked in Bishop Tempier's condemnation was at home in the arts faculty and hence concerned philosophical rather than theological errors. Toward the middle of the century Averroes had supplanted Avicenna in the scholarly world as the commentator of Aristotle. The turning of the philosophers to him developed at Paris into a vigorous movement. The doctrine of the eternity of the world, the proposition of the double truth, and monopsychism became characteristic of it. Its leader was Siger of Brabant (1235–84), one of the most important interpreters of Aristotle of that time, independent in judgment and of constructive intellectual powers. He later freed himself from an originally radically Averroistic understanding of Aristotle through the influence of the works of Aquinas and accepted the latter's interpretation of the Stagirite. He abandoned monopsychism and never formally defended the doctrine of the double truth. If he had earlier been a determinist, in his later years he defended the freedom of the will.

England's contribution to the history of High Scholasticism matched that of France. Especially in the Franciscan Order were found many scholars of English nationality. One need only recall Alexander of Hales, founder of the Franciscan school at Paris. There and even more at Oxford was established a school of a unique character. Robert Grosseteste, who introduced the Franciscans to Oxford, was also the one who founded that university's fame in science. He was chancellor of the university until his promotion to the see of Lincoln. At first profoundly influenced by mediaeval Augustinianism, he was the first Englishman to adopt Aristotle's philosophical system and sought to assimilate the whole wealth of the onrushing stream of science in the Greek, Arabic, and Jewish tradition. In contradistinction to the Paris scholars he also placed great stress on the cultivating of the sciences of the *quadrivium,* above all mathematics. His scriptural study was bound strictly to the text, his knowledge of Greek being here of use to him, and was critically oriented. On the other hand, like his contemporaries, he was not a humanist. It was not until 1247 that Franciscans took over the direction of their own house of studies. The first to do so was a close collaborator and friend of Grosseteste, Adam Marsh.

The greatest name among the English Franciscans was that of Roger Bacon (ca. 1214–92). Influenced by Grosseteste, Adam Marsh, Thomas of York, and other Oxford scholars, Bacon himself was not a professor and perhaps not even a priest. He turned from speculation to encyclopedic, comprehensive research in the field of mathematics, natural science, and social science. He pursued positive science not only for its own sake but for the service of theology. Independent and self-willed, intuitively gifted and endowed with critical precision, in his literary works he developed ideas whose significance in intellectual history must be seen not so much in themselves as in their ability to stimulate others. He deplored the separation between speculative thought and experimental science and the uncertainty involved in the uncritical use of traditional texts. An unstable wanderer, he was commissioned by Clement IV to draw up a plan for the reform of ecclesiastical studies; but he made so many enemies that he spent more than ten years, till shortly before his death, under house arrest. His chief work was the *Opus maius,* in which he asked that science be put at the service of practical life. Revolutionary was his demand for the introduction of experiment. In theology he remained bound to the Augustinian tradition.

The great importance of English scholars of the mendicant orders is especially to be seen in the two eminent personalities who successively ruled the archbishopric of Canterbury: the Dominican Robert Kilwardby (ca. 1210–79) and the Franciscan John Pecham (ca. 1220–92).

After the Paris judgment of 1277, which Pecham also adopted for England, the Thomist school and the Franciscan followers of Saint Bonaventure drew farther apart. He is perhaps to be regarded as a precursor of the greatest English theologian, John Duns Scotus (ca. 1266–1308), whose beginnings and early death belong in this period. He studied and taught at Oxford and Paris in turn. He was sent to Cologne in 1307, and died there the next year. As a Franciscan he remained attached to the Augustinian tradition, but his eclectic Aristotelianism went far beyond what Bonaventure and Pecham had allowed. The Oxford school gave him his interest in mathematics and in experiment. His keen critical faculty likewise distinguished him from the Augustinian and Thomist-Aristotelian visual range. But he too applied himself to the unity of faith and knowledge to a synthesis of metaphysics and theology.

In Paris and elsewhere on the continent the great condemnation of Aristotelianism in 1277 meant a splitting of minds. While a certain trend toward a conservative reaction displayed itself, on the whole the development continued on the routes previously pointed out by the great masters of synthesis.

Scholarly life became even more intense and richer and a great number of noteworthy teachers and investigators appeared, who devoted themselves to philosophical and theological problems in a personal, independent, and critical method.

Shortly after 1277 appeared the *Correctorium fratris Thomae* of William de la Mare, the manifesto, so to speak, of the neo-Augustinian Franciscan school, in which 117 Thomistic theses were critically examined. Richard of Middleton belonged to this school, even though he approached Thomas in his epistemology.

Parallel to this neo-Augustinian tendency, represented mostly by Franciscans, there grew up the young Thomist school, whose spokesmen belonged mainly to the Dominican Order. Remarkably enough, Saint Thomas' immediate disciples were not very prominent in it.

The thirteenth century can be summarized as an epoch of philosophical and theological culture, and Maurice de Wulf called it the Golden Age of Metaphysics. Through it theology became speculative without losing its contact with Holy Scripture and the patristic tradition. It not only enriched the Greek-Jewish-Arabic legacy; it also made it capable of confronting the world of Judaism and Islam in apologetics.

The literary culture of the twelfth century was replaced by the cultivation of the particular disciplines, which formed their own languages. While the great scholars, especially Bonaventure and Thomas, mastered a distinct literary style, it did not achieve the rich brilliance and vivacity of the twelfth century.

A certain ambivalence of the age revealed itself in the development of a heterodox Aristotelianism in the arts faculty: the danger of rationalizing naturalism made itself felt. Siger of Brabant became its exponent and against him Bonaventure, Pecham, and Aquinas entered the lists. But Aquinas himself did not escape criticism on the part of almost the entire theological faculty of Paris. By means of his critical study and assimilation of the Aristotelian stock of ideas, especially its concept of knowledge, he had created the first original Christian philosophy, but it was precisely here that, according to his critic, John Pecham, the future dangers lay for theology; he felt that in Thomas there could be detected a surrender to Siger's positions — too far-reaching concessions to a heathen philosophy. And yet from the historical viewpoint the figure of Saint Thomas dominated his century. His work presupposed the exertions of the first century and a half and built on them. The philosophical and theological disputes which filled his lifetime stimulated his thought and promoted its development. The violent reaction against his total view and the sharp criticism of Duns Scotus compelled his pupils and successors to penetrate his work more deeply and make it better understood. The enduring and timeless value of Thomas' synthesis, however, was not to be appreciated fully for centuries.

CHAPTER 34

The Cardinals and the Curia in the Thirteenth Century

The Emperor Frederick II had addressed the cardinals as "successors of the Apostles" when in 1239 he suggested to them the summoning of a council at which his quarrel with Gregory IX should be arbitrated. And at the end of the century King Philip IV of France used the same phrase in an analogous context. Even if the canonists soon stressed the distinction between a "succession" of that sort and the recognized position of the bishops as *successores apostolorum,* it became clear in other ways how exalted a rank the cardinalate had acquired in the awareness of the age together with the papacy in its rise in esteem. The origins of the cardinalate from the Roman clergy belonged to the remote past. Innocent IV said without affectation that the cardinals possessed the authority of senators. As the Pope's advisers and participants in the government of the Church they met under the Pope's presidency in the consistory, which had replaced the Roman synods. They were early called *pars corporis papae,* as the princes of the Empire were regarded as *pars corporis imperatoris.* While the *Descriptio sanctuarii Lateranensis* (ca. 1100) still knew fifty-three cardinals, — seven bishops, 28 priests, 18 deacons, — this number fell in the thirteenth century to fewer than twenty and occasionally to even fewer than ten. Furthermore, by virtue of the corporative thought of the age, the cardinals appeared ever more clearly as a *collegium* and a corporation. The beginnings of their own financial administration went back to the pontificate of Calixtus II (1119–24). In the thirteenth century it was directed by a Cardinal *Camerlengo.* In 1289 Nicholas IV granted the college one-half of the income of the Holy See. Especially in view of the prolonged vacancies during this period — together they amounted to almost ten years in the thirteenth century — it was not possible to evade the question of what authority pertained to the college in the government of the Church. The leading decretalist, Hostiensis, himself Cardinal Bishop of Ostia and hence *prior et decanus* of the college, held that the college and the Pope constituted a unity, "unum et idem est," and hence it participated in the *plenitudo potestatis.* Others, however, limited the cardinals' proper authority to their right and duty of electing the Pope, while all other authority came to them from the Pope, for they are what they are through the Pope, who named them, bestowed their privileges, assigned their duties, and, if necessary, deprived them of their dignity. As a matter of fact, during the vacancies of the Holy See the cardinals acted so consistently in regard to decisions of law and of administration that they did not lay claim to the papal primatial power. In the consistory they were advisers but not real codetermining participants. The cardinals' signatures on especially solemn papal decrees must be similarly understood. Whatever accrued to the cardinalate in authority and dignity came through a grant by the Pope and was therefore of positive ecclesiastical law. The cardinals received no order and were not necessarily bishops, even though they outranked bishops in the course of time and, like them, had a seat and a vote at council.

In the thirteenth century, as earlier, the Pope made extensive use of the cardinals in the government of the Church and of the *Patrimonium,* where they obtained the most important rectorships, that is, the administration of the provinces. When acting as legates they received far-reaching powers, including judicial, and on such occasions appeared in almost papal dress and with papal ceremonial. In 1245 Innocent IV granted them the red hat. At Rome they became a sort of council of state during the Pope's lifetime and they assumed the government after his death. Their honorary rights began to multiply. The Pope was their only judge, and, placed on an equality with the electors in the secular sphere, they ranked immediately after him.

If the cardinals, under the direction of the Pope in the consistory, represented, in a sense, the highest organism for justice and administration in the Church, the Curia developed on its own alongside the college. The departments of the Curia, so far as they were constituted in the thirteenth century, were by no means directed by cardinals, except for the *Penitentiaria.* Perhaps the number of cardinals was too small; some of them were absent from Rome for rather long periods as legates. Perhaps the Popes felt that in this way they could retain the organization of the Curia directly at their own disposal.

The Curia

The epoch of the great jurist Popes, from Innocent III to Boniface VIII, brought to the elaboration of the Curia a growth and at the same time a simplification. It became the administrative and judicial organ of a spiritual commonwealth, to which the development of canon law, especially through the codifications of the thirteenth century from the decretals of Gregory IX to the *Liber Sextus* of Boniface VIII, had given a uniform order applying to all lands in Christendom. To watch over and perfect it became one of the more essential tasks of the Curia, which thus had to carry out governmental, administrative, and judicial functions. The final decision, of course, lay always with the Pope, who usually reached it in consistory.

The administration fell under the two offices of chancellor and *camerlengo.* Judicial matters were divided between the *Penitentiaria* for the forum of conscience and the *Audientia causarum* or *Audientia Sacri Palatii,* from which was to emerge the *Sacra Rota Romana* from the end of the thirteenth century. Besides these offices, whose activities could not as yet always be clearly distinguished, the papal court also disposed of the *capella,* whose development had been similar to that of its secular counterpart.

The Chancery

The name *cancellaria* appeared as early as 1182. Basically, the chancery was supposed to take care of all the correspondence between the Pope and Christendom. However, separate records for the *Penitentiaria* and for the *Camera* soon branched off. The vice-chancellor was not a cardinal until the end of the thirteenth century. The organization of the chancery was still in full process of development at this time. Under the vice-chancellor worked the notaries, the *corrector,* the *auditor litterarum contradictarum,* the *abbreviatores,* the *scriptores,* and the *bullatores.* The seal had to be left with the *camerlengo* over the weekend. From around the middle of the thirteenth century the notaries' chancery activity slowly declined, while the vice-chancellor, previously merely *primus inter pares,* increased his authority.

In addition to charters, which corresponded to initiatives of the Pope himself, the chancery especially took care of petitions, *supplicia,* coming in writing to the Curia from everywhere; they dealt with questions from the most varied aspects of ecclesiastical law.

The Camera

The *Camera* provided the financial administration of the Holy See. The Pope had had to assume immense tasks, above all in regard to the organizing of the crusades, in the conflicts between the Holy See and the Empire, and in the matter of subsidies, which proved to be necessary everywhere because of the tensions within Christendom. Furthermore, there was the increasing burden of supporting so expanding an administrative organism as the Curia itself. Hence a special bureaucracy for financial administration became necessary. Cluny was perhaps the model for the origins of the *camera apostolica.* The revenues came from the tax yield of the *Patrimonium,* from the proceeds of Peter's Pence, from the gifts brought by prelates visiting the Curia. From Innocent III these last were converted into fees and specific services. *Servitia communia,* amounting to one-third of a year's income, were payable on the occasion of the nomination and confirmation of bishops and abbots, and the dispatch of chancery *acta* was connected with the payment of various fees. From the crusade tithes there gradually evolved a system for a general taxation of Christendom.

The direction of the *camera* always pertained to a bishop and occasionally even to a cardinal, who should not be confused with the *camerlengo* of the College of Cardinals. Under him were the collectors, sent out to gather on the spot the monies due or, in the case of taxes paid in kind, to convert them into money and to remit them. When, from the middle of the thirteenth century, to the *servitia communia* for the higher benefices were added for the lower benefices the annates, or one's year income, usually paid in kind, the work of the collectors was increased.

Since there was as yet no distinction between the direction of the papal treasure and that of the Church, the *camerlengo* was one of the Pope's closest collaborators. His correspondence was recorded since the days of Urban IV in the *camera* register; *camera* clerics took care of the correspondence, examined contracts, and checked the receipts of the collectors. The *camera* had its own judicial officials as the number of processes increased. For the exchange of money the *camera* made use of the banking firms of Florence, Genoa, and elsewhere. Under the *camerlengo* was the actual administrator of the treasure, *thesaurarius,* who guarded the cash on hand.

Judicial Offices

Whereas in the twelfth century the consistory, presided over by the Pope, was able to settle disputed cases and appeals, in the course of the thirteenth century special offices were constituted, which were not fully established until the fourteenth century. The first was the *Penitentiaria,* for the forum of conscience. For a long time, perhaps from the seventh century, the Pope had made use of the services of a *penitentiarius,* but the latter's activity had grown so extraordinarily by virtue of the frequency and abundance of reservations and dispensations that he had to receive corresponding assistance. Thus appeared the *Penitentiaria,* whose structure was organized under Gregory IX (1227–41) and constantly perfected into the fourteenth century.

The *Penitentiaria* absolved from sins and censures that were reserved to the Pope, granted dispensations from irregularities and marriage impediments, could quash illegal and unfair decisions, dispense from vows, commute them, or postpone their fulfillment, dispatched indults, conferred privileges, mitigated penances. The grand *penitentiarius* was the confessor of the cardinals and of prelates staying at the Curia. Under Boniface VIII there were as many as twelve *sub-penitentiarii;* often they were religious of various nations.

The public administration of justice pertained to the *Audientia Sacri Palatii,* from which the *Rota* developed in the fourteenth century. When in the course of the twelfth century the legal cases which reached the Curia directly or by means of appeal grew more and more in number, even more *auditores* were commissioned to introduce the processes and lay them before the Pope, together with the cardinals, for decision; sometimes they were themselves authorized to render decisions. The Pope also reserved *causae maiores* and disputes over elections to himself and the cardinals. This papal judicial office only obtained a stable organization in 1331 in the bull "Ratio iuris"; it was later called the *Rota.*

Alongside it worked the so-called *Audientia litterarum contradictarum,* which belonged to the chancery. Authorized by Innocent III, it was concerned with legal documents and with grants of favors by the Curia which had been challenged by opponents of the recipients. In general, it was intended to exclude foolish issues from the outset, and to seek an arbitrated compromise before the starting of a process. This could be achieved by revision of records and elimination of bureaucratic chicanery and of delays in trials. Chancery rules and legal structures were set up and published by the *Audientia publica.*

In addition to the offices of the Curia in the strict sense there appeared the college of papal *capellani.* These devoted themselves not only to the liturgy at the papal court but also to various types of diplomatic and judicial tasks. Already numerous in the twelfth century, their number increased to almost 200 under Innocent IV. They served as *penitentiarii,* distributors of alms, sacristans; they were also chamberlains, treasurers, or lectors in the circle closest to the Pope.

A mighty mechanism for the business of ecclesiastical law and administration, which of course also had to perform corresponding functions in the government of the Papal State, made it clear toward the end of the thirteenth century how extensive the practical direction of the Church by the Pope had become. Weighed down by all the weaknesses of large bureaucracies, but also distinguished by astonishing achievements in tribunal, *camera,* and chapel, the thirteenth-century Curia was one of the most impressive phenomena of Church life in the High Middle Ages.

CHAPTER 35

Celestine V and Boniface VIII

The Second Council of Lyons in 1274 was, in its achievement if not in its enduring effect, a convincing sign of the still unruffled ecumenical prestige of the papacy, above all of course in the West. The narrow partisanship amongst them kept the cardinals from uniting around a strong candidate for Pope, who, like Gregory X, coming from outside their numbers, uniting breadth of vision and freedom from factional ties, would have been able to direct the helm toward greater goals. As a matter of fact, the election of 5 July 1294, two years and three months after the death on 4 April 1292 of Nicholas IV, fell on a man who did not belong to the college, where the rivalry of Colonna and Orsini would not allow anyone to obtain the required two-thirds majority. But it was not a happy choice. Piety could certainly be expected in the hermit, Peter of Murrone, and this was probably what motivated the Franciscan Cardinal Latino Malabranca to suggest him. The Pope-elect had been a Benedictine, but later, as a hermit, he had founded an eremitical community, which had been incorporated into the Benedictine Order by Urban IV. The members later called themselves Celestines, from the name which the Pope from their midst had assumed. He only accepted the election under much pressure and despite his own great hesitations. A year earlier the founder, more than eighty-years old, had relinquished to others the direction of his community, whose principal monastery was Santo Spirito near Sulmona. In the Spiritual circles the new Pope was hailed as the "Angel Pope" expected by the Joachimite movement; it was believed that a new era was beginning for the Church. Extraordinary as the election was, the end of the brief pontificate was equally extraordinary: at the end of the same year, Celestine V abdicated.

Charles II the Lame, King of Naples, who had already exercised a determining influence on the conclave, believed himself authorized to exert the decisive impact during the pontificate. He was not only able to prevent the new Pope from transferring his residence to Rome, as the cardinals wanted; he even succeeded in having him take up residence at Naples in the Castel Nuovo, placed at his disposal by the King. Celestine V had been crowned on 29 August 1294 at Aquila in Santa Maria di Collemaggio, a church of his own congregation. Charles II induced him to renew Gregory X's strict rules for the conclave and had himself appointed guardian of the next conclave. The Pope named twelve cardinals.

Against the opposition of the cardinals the Curia moved from Aquila to Naples, arriving on 5 November. The most important posts were occupied by Charles' creatures, who also succeeded in taking over the key positions in the Papal State. The overhasty measures of the pontificate included the rich grant of privileges to the Celestine congregation, whose confirmation the Pope renewed. The actual administration of the Church fell into hopeless confusion, especially since an insight into the situation was not granted to the Pope and he did not have the strength to exercise supervision. Benefices were given simultaneously to several petitioners. Efforts were made to incorporate the greater abbeys into the Celestine congregation; even Montecassino was threatened. Charles II obtained a ratification of the peace with Aragón and the grant to himself of the tithes from France and Burgundy for four years and from England, Ireland, and Scotland for one year. He was eventually also named Senator of Rome. When the cardinals, to whom Celestine allowed no say, came with their grievances and complaints, the Pope became aware of his very difficult situation. After having consulted with Cardinal Benedict Gaetani, he had it ratified in consistory that abdication was possible. On 10 December he issued a constitution dealing with abdication by a Pope and decreed the legal validity of Gregory X's conclave regulation also for the case of resignation. Then, on 13 December, he laid down his office.

His successor did not permit him to return to his old hermitage, fearing that his own opponents and Celestine's disillusioned friends might exploit the person of the resigned Pope to bring about a schism in the Church. At first, to be sure, Celestine did manage to flee, but he was overtaken and placed in honorable confinement in the Castel Fumone near Ferentino, where he died on 19 May 1296. He was buried in the church where he had been crowned. Clement V canonized him in 1313 under pressure from King Philip the Fair in the course of the struggle over the memory of Boniface VIII. Pious asceticism was not enough to qualify one to rule the Universal Church. All of these qualities were brought to the papacy by Celestine's immediate successor, Boniface VIII.

The conclave following Celestine's abdication began on 23 December — there was a ten days' interval, just as at the death of a Pope. Then Benedict Gaetani was unanimously chosen. Boniface VIII (1294–1303), as he styled himself, came from a Roman family that had branched far out, to Anagni, where he was born, to Pisa, and to Spain. His mother was a niece of Alexander IV, and the mother of Nicholas III was also related to him. He was also connected with the houses of Orsini and Colonna. Born at Anagni around 1240, he was raised by his uncle, the Bishop of Todi, and studied law at Bologna. He became a notary at the Curia and, as secretary, accompanied the future Popes Martin IV and Adrian V on embassies to France and England. He was entrusted with important business at the Curia and, despite the Ghibelline tradition of his family, was oriented toward France, and hence Martin IV created him a Cardinal. His legateship in France in 1290–91 became his most important activity. He succeeded in mediating the Treaty of Tarascon with Aragón and in preventing the outbreak of a war with England and restoring good relations between France and the Curia. At the University of Paris he stood up for the rights of the mendicant orders; it had been charged by the diocesan clergy and the University that their excessive privileges disturbed the orderly care of souls in parishes. As a friend of popular piety — he was not a specialist in theology — the Cardinal inclined to the ideal of the mendicant orders. His harsh and intemperate manner of speaking gained him no friends. If, nevertheless, his fellow cardinals elected him, they did so because of the qualities which made him seem suited for the papacy, so seriously compromised by Celestine V: trained intellect, knowledge of the world, experience in business, intrepid boldness, an iron will, and amazing energy.

The new Pope dismissed the curial officials imposed by Charles II and moved to Rome, where he was crowned on 23 January. He had annulled all favors granted by his predecessor; only the prelates appointed by Celestine retained their dignity. All grants of benefices that had not yet been effected and all expectatives were also cancelled. The administration of the Curia's finances was transferred to three Florentine banking firms; hence the *Camera* became only an accounting office, and abuse and suspicion on the part of both payers and receivers were eliminated. The financial administration was tightened and regulated, the returns from public finance increased, and at the end of the pontificate there was an important cash reserve on hand. The city of Rome remained calm under Boniface VIII and the Papal State felt his strong hand. Risings in the Marches could be put down, Orvieto submitted within a year, and only Romagna continued restless. In many places the Pope had himself elected as city lord. The Papal State had not had a more powerful master since Innocent III.

At the same time a war was in progress between England and France. In the summer of 1296 Boniface was asked to mediate, not in his capacity as Pope but personally as an arbiter. Both Kingdoms had demanded taxes from the clergy for the prosecution of the war. Since on the outbreak of war a Pope had not yet been elected, the necessary consent of the Curia, as provided by the Fourth Lateran Council for taxation of the clergy, had not been sought. When at the beginning of 1296 new tithes had been announced for a year, two for the North and four for the South, the clergy, led by the Cistercians, had protested, but the bishops had not. Boniface complied with this protest in the bull "Clericis laicos" of 24 February 1296, which was entered in the chancery register as "Statute on Ecclesiastical Freedom." It renewed the enactment of the Fourth Lateran Council and made it stricter in the sense that any tax not expressly authorized incurred the penalty. Promulgated as a general law, it was directed equally at France and England and intended to make unambiguous a law that had become doubtful. Thereby the Pope intervened as legislator in important areas of the life of the state, which was becoming ever more keenly conscious of its autonomy. In practice kings in their wars would have become dependent on the good will of the Pope, who could permit the paying of war taxes.

Did Boniface intend to further his peace efforts by this decree? In any event, the English clergy refused further contributions, appealing to the bull, and the barons followed their example. There ensued a constitutional conflict, which, as in 1215, ended in 1217 with the submission of the King and the confirmation of Magna Carta. In France the episcopate at first withdrew its consent to the tithe, but at an assembly at Paris in June 1296 it asked the Pope for authorization. At the same time Boniface was asked by both belligerents to mediate personally in the war. Surprisingly, there quickly followed, on 18 August 1296, a prohibition of the export from France of precious metal, money, and bills of exchange. This was explained as an ordinary war measure, but the Pope was the one chiefly affected by it, for his budget was dependent on French dues. He reacted on 20 September with a sharp note to King Philip the Fair. He accused him of violating the liberties of the Church and reminded him that the edict contained nothing new; it authorized the Pope to protect the clergy but by permitting particular taxes it did not exclude support for the King. Boniface had always been particularly friendly to France, but the letter ended with certain threatening admonitions: the Pope would see himself compelled to have recourse to extraordinary means in the event that France did not comply. There then began in France a journalism, probably managed by the court, which discussed in a polemical fashion fundamental questions of the relations between laity and clergy within the Church, understood as Christendom. The French Church, it was said, had special obligations toward the "political" community because of its wealth, which came from the laity, and the penalties threatened by the Curia were felt to be unjust. In the widely circulated *Dialogue Between A Cleric and A Knight* it was admitted that the secular was bound to assist the spiritual, but the superiority, deduced from this, of the spiritual power to the secular power was denied. The Church of the clergy was advised to undertake an extensive spiritualizing process: the Word and the Sacrament and Sacrifice were her vocation, and she should be concerned for the heavenly rather than the earthly kingdom. The territorial Church was obliged to aid the King, since he was constituted as her protector.

In the course of this polemic the political powers regrouped themselves. Flanders, threatened by France, allied with England. The Burgundian princes again made contact with Germany. An understanding with the Pope rather than a fight against him now seemed to be what was needed by the French crown and its advisers. The non-arrival of the French dues so crippled the Curia's policy, especially that against Sicily, that it too was for an understanding. A Florentine banker, John Francesi, nicknamed Musciatto, undertook to make the contacts. In a letter to the French King, Boniface declared that the bull "Clericis laicos," as a universal law, was not directed specially against him, complained of the export prohibition, and stated that he was prepared to accommodate the King. An accompanying interpretation of the law explained that voluntary contributions by the clergy were not bound by the requirement of authorization and that, in emergencies, when the Pope could not be approached in time, such authorization was to be presumed.

An embassy led by Peter Flotte, the chancellor, went to Rome for negotiations, since a favorable situation had arisen there: from May 1297 the Pope was occupied with the revolt of the House of Colonna.

This took place *consensu fratrum* but without any judicial procedure and corresponding judgment; this had been reserved, in the event that the cardinals concerned should, as Boniface had demanded, personally arrange for proceedings. The Colonna undertook counter-measures. On the altar at Saint Peter's they laid a solemn protest, in which it was stated that Boniface was not a legitimate Pope; the judgment of a general council was demanded, at which Boniface should be called to account for the murder of his predecessor. On 23 May the Pope renewed his sentence on the Colonna, and on 9 July the Inquisition was directed to begin a process against them and two of their adherents. The resistance of the Colonna to the Pope's measures found support in the French crown. In a comprehensive memorial they summarized all the charges against the Pope and invited the Universal Church — kings, princes, prelates — to have a general council decide on the punishment and removal of the Pope. Copies were sent everywhere. The French embassy was informed of it. The memorial provided it with a favorable point of departure in its negotiations with the Curia. These could be concluded to the advantage of France on 31 July. It was agreed that the bull "Clericis laicos" did not apply to France. The crown was qualified to decide when an emergency existed which made recourse to the Pope pointless. A group of further privileges was added, and the canonization of Louis IX was promised. The extraordinary success of the French agents can only be grasped if one assumes that they had threatened to join the Colonna in the event that the Curia should not return a favorable answer. And despite the restoration of friendly relations with France this shadow remained.

The price of the understanding had to be paid by the Colonna, who now did not find in France the expected support. Peter Flotte held himself aloof from them. The front that had been forming against Boniface fell to pieces. The cardinals were ready to declare their solidarity with Boniface. The minister general of the Franciscans demanded submission from his subjects. The Dominicans were commanded by their general publicly to recognize Boniface as true Pope. At the same time they were forbidden to join the Colonna. A crusade was preached against the Colonna. It lasted only until October 1298, when their chief fortress, Palestrina, fell and was razed to the ground. The Colonna submitted, but when the two Cardinals were freed only from excommunication and not from the other penalties, they again took up resistance. However, it did not become a reality until they allied with France after the beginning of the new century.

Imperial Italy played an important role in Papal relations with Germany. Boniface was less interested in Lombardy than he was in Tuscany, which he would have liked to incorporate into the Papal State. Boniface had close ties with the chief city of Tuscany, Florence. Important Florentine banking houses were in the service of the Curia. In Florence the Blacks and the Whites vied for control of the government; both factions belonged to the wealthy class, which had imposed its rule on the lesser folk. The Pope decided for the Blacks, who included the papal bankers.

Adolf of Nassau had been King of Germany since 5 May 1292. But in the course of the years he had so alienated his electors that in June 1298 he was deposed. Duke Albert of Austria, son of King Rudolf I and center of the opposition to Adolf, was chosen to succeed him. On 30 April 1303 in the bull "Aeterni Patris" he solemnly recognized Albert of Austria as King of Germany and future Emperor. Albert now broke off his alliance with France and bound himself not to appoint an imperial vicar in Lombardy and Tuscany for the next five years without the Pope's consent and after that to name only a vicar acceptable to the Pope. Herein lay a recognition by the Curia that this was imperial property.

The Jubilee of 1300 formed a sort of caesura in the pontificate of Boniface VIII, at least in regard to the relationship with France, which had calmed in this year. Rumors at the end of 1299 had told of ample grants of indulgences which persons could gain at the beginning of the new century in Saint Peter's. And so from the start of the year great crowds of pilgrims arrived in Rome. Only because of these was the Pope induced after consultation with the cardinals, to issue the bull "Antiquorum habet fidem" on 22 February 1300. Anyone who in this year, a year of jubilee, such as was thereafter to be celebrated every hundredth year, should after contrite confession, visit the basilicas of the two Princes of the Apostles, received a plenary indulgence for the temporal punishment due to his sins. Enormous crowds of pilgrims came, attracted by this indulgence, hitherto not granted. A great need for expiation, penance, and conversion seemed to fill Christendom. At Rome arrangements had to be made to take care of the stream of visitors. The pilgrims' offerings were considerable; they profited not the papal coffers but those of the churches visited. For the Pope the jubilee brought a gain in prestige *vis-à-vis* the Western kings with whom he was engaged in a political confrontation. The unchallenged esteem of the Apostolic See and its religious authority found an unexpected confirmation. The self-assurance of Boniface VIII increased. It also led him to disregard a proper judgment of the political reality. This would soon be made crystal clear in the renewal of the conflict with France.

An insignificant incident started it. Bernard Saisset, provost of the collegiate chapter of Saint-Antonin, had become first Bishop of Pamiers, created by Boniface VIII in 1295. The King had not been consulted, nor had the Bishop of Toulouse, from whose diocese Pamiers had partly been carved. As provost the new Bishop had had difficulties with the King. Careless remarks by the Bishop that were critical of the King led to Bernard's being cited before the *conseil* after his property had been sequestered on 24 October 1301. He was prosecuted under the direction of the chancellor, Peter Flotte, on charges of defamation of the King, sedition, high treason, simony, and heresy. He was judged guilty and turned over to his metropolitan, the Archbishop of Narbonne, for imprisonment. The Pope was informed of the outcome and asked to depose and punish the Bishop of Pamiers. Without studying the dossier, Boniface demanded the Bishop's release on 5 December 1301. By the bull "Salvator Mundi" he withdrew the privileges granted to the King, because the freedom and immunity of the Church had been violated. In effect, the bull "Clericis laicos" was again made binding for France. The Pope summoned the French episcopate, the deans of the cathedral chapters, and the doctors to a special synod, to be held at Rome on 1 November 1302. The King was also invited. The bull "Ausculta Fili" contained all the grievances of the Church against the crown and its agents. They were to be the object of the discussions at the synod. There was also mention of the unconditional superiority of the papal over every secular power. A notary carried the bulls to Paris. Instead of justifying himself, King Philip had decided to fight. It was forbidden to publish the bull "Ausculta Fili." In its place Peter Flotte circulated a forgery, "Deum Time," in which, over the Pope's name, the content of the suppressed bull was made known in a distorted and sharpened manner. At the same time an alleged reply of the King was sent out with it — "Sciat maxima tua fatuitas." This maintained that in secular matters the King was subject to no one. Thus was French public opinion formed. In order to win the leading circles of the nation, a meeting of the Estates General was summoned to Paris; in addition to the nobility and prelates the cities were invited for the first time. The meeting took place on 12 April 1302. Peter Flotte read "Deum Time" and defended the King's case. The estates were persuaded to defend the King and to write to Rome in this sense. Only a few of the bishops attended, but they conformed after some hesitation. The nobility and the cities received a reply from the cardinals; the episcopate received theirs from the Pope. A consistorial discourse exposed and condemned the intrigues of Peter Flotte. It then declared that the Pope claimed no feudal suzerainty in France but could take the King to task *ratione peccati.* However, he threatened Philip with deposition and repeated the summons to the announced synod.

In spite of a royal prohibition, thirty-nine prelates appeared, but no decrees were issued. The bull "Unam Sanctam" may have been discussed, for it was published soon after, on 18 November 1302. It became the most debated document of this pontificate, perhaps even of the mediaeval papacy in general. There is only one Church, so it explained, outside which there is no salvation, with only one head, who is Christ, and his vicar Peter and Peter's successors. Both swords, the spiritual and the temporal, are in the power of the Church, the spiritual wielded by her, the temporal wielded by the hand of the king but according to the priests' instructions. The spiritual power surpasses every secular power in dignity. The spiritual power can institute the secular and judge it, if it transgresses. The highest spiritual power can be judged only by God. Whoever opposes it resists God. Hence it is necessary for the salvation of every man that he be subject to the Roman Pontiff.

None of this was new. The celebrated concluding sentence comes from Thomas Aquinas. The bull's train of thought followed the treatise *De ecclesiastica potestate* by the Augustinian Hermit, Aegidius Romanus (Giles of Rome), which had appeared only shortly before. In 1295 Boniface had promoted this master of theology at Paris, who had become general of his order, to the archiepiscopal see of Bourges. However, not he but the Franciscan Cardinal Matthew of Aquasparta was probably the one who drew up the bull. The violent reaction to this document was directed, not especially against the theological and canonical doctrines of the century just ended which were summarized in it, but against the supposed political program which persons thought they had to see in it. Dogmatic significance attaches only to the concluding sentence, which obtained its importance through its confirmation by the Fifth Lateran Council.

Attempts to reach a compromise with the French King continued even after the promulgation of the bull. Cardinal Le Moine, or John the Monk, was commissioned as legate to lay the Pope's demands before the King. At first Philip refused to commit himself, but then he decided on a more vigorous fight. Responsible for this turn was William of Nogaret, who had taken the place of Peter Flotte after the latter had perished in the battle of Courtrai, which France had lost to the Flemings on 11 July 1302. Through Nogaret the Colonna cardinals now gained influence on the further course of events. And the legate, Le Moine, now abandoned the side of the Pope, one of whose most trusted advisers he had been, and treacherously joined the French faction. In the *conseil* on 12 March 1303 Nogaret brought forward the grievances against Boniface VIII, which were substantially the same as the accusations made by the Colonna in their memorials. The King's consent was obtained. There was propaganda for a general council at which the Pope would have to justify himself. Nogaret received authorization for an expedition to Italy. Apparently the plan was to arrest the Pope and take him to France, where it was intended that he should be presented to the projected council.

Boniface considered inadequate the French reply to his demands as made known by Cardinal Le Moine, and on 13 April 1303 he declared the excommunication of the King. The bearer of the document was imprisoned in France, and the information was suppressed. In mid-June Philip again had charges brought against the Pope before the Estates General, this time by William of Plaisians. The King declared the necessity of a council and spoke in favor of convoking one. The consent of the assembly was general, though there was some reservation among the bishops. The record of the discussions was circulated, and meetings to obtain consent were held. Only the Cistercians and a few houses of mendicants refused. Ever imprisonment and banishment were resorted to. A great popular gathering at Paris on 24 June 1303 was prepared to give consent, letters were dispatched to foreign princes and to the cardinals, and a messenger even went to the Pope. From Anagni Boniface rejected the charges, issued a series of bulls against Philip and his councillors on 15 August 1303, and finally began work on the bull "Super Petri Solio," in which the solemn excommunication of the King was proclaimed and his subjects were released from their oath of loyalty. It was to be published on 8 September 1303.

On the previous day occurred the well known attack at Anagni, perpetrated by Nogaret in association with Sciarra Colonna, head of that family of enemies of Boniface. The residences of the cardinals and the papal palace were stormed. It was demanded that the Pope should lay down his office, restore offices and possessions to the Colonna, turn over the treasure of the Church to several older cardinals, and submit to imprisonment. Boniface rejected the demand and even offered his life. Nogaret did not permit Sciarra Colonna to go along with this suggestion; he was concerned only for the living Pope, who was to be judged in France. In the city, which at first had aided the conspirators, the mood changed, Boniface was rescued, and the conspirators were driven out. Boniface left insecure Anagni for Rome, and the Orsini undertook to protect him. He arrived there on 25 September but on 12 October he succumbed at the Vatican to his sufferings and the disillusionment of Anagni. He was laid to rest in the chapel of Saint Peter which he had constructed, in a tomb which he had had built by Arnolfo di Cambio in his lifetime.

His political measures turned out for the most part unsuccessfully or critically for the Curia. On the other hand his activity within the Church was to survive the pontificate: first, the publication of the *Liber Sextus,* a supplement to Gregory IX's collection of decretals, then the introduction of order into the chaotic state of affairs in the curial administrative system brought about in the previous pontificates, and finally the decision in the question of the relations between the mendicant orders and the diocesan clergy in the bull "Super Cathedram" of 18 February 1300.

The mendicants were permitted to preach freely in their own churches and in public squares, but in parish churches only with the permission of the pastor. They had to ask faculties for hearing confessions from the local bishop, and these were limited to the territory of his see. The number of confessors thus licensed was determined by the needs of the diocese. The denial of such faculties by individual bishops could, if necessary, be righted by a papal decision. In regard to reserved cases the mendicants were not to have more authority than the parish priests. The right of burial was conceded them; that is, they were allowed to bury in their churches whoever asked this, but one-fourth of the fees falling due pertained to the proper pastor as his canonical share. This was a carefully weighed regulation, distinguished by impartiality. The respective legal competences were exactly determined. The preeminence of an orderly care of souls was assured, and the orders gave extraordinary assistance which was to be understood as supplementary.

In June 1303 the Pope founded a university at Rome, the later Sapienza, as a *studium generale.* He bestowed careful attention on the library and archives of the Vatican. A university was also to come into being at Avignon.

The fate of the Pope was not decided by his death, and the process concerning him did not preoccupy only the succeeding pontificates. It has been said that even today his records are not yet closed. His outstanding juristic and administrative gifts, his energetic direction of the Curia, the intensive work which he demanded of himself and of his co-workers — these remain unchallenged. His broad education and his knowledge of Holy Scripture were famed. But his arrogant bearing, which people labelled pride and contempt, made him no friends. The failures of his political enterprises raised the suspicion of a lack of judgment, which seemed to plague him even in the formulating of his fundamental bulls. His nepotism placed him beside many of his predecessors, but with him everything assumed immoderate forms. As a legislator and judge he remained for all contemporaries a vast and enduringly influential figure, but people were unable to venerate him as the Father of Christendom. The Spirituals continued to be hostile to him because of Celestine. His memory remained overclouded by the unrestrained propaganda of his opponents and the repeated attempts to have him tried posthumously as a heretic. He was not guiltless in regard to some charges, which, however, were completely distorted in the light of an excessive hostility. All things considered, he was an important Pope.

CHAPTER 36

The End of the Crusading Epoch

The fall of Acre in 1291 ended the rule of the crusaders in Syria and Palestine. After the taking of the city in May the Sultan al-Ashraf Khalil, with his Mamelukes, completed the mopping up: Tyre was taken as early as 19 May, Sidon at the end of June, Beirut surrendered in July, and the Templars handed over their remaining strongholds, Château Pèlerin and Tortosa.

There remains the astonishing fact that the conquests of the First Crusade — the Kingdom of Jerusalem and its vassal principalities — could be maintained at all for almost 200 years, even though in a constantly diminishing extent. Pilgrims, merchants, knights, princes, and kings had traveled beyond the sea almost without interruption. The classical crusades were only moments of special energy in this movement. What is most astounding is that in the crusader states, small lordships in the sphere of influence of port cities, the circumstances of government had to be constantly revised and kept in balance in accord with the model of Western feudal relationships, a strong kingship was for the most part lacking,the military orders did not co-operate, and the commercial colonies of Venice, Genoa, and Pisa at Acre, Haifa, Beirut, and Tripolis were basically concerned only for assuring their own mercantile interests.

More than ever, the crusade dominated the program of councils from the Fourth Lateran Council in 1215 to that of Vienne in 1311–12. It had become a virtually essential task of the Popes to be concerned for its continuation, to plan great expeditions, to organize them, to help finance them, and occasionally to assume even their direction. Anxiety over the maintaining of the Latin Empire (1204–61) was drawn into the papal crusade policy, even though it constantly compromised the accumulated effort on behalf of the Holy Land.

At the Fourth Lateran Council in 1215 Innocent III had endeavored to mobilize all the resources of the West in order to make good the failure of 1204. He died in 1216 during the proximate preparations, and so the implementation of his project had to be left to his successor, Honorius III. The mighty enterprise that was the Fifth Crusade, in which almost all the nations of Christendom took part, with in some cases very large contingents, lasted from 1217 to 1221. The first to set out were

King Andrew II of Hungary and Duke Leopold VI of Austria with German nobles and bishops; later came those from the Lower Rhineland and Frisia, under the direction of the successful crusade preacher, Oliver, *scholasticus* of the Cologne cathedral. Then came Flemings, Englishmen, Frenchmen, Scots, and finally Italians from the cities and the knightly class. From 1218 the enterprise was directed by the Cardinal Legate Pelagius. His big success was the taking of Damietta, the key to Egypt, on 5 November 1219. But in August 1221 the legate was responsible for the defeat at Mansurah, which ruined the earlier achievement. The history of this crusade became a tragedy of Christian disunity, of heroic effort, and of diplomatic folly. At times the Sultan al-Kamil had been ready to surrender the entire Holy Land in return for peace, but the obstinate greed for conquest in the Spanish Cardinal Legate led to the breakdown of all offers and hopes.

The often promised and just as often postponed crusade of the Emperor Frederick II — a part of his forces had taken part in the Fifth Crusade — was finally led in 1228 when the Emperor had already incurred excommunication. Negotiations with the Sultan al-Kamil were successful, and Jerusalem, Nazareth, and Bethlehem were restored, together with a corridor to enable pilgrims to reach the coast. A ten-years' armistice was concluded in 1229.

A further territorial gain accrued from the curious double crusade, expressly forbidden by Gregory IX, of Count Theobald of Champagne, King of Navarre, and Earl Richard of Cornwall: Galilee was recovered from Damascus. The public crisis between Gregory IX and Frederick II had impeded the preparation and implementation. The two phases of this crusade of 1239–41 followed in such a manner that the two leaders did not meet, but Richard managed to conclude favorably the negotiations prepared by Theobald with the Sultans of Damascus and Cairo. While there was fighting at various times, there were no crucial battles. The model of the Emperor in 1228–29 was decisive.

A few years later, in 1244, all was again lost. Jerusalem fell, this time forever, and the hosts of the military orders and crusaders were overwhelmed at Gaza. The First Council of Lyons in 1245 concerned itself, as expected, with the distress of the Holy Land, but the needs of the Latin Empire obtained preference in the discussions. And, even after the Council, the quarrel with the Emperor Frederick II continued to eclipse all other concerns of Innocent IV.

King Louis IX of France, representing, as it were, a Christendom which was implicated in so many other distractions, assumed the duty of assisting the Holy Land. The expedition, which he carefully prepared for years and on which he set out in 1248, was the last grand-scale crusade of the century. Damietta was captured; then followed, as in 1221, an overwhelming defeat at Mansurah, in which Louis IX was captured. Set free on the payment of a high ransom, he stayed until 1254 in the Holy Land in order to do what he could to regulate the political situation and to unify the rival resources of tradesmen, knights, and orders on the one goal of defense. Only so long as he was there, personally intervening, reconciling, and punishing, was there the appearance of inner peace. It ended as soon as he had departed.

Once more, in 1270, Louis went on crusade. He landed in Tunis, but pestilence and hunger destroyed his army, and the King himself died on 25 August 1270. His brother, Charles of Anjou, arrived in time to liquidate the enterprise in a peace advantageous to his Kingdom of Sicily. Other expeditions of this century were without importance.

The *reconquista* in the Iberian peninsula had long borne the character of a crusade, so that during the Second Crusade the Frisians *en route* to the Holy Land could, with a good conscience, take part in it at Lisbon. From the time of Innocent III the struggles for the conquest of the Baltic area were also endowed with crusade privileges, on the model of the Wend Crusade of 1147–48. At the same time there was added the Albigensian Crusade to overcome the serious threat from the Cathari in the Midi. This crusade turned into a war and finally a merely political affair of the French crown. The Stedinger crusade (1232–34) of Archbishop Gerard II of Bremen against peasants on both sides of the lower Weser for non-payment of tithes is an example. Gregory IX issued the requisite bulls and granted the crusaders the "great crusade indulgence." More hotly disputed by contemporaries were the crusades of Innocent IV against the excommunicated and deposed Emperor, in which Germany, Lombardy, and Sicily were summoned to participate. In the Albigensian War he had developed the theory and practice of the political crusade. But Gregory IX, in the last phase of his quarrel with Frederick II, was the first to permit his legates in Lombardy and Germany to preach the crusade in order to be able to raise troops for the fight against the Emperor. Following his example, Innocent IV, after the First Council of Lyons (1245), had recourse to this means against Frederick II in Germany and Italy. And he also had a crusade preached in Germany against Conrad IV in 1253 and 1254.

Urban IV granted boundless crusade privileges to Charles of Anjou for the latter's struggle to gain the Kingdom of Sicily from Manfred, and in order to finance it and to make up for losses sustained he had the crusade preached in France and Italy. He took similar steps against Byzantium in 1263 and against Manfred's friends in Sardinia. Clement IV continued this policy, notably during the expedition of young Conradin to Italy and the Sicilian Kingdom in 1268.

The Sicilian Vespers of 30 March 1282 made the island a bone of contention between the Houses of Anjou and Aragón. Pope Martin IV, a Frenchman, opposed Aragón and deprived King Peter III of his crown, which was held in fief of the Holy See. Charles of Valois, a son of King Philip III of France, was to receive it and to conquer the Kingdom. The expedition of 1285 was financed and endowed with privileges, just like a crusade.

The last of these political crusades was raised by Boniface VIII in 1298 against the Colonna.

The original idea of the crusade was determined by the wish to defend the Christians of the East, who were hard pressed by Islam. Hence the crusade became a war against Muslims (the "infidel"), wherever Western and Eastern Christianity had their frontiers. If the evangelization by the sword in Central Germany and the Baltic area assumed a crusade character, the enterprise remained basically true to the original notion of military defense of the faith, even though the element of extending the sphere of the faith had been added. Here the unforgotten duty of proclaiming the faith was put forward in forms suitable to the age. Even the political crusades of the thirteenth century, just mentioned, were theoretically justified as struggles for the faith. This was more apparent in the Albigensian Crusades than in those against Frederick II. But here too it must not be overlooked that the concept of heresy at that time included obstinate opponents of the Roman Church.

The crusade organization drawn up by Innocent III stood the test, especially with regard to the preparing of planned journeys. A plenary indulgence, presupposing sincere repentance, confession, and satisfaction, was promised on setting out. Efforts were made to raise money in the form of income taxes, testamentary bequests, and even commutation of crusade vows. From all this developed the crusade taxes, laid first on the clergy, then on the laity also. The deciding of the amount pertained to councils and also to the Pope in agreement with kings and princes. The collecting of these taxes brought into being a real financial organization, which became useful not only to the Curia but also to state administrations. Toward the end of the century, when real crusades to the Holy Land had long since ceased to materialize, the taxes were still repeatedly demanded, especially by King Philip IV of France, and their levying was granted. This preoccupation of the crusade idea with finance contributed greatly to the decay of the notion.

Legates were named and preachers were commissioned specifically for the propaganda preparation of the crusade. The history of preaching was thereby greatly enriched. Entrusted ever more in the thirteenth century to the mendicant orders, this preaching developed into the popular mission in a liturgically oriented *milieu*. The success of this preaching, even though in particular cases it is difficult to show it because of the meager information in the sources, was sufficiently extensive and profound to cause the flow of pilgrims and fighters to continue without interruption till the end of the real age of the crusades and to revive and deepen the crusade spirituality of both those who undertook the journey and those who remained home.

The growing number of voices expressing disillusionment and doubt, criticism and abhorrence, was basically unable to change much of this. Disillusionment grew by virtue of the failures, especially of the big expeditions, whose returns seemed in no way to correspond to the mighty output in money and manpower. Doubt was expressed chiefly because in these failures people felt they were abandoned by God, whose business they had undertaken to defend in the crusade vow. Criticism was directed not only against poor leadership and the disunity of the political authority in the Holy Land, where there was a readiness to ally with the infidel and thereby the impression was created that in the Holy Land the constructing of positions of political power was at stake. But criticism was also turned on the growing preoccupation of the crusaders with finance and the Curia's share in creating this atmosphere.

It is astonishing that the collapse of Frankish rule in the Holy Land still evoked a flood of literary propaganda, as though persons in the West regarded such an outcome as shameful. But at the same time one can see in it an aspect of the reflection that seems to follow every period of emphatic action. No longer the preachers but scholars and writers took the floor.

It may be held that, with this chiefly meditative pursuit, which was at the same time an examination of conscience and a planning, the strictly classical Age of the Crusade had come to an end, only to make ready the epochs of the late mediaeval expeditions against the infidel.

Part Two

The Late Middle Ages

Section One

The Popes at Avignon

Chaps. 37–40: Karl August Fink
Chaps. 41–44: Erwin Iserloh
Chap. 45: Josef Glazik

Chapter 37

The Situation after the Death of Boniface VIII: Benedict XI and Clement V

When, a few weeks after the outrage at Anagni, Boniface VIII died in Rome, the city and the Papal State were filled with unrest, and the strife between the Gaetani and the Colonna was raging even more violently than before. But the supporters of the dead Pope in the College of Cardinals, led by Matthew Rosso Orsini, succeeded in opening the conclave at Saint Peter's on the expiration of the appointed interval and in rejecting the demand of the deposed Cardinals, James and Peter Colonna, to take part in the election. The French envoys and Nogaret actively supported the Colonna, but King Charles II of Naples used his troops to thwart all attempts to enter the Eternal City by force. Hence, from the outset, the validity of the papal election was placed in doubt.

Despite serious difficulties, due to the existence of two factions of equal strength in the conclave, the election was completed on the first ballot, when the Cardinal Bishop of Ostia, Nicholas Bocassini of Treviso, former master general of the Dominicans, was chosen pope. But this did not resolve the severe tensions nor close the split between the quarreling groups. Quite the contrary: the situation required of the new Pope discretion and strength, qualities in which Benedict XI was not especially outstanding. His having begun to reconcile opponents was often construed as weakness. But how would he have been able to act otherwise in view of the excessive influence of France throughout Italy and of the agitation in the Papal State? These, however, were only the external difficulties. Boniface VIII's new style had altered the papacy as an institution and evoked opposition which went far beyond the political sphere, as would become evident in the process against him and the repeated demands for a council. To oblige France as far as possible without total surrender seemed to the new Pope to be politic, but it involved great risks.

As a Cardinal, the new Pope had clearly been a success in the capacity of legate and had behaved courageously at Anagni. But he was not quite equal to the demands of his new, burdensome office. If he would do nothing without the cardinals, he was presumably returning to a collegial administration of the Church and thus abandoning the methods of the Gaetani Pope. Insecurity and narrowness are evident in the fact that the three cardinals created by him were Dominicans and in the further fact that he spoke "only to Dominicans and Lombards." When Arnald of Villanova, Boniface VIII's physician and an ardent Spiritual, sent him admonitions and threats in apocalyptic dress, he had this opponent of Thomistic philosophy imprisoned without trial. But Arnald's prophecies were fulfilled. On 7 July 1304, after an eight-months' pontificate, the Pope died at Perugia and was buried there in the church of his order.

In an extremely difficult situation, the cardinals, according to regulations, entered the conclave ten days after the death of the unhappy Benedict XI and in the place where he had died. Contemporaries were, of course, in no position to grasp the full significance of this conclave, which was to be one of the most momentous in Church History, for it was to result in the Avignon residence and eventually in the Great Schism. Hence the history of this conclave has been the object of ever more research. When it opened in the summer of 1304 it comprised nineteen members, eight of whom were religious. In the course of its eleven months four cardinals left because of sickness, but they remained in the city and were kept informed of the proceedings. Fifteen cardinals took part in the actual election. Of the two almost equally strong factions, one demanded the energetic punishment of the criminals of Anagni, not excepting the French King, and the safeguarding of the memory of Boniface VIII, still under attack after his death. The leader of this faction, the worthy Cardinal Dean Matthew Rosso Orsini, was considered its candidate from the start. His nephew, the Cardinal Deacon Napoleone Orsini, leader of the opposing group, regarded respect for French might and hence reconciliation with the Colonna, as necessary. Common to both factions was the desire, it seems, that the tiara should not go again to so strong a personality as Boniface VIII. Since the Colonna were also regarded as friendly to reform, the mendicant friars in the Sacred College were on the side of Napoleone Orsini.

Almost every time that the cardinals met for the business of election, — and such gatherings were not numerous, — there were violent quarrels between the two Orsini. Toward Christmas of 1304 it was plain that no member of the college could muster the required two-thirds of the votes and hence it was necessary to seek candidates from the outside more earnestly than ever, while external influences grew stronger or at least became more evident.

Shortly after the beginning of the conclave, in August 1304, the cardinals had sent the Patriarch of Jerusalem to King Charles II of Naples to ask him to come, for he was regarded as *advocatus ecclesiae* and a neutral mediator. When, toward the end of February 1305, he finally arrived, he was enlisted in the French ranks. But he was admitted to the conclave only after a prolonged delay. After a stay of three days with the cardinals and many conversations he was evidently able to accomplish nothing, for the faction of the cardinals favorable to Boniface VIII now regarded him as too biased. At this time there also appeared a French embassy, which, according to its official declarations, was supposed to conduct discussions between the Gaetani and the Colonna for reconciliation and settlement of their differences. It lingered in Perugia for several months, and the city officials could not but be concerned with its suspicious behavior.

In the first weeks of the conclave the name of the Archbishop of Bordeaux, Bertrand de Got, had been brought up by someone of the "Bonifacian" party. He was regarded as one to whom the memory of Boniface VIII was sacred and who would not go too far in appeasing the French King. Napoleone Orsini had not forgotten this name; on the contrary, in the utmost secrecy he had got in touch with him, probably through the French embassy that was staying in Perugia. Apparently his inquiries turned out favorably, and the Bonifacians were tricked in a subtly devised scheme after the aged Matthew Rosso had had to leave the conclave because of sickness. By exactly a two-thirds majority Bertrand de Got was elected on the Vigil of Pentecost, 5 June 1305, in spite of the emphatic protest of the remaining five Bonifacians, who then accepted the result.

Following this curious conclave of eleven months, who was the newly elected Pope on whom the direction of the Church was laid in so uneasy a time? Bertrand de Got was from Gascony in southwestern France. Bertrand himself had become Bishop of Comminges in 1295 and Archbishop of Bordeaux in 1299; since 1303 his city had again come under English rule. He could be regarded as an adherent of Boniface VIII. But Napoleone Orsini knew very well that, in the person of this man, he had provided the French King with a compliant Pope.

The newly elected Pope accepted the notification made to him at the end of June, styled himself Clement V, and prepared for the journey to Rome *via* Provence. But then he ordered six cardinals to attend his coronation at Lyons on All Saints. During the solemn coronation procession on 14 November a wall collapsed, killing several persons of high rank; the Pope fell from his horse, and the most expensive jewel in the tiara was lost. People read these happenings as an evil omen.

Now was the time to set out for Italy. It is not to be doubted that at the beginning of his pontificate and even later Clement did intend to go to Rome. In any case he never considered transferring the seat of the Curia from Rome. His inability to make up his mind during the nine years of his reign was due to his weakness and the ever increasing pressure of the French King. His first creation of cardinals, in December 1305, makes this clear enough: nine, including four nephews, were French and one was English. Thus the Sacred College, long overwhelmingly Italian in composition, had changed its appearance. It abandoned the Roman tradition for the narrowness of a region hitherto hardly noticed. And the Pope was even more confined to his homeland.

After his coronation he stayed for quite a long time in his native plain, in Poitiers alone for sixteen months. It was not until 1309 that he went to Avignon, because of its proximity to Vienne, where the Council was soon to meet. Still, Avignon was not his permanent residence. From 1309 till his death he spent most of his time outside the city on the Rhone. French scholars have rightly referred to the absence of a *stabilitas loci* in the thirteenth-century Popes. If he was no Roman Pope, neither was he an Avignon Pope. A sick man, always dependent on place and season, always in search of the spot most advantageous to his health, for weeks at a time he granted no audiences and only the Cardinal-nephews could speak with him. His army of relatives brazenly exploited their kind uncle. The riddle of his personality lies in its hypochondriac nature. Though intelligent to the point of craftiness and at times even obstinate, he was basically a good-natured and vacillating man. This weak personality was forced to deal with men such as Philip the Fair and his councillors. In his relations with France the Pope's dependence was especially clear in two matters: the process against the dead Boniface VIII and that against the Templars.

The Process against the Memory of Boniface VIII

The process instituted by the French king and the crown jurists against Boniface VIII was intimately connected with the very obvious collision of the two powers in the outrage of Anagni. Nogaret, excommunicated by Benedict XI, was especially interested in it and had to be, for his fate — condemnation or rehabilitation — depended on the settlement with the deceased Boniface. Since, according to the general opinion, only a council could judge the Pope, efforts to hold one had been made ever since Anagni. But outside France voices were raised against a defamation of the memory of the great Gaetani Pope. As early as the coronation in Lyons a council and proceedings against Boniface were discussed, and again during the brief meeting of Clement and Philip at Poitiers in April 1307. Several extant memoranda make clear how painstakingly the matter was prepared. For example, it was to be emphatically demanded of the Pope that all measures of Boniface VIII against France and against his assailants at Anagni be annulled, that full compensation be made to the Colonna that the corpse of the Pope be disintered, and that the sentences issued by Benedict XI be recalled. Precise directions were even given for the formulating of the bull to be issued by the Pope. If these demands were met, then the case could rest for some time. At the Curia the demands caused consternation.

In the long interview between King and Pope, again at Poitiers a year later, the topic of discussion was chiefly the Order of the Templars. As an introduction to the conversations the King had his entire program submitted: permanent settling of the Curia in France, condemnation of the Templars who had been cross-examined in France, holding of the projected general council in France, canonization of Celestine V, condemnation of Boniface VIII, burning of his remains, and absolution of Nogaret. The most dangerous accusation, that of heresy, revealed the political intent of the process: to render the weak Pope pliable for other purposes. It was probably the influential Enguerran de Marigny who proposed the discontinuance of the trial, once the Pope, in the Bull "Rex Gloriae" of 27 April 1311, had acknowledged the King's praiseworthy zeal in his proceedings against Boniface and had absolved Nogaret *ad cautelam.* The cancellation in the official register of the bulls issued by Boniface VIII against France was a serious humiliation.

Ruin of the Templars: The Council of Vienne

The downfall of the Order of Knights Templars was one of the most dramatic happenings in the Church History of the early fourteenth century. To contemporaries the loss of Acre, the last Latin foothold in the Holy Land, in 1291, did not imply the end of the crusades. The idea above all persisted, even though in actual fact it served only as an excuse for prescribing tithes in most states. Even before the pontificate of Clement V the French King had been concerned with the Templars. He had planned the merging of all the military religious orders, with himself as grand master, and in Lyons, at the time of the Pope's coronation, he had brought forward his complaints. Complaints were also expressed by others.

The real motive for the prosecution and destruction of the Templars eludes us to a great extent. Certainly the independence of the military orders and their great wealth in landed property and money were irksome to the growing power of the so-called national states. No doubt they were defamed to some degree. Evil rumors were nourished by Esquiu de Floyran, the well-known betrayer of the order, who first denounced it to the King of Aragón and then, with more success, to Philip IV of France, and by the spies introduced into the order by Nogaret. Damaging reports about the order were also carried to the Pope, who became quite worried. But there was general consternation when, early on 13 October 1307, all French Templars were arrested at the King's order and then subjected to strict interrogations by royal officials, who made abundant use of torture. In this way were extorted confessions, the repudiation of which could lead to the pyre, in accord with the procedure of the Inquisition. Somewhat later, inquisitors continued the investigation, while accepting for the most part the numerous confessions already obtained.

What did the tortured Templars admit? Rejection of and spitting on the cross, indecent kissing and exhortations to commit sodomy, and even the adoration of an idol in the ceremony of admission to the order. Matters were further complicated at the end of the month by the confession of the grand master, James de Molay, and his circular to the imprisoned knights, who were also asked to confess. These avowals were handed to the Pope. Impressed by them, he ordered the arrest of the Templars in all countries. In so acting he had no doubt kept in mind that it belonged to the Church and its head to pass judgment on an exempt order of such importance and under so serious an accusation and to control the disposal of its property. But when he had been apprised of the nature of the proceedings and of the repudiation of many of the confessions, he suspended the delegated authority of the bishops and inquisitors in February 1308. Nevertheless, the imprisoned Templars remained under the custody of the King and his officials.

It was necessary to start again in order to achieve the goal: the extermination of the order. The celebrated meeting at Poitiers in the summer of 1308 followed upon accusations against the Pope as an abettor of heresy, notably at the Estates General of Tours. Accompanied by the delegates of the estates, the King arrived in Poitiers on 26 May and remained there until 20 July. In solemn consistories the Pope was shockingly attacked in speeches outlined by Nogaret and was overwhelmed by threats. And carefully selected Templars repeated their previous confessions in the presence of Pope and Curia. On the other hand, the King did not allow the grand master and the chief officials of the order to come to Poitiers; they were questioned in the vicinity by accommodating cardinals, with, of course, the expected result.

At Poitiers the Pope's will to resist was completely broken. He had to agree to hold a council in France, to open the process against the memory of Boniface VIII, and to lift the suspension of the authority of bishops and inquisitors in regard to the Templars. It seems pretty certain that he gradually came to doubt the order's innocence. And so he cited the Templars before the Council, which was to meet at Vienne on 1 October 1310, and appointed two investigating committees. One of these, a papal commission to deal with the entire order, was to operate in larger areas; the King nominated its members for the investigations, not in France alone, but also abroad. These commissions were to concern themselves with the guilt of the order as such and with its highest ranking dignitaries. The Templars were to be interrogated as individuals in every diocese on more than a hundred questions by means of the episcopal commissions, and the material thus amassed was to be laid before the provincial council. The King also had an influential voice in the composition of the local commissions. Many fragments survive of the activity of these two committees. They give a manifold picture of the proceedings, in which as far as France was concerned the goal was clear: to extort confessions and prevent the repudiation of previous avowals by threat of the stake for the relapsed. When, especially outside France, confessions were slow in coming, the Pope ordered the universal application of torture. Just the same, in many places there were heroic scenes, when whole groups of imprisoned Templars publicly declared their innocence and that of the order. Since material was arriving only slowly, the opening of the Council was postponed a year, till 1 October 1311, in order meanwhile to be able to prepare from the urgently requested records summaries for its deliberations.

Outside the Kingdom of Philip the Fair we are especially well informed about the proceedings against the Templars in Aragón. King James II eagerly seized the opportunity to take possession of the order's many strong castles, but in an opaque and not entirely unobjectionable manner. At the news of the start of the prosecution, the Aragonese Templars put their castles in a state of defense, and their resistance was broken only after a long siege and starvation. Occasionally torture was resorted to here also, but recent evidence from Barcelona shows that, despite repeated torture, confessions could not be extracted. In the other countries of Europe, such as Italy, Germany, and England, and especially at its headquarters on Cyprus, the order's innocence was unquestioned, despite the use of torture. Because of his proceedings against the few Templars in his territory the Archbishop of Magdeburg incurred the indignation of the other German bishops. Thus, nothing had been definitively decided when the Council convened at Vienne on 16 October 1311.

The Council had been summoned chiefly because of the affair of the Templars; other tasks mentioned in the bull of convocation — crusade and reform — were only platitudes. The summons was formally directed to all possessed of jurisdiction in the Church, but only those bishops were supposed to come who were specified by name. Of importance is the summoning of all archbishops, usually with one or two of their suffragans, who should then represent the Universal Church — an idea to be met again at the period of the reform councils. For the strengthening of the Pope's stand it must have been of importance that at least those bishops who were personally invited should actually come. But outside France there was little desire to cooperate in such an affair.

At the opening session on 16 October, Clement referred to the settlement of the question of the Templars as the chief task. At the Pope's suggestion the Council selected from among its members a large committee, to which the records and summaries were submitted for examination. A smaller working committee saw to the necessary preliminaries. In addition, a committee of cardinals seems to have concerned itself with the special problems of the Templars, and there was frequent discussion of the subject in consistories. The appearance of several Templars before the full committee brought up the question of the order's defense. An oral and written questioning of the members of the committee by the Pope showed that at least four-fifths were in favor of granting the order the possibility of defending itself, to the great chagrin of the Pope and the anxiety of the Council Fathers on account of the King's "intense anger." For Clement, out of regard for the King, had by now apparently decided to dissolve the order in any case. While the Council, awaiting the further development of the case of the Templars, was preoccupied with plans for a crusade and was granting extensive tithing authority to the French King in anticipation of it, secret negotiations were in progress between the Curia and the *conseil;* they represent the climax of the "conciliar activity." The French envoys, headed by Enguerran de Marigny, contrived, presumably by threatening to renew the process against Boniface VIII, to extract from the Pope the suppression of the order by an administrative action, a result probably gratifying to both parties, in view of the mood of the Council. Immediately following, there occurred at Lyons a meeting of the Estates General — the customary means with the customary result. Accompanied by the estates and by his own large retinue, the King then arrived at Vienne on 20 March. Two days later the large committee met — and by a large majority accepted the Pope's proposal that the order should be dissolved by an apostolic decree. Finally, on 3 April, in the Council's second public session, the suppression was announced by the Pope.

Then began the struggle for the Templars' property. Most prelates wanted it to be transferred to a new military order, yet to be founded. But the Pope and the French government, influenced by Marigny, the official expert in this matter, were for assigning it to the Hospitallers. From the Aragonese diplomatic dispatches we are well informed about the discussions concerning the Templars' fortresses. On 2 May, shortly before the close of the Council, the transfer of the Templars' property to the Hospitallers, except in Castile, Aragón, Portugal, and Mallorca, was published.

Several dogmatic discussions were occasioned by the continued discord between the two Franciscan factions. They centered on the person and teaching of Peter John Olivi, whom the so-called Conventuals had long persecuted and whose condemnation they aspired to extort from the Council. It seems that an effort was made to dispose of the difficulties by a suitable compromise. The Constitution "Fidei catholicae fundamento," read in the closing session on 6 May, proclaimed:

> The side of Christ was not opened until after the Lord's death. The substance of the rational human soul is, of itself, really the form of the human body. Children and adults obtain in baptism sanctifying grace and the virtues in the same manner.

Since Olivi was not named in the decree, violent quarrels would later arise in regard to the import of these words. But the difficulties could not be eliminated because of the unfavorable state of the transmission of the sources. Furthermore, the quarrels in the Franciscan family over the meaning of *usus pauper* occupied much space. The controversy ended with the publication of the Apostolic Constitution "Exivi de Paradiso," also in the closing session of the Council. It prudently followed the middle path and gave a detailed explanation of the rule, without touching the dogmatic side of the controversy.

Opinions vary as to whether the Council of Vienne can be termed a "reform council" in the same way as others of the late Middle Ages. The Council does not seem to have been summoned for the sake of reform, but from the start the Pope had asked for testimonials on the subject. Since the Council ended right after the settlement of the affair of the Templars, the consultations on reform had to be broken off abruptly. Only a few decrees were ready. These were read on 6 May in the third and final session. A subsequent reading and putting into force at a later time were announced for all reform decisions. A reading actually did take place at a public consistory in the Château Monteux four weeks before the Pope's death. Thereafter, the decrees, partially revised after the Council, formed part of the *Corpus Iuris Canonici* as the "Clementines." Prominent in the reform material are several testimonials of general importance. Of significance for the missionary work of the late Middle Ages were the decisions issued, at the urging of Raymond Lull, in regard to establishing schools of languages.

In accord with the instructions of the Council, the property of the Templars should have been turned over to the Hospitallers, but the execution of this regulation proceeded very slowly and was dragged out for decades. In France the greatest part of it apparently landed in the King's hands, since he claimed an adequate compensation for having brought the case to a conclusion.

Italy and the Papal State

In an effort to justify the stay of Clement V and his successors at Avignon the political situation in Italy and in the Papal State has been depicted in the blackest colors. But it was scarcely worse than it had been in the decades following the downfall of the Hohenstaufen. The House of Anjou was in firm control of the south, except for Sicily, where under Frederick II, of the House of Aragón, a new type of government was developing. And under Robert of Naples the Angevin influence extended far beyond the Papal State into Central and Upper Italy. In addition to Florence, Milan especially had become a power center of great attraction with an incessant change of conditions and relationships virtually impossible to estimate. This is especially true of the internal life of the numerous cities, of the rapid changes of government and the consequent difficult problem of the exiled. The strongest external influences came from France, but on the other hand the seizure of Corsica and Sardinia stands out in the execution of the investiture of James II of Aragón, arranged by Boniface VIII as far back as 1297.

For the new Pope the situation in the Papal State was, of course, of special importance. For a long time it had not been a real state at all, but a conglomeration of many lordships. There were striking differences between the baronial feudal *Patrimonium*, including Rome, and the Marches of Ancona and Romagna, with their new *signorie.* Boniface VIII made allowances for this state of affairs in a series of excellent reforms, which, however, were cancelled in the brief reign of his successor. The sequel was revolts lasting for years, and Clement V had to try to crush them. The pacification of the northern parts of the Papal State was one of his principal tasks, and he devoted himself to it with energy and some success. That he first inclined to the Ghibellines, only to rely later almost exclusively on the Guelfs, is a theory that goes too far in simplifying the tides of history. Very damaging to an orderly administration was his unrestrained nepotism in filling the important and lucrative rectorships in the provinces. In the war with Venice over Ferrara, which had long been ruled by the House of Este and which the Pope at a favorable opportunity claimed for the Papal State by virtue of the alleged Donation of Constantine, Clement displayed a really inhuman harshness. He succeeded in acquiring the city and the territory of Ferrara and in humiliating proud Venice, but his achievement was of brief duration.

Clement V and the Empire

After the new Pope had called upon the German King to go on crusade, a solemn embassy was sent to Lyons by Albert I to request his imperial coronation and to ask that the tithes collected in Germany not be spent elsewhere (that is, not in France) and that persons suspected by the King be excluded in the filling of German sees. Like Boniface VIII, Clement could not but see in the Empire and in the German King a support against the overmighty influence of France. But this was possible only so long as France itself did not assume the *Imperium* — an idea toyed with by Philip and his advisers. The question became pressing when in 1308 Albert was assassinated. Now the pressure on the Pope increased greatly, especially during the discussions at Poitiers in the summer of 1308, and it seems that only by some stratagem did he evade an effective direct recommendation of Charles of Valois.

The new King Henry VII, of the House of Luxembourg, brother of Archbishop Baldwin of Trier, also came from the French sphere of influence, but, with all his deference to France, he always honorably defended the interests of the Empire. He was able to obtain recognition in the manner of the Habsburg submission of the *Imperium* to the Roman Church. The Pope intended to officiate personally at the imperial coronation, perhaps in 1312, but only after the settling of outstanding ecclesiastical matters, such as the Council of Vienne. However, the Emperor-elect's journey to Rome was decided in the summer of 1309 and began in the autumn of the following year. At first joyfully received in Italy, the German King quickly came of necessity into conflict with the interests of Anjou and hence of France, a situation that could lead to trying developments, especially if the new Emperor should lay claim to the customary imperial rights in Italy. The coronation was performed by three cardinals in the Lateran on 29 June. Meanwhile, the Pope had succumbed to French pressure also in this area. When after his coronation the Emperor moved against Robert of Naples and instituted proceedings against him, the Pope openly espoused the cause of the Guelfs. Once again a great controversy of theory concerning the power of the Emperor and the imperial institution itself began to keep public opinion busy. Because of his depth of thought, Dante deserves, unchallenged, the first place in these considerations. Having rapturously hailed the King on his journey to the "garden of the Empire," he discussed in the three books *De Monarchia,* which were probably composed at this time, the theological necessity of the *Imperium* and the legitimacy of Rome's claims to the imperial office and then demonstrated the direct dependence of the *Imperium* on God, without any mediation of the Pope. The aim of his great work was to prove the Emperor's independence in the political field. On the other hand, in the Neapolitan opinions the *Imperium,* as *de facto* German, was attacked and repudiated as an institution.

After the early death of the Emperor at Buonconvento near Siena on 24 August 1313, Clement made his position clear in the famous bull "Pastoralis Cura," written between the fall of 1313 and the spring of 1314, probably with the assistance of Robert of Naples. He carried further the theocracy of Boniface VIII by declaring null the imperial sentence against Robert and claiming for himself the right to name imperial vicars during the vacancy of the Empire. Significant in this decretal is the limitation of the *Imperium* in extent and hence the denial of its universality. Then in 1314 he named Robert as imperial vicar for all of Italy. The unlucky Pope bequeathed an evil legacy to his successor: Rome abandoned, the government of the Church shamefully dependent on France, a College of Cardinals consisting mostly of Frenchmen, and a Curia bloated and plundered by narrow nepotism.

CHAPTER 38

From John XXII to Clement VI

John XXII (1316–34)

The difficult situation of the cardinals at Carpentras was due to the factions within the college — ten or eleven Gascons, six other French or Provençaux, and seven Italians. The creations of Clement V had contributed not only an excessive growth of French influence in general, but so strong a group of relatives and tightly knit countrymen as had never existed previously.

On 7 August 1316 accord was reached on the Cardinal Bishop of Ostia, James Duèse of Cahors, seventy-two years old and seemingly in poor health. Of vast experience in all questions of politics and administration, he found the papal Curia in utter chaos, as a result of the weak, not to mention confused, government of his predecessor and of the two-years' vacancy. His fear of assassination seems to imply a strong opposition to his election. His coronation, performed at Lyons on 5 September, was more solemn than was customary and was attended by the French King. The new Pope arrived in Avignon in October.

With good reason qualified judges have termed this period the age of the avowedly political papacy, adding that little time for things purely religious was left to the Popes. With the election of John XXII the choice was made for the priority of politics over every other point of view. And on that, as would become apparent, depended the decision whether a return to Rome was seriously considered or whether persons were willing or forced to continue the provisional arrangement bequeathed by Clement V. If Clement was always in need of being pushed, John brought an entirely different sort of personality to the government, which successfully influenced the course of history during his long pontificate. Certainly the new Pope did not from the first exclude a return of the Curia to Rome or Italy; he repeatedly expressed the desire, even before the close of the year in which he had been elected, to go to Rome. But, captivated by the notion of a Guelf-French Italy, he regarded a return as possible only after this aim had been realized. The longer the delay lasted, the more serious became the psychological difficulties confronting a transfer of the Holy See. As would later appear, the situation in Italy could have been corrected only by a Pope functioning in the Papal State.

At the very center of this pontificate, too, loomed always its relationship with France and its Kings and with the Angevin Dynasty that dominated South and Central Italy. The aim was obvious: the continuation of the curial policy, followed from the latter half of the thirteenth century, of consolidating Angevin power throughout Italy and, correspondingly, of routing and eliminating the *Imperium* and Frederick of Sicily. To employ the then current terms for the political factions — Guelfs and Ghibellines — John XXII was certainly the Guelf chief, far more effectively than was Robert of Naples, whose attitude and activity did not always meet with the Pope's approval.

The situation in the Empire was not unfavorable to the new Pope. The premature death of Henry VII at Buonconvento was followed by a double election, with Louis the Bavarian and Frederick of Habsburg claiming the throne. Both applied to the Pope, who treated both as Kings-elect and claimed the right to give the decision. His first measures in Italy were based on his duty to mediate a general peace, but before long the Pope referred in a constitution to the claim made by his predecessor to act as imperial vicar and forbade the vicars appointed by the late Henry VII to exercise their functions. He then made Robert of Naples Senator of Rome and Imperial Vicar of all Italy.

Matters did not remain in the realm of theory. There now began strong measures against all who were not in agreement with the papal policy, in the form of canonical Inquisition processes with various degrees of penalties, including the branding of persons as heretics and the laying of interdict on cities and territories. A relative of the Pope, Cardinal Bertrand du Poujet, appointed legate for Lombardy in 1319, entered upon his assignment in the summer of the next year. Until his unhappy departure in 1334, he had as his task to topple the tyrants, a term used by the Pope to denote all non-Guelfs. The wars now erupting dragged themselves out for years, with rapidly changing political groupings but without any real decision. Of particular importance were the interventions of French troops in North Italy. Though the French government regarded a change in the political views of the Visconti as possible and worth seeking, the Pope inexorably demanded the forcible overthrow of their authority in Milan and Lombardy. He went so far as to grant the crusade indulgence "contra hereticos et rebelles partium Italiae." All bishops were required to proclaim it and to provide separate collection boxes for this purpose. The cardinals were apparently not consulted about these measures and not all of them approved.

More portentous and decisive for events in Italy till the end of the pontificate was the intervention of Louis the Bavarian after the battle of Mühldorf in 1322, which was supposed to have established him as sole King. But the Pope in no way changed his earlier alleged neutrality; so far as he was concerned, Louis was still only King-elect. Since the King, now triumphant in Germany, laid claim to the customary royal rights, which also covered Italy in varying degrees, there once more broke out a bitter war between *Imperium* and *Sacerdotium,* but now the *Sacerdotium* no longer in Rome, was in the immediate vicinity of France and strongly dependent on it. Approached for help by the Ghibellines, King Louis in the spring of 1323 dispatched a delegation to Italy. Having first bound several wavering Ghibelline leaders by oath, it contributed decisively to the relief of Milan, besieged by the legate's army. Thereby were ruined the Pope's prospects for an imminent victory over the Visconti. Hence his violent wrath and his proceedings against Louis from the autumn of 1323, despite the strong opposition of some of the cardinals, are understandable.

Only after long hesitation did Louis decide to resist. First at Nürnberg in December 1323, and then, following his excommunication in March 1324, at Sachsenhausen near Frankfurt in May, in the Chapel of the Teutonic Knights, Louis lodged an appeal against the Pope's rebukes and sentences. He first protested against the reproach of illegally bearing the royal title and exercising the royal rights and then against the charge of patronizing heretics, and concluded with the request for the convoking of a general council. More calculated for a public reaction against the adroitly publicized papal proceedings was the so-called Declaration of Sachsenhausen, which charged the Pope with a prejudiced recourse to ecclesiastical censures for the struggle against his political opponents and in particular branded as clear heresy John's stand in regard to the Spirituals' ideal of poverty. Here were the accusations of heresy, familiar since the days of Philip the Fair, for which even a Pope could be prosecuted by the whole Church at a council.

The conflict became more acute when Louis, invited by Ghibelline circles, began in 1327 to intervene personally in Italy. In many respects his journey to Rome differed from previous journeys of German kings and emperors. He did indeed go to Rome but found there no ecclesiastical dignitaries who would officiate at his coronation. Appealing to the imperial idea of antiquity, old Sciarra Colonna conferred the crown on him in the Lateran.

But the last years of John XXII saw new complications. The Pope's harsh stand in the controversy over poverty not only exasperated the Spirituals and made him implacable enemies but likewise incensed wide circles of ecclesiastics and lay persons against him, notably King Robert of Naples and Queen Sancia. Grave dissensions ruined hitherto intimate relations, especially when differing political views arose in regard to domination in North Italy. In addition, the Pope became embroiled with a part of the Sacred College, which, led by Napoleone Orsini, tried earnestly to have a general council put him on trial and got into contact with the Emperor Louis and the German bishops. Toward the close of his pontificate the

Pope even gave scandal in the purely dogmatic field by defending in his preaching a quite unusual view of the beatific vision but one not unknown to early Christian thinking: that the souls of the just do not enjoy the full vision of God immediately after death but only after the general judgment. The ensuing controversy affected a large audience, and the greater number of theologians opposed John. These problems were discussed in many meetings and extensive disputations, and a series of expert opinions were handed down. In Paris the government unequivocally opposed the Pope and threatened to prosecute him for heresy. On the eve of his death he is said to have abandoned his peculiar opinion.

It has long been known that the Pope liked to preach and often did so in the presence of cardinals, bishops, and curial prelates, using this opportunity to make known his theological views and positions, which were further publicized by official transcripts. It has recently been shown that he carefully studied collections of sermons and annotated them for his own use. And we know of more than thirty of his sermons, some *verbatim,* others in outline. As regards content, they deal mostly with the Blessed Virgin, including unambiguous remarks against the Immaculate Conception, and with political views, as is to be expected from the greatest politician in Avignon. Many extant codices of his personal library and of the papal library prove him to have been an attentive reader, as the marginal notes on requested expert opinions indicate. They also reveal a thorough knowledge of the theology of Thomas Aquinas, in preparation for his canonization. On the whole, the Pope favored the collecting of material and possessed many such *tabulae.* Probably most important in his eyes were legal questions, and a group of these in his own hand has survived. While in general the only fourteenth-century papal autographs that we have are the notes of approval on the few extant original petitions, the scarcely legible hand of John XXII has been preserved in many places, for example, in his outlines for political writings of great importance. They show the Pope at work, the repeated efforts of the aged and trembling hand for a new wording; he even took part personally in the composing of weighty political *cedulae,* using a cipher.

If any Pope deserves the label of politician, it is John XXII. In the years when his own views were being formed and were acquiring their constituents, he was at the Angevin court in Naples with the there dominant Guelf doctrine. Thus he established the Angevin political style even for his successors and thereby caused untold harm. For achieving his ends he ruthlessly made use of all the means at his disposal as Pope. He stubbornly continued along the road taken by Innocent IV and Boniface VIII in the high-handed setting up of new rights and through his decretals became the prototype of the brutally political Pope. The rights claimed by the Curia from the thirteenth century in the matter of matrimonial dispensations were exploited by John XXII in a completely biased manner for his political goals, the advice of the cardinals being sought only to cover up a refusal. The imposition of ecclesiastical censures on purely political grounds and the arbitrary granting or refusing of dispensations were garnished as *necessitas et utilitas ecclesiae* or *utilitas publica,* in an arrogant identification of his politics with the Church, of the hierarchy with religion. He was irresponsible in dealing with benefices and with the Church's financial system for the completion of the administrative primacy will be examined later. His pontificate was the climax of the hierocratic system.

Benedict XII (1334–42)

The conclave, meeting in the episcopal palace at Avignon at the appointed time after the death of John XXII, faced not only personal but also great material decisions. On it depended a return to Rome or a staying on for the time being at Avignon. The quickly accomplished election of the "White Cardinal" on 20 December 1334 is said to have caused surprise. Perhaps, following the anxiety caused by the *dilettante* theologian, a real specialist was desired, and such was James Fournier, who became Benedict XII. As a youth he had entered the Cistercian Order, in which his uncle was an abbot, and in 1311 he became his successor at Fontfroide. In 1317 he was Bishop of Pamiers, in 1326 of Mirepoix, and in 1327 a Cardinal. In Paris he had engaged in profound studies and had earned the degree of master in theology. As Bishop and even as Cardinal he paid special attention to the fight against heresy. Significant also was his activity as a theological expert. Our present knowledge of his views in the process against the *postille* on the Apocalypse of Peter John Olivi, against William of Ockham and Master Eckhart, has been extended by new discoveries. He took a stand early in the dispute over the beatific vision. John XXII entrusted him with a study of the question, the result of which is found in a large unprinted work. He presided at the trial of the Dominican Thomas Waleys. This thorough familiarity with problems facilitated for him as Pope the settling and provisional ending of the discussions in the usual manner.

Difficult to assess is his position in regard to the return of the Curia to Rome, in particular whether he was really in earnest when he held out to the envoys of the Roman people the prospect of a speedy return and yet in the first months of his pontificate undertook the building of the great palace at Avignon. Thereby an important decision had in effect been made and no more thought was given to a departure for Italy. Rather detailed reports give information about the exertions for order in the Papal State. Archbishop Bertrand of Embrun, sent to Central Italy by John XXII, continued his activity under Benedict until 1337. He was followed by John de Amelio as *reformator generalis,* who is known chiefly for his having transported the papal archives to Avignon. Repeated peace edicts endeavored to check the quarrels in Rome between Colonna and Orsini over the Tiber bridges and fortresses in the city.

Benedict too had to travel the way of dependence on France, marked out by John XXII. The French Church was again and again seriously burdened for the political needs of the government, a situation that repeatedly gained for the Curia the reproach of partiality as the war against England got under way. Furthermore, Avignon's intelligence service was at the disposal of the French King. In an effort to mediate peace the Pope sent two cardinals to England, but they obtained only transitory results. To the people of northern France, severely tried by the war of devastation in 1339–40, the Pope sent generous financial help. Throughout his pontificate Benedict was unable to free himself from the strong bonds linking him to French policy.

Peaceable remarks at the beginning of his reign awakened the hope of a settlement of the strife with the *Imperium.* In any event, as early as the spring of 1335 the Emperor got into contact with the Curia in order to ascertain the conditions for a peaceable solution of the affair. No agreement was reached, for it was not in accord with the political line of Philip VI, who was kept abreast of the complicated discussions by the Pope in all details. On the whole, Benedict was even more subservient to French policy than his predecessor had been. And so there had to be a new break.

But the attitude in Germany was now quite different from what it had been under Benedict's predecessor. Many Imperial Estates — Electors, nobility, the higher clergy, and especially the cities — were alienated by this policy of the Curia. The desertion of the papally provided Archbishop of Mainz, Henry von Virneburg, was of great advantage to the Emperor's cause. At the end of March 1338 a synod of the province of Mainz at Speyer rallied many bishops around the Emperor and interceded in his behalf with the Curia, only to receive the reply that the Pope was unwilling to throw his cardinals to bears and lions. Important rallies rapidly followed one another this same year. In May at the first Diet of Frankfurt was published the celebrated manifesto "Fidem Catholicam," produced with the vigorous co-operation of the Franciscan court theologians. It solemnly proclaimed that the imperial authority derives directly from God and not from the Pope, and that the Emperor-elect, even without having been crowned, can rule the Empire. Accordingly, John XXII's institutive proceedings were unjust and must not be obeyed. The Empire itself took its stand in the declarations made by the Electors around the royal throne in Rhense, where, after uniting in the Electoral Union for the protection of their traditional rights, they made the following proclamation with legal force: the one elected King of the Romans by the Electors, or by a majority of them, needs no nomination, approbation, confirmation, consent, or authorization of the Apostolic See for administering the property and rights of the Empire or for assuming the royal title. A second Diet of Frankfurt in August of the same year produced the imperial law "Licet Iuris," which, expanding the Rhense decrees, conceded also the imperial dignity to the one properly elected, without the need of any approval or confirmation by the Pope. The Franciscans of the "Munich Academy" had shared in the preparation of these momentous proclamations by numerous opinions and day-to-day consultation. There immediately followed, in September, the Diet of Koblenz, where the alliance with King Edward III of England was concluded, despite the opposition of the Curia. Five imperial laws prescribed the implementation of the great decrees of this year.

In the face of this unexpected development in the Empire, the Pope, in the interests of France, sought to resume and drag out the discontinued negotiations and especially to dissuade the English King from the German alliance. Anti-curial feeling in Germany was growing, and the announcement of trials and observance of censures imposed were almost out of the question. In the spring of 1339, again at a Diet of Frankfurt, the Electors, in a new proclamation, went beyond the Rhense formulation and unconditionally acknowledged Louis' imperial dignity. The ecclesiastical anarchy grew worse than before. Differing from the tactically more clever John XXII, Benedict scarcely allowed any suspension of the interdict. And so now, to a far greater degree than before, there was recourse to self-defense, to the very great prejudice of the ecclesiastical authority. The state of affairs is described in chronicles of that age.

Benedict XII is reckoned among the reform Popes, not because of the customary statements on the subject at the outset of his pontificate but because he actually started a comprehensive reform activity. A few days after his coronation he sent back to their benefices all ecclesiastics who could not satisfactorily justify their sojourn at the Curia. In the government of the Curia he took up and extended the principles of his predecessor but differed from him in a strict control of the full authority to issue decrees in order to avoid the many abuses that had crept in. He abolished the unfortunate and odious system of expectatives and the *commenda* for high ecclesiastical dignitaries other than cardinals. Contrary to the prodigality of his predecessor, he was sparing in the granting of dispensations.

The religious orders were the special concern of the Pope, who as a Cardinal had continued to wear his Cistercian habit, and his most important and most thorough reform measures were devoted to them, but not to their great joy. In the bull "Fulgens sicut Stella" he began with his own order, which had already preoccupied John XXII. There was also a bull for the reform of the Benedictines, "Summi Magistri." The Dominicans very skillfully contrived to escape the Pope's zeal for reform. On the other hand, the bull "Redemptor Noster" for the Franciscans, drawn up in an authoritarian tone, produced great alarm, above all because of the unprecedented character of the Pope's stand, which displayed no particular regard for the order's tradition and insufficient insight into its internal difficulties and a situation that had been exacerbated by John XXII's rough dealings with the Spirituals. Prepared by a commission of specialists — including not only cardinals and bishops but expert theologians, — it was felt by many contemporaries to be too monastic because of its regulation of even small details and it was cancelled in part by Clement VI. Many of its prescriptions, changed in their wording, were preserved essentially in the statutes of the order or were of significance for all religious orders, such as the directions in regard to the fostering of studies and the central training of the novices.

Estimates of Benedict XII's personality vary. No one denies that he was inspired by lofty motives. In his first *"sine nomine"* letter Petrarch judges him quite severely, characterizing him as a totally unfit, drowsy, and drunken helmsman of the ship of the Church. He is alluding especially to Benedict's continued stay at Avignon, his momentous erecting of the palace, his dependence on the French government, and his scarcely flexible, often even unwise policy. In regard to theology he was rightly considered scholarly but of inquisitorial harshness. Ockham may be exaggerating when he characterizes him as master over the faith, even against the authority of Scripture. He unflinchingly fostered the growth of papal power in the government of the Church — a spiritual autocrat but a firm preserver of legality.

Clement VI (1342–52)

King Philip VI of France sent his son, the Duke of Normandy, to Avignon for the election of a successor to Benedict XII. A direct influence on the election of Peter Roger cannot be proved, but certainly a candidate unacceptable to France could have been stopped. The election of the Cardinal from the Limousin took place on 7 May 1342, his coronation on 19 May.

At an early age he had become a Benedictine at La Chaise-Dieu, and extended studies at Paris had equipped him with a broad education. Known early for his oratorical gifts, he was soon regarded as one of the best speakers of his time, but this reputation refers to form rather than to content. Many testimonies are extant in regard to his course of studies and his literary activity. Hundreds of "pages in his autograph" fill in details of the picture of Clement VI, something true of hardly any other person of the age.

Even more than his predecessors at Avignon, Clement VI was a French Pope, and, altogether apart from the intensification of the opposition between England and France at the beginning of his pontificate, a return of the papacy to Rome was not to be expected from him. Like his predecessors, he exerted himself, chiefly in the interests of France, for a settlement of the conflict. He was unable to prevent military engagements, but through his legates he played a decisive role in achieving the truce of Malestroit in 1343; the long negotiations were conducted at Avignon. By means of loans, grants of tithes and subsidies, and the making over of crusade contributions, occasionally in very great amounts, he embraced the French cause. The very active relations between Clement and King Philip retained a personal stamp. Most of the harshness in the disputes over the freedom and privileges of the Church and most of the success were on the side of the royal government.

In this state of affairs a reconciliation with Louis the Bavarian was unthinkable, unless he totally renounced his rights as recognized by Electors and Empire. The Pope was deeply interested in the deposition of Louis and the holding of a new election in Germany after there had been a rumor that Louis was planning a new journey to Rome. In 1346 the papal-Luxembourg party contrived to have the young Bohemian King Charles elected by a part of Electoral College. Louis' death in the following year soon brought general recognition of Charles IV. His subservience to the Curia gained him the nickname of the "Priests' King," but not quite fairly. Naturally, at the beginning of the negotiations he abandoned the prevailing attitude in regard to papal claims to approve the election and made very extensive concessions. Then he slowly but consistently took them back by means of a very cunning diplomacy. This development in Germany was made possible by the course of the war with England, which was unfavorable to France, and by events in Italy.

In Italy Clement at first followed the method of negotiations with varying success. When the warlike Archbishop and *Signore* of Milan, John Visconti, invaded Piedmont and was threatening Provence, Clement too passed to the offensive. In the struggle for the possession of Bologna, however, he was the loser in dealing with the more cunning Visconti. In a treaty concluded after stubborn bargaining the Visconti submitted to the Pope but received Bologna from him in fief for twelve years — and was the real winner.

The news of the purchase of Avignon and of the Comtat Venaissin from Queen Joanna I of Naples by Clement in 1348 and the magnificent construction of the *palais des papes* disappointed all Italian hopes of a return of the Curia. The death in 1343 of King Robert of Naples was followed by a seriously troubled state of affairs during the long reign of his granddaughter, Joanna I. Her first husband, Andrew of Hungary, was not acceptable to the Curia, and the papal legate received orders to crown only the Queen. The murder of Andrew was followed by an expedition for revenge led by his brother, King Louis I of Hungary. As a result,

Joanna, who had meanwhile married Louis of Taranto, fled to Avignon. Her return was made possible by a great Italian league in which the Pope took part. Despite great difficulties, the marriage of the King of Castile with the daughter of the Duke of Bourbon, urged by French policy and hence also by the Pope, materialized.

Clement ranks as the most splendid representative of the Avignon regime, if by this expression are understood grand-scale expenditures, a court of princely luxury, and unbridled favoritism of relatives and countrymen. With him begins the age of three Limousin Popes, who gave to the papacy a South French stamp even stronger than had been the case in the first half of the century. Under Clement the Curia was scarcely to be distinguished from a secular court. He delighted to display his sovereign power through a gorgeous retinue, quite in accord with the saying ascribed to him — that his predecessors had not known how to be Popes. For the honor of his name, no petitioner should go away discontented. His pontificate bore a worldly character and even contemporaries saw divine judgment in the Black Death that fell upon all of Europe in 1347 to 1352.

CHAPTER 39

From Innocent VI to Gregory XI

Innocent VI (1352–62)

The conclave following the death of Clement VI, in which twenty-five cardinals took part, lasted only two days. Hence there was no need to have recourse to the mitigation of the strict prescriptions for the conclave, enacted the previous year by the deceased Pope. More important is the information concerning the first known election capitulation, which was intended to assure the growing influence of the College of Cardinals in the government of the Church and was sworn to by all the cardinals, in some cases with reservations. According to it, the Pope could create no more cardinals until their number had dropped to sixteen and there could be no more than twenty of them. The Pope was bound in this matter by the consent of all or at least of two-thirds of the cardinals; such consent was also required for any procedure against individual cardinals and for the alienation of any part of the Papal State. The revenues allotted by Nicholas IV to the College were to be guaranteed. The consent of the cardinals was to be obtained in filling the higher administrative posts, in granting tithes and subsidies to kings and princes, and in demanding tithes for the benefit of the *Camera Apostolica.* The Pope was not to hinder the cardinals' free expression of opinion. As was to be expected, half a year after his election the new Pope declared this capitulation null, as being incompatible with the *plenitudo potestatis.*

The choice of the conclave, Stephen Aubert, from the Limousin, had studied canon law and had become Bishop of Noyon and Clermont. In 1342 his countryman, Clement VI, made him a Cardinal and later Bishop of Ostia and grand penitentiary. Judged by the brilliant show of the previous pontificate, he was considered a "rough Pope," and his health was not too good. If he began at once with reforming the papal court, sent many curialists back to their benefices, reduced the size of his retinue, and intended to be a thrifty steward of ecclesiastical property, still his reform endeavors have often been exaggerated by comparing him with his predecessor. His reforms affected the orders also, especially the mendicants and the Hospitallers. His undertakings in Italy were relatively successful, and they were his real preoccupation.

Since the mid-century the idea of a return to Rome had acquired momentum, stimulated by the deteriorating situation in the Papal State and throughout Italy as well as by the serious threat posed by wandering mercenary bands to the hitherto so peaceful stay in Provence. As a rule it was possible to induce the companies to depart on payment of blackmail or to hire them for the papal armies in Italy. Soon after his election the Pope had decided to send there a vigorous personality, and he did so in selecting the former Archbishop of Toledo, now Cardinal of San Clemente, Gil de Albornoz.

Provided with almost unlimited authority, the Cardinal set out in August 1353. He was to spend thirteen years in Italy, with a brief interruption, and, in spite of the Pope's lack of political judgment and the Curia's failure to supply funds, to become the second founder of the Papal State. He began the work of reconstruction in the *Patrimonium* proper.

Once the *Patrimonium* had been gained, Albornoz devoted himself to the Duchy of Spoleto and then to the Marches of Ancona and Romagna, where success was possible only after years of effort. Through the intrigues of the Visconti the legate even had to withdraw from Italy for a while, but after the renewal of his commission he won back for the Papal State the important city of Bologna. If the papacy could now be restored from Avignon to Rome, this was due to the military and administrative gifts of the Cardinal. The *Constitutiones Aegidianae,* or *Liber constitutionum sanctae matris ecclesiae,* published at the Parliament of Fano in 1357, provided a sure legal basis for administration, while the many fortifications erected at his orders were adequate strongholds for suppressing local risings. The Spanish College that he established at Bologna testifies to his interest in learning. According to all information, however, he never set foot in the Eternal City. But the prematurely aged, sickly, and indecisive Pope could no longer realize his often expressed desire to go to Rome. He died at Avignon on 12 September 1362.

Urban V (1362–70)

The factional division in the Sacred College was apparently so complicated that the candidacy of a cardinal seemed hopeless. And there was talk of seeking to come to an agreement by compromise. William d'Aigrefeuille seems to have directed the attention of the electors to the Abbot of Saint-Victor de Marseille, who was thereupon chosen after a conclave of five days. Since at the moment he was acting as legate in Naples, it was necessary to recall him before obtaining his consent to the election and publishing the result.

William Grimoard, from the vicinity of Avignon, was regarded as a fine canonist. He had been a professor at Montpellier and Avignon and shortly before his election had become Abbot of Saint-Victor. The new Pope retained his monastic habit and even more so his monastic way of life. He understood the importance of studies, which he promoted by founding colleges and burses, while a large number of students were indebted to him, even for information. It should cause no surprise that he took steps against the luxury of the papal court and sent many curialists packing. As a monk and never a cardinal, he found it difficult to maintain a frank relationship with the self-assured College of Cardinals and was often insecure *vis-à-vis* the great lords. This explains his frequently abrupt expressions and measures, for example, the creation of young William d'Aigrefeuille at Marseilles immediately before the departure for Italy. To the remonstrances of several members of the Sacred College he rejoined that he had even more cardinals in his capuche. A man of a deep interior life and somewhat ignorant of the world, he did not always see through the diplomatic game and, curiously enough, fell prey to the allurement of political power.

At the beginning of Urban's reign the situation in Italy was not unfavorable, but only because of Albornoz, whom he confirmed in office. As Abbot of Marseilles and even earlier he had known the state of Italian affairs to some extent from several missions and he had personal experience of the despotic rule of the Visconti. Hence he immediately resumed the proceedings against Bernabò Visconti, uttered all possible condemnatory sentences against him in March 1363, and summoned a crusade against him. It quickly became clear to him that only in Italy could he realize his great plans — elimination of the mercenary companies, crusade, union with the Greek Church, — once Italy had been pacified and all the forces of the peninsula brought together. Thus he made a change of policy, contrary to that followed by the great soldier and politician Albornoz.

The new policy involved secret negotiations with the Visconti behind the back of the Cardinal Legate and the appointment of Cardinal Androin, former Abbot of Cluny, an opponent of Albornoz and friend of the Milanese. The resulting peace with the Visconti burdened the Church with enormous payments to Bernabò for the evacuation of Bologna and was felt even by contemporaries to be pernicious and unworthy. A meeting of Pope and Emperor at Avignon in the spring of 1365 was intended to further the achieving of the goals and, by means of an imperial journey to Rome, to assure the return of the Curia. Urban, however, quickly adopted the plan of going to the Eternal City without the Emperor. Objections to the Pope's intended journey to Italy came from all sides — from France and from the College of Cardinals — but he could not be dissuaded. After changing the date of departure several times he left Avignon on 30 April 1367 and on 4 June landed at Corneto in the Papal State, to be welcomed by the one who had restored his principality. After a brief rest the Pope proceeded to the security of Viterbo in preparation for entering Rome, with a strong military escort, on 16 October.

In Italy the Pope's political aims quickly changed. In an extensive league of the

Curia with the smaller Lombard states the Visconti was defied. The Emperor, the Queen of Naples, and even several cities of Tuscany joined, but not Florence.

The Pope, finally residing in Rome after many decades, devoted special attention to the repair and adornment of the Roman churches, especially the Vatican and Lateran basilicas. There were long discussions of the political situation in North and Central Italy. The Pope's intention of exercising greater influence in Tuscany was only reluctantly encouraged by the Emperor, and it was observed by Florence with much anxiety. In general, in conformity with the Emperor's policy, the delineation of the power system continued as it had been since the middle of the century. For the Pope this was a great disappointment, and gradually he became obsessed with the notion of a return to Provence.

Urban left Italy on 5 September 1370 and on the twenty-seventh of the month reentered Avignon. He was not long to enjoy that city's jubilation, for on 19 December he died. Not until five centuries later was he beatified.

Gregory XI (1370–78)

The conclave, which began on 29 December with seventeen cardinals, ended the following morning with the election of Cardinal Peter Roger, nephew of Clement VI. Gregory XI was crowned on 5 January 1371 and, in contrast to his predecessor, appeared on horseback in a colorful procession in Avignon. Thus the so-called Limousin faction had provided its third Pope. Elected at the age of forty-two, Gregory had been in the Curia for more than twenty years and so had ample opportunity of training and activity in ecclesiastical policies. When only nineteen, he had been made a Cardinal-Deacon by his uncle in 1348, but he continued his studies and acquired a solid and comprehensive education. As Pope he too remained strongly attached to family and homeland. Of the twenty-one cardinals he created, eight were from his own land; there were eight other Frenchmen, two Italians, and one each from Geneva, Castile, and Aragón.

Judgments of his personality and character vary greatly. In poor health and very sensitive, he is said to have been an indecisive brooder, a weak and easily influenced man, who liked especially to seek the solution of difficult problems in mystical enlightenment. All this was certainly present in this rich personality, but there were also other traits, including tenacity and energy and even unrelenting severity, as in his procedures against Milan and Florence, which can hardly be understood from a religious viewpoint.

Gregory was experienced enough to comprehend, from the beginning of his pontificate, the necessity of the papacy's return to Rome. But to the reasons hitherto in favor of Rome was now added the growing insecurity in the Midi because of the Hundred Years' War, and from 1372 official announcements of the impending journey to Rome were multiplied. But first the situation in North Italy had to be clarified. Gregory soon was resolved to make a clean sweep of the Visconti, as the chief enemies of the Papal State. A great league against Milan was formed in August 1371, a new cardinal legate proceeded to Lombardy, and Amadeus VI of Savoy assumed command of the troops, which were to be reinforced by a contingent from France under the Pope's brother, the Viscount of Turenne.

The institution of processes against the Visconti was proclaimed at the beginning of 1373 and then a crusade was preached against them. Considerable sums were demanded of cardinals and curialists, and contributions were imposed on all countries. The journey to Italy now seemed to the Pope necessary for the destruction of the Visconti, and the spring of 1375 was considered. Many cardinals arranged lodging for themselves in Rome, the Pope's *magister hospitii* was sent there, and galleys were requested from Venice and Naples for September. The Pope's tenacity attracted general attention, as when, in the consistory of 7 February 1375, the Duke of Anjou in a powerful speech advanced ten reasons why the Curia should remain at Avignon. The reply, made by Cardinal James Orsini, referred emphatically to the Papal State as the Pope's country and maintained that its confused situation was due to its sovereign's tarrying abroad. Even the pleas of the Pope's closest relatives and of the people of Avignon were ineffectual; but the date of departure was postponed in August until Easter of 1376.

Earlier, in June 1375, the Curia had been obliged to make peace with Milan because of the defection of several of its allies, but presumably the Pope did not regard it as a real peace. No good was to be expected of the league made between Milan and Florence in the summer of the same year. Florence succeeded in gaining many cities of Tuscany and parts of the Papal State and in inciting revolt against papal rule, for the extravagant demands for subsidies had contributed seriously to a lowering of morale. In addition to Viterbo, Perugia, and Città di Castello, many other cities and territories were in open revolt. Nevertheless, the Pope held to his plan and, as he put it, if at least a foot of ground in his state was left, he intended to be in Italy in the spring. Therefore, extensive preparations were made, mercenary captains were hired, long consistories were held, and all-out war against Florence was decided. The preparations included the issuing of a bull on annates, pawning of papal treasures, and extensive striking of coins in Avignon. In the summer the direst threats were directed at Florence: interdict, prohibition of clerics' staying there, suppression of the episcopal see and deprivation of civil rights, confiscation of all property of Florentine citizens in foreign lands, and hence the paralyzing of commerce. Meanwhile, *taxatores domorum* and the papal *capella* set out for Rome. On 13 September he left Avignon forever.

On 2 October 1376 the papal fleet at Marseilles put to sea, but persistent storms forced frequent landings, and it was not until 6 December that Gregory reached the Papal State at Corneto. With thirteen cardinals he made his solemn entry into Rome on 17 January 1377. It was high time. Revolts and general unrest had reached dangerous proportions. Hatred against the foreign governors and their fortresses had broken out with unlooked-for violence, nourished by the probably exaggerated dread of the establishing of an Angevin State in Lombardy and Tuscany. The worst, then, could at least be prevented. Florence, affected less in the spiritual than in the commercial sphere, utilized the mediation of Milan, and the Pope followed suit. A great congress was summoned to Sarzana for February 1378. But before it had completed its work death overtook the Pope on 27 March, and the conclusion of peace with Florence and Milan was reserved for his successor in Rome, Urban VI.

CHAPTER 40

The Curia at Avignon

Avignon, on the banks of the Rhone in Provence, occasioned the expression "Babylonian Exile." For almost seventy years it was the Papal residence, though the seat of the papacy was never transferred there. The term "Babylonian Exile" refers to the desolation of Rome and implies an accusation. In the immediate vicinity of the French Kingdom as it then existed, the city, by its size and favorable location, afforded a respectable site for a court. And, following the purchase of the city and of the surrounding territory by Clement VI in 1348, Avignon was considered a part of the Papal State.

The *palais des papes* was erected over a period of two decades at the mid-century. Begun by Benedict XII soon after his election, at first a gloomy, monastery-like fortress, it was completed by Clement VI as a princely palace. The mighty exterior was designed by French architects; the interior was decorated mostly by Italian artists. The cardinals and the high curial officials and their offices were at first lodged in leased or sequestered houses. But there was soon much constructing of palaces, monasteries, hospitals, hospices, business houses, and the now greatly expanded city was protected and defended by a powerful ring of walls.

The large incomes of the cardinals were used not only for maintaining princely courts but for art and learning and the building and adorning of churches and chapels in Avignon. The account books of the *Camera Apostolica* occasionally provide glimpses of the carefree life and bustle at this ecclesiastical court. If the extent or excess of the princely household depended on the personality of the reigning Pope, in any event there gradually developed an elegant, even magnificent, style, which was at its best in the great Church solemnities, in consistories, and in the reception of numerous kings, princes, and ambassadors. For the city of Avignon the papal stay meant great structural changes, a large increase in population, an extraordinary stimulus to commerce, and a cosmopolitan mode of life.

In it the Papal Curia constituted a special state in stark contrast to the city population, despite common interests and mutual influence. There was a Curia in the sense of a princely court at Rome already in the High Middle Ages; the household of Boniface VIII is known in detail. But now it was further enlarged and, more important, we have exact information about it. At first Italians still predominated in the higher posts and offices, but the middle and lower personnel were at once recruited from countrymen of the reigning Pope. Thus, Clement V enlisted a sort of bodyguard from his immediate homeland. The systematizing mind of John XXII applied itself even to the household and regulated everything more exactly. More than in the case of other princely courts, a change of pontificate involved a change of personnel and practice, even in the operation of the offices.

The management of the Apostolic Palace was the charge of the *Magister hospitii papae. Clerici capelle* and *cantores* took care of the liturgical rites in the papal *capella.* The *capellani commensales,* whose duties were not always strictly defined, were influential persons, who were frequently promoted to episcopal sees. In immediate attendance on the Pope were the *cubicularii,* among whom physicians were specified, and the *Magister sacri palatii,* usually a Dominican. Even in periods of severe financial strain the office of almoner (*panhota*) got large contributions from the papal chest for feeding and clothing many hundreds of poor persons. In addition, there was a lay personnel of probably the same number: porters, soldiers and police, and a sort of Noble Guard. Some 500 persons were employed in the household.

The French orientation is seen clearest in the College of Cardinals. Shortly after his coronation at Lyons, Clement V created ten new cardinals — nine Frenchmen and one Englishman. The ratio of preponderance was thereby decisively shifted to the disadvantage of the Italians and so it remained. Particularly obtrusive in all the Avignon pontificates, except that of Benedict XII, were relatives and countrymen from Gascony, Quercy, and the Limousin. A representation of the Universal Church was out of the question; the influence of the French crown was constant and unabated, and several members of the Sacred College had formerly been in the service of that crown. In the Avignon period the revenues of the College were considerable, especially those accruing from prodigal gifts at papal elections and from numerous benefices, but on the outbreak of the Great Schism they declined.

Participation of the cardinals in the government of the Church was manifested principally in the consistory, in judicial commissions, and in legations. In general the Pope's freedom of action was restricted by the College of Cardinals. The number of cardinals stayed at about twenty.

The term "Avignon Papacy" connotes also the centralized system of Church government, which was decidedly different from the previous regime and created new forms in the ecclesiastical constitution and the papal system of finance and an unqualified Church bureaucracy.

The juridical basis for the *plenitudo administrationis* had been laid in the thirteenth century. The Popes at Avignon accepted it and developed it in masterful fashion in the so-called reservations. Urban V in 1363 reserved to the Holy See the filling of all patriarchal and episcopal sees and of all monasteries of men and women of a specified income level. Thereby was attained in theory the complete bureaucratic supremacy of the Curia.

The implementation of these important constitutions required numerous offices and a powerful civil service. The Apostolic Chancery was responsible for the technical aspect. Its chief, the vice-chancellor, belonged to the College of Cardinals. The regulations and rules of the chancery determined even the details of its routine.

In spite of many losses, the series of registers of the Vatican Archives for the fourteenth century include hundreds of thousands of documents — for example, for John XXII about 65,000 in the local Registers alone, for Clement VI about 90,000, for Innocent VI 30,000, for Urban V 25,000, for Gregory XI 35,000. The enormous quantity of written documents proceeding from the Curia, especially the routine affairs of the Apostolic Chancery, posed serious problems in regard to their dispatch. A great part, possibly half, was taken along by the petitioners themselves; a further considerable percentage by persons traveling from Avignon to the areas in question. Neither sort went at the expense of the Curia. Much was conveyed by means of the world-wide business connections of banking firms which had an establishment in Avignon.

Only in regard to especially important documents, chiefly political and urgent, was recourse had to the Pope's *cursores* or to high ecclesiastics or religious, chiefly Dominicans.

The most important administrative body was the *Camera Apostolica.* It was presided over by the *camerlengo,* usually an archbishop, who in the past had been employed in the Curia and as collector outside. The *camerlengo* and a small staff of cameral clerks and secretaries took care of political correspondence, and the personnel of the papal court took the oath of office in his presence. We know relatively little about the *Camera's* secret policies but a great deal about its administration of finance.

The most important types of income were *servitia,* annates, tithes, subsidies, and *spolia.* Since the High Middle Ages, Pope and cardinals had received an increasing amount of money gifts, which were gradually stabilized and regarded as of obligation. Registers of *servitia* due are extant from 1295. This amounted to one-third of the first year's income and could be required only once in a year.

Annates first made their appearance at the Curia when in 1306 Clement V demanded the first year's income of all benefices, vacant or to be vacated, in England, Scotland, and Ireland, without regard to the type of nomination. He based this on the classical statement: *quia quod postulat inferior, potest etiam superior.*

Compared with the previous century, the proceeds from the still frequently demanded tithes had greatly decreased. The great crusade tithes of the Second Council of Lyons and those of Boniface VIII had still not been entirely paid and settled when the Council of Vienne demanded from all Christendom another crusade tithe for six years.

Originally a spontaneous donation in return for a specific thing, the *subsidium caritativum* was regulated in the fourteenth century in regard to the amount and made obligatory. For the most part it was collected in locally restricted areas, chiefly for the unending wars in Italy.

The direction of the treasury at the Curia was the duty of the *thesaurarius,* whose office was sometimes shared by two men. Working closely with the treasurer were the *depositarii,* the representatives of the banking firms which gave credit and made loans and saw to the transfer of money. In spite of the imposing mass of account books for the fourteenth century, the question rises whether they afford a complete picture of the Curia's conduct of finances and its background. In any case, in addition to the ordinary administration there were secret funds, which were also called the Pope's privy purse.

It has been estimated that John XXII had an average annual income of 230,000 gold florins, Benedict XII 165,000, Clement VI 190,000, Innocent VI 250,000, Urban V 260,000, and Gregory XI 480,000.

Unlike the government of individual states, the Curia had a thoroughly international character with a ceaseless coming and going, to and from all parts of Christendom. Later Avignon became a first-class commercial center as probably the third city in size at that time, with some 30,000 inhabitants, where most of the great commercial houses set up offices. Though the revenues of the Curia were smaller in comparison with those of the Kings of France, England, and Naples, they were nevertheless always imposing sums.

It is difficult to resist the impression that at Avignon the Curia felt free to dispose at its discretion of the money gathered from the whole Christian world. This state of affairs did not escape criticism from those affected. The Council of Vienne summed up much that earlier had been expressed only by complaining voices. Throughout the century, especially during the Great Schism, bishops and abbots and even entire ecclesiastical provinces sought to defend themselves against being rendered impotent by the Curia. Above all the unceasing and inconsiderate demands for money and the defective administration of the systems of benefices and finances gave scandal. It is true that the initiative did not always lie with the Curia, yet it did bear the responsibility when it yielded to the often very importunate and menacing wishes of kings and princes in nominations to offices and in demands for tithes. Every possibility for the obtaining of money was exploited ruthlessly. Irresponsible was the manipulation of ecclesiastical censures when payments promised under oath were not made on time. The infliction of suspension, excommunication, and interdict followed automatically.

The unclerical management of the Avignon government, which was continued and multiplied during the Great Schism in two and then in three obediences, led to a serious decline of confidence in the Curia and in ecclesiastical authority. Thus the bitter reproaches hurled at Popes and cardinals during the Schism and the obstinate struggle for a true reform of the Church at Constance and Basel become intelligible. For, if not directly simoniacal, these money transactions were at least incompatible with the predominantly spiritual character of the papacy and introduced a dangerous secularization of the highest Church posts.

CHAPTER 41

Nominalism: The Universities between Via Antiqua and Via Moderna

The beginning of the fourteenth century marked a turning point in philosophy and theology. In general this can be characterized as the dissolution of the universalism and objectivism which had found their imposing expression in the *summae* of High Scholasticism. The philosophical and theological syntheses were supplanted by the critical investigation of individual problems. If everything had hitherto been referred to the universal in which individual things participated, interest was now concentrated rather on the concrete thing; it is perceptible directly and does not stand in need of the roundabout recourse to the universal. The individual was more strongly stressed, and the perceiving subject became its own object to a much greater extent. Precedence was given to reasoning and, in contradistinction to doctrinal authority and tradition, the right of criticism was claimed more than hitherto. Epistemology and formal logic thus attained to greater importance. In fact, the great achievements of the century lay in the field of logic. Recognition of this fact is not incompatible with the view that this shift from metaphysics to logic implies the dissolution of the Middle Ages.

After Duns Scotus, the critical attitude was especially clear in the Dominican Durandus of Saint-Pourçain (d. 1334) and the Franciscan Peter Aureoli (d. 1322), both of whom turned against the great authorities of their respective orders, Thomas Aquinas (d. 1274) and Duns Scotus (d. 1308). For human authority should be given little weight in comparison with clear rational knowledge. For it no principle of individuation is needed to bring the individual into existence, no species to recognize it. Peter Aureoli distinguished the thing *in rerum natura* and the thing in so far as it is grasped by our intellect (*res apparens in intellectu*). The universal concept is the product of our cognition (conceptualism).

What was, so to speak, in the air and was variously advertising its presence received its definite impetus, and the form that would characterize the future, in William of Ockham. We are accustomed to label the attitude brought about by him as nominalism, but it is much disputed whether Ockham was a nominalist. A crass nominalism, such as Anselm of Canterbury (d. 1109) attributed to Roscelin of Compiègne (ca. 1050–1120), was hardly thinkable in the fourteenth century. The great tradition of the thirteenth century had left an imprint which was too deep and strong to allow it. More important is the fact that, in the term nominalism, the epistemological aspect, that is, the controversy over universals, is too much in the foreground, whereas the mentality characterizing it operated with even more serious consequences in metaphysics, ethics, and sociology, and was even more destructive in theology than in philosophy. To speak simply of Ockhamism is equally not permissible, for a certain nominalist trend was inherent in all theology in the fourteenth and fifteenth centuries and characterized not only Ockham's pupils but also many a theologian actually belonging to the schools of Thomas Aquinas and Duns Scotus. Thus characteristic views of Ockham, such as those of the sovereign omnipotence of God, the acceptance of man, or the act of natural and of supernatural love, were expressed before him and in an even more extreme form by contemporaries.

The nominalism of the fourteenth century is described correctly but not adequately, by designating "as its essence an unrestrained craving for novelty allied to a strong inclination toward a purely skeptical and destructive criticism." (F. Ehrle) This description is too formal and too unsatisfactory in regard to content. For the epistemological starting point of nominalism, which implied a separation of thought and essence, affected all other fields much more directly than at first it seemed to. The often presumptuous speculation with its subtle and hair-splitting questions, which characterized the thinking of the age, was the result of a science which was concerned only with ideas, not with essence. The more the ideas lost ontological significance, the more easily could they be manipulated and the less persons felt the obligation of examining the results of thought in the reality. The separation of thought and essence led in theology to a preference for the investigation of all imaginable possibilities on the basis of the *potentia dei absoluta* and to a neglect of the way of salvation, which was effectively pointed out and binding in the sources of revelation. If the genuine symbolic nature of word and idea was surrendered, soon there was no further place whatsoever for symbols. Thus the approach to a deeper understanding of the Sacraments was barred. In ethics a radical separation of essence and duty and the allied formalism and voluntarism indicated the main feature of nominalism.

William of Ockham represents in its original radicalism that which characterized the two following centuries but which, as they ran their course, was variously covered over or set straight by the traditional theology of the schools. Born in England around 1285, he became a Franciscan and in 1306 was ordained a subdeacon. In regard to his higher studies at Oxford we can determine only that around 1317–18 he prepared an *ordinatio* on the first book of *The Sentences* and in 1318–20 lectured on *The Sentences;* the commentaries on Books II–IV are preserved. As *baccalaurens formatus* he had fulfilled the requirements for *magister regens* but never took the degree and hence found his way into history as *venerabilis inceptor.* His career was interrupted when his philosophical and theological teaching became the subject of a violent controversy at Oxford. John Lutterell, chancellor of the University, sought to end Ockham's teaching by disciplinary measures. Perhaps out of concern for their academic freedom, the professors induced the Bishop to deprive Lutterell of the chancellorship. Then, in an extensive polemical treatise Lutterell in 1323 accused Ockham to the Curia at Avignon of heretical or at least dangerous doctrines. Proceeding from the scriptural text, "see to it that no one deceives you by philosophy and vain deceit" (Col. 2:8), Lutterell charged Ockham with misuse of logic. In so doing he himself employed logic as an instrument of theological proof, aware that this was regarded as a peculiarity of English theologians. His charges in regard to content were especially directed against immoderate speculation *de potentia dei absoluta* in Ockham's teaching on the Eucharist, man's acceptance, and grace.

Pope John XXII summoned the *venerabilis inceptor.* He appeared at Avignon in 1324 and had to defend himself before a commission, which filed two expert opinions against him. Apparently, however, the judges, including so controversial a figure as Durandus, could not agree, and the case was drawn out. By his flight on 26–27 May 1328 to Louis the Bavarian at Pisa, along with Michael of Cesena and Bonagrazia of Bergamo, who were being detained at Avignon because of the poverty controversy, Ockham escaped the court. No condemnation of his philosophical and theological views would be forthcoming, for thereafter the question of poverty and the quarrel between Louis the Bavarian and John XXII claimed the Curia's interest. And Ockham's writings would now be exclusively preoccupied with these matters until his death at Munich in 1349 or 1347. He was never reconciled with the Curia. Thus the philosophical and theological works of the *venerabilis inceptor* all appeared before 1324 or, at the latest, 1328. In addition to the commentary on *The Sentences,* or rather the *Quaestiones on the Sentences of Peter Lombard,* and the *Quotlibeta septem,* there were the *Summa logicae,* the exposition of the logical treatises of Aristotle published in 1496 as the *Expositio aurea,* the writings on physics, and several smaller treatises, including two *De sacramento altaris* or *De corpore Christi.*

According to Ockham we have a direct intuitive knowledge of the particular thing. As soon as we make statements we make use of ideas which our mind forms. No universality in things, no universal nature corresponds to universal concepts. At first Ockham looked upon universal ideas as mere figments of thought (*ficta, figmenta*), but later he identified them with the act of knowing. In the passive intellect the particular thing produces an image similar to itself. The universal is the things imagined and inheres in the soul as its subject. Thus ideas are based on the reality, not of universal substances, but of the particular things. There is no need of a third element, of a means of knowing between subject and intellect and it is precisely in the fact of the passivity of the intellect that the objectivity of knowing is assured.

In his teaching on God Ockham especially stresses God's freedom and omnipotence. He can do whatever does not involve a contradiction. God's will is bound neither externally nor internally. He acts when and as he will. The almighty divine will suffices to explain the *de facto* situation. The good is what God ordains, and even in regard to the order established by him he is entirely free. He could annul the commandments and command theft, unchastity, even hatred of himself.

If God's own action is subject to no necessity, it was the more repugnant to Ockham to assume that God should in any way be bound by man's being and conduct. Even if he strongly emphasized the freedom of man and was confident of man's natural capability, — for example, that man can of himself love God above all things, — in doubt he would always decide in favor of the sovereignty of God. God can save a man in sin and condemn a person in the state of grace. More than once Ockham used the following example for the transition *a contradictorio in contradictorium* by the mere lapse of time: God can decide that all who today are at a specified place will be damned and that all who are there tomorrow will be saved. Now if anyone stays there two days, he who was yesterday rejected is today accepted into favor, without himself or anything in him having been changed (*IV Sent.*, q.4,L ad 2).

But God has bound himself by his dispositions, which he observes and which acquire their necessity for man from God's *fiat*. What God can do in the abstract, he cannot do in consequence of the order decreed by him; what he can do *de potentia sua absoluta,* he cannot do *de potentia sua ordinata.* In the effort to make clear the contingency of the actual order, Ockham found delight in showing the possibilities which exist on the basis on the *potentia absoluta dei* and deducing further possibilities from them. In these daring speculations concerning *potentia dei absoluta,* which often went beyond the limits of what could be tolerated, he developed a theology of the "as if" and lost sight of the way of salvation actually traced out by God. Moreover, no attempt was made to establish this way of salvation nor to inquire reverently into the wisdom of the ways of God. The presentation of sacred history gave way to the discussion of mere possibility, and theology became a practicing ground for logical and dialectical dexterity.

It is in keeping with this attitude that Ockham preferred extreme cases or exceptions and deduced further possibilities. Since God can produce directly whatever he can produce by secondary causes, it can, for example, not be proved that something was produced by a particular secondary cause. Only a *post hoc* but no *propter hoc* can be established. For example, from the fact that, on being brought into contact with fire, something burns, it cannot be proved that fire was the cause of the burning. For God can arrange precisely that, whenever anything is brought into contact with fire, he alone produces the burning, just as he has arranged in regard to the Church that at the uttering of specified words grace is effected in the soul (*II Sent.,* q. 5, R).

Hence one can speak of a causality of the Sacraments only in so far as the sign is a mere condition of the direct action of God. Furthermore, these signs were established quite arbitrarily. God could link the grace of baptism to contact with a piece of wood and determine that confirmation should be conferred with baptismal water (*IV Sent.,* q. 1, G).

The reaching of conclusions by means of exceptions becomes especially clear in Ockham's teaching on the Eucharist, which he restricts to the doctrine of transubstantiation, in fact to the discussion of questions of natural philosophy, such as the relationship of substance and quantity. Ockham would prefer the coexistence of the bread and the body of Christ, or this doctrine in his view opposed neither reason nor Scripture. In fact, he held, it was *rationabilior* and easier to reconcile with the principle of economy, according to which as few miracles as possible were to be posited. For then the greatest difficulty would disappear: the existence of accidents without a supporting substance (*IV Sent.,* q. 6, D). But since the judgment of the Church requires it, Ockham clung to transubstantiation. The accompanying miracle of the continued existence of the accidents after the destruction of the substance became for him the chief proof that corporeal substance is extended in itself and has no need of a really distinct accident of quantity. For if, so he argues, God can permit accidents to exist of themselves, then he can also certainly destroy them and preserve the substance without any local motion of its parts. But then substance would be extended without quantity (*De sacramento altaris,* cap. 25). Furthermore, if God can destroy the accidents of the bread and preserve the body of Christ, the latter must be in the place directly and not by means of the species (*IV Sent.,* q. 4, N, Resp. ad 2 dubium).

Another case of the suspension of the *causa secunda,* namely, that God produces in me the intuitive knowledge of something non-existent, became the point of departure for the proof of the possibility of seeing Christ in the Sacrament in a natural manner (*IV Sent.,* q. 5, D).

For Ockham there was no basic distinction between a natural and a supernatural act; they are "eiusdem rationis" (*I Sent.,* d. 17, q. 1, K). By purely natural power man can love God above all things. In this and in his extravagant speculation to the effect that, in the abstract, habitual grace is not necessary for salvation, Ockham incurs the suspicion of Pelagianism. On the other hand, he claimed to be protected from any Pelagian tenet because, according to him, God is independent of every created thing, is no one's debtor, and nothing in man, neither anything good nor anything evil, and no supernatural form inhering in the soul can compel God to save or to damn anyone (*I Sent.,* d. 17, q. 1, M; q. 2, E; *III Sent.,* q. 5, L; *Quotl.,* VI, q. 1). No act is meritorious because of any quality proper to it, even though it may have been produced by God; it is meritorious only on the basis of divine acceptance. For Ockham grace is not a power which is communicated to man, renews him, and qualifies him for meritorious actions, but God's indulgence, whereby he accepts man or not, as he pleases.

Hence the importance of Ockham and his impact of future generations lie not so much in his particular teaching as in the nature of his theological speculation. The significant and passionate logician failed to place his skill at the service of theology. Instead, theology furnished the occasion for showing off his acrobatics in logic. An inner relationship to the subject was wanting. Theology was no longer the doctrine of salvation, and the theologian could the more easily abandon himself to daring speculations, the less he regarded his salvation as at stake in his theological endeavors.

In Ockham's own lifetime a school of thought was attributed to him which quickly captivated the universities, Paris at their head; but this school of thought was likewise quite early violently attacked as an innovation. Its adherents were called *nominales* or *moderni* in contradistinction to the *reales,* and the method they represented was called *via moderna.* Immediate disciples of Ockham were Adam Wodham (d. 1358) and John Buridan (d. after 1358). The latter maintained a moderate attitude and, rector of the University of Paris, even signed a condemnation "of the new teachings of certain Ockhamists" in 1340. He was especially preoccupied with the Ockhamist logic and took up the new efforts for a natural science. The Dominican Robert Holkot (d. 1349), on the other hand, became prominent under the spell of Ockham for his extreme radicalism in the use of nominalist principles and delighted in oversubtle formulations. He questioned the validity of Aristotelian logic in the realm of faith and regarded the existing order as based solely on God's free determination.

Around the middle of the fourteenth century the Ockhamist method had established itself at the University of Paris. As early as 1339 and 1340 the faculty of arts was induced to proceed against abuses of Ockhamism, and the Parisian masters, Nicholas of Autrecourt (d. after 1350) and John of Mirecourt, were personally condemned. The first named became in 1340 the subject of a process at Avignon, which ended in 1346 with the condemnation of sixty propositions. He was especially charged with denying the principle of causality. At the same time a papal bull was directed against the luxuriant growth of disputations in formal logic. Theologians were exhorted to keep to the texts of the old masters and not to neglect the Bible and the Fathers in favor of entirely useless philosophical questions, subtle disputations, and suspected doctrinal views.

The Cistercian John of Mirecourt was denounced for sixty-three suspected propositions in his commentary on *The Sentences.* Despite his written justification, forty-one of his theses were condemned at Paris in 1347 because of their exaggeration of God's arbitrariness and the dangerous consequences resulting for ethics.

Nominalist tendencies in epistemology and harsh anti-Pelagianism in the doctrine of grace characterized Gregory of Rimini, general of the Augustinians, who died at Vienna in 1358. He had studied and taught at Paris, where he became a master in 1345. In the doctrine of acceptance he showed his dependence on Ockham, whose optimism, however, in regard to naturally good works he did not share. Here, as in the doctrine of original sin, he was fascinated by the "founder" of his order, Saint Augustine. Without a special divine aid man cannot overcome temptation to sin, do any naturally good work, or even know what constitutes a morally good life.

Already from the middle of the fourteenth century onward, the originally excessive radicalism gave way to a more moderate view. Characteristic of the second half of the century, the epoch of the establishing of universities in Germany, were German theologians. They were eclectics, who "were able to deflect the pernicious tendency of nominalism and, almost unnoticed, to regain the connection with the scholastic traditions" (A. Lang). And such a series of important theologians is found in this period that one can refer to it as the climax of nominalist-influenced scholasticism, "a climax the more important in that it was followed only by extracts and epitomes in the fifteenth century, which turned into current coin the achievements of the fourteenth century" (F. Ehrle).

In addition, the fifteenth century was, in Harnack's term, decidedly "untheological." Edifying writings, practical moral instruction, and the treatment of rubrical and canonical questions became predominant. Characteristic of this change was the transition at Paris from Pierre d'Ailly (d. 1420), a leading representative of "undiluted Ockhamism," to his pupil, John Gerson (d. 1429), who in 1395 succeeded him as chancellor of the University. "It was this nominalist, with his edifying scholarly writings, his combination of mystical, Ockhamist, and Thomistic ideas, who became the prototype of an extensive, half-popular, syncretistically inclined theological literature, which was characteristic of the whole fifteenth century" (G. Ritter). He directed sharp criticism at theological scholarship, with its sophistical-logical ballast, and attacked those who dealt with useless and sterile doctrines while neglecting the truths necessary for salvation and scorning Scripture. He assailed the one-sided preoccupation with the first book of *The Sentences,* which offered more scope for interest in logic and purely formal theologizing, and demanded full treatment of the second to fourth books with the mysteries of salvation history. Considering the need of the age and the danger to souls, it was wrong, he said, to take delight in playing with or even indulging in reveries of superfluous things. No one should deem it beneath him to instruct the uneducated simple people in the faith. It was no mere chance that this nominalist, strictly geared to practice, who stressed the preeminence of mystical over scholastic theology but also warned against the dangers of a too presumptuous mysticism, stood up for the *devotio moderna* at the Council of Constance.

At the universities, of course, the conflict between the two "ways" was prolonged throughout the fifteenth century. In the course of these developments the *via antiqua* recovered ground. For example, at the University of Cologne, founded in 1388, both ways were allowed by the statutes, but at first nominalism predominated. As early as 1414 the faculty of arts had to resist the efforts of the *antiqua* to suppress the modern methods. But, soon after, the adherents of the *via antiqua* acquired the ascendancy. In 1425 the Electors urged the city of Cologne to reintroduce the modern methods at the University. They regarded Thomas, Albert, and the other teachers of the old school as profound but too difficult for the students, who would be seduced by a lack of understanding into errors and heresies, as the chaos at Prague testified. Tactfully but decisively the University refused, and under men like Henry of Gorkum (d. 1431) became the forerunner of a Thomistic renaissance, which gradually replaced *The Sentences* of Peter Lombard with the *Summa theologiae* as the textbook. In his *Compendium Summae theologiae Sancti Thomae,* printed in 1473, Henry of Gorkum gave an excellent summary of its arrangement and content. Quarrels in the camp of the realists produced temporarily at Cologne a third doctrinal school, the Albertists denied the real distinction between essence and being and maintained a Neoplatonic dynamic notion of being.

Vienna and Erfurt were the only German universities that were exclusively nominalist. Others had been so at first but later opened their doors to the realists. At Heidelberg, where the realist John Wenck (d. 1460), rector in 1435, 1444, and 1451, demanded a sober biblical theology, free from all sophisms and inventions of human ingenuity, the Elector Palatine in 1452 decreed the admission of the *via antiqua* and the equalization of the two ways. This was achieved at Basel in 1464, but at Freiburg not until 1484.

Like Cologne, the Universities of Cracow, Leipzig, Greifswald, Ingolstadt, Tübingen, and Wittenberg gave equality to both ways. If the arts faculty was nominalist, then the theological faculty did not have to be. Here the pressure of tradition was stronger and the influence of professors bound by the school of their order operated in many ways. Indeed, "many teachers who were devoted to the innovation in logic remained conservative in theology" (A. Lang). At Paris the conflict of the ways led toward the close of the fifteenth century to the prohibition of nominalists.

In the course of time the originally basic philosophical opposition in epistemology, especially in the solution of the problem of universals, played a more subordinate role, which in many ways was merely artificially maintained. More important were differences in the content of instruction and in the method followed. In the faculties of a nominalist hue more value was set on "terminist" logic. This logic regarded the concept rather than the judgment as the central point of reflection and in the exposition of a text was not content with presenting the actual content but was more logically concerned with the terms employed.

The *via antiqua* brought the text of Aristotle, of Peter Lombard, or of Aquinas again into the foreground and was content with an exegesis or paraphrase instead of debating in subtle details special problems in the questions on the text. If the *moderni* could be accused of sophistry and a craze for novelty at any price, the *antiqua* could be reproached for having renounced independent study of the thought contained in the "ancients" and for failure to develop ideas of their own. The orientation to the text and the simplification of theological teaching methods were not the exclusive property of the *via antiqua;* at the middle of the fifteenth century they were shared also by humanism and the Church reform efforts of the age and to some extent by the *devotio moderna.* In any event, humanism did not level its criticism at a scholasticism characterized by special radicalism and the subtlety of its theses — in this respect the climax had been reached ca. 1350. Rather, it attacked a school theology already groaning "under the weight of the literary tradition which in the course of the centuries had accumulated an immense mass of 'authorities,' opinions, and controversies, whose eternal ruminations, comparisons, and manipulations for new, and yet basically old, 'conclusions' [had] become an unending business" (G. Ritter).

CHAPTER 42

Concept of the Church and Idea of the State in the Polemics of the Fourteenth Century—The Laicized State in Marsilius of Padua

The claims of Boniface VIII and John XXII to authority in the secular domain were excessive and not in accord with the doctrine of the two powers developed from the time of Pope Gelasius I (492–96) and still accepted by Innocent III. According to this theory, the ecclesiastical and secular powers are mutually independent but related to each other; the spiritual power is nobler but it is not possessed of superior authority. The pretensions of Boniface VIII and John XXII were likewise historically obsolete, for the West had achieved maturity and the age of a universalism and clericalism occasioned by the situation was past. In 1286 the Dominican John Balbi of Genoa (d. 1298) in his lexicon of the liberal arts could still define the layman as *extraneus a scientia litterarum,* lacking in a literary education. In the meantime, in that very thirteenth century, a far-reaching process of individualization was under way; the individual had been discovered in the universal, and vast intellectual, artistic, and religious forces had been released. Related to this were the awakening of a responsible laity, the growth of cities, and the formation of national states. There was no longer a question solely of the relations of Emperor and Pope, but of the clerical and lay community and the place of man, who was both believer and citizen, in them.

The question was to what extent the Church was able to yield to the new claims and how far her religious nature was adequate to bind these driving forces individually and collectively to her own center. Mere resistance was no solution; an exaggeration of her own position was bound to produce a contrary effect. Statements such as Boniface VIII employed in the introduction to the bull *Clericis Laicos* (1296), "that the laity are hostile to the clergy is proved abundantly by antiquity and is clearly taught by the experiences of the present," did not do justice to reality. It was to be feared that developments, in themselves legitimate, which the Church failed to take promptly into account and in fact opposed, would forcibly find a place for themselves. In this respect the arrest of Boniface VIII at Anagni in 1303, in which the national state and the lay world represented by Nogaret and Sciarra Colonna acted jointly, was a warning signal. If Popes offered the political forces a legitimate ground for resisting them on account of obsolete and exaggerated claims, then it was obvious that the fight would soon be directed against the papacy itself. This struggle was not merely literary, but it was to a great extent prepared and waged by polemical writings and bulky treatises.

On behalf of Pope and Curia the polemic was especially conducted by the Augustinians Aegidius Romanus (1243/47–1316) in *De ecclesiastica potestate* (1302), James of Viterbo (d. 1308) in *De regimine christiano* (1302), and Augustinus Triumphus (1243–1328) in *Summa de potestate ecclesiastica* (1320).

According to Aegidius Romanus, or Giles of Rome, the Church has universal dominion. If she does not ordinarily exercise this directly over worldly things, no fundamental limitation is to be inferred from this fact. At any time she could monopolize secular dominion. In ordinary circumstances, in accord with 2 Timothy 2:4, the sword is to be wielded, not by the Church, but for her and at her bidding (III, 11, p. 205). Outside the Church there exists no right in the full sense. Only baptism makes one a lawful ruler and owner of earthly things. Outside the Church no one can possess in full right a field or vineyard or anything else (III, 11, p. 201). In brief, "the secular power is established through the ecclesiastical and by the Church and for the attaining of the Church's ends."

The work of Aegidius Romanus acquired a far-reaching importance, since it served as the basis of the bull "Unam Sanctam." James of Viterbo did not adopt these extravagant theses of his confrère in *De regimine christiano,* despite his effort to justify the policy of Boniface VIII. In his eyes the secular power does not stand in need of any consecration by the Church to gain legitimacy. It is certainly formed and perfected by the spiritual power. But if the spiritual power is the form of the secular power, as light is the form of color, then, despite all of James' efforts to maintain the legitimacy of the secular power according to natural law, the door is opened to unilaterally curialist conclusions.

In addition, it is to be realized that we are at the beginning of the fourteenth century, when formal logic acquired a leading role. An excessive confidence in the accuracy of their logic induced the two Augustinians, like many of their contemporaries, to push to extremes, even to "absurd conclusions," hitherto current axioms, which had been prudently and carefully applied earlier with regard to a living reality, and then not even to test the result of thought by the reality. This is to be regarded also as nominalism, or at least as conceptualism. Major terms of this sort were, for example the principle of the subordination of the imperfect to the perfect, of the body to the soul, of the temporal to the eternal, of the secular power to the spiritual power, and of the unity of social life. The comparison of secular and spiritual powers to body and soul acquired an entirely different impact after the decision by the Council of Vienne (1311–12) that the soul is the single immediate essential form of the body. For in accord with this the secular power would be an authentic power only through the spiritual power. Thus the same image could acquire in the fourteenth century a significance entirely different from what it had in Augustine, for example, or in the eleventh century. From the "one Lord . . . one God" of Ephesians 4:5, James of Viterbo deduced "unus princeps, unus principatus, unus rector, una res publica," and Aegidius Romanus concluded:

> In the Church Militant there can be only one source of power, only one head, which possesses the fulness of power . . . and both swords, without which its power would not be complete. From this source all other powers are derived. (De ecclesiastica potestate III, 2)

In opposition to Aegidius Romanus, Augustinus Triumphus in *Summa de potestate ecclesiastica* stressed the independence of the natural order. But it is oriented to the order of grace and is enlisted in its service. The Pope does not establish the secular power but involves it in the economy of salvation by virtue of his spiritual power. However, he can do so only on the basis of the relationship of the princes or citizens concerned to the Church. The state as such does not become a part of the Church, but to the extent that its members belong to the Church and render the Church's standards operative in it, it becomes a social structure in the *populus christianus.* In the worldly sense the king has no superior (q. 45, 1 ad 2), but only in so far as his power as a Christian authority is an integral part in the economy of salvation. This latter is Augustinus Triumphus' real concern, and his papalist claims are to be understood from this point of departure. It is a question of the "inclusion of the secular order in the economy of salvation and of the proper permeation of the world by the redemption" (W. Kölmel).

The extreme formulation of the curial viewpoint encouraged the development of the contrary doctrine of the independence of the state and of its claims to direct the Church. The legists likewise proceeded from the oneness of power and in this they were supported by Roman Law. The power attributed by it to the Emperor they ascribed to the King of France, who "is Emperor in his Kingdom." The supreme power of emperor or king respectively is inalienable. Therefore, the Donation of Constantine is to be regarded as unauthentic and the privileges of the clergy in regard to taxation and courts are to be abolished. The clergy, who "have become fat and obese because of the piety of princes," must have their recompense. But if the laity place the means at their disposal, then the laity must be permitted to supervise them to see whether such means are used properly. As a matter of principle they state that "Holy Mother Church consists not only of clerics but also of lay persons." Did Christ not die for all the faithful?

If the Pope has an indirect power in the temporal sphere, then, according to John of Paris (d. 1306), an advocate of the doctrine of the two powers, the king has the same in the spiritual domain. He can "indirectly" excommunicate an unworthy Pope and *per accidens* depose him, by himself or through the cardinals.

Laity and state emerged from these disputes with a more vivid sense of their independence and a growing awareness of their rights and duties, even with regard to the spiritual. Whereas the defenders of the Curia, frequently in a most presumptuous manner, advocated an abstract system that did not correspond to the Church's past nor take account of her future, and thus missed the reality and the opportune moment, the representatives of the state registered such elementary rights as sovereignty over property and persons, judicial supremacy, autonomy in legislation, and a certain control of the intellectual life of the nation. Though individual demands may have been expressed obscurely and exaggerated, a justified concern was present in them and the future was to belong to it.

Marsilius of Padua

The struggle of the legists, in the name of princes and cities, or the autonomy and independence of the secular power against encroachments of the spiritual did not terminate in a separation of Church and State in the modern sense but rather in a State Church or at least an extensive control of Church life by the secular power. In the *Defensor pacis* of Marsilius of Padua this attitude led to the total destruction of the ecclesiastical power and the total control of all aspects of life, including the Church, by the purely secular laicized state, so called because in final analysis deprived of authoritative values.

Marsilius was born at Padua probably between 1275 and 1280 and there began his studies. The first certain date is that of his rectorship as master of arts from December 1312 to March 1313 at the University of Paris. As a partisan of the Ghibellines he seems to have taken part in the Italian factional strife from around 1314, and he carried out diplomatic tasks for Can Grande della Scala and Matthew Visconti. Between times he tried to obtain a benefice at the Avignon Curia. From 1320 he again concentrated on study at Paris in natural philosophy, medicine, and perhaps theology. Here he was intimately associated with the leader of the Parisian Averroists, John of Jandun (d. 1328), who probably inspired the *Defensor pacis* but cannot be called its coauthor. Marsilius completed this, his chief work, in June 1324, shortly after the Sachsenhausen Declaration of Louis the Bavarian. This great book was probably intended from the outset to play a role in the antipapal activity to which had rallied Ghibellines, cardinals of the opposition, and Spirituals. But it was not until 1326 that Marsilius fled with John of Jandun to the court of Louis the Bavarian in Germany, probably because his authorship had become known. At first Louis apparently did not want to compromise his case with the work of these men, who were to be condemned as heretics on 3 April 1327. But during the Emperor's journey to Rome (1327–29) Marsilius and his friend were the influential advisers. Events such as the imperial coronation in the name of the Roman people and the installing of the Antipope appear to be the realization of the basic ideas of *Defensor pacis.* Following the collapse of the Emperor's Italian policy, Marsilius lived at Munich as a physician. His influence seems to have been insignificant in comparison with that of the more moderate William of Ockham and the other Franciscans. His death must have occurred soon after the appearance of the *Defensor minor* (1342), for on 10 April 1343 Clement VI referred to him as lately deceased.

According to the *Defensor pacis,* peace, the principle of order in the state and the basic presupposition for human happiness, is greatly disturbed. In an effort to inquire into the causes of this and to indicate the fundamental principles for the assuring of peace, Marsilius develops his theory of state and society. In this he is guided by his experiences in the North Italian city states, the writings of the French legists, and the Averroist interpretation of the Aristotelian political doctrine. According to him the fundamental evil is the papal pretension to the fulness of power, to a *vis coactiva* over Church, princes, and kingdoms; as a matter of fact, that, in addition to the state, another principle of power should claim the right to exist. Opposing this, Marsilius stresses the unity of power. "The multiplicity of sovereign powers... is the root and origin of corruption" (II, 23, 11; *cf.* I, 17, 1–9).

The state is the union of men for the sake of a satisfying existence (I, 5, 5). What the individual cannot do, the state accomplishes in its various professions. Among these is included also the priesthood, for the state must assure the earthly and the supernatural welfare of man. "The legislator or the first and specific efficient cause of law is the people or the totality of citizens or a majority of them" (I, 12, 3). The people, as *legislator humanus,* commits the exercise of power to a ruler (*princeps*) who has to preserve and guarantee peace, which makes possible the good life for the citizens.

Every other power, and hence that of the Church, is delegated. Inasmuch as priests and bishops exercise power, they receive it from the believing human legislator, that is, from the lay hand. The Church is "the totality of the faithful, who believe in Christ's name and invoke him" (II, 2 3).

> Therefore all Christ's faithful are churchmen (*viri ecclesiastici*) in the truest and most proper meaning and must be so called, priests and those not priests, for Christ has acquired and redeemed all by his blood...; hence bishops or priests and deacons are not exclusively the Church, which is the bride of Christ (II, 2, 3).

The priesthood is a divine institution. "Christ gave priestly power to the Apostles and he still gives it today, whenever one of them invests his successors with full powers through the imposition of hands" (II, 15, 3). "This power, inseparable from the priest as priest,... this priestly character is possessed by all priests in the same manner, and neither the Bishop of Rome nor any other possesses any more comprehensive power than any so-called simple priest" (II, 15, 4; *ibid.*, 15, 5, 7). Hence the hierarchy is of human law; "not God directly but the human will and mind" (I, 19, 8; II, 15, 6) created it for the sake of order, "like the other offices of the state." The attempt to deduce a special dignity of the Bishop of Rome from the Petrine succession runs aground on the impossibility of proving Peter's being in Rome (II, 16, 15). No real external power is, however, given along with the priestly character bestowed by God. In confession the priest can merely "declare to whom God has retained or pardoned sins" (II, 6, 7). He has no *vis coactiva*, for offenses against the divine law are not punished in this world (II, 9, 3–10; III, 2, 3), unless they are also forbidden by human law. But then it is the business of the state to prosecute and excommunicate the heretic. At the most the priest is called upon as a specialist for an opinion.

In disputes over doctrinal questions or uncertainties as to the meaning of a scriptural passage the decision pertains "to a council of all the faithful or of their delegates" (II, 18, 8). As the rule of faith Marsilius laid down: "Only the divine or canonical Scripture and every interpretation that is convincingly deduced from it and that which is handed down by a general council is true; it is necessary for eternal salvation to believe these" (III, 2, 1). But the council is not an autonomous body beside the state; on the contrary, it is instituted in it, so to speak, as an organ for definite questions. Only "the believing human legislator or the one who rules through it by proper authority" has the power "to convoke or direct a council, to choose and determine suitable persons for it, command the observance of the conciliar decrees, and punish transgressors" (II, 21,1; II, 18, 8). The decisions of the council have their truth from the Holy Spirit, "but from the human legislator the authority which enforces their acceptance and their propagation by priests" (II, 19, 3). If, "by a council or the believing human lawgiver," a bishop or a church is appointed as head and ruler of the others, then this bishop together with the college of priests assigned to him by the legislator, can, in case of necessity, ask for the summoning of a council (II, 22, 6).

Accordingly, there exist no clerical person and no college which were not delegated by the *legislator humanus*, that is, by the totality of citizens. The frequently recurring phrase, *concilium generale vel fidelis legislator humanus*, shows to what an extent *universitas fidelium* and *universitas civium* are identical for Marsilius and that the council is not a separate entity. For Marsilius, the Church is directed neither monarchically by a Pope nor collegially by the episcopate nor democratically by a council. She is also not purely spiritualized but fully disintegrated. She is devoid of any character as a society and has become a mere function of the state. From this arise two difficulties. For Marsilius the universal state is not the ideal; in his view peace and the public welfare are better guaranteed in several states (*cf.* for example, II, 28, 15). But if the *universitas civium* and the *universitas fidelium* are to him identical, then the council, which is conceived as a universal institution, must have its counterpart in a realm which unites all Christendom and in which the conciliar decrees have the force of law. Can the prince of a national state be the "believing human lawgiver, who recognizes no higher power," or is an emperor or a world state still postulated? Marsilius ignores this question. But he does not wish to pass over the second question in silence (II, 22, 12). If the believing human lawgiver alone renders the Church capable of functioning, if he summons the council, appoints priests, looks after worship, and so forth, who assumes these tasks when believers are subjects of unbelieving lawgivers? In the age of the persecutions, so Marsilius claims, the Church was charismatically guided. Believers were prepared to obey the bishops, and in particular the Roman Bishops, who excelled in love of God and exemplary poverty, in order to preserve the unity of faith and peace. For this could "be achieved neither by coercive power nor in any more appropriate manner, because the human legislator was at that time almost everywhere an unbeliever" (II, 25, 3). Hence, the Primitive Church was a state of emergency, which was ended only by Constantine.

On 23 October 1327 five propositions of the *Defensor pacis* were condemned as heretical: 1. That Christ by paying the tribute money intended to testify to his subordination to the secular power. 2. That Peter had no more authority than the other Apostles. 3. That the Emperor can appoint, depose, and punish the Pope. 4. That all priests are equal in degree. 5. That priests have no penal authority of themselves but only by grant of the Emperor. Despite this condemnation the book and its ideas continued to be influential. Louis the Bavarian had it read to himself and his Italian policy determined by it. However, a moderating tone gained ground at the court of Munich with the Franciscans Michael of Cesena and Ockham. In the fifteenth-century struggles over the constitution of the Church the *Defensor pacis* again became influential. While the heretic and determined foe of the papacy was rejected and his doctrine of the laicized state was not accepted, his historical and moral criticism of the abuses in the Church were. This is true of Nicholas of Cusa (d. 1464) in his great reform treatise *De Concordantia Catholica* (1432–33). In summary it can be stated that the *Defensor pacis* was too radical to exert an immediate influence, but indirectly it had a great and far-reaching effect.

William of Ockham

It was not until his Munich period that William of Ockham was concerned with the poverty dispute and the relations between the spiritual and the secular powers. His philosophical and theological works appeared before his flight from Avignon in 1328; his fifteen ecclesiastico-political writings, without exception, after it. "Emperor, protect me with your sword; then I will defend you with my pen," he is alleged to have said as a refugee in the train of Louis the Bavarian.

The Pope had already taken a final stand in the poverty dispute with "Quia

Vir Reprobus" (1329), the *Defensor pacis* had appeared, and the decisive events had taken place during Louis the Bavarian's journey to Rome — the imperial coronation and the appointment of the Antipope — when Ockham intervened in the discussion in 1333–34 with his *Opus nonaginta dierum,* so called because he claims to have composed the voluminous work in ninety days. Ockham could merely establish and defend what was already an accomplished fact. He was and continued to be a philosophical and theological thinker, accustomed to pursue questions to their ultimate possibilities in a critical and biased speculation and as far as possible to go back to principles and sources.

The great ecclesiastico-political writings, the *Opus nonaginta dierum* (1333–34), his extensive but still incomplete principal work, *Dialogus inter magistrum et discipulum de imperatorum et pontificum potestate* (1333–38), and the *Super potestate summi pontificis octo quaestiones* present the difficulty that the author does not clearly come forth with his own opinion but lets the several sides speak and refers to himself only as the narrator. For the sake of the disputation, a sort of school exercise, he can expound the most audacious theses without identifying himself with them and he cannot be tied down to them. As evidence for Ockham's view these writings can be used only with caution.

As with his image of God and man, Ockham's doctrine of state and Church and of their mutual relations is determined by freedom — the freedom of the individual in Church and state and the freedom of the secular ruler *vis-à-vis* the Pope. The principle of economy of his philosophy attests the sociological doctrine that no more obligations and norms should be permitted than the public welfare requires. In particular it is important to safeguard freedom against "the Church of Avignon, which stubbornly maintains errors, indeed manifest heresies, . . . and is currently guilty of the gravest injustices against the rights and the liberties of the faithful, great and small, lay and cleric. . . . "

Opposing the monism of both the curialists and Marsilius of Padua, Ockham defends a theory of the two powers, in which both powers are mutually complementary, are even "allied in a mutual dependence." Apart from the divine law, Emperor and Pope in their respective sphere; have no such absolute power that it could not be limited by the freedom of the individual and by the public welfare. Ockham firmly emphasizes the independent status of the secular power. There was a lawful worldly order before Christ and before the Church. The Empire was not first made legitimate by the baptism of Constantine; the pagan Roman Empire already had real jurisdiction and hence was acknowledged by Christ and the Apostles (*Breviloquium,* IV, 10; III, 2). Like private ownership, the political order also, "the power to appoint rulers who have secular powers of government," is derived from the divine arrangement. After the fall the liberty of the primeval condition, like the absence of ownership, could not be maintained any longer, and for the sake of *bene et politice vivere* governmental power was necessary (*Brev.,* III, 7). And though this is transmitted by means of men, it comes from God. "All mortals who were born free and have not been subjected to another by human law derive from God and nature the right freely to elect a ruler" (*Brev., IV,* 10). If peoples are forcibly subjugated, dominion becomes legitimate only through their inner assent. Ockham is unable to say when such was the case, for example in the Roman Empire. Anyhow it is true that "the power to make laws and establish human rights lay first and originally in the people, who transferred it to the Emperor" (*Brev.*, III, 14). But the transmission of power by the totality of the citizens does not include the right to terminate allegiance. And if the authority of princes is termed dominative, in contrast to the ministerial office of the Pope (*De potestate,* c. 6 and 7), it is still not unlimited. It finds its limits in the liberties of man, which are of an earlier origin than the state, and in the public welfare, for which authority is instituted (*Brev.*, II, 5).

The Church is the community of all the faithful. To the nominalist, who does not recognize the relation as real and for whom the totality is only the sum of its parts, the Church is a multiplicity of individuals. In fact, she is a phantom and a chimera. To be exact, just as there is not an order apart from the Franciscans subject to the law of poverty but only a *persona repraesentata,* which possesses a *ius utendi,* so it is a fiction to speak of the Church as a legal person. As the community of the faithful, she has, according to Christ's will, a monarchical form of government. He appointed Peter as his vicar. Differing from Marsilius of Padua, Ockham concedes to the Pope real power transmitted by Christ. "Christ would not have taken sufficient care of the Church and would have neglected something necessary" (*De potestate,* c. 8), if he had not given her in the Pope the principal who should see to all things necessary for the salvation of the faithful and guide them. But Christ did not invest Peter with full power, either in the secular or in the spiritual sphere (*De potestate,* c. 2). It is entirely clear that he did not give him absolute power *in temporalibus,* for otherwise he would have made slaves of all and there would no longer be any "evangelical liberty" (*De potestate,* c. 1). But the spiritual power also has its limits. Ockham speaks of the "ancient boundaries" (*De potestate,* c. 15, 1) to which the Church of Avignon should be again reduced. The Pope is not allowed to command everything which is not contrary to the divine precept and natural law (*De potestate,* c. 1). For example, he is bound to respect the legitimate tithes of kings, whether Christian or non-Christian. Furthermore, liberty must be not unnecessarily restricted. The Pope's full authority extends only to what is necessary for the salvation of souls and the guidance of the faithful. "All else, even though it be spiritual, he must not command, lest the law of the Gospel become a law of slavery" (*De potestate,* c. 10; *Brev., II, 4).* The Pope's power is one, not of dominion, but of service.

Despite the rigorous inclination to confine the Pope within his limits, Ockham foresees the case in which he directly assumes secular duties. In an emergency, when the proper authorities fail or break down, the Pope may and should intervene in worldly affairs for the sake of the common welfare. Without using the expression, Ockham is thereby championing the theory of the *potestas indirecta in temporalibus.* There are no rules for such a case. The greatest discretion is indicated and the counsel of experienced and impartial men is necessary (*De potestate,* c. 13).

Eminent as is the Pope's dignity as Christ's deputy, above him is the *Ecclesia Universalis.* Not to be identified with the contingent aspect of *Ecclesia Romana* or *Avionica,* she will never fall into error. But every individual in her can err, Pope as well as layman. Even a council is not protected from error. This *Ecclesia Universalis,* guided and kept free of error by the Holy Spirit, could eventually be represented in an individual man, a woman, or even in children under age.

Accordingly, Ockham cannot without more ado, be termed a precursor of conciliarism. In any event, it cannot be an absolute standard in matters of faith. Final resort is Holy Scripture and reason. Pope, clergy, and council must answer to them.

In his last work, *De imperatorum et pontificum potestate,* he appeals to the public, because there could no longer be any question of the Pope as a judge and the "Church of Avignon" had succumbed to the greatest heresies. He does not want to submit to the majority but only to rational insight and the clear testimony of Scripture. The crowd, he said, has quite often erred and more than once in the history of the Church truth has been found in an individual (c. 1). It can be the Emperor. In a state of emergency in the Church the Emperor can intervene in the spiritual realm, just as the Pope in cases of necessity can intervene in the temporal. For example, the Emperor can convoke a council or even depose the Pope. But he can do so, not by virtue of his office, but only as a believing member of the Church (*De potestate,* c. 12). For if the clergy fail, the laity bear responsibility for the Church. But there is no tribunal to decide when they must intervene on behalf of the faith and of the public good.

In case of necessity the Emperor may, on his own authority, requisition Church property for worldly tasks. Ockham distinguishes between the temporal property necessary for the support of clerics — this belongs to the Church *iure divino* — and whatever, over and beyond this, is entrusted to the Church *iure humano,* from the generosity of kings and laity, *ad pias causas:* care of the poor and strangers, construction of churches, and so forth. The donor can determine the use, and the Pope has no authority over this. On the other hand, the King can dispose of the Church property donated by himself or his predecessors without consulting the Pope. He can "on his own authority in case of need demand subsidies from the churches for pious ends" (*De potestate,* c. 24). According to the treatise *An rex Angliae,* among these *piae causae* is included the defense of the country, for the welfare of the father-land is superior to that of its poor. Now the clergy must make the goods of the Church available for the poor and hence all the more for the defense of the fatherland.

Ockham's efforts for a definition of the competence of the secular and spiritual powers are noteworthy. In emphasizing their mutual independence in reciprocal assistance he could have prepared for an adjustment in accord with reality. But his polemical stand in the struggle for the Emperor's rights against the Curia and the opinion he championed in the poverty dispute, according to which the Church, emulating Christ's poverty and powerlessness, should, as far as possible, renounce all functions in the world, caused him to underestimate the danger of state absolutism and so to expand the absolute powers of the secular authority that he promoted an *étatisme.* He stressed the liberty of the individual and of princes, but on the other hand did not even concede to the Pope the defense of the liberty of the Church as a justification of his actions, "for the liberty of the Church and her honor in this world are to be reckoned among the least important goods" (*De potestate,* c. 23).

CHAPTER 43

The Spiritual Movement and the Poverty Dispute

In the very lifetime of Saint Francis there had begun among his friars a vehement struggle over the ideal of absolute poverty. In it victory had soon gone to the circles which, because of the necessity resulting from the order's world-wide expansion and in the interests of a fruitful care of souls, modified the saint's ideal by means of papal privileges and interpretations of the rule to such an extent that absolute poverty was abandoned. In 1245 Innocent IV (1243–54) had declared the movable and immovable property of the Franciscans to be the property of the Roman Church, and in 1247 he had allowed them procurators who could take care of legitimate business affairs according to the will of the friars, that is, "they are permitted to collect, sell, exchange, alienate, trade, spend, . . . and use for the needs of the friars." If this development was necessary, it was also ominous and the source of criticism and unrest that officially the founder's ideal was adhered to and the order claimed to practice the poverty desired by Francis. It was only a matter of time until the friars would be reproached on the ground that their poverty was a legal fiction.

Around the same time, at the middle of the thirteenth century, the spiritualism of Joachim of Fiore (d. 1202) gained a foothold in Franciscan circles. Saint Bonaventure, minister general of the order from 1257 to shortly before his death in 1274, had thus to defend Franciscan poverty and at the same time to fight the Joachimite apocalyptic currents in the order. He sought to save the ideal of poverty and to restrict the use of property as much a possible. In accordance with Bonaventure's ideas, Pope Nicholas III (1277–80) issued an authentic explanation of the rule in the Constitution "Exiit qui seminat" of 14 August 1279. It stressed the sanctity of evangelical poverty and the obligation to its observance on the basis of the rule, but, by distinguishing between property or the right of usufruct and simple use (*usus moderatus*), enabled the Franciscans to retain their houses and the use of their properties. As a result the stricter element was rendered all the more unhappy, for even this modified ideal of poverty was not observed by a great part of the order and since the death of Bonaventure a decline of discipline was becoming widespread. Hence the dispute over poverty continued.

Spokesman was Peter John Olivi (d. 1298). The point in controversy was not whether there could be property or not, but the restricted use of earthly goods, the question whether an *usus pauper* was desirable and whether it was implied in the order's vow. Olivi gave his support for it and demanded this "use of things in a spirit of poverty" even by bishops belonging to the order. Renunciation of earthly possessions without a real life of the poor was, he said, similar to matter without form and brought the members of the order the scorn of the world. Nevertheless, in Provence and in Italy a growing circle of zealots for poverty was forming around him. People were beginning to call them the "Spirituals" in contradistinction to the "Conventuals," who tried to adapt themselves to the situation and to achieve a mitigation based on the interpretations of the rule by Gregory IX and Nicholas III. The Conventuals were thereafter in a difficult position because all abuses were laid at their door and they were held responsible for the decline of fidelity to the rule, although they also struggled against it.

With the pontificate of Celestine V (1294) the Spirituals felt they had achieved their goal. He permitted a group of them under Angelus of Clareno and Peter of Macerata ("Liberatus") to live the rule in its full austerity according to the last will of Saint Francis, as a special branch of the order. Great was their disappointment when this "Angel Pope" gave way to the totally different Boniface VIII. Ubertino da Casale, who became leader of the Spirituals after Olivi's death in 1298, later branded the new Pope as the beast of the Apocalypse, the "mystical Antichrist."

The quarrel in the order continued. The harsh proceedings of the Conventuals, under the general Gonsalvo de Valboa (1304–13), against the Spirituals and the latters' charges against their persecutors and the presence of their influential patrons among princes and cardinals made it impossible for Clement V not to concern himself with the poverty question. As spokesman of the Spirituals at the Avignon Curia, Ubertino da Casale in his memorandum "Sanctitas Vestra" at the end of 1309 emphasized that the order had declined profoundly because of various offenses against the letter and the spirit of the rule, particularly the view that the *usus pauper* was not binding on the basis of the vow of poverty. He asked the Pope that those who wished to practice poverty in all strictness should be allowed to live in peace and that the others should at least abide by the papal interpretations of the rule. Ubertino therefore urged the separation of the Spirituals from the Conventuals.

In view of the favorable attitude toward the Spirituals at the Curia and the not unjustified reproach of laxity in the observance of the rule, the Conventuals were now hard pressed. In a counterattack they accused Peter John Olivi, already twelve years dead, of heresy and the Spirituals of fostering his heretical doctrines. The Pope wanted to have these questions, for the most part purely dogmatic, discussed by the approaching Council. Thus the poverty dispute came before the Council of Vienne (1311–12), which on 5 May 1312 decided in general in favor of the stricter view. According to the bull "Exivi de Paradiso," the precepts of the rule were binding under serious sin. Prescriptions which were regarded as equivalent to such precepts were individually specified. "The friars, by virtue of their profession, are obliged to a truly poor use in those things which are expressly specified as such in the rule." Individually and as a community they were not capable of receiving inheritances, they were not permitted to bring suit, possess vineyards, or build storehouses, and they were to be content with unpretentious churches and monasteries. The bull intended to provide a practical decision. The effort to connect the friars' poverty with the dogmatic question of the import of Christ's poverty and to brand the opposing view as heretical, according to whether one regarded the *usus pauper* as included in the vow of evangelical poverty or not, was expressly designated as "presumptuous and insolent." The bull said nothing about a return of the Spirituals to their original convents under obedience to the superiors of the order.

This omission led to new difficulties. Michael of Cesena, elected minister general in 1316, tried, with the assistance of John XXII, to reduce to obedience high-handed and refractory Spirituals in Tuscany and Provence. The Pope summoned a number of them to Avignon and in the Constitution "Quorumdam Exigit" of 7 October 1317 forbade the Spirituals all unauthorized actions. He stated that obedience was superior to poverty and that the superiors of the order had the final say in regard to clothing and stocks of provisions. Obstinate Spirituals were handed over to the Inquisition and on 7 May 1318 four of them were burned at Marseilles. In other writings John XXII again dealt with the Spirituals, whom he labelled *fraticelli,* and deprived them of their own monasteries, among other things.

But soon the Pope was destined to oppose the entire order. In this conflict, the dispute over the theory of poverty, the question at issue was whether Christ and the Apostles, individually or as a group, had possessed property. Thus the poverty dispute affected all Christendom much more deeply and acquired a direct bearing on the relationship, then a subject of controversy, between the spiritual and the secular powers. If Christ as man had renounced property and the exercise of authority over men and things and had subjected himself to Caesar, then this had to have consequences for his vicar on earth and for all who exercised spiritual authority in his name. It was further controverted whether private ownership had come into existence only as a result of the fall or was in accord with a divine ordinance from the very beginning.

The Dominican John of Belna, as inquisitor, had declared as heretical in a trial of Beghards the proposition that Christ possessed absolutely nothing. The Franciscan Berengar of Perpignan protested against this decision, citing Nicholas III. Thus the question came before the papal tribunal. When in the bull "Quia Nonnumquam" of 26 March 1322 John XXII annulled Nicholas III's prohibition of discussing "Exiit qui seminat," the Franciscans became afraid that he would decide the question according to the interpretation of the Dominicans. The general chapter at Perugia under the direction of Michael of Cesena, anticipated such a papal decision by declaring in an encyclical of 6 June 1322 to all Christendom that "it is sound, Catholic, and orthodox teaching that Christ and the Apostles owned nothing as their own." In doing so it cited Nicholas III, Clement V, and even John XXII himself.

The indignant Pope's first reaction was to renounce ownership of the order's property and forbid the naming of procurators. Bonagrazia of Bergamo was imprisoned for protesting this measure. In the bull "Cum inter Nonnullos" of 12 November 1323 John XXII declared heretical the assertion that Christ and the Apostles had possessed neither as individuals nor as a group. The entire order was enraged, and some of the members labelled the Pope a heretic. The situation became all the more inflamed when Louis the Bavarian adopted this charge in his Declaration of Sachsenhausen on 22 May 1324. However, the majority of the Franciscans returned to loyalty and the Pentecost Chapter at Lyons in 1325, under Michael of Cesena appealed for respect for the papal decrees. But the Pope apparently did not feel sure of the attitude of the minister general. He summoned him to Avignon in 1327 and, not finding him submissive, detained him there. During the night of 26–27 May, 1328, Michael of Cesena succeeded in escaping from Avignon together with Bonagrazia of Bergamo and William of Ockham. The last named had had to defend his philosophical and theological teachings at the Curia. At Pisa they joined Louis the Bavarian, in whose retinue was already Marsilius of Padua. Thus Louis' quarrel acquired much more an ideological character through becoming involved with the poverty dispute.

Michael of Cesena preached against John XXII and from Pisa released voluminous and scholarly appeals against the Pope, who on 6 June 1328 had deposed and on 20 April 1329 had excommunicated him along with his companions. In the bull "Quia Vir Reprobus" of 16 November 1329 John XXII gave a definitive expression of his views against Michael of Cesena. He stressed that Christ had had a *dominium* over worldly goods. Even in Paradise property was assigned by God to our first parents; it was not a mere human institution after the fall. At that time it required only a regulation by positive law. A general chapter at Paris declared the deposition of Michael of Cesena legitimate and elected Geraldus Oddonis as his successor.

Geraldus wanted to dispense from the prohibition of money and other precepts of the rule. Hence both he and the Avignon Curia were bitterly reproached by Michael of Cesena during the rest of his life in numerous polemical pamphlets.

In his *Literas plurium,* which he sent to the general chapter at Perpignan, Michael declared that he was an orthodox Franciscan and the legitimate general and that John XXII was a heretic. Unfortunately, the Pope was destined to provide further substance for this charge in his teachings on the beatific vision. The chapter expelled from the order the Franciscans at the court of Munich. There they were more and more involved in the ecclesiastico-political struggle and became champions of the lay power against the Avignon papacy. Thus, almost exactly a century after its establishment, a part of the Franciscan Order became the chief prop of resistance to the Holy See.

The poverty dispute itself, the further decline of the ideal of poverty, and the universal abuses evident in Christendom, such as the prolonged interdict occasioned by the quarrel between Pope and Emperor, the Hundred Years' War (1337–1453), and the Western Schism produced a further decay of the order. The endeavor to supply as quickly as possible for the inroads of the plague (1348–52) — it is said that two-thirds of the members of the order fell victim to the Black Death — did nothing to advance religious discipline. But it is a testimony to the vitality of the order and the strength of its ideal that, in an effort to correct evils, reform circles were established again and again and in all the provinces. Thus there occurred in the second half of the fourteenth century and in the fifteenth the Observant movement, which led to the dividing of the order into Observants and Conventuals. While the former clung to the non-possession of property even by the community and wanted to renounce any regular income and real estate, the latter accepted common property, income, and estates.

The Council of Constance (1414–18) granted to the Observants of France their own provincial vicars and a vicar general. Continuing efforts to reform the order as a whole and thus to preserve its unity were futile. In 1443 Pope Eugene IV gave the Observants two vicars general, one for their cismontane and one for their transmontane communities, and their own chapter. In 1446, at the suggestion of John Capestrano, he made the position of these vicars general so independent of the minister general that in actuality the Observants had become independent, even though the legal connection was still maintained. The complete division of the order occurred in 1517 when the Observants already constituted a majority. At the general chapter Leo X excluded the Conventuals from the election of the minister general and united all branches of the Observants as the *Ordo Fratrum Minorum Regularis Observantiae.* The new arrangement was confirmed in the bull "Ite et vos in vineam" of 29 May 1517, and on 1 June a new minister general was elected, to whom the minister general hitherto in office had to surrender the seal of the order. The Conventuals elected their own general, who, at the command of the Pope, had to assume the title of master general.

CHAPTER 44

The German Mystics

In the scholasticism of the thirteenth century speculative discursive theology, which Bernard of Clairvaux had felt called upon to assail as arrogant learning (*stultilogia*) in Peter Abelard, had carried off the victory. Just the same the tide of the theology of practical acquisition and prayerful achievement, advocated by Bernard, never ceased. Neoplatonism too continued to exert its influence beside and within the Aristotelian trend of thought.

In addition, the increasing coming of age of the laity brought along a great yearning for education and a religious interest which had to be met more fully and more deeply. In particular, women made widows as a consequence of the crusades, other wars, and plague, and unmarried women longed for religious and theological instruction. Many religious houses for women were founded in the thirteenth century, especially for Dominican nuns. In Strasbourg alone there were seven. Thus was called into being a more practical theology, cultivating the spirituality of the heart and leading directly to union with God. Naturally, it was expressed in the German tongue. The presupposition for the rise of German mysticism was, then, the "combination of Dominican theology and pastoral care, vernacular preaching, feminine piety, and Germany's special position in the religious movements of the thirteenth and fourteenth centuries" (H. Grundmann). It presented itself as a doctrine of the experimental knowledge of God in the soul, as a guide to this, and as a witness of the mystical experience itself. We must not understand too narrowly the circle of persons termed mystics. In the fourteenth century we may include among them not only those favored with extraordinary gifts and visions but all who wrote on piety in the vernacular.

The Dominican Henry of Halle collected from 1250 the notes of Mechtilde of Magdeburg (ca. 1212–85 or 1294), who, after a penitential life of more than thirty years as a Beguine, spent her last days in the Cistercian convent of Helfta. This collection, *Das fliessende Licht der Gottheit* (*The Streaming Light of the Godhead*), is the first great mystical work in German. Its Low German original is lost and has come down to us only in a free Latin translation and in the High German text of Henry of Nördlingen (d. after 1379). In daring but fervent images, determined by the *Minnesang,* Mechtilde beholds in her meditations, sayings, and verses the birth of the soul from God the Father, beyond the whole world and all time. The supernatural union with God is thus the vital element, the true "nature" of the soul (I, 44). Christ is the bridegroom destined for it, to whom it surrenders itself without disguising or reserving anything, and the Holy Spirit is the "lavish outpouring of the Father and the Son" (VI, 32), "the blessed gushing fountain of love" (VII, 24). The soul living in the streaming light of divine grace breaks out of its bounds, belongs to Christendom and to the world, lives and suffers for them. Unlike the Neoplatonic formula of purgative, illuminative, and unitive ways, for Mechtilde love is fulfilled in this earthly life in suffering, in patient longing, even in descent with Christ into hell. "It is the nature of love that it first proceeds in sweetness, then becomes rich in perception, and, thirdly, becomes desirous of and eager for abandonment" (IV, 20).

Master Eckhart

Master Eckhart was the most important and most daring representative of speculative German mysticism. He was German in the deep fervor of his thought, in the radicalism, even extravagance, with which he sought to carry his speculations to their ultimate consequences, even to paradox, and in the vigorous style with which he was able to express them in German. Born at Hochheim in Thuringia around 1260, he became a Dominican and, following studies at Cologne and Paris, was made, while still young, prior at Erfurt and vicar of the provincial, Dietrich of Freiberg, for Thuringia. As such he delivered to the young members of the order the *Reden der Unterscheidung* (*Discourses on Discrimination*). In these he outlined the criteria of genuine piety and taught "the total divesting of self for God" in obedience. Thus was sounded the keynote of his later preaching: solitude as the prerequisite of union with God. In 1302 he became master of theology at Paris, and, after the division of the German province, provincial of the new Saxon province (1303–11), with forty-seven houses of friars and more than seventy of nuns. In addition, he became vicar general of the Bohemian province in 1307. When Eckhart's election as provincial of the South German province was annulled, the general sent him to Paris as master for the school years 1311–12 and 1312–13. From 1314 he was at Strasbourg, his headquarters for supervising the spiritual care of the convents of nuns in Alsace and Switzerland until 1322. During the last five years or so of his life he was director of studies at the house in Cologne and a zealous preacher.

Transcripts of his German sermons provided the material which induced Archbishop Henry von Virneburg to institute a process in 1326 because of the propagation of false teaching. Eckhart declared on 26 September 1326 that the archiepiscopal court had no jurisdiction over him as a Dominican and a master, but he nevertheless answered the charge in an "essay of vindication." On 13 February 1327, in the church of the Dominicans, he protested his orthodoxy and his readiness to repudiate ascertained errors. In spite of the rejection of his appeal on 22 February 1327, the case was referred to Avignon, where he personally undertook his defense. It was only after his death, which occurred before 30 April 1328, that seventeen propositions were condemned as heretical and eleven declared suspect in the bull "In agro Dominico," issued by John XXII on 27 March 1329. Only the third part of the projected *Opus tripartitum* was finished: scriptural exegesis — Genesis, Exodus, Wisdom, and Saint John's Gospel — and sermons on biblical texts. More controversial, but also more influential, were his German writings: *Reden der Unterscheidung, Buch der göttlichen Tröstungen* (*Book of the Divine Consolations*), with the sermon "Von dem edeln Menschen" ("On the Noble Man"), and some 160 sermons which have been handed down only in transcripts; it is difficult to prove that all are genuine.

With a grandiose partiality Eckhart repeats some fundamental notions of God as the basis of all being, of the birth of the Son from the Father in the spark of the soul, and of solitude of soul whereby it is able to contain God.

> When I preach, I am accustomed to speak, first, of solitude and that man should be devoid of self and of all things; second, that one should be reformed into the one good, which is God; third, that one should be aware of the great nobility with which God invests the soul in order that man may thereby enter into the wonderful life of God; fourth of the purity of the divine nature (F. Pfeiffer).

Proceeding from the scriptural texts, "I am who am" (Exodus 3:14) and "In the beginning was the Word" (John 1:1), Eckhart stresses perceiving as the basis of God's existence. If existence follows the divine perceiving, God is something higher than existence. "And hence whatever is always in God is above existence itself and is exclusively perception." Thus Eckhart is able to say "that in God non-existence is still existence," for he is the source of all existence. "Accordingly, existence is not within God's province, unless you should wish to term such purity existence." That which perceives this knowing, supporting and embracing all existence, is its own self, which the Father beholds and expresses in his Word, the Son. At the same time he comprehends in it all ways in which creatures can portray his essence. "The Father perceives nothing except this same Word and himself and the whole divine nature and all things in this same Word, and whatever he perceives in it is equal to the Word and is the same Word by nature in truth" (Pfeiffer).

Thus Eckhart endeavors to safeguard God's distinction from the world and at the same time to make clear his presence in the world. God calls creatures to himself out of nothing, and hence they obtain and have existence in him and only in an enduring relationship to him. Because their being depends on God's presence, they are nothing if left to themselves. Thus Eckhart can say in exaggeration that all creatures "are pure nothingness." But if the existence of creatures depends on God's presence, then there must be a point of contact with him. In man this is located in the depths of the spiritual soul in the state of grace. Here man is responsive not only to God's action but to God himself.

> I have a power in my soul which is fully responsive to God (Quint 323). God is in all things; but... nowhere so really as... in the innermost part and the highest part of the soul (Quint 356). It is the castle which Jesus enters, more according to his existence than according to his activity: by giving to the soul a divine and godlike existence through grace, which is oriented to

> essence and existence, according to the text: By the grace of God I am what I am . . . God has no more fitting abode than a pure heart and a pure soul; there the Father brings forth his Son, as he brought him forth in eternity, neither more nor less (Quint 175).

Hence on man is enjoined the duty of becoming "God's son by grace." "The image of God, the Son of God is in the soul as a living fountain." It must be freed of all concealing layers. Man must separate himself from all that is not God, especially from his own will. "That is pure which is detached and separated from all creatures, for all creatures defile, since they are nothingness" (Quint 175). Man is he "who submits himself to God with all that he is and has, obeys him, and gazes upward at God" (Quint 145). In keeping with the Gospel (Mark 8:35, and elsewhere), man must practice humility, poverty, resignation, seclusion, and self-denial in order to become free for the encounter with God in the depth of the soul. He must progress from distraction to recollection, from diversity to unity.

> Hence I say: If man renounces himself and all created things — to the extent that you do so, you will be united and blessed in the soul's little spark, which knows neither time nor place. This spark rejects all creatures and wants nothing but God, revealed as he is in himself (Quint 315f.).

Though mystical union in the depth of the soul is the highest stage that man can attain to, he is not permitted to remain satisfied with it. No creature can be man's beatitude and perfection, and so he must keep himself aloof from finite being in order to permit himself to be seized upon by God. But once man has become aware of God, then he can rightly know and love his fellowmen and things. In fact, whoever is most intimately united to God, "whoever does right," finds God in all things and deeds "Such a man bears God in all his works and in all places" (Quint 59). "Whoever thus has God in his existence understands God as God, and God radiates in him in all things; for in all things there is for him the taste of God, and the image of God becomes visible to him in all things" (Quint 60). Virginity must be realized in the fecundity of woman. "It is good that man receives God in himself and in this receptiveness he is a virgin; but for God to become fruitful in him is better, for to become fruitful with the gift is the only gratitude for the gift, and the spirit lies in gratitude returned. . . . " Contemplation and the active life thus call for each other. Mary at the Lord's feet was only at the beginning.

> For when she was [still] sitting at our Lord's feet, she was not [yet the true] Mary; she may have been in name but not [yet] in her being. For she [still] sat in pleasant feeling and sweet sensation and was being taken in hand and was [now] learning life. But Martha was fully real there (Quint 288).
>
> If a man were in ecstasy as was Saint Paul and knew of a sick man who wanted a bit of broth from him, I would deem it far better for you to surrender the ecstasy out of love and serve the needy one in greater love (Quint 76).

The condemned propositions extracted from Master Eckhart's works, in so far as they clearly reflect his views, can be shown to be orthodox in the context of his doctrine. We must also bear in mind the difficulty of the mystic, who must express subtle knowledge and experiences of the spiritual life in human speech, particularly in a vernacular hardly developed for this. Yet, the charge of "having propounded many doctrinal propositions which laid a smoke screen over the true faith in many hearts, which he taught above all in his sermons to simple people, and which he also put in writing," is not wholly wrong. The cause here lay in his boundless and ever more extravagant eagerness to express himself even to excess and in paradox, which in his exalted solitude saw no need to have regard for the many who did not understand him, who in fact could not but misunderstand him. "If, however, there is anyone who understands this word incorrectly, what can be done by one who correctly utters this word which is correct?" (Quint 139). But if truth is to be expressed in love (Ephesians 4:15), the theologian, and in particular the preacher, must be guided by a pastoral consideration. It was also dangerous that Eckhart in his speculation on the Logos lost sight of the historical Christ and did not accept the literal sense of Scripture as his standard, while the Church and the Sacraments, though not denied, were not given their proper place. At that very time the Church was concerned with rejecting the extravagances of the nominalists.

John Tauler

Master Eckhart's most important disciples were John Tauler (ca. 1300–1361) and Henry Suso (1295–1366). While avoiding bold formulation, they aimed to make clear the orthodoxy of Eckhart's ideas and to prevent their being misused by enthusiasts.

Tauler was probably never a lecturer and hence it is unlikely that he attended the *Studium generale* at Cologne. He probably studied at Strasbourg or elsewhere in southern Germany. He may have known of Eckhart through his writings, which were available to him in 1339 at Cologne or Strasbourg. Perhaps he met the master personally when the latter was on the upper Rhine carrying out his function in the order. From 1330 Tauler was a preacher in Strasbourg, his native city. In the conflict between Louis the Bavarian and John XXII the city sided with the Emperor and hence lay under interdict from 1329 to 1353. When the conflict reached its critical stage and Louis ordered the public celebration of Mass, Tauler and his community withdrew to Basel in 1338–39. Here he was in touch with Henry of Nördlingen and the "friends of God." He spent some time in Cologne in 1339 and 1346. In 1342 he must have returned with his community from Basel to Strasbourg, where thereafter he was chiefly concerned with popular preaching and the spiritual care of nuns and Beguines. He died at Strasbourg on 16 June 1361.

There is still no critical edition of Tauler's works. Only his German sermons are undeniably authentic, and only about eighty of the 144 ascribed to him. His mysticism is based on Eckhart's speculations but it has a more ethical and psychological orientation, is far more practically concerned for day-to-day living, and places more strongly in the foreground the exertion of the will in the purgative way. In Tauler the divine birth is not so much a participation in the divine knowing as an assimilation to the divine will after the example of the suffering and life of Christ. Tauler, the practical mystic, pastor of souls, and cheerful master, gained through his preaching enthusiastic listeners in the circles of the "friends of God."

Tauler frequently admonishes that contemplation should be rendered effective in active love. The active life, then, is not merely a preparation for the contemplative life but just as much its fruit.

> You should know that, if I were not a priest and did not live in an order, I would regard it as a great thing to be able to make shoes and I would do it better than anything else and would be happy to earn my bread with my hands.... I know one of the most honored friends of God. He has been a farmer all his days, more than forty years, and that is what he still is. He once asked our Lord whether he should stop work and go to the church. But the Lord said: No, he should not do that; he should earn his bread in the sweat of his brow in honor of the Lord's precious blood.

Henry Suso

If daring and lonely speculation was characteristic of Eckhart and practical ethical striving of Tauler, Henry Suso was noteworthy for the warmth and depth of his feeling. He was born around 1295 at Constance of a knightly family. Having become a Dominican at the age of thirteen, he studied at the house in Constance and then around 1322 was sent to the *Studium generale* at Cologne. Here he was an enthusiastic disciple of Eckhart and was with him during his trial. From around 1327 he acted as lecturer at Constance, but around 1330 he was reprimanded for his association with Eckhart. Hence he did not continue his academic career but devoted himself entirely to the care of souls, chiefly in the houses of nuns on the upper Rhine and in Switzerland. He was in contact with the "friends of God" and engaged in a lively correspondence with them and with his spiritual women disciples, especially Elsbeth Stagel, who edited his autobiography. In the *Büchlein der Wahrheit* (*Little Book of Truth*) Suso defended Eckhart's mysticism and sought to protect it against misunderstandings. In the *Büchlein der ewigen Weisheit* (*Little Book of Eternal Wisdom*), and its expanded and widely disseminated Latin version, the *Horologium Sapientiae,* Suso provided a practical mysticism of the following of the suffering Christ and union with his Mother beneath the Cross. He expresses his mystical doctrine in the words: "A detached man must put off the image of the creature, be formed into the image of Christ, and be further formed into the image of the God-head." Thus Suso was in the school of Eckhart. But in the manner of his mystical way, with its orientation to the tangible events and situations of the life of Christ, accessible to contemplation and actual imitation, he is far removed from his master. This moulding and this very detailed description of sacred history call directly for artistic representation. Thus Suso's mysticism stands in an especially close, perhaps reciprocal, relation to the pictorial art of his age. As the minnesinger and poet among the mystics, he combined sensitivity and warmth of feeling with chivalrous magnanimity. This investing of the "mystical devotion to God with the symbolism of courtly love," to use the words of Kunisch, caused him to stress clearly the relation to the beloved "thou" and preserved him from a pantheistic misunderstanding.

Mysticism was not confined to the few great masters from the ranks of the Dominicans. But the diocesan priest Henry of Nördlingen (d. after 1379) lacked their independence and depth. His significance lay in his tireless activity in many places, as leader and adviser of the "friends of God" in the world and in the cloister, for the spread of the notions and practice of the mystical life. His correspondence with Margaret Ebner (d. 1351) and her circle is the oldest extant collection of letters in German. It affords a glimpse into the life of the mystical circles of the fourteenth century.

Jan van Ruysbroeck

In the area of the Netherlands and Flanders German mysticism reached its peak in Jan van Ruysbroeck (Ruusbroec). He was born in 1293 in the village of Ruysbroeck between Brussels and Hal. After his ordination in 1318 he acted as vicar of Saint Gudula at Brussels, but at the age of fifty (1343) he withdrew with some like-minded canons into the solitude of Groenendael. They lived here as a community of hermits until 1350 when they adopted the rule of the Augustinian canons. Ruysbroeck became prior of the new monastery. He was in close relationship with mystics and reform circles, and Gerard Groote and perhaps also Tauler came to see him. He died in 1381 at the age of eighty-eight.

His eleven authenticated writings were composed in great part while he was still a diocesan priest. The urban population of the economically and culturally highly developed Netherlands was prepared for a deeper religious life in keeping with its greater maturity and independence and set higher standards for itself as well as for preaching and pastoral care. This is evident in the numerous communities of Beguines and Beghards, Men and women of deep religious sensitivity but of insufficient theological training were exposed to the danger of falling victim to an unenlightened heretical exuberance in their mystical religious aspirations. If in addition it was not always easy to distinguish between genuine religious striving and experience and an ecstatic pseudo-mysticism, it was especially hard to determine the boundaries between, on the one hand, Beguines and Beghards, who, unlike the orders, were not clearly indicated by organization and theological education, and, on the other, such heretical groups as the "Brothers and Sisters of the Free Spirit." Time and again the former had been confused with these sectaries, who subscribed to a monistic pantheism, aimed to participate in the vision of God even in this world by being merged into the universal oneness of God, and fancied themselves to be above all laws and sinless. Closely connected with them was the visionary Blommaerdine (d. 1336), who in Ruysbroeck's day caused a great stir at Brussels through her teaching and writing and was idolized by her followers.

The young vicar of Saint Gudula sought by his writing to satisfy the genuine hunger for spiritual guidance and at the same time to counteract Blommaerdine's false mysticism. Hence in 1330 he wrote his treatise *Von dem Reich der Liebenden* (*The Kingdom of Lovers*) and soon after his most admired work, *Zierde der geistlichen Hochzeit* (*The Spiritual Espousals*). To this period of his pastoral activity at Brussels belong also the works *Vom glänzenden Stein* (*On the Sparkling Stone*), *Von den vier Versuchungen* (*The Four Temptations*), and *Vom Christenglauben* (*On the Christian Faith*), an explanation of the creed for the use of priests. The very large, *Buch von den geistlichen Tabernakeln* (*Book of the Spiritual Tabernacles*) was completed at Groenendael. It was strongly critical of the Church and clergy of the day. *Von den sieben Einschliessungen* (*On the Seven Enclosures*) was intended for nuns. In the *Spiegel der ewigen Seligkeit* (*Mirror of Eternal Happiness*) Ruysbroeck provides a comprehensive instruction in the spiritual life. The *Buch von den sieben Stufen auf der Treppe geistlicher Minne* (*Book of the Seven Steps on the Ladder of Spiritual Love*) strongly emphasizes asceticism, while *Das Buch von den zwölf Beginen* (*Book of the Twelve Beguines*) is a collection of pious meditations. In order to counteract all misunderstandings, Ruysbroeck, when almost seventy, once more took up his pen and, at the request of friends, gave a condensed explanation of his doctrine in *Samuel oder das Buch von der höchsten Wahrheit* (*Samuel or the Book of the Sovereign Truth*).

The starting point and the final goal of Ruysbroeck's mysticism is God, one and three-in-one. His idea of the world and of man and even more his doctrine of grace and the spiritual and mystical life are oriented to the Trinity. God's being exceeds all limits, is *wijselos,* is "inaccessible height, abysmal depth, incomprehensible breadth, eternal length, a gloomy silence, a sumptuous desert." But his nature

> is fecund. Hence it does not remain in the oneness of fatherhood but must generate unceasingly the Eternal Wisdom, the Son of the Father.... Since the Father beholds his Son, the Eternal Wisdom, and all things in this same Wisdom, he was born and is a different person from the Father.

However, this self-contemplation of Father and Son is at the same time a mutual affirmation of self, is love. From the fact

> that the Son is born as a different person from the Father, since the Father beholds him as born and all things in him and with him, as a life of all things, and that the Son in turn beholds the Father as giving birth and fecund and himself and all things in the Father, proceeds a love, which is the Holy Spirit and the bond from Father to Son and from Son to Father. This giving birth and returning to unity is the work of the Trinity — unity of nature, trinity of persons.

This union of fruitfulness of nature and singleness of essence, of becoming and being, of activity and blessed enjoyment, of overflow into multiplicity and discharge into oneness, of beginning and completion, is the goal of the mystical life.

> The Holy Trinity has created us according to this eternal image and this parable. Hence God intends that we move out of ourselves in this divine light and seek to attain supernaturally to this image, which is our real life, and possess it with him, working and enjoying in everlasting blessedness.

As image, as mirror of the Triune God,

> the substance of our soul [has] three properties, which according to their nature are one. The first property is the formless and essential nakedness (*blooetheit*) whereby we are like the Father and his divine nature and united with him. The second property can be called the higher reason of the soul. It is a reflecting clarity in which we receive God's Son, the Eternal Truth. In the clarity we are like him, in receiving him we are one with him. The third

property we call the spark of the soul; it is a natural inclination of the soul for its origin, in which we receive the Holy Spirit, the love of God. In the inclining we are like the Holy Spirit, in the receiving we become one spirit and one love with God.

These three properties are at the same time the organs of the efficacy of the divine persons on the soul. We are created "to" the image of God, that is, the essence of the image is both giving and surrendering. "God has created us that we may find, know, and possess this image in our being and in the purity of the depth of our soul (*in puerheit onser ghedachten*)." In the spark of the soul God touches man, so that man feels him self drawn by God and begins his return to the purity and oneness of the spirit. This return to God in grace and the virtues, in the contemplative life and moral exertion, follows in three stages, the "active," the "intimate," and the "contemplative" life. These stages roughly correspond to the three ways of mysticism in general, and hence in Ruysbroeck the practical and personal feature is especially stressed.

In the "active" life there is question not so much of acquiring and practicing various virtues as of the "advent of Christ," to whom the pious person is betrothed, and of union with and likeness to the manner and work of Christ.

The aim and end of the "intimate" exercise is the mystical recognition of the bridegroom as he is in himself and the mystical union with him in the depth of the soul, which is made ready by the grace of God and the virtuous deeds of the "active life."

Likeness to and union with the Son leads to the Father, the source of the Godhead. Just as the Son proceeds from the Father in the eternal birth and flows back in love to unity, so does he speak to the soul united to him: "Follow me to my Father." Hence all holiness and beatitude consist in our being led to the Father, that is, to repose in the essential oneness. But as God, by virtue of his unity, abides in blessed repose and, by virtue of his trinity, works in active love, so the loving soul in the "God-seeing life" is one with God in repose and like him in works of love. In connection with Psalm 41:8 it is said:

> And the abyss [of God] calls to the abyss.... This calling is an outpouring of the essential light, and this essential light causes us to lose ourselves in the embrace of an unfathomable love and to escape into the wild darkness of the Godhead. And hence, one with God's spirit in a direct union, we can meet God through God; that is, like God and made in his image by God himself, by union and likeness with he Holy Spirit, the Son, and the Father, we can now take possession of God also in his oneness and repose, and hence of the divine nature as such. (G. Dolezich)

To this contemplation, this nearness of the depths of the soul with the depths of the Godhead,

> no one can attain by means of learning and cleverness nor by any sort of practice. But only he whom God wishes to make one with his Spirit and to illuminate with himself can seize upon God in contemplation — no one else.

This doctrine of God-seeing love in the third book of *The Spiritual Espousals,* according to which "the soul receives the clarity which is God" and "it becomes itself the clarity which it receives," and similar pantheistic-sounding sentences were attacked by John Gerson soon after 1400. But from the first Ruysbroeck anticipated reproaches of this sort, by often emphasizing in his later writings, as protection against misinterpretations, that this oneness of being with God must be understood as

> one with him in his love but not in his nature. For otherwise we would be God, annihilated in ourselves, which is impossible. Indeed, we are further formed by the Spirit of God, as iron by fire, so that, as far as there is iron, there is also fire, but the fire does not become iron and the iron does not become fire.

To what extent mysticism, as a movement of renewal, embraced large circles appears from numerous memoirs and *vitae* from the monasteries of women of the period. The most precious of these accounts of mystically gifted nuns are those of the sisters of Töss near Winterthur by Suso's friend, Elsbeth Stagel (d. ca. 1350–60), and of the nuns of Engelthal, which Christine Ebner (d. 1336) relates in the *Büchlein von der Gnadenüberlast* (*Little Book of Overflowing Grace*).

Lack of self-criticism and self-discipline then led easily to sensuous emotional excesses, to self-deception, and to extravagances in poor taste. John Gerson (d. 1429) came out against such aberrations in the mysticism of his time. In his chief work, *De mystica theologia* (1408), he gave to mystical theology pre-eminence over scholastic theology and termed it the source of the complete knowledge of God. But he warned against a deviation of mystical love into sensuality and feasting on sweetness and showed the way to a practical piety.

Of the Dominicans who kept up with the spiritual legacy of their order in the fifteenth century, John Nider (d. 1438) is especially noteworthy. In his writings, for example *Vierundzwanzig guldin Harfen* (*Twenty-Four Golden Harps*), published at Strasbourg in 1493, and *Formicarius* (Strasbourg 1417), are found many phrases and ideas from fourteenth-century mysticism and resemblances to Henry Suso and John Tauler especially. But precisely because of the far-reaching agreement, the quite different attitude of the fifteenth century and the change in meaning of basic ideas become especially clear. Mystical speculation has yielded to guidance for pious living, determined by the care of souls. This turning to the ethical, the practical, and the concrete, joined to a stricter withdrawal from the world, is characteristic of the fifteenth century in general.

In the first half of the century a so far unknown "priest and guardian of the Teutonic Knights at Frankfurt," as the introduction styles him, provided in his *German Theology* a "summary of the intellectual output of German mysticism" (J. Bernhart). Prudent in speculation, he was, like Tauler, concerned for the practical and pastoral. He would like, as a defense against "unauthentic, false, free spirits, who are harmful to Holy Church," to lead to the true and proper "friendship of God." In this book, which Luther edited for publication in 1516 and 1518, German mysticism acquired a direct influence on the reformer and on Lutheranism.

In mysticism we have before us a first initial effort of some importance toward a German theology, that is, the attempt to penetrate revelation on the part of German thinkers and with the possibilities of the German tongue. This endeavor did not get beyond the first starts, imposing as they are. Eckhart was condemned;

Tauler was slandered in connection with the Reformation and in 1559 put on the Index. Then the stream of German mysticism was sealed off, at least within the Catholic Church, and the chasm between spirituality and theology in the West became deeper still. At the Council of Trent and thereafter theology acquired an exclusively Romance coloring, and in it and in the liturgy the Latin language virtually took on the character of orthodoxy.

CHAPTER 45

Missionary Work of the Mendicants outside Europe

It was especially the two great mendicant orders, Dominicans and Franciscans, who were most responsible for carrying missionary work beyond Europe. As the first founder of an order, Francis of Assisi devoted to the missions a special chapter in his "Regula prima." Dominic "only gradually advanced into the great commitment of a world-embracing action" (Altaner), but the Preaching Friars were sent forth to evangelize not much later than the Friars Minor (1217–18).

When in 1219–20 Francis of Assisi proceeded to the camp of the Sultan of Egypt in order to preach Christianity to him, his action stimulated the emergence of the realization, slowly awakening during the crusades, that Christianity should not be spread by force of arms but only by preaching and love. At any rate, the missionary concept moved on equal terms alongside the crusading idea, even though it still needed a long time before its implications were fully clarified. Thus Roger Bacon (d. 1294) represented the view that it is better to convert infidels by means of knowledge and wisdom than by wars, whereas his confrère, Duns Scotus (d. 1308), demanded the severest punishment of idolators and allowed princes the right to spread God's Kingdom by force. In his *Defensor pacis* (1324) Marsilius of Padua taught that the Church has no coercive power against heretics and infidels, but the Council of Basel still held that Jews could be compelled to listen to Christian sermons.

Like theory, practice oscillated between the extremes. The mendicant orders offered their services not only for evangelization but for crusade preaching as well. Again and again events tempted Christendom to take up the sword. The victory of Alfonso VIII of Castile over the Muslims at Las Navas de Tolosa in 1212 was an inducement to transfer the war to African soil, and Honorius III granted the same indulgences as for a crusade. And the appearance of the Mongols raised the hope of finding in them allies against the Muslims. People regarded their Khans as successors of Prester John, whose image had excited the West for centuries.

Against public opinion, the mendicant orders gave preference to the missions.

It is true that in North Africa and the Near East their activity was missionary in intention rather than in reality. For in North Africa it was restricted to caring for the needs of Christian merchants, mercenaries, and slaves. Neither the Popes nor the Christian commercial city states could obtain from the sultans more than freedom of worship for Christians. Preaching to Muslims remained forbidden, and when the preachers violated the prohibition they risked their lives, as did the first Franciscan martyrs in Morocco, who even felt that they could preach as they did in Italy and harshly refuted the teachings of Islam. Still, the two sees of Morocco and Fez could be erected in North Africa.

In the Near East the mendicants were chiefly interested in bringing back the schismatics and they were so successful that Gregory IX in 1238 admitted that it is just as good to lead unbelievers to the praise of God as to overcome them by armed force. This activity among schismatic Christians was regarded as preliminary to missions among Muslims, and the Popes supported the mendicants in this view. They even gave them letters for the sultans in which the Christian faith and its messengers were commended. We thus hear of mission journeys to Aleppo, Damascus, Cairo, and Iconium. William of Tripolis who claimed many converts based them on an indication of his method: he had obtained his successes "by the simple Word of God, without philosophical arguments and without force of arms." This allusion was not unintentional, and it contradicted the prevailing opinion that Muslims could not be converted. The mission work of the mendicants among them made it clear that the reasons for the sterility of efforts thus far made were to be sought not only on the side of Islam but equally in the missionaries. Since a command of languages is the first requirement for properly facing the missionary project, the mendicants, and in particular the Dominicans, established their own schools of languages and eagerly pursued Islamic studies. In this connection can be mentioned Aquinas' *Summa contra gentiles.* Among the Franciscans Raymond Lull (1234–1315) is especially deserving of mention. Through various memoranda to the Popes, the King of France, and the University of Paris, he exerted himself to appeal to the conscience of Christendom and to draw attention to the duty to the missions. Besides the erecting of mission colleges, he suggested the founding of a supreme missionary authority, which, directed by a cardinal, should co-ordinate the mission efforts of the various orders.

The appearance of the Mongols in Eastern and Central Europe contributed directly to the expansion of mission work outside Europe. At first consideration was given to meeting them also with crusade methods. But once the gravest danger seemed to have been warded off from the West — after their victory at Liegnitz in 1241 the Mongols returned to Central Asia to arrange the succession to the khanate, — other ways of reaching them were sought. Among those who set out for the Mongol in the course of the following years, the most important was William of Ruysbroeck, who reached Karakorum and left a detailed account of his travels, which is generally reliable and valuable. The missionary aims of all these journeys are unmistakable, but in the final analysis they were not the appropriate means of effecting lasting conversions. William of Ruysbroeck had not yet returned when the Dominicans and the Franciscans, with papal encouragement, undertook direct missionary work. To what extent the mendicant friars were regarded as the real representatives of the Church's missionary work is shown by the resolution of the Cistercian general chapter to ask prayers for the heralds of the faith who were going to the Tartars. Not incorrectly has this directive been termed "the order's charter of resignation of its missionary activity" (B. Altaner).

Of special importance for the effectiveness of the mendicant orders was the jurisdictional organization of their mission work. Not only did the authority to dispose of the individual friars no longer lie with the respective superiors of the several houses but rather with the generals of the orders; the friars who chose the missionary vocation themselves constituted special missionary communities within their order. Even so, the ecclesiastical mission was received, not by these groups but by the order as such. The general handed over the mission by appointing prefects or vicars, who, at the orders of the general and as his representatives, were to supervise its implementation. Hence, unlike the later vicars apostolic, these prefects or vicars were not ecclesiastical authorities but religious officials. This arrangement is especially striking among the Franciscans. Their mission fields were divided into six vicariates: those of Tataria Aquilonaris, Tataria Orientis. and Cathay, embracing the lands of the Mongols, the Vicaria Marocchii for North Africa, and those of Bosnia and Russia for Southern and Eastern Europe. The Dominicans adhered in their mission territories to their familiar division into provinces. But toward the close of the thirteenth century there arose the *Societas fratrum peregrinantium propter Christum in gentes,* which seems to have included chiefly the Dominicans working in the Orient.

Activity among the unfamiliar peoples of Eastern Europe must be regarded as the starting point for the mission in the interior of Asia. As early as 1211 King Andrew II of Hungary had called upon the Teutonic Knights for protection from the invading Cumans.

It was not until 1253, after the diplomatic visits to the Mongols, that the missionary journeys to Eastern Europe were resumed. The first quarter-century of this new start is shrouded in darkness and only in 1278 do we discover efforts to reestablish the Cuman bishopric in connection with an account of the Franciscan missionaries working in Qipčaq, the Khanate of the Golden Horde. The Franciscans succeeded in baptizing the "Empress" Yailaq and eventually even the Khan Toqtai (1300–1312) and several members of his household. Around 1320 Franciscans were working even among the Bashkirs, but unfortunately the conversion of the Khan Uzbek (1312–40) to Islam soon forced the greatest part of the Golden Horde to embrace the religion of The Prophet. At the beginning of his reign the Vicariate of Tataria Aquilonaris counted seventeen settlements and between 1318 and 1321 Sarai became the see of a Latin bishop.

Political events contributed substantially to the development of the mission in Tataria Orientis, where the Mongols' originally hostile attitude to Islam roused great hopes. The incentive was provided by the taking of Baghdad in 1258 by Hulagu, a brother of the Great Khan Mangu. The Abbasid Caliphate in Persia came to an end, and Hulagu established the dynasty of the Il-khans (1256–1335). His empire embraced Iran, parts of Turkestan, Armenia, and eastern Anatolia, and Azerbaijan and Iraq. His warfare was aimed chiefly at the Mameluks of Egypt. Thus he established numerous contacts with the Christians of Syria and as a consequence there were missionary undertakings in the empire of the Il-khans and the neighboring lands.

Less stress was laid on the conversion of Muslims and pagans than on reunion with the Nestorian Church, which had benefited by Mongol toleration to reorganize itself in Asia. Efforts for union reached their climax when in 1287 the Catholicos Jahballahā III of Baghdad (1281–1317), an Ongüt, sent his confidant, the Uigur Bar-Sauma, to Rome. Bar-Sauma had no scruples about recognizing the papal primacy and in 1304 Jahballaha followed suit. But matters proceeded no further. Under the Il-khan Gazan (1295–1305) Islam gained the upper hand and the conflicts between Shi'ites and Sunnites contributed to the decline of the Il-khan empire. From 1295 the preaching of the faith to Muslims caused persecution and bloody martyrdoms. But the fact remains that in 1314 Dominicans and Franciscans each had fifteen monasteries in these areas.

Greater significance attaches to the missionary work on the farthest edge of the then known world, in China. The earliest contacts with the Mongol dynasty in China were made by Venetian merchants, the Polos, in 1261–69. They delivered to the Pope a message from the Great Khan Kublai (1260–94), in which he asked for 100 missionaries. But two expeditions sent by the papacy did not reach their goal. The first to arrive in China was the Franciscan John of Montecorvino, dispatched by Nicholas IV in 1289. He was the first to select, not the land route through the interior of Asia, but the sea route from the Persian Gulf. He delivered the papal letter to Kublai's successor Timur (Ch'eng-tsung, 1294–1307) and then began his apostolate, first among the Nestorian Ongüt in Northern Tenduc. He was able to bring their King George into union with Rome and in the latter's capital built a church, where the Latin Mass was celebrated in the Mongol tongue. Unfortunately, George died in 1298 and the strong opposition of the Nestorians induced John to seek out Khanbaliq, "city of the Khan," later Peking, where he began missionary work in the proper sense. After some setbacks he was able to establish a numerous community of Mongols and Chinese. In a letter of 1305 he recounted his successes and asked for assistance. In regard to mission procedure the letter is unusually rich in information. John emphasized catechetical and liturgical formation and excelled in intelligent and generous adaptation. His achievements induced Clement V to name John Archbishop of Peking in 1307, with Khanbaliq as metropolitan see for all the Mongol missions. Six bishops were sent by the Pope to China to consecrate John and then to be assigned by him to the suffragan sees of Zaitun (Fukien), Almaligh (Jagatai), Kaffa, Sarai, Tana, and Kumuk (Qipčaq). John directed the mission until 1328. At his death Catholic Christianity in China counted some 30,000 faithful, including about 15,000 Alans, whom the Mongols had transferred from the Caucasus to China. (The first Chinese plenary council, held at Shanghai in 1924, proposed the beatification of John of Montecorvino.)

John's accomplishments stand out in even greater relief when it is remembered that for years he worked alone. It was not till 1303 that he obtained an assistant. When John was appointed Archbishop, many mendicant friars tried to hurry to his aid, but how many of them reached their goal is not known. Still, there must have been several monasteries in China.

In the meantime Pope John XXII had reorganized Church affairs in Asia. In 1318 he erected the province of Sultaniyah, to which he assigned six suffragan sees, entrusting them to the Dominicans. His principal concern here was the promoting of reunion with the schismatic Armenians. Monks of the monastery of Qrna, having returned to Rome in a body, formed a special community and, with reference to their aim, called themselves the *Fratres Unitores.* They were loosely connected with the Order of Preachers and existed into the eighteenth century.

To the province of Sultaniyah belonged two sees located outside the area just referred to. One was Samarkand, in the province of Sogdiana in the Khanate of Jagatai. The other was Quilon (Kollam) in South India, which owed its origin to the circumstance that missionaries *en route* by sea to China transferred here to Chinese junks. The interval was filled with missionary work. From Quilon arose the first connections with Ethiopia.

Then disaster overtook the late mediaeval missionary work. The Black Death, which in 1348 carried off almost all the missionaries in Persia, on its progress through Europe also depopulated the monasteries of the homeland so that it became impossible to supply the required number of apostles for distant lands. To this was added the unceasing Islamization of the Mongols, forcibly completed under Timur-Leng (1336–1405). The religious toleration practiced by the Mongols was succeeded by intolerant Sunnite fanaticism, which met all missionary endeavors with bitter hostility. In addition, all travel was prevented by the wars with which Timur-Leng filled Asia for a whole generation.

For the Church in China matters were decided when in 1308 the Mongol Dynasty was overthrown by the nationalistic Ming. Until the beginning of the fifteenth century occasional reports concerning Christianity in China are found, but thereafter the final remnants seem to have perished. In 1410 the archbishopric of Sultaniyah was united with Khanbaliq, but in 1473 the Venetian Contarini found there neither churches nor Christians.

Success had been achieved neither in direct missionary work among the Muslims of North Africa nor in the endeavor to gain the Mongols as allies against Islam. On the contrary, the barrier which Islam had erected between Europe and Africa had been extended from the Near East into Central Asia when the Mongols turned to Islam. More than ever Christendom was eager to breach this barrier, and to do so became the goal of a community of Portuguese Knights who had united after the suppression of the Templars and in 1319 had been recognized by John XXII as the "Militia Iesu Christi." The bull "Ad ea ex quibus cultus" is not only the Magna Carta of the Order of the Knights of Christ. It is equally the basis for Portugal's colonial expansion, for ecclesiastical jurisdiction in the conquered territories, and for the future Portuguese royal *padroado* in the missions.

In contrast to the other military orders, the Order of Christ had to conduct the war against the Muslims chiefly on the sea. Since Southern Spain was still under the rule of the Moors, it was important to gain a foothold in North Africa and attack the enemy from the rear. This tactical idea was maintained when Prince Henry the Navigator (1394–1460), after the victory of Ceuta (1415), laid the ground for the Portuguese voyages of discovery. The Holy See did everything possible to promote these undertakings. In 1418 Martin V summoned all of Portugal to the crusade against the Muslims and to the spread of the faith. In 1443 Eugene IV awarded all islands, conquered or to be conquered (!), to the Order of Christ. In the bull "Romanus Pontifex" Nicholas V gave voice to the expectations of all Christendom: that the voyages of discovery on the African coast should help to find the sea-route to India, to enter into an alliance with the Saint Thomas Christians living there, and to lay hold of the Muslims from behind. The bull awarded

Portugal a monopoly of conquest and trade on all seas and islands. In return, Portugal had to do all in its power for the spread of the faith. A protest by Castile was rejected by Calixtus III in 1456 and quasi-episcopal jurisdiction over all lands still to be conquered was given to the Order of Christ in perpetuity. This was to be of exceptional significance for evangelization in the following epoch, since all authority granted for the mission was to be regarded only as delegated authority. The vicars and prefects of the contemporary sources were not ecclesiastical officials but deputies of the Order of Christ. This meant also that missionary activity could develop only on the Portuguese firing line.

Section Two

The Western Schism and the Councils

Chaps. 46, 48–50: Karl August Fink
Chap. 47: Irwin Iserloh

CHAPTER 46

The Western Schism to the Council of Pisa

The premature death of Gregory XI placed the Church in a difficult situation. The Curia, back in Rome, and in particular the many French cardinals were not yet acclimated to Italy, and six cardinals were still at Avignon. The anxiety of the Romans lest they might again lose the recently recovered papacy makes it easy to understand their exertions to obtain a Roman or at least an Italian as the new Pope. These exertions were not confined to requests and expostulations; they took on the forms of violence.

Even during the obsequies for Gregory XI there were riots in the city, and after the sealing off of the conclave in the Vatican Palace on the evening of 7 April 1378 the excitement and pressure increased notably. Thousands of Romans noisily demanded someone from Rome or at least a native of Italy as Pope. It was only with great effort that armed bands could be removed from the area of the conclave. On the same evening the desire for an Italian Pope was presented to the sixteen cardinals — eleven French, four Italians, and one Spaniard — by the heads of the urban "regions." The cardinals gave them an evasive reply.

Even apart from these external troubles, the usual factional groupings gave reason to expect that the course of the business would be unpleasant. The strongest faction comprised the so-called Limousins, who were interested in continuing the tradition of the three recent Limousin Popes. Opposed to them was the small so-called French faction, determined to thwart this project at any cost. With this in mind, outside candidates had already been mentioned, including the Archbishop of Bari, Bartholomew Prignano, regent of the papal chancery, since the actual vice-chancellor was still at Avignon. He may have seemed acceptable to both French and Italians, for he came from Angevin Naples and had spent many years at Avignon.

A proper election procedure soon proved to be impossible. The very next morning, following a restless night, the disturbances were renewed. Again and again the guardian of the conclave, the Bishop of Marseilles, had to send for the seniors of the three orders of cardinals to have them calm the mob by holding out the prospect of a Roman or an Italian Pope in the course of the day. In the early morning a part of the cardinals decided to vote for Prignano. Whether this was with a general reservation is not entirely certain, but it is attested for a few cardinals. In the afternoon, some, but not all, of the cardinals sought to repeat the voting in regard to Prignano and to question the candidate, who had meanwhile been sent for, as to his acceptance of the election. But they were unable to finish, for then ensued an invasion of the conclave. It was calmed for the moment when it was declared that the aged Roman Cardinal Tebaldeschi had been elected. Despite his resistance he was enthroned before the altar of the chapel by the mob. The other cardinals profited by the break to flee, six to Castel Sant'Angelo, the others to their residences or outside Rome. On the next afternoon twelve cardinals returned voluntarily or were called to the Vatican to complete the election procedure.

The real problem begins after this very dubious election, since the cardinals took part in the enthronement, treated Urban VI (1378–89) as Pope, at least outwardly, presented their petitions to him, and sent notification of the election to the princes. Thereby tacit consent was given and the cardinals lost their right of protest against "pressure" in the election.

Consideration must be given above all to the collection of about sixty manuscripts preserved in the Vatican archives under the title *Libri de schismate.* This comprises a many-layered material, which goes from the beginning of the Schism to the turn of the century and was compiled by a loyal adherent of Benedict XIII, Martin de Zalva, Bishop of Pamplona and Cardinal. Later it passed into the possession of Benedict XIII, who had a *tabula* prepared for ready use. Hence the collection served the practical purpose of defending legitimacy, but it was more far-reaching and took the opposing side into full consideration. It has often been utilized, and is the basis of a variety of interpretations.

The first really important hearings took place in Rome in March 1379 and were in favor of Urban. A second hearing was arranged at Barcelona in May and September 1379 by the royal council, and it supported Clement. The twenty-three witnesses interrogated at Rome in November 1379 decided for Urban. We are best informed about such efforts in the Iberian peninsula and in most detail for Castile, where King Henry II was kept very well informed by his envoys then staying in Italy; in view of the difficult circumstances the strictest secrecy and the utmost circumspection were maintained. Then, by order of the new King John I, extensive hearings were conducted at Avignon in May 1380 and at Rome in the following July as the basis for the great judicial procedure at Medina del Campo from November 1380 to May 1381; further written material was submitted here and oral testimony received. More than 100 declarations of all tendencies were here considered and, after months of deliberations, they resulted in the Kingdom's deciding for Clement VII. Much later, in the summer of 1386, the King of Aragón had forty more persons questioned at Avignon, and, as expected, they pronounced in favor of the Pope there resident. These late declarations also, despite the great lapse of time and the consolidation of the obediences, are not without value, but the organization of the process in Castile excels all the others.

What, then, is the result of these efforts to ascertain the *factum?* This *dubium in facto* was examined from all points of view with the aim of investigating the events in Urban's election down to the least detail and, as far as possible, the intention of the electors. The opinion of the election is virtually unanimous. The election was not free but resulted from *impressio,* from *metus qui cadit in constantem virum,* neither absolutely valid nor absolutely null, but in any event controvertible. If an effort is made to form a picture out of this thicket of numberless declarations (*depositiones*), it does not favor Urban, not merely in view of the events of the election and his personality but also in regard to the period immediately after the election.

The first reports reaching the outside carried chiefly only the news of the completion of the election and with it the acceptance or recognition of the one elected. But, before long, details of the happenings in Rome were known in various places, and these urged caution if not reserve n regard to recognizing the new Pope. Everything now depended on how the new Pope conducted himself and whether the defects in the election could be eliminated by actual subsequent consent.

But matters did not turn out that way at all. Soon there were quarrels and collisions with the envoys of princes, with cardinals, bishops, and curial functionaries, and politically very unwise behavior toward such persons as Queen Joanna I of Naples and the German King Wenceslas. Furthermore, basic reforms were at once announced — to begin with the cardinals. It was not so much the question of reform that was important but rather of the unfortunate style and method of an authoritarian, dictatorial government by a hitherto subordinate curial *archiepiscopellus,* as one cardinal called him to his face, of a morbidly exalted notion of his new office, no longer corresponding to the actual status of the papacy, and of an offensive arrogance gushing from this. All this confirms the impression of a pathological personality.

What had previously been active only in the background and had been expressed only with the utmost caution quickly put in an appearance after the beginning of the summer *villeggiatura.* In quick succession the cardinals left Rome in June with the Pope's permission and came together at Anagni. The Curia had been transferred there and the Pope intended to follow. Now voices were multiplied, speaking of an invalid election, of new discussions to take place at Anagni, of a second election under normal circumstances, and also of a council and of a sort of tutelage for the not completely qualified Pope. These voices did not remain concealed from Urban; even cardinals now made known to him their misgivings. Though he was not fully aware of the gravity of the situation, he put off going to Anagni and at the end of July went to Tivoli. Shortly before this there had appeared in Rome an official representative of the cardinals assembled at Anagni to make known to him their opinion: that he had no right to the papal dignity and would either be reelected or otherwise provided for.

The three Italian cardinals, still in Rome and as yet undecided, were thereupon sent by Urban to Anagni with compliant proposals that betrayed weakness. But before long he returned to his usual obstinacy and rejected the considerations put forth by a new embassy from the cardinals as well as those of the Italian cardinals, who returned to him at Tivoli. He would not consent to one or more coadjutors who would cover up his incapacity, but demanded unconditional recognition of the validity of his election. The declaration of the French cardinals of 20 July with regard to the nullity of the election and hence of the vacancy of the see rendered further negotiations complicated, while the three Italians, who continued to regard a council as the final remedy, did not return to the Pope again but maintained relations only in writing. Submission on Urban's part was less and less to be looked for.

Decisive discussions among all the cardinals took place in mid-September at Fondi. Once again the Italians referred to a council, which need not include all bishops but could consist of representatives of each province. Venice, Pisa, and Naples were suggested, or even the Piedmontese area because of its proximity to France. These considerations foundered on the difficulties attendant upon the convocation and the interim administration, and it required decades of discussions before the matter was clarified.

These consultations at Fondi concluded with a new election. Presumably, the Italians had been given reason for hope and so they took part in the conclave of 20 September. None of them, however, was elected, but instead Cardinal Robert of Geneva, who had long been considered. If one so desired, one could see in him a neutral, between France and Italy. He was elected on 20 September, the election was proclaimed on the twenty-first, and on 31 October he was crowned as Clement VII (1378–1394). The Schism was a reality.

As regards the Curia and its staff, Robert's election was for the most part hailed. Whoever could escape from Rome did so, along with official books, registers, and the impressions for the seals. The highest ranking officials of the curial administration went over to Clement VII and hence Urban's position appeared very precarious. Both claimants endeavored by means of numerous letters and embassies to kings, princes, bishops, universities, and cities to prove their legitimacy and to acquire recognition. At first the political climate seemed to favor Clement, but he was unable to take possession of Rome and of Urban's person. On the contrary, following the victory of Urban's mercenaries near Marino on 29 April 1379 and his acquiring of Castel Sant'Angelo, Clement had to withdraw from Italy, in spite of the support of the Queen of Naples, and retire to Avignon in May 1381. From this last point persons have rashly inferred a close understanding with the French King at the time of the events in Anagni and Fondi. But at the start France seems to have held back, even if its sympathies were with Clement.

For Urban it was important to organize a new Curia. Urban was almost universally recognized in Italy, with its many large and small lordships. When a quick decision between the *primus electus* and the *secundus electus* and the holding of a council did not materialize, the Great Schism began to come clearly into view. It was consummated mainly under political aspects. On Urban's side, in addition to Italy, were ranged especially the Empire and King Wenceslas, the eastern and Nordic countries and Hungary, and, of the western states, England, the enemy of France. After a brief neutrality France became Clement VII's chief support, along with its dependent territories, Burgundy, Savoy, and Naples, and Scotland, the foe of England.

There were likewise political areas where a decision for one claimant or the other did not occur so rapidly. Since the call for a council, raised early, could not be realized, or at least not soon, efforts were made to form a judgment on the basis of the most exact possible examination of the facts. The careful endeavors in Castile have already been mentioned; they resulted in the recognition of Clement VII in 1380. More so than in previous schisms an attitude of reserve appeared, the so-called indifference, which does not mean unconcern or a lack of interest, but a neutral waiting for a universally acceptable solution of the extremely difficult canonical questions. Meanwhile, the administration of Church benefices and finances in the "indifferent" territories required a competent authority. It was not merely financial aspects which led in Aragón especially to the organizing of a royal *Camera Apostolica;* in many places a similar expedient was resorted to. More so than in these large states there were difficulties on the frontiers of the obediences, where the Schism often assumed bizarre forms, above all on the western boundary of the Empire, which did not even present a stable line and hence produced frequent changes.

At the beginning of the Schism Clement displayed a feverish activity in an effort to secure influence in Germany, an area lacking a strong central power. Many provisions, expectatives, and interventions in disputed cases have come down to us but we do not always know the outcome. The upper Rhine sees of Constance, Basel and Strasbourg, Duke Leopold of Austria, Count Eberhard of Württemberg, Margrave Bernard of Baden, and lower Rhine princes and cities inclined to Clement. But apart from the borderlands, the Roman obedience clearly consolidated itself in the Empire, chiefly through the activity of King Wenceslas and the Urbanist alliance brought about by the efforts of the Count Palatine Rupert I, as well as by the successful legation of Cardinal Pileo da Prata. But not even all the German bishops entered the Urbanist alliance; in spite of the prevailing sympathy for Urban, imperial unanimity was unthinkable.

The split also affected the centrally organized religions orders, which soon had a duplication of superiors and of general chapters. For the same reason there was schism in the cathedral and collegiate chapters, and dissension even invaded families, though, of course, we do not know much about the distress of consciences. Only in the field of international finance was there little evidence of the split in Christendom, since most banks served both obediences.

Clement VII, an extremely able politician, was not content with drawing up the Mass *De schismate tollendo* and arranging processions for ending the evil; he stubbornly strove for the *via facti,* so that Italy would have come entirely under French rule or influence. Here again it was high politics that impeded the realization of the *via facti,* above all the opposition between England and France, which had its effect also on the situation in Italy.

At scarcely any other period of the peninsula's history was it so confused and were alliances and treaties so fragile. This was the age of the greatest ascendancy of the Visconti at Milan. Virtually all undertakings of the Italian *signorie* took place under the proud banner of *Italianità,* but in reality this mostly constituted the trimmings for selfish political ends. But interventions by France and the German King had to be avoided if a balance of power was to be maintained.

The two papal claimants were to a great extent mere figures in the high politics of Europe and of the small Italian states. Again and again one comes across a readiness to switch obediences at a favorable opportunity. But the situation existing shortly after the outbreak of the Schism was maintained for a long time. Because of his unfortunate policy Urban VI repeatedly ran into difficulties. His expedition to Naples, undertaken from considerations of nepotism in addition to other reasons, ended with his being detained at Nocera. He escaped to Genoa only by great exertions and there had some discontented cardinals cruelly executed. After a long absence he returned to Rome in 1388 and died there a year later.

When the prescribed interval after Urban's death had ended, the conclave began at Rome without any serious consideration of postponing an election. After a few days, agreement was reached on the still youthful Neapolitan Cardinal Peter Tomacelli, who became Boniface IX (1389–1404). He at once turned against Louis I of Anjou and hence against France, from where loomed the gravest danger in the repeatedly projected campaigns into Italy, now in agreement with Milan, now with Florence. Many cities in the north of the Papal State were openly sympathetic toward Avignon, and even Viterbo was for a while Clementine. But Boniface IX contrived to establish himself in Rome and then in the Papal State. His pontificate was without great significance in the general field of politics. Much as he frequently and willingly had recourse to arguments common to Italians a large or decisive role in the maintenance of the balance of power can probably not be ascribed to him.

Two weeks after the death of Clement VII, the Avignon College of Cardinals elected a successor on 28 September 1394, even though the desire of the French government that there be no election immediately had been made known to the cardinals while still in conclave by protagonists of the *via cessionis.* Peter de Luna, now elected and styling himself Benedict XIII (1394–1423), was certainly the most outstanding figure in the Avignon College and fully conversant with all the theological and canonical problems of the Schism. With most of his colleagues in the conclave he had signed under oath a statement that he would devote himself to union with all zeal and would even abdicate in the event that the cardinals should regard this as necessary. This *via cessionis* had for years been prominent in discussions and considerations for the ending of the Schism. It had been frequently brought up under Clement VII and possessed a notable majority in both Colleges of Cardinals.

In many respects Benedict XIII was the heir of the policy of Clement VII, such as in his confidence in the *via facti,* that is, the settling of the question in a practical manner by a campaign in Italy. But Benedict displayed an incomparably greater energy and diplomatic skill. In his first close contacts with the court of Paris for the liquidation of the Schism in October 1394 he was very courteous, but in January 1395 he precisely stated his views and later rejected the decrees of the first Council of Paris, held in the spring.

After there had been discussions at Paris for years on the ways of restoring unity, there began also at Avignon a feverish activity in this direction. Opinions and pamphlets circulated, predominantly in the sense of the *via discussionis* (*conventionis, compromissi, iustitiae*), but also of the *via cessionis* as a last resort. Meanwhile, the so-called first Council of Paris (3–8 February 1395), under the influence of a few cardinals and of the extreme factions at the University, had declared abdication to be the only way to be adopted. This was contrary to the moderate proposals of d'Ailly, who returned from an embassy to the Pope. Then in the summer of 1395 (22 May–9 July) there appeared at Avignon a "high embassy," consisting of the King's uncles, and his brother, the Duke of Orléans, with many experts and delegates of the University. In several audiences they made known to the Pope the King's vigorously formulated desire but were able, of course, to obtain from Benedict only an evasive reply which rejected the *via cessionis.* The embassy had more success with the cardinals, most of whom in personal interviews consented to the *via cessionis.* The government at Paris exerted itself in numerous embassies to the German princes and to Kings Wenceslas and Sigismund, to King Richard II of England, and to Spain to gain support for this plan.

A second synod of the French clergy at Paris, from 16 August to 15 September, was again preoccupied with the unsatisfactory situation. In accord with the royal instructions the deliberations were to deal no longer with the *via cessionis,* but only with the best method of realizing it. The majority favored a withdrawal of obedience, but one more admonition should be directed to the Pope before suitable measures were taken. Meanwhile, he had not been idle. He eagerly sought to promote the *via conventionis* by negotiations with the Roman claimant and even more to effect the elimination of his rival by the *via facti.* Benedict's envoy, the Bishop of Elne, was able to bring about a dangerous conspiracy against Boniface IX. The Bishop of Tarazona, received at Rome as Benedict's ambassador in the summer of 1396, had very interesting discussions with Boniface and a few cardinals, including the events in the election of Urban VI, in which he had taken part as a conclavist. The repeated offers for an encounter of the two rivals or at least for negotiations by plenipotentiaries were repulsed by Boniface. Boniface's apprehensions were not unfounded, for Benedict had many adherents in Italy and enjoyed much sympathy even in Rome.

En route from Sicily to Aragón, King Martin I had visited Benedict at Avignon and had been won to his policy. Hence he participated in Benedict's efforts to enter into serious discussions with his rival or to reach a decision by the *via facti.* The Aragonese King, loyal to Benedict, wanted to gain also the King of Castile for this policy, but without success, since political developments bound Castile ever more strongly to France. And in the meantime France had succeeded in finding sympathy for the *via cessionis* in England, hitherto belonging to the Roman obedience. To what degree politics decided ecclesiastical questions is evident from this procedure of England, which resulted automatically from its *rapprochement* with France. Envoys of the Kings of England, France, and Castile went to Avignon and Rome but could accomplish nothing definite.

Of great importance for theory and practice was the third Council of Paris, which sat from the middle of May till the beginning of August 1398 and declared the withdrawal of obedience. Estimates of it differ greatly, but two notions seem especially pertinent. By being deprived of his income from France the Pope should be forced to resign and on this pretext the influence of the government in the administration of the French Church, naturally including the financial aspect, should be further strengthened. The decree of withdrawal was dated 27 July, and on the following day it was solemnly published by the King. In the next weeks instructions were issued to the officials. Almost no one in the Kingdom resisted the decrees of the synod, and at Avignon itself eighteen cardinals, one after another, abandoned the Pope and betook themselves to French territory at Villeneuve-lès-Avignon. There they made preparations for impeding Benedict in the exercise of his office and for getting him into their power if possible.

Thus began the memorable siege of the papal palace, which the Pope had some time before converted into a fortress, well provided with all war equipment. The shelling and assaults made in the fall of 1398 by the troops engaged by the cardinals, were at first without effect. Though a fleet sent by the King of Aragón was unable to get as far as Avignon, there ensued a truce in May 1399 and the departure of the greater part of the garrison. However, Benedict was isolated in the palace by a zone of stockades until 1403 and only scantily supplied, despite several safe-conducts which the Duke of Orléans had secured from the King. By secret protests in the summer of 1399 Benedict had in law repudiated all concessions wrung from him. On 12 March 1403 he made a fantastic escape from the papal palace down the Rhone to the Château-Renard in the territory of the Count of Provence. With this there began a new episode in the troubled history of the Western Schism.

An almost incalculable number of discussions and embassies had prepared, accompanied, and effected this result. Even during the siege Benedict was in contact with the disloyal cardinals and Paris. There the difficulties attendant upon the withdrawal had become greater and greater in the administration of benefices and in the Church's financial system. If the bishops had expected more independence by virtue of the "liberties of the Gallican Church," they felt greatly deceived. The court and the government took the place of the papal Curia. Wide circles doubted the legitimacy of the proceedings against one who till now had been defended as the only lawful Pope, and his inflexibility created a profound impression. Apparently he was not to be subdued by military measures. Withdrawal by the government and siege by the College of Cardinals were not regarded as legitimate means for liquidating the unsatisfactory state of things. For this a judgment of the Church, and hence a council, was qualified. And representatives of the French government discussed such a council at Metz and Mainz with Rupert of the Palatinate, elected King of Germany on the deposition of Wenceslas.

Provence had returned to Benedict in 1402 and in Paris Castile was working for a restitution of obedience as the best way out of the hopeless situation. To Château-Renard went the cardinals, to obtain reconciliation with Benedict. Then faithless Avignon also submitted to the now liberated Pope. But still certain concessions on Benedict's part had to be discussed with the Duke at Tarascon. Absolution was granted to the King *ad cautelam* and the new peace was sealed by a compact of the Pope with the King, the Queen, and the Duke.

Soon after his liberation, Benedict sent important proposals to Rome: (1) for a meeting of the two rivals on the borders of their respective obediences or in Italy, for example in the territory of Genoa; (2) for negotiations by plenipotentiaries in the event that the claimants could not meet personally (3) for resignation. All of this was rejected by Boniface. Even considering the tendencies of the reports that have come down to us in a biased form, Boniface does not cut a fine figure. His death, occurring while the Avignon envoys were in Rome, interrupted the contact, and the new Pope Innocent VII, Cosimo Migliorati (1404–6), did not take part in discussions.

However, Benedict stubbornly pursued his projects in missions to Sicily and to many Italian cities and lordships. He gained for his obedience a great part of the Riviera with Genoa, which was then ruled by Marshal Boucicaut, and proceeded as far as Genoa, but was then forced by the outbreak of an epidemic to return to

Marseilles. In Paris this move into Italy was regarded with a certain amount of fear that the Pope, if successful in his Italian schemes, might be able to reside in Rome.

The death of Innocent VII in 1406 seemed to open up another solution when Benedict asked the Roman cardinals not to proceed to an election. But before his envoys arrived the new Pope had been elected: the Venetian Angelus Correr, who became Gregory XII (1406–15). Just as earlier at the election of Benedict XIII at Avignon, now too each cardinal had bound himself, in the event of his election, to resign if the same thing were to happen on the opposing side; specific regulations concerned the naming of new cardinals in order to maintain both colleges at numerical equality. This was a step in the direction of a meeting of the two rivals or at least of the two Colleges of Cardinals.

During the night following his election Gregory had solemnly accepted these stipulations and in numerous letters to kings, princes, and cities he had proclaimed his willingness to resign. Then on 21 April 1407 was signed the Treaty of Marseilles, in which, as its principal item, the meeting of the claimants at Savona near Genoa on Michaelmas was agreed to. But from now on Gregory's behavior is difficult to understand. His postponing the fulfillment of the treaty, in fact his downright refusal to do so, has been interpreted as due to the unfortunate influence of his nephews. But the danger of his position was sufficiently well known to him and his fear of a trap was not entirely groundless. His words and deeds, however, hardly display greatness in comparison with the dignified, learned, and very skilful diplomatic procedure of Benedict, who was apparently more profoundly convinced of his legitimacy and of the success of his plans. Benedict was in a far better situation than Gregory. The King of Aragón, with his considerable strength in the Mediterranean, clung loyally to him, and in the Midi he had many adherents. In the reports of the negotiations the mutual regard of the two rivals is astonishing and perhaps implies secret arrangements; such at least was the reproach often hurled at both pretenders at the Council of Pisa.

Not until the beginning of August did Gregory quit Rome, indecisive and already too late to reach Savona at the date agreed upon. He was with his Curia at Siena from the beginning of September till January 1408. The advance of King Ladislas of Naples on Rome created for Gregory a really threatening situation, for then the Romans themselves applied to Benedict for subsidies. The fleet that had put to sea on his orders arrived too late to prevent the capture of Rome, and it probably had other assignments than merely that of supplying the Romans with money. In conformity with the stipulations of the Treaty of Marseilles, Benedict set out, arrived at Savona before the appointed day, and left half the city for Gregory. From the latter came messages with excuses and requests for another place of meeting. Meanwhile, Benedict sailed with his galleys to Portovenere, while Gregory appeared at Lucca at the end of January 1408. Negotiations were drawn out for months.

The negotiations, unceasing and unsuccessful, dragged themselves out but then came to a sudden end with the defection of Gregory's cardinals and the simultaneous renewal of proceedings against Benedict by France. Wide circles in Christendom had familiarized themselves with the notion of neutrality and council. And so, after their departure from Lucca, the cardinals of the Roman obedience at once appealed to a council, but without destroying all bridges to their Pope. Relations with Benedict's cardinals now became more intense, especially after the new withdrawal of obedience by France. The assassination of the Duke of Orléans in 1407 had deprived Benedict of his strongest supporter. When in the spring of 1408 France resumed its neutrality, Benedict replied in April with the publication of the long ready bull of excommunication. It seems that the French envoys, led by the Patriarch Cramaud, intended to seize Benedict's person. Benedict then decided to leave Portovenere, after he had summoned a council to meet at Perpignan on the coming All Saints' Day. On 15 July his fleet put to sea and, after some unfriendly treatment at the Riviera ports, made its way to Perpignan at the end of the month. Most of his cardinals had not followed him and in August they joined Gregory's cardinals.

When all of Gregory's attempts for a resumption of negotiations had collapsed, his rebel cardinals had resolved, probably as early as the beginning of June, on a council which they would summon. February of 1409 was proposed as the date; Pisa was decided on as the place of the council. Publicity for the council was undertaken in the grand manner.

Meanwhile, Benedict's council got under way at Perpignan in November 1408; it was mainly occupied with the reading of the *informatio seriosa,* a detailed exposition of Benedict's efforts for unity. The Council of Perpignan was well attended from Spain and the Midi. In spite of all the admonitions to the Pope to resign, the only tangible result was the dispatch of an embassy to the Council of Pisa. Then, on 26 March 1409, the session was interrupted and again and again prorogued into 1416.

The Council of Pisa (1409)

The exertions of the united College of Cardinals for a good attendance at the announced Council were a complete success. In addition to twenty-four cardinals and four patriarchs, there were more than eighty archbishops and bishops, an equal number of abbots, the proxies of more than 100 bishops and over 200 abbots, many deputies of princes and universities, the generals of the important orders, and numerous doctors of theology and canon law. Pointedly absent were the German King Rupert and the kingdoms of the Iberian peninsula. On 25 March the Council was opened with the traditional solemnities in the cathedral of Pisa.

In view of the fact that the cardinals rather than the papal rivals had convoked the Council, the external conduct of business naturally differed from preceding mediaeval councils. Furthermore, the purpose of the gathering was to institute proceedings against both *pro papa se gerentibus* and thus the trial formalities were in the foreground. The question of the Council's presidency was solved in a very different manner. The College cf Cardinals in its entirety was regarded as holding this office, but this was not emphasized. After the papal election it goes without saying that the new Pope assumed the direction of the Council.

The assembly completed its work in twenty-two sessions, usually following close upon one another. In preparing for them the members met in what they called "nations" — German, French, English, Italian, and a small Provençal "nation" — while the cardinals met as a college, frequently with representatives of the "nations." At the first session, on 26 March, the Cardinal of Milan delivered the opening sermon, which propounded sixteen important propositions on the cardinals' right to convoke the Council in view of the refusal of the papal rivals — theses which reproduced what had been held and taught by a great many theologians and canonists, for years and decades now, as the correct doctrine of the constitution of the Church.

The Council's principal task, the process against the two pretenders, was provided for by the appointment of an investigating committee, which was resolved in the seventh session, on 4 May, at the suggestion of the "nations" and of the envoys of princes, prelates and universities. But before the process began there arrived envoys of the German King Rupert, a loyal adherent of the Roman obedience, who protested both in lengthy speeches and in writing and at once left the city. Later appeared envoys of King Martin of Aragón and of Benedict XIII, who were also heard. The thirty-seven articles of accusation against both claimants were publicly read at the fifth session, on 24 April, and the introduction of the process was moved. Later, further articles were added. On 4 May, in the seventh session, the proposed committee was approved by the Council. It consisted of two cardinals, four representatives of the German nation, five of the French, one of the English, five of the Italian, and one of the Provençal.

As early as 7 May occurred the public citation of the witnesses, who were sworn by the committee on 9 May in the sacristy of the Carmelite church. The hearing of the witnesses began on the same day; a total of sixty two witnesses were interrogated on the chief points.

On 22 May the Archbishop of Pisa began his report on the result of the inquiries. Since such processes pursued a definite goal, in this case the deposition of both rivals, their lack of an intention to resign was especially emphasized — matters which had been long known and whose notoriety was to be made clear and stressed. Of course, in this process, as in that against John XXIII at Constance, a great deal of gossip was in circulation and some common views or impressions were transmitted only by hearsay. But among the witnesses were many prominent men, persons in high positions of responsibility at both Curias, who reported things in which they had participated. Above all, many of the things now brought forward belonged to the quite recent past, and so were different from a part of the investigations into the events of 1378.

Benedict, of course, never seriously considered abdication, though as a Cardinal he had been energetically in favor of it and in the conclave had obliged himself to it under oath. But it is reported that in the first year of his pontificate he had stated that he would rather have himself burned than resign. It was claimed that he dismissed all advocates of the *via cessionis* and advanced those who said what he wanted to hear. To Gregory's clear offer to resign he returned evasive replies. At Portovenere he was said to have first agreed to the plan for a general council, then to have rejected it, only to retire to Perpignan and summon a council there. There were many specific charges: acts of violence, execution of clerics in major orders, arrest of priests and of superiors of orders for service on his galleys, favoring of heretics, and of course magic, which finds a place in all the contemporary trial material.

And Gregory XII was no different. A long list of omissions and intrigues was laid to his charge. Advocates of resignation were also ill-treated and imprisoned by him.

All these charges probably have an historically true basic element, but they must have been often exaggerated in the drawing up of the accusations and in the depositions of the witnesses. Some things were pure fabrications, others were reported inexactly, torn from their context, and thus altered. On one very weighty point, the so-called *collusio,* or secret dealings and understandings between the two rivals, full clarity will never be obtained. The many secret conferences in the dead of night in the rooms of the claimants or in the cathedral sacristy at Siena between Gregory's nephews and Benedict's envoy supplied plenty of material for fantastic conjectures.

A quick winding up of the hearings was agreed to by the Council because of the threat from King Ladislas and on 1 June the accepting of reports ceased, while copies were made accessible for further information. Meanwhile, the two papal claimants had been repeatedly cited by the Council and on several occasions solemn deputations proceeded to the doors of the cathedral to call in a loud voice the pretenders or their representatives — everything according to the precise rules of trial procedure. Then the process was quickly concluded and in the fifteenth session, on 5 June, the judgment was publicly read by the Patriarch of Alexandria, sitting as judge and attended by the Patriarchs of Antioch and Jerusalem. Gregory XII and Benedict XIII were cast out of the Church as notorious schismatics, promoters of schism, and notorious and obdurate heretics and perjurers, obedience was withdrawn from them, and the vacancy of the Holy See was confirmed. The sentence was signed by almost all members of the Council; the list of signatures comprises 213 entries, including twenty-four cardinals.

At once preparations were made for the conclave. Part of its task should be to bind the future Pope to a wise and adequate reform of the Church at this very Council. Apparently an agreement had been made among the cardinals that for the validity of the election at least two-thirds of the votes of the cardinals of each obedience were necessary. The conclave began on 15 June in the archiepiscopal palace and ended on 26 June with the unanimous election of the Cardinal of Milan, Peter Philarghi, who called himself Alexander V (1409–10). The electoral protocol, with the signatures of all the cardinals, was read in the next session.

Peter Philarghi, born in northern Crete of Greek parents and educated by Franciscans, had entered the Franciscan Order. He soon went to Italy, then to Oxford for study, and later to Paris and Pavia. To this period belong his widely known commentary on *The Sentences* and his reputation as a humanist. Galeazzo Visconti arranged his promotion to the sees of Piacenza, Vicenza, and Novara in succession. From 1392 he carried out diplomatic missions for the Visconti and in 1395 procured the ducal title for him from King Wenceslas. In 1402 he became Archbishop of Milan, in 1405 a Cardinal and Legate in North Italy. He had taken a prominent part in arranging the Council of Pisa, and his election as Pope had been strongly promoted by Cardinal Baldassarre Cossa. Though the French court had relinquished its demand for a French candidate and for residence at Avignon, the new Pope owed his elevation to France. After his coronation on 7 July the Council quickly finished its business. And first of all, the Pope confirmed in favor of the adherents of the Council all measures taken during the Schism in the administration of benefices. A reform committee did not actually take up any business; for this purpose a new council was announced for 1412 and provincial and diocesan synods were directed to prepare for it. The Council ended on 7 August.

The Conciliar Idea

Following the outbreak of the Western Schism and the first unsuccessful efforts to end it, it was natural to look about for a fundamental remedy for the now disjointed *corpus politicum* of the Church. Then the conciliar idea suggested itself as an aid. In an almost limitless profusion of still mostly unprinted treatises and testimonials the council was again and again recommended as the saviour in the emergency. But it should finally be admitted that most of the testimonials, memoranda, and theological treatises were predominantly political in character and, despite all the scholarly embellishments, had to conform to their current sphere of influence. First of all, the Italian cardinals demanded the convoking of a council, before which Urban VI should appear, and then also Clement VII after his election at Fondi. Even Peter de Luna, who later as Benedict XIII was bluntly to reject a council as a means of uniting the two or later the three obediences, is said to have desired a council at the beginning of the Schism. The conciliar idea encountered powerful opposition from Clement VII's cardinals, especially from the important jurists Flandrin and Amelii. But there were demands for a council in Castile and Aragón, notably by the forceful inquisitor Nicholas Eymerich and the fiery Vincent Ferrer.

At the basis of the conciliar idea, which found at times stronger and at times weaker expression, according to the political situation, lay the concept that the Pope is not the absolute master of the Church. In normal conditions he or the *Ecclesia Romana* in the narrower sense governs the visible Church. But in special cases — schism, heresy, "contra bonum commune ecclesiae" — the Universal Church comes to the fore — *ecclesia universalis, congregatio fidelium, corpus Christi mysticum* — in accord with the frequently recurring proposition: "quod omnes tangit, ab omnibus approbari debet" or "maior est auctoritas totius orbis quam urbis alicuius." According to this opinion, the power of the whole Church is greater, and she alone is infallible. Numerous concepts sought to clarify the complicated problem of the *plenitudo potestatis, potestas actualis* and *habitualis.* The favorite set of terms, *potestas — exercitium,* generally meant that the *exercitium,* the *potestas actualis,* is ordinarily vested in the Pope and Curia — *minister, dispensator, procurator, caput ministeriale* — but in emergencies the greater *potestas, habitualis* of the Universal Church is actualized in the council as the great regulator.

The emphasis on the extremes, papalism — conciliarism, which was up to this time often the favorite approach, caused the broad middle course to fade into the background. According to it the Pope's will is not the supreme law of the Church; or, the Pope is really the Church, but his power is hemmed in by the higher power of the Universal Church. But this is not to be understood in the sense that he has nothing further to say and has only to execute the conciliar decrees. From this body of theories the proper means had to be selected and applied on the occasion of the first great practical case, the double election of 1378 and the subsequent years, in the event that a quick political solution should prove to be impossible. There was no doubt that the Pope or, now, the two claimants could be examined by the Universal Church in regard to legitimacy. But who sets the Universal Church in motion? Who acts for her? How will she appear and act?

Among the views on the distribution of powers in the Church a very great importance was attributed to the College of Cardinals, at least at the beginning of the Schism, when there was question of finding a supreme authority for judging the legitimacy of the elections. In the great and, despite their length, important treatises of the cardinals of Clement VII, the College itself was the competent judge of the papal election. The comparison of the bishop and his chapter and the widely held opinion that the cardinals, and not the bishops, are the successors of the Apostles served as the basis for this view. The authority to convoke the council had occasionally been attributed also to the patriarchs and, to a much greater degree, to the princes, especially to the Emperor or the King of the Romans. Just as the secular princes must force the cardinals to elect a Pope, so in a case of schism they must force the Church to hold a council. Various kinds of councils are to be distinguished here: a general council in each obedience or the *conventio universalis utriusque partis* or the *congregatio universalis* under the direction of the College of Cardinals. And the idea of a council made up of cardinals alone was mentioned more than once, as was also one consisting of a few but well chosen representatives of all ecclesiastical provinces.

Furthermore, there was need of a council for the already long overdue reform of the Church. As early as the Council of Vienne, Durandus the Younger had demanded the holding of a general council every ten years. It became an increasingly universal conviction that reform could not be realized without a council.

And so there was a variety of opinions in regard to the council and the constitution of the Church. Therefore, it will not do to speak of an exclusively correct "divinely willed monarchical structure" of the Church in the late Middle Ages.

CHAPTER 47

The Devotio Moderna

Devotio moderna is the descriptive term, occurring already in Thomas à Kempis (1380–1471) and John Busch (1399–1479), for the spiritual movement which began in the Low Countries at the end of the fourteenth century and spread throughout Europe, especially Germany, during the fifteenth century. This form of piety was "modern" in its orientation to practical experience, in its activation of the affective powers, and in its instruction for self-control. It "would rather feel compunction than know its definition" (*Imitation of Christ,* I, 1, 9). In this empirical trait the *devotio moderna* takes its stand in the *via moderna* of late scholastic nominalism. But simultaneously disgust with nominalism's extravagant speculation, unrelated to life, led in the *devoti* to an estrangement from theology in favor of virtue made good in humdrum day-to-day living.

> Of what use is it to discourse loftily on the Trinity, if you lack humility and hence displease the Trinity? Truly, lofty words do not make one holy and righteous, but a virtuous life makes one dear to God (*Imitation,* I, 1, 7f.).

With this in itself sound and justified criticism of a decadent scholasticism was opened up a chasm between theology and piety in the Western Church. The devout even rejected the speculative mysticism of a Master Eckhart and sought intimacy with God on the path of active penance and love. However, the ideas of the great mystics were variously utilized and made productive in circles which had no access to lofty speculations.

Gerard Groote

The father of the new devotion was Gerard Groote (1340–84). Born at Deventer in 1340, the son of a draper patrician, he became a rich orphan at the age of ten, as a result of the plague. He soon found the Latin school of his native town inadequate and in 1355 went to the University of Paris, where in 1358 he became master of arts. The study of law, medicine, and theology was now open to him. In his eager thirst for knowledge and in his own impetuous manner he seems to have devoted himself to all three and in addition to have occupied himself with magic. But he concentrated on canon law. As a student, fond of all intellectual as well as sensual delights, and in diplomatic missions he spent time not only at Paris but at Prague, Cologne, Avignon, and Aachen. At Aachen he sought a canonry in 1362 and obtained one in 1370; he acquired other benefices at Soest, Nordmünster, and Utrecht. But even these honors and successes were as little satisfying to him as had been his restless studying and life previously.

An encounter after 1370 with his friend of student days, Henry Eger of Kalkar (1328–1408), prior of the Carthusian monastery of Monnikhuizen near Arnheim, produced a profound change. The Carthusian showed him the way to a spiritual life. As a consequence, he spent a few years in Eger's monastery, where, as a *donatus,* or brother without vows, he laid the foundations of the new devotion in useful work and reading, especially the mystics Hugh of Saint-Victor, Henry Suso, Gertrude of Halfta, Master Eckhart, Ludolf of Saxony, and John Ruysbroeck. But in the long run his way to becoming one with God was to include the active life in the world; for him self-sanctification was to be connected with the service of his fellowmen. "It would be wrong, for the sake even of contemplative prayer, devotion, and righteousness, to disregard what cannot be done by another and the good of your neighbor, which is pleasing to God," he wrote in his notes "Resolutions and Intentions, Not Vows."

Gerard Groote resigned his benefices and made over his town house at Deventer in September 1374 to some pious, God-seeking ladies, who aimed to lead a quasi-monastic life under a superioress and also to support themselves by the labour of their hands. Groote did not give away all his property, but retained what he needed, including two rooms in this house, and from here he tended to his foundation. To this community, the nucleus of the Sisters of the Common Life, he gave in 1379 an organization or, in a sense, a rule. Particularly in such a loosely constructed community it was important to assure discipline and orthodoxy and to protect the members from being mistaken for the "Brothers of the Free Spirit" and other enthusiasts.

At the same time a similar community of brothers was formed at Deventer in the vicarage of Florens Radewijns (1350–1400). After studying in Prague, the latter had been converted in 1380–81 as a result of a sermon by Gerard Groote. He was the only one to whom the master suggested ordination to the priesthood; he sent him for this purpose to Worms in order to find a bishop with clean hands. Groote himself received only the diaconate (ca. 1379) in order to be able to preach in public. He shrank from the priesthood because of his unworthiness and in view of the simony and concubinage prevailing among the priests of his day. As a preacher of penance he led a strong fight against superficial piety, the immorality of the cities, the heretical movements, against simony and concubinage in the clergy, and against the disregard of the vow of poverty by religious. When in 1379 Florens of Wewelinghoven became Bishop of Utrecht, Groote at first obtained his support. He received a personal license to preach and was appointed synodal preacher, and as such, on 14 August 1383, delivered his *Sermo de focaristis.* In the form of a pamphlet, it became his most widely known work. Together with the Prague canonist, Conrad of Soltau (d. 1407), he held it to be a mortal sin to attend the Mass of a notorious concubinary, even if a bishop allowed such a priest to celebrate Mass. The opposition of the clerics concerned and of the mendicant orders, which saw themselves threatened by the rejection of begging and by the new way of life of the brothers and sisters, became so stiff that the Bishop had second thoughts. Apart from his rigorism of manner, no charges could be brought against Groote and so he was indirectly silenced by a prohibition against preaching by deacons. This was sufficient to bring down on the master and his brethren the stigma of heresy. Groote had a *protestatio fidei* posted on church doors at Deventer and Zwolle and asked Pope Urban VI for a personal license to preach. Until it was granted he could only live according to his sermon on painful obedience (*Imitation,* III, 19; III, 49, 18–27). He induced Florens to stay at Deventer and thus prevented a dispersal of his community of brothers.

Groote died of the plague on 20 August 1384, without having been rehabilitated. The new devotion that he had established was developed in the communities of brothers and sisters of the Common Life and in the Augustinian Canons of the Windesheim Congregation. He gave their spirituality its characteristic stamp. But his austerity, inclining to rigorism, was of less significance than his practical style and his following of Christ in daily life, determined by the unremitting contemplation of the life and sufferings of Jesus.

The Brothers of the Common Life

The Brotherhood of the Common Life was already so firmly established by the death of Gerard Groote that its continued existence was assured and its further growth made good progress. In the spirit of their master, who rejected begging and regarded manual labor as an aid to virtue, the brothers, following the example of Saint Paul, earned their common livelihood — in their case, by copying and binding books. Hence they had at the same time the opportunity for spiritual reading, did not have to leave the community or the house, and contributed to the spread of Christian doctrine and education. However, there was not much possibility of exterior apostolic work. Perhaps that is why Gerard Groote in 1383 had accepted an endowment for the support of two or three priests who should be active in the care of souls. Otherwise, the seeking of the priesthood was regarded at first as contrary to humility. They aspired to help their fellowmen by prayer, silent example, and encouragement.

Spiritual reading, chiefly of Scripture, meditation, and prayer occupied their day in addition to manual labour. Fraternal correction and common examination of conscience were intended to aid in observance of the rule and to foster humility. Radewijns advised his disciples: "Persevere in humble simplicity, and Christ will be with you." The following of the humble Christ was the central idea of their piety. In the midst of the late mediaeval urban middle class they wanted to live the life of the fathers of the desert in prayer and work. Differing from the Beguines and the Beghards, the Brothers and Sisters of the Common Life had all property in common. Following the example of their master's "Resolutions and Intentions," many brothers drew up their own rule of life and wrote spiritual diaries with the results of their edifying reading. A great part of the devout literature was composed or compiled as such, in the first place for edification, or consisted of letters intended to introduce others to the spiritual life.

From the *Exercitium* of John Kessel (d. 1398), a lay member of the Deventer community, which comprised four priests, eight clerics, and a few lay brothers, we can obtain a picture of the order of the day. The day began with meditation at 3:00 A.M., followed by Matins and scriptural reading. To guard against drowsiness it was recommended that the brothers make notes. At 5:00 o'clock each went to his work, which lasted until the bells of the parish church rang for Mass. On the way the brothers prayed the psalms of Terce; returning, those of Sext. During Mass they were to meditate on the life and sufferings of Christ. Back home, they resumed their work. The common meal was not eaten before 10:00 o'clock, accompanied by reading. Then each retired to his cell until None. The time between None and Vespers was again devoted to work, and after Vespers there was meditation. The work that followed until Compline was interrupted by the common supper, the second meal. The day ended at 8:00 o'clock with the examination of conscience, in which each jotted down the day's faults. Bedtime was at 9:00 P.M. unless, in conformity with the example of the desert fathers, they engaged at night in spiritual discourses.

They did not themselves found and accept schools but they devoted themselves to the religious education of pupils apart from their formal lessons. Nevertheless, they acquired an influence on the educational system of the age.

It was not until the second half of the fifteenth century that the Brothers of the Common Life participated directly in education in a few cities, such as Utrecht, Liège, and Groningen and, in Germany, Magdeburg and Trier.

If any of their pupils were thinking of the priesthood or the religious state or were suited for them, they were admitted into their houses. Others they lodged with reliable townsmen. They gathered the pupils for spiritual conferences and were at their disposal for discussions and confession. When in 1391 the brothers at Deventer were able to acquire a larger house of their own, they adapted the one hitherto used as a house for the pupils. The brothers' house at Deventer under the direction of Florens Radewijns became a model for many others but it can hardly be said to have contributed directly to their establishment. In fact, it was still without ecclesiastical approbation. In Kampen and Zwolle citizens affected by Gerard Groote's sermons founded similar religious houses. Under its rector, Dirc van Herxen (1381–1457), the "father of all the *devoti,*" this house at Zwolle acquired great prominence and after 1420 was the site of the annual chapter.

But the ecclesiastical status of the new communities was still not settled. The brothers were not an order — the Lateran Council of 1215 had forbidden the founding of new orders — but they lived a quasi-monastic life. The most important product of the dispute was the *Libellum super modo vivendi hominum simul commorantium* of Gerard Zerbolt van Zutphen (1367–98), who sought to prove that, despite the deviation from the traditional form of monastic observance, the life of the brothers was a school of perfection. It was only in 1401, after the death of Florens Radewijns (24 March 1400), when the direction of the house had passed to Emil van Buren, that the long sought confirmation of the Brotherhood of the Common Life was forthcoming in an apostolic mandate obtained by the Bishop of Utrecht. The brothers were permitted to maintain their common meals, to make common property out of their possessions and the proceeds from their work, and perform pious exercises together, but they could not found a new order or adopt a new habit.

The Windesheim Congregation

In addition to the association of the Brothers of the Common Life, which represented something new between cloister and world, the *devotio moderna* led to a monastic reform movement. If we can rely on Thomas à Kempis, Gerard Groote, following his visit to Ruysbroeck at Groenendael, had already given thought to the establishment of a cloister or canons for such of the brothers as inclined to the monastic life. In view of the difficulties of 1383–84 it was natural to seek support in one of the old orders and to assure the continuance of the movement of the *devoti* by means of a monastery. Accordingly, John Busch relates in the *Windesheim Chronicle* that Groote, on his death bed, recommended to his brothers the founding of a monastery in which all the brothers and sisters could find refuge, aid, and protection. The so-called Augustinian rule presented itself as the most appropriate for this purpose. Certain as it is that Gerard Groote, Florens Radewijns, and other brothers purposely rejected the official monastic form of life for themselves and aimed at closer contact with the world, apparently there were also among their pupils some who felt themselves called to the religious state. For many the brothers' houses became places of preparation for the cloister.

To provide models of true claustral life and also to preserve the special character of their own form of life, it was natural to found a monastery for the brothers with an inclination to the religious state. Within its shelter they could assure protection for the real offshoot of the *devotio moderna,* in still so precarious a situation in regard to canon law and the recipient of so much enmity.

And so from Deventer occurred the founding of the Canons of Windesheim near Zwolle. On 17 October 1387 the church was consecrated and six pupils of Gerard Groote made their vows. Previously they had familiarized themselves with the traditions of the Augustinians at the monastery of Emstein, founded from Groenendael in 1382, where at the same time they had come into contact with the spirituality of Jan Ruysbroeck. Before long, in 1392, two more monasteries were founded, at Marienborn near Arnheim and at Neulicht near Hoorn. With these and Emstein, Windesheim established a congregation under the "Prior Superior," John Vos van Heusden (1391 to 1424), in 1395. By 1407 twelve monasteries belonged to it, including Agnetenberg, of which Thomas à Kempis was a member. Union with the chapters of Groenendael (1417) and Neuss (1430) brought a great increase in numbers. By 1500 this number was to grow to eighty-seven houses. The spirit was purely contemplative. The very location of Windesheim and other houses outside cities indicates that they were not adapted to pastoral work, and in the statutes from the pre-Reformation period we find no reference to apostolic or educational activity, apart from the copying of books and monastic reform.

The last mentioned became the specific historical achievement of the Windesheim Congregation in the fifteenth century. In 1435 the Council of Basel entrusted Windesheim with the reform of the German Augustinian monasteries.

If we note the absence of proper religious depth, and if external fidelity to the rule apparently replaced the pious sentiment which characterized men like John Vos and his successor, still the Windesheim Congregation, even in the latter half of the century, represents a flourishing and vigorous monastic life, which acted as a model for other communities.

The monasteries, gathered into so compact a congregation, were naturally much stronger and more secure in regard to their institutions than the less firmly united houses of the brothers. Entirely on their own, they moved into the foreground, assumed leadership,and represented themselves in literature, with Thomas à Kempis and John Busch, as the true heirs of Gerard Groote. On the other hand they afforded support and protection to the communities of the brothers. Thus, on 19 March 1395, the superiors of the monasteries of the Windesheim Congregation issued a solemn declaration on the orthodoxy and proper manner of life of the Deventer brothers.

The Brothers of the Common Life in Germany

The "Brother Movement" in Germany also originated at Deventer. In April 1400, soon after the death of Florens Radewijns, Henry von Ahaus (d. 1439), vicar of the Münster cathedral, visited Deventer. He was deeply impressed by the primitive

Christian spirit in the house and shared its life for more than a year. Having returned home, he founded at Münster on 26 October 1401 the first house of the Brothers of the Common Life. According to the foundation charter, "two or more priests, with a few clerics and one or more lay brothers" should live in it permanently with common ownership of books and other property; they should be such as "were unable to enter an order because of some impediment or did not regard that as their vocation, but, remaining in the house to the end and living in humility, chastity, and the other virtues, were desirous of serving God and assisting one another in a common life." Henry seems not to have been the rector at first of this still loosely organized community. It took him perhaps fifteen years to consolidate the house in the Deventer spirit and to overcome the opposition of the "rude and uncouth Westphalians" ("groven ende onbesnedenen Westphalen"). But in the later fifteenth century Westphalians were the chief representatives of the German aspect of the movement. At that time they were found in all the houses of western and central Germany.

Henry von Ahaus founded another house at Cologne in 1416, which he directed for three years until his return to Münster in 1419. Shortly before his death he founded one at Wesel in 1435. In addition, there were houses of sisters. Henry von Ahaus was not satisfied with the founding of individual houses. It was important to assure their existence and to maintain the proper spirit in them. To these ends he worked for a union among the houses, and in 1425 it was realized in the case of Münster and Cologne. From it developed the so-called Münster Colloquy of 1431. Every year, on the Wednesday preceding "Cantate" Sunday (the fourth Sunday after Easter), the superiors of the houses of brothers and sisters in northwest Germany were to meet at Münster to discuss common affairs, such as the installing of rectors, the appointing of confessors and visitors new foundations, and so forth. The connection with the brothers in the Netherlands was maintained by the interchange with the Zwolle Colloquy of two representatives of each group. From 1479 Hildesheim instituted a colloquy of its own with Kassel and Magdeburg. Aspirations for union finally led in 1499, under the influence of Jasper (d. 1502), rector of Deventer, to a general chapter.

The growth of the Brothers of the Common Life in Germany presents itself in four centers, which are to some degree definable in time and geography.

1. The West German or Münster circle, with houses at Münster (1401), Cologne (1416), and Wesel (1435). Not established by Münster, but closely connected with it, were Osterberg near Tecklenburg (1409–27), Osnabrück (1410–30?), and Herford (1426). Later Rostock (1462) and Marburg (1477) were founded from Münster, and Emmerich (1467) from Deventer.

2. The Hildesheim circle, with the central German, chiefly Hessian, houses: Hildesheim (1440), Kassel (1455), Kulm (1472), Magdeburg (1482), Berlikum in Friesland (1483), and Merseburg (1503). Of these, Kulm and Berlikum, like Emmerich, were at first oriented to Holland.

3. The Middle Rhine circle, proceeding from Cologne: Marienthal in the Rheingau (1463), Wiesbaden (1465, but it probably never actually came into existence), Königstein (1466), Butzbach in South Hesse (1468), Wolf on the Moselle (1478), and Trier (1499).

From 1471 these Middle Rhine foundations formed, against Münster, a special union with its own general chapter, which in 1477 was joined also by the Württemberg houses. The communities of this "South German" union strongly resembled the communities of canons. Their members were "Canons of the Common Life" and the term was not a camouflage. They were headed by provosts; Gabriel Biel, for example, was provost of Butzbach in 1477 and of Urach in 1479.

4. The Württemberg circle. From Butzbach, Gabriel Biel (d. 1495) founded Urach in 1477 on the initiative of Count Eberhard the Bearded. Then arose Herrenberg (1481), Tübingen (1482), Dettingen (1482), Dachenhausen (1486), and Einsiedel in the Schönbuch (1491). Gabriel Biel exerted the decisive influence in the establishing and in the internal and external organization of the Württemberg houses. And even when he was no longer provost of Urach, this house occupied a leading position among those of Württemberg.

To these twenty-six German houses of the brothers are to be added the even more numerous houses of sisters, which were under the pastoral care of the brothers. Because of their cowl, the brothers were often referred to as Kogelherren or Kugelherren or, in Württemberg, as Kapuziaten or Kappenherren.

Opposition: Matthew Grabow

The new form of life, between world and cloister, encountered various kinds of lack of understanding and opposition. These came from the old orders, especially the mendicants, who felt themselves under criticism or even defamed because of the rejection of begging; from the diocesan clergy, who at times were unwilling to relinquish to the brothers the care of souls in the sisters' houses; and from trade circles, who saw an unwanted competition in the brothers and sisters who lived from the proceeds of their labour.

Offense was also given by the translating of the Bible into the vernacular and the using of such versions in the houses of the brothers and sisters. Gerard Groote had spent the last days of his life in translating parts of the breviary in order to make possible for the sisters and others who were uneducated a meaningful participation in the liturgy. At the monastery of Windesheim there was a special *Librarius teutonicorum librorum.* To what extent the *devoti* thus fell under suspicion is clear from the *apologiae* attributed to Gerard Zerbolt van Zutphen (d. 1398), *De libris teutonicalibus* and *De Precibus vernaculis,* or the opinion handed down by Abbot Arnold, of the Dutch Benedictine monastery of Dickeninge, on 2 December 1397, in favor of the brothers. In it the question, is it lawful to read and to have books of the Bible in the vernacular, was answered in the affirmative.

The opposition to the Brothers and Sisters of the Common Life found expression in principle in the work of the Dominican Matthew Grabow. A member of the friary at Wismar, he was a lector in theology at Groningen and in 1400 is mentioned as inquisitor. He delivered to the parish priest of Deventer a treatise against the brothers, of which only the conclusions are extant. The brothers defended themselves in a counter-complaint to the Bishop of Utrecht, who condemned Grabow. He thereupon brought the case before the Council of Constance. Here Pierre d'Ailly and John Gerson attacked his thesis, that no one can meritoriously or even sincerely observe the universal counsels of obedience, poverty, and chastity if he remains outside the true and recognized religious orders. Appealing to Thomas Aquinas, Grabow held that the renunciation of all ownership in the world was sin and murder. In 1419 his theses were repudiated by Martin V at Florence, his writings were consigned to the flames, and he was himself condemned to imprisonment. Despite his abjuration, he was still confined in Castel Sant'Angelo as late as May 1421.

How difficult it was to understand the special character of the Brothers of the Common Life and how natural to count them among the traditional orders or how necessarily they had to sail under the "standard of a false canon law" in order to obtain recognition is evident from the bull of 18 April 1439, in which Eugene IV granted papal confirmation to the houses in Münster, Cologne, and Wesel. In this the houses are declared to be monasteries of canons, the brothers become canons, their rector a provost.

Literature and Spirituality

The *devotio moderna* produced no great theologians. It aimed to avoid theological disputations, held speculation in no esteem, and even in regard to mysticism was on the whole reserved. Its significance lay in the practice of the spiritual life, and its literary output served this end. The communicating of one's spiritual, practical experience in letters, diaries, or rules of life for the guidance of others occupied a large place. There were also edifying teachings and idealizing biographies of the founders, whom the brothers wished to emulate in the following of Christ. In addition to Scripture and the Fathers, especially Augustine, Gregory the Great, pseudo-Dionysius, and John Cassian (*Collationes*), the *devoti* preferred as the sources of their spirituality the works of Bernard of Clairvaux (d. 1153), the Franciscans' Bonaventure (d. 1274), especially his *De triplici via,* and David of Augsburg (d. 1272), in particular his *Profectus religiosorum* and *Speculum monachorum,* Henry Suso, and the *Life of Christ* by Ludolf of Saxony (d. 1378).

The center and root of the *devotio moderna* was the Christ of history. "Our first effort should be to become absorbed into the life of Jesus" (*Imitation,* I, 1, 3). "The life of our Lord Jesus Christ, which he has held up as an example to us, is the source of all virtues and the model of all sanctity," declares the *Epistola* attributed to John Vos van Heusden.

The aim was to nourish oneself by meditation "on the soul's true food of the most holy life of our Lord Jesus Christ." It is above all important to imitate his humility, his obedience in the degradation of his Passion. The imitation of the humanity of Christ gives access to his divinity.

This attention to systematic meditation and the development of its method characterized the *devotio moderna.* In it were sought, not transporting ecstasy nor even mystical union, but rather the simple narrating and experiencing in loving contemplation of the life of Christ and the sorrows and joys of his Mother. Gerard Zerbolt van Zutphen (d. 1398), the most prolific author among the Brothers of the Common Life, in *De spiritualibus ascensionibus* provided guidance in reflecting on what had been heard and read and in applying it to one's own life in the practice of love and humility.

The special care of the *devoti* for the young was expressed in the four pedagogical writings of Dirc van Herxen. This spiritual literature of the *devotio moderna* originated for the most part in the communities, was destined for their aims, for example, biographies for reading matter during the common meals, and was regarded as their common property. Hence our notion of authorship cannot in numerous cases be applied to it strictly. This explains the anonymity of so much of the literature and probably also the fact that even in regard to works so well known and influential as the *Imitation of Christ* and the *Epistola de vita et passione Christi* the authorship is disputed.

The Letter on the Life and Passion of our Lord Jesus Christ and other devout exercises, according to which the brothers and laymen at Windesheim are accustomed to arrange their exercises, has come down to us in a Latin translation. The *Epistola* is intended as a handy guide for the weekly religious exercises of persons practicing this devotion. The material for meditation is arranged for the week. Three meditations are provided for each day. In the first, one considers a mystery from the youth of our Lord; in the second, from his passion and death; while in the third attention is centered on a saint.

> What is sweeter, more comforting, more pleasing to God more salutary for the simple dove than to dwell devoutly in the cleft of a rock, that is, in the wounds of our Lord Jesus Christ? May your sweet Lord and lovable bridegroom grant you the favor not merely to dwell there daily and to repose in joy but also to die daily, while still alive, in the same love with which he accepted wounds and death.

Here is indicated the same *via regia* of meditation on and following of the passion of Christ as in *The Imitation of Christ.*

The Imitation, comprising since 1427 four perhaps originally independent works, is not only the best known book of the *devotio moderna* but, after the Bible, of world literature in general.

The question of authorship is of significance only to the extent that it is not unimportant for an evaluation to ascertain whether the author was a worldly-wise and active man like Gerard Groote, who had experienced the temptations of the world in his own body and was calling for renunciation of the world, or an awkward, introverted, pious man, ill at ease in the world, who like Thomas à Kempis had proved to be useless in practical business and for whom activity in the world was never a serious temptation. More important is the question of the content and spirituality of the work. It offers no systematic doctrine of piety or even of the mystical life. It is rather a spiritual diary or, better, a collection of pithy sayings about the spiritual life, a so-called *rapiarium.* The author seems to have written it over a somewhat long period of time, chapter by chapter, without being particularly concerned for their coherence and logical order.

Book I aims to lead to humility and inner peace through contempt of the world and of vain knowledge, through self-control and contrition of heart. A glimpse of death and judgment is intended as a further lid. Book II shows how we "must enter the kingdom of God through much affliction" (II, 12, 62). This kingdom of God is within us. The devout man feels that he is unjustly treated by men; he is disappointed in them. He finds comfort in the friendship of Christ (II, 8, 18ff.).

For the sake of this friendship sufferings are glorified (II, 3, 19), cheerlessness and loneliness are accepted (II, 9), the cross is loved. But, despite all longing for inner consolation, the devout man of *The Imitation* knows also that mature love for Christ proves itself in cheerlessness, when one perseveres with Jesus in the abandonment of the cross (II, 11, 1–11).

Books III and IV are in the form of a conversation which the Lord has with his servant, Christ with his disciple. If the human will is stressed in Book I, grace is predominant in Book III. Man of himself has nothing that is good (III, 49). The more he is stripped (III, 37, 6, 16) and abandons himself (III, 37, 17ff.; 42, 9; 49, 9ff.; 54), he acquires true liberty in grace. Book IV presents "pious exhortations for holy communion" in three exercises (chapters 1–5, 6–11, 12–18). *The Imitation,* like mysticism, wants to lead to union with God (III, 31, 5ff.). But this union is genuine and real only if it grows out of virtue (II, 10, 5f.) and it does not absolve from persevering moral effort. The unassailed, peaceful possession of God is reserved for the next world; here the *militia Christi* is our portion (III, 25, 8; 6, 27). In this struggle Christ under his cross is both model and help (III, 56, 28). Seeking God's will and concern for a pure conscience take precedence over contemplation in this world (I, 3, 23; 20, 14). In addition to this strongly ethical orientation, the mysticism of *The Imitation* is dominated by the opposition between the spiritual and the material, the internal and the external.

> Be intent on setting your heart free from an inclination to the visible and raising it to the invisible. Whoever follows his senses stains his conscience and loses God's grace (I, 1, 20).

For the sake of this inner life, external exercises of piety are underestimated, and pilgrimages and the cult of relics are criticized (I, 11, 13; 23, 25; III, 58, 9f.; IV, 1, 38f.). By virtue of this criticism of the externalization of late mediaeval piety through the multiplying of external forms at the expense of depth and the mean, by virtue of this struggle against a piety of good works and for a better inner righteousness, *The Imitation* is in the lineage of both the Catholic Reform and the Reformation of the sixteenth century.

But because its intensification of inner feeling was connected with a disregard for the mystery of creation as well as of the Incarnation, the piety of *The Imitation* threatened to lose its context to the world. In contradistinction to German mysticism, the "imitation of Christ" did not see that the dignity of things is based on creation. They are experienced only as seductive glamour and not as symbols pointing to God. The world is fit only to impede the glimpse of God. "If you look at creation, the creator withdraws from you" (II, 42, 10).

Toward the close of the century one encounters a union of mysticism, humanism, and *devotio moderna* in one of the Münster brothers, John Veghe (d. 1504). After a short time at Rostock, he became rector of the brothers' house at Münster in 1475 and in 1481 of the local Niesink convent of the Sisters of the Common Life. In his Low German treatises, *Gheystlike jagd, Lectulus noster floridus,* and *Wyngaerden der sele,* and his sermons or conferences, twenty-four transcripts of which are extant, he offers, in connection with the Canticle of Canticles, a mysticism directed to practical ends and thus makes the teaching of the mystics fruitful for the various levels of Sisters of the Common Life. All are called to be God's brides. "God has created mankind that he may make use of it." This union with God, the participation in the divine joys, begins already in this life but finds its fulfillment only in the next. Man must exert himself to achieve it. This blessed union of man with God in love is explained by Veghe under the symbol of sacramental communion and of the union of spouses.

The last important spiritual writer from the Windesheim circle was John Mombaer (Johannes Mauburnus). Born at Brussels around 1460, around 1480 he became a canon at Sankt Agnetenberg. Important and entirely too little esteemed is his significance as a monastic reformer in France at the end of the century. There he became Abbot of Livry in 1501, but he died at Paris soon after, possibly on 29 December of the same year. Like Wessel Gansfort (d. 1489) and following his example, Mombaer wanted to indicate ways to the interior life, especially to devotion during the canonical hours, at the reception of holy communion, and in meditation — in other words, the most important spiritual exercises of the *devoti*. But in so doing he developed the method of the spiritual life to such a degree that the danger of mechanical routine, which he, like the *devotio moderna* in general, aimed to combat, became acute again in a new form.

Through the *Rosetum,* the *devotio moderna* acquired a stronger influence in France and, *via* France, in Spain, for example, on Abbot García Jiménez de Cisneros (d. 1510) of Montserrat. His writings, which aimed to provide a help for the interior performance of the choral liturgy (*Directorium horarum canonicarum,* Montserrat 1500) and for meditation (*Exercitatorium spirituale,* Montserrat 1500), are strongly dependent on the Rosetum. Whether Ignatius Loyola obtained the stimulus for his method of meditation through this Benedictine Abbot or directly from John Mombaer cannot be definitely determined. In any case, at Manresa he had *The Imitation of Christ* at his side and thereafter is said to have preferred it to any other devotional book. Thus was established the direct connection of the *devotio moderna* with the Catholic Reform of the sixteenth century.

CHAPTER 48

The Nationalist Heresies: Wyclif and Hus

Ideas regarded as heretical, which were maintained in England and Bohemia toward the end of the fourteenth and at the beginning of the fifteenth century, acquired a universal importance because they expressed revolutionary views in the quarrels over the constitution, structure, and life of the Church.

John Wyclif, born near York around 1330, spent most of his life at Oxford as master of theology following his studies at that University and held several benefices.

While he has until now been regarded chiefly as a philosopher and politician, numerous recent studies point up his interest as primarily theological and especially biblical. Though he has often been referred to as a nominalist, an emphasis on his extreme realism seems to correspond better to reality. Detailed commentaries on Holy Scripture and the treatise *De veritate sacrae scripturae* gained him the title *Doctor evangelicus.* After he had become professor of theology, he composed a sort of theological *summa* in several treatises. Moved by the deplorable situation of ecclesiastical administration and by the insecurity consequent upon the outbreak of the Western Schism, he now came forward as a reformer of more aggressiveness than had been indicated in his biblical exegesis. His theses, regarded as dangerous, gave the competent ecclesiastical authority the excuse to intervene, especially since denunciation; came from several quarters. Wyclif had to give up his teaching position and retired to his parish of Lutterworth, where he remained unmolested until his death on 31 December 1384. To this period belong a group of important writings, such as the *Trialogus.* When Urban VI cited him to the Curia he replied in a work that was hardly submissive and then in his *De citationibus frivolis.*

Wyclif's criticism of Church and theology soon found a response in wide circles and imitation through the so-called "Poor Priests." After Wyclif's adherents at the University of Oxford had been expelled by the Archbishop and the state officials or had submitted, a cruder Wyclifism remained active in the middle and lower strata of the population for several decades more. They went into the catalogue of heretics under the old label "Lollards," and the translation of the Vulgate into the vernacular, suggested by Wyclif, was called the "Lollard Bible." Energetic steps were taken by state and Church to prevent the survival of Wyclif's doctrines. The at first strong opposition to the visitation was less an advocacy of Wyclif than a protest in favor of the University's freedom. At Rome on 10 February 1413 John XXIII's bull of 2 February was published in the single solemn session of the Council of Rome. This contained the condemnation of all Wyclif's writings, especially the *Dialogus* and the *Trialogus,* and also the demand that anyone who intended to defend Wyclif's memory had to appear at the papal court within nine months. At Constance, right after the opening of the Council in 1414, persons were also concerned with Wyclif and Hus. The Council condemned Wyclif's theology in nearly every respect. While yet at Constance the new Pope, Martin V, issued a series of decrees on the religious situation in Bohemia, which included an enumeration of Wyclif's forty-five articles and thirty articles of John Hus; these too were condemned in the fifteenth session. He addressed himself to England in repeated documents and demanded the destruction of Wyclif's writings and the suppression of his errors. Finally, in December 1427 the Bishop of Lincoln was commanded to have Wyclif's remains disintered and burned; this was carried out.

An evaluation of Wyclif's personality was from the start a cause of dispute, since his strictly scholastic style, a certain obscurity in his caustic criticism, and the frequent repetition of his pet ideas impeded the study of his writings. It must be said, however, that he did not rest content with a criticism of external and superficial things, such as the veneration of relics and saints, auricular confession, purgatory, indulgences, and monasticism, but, proceeding from the *lex Dei* in Scripture, attacked the theological bases of the mediaeval Church and hence was regarded as one of the worst enemies of the hierarchy. As an extreme Augustinian he represented in a radical manner a Church of the predestined in which there was no room for the hierarchy and ecclesiastical property in their contemporary forms to the Church of his day — *lex ecclesiae, epistulae papales* — he opposed the ancient Church in his indictment. If the papal bulls compared him to Ockham and Marsilius of Padua, this probably referred less to his philosophy than to the practical danger he implied for the structure of the late mediaeval Church.

A powerful reform movement was in progress in Bohemia from the middle of the fourteenth century, even before Wyclif's ideas became known and obtained a wide circulation there. As everywhere else, the usual reproaches were directed against the wealth and privileges of the clergy. Protagonists of such reform ideas were quite numerous among the theological masters of the University. Hence it is not difficult to understand that Wyclif's doctrines and writings fell on a well prepared soil. Through the marriage of Anne, sister of King Wenceslas IV of Bohemia, to King Richard II of England intellectual interchange, especially through the activity of Bohemians studying at Oxford, became very lively. It is significant that more manuscripts of Wyclif are found in Bohemia than in England.

Into this situation, politically excited by the opposition between Germans and Czechs, came John Hus, who was born around 1370. He had obtained the master's degree in the Prague arts faculty and, after receiving the priesthood in 1400, devoted himself to the study of theology. The period up to his public appearance is obscure. In the first years of the new century he appeared as one friend of reform among many. Appointed by the Archbishop of Prague as synodal preacher, he began with remarkable asperity to denounce the vices of the clergy and in the Bethlehem Chapel, established for vernacular preaching by some lay enthusiasts for reform, he addressed the ordinary people. He rejected the wholesale condemnation of Wyclif, since, he said, there was much that was orthodox in his formulations. Minor collisions with the Archbishop and the University were followed by a process against Wyclif's adherents, instituted by the Prague curia in accord with the instructions of Alexander V, the public burning of his writings, and the forbidding of preaching in private chapels. The result was an open break and Hus' excommunication. As he had done earlier, he now appealed to the new Pope, John XXIII. The matter was turned over to Cardinal Colonna for consideration and decision; he approved the Archbishop's measures and sent Hus an invitation to appear at the Curia; he rejected the excuses submitted by proxies and in February 1411 excommunicated Hus. Before long an interdict was laid on Prague. But then Hus' preaching in the summer of 1412 against the crusade indulgence which John XXIII had offered because of King Ladislas of Naples brought the strife to a climax. A great part of the clergy, many masters of the University, and finally even the King withdrew their earlier support. Cardinal Brancaccio renewed Hus' excommunication and threatened his followers with excommunication and interdict. Hus had to leave the city and stayed with friendly Bohemian nobles. At this time he composed a work entitled *De ecclesia.* In this unsystematic polemic, which also borrowed from Wyclif, against the Prague theological faculty the Englishman's notion of the Church as the community of the predestined was very prominent, and hence the prevailing structure of the hierarchical Church and the obedience due to her were brought into question. It is not surprising, then, that there was a powerful opposition to it and that most of the points of the indictment could be taken from this document. The situation in the Bohemian Kingdom was now so tense that even King Sigismund, as heir of Bohemia, looked to the coming Council for the solution of the political and ecclesiastical difficulties and suggested to Hus that he appear there.

CHAPTER 49

The Council of Constance—Martin V

The Council of Constance (1414–18)

In spite of the great successes of the Council of Pisa union had not yet been entirely achieved, especially in the obedience of Benedict XIII in the Iberian peninsula. Once again politics determined the further development of ecclesiastical matters. The fate of the envisaged synod hung upon the attitude of the European states.

The extremely complicated prehistory of the Council of Constance is best grasped in the activity of the German King Sigismund. Already as King of Hungary he had early taken the part of the Council of Pisa and its Popes, Alexander V and John XXIII. Since his unanimous election as German King in June 1411, his actions and influence had concentrated especially on the unity of Christendom. It was clear to him from the start that, despite the extensive Pisan obedience, only a radical solution, namely, the withdrawal of all three pretenders, could lead to the desired goal. The difficulties connected with union lay chiefly in the political field. So long as John XXIII, elected at Bologna in 1410 as successor of Alexander V, was able to maintain himself in Italy, any rapid progress on the road to union was out of the question. This crafty man, who was not particularly choosy about means, succeeded in establishing himself in Rome through the instrumentality of Louis of Anjou and in expelling the Pope of the Roman obedience from South Italy. Thus Gregory XII had only a few adherents in the lordship of Prince Charles Malatesta of Rimini and, in Germany, in the territory of the Count Palatine of the Rhine and in the dioceses of Trier, Worms, Speyer, and Verden.

In conformity with the decrees of Pisa, John XXIII summoned a council to meet at Rome on 1 April 1412. But this was announcement rather than fulfillment, although the peace made with Ladislas of Naples in June 1412 introduced a brief interval of peace in Italy's agitated political situation. Especially France, but also Italian circles, Malatesta in particular, displayed great interest in the meeting; the Pope was less interested. After the opening on 14 April there took place, apart from several rather insignificant sittings, only one solemn session, in which occurred the condemnation of Wyclif's propositions. When in March 1413 this gathering was adjourned, a new council was simultaneously announced but without any mention of where it would meet. As early as June, however, the Pope, again seriously menaced by Ladislas, had to abandon Rome in great haste. He found shelter outside the gates of Florence, while his Curia was lodged in the city.

Now Sigismund's hour had arrived. The developments in Central Italy caused John to look around for a protector, since Ladislas was beginning to push northward *via* Rome, and even Florence decided to seek a *rapprochement* with the King of Naples. After lengthy consultations with his Curia, John XXIII at the end of July 1413 announced the dispatch of cardinals for negotiations in regard to the time and place of the future council. Also envisaged was a meeting with the King at Genoa or Nice. But then the cardinals met with the King at Viggiù near Como from 13 to 31 October. The outcome of these detailed conversations was the announcement by Sigismund on 30 October of a council which was to meet on 1 November 1414, at Constance, as Sigismund had proposed. On 9 December the Pope issued the bull convoking the council to Constance.

In contrast to Gregory XII, Benedict XIII was a dangerous rival; his obedience was still solid and he was planning to enlarge it and even to invade Italy. Only the Aragonese King's eagerness for union brought about the great gathering at Morella on the frontier between Catalonia and Valencia. In the discussions, lasting from June to September 1414, Benedict and his Spanish obedience showed themselves to be unprepared to yield, despite many obliging words. Nevertheless, envoys of the Pope and of the King of Aragón were sent to Sigismund with the suggestion of a meeting of Benedict and Ferdinand with the German King. The previous crude refusal was now succeeded by a close contact and as a result very much was gained. Following these circumspect preparatory steps, everything now depended on whether the states, especially the great powers, would really take part in the Council. For this Sigismund had to display all his mastery of politics and diplomacy. The greatest difficulty was the war, or at least the hostility, between England and France, together with the changing and uncertain attitude of Burgundy. Even before issuing the official invitation to the Council, Sigismund had simultaneously conducted negotiations for an alliance with England and France; then, in June 1414, he had signed with France the secret Treaty of Trino, directed less against England than against Burgundy. The usual rapid change in the coalitions at this period was already apparent in September in France's *rapprochement* with Burgundy in the Peace of Arras. Although the negotiations and the plans for an alliance with England were more in keeping with Sigismund's policy, here too the idea of the Council held the first place. Accordingly, it was a question of preventing the outbreak of hostilities until the Council could get under way and then of preventing the forsaking of the Council by the powers. Sigismund's diplomacy and his temporizing were successful in both matters and so to him belongs the chief merit for having brought the Council into being and for its accomplishments. His policy before the Council was as important as that at the Council. The Council of Constance was essentially a political event and can be understood and appreciated only from this viewpoint.

The Pope entered Constance on 28 October and on 5 November solemnly opened the Council. At first the number of participants was slight, because many wanted to see whether the Council would meet at all. The German King arrived at Constance on Christmas, and with the new year, 1415, the attendance rapidly grew: cardinals, archbishops and bishops, abbots, generals of orders, the grand masters of the military orders, many proxies of the higher clergy, deputies of chapters, professors of theology and of canon law, envoys of kings, princes, free cities, cities, and, not least, universities. The lay element was very strongly represented, especially the German princes, counts, and other nobles. Another class appeared in large numbers at a general council for the first time since Pisa: the scholars, for since the High Middle Ages the universities, Paris at their head, had assumed the tasks of the *magisterium ordinarium.* Present at this great congress of the Middle Ages was the whole of contemporary Christendom, including the Eastern Church. The importance of this gathering of peoples for the spread of humanism can scarcely be overestimated. A new style made its appearance in sermons, treatises, and especially pamphlets. All the weighty questions of the age were treated at the Council. In its three-and-one-half years there occurred forty-five solemn sessions and hundreds of general congregations and meetings of the nations and of the various committees. The Popes, John XXIII and then Martin V, presided over the Council. From the spring of 1415 voting in the solemn sessions was by nations, the College of Cardinals occupying the position of a nation. In the nations themselves, following the precedent of Pisa, voting was by heads.

By contemporaries themselves the tasks of the Council were designated pointedly in the brief summation: *causa unionis, reformationis, fidei.* All three tasks continuously occupied the Council, sometimes in the foreground of the discussions, sometimes only in committees, depending on the political situation. Unquestionably, the restoration of unity was the most important and most pressing task. The difficult struggle for it was not lacking in drama. Although the legitimacy of the Council of Pisa and of the election of John XXIII was recognized almost unanimously, only the resignation of the Pisan Pope also and of the two deposed at Pisa seemed to give hope of success. This was also Sigismund's plan and that of most of the nations. Then, in the night of 20–21 March 1415, he left the city secretly and in disguise and, under the protection of Frederick of Habsburg, went to Schaffhausen; from there he fled to Freiburg and to the Rhine, where, on the other side, Burgundian knights were awaiting him. He intended that his flight should disrupt the Council, but the German King kept it together with all the means at his disposal. In these fateful days, when the existence or non-existence of the Council and hence of union was at stake, the assembly, in the fifth session on 6 April, promulgated the decrees, later so controversial, on the superior power of the general council in the Church. It then instituted the process against the fugitive Pope. He was brought back as a prisoner and deposed. He accepted the Council's sentence.

The proceedings against John XXIII belong in the series of famed papal processes of the Middle Ages. From the many abominations noised about in the Council seventy indictments were compiled in all haste, and in barely two weeks numerous interrogations of cardinals, bishops and high ranking prelates of the Curia took place. As was customary in such processes, some articles referred to facts already well known, which were supposed to be attested by as many witnesses as possible. Much else was reported only by hearsay. Even if some points were then dropped, still the defamation was general and uncontested, and that is what especially mattered.

What is to be thought of this trial and the shocking accusations? First of all, the desired goal of a quick elimination of the Pope stands out clearly in the hasty and perhaps even precipitate procedure.

Much was charged to him for which his predecessors and the system were responsible. Deposition followed because of "unworthy life, notorious simony, incorrigibility, misgovernment of the Church, fostering of the Schism, and much scandal given to the Church." Hence he was regarded as an unworthy but not as an unlawful Pope.

Envoys of Gregory XII had arrived in Constance very soon after the opening of the Council. It was more than a trifling incident that the arms of their Pope, displayed at their lodgings, were torn down. It gave rise to a spirited discussion about the retirement of all three claimants in a kind of cancellation of the Pisan sentences. But then Gregory would be unable to come to a synod convoked by John XXIII; rather, he must summon it himself. This was granted to him. In the fourteenth solemn session, 4 July, his Cardinal John Dominici convoked the Council, whereupon Charles Malatesta announced Gregory's resignation. The Council appointed him Cardinal Bishop of Porto and Legate of the Marches of Ancona.

All these events lay within the bounds prescribed by politics. Following the now realized union of the Roman and Pisan obediences, there still remained the definitive elimination of Benedict XIII and the winning of his adherents in Spain and the Midi. Here too the Council wanted to complete the job before proceeding to the election of a new Pope.

Quite soon after the opening of the Council, envoys of Benedict XIII and of King Ferdinand of Aragón had appeared in Constance. They held out the prospect of a meeting with Sigismund at Nice. But it was not until July that a large delegation from the Council, Sigismund at its head, set out for Perpignan. Long and stubborn negotiations were unable to move Benedict to retire, but the kingdoms of the Iberian peninsula were won for the Council in the Treaty of Narbonne of 13 December 1415. The form of a reciprocal invitation betrays the primacy of politics here too. Thereby the Council, which had already been in session at Constance for more than a year, was to become a lawfully convoked Church gathering also for the former obedience of Benedict XIII. Even so, it was almost two years before all the Spanish states were represented at the Council as the fifth nation. The withdrawal of obedience also proceeded slowly and it was only in the thirty-seventh session, on 26 July 1417, that Benedict XIII was deposed, following a detailed process in which ninety charges figured. Till his death in 423 the aged Pope, in his fortress of Peñíscola near Tortosa, regarded himself as the only legitimate successor of Peter.

The political amalgamation of all the former obediences finally opened up the way for the election of a new Pope. The form of the election was already the subject of detailed discussions. It had been said for some time that, in the event of the vacancy of the Holy See during a council, this council should certainly take part in the election of the new Pope. In view of the political structure of the Council of Constance, the cardinals were in no sense considered as the sole papal elector. The College had already made concessions in this regard in the deposition of John XXIII and in the resignation of Gregory XII, but it now sought to recover as much influence as possible. And so at Pentecost 1417 it submitted the celebrated *cedula* "Ad laudem," which, by way of exception, proposed the admission of representatives of the individual nations, with the proviso that, in comparison with the College of Cardinals, they must constitute a minority. Two-thirds of the votes in each of the two groups would be required for the validity of the election. Meanwhile, the German King succeeded in achieving the deposition of Benedict XIII and in assuring Church reform by a conciliar decree to the effect that what had so far been accomplished in regard to reform would be promulgated in a decree and the future Pope would be obliged to further reform before the close of the Council. The new Pope, as the Pope of the now reunited Universal Church, should be elected by the College of Cardinals and six representatives of each of the five nations. His position would be politically unassailable, for the customary two-thirds would be required not only from the College of Cardinals but also from the representatives of each individual nation. The election thus carried out would be assured against any later objection. And so it was decided. This method of election was decreed in the fortieth session, on 30 October, and the opening of the conclave was set for within ten days.

In rapid succession occurred the selecting of the deputies in the nations, — not always without difficulties, — the appointing of the guardians of the conclave, the preparing and sealing off of the place of the election in the Merchants' Hall on the lake. The electors entered the conclave on 8 November and on the following day they began the deliberations. Faithful to the political mandate, the election could not be secret. On the reading of the ballots aloud, each elector was carefully asked whether it was his ballot and whether he wished to vote thus.

The first voting took place on 10 November, the votes being rather widely scattered. In the afternoon it was decided to allow the customary *accessus,* but only in writing. The decision was reached as early as 11 November. Serious candidates were the Cardinals of Ostia and Saluzzo, Colonna, and the Bishop of Geneva. If Colonna obtained only eight votes from the cardinals, he also had votes from each nation and the required number from the Italians and the English. While the *accessus* was taking place, the daily procession came to the conclave and sang the "Veni Creator Spiritus." Even the dull chroniclers mention the emotions thereby produced and the admonition to unity. Before noon Cardinal Oddo Colonna obtained two-thirds of the votes of the cardinals and of the delegates of each nation, accepted the election, and took the name of Martin V in honor of the saint of the day. No one had expected so quick an election, considering the extremely difficult mode of election. All the greater, then, was the general rejoicing in the conciliar city. Following his ordination to the priesthood, the new Pope was consecrated a Bishop and crowned on 21 November. From now on the Council was under his direction.

To the area of the *causa fidei* belong the controversial granting of the chalice to the laity, the attitude toward Hus and Wyclif, the question of the lawfulness of tyrannicide, and the dispute between the Teutonic Order and Poland.

The method of administering communion, actually a question of liturgical practice, acquired the greatest political importance because of special circumstances. Well into the High Middle Ages the Eucharist was ordinarily administered to the faithful under both species, but from about the middle of the thirteenth century for the most part under the species of bread. Apparently the introduction of communion *sub utraque* in Bohemia can be dated rather exactly to the autumn of 1414 and can be ascribed chiefly to the Prague master, James of Mies. Hus was not involved. But on being questioned by his followers in his first weeks at Constance, he expressed himself prudently in favor of it in the pamphlet "De sanguine Christi sub specie vini a laicis sumendo." Later he came out publicly for it.

The treatment of this question proceeded together with the process against Hus. Reports on the granting of the chalice in Bohemia had piled up and the Council occupied itself with the question in the spring of 1415. On 15 June, in the thirteenth session, the lay chalice was forbidden by a synodal decree. When the report of this reached Bohemia together with the news of the condemnation and execution of Hus, the really disciplinary question of the chalice became a prominent sign of opposition and also, for wide circles, an intelligible symbol of the Hussite Revolt. After long negotiations and internal discussions the University of Prague — now the highest ecclesiastical tribunal in Bohemia — approved the lay chalice in the spring of 1417. This decision, together with an extensive historical demonstration of communion under both species, was transmitted to the Council through the good offices of King Sigismund. This was, then, an effort to induce the Council to a reexamination of the decision already rendered. This negative attitude was then confirmed by the bulls "Inter Cunctas" and "In Eminentis" of the new Pope on 22 February 1418. It took the frightful experiences of the Hussite wars to bring the Council of Basel to an accommodation.

The Bohemian reformer, John Hus, set out on 11 October 1414 and arrived at Constance on 3 November. The journey passed without incident, even though Hus had not yet received the royal safe-conduct. From the outset he did not find the atmosphere favorable at Constance. To Gerson and many doctors of Paris he was a dangerous heretic, against whom measures had to be taken. Out of regard for the King, John XXIII was mild, lifted the censures, and allowed Hus to celebrate Mass. But already at the end of November, despite energetic protests by the knights who were guarding him under the King's commission and despite an appeal to the royal safe-conduct, he was imprisoned. Attempts to treat his case in a small committee and to settle it there were frustrated by his demand to speak before the whole Council. The committee appointed on 4 December to handle his case consisted of the Patriarch of Antioch and the Bishops of Castellammare and Lebus. It set to work at once, relying on the often dubious charges of his Bohemian adversaries; many of these articles were later rejected by the committee. Until John XXIII's flight Hus was in custody in the Dominican monastery on the island, busy with replies to the questions of the members of the committee. After the Pope's escape, the Bishop of Constance had to take charge of the prisoner; he let him stay at his castle of Gottlieben.

The King's demand that Hus be given a public hearing was complied with at the beginning of June. On 5, 7, and 8 June he stood before numerous prelates and theologians in the Franciscan refectory. While the first session was stormy, the two others were devoted to the quiet interrogation of the master. Hus rejected many articles that were falsely attributed to him, especially in regard to the Eucharist, but without much success, for, now just as earlier, he was regarded as Wyclifite. This was all the more unfortunate, since shortly before, Wyclif and his writings were again condemned. Hus refused to accept the judgment of the Council, and the King's kind exhortations were unsuccessful. Thus his fate was sealed, despite many efforts to get him to change his mind.

The decision was reached in the fifteenth session on 6 July, before the King's departure for Perpignan. Several previous attempts to save him foundered on his opposition. On the very eve of the session Cardinals d'Ailly and Zabarella, with many prelates and doctors from all the nations, submitted to him a very moderate formula of abjuration, but Hus rejected it. That evening there arrived, by order of the King, Duke Louis of Bavaria and the Count Palatine, with the Bohemian knights who were his friends, to persuade him to yield, but in vain. And so fate took its course. After the Mass preceding the solemn session, Hus was led into the cathedral to hear the reading of the indictment and the sentence. Again and again he interrupted the solemn action with challenges, protests, and prayers, but he gave no sign of submission. Two sentences had been prepared, one for the case of his recantation, the other for that of his persisting in his previous attitude. It was the second that was read. Hus was immediately degraded and surrendered to the secular arm, and the judgment was thereupon executed by burning. Hus died a martyr to his convictions.

The position of the German King has often been investigated and usually blamed. There is no doubt that he intended by means of the Council and the anticipated justification of John Hus to master the difficulties in Bohemia. He had probably not given a thought to an unfortunate outcome and had long sought earnestly to prevent one. He thus protested energetically against the imprisonment and forced the three great interrogations and the submitting of the authentic and unfalsified writings of the master. It was some time before he became convinced of heresy, and still longer in regard to dangerous fanaticism. Only for a time was it possible to insist, against the verdict of the Council, on the promised safe-conduct. He could not and would not protect a heretic.

A year after Hus' death, Jerome of Prague also had to mount the pyre at Constance. Less a theologian than his master, on many academic travels he acquired a comprehensive knowledge of philosophy and brought Wyclif's works from Oxford to Bohemia and Poland. As a Czech nationalist and patriot he defended Hus at Constance but left the city, was arrested *en route* to Bohemia, and was brought back to the Council. After a first submission he disavowed his action and was burned on 30 May 1416.

In the area of the *causa fidei* the question of the lawfulness of tyrannicide occupied the Council the longest and agitated it the most. To begin with, it concerned a problem of urgent political relevance. The occasion went back some years, to the assassination of Duke Louis of Orléans, brother of the French King Charles VI, in the fall of 1407 at the instigation of John the Fearless, Duke of Burgundy. In the following spring the Parisian master, John Petit, a Franciscan, justified this deed in the presence of the court and of an illustrious gathering in his famous, and soon to be infamous, *Iustificatio ducis Burgundiae.* When there occurred a change in France's internal politics a synod at Paris and the Bishop of Paris, at Gerson's urging, condemned the *Iustificatio* in the spring of 1414, whereupon the Duke of Burgundy appealed to John XXIII at the beginning of March. The Pope entrusted the case to Cardinals. Since there was no immediate decision, this matter also came before the Council.

And so the problem was not brought up until after the deposition of John XXIII. It is true that the commission of cardinals, instituted earlier, was still competent, but soon the committee on the faith became interested. The result was the condemnation of the thesis "Quilibet tyrannus" in a general form, with no mention of John Petit, in the decree of the fifteenth session, 6 July 1415. The struggle of the two factions continued during the preparation of this decree and, even more, afterward until the end of the Council.

The majority of the testimonials requested by the committee and still known to us belong to the period from the autumn of 1415 to the spring of 1416. However, in a question of such political significance and such dogmatic importance, it is remarkable that a strong majority opposed Gerson: sixty-one opinions against condemnation and only twenty-six for it. Of course it would have been best, so many felt, if a decision were postponed to the next council. The annulment of the Parisian verdict, pronounced by the committee of three cardinals on 15 January 1416, was in accord with this frame of mind. Hence the outcome was a retreat, without any direct approval of either side. The difficulties were not only political. The fundamental texts were disputed at Constance, just as they had been earlier at Paris. The particular case defended by Petit had been made into a universal in order thereby to arrive more easily at a condemnation and still to spare the Duke of Burgundy. If by "tyrant" Petit apparently understood only a traitor, then in addition there was a widely divergent terminology.

The quarrel between the Teutonic Order and Poland also led to a dispute over principles. As in all great and undecided questions, here too the Council was supposed to be the final and highest court, especially since the attack on the Order and its justification of its existence had been introduced on a broad theoretical front. Just the same, the Order's procurator, Peter of Wormdith, obtained the confirmation of its most important privileges by the Council and thus recognition of its past and future activity. The quarrel was aggravated by the *Satyra* of the Prussian Dominican, John Falkenberg, which was very hostile to the Polish King and nation. All motions by the Polish delegation, which also enjoyed Sigismund's support toward the close of the Council, for the condemnation of the Falkenberg theses as heretical were fruitless.

To the subjects treated at Constance in regard to faith belonged also the case of another Dominican, Matthew Grabow, a native of Wismar. He was active in Utrecht and had repeatedly lodged serious charges against the Brothers of the Common Life and all similar groups. He appeared before the Council with his accusations but was forced into the defensive by the accused and had to remain at the Council to justify himself. He submitted his views to the new Pope, but they were rejected by several who studied them, including d'Ailly and Gerson, and branded as heretical. However, it was not settled at Constance but during Martin V's long stay at Florence. Condemned on 6 May 1419, Grabow recanted on 22 October.

If reunion was the most important, even though a strictly limited task of the Council, the reform of the Church or at least of the Curia was the broadest program. It was the special theme of the late Middle Ages and not merely a vague or mystical notion. It was widely held that the long desired unity could be reestablished only on the basis of an equally long desired and demanded reform. The notions of council and reform were inextricably linked in the fourteenth and fifteenth centuries.

In the *De Modus* of Dietrich von Niem are summarized all of the reform proposals then desired, and in it there recurs the statement, short and to the point: "concilium ergo generale... limitet ac terminet potestatem coactivam et usurpatam papalem." This meant the abolition or at least an extensive curtailing of expectatives, reservations, dispensations, exemptions, the *commenda,* annates, tithes, *subsidia,* and *spolia* in order to avoid simony and the simplification of the curial administration and of the chancery rules. Reform must begin at the top, for now there is no longer the *servus servorum Dei,* but rather the *dominus dominorum.*

This brief glance at the universal desire for reform is necessary for an understanding of the Constance reform. Prior to the Council it is expressed in the *de squaloribus Romanae curiae* (ca. 1401) of Matthew of Cracow, Bishop of Worms, in the *Aureum speculum de titulis beneficiorum,* in the reform work of the Bishop of Senez (ca. 1406), in the pamphlet *De ruina et reparatione eccelsiae* by Nicholas of Clémanges, in Andrew of Escobar, in the *Capitula agendorum,* and in the pamphlet *De materia concilii generalis* by Cardinal d'Ailly. At the Council itself it was heard in numerous sermons and motions, above all in the *Avisamenta* of Dietrich von Niem and in Gerson's treatises *Tractatus de simonia* and *Ad reformationem contra simoniam.*

Reform writings also criticized the form of the papal election. Not only the cardinals should have a vote; in alternate elections there should be another electoral college, to be determined by the Council. The Pope must not be always chosen from the same nation; and under no circumstances might two Popes in succession come from the same nation. It would be best to alternate between cisalpine and transalpine candidates. Intimately connected with the preceding was the reform of the College of Cardinals, which, according to some very critical voices, should be entirely abolished. The cardinals should not always come from the same country but from the various ecclesiastical provinces; from no nation should there be enough to give it a majority of the votes. The number of cardinals should be decreased, so that there should be, for example, between eighteen and twenty-four and never more than thirty. Their creation should take place by means of a vote in consistory, and for the future they should no longer obtain the *commenda* but only minor benefices. The income allowed them fluctuated between three and four thousand gold florins.

The Council of Constance was very much preoccupied with this reform program and the old and often repeated assertion that it did little for the reform of the Church is completely unjustified. Three commissions and, according to need, a group of smaller committees were instituted for handling reform questions.

Out of the wealth of reform proposals, what was decreed by the Council? Here, more than in the other tasks of the Council, general politics were the determining factor. When, following thorough preliminary work by the first and second reform commissions, much material was ready for formulation and voting, the reform got bogged down in the so-called "priority controversy" in the summer of 1417.

It is entirely understandable that at last, following the deposition of Benedict XIII, persons wanted to proceed to the election of a new Pope, especially since the Council was already in its third year. Equally understandable are the exertions of Sigismund and his adherents somehow to bring reform to a conclusion, since only through reform did it seem possible to avoid a new schism. The outcome was a compromise: the reform articles already approved by all the nations were to be published by a conciliar decree and put into effect before the papal election.

In the five decrees under these headings were contained these regulations: the holding of a general council, at first after five, then after seven, and thereafter every ten years; precautions against the future occurrence of a schism; the making of a profession of faith by every newly elected Pope; the non-transferability of the higher clergy; and the suppression of *spolia* and procurations. Moreover, in the compromise the future Pope, soon to be elected, was obliged to Church reform "in capite et curia Romana" at this very Council.

On 30 October, in the fortieth session, the Council decreed the implementation of these stipulations.

The activity of the third reform commission was under omens different from those of its predecessors, since now the Pope also had something to say. In conformity with the obligation imposed on him, he treated with the commission and the individual nations. The difficulty of adjusting general decrees to the peculiar wishes of the nations was solved in such a way that seven reform decrees were promulgated by the Council in the Pope's name in the forty-third session on 21 March 1418. In addition, the concordats agreed upon by the Pope with the individual nations but not yet formally concluded were read at this time.

The reform decrees were approved *conciliariter,* the concordats *nationaliter,* and the execution of the version agreeable to the Pope was certified. The separate arrangements with the five nations were drawn up in three versions, with the German, the English, and the three Romance nations. All except the English concordat were concluded for a period of five years, namely, until the next council, at Pavia, which was to continue the work of reform. Already in the autumn of 1416 the Bishop of Lodi had demanded that, in order to continue the reform discussion and to prepare for the next council, a commission, to be set up now, should obtain opinions from the universities on important questions; the representatives of the universities should then report at the next council. However, very much or everything depended on the attitude of the new Pope and his successors to the decree "Frequens."

The importance of the Council of Constance has been variously estimated down to the present, and the evaluation extends from full or partial recognition to rejection. The Council of Constance, like that of Basel, was not contained in the enumeration of the general councils current from Bellarmine on. This computation sprang, not from scholarship, but from a preponderantly apologetic effort and hence it has little claim to objectivity. Constance and Basel belonged to the group of synods that were only partially to be recognized, because they did not correspond to the canon provided for an evaluation of the past. But a part of the decrees of Constance are contained in the fourth volume of the *Editio Romana* (1612), the official Roman edition which was prepared in a congregation set up for this express purpose. This one-sided viewpoint and the effort to decide historical facts by ecclesiastical authority were opposed by scholars who were less apologetically oriented. The evaluation depends especially on the attitude to the so-called "decree on superiority" of the fifth session. The question withdraws behind the perhaps necessary and express approval of the decrees by Martin V and Eugene V. That the new Pope exerted himself to maintain the position gained in the thirteenth and fourteenth centuries is understandable, but his striving, found a limit in the almost universal teaching of the theological world on the higher power of the general council. But there is no doubt that the higher position of the general council had already been represented for a long time and by a much larger portion of theologians. The flight of John XXIII was only the occasion for actualizing and confirming, at this very moment, the previously more habitual power of the council. Everything connected with reform — "without a council, no reform" — points in this direction, especially the decree "Frequens."

Martin V (1417–31)

The first and only Pope from the Colonna family was a Roman in the full sense of the word. Always at the Curia, as a Cardinal from 1405, under Popes Boniface IX, Innocent VII, and Gregory XII he had abundant opportunity to become conversant with the confused situation in political and ecclesiastical life. He went to Constance with John XXIII, stayed with the refugee Pope for a short time, and then returned to the Council. Busy on many committees, he was not very prominent to outsiders and in the conclave he was regarded as one who, while perhaps having few friends, had scarcely an enemy; hence he was a genuine compromise candidate. With his election the Council acquired a new appearance, for, in accord with tradition, the Pope assumed its direction.

The Pope proceeded at once to construct a Curia. The announcements of the election were received in a friendly manner for the most part, though in some cases their reception left something to be desired. In a skilful, reserved, and apparently accommodating manner Martin V had achieved a great deal without any great conflicts. The general exhaustion of the Council did the rest, so that some still unsettled questions could be postponed until the next council, to meet in five years. His task was now to salvage as much as possible from the new situation, and for this he needed a certain independence in ecclesiastical and political matters.

But how was this to be achieved? From the political viewpoint, Martin V was the right man for the papacy. Since he was regarded as Pope of the Germans and the English, he had to repulse all of Sigismund's efforts to keep him in imperial territory for a while. From the start of his pontificate he pushed for a return to Rome. He felt that only in Rome could he escape the often overwhelming influence of the states and the predominance of the Council. In addition, for a merely relative independence a financial basis was required, and only one territory offered it. But almost insuperable obstacles stood in the way of a quick return to Rome.

Together with the establishing of a Curia and the sending of cardinal legates to Aragón and France, Martin's first instructions had to do with the situation of the Papal State, where he appointed rectors and officials. The Council and the new Pope had issued decrees on the administration of the Papal State, the recovery of the lost territories, and the duration of the vicariates. The goal — the reestablishment of papal sovereignty — was clear, but it was difficult to realize, especially from afar. Hence, for all his seeming patience, Martin worked for the quick liquidation of the Council and his departure from Constance. There began at once a vigorous diplomatic activity, which was to last throughout the pontificate. In view of the rapidly changing balance of power in Europe and especially in Italy at that time, this meant a ceaseless tension, which filled the entire reign.

The first task was to clear the road to Italy. When on 16 May 1418 Martin V left Constance and went through western Switzerland toward Geneva, the remainder of his route was not yet visible. The procession moved to Florence, where the Pope had to wait for almost one and a half years before he could finally enter the Eternal City on 28 September 1420.

The chief difficulty was the *condottiere* in the grand style, Braccio of Montone, with his supremacy in Perugia and far beyond Umbria; a great part of the Papal State had become financially subject to him. That the Colonna Pope could only take a dim view of Braccio's "state" was clear to the *condottiere,* and so recognition came only reluctantly in the areas dependent upon him. While still at Constance the Pope began the process of isolating Braccio by making contact with Milan, Florence, Naples, and many smaller *signorie.* From the outset he decided to get rid of the dangerous *condottiere* by military action, especially when the first negotiations were not very favorable. Only the extensive promises which Martin had to make at Florence in February 1420 opened the road to Rome. But they implied no more than an armistice, and the great confrontation was yet to come. Uprisings at Bologna, which Martin suppressed with armed force, and the struggle for Naples postponed the reckoning with Braccio. It occurred in May 1424, when Braccio was defeated and found death at the siege of Aquila. The Pope at last had a free hand in domestic matters and could turn with more success to the recovery and reorganization of his state.

His relationship with Naples was of great importance. In order to bring about the evacuation of Rome, which was occupied by Neapolitan troops, the Pope made great concessions in this regard too. The strength of his forces saved him from defeat in the field and, through the good offices of Florentine envoys, there occurred in the fall of 1421 an armistice, which was followed by further negotiations. The Pope had succeeded in keeping the Aragonese great power away from Italy and the Papal State.

In addition to diplomacy, of which the Pope was a real master, he also displayed, as we have seen, an occasional resort to force, as in Bologna's first great revolt in 1420 and in the second, which involved all of Upper Italy in 1428–29. By means of a considerable military levy he compelled the refractory city to yield and thus retained the important northern pillar of his state. This state was not a centrally administered territory in the modern sense. A variety of bonds held it together: direct subjection to the Curia by means of legates, governors, and rectors, and short-term enfeoffments with vicariates. The decisive factor, however, was that the finances of these areas were largely at the disposal of the Curia. To the extent that the sources provide reliable information, two-thirds of the income of the pontificate came from the Papal State — and were in turn expended on it. Because of the importance of finance, the *Camera Apostolica* was the highest administrative department of the Papal State. Rome, formerly so restless, was under the Pope's absolute rule from the time of his entry there, even though the forms of administration might appear otherwise. In return, the dilapidated city was splendidly renovated, especially the great basilicas, streets, and bridges and the fortifications of the city and its immediate vicinity. It goes without saying that the Colonna family in its many offshoots was much used in the administration of the Papal State. Considering the uncommonly difficult situation in which the Pope found himself after his return from the Council, he needed absolutely trustworthy people if he was to realize his plans. But this nepotism and its attendant enrichment went too far, led to conflicts with other great families, especially the Orsini, and was the motive for reprisals after the Pope's death.

What about the spiritual power, the relationship to Church and council? In many respects the Council of Constance had sketched the further development, but the details were not yet visible. Following the achievements thus far it was natural that here too the Pope would take matters into his own hands in the sense of restoration — nothing less could be expected of a Colonna. This was obvious in the prudent but unambiguous efforts at the close of the Council. In the limits drawn by the conciliar decrees he tried to regain as much as possible in rights before the new general council, to be convoked in about five years, could undertake new measures. The customary chancery rules were published at Geneva with the traditional dating from the day of coronation. But a beginning had already been made at Constance with the granting of expectatives. In this context belong also the less well known reform proposals of two commissions of cardinals; for the most part they were rejected by the Pope. They were made before the Councils of Pavia and Basel, probably to anticipate the tumultuous reform desires that were to be expected. If Martin V was not a friend of conciliar reform which might lay a hand on the organization that he was defending, he did everything to guide the implementation of the rights pertaining to him in orderly paths; hence a reform of administration. He honestly exerted himself to see to it that the cardinal legate in Germany observed the principles communicated to him in regard to the filling of benefices. This is apparent in several reform decrees for the curialists and the curial offices and can be demonstrated from the numerous volumes of registers of his pontificate. On the expiration of the concordats after five years he reverted without more ado to the old system of reservations and provisions in so far as no general decrees of the Council stood in the way and the countries concerned were agreeable. Thus the revenues of the *Camera Apostolica* from *servitia* and annates were not inconsiderable.

With regard to the Council he observed the decree "Frequens," even though he was reluctant and was forced by public opinion. Accordingly, the Council that was due to take place in five years was summoned to Pavia but it was soon transferred to Siena. The attendance was quite small and the political situation was extremely dangerous. It cannot now be determined whether the Pope seriously intended to go to the Council. The fear that, in the midst of the Neapolitan conflict, it would be used by the King of Aragón as a means of pressure was certainly not unfounded. Determined not to tolerate any revival of the Council at the height of the crisis with Braccio, he proceeded to dissolve it before it could show its possibilities. Decrees on lessening the Curia's income were at this point unacceptable to him. Hence all conciliar discussions were deferred for seven more years, since the letter of "Frequens" had been sufficiently respected. Shortly before his death Martin summoned, but not voluntarily, the Council of Basel and appointed Cardinal Julian

Cesarini as president with authority to dissolve it. Hence it came about that a continuous curial administration was and is more than a match for a council meeting only at infrequent intervals. The Pope greatly exploited this advantage. It makes little sense to deduce from this procedure a theological concept, just as it would seem hopeless to include Martin in one of many tendencies and to label him, for example, a moderate conciliarist. He was only a politician, though a great politician with a bent for power, and such was what the Church and the Curia needed in order to be able to exist again, in the old style, after the confusion of the Western Schism and the Council of Constance. A man of very simple life, he used all the means which his state and the government of the Universal Church offered him for reestablishing the Papal State, whose third founder he is rightly called. If his sepulchral inscription in the Lateran extols him as *temporum suorum felicitas,* this may be correct for Rome and the Papal State. When he died on 20 February 1431 he left to his successor, despite all the tensions, a state in relatively good order and hence a basis on which the Roman Curia could look forward to further political and conciliar developments more calmly than had been possible hitherto.

CHAPTER 50

Eugene IV and the Council of Basel-Ferrara-Florence

While Martin V at his death had left a Papal State that was in a peaceful condition, still the conclave that met to choose his successor heralded new difficulties. The cardinals gathered in Santa Maria *sopra Minerva,* but not all of them were present. Accepting election, Gabriel Condulmer, a Venetian and nephew of Gregory XII, called himself Eugene IV (1431–47); his pontificate was not one of the happiest. Since the cardinals had been dissatisfied with Martin V's authoritarian administration, an election capitulation had been decided upon and signed by all the cardinals. It demanded not so much a change in the constitution of the Church as it did an implementation of the Council of Constance. In it were unequivocally expressed the aspirations of the College of Cardinals for a share in the government of the Church. This election capitulation was again sworn to by Eugene IV after his election and confirmed by apostolic constitutions after his coronation.

Martin V had been skillful as a politician and as ruler of the Papal State. His successor, Eugene IV, a former canon regular, was to an equal degree incompetent. His rash proceedings against the Colonna produced long lasting troubles in all parts of the Papal State. Risings in individual provinces and in Rome itself could be put down only by great exertions. In 1434 the Pope had to flee from the Eternal City. He was not able to return to Rome until 1443.

The pontificate of Eugene IV was entirely overshadowed by the Council of Basel. The date of its opening had been determined by Martin V, and the new Pope at once confirmed the appointment of the Cardinal Legate in Germany, Julian Cesarini, as legate and president of the Council. Since Cesarini was still involved in the anti-Hussite campaign, he had the Council opened at Basel on 23 July 1431 by his vicars, John of Ragusa and John of Palomar. The number of those present was still quite meager when Cesarini reached Basel in September. Contrary to the election capitulation that he had sworn to observe, Eugene IV opposed the Council from the start. Following the example of Martin V, who had managed to dissolve the previous Council of Siena, Eugene, through his unsure, vacillating, and even dishonest conduct, led himself, the Curia, and all of Christendom into the worst difficulties.

In the bull "Quoniam alto" of 12 November 1431 which only ten cardinals signed, he dissolved the Council and summoned a new synod, which was supposed to meet in Bologna eighteen months later. But before anything could be done at Basel, the Pope, at the consistory of 18 December, published the bull of dissolution, even though some of the cardinals were not in agreement with this procedure and challenged the Pope's right to dissolve a legitimately meeting Council. Meanwhile, the first solemn session had taken place at Basel on 14 December, with the reading of the decree "Frequens" and of the bull of convocation. The Council organized itself in the second session, held on 15 February 1432, following the pattern of the Council of Constance and the decree "Frequens." The Pope was pressed to withdraw the dissolution and it was demanded that he and the cardinals must appear at Basel.

To appreciate the situation it is important to note that the majority of the cardinals adhered to the Council; only six out of twenty-one were on the Pope's side. From then on Pope and Council were hostile to each other, and, as at Constance, the future fate of the Synod depended essentially on the politics of the various states. On the Council's side were at first the King of the Romans, France, England, Scotland, Castile, Burgundy, and Milan. At this time the Pope could count on only Venice and Florence as loyal adherents. But the attitude of the powers to the Council continually changed. During the tedious negotiations with the Pope the Council, now better attended, arranged its own organization and personnel. They set up of permanent committees, the so-called "deputations," with the College of Twelve as the group of presidents. The political situation, above all the unrest in the Papal State, forced the Pope to give in. Since a new schism was becoming a distinct possibility, most states advised yielding and compromise. The Council was unmoved. The presidents sent by the Pope were admitted only with great restrictions and took the required oath to the decrees of Constance. The long and unpleasant jockeying had led to an armistice rather than to peace; it had also led to a hardening of positions, in particular on the part of the Council Fathers. The Pope was mostly to blame for the situation that had arisen.

The question of union with the Greek Church decided the contest between Council and Pope. Martin V had reached an agreement with the Byzantine court relevant to a council in the West, and in the first year of his pontificate Eugene IV obtained assurances of Greek attendance at a Western council, for example in Bologna. Aware of the political importance for whichever succeeded in restoring union between the separated Churches, both Pope and Council took great pains in regard to the Greeks. From the spring of 1433 embassies of the Council as well as of the Pope went to Constantinople, and Greek envoys traveled to the West. The means resorted to in order to gain the Byzantine Emperor and to outdo the other side were not exactly edifying. The final voting produced a schism. More than two-thirds of the members held to the proposal of the Council. Despite many efforts for an understanding, the Pope, in the bull "Salvatoris et Dei nostri" of 30 May 1437, confirmed the minority decision, and, after long debates and recourse to not unobjectionable means, his envoys at Constantinople succeeded in winning the Greeks for the minority and hence for the holding of the council in Italy. On 18 September 1437, in the bull "Doctoris gentium," recognizing the minority as the *pars sanior,* Eugene IV transferred the Council to Ferrara. Thus ended the first phase of the Council of Basel. The question of what it achieved naturally presents itself.

The repeated defeats of the anti-Hussite crusade armies suggested the idea of negotiations. Hence it is not surprising that after the defeat at Domažlice in August 1431 the Cardinal Legate and one so familiar with the Hussite danger as John of Ragusa pressed for an invitation to the leaders of the Hussite factions. As early as 15 November 1431, and hence shortly after the opening of the Council, there was issued a message to appear in Basel. Many discussions relevant to safety and free discussion led to the very accommodating letter of safe-conduct of 20 June 1432, in the fourth session. The Bohemians left Basel on 14 April, but the negotiations were continued at Prague and led to agreement on the four articles of Prague, which had in the meantime been frequently modified, concerning the chalice for the laity, free preaching, the punishment of those guilty of serious sins, and a far-reaching renunciation of ecclesiastical property. This agreement, the so-called Prague *Compactata,* was promulgated on 5 July 1436 in the presence of the Emperor at the Diet of Iglau, and was ratified by the Council of Basel on 15 January 1437. The *Compactata* were not ratified by the Curia and were annulled in 1462. But this settlement of the Bohemian affair was a great success for the Council.

Despite some accomplishments, the reform of the Church could not be brought to a conclusion at Constance. A glance at the enormous reform literature makes this clear, and the decree "Frequens" had been issued for the very purpose of assuring the reform. And there have come down proposals which envisaged the thorough study of specific matters, such as union with the Greeks, by commissions of cardinals and university professors in the interval till the next council. As was the case with the Council of Constance, three tasks were assigned to that of Basel in Martin V's bull of convocation of 1 February 1431: concern for the Christian faith, the restoration of peace in Christendom, and the reform of the Church. It is beyond doubt that the last of these was regarded as the most important.

Soon after the opening of the Council a reform commission of twenty-four members was set up. The well known eighteen articles of the Constance reform demand had been discussed and passed only in part. This work was now resumed at Basel, but it required a long time before any order could be discerned in the reform motions, while again and again the effort for reform was interrupted by the conflict with Pope and Curia.

The filling of the higher benefices was once more an open question. In addition, a group of proposals and memoranda were soon presented to the Council with the aim of completely eliminating papal reservations. This was a theme that had been for decades at the very center *of reformatio capitis et curiae Romanae* and was intended to lead back to the ancient law. The so-called election decree, published on 13 July 1433, in the twelfth solemn session, is rightly termed moderate. It abolished general and specific reservations of bishoprics and monasteries and prescribed election by the qualified bodies according to earlier usage. The Pope could decide otherwise only in exceptional cases and with a precise listing of his reasons. Upon assuming office each Pope had to bind himself under oath to observe the decree.

The question of the payments made to the Curia, summarized under the term "annates," had also to begin over again. Here too there was a two-way split: Germans and French opposed annates, while Spaniards and Italians were uninterested. The question of indemnification of the Curia for the loss of annates occupied an important place. In view of the Pope's very difficult, even if not unmerited, situation this was understandable. The discussion was heightened and also prolonged by the preparation of a fundamental decree on simony with the decisive participation of the Cardinal Legate. The decree on annates, on 9 June 1435, peremptorily forbade all payments at the filling of benefices by either the Curia or the ordinaries. Thus was the late mediaeval development ended and, above all, a serious blow was given to the Curia.

Long in need of reform was the curial system of procedures, which had assumed a downright colossal magnitude. Since not much had been accomplished in this area at Constance, the old demands for limiting the Roman jurisdiction in favor of the ordinary courts were renewed at Basel. In several decrees of the Council there was enacted a restriction to *causae maiores* as in the old law, appeals were curtailed, and precautions were taken against the harassing of occupants of benefices.

Of special importance in the reform of the Curia were the decrees on the papal election and the College of Cardinals. They were a balanced product of earlier reform literature and searching consultation. Whereas the election of the Pope of unity at Constance took place outside what had hitherto been customary and the prescriptions laid down by conciliar decrees and papal directives for their implementation, the Council of Basel reverted to the old practice, allotting the election once again to the cardinals alone, despite many contrary voices. New, however, was the rule in regard to voting: that at most three candidates might be named; if more than one candidate was written on the ballot, one of those named had to be a non-cardinal. In this way the much complained of inbreeding in the College would be at least theoretically limited.

To what extent Basel was strictly a continuation of Constance appears above all in the oath to be taken by the newly elected Pope. The proposals at Constance required, besides the making of the so-called profession of faith of Boniface VIII, a whole series of promises relating to the government of the Church and of the Papal State. The Pope's oath as prescribed by the Council of Basel retained completely the brief version used at Constance except that, understandably, it included also the General Councils of Constance and Basel and their decrees, especially in regard to the observance of the decree "Frequens."

The decrees of the twenty-third session *de numero et qualitate cardinalium* likewise adhered closely to the Constance proposals, reform acts, and concordats. The number of cardinals was to be at most twenty-four and they were to be doctors of theology or of canon or civil law. The Constance prescriptions that cardinals must no longer be elevated merely by oral expression of opinion were extended at Basel to include the requirement of a written consent of a majority of the College. The so difficult and much discussed problem of the representation of all countries in the Senate of the Church was prudently decided in the sense that no nation might have more than one-third of the cardinals at any one time.

Ferrara and Florence

The Council that Eugene IV had summoned to Ferrara was opened in January 1438, though without the Greeks. They only arrived at Ferrara at the beginning of March. While the Curia pressed for quick action, the Greeks worked for delay in order to await the Western princes or their envoys. And so an interval of four months was first agreed upon. The hopes of the Pope and of the Byzantine Emperor John VIII for representatives of the Western states were not realized; only the Angevins and the Duke of Burgundy sent official envoys. In June began the theological discussions.

Because of an alleged danger of pestilence, but really for financial reasons, the Synod was transferred to Florence in January 1439. The expenses of the conciliar meetings were a burden on the Curia. After long and fruitful discussions, conversations between Emperor and Pope, and repeated threats of departure by the Greeks, there finally took place on 6 July 1439 the promulgation in both languages and signing of the union decree "Laetentur coeli." Soon after the Greeks left, and on the very return voyage many of those among them who had taken part in the Council withdrew their consent. The union was scarcely acknowledged in the East, even though other smaller groups of Oriental Christians — Armenians, Copts, Syrians, Chaldees, and Maronites — reached an understanding with the Curia. On the Pope's return to Rome in 1443 the Council was transferred to the Lateran; it quickly declined in importance and was never officially concluded.

The points of theological controversy were the *Filioque,* purgatory, the matter and form of the Eucharist, and the interpretation of the papal primacy. For the Greeks the *Filioque* was the most important and really decisive point. Nevertheless, the theological conversations first took up the doctrine of purgatory. The Greeks especially took issue with the Latin notion of a purifying fire, since Scripture and the Fathers had nothing to say about it. The union decree evaded an exact definition and confined itself to the statement that the souls in question had to undergo a cleansing penalty after death: penis purgatoriis post mortem purgari."

The question longest discussed was the *Filioque,* which had been inserted into the Nicene Creed in the early Middle Ages. The Greeks took as their point of departure the decree of the Third Ecumenical Council at Ephesus, according to which the creed was not to be altered by additions; in the *Filioque* they saw a modification in content. In the long and bitter discussions, the difference in the development of the two halves of the Church was clearly exposed. The Greeks especially rejected the scholastic deductions of the Western theologians. It was easier to convince them on the basis of patristic theology that the addition they so disliked had a certain basis in the Eastern and Western Fathers. But since they regarded the *Filioque* as the cause of the Schism, their resistance was stubborn. Again and again they said they would sooner depart than yield. The axiom, theologically doubtful but enthusiastically hailed as a way out, that "between the Western and Eastern Fathers there can be no contradiction, since they are all illuminated by the Holy Spirit," quickly produced agreement but no solution of the theological question. In the decree of union the accord and the permissibility of the accepting of the *Filioque* into the creed were defined with many words but it was not said who could lawfully make such an addition, and the Greeks were not obliged to insert the Western addition.

There were likewise grave difficulties in the discussions on the Eucharist, although there seemed to be reasonably close agreement as to essentials. A compromise got around the difficulties by recognizing unleavened and leavened bread as the matter but there was no decision relevant to the form, that is, to the words of consecration and the *epiclesis*.

The papal primacy came up as the final topic of discussion at the demand of the Latins and especially of Eugene IV, but too hastily. The Emperor opposed the discussion but in the interests of union he had to exert considerable pressure on the Greek participants. The Greeks regarded as the highest tribunal in the constitution of the Church the pentarchy, the traditional Five Patriarchates of Rome, Constantinople, Alexandria, Antioch, and Jerusalem. They were fully prepared to concede to the Patriarch of Old Rome the privileges he had enjoyed before the outbreak of the Schism. There could be no question of a primacy of jurisdiction. But in barely three weeks the Greeks were compelled to yield on a broad front. However, this was not a genuine solution, as the various possibilities of interpretation showed and still show.

It must be noted that the dogmatic discussions and decisions that took place in a politically conditioned climate and that the participants kept fully concrete political goals before their eyes. Pope and Emperor needed the union. The Emperor wanted the military assistance of the West in exchange for the slightest possible dogmatic concessions; the Pope wanted aid against Basel and hence demanded recognition of the primacy. The confrontation between the Curia and the Council of Basel was also of great influence on Ferrara-Florence. Both at Basel and in the papal camp persons entertained ideas in regard to the Byzantine Church that were erroneous because they were preponderantly idealistic. But the Pope and Curia displayed greater skill, made many otherwise unusual concessions, and played off union against Basel. More important than the subsequent "union" was the exposition of standpoints and the constant referring by the Greeks to Scripture and the Fathers as the unique source *vis-à-vis* the Latins' deductive theology.

It goes without saying that the ecumenical character of the Council of Ferrara-Florence was accepted on account of the personal attendance of Pope and Emperor. But it must be noted that relatively few bishops, and those almost entirely Italians, represented the Latin Church. And so there could be no question of a representation of the Universal Church or of the European states, and that at a time when Basel again obtained recognition from numerous quarters.

The position of France in regard to Basel was important for the reason that most of the participants and the most influential personalities came from France, and from them came, to a great extent, the proposals for the reform discussions. Even if one admits annoyance over the loss of the papacy after the Council of Constance as a powerful stimulus to the anti-curial policy, without the Neapolitan question the changing attitude of the French King would be inexplicable. If France had favored a transfer to a French city, the *rapprochement* with the Curia began in 1435 when Eugene IV made the enfeoffment of René of Anjou as King of Naples dependent on his abandoning the Council of Basel. But the Pragmatic Sanction of Bourges in 1438 was the reply to the miscarriage of this plan. In this the French Church in twenty-three articles adopted, with some modifications, the reform decrees of Basel, in particular "Frequens" and the decrees on the authority of the Council: the election decree, that on the abolition of annates, and a group of prescriptions on reform of the liturgy and of the clergy. But the suspension of the Pope was not recognized and relations with the Curia were not broken off; in fact, a few years later they were again rather lively. But attendance at the Council of Ferrara was not permitted; on the other hand, while France had no share in the deposition of Eugene IV, any molestation of the Council at Basel was forbidden.

At first Aragón was represented at Basel only by one envoy as an observer. It was not until the death of Joanna II of Naples in 1435 had opened the question of the succession and Alfonso V of Aragón had become first the prisoner and then the ally of Milan that a rather large embassy arrived at the Council. Since the Pope apparently wanted to confiscate the escheated fief and incorporate it into the Papal State, the task of the Aragonese embassy consisted chiefly in inciting the Council to sharp measures against the Curia. When the effort, sanctioned by the Council, to deprive the Pope of the Papal State misfired, the Aragonese at Basel at least worked eagerly for the trial, suspension, and deposition of Eugene.

The policy of Castile was strictly dependent on France. John II inclined to the Council but no embassy went to Basel until 1434. In the struggle with England for the place after the French in June 1434 Castile was victorious. From 1437 Castile's attitude was one of reserve, although the Fathers at Basel went to great pains to be accommodating. The envoys left the city in 1438 and, after visiting the new German King Albert II at Breslau and attending the Diet of Princes at Mainz in 1439, returned home. Thereafter Castile was on the side of Eugene IV.

Philip the Good, Duke of Burgundy, was for a long time neutral. He made promises to both sides and obtained the approval of the Treaty of Arras from both Eugene and the Council of Basel. From 1435 he inclined to the Curia, recalled his embassy from Basel, and was represented at the Council of Ferrara. But his policy was always very cautious.

England did not play a decisive role in the history of the Council of Basel. Its championing of the Curia was to a great extent determined by opposition to France, even though the Fathers at Basel tried again and again to draw the English King to their side. Yielding to the insistence of the Council, a small but highly qualified embassy appeared at Basel in 1433, probably chiefly motivated by the hope of bringing back the Hussites to the Church. However, the envoys did not permit themselves to be incorporated and demanded an organization by nations, as at Constance. A second embassy came in 1434 to discuss peace with France. English prestige suffered a severe blow at Basel in the strife with Castile over precedence. The deposition of Eugene IV and the election of Felix V were not recognized in England. What France and Germany adopted of the reform decrees the English King had long ago attended to on his own.

So from 1438 there faced each other two hostile general councils, each exerting itself to obtain recognition by the states. If the Western Schism had to do with the *papa indubitatus,* now the problem was the *concilium indubitatum.*

After the German Emperor Sigismund's disappearance the ecclesiastical question was treated at numberless diets, but, despite detailed discussion by representatives of both sides, it remained undecided. The indecision found expression in what was called neutrality, which was extended from meeting to meeting. The proclamation of neutrality was intended especially as a protection against the censures of both Pope and Council and a means of preventing unrest among the faithful and of assuring the possession of benefices. The Mainz *instrumentum acceptationis* of 1439, in which, following the French model, the Council's reform decrees were declared valid with certain modifications, was a taking of a stand for the Council and its teaching but without an adopting of the Council's policy. Since, as earlier, both the Curia and the Council were applied to by the higher and the lower clergy, there could be no question of strict neutrality. Thus the representation of German sees at Basel reached its high point around 1440, while suits at the Curia strongly declined. The ecclesiastical Electors of Mainz and Cologne supported Basel and were unsuccessfully deposed by the Curia in 1446. An escape from the complicated situation seemed to be offered by the plan for a new, third council, which was eagerly defended in Germany; but, despite a seeming willingness, it was rejected by the Curia. Since the Council, in contrast to the Pope, possessed no real power, its importance steadily declined. No change was made by the promulgation on 16 May 1439, in the thirty-third session, of earlier formulated propositions as *veritates catholicae:* The proposition concerning the power of the Council over the Pope and every other person among the faithful is a truth of the Catholic faith; the proposition that the Pope cannot dissolve a general council without its consent is a truth of the Catholic faith; whoever obstinately opposes these truths in word, deed, and writing is to be regarded as a heretic.

The Council of Basel deposed Eugene IV in June 1439. In November it elected as Pope Felix V (1439–49). He was able to obtain recognition only in a very restricted area. The Council continued at Basel until 1447, when it was transferred to Lausanne. The greatest danger for the Curia was over when King Alfonso V of Aragón, after conquering Naples, went over to the Pope in 1443 in exchange for far-reaching concessions and recalled his bishops from Basel. And the new German King, Frederick III, let himself be won over by the promise of the imperial crown and much ecclesiastical patronage. It was more difficult to reach an agreement with the Electors, the real imperial government. Their demand for the reinstatement of the Archbishops of Mainz and Cologne, recognition of the Basel reforms and of the decrees of Constance and Basel, and the convocation of a third council was accepted in the Concordat of the Princes in 1447 in a veiled form that still remains obscure.

Eugene died on 23 February 1447, just after envoys of the German King and of some German princes had taken the oath of obedience to him. His successor, Nicholas V (1447–55), at once ratified the settlement with the German Church. More adroit than his predecessor, he reached an agreement with Frederick III in the so-called Concordat of Vienna and was able to effect considerable modifications in the Basel reforms. Negotiations for the ending of the schism were conducted by France as early as 1447. But it was only in 1449 that it was possible to induce Felix V to retire and the Council of Basel to decree its own dissolution after it had been allowed to elect Nicholas V. Without any condemnation of the theological views, the mutual censures and processes were annulled, the possession of benefices was confirmed, some of the cardinals of the Basel obedience were admitted into the Roman College of Cardinals, and Felix V was allowed to exercise papal rights in his former obedience.

The great quarrel was thereby ended for the moment, not by a theological solution of the vexing questions but under political auspices.

From the political viewpoint the Council of Basel, a gathering of solely intellectual power, was more dependent than the Roman Pontiff on the princes, who sought to extract as much as possible from both sides. Not only were political disputes brought before the Council, but in its competition with the Pope the Council sought political successes by mediating peace or, especially clearly, by arranging union with the Greeks. Always dependent on the good will of the secular lords, great and small, the Council had to move very circumspectly in its administration. Reform questions were important at Basel because of the time limit in the Constance concordats. The discussions and treatises, though theologically and philosophically sound, could change nothing there, since the envoys and proxies had to uphold the changing policies of their lords and did so with great skill. In this controversy, conducted by both sides with distasteful means, the Curia managed to a very great extent to rescue its situation. This was a considerable political achievement, but far removed from a genuine reform will. It purchased its own recognition by means of great compromises and withdrew into the Papal State as one of the *cinque principati* of Italy. In this way its world-wide impact was powerfully obstructed and reform was frustrated. But one must distinguish between adhering to the Council of Basel and defending the conciliar idea. The Council of Constance presented so many complications to the Roman *Congregatio super editione conciliorum generalium* that the congregation decided to remove the Council of Basel from the list of general councils. Such a procedure attests, not a scholarly outlook, but bias.

The person of Eugene IV must be evaluated in the same manner. Judgments by contemporaries were in general quite reserved. He was blamed for the harshness of his procedures, his quick recourse to force, and the incessant stressing of his position as ruler of the Church. One may be happy to regard him as the papacy's saviour from the danger of "conciliarism," but the failure of reform is also his responsibility, for it had become all too clear that without a council there could be no reform. From the viewpoint of Church history the decisive turning from the Middle Ages to modern times occurs around the middle of the fifteenth century. Rome had prevented reform and in return soon received the Reformation.

Section Three

The Byzantine Church: The Age of Palamism

Hans-Georg Beck

CHAPTER 51

From the Second Council of Lyons to the Council of Ferrara-Florence

Probably at no other period were relations between the Orthodox Church of the Byzantine Empire and the papacy in so deplorable a state as during the long reign of the Byzantine Emperor Andronicus II (1282–1328). The great gamble of his father, Michael VIII, to assert power *vis-à-vis* Charles of Anjou depended on his playing with high stakes — the policy of reunion, — even if one is not justified in denying an inner sympathy on the part of the Emperor, who had grown up in an atmosphere favorable to union. With Michael's death in 1282 the game ended for a long time, for his successor did not have to play. The Sicilian Vespers had relieved the Empire for years to come from a severe direct pressure. And so Andronicus annulled the union, even though he had subscribed to it under oath as recently as 1279. His decision was, to be sure, no mere caprice. Michael VIII, who had concluded the Union of Lyons on his own, had never contrived to break popular resistance. Part of the higher clergy had adopted a passive attitude, and the Patriarch John XI Beccus, favorable to the union and a theologian of importance, had known how to remove many obstacles. But all the more obstinate was the opposition from monastic circles, whose influence prevailed not only with the people in the streets but to a degree even with members of the imperial family. Furthermore, the Popes plainly cherished false views of the Emperor's real power and in their demands actually recognized and furthered that very Caesaropapism which the union was supposed to eliminate. Finally Pope Martin IV, completely under the influence of the House of Anjou, excommunicated Michael and his associates for schism and heresy.

For the Emperor the situation was all the more dangerous in that the opposition to the union was secretly associated with repudiation of the legitimacy of the imperial house. When he seized the throne, Michael VIII had first reduced the lawful heir, John IV Lascaris, to second place and then, by blinding him, had disqualified him for the imperial office. Arsenius, then Patriarch (1255–60 and 1261–63), at first assumed a vacillating attitude to the situation. But under pressure from a strong opposition in Asia Minor to the Palaeologi and in favor of the Lascarid, he finally became the leader, at least passively, of this very group. There was formed the Arsenite faction with no real program except to keep faith with Arsenius and to reject all new patriarchs. The theory of the Emperor as master of the Church remained unquestioned in official circles, the practice of communication between palace and *patriarchium* was unchanged, but both Emperor and bishops had to admit in the end their powerlessness against pressure from the masses led by the monks. It is a characteristic of the new Emperor's insight that he gave the Arsenite problem his full attention. Not for some decades were they inclined to make peace. In 1310 the schism was ended.

Meanwhile, affairs in the West had worked to the benefit of the Byzantines. The Popes were still trying to keep alive the crusading idea, and again and again the planning of the crusade advocated by them was directed against Constantinople for the restoration of the destroyed Latin Empire. But the preaching of the crusade evoked no response. Acre, the last foothold of productive activity in Syria, fell in 1291. The commercial interests of the Italian cities were more concerned with the *status quo* than with the risks of a campaign. The indulgence found hardly any response, and the Western kings were too much engrossed in the consolidation of their national states to listen with both ears to the preaching of the Pope and his legates. Theorists, it is true, were not satisfied.

In these and similar undertakings, which served, not the crusading idea, but the dynastic policies of *la France outremer,* Andronicus could wait calmly for the opposing forces in Achaia to dissipate themselves. The danger again assumed a serious nature with the more extensive plans of Charles IV of France (1322–28) in favor of the Kingdom of Armenia. That this expedition could have been diverted to Constantinople was not to be denied. And so Andronicus reverted to his father's policy, proposing negotiations for union. But with the fading of the danger and because of the civil war between Andronicus and his grandson they were soon shelved.

Meanwhile, circumstances occurred which forced upon the Curia a reorientation of its reunion policy and, in fact, caused all interested Western powers to look for an entirely new approach in the Eastern policy. It suffices to mention the key phrase, "the Turkish danger," to indicate a factor which remained in the foreground of Church History for the next four centuries.

The capture of Constantinople by the Byzantines in 1261 and the return of the imperial court had again necessarily shifted the emphasis in Byzantine policy much more sharply toward the West. After the reconquest there were not sufficient forces to keep a determined and watchful eye on the East at the same time. Asia Minor was neglected, the frontiers were left exposed. The welfare of the eastern provinces yielded to general decline, and the Lascarid legitimists reduced the provinces to disorder. Danger from the Seljuks was no longer serious, since their power had been broken by the Mongols in 1243. But a result of this event was the rise on the edges of the Seljuk empire of Turkish tribes which made themselves independent and on their own not only threatened the dominions of the Sultan but also pressed against the inadequately tended frontiers of the Byzantine Empire. Like an avalanche, Ottomans and Seljuks fell upon the Byzantine provinces in Asia Minor. Around 1300 virtually all of the countryside had become Turkish and it was not long before the famous old metropolises of Asia Minor fell to them: Prusa in 1326, Nicaea in 1331, Nicomedia in 1337. Meanwhile there occurred the first offensives against the Aegean islands, Thrace, and the environs of Constantinople. At first only desultory raids, these expeditions were soon systematically managed, and in 1354 Kallipolis (Gallipoli), the key to the Dardanelles, became a firm Turkish foothold in Europe. Adrianople (Edirne) became Turkish in 1362, and there, around 1365, the Ottoman Sultan established his capital, about 100 kilometers to the rear of Constantinople.

Since the Arab attack in the seventh century no invasion had brought greater losses to the Church than that of the Ottomans. In the earlier onset Syria, Palestine, Egypt, and Africa had been lost and the Christian communities in those lands could maintain themselves only in precarious circumstances. But now the ancient Christian metropolises of Asia Minor were swallowed in the Islamic desert and before long the Balkans would share their fate. In these circumstances the political problem of the Western powers was not so much to reestablish the Latin Empire, for which it was difficult to find a serious aspirant, but rather to defend Europe from the infidels in union with the beleaguered Greeks. Such an association would inevitably involve discussion of Church union, but now with far less political justification. And for the Greeks the difficulty no longer consisted in keeping the Latins out of the Sea of Marmora but in gaining them as auxiliaries, even at the price of union. So long as the danger was only dimly in the consciousness of the West, it was felt that the idea of union could not be disregarded, and political circles in the Byzantine Empire reckoned with this condition. The East insisted on a truly ecumenical council, a suggestion now more strongly supported in the West, not at first by the Popes but by those circles representing the conciliar movement. Unfortunately, the problem of union thereby became a political question between papacy and conciliarism.

Despite everything, the difficulties remained almost insuperable. To a great extent they were psychological. The East until now knew Westerners either as conquerors who, with a cross on their shoulders, wanted to establish a domain of their own and for whom the problems of Church union, if they were important at all, were to be solved in the manner of conquerors, or as mercenaries, adventurers, and traders, who with skill and money had deprived the Byzantines of all positions of commerce and trade. The intellectual forces of the West were virtually unknown to the East until the middle of the fourteenth century. Potentially effective influences, such as the activity of the Franciscans and the Dominicans, were unrealized because of reciprocal charges of heresy. And the information that the West had concerning the East derived almost exclusively from those who represented the West in the East. Relations thus revolved on a not very high plane. The standard bearers of Orthodox theology compiled long lists of heresies which were prevalent in the West and multiplied them further by several enticing new numbers, such as the questions of the *epiclesis* and purgatory. With equal ardor their Western counterparts made the Greeks responsible for dozens of heresies.

The amazing thing in all this is that the Union of Florence was eventually achieved. To be sure, it took a whole century.

Thus Barlaam, who amazingly foresaw much of what would eventually happen, failed, but behind his mission stood the grand chamberlain John Cantacuzene, who, as the Emperor John VI (1347–54), further pursued his lofty goal. Around 1350 one embassy after another set out for Avignon. The council, according to the Emperor's wish, ought to meet at a place equally distant from Rome and Constantinople. Pope Clement VI was not at first opposed to the idea, but eventually the plan miscarried. However, Cantacuzene did not cease his exertions and his successor, John V Palaeologus (1354–91), walked in his footsteps, though probably without much genuine dedication. New discussions took place in 1367, with the co-operation of the former Emperor Cantacuzene, the Latin Archbishop Paul, papal legate and titular Patriarch of Constantinople. The outcome appeared favorable, and even the Patriarch Philotheus Coccinus of Constantinople (1353–54 and 1364–76) seems to have accepted it. In any event, the first moves for convoking the council were made. But, unfortunately, John V had in the meantime decided, like Michael VIII, to go it alone. In 1369 he became a Catholic at Rome, a step which certainly enhanced the Pope's prestige in regained Rome but without significance in the overall picture of the relations between the Churches, if indeed, as it is described, it could have had any significance. In an encyclical to the Churches the Pope once more rejected the idea of a council on the ground that it was absurd to make defined truths a subject of controversy again.

But before long the Western Schism and the resulting Conciliar Movement produced a change along the entire front. Now the West almost forced a council upon the East and the retarding factor was the Byzantine Emperor Manuel II Palaeologus (1391–1425). A genuinely religious man, he knew exactly how difficult, if not impossible, it would be to make union palatable to his people. A miscarriage would aggravate the schism and deliver Byzantium to the mercy of the Turks, whereas the threat of union would continue to be a means of impressing the Turks. Hence the Emperor was determined *a priori* not to draw the final conclusion from the union discussions but to seek the Empire's safety in the purely political sphere. But meanwhile the situation had become still more threatening and he may have hoped that it would open the eyes of the Western princes. Bulgaria became a vassal state of the Turks in 1371. In 1389 occurred the celebrated First Battle of Kossovo, which made the Turks masters of the entire Balkan peninsula. The remnant of the crusading states in Greece had long been dependent on the favor of the Turkish overlord. Theological prolegomena were now too late. Still, chiefly on the initiative of the French King Charles VI and of King Sigismund of Hungary, an army of crusaders was actually assembled, but the Battle of Nicopolis on 26 September 1396 was a Turkish victory and proved, to quote Runciman, "that the Crusaders had learned nothing in all the centuries."

In these circumstances the Byzantine Emperor Manuel made a desperate attempt to arouse the Christian West to a new expedition by means of a personal visit to Western Europe. But the actual result was at most a vague promise here and there. That Byzantium did not then become the spoil of the Turks was due solely to the fact that at that very moment (1402) the Mongols under the Khan Timur-Leng decisively defeated the Ottoman Sultan at the Battle of Ankara and thereby gave the Empire a breathing spell.

The project of a union of the Churches was now more animated in the West than in the East. Manuel was invited by the cardinals to send delegates to the Council of Pisa (1409). The Emperor Sigismund informed his colleague in Constantinople that the Council of Constance (1414–18) aimed "contra infideles paganos et praecipue Turcos remedia vobisque et predicte civitati Constantinopolitane... providere" and invited him to send representatives. Manuel complied, but his highly esteemed agent, Manuel Chrysoloras, died at the Council in 1415 and since the Synod soon realized the impracticability of its too detailed program the *reductio Graecorum* was put on the waiting list.

But in the interval new imperial envoys had arrived. They submitted thirty-six articles in which the Greeks had specified their notions of the preparations for union. The embassy seems to have been optimistic in all regards. To its superiors it painted in glowing colors the readiness of the Council and of the Curia to meet every advance half-way and with the same palette depicted the inclination of the East to return to Rome's obedience in both faith and ritual. It must have been these brilliant hues that induced the new Pope, Martin V, to agree to the Greeks' demand that he be represented at a union council to be convoked to Constantinople by the Emperor, just because in such a council he apparently saw nothing more than the solemn framework for the ratification of a unity already established *de facto.* But the realization was slowed down, because in the thirty-six articles it was stipulated that the Pope should finance the undertaking and at the moment he did not have the necessary means. And once the papal till had been replenished, a Turkish attack on Constantinople thwarted the projected meeting (1422). Hence Martin V first sent a nuncio to Constantinople to make the preparations. At that time, however, it soon became clear how misleading had been the optimism of the Byzantine envoys. The Greeks were far from agreeing to an unscrutinized union and had no intention of viewing an ecumenical council as a mere backdrop for submission. The Emperor flatly disavowed his envoys and demanded a council at which the disagreements between the Churches should be taken up point by point. Thereupon, quite understandably, the Pope's readiness for what was basically a Greek Council at Constantinople with a single representative of the Latin Church quickly disappeared.

Just the same, the way was opened for a compromise Martin V, however, died and his successor, Eugene IV, had his hands full in dealing with conciliarism, which now exploded at the Council of Basel. But eventually it was this very power struggle that brought the idea of union to maturity. For both sides the gaining of the Greeks could only mean a powerful rise in prestige and so both sides wooed them. All cities that were adequate were suggested as the meeting place; Constantinople was repeatedly considered, as were Vienna and Buda and finally preference was given to Avignon or Florence or Ferrara. Even just before the departure of the Greeks it was not clear whether they would board the squadron sent by the Council of Basel or that sent by the Pope, and when at last they reached Venice in the papal flotilla it was even then probably only the political advice of the Most Serene Republic that definitely induced them to go to Ferrara.

The story of the Council of Ferrara-Florence (1438–39) contains in part the following. For an appreciation of the fate of the union in the East only what follows need be noted here. Since the victory of Eugene IV over his opponents at Basel, far from being achieved at the beginning of the Council, needed a real union to crown it, the Pope was prepared for every imaginable concession. The Synod was a papal epic *par excellence.* Any forced union, any lack of freedom of debate, even any cutting short of disputes by means of dictation from Rome was out of the question. It was the sort of council the Greeks had always wanted. But the pressure of political circumstances? With this the Emperor John VIII (1425–48) had primarily to reckon. He took part in the Council in person and switched signals on several occasions. But one almost feels that, the longer the Council lasted, the more precisely he got to know the Pope's financial difficulties and mortgaging, and the more disillusioned he must have become because of the slight participation of the secular princes, so much the less was he convinced of the political success of a Church union. Even at the very end he hinted at his readiness to return to Constantinople without a settlement. At last, on 6 July 1439, the union was promulgated in the decree "Laetentur Caeli" and all the Greeks who were entitled to do so signed it, except the Metropolitan Mark Eugenicus of Ephesus. The signatures were not coerced and were probably sincere.

Nevertheless it is impossible to maintain that one side had convinced the other by arguments. If, for example, both *a filio* and *per filium* were considered valid and accepted as expressing one and the same dogmatic truth, this happened not from philological and primarily also not from dogmatic considerations, but because both formulations were found in recognized Fathers and because all held to the axiom that the Fathers of the Church, being inspired, could not err and accordingly the different formulations had to mean the same thing. Even Mark Eugenicus could not escape this argument, and hence he again and again hinted that the writings of the Latins were probably falsified. Thus, except for men like Bessarion of Nicaea and Isidore of Kiev, the Greeks were coerced by the possibility of union to a "notional assent," but they were unenthusiastic over the achievement of union, because the last inner resistances had by no means been broken — a mood that could not long withstand the cool reception that was theirs at Constantinople in February 1440. More serious was the fact that the Emperor himself died in 1448 without having been able to decide to promulgate the union.

Yet the achieving of union had, in the meantime, brought about even political consequences. The new, and last Byzantine Emperor, Constantine XI Dragases (1448–53), a man of political ability, saw in the union, in spite of everything, a better basis of further exertions for the defense of Constantinople than had been the case with the delaying tactics of his dead brother, John VIII. Finally, on 12 December 1452, a solemn liturgy with a commemoration of the Pope could be celebrated in Hagia Sophia, and during it the decree "Laetentur Caeli" was promulgated. But this had no effect on the fate of Constantinople. And the first Patriarch under Muslim rule, Gennadius Scholarius, governed the remnant of his church as though the act of 1452 had never taken place.

CHAPTER 52

Hesychasm and Palamism

Once again, before the history of the Byzantine Empire came to an end, the structure of the Imperial Church was convulsed by a quarrel that recalls the iconoclast strife of the eighth and ninth centuries. It was a dispute in regard to a mysticism, fought out on dogmatic ground,. Hesychasm may be understood as Byzantine mysticism in its entirety, with its striving for *apatheia* (resignation) and peace of soul. By reason of expediency in regard to terminology, however, it is best to restrict the term Hesychasm to one facet of this mysticism, which cannot be separated from the whole but shows specific trends. In the classical threefold ascent to God — practice (asceticism), "natural theology" (comprehension by means of meditation and contemplation of the ultimate cause of things and of their history in God), and *theoria* or *theologia* (union with God) — the emphasis shifts slowly but constantly. The great ascetical subject of "practice" is displaced, not completely but nevertheless energetically, by a psycho-physical technique of recollection and prayer. The rhythmic repetition, carried out in a Yogi-like position, of a prayer formula — the "monologue" usually called the "Prayer of Jesus" today — has the task of completely "emptying" the mind, of transcending not only every meditative representation of the imagination but also every *logismos,* every formation of concepts, to arrive at full "nakedness" of mind upon which shines the vision of the Godhead in light, a vision which seizes upon the whole man and comes to rest in an undefined sphere between corporal visibility and invisibility. That which the classical Byzantine mystics, and especially Maximus Confessor, had cultivated, "natural theology," declines more and more in importance, even if it is dragged into the terminology. There thus disappears one of the chief connections between mysticism and Christian humanism, because this natural theology was the sphere of a spiritualized universal sympathy, a universal embrace, a universal emotion. The Hesychasts' impatience could not endure stopping at this level.

The age of the first Emperors of the House of Palaeologus was the period of the triumphant progress of this method of prayer, which possessed the inherent desire to establish itself absolutely. Political difficulties on Athos — raids by the Turks, arguments with the Serbs, and so forth — again and again led masters and disciples to more distant surroundings, especially to Thessalonica. Devout circles were formed, in which the Hesychasts passed on their method, and quarrels with the still active Bogomilism intruded themselves. The more this mysticism spread, naturally the more it was exposed to misinterpretation and misuse. The terminology of the masters, going back to Simeon the New Theologian and even to a Messalian origin, in regard to the vision of light strongly scintillated between metaphor and matter and thus gave support to those who were inclined, contrary to the counsels of Gregory Sinaites, to identify every light experience and every by-product of their rigorous psychotechnique with a specific grace of God and his own proper light.

Conflict was not long in coming. It found its occasion at last in the susceptible vanity of the protagonists. The monk Barlaam of Calabria, born in Orthodoxy and raised a Greek, but even so hailing from the "Latinizing" fringes of the Empire —

this was one of the chief reasons for the antipathy that he encountered everywhere — had energetically defended the Byzantine view in his treatises on the procession of the Holy Spirit, but a monk of Athos, Gregory Palamas, took exception to the form of his syllogistic reasoning. Barlaam, easily offended and greatly infatuated with his Aristotelian education, thereupon attacked Palamas' method of argument. The quarrel rapidly and noticeably became envenomed and Palamas soon fell back upon a fundamentally anti-dialectical procedure, that is, to a type of theology that is no longer rational but mystical in nature. Thereupon, Barlaam felt obliged to throw light on his opponent's intellectual background and in so doing he quickly met something of which he had hitherto been unaware — Hesychasm, of which Palamas was an ardent protagonist. He was told by Hesychasts — by immature pupils, so the Palamites later claimed — that they were in possession of an infallible method which helped them to see with bodily eyes that uncreated light which suffused Jesus on Mount Tabor and is identical with the divinity itself. They told him about their exercises of concentration and their technique of prayer — and soon Barlaam knew enough. In the Hesychasts he saw a return of the old Messalians, people who apparently sought the seat of the soul somewhere in the region of the navel — that is why he gave them the derisive label of "Omphalopsychists," — above all, men who either materialized God in order to see him or introduced an unlawful distinction between God's essence and operations.

A friend of both Barlaam and Palamas, the Athos monk Gregory Akindynos, warned the Calabrian against rash attacks on the sacrosanct Athonian monachism but Barlaam refused to be deterred any longer and from 1338 proceeded to denounce this mysticism in treatises and at a synod in Constantinople. Palamas took this deeply to heart and in a steadily rising spiral developed in an anti-Barlaamite pamphlet literature, the essence of a theology that was fittingly termed "Palamism." At intervals this theology also had recourse to syllogisms but fundamentally it recognized is the basis of theology only the tradition of the Fathers and the personal mystical inspiration of the theologian. Central, precisely in order to safeguard the light visions of the Hesychasts, is the real distinction between God's completely inaccessible essence, invisible even to the blessed in heaven and his operations, the chief of which is *gratia increata* and to which belongs the light of Tabor, identical with it. Nothing was farther from Palamas' thought than to introduce a "division" in God but he merely succeeded in establishing an antinomy between unity and real distinction. The attempt to trace this doctrine to the patristic tradition was based, at least as regards the much quoted Maximus Confessor, on a misinterpretation. But his adherents were basically by no means hesitant to waive the proofs from tradition and to expound their theology as something new: a legitimate continuation of the New Testament revelation through their inspired master.

Barlaam submitted his writings to the Patriarch John XIV Calecas (1334 to 1347), a theologically indecisive and politically wavering prelate, who doubtless found Palamas' theology intrinsically foreign, although he was not favorably disposed toward Barlaam. He wanted to dispose of the quarrel and understood exactly how dangerous it would be to run afoul of the Athonians. Monachism had indeed become a dread power, especially since the Second Council of Lyons and the abortive union, and in comparison with it the union of patriarchal and imperial authority counted for rather little. Meanwhile, inspired by Palamas himself, a large majority of the Athonians had issued a *tomos,* a dogmatic manifesto, which set forth the basic tenets of the Palamite doctrine as the original proper ingredient of Orthodoxy and anathematized Barlaam as a heretic. The matter pressed for a decision.

Details of the two synods held in Constantinople in June and August 1341 escape us. The first session took place on 10 June in Hagia Sophia, with the Emperor Andronicus III (1328–41) presiding. Barlaam was not permitted to advance his dogmatic contentions, since, as he was told, this was the affair of the hierarchy. Palamas, on the other hand, was absolved of the charge of ditheism, the doctrine of the real distinction between God's essence and operation was considered rather *en passant* than expressly, and the reproaches levelled at the Hesychasts' method of prayer were rejected. The questions were in no sense probed by the members of the synod, but Barlaam observed that he could count on no sympathy and submitted to the prohibition of again attacking Palamas and the mystics. Thereupon the session ended, and the Emperor died a few days later. Barlaam now felt no longer bound by his promise, but he returned to the West and eventually became a Catholic and Bishop of Gerace. He died in 1350.

A new opponent, who remained behind, was Gregory Akindynos. He had not become disloyal to the monastic ideals of the Athonians but he now rejected the theological argumentation of his friend Palamas. The synod again met, presided over by the grand chamberlain John Cantacuzene, a member of the Council of Regency for the Emperor John V Palaeologus, who was under age. But political complications began to play a role. In the Council of Regency the Patriarch and the grand chamberlain were struggling for the decisive influence, and above them both stood the widowed Empress, Anne of Savoy. This rivalry, rather than any particular internal affinity, may have been the reason why Cantacuzene now resolutely embraced the Palamite faction *vis-à-vis* the half-hearted Patriarch. And thus Palamism was dragged into the conflict about to explode between Cantacuzene and the Palaeologi and at the same time into the corresponding social struggles in the Empire; yet no inner connection can be established. At any rate, Akindynos was condemned (August 1341). Then the synodal decree (*tomos*) of both sessions was to be prepared, but the Patriarch refused to participate unless action was limited to a *tomos* which would ignore the August session, over which, in his opinion, Cantacuzene had unlawfully presided, and the condemnation of Akindynos. The *tomos* was drawn up anyhow, but displayed great restraint. The struggle in the Council of Regency continued to smoulder, and the Patriarch joined with Alexius Apokaukos in an effort to hamstring Cantacuzene. When a campaign kept the grand chamberlain away from the capital, Apokaukos and the Patriarch finally usurped power. Palamas had reason to fear that in these circumstances the successes of 1341 would be lost to him, and so he definitely joined the faction of Cantacuzene, who thereupon had himself acclaimed as Emperor on 26 October 1341. He obviously found in the Palamites a suitable instrument for his plans and thereafter energetically favored them, though he had originally supported Barlaam.

Palamas continued to develop his theories in writings, thereby affording the Patriarch an opportunity to charge him with violating the *tomos* of 1341. On the other hand, he allowed Akindynos more and more leeway for his attack on Palamas. At several conferences in 1342 and 1344 the writings of Palamas, who was arrested at the behest of Calecas, were condemned and he was personally anathematized. But the Patriarch's days were numbered. Cantacuzene approached the capital in a menacing mood, and Anne of Savoy considered sacrificing the Patriarch and reaching an amicable settlement with Cantacuzene. Only in this way could the Palamites be won over and the Dynasty of Palaeologus saved. Since Calecas had meanwhile raised Akindynos, who had earlier been condemned, to the diaconate, there was at hand a canonical reason for deposing him. This took place the day before Cantacuzene triumphantly forced his way into the capital on 2 February 1347 and was crowned Emperor. At once Palamas was set free and Akindynos was excommunicated. Isidore, former Bishop of Monembasia, a staunch Palamite, was chosen Patriarch (1347–50).

Still, the victory of Palamism was not yet assured. The opposition was active. Not a few prelates and clerics regarded the theology of Palamas as merely an unlawful *neoterismos,* and not a few monks were unwilling to be identified with the behavior of the Hesychasts. And finally, the opposition had its chief center in the intellectuals and humanists of the capital. These circles must not for that reason be charged with "agnosticism." They were as orthodox as their opponents claimed to be, but in Hesychasm and Palamism they saw threats to far too many values which had hitherto flourished peacefully in the shadow of Orthodoxy. Thus all questions were supposed to be settled at a general synod which met on 28 May 1351 in the imperial palace. John VI Cantacuzene presided. The opposition was only meagerly represented. Its leadership had meanwhile been assumed by the historian and polyhistor, Nicephorus Gregoras. Finally, at the fifth session, all were excommunicated who refused to recognize the orthodoxy of the Palamite doctrine. A long synodal *tomos* was drawn up, which contained an account of the proceedings and the dogmatic decisions. On 15 August it was published over the signatures of the Emperor John Cantacuzene and the Patriarch, and later that of the coemperor, John V Palaeologus, was added. It was the greatest triumph which Palamas, who had in the interval become Metropolitan of Thessalonica, could have hoped for. And hardly ever had it put its fundamental principle of traditionalism to so severe a test as now. No change in the situation occurred when Cantacuzene, the protector of the Palamites, had to give place to the legitimate Palaeologus in 1354. John V could scarcely afford to antagonize the large Palamite party by an opposing religious policy and besides he was apparently uninterested in theology. Furthermore, Cantacuzene, as earlier, was still a towering personage, whom John V could not ignore. Hence the Palamite hierarchy had a free hand.

In no sense was Palamism the result of a conflict between Latin scholasticism — Barlaam was not a Latin scholastic — and Greek patristic thought. Its victory was easy for the very reason that its strongest opponents, Barlaam and Akindynos, were quickly reduced to silence and thereafter the opposition lacked qualified leaders. The situation did not change until, through the translations of Demetrius Kydones and his brother Prochorus, the writings of Thomas Aquinas and other scholastics became known in Byzantium and exercised an influence. Aquinas' rigid theology provided the opponents of Palamas with strong weapons not available in the limited arsenal of fourteenth-century Byzantine theology. It is true that Prochorus Kydones, a monk of Athos, did not escape excommunication at the hands of the Patriarch Philotheus (1368), but from the *tomos* condemning him it is evident how far Prochorus had driven his opponents into a corner, and from the writings of Demetrius Kydones it appears that the victory was not achieved by the Palamite doctrine exclusively. Other theologians, John Kyparissiotes and especially Manuel Calecas, stiffened the opposition. Then the Palamites themselves abandoned certain daring formulations — even Cantacuzene, who had meanwhile become a theological author in his monastic retreat. The light of Tabor played an ever less prominent role, the teaching on the distinction was made more refined, and scholars have referred to a *palamisme mitigé* among the later Palamites. Furthermore, a man such as Cantacuzene, even as a monk still a politician, clearly perceived the urgency of Church reunion and was smart enough not to aggravate further the points of controversy between East and West by anything so serious as the Palamite teaching on God. Thus intransigent Palamism was recalled from the front line of battle and intentionally kept outside the negotiations with Rome, especially at the Council of Ferrara-Florence.

But the mystics, including the Hesychasts in the strict sense, had fundamentally no need of the support of Palamism. Palamism proper almost completely died out for centuries around the middle of the fifteenth century, while mysticism, the source for its rise, continued on undisturbed.

A comprehensive evaluation of the movement is difficult to reach, since as yet too few sources have been edited and published and we are only meagerly informed about its sociological stratification. Palamas undoubtedly had recourse to an ancient basic concern of Eastern theology and in addition possessed a refined sensitivity to the limits of theological testimony. His mistake was to have ignored — or not to have taken seriously enough — the warnings of the classical Byzantine mystics against such phenomena. And his mystical polemic urge kept him from appreciating the proper scope of a rational theology. That he decisively influenced Orthodox theology, that he again opened up recourse to the mystical sources and heightened the skepticism in regard to rational theology cannot be denied. He gave to Orthodoxy a coloring which has become integral to it.

CHAPTER 53

Intellectual Life in the Late Mediaeval Byzantine Church

The great doctrinal controversy over union of the Churches in the second half of the thirteenth century had summoned theologians of all trends and shades to the battle field and had finally exhausted them. Thus at the beginning of the fourteenth century there was everywhere an unmistakable lack of interest in dogmatic questions and several contemporary representatives of the Byzantine intelligentsia made no secret of this. On the other hand, these decades were a great and auspicious age of Christian humanism in Byzantium. It was not only that in this period the output of studies dealing with ancient authors was especially large, as evidenced by the manuscripts extant. This was no mere accident but an expression of the pains taken by the intellectuals. Far more significant is the fact that the pagan cultural tradition was now interpreted and made available in terms of Christian standards by means of new ideas, a new receptiveness, and new theological categories. In other words, the mere acknowledgment of these treasures, their existence in mutual isolation, gave way to a synthesis, however risky this may have been in individual cases. For the first time in Byzantine intellectual history even churchmen no longer regarded the legacy of antiquity as mere decoration in comparison with the strictly Christian inheritance, something merely tolerated for possible use. This was the age when the term "Hellene" no longer referred almost exclusively, as earlier, to pagans but was used proudly by the "Romaioi" as an expression of their history and of their zeal for education.

Many names could be given. Let it suffice, however, to treat of Maximus Planudes, Theodore Metochites, and Nicephorus Gregoras, while mentioning at least some others in passing. Their activity was versatile, each was something of a polyhistor, and as a group they formed a not unimportant class of sensitive humanists, who, guided by Christian categories of thought, allowed the abundance of the legacy to take its effect on themselves, not, however, forcing a compromise but striving for it by means of a calm development—*viatores in hoc saeculo.*

With Maximus Planudes (d. ca. 1305) we are not merely in the very midst of the best period of the transmission of classical literature but likewise at the start of a vast extension of the content and horizon of culture, achieved by the reception of the Latin heritage also. Planudes translated into Greek not only the *Somnium Scipionis,* not only Ovid and Macrobius, but Boethius' *De consolatione Philosophiae* and Augustine's *De Trinitate.* It is revealing that the last mentioned translation had no direct connection with the theological controversies of the day but, together with the other translations, was an expression of a happy curiosity, stirred by a universal interest in the good and the beautiful, even though this emanated from a "Church" which till then had been faced as something foreign.

Nicephorus Chumnus (ca. 1250–1327), for years imperial chancellor and high court dignitary, frequently wrote, it is true, against Plato's seductive tricks and regarded Aristotle as the genuine philosopher of humanism; but this was more a warning against those doctrines of Platonism and Neoplatonism that were irreconcilable with Christianity than a war against Platonism as such. He too lived to a great extent on the heritage of antiquity, even though he was certainly prudent and petulantly guarded. And in fact the many controversies in which he found himself involved because of his writings show how actively problems engaged the minds of the age. His chief opponent, Theodore Metochites (ca. 1260–1332), belonged, like Chumnus, to the lay class which was the backbone of public service and of culture. He too made his career at the court of the Emperor Andronicus II and rose to the highest dignity, that of *megas logothetes.* No systematizer, his thought unfolded itself in the *aperçu,* his literary form was the essay. More than is true of the other Byzantines, his literary output was marked by the prevailing internal insecurity and frequently he could not offer more than to set one solution in opposition to the others. The problematic order of precedence between *vita activa* and *vita contemplativa* permeated his entire creative activity and obviously his very existence, to the prejudice of the policy of his Emperor, for which he must bear responsibility to a great extent — a central problem of any intellectual history, but an absolutely elementary problem of Greek Orthodoxy. His views on the value and prestige of practice were more progressive than those of his contemporaries and, without even making mention of it, he had attained, better than they, to the proper balance postulated by Christianity, not least because he left the balance there, exposed and with all its susceptibility. He was not a theologian, but he did theology a service precisely because he did not presume to force this system of thought into the theological categories of his Church, to which he was devoted. In view of the nature of this terminology, such a situation would have involved the collapse of the desired intellectual progress *a priori.*

Metochites refers again and again gratefully and respectfully to the monk Joseph, known as the Philosopher (ca. 1280–ca. 1330), author of a broadly planned "Encyclopedia." In this work he gave full recognition to the individual fields of knowledge, but then in treating of the four cardinal virtues he directed these fields to the contemplation of God and of the Trinity.

Metochites' pupil, Nicephorus Gregoras (1295–ca. 1360), belonged to the period when the halcyon days of Byzantine intellectual history were already over. He is first and by predilection the historian of his age. And if he was not at his best as protagonist of the anti-Palamites he nevertheless proved himself to be a humanist who, in defense of his intellectual ideals, entered the arena against Palamite intransigence. Particularly, his rich output in hagiography demonstrates that these humanists wanted to operate within the Church and using the Church's means.

But if the great generation of humanists was buried with him, this was surely not due primarily to the victory of Palamism. Equally responsible was the hopeless situation of the Empire: civil strife, social revolution, and the steadily increasing danger from the Turks. The intellectual forces were, it is true, powerfully engaged by the Palamite controversy. But in the very midst of this struggle occurred an event of far-reaching importance: the translating of Latin theologians into Greek. In this respect *facile princeps* was Demetrius Kydones (ca. 1324—ca. 1398), a highly cultured citizen of Thessalonica, for many years chancellor of Emperors and the leading personality of the second half of the century. Dependent in the foreign ministry on the inadequate knowledge of Latin possessed by his interpreters, he decided to learn Latin himself and studied under a Dominican, who made him thoroughly familiar first of all with the *Summa contra Gentiles.* Struck by the lucidity of this Latin, he set about translating it and on 24 December 1354 completed the task in an equally lucid classical Greek. Then he took up parts of the *Summa theologica,* besides the brief *Ad cantorem Antiochenum* and other short works. Delight led him on to Augustine, Anselm of Canterbury, Peter of Poitiers, and Ricoldo da Monte Croce. At first Kydones had no theological aim in mind. And when people discovered the treasures of Greek thought in Latin dress, the translations were a huge success. John Cantacuzene and others were enraptured.

But it was not long before the theological content was discovered, before advocates of union ascertained how valuable an alliance they had found and enemies of union how difficult it would probably be to argue against them. The translations thus intensified the Byzantine discord — from the time of the Second Council of Lyons there had been a not insignificant group of "Latinophrones" — and the controversy could only become worse. The wealth of Latin scholasticism now saw service in the conflict with the Palamites, and Demetrius bore the entire brunt. While it is true that he was not personally attacked, he had to look on while his brother Prochorus, who had shared the work of translating and was the first to draw the theological conclusions, was accused of heresy, while his many other students, several of whom thus found the way to the Catholic faith, had to go into exile, and he himself was driven into an increasing isolation. His autobiographical writings are the deeply human expression of the intellectual situation in dying Byzantium.

In John Kyparissiotes, one of the most important of the anti-Palamites, an acquaintance with the Kydones translations probably exerted very little influence. But Manuel Calecas (d. 1410), a pupil of Kydones, followed in the steps of his master and composed a brief *Summa* of the faith, in which Augustine and Aquinas obtain full recognition. It is significant for the extent of the interchange that Ambrose Traversari now translated his work against the heresies of the Greeks into Latin, just as it is no longer a matter for surprise that Calecas died a Dominican after imitating Kydones by translating Anselm, Aquinas, and other Latin writers. Still to be mentioned are the brothers Chrysoberges. Of these, Maximus (d. ca. 1429), a pupil of Kydones, also became a Catholic and a Dominican; Andrew (d. 1456) was interpreter of the Greek envoys sent to Pope Martin V, worked tirelessly for union, acted as papal nuncio to the Emperor John VIII, and finally became Archbishop of Nicosia on Cyprus. And by no means least of the pupils of Kydones was the framed humanist Manuel Chrysoloras (d. 1415), the first teacher of Greek in Florence.

Opposition to the Kydones translations grew slowly. The most striking example is provided by Neilus Kabasilas, Metropolitan of Thessalonica (d. ca. 1363), Kydones' deeply revered teacher. On the appearance of the first translations of Aquinas he had nothing but praise for his pupil's achievement. But when he recognized that here was an arsenal which the Byzantines could match only with great difficulty, he tried to dissuade Kydones from his undertaking. In this effort he brought forward the patriotic argument that would become increasingly decisive in the course of the next years: Whatever may be thought about the opinion of the Latins, one must not on their account sacrifice the teaching inherited from one's ancestors; "it is not safe to take up arms against Emperor, Patriarch, and people." When this argument proved unavailing, Kabasilas undertook to compose a voluminous refutation of Aquinas, which included a sharp attack on the scholastic method altogether.

The sequel to all this was a great uneasiness. Some simply rejected the scholastic method.

> Go ahead and use your syllogisms and unsheathe them against us. . . . If I so wished, I could hold far better syllogisms against your sophistic considerations. But I do not care to. I obtain proofs from the Fathers and their writings.

> You come with Aristotle and Plato; I oppose you with the Galilean fishers and their candid word. The cross has not yet lost its power, even though for some it is regarded as folly to preach it Simeon of Thessalonica.

Others suffered greatly from the inferior state of theological refinement in Byzantium and reproached their fellow countrymen for this. George Scholarius, for example, did so expressly at the Council of Florence:

> There are people with no qualifications who want to compete with the Latins in theology and philosophy. For among us matters are not at their best. A person can attain to the highest posts even if he knows just enough theology not to give the impression of a complete lack of education. You see, classrooms are lacking, zeal for study has disappeared, and what does take place is subject to the circumstances.

Kydones himself expressed the uneasiness of the opposite side:

> We exhaust ourselves with these quarrels and make it clear to the others that they should keep at a distance so that they will not be infected by contact with us.... Is there anything imposing about our Empire — the only thing we can do is to complain!

If intellectual life in the Byzantine Empire had more and more to suffer from the growing malice of external circumstances, this situation was still unable to cripple its intellectual powers, and it may be emphasized that in this very period churchmen gave increasing thought to their social tasks. Most important were the social and ethical treatises of the great mystic Nicholas Kabasilas (d. before 1391), nephew of Neilus Kabasilas. He preached against usury and exerted himself at the imperial court for a more equitable system of taxation. In a long squib he also attacked the judicial deterioration evident in state and Church. Also to be mentioned is Joseph Bryennius (d. ca. 1431), who, as a missionary of Orthodoxy on Crete and Cyprus, not only energetically defended Orthodox doctrine against the Latins but just as zealously lashed out against the moral degeneration of clergy and people, so that the nickname "terror of priests" stuck to him. The abridged collection of his missionary sermons is one of the most eloquent sources for the cultural history of the age.

Even in the domain of mysticism neither the Palamite controversy nor Hesychasm held a monopoly. In fact, it really seems as though the over-simplification of Hesychasm and Palamism evoked a reaction connected with the name of Nicholas Kabasilas. His aim too was participation in God and deification, but the road leading to this included everything that fared badly with the Hesychasts, not only "natural theology," that is, mystical absorption in the world of creation, but especially the liturgy and not least an active mystical union with Christ. Meditation on the life of Christ, the imaginative submersion into his teaching, life, and example in a Franciscan fervor, the conscious contemplative junction with all phases of the liturgical celebration — all these elements clearly made his mysticism appear as necessarily anti-podean to the Hesychasts' abrupt seeking of God. It preserved both the human nature of Christ and Christian humanism.

The Empire's closing decades encroached day by day upon the foundations of its intellectual life without bringing it to destruction. The intensified controversy with the West brought ever new impulses, and the gravest danger finally induced recourse to desperate means. Three representatives of this period brought this into clear awareness: Bessarion of Nicaea, George Scholarius, and George Gemistus Plethon.

Bessarion (ca. 1403–72) was the Byzantine who, in exile, did most, next to Plethon, to keep alive the intellectual treasure of his nation. His development from the convinced Orthodox to the Catholic and the Cardinal was accomplished without any break, in a healthy, slow movement, and because his breadth of knowledge was already that of a Renaissance-type. Pupil and intimate of the paganizing Plethon, his heart was centered on Church union not only for political but for theological and religious reasons. His intellect submitted to the Latin arguments, but even as a Cardinal he never forgot the distress and the need of his homeland. His work *Contra calumniatores Platonis* attempted to do for Plato nothing less than what Albertus Magnus and Thomas Aquinas had actually done centuries earlier for Aristotle.

George Scholarius (ca. 1405–ca. 1472) went the opposite way. Active first as a teacher and a lawyer, he soon became an imperial supreme judge and councillor and in this capacity accompanied John VIII to Florence. In their fulness his literary works show what the Byzantine mind was still capable of. Aquinas was scarcely less important to him than to Kydones. He translated the *De ente et essentia* and epitomized the *Summa contra Gentiles* and parts of the *Summa theologica,* he wrote the most distinguished Byzantine treatises on divine providence and predestination, and attacked simony, Judaism, and atheism. His formation was solid and he deplored nothing so much as the intellectual decay of his country. The sarcasm to which he gave vent at the Council of Florence was not directed against the Latins. He said that some persons had come to Florence convinced that they would have an easy time with the ignorance of the Latin, but matters had actually turned out quite differently. The Latins had brilliantly defended their faith; the Greeks could contribute only words which were without any importance. Why, then, should they not simply yield and conclude the union? And yet, at the death of Mark Eugenicus in 1445, this same Scholarius assumed the leadership of the antiunionists. His desperate patriotism clung to the "faith of the Fathers" as to the only thing left to the Byzantines, and his old love of Aquinas caused him now to exclaim, "O Thomas, if only you had been a Greek!"

The most singular road of all was that traveled by George Gemistus Plethon (d. 1452). He belonged to one of those families which by custom held the high patriarchal posts at Hagia Sophia. He had to leave Constantinople quite early because of ideas which he had spread among his pupils, but he found refuge at the court of the Despots in Mistra, where Hellenism could still breathe somewhat freely. No less than Scholarius did he suffer from the misfortunes of his homeland, but, born reformer that he was, he thought to find in Hellenic antiquity enough material for a religious and political rebirth of the Greeks. Thus the road led him away, from Christianity, especially from the monastic Byzantine Christianity of his day, to a Plato interpreted from the point of view of politics and reform. All this was a serious and carefully planned reform project. We know that Plethon was not alone; he was able to gather around him a not unimportant circle of enthusiastic disciples. Furthermore, similar paganizing tendencies were to be observed in other parts of the Empire. They had no future, but they are of historical interest because they drew an arc whose ends often moved apart only in appearance throughout the Byzantine centuries.

CHAPTER 54

Patriarchate — Emperor and Church — Missions — Monasticism

The collapse of the Empire, in progress during the fourteenth and fifteenth centuries, involved frightful losses for the Orthodox Church. Not every Seljuk or Ottoman conquest of a strip of territory meant the annihilation of Orthodoxy and the elimination of Church government, but the unceasing raids of undisciplined tribes and the changing religious policy of the conquerors produced great insecurity and complete impoverishment. We constantly hear of complaints that now even great and wealthy ancient cities were no longer able to maintain a cleric, let alone a bishop. From time immemorial the Greek metropolitans had preferred residence in the capital rather than in their own provinces. What had once been a pretext had now become a necessity. In the *Notitiae episcopatuum,* which in their several revisions reflect the actual importance of the sees, we learn how one after another of the metropolitan sees of Asia Minor had to be transferred to dioceses that had not been especially important earlier but were more fortunately located. *De facto,* however, the synod at Constantinople for the most part had no alternative but to unite two or more bishoprics under one bishop, even if they were far apart, so that the more abundant resources of the one might provide for the administration of the other. The ruin of the churches in the conquered territory could thereby be arrested for a while, but in many cases the course of events could be retarded no longer. Even clergy and bishops who remained behind adapted themselves to circumstances here and there, and thus the total picture of the Orthodox Church in Asia Minor grew ever more bleak.

In a great part of the interior of Asia Minor celebrated metropolises were without their own bishop for decades. Impossible though it was, their administration was entrusted to a single person, the Metropolitan of Caesarea in Cappadocia. This happened in 1327, and by 1365 the situation was virtually unchanged. Better off were the cities on the northern fringes of Asia Minor, in particular Trebizond, which was actually under the protection of an Emperor of its own, and Amaseia and Sinope in Helenopontus. Special efforts were made to keep the ancient apostolic see of Ephesus alive. This bishopric contrived to have a bishop throughout almost the entire fourteenth century but only by amalgamating most of the sees of its former extensive province, which for decades and even centuries had been autonomous metropolitan or archiepiscopal sees. At the same time the inhabitants of Nicaea seem to have gone over to Islam in large numbers. In 1338 the Patriarch offered to accept them back into the Church if they were repentant. He even went so far as to dispense them from the public exercise and the public profession of Christianity in so far as fear of the Turks made such behavior seem necessary — something unique in Orthodoxy.

The Patriarch was scarcely in a position to support the needy churches financially. Hagia Sophia had, as a result of the Fourth Crusade, lost most of its real estate and had been given back only a small amount since 1261. In 1324 the metropolitan and archiepiscopal sees, Monembasia at their head, pledged themselves to support the Patriarch by special contributions. The more the metropolitan sees themselves now ran into difficulties, the less effective was this resolution. As early as 1381 the complaint was heard that no metropolitan see of the Orthodox Church was poorer than the "Great Church."

But despite everything, to the last Constantinople did not fail to recall emphatically the territorial, juridical, and spiritual rank of its Church.

The smaller the actual extent of the patriarchate grew and the more vigorous the dispute over the Roman primacy became, the more strongly did Constantinople move toward a concept of centralization that was nourished by reflection on the universal primacy of its own church. On this point too the patriarchal records of the age are clear. The concept of a pentarchy, that is, the idea that the essence of the constitution of the Church consists of a loose co-operation of five actually autocephalous patriarchates, is found not only in the middle but also in the late Byzantine age. But more and more the Patriarchs of Constantinople stressed their special position, using for this purpose a papal vocabulary, so to speak. The Church of Christ has its head in Constantinople, the foundation of Andrew, the "first called." The Bishop of Constantinople is "the common father of all Christians on earth"; the metropolitans are his vicars. Every Christian has the right to appeal to him. He is also the "universal teacher" of the world and vicar of Christ, on whose throne he sits.

In all this, his relationship to the Emperor had scarcely changed in theory. *In hoc discrimine rerum* the two powers were more than ever bound to work together. As people became more familiar with the situation in the West, the more they adjusted themselves in the discussions to the Western body of ideas on the relations between Church and state. The best example of this is the attitude of the Emperor John VIII at the Council of Ferrara-Florence. While never letting the control of the conduct of negotiations out of his own hands, he allowed the Patriarch and the bishops more freedom in the theological discussion than any of his predecessors had and did not object when churchmen insisted on the independence of their authority. Nevertheless, to Pope Eugene IV the position of the Church *vis-à-vis* the Emperor seemed deplorable, and the Patriarch Joseph II had hopes of strengthening the Church's liberty with the Pope's assistance by establishing the union. Moreover, the Church had to acknowledge in writing this absence of freedom in this very period. The Emperor John V demanded of the patriarchal synod between 1380 and 1382 a decree which sanctioned the principal rights thus far exercised by him in matters of Church government. The crucial point was, of course, that now, contrary to the legalist theories of the past, the Emperor's rights were specified as a privilege granted by the Church rather than as innate rights, but the irony that the Emperor could compel such a grant of privilege shows the real distribution of powers. But it can be said that, obstinately as the Emperors clung to their rights over Church government, they more and more yielded the rights hitherto made use of in matters of faith and dogma, guaranteed by the proviso of 1380–82 that the synod and the Patriarch could not excommunicate the Emperor and court.

The activity of the patriarchs at this period did not envisage merely the prestige of their own position. It also followed attentively the consolidation and extension of Orthodoxy wherever there remained such a possibility. At times it seemed that parts of the Mongol dominion, which extended far into former imperial territory, might become Christian. The Mongols of Persia, in particular, were inclined toward Christianity, especially in its Nestorian form. The Orthodox benefited from this toleration. Even if this success was not lasting — Chioniades seems soon to have been imprisoned — the Patriarch applied himself all the more energetically to that former imperial territory where the weakening and incipient collapse of Latin rule gave great hopes to Orthodoxy, especially Crete, Cyprus, and the Peloponnesus.

On Crete the Greek Church was nominally united to the Latin Church, but the Venetians would not allow a Greek bishop on the island. The direction of the Greeks was in the hands of the archpriest (*protopapas*) of Chandax, who was responsible to the Latin Archbishop of the island. No ecclesiastical relations with Constantinople were permitted and, after being examined by the Latin bishops of Crete, Greek clerics were ordained by Greek bishops of the Venetian possessions, Modon and Croton, in the Peloponnesus. Just the same, Orthodoxy maintained an uninterrupted existence and even contrived to gain not a few Venetian colonists in the interior of the island. Constantinople again and again undertook efforts for direct influence. And soon afterward Joseph Bryennius (d. ca. 1430) went to Crete for twenty years, doubtless at the order of the Patriarch, though this was not stated publicly. At that time Crete was the refuge of a number of Catholic converts who had left Constantinople, and Bryennius exerted himself to check their influence as well as to encourage the Orthodox, especially monks and clerics, in their moral life, which, in the twilight zone between the two confessions, apparently needed a vigorous strengthening.

The situation of the Orthodox Church on Cyprus was desperate. It managed as well as it could under the legal provisions of the *Bulla Cypria* of Pope Alexander IV of 1260. There were four Greek bishops but each had his Latin counterpart and the one metropolitan was the Latin Archbishop. A newly elected bishop was examined and approved by the Latin hierarchy and had to take an oath of loyalty to the Pope. Disputes between Orthodox clerics were decided by an Orthodox court but had to be reported to the Latins, while mixed cases fell exclusively under the canonical judgment of the Latin hierarchy. Thus the Greeks on the island were not only fully dependent on the Latins but were held in contempt by the Orthodox world, and especially by the patriarchate. Under these circumstances the Greek bishops at the beginning of the fifteenth century resolved, though not unanimously, to become again subject to Constantinople. Joseph Bryennius, acting again as the Patriarch's deputy, went to the island and held a synod. His instructions demanded that the Cypriot bishops should renounce obedience to the Pope and discontinue their collaboration with the Latin bishops. When the bishops, from fear of their masters, proposed a secret understanding with the Patriarch with no change in externals, Bryennius recommended that the synod renounce the union.

In the Peloponnesus Orthodoxy made real progress. The successful campaigns of the Despots of Mistra enabled the Greek hierarchy to take effective possession of several of the great ancient metropolitan sees such as Patras and Corinth. The reorganization of the church of Patras had been under way for decades when the city again became Greek in 1429–30. In the meantime the Metropolitan was forced to rule the see from the Mega Spelaion Monastery. Corinth became Greek once more in 1395. The restoration of the metropolis around the middle of the fourteenth century did not fail to bring about serious disputes over rank with Monembasia, which in the interval had become important and now energetically resisted the ancient privileges of the first see in the Peloponnesus. Mistra too, in the course of these decades, presented itself as a new center of Orthodoxy with full external splendor. Here lived the Bishop of Sparta; here sprang up new churches and monasteries. Around 1300 arose the imperial Brontochion Monastery, the Zoodotu Monastery, and the Pantanassa. Mistra was also the stage of a brisk intellectual life in which theology played a role and of a rising Greek nationalism with regenerative strength — until Muhammad the Conqueror brought it to an end.

The victory of the Palamite theology in the fourteenth century was at the same time a victory of Hesychast monachism and, *a potiori,* a victory of Byzantine monachism in general. The controversy, it is true, showed that this monasticism was even at that time a sort of sacrosanct national institution and that the condemnations then uttered were often based, not on an exact analysis of the theological views of the anti-Palamites, but simply on the fact of *crimen laesae religionis.* But anti-Palamism, notably as expounded by Barlaam, but also by Gregoras, was precisely an attack, though the final one, on Athos. Simultaneously the victory meant an enhanced political influence, if such were possible. This development had been in the making for many decades. In places where the Greek hierarchy had been expelled by the Latin conquerors, the Greek monks frequently remained. For within the Byzantine Empire they had been cultivating their ideals in a substantially greater independence of externally monastic ways of life than was the case, for example, in the contemporary West. Hence, in the occupied part of their homeland they could easily submerge themselves in order to supervise the resistance to Latin rule in administrative and Church matters, as leaders and advisors of the people. And they carried the resistance into the interior of the Empire, against the Emperor or the higher clergy and Patriarch, as often as there appeared an inclination to come to an agreement with the Western Church. The prestige of the monks was shored up by the great landed wealth and small farms, accruing for years to most of the monasteries from pious donations, demonstrations of imperial favor, solicited patronage, and clever economic policy. However, the economic position of the Emperor and the higher nobility was, in the fourteenth and fifteenth centuries, no longer such that the number of great monasteries could be substantially increased. What foundations there were seem to have been all of quite modest proportions.

In the fourteenth century occurred the chief phase of that development which gradually led to the victory of *idiorrhythmia* in the older monasteries. This word had long formed part of the terminology of asceticism and meant self-will bound by no yoke of obedience — always an evil. In this later period the idea retained this meaning, judged now favorably, now unfavorably, while acquiring also in the strict sense the meaning of a form of monastic life resulting from the decay of the *koinobion.* The great monastic family broke up into very small groups, which, apart from the general outlines of the monastic ideal, regulated their own life, acquired property, bequeathed it, and scarcely needed an abbot. In his place soon appeared the so-called *epitropia,* a directing committee made up of representatives of these tiny communities and headed by a person soon called the *dikaios,* who was only *primus inter pares.*

The most varied theories have been advanced to account for the origin of this manner of life, but not to be overlooked are the facts that strict cenobitism always encountered resistance in Byzantium. The numerous monastic *vitae* indicate again and again that the actual state of affairs far exceeded what legislators allowed. And the growth of the Hesychast mysticism could not but directly favor the tendency toward *idiorrhythmia.* Just as the liturgy, the "psalmody," played at most a nominal role in the life of the Hesychasts, and was actually rejected by many enthusiasts, so could a small group of Hesychasts break up the cenobitic life altogether. Their mysticism was incompatible with the formation of larger groups in which the idea of the community ought to be predominant.

But there was one voice in late Byzantium which wanted to make a clean sweep of this and every kind of monasticism, the voice, however, of an outsider, Gemistus Plethon. His reform writings, dedicated to the Palaeologi, were meant to reorganize the Byzantine State. To the monks, "who on the pretext of spiritual contemplation lay claim to a rich share of state property," he denied any right to it, "because they contribute nothing to the common welfare." They should work for their own support rather than extort it from others. "If the state's total income scarcely suffices to defray the expenses of defense, what will be left if a swarm of drones has to be fed, of whom some allegedly devote themselves to spiritual contemplation and others are idle."

Flexible criteria must be sought in determining the social contribution of the Byzantine or any other monasticism to the life of people and state. But whenever Byzantine monachism intervened in Church-State questions of the time, it did so stubbornly and intransigently, with the result that, from the start, legitimate reflection, rational absorption in the question, and a balanced judgment were all lacking.

Section Four

From the Middle Ages to the Reformation

Chaps. 55–57: Karl August Fink
Chaps. 58–61: Erwin Iserloh

CHAPTER 55

Renaissance and Humanism

The events of the mid-fifteenth century — the end of the Council of Basel, the reassurance appearing in the European states, especially in Germany, as a result of Nicholas V's willingness to oblige, the restoration of the Papal State, with the abandoning of a genuine reform of Church and Curia, — point to a decisive turning point in the history of the Church. The age now getting under way, that of the Renaissance and of the Renaissance papacy, led rapidly from the Early to the High Renaissance. This revolutionary change on a vast scale was attended by phenomena of critical importance and has been variously estimated in presentations of Church History.

The beginnings of the Renaissance and of humanism as literary movements are variously stated; in the designations of a Christian or un-Christian Renaissance of believing or unbelieving humanists the evaluation fluctuates from a condemnation as being anti-Christian to the notion of a reform movement. The turning from Aristotle and the late Scholasticism and the trend to Plato and Augustinianism could in many respects signify a renewal. The Renaissance of classical studies was at first a predominantly Italian affair. From Florence, Rome, and the petty princely courts of fifteenth-century Italy it became, in its radiation over all Europe, a new bond, which might have substituted for the bond of the Christian Empire that had weakened as a consequence of the rise of national states.

The humanist movement in Italy was strongly fostered by Greek scholars who came to the West around the turn of the fourteenth-century, at the time of the reform councils, and after the fall of Constantinople: Chrysoloras, Gemistus Plethon, Bessarion, and others. But so-called Christian humanism acquired its special importance from figures such as Lorenzo Valla, Marsilius Ficinus, Pico della Mirandola, and the Platonic Academy at Florence. Lorenzo Valla (1407–57), a Roman by birth, was active at Pavia for some years until a quarrel with local jurists forced him to leave. He then spent eleven years at the court of the great patron of humanists, King Alfonso the Magnanimous of Naples, and during the pontificate of Nicholas V returned to Rome. The most richly endowed of the Italian humanists of the first half of the fifteenth century, he was not satisfied with the philological discussion of texts already known or recently discovered but drew conclusions in the philosophical and theological sphere. He became especially well known for his acrid and clever attacks, based on Nicholas of Cusa, on the *Donation of Constantine,* with his demand for the renunciation of the papacy's secular power. The *Declamatio* also expresses a great understanding of the religious concerns of the reform synods, above all of the Council of Basel. The denunciation, usual among the humanists, of the avarice of the clergy and the duplicity and wickedness of the monks proceeded in Valla's *De voluptate, De vero bono,* and *De professione religiosorum* from a deep layer of genuine religious feeling and true Christianity. Like Nicholas of Cusa, he wanted religious peace, *pax fidei,* in the one religion, even though this religion might be characterized by different rites. From the many philological disputes grew a critical historical sense, which turned away from the traditional scholastic theology, led back to Saint Paul and the Church Fathers, understood the new religious needs of its time of change, and also extended to the noblest Christian transmission, the New Testament. The comparison of the Vulgate with the Greek text in the *Collatio Novi Testamenti* of 1444 yielded a wealth of new theological knowledge and questions, which were to exert an influence for a long time. The *Annotationes,* first published by Erasmus in 1505, went through numerous editions and were of great influence on the biblical criticism of the sixteenth century. Of course, they encountered strong resistance and were placed on the Index by Paul IV in 1559; the other works were consigned there in 1590. But by then they had made their impact, brought about a new type of discussion, and awakened a zest for life that was opposed to the *miseria humanae conditionis* of the Middle Ages.

But, despite the exertions of Nicholas V and the grand-scale patronage of humanists by Sixtus IV, Rome did not continue to be the center of humanism and of the Renaissance, at least not in the purely intellectual field. At Florence Christian humanism came to full development as Platonism. Even the first half of the fifteenth century witnessed a lively scholarly activity in the city on the Arno. At first, it is true, Aristotle was still reckoned as the real teacher; he was explained especially by John Argyropulos, who had fled to Italy and been given a position at the Florentine studio. The Academy, fostered by Cosimo de' Medici, arose soon after the mid-century and at once devoted itself almost exclusively to Platonism. Even though Plato's writings had already been translated into Latin, there now came to the Academy, especially through Marsilius Ficinus (1433–99), a philosophizing philologist who had pledged himself in the entirety of his teaching and manner of life to the Athenian philosopher. Besides the translation of almost all the writings of Plato and of the Neoplatonists there appeared his chief work, *Theologia Platonica seu de animorum immortalitate* (1469–74). Hence the interest of this Academy embraced not only Plato in the stricter sense but the intellectual currents of antiquity and late antiquity that he had stimulated and was not restricted to philosophy properly speaking. According to the general view, the Florentine Academy reached its high point under Ficinus' pupil, Giovanni Pico della Mirandola (1463–94), who in his brief career sought to combine the religious traditions of all peoples and to use them for an understanding of the Christian religion; this was the aim of his *Heptaplus* and *De ente et uno*. Best known was the discourse on human dignity, *De hominis dignitate*, with which he intended to inaugurate the congress that he had planned for 1436 in Rome for a disputation on 900 theses. The esoteric, the hermetic, the Cabala, and the Areopagite played a big role in his train of thought. His non-dogmatic outlook, which frequently rejected the Church's teaching authority, gained him the reputation of being a syncretist and a man living outside the Church, but this is probably refuted by his close relations with Savonarola. Here, as elsewhere in this period, it should be noted that paganizing formulations of Christian truths sought especially to provide proof of a classical education and not to act as a religious profession of the ancient gods. As regards radiation and continued influence, he was the most important figure in Christian humanism.

Irrespective of this religious striving, which must be taken seriously, at Rome the Papal State more than ever appeared as the representative of the Church. The Pope thus became chiefly the ruler of a territory which, like the other Italian states, was developing from a feudal state into a *signoria* but with considerable differences from the Italian and foreign dynasties. While it is true that *condottieri* often obtained permanent princely rank, at the Curia it usually happened that the death of the reigning Pope produced a new faction; hence the too frequent changes of political orientation and the so much deplored but mostly misunderstood nepotism. In the nationalist Italian view it was the duty even of the Papal State to keep the great European powers, especially France and Spain, out of the peninsula or not to tolerate an increase of their existing territories. This became particularly clear in the pontificates of Alexander VI and Julius II. Within Italy itself it was important to maintain the balance of power of the *cinque principati* that had been achieved by the Peace of Lodi in 1454. And so the Papal State was compelled to co-operate in this subtle diplomatic game with its ceaseless change of treaties and alliances in the hope of outwitting the partners of the moment. In addition the Curia had at its disposal a superior weapon, that of ecclesiastical censures, which, employed rapidly and ruthlessly, probably caused little spiritual harm. But, even as spiritual weapons, they could be quite effective in the temporal sphere, if the laying of an interdict led to an interruption of commerce and a seizure of the property of outsiders by competitors.

The enemy from the East, the Turks, kept the Popes preoccupied. More than all other powers, the Curia sought to halt the advance of the Christians' born enemy, though not always with the utmost exertion. The old crusading spirit had died out in the age of the nationalist states and no one could fan it to new life.

In comparison with politics the papacy's proper religious tasks retired shockingly into the background. If since the fourteenth century the autonomy of the states with regard to the Church had powerfully increased, in the following century the celebrated phrase, "superiorem non recognoscens," achieved its complete practical form and implementation in England, France, Spain, Venice, Milan, Florence, Naples, and some German territories. Since the greatest part of the revenues now came from Rome and the Papal State, this situation could be endured and it made the Curia quite independent, but with regard to the so-called spiritual income there was still question of large sums. These spiritual revenues consisted chiefly of *servitia* and annates, though these were greatly reduced in comparison with the age of the reform councils. The falling off of many sources of income from the Universal Church forced the reorganization of the fee-system and of the *Dataria,* now functioning as the most important financial department with its often quite dubious compositions. Through the higher assessment of vacant benefices and the increasing of the fees for dispensations further gains could be made in extraordinary cases. The great multiplication of marketable posts, *officia vacabilia,* which were to be regarded as a sort of state loan, endeavored to keep the mounting debt balanced. In the pontificate of Leo X there were about 2,000 marketable posts with a capital value of about 2.5 million gold florins and an interest of 300,000 gold florins. A real reform of the curial administration was rendered impossible by this system. The alum mines discovered at Tolfa in the pontificate of Pius II were an unexpected and copiously flowing source; as a monopoly industry they brought in important sums and were supposed to be applied to the Turkish war.

As an Italian princely court, the Curia had its full share in the so-called Renaissance culture. Because of the extravagant display, the papal household became a very costly business, with the usual expenditures on building, works of art, books, music, the theater, and gorgeous festivities, with the salaries for the large number of *curiales,* who also obtained part of their support from benefices.

The College of Cardinals occupied a special position. The Western Schism and the reform councils had greatly tarnished its reputation, but the much demanded reform did not materialize, despite numerous splendid reform drafts. The return of the Holy See to the Papal State, made by Martin V, also assured the existence of the College of Cardinals in its traditional form, even if now and then, under pressure from foreign powers, persons less suited to the tastes of the College had to be accepted. In the text of the decrees and arrangements of the Council of Constance these ideas constantly recur: the obliging of the future Pope to summon a crusade against the Turks; reform of the Curia, which, taken up three months after the coronation, must be carried through and observed for the future; the holding of a general council within the space of three years or "quam primum commode fieri potest"; at it the summons to the crusade must be given and the reform of the Universal Church introduced; the number of cardinals must not exceed twenty-four, only one of them could be a relative of the Pope, each creation must have obtained the consent of two-thirds of the College, the nominees must be more than thirty years old, the incomes and possessions of the cardinals and their share in the administration of the Papal State must be guaranteed; war or alliance with foreign princes for war against another prince must have the consent of two-thirds of the College; the most important fortresses of the Papal State, especially the Castel Sant'Angelo, must be commanded, not by relatives of the Pope, but only by ecclesiastics. Of great importance could have been the concluding decrees, if they had been observed: that the capitulations were to be read in the first consistory of every month, and later of each quarter of the year, in the presence of the Pope, and the cardinals were to ascertain twice a year, on 1 November and 1 May, whether the stipulations were being observed by the Pope; if they were not, he was to be remonstrated with to a third time.

More recent research has shown that the income was subject to severe fluctuations, that there were rich and poor cardinals.

The election capitulations contained also a group of general commitments, which in time were often included in a merely schematic way and placed at the beginning: Turkish war, reform of the Curia, calling of a general council within a short time. But the conciliar idea was still alive within the ecclesiastical sphere itself; several of the prohibitions issued by the Curia against appealing from the Pope to a general council were interpreted only as the opinion of a faction. Renowned canonists stressed the superiority of the council, at least in some important cases, into the sixteenth century. Through the Reformation the conciliar idea obtained a different ecclesiastical and political importance.

A special source of irritation was the persistent disregarding of the undisputed decree of the Council of Constance on the periodic holding of general councils, the celebrated decree "Frequens," according to which a council should have been summoned every ten years from the middle of the fifteenth century at the latest. Even Popes saw in the neglect of this conciliar decree the real cause of the crisis in the Church and of the secularization of the Curia.

CHAPTER 56

The Popes of the Early Renaissance

Nicholas V (1447–55)

When Eugene IV died on 23 February 1447, he left a heavy legacy. While a group of questions had been settled in a manner satisfactory to the Curia shortly before his death, there was still needed a person of moderate views to bring about a suitable adjustment. The conclave again met in Santa Maria *sopra Minerva;* whether an election capitulation was drawn up or that of 1431 was renewed is unknown. The traditional strife between Colonna and Orsini prevented the election of Prospero Colonna, who lacked only two votes for the necessary two-thirds majority. To his own and the general surprise Thomas Parentucelli, the Cardinal of Bologna, was elected in a compromise solution.

A native of Sarzana and the son of a physician, after studies pursued amid severe privations he was long in the entourage of the famed Cardinal Albergati. After his patron's death he stayed on at the Curia and in 1444 became Bishop of Bologna, but, because of political troubles, he was unable to enter upon his duties. He was esteemed as highly educated without being a real scholar, as a friend of humanists and of humanistic studies, and, above all, as a lover of peace. The Church and the Roman Curia needed such a man in order to make good the blunders of Eugene IV.

In Rome and the Papal State he began with pacification and in a short time succeeded in calming the quarreling factions and in winning back a number of cities, among them the important town of Jesi, which he repurchased from Sforza. The political situation in Italy was upset some months after the Pope's election by the death of Philip Mary Visconti, Duke of Milan, in August 1447. The question of the succession was of the greatest importance for all Italy, even the Papal State, since, in addition to France and Naples, Venice and the *condottiere* Francis Sforza laid claim to it. In 1453 the Pope summoned a congress to Rome for the settling of the smouldering crisis and the pacification of Italy, since, with the fall of Constantinople, it was important to husband all resources. At length, secret negotiations between Venice and Milan led to the Peace of Lodi, 9 April 1454; Florence also joined, after long hesitation, and later so did the Neapolitan King, though with some reservations. Despite his annoyance that he had thus far been ignored, the Pope in February 1455 adhered to the comprehensive treaty as *Protector et Custos.*

The Treaty of Lodi was intended to assure the inner peace of Italy in accord with the current state of territorial holdings and to protect the peninsula from outside interference. Fixed troop contingents, the creating of courts of arbitration, the peaceful settling of all conflicts, and the avoiding of foreign intervention were the chief points of the treaty, which appears so modern. In the midst of this political tangle occurred the journey to Rome of the German King, Frederick III, for his imperial coronation in 1452. It had only a slight impact on the Italian situation, and the Pope's fears proved to be groundless. Nicholas V showed himself to be a good politician, to whom what especially mattered was peace and who, to achieve this goal, made great concessions. And so in 1450 he could solemnly celebrate the year of jubilee and display the Pope's spiritual power to the Christians who flocked to Rome in great numbers.

Because of the jubilee the Pope inaugurated a series of important reforms and measures, which began to alter the structural appearance of mediaeval Rome, but only a small part of his great project for the papal city could be realized because of the brevity of his pontificate and the vastness of his plans. He regarded especially the Leonine City and the Vatican palace as a gigantic center of resistance against dangerous uprisings; from it unrest could be controlled and its inner area could be adorned according to the new methods. To Nicholas goes back also the grandiose plan of replacing the ancient and dilapidated basilica of Constantine by a new construction of splendid proportions.

Ample justice has been done to this Pope's concern for humanistic studies. At his court he gathered hundreds of scholars, who were especially to devote themselves to the translating of Greek authors into Latin. This undertaking was promoted by the many Greeks who fled to the West after the fall of Constantinople. In this regard Nicholas and King Alfonse of Naples rank as the greatest Maecenases of their century. The Vatican Library can look to Nicholas as its real founder. He avoided no expense for the purchase of manuscripts, and in a short time his collection became Italy's greatest treasury of books. It was pointed out to him that he might have used this money better for the defense of the East. But he tried again and again to bring about a union of princes for resistance to the ceaseless advance of the Crescent. The realization of this goal was denied him and most of his successors. An obstacle was the priority which was attributed to Church union.

Nicholas was greatly hindered in the last year of his pontificate by a chronic illness. With him died the first Renaissance Pope, but he was a Renaissance Pope in the best sense.

Calixtus III (1455–58)

Nicholas V died during the night of 24–25 March 1455. The next conclave was again overshadowed by the rivalry of Colonna and Orsini but it could be held in the Vatican. Its outcome was totally unexpected. The seventy-seven-year-old Catalan Cardinal, Alfonso Borgia, obviously a compromise and intended as a "caretaker" Pope, was elected; he called himself Calixtus III. As a young professor at Lérida he had been regarded as an eminent jurist and especially as an outstanding canonist. Borgia was admitted to the College of Cardinals in 1444.

The chief activity of the new Pope, who reigned only three years, was devoted to the crusade. With an energy amazing in a man of his advanced age he tirelessly directed all his thoughts and endeavors to this duty. Well known is the vow he made on assuming office: not to rest until he had taken Constantinople from the enemy of the Christian faith, had liberated the imprisoned Christians, and had exalted the faith. Resounding appeals, the dispatch of legates to the most important countries and to threatened frontiers, and the proclamation of ample indulgences for all participants in the campaign against the Turks are always recorded. In particular he himself began preparations. Thus at Rome the keels of large vessels were laid on the Ripa and the matter was entrusted to a commission of competent cardinals. Great sums of money were constantly sent to the Balkans, Hungary, and Albania, and many gold and silver works of art from the papal treasure ended up in the furnace. Two such important figures as Cardinal Caravajal and John of Capestrano carried the Pope's enterprising spirit into the various lands, but the response to their ardent preaching was for the most part inadequate or only ephemeral. The Pope was permitted to experience one great success: the relief of the Serbian capital, Belgrade, which was besieged by Muhammad II with a great army and was close to falling. Significant for the crisis of Christian awareness is the fact that in this case and elsewhere Christians, and not under compulsion, served in the Turkish army and that the cannon-founders, the cannoneers, and the builders of siege machines were almost always Westerners; there is no need to mention the secret intrigues of the Italian port cities at the Sultan's court. In July 1456 a motley army led by John Hunyadi and John of Capestrano succeeded in breaking the ring around the besieged stronghold and in forcing the Sultan to a retreat that resembled flight. This really great success was much exaggerated and was not exploited, even though the Pope through legates called for a decisive struggle. And, over and above his military plans, the Pope showed a warm, though perhaps not always enlightened, interest in Christians under Turkish rule and in reunion with the remnants of Eastern Christendom.

His relations with his former master, King Alfonso V of Aragón and Naples, were from the first not good and they grew increasingly worse, for the King did not share the Pope's zeal or in any event pursued other goals in the East. Alfonso died a few weeks before Calixtus, who rejected the succession of the King's natural son, Ferrante. In any event, Peter Louis was enfeoffed with Benevento and Terracina in the last days of the dying Pope. Against the *condottiere,* Piccinino, who had been rendered unemployed by the Peace of Lodi and intended to pursue his calling before Siena, Calixtus sent an army and thereby preserved peace in the peninsula. To be on the safe side, he garrisoned most of the castles and strongholds of the Papal State with Catalan commanders, while his nephew, Peter Louis, became Captain General of the Church and governor of Sant'Angelo.

Pius II (1458–64)

The death of Calixtus III was followed by a prosecution of the Catalans who occupied many posts in Rome and the Papal State. The conclave was from the start overshadowed by the French Cardinal d'Estouteville, who was able to gain a considerable number of votes because of his enormous wealth. By contrast the candidate of the other Italians, Aeneas Silvius Piccolomini, Cardinal of Siena, could offer only his education and experience; but he was a widely traveled man and knew most of the European countries from many political tasks he had performed for the Council of Basel, the Emperor, and later the Roman Curia. After a short but tense course of balloting he was elected or 19 August 1458 and took the name Pius II, not from religious but from classical considerations. An election capitulation that was in some respects borrowed from that of 1431 was decided on and sworn to in the conclave.

The previous career of the humanist Pope had long interested his contemporaries. In the retinue of Cardinal Capranica, who was seeking justice at Basel, and later as secretary of the Pope set up by the Council of Basel, he came forward as champion of the conciliar idea and was repeatedly sent by the Council to several European states and to German diets; then he passed over to the imperial chancery and, at the opportune moment, to the Curia. He successfully conducted the negotiations for the ending of the Electors' neutrality and was rewarded with the bishoprics of Trieste, Ermland, and Siena. In 1456 he was created a Cardinal. In general, his election to the papacy was well received.

On the very first day of his pontificate he made it clear that he intended to adopt and to intensify his predecessor's zeal for the crusade. Scarcely a month after his coronation he summoned a European Congress to Mantua for the following summer and issued a crusade bull that, with regard to style, was unusually impressive. From his youth he had been conversant with questions relating to the Turkish war and in powerful discourses before Pope and Emperor and at German diets he had called for a struggle against the infidel. But, for all his knowledge of the political situation in Italy and the rest of Europe, he probably did not reckon with the great disappointment that was in store for him at Mantua. At Rome persons tried to detain the Pope with the gloomiest predictions, but no remonstrances, even in regard to his weak state of health, were able to divert him from his plan. First, however, the political tension had to be relaxed.

Entering upon his pontificate, Pius II adopted the violent hostility of the Curia for Ferrante of Naples. This claimant, not yet fully recognized in his Kingdom, was especially supported by Francis Sforza, Duke of Milan, from quite obvious reasons, for by conquering that realm France could not but threaten Milan also. The new Pope was now faced with the choice of Sforza and Ferrante or France; he decided for the Italian solution and the keeping of the foreigner at a distance. For this reason he has been praised for his Italian nationalist spirit, but his decision was a political act, springing from the justified fear of the hemming in of the Papal State. His attitude was also in conformity with the Peace of Lodi, which had achieved a balance of power in the Italian peninsula. And so, under strong pressure from Sforza, the Pope chose Ferrante and arranged his enfeoffment and coronation and the engagement of the papal nephew, Anthony Piccolomini, to a natural daughter of the new King. This decision was of great importance and, despite frequent vacillation in extremely critical situations, Pius remained faithful to it throughout his pontificate.

As early as the end of January 1459 the Pope left Rome for Mantua; Nicholas of Cusa remained behind as *Legatus Urbis.* The party moved slowly through the Papal State. He entered the city of the Gonzaga on 27 May and in 1 June opened the Congress. One disappointment after another awaited him. Months later no prince had appeared, and only a few envoys gradually arrived for the Congress; the first session could not be held until the end of September. Again and again the Pope sent earnest appeals to the Italian and foreign princes to meet in view of the threatening peril. But the Emperor and the King of France had already declined, and the Duke of Burgundy, who was supposed to assume the leadership, then went back on his crusade vow. Of the Italian powers none thought seriously of taking part, and even the collecting of the tithe from the clergy, the twentieth from the Jews, and the thirtieth from the laity, agreed to in the face of great opposition, was rejected in most countries and city states. The attitude of Venice was generally blamed and branded as treason against Christian interests. After long hesitation and repeated unambiguous demands envoys of the Most Serene Republic came to Mantua. Shortly before Venice had made peace with the Sultan. The excuses offered by Picotti for the delay are really striking. Without the Venetian fleet an undertaking of any magnitude was unthinkable, but Venice was the most seriously threatened, especially in its trade, which was after all the backbone of the state, and in its Greek possessions. Hence, while the policy of sensible reserve was not very heroic, it did correspond to the political situation. He finally appeared in Mantua in September and made great promises. In his case the fear of a French invasion of his territory was understandable. The Italian states took a realistic view: one feared another, and before a genuine reconciliation the risk of a crusade was too great. France, once the proud champion of the crusade idea, refused any cooperation with the Pope, his Congress, and his eloquent and fervent appeals. And so the Congress moved slowly to its conclusion without any visible success. Nevertheless, the papacy had sought to place itself at the head of Europe and had registered its claim to leadership.

After his return from the Congress of Mantua Pius II found himself involved in the usual disputes with unruly *signori* and Roman barons. Sigismund Malatesta of Rimini rebelled against the papal temporal authority and could be subdued only with difficulty; in this quarrel considerations of nepotism played a decisive role, for a part of the holdings of the Malatesta was intended for the nephew Anthony. With the Pope's aid Ferrante finally established himself at Naples and compelled the Angevin to withdraw, but Pius now had to experience the hostility of Louis XI of France. As dauphin Louis had opposed his father and had to flee to Burgundy; he there promised the Pope that he would annul the Pragmatic Sanction of Bourges when he succeeded to the throne. The annulment actually took place in the autumn of 1461. But it was purchased by the creation of two French cardinals and was intended to win the Pope from his alliance with Ferrante. It was reintroduced in practice by a royal ordinance.

His anxiety for the Papal State and his involvement in Italian politics did not cause the Pope to forget the chief task of his pontificate: the crusade. He again appealed for a crusade in October 1463 and appointed Ancona as the place of gathering in the next summer. Despite his poor state of health, he said that he would himself take part. His appeal found a response among the lower classes throughout Europe. They set out for Ancona in considerable numbers but soon had to turn back. There was no response from the princes, on whom the matter chiefly depended. Meanwhile, on 18 June 1464 the seriously ill Pope left the Eternal City and, with many cardinals and curialists, made his way to Ancona. To his great disappointment he found there only a few crusaders and eagerly awaited the arrival of the Venetian galleys. As they came in sight, he died on 14 August and the great enterprise was ruined.

In the period beginning with the autumn of 1461 occurred the work on a remarkable document by the Pope: the so-called letter to Muhammad II. The content and fate of this long treatise are still a puzzle. Presumably, the "letter" was never sent and never reached the addressee. The letter to Muhammad is an extremely important document for an explanation of the personality of Pius II.

In the pontificate of Pius II began the long quarrel with Bohemia and its King, George of Podiebrad. As always, this struggle was dependent on the political situation in Italy, the Empire, Poland, and Hungary. When in 1458 Podiebrad obtained the Bohemian royal crown, he took in the presence of the two Hungarian bishops who crowned him and of a small group of witnesses an oath, whose not entirely clear text apparently denied the further validity of the *Compactata* of Prague, which had granted free preaching, the lay chalice, the abolition of the temporal authority of the clergy, and the punishment of mortal sin. In view of the religious situation in Bohemia and Moravia this promise could hardly be kept. And when Podiebrad in 1462 applied for the confirmation of the *Compactata,* the Curia annulled them. But since they had been agreed to by the Council of Basel, no further confirmation was needed. Thus was the break made complete and shortly before the Pope's death the King was cited to Rome.

In 1462–64 Podiebrad came forward with a great project. In the twenty-three chapters of the text it was proposed that a sort of European League of Nations, under the motto *Pax et Iustitia,* should be formed for a successful attack on the Turks. It is clear that in this plan the initiative was to be removed from the two swords, the Pope and the Emperor, precisely because the text exhibits a form that frequently recalls curial documents. Beside the program of Pius II there now stood a great vision of a united and pacified Europe. Gregory Heimburg, well known as a bitter enemy of the Curia, was active as advisor and envoy in the quarrel with the Pope, especially in the next pontificate; he also played an important role in the revolt of Dieter von Isenburg, Archbishop of Mainz.

Pius II is justly regarded as a reform-minded Pope. More than any other Pope of his century he had the opportunity to become acquainted with the *gravamina* against the Curia in all of Europe and to inform himself on the anti-curial sentiment. He had viewed the reform work of the Council of Basel from close at hand and had worked eagerly for its implementation. Right after his election he began comprehensive preparations for general reform and for the reform of the Roman Curia, called for expert opinions, and worked hard on the drawing up of a great reform bull, which, however, did not succeed in being promulgated in his lifetime. In it he did not exhibit any great difference from his predecessors and successors, but he cannot be denied the genuine reform will which was quite often lacking in other Popes. His ideas of reform, especially in regard to the constitution of the Church, had changed very much since the Council of Basel, and it was only natural that as Pope he no longer defended views pertaining to the conciliar theory but rather intended to maintain his primatial prerogatives. In this context belongs his prohibition of appealing to a council in the bull "Execrabilis," a measure which was intended to control the widespread practice, even approved by canonists, of appealing to a council against the Pope.

In the outline for the bull "Pastor aeternus" the two still extant testimonials of Dominic de'Domenichi and Nicholas of Cusa were abundantly used, as were passages from earlier election capitulations and especially from the reform ordinances of the Councils of Constance and Basel and the reform decrees since Martin V. This projected reform bull was very much in accord with the concerns of the age, but, like almost all the reform demands of the fifteenth century, it remained merely a sketch. Reforms affected also the City of Rome and its administration and the Papal State. To safeguard his position Pius II was forced to admit several relatives to the College of Cardinals and to confide important posts to Sienese fellow countrymen.

Hardly any other Pope has so engaged the attention of historians and of others as has Pius II, chiefly because until the most recent period we do not know as much about the personal lives of the Popes as we do about his. A group of treatises, poems, numerous letters, reports, and the *Commentarii* afford a good insight into the interior of this man, who was not only a patron of humanism, as was Nicholas V, but was himself a humanist as this word was understood in the fifteenth century. A man of broad, though not always deep, scholarship, with an eye alert for nature, beauty, and form, he was able to do justice to the demands and expectations of his time and had in his heart "room for varied strata and ideas." Thus his passage from the Council of Basel and its Pope to the other camp was not accomplished without its guarantee. With the strength of his intellect and the fluency of his linguistic formation he proclaimed a united Christian Europe and the superiority of its culture, and yet he was aware that his message was utopian, he knew from bitter experience that his lofty plans and soliloquies were bound by the realities of the Italian and European political systems, by which they were decisively checked. His passing at Ancona was the tragic end of a magnanimous soul.

Paul II (1464–71)

The preparations for choosing a successor to Pius II began in Ancona. The conclave met in Rome and, after some negotiations, in the Vatican. On the first ballot the Venetian Cardinal Peter Barbo, a nephew of Eugene IV, obtained the required majority; he assumed the name Paul II. Once again the election was preceded by the drawing up of a capitulation, which to a great extent utilized the text of the previous capitulation, but, because of the experience with Pius II, it included more detailed regulations.

Certainly it was difficult to be the successor of Aeneas Silvius Piccolomini, and the judgments of the envoys on the new Pope were not exactly friendly in regard to his intelligence and manners. He tried to get his way by force and hence was feared rather than loved. On the other hand he exerted himself to win the lesser folk by splendid entertainments. As a Cardinal, he had used his immense wealth to begin constructing the huge Palazzo Venezia and planned great collections. He was not uneducated but he was likewise not a narrowly literary type. An aesthete and bibliophile, he pursued predominantly antiquarian interests and laid great stress on magnificent display. He issued a series of practical rules for the administration and care of Rome and the Papal State.

An insuperable distrust of humanists and literary men brought him into a serious conflict with the then modern educational level and damaged his memory. He abruptly abolished the seventy posts of *abbreviator* which Pius II had created as marketable offices; he thereby made bitter enemies out of a large number of humanists. When their spokesman protested in violent turns of expression and threatened to appeal to a council, he was consigned to Sant'Angelo and tortured.

As sometimes happens, there occurred at the change of pontificate also a change in the leading personalities and in politics. While in ecclesiastical matters Paul II did not enjoy good relations with his native city, he was at first devoted to it and also to Florence in Italian politics and abandoned the former close connection with Milan and Naples. New quarrels erupted. A general alliance, concluded at Rome in 1470 under pressure from the Turkish threat, brought a temporary calm. But the spirit of Lodi could not be reawakened, and, despite his claims, the Pope played a subordinate role.

Shortly before his death Pius II had summoned the Bohemian King, George of Podiebrad, to Rome. With the accession of Paul II the affair came to a standstill and at first efforts were made to settle it amicably. The Emperor, powerfully supported in his difficulties by Podiebrad, interceded for him, as did a group of German princes. However, after the Bohemian had quarrelled with the Emperor and with King Matthias Corvinus of Hungary, the Pope pronounced his excommunication and deposition at the end of December 1466 and called for a crusade against the heretic. Despite threats from within and without, the Bohemian King managed to maintain himself until his death in March 1471, when at Rome there was a willingness to reach an agreement through negotiations.

The project of a general council became ever more prominent under Paul II in his constant disputes with France. In his election capitulation the holding of such a council within three years had been demanded. It was not only the understandable dislike of the Curia for a council, which it feared would seek reform of the head, that posed obstacles; with Peter Barbo there was added his own authoritarian and aristocratic concept of his office. Quite unexpectedly the Pope died in July 1471 at the age of only fifty-three.

CHAPTER 57

The Popes of the High Renaissance

Sixtus IV (1471–84)

With the pontificate of the former minister general of the Franciscans, Francis della Rovere, one may correctly say that the High Renaissance had begun. For, contrary to all expectations, this son of Saint Francis did not emulate his master. This appears in the election itself, which occurred on 9 April 1471 after a conclave of three days. The election capitulation is extant and offers the usual picture of the last two decades. These regulations, though sworn to by the one elected, were hardly observed by the Popes, and Sixtus IV was no exception. His election was especially promoted by the Duke of Milan, and rich presents were made to him and all the electors. The Franciscan, a native of Liguria, was regarded as an outstanding theologian, who successfully devoted himself to timely controversies, and was a well known and much sought preacher. People were thus all the more amazed at the rapid change in his views, at the preeminence of politics which could not be reconciled with the papacy's religious tasks, at the making of the Papal State into an Italian principality by recourse to all means, lawful and unlawful, and at the unseemly promoting of the Pope's relatives.

As early as two weeks after his election, the Pope, in flagrant disregard of the sworn election capitulation, raised two nephews, the Franciscans Peter Riario and Julian della Rovere, to the cardinalate. If the creation of Julian della Rovere, later Pope Julius II, can be defended, the papal favor shown to Peter Riario fell upon one who was unworthy, who after a life of luxury and vice died in 1474. His position of influence was assumed by still another nephew, Jerome Riario, who became the Pope's evil genius. He bears most of the guilt for a policy that was unbecoming to a Pope and that was also unfortunate.

The Pope's strained relations with Florence, which could only regard the consolidation of the neighboring ecclesiastical political power with opposition and suspicion, came to a climax in the so-called Pazzi conspiracy.

Two groups now stood in confrontation: Florence, Naples, Milan, and Ferrara on the one side, and on the other the Pope, Venice, and the Angevins, who now renewed their old claims to Naples with favorable prospects. And Jerome Riario, who, like the Borgias later, intended to construct for himself in Romagna a state of his own that should, so far as possible, survive the death of his uncle, was once again the author of a new war in Italy. The year 1482 saw almost all the Italian powers engaged in the new war. The Peace of Bagnolo in 1484 confirmed the *status quo* and brought the Pope and his nephew, not the expected acquisition of territory in Romagna, but instead dangerous risings in Rome and Latium and strife between Colonna and Orsini. The eventful years 1482–84 also witnessed the threat of an attempt to convoke a council.

The election capitulations made it clear that the decrees of the reform Councils of Constance and Basel were not forgotten, even though here too they gradually became a *topos*. The opinions on the conciliar idea that were often defended in the course of the fifteenth century, the numerous appeals to a council, and the efforts to convoke one also showed this. The threat of a reform council was one of the means resorted to in the political struggle with the papacy and the Papal State, but it seldom materialized. However, it did go that far in the pontificate of Sixtus IV.

The first task of the new Pope mentioned in the election capitulation of 1471, the crusade against the Turks, was taken very seriously by Sixtus IV in the first years of his pontificate, and immediately after his accession he issued a solemn summons and dispatched five cardinal legates to all the greater states of the West. A fleet was equipped at great expense, but after modest successes on the coast of Asia Minor it returned to Italy. The succeeding undertakings were not in keeping with the great plans at the beginning. This procrastinating attitude of the West did not change during the remainder of his pontificate, and Italian politics and the effort to provide for his importunate relatives claimed his energies to an ever greater degree. The outcome was actually a landing of Turkish troops in Apulia, where Otranto was occupied by them for more than a year. The news of the Muslim invasion of the Italian peninsula aroused fear and dread. However, even this extremely grave situation was unable to induce Western Christendom to a common energetic action against the infidel.

From the religious viewpoint also the pontificate of Sixtus IV cannot be described as fortunate. The thirty-four cardinals — six of them were his nephews — whom he created contrary to the electoral capitulations were for the most part hardly worthy men and carried further the secularization of the papacy and of the Sacred College. Reckless multiplication of curial posts and the increase of the Roman court also belong to the shady side of his reign. The Curia's fiscality mounted rapidly under Sixtus IV, as the need for money for the numerous costly undertakings and the paying of the mercenaries required for these, the expenditures on art and luxury, on the maintenance of the court, and on providing for the papal relatives increased just as rapidly. With the name of Sixtus IV is forever connected the transformation of mediaeval Rome into a Renaissance city. This includes the new streets, as the need for these was made clear by the crowds of pilgrims in the Jubilee of 1475, the Ponte Sisto over the Tiber, the churches of Santa Maria del Popolo, burial place of the della Rovere, and Santa Maria della Pace, the new hospital of Santo Spirito, numerous palaces of cardinals and other high prelates, and especially the great new palace chapel in the Vatican, the Sistine Chapel, which received its first decorations from the Umbrian masters. The

Pope's bronze monument by Pollaiuolo, now in the crypts under Saint Peter's, is one of the finest of papal graves.

The stressing of the personal goodness and piety of Sixtus IV cannot prevent our seeing in him the one who upset the Italian balance of power by his unfortunate political enterprises. And he bears the chief guilt for the further progress of the Roman Curia into unbridled nepotism and worldliness.

Innocent VIII (1484–92)

The death of Sixtus IV was followed in Rome by a storm against the "Genoese," who, so the Romans and the inhabitants of the Papal State thought, had occupied all the good positions under the Ligurian Pope. The chroniclers do not tire of reporting the insecurity, the unrest, the plundering, and the street fighting during the vacancy, but these lasted throughout the reign of the new Pope. The conclave could begin in the Vatican. It lasted only from 26 to 29 August. After it had become clear that he had no prospects, Cardinal Julian della Rovere managed to carry the election of Cardinal John Baptist Cibò, Bishop of Molfetta, who belonged to a Genoese noble family and was sickly and totally dependent on him. His having signed the petitions of several cardinals in his cell on the night before his election can scarcely be regarded as other than transparent bribery and simony. Formally elected on the following, morning, he called himself Innocent VIII, thereby acknowledging the Roman line of claimants in the Western Schism.

In politics the Pope, who was a lover of peace, opposed the great league of Naples, Milan, Florence, Siena, Lucca, Spain, and the Orsini, while Venice remained neutral. Peace and an understanding with Naples were reached shortly before the Pope's death in 1492.

The chronically ill Pope was subject to the influence, really to the domination, of the strong personality of Julian della Rovere. Only during the Cardinal's absence from Rome did the Pope make any decisions of his own, and for the most part these sought weakly to effect compromise. The constant lack of money could not be corrected even by the multiplying of marketable offices and similar practices.

A remarkable figure arrived at the Curia in the person of the Turkish Prince Dschem, son of Muhammad II and brother of the reigning Sultan Bajazet II. He fled from snares laid by his brother, who rightly saw in him a rival to his authority. The Sultan paid a large sum annually to keep him confined and abstained from direct undertakings against Italy. The reign of the Cibò Pope was almost constantly filled with disturbances in Rome, and it was necessary to fortify the Vatican and the palaces of the cardinals. On the whole it was an unfortunate and weak pontificate in an age which needed a strong, reform-minded personality.

Alexander VI (1492–1503)

Innocent VIII died on the night of 25–26 July 1492. Because of his poor health and his repeated sicknesses there had been much concern about the succession in both the Sacred College and the chanceries of Europe. Among the twenty-three cardinals who entered the conclave at the Vatican on 6 August there can be discerned two factions, one of them centering on Ascanius Sforza and the Vice-Chancellor Rodrigo Borgia, the other on Sixtus IV's nephew, Julian della Rovere, who had exercised the greatest influence on Innocent. Neither faction could expect a quick achieving of the two-thirds majority. But then, in the late evening of 10 August, the election of the Vice-chancellor was assured for the following morning. Since the Dean of the Sacred College, Cardinal Borgia, was not at first regarded as a serious candidate — though from national rather than moral considerations, — an explanation of the sudden turn of events is desired. It is hardly possible to doubt that simoniacal intrigues produced the change. In this election simony was openly admitted by contemporaries and was mentioned as a possible point of attack on the new Pope in case of need.

Not much exception was taken to his moral defects in the conclave and just as little in the chanceries of kings, princes, and cities when the outcome of the election was made known. The obedience and joy over this election, as expressed by numerous embassies, indicate, even while taking into consideration the formalities and flattery usual on this occasion, the gratification that, after the sickly Innocent VIII, an important politician and a capable statesman was elected. If difficulties should occur, one could always go back to the simoniacal election and the unspiritual manner of life.

Alexander VI, as he styled himself, was born around 1430 at Játiva near Valencia. When his uncle had become Pope Calixtus III, he was admitted to the Sacred College, with the assent of all the cardinals present, and later he obtained the very lucrative post of Vice-Chancellor of the Roman Church. Because of the large number of his benefices, among them several bishoprics and rich abbeys, he was regarded as being the richest Cardinal of his time next to the French Cardinal d'Estouteville. Corresponding to this wealth was a mode of life that was decidedly not exemplary. Since, as Cardinal and even as Pope, he had no concern for popular gossip, the curiosity of those responsible for the *chronique scandaleuse* then and later could amply occupy itself with the alleged or real number of his children. In the years 1462–71 were born to him Peter Louis, Jerónima, and Isabella, the names of whose mothers have not come down to us. Best known are those born of his liaison with Vannozza de Cattaneis, Caesar, John, Geoffrey, and Lucretia, who, after his election to the papacy, were at once provided for in the manner of princes and who claimed an excessive share of the Pope's interests.

Great difficulties await any effort to pass judgment on Alexander's relationship with Julia Farnese, sister of Cardinal Alexander Farnese, the later Pope Paul III. As a Cardinal he had himself blessed her marriage to Orsino Orsini. And the two boys born during Alexander's pontificate, John, the *Infans Romanus,* in 1498 and Rodrigo in 1503, very probably had the Pope for their father.

Alexander's policies as ruler of the Papal State were generally shrewd. This was of great importance, since in the epoch of the Renaissance papacy, far more so than previously or later, the administration of the Papal State was regarded as a standard for evaluating a pontificate. The Italian peninsula was the site where the great European contests were decided. The political entities of Italy were, despite their widely divergent interests, deeply concerned for the preserving of the laboriously achieved balance of power and reacted very sensitively to outside interference. As interference must be understood the constant wrangling between Spain and France, which had gained a footing in Naples and Milan. After first inclining toward the Sforza of Milan, the Pope veered to Naples and maintained this position when Charles VIII of France in 1494–95 undertook his famous but ill-starred expedition through Italy *en route* to Naples. Although the French King put strong pressure on the Pope at Rome, Alexander did not yield to the demand for investiture with the Neapolitan Kingdom; he alone energetically represented an Italy free from foreigners. When the French army decided to withdraw because of the concluding in March 1495 of the Holy League between the Pope, Venice, Milan, the Emperor Maximilian I, and Spain, the Pope avoided a meeting with the foreign King and vanished into the strongholds of Orvieto and Perugia. In the second half of his pontificate he moved ever closer to France under Caesar's influence and agreed to the partition of Naples between France and Spain. The enduring quarrels of the petty lords in the Papal State, especially the rivalries of the Roman families of Colonna, Orsini, and Savelli, caused him great difficulties. Quite often the Pope had to seek shelter in Sant'Angelo, and he did not hesitate to proceed with severe ecclesiastical penalties against the disturbers of peace. He was not prudish in his choice of means and in this respect conformed to the style of other princely courts. This is the explanation of his dealings with the Turkish Sultan Bajazet II to keep the French out of South Italy.

With regard to the figure of the Prior of San Marco at Florence, Jerome Savonarola, historians are greatly divided, and on their interpretations depends to a great extent their judgment of the Borgia Pope. A learned and mystically gifted theologian and ardent advocate of a strict religious discipline, he was drawn into politics as a passionate preacher of reform and was especially involved in a leading capacity in the upheavals at Florence in the last decade of the fifteenth century. His prophetic preaching, originating in a consciousness of a special mission, seemed to be confirmed in the French King's expedition to Italy and the ensuing overthrow of the House of Medici. The religious and democratic system of government that he brought about at Florence and the conversion of large groups to an edifying life were, however, of only brief duration. His clash with the Pope had political rather than theological causes, namely, his support of the refusal by the Florentine *signoria* to join the great Italian league against France. For the King of France was intended, in a total misunderstanding of reality, the task of reforming Church and Curia by the convoking of a general council and of replacing Alexander by a more worthy Pope. After long and patient waiting the Curia took action by excommunicating Savonarola and threatening Florence with interdict. The disregard of the ecclesiastical censures and the ordeal by fire, which was tensely awaited by the public but which did not materialize, produced a quick revulsion and imprisonment, torture, and execution in May 1498, after an obliging ecclesiastical court had condemned Savonarola as a heretic. The controversial Dominican was obviously a victim of the rapidly changing sympathy of the Florentine masses, of the hostility of some of his own confrères, and of the rivalry of other orders.

Despite all the evil that can be said of Alexander VI, in the external ecclesiastical sphere he can seldom be taken to task. Alexander appointed a reform commission of worthy and learned cardinals and competent theologians. It worked hard and drew up an admirable program for reform of head and members, but the reform bull that was prepared was never issued. Its draft holds an important place in the long series of reform testimonials. Patronage of the religious orders, especially of the Augustinians and the Minims, lay very close to the Pope's heart.

The drawing of the famous line of demarcation 100 leagues west of the Azores between Spanish and Portuguese possessions and newly discovered areas confirms the prestige enjoyed by the Holy See and even by Alexander. Agreements over the lands wrested from the Muslims and the recently discovered islands had been reached earlier by the two seafaring powers and were ratified by the Curia. The bulls issued in 1493, shortly after the discovery of America by Columbus, dealt with what was clearly an act of investiture in favor of Castile, and in 1494 this was followed by the important Treaty of Tordesillas. An expert knowledge of the questions at stake seems not to have been present at the Curia or anywhere else.

In regard to the Pope's death in August 1503, following a severe fever, there are varying reports and varying interpretations. Many historians, however, defend the more probable view that the dangerous Roman fever was the cause of death.

No other pontificate has evoked so much lively discussion and disagreement. Of fundamental importance is the question of the reliability of the data in the diary of the papal master of ceremonies, Burckard of Strasbourg. His statements on Alexander were certainly prompted by hatred and hence require a careful investigation to the extent this is possible from the sources. During Alexander's own pontificate there were many critical voices, which, it is true, often held a political origin.

The Renaissance papacy reached its climax in the remarkable personality of Alexander VI, for evil practices that had been hitherto customary were now present in abundance and were tolerated by the cardinals: a failure to observe celibacy even as Pope, dissolution of marriages from purely political motives, granting of high ecclesiastical office, including the cardinalate, in return for considerable sums, extremes of nepotism in the providing for children to the detriment of the Papal State, the administering of the apostolic palace by the Pope's daughter Lucretia, who was also regent of Spoleto for a year, — and yet Rodrigo Borgia refused to be outdone by anyone in the firmness of his faith.

Pius III (1503)

The unexpected death of Alexander VI produced much commotion in Rome and the Papal State. The conclave of 16–21 September, however, could proceed calmly with its business in the Vatican. This time, however, the election capitulation of 1484 was adopted with the express injunction that a general council had to be convoked within two years, and then one was to meet every five years, especially for the reform of the Church. The candidates with the best prospects were Julian della Rovere and the French Cardinal George d'Amboise, Archbishop of Rouen. But since neither could gain the required number of votes, Pius II's nephew, Francis Todeschini-Piccolomini, who was seriously ill, was elected as a "caretaker" Pope. The pontificate of Pius III lasted only twenty-six days. Contemporaries and posterity regarded the briefness of his reign as a great misfortune, since the convoking of a general council and serious reform measures could have been expected from him.

Julius II (1503–13)

Matters were to turn out quite differently and a man was to obtain the tiara who would be reckoned among the forceful and great Popes, at least from a worldly viewpoint: Julius II.

The few days of the pontificate of Pius III did not suffice to alter the general situation and so the same groups confronted each other in the new conclave. But now Julian della Rovere, whom people on all sides wanted as Pope, succeeded in outwitting the crafty Caesar Borgia while assuring him of his good will. This got him the votes of the Spanish cardinals. Without doubt the election must be called simoniacal. One of the shortest conclaves in papal history ended on the very first day with the election of della Rovere, who styled himself Julius II. Although, as was customary after the completion of the election, he swore to abide by the arrangements of the Sacred College, he had no intention of keeping these and other promises, as Caesar Borgia especially was to learn. With a firm grip the new Pope took hold of the reins and inaugurated a pontificate which was filled with great policies and military enterprises such as no other could claim. He was now sixty years old and had been made a Cardinal by his uncle, Sixtus IV, as long ago as 1471 when he was a young Franciscan. He had had great experience in all secular affairs and ways of life and was brilliantly gifted.

Building on the political successes of the Borgia in the Papal State, his goal was the consolidation of his state — something which could be achieved only by keeping the great powers out of Italy. His policy was pursued in three stages: the assuring of papal authority in Rome and the Papal State, the winning back of lost territories, and the expelling of the "foreigners" from the Italian peninsula. And so he is regarded in Italian historiography as a proponent of Italian unification. To counter the threatening danger to himself and to his policies, the Pope now summoned the Fifth Lateran Council to meet at Rome in 1512.

This year did not at first grant the Holy League the desired success. Quite the contrary: under the leadership of the young and capable Gaston de Foix the French inflicted a severe defeat on the Spanish and papal army at Ravenna on Easter Sunday, and the papal legate, Cardinal Giovanni de' Medici, was captured. But luck changed sides after the death of the French general, and some months later the troops of France had to leave Italian soil. The Medici returned to power at Florence, Maximilian Sforza, son of Louis *il Moro,* at Milan, and the Emperor deserted the schismatic Council of Pisa of 1511 and recognized the Lateran Council. The latter continued in several sessions until 1517, but with the collapse of the schismatic synod it had really accomplished its intended task.

To what extent politics dominated all else appears in the Pope's relations to the Emperor Maximilian. Julius sought in every way to keep him out of Italy and from his imperial coronation, even if he occasionally had to ally with him for the sake of his Italian policy. He was not displeased by the obstacles which Venice put in the way of a journey to Rome. He agreed when in 1508 Maximilian had himself designed as "Roman Emperor-elect" at Trent. The Emperor was unwilling to renounce the rich provinces of Italy and the financial power of the German Church and hoped to achieve his goal in the ecclesiastical sphere. Hence a matter which has received very different evaluations becomes understandable: the Emperor's plan of acquiring the tiara. New finds have confirmed the seriousness of the plan and of the steps taken. When in the summer of 1511 the Pope became seriously ill and his end was expected, Maximilian, like everyone else, readied himself for the impending conclave, but in such a way that he himself appeared as a candidate. An old desire seemed about to be fulfilled. Since as early as the last decade of the fifteenth century it had been heard of Maximilian's intention of controlling at last the German Church, on the French model, either through a reform council or through a withdrawal of obedience and a schism. The schismatic Council of Pisa was a favorable opportunity for such an undertaking. But now, with the serious illness of the Pope, it was important to act quickly in order "to arrive at the papacy" or at least to acquire the disposal of the rights and finances of the German Church. In a detailed letter, whose authenticity has recently been proved, several possibilities emerge: that Maximilian should become the coadjutor of the reigning Pope or of an Antipope, that he should himself become Antipope or even, the lawfully elected Pope after the death of Julius II. There were long discussions on the subject with France and Spain, with the intention on both sides of outwitting the other partner. The masterful diplomacy of the Spanish court, *vis-à-vis* the imperial intermediary, Bishop Matthew Lang of Gurk, succeeded in dragging out the business and, after the Pope's recovery, in detaching the Emperor from the alliance with France and from supporting the Council of Pisa. Hence it hardly modifies the well known remark of the Florentine historian. Guicciardini, that Julius II had nothing of the priest except the dress and the name. The four solemn sessions of the Fifth Lateran Council in his pontificate were devoted essentially to combatting the Council of Pisa and counteracting its encouragement by France. The important prohibition of simony in future papal elections would have acquired a great significance if it had been heeded.

Although he was personally neither a theologian nor a man of letters, the Pope acquired immortal fame as a Maecenas. The rebuilding of Saint Peter's and the ruthless tearing down of the venerable Constantinian basilica, the painting of the ceiling of the Sistine Chapel by Michelangelo, and the frescoes of Raffael in the *stanze* of the Vatican palace must especially be mentioned here. The plan for his tomb in Saint Peter's can be called gigantic but also daring; of it there survives the always impressive moment in his former titular church of San Pietro in Vincoli with the figure of Moses, in which is materialized the overwhelming personality of the Pope. If the Papal State became temporarily through the policy and military abilities of its kingly ruler the first power in Italy and for a while played a leading role in European politics, this situation changed in the last weeks of the second Rovere Pope with the *rapprochement* of Venice to France and the growth, dangerous for the "freedom of Italy," of Spanish influence.

Leo X (1513–21)

Julius II left a conflicting legacy: on the one hand, the Papal State in a position which again deserved the name of state and a considerable treasure in the Castel Sant'Angelo; on the other, the enmity with France and an ecclesiastical opposition, called into being for political reasons but not without its dangers. In addition was the fact that really nothing had yet been done in the ecclesiastical sphere for the reform that was so urgently necessary and was being energetically demanded on all sides.

Twenty-five cardinals took part in the conclave, which began in the Vatican palace on 4 March 1513; the schismatics of Pisa, whom Julius had deposed, were not admitted. Two factions, the "old" and the "young," confronted each other. But agreement quickly occurred, and on 11 March the thirty-seven-year-old Giovanni de' Medici was elected. The fact that he was carried into the conclave ill and at once had to undergo an operation is said to have made it easier to gain the assent of the old cardinals; but, more than this acute illness, the zealous but probably not simoniacal activity of his secretary, Bibbiena, seems to have gained the decision for him. His great political experience and his activity as ruler of Florence made him probably the most qualified candidate.

His home was Florence, his father was Lorenzo *il Magnifico.* Admitted to the clerical state by receiving the tonsure at the age of seven, he soon obtained a series of lucrative benefices, including the abbey of Montecassino. When not yet fourteen he was secretly named a Cardinal by Innocent VIII and in his seventeenth year, as the Pope had arranged, he entered the Sacred College.

Because of a careful education the young Cardinal had the aristocratic culture and manners of a Renaissance prince. And such he remained when, following the death of the forceful Julius II, he was elected Pope. He was above all the prince in politics, the chief activity of a Pope in the age of the Renaissance. Not without skill in all the arts of diplomacy, he sought to keep the Papal State and his own Florence out of the struggle of the great European powers, France, Spain, and Austria, over Italy and to acquire for his family at the favorable moment a position of predominance in Italy, even outside Florence. If his political practices — simultaneous negotiations and alliances with different and mutually hostile partners and equivocal treaties — were often condemned, still, despite deceit and double dealing, the concern for peace in his balance of power policy was prominent. He deviated from it only in a few cases.

From the ecclesiastical viewpoint the discussions at Bologna in December 1515 were of special importance because of agreement on a concordat and the annulling of the Pragmatic Sanction of Bourges. The concordat made hitherto unprecedented concessions to the French crown. The King obtained the full right of nomination to almost all benefices that were conferred in consistory, that is, bishoprics and abbeys. The Pope could fill only a small number of lesser benefices. Expectatives and reservations were abolished for France, and only *causae maiores* could be carried to the Curia. In addition, the King personally received a number of privileges. The Pope had great difficulty in having so far-reaching a concordat approved in consistory, and only the fear that the French Church would separate itself entirely from Rome facilitated the consent of the cardinals. Nevertheless, the French *parlements* were not satisfied with the concordat. In the course of the pontificate and especially in its last years relations with France grew worse. Apart from Venice it was chiefly the French King who obstructed Leo's serious efforts for a crusade against the Turks, even though he collected large sums in crusade tithes and managed to use them for his enterprises in Italy. The religious situation in Germany brought the Pope to an understanding with the new King of the

Romans, with the result that the French troops in North Italy were compelled to withdraw.

After his earlier mishaps, especially in the war against Venice, the Emperor Maximilian had been able to take only a slight part in the struggle for predominance in Italy. When the question of the imperial succession became acute, the Curia acquired an important role because the candidates were Francis I of France and Charles I of Spain. Because of their great power and their position in Italy both presented a danger to the Papal State, especially Charles as ruler of Naples. Hence Rome desired a candidate from among the German princes and thought of the Elector Frederick of Saxony. When he declined, the three spiritual Electors were to be gained for the French King by tempting offers. Not until Charles' election was certain did the Curia yield. The Pope's simultaneous treaties of alliance with Francis and Charles have gone down in history as masterstrokes of diplomacy.

A great sensation was produced by the proceedings against several cardinals on the charge of conspiracy. The Sienese Cardinal Alfonso Petrucci was alienated by the expulsion in 1516 of his brother from Siena, in which the Pope had played a role, and he was soon regarded as the head of a dangerous *fronde* of cardinals. He is said to have tried to have the Pope poisoned by a Florentine physician. As a result of confessions obtained by torture from Petrucci's servants, he and Cardinal Sauli were arrested as they entered the Vatican and imprisoned in the dungeons of Sant'Angelo. Petrucci was executed; the other accused cardinals were deprived of their dignities, benefices, and revenues for a long time and punished with enormous fines.

Church History has taken Leo X severely to task for his nepotism. Since he was actually ruling Florence also, his concern for the Medici family is understandable. He rejected many demands of his relatives, such as their claims to Piombino and Siena. That he wanted to obtain Parma, Piacenza, Modena, and Reggio, and perhaps Ferrara also, for his brother Julian can be regarded as means of guaranteeing the Papal State, but less can be said for his covetous glances at Naples. The finances of the Papal State endured an enormous burden because of the gigantic expenses for politics, for the luxurious court, and for the grand-scale patronage of art and scholarship. According to a contemporary saying, he squandered the treasure amassed by his predecessor, the income of his own pontificate, and that of his successor's reign. Leo X was an almost unfathomable personality, a refined gourmet, a Maecenas, but without creative qualities. He took particular delight in festive cavalcades and pageantry. The theatrical performances in the papal palace did not, for he most part, correspond to a spiritual mode of life, and Leo's predilection for hunting has often been censured. And yet the blame affects not so much his person as the system that he took over and further developed, a system which could not be justified from a religious viewpoint.

CHAPTER 58

The Inner Life of the Church

The Urban Parish

The Church life of the late Middle Ages, like that of the early Church, once again was centered around the urban parish. Cities had experienced a vigorous growth in the thirteenth and fourteenth centuries. If there were some 250 cities in Germany around 1200, about 800 more were founded during the thirteenth century alone, and by the close of the Middle Ages approximately 3,000 places possessed city rights. The European city owes its growth to commerce rather than to the trades. As soon as and so long as commerce linked the lesser economic systems to an extensive area — the Hansa is the prime example, — cities flourished, whereas they stagnated wherever the gilds with their efforts for self-sufficiency prevailed.

Notwithstanding their importance, their inhabitants were not numerous. Of the 3,000 German cities, 2,800 had fewer than 1,000 inhabitants, and 150 between 1,000 and 2,000. Only the remaining 50, with more than 2,000 citizens, were of real significance for the economy. A mere fifteen of them exceeded a population of 10,000; the largest, Cologne, surpassed 30,000. Then came Lübeck with about 25,000. Next, probably only Nürnberg, Strasbourg, Danzig, and Ulm reached a figure of 20,000. In 1493 the population of Erfurt was reckoned as about 18,500, whereas that of Leipzig was estimated as only 4,000 in 1474. Among the inhabitants of the cities women predominated. The causes of this were male military service, greater male licentiousness, and the greater susceptibility of males to contagious diseases. Also responsible is the fact that a relatively large number of males were out of the question as far as marriage was concerned because their were diocesan or religious priests. With this surplus of females the convents and, in the case of the middle and lower classes, the houses of Beguines had a considerable social importance as places for the support of unmarried women.

The large number of priests and religious in the cities, constituting as much as one-tenth of the total population, gave rise to serious social and economic problems. Clerics and religious claimed immunity from taxation for themselves and for the property of their church or monastery. Yet they not infrequently possessed as much as half of the real estate in a city. They claimed the advantages of urban life, for example its security and commerce, without contributing a corresponding share to bearing the city's burdens. In the country too efforts were made to restrict the exemption of ecclesiastics from taxation or at east to guard against its consequences. Hence in the fifteenth century clerical privileges declined increasingly in importance.

Special grounds for conflict developed in the episcopal cities. In contrast to most secular princes, bishops resided in cities and sought to maintain their supremacy against the townsmen's aspirations for freedom. Probably no episcopal city was spared a struggle with its bishop. Cologne obtained its independence in 1288 as a result of ceaseless bitter quarrels with its archbishops, but only in 1475 was it formally recognized as a Free Imperial City by Frederick III. By the close of the thirteenth century most of the important cities of Germany and of the

Low Countries had self-government. As in the case of immunity from taxation, the conflict in the cities was concerned also with clerical freedom from lay courts.

The development of the parochial system in the cities was essentially complete in the thirteenth century. For a long time the cathedral had ceased to be the only parish church in the city. Collegiate churches and at times even abbeys had obtained parochial rights in the cities and their own parishes. But the self-reliance of the now independent *bourgeoisie* went beyond this to demand its own parish churches or at least its own priest from its own ranks (*plebanus*, people's priest). This priest and often also the pastors were frequently considered to be city officials, like the justice of the peace, schoolmaster, and councillors. This led logically to the demand on the part of the citizens or of the party in political control in the cities to elect their pastor like other officials. The right of electing the pastor was granted especially to newly founded cities, but it was not universally established. Frequently the citizens contrived to acquire patronage over their city churches and hence the right to name or to present the pastor. The citizens took care of their churches and in accord with the cooperative principle wanted a share in the administration and supervision of church property. For this purpose they made use of the church custodian, whose function more and more became part of the urban administrative system and was subject to the council. Cities made the building of their churches and the administration of the church property their own monopoly and responsibility.

But the city council not only supervised the church plant and controlled the offerings and other donations of the faithful through the custodian. It also exercised a decisive influence on the appointment of clerics to Mass benefices and the administration of the endowment funds. Hence there existed quite often a close bond of life and interests between *bourgeoisie* and clergy.

The absorption of the ecclesiastical organization into the *bourgeoisie* included also the school and the care of the poor and the sick. These passed increasingly into the hands of the laity or of the secular officialdom. The hospital organization was probably the starting-point of this development. The office of the city hospital custodian appears to be older than that of the church custodian. The close connection of hospital and religious corporation or monastery dissolved, and led to the transformation of the church hospital into a municipal institution.

The establishing of city schools meant that the school system also passed from the clergy to control by the city. But even so, the post of schoolmaster, like that of town clerk, frequently continued to be filled by clerics. Cities founded universities by papal privilege: Cologne in 1389, Erfurt in 1392, Basel in 1460, and Breslau in 1507. At Trier the university was able to become a reality in 1473, once the Archbishop had ceded to the city the right of foundation granted to him by the Pope in 1454.

Even "the monasteries became more *bourgeois*" (Schiller). The cities increasingly secured control of monastic property and in many cases monasteries were regularly included in the sphere of city government. In the pastoral care of the city populations great credit belongs to the mendicant orders of Franciscans and Dominicans, whose houses were to be found in every city of any importance. Because they carried out their care of souls among the people without regard to the boundaries of dioceses or parishes, they came into conflict with bishops and diocesan clergy. The less the parish priests took into account the new needs and, because of pluralism and disregard of the duty of residence, did not even carry out their traditional obligations, the mendicant orders gained popular favor.

The Liturgy

The Church's worship, with the Mass as its center and climax, underwent a further elaboration, not in the sense of a real enrichment but rather of a multiplication and continuation of the existing rite. New starts cannot be ascertained, but, all the more, a proliferation of external forms. The personal and the subjective elements came into prominence, the tangible and concrete and the particular that could be counted were stressed. The community nature of the celebration of the Eucharist became constantly less clear, and the "private" Mass more and more preempted the field. It gradually determined the very form of the solemn Mass.

From the thirteenth century, when the complete missal superseded the sacramentary, the priest had also to read, for himself, the parts sung by the choir and soon even to read the Epistle and the Gospel while they were being sung by the sacred ministers. The liturgy was no longer understood as the service of the whole Church, whose membership was expressed in the distribution of functions among priest, choir, and community, but was a clerical or even a priestly liturgy. Only what the priest did was "valid," and hence he had to recite everything himself. The people were even debarred from the readings. No effort was made to translate them, and frequently they were drowned out by the playing of the organ. The Mass had ceased to be a proclamation of the word. The unintelligible language barred any approach by the people to an understanding. All the more importance was attached to the ritual — the external ceremonies and the sacramental signs — but without the word this threatened to become a splendid but empty covering. The liturgy became a performance — beautiful and intricate but really mute. From outside it efforts were made, by means of allegory, to give it an artificial voice. Sermons on the Mass, which could have unlocked the mystery, were inadequate as regards both number and content. Thus the Eucharistic celebration was able to exercise a fruitful influence on popular piety only in a very limited sense.

Popular piety invented substitutes for the liturgy, and these succumbed all the more easily to the danger of superficiality to the extent that they were no longer connected with the center of the mystery. What was unfamiliar and inaccessible had to be praised. Sermons and speculation on the fruits of the Mass and the value of attendance at Mass dominated the otherwise jejune theology of the Mass and the instruction in it. The fruits of the Mass were understood at the close of the Middle Ages in an increasingly massive and this-worldly manner.

If there was nothing to listen to, even greater prominence was given to seeing. Popular devotion at Mass concentrated on gazing at the Host at the elevation following the consecration, and this became of the greatest importance from the thirteenth century. William of Auxerre (d. 1230) had already taught: "Many prayers are answered while looking at the Lord's body, and many graces are poured out." Synods urged priests to elevate the Host so high that it could be seen by the people. The elevation acquired such importance that in some places "to go to

Mass" meant to arrive for the consecration and to look at the Host. The popular demand for looking was met from the fourteenth century by numerous Eucharistic processions, exposition, and benediction with the Sacrament. All of this caused the Eucharistic celebration as sacrifice and banquet to retire more and more into the background.

In the fifteenth century there were not lacking voices protesting the multiplication of processions and expositions. The Papal Legate Nicholas of Cusa emphasized that the Eucharist "was instituted as food and not for show," and in his reform decrees he forbade processions and expositions outside the octave of Corpus Christi. His prohibition of venerating bleeding Hosts and of the pilgrimage to Wilsnack foundered on the resistance of local authorities, which obtained support at the Curia.

Abuses and superstition in regard to the Blessed Sacrament could spread all the more since the word, the *verbum sacramenti* in the strict sense and that of the liturgy in general, was not only not understood but was not even heard. The word is of course intended to remove from the sensible element its ambiguity and elevate it to the clarity and precision of the intellect. Without the accomplishing of the word there is the risk of missing the meaning of the Sacrament or even of falsifying it. Too easily what took place ran the risk of magic.

As a matter of fact, in the later Middle Ages the Mass was stamped by individualization and multiplication. Every gild and confraternity, even a family which thought highly of itself, wanted to have its Mass and, so far as possible, at its own altar. This striving was encouraged by a theology which taught the finite value of the Mass and defended the view that an *a priori* determined number of Mass fruits was divided among the participating group; hence it was better to live in a smaller parish because then the share in the Mass offered by the pastor on Sundays for his flock was greater. To satisfy all these demands the number of Masses and of altars had to be greatly multiplied. This also led to an unhealthy growth in the number of Masspriests — those who had nothing else to do but celebrate Mass and on occasion take part in the choral office. Parish churches, like cathedrals and collegiate churches, had a large number of altars, for which, to some extent several priests were beneficed.

The duties of Mass-priests were not sufficient to keep them occupied, and the income was not enough to assure them adequate support. The only natural attempt to escape pauperization by means of pluralism led to further abuses.

The multiplication of Mass-endowments made necessary a rapid succession of the most varied services. If there was a question of chanted Masses, then, even with so many altars, it was difficult to celebrate them. Hence there arose abuses such as "curtailed Masses," that is, sung Mass became a low Mass from the Creed to enable another sung Mass to begin, or *Missae bifaciatae* or *trifaciatae* were held. In these several "liturgies of the Word" were combined with one sacrificial Mass. The "dry Mass," that is, Mass without the Canon and the narrative of the institution of the Eucharist, which had some meaning as the administering of communion in a sick-room, was debased in order that a priest might accept a stipend without having celebrated the consecration and communion.

Criticism of the practices in regard to Mass was not wanting. This notion of the Mass, connected with the characteristic late mediaeval inclination to the individual and the subjective, led to the endeavor to put it as far as possible at the service of the individual's needs and desires. The result was a tremendous increase in the number of votive Masses.

> There were votive Masses of the twenty-four patriarchs or elders; of the fourteen, fifteen, and more "holy helpers"; of the seven joys and sorrows of Mary; votive Masses against sicknesses, including one against pestilence, one of Holy Job against syphilis, one of Saint Christopher against sudden death, one each of Saint Roch and Saint Sebastian against pestilence, one of Saint Sigismund against fever; votive Masses for special requests: in honor of the Archangel Raphael or of the Three Magi for a safe journey, a Mass to keep away thieves and to recover stolen property, a Mass before a duel or ordeals, one against Hussites and Turks and against witches; the seven-day, thirteen-day, or thirty-day Masses of emergency, which had to be offered by one priest for seven, thirteen, or thirty days respectively, at the end of which interval guaranteed liberation from sickness and distress was expected, and in addition the three Masses of Saint Nicholas for needs. (L. A. Veit)

These series of Masses, which increased to forty-five in number for all possible concerns, were all the more dubious in that they held out the prospect of a guaranteed outcome for the living and the dead on the eve of the Reformation the gloomy statement is true, that

> The holiest of the Church's possessions remained, it is true, the center of genuine piety. But alas, the clouds and shadows surrounding this center brought matters to such a pass that the Institution of Jesus, that well of life from which the Church had drawn for fifteen hundred years, became an object of scorn and ridicule and was repudiated as a horrible idolatry by entire peoples. (Jungmann)

Preaching

If, because of the Latin language, the liturgy itself was in no position to introduce the faithful to Christian doctrine, this assignment became the monopoly of preaching. There was much preaching in the late Middle Ages, perhaps more than in more recent ages. Preaching in German on Sundays and holy days, during or before Mass, was probably the rule in city and country. In addition there often were also special afternoon preaching services. Before or after the sermon the feasts of the coming week and the annual commemorations were announced, the names of the dead and of benefactors were read out, prayers of intercession for all classes in the Church, the Our Father, the Hail Mary, the Creed, and the ten commandments were recited. To the sermon were added, though in some places only on specified days, a general confession of sins and absolution. There was preaching on week-days too, especially on the Wednesdays and Fridays of Advent and Lent. The duty of preaching on the part of clerics occupied in the care of souls goes without saying, but the frequent insistence on this duty by synods proves that it was not seldom neglected, less in cities than in the country. If it was demanded time and again that the priest must recite the Our Father, the creed, and the commandments to the people in their vernacular on Sundays, then we should probably not entertain any high expectations of pastoral preaching. It is difficult to form a picture. The material left by diocesan priests is naturally scanty.

The basic source of these shortcomings was the inadequate education of priests, especially of the poorly paid vicars, by whom the frequently absentee holders of pastoral benefices had their functions performed. The dearth of a priestly spirit and of a pastoral sense of responsibility in the bishops had an especially unhealthy effect in this regard. One could obtain ordination from a bishop, usually without any special examination. The cathedral *scholasticus,* and in the fifteenth century also a special cathedral preacher, had charge of the instructing of clerics and of the examining of candidates for ordination. Only a small percentage of clerics attended a university; a high estimate gives one-fifth. But most of these did not continue the study of the liberal arts more than one or two years, and so they obtained no special preparation for the clerical office.

Shockingly slight was the indispensable minimum of knowledge which thirteenth-century theologians required of the priest and with which persons were probably satisfied in practice. The Dominican Ulric of Strasbourg (d. 1277) expressed it in the following manner and this was adopted by the canonists:

> To the extent that the priest is obliged to the celebration of the worship of God, he must know enough grammar to be able to pronounce and accent the words correctly and to understand at least the literal sense of what he reads. As minister of the Sacraments he must know the essential form of a Sacrament and the correct manner of administering it. As teacher he must know at least the basic doctrine of faith proving itself effective in charity. As judge in matters of conscience he must be able to distinguish between what is sin and what is not and between sin and sin.

It was certainly no mere chance that the mendicant orders, which were especially concerned for the extensive theological education of their members, assumed in the thirteenth and fourteenth centuries the task of preaching, rendered more urgent by the enhanced religious interests of the city populations and because of the sects. From the end of the fourteenth century they were joined by educated priests from the diocesan clergy. At that time in many places, especially in South Germany, a few preaching offices were created for them by private bequests or by action of a city council. They were supposed to satisfy the more rigorous claims of their listeners and hence as far as possible were to have earned a degree in theology. But this *sine qua non* stipulation again made it difficult, considering the educational status of priests, to fill the posts. These preachers were not to replace the customary preaching in the parochial liturgy. Frequently in the foundation charters a defining of rights and duties was envisaged or it was specified that this preacher had to withdraw if the pastor himself wanted to preach. When the canons would not accept John Eck, presented for the preaching office at Sankt Moritz on 29 January 1518, James Fugger wrote: "A parish is in greater need of preaching and hearing confessions than of the choral chanting of the entire chapter." He thereby expressed vividly the esteem in which preaching was held by the upper *bourgeois* and the responsibility which they felt for it.

In addition to the principal categories of sermons for Sundays (*de tempore*) and for feasts of saints (*de sanctis*), in the late Middle Ages there appeared sermons on the Passion, Lenten sermons, and catechetical sermons, that is, on the various points of Christian doctrine which were later compiled in the catechism under the headings: articles of faith, prayers, the ten commandments, and the seven Sacraments. There were also sermons on the seven capital sins, the cardinal virtues, and other moral questions. The sermon based on the scholastic method was fostered by scholars such as Robert Holcot (d. 1349), John Gerson (d. 1429), Nicholas of Dinkelsbühl (d. 1433), Nicholas of Cusa (d. 1464), and Gabriel Biel (d. 1495). More popular and more adapted to ordinary Christian life were the great itinerant preachers of penance, like Jerome Savonarola (d. 1498), probably the most powerful and ardent preacher of the Middle Ages. To precision of thought Savonarola joined mystical depth and warm emotion. Disregarding all scholarly and ornamental formality, he preached Holy Scripture and with unheard of prophetical frankness arraigned before its tribunal life in the world and in the Church. In the area of German speech the most important popular preacher at the end of the Middle Ages was Johannes Geiler von Kaysersberg (d. 1510). Before going to the Strasbourg Münster as preacher in 1478, he had taught at Freiburg (1465–70) as a master of philosophy and had received the doctorate in theology at Basel in 1476. He understood both life and man and had the special gift of expressing himself in a clear and down-to-earth and oftentimes coarse manner. With great frankness he condemned the immorality of the people and that of persons of high rank in Church and State, humorously but frequently with biting irony and devastating ridicule. In him the proclaiming of the faith very definitely took a second place after moral teaching — something characteristic of late mediaeval religious instruction generally.

An influence was exercised on preaching by various reference books for homiletics: preaching cycles, collections of topics and examples, lives of saints, and postils. Furthermore, textbooks of homiletics were not lacking. While church records were kept in Italy and the Midi already in the fourteenth century, this was not the practice in Germany. At the end of the fifteenth century synods more and more frequently admonished or obliged pastors to keep lists of the baptized, the dead, those going to confession, and the excommunicated. But it was not until the Council of Trent that it became a duty to keep records of baptisms and marriages.

Catechesis

The baptism of infants put an end to the catechumenate of adults, but in the Middle Ages no regular Church instruction of children took its place. Only sporadically and rather late do we find synodal decrees that oblige pastors to instruct the young in faith and morals, for this was regarded as the duty of parents and godparents. They were supposed to teach the children the creed and the Our Father, and in the late Middle Ages care was taken to include the Hail Mary and the ten commandments. Works of edification, urged parents to carry out this duty. How meager religious knowledge was can be gathered from the fact that Nicholas of Cusa, as Cardinal Legate in Germany in 1451–52, felt obliged to have wooden tablets giving the Our Father, the creed, and the ten commandments set up in the churches for the religious instruction of the people.

Because of this lack of direct and systematic instruction, this "catechetical vacuum of the Middle Ages" (R. Padberg), people were for the most part left to learn the Christian faith by life and experience in a Christian environment. The paintings on the walls, in the windows, and on the altars were the Bible of the illiterate. Mystery plays, Christmas, Holy Week, and Easter plays, and other dramatic presentations brought sacred history to men and held up to their gaze morally good conduct. An abundance of religious customs attended the day-to-day life of the individual and the community from cradle to grave. The educative power of Christian morality and a Christian *milieu* must certainly not be underestimated. But there is also no question that such a Christianity of mere custom, without adequate clarification by knowledge and understanding, was particularly susceptible to mass-suggestion and superstition and was hardly a match for serious crises.

The vast deficiency in personal instruction and formation of consciences lent an enhanced importance to the annual confession, the preparation for it, and the actual making of the confession. Helps were provided by the outlines for examining the conscience and, at the end of the Middle Ages, the confession brochures. About fifty printings of such little books are known for the period 1450 to 1520. This clearly indicates the new possibilities for religious instruction latent in the invention of printing. There had already earlier been such compilations of the chief catechetical points for the use of pastors and teachers, such as the *Opus tripartitum de praeceptis decalogi, de confessione et de arte moriendi* of Jean Gerson (d. 1429).

Printing was of special importance for the spread of the Bible. Around 100 printings of the Vulgate had appeared by 1500. From the first printed German translation in 1461, or at the latest in 1466, e.g., until Luther's edition of the New Testament in 1522 fourteen High German and four Low German complete Bibles appeared in print, in addition to a large number of German psalters, other printings of parts of Scripture, and editions of Gospels and Epistles (postils and *plenaria*).

Religious Orders

The religious institutes of the late Middle Ages were in a state of decay, arising from many causes. Its progress in the individual orders was also quite varied and did not follow one pattern. When the mendicant orders experienced their tremendous growth early in the thirteenth century, the Benedictine family was in decline, and it was the mendicants that responded to the needs of the new situation. Hence they exerted a powerful attraction on the young, whereas the old orders were in no position to proclaim and to live their ideal in a manner adapted to gaining in any great numbers young men of deep religious convictions. Too closely identified with feudalism, the Benedictine order had as slight a connection with the new social and economic conditions as with the new educational system of *studia generalia* and universities. The nobility saw the monasteries as places for providing for younger sons. But these wanted to continue in the monastery to live the life of their own social class and frequently disregarded the vow of poverty as well as inclosure. It became more and more common for the monastic property and income to be divided between abbot and community, with the abbacy and the claustral offices being regarded as benefices and the monks being allowed to have property (*peculium*) for their personal use. Abbeys were conferred *in commendam* on cardinals, bishops and even lay persons, who drew the income without being concerned for the internal life of the monasteries.

The Black Death of 1348 involved grave material distress in most religious communities and carried off a large number of the members. In general it produced a serious breakdown of religious and moral discipline. Monks who had fled from the plague and had lived in freedom in the world were no longer willing to submit to the rule as formerly. In an effort to replenish the thinned ranks people ceased to be very particular about accepting candidates. Before long the Western Schism gave rise to serious shocks in the orders as well as in the Church at large. The split showed itself in the orders and at times in individual monasteries. Some orders, like the Carthusians, Cistercians, and Carmelites, split into two branches, each with its general.

All this naturally caused grave damage to the spiritual life and discipline of the monasteries. Under these circumstances reform was not possible, because its opponents contrived to play off the one authority against the other. But reform efforts were made in the fourteenth and fifteenth centuries. The quarrels in the Franciscan family, which resulted in 1517 in the separation of the Conventuals and the Observants, were fierce and also of the reform congregation of the Windesheim Augustinians. In other orders, too, observant circles were formed to live the rule in its original austerity. Among the Augustinian Hermits the reformed houses united into a special reformed congregation directly subject to the general.

Benedict XII (1334–42) seriously sought a reform of the orders. Although the Pope personally tried to implement his reform decrees in practice, he had no success.

If the "Benedictina" had had hardly any effect, the idea of merging individual monasteries into provinces or congregations remained alive, and all reform efforts of the fifteenth century were characterized by it. From Santa Giustina at Padua Abbot Louis Barbo founded in 1419, under Martin V, a reform congregation which obtained its definitive form in 1432 under Eugene IV. All authority was vested in the annual general chapter of delegates and superiors of the monasteries. The individual abbey was a member of the congregation and was administered by it. The abbots were elected for life but they changed monasteries every year and later every six years. The monks were professed for the congregation rather than for a particular monastery and could be transferred to another monastery by the president of the congregation or the visitor. Thereby the abbatial dignity and the claustral offices were stripped completely of their character as benefices and the abuses of *commenda* and prebends were effectively obviated. In the course of time almost all the Italian monasteries, including Montecassino, Subiaco, La Cava, and Cervara, themselves reformed houses, joined the Congregation of Santa Giustina. And though it continued to be restricted to the peninsula, it still exercised a great influence on the organization of many other congregations.

In Germany the reform movement received a stimulus from the Council of Constance, in which, among the numerous regulars, many Benedictines took part. Under the very eyes of the Council Fathers, as it were, there took place at the Abbey of Petershausen near Constance in 1417 a chapter attended by the Benedictines present in Constance and the superiors of the Mainz-Bamberg province. The "Benedictina" was again to be observed and, above all, poverty and the common life were again enjoined. Furthermore, the chapter issued decrees against the nobility's monopoly of certain monasteries. But there was no central tribunal to see to the implementation of the decrees. Many abbeys resisted the reforms, and some sought to escape them by having their monks transformed into secular canons. Just the same, the idea of reform had awakened. Centers of renewal were the abbeys at Kastl in the Upper Palatinate, Melk on the Danube, Sankt Matthias in Trier, Tegernsee, the Vienna Schottenkloster, and Bursfeld on the Weser.

The customs of Kastl, which, in addition to the liturgy, especially stressed silence, poverty, and obedience, determined the monastic reform decrees of the Petershausen Chapter and of the Council of Basel. Twenty-five abbeys were revived by Kastl, directly or indirectly. The establishing of a congregation was initiated by German monks from Subiaco and spread from Melk to monasteries in Austria, Bavaria (Tegernsee), Swabia, and Hungary. The starting point of reform in North and West Germany was the monastery of Bursfeld near Göttingen. From Abbot John Rode of Sankt Matthias, the new Abbot of Bursfeld, John Dederoth, obtained the reform statutes and four of his best monks. Thus Bursfeld was able to experience a new flowering and to become under the direction of Abbot John von Hagen from 1439 the nucleus of a strictly organized congregation with a chapter that met annually from 1446. In 1469 thirty-six monasteries, including Hirsau, belonged to it; in 1530, ninety-four. The Bursfeld reform received stimulation and encouragement from the Cardinal Legate Nicholas of Cusa (d. 1464).

Religious life in France sank to its nadir in the fifteenth century as a consequence of the Hundred Years' War and the far-reaching encroachments of the secular authorities, notably through the Pragmatic Sanction of Bourges in 1438. Within the Benedictine Order there were reform endeavors at Cluny, Tiron, and especially Chezal-Benoît in the diocese of Bourges. But the Concordat of 1516 hurt reform by giving the King the right to name the abbots.

In Spain the monastery of Valladolid, founded as recently as 1390, became the center of a reform congregation which almost all the Spanish monasteries joined. To avoid the abuses of *commenda* the abbatial title was abolished and the duration of office of the claustral appointments was restricted to a few years.

In the Cistercian Order the symptoms of decay were not so alarming, and the twenty-four new foundations of the fifteenth century testify to a certain vitality. The Carthusian order experienced a real flowering in the fourteenth and fifteenth centuries. Despite numerous afflictions and persecutions at the hands of Hussites and Turks, in 1510 there were 195 charterhouses in seventeen provinces.

The founding of new orders and of communities and confraternities resembling orders proves that the seeking of Christian perfection was still alive. In addition to the Brothers and Sisters of the Common Life, still other lay confraternities were formed to devote themselves to active charity for the neighbor in the care of the poor and the sick and the burial of the dead. The Alexians, also called Cellities, Lollards, or Rolibrüder (Burial Brothers), came together after the Black Death of 1348–49 in Flanders and on the Lower Rhine. Those of Aachen made vows in 1469. In 1472 Sixtus IV gave them the Augustinian rule.

Originally a lay confraternity founded by John Colombini at Siena in 1360, the

Jesuates aimed to devote themselves to the salvation of their fellowmen by prayer, mortification, and the care of the sick. They lived at first according to the Benedictine rule but later adopted that of the Augustinians. They were called "Apostolic Clerics of Saint Jerome," after their patron.

As patron of hermits he also gave his name to the Hieronymites, who followed the Augustinian rule as expanded by ideas from Jerome. There were originally four congregations in Italy and Spain. Confirmed as an order in 1373, they were subordinated in 1415 to a superior general in Spain.

The Minims are a mendicant order founded in Calabria in 1454 by Francis of Paula under the title of "Hermits of Saint Francis." Their rule is the Franciscan, but made more austere in regard to diet. Referred to as Paulans from their founder, they were called "Bons hommes" in France and "Fratres de Victoria" in Spain in connection with the victory over the Muslims. In 1520 they had around 450 monasteries.

The Birgittines, or Order of the Saviour, were founded by Saint Birgitta of Sweden (1303–73). She lived a happy married life with a noble to whom she bore eight children, among them Saint Catherine of Sweden. Following a pilgrimage to Santiago de Compostela (1341–42), her husband retired to a Cistercian monastery, where he died in 1344. Around this time began the "heavenly revelations," which she recorded in Swedish language and which her confessors translated into Latin. She founded the first monastery at Vadstena in 1346 and in 1349 went to Rome to secure the establishment of her order. In burning words she lashed out at the abuses in the Church and implored the Popes in the name of Christ to return to Rome. The constitutions of her foundation were confirmed by Urban V in 1370; but the definitive approval did not come until 1378, after her death, when Urban VI added them as a supplement to the Augustinian rule. Like Vadstena, the houses were to be double monasteries, both being under the direction of an abbess. For sixty nuns there were to be thirteen monks, four deacons, and eight lay brothers. The order spread quickly throughout Europe and is said to have soon comprised seventy-nine monasteries, which were of great religious and cultural importance, especially for Scandinavia. Birgitta died at Rome in 1373, after a pilgrimage to the Holy Land. She was canonized by Boniface IX in 1391.

CHAPTER 59

Theology in the Age of Transition

Nicholas of Cusa

At the point where the Middle Ages gave way to modern times there was in Nicholas of Cusa a mind which, with headstrong and obstinate will power to create a whole, compelled the antagonistic forces of his day into a "Catholic concordance" and at the same time held out the creative beginnings of a possible bridge connecting with a new age.

Nicholas was born in 1401 at Kues (Cusa) on the Moselle. He matriculated at Heidelberg as a *clericus* as early as 1416 and became bachelor of arts in 1417. In the same year he took up the study of canon law at Padua, where he became acquainted with the doctrine of consent which according to what affects all must be approved by all. At the same time he came in contact with Italian humanism and studied mathematics, physics, and astronomy. In 1423 he became *doctor decretorum.* Back home he obtained the parish of Altrich in 1425, without having received the priesthood. From Easter 1425 he lectured on canon law and studied theology at Cologne. His teacher, or rather his stimulating friend, was Heymeric de Campo, the chief protagonist of the Albertists, a strongly Platonic version of scholasticism, which gave him the intellectual treasures of pseudo-Dionysius and Raymond Lull and probably of Master Eckhart.

The discovery of twelve comedies of Plautus and of other Latin classics, his demonstration of the spuriousness of the Donation of Constantine by a critical investigation of its sources, and his doubts as to the identification of the highly esteemed Dionysius with Dionysius the Areopagite made him a pioneer of German humanism.

At Trier, he finished his *De concordantia catholica.* Originally this seems to have been projected only as a "Libellus de ecclesiastica concordantia," which was to treat in two books of the Church, her nature, her reform, and the tasks of the council. The adding of a third book on reform of the Empire produced a significant work on the all-embracing Christian concord in Church and Empire.

In the *Concordantia catholica* and in the testimonial "De auctoritate praesidendi in concilio generali" (1434), Nicholas of Cusa was a moderate conciliarist. The Roman Pontiff, who is a member of the Church, even though the highest ranking in administration, is subject to the general council." The council represents the Universal Church more truly than does the Pope alone. The Pope represents the Church only in an indefinite manner ("confuse"). Hence the Church, "for the sake of her own welfare or in urgent need, [can] dispose of the papacy at her discretion." The Pope holds the first place at the council and must be regarded as its head and judge. Hence he or his legates must be allowed to participate in the council. In fact, if he wishes to attend and is able to do so, no council can take place without him.

The unity, or *consensus,* of pope and council is for Nicholas the sign of truth. And so his sudden *volte-face,* his change from the Council of Basel to Eugene IV, was not so radical as it seemed, for the Pope offered a Council which promised unity with the East, whereas at Basel controversy and uproar became increasingly open. To leave Basel meant to decide for Pope and Council. Because unity is the proof of truth, and the Council of Basel on the other hand was working for a schism, "the Holy Spirit could not be there."

For Nicholas the unity of the Church was more and more guaranteed in her single head. "The Christian people, united to the one Shepherd of the one *Cathedra Petri* and to the one High Priest, constitutes the one Church, just as man is one because all his members are united to one head." His previous view, that the unity of the Church is the result of the orderly cooperation of the various degrees of the one priesthood and of the consent of all believers (*concordantia catholica*), was replaced, in connection with the philosophical insights of the *Docta ignorantia* (1440) in the sign of the double concept "complicatio-explicatio," by the knowledge that plurality is the unfolding (*explicatio*) of unity, which precedes everything as *complicatio*. Folded up in unity in God is everything that in the world is unfolded in plurality and differentiation. Because all things are in him as their effective and formal cause, though not in their multiplicity but in unity, he is the "coincidentia oppositorum." He, however, does not comprise the contradictories in their opposition; rather he is above every opposition. This one and first before all else is beyond our intellect.

Just as now the plural is explained only by the one, and the beneath can be understood only by the above, so the unity of the Church is based also on the one supreme head. His authority is the *complicatio* of all powers requisite for the maintenance and guidance of the Church.

Nicholas distinguishes the mystical body of Christ as the invisible Church, which is nothing other than the unfolded grace of Christ, from the visible Church, the *ecclesia coniecturalis*. The latter embraces good and bad, but it can be recognized as the Holy Church, and to some extent comprehended, by its marks. It possesses a visible head in the Pope. In him the Church is given *complicative*, and, vice versa, the Pope is in her in so far as she has developed on the basis of Peter's confession and preaching.

"The Hercules of the Eugenians" — so he was called by Aeneas Silvius Piccolomini, later Pope Pius II, — Nicholas of Cusa in the succeeding years fought for the recognition of the papal authority and at imperial and princely diets came out for the reconciliation of Pope and Empire. His exertions had their successful conclusion at the Princely Diet of Aschaffenburg in 1447, where Nicholas V obtained general recognition and the Vienna Concordat of 1448 was arranged.

He traveled through the Empire as papal legate for a year and a quarter, from Vienna to Brussels, from Magdeburg to Trier, preaching the jubilee indulgence. To effect in clergy and people a religious and moral renewal, to visit monasteries, to make peace, to summon aid against the Turks, in brief to reform the German Church and activate its forces — such was his task. The decrees published at the synods ordered prayers for Pope and Bishop at Mass, gave directions for the dignified celebration of the liturgy and the honoring of the Eucharist, forbade the founding of new confraternities, the venerating of bleeding Hosts, and the laying of an interdict in order to collect debts, attacked simoniacal intrigues in the conferring of benefices, clerical concubinage, and the disregard of the inclosure of nuns, and required in general a reform of religious orders by strict fidelity to the rule within one year. Jews were to make themselves known by special badges and thereafter they were no longer to engage in lending money to Christians. He dispensed from pilgrimage vows and ordered those thus dispensed to visit instead the Blessed Sacrament in their parish church; here divine power really lay concealed.

But the Legate did not only encounter hidden resistance. The opposition in Liège was especially serious.

If the refractory refused to change their mind, Nicholas threatened with the secular arm. In general he had few reservations in regard to calling upon political power for the sake of reform, though he must have known from his own bishopric that to allow the secular authorities to intervene within the ecclesiastical sphere was to draw a two-edged sword. In the next years monastic reform in Brixen would be tedious and finally collapse, precisely because circles unwilling to be reformed found support in the territorial nobility against the Bishop. On the other hand, Nicholas had to restore his own territorial authority as a Prince-Bishop if he wished to carry out his reform. This in turn entangled him in a disastrous political power struggle.

In these very years of controversy over his bishopric (1453–60), a time of exasperating disputes over reforms and feudal rights, over spiritual and secular judicial supremacy, which were carried on by means of force on the one side and excommunication and interdict on the other, Nicholas of Cusa found time and leisure for speculative writings such as *De visione Dei* (1453), *De Beryllo* (1458), and *De principio* (1459). The fall of Constantinople in 1453 and the impotence of divided Christianity, made clear in the event, provided Nicholas with a sad opportunity to ponder more deeply *On Peace and Unity in the Faith* (1453). In a vision he has seventeen representatives of the various nations and religions discuss the differences and similarities of all religions before the throne of God. In them is sought, in different ways and under manifold names, the one God, who remains concealed and ineffable in his true essence. The aim of this is the understanding, made possible by the mercy of God, "that amidst the diversity of religious customs there is only one religion" (chapter 1).

> To strive for exact uniformity in everything would be rather to disturb peace.... Where a uniformity cannot actually be realized, the nations may retain their own forms in the exercises of piety and ceremonies, to the extent that faith and peace are preserved. (chap. 20; chap. 17).

In all forms of divine adoration the one true God of Jesus Christ is meant and in Christianity the religious concerns of all are capable of realization. Nicholas later sought to prove this in regard to Islam.

With the pontificate of Pius II (1458–64) Nicholas of Cusa obtained the opportunity to escape from the increasingly hopeless guerilla warfare over his bishopric and to make his energies and reform will available to the entire Church. As early as the beginning of 1457 he had received from Aeneas Silvius Piccolomini, just made a Cardinal, the pressing invitation to come to Rome so that they might bear the burden of responsibility together. The future Pope wrote:

> Unacceptable is the excuse, "I am not listened to, when I urge to what is right." Fortunes change, and he who was once scorned is now especially honored. Come then, I implore you, come. For it is precisely your strength that must not languish there, inclosed in snow and dark vales. I know that there are many who wish to see, hear, and follow you, among whom you will always find me as your obedient listener and pupil.

On 30 September 1458, after the accession of Pius II, Nicholas arrived in Rome. Frustrated in his bishopric, he seemed to have come to his exile, but in reality he experienced at the side of Pius II a climax in his ecclesiastical and reform activity.

He was a member of the reform commission of cardinals, bishops, and prelates, appointed by the Pope in the autumn of 1458 to determine and report on what needed changing and reforming at the Curia.

As early as 11 December 1458, Pius II, before his departure for the Congress of Princes at Mantua, had confided the reform of the Roman clergy to Nicholas of Cusa by naming him *Legatus Urbis* and governor of the part of the Papal State south of the Apennines. The Cardinal had at once taken up the task at a synod but he was hardly successful. Failure, however, was unable to break his reform will. In order to gain a free hand with regard to France and Germany, in 1461 he recommended a council at Mantua, which should deal with crusade and reform. If as legate in Germany he had impressed upon visitors always to begin the reform of a monastery with its superior, so, according to the *Reformatio generalis,* the reform of the Universal Church should begin with the "Church of Rome and the Curia." The visitors should not even hesitate to visit the Pope. Though he is the Vicar of Christ, he is also a sinful and mortal man. The cardinals should be exemplary men and faithful advisers of the Pope, subject to no one. As a continuing council in miniature, at the Pope's disposal, the College should have a share in the government of the Church.

The general rules given to the visitors aimed to lead every member of the Church, from the baptized Christian through monk, priest, canon, and cardinal, to Pope, to the manner of life which his name signifies and which he assumed in solemn promise. Steps should especially be taken against any pluralism, which impedes the celebration of the liturgy and the care of souls, against embezzlement of the property of hospitals and parishes, against humbug on the part of indulgence dealers, against false relics and allegedly miraculous Hosts, invented for the sake of indecent profit.

> It should be sufficient for Christians to have Christ really in their churches in the Sacrament of the Eucharist. In it they have everything that they can desire for their salvation.

Nicholas sought, not radical changes, but reform, a leading back to Christ, the archetype of all Christians. "We who wish to reform all Christians can provide them with no other model for their imitation than Christ, from whom they have obtained their name." God the Father, so we read at the very beginning of the introduction to the reform treatise, has revealed himself in the Word, his beloved Son, full of grace and truth, in order to enable all who accept him to share in his life.

> The Father's only commandment is to believe in his Son and ambassador, who is his Word.... This faith bestows all sanctity, wisdom, justice, and beatitude. For he who truly believes this keeps his commandments and does not sin.... He knows that true life is found only in the promises of Christ and no one is justified whom he does not justify by the merit of his death. He can say with the Apostle that he knows only Christ, and him crucified, in whom he achieves the highest and perfect faith, the faith whereby the just man lives.

If a person seizes hold of Christ

> as the unique teacher of life, to him he gives in faith and work the figure which qualifies him for eternal life.... However, Christ must impart and give

> it.... For we are appointed out of grace to the inheritance. We can acquire it only by justice [based on] the merits of Christ.... Hence he became justice for us.... And so it is only from him that we have everything necessary for perfect bliss, whether it be grace or justice. And he is the sole mediator in whom is everything and without whom we cannot possibly be truly happy.

Justification by faith can probably not be more clearly formulated, rejection of all justification by works cannot be more firmly stated. This is especially noteworthy in a summons to reform, in which one would expect to find stress placed rather on human activity. There is no question here of any isolated expression in Nicholas. For example, there occurs in *De pace fidei* (1453): "For man's justification consists in this — that he obtains the promise on the sole ground that he believes God and hopes for the fulfillment of God's word" (chapter 17).

If it is desired to represent the Cardinal as a reformer before the Reformation because of this teaching of his on justification by faith, then it must be said simultaneously that at that time the Reformation was still a Catholic possibility.

Impressed with the stamp of a realistic scholasticism that was influenced by Platonism, Nicholas of Cusa freed himself in method from the procrustean bed of the questions, objections, and responses of the philosophy of the schools and its cult of authorities. Related to humanism in this respect as well as in his renewed connection with antiquity and in his inclination to historical criticism, on the other hand he pressed too much for a speculative grasp of being in its unity and totality to be satisfied with the world of rhetorical literature of the humanists as he had encountered these in Italy. With Nicholas the philosophy of being became a philosophy of consciousness, of knowledge, even of the knowledge of not knowing. In this reflecting of the mind upon itself, in the question of one's own subjectivity and of the personal mind seizing hold of and touching upon everything, Nicholas probably most unambiguously showed himself to be a modern thinker. Furthermore, he took up the initial steps, later on so significant, toward mathematical and scientific thought in late scholasticism and in the Byzantine mathematicians and carried them forward creatively.

Above all, Nicholas of Cusa was a churchman, for whom the receptacle of all philosophy, all exertions of the mind, was theology; in the final analysis they had to serve to conduct man and history back to their divine origin. On the other hand he also again and again withdrew himself from the leisure of speculation in order to intervene in a responsible fashion in the exasperating real world of Church and Empire, though here compromises were at most to be expected. He stood in the "autumn of the Middle Ages," but also in the spring of the modern world. He proved that it would have been possible for the latter to come forth in continuity with the Middle Ages and in harmony with the Church and that, accordingly, the revolution was as yet not an unconditional historical necessity. It was all the more portentous that, after Pius II, began the series of Renaissance Popes in the bad sense and the papacy long refused to have anything to do with the reform that was so urgently demanded.

Johannes von Wesel

Compared with Nicholas of Cusa, the men who, like Johannes von Wesel, Johannes von Goch, and Wessel Gansfort, have been called "reformers before the Reformation," seem small in regard to religious depth, reform *élan,* and inner proximity to Luther, unless the essence of the reform movement is understood simply as criticism of the Church. As has already been said, the fifteenth century was characterized by a looking back to tradition. Aquinas and the *via antiqua* experienced a renaissance. People were weary of the extravagant sophistries of the *via moderna* and found it painful that what had been achieved should again and again be questioned.

This explains the fate of a mind, hardly original and rather mediocre, condemned by the Inquisition and regarded by later generations as a "reformer before the Reformation": Johannes Rucherath von Oberwesel. From 1441 he studied at Erfurt, where he became master of arts in 1445 and doctor of theology in 1456. Immediately afterward he was rector of the University. From his Erfurt period came his commentaries on the *Physics* of Aristotle and on *The Sentences* of Peter Lombard, which offered a simple and shallow Ockhamism. "The infinite mass of learned ballast drives out the spirit at the same time" (G. Ritter). For unknown reasons Johannes von Wesel went to Worms, where in 1460 he was a canon. In the spring of 1461 he took up at Basel a professorship in theology that had been offered him. But he soon (1463) returned to Worms as cathedral preacher. As an author he directed an often bold and challenging criticism to Church life and institutions, but there is no trace of a deeper religious concern, not to mention the proclaiming of a new, reforming sense. Decisive for him were the Ockhamist viewpoints of the sovereignty of God and the freedom of man. This caused him above all to place limits to the legislative authority of the Church. He clearly expounds the difference between the divine and the merely ecclesiastical law. God bestows grace in absolute freedom; but he can even grant it when man does not do "what is in him." Grace places man in a position to gain eternal life. God acts directly in the Sacraments if the priestly minister effects the sign. Johannes von Wesel rejects indulgences because the temporal punishments for sin have to be endured and only God can dispose of the merits of the saints. According to God's determination, the Church's power of the keys refers only to the guilt of sin. To conclude from the *de facto* instituting of indulgences by the Church a justification of the practice is unlawful, for the Church, like councils, can err. Only the Church of Christ, contained in the Universal Church but not empirically demonstrable, is holy and immaculate. According to Matthew 28:20, Christ himself is always with his Church and guiding her. He needs no vicar, and he alone, in the final analysis, has the power of the keys. The Pope is the executor of his commands. Ultimately authoritative is the truth recorded in Holy Scripture. This truth is authority; in comparison with it knowledge acquired by reason and revelation by means of miracles have only a secondary importance. What is necessary for salvation is contained in the Bible.

According to Johannes von Wesel, a scriptural proof of transubstantiation cannot be given. Though, like Ockham, he inclined to consubstantiation, also like Ockham he held to the substantial change as being the teaching of the Church.

And he adhered to the Ockhamist school also in the doctrine of original sin. With Anselm he saw its essence in the absence of the justice of the original state of man, with no further injuring of nature which would be transmitted by procreation. Because original sin is thus the mere lack of something not of itself belonging to man, Johannes von Wesel could designate it as a "nothing"; but this does not imply that he denied it. Apart from the denial of the *Filioque,* for which he saw no scriptural basis, in his trial for heresy he could not really be charged with any formal heresies, but only with brazenly formulated opinions which had already been expounded for decades. But is was fatal to him that, he brought everything into the pulpit before the people and brought suspicion upon himself through his relations with the Hussites.

In 1477 he was dismissed from his posts as cathedral preacher and canon at Worms, but found temporarily a situation as rector of the cathedral at Mainz; however, he was soon again accused of heresy and of relations with the Hussites. In February 1479 he had to defend himself before a tribunal of the Inquisition, consisting of professors from the Universities of Heidelberg, Cologne, and Mainz and of members of the Mainz cathedral chapter. The presidency was exercised by the Cologne Dominican and Inquisitor Gerard von Elten, together with the Dominican Jakob Sprenger, the future coauthor of the *Malleus Maleficarum* (Cologne 1489). After almost fourteen days of discussion, when he had recanted nineteen propositions that had been branded as heretical and his books had been burned, he was condemned on 21 February 1479 to life-imprisonment among the Mainz Augustinians. There he soon died, probably in 1481, after reception of the Sacraments.

Wessel Gansfort

Wessel Gansfort (1419–89) came from the world of the *devotio moderna.* Born at Groningen, he studied there with the Brothers of the Common Life and then taught at Zwolle (1432–49). His profound uneasiness drove him into the world. He studied first at Cologne (1449) and then at Heidelberg (1456–57); in 1458 he was in Paris and around 1470 he went to Italy. He zealously applied himself to languages, learning Greek, Hebrew, Aramaic, and Arabic. But he found as little satisfaction in early humanism as he had in scholasticism. He had started out as a champion of Cologne Neo-Thomism; then, one after another, he took up all the schools of the existing universities and learned to scorn them all together. Externally he included himself in the Ockhamist school, without sacrificing his independence to a professorial chair. He was critical of the authority of Pope and council, of the Church's power of binding and loosing, of indulgences and purgatory, of the efficacy of the Sacraments. Only Scripture is binding. The apostolic traditions interpret the content of the canonical Scriptures. We believe "with" the Church, not "in" the Church.

It cannot be said that Wessel Gansfort in his teaching overstepped the limits of what was then possible within the Church. He actually proved how much latitude there was in the fifteenth century or how extensive was the dogmatic uncertainty. After long years of traveling — he had to leave Paris in 1475, probably because of the royal prohibition of nominalism — he returned to his point of departure, the world of the *devotio moderna.* From 1477 to 1482 he lived on the Agnetenberg, enjoying the protection of Bishop David of Utrecht. In his last years he devoted himself at Groningen to study and meditation.

Though a layman, he composed for the pious canons of Agnetenberg a series of treatises as an introduction to prayer and meditation. He was concerned about the encounter with Christ, especially with him crucified, in the faith given by God. "God has been pleased to impart justice to those who believe, to bestow on them a greater righteousness and integrity than the justice of the angels." Also in the Eucharist Christ wants to be received in faith. Hence a purely spiritual communion in faith and love can produce more fruit than a sacramental reception which is lacking in disposition, in a real spiritual hunger and thirst. Through his introduction to meditation Wessel Gansfort became one of the teachers of the *devotio moderna,* especially influencing John Mombaer (d. 1501) and his *Rosetum.* Luther felt a spiritual relationship with him. In 1522 Luther published *Farrago rerum theologicarum,* a collection of essays, and remarked in the introduction that the malicious might be able to think that he had taken everything from Wessel Gansfort, "so much were both minds in accord" (*WA,* 10, II, 317). But we have to see in Wessel Gansfort a connecting link from the *devotio moderna* to criticism of the Church and to the spiritualistic Bible Christianity of Erasmus.

Gabriel Biel

Gabriel Biel (d. 1495) represents the direct connection between late mediaeval theology and piety and the modern age. He ranks as the "last of the scholastics" of the Middle Ages and exercised a strong influence on both Luther and Luther's Catholic opponents. At the same time as Luther was doing so at Erfurt, his future opponent John Eck was lecturing at Freiburg (1509–10) on *The Sentences* of Peter Lombard, following Biel.

Gabriel Biel was born at Speyer around 1410. As morning sacristan of Sankt Peter there, he matriculated at Heidelberg in 1432, becoming master of arts in 1438. In 1442–43 and again in 1452 he was on the theological faculty at Erfurt and in 1453 on that at Cologne. He got to know not only Ockham at Erfurt but also Aquinas and Albert at Cologne. At the beginning of the sixties he became vicar and cathedral preacher at Mainz. Around 1468 he joined the Brothers of the Common Life at Marienthal in the Rheingau and soon became provost of Sankt Markus, their house at Butzbach. From 1476 he collaborated with Count Eberhard the Bearded in the Württemberg Church reform initiated by the latter, and in 1479 he became provost of Eberhard's foundation, the monastery at Urach. On 22 November 1484 he assumed a professorship at the University of Tübingen, founded in 1477; he made possible there the breakthrough of the *via moderna.* Following his retirement in 1491, he directed the new house of the Brothers of the Common Life, Sankt Peter at Einsiedel in the Schönbuch near Tübingen, and there he died on 7 December 1495.

Gabriel Biel was not especially independent. He communicated to his epoch the nominalist theology in a form supplemented and toned down in accord with a pastoral outlook. His works are compilations, very popular because of their practical usefulness.

The commentary on *The Sentences* is a summary of and addition to Ockham's *Quaestiones in IV libros Sententiarum* and hence is also called the *Epitome* or *Collectorium.* Biel finished the first book before 1 May 1486 and the third on 13 August 1488, while the fourth probably preoccupied him until his death.

But the crucial point of Biel's work is found in the religious and pastoral sphere, in his sermons and his explanation of the Canon of the Mass. His lengthy sermons prove a high opinion of the dignity and importance of the word of God. He who does not devote a proper attention to preaching is no less guilty than one who out of carelessness lets the body of Christ fall to the ground. Preaching is really more important than the Blessed Sacrament, for the former leads to faith and penitence and hence is necessary for salvation, whereas the latter only increases grace. The *Canonis missae Expositio,* completed on 4 November 1488, is a lecture, closely dependent on the discourses which his friend, Master Egeling Becker of Braunschweig, had delivered at Mainz at the close of the 1450s. Biel claims he omitted only a little but "added or changed some." A comparison of both texts shows "that more than three-fourths of the *Expositio* belongs to Master Egeling" (A. Franz). This work, at the reading of which Luther had felt his heart bleed from emotion, stands between scholastic theology and pastoral theology.

In his theology Biel closely follows Ockham. But he does not propound it so defiantly and takes care that its philosophical permeation does not undermine faith. Throughout, he has rather the actual way of salvation in mind. *De potentia dei absoluta* God can accept anyone for salvation without *caritas creata,* but conversely he does not have to bestow eternal life on anyone who possesses *caritas.* He is absolutely free and not bound by any form or available gift. Thus Biel, like Ockham, seeks to exclude any Pelagianism. The divine will has no superior rule to which it must conform itself. A thing is right and just because God wills it to be so. He can do something which in itself is unjust. If he were to do it, then it would be just for it to happen. One can rightly speak here of a "divine caprice." But actually God has bound himself. Since Biel now discusses the actual way of salvation in more detail and treats the question of preparation for grace by applying the proposition: "God does not deny grace to one who does his best," he succumbs to the danger of Semipelagianism. For now the initiative lies with man. *Facere quod in se est* is understood as natural activity with the exclusion of actual grace. Man for his part is in the position of doing his first duty, and God, because he has so bound himself, is obliged to give his grace to everyone who does his best. Thus, grace is "not the root but the fruit of the preparatory good works," God's reply to man's free act. Here Gabriel Biel finds himself opposing Gregory of Rimini, who credits man's free will with too little (II *Sent.,* d. 28, q. 1, A). Man does his best if he loves God above all. As Ockham had already taught, this love lies in the possibility of man's natural powers. All the more must man struggle for it or be anxious about possessing it. Accordingly, in such a strongly Pelagian system anxiety over salvation is not less but greater. "The dialectic between fear and love is [also] the general topic of Biel's preaching" (Oberman). Thus Gabriel Biel became Luther's chief opponent in the latter's "Disputation against Scholastic Theology" of 4 September 1517, in which Luther sought to prove that modern theology was Pelagian. "All the antitheses which dealt directly with the theological theme of the disputation were either directly taken from Biel's *Collectorium* or at least are to be found there" (Grane).

In his explanation of the Canon of the Mass Biel emphasizes that the Mass is not a repetition of the sacrifice once directly offered by Christ on the cross, but a calling to mind and representation of it. The related concepts, *memoria, recordatio,* and *repraesentatio,* are not explained with regard to content. There is no question in all this of an identity with the sacrifice of the cross but of a difference in the manner of offering. The Mass is a symbol of the sacrifice of the cross, a recalling of the historical past as a psychological representation. The "moment of truth" and the unity of the sacrifice are based on the sacrificial gift which is offered by the Church in the Mass. Since the Mass is "only" a symbol, in value it is far inferior to the sacrifice of the cross. Biel understands the "once for all" of Hebrews (7, 27; 9, 11; 10, 10) to refer to the bloody sacrifice on the cross and not to the daily sacrifice under the appearances of bread and wine. Hence it is unexplained how the Church can have a sacrifice without the unity of the New Testament sacrifice being jeopardized — a question which, a few decades later, would come decisively between Luther and the Church.

Chapter 60

The Jews in Mediaeval Christendom

Despite national and political variety, Western Christendom was, until the beginning of modern times, united in the one faith in Christ in the one Church. In day-to-day consciousness the world as a reality determined and formed by religion was identical with Christianity. The Jews were an exception, constituting a special religious and national group and, as such, exposed to all prejudices and resentments. Unintelligible rites, not open to everyone, increased the mistrust and dread. In the abstract Judaism was far closer to Christianity than was paganism. According to the mosaics in the apses of Christian basilicas, the Christian congregation even in the early Middle Ages regarded itself as the Church of Jews (Jerusalem) and pagans (Bethlehem). In crucifixion scenes in manuscript illuminations and on the portals or in the narthex of Gothic cathedrals the synagogue proclaimed through the majesty of her aspect the dignity of the Chosen People, while the blindfold and the broken lance indicated that this people missed its destiny and in its obstinacy called down the blood of the Messiah upon itself and its children. The less this understanding was dominated, in the course of the Middle Ages, by the Pauline message that God had not retracted his promise to Israel but rather that finally this nation, whose "rejection had brought the reconciliation of the world," would be saved as a whole, and the less people took to heart with Gregory the Great the reflection that the death of Jesus was caused by all mankind, the accusation of deicide became the root of a religiously determined anti-Semitism.

Patristic theology established the notion of Jewish servitude. According to Augustine, who was here following Tertullian and Justin, the older (Esau) shall, according to Genesis 25:23, serve the younger (Jacob), and the Jewish people, having forfeited its inheritance, had become the slave of the younger Christian people. This idea was adopted by mediaeval theologians, including Rupert of Deutz (d. 1129), Peter the Venerable (d. 1156), Bernard of Clairvaux (d. 1153), and Thomas Aquinas (d. 1274). The Jews were scattered among the nations as witnesses to the prophecies and are reserved for the end. They are "bookkeepers of the Christians," as slaves they carry the Holy Scripture for them but without understanding it. Thus the pagans cannot assert that the Christians had invented the prophecies. These theologians envisaged only individual conversions; the people as a whole will not be converted and will persist in its blindness and slavery till the end of the world as witness of Christ's death, and hence no one is allowed to do violence to it.

At first this "servitude of the Jews" was valid only in the spiritual and not the legal sense. Decisions in Roman Law in regard to the Jews, made last of all under Justinian (527–65), were transmitted into the Middle Ages and were not expressly abolished. According to these, religious toleration was basically accorded them, but it was subjected to various restrictions. Conversion to Judaism was forbidden. The Jews were free and could possess property, but they were excluded from public office and military service and could not keep Christian slaves or domestics. At first in the Middle Ages they could freely engage in commerce and industry and did not have to reside in ghettos. Perhaps the common practice of their religion in a hostile environment induced the Jews on their own to live in special residential quarters. But it was only in the late Middle Ages that the Jewish quarter became a ghetto, walled in and sealed off by gates. In the early Middle Ages Christians and Jews lived together on relatively friendly terms. Bishops and kings issued letters of safe-conduct for the Jews, who in return paid fees.

Shortly afterward severe persecutions of Jews occurred in connection with the crusades. As early as 1063 when aid was being hurried to the Christians of Spain in their war against Islam, *en route* attacks were made on Jews. Pope Alexander II censured the blind passion which then raged against those whom the divine goodness perhaps destined for salvation. And the same Pope cited greed as the motive for persecution of Jews. Frightful excesses took place when the crusaders from northern France moved up the Rhine toward the southeast. In the Jews people saw "enemies of Christ" who had to be liquidated in one's own country before the Holy Land could be set free. The chronicler Ekkehard of Aura, who took part in the crusade in 1101, reported:

> In all cities through which they went they either completely exterminated or forced baptism on the remnants of the wicked Jews, those internal enemies of the Church. But very many of them returned to their former faith, as the dog to his vomit.

These excesses became still worse in the next crusades. The Cistercian Radulf, who was inciting religious fanatics and the economically discontented to murder the "enemies of the Christian religion," encountered opposition at Mainz from Saint Bernard of Clairvaux. According to the latter, the Jews must be neither persecuted nor banished; for they are living witnesses of our redemption, who set the Lord's sufferings before our eyes.

Bishops and Emperors undertook the protection of Jews and in times of persecution placed their castles and strongholds at their disposal. They punished extravagances. The public peace promulgated at Mainz in 1103 subjected any attack on the life and property of Jews to the threat of punishment, including the death penalty. On the occasion of the pogroms in connection with the Third Crusade, Frederick I issued an edict whereby the hand that injured a Jew was to be cut off and murder of a Jew was to be punished by death. This Emperor considered the Jews as belonging to the imperial fisc.

In the thirteenth century the legal situation of the Jews deteriorated. Their "servitude," originally understood as spiritual, became legal, and, as "slaves of the imperial chamber," the Jews were placed under a particular law. The privilege of the Emperor Frederick II for Vienna in 1237 states:

> Faithful to the obligations of a Catholic prince, we exclude the Jews from public office so that they may not exploit the power of office to oppress Christians. For the imperial authority from time immemorial has imposed perpetual servitude on the Jews as punishment for Jewish crime.

As slaves of the chamber the Jews and their belongings were the possession of the Emperor, taxable by him and at the same time under his protection. Protection of the Jews thus became a source of revenue, which, with the decay of the central power, was claimed by bishops and princes also or was regularly sold or pawned to them. In the fourteenth century the right to protect the Jews became more and more an object of traffic.

The Jews' route into bondage from the thirteenth century onward was accompanied by fearful pogroms, for which the charge of ritual murder and of desecration of the Blessed Sacrament supplied the pretext. According to this the Jews were said to have given vent to their hatred of Christians by outraging the Host and innocent members of Christ's body.

Besides religious fanaticism and naked greed, which afforded a pretext for the pillaging of Jewish property or for the cancelling of debts, superstition led to this charge of murder. From Innocent IV (1243–54) the Popes had repeatedly opposed this, but their voices, like the voices of Emperors and bishops, went unheeded. They could not prevent persons "from maliciously charging the Jews with murder whenever a corpse was discovered" or from

> stirring fury against them by these and many other atrocity stories, depriving them of all their property without accusation, confession and conviction . . . against God and justice, oppressing them with hunger, imprisonment, and many tortures and torments . . . and condemning as many as possible to a shameful death. (Innocent IV)

In the often renewed bull "Sicut Iudaeis" the Popes assured the Jews of freedom of religion, forbade compulsory baptism, and under threat of excommunication demanded unqualified respect for property and life. Thus at the end of the Middle Ages the Jews in Italy were relatively very secure.

However, at most the Church tolerated the Jews; in other respects she restricted them as far as possible. There could be only one synagogue in one place and this had to be as unassuming as possible. Ecclesiastical regulations which sought to prevent endangering Christians by means of Jewish teaching and the association of Jews and Christians, above all in mixed marriages, contributed much to the hatred of Jews. The Fourth Lateran Council (1215) decreed that "Jews and Saracens of both sexes in every Christian country and at all times should be distinguished in public from other persons by their dress, especially since Numbers 15:37–41 has already imposed this on them." These prescriptions in regard to dress were not applied in Germany, however, before the fifteenth century. Cardinal Nicholas of Cusa had them prescribed during his legatine journey of 1451–52 by the provincial councils of Salzburg, Bamberg, Magdeburg, Mainz, and Cologne as canonical regulation and as the legal usage in Rome and at the same time had all money-lending by Jews to Christians forbidden.

As a result of the remonstrances of the Emperor and the Archbishop of Salzburg this last prescription was annulled by the Pope, because it was too harmful to their private interests. For money-lending, to which the Jews were reduced after they had been excluded from the wholesale trade and in the late Middle Ages also from acquiring real estate, was thoroughly exploited for the public treasury by the Emperor and the princes, not excluding the bishops. These last often determined the excessive interest which branded the Jews as usurers.

In the fifteenth century the Jews were almost completely annihilated in the Rhineland and many cities of South Germany. As early as the mid-fourteenth century frightful pogroms had occurred throughout Germany. The occasion was, among other things, the Black Death of 1348–49, which was attributed to the poisoning of wells by the Jews. The real cause was envy and greed and the driving forces were often the gilds. In Basel the city council was forced to burn the Jews, and in Strasbourg the majority of the approximately 2,000 Jews were delivered to the flames in their cemetery. This example was followed at Speyer, Worms, Cologne, and many other places. At Mainz, which had the largest Jewish community in Germany, the Jews, after a fruitless defense, surrendered themselves to the fire. Although many cities again allowed them to take up residence and even exerted themselves to this end for the sake of financial gain, the Jewish communities never recovered after the Black Death. They were unable to cope with financial demands from three quarters: king, territorial prince, and city. Controversy between bishop and city council in regard to the protection of Jews led to new expulsions of Jews at the end of the fourteenth and the beginning of the fifteenth century. Many of the Jews who were banished from western and southern Germany settled in lands east of the Elbe and in Italy.

Jews were expelled also from England, France, and especially Spain. After the fall of Granada in 1492 the *reyes católicos* enacted a law whereby everyone who did not attend proselytizing sermons and was unwilling to receive baptism within four months had to emigrate. Some 50,000 may have avoided loss of home and property by means of baptism, but the majority left Spain. Feigned baptisms, however, were the source of new misgivings and of suspicions which went so far as to call for Inquisition procedures.

The Popes of the Renaissance, especially those of the Medici family, were kindly disposed to the Jews, and Leo X took Reuchlin under his protection. But a reaction began under Julius II when there was mention of a condemnation of the Talmud. It was completed by Paul IV, who in the bull of 14 July 1555 confined the Jews of Rome and of all other cities of the Papal State to ghettos, forbade them to possess real estate, and forced them to wear the yellow "Jewish hat."

Jewish Philosophy and Theology

Of special significance for the intellectual life were the Jews of Provence and Spain, where Christian and Muslim cultures were in contact and where especially Jewish and Arabic intellectual endeavors were in competition. Not only Arabic philosophers such as Averroes (d. 1198) but also Jews handed on to the West the writings and intellectual legacy of Aristotle.

The most significant representative of Jewish theology and philosophy in the Middle Ages was Moses Maimonides, who was born at Córdoba in 1135 and died at Cairo in 1204. He sought by means of commentaries on the Talmud and systematic presentations (*Recapitulation of the Law*) to explain Jewish doctrine and make the simple Jew acquainted with it. In his chief philosophical world, *Guide of the Wavering,* he wanted to demonstrate the reasonableness of the faith of their fathers to those of his fellows who had been made unsure of it by Arabic philosophy. Philosophical knowledge, whose highest authority is Aristotle, is independent of revealed faith; it does not contradict it but rather helps to grasp it more deeply. Himself strongly affected by the Arabic Aristotelian philosophy, Maimonides acquired an influence on thinkers and mystics such as Albertus Magnus, Thomas Aquinas, Master Eckhart, and Nicholas of Cusa.

Chasdai ben Abraham Crescas (1340–1412) in his *Light of God* definitely rejected Moses Maimonides and his Aristotelianism. For Crescas God is especially the supreme love and not the supreme reason. The route to God leads, for man, not by way of knowledge but of love.

Opposed to the rationalism of a Maimonides was likewise the *Cabala,* or tradition, a mystic and theosophic secret doctrine of Judaism. It originated in Provence between 1150 and 1250, spread to Spain, and, following the expulsion of 1492, became a national religious movement. Its chief work, *Zohar* ("Brilliance") must be regarded as composed by Moses de León (d. 1305) from Castile. According to it, the hidden God ("En Soph," the infinite, the first cause) reveals and unfolds himself in the ten "Sephirot" (spheres). Through them, as though through doors, the devout one, by proper fulfillment of the law, prayer, and contemplation, can gain access to the mystery of God and contribute to the restoration of the fallen world. In itself the world was created according to the model of the Sephirot and hence is a mirror of the divine wisdom revealing itself in them. Man and world are evil only to the extent that they have broken the connection with divine love and grace and depend upon themselves alone. The expanding of the *Cabala* from an esoteric teaching to a national movement after 1492 gave a new stimulus to messianism and contributed to intensification of internal life, but it also led to magic and to abuses of superstition. Beyond Judaism, the *Cabala* also influenced humanists such as Pico della Mirandola (d. 1494) and Johannes Reuchlin (d. 1522).

Efforts to Convert the Jews

With all the persecuting of the Jews, efforts were made time and again to win them to Christian truth. One means of this was the religious discussion. Far too often, it is true, this became an argument or dispute in which the important thing was to vanquish the opponent rather than to understand and win him over. Occasionally, especially in the earlier Middle Ages, there were real discussions. The most celebrated example of such a conversion was Hermann Judaeus. He had money transactions with the Archbishop of Cologne and thereby came into contact with Abbot Rupert of Deutz. This led to exhaustive religious discussions. After severe struggles he had himself baptized, became a Premonstratensian at Kappenberg, and finally was made first prior of Scheda, founded in 1143. In his account of his conversion he laments that Christians' hatred for Jews kept Jews from belief in Christ.

From the thirteenth century ecclesiastical authorities regarded religious discussions between Jews and Christians with an ever growing distrust. Jews were often ahead of Christians in a knowledge of the Old Testament, and they did not find it difficult at all to refute irresponsible charges by means of the Talmud. Hence the Trier Provincial Council of 1227 forbade uneducated priests ("sacerdotes illiterati") to engage in such conversations. Alexander IV's prohibition of disputes by the laity with heretics, which in 1298 became a part of the common law, covered also colloquies with Jews. Rules of this sort were not intended to prevent disputations in which persons who had studied theology and clerics familiar with Hebrew and with the Talmud took part and which held out the prospect of demonstrating the superiority of the Christian faith.

Polemical writings were often not real dialogues, even though they were often so called. The Jewish participants were for the most part invented in order to demonstrate the truth of the Christian faith by their objections. The farther we get from the early Middle Ages, the more inconsiderate, contemptuous, and ironical becomes the tone of the discussion.

Mediaeval theologians and canonists forbade Jews to attend Christian worship. For Thomas Aquinas it was not fitting that infidels and Jews should look at the sacred Host (*S. th.*, III, q. 80, a. 4). Jews were, however, allowed to hear sermons.

If the number of converts remained extremely slight, the explanation is not to be sought only in the curious missionary methods or lack of a genuine missionary spirit in accord with the Gospel among Christians nor in the loyalty and love of the Jews for the faith of their ancestors and their tradition. Not the least important reason is the fact that their conversion was opposed to the financial interests of the princes, not excluding the bishops, and these made it almost impossible by legal measures. The source of revenue which every Jew represented on the basis of the right of protection and especially of the cameral servitude dried up with his baptism. To balance matters converts were to renounce their property.

Naturally, this total loss of property kept many from being baptized. That from Alexander III in 1179 the Popes took measures against this practice and threatened excommunication for those who caused converts to lose their inheritances or confiscated their property seems to have had little effect. The Council of Constance forbade under excommunication the seizing of the goods of the newly converted.

CHAPTER 61

German Humanism

Much more so than south of the Alps, in Germany humanism was a matter of education, the concern of scholars and restricted circles. Hence it appears more independent in comparison with the general cultural movement of the Renaissance, of which it was actually the effect in the field of literary culture, language, and education. Indeed, German princes and German cities also made use of the writers, jurists, and medical men trained by the new lay education, but this did not result in a Renaissance state or a Renaissance society as in Italy, or a corresponding political theory similar to that of Machiavelli. In regard to German territory one cannot speak of a "Renaissance culture" but of German humanism. The connection with antiquity was not so direct here; there was no unbroken continuity. Therefore the encounter with antiquity was also not so elementary but rather the object of the educational endeavor, and the temptation to paganism was less real than in Italy. In art Gothic was so deeply rooted and still so alive that the new style had a difficult time establishing itself.

Already at the Council of Constance (1414–18) and especially at Basel (1431–49) closer contacts were made with Italian humanism. The new education had its first center, not at the universities, but in the chanceries of princely courts and cities, the living quarters of scholars, the monasteries, and a number of city schools. The universities were too institutionalized and too dominated by the traditional scholasticism. The liberal arts were above all preparatory stages for the other sciences, especially theology. Little wonder that homeless poets and *rhetores,* who as itinerant teachers gave only occasional lectures and courses, became the most active opponents of scholasticism. It was not until the turn of the century that special chairs were established within the faculty of arts or even special courses in poetry were given, as at Vienna under the direction of Conrad Celtis (1459–1508). This "German arch-humanist," as David Frederick Strauss termed him, the vintner's son, Conrad Bickel of Wipfeld near Würzburg, was crowned at Nürnberg in 1487 by the Emperor Frederick III with the laurel of the poet, the first German to be so honored. In the course of his restless wandering he founded learned societies in many places, such as Cracow, Prague, Bratislava, Buda, Heidelberg (1491), and Vienna (1497). At Vienna he also established, at the request of the Emperor Maximilian I, a college of poetry and mathematics in 1502, and as its president he had the right of conferring the poet's laurel. With his edition of the *Germania* of Tacitus and the discovery of the *Tabula Peutingeriana,* of the works of Roswitha of Gandersheim, and of the Barbarossa epic *Ligurinus,* Celtis laid the foundation for the study of German history and antiquities. He is an early example of the manner in which the German humanists, in a sort of hate-love for Italy, which had handed on to them the treasures of ancient civilization, came to extol extravagantly the value of German nationality and of German history in order to give the lie to the charge of barbaric origin. His polemic against abuses in the Church, against indulgence fraud and "stinking cowls," was conditioned by the struggle against the foreign spiritual domination and material exploitation by the Roman Curia.

A break with the Church never entered his mind. Above all, what the circle of the initiated was free to choose to do and think should remain forbidden to "the people."

The men who in Italy became enthusiastic over antiquity, its language, art, and way of life, and sought to pass on these treasures to their countrymen were first in the circles of the patrician class of the cities. Through the stimulation they provided and their work the Free Cities of South Germany became Centers of humanism.

The strongly pedagogical character of German humanism is made clear in a group of scholars from the Netherlands and Westphalia, who were often closely connected with the *devotio moderna.* The Frisian Rudolf Agricola (1444–85) had studied philosophy at Erfurt, Cologne, and Louvain in the traditional way, then had concentrated on humanistic studies in Italy, and finally in 1484 went to Heidelberg. Here he delivered talks and lectures in connection with the University, learned Hebrew, and developed a program for the reform of university studies. He himself never sacrificed his freedom as a man of letters to a set teaching assignment, regarded marriage as an intolerable restraint, and even considered his obligation to his benefactor, Bishop Dalberg of Worms, as a grievous slavery.

Alexander Hegius (1433–98) learned Greek from Agricola. According to his pupil Erasmus, Hegius raised the school at Deventer from a barbaric educational establishment to a humanistic school. He was one of the early Christian humanists, who emphatically sought the association of scholarship and religion. He considered any "knowledge injurious which [was] gained at the cost of integrity."

The patriotic tendency in German humanism found a congenial environment especially in Alsace. In addition to the pleasure derived from collecting the antiquarian and historical evidence of the German past and criticism of the Roman Curia, here in the west the resistance to French claims afforded a special stimulus to enthusiasts for German greatness and the declaration of national interests. The poet and journalist Sebastian Brant (1457–1521), born in Strasbourg, who had served in his native city as legal adviser and clerk from 1500, was still strongly attached to scholasticism. In popular legal collections in religious poems, and in moral treatises he developed a heavily didactic method. He became famed for his *Narrenschiff* (1494), in which, in popular language, he provided a mirror of the failings and vices of all contemporary classes and professions.

The Alsatians Geiler von Kaysersberg (1445–1510), Sebastian Brant, Thomas Murner, James Wimpheling, and Beatus Rhenanus (1485–1547) are to be regarded as representatives of a moralizing humanism, which was concerned not only for the reform of the Church but equally for the maintaining of the old order.

The anticlercial spirit and radical criticism, aloof and sarcastic, gained the firmest foothold in the humanist circle at Erfurt.

The occasion for open war against scholasticism and the hollow ecclesiasticism was provided by the Reuchlin dispute. Johannes Reuchlin (d. 1522) had, while pursuing studies at Paris and Basel in 1474, learned Greek through association with Byzantine emigrants, and, after 1482, Hebrew also from Jews in Italy. Through his *Rudimenta linguae Hebraicae* (1506) he became the founder of Hebrew linguistics in Germany. He took great pains with the study of the *Cabala*. In 1482 he entered the service of Count Eberhard V of Württemberg as a jurist, accompanied him to Italy, and served him as adviser and agent. From 1499 he lived at Stuttgart as a private scholar and was acting as a judge of the Swabian League (1502–13) when his name became the war-cry of the younger humanists in the struggle against scholasticism.

The convert's zeal of the ex-Jew, Johannes Pfefferkorn, baptized at Cologne in 1507, was not satisfied with working for the conversion of his former co-religionists by writings only. In 1500 he secured an imperial order for the confiscation of all Jewish works of a theological content. In an opinion sent to the Emperor in 1510 Reuchlin proposed that only those Jewish writings should be destroyed which contained clear defamation of Christianity. The Talmud and the *Cabala* could be used to support the Christian faith. Against this Pfefferkorn wrote the *Handspiegel*, to which Reuchlin replied with the *Augenspiegel*. Meanwhile, the theological faculty of Cologne had become involved in the question. In the Dominican Inquisitor Jakob von Hoogstraeten (1460–1527) an important man sided with Pfefferkorn. He declared the *Augenspiegel* heretical and instituted a process against Reuchlin. The Pope referred it to the Bishop of Speyer. The humanist was acquitted at this tribunal and silence was imposed on his opponents (1514), but Hoogstraeten appealed to the Pope.

In the meantime attention was less centered on Jewish writings, for in Reuchlin the humanists saw themselves and the new style of thought and scholarship attacked. As proof of his integrity, Reuchlin in 1514 published under the title *Clarorum virorum epistolae* letters which the most illustrious minds of the day had written to him. The preface was written by his great-nephew and pupil, Philip Melanchthon. More attention was attracted the next year by another collection of letters, the *Epistolae obscurorum virorum* (1515–17), addressed to Master Ortwinus Gratius, spokesman of the Cologne scholastics. These "letters of obscure men" are fictitious and composed in barbarous "kitchen Latin." They were supposed to make Reuchlin's opponents look ridiculous and to present them as uneducated and hypocritical. Ultimately all monks appeared as stupid, vain, untruthful, and lewd, and theologians got their delight in empty and ridiculous subtleties. In coarse and obscene humor the Church and what is sacred were exposed to ridicule, along with the orders, relics, and indulgences. Here humanism stood in hostility to the Church, but this hostility was originally foreign to it. The proceedings against Reuchlin were long drawn out and were finally affected by the case against Luther. Hence the *Augenspiegel* was condemned under Leo X in 1520. Nevertheless, Reuchlin, who was active in his last years as professor of Greek and Hebrew at Ingolstadt (1520–21) and Tübingen (1521–22), remained loyal to the ancient Church. He died at Stuttgart on 30 June 1522.

German humanism reached its zenith in Desiderius Erasmus. The second illegitimate son of the priest Rotger Gerard, he was born at Rotterdam on 28 October 1466 (or 1469). At about the age of fourteen he lost his parents. The taint of illegitimacy, which he never overcame, and the lack of family and home contribute much to make his restlessness, his suspicious withdrawal, his fear of committing himself, his sensitivity, and his need to be accepted understandable.

His schooling at Deventer and 's-Hertogenbosch was marked by the spirit of the *devotio moderna.* He claims that he was forced by his guardian to enter the Augustinian monastery at Steyn near Gouda (1486–88). However, his enthusiastic friendship with a former fellow student from Deventer and the opportunity for abundant reading of the ancient and patristic authors at first reconciled him to the monastery. Jerome became his ideal as a synthesis of Christianity and classical culture. Later (1496) he adopted the name of Jerome's friend, Desiderius. Soon after his ordination to the priesthood on 25 April 1492, Erasmus became secretary of Henry von Bergen, Bishop of Cambrai. The trip to Italy, which he had hoped for as the Bishop's companion, did not materialize, but the Bishop made it possible for him to study at Paris from the autumn of 1495. The barbarous severity at the Collège Montaigu pleased Erasmus as little as did scholasticism and its "barbarous" Latin. His humanist writings, which were printed later, *Antibarbari* (1520), *Adagia* (1500), *Colloquia* (1518), and others,took form in these years. Following a wandering life Erasmus went to England in 1499. This first stop there was of decisive importance, for in men such as John Colet (1466–1519), Dean of St. Paul's at London, Thomas More (1478–1535), and John Fisher (1469–1535), he met a Christian humanism and a theology based on the Bible and the Church Fathers. His enthusiasm found expression in the words: "For one who knows England a journey to Italy is superfluous." Erasmus achieved a conscious turn to theology. Thereafter he wanted to "apply himself with all his heart to Holy Scripture" and to "dedicate the rest of [his] life" to it.

The first result of his turning to theology was the *Enchiridion militis Christiani* (1503), the manual or small weapon of the Christian warrior, intended as an introduction to Christian life for the laity. In the foreword Erasmus summarizes the basic ideas of the *Enchiridion* and gives an insight into his own religious outlook. For the simple man, who is unable to pour over the thick and detailed volumes of the scholastics, but for whom also Christ died, one should "condense the entire philosophy of Christ in its fundamental traits from the purest sources of the Gospels and the Apostles, from the most trustworthy exegetes, and this should be simple but scholarly, brief but clear." Clarity, simplicity, and purity through going back to the sources, Holy Scripture and the Fathers — such are the goals of Christian humanism as Erasmus advocated it.

> The goal is thus one: Christ and his holy teaching.... No type of vocation is excluded from this goal.... One must not stain the heavenly philosophy of Christ with man's work.... He who kindles love for Christ teaches the essence of Christian piety.

Christian perfection is not a matter of subtle reflection but of a loving act. "It manifests itself in warmth of feeling, not in a special state [monasticism], in the heart, not in holy garments or foods." All ceremonies are only helps for those not of age; the perfect is the invisible, the religion of the heart. The spiritual man no longer needs the aid of the external.

This criticism was expressed in a particularly clever manner, but also especially frivolously and maliciously, in the "intimate conversations" which Erasmus had written at Paris in 1500 but which only appeared in Basel in 1518 under the title *Familiarium colloquiorum formulae.* This work was intended as a school textbook; as a collection of Latin idioms and of examples of cultured conversation it was to instruct the pupil in Latin eloquence and impart to him proper conduct of life. The Italian sojourn of 1506–9, during which he became doctor of theology at Turin, did not have for the great humanist the significance that we might suppose. It was only the finishing touch in his humanist education. At the beginning of his third visit in England (1509–14) Erasmus wrote *Encomium Moriae* (1511), the *Praise of Folly,* in the house of Thomas More, who was bound to him in a close friendship. In it folly has its say. This literary artifice made it possible to say serious things without committing oneself. If the author even wanted to express risky views, he could not be pinned down but always had an alibi. It was only folly speaking.

As early as 1504 Erasmus had discovered Lorenzo Valla's *Adnotationes* to the New Testament, which he published in 1505. Thereafter he had eagerly studied Greek and preoccupied himself with the text of Scripture. These studies bore fruit when in 1514 he moved to Basel for two years and in John Froben found a qualified printer and publisher for his *Novum Instrumentum.* Appearing in 1516, this was the Greek text of the New Testament with notes and a Latin translation differing from the Vulgate. In the introduction, Erasmus outlined a biblical theology, his "Philosophia Christi," which, as "renascentia," that is, as "the renewal (*instauratio*) of the originally good nature," should be simple, clear, devout, and practical. In the dedicatory letter to Leo X he wrote:

> ... since I see that that doctrine of salvation is found much purer and more alive in the veins themselves, from which sources it is drawn, than from pools or drained-off streams, I have revised the entire Greek New Testament in fidelity to the original text, not frivolously or with slight exertion but by recourse to several Greek and Latin manuscripts, and those that are the oldest and the best, not those that are entirely more agreeable.

In the admonition to the pious reader, he wrote:

> At best few can be scholars, but everyone can be a Christian, everyone can be devout, yes, I will boldly add, everyone can be a theologian. What is in conformity with nature easily becomes common property. But what is Christ's philosophy, which he himself calls a rebirth (*renascentia*) but a renewal of the originally good nature?... That rich and genuine philosophy

> of Christ is obtained nowhere more happily than from the Gospels and the other Apostolic writings.

Erasmus demands:

> The young theologian must learn to quote well from Sacred Scripture, not from manuals, musty tomes, or God knows what kind of *collectanea* which have already been shaken together and hodge-podged hundreds of times, but according to the sources themselves.... Make your own heart a library of Christ; from it, as from a treasury, bring forth new or old, as the matter requires.

With the edition of the New Testament and that of the works of Jerome (1517 ff.), "by far the first and most learned" of the Church Fathers, Erasmus moved into the front rank of theologians of his day. At the same time, having taken up residence in the Netherlands again in May 1516 and having become a princely councillor, he entered upon the political scene with his *Institutio principis christiani* (1516) for the future Charles V and with the *Querela pacis* (1517). Through his English connections in 1517 he obtained from Rome the privilege of living free in the world without his religious habit and of accepting benefices unimpeded by his illegitimate birth. In accord with his demand that theologians should open up Scripture instead of treating silly questions, he wrote paraphrases of Romans (1517), the other Epistles (1517–21), the Gospels (1522 ff.), and Acts. At the same time he worked on the writings of the Fathers. Their printed editions were to occupy the rest of his life: Cyprian (1521), Arnobius (1522), Hilary (1523), Irenaeus (1526), Ambrose (1527), Origen (1527), Augustine (1527–29), and Chrysostom (1530).

In the years 1516–18 Erasmus was at the height of his reputation. By means of scholarship and education and more particularly through his exertions in regard to the text of the Bible and of the Fathers — *"ad fontes!"* — he expected to bring about renewal, and not a few contemporaries looked to him as the man of the longed-for reform. Then, with the appearance of Luther, forces emerged which were strange and even repugnant to the prince of humanists in their elemental power and existential importance, especially since they did not remain within the sphere of the "good sciences" but appealed also to the man in the street and demanded of Erasmus, "vir duplex," a clear taking of sides.

Book Five

REFORMATION AND COUNTER REFORMATION

Translated by Anselm Briggs and Peter W. Becker

Part One

The Protestant Reformation

Erwin Iserloh

Chap. 88: Hubert Jedin

Section One

Martin Luther and the Coming of the Reformation (1517–1525)

CHAPTER 62

Causes of the Reformation

When we ask about the causes of the Reformation, we admit that this event of such tremendous importance was not the work of one man, such as Luther, and that it did not first begin with the ninety-five indulgence theses of 31 October 1517. Long before the outbreak of the Reformation things occurred, facts were provided, steps were taken, ideas were spread and emotions were stirred, which facilitated, made possible, provoked, and even made unavoidable the coming of a revolt against the Church — so unavoidable that we can speak of an inner historical necessity. This does not mean that it could not have happened differently.

No one desired a reformation that would lead to a division in Western Christendom. The reformers wanted the reform of the one Church common to all. Because this reform in head and members was thwarted, the split occurred. Consequently the Reformation would be the revolutionary rejoinder to the failure of reform in the fourteenth and fifteenth centuries. The causes of this were all the conditions and attitudes in need of reform, in particular everything that stood in the way of the realizing of reform at the proper time.

Certainly the disgust of the time over the "wretched conditions," to use Zwingli's words, gave great impetus to the Reformation, but its enticing appeal was contributed by the circumstance that to the men of the new age it seemed to lead the way out of outmoded medieval attitudes and conditions, and promised to give man what he had long demanded or unconsciously yearned for in vain. Not by chance was the "freedom of the Christian man" the great shibboleth of the Reformation, laden with portents for the future and frequently misunderstood.

The so-called abuses were certainly no greater at the end of the fifteenth century than in the second half of the fourteenth century. But people put up with them much less easily, for they had become more alert, more aware, more critical, and in the good sense more demanding and hence more sensitive to the contradiction between ideal and reality, teaching and living, claim and achievement.

The fact that this augmented religious need, this greater maturity of the laymen, was not sufficiently taken into account, or that an attitude typical of the Middle Ages, and at that time justified by circumstances, was not definitely put aside early, was consequently more disruptive than any failure, however regrettable, on the part of individuals.

Accordingly, a cause of the Reformation in the broader sense is the dissolution of the medieval order and of the fundamental attitudes proper to it or the failure to replace it at the proper time with new organizations in keeping with the times. Here must be mentioned first the disruption of the unity which embraced the totality of political, intellectual, and religious life. The one Church in the one Christendom, expressed in the unity effected through the counterbalancing of *Sacerdotium* and *Imperium,* was the most striking characteristic of the Middle Ages. The papacy itself contributed to severing this unity. For the sake of the independence and autonomy of the Church, it saw itself forced to weaken the power of the *Imperium.* For a while it seemed as though the Pope could also assume political leadership. But the more he exercised his fullness of authority on the secular political sphere, the more decidedly he encountered the justified resistance of a world becoming ever more strongly divided into nations and conscious of its autonomy. Soon, together with its unjustified claims, people were attacking the papacy itself, and its religious guidance was rejected along with its political leadership. It was frankly a warning signal that Boniface VIII, who replaced the traditional two-powers theory — that the secular and the spiritual power are autonomous and both come directly from God — with the monism of the Bull "Unam Sanctam," became at Anagni in 1303 the captive of the modern national state, represented by Nogaret, and of the laicized democratic forces, symbolized by Sciarra Colonna.

The sequel was the so-called Avignon Exile of the Popes and their far-reaching dependence on France. The papacy seemed no longer to consider the interests of the Universal Church but all the more to be exploiting the nations of Europe in a thoroughly organized fiscal system.

Especially in Germany this charge would henceforth never cease to be heard. In France, Spain, and England the national state, which more and more dominated the territorial Church and made the Church's sources of income useful to itself, was able to a great extent to thwart the exportation of money. The Western Schism obscured the unity of the Church as expressed in the Pope to such a degree that not even saints knew who was the lawful Pope. Conciliarism seemed to be the only escape from the difficulty of the "damnable trinity" of Popes.

After the Council of Constance (1414–18), conciliarism was not overcome from within nor fundamentally but *via facti* and largely by political means. By means of concordats — agreements with states — the Popes sought to protect themselves against democratic currents and in addition to avoid the reform that was in many ways embarrassing for them. Indeed, when schism again loomed at the Council of Basel in 1437, the fate of the Church seemed, according to Halle to have been handed entirely to the secular powers. The Pope had to pay dearly for recognition by the German princes, the Emperor, and the King of France and allow the state extensive power over the Church. The result was the territorial Church — the dependence of the Church on the secular powers, whether royal, princely, or city, with the possibility granted to these of interfering on a large scale in the life of the Church. Without this sovereignty over Church government it is difficult to conceive of the victory of the Reformation. The papal policy of concordats also brought it about that, in the course of the fifteenth century, the Popes, instead of stressing their proper religious mission in view of the secularization, became more and more princes among princes, with whom alliances could be made and against whom war could also be waged, as against any other prince. This entanglement in politics enabled Leo X to become the savior of the Reformation by neglecting for two years to proceed vigorously against Luther and thus capture the foxes while they were small, as Johannes Cochläus put it.

Also characteristic of the Middle Ages was a clericalism based on the monopoly of education by clerics and on the privileges of the clerical state. To the young and intellectually immature Germanic peoples the Church had to transmit not only the revelation of Jesus Christ but also the cultural treasures of antiquity. This led to a preponderance on the part of clerics, which went beyond their specific duty of religious leadership. The day had to come when medieval man attained his majority and was both able and willing on his own to distinguish between the treasures of faith and of culture held out to him. This required of the Church that at a given time she should relinquish all the fields of activity which she had assumed only in a subsidiary way and the rights not directly connected with her function, which was based on divine institution, and that she should make her religious mission all the clearer.

As consideration of the late Middle Ages has shown, this peaceful change did not take place. The movements in which the striving of the laity for independence was at stake involved revolutionary features. The Church maintained outdated claims, and the world — the individual as well as the state and society — had to extort its autonomy. Thus the process of secularization was carried out against the Church under the standards of subjectivism, nationalism, and laicism.

In the encounter with antiquity and through his own investigation and experience, man discovered realities which had not grown in the soil of Christianity or were self-evident and not in need of confirmation by authorities. The representatives of the new scholarship wanted indeed to be Christians also, but the more the Church seemed to identify herself with the old and the traditional, the more did the new, brought forward with all the fervor of the joy of discovery, have to act on her as critic. The circles of the humanists frequently produced an antischolastic, anticlerical, anti-Roman, and, in the final results, if not an antiecclesiastical, at least a nonecclesiastical atmosphere.

As immediate causes of the Reformation there must be mentioned the abuses among clergy and people, a far-reaching dogmatic uncertainty, and the venality of religious life. When abuses in the Church on the eve of the Reformation are discussed, one thinks especially of "bad Popes," in particular of Alexander VI. But perhaps the decay was even more dangerous in the reign of Leo X. He cannot be charged with the enormous misdeeds by which Alexander VI sullied the throne of Peter; instead he was guilty of shocking negligence, irresponsible frivolity, and prodigal love of pleasure. One does not find in him an awareness of duty and of the responsibility of the supreme shepherd of Christendom and a manner of life in conformity with this responsibility. The deterioration of the Christian is achieved not only in an openly wicked life, but also furtively and hence more dangerously in an inner wasting away, a slow loss of substance, an imperceptible secularization, and a confused lack of responsibility.

The situation of the clergy, high and low, was no better than that of the papacy. Here too we should not direct our attention exclusively to failures in a restricted moral sphere, such as clerical concubinage. In some areas concubinage was so widespread that parishioners were hardly seriously scandalized in this respect by the lives of their pastors. If only they had really been pastors! Certainly in the late Middle Ages there was holiness in the Church, and much sincere and loyal devotion to duty. But there were also many manifestations of neglect.

Without exaggeration it can be said that the Church appeared altogether as the property of the clergy, property intended to bring economic advantage and profit. In the establishing of positions the needs of divine worship and of the care of souls were often far less decisive than the desire to do a good work in order to gain for oneself and one's family a share in the treasures of grace. Consequently a person would, for example, erect an altar with a benefice for a priest to celebrate Mass. And so there existed revenue which sought a beneficiary. Considering the great number of positions, one could not be very selective in choosing candidates. Bishops and pastors did not regard themselves primarily as persons who held an office for whose exercise the necessary livelihood was provided. They regarded themselves as holders of a benefice in the sense of Germanic feudal law. This benefice was a profitable right to which were attached certain obligations of service. But these could be turned over to a poorly paid substitute, a vicar, a hireling, to whom the sheep did not belong, to paraphrase the Lord's words (John 10:12).

Thus to the detriment of the care of souls, several bishoprics or other pastoral offices could be united in one person. As late as 1556 Cardinal Alessandro Farnese, grandson of Paul III, possessed ten episcopal sees, twenty-six monasteries, and 133 other benefices — canonries, parishes, and chaplaincies. An especially pernicious aspect was that in Germany the episcopal sees and most abbacies were open to members of the nobility only. Thus they became the means of providing for younger children of noble families, who often never gave a thought to leading a clerical life or even engaging in the care of souls. What concerned them was a carefree existence, as enjoyable as possible. If a bishop seriously desired to improve the inner state of his diocese, he was in no position to do so, because he did not control his territory. For his jurisdiction was to a great extent limited, from above by many sorts of exemptions, and from below because most pastors were named by secular patrons, ecclesiastical corporations, and monasteries, and the archdeacons had usurped other episcopal rights.

The lower the religious spirit and zeal for the care of souls sank at the Roman Curia and in the rest of the clergy, the more unpleasant the pursuit of money became, and the preoccupation with financial matters heightened the scandal. At the Curia men sought to fill up the coffers by means of an elaborate system of fees, taxes, more or less voluntary contributions, and finally even indulgence offerings. The prodigal and worldly papal court, the extensive building activity, and the great expenses of war brought about a continuing need for money. It was certainly not accidental that the scandal of Tetzel's dealings in indulgences, which provided the immediate occasion for the outbreak of the Reformation, was connected with this concern for money.

The abuses described resulted in a far-reaching dissatisfaction with the Church, which more and more grew into a resentment and even a hatred of Rome. The *gravamina* of the German nation were expressed for the first time as early as 1455 by Dietrich von Erbach, Archbishop of Mainz. This listing of German grievances against the papacy was thereafter renewed again and again, but the less successful it was, the more it increased the anti-Roman feeling in Germany.

In his *An den christlichen Adel deutscher Nation* (*To the Christian Nobility of the German Nation*) Luther made these complaints his own and thereby became a national hero. Zwingli too knew how to exploit the dissatisfaction. He directed his disciples not to preach chiefly about doctrine but about the wretched conditions and the necessity of restoring righteousness.

The call for reform and the related opposition to the Church thus brought it about that many a person who had absolutely no involvement with their teaching acclaimed the reformers merely because they seemed to be bringing the long-desired reform. There was a great readiness for anything new that announced salvation.

Deplorable as the abuses were and however much they contributed to the origin and success of the Reformation, they are not the most significant factors in this context. More decisive than the personal failings of Popes, priests, and laity is the question whether the truth given by Christ and the order established by him were attacked, whether the moral decay was an expression of a falling off in matters touching the essence of religion.

We must ask, "Precisely what were the strong and weak points of the Church as it entered the era of the Reformation?" To what extent was the external religious activity, which was so rich and varied, a façade or a reality? In the many-colored picture of popular devotion, veneration of saints, pilgrimages, processions, Mass foundations, and so forth, how much was really genuine and to what extent did superstition, a desire for pious activity, or a mercenary spirit hold sway?

Another question to be asked is: Was this external practice, based on a sound theological doctrine, explained by it, and illuminated by it? And special mention must be made here of an extensive dogmatic uncertainty as a manifestation of failure fraught with dire consequences. The areas of truth and error were not delineated with sufficient clarity. Men fancied themselves in accord with the Church, although positions had long been adopted that contradicted her teaching. Luther thought that he was still in the Church when he reviled the Pope as Antichrist, and in 1530 Melanchthon in the Augsburg Confession could still try to have people believe that in that teaching there was no opposition to the "Roman Church" and that persons were of different opinions merely in reference to a few abuses. (Article 21). Uncertainty was particularly great in regard to the concept of the Church. Because of the Western Schism — the last antipope, Felix V, had abdicated only in 1449 — it was no longer generally clear that the papacy established by Jesus Christ was essential to the Church. Unable to ascertain who was the legitimate Pope, many people had stopped asking this question and had grown accustomed to getting along without a Pope. Great impetus was given to the Reformation by the fact that many felt Luther was merely bringing about the reform long due and did not notice at all, or only belatedly, that he was questioning essential doctrines of the Church.

If Luther became a reformer — not the least reason being that he was unable to reconcile his understanding of revelation, gained in severe and perilous religious struggles, with the theology and practice of his day — the cause lay especially in the fact that this theology was the one-sided doctrine of nominalism, while the depth and wealth of an Augustine or an Aquinas, and especially of Scripture, were lacking. Consequently nominalism, going back to William of Ockham and communicated to Luther in the shallow form of Gabriel Biel, who had given it a moralizing tendency, must be named among the decisive causes of the Reformation. Manifestations of failure showed themselves to be especially fateful in the theology and practice of the Mass. If the Mass, which occupied so much of the life of piety in the late Middle Ages, could in so short a time thereafter be abolished as the worst idolatry, must we not suppose that often it was performed only as an external ritual, something not really grasped, not performed from within?

In the lack of inner strength and life, which can be connected very closely with correctness and legalism, is also to be sought the reason why the Fifth Lateran Council (1512–17), referred to by Jedin as the last "papal reform effort clothed in the guise of a council" before the Reformation, was of only meager effectiveness. The new spirit was lacking. For of what use can one or another well-meant measure be? Nothing sheds more light on the situation than the fact that in 1514, together with the papal bull on the reform of the Church read at the ninth session of the Council, there was sent to Archbishop Albrecht of Magdeburg and Mainz the Curia's offer, which provided the immediate occasion for the Reformation: for a fee of 10,000 ducats the archbishop would be allowed to hold the two sees simultaneously, and for the financing of the fee, half of the indulgence offerings for Saint Peter's would be made over to him. "Theory and practice were in such glaring contradiction!"

A lack of seriousness and determination in the leaders, beginning with the Pope himself, condemned the Council to ineffectiveness. And so, after the many useless calls to reform and the many lost opportunities, a revolutionary confrontation, similar to that which actually occurred in the Reformation, was almost inevitable.

CHAPTER 63

Martin Luther: The Early Years

None of the suggested causes of the Reformation really "explains" it. The far-reaching deterioration of religious and moral strength, the want of precision in central questions of faith, and the lack of a sense of pastoral responsibility in the clergy, along with so many lost opportunities for reform and in view of widespread criticism of the Church, make an upheaval quite intelligible. But the fact that it occurred as it did, in what we know as the Reformation, depended to a great extent on Martin Luther himself and hence is steeped in the mystery of the human person. If every *individuum* is something "ineffable," this is especially so of Luther.

If the reformer's image has remained controversial, this is so not only because a judgment on his person and work is bound up with a decision in regard to the Reformation's claim to truth. For one side he is the hero of the faith; for the other the archheretic, the destroyer of the Church's unity. Actually, however, the reason for the difficulty of assessing his person and work and of correctly portraying them is found in Luther himself. We have an abundance of writings from his pen and of his own testimony about himself and his aims. Even though an inner cohesion is not missing from all these statements and all of Luther's questions fit under a rather small number of viewpoints and are answered accordingly, nevertheless he was not a systematizer. He was far too dependent on his experience and will. This makes it even more difficult to grasp the richness and versatility of his being, and he often seems to be vacillating and contradictory. He experienced a profound change in developing from friar to reformer. Because his career was so intimately connected with experience, he was unable to look back without bias on earlier stages of his development. And so he himself had a decisive share in the origin of the "Luther legend," whose gradual deflation has occurred only in recent decades, thanks to the learned and painstaking study by men such as Otto Scheel. Furthermore, everything that Luther wrote and said is a confession or realization which was paid for in his own experience and suffering and which he had to communicate to others. But again it was uttered in a distressing way, in which he did not shrink from violent language for the sake of clarity, and even the paradox became for him a suitable manner of expression. Luther always asserted things; a cautious consideration for and against seemed to him to be skepticism. No wonder he all too often succumbed to the hazards of his irascible temperament and his polemical ability. All this made it difficult to assess his character and his work, which to a great extent fashioned the German Reformation.

Home and Youth

Martin Luther was born at Eisleben on 10 November 1483. His peasant ancestors came from Mohra, on the western edge of the Thuringian forest. His father, Hans Luder, lacking hereditary title to land, had to earn his living in the copper mining industry. In 1484 he moved to Mansfeld, where by stubborn hard work he slowly rose from simple miner to partner in mining companies and small entrepreneur. The community repeatedly selected him as one of the board of four who had to defend the rights of the citizenry against the town council. Luther's youth in this aspiring lower-middle-class family of numerous children was thus marked by hardship, sobriety, and severity. In the parental home, of course, there prevailed a Catholic piety which, with its colorful customs, was a part of the world of peasants and miners, but which was also laden with superstition and apparitions of witches and devils. The ambitious father wanted a better career for his son and sent him quite early to the Latin school at Mansfeld (1488–97). Here, in addition to reading and writing, he especially learned Latin and ecclesiastical song. Even more severely and perhaps with more justice than Erasmus did, Luther later complained of his teachers' crudeness. He claims "to have been once flogged fifteen times in a morning for no fault. This harsh upbringing at home and at school to a great extent fashioned the uncommonly sensitive youth's image of God. "From childhood I was so trained that I could not but turn pale and become terrified if I merely heard the name of Christ mentioned, for I was taught only to regard him as a stern and angry judge."

In 1497, at the age of fourteen, Martin and a fellow student went to Magdeburg, to the school of the Brothers of the Common Life. Both there and at Eisenach, to which he transferred after a year (1498), he had to earn his bread, according to the custom of the time, as an itinerant singer, or "Partekenhengst," outside doors. At his "beloved city" of Eisenach he had a number of relatives. Especially in the Schalbe-Cotta family a warm, genuinely Christian environment embraced him.

University and Monastery

In the summer term of 1501 Luther entered the University of Erfurt and began the basic course in the liberal arts. He was enrolled in the Sankt Georgenburse. Manner of life and curriculum were determined for him. The arts faculty belonged entirely to the *via moderna,* the nominalist philosophy deriving from William of Ockham. Following the course in the trivium — grammar, dialectic, rhetoric — he became a bachelor of arts in the fall of 1502. In this capacity he had to give lectures of his own while continuing his required courses. In addition to the quadrivium he had to attend lectures on cosmology, metaphysics, and ethics. Having become a master of arts on 7 January 1505, he could choose one of the special fields, theology, medicine, or law. His father's ambition destined him for the study of law, which he began on 20 May 1505. But on 20 June, for reasons not clear, he went home for a vacation. On his way back, on 2 July, a powerful electric storm took him by surprise at Stotternheim near Erfurt. Thrown to the ground by lightning striking very close to him, he cried cut in great anguish, "Saint Anne, help me and I will become a monk!"

Despite the consternation of his friends and the extreme disapproval of his father, Luther fulfilled this vow, probably wrung from him by terror, and on 17 July entered the monastery of the Hermits of Saint Augustine of the Observance at Erfurt. Of the numerous monasteries in the city, this one may have recommended itself to him, apart from its serious asceticism, because of its Ockhamist bent, which offered Luther an organic continuation of his studies in the arts faculty.

The choral office and the scriptural reading prescribed by the rule made the young Augustinian thoroughly familiar with the Bible. After a year's novitiate he was professed in September 1506, and only a few months later, on 3 April 1507, he was ordained a priest. Anxieties experienced during his first Mass, which almost caused him to flee from the altar, show to what a degree he was impressed by the overwhelming majesty of God and how little he was able to attend to and understand liturgical texts such as "clementissime Pater." This is important for a judgment on Luther's claim that in the monastery he had been taught "to expect forgiveness of sins and salvation through our works." For the texts that had been spoken at his reception as a novice and that he prayed daily from the missal were, in their constant assertion that man can do nothing of himself and that God supplies the will and the accomplishment, an impressive disavowal of all justification by works.

Marked out to be a teacher of theology, Luther studied at his Order's *studium generale* in Erfurt, which was connected with the university. Here he again came under the influence of Ockhamism, as presented in the commentaries on Peter Lombard's *Sentences* by Pierre d'Ailly and Gabriel Biel. At the same time he was lecturing in the liberal arts. In the autumn of 1508 he obtained the post of lecturer in moral philosophy at the recently founded University of Wittenberg, and continued his study of theology there. In March 1509 he obtained the baccalaureate and, after that, delivered lectures on the Bible. Before he had reached the position of *sententiarius* he was transferred back to Erfurt, where he lectured on *The Sentences.* In the autumn of 1510 he became *baccalaureus formatus* as he began the third book — that is, he had completed the requirements for the master's degree.

In his marginal notes on the text of Peter Lombard and those made at the same time on the writings of Saint Augustine we have the first theological observations from Luther's hand. In the notes on Augustine he shows himself to be an Ockhamist on the question of universals and in his concept of God. He interprets Augustine in this sense but at the same time regards himself as confirmed by him in his criticism of philosophy and of philosophers, in their sterile disputations.

At the beginning of his comments on *The Sentences* Luther emphasizes that he does not intend to deny all usefulness of philosophy for theology, but that he would rather, with Peter Lombard, rely more on the doctors of the Church, especially Augustine, instead of seeking support in the discussions of the philosophers and the views in which they attack one another. If we want to speak of divine things, we need only the word of God itself. Otherwise we are groping in the dark, but the oversubtle philosophers will not admit to this. Whereas the master of *The Sentences* stresses with Augustine that: our words lag behind our thoughts in regard to God, and our thoughts on the other hand are unable adequately to grasp God's being, the philosophers act as though everything could be comprehended and expressed by them. To the opinions of the "highly esteemed doctors," who can claim only human traditions, Luther opposes Holy Scripture and thereby first sounds the note of the principle of Scripture.

In these marginal notes Luther was already preoccupied with the questions that would later be so urgent for the reformer — original sin and the justification and sanctification of man by faith and charity. In relatively great detail he concerned himself with the problem of the relationship of the Holy Spirit and charity, discussed in the seventeenth distinction of Book I of *The Sentences.* He distinguished our love, *caritas creata,* from the Holy Spirit, *caritas increata.* The latter is the efficient cause of our love, but not its formal cause, not that whereby we love. This is not the Holy Spirit himself but rather his gift. In the actual order of salvation, however, created love is given and returned with the Holy Spirit.

Just as "for us Christ is faith, justice, grace, and sanctification," but at the same time these are created gifts, which become our own, so love is on the one hand the Holy Spirit and on the other hand the act of love which the Holy Spirit produces by means of our will. Hence Luther did not want to assume a specifically created *habitus* of love but only an actual created love, again and again produced in us by the Holy Spirit, who, as the principle of love, plays the role of *habitus.*

Luther did not accept from Peter Lombard the identification of supernatural charity with the person of the Holy Spirit, according to which he himself would be our love immediately. But he defended the master of *The Sentences* against the scholastics. He could not appreciate the reasons for their criticism of Lombard. Their intention was to preserve the distinction between creator and creature and to stress that the sinner needs a new disposition in order to enter upon the new relation and the new dealings with God. For Luther this is a chimera; the scholastics are simply determined by the teaching on *habitus* of that "rancid philosopher" Aristotle. Hence he stood by the doctrine of the Ockhamists, who would have preferred most of all to do without habitual grace in order to eliminate in man every reason which might oblige God to make man happy.

According to Luther, the love effected by the Holy Spirit is not only a good disposition in man; rather it makes "the entire person pleasing" — all its acts and attitudes. "It alone is virtue and makes all else virtue"; it is "the mistress of virtues and the queen of merits." But this love exists only in connection with faith and hope. On the other hand, justifying faith is possible only in connection with love and hope. But one in mortal sin also believes! Is this another faith and not the same, lacking only the form provided by love? Luther assumes two kinds of faith. Infused faith comes and departs with love and hence is identical with *fides formata. Fides informis,* on the contrary, is to be identified with *fides acquisita et naturaliter moralis.* Accordingly, as supernatural virtues, faith, hope, and charity are inseparable. They are infused together. They are based on no habitus except the Holy Spirit himself, who effects them in us and in whom they must be constantly activated by us. Justifying faith, which makes us do what the law commands, is thus always a faith produced in love. All merit is preceded by grace, and in his rewards God crowns his own gifts.

In regard to the preparation for the grace of justification, Luther, along with Peter Lombard, stresses against the theology of the Biel school that good will is already a gift of grace and that faith precedes it, not indeed in time but causally and by nature. In his doctrine of original sin Luther turns somewhat sharply against Lombard, whose opinion "that original sin is tinder is not to be held." Original sin consists in the deprivation of the supernatural justice of man's original state and is totally obliterated in baptism. Concupiscence remains as a punishment; it is the "tinder" which kindles sin and consists in the insubordination of the flesh. Reason, deprived of grace and virtue, can no longer restrain the flesh, whose nature it is to run wild, just as a horse whose reins are broken no longer submits. After baptism the state of concupiscence is weaker (*debilitatur*) but it is not eliminated. As a punishment man encounters the resistance of the flesh; he can control it and fulfill God's commands only with difficulty. Original sin is, to be sure, transmitted by means of procreation. Its cause, however, is not carnal desire but divine punishment. Against Peter Lombard Luther insists: "Even if the flesh were totally pure and were reproduced without carnal desire, still, by virtue of God's judgment on Adam, the soul would necessarily have to be devoid of the original justice and hence it would be in original sin." In these views Luther was still within the framework of the theology of his day. Of a particular pessimism, based on his own struggles and sad experiences, and of a noteworthy dependence on Augustine there is hardly a trace.

Luther's Visit to Rome

Conflicts within his Order took Luther to Rome at this time. In 1510 Johann von Staupitz, the German vicar general of the Observant Augustinians, also became provincial of the Saxon province of the Conventual branch of the Order. In keeping with the desire of the Curia, Staupitz sought to unite the two branches, but seven houses of the Observance, including that at Erfurt, resisted, fearing a dilution of the reform through concessions made to the Conventuals. Luther's teacher, Johann Nathin, with Luther as his companion, was sent to the Curia as spokesman of the strict Observance, but very little was accomplished.

What was the significance of this encounter with Renaissance Rome for Luther's development into a reformer? Did he there perhaps receive the decisive impulse for his war against the Curia? Not at all. Luther's experience of Rome was like that of other devout pilgrims of the time. Sacred Rome, with its places of pilgrimage, so monopolized him that unfavorable impressions could scarcely make themselves felt. "The main purpose of my journey to Rome," Luther explained later in one of his Table Talks, "was to fulfill my desire of making a complete confession from my youth and to become devout." But he was disappointed in this expectation of being delivered from his inner distresses by a general confession in Rome. He found uneducated and, so he felt, unsympathetic confessors.

Doctor of Holy Scripture

When by the "Compact of Jena" a compromise was found for the conflict in the Augustinian Order which prevented the observance being outvoted in the chapter, Luther no longer had any reason for opposition to Staupitz, and in the summer of 1511 the latter recalled him to Wittenberg. He now was to prepare to assume the post of professor of Scripture, hitherto filled by Staupitz. In June 1512 Luther was appointed preacher in the Order and on 19 October he became a doctor of theology.

He was now qualified to take over the lectures on the Bible. This post, which he retained until his death, was to determine his lot and to push into the center of world interest the little university town of Wittenberg, lacking in every sort of tradition and "on the edge of civilization." His lectures, transmitted in autograph or in transcripts by his pupils, were in part discovered only at the turn of this century, but thereafter they were more and more taken into consideration, since they are the most important source for Luther's development into a reformer. They comprise his lectures on the Psalms (1513–15) and on the Epistles to the Romans (1515–16), the Galatians (1516–17), and the Hebrews (1517–18). With his arrangement of the lectures in glosses and *scholia* and his use of the fourfold sense of Scripture, Luther was within the framework of the traditional exegesis. But at the same time he appropriated the new humanistic linguistic studies, for example in his use of the *Psalterium Quincuplex* (1509) of Lefèvre d'Etaples (c. 1450–1536) and the latter's translation and exegesis of the Pauline Epistles (1512). Although these editions may actually have determined the choice of material for the lectures, more decisive is the fact that it was precisely the Psalms and the Pauline Epistles that were best qualified to bring out Luther's strongly experienced theology.

It was in his Order that Luther had been brought early and intensely into contact with Scripture. He bears witness to this in the Table Talks: In the monastery the friars gave him a Bible bound in red leather. He became so familiar with it that he knew what was on every page and could immediately open to any passage. Thus Luther attained a remarkable grasp of the Bible, which enabled him to quote it at length from memory. But more important than this formal mastery of Scripture was the personal relationship which he developed with it and as a consequence of which he could call it his bride. For him the Bible was not a cultural experience, as it was for some of the humanists, nor a theology in contradistinction to the direct religious encounter with the word of God. To Luther there was no such separation.

The Lectures on the Psalms (1513–15)

The *Dictata super Psalterium,* the written version of the lectures on the Psalms which Luther delivered from August 1513 to October 1515, constitute the earliest comprehensive record of his views. Hence in recent decades they have been repeatedly discussed, but unanimity about their role in Luther's development into a reformer has not yet been achieved.

The young professor, relying on the *Psalterium Quincuplex* of Lefèvre d'Etaples, had a text of the psalter printed expressly for the use of students, with wide margins and considerable space between the lines. The edition was preceded by a preface written by him, and each psalm by an account of its content. Luther's personal copy, with its linear and marginal glosses, is preserved in the "Wolfenbüttel Psalter"; the detailed textual exegesis, the *scholia,* in a Dresden manuscript. Luther began to prepare the lectures for printing in the fall of 1516, but he got no farther than the earliest steps — Psalms 1, 4, and 22 to 24. Nevertheless, we encounter difficulty with the chronology of individual passages, for we do not know whether we are dealing with an expression of Luther's from the time of the lecture series or from the later revision.

Loyal to the exegetical tradition, Luther adhered to the fourfold sense of Scripture. In his view the literal sense was a reference to Christ as already manifested, but this Christ was seen in union with his mystical body. "What can be understood of Christ as the head can also be understood of the Church and of faith in him." Hence assertions in regard to Christ can be applied allegorically or mystically to the Church and morally or tropologically to the Christian. Thus there is found in Luther a close connection of Christology, ecclesiology, and soteriology. But though the Church is obviously regarded as the body of Christ, and her function as an instrument of salvation in the administration of the Sacraments is important — above all in her preaching of the word of God — emphasis is placed on the identification of the Christian with Christ, based on the mystery of the mystical body. "Every scriptural passage that speaks of the advent of Christ in the flesh can appropriately, or rather must be understood of his spiritual advent through grace." "Hence, as Christ was conceived by the Holy Spirit, so too every believer is justified and reborn without any human action by the grace of God alone and the operation of the Holy Spirit."

God has revealed himself in Christ, the *opus Dei,* but he is still the hidden one, *Deus absconditus.* Though he cannot in any event be comprehended by us, he has concealed himself in a special manner in the Incarnation; indeed, in the wretched human figure on the cross he has hidden himself under the very opposite of his true form. In the Crucified the contrast between God and man, heaven and earth visible and invisible, present and future, spiritual and carnal, judgment and grace, justice and mercy, death and life, was intensified to the point of contradiction, but at the same time all contrasts were reduced in him to a higher unity. By means of the Cross God kills in older to awaken to life, he destroys in order to save, he condemns in order to bless, he judges in order to pardon, in *opus alienum* he effects his *opus proprium.*

Christ's Cross and death are a judgment on sin; on the Cross Christ assumed our condemnation and rejection. However, God punishes, not to destroy, but to lead to life. God accomplishes marvels in his saints (Ps. 4:4), because he subjects Christ to every temptation of suffering and death and by this very means saves him. He embraces him the most powerfully where he abandons him the most. He leads him to salvation where he condemns him. Christ, who appears to be the most depraved and accursed, is blessed. Thus on the Cross is ended the tension between judge and redeemer, between divine anger and grace, and the unity of God's holy wrath and grace-bestowing love becomes visible.

What is now true of Christ by origin (*radicaliter*) and cause (*causaliter*), what happened to him as exemplar, is affirmed in the tropological sense of the Christian, who through his faith is included in salvation history. The *opus Dei* Christ thus becomes the *opus Dei* faith in Christ. Christ is Sacrament, that is, a sign pointing beyond him; "he is our *abstractum,* we are his *concretum,*" that is, Christ, so to speak, aspires after realization in the believer; "we must all be fashioned according to his example."

The applying of the work of salvation occurs in word and in Sacrament: the words of the Gospel are the "vehiculum" on which the truth comes to me. This word is not merely a communication but a living word; in it the judgment of God is continued through history, the cross is made contemporary with us. This cross, as the judgment and justice of God, means tropologically *humilitas* or, better, *humiliatio* and *fides.* In humility the just man becomes his own accuser. Thus the divine summons to judgment becomes effective; we renounce our justice, acknowledge our sins, and admit that God is right, even when he seems to be unjust. Thus "all our ardor must be directed to making our sins great and serious."

This self-judgment, the "crucifying of the flesh, is an effect of the word of God." It is no mere prerequisite of justification, but, as "humilitas fidei," it is justification itself. "For not he who considers himself humble... but he who thinks himself to be abominable and worthy of damnation is just." Tropologically understood, judgment is the *humiliatio,* self-condemnation beneath God's word, and justice is faith. For according to Romans (1:17), the justice of God is revealed in the Gospel and proceeds from faith to faith. *Humilitas* and *fides* can be distinguished as concepts, but they are as inseparable as two sides of the same thing.

Judgment and justification must be understood as one, and judgment must be identified with the Gospel and with grace — for Luther this is the great marvel. Justification is not completed, however, it is a process. If we come to a standstill we cease to be good. We who are just are still in need of justification and never reach an end. To advance means always to begin anew. So far we are only redeemed as a result of hope. Justification is not visible; it is imparted only in faith. We who are saved "in spe" are not yet saved "in re." In this world we have not the "res" itself, but only evidence or signs of it, for faith is, of course, not the "res" itself, but the conviction of invisible realities.

This antithesis of *res* and *spes* can be understood only against the background of Luther's Christology and doctrine of *absconditas.* In a gloss on Psalm 113 he says that Christ has two natures, one of which is manifest "in res," while the other is given only in faith and will be manifest "in re" only in the future. The contrast between "in re" and "in spe" is, then, not that between "real" and "unreal" but between "manifest" and "hidden," between "visible" and "invisible." In this life we have Christ, salvation, justification, and so forth, not "in re" — that is, not in the brilliance of the final state — but in the hidden state of the "absconditas sub contraria specie." Hence the hidden reality is accessible to us only "in fide et spe." It must be our concern not to lose what has been given to us only in hope and not permit sin again to obtain power over us. For even after the forgiveness of guilt there remains much of what sin has done to us — weakness of the memory, blindness of the intellect, concupiscence or disorder in the will. Every sin derives from these three as its source. They are the remains of sin, which was itself remitted in baptism. Thus even the baptized remain in need of sanctification.

In the earliest period of his monastic life Luther had learned by experience that "we fall again and again and are always unclean." In addition, the lectures on the Psalms are full of the recognition that the Christian, like Christ on the Cross, is closest to God in the depths of his abandonment by God; he is saved when he regards himself as lost, justified when he is dead (Rom. 6:7). Accordingly it is of no avail to be free from temptation, but rather one must accept it in faith in God, who "alone is just and justifies all in Christ."

The Lectures on the Epistle to the Romans (1515–16)

The ideas on judgment and justification expounded in the *Dictata super Psalterium* were further clarified and developed in the lectures delivered from November 1515 to September 1516 on the Epistle to the Romans. If Luther was already inclined to paradox in thought and expression, he was challenged by the language of this Pauline Epistle to thinking in paradoxes to a shocking extent. In the introduction to the *scholia* he formulated the fundamental idea of the lectures, the persistence of sin and the external character of justice.

> The sum total of this Epistle is: to destroy, to extirpate, to annihilate all the wisdom and justice of the flesh... so far as may be done by the heart and the honest mind, and to plant, raise, and make sin grow. For God wants to save us, not through our own, but through an external justice and wisdom, through a justice which does not come from us and grow out of us, but comes to us from elsewhere, which does not spring from our earth but from heaven. Thus one must teach a justice which comes entirely from without and is an exterior justice. Therefore, first our own justice, which abides in us, must be extirpated.

The question at issue is the acknowledgment that we are sinners, and in this sense we must "become sinners." By this sin, which Luther experienced as persisting and against which the baptized must struggle throughout life, was not meant actual sin but radical sin, which precedes all wicked individual acts — evil concupiscence. Its innermost nature is self-righteousness, self-complaisance, and selfishness. We have grown crooked and bent back upon ourselves. This reference to self threatens to gnaw away and ruin our best dispositions and actions. " 'You shall not covet,' that is, you shall direct nothing to yourself and seek nothing for yourself, but in all things live, act, and think for God alone." Everything — knowledge, virtues, property — though it may be good in itself, is perverted because of this false reference. "Hence, if faith does not enlighten man and love does not free him, he cannot will or possess or do anything good; he can do only evil, even when he does good." This evil concupiscence is for Luther not only the remains of sin, as it was in the lectures on the Psalms, and not only the tinder for new sins, but real sin. Luther reproached the scholastic theologians for "imagining that the totality of original sin as well as actual sin is taken away, as if they were certain things which one could remove from sight, as darkness is expelled by light."

Guilt may be remitted, but sin as the perverted fundamental disposition of man is eliminated only by grace as a result of a slow process. Luther says that he was not aware of this in the struggles of the years behind him. Whoever admits this sin as his own and "voluntarily acknowledges his damnation" has "satisfied God and is just." "This happens through faith, when man surrenders his intellect to the word of the Cross and renounces himself and abandons all things, dead to himself and to everything."

This persisting sin does not prevent a real unity of the believer with Christ, nor does it exclude the transfer to him of the justice of God in the sense of an objective justification. "Through his faith, which is Christ's faith, bound up to his death on the Cross and therein accepting the condemnation of his sin in God's sentence, he is transformed in his innermost being and justified before God." Luther's oversubtle formulas and frequent recourse to the words *imputare, reputare,* and *nonimputatio* have led to the erroneous belief that Luther knew no justification of man in the sense of an inner transformation and real remission of sins. External justification does not mean that it remains merely external, but that it comes from without, is bestowed by God, is achieved not through man's strength but only through faith in God's word. In fact Luther stresses that it is above all not a question of the elimination of individual sins but of the elimination of the old man and the creation of a new man. According to human speech, sins would be taken away, while the man remained. But for the Apostle it is quite different:

> It is man who is removed from sin, while sin persists as remains. . . . Grace and spiritual justice elevate man himself, transform him, and alienate him from sins, though they may leave the sin behind. Hence Samuel also says, "You will become another man" [1 Sam. 10:6], that is, another human being. He does not say, "Your sins will be changed," but "You will first become another, and only when you have become another will your works be other."

Justice does not result from righteous acting, as Aristotle teaches, but precedes it. As the official acts of the priest presuppose ordination, so the works of faith presuppose justification by faith. This grace of justification is not a habit or quality which adheres to man as whitewash adheres to the wall, but it is the state of being touched by the strength of God, by the Holy Spirit, who receives power over us and adjusts our whole existence toward God in faith, hope, and charity. To the extent that we allow ourselves to be actually seized upon by the Holy Spirit, we are just. Man is freed from sin, actual and radical, when "he permits God to act and himself keeps still." For the sake of this actualism and to exclude any disposal of grace by man separated from the Holy Spirit — this was Luther's wrong interpretation of scholasticism — he, like Ockham, rejected habitual grace. He saw Christians in danger of wishing to please God independent of Christ, as if they no longer needed Christ after they had received justifying grace. Life by faith is thus an ever new beginning, an ever new delivering of self to Christ. But it is also a continuous process, "a renewal of the spirit day by day and more and more (2 Cor. 4:16)."

Luther regarded the justified man as a sick man in the presence of his physician, who promises health and has already begun to cure him. Christ, the good Samaritan, has "taken the half-dead man into the inn and begun to heal him after he has promised him complete health for eternal life." Meanwhile he denies him anything that could delay recovery.

> Is he thereby completely just? No; he is simultaneously a sinner and just [*simul peccator et iustus*]; a sinner in reality, but just by virtue of the consideration and the sure promise of God that he will redeem him from sin until he completely saves him. Accordingly, he is fully saved in hope [*in spe*], but in reality [*in re*] he is a sinner. Still, he possesses the first gift of justice in order that he may continue to seek, always in the awareness of being unjust.

"Iustus ex fide" then means not merely "I am just because of faith," but that justice is the object of faith. It is not visible and empirical ("non in re"). In fact it must remain concealed; like the divine glory in Christ, it must not become visible. It is established in me and aspires slowly to obtain dominion over me. "For our whole life is a time in which a person wants justice, but it is never completely attained; this occurs only in the life to come." In a sense God already has the outcome before his eyes. He beholds man as just and does not impute his sins to him.

Luther thus distinguishes between justification, which is indivisible, like faith, and sanctification, which proceeds slowly. In this lecture series, however, he does not yet speak of "double justice" but, following Romans 5:15, of grace and gift. *Gratia* means that whereby God justifies us, or rather that which has been given in Christ as the source, while *donum* signifies that which Christ infuses into us. "That expression, 'through the grace of this one man,' is to be understood of the personal grace of Christ, corresponding to the proper and personal sin of Adam, but the 'gift' is the justice which is given to us." Luther emphasizes that grace and gift are "one and the same" and does not further define the relationship between them. Even the relationship between *gratia operans,* the only efficient "first grace," and *gratia cooperans,* which knows growth and degree, is not explained. Especially obscure is the subject, which is flesh and spirit, just and sinner, which does the works of the law and of faith, which is passive in regard to the only efficient grace but nevertheless must believe, hope, and love, must even cooperate with grace and grow in it and become holy.

Whereas Paul, besides flesh and spirit, admits also the *nous,* the inner man, which can be carnal and spiritual, Luther knows only *caro* and *spiritus* and is tempted to identify them with man's body and spirit. "The same man is both spirit and flesh" Luther compares this unity to that of the two natures in Christ, and in both cases the *communicatio idiomatum* is valid.

> But because one and the same man, as a whole, consists of flesh and spirit, Paul assigns both elements to the whole man, though they are opposed to one another and arise from mutually opposing parts of his being. Thus there results the common possession of properties [*communicatio idiomatum*] — that one and the same man is spiritual and carnal, just and sinful, good and evil. As one and the same person of Christ is simultaneously dead and alive, simultaneously suffering and happy, simultaneously active and inactive, and so forth, because of the common possession of properties, even though neither of the two natures acquires what is proper to the other, but the most absolute contradiction persists between them.

According to this comparison the human person ought to be the bearer of *caro* and *spiritus;* though indeed it is inclined to evil, it is not so totally evil "that not even a remnant would remain which is oriented to the good, as becomes clear in our conscience."

Thus man must work with the *donum;* or, better, the man seized by the divine Spirit, the *homo spiritualis,* must oppose concupiscence in order that sin, remaining in us, may destroy in us that which formerly prevailed over us, that man may endure it until the spirit removes it. Thus through *concupiscentia* man is a sinner, but because he asks for the justice of God he is just. This is not something static, but an enduring process of improvement.

If Luther is in many respects lacking in theological accuracy and care, he is exceedingly serious in regard to man's "being on the way" and to the "typically Pauline problem of being and becoming, of having and aspiring, of indicative and imperative" (O. Kuss). This led easily to the first indulgence thesis, according to which the entire life of a Christian should be a repentance.

The Lectures on the Epistle to the Galatians (1516–17)

After the Epistle to the Romans, Luther expounded the Epistle to the Galatians in the winter of 1516–17 (27 October to 13 March). These lectures have been preserved in only one student manuscript. In 1519 Luther or Melanchthon prepared the series for printing as a "Commentarius." The Epistle to the Galatians was to occupy Luther quite often. In it Luther found confirmation of his concept of justification by faith, of the works of the law and the works of faith, of flesh and spirit, of continuing sin. "The wonderful new definition of righteousness" is as follows:

> Righteousness is faith in Christ.... According to a saying of Jerome, the believer does not live by righteousness, but the just man lives by faith; that is, he does not live because he is just, but he is just because he believes.

By faith we become "one with Christ." Faith is righteousness taken collectively ("universalis iustitia"). Thus every sin can be reduced to unbelief in Christ. To the objection that in that case faith suffices and I no longer need to do good and abandon evil, Luther retorts: In itself faith suffices, but no one has so great a faith that it cannot be increased. Hence works serve to increase faith. Moreover, they are to be done as a free service to the Lord Christ.

In connection with Galatians 2:17 the question is posed how the Apostle could deny that even believers in Christ are found to be sinners (Rom. 6:2, 10ff.). Accordingly, for Luther, justification is really instituted in me but is not yet completed. It is a process of becoming conformed to Christ. Sin persisting to the end is not imputed because God, so to speak, looks to the end, which is already anticipated in faith.

The Lectures on the Epistle to the Hebrews (1517–18)

The final lectures, those on the Epistle to the Hebrews, have also come down only in transcripts. Luther delivered them from the spring of 1517 to the spring of 1518, and so they fall in the period of the indulgence controversy and the first months of the reform struggle. Little of this is noticeable, however. Criticism of the external image of the Church is no more striking than in the preceding lectures. On the other hand, Luther's philological and humanist interests are much more prominent. Justification has a sharper Christological tone. Union with Christ is given to us in faith. Faith is the cement between the heart and the word of God; by faith they are joined in one spirit and "man becomes like to the word of God, but the word is the Son of God; and so it finally comes about that everyone who believes in him is a son of God (John 1:12)."

The idea of the death of Christ as *sacramentum* and *exemplum*, explained in the marginal notes on Augustine's *De Trinitate* (IV, 3) and later quite frequently taken up again, among other things, in the lectures on Romans, was worked out in detail by Luther and brought into close connection with justification. Christ's passion is a divine sign (*sacramentum*) of death and the remission of sins. Man must die with Christ in faith so that Christ can live and act and even rule in him. "Then, of themselves, works flow out from faith." In the exegesis of Hebrews 10:19, the death of Christ and his entry into the glory of the Father are the sign and Sacrament of the imitation of Christ. The death of Christ is the divine sign of the mortification of concupiscence, even of its death, and his entry into heaven is the sign (*sacramentum*) "of the new life and the way on which we now seek and love what is heavenly."

However, Christ is not only the model for our passover, not only our leader, but our helper, our ferryman. In the death of Christ God allowed the devil to have his way, but thereby death over-reached itself against the divinity of Christ. In slaying him the devil was overcome and by death he could create nothing but life.

Just as Christ, by his union with the immortal Godhead, overcame death by dying, so the Christian, by the union contracted in faith with the immortal Christ, overcomes death by dying. Justice is not done to this argument on the basis of the Anselmian doctrine of satisfaction. It must be understood in conformity with the patristic doctrine of redemption against the background of Philippians 2:7ff. Christ divested himself of his divine form, that is, "of justice... glory, peace, joy," and assumed what "is ours: sin, folly, perdition, humiliation, the Cross, sorrow, and so forth," and thereby took away the power from all this from within. Because he thus became conformed to us lost men, we can be brought into likeness to him. He took our injustice upon himself and gave us his justice.

According to this exegesis Christ would not communicate his justice to me, but an exchange of subjects would take place. Man would emerge from his own personality and put on the person of Christ, just as in Christ the human nature put on the divine person. Then the properties of Christ could be predicated of man in a *communicatio idiomatum*.

What is new in the lectures on Hebrews is the discussion of the relations of faith and sacrament and the presentation of a relatively detailed doctrine of the Lord's Supper. As previously in the lectures on Romans, in the same words and with a reference to the same passage in Bernard of Clairvaux, Luther maintains: "Faith in the remission of sins does not suffice if you do not believe with absolute certainty that your sins are remitted." This granting of the forgiveness of sins to me personally is effected in the sacraments. "Hence it is that no one obtains grace because he receives absolution or baptism or communion or anointing but because he believes he obtains grace through absolution, baptism, communion, or anointing."

The statement quoted by Thomas Aquinas from Augustine, that the sacrament operates by virtue of the word, and not because the word is uttered but because it is believed, is cited by Luther in a somewhat abridged form in which he stresses the necessity of the preparedness of the heart, that is, of faith, for the fruitful reception of the Sacrament. To present no obstacle is not enough.

> Even today a child is not baptized unless someone answer for him, "I believe." The Sacraments of grace help no one, but rather they harm anyone who does not approach in full faith. No, faith is already a justifying grace.

Especially urgent for Luther, as for the late medieval theologians, was the question of why there are sacraments, if faith already justifies. "External word and sign are common to worthy and unworthy; they do not suffice unless we also savor Christ concealed in them." When Luther stresses that "in the New Testament it is not the sacrament but faith in the sacrament that justifies," he does nor intend to deny the *opus operatum* nor to deny that the sacrament is effected independently of the worthiness of minister and recipient, but to emphasize that the mere sacramental reception without a spiritual reception, that is, without faith, is of no avail.

To be mindful of Christ's passion does not mean to take pity on him — even the pagans can do this — but to believe that Christ shed his blood for my sins. "For that means to drink and eat spiritually, by such faith to be plunged into Christ and incorporated into him." For Luther the Eucharist is a testament — the bequest of the dying Christ. In it the remission of sins is promised to me. The testament became valid by the death of the testator. This death is the sacrifice of the New Covenant, offered once for all time. "What is sacrificed by us daily is not so much a sacrifice as the memorial of that sacrifice, as he said: 'Do this in memory of me.' "

If we disregard the development in the lectures on the Psalms, which is difficult to determine because of the later revision, and keep in mind Luther's dependence on his current subject and the central ideas formed under its inspiration, we can say that the exegetical lectures of 1513–18 are based on the same fundamental concept: justification through Jesus Christ, who assumed our weakness and gives us his justice in faith. Faith as communion with Christ, in whom we gradually overcome persisting sin, is a process which will be completed only with death.

Luther's Reform Understanding of *Iustitia Dei*

From 1532 Luther referred frequently in the *Table Talks* and in his lectures to an understanding, even an experience, which had given him an entirely new insight into the Gospel and, after hellish suffering, had opened to him the gate to the joy of paradise and to life and salvation. In substance the understanding of the justice of God was involved. Until then he had been frightened when he read in Psalms 31(30):2 or 71(70):2 or Romans 1:17 the words the "justice of God." This expression had struck him like a flash of lightning. Then it had dawned on him, thanks to the illumination of the Holy Spirit, that the meaning was not punitive justice but the justice through which God makes us just in his grace. Thereupon, he says, "all of Holy Scripture and heaven itself was opened up" to him, who had previously hated the Psalms and Scripture because of this anxiety.

According to Luther's remark in early 1532, one of the *Table Talks* which was written down in almost identical words by Cordatus, Kumer, Schlaginhaufen, and Rorer, this can be described as follows:

> These words, just and justice, had the effect of lightning on my conscience. When I heard them I was horrified. If God is just, he will punish. However, thanks be to God, when I was once meditating in this tower and in my study over the words "the just man lives by faith" [Rom. 1:17] and "the justice of God," I thereupon thought: If we, as just, must live by faith and if the justice of God must bring about salvation in everyone who believes, then it must be not our merit but the mercy of God. In this way my spirit was lifted up. For the justice of God consists in our being justified and redeemed by Christ. And those words then became more pleasing to me. The Holy Spirit revealed Scripture to me in this tower.

As the place of this experience Luther specified the heated room (*hypocaustum*) in the tower of the Wittenberg monastery, which served as his study. For this reason it is referred to as the "tower experience."

More controversial is the time to which Luther attributed the experience, and on this depends its content. The dispute broke out over Luther's last and most detailed report of his experience in the introduction to Volume I of his Latin works in 1545. In it Luther intends to show the reader that in his earlier writings are found "many important concessions to the Pope," which he, Luther, "now regards and condemns as the greatest blasphemy and abomination." It was, he says, quite difficult "to extricate himself from such errors." Luther would like, so to speak, to ask his "Protestant" reader's leniency and to give him the theological keys to the correct idea. These keys are justification through faith in Christ and the justice of God as *iustitia passiva.* Both dawned on him only in a long, severe struggle. He shows this in two digressions, which he includes in the report of the external events, with allusion to the past by use of the pluperfect tense. The second digression is as follows:

> Meanwhile during the meeting with Miltitz and the Leipzig Disputation in that year 1519 I had returned to the explanation of the Psalms, confident that I was better prepared after having treated Saint Paul's Epistles to the Romans, Galatians, and Hebrews in lectures. I had been seized upon [*captus fueram*] by a certain wonderful desire to understand Paul in Romans. No lack of seriousness had hitherto stood in my way, but only a single statement in the first chapter: "The justice of God is revealed in the Gospel." I had, of course, conceived a hatred of this phrase, "justice of God," because, in conformity with the custom of all theologians, I had been taught to understand it philosophically as formal or active justice, whereby God is just and punishes sinners and the unjust.
>
> Though as a friar I had led a blameless life, I felt myself to be a sinner before God, with a totally restless conscience, and I could not be confident that I had reconciled God by my satisfactions. Hence I did not love, but rather I hated the just God who punishes sinners. Thus I was angry with God, if not in secret blasphemy, at least in strong grumbling, and I said: It is not enough that wretched sinners and those lost forever because of original sin should be oppressed according to the law of the Old Covenant with every sort of calamity. No, God also intends to heap affliction upon affliction by the Gospel, while menacingly holding out to us his justice and his anger through the good tidings. And so I was frantic, upset and raving in conscience, and struggled relentlessly with that passage of Paul, filled with an ardent desire to know what Paul meant.
>
> After days and nights of meditation God finally took pity on me and I noted the inner connection of the two passages: "The justice of God is revealed in the Gospel, as it is written, 'The just man lives by faith.' " Then I began to understand the justice of God as that by which the just man lives, thanks to the gift of God, that is, by faith; that the justice of God, which is revealed by the Gospel, is to be understood in the passive sense; that God in his mercy justifies us by faith, as it is written: "The just man lives by faith." At once I felt

myself to be reborn and as though I had entered paradise through the opened gates. Holy Scripture immediately showed me another face. I then went through Scripture, as my memory presented it, and found a corresponding meaning in other passages. For example, the "work of God" is what God works in us; the "strength of God" is that whereby he makes us strong; the "wisdom of God" is that by which he makes us wise. In a similar manner are to be understood the "power of God," "salvation of God," "glory of God."

Just as great as was my hate with which I had previously encountered the phrase, "justice of God," so great was now my love with which I glorified it as the sweetest word of all. Thus did this Pauline passage really become for me a gate to paradise. Later I read Augustine's *De spiritu et litera,* and there I unexpectedly found that he too understood the justice of God in a similar manner, as that with which God clothes us by justifying us. And though this is said defectively and Augustine does not clearly develop everything concerning imputation, I was pleased that here the justice of God was taught as one whereby we are justified.

Better equipped by such reflections, I began for the second time to expound the Psalms.

Luther established the point of time of his basic understanding with the remark that he had afterward read Augustine's *De spiritu et litera.* But he had already quoted abundantly from this work at the beginning of his lecture on Romans in order to prove his idea of the *iustitia Dei passiva* in connection with Romans 1:17. Hence we should have to place the reform understanding, so important for Luther, at the period of the first lectures on the Psalms and at the latest before Easter of 1515. On the other hand, Luther himself seems to indicate as the point of time the days before the beginning of the second lectures on the Psalms, the autumn of 1518. For his account is fitted into the second reference to the second lectures on the Psalms. This does not mean that the events related could not have occurred much earlier; in fact the double pluperfect, *redieram* and *captus fueram,* even demands this. Luther aims to show that his lectures on the Pauline Epistles had better equipped him for the lectures on the Psalms, and so, in describing his realization, he goes back beyond the beginning of the lectures on the Psalms. He certainly does not mean that he had lectured on this Epistle for a year without a correct understanding of Romans 1:17. In fact he there interpreted the justice meant in Romans 1:17 as that whereby God makes us just "per solam fidem, qua Dei verbo creditur." In a letter of 8 April 1516 to the Augustinian Georg Spenlein, he developed his doctrine of the "justice of God, which is given to us most abundantly and gratuitously in Christ," with the indication that he had fallen into error in this regard. Accordingly, a basically new understanding had meanwhile become his. If Luther were specifying the year 1518–19, he must have been mistaken in regard to the time, as some scholars indeed hold.

Are we to think of an experience in the sense of a realization flashing like lightning? The *Table Talks* give this impression, whereas the 1545 retrospect presents the new understanding rather as the result of long, stubborn, and quiet struggling with the meaning of Holy Scripture. Luther, in fact, expressly invites the reader to keep in mind that he, as Augustine says, was one of those who seek to advance themselves by writing and teaching and not one of those who suddenly rise from a nonentity to be everything, and who "at the first glance fathom all the meaning of Holy Scripture." Accordingly, he means that he "has begun to understand." In another passage he says of himself: 'I did not learn my theology all at once, but I had to dig deeper and deeper."

We certainly must not claim to find in the lectures any direct reference to a "tower experience." But we can inquire when Luther first made fruitful use in his exegesis of the new understanding, so revolutionary, so decisive for his self-knowledge and for his idea of Scripture. The answer must be in the *Dictata super Psalterium*, in the first series of lectures on the Psalms. In them the *scholia* of Psalms 1 and 4 must first be eliminated as the result of a later revision of the series for printing.

In the exegesis of Psalm 30(31):2, where the bitterly hated expression "In iustitia tua libera me" was to be explained for the first time, the new understanding of God's justice is not yet present. There is likewise no trace of the "thunder bolt" by which Luther claimed to have been struck when reading this verse. In the exegesis of Psalm 71(72):2, which Luther tackled twice, he clearly defines *iustitia Dei* as *fides Christi*, referring to Romans 1:17. To his exegesis of Psalm 71:2 he adds as a general rule of hermeneutics:

> If one wishes to understand wisely the Apostle and the other Scriptures, one must explain tropologically all these concepts: truth, wisdom, virtue, salvation, justice, as that whereby he makes us strong, saved, just, wise, and so forth. Thus the works of God are the ways of God. In the literal sense everything is Christ; in the moral sense, everything is faith in Christ.

Luther commented on Psalm 71 in the autumn of 1514. At that time, then, he would already have made use of his discovery, that *iustitia Dei* is not punitive justice but that of faith given us by God, not *iustitia activa* but *iustitia passiva.*

But there is hardly a trace of an immediately previous liberating discovery, of the "entry into paradise" after distressing anxiety. Certainly Luther speaks later of the wonderful new definition of justice and of the fact that the Lord accomplishes marvels in his saints.

Luther's discovery in regard to *iustitia Dei* is fundamentally Catholic. And he accordingly "was struggling against a Catholicism that was no longer Catholic in the full sense of the word." Luther routed, as religiously inadequate and not in accord with the Gospel, positions which had been handed down to him from late medieval practice and Ockhamist theology. The latter is not quite scholasticism; in fact it is not readily to be identified even with the teaching of William of Ockham himself. The *venerabilis inceptor* did indeed sharply stress human liberty alongside the divine sovereignty, but he no less unequivocally expounded that everything lies in the *acceptatio divina* and neither a naturally nor a supernaturally good work of man can bind God and limit his free choice of graces. Ockham's pupils had no longer been able to maintain this strong tension, exaggerated to paradox, between human freedom and divine caprice. With Gabriel Biel, who directly influenced Luther, they bent Ockham's theses to conform with morality and understood a sentence such as "Facienti quod est in se, deus non denegat gratiam," which is not in the works of the Franciscan, to mean that man by himself can and must dispose himself for grace and that there exists a synchronism, even a causality, between this disposition, effected by man's power, and the infusion of grace, in so far as God, on the basis of his arrangement, necessarily bestows the supernatural *habitus* on whoever loves him above all things *ex puris naturalibus.* But in Catholic doctrine, according to Aquinas as well as Augustine, every disposition — that is, every act directed toward God — which is answered by God with justifying grace, is already a work of prevenient grace, the gift of him who produces the will and the accomplishment (Phil. 2:13).

Luther's *Disputatio contra scholasticam theologiam* of 4 September 1517 was an express and official confrontation with the Ockhamist school of theology. He attributed great importance to it and intended to make it available to far wider circles than would be the case in regard to the indulgence theses of 31 October.

With the individual theses their opponents were named at the same time. They were Scotus, Ockham, Pierre d'Ailly, and Gabriel Biel, and the last named was the chief opponent. He was cited most and was also dealt with in passages where the others were specified by name. The matter was taken from Biel's commentary on *The Sentences* and his *Collectorium.*

Luther first objected to any attempt to explain away Augustine's theses on the wickedness of man. Without grace man can will and do only evil (1–4). He has no liberty to turn in both directions (5), but, without grace, necessarily chooses the evil act (6), and to assume that man of his own power can love God above all things is a pretense (18). The *amor amicitiae* is a work of prevenient grace (20). Thus the initiative lies with God, and his choice and predestination constitute the sole disposition for grace (19). It is false to say that man eliminates obstacles when he does what lies in his power (33). Left to himself, he has neither right understanding nor good will (34).

There is no natural morality. Externally good works are sins because of our pride or our bad disposition (37–38). Hence we cannot become just through just works, but we must be just in order to be able to do just works. In connection with this attack on moral philosophy Luther turns in general against Aristotle and the use of logic and metaphysics in theology (43–53).

He then emphasizes that grace is not something in man; it determines his entire existence. It is always effective and is not to be separated from love of God, just as love of God is never without grace (54–56) and God cannot accept man without justifying grace (57). As early as the lectures on Romans, Biel's doctrine that man of his own power can love God above all things and fulfill the law in fact (*secundum substantiam facti*), even if not according to the mind of the lawgiver (*ad intentionem praecipientis*), had driven Luther to exclaim, "O fools, O piggish theologians!" In the *Disputatio* too this is the chief reproach against scholastic theology. Just as one must not separate love and grace, so also the fulfilling of the law and grace. Grace requires no new work in addition to the observance of the law by natural strength, but it makes possible the spiritual fulfillment of the law (58–60)."

For "not to kill is not a sin because of the mere absence of the grace prescribed by God but because a false disposition — pride, anger, or greed — is at the basis of this external right conduct (61–63). To fulfill the law means to overcome hatred and greed, which inspire the external act, and the will, which rebels against the law (64–73). Only grace, or, better, "the child who is born to us," can do so (74). Only love, which is poured out in our heart by the Holy Spirit, can reconcile the will, which hates the law, with the law (85–90). At the end Luther once more turns on the Ockhamist understanding of the love of God. Grace does not facilitate the act of love, but rather makes it possible at all. We cannot by the same act love God for his own sake and creation for God's sake (94); that is, love of God and love of creature are irreconcilable (95). To love God above all else means to hate self and to know nothing except God (96).

Luther is here opposing a concept which, so to speak, sees man in a neutral zone where he is not challenged by God, does not face him in faith or in defiance, or where neither the anger nor the mercy of God is the power fundamentally determining him. In this disputation it is clear that the scholastic theology attacked by Luther is Ockhamism of the Biel type. With his stressing of prevenient grace, with his requiring of the grace of justification as the basis for *acceptatio divina,* and with his teaching that grace is not added as a condition to an already good natural activity but that it forms man's activity from the very beginning and leads to God, Luther contests what would have been censured by Thomism too and above all by Augustinianism. But at the same time Luther remains dominated by Ockhamism. And therefore he does not succeed, for example, in showing the relationship of the love of neighbor and of God and in seeing creation as an image of the divine nature.

CHAPTER 64

The Indulgence Controversy

History and Use of Indulgences

An indulgence is a remission of the temporal punishment of sins, granted by the Church and effective before God. The practice of indulgences in the Church, going back to the eleventh century, preceded the theological justification. Several factors contributed to the rise of indulgences. Private penance in the early Middle Ages brought about a connection in time between confession and absolution, whereby the subjective performance of penance followed reconciliation and the distinction between guilt and punishment became clearer. And in the atonements and commutations — that is, the adaptations whereby penitential works were adjusted to the circumstances and abilities of the penitent — it became evident that various kinds of penance could be substituted for one another and that the Church could decide such matters. Earlier the Church had already provided assistance outside the Sacrament in the penitential efforts of individuals by means of the intercession of martyrs and the official liturgical prayer. In the early medieval "absolutions" this aid acquired a more official form. These were prayers or benefits of the Church, which were to some extent connected with a summons to a particular work, such as the building of a church or participation in a crusade. Because it had been expressed by the bearer of the power of the keys, such an intercession was regarded as of special efficacy with God.

Whereas the atonement was concerned primarily with the canonical penalty, the absolution referred to the punishment in God's sight. The indulgence united them. But the indulgence differed from the atonement, because in the latter the substituted penitential work had to be equivalent, and also from the absolution, since this was not a judicial act. The indulgence, as a jurisdictional act, concerned the remission of ecclesiastical penance. But it was connected with prayer for the remission of the penalties for sin before God, a prayer which, because of its official character, one could be especially sure would be granted. The transition from a mildly administered atonement to an indulgence is naturally not clear. Still, the mitigation afforded by an indulgence was so well understood that even up to the thirteenth century it was regarded as a kindness toward the imperfect, a kindness that serious Christians were not to claim.

The theological justification of indulgences followed their use. The canonist Huguccio (d. 1210) was the first to describe an indulgence as a jurisdictional act relative to the penalties for sin before God. The question as to the source of the substitute for the remitted penance was answered after Hugh of Saint-Cher in 1230 with the doctrine of the *thesaurus ecclesiae,* of which the Church lawfully disposes. The more its efficacy was derived from the treasury of the Church, the more the indulgence became reserved to the Pope, who alone had power over this treasury, but the penitential work lost its significance in regard to the degree of the remission of punishment. If, besides, the punishments of sin were regarded as merely vindictive penalties, which as such had no meaning for the purification of man, then there was the further danger of disregarding man's susceptibility to the remission of penalties granted him and of neglecting pastoral responsibility for man's inner penitential spirit. Thus it was that the late Middle Ages saw a multiplication of indulgences and ever lighter works of indulgence and an unscrupulous financial exploitation of them.

The indulgence for the dead provided a special opportunity here. As early as the thirteenth century theologians and canonists had taught that indulgences could be applied to the dead, and indulgence preachers had proclaimed such indulgences on their own authority. We do not have genuine papal grants of indulgences for the dead until the middle of the fifteenth century, such as that of Calixtus III in 1457 for a crusade against the Muslims and that of Sixtus IV in 1476 for Saint-Pierre de Saintes. An efficacy *per modum suffragii* was attributed to indulgences for the dead, but this did not keep many theologians and, above all, preachers of indulgences from ascribing to them an infallible effect and from teaching that they could be gained even by one in the state of mortal sin and hence that only the prescribed monetary contribution was necessary. Despite the objections of several theologians, such as Cajetan, these views were prevalent around 1500, and indulgence preachers further exaggerated them in the pulpit. As early as 1482 there was submitted to the judgment of the Sorbonne a proposition which was identical in content with the notorious lampoon: "As soon as the money jingles in the chest, the soul springs out of Purgatory."

The strong financial exploitation of indulgences by the Curia led to similar practices by the territorial lords. They aspired to a direct share in the financial results; otherwise they forbade the preaching of the indulgence.

The Trafficking in Indulgences by Albrecht of Mainz

In 1505 Pope Julius II (1503–13) had begun the rebuilding of Saint Peter's basilica, and in 1507, according to custom, he had announced a plenary indulgence to finance this immense building project. The indulgence had been renewed by Leo X (1513–21). Because of considerable resentment at the financial exploitation by the Curia, as well as the efforts of territorial lords to permit only the preaching of indulgences in which they would have a financial share or which would benefit the churches of their territories, the proclamation of an indulgence did not necessarily assure its being preached. But a special opportunity presented itself in the territories of the Archbishops of Mainz and Magdeburg, the Bishop of Halberstadt, and the Margrave of Brandenburg. In 1513 Albrecht of Brandenburg, a twenty-three-year-old youth, became Archbishop of Magdeburg and administrator of Halberstadt. And in the very next year the chapter of Mainz also postulated the easygoing prince as Archbishop-Elector of Mainz. For Albrecht proposed to pay personally the *servitia* and the pallium tax, which had fallen due now for the third time within one decade. They amounted to 14,000 ducats. In addition there was owed a dispensation fee of 10,000 ducats, since, along with the great Mainz archbishopric, Albrecht wanted to retain his present sees of Magdeburg and Halberstadt — an illegal accumulation of pastoral benefices. The archbishop borrowed 29,000 Rhenish gold florins from the Fugger banking house, and the Curia itself indicated how this burden of debt could be paid. The archbishop was to undertake the preaching of the indulgence for Saint Peter's for eight years and be allowed to retain half the proceeds. Including the tax of 2,143 ducats which the Emperor had reserved for himself, Albrecht had to raise 26,143 ducats. Accordingly the indulgence had to raise 52,286 ducats if it was to achieve its goal. Representatives of the Fuggers accompanied the indulgence preachers in order to take their share on the spot. Thus did the indulgence, which Leo X granted by the Bull "Sacrosanctis Salvatoris et Redemptoris" of 31 March 1513 become an "object of barter in a wholesale commercial transaction," as Lortz stigmatizes the deal.

As papal agent for this indulgence, Archbishop Albrecht issued for his deputies and the indulgence preachers a comprehensive set of instructions, the *Instructio Summaria.* Despite certain obscurities, the doctrine of indulgences contained in this is correct, but in its recourse to pious formulas and superlatives it resorts in practice to a commercialized extolling of the indulgence in order to realize the highest possible monetary profit. The remission of future sins was not promised, contrary to what Luther claimed in 1541. But one could purchase a confession certificate, by virtue of which one could confess to any priest at any desired time in his later life sins reserved to the Pope. The indulgence preacher had to make it clear that a person did not need to confess at the moment of buying such a confession certificate, which procured for him, among other things, then and forever a share in the spiritual goods of the Church Militant. Likewise, one could gain a plenary indulgence for the dead without contrition and confession but merely by the paying of the money. And especially this indulgence was represented as "efficacissime" and "certissime," and sermons of a content such as that referred to in the lampoon mentioned above were thus abetted by it. The faithful were invited to postpone repentance, and the impression was strengthened that what was at stake was money rather than the salvation of souls.

On 22 January 1517, Johannes Tetzel (c. 1465–1519), a Leipzig Dominican, was appointed one of the two deputies for the preaching of the indulgence in the province of Magdeburg, and a high compensation was granted him. He quickly took up the task. He is reported to have been active in Halle in March and at Jüterbog on 10 April; according to Luther's statement people flocked to him from Wittenberg also, as though they were "insane" and "possessed." Frederick the Wise had not given leave for the preaching of the indulgence in Electoral Saxony, for he was unwilling to permit his subjects' money to profit Albrecht of Brandenburg, the rival of his dynasty, or to allow the pilgrimage to his Wittenberg Church of All Saints, so richly endowed with relics and indulgences, to suffer any falling off. The store of relics which the elector had assembled there, and the multitude of indulgences which he acquired for those venerating them, show clearly that Frederick the Wise was in no sense an opponent of indulgences.

In regard to his personal life Tetzel provided no reason for any special complaints. He was not one of those indulgence preachers about whom not only Luther but also Johann Eck himself, in his opinion on reform for the Pope, said that they paid off their prostitutes with indulgence certificates. But he was one of those who, as Johannes Cochläus, Duke Georg of Saxony, and his court chaplain Hieronymus Emser complained, emphasized the money at the expense of contrition.

As a confessor, Luther had occasion to deal with indulgence preaching and with the expectations and ideas it aroused in the minds of his penitents. He had already directed criticism at indulgences in the lectures on the Psalms and on Romans, and in a sermon usually assigned to 31 October 1516, he came out specifically against the indulgence Tetzel had preached on the Feast of Saint Matthias in 1517. He maintained that as a consequence of indulgences the people learned to flee and abhor the penalties of sin but not sin itself. It would be far better to admonish them to love the punishment and to embrace the Cross. In a sermon on the occasion of a church dedication, which he delivered in April 1517 or later, he came out against the "big show" of Tetzel's indulgence preaching. In this he emphasized that indulgences merely free from the conditions of private penance and not infrequently stand in the way of inner repentance. The genuine penitent, he said, did not wish to be freed from punishment by indulgences.

Luther presented his idea in detail in the treatise *De indulgentiis.* According to this, an indulgence is the remission of the satisfaction imposed in confession by the priest. In itself it does not lessen concupiscence nor does it increase love and grace. In Luther's opinion the faithful should be directed to genuine penance, that is, to inner conversion and the eradicating of radical sin. One cannot buy oneself off from it by an indulgence. Hence an indulgence is to be rejected if it provides the occasion for false security and spiritual laziness and does not promote the allaying of concupiscence and a longing for God. "We have to seek God's healing grace incessantly" — so runs the last sentence of this far too little noticed treatise. Till then Luther had regarded the indulgence doctrine expounded by Tetzel as the latter's private opinion and had ascribed its excesses to his charlatanry. But acquaintance with the *Instructio Summaria* of the Archbishop of Mainz showed him that Tetzel's sermons were based on official instructions. This may have induced him to turn to the prelates responsible — the Bishop of Brandenburg as local Ordinary and the Archbishop of Magdeburg and Mainz as the papal agent for the indulgence.

In a letter of 31 October 1517 to Albrecht of Mainz, Luther complained that the indulgence preachers "by deceiving stories and promises about indulgences lull the people into security and lack of fear." The archbishop should withdraw his *Instructio* and give other directions to the preachers; otherwise great shame and dishonor would ensue. From the accompanying theses he would be able to ascertain how unsettled the doctrine on the indulgence really was. The reference here was to the celebrated ninety-five theses. Luther actually sent them to the bishops directly concerned on the eve of All Saints. Only when these prelates did not reply, or replied in an unsatisfactory manner, did he, as he maintained throughout his life, distribute them to learned men in and outside Wittenberg. A posting of the theses at the Wittenberg castle church on 31 October 1517 is incompatible with these statements of Luther. Neither Luther himself nor any other of the numerous contemporary sources refers to such a move.

Luther's Ninety-five Theses

Apart from numerous other inconsistencies, the posting of the theses on the eve of the titular feast of the castle church, in view of the great concourse of people attracted by the rich indulgences to be gained there, would have had the character of a public spectacle, despite the fact that the theses were written in Latin. But as he repeatedly insisted, Luther sought a discussion among scholars for a clarification of the doctrine of indulgences, thus far not officially defined. The colleagues to whom Luther forwarded the theses after 31 October — Johann Lang in Erfurt, for example, on 11 November — passed them on. Thus in both longhand and print they acquired in a few weeks such a rapid and extensive distribution as no one, not even Luther, could have foreseen.

"Our Lord and Master Jesus Christ in saying, 'Do penance...' (Mt. 4:17), desired that the whole life of the faithful should be a penance" (Thesis 1). Here is expressed Luther's anxiety lest the faithful be lulled into a false assurance of salvation. Rather they should be "admonished to follow Christ, their Head, through suffering, death, and hell" (Thesis 94; 92–95). Indulgence preachers who by "extravagant and unrestrained" words (Thesis 92) commend indulgences far beyond their value (Thesis 24; 73–80) promote a lazy peace (Thesis 95), at the expense of contrition and penance (Theses 39–41). In this connection Luther later wrote in his *Resolutions:* "See the danger! Indulgences are preached to the people in direct opposition to the truth of the Cross and the fear of God." Indulgences are not to be rejected in principle (Thesis 71), but people are not to put their trust in them (Theses 49, 52, 32), and works of charity and prayer especially are superior to them (Theses 41–47). In opposition to the *Instructio* and the indulgence preachers, who give the impression that only by means of indulgences do we obtain remission of the penalties of sin and a share in the goods of Christ and the Church, Luther overemphasizes that every Christian finds full remission of penalty and guilt in true contrition (Thesis 36) and, even without indulgences, has a share in all the treasures of Christ and the Church (Thesis 37). The true treasury of the Church is the Gospel of the glory and grace of God. (Thesis 62). Hence only enemies of Christ can, like the *Instructio,* forbid the preaching of the word of God in the churches during the time of indulgence preaching (Theses 53–55). In Theses 14 to 19 Luther stresses the uncertain character of the statements of theologians in regard to the souls in purgatory. In any case, the indulgence for the dead is granted only in the form of an intercession (Theses 26, 25), and so one must not speak of an infallible effect (Theses 27–29).

All these topics can be understood as orthodox, as legitimate criticism of abuses in the indulgence system, and as a contribution to the discussion of theological questions not yet defined. Even Luther's idea of the declaratory nature of absolution — that the Pope can remit guilt only by the declaration and the acknowledgment that it is remitted by God (Theses 6, 38) — was in line with contemporary nominalist theology, according to which the sacramental absolution does not cancel "guilt and eternal punishment, but only indicates a cancellation that has already taken place."

Luther also stresses the intention of confessing as a condition of forgiveness by God (Theses 7, 38), and he even allows the Pope a right, efficacious with God, to reserve sins (Thesis 6). But he questions the nature of indulgences, especially according to the prevailing opinion of the time, when he restricts them to the remission of the canonical penalties (Theses 5, 11, 20, 21, 31) and does not concede that ecclesiastical penalties correspond to those imposed by God. In the declaration of these theses, however, he repeatedly affirms that he does not desire to make claims but wishes to dispute and would willingly be corrected.

Although, he says, the views of Thomas and Bonaventure are against him, no canon of law and no passage of Scripture is, and no doctrinal decision by the Church has yet been issued. Luther is convinced that he is within the limits of theological opinions that are defensible. That he was correct in this view is proved by the fact that his *Resolutions,* or explanation of the theses, was submitted to his Ordinary, the Bishop of Brandenburg, whose *placet* it obtained.

If we are not satisfied merely to establish the facts, if we inquire historically and causally to determine what the theses were aiming at and what development lay imminent in them, then we will attribute to them a greater significance. In so inquiring we have to keep in mind that in the nominalist theology divine and human activity were already separated to a great extent, in the sense that God accepted the action of the Church only as an occasion for his own saving action, without actually entering into it. Luther pushed this separation of the human and the ecclesiastical from the divine so far that he no longer attributed to the ecclesiastical penalty or its remission even an interpretive significance with regard to the penalties for sin imposed by God. In my view this seems to be a root of Luther's proximate rejection of the hierarchical priesthood as a divine institution.

But this theological impact of the theses was not immediately effective. The secret of the inflammatory effect and rapid spread of the indulgence theses lies in their polemical and folksy tone. With them Luther touched long-smoldering questions, grievances, and resentments which had already often become vocal; he made himself the spokesman of many disillusioned hopes and of a widespread discontent. In Theses 80 to 91 he took up, as he himself said, "the quite pointed and critical objections of the laity" (Theses 30, 81), which were not to be "silenced by force" and not to be appeased by cheap excuses. Many contemporaries felt as Prior Johannes Fleck did when, on becoming acquainted with the theses, he said to his confreres, "This is the one who will do it." And even such determined later opponents of Luther as Johannas Cochläus, Hieronymus Emser, and Duke Georg of Saxony hailed the theses. The Duke's councillor, Caesar Pflug, told him of a remark by Bishop Adolf VII of Merseburg to the effect that the prelate thought the theses "should be posted in many places" to warn the poor "against Tetzel's humbug."

The rapid circulation of the theses was for Luther himself a proof that he had expressed what many had kept quiet about because of "fear of the Jews" (John 7:13). But he deplored this turn because the theses had been intended, not for the people but for a few scholars, and because they contained some doubtful propositions (letter to Scheuerl of 5 March 1518). Hence he hastened to put his basic ideas on indulgences in writing for the people in the "Sermon on indulgences and grace" in March 1518. In 1518 alone thirteen printings of this appeared, an indication of the possibilities afforded to Luther and the Reformation by the printing press. At the same time, in his *Resolutiones disputationum de indulgentiarum virtute* Luther provided a detailed case for his indulgence theses, but this did not appear until August 1518. In it Luther was concerned to protect himself against misunderstandings and distortions and to give his superiors — Leo X, Staupitz, and the Bishop of Brandenburg — a first-hand account of the motives for his action. In the accompanying letter to the Pope Luther alludes to the unprecedented success of his theses. He says that he deplores this because they were unsuited for a circulation of this sort. However, they cannot be withdrawn now, and so he is issuing this explanation of them. In this way it should become clear that he is honestly concerned for the power of the Church and the respect due to her keys. At the end he wrote: "Therefore, most holy Father, I cast myself at the feet of Your Holiness and commit myself to you with all that I am and have." In the *Protestatio* introducing the *Resolutiones* he affirmed: "I first of all declare that I intend to say and to assert nothing except what is contained primarily in Holy Scripture and then in the Church Fathers acknowledged and preserved by the Roman Church and in canon law and the papal decrees. . . . " But he declined to be committed to the opinions of the theological schools: "Through this *Protestatio* of mine it is, so I hope, made sufficiently clear that I can err but that no one can make me out to be a heretic. . . . " The letters accompanying the *Resolutiones,* with their quite singular mixture of candid humility, prophetic self-assurance, and bold avowal, are not adequately characterized when they are referred to as "first-rate chess moves." Be that as it may, they prove — especially if the posting of the theses did not take place — that there was a real possibility of binding the Wittenberg friar, zealously striving for the honor of God and the salvation of souls, to the Church and of making him productive in her.

Of course there was also required on the part of the bishops concerned and of the Pope an approximately equal measure of religious strength and of apostolic and pastoral responsibility. That such was unthinkable reveals the radical weakness of the Church of that time. In this failure in the sphere of what is proper to the priesthood rather than in all the abuses lies her part of the guilt for the Reformation.

CHAPTER 65

Rome's Proceedings against Luther and the Leipzig Disputation

The first person affected by Luther's theses was Archbishop Albrecht of Mainz, who requested an opinion from his university at Mainz. The university returned an evasive reply and suggested that the matter be submitted to the Pope, since his authority was at stake. Even before this answer reached him, Albrecht informed his Magdeburg advisers on 13 December 1517 that he had sent the theses to the Pope and suggested that they should institute a *processus inhibitorius* whereby Luther would be summoned and called upon, under threat of punishment, to refrain in future from all attacks on indulgences in preaching, writing, and disputation. But apparently the advisers did not comply. The denunciation of Luther at Rome for spreading new doctrine was the archbishop's only strong weapon. He obviously did not want to be bothered further with the affair, and so his advisers shelved the *processus.*

The efforts of Tetzel and the Dominicans were more effective, but their activity only too easily created the impression that this was a case of a dispute between rival orders. In January 1518, at the chapter of the Saxon Dominican province in Frankfurt on the Oder, Tetzel debated either ninety-five or 106 theses — the sources differ — against Luther, drawn up by Konrad Wimpina, rector of the university. Here he frivolously defended the lampoon: "As soon as the money jingles in the chest, the soul springs out of purgatory." In fact he stressed that the soul would be freed even more quickly, for the money took time to fall. But even he was outdone by his confrere Sylvester Prierias, the Pope's own theologian. According to Prierias, a preacher who taught this was no more blameworthy than a cook who makes food more attractive to a satiated stomach by adding condiments.

Just as grave as this lack of religious seriousness was the thoughtlessness with which opinions of the schools were passed off as dogmas and their opponents were branded as heretics. The opinion so offensive to Luther, that the state of grace was not necessary for gaining indulgences for the dead, was put forth by Tetzel in Thesis 42 as a "Christian dogma." It was for this reason that Cardinal Cajetan, in a treatise on indulgences of 20 November 1519, attacked preachers who pass off private opinions as teachings of the Church. This arbitrary method of making dogmas out of questions still open to debate was a no less dangerous variation of the "theological vagueness" which was one of the most decisive causes of the Reformation.

The Dominican chapter agreed to denounce Luther at Rome of suspicion of heresy. This was done in March 1510, and, considering the great influence of the Preaching Friars at the Curia, it was not without danger for Luther.

Johannes Eck's rather hastily scribbled *Obelisci,* comments on the indulgence theses, were intended for the private use cf Gabriel von Eyb, Bishop of Eichstätt. In March 1518 they came into Luther's hands through Wenceslas Link of Nürnberg but obtained about as little publicity as Luther's *Asterisci* did. In addition to his eagerly pursued amusements — the hunt, comedies, banquets — Leo X was fully occupied with plans for filling his always empty coffers, with the family politics of the House of Medici, and with at least one serious enterprise, the defense of Christendom against the Turkish threat; and so he was disinclined to take seriously the "squabble of monks" in Germany. On 3 March 1518, Gabriel della Volta, general-designate of the Augustinians, was directed "to calm down the man" and to put out the rising flame in time. But nothing more than a fraternal admonition by Staupitz seems to have resulted. On the contrary, the Augustinian chapter meeting at Heidelberg in April and May of 1518 turned into a pro-Luther demonstration. Theses composed by Luther on original sin, grace, free will, and the power of the natural man for the good were debated under his direction, with his pupil Leonard Beier as *respondens.* The Heidelberg meeting showed that the German Augustinians were backing Luther. In addition, he was able to gain the support of several of the younger theologians, such as Martin Bucer, a Dominican, and Johannes Brenz, the future reformer of Württemberg.

On 17 May, the day after he returned to Wittenberg, Luther preached on John 16:2: "They are going to put you out of the synagogue." Whoever dies under an unjust excommunication is saved, even though he dies without the Sacraments. Excommunication can deprive one only of external membership in the Church, not of a share in heavenly treasures. At the same time Luther composed the very submissive accompanying letter to his *Resolutiones* for Leo X.

The Dominican general chapter at Rome became important for the start of the proceedings against Luther in May 1518, when Tetzel was promoted to doctor of theology by authorization of Leo X. In mid-June, at the Pope's request, Sylvester Prierias drew up an opinion, *In praesumptuosas Martini Lutheri conclusiones de potestate papae dialogus.* This hastily composed polemic rightly began with the authority of Church and Pope as the crucial point of controversy, but exaggerated the extent of the infallible doctrinal authority and made so slight a distinction between binding Church teaching and the practice of indulgences, or rather the views of theologians, and was furthermore so biting in tone, that from the outset it rendered any "dialogue" impossible. The *Dialogus* was printed in June and attached to the notification with which, at the beginning of July, the Auditor of the *Camera Apostolica,* cited Luther to Rome for hearings.

The summons reached the reformer on 7 August through Cardinal Cajetan, who had been at the Diet of Augsburg since 7 July in an effort to win the German estates for the Turkish war. The next day Luther requested the Elector Frederick the Wise to induce the Emperor to have the Pope allow the proceedings to take place in Germany. If Prierias had allegedly jotted down his *Dialogus* in three days, then Luther claimed to have prepared his *Responsio* in two days. A work of poor quality, wrote Luther to Spalatin on 31 August 1518, did nor deserve a more serious consideration. Thus Luther likewise failed to do justice to the gravity of the situation in style and content. "Both the Pope and a council can err." Scripture, as Augustine writes, is without error. To be sure, up to now the Roman Church, Luther gratefully admits, has actually not deviated from the true faith in her decrees and has clung to the authority of the Bible and of the Fathers. Luther regards himself as bound by her decrees. He will not, however, submit to the opinions of the Thomists but will await the decision of Church or council in the question of indulgences.

Luther could not count on the good will of Maximilian I. For on 5 August the latter had pointed out to the Pope the danger to the unity of faith caused by Luther's appearance and had promised to back up in the Empire the measures to be taken by the Church. Without respecting the period of time specified in the summons, Leo X on 23 August issued a brief for Cajetan at Augsburg: the legate was to summon Luther as a notorious heretic. If he should recant, he was to be graciously received. If he failed to appear voluntarily or refused to recant, Cajetan was to arrest him and send him to Rome. In the event that he was unable to arrest him, the legate received authority to declare Luther and his adherents excommunicated.

At the same time the request was made that Frederick the Wise should surrender the "son of wickedness" to Cajetan or to Rome. The elector exerted himself to have Luther's case dealt with by a court in Germany. From Cajetan he obtained a promise to deal with Luther at Augsburg "paternally" and to release him even if Luther refused to recant. The legate agreed to this concession for political reasons. On 27 August five of the electors — those of Trier and Saxony were not included — had pledged themselves to elect King Charles I of Spain as Maximilian's successor. The Elector Frederick had violently opposed the election of the Habsburg and had thus become a partisan of the Pope, who at any cost wanted to prevent the encirclement of the Papal State by the united Habsburg lands.

On 3 September Leo X announced in consistory his intention of bestowing the Golden Rose on Frederick the Wise. On 10 September the delivery of the distinction to the elector, together with rich indulgences for the Wittenberg castle church, was assigned to a papal notary and secret chamberlain, Karl von Miltitz, a young Saxon noble. But this mission was halted by the arrival of a message from Cajetan reporting Frederick the Wise's opposition to the election of Charles I, as well as his personal intervention in Luther's favor. The Curia agreed to the legate's arrangement about Luther's hearing in Augsburg, but in the brief "Dum nuper" of 11 September placed the responsibility on Cajetan by giving him judicial authority over Luther's case. He was to give the Wittenberg friar a careful interrogation, avoiding any disputation, and, in accord with his findings, acquit or condemn him.

At the end of September Luther received orders from his prince to appear before Cajetan at Augsburg. He arrived there on 7 October 1518. He first waited for the imperial safe-conduct and on 12 October and the two succeeding days went to Cajetan. If any contemporary theologian did, then Cajetan possessed the qualifications for gaining Luther for the Church. He had already written on indulgences in 1517, making it clear that the opinions of canonists and theologians on the subject were widely divergent. At Augsburg in the weeks preceding Luther's interrogation he had composed five more *quaestiones* on the subject. He took the trouble to read Luther's writings, and his views on indulgences were moderate. Of course, for Cajetan an indulgence could not be a mere remission of ecclesiastical penalties; it must also free us from the penalties which we have incurred for our sins before the divine justice. Otherwise it would be a dangerous misleading of the faithful. To be concerned about indulgences was not a mark of imperfection. However, it was to be conceded to Luther that an alms is preferable to an indulgence and that anyone who neglects an obligatory alms for the sake of an indulgence commits a sin. Although indulgences for the dead are also based on the Church's power of the keys, they take effect only *per modum suffragii.*

A more detailed study of Luther's writings by Cajetan at Augsburg is attested by several treatises on the sacrament of penance, excommunication, and purgatory. In a *quaestio* completed on 26 September 1518, Cajetan asks whether, for the fruitful reception of penance, the penitent must have the certainty of faith that he has obtained from God the forgiveness of his sins. After six affirmative arguments, mostly taken *verbatim* from Luther's sermon *De Poenitentia,* Cajetan stresses that the penitent need not necessarily have faith that he has actually been absolved, but he must believe that the grace of absolution is given to us through the sacrament of penance. Luther's requirement of the certainty of faith by the one receiving the sacrament that his sins have been pardoned is regarded by Cajetan as unheard of and of great significance; for him it implies "the establishing of a new Church." It is not the necessity of faith for a fruitful reception of the sacrament that is questioned. Cajetan rejects the faith that is referred back to the recipient; that is, the uncertainty of faith that pardon has been obtained as the constitutive element in justification.

This "reflexive faith" (P. Hacker), together with the doctrine of the *thesaurus ecclesiae,* was the chief topic of the interrogation in Augsburg. According to Luther's description, he was received on 12 October "very graciously by the Lord Cardinal Legate, almost with too much deference." Cajetan could nor and would not engage in a disputation. He demanded recantation and a promise to keep the peace thereafter. In him Luther saw not the legate of the Church but the Thomist, a "member of the opposition," by whom he refused to let himself be committed to "the hallucinations of scholastic opinions." And so a heated dispute arose, nevertheless. The Cardinal demanded the withdrawal of Thesis 58, according to which the treasury of the Church is not identical with the merits of Christ and the saints. Luther refused and insisted upon the thesis: "That the merits of Christ are not the treasury of indulgences, but rather they have amassed it," or, as he expressed it in the *Resolutiones:*

> . . . since Christ is the ransom and the Redeemer of the world, he is therefore truly the only treasury of the Church. But I deny, until shown otherwise, that he is the treasury of indulgences.

It cannot be said that this decisive conversation foundered on hairsplitting distinctions. Luther wanted to make sure that access to the merits of Christ is not restricted to indulgences and even that an indulgence is not the closest and best route to them. But would not and could not the Cardinal concede this? Luther, however, saw a difference between the "treasury of indulgences" and the "treasury of the life-giving grace of God," between what is granted to us on the basis of the "cooperation of the power of the keys and of indulgences" and what we obtain only "through the Holy Spirit and on no account from the Pope." Thus the fundamental difference lay in the concept of the Church. For Luther the Pope is "authority," to whom he subjects himself, as he does to political authority, on the basis of Romans 13:1, and not of Matthew 16:18, so long as such submission is pleasing to God. In the same breath Luther emphasized that he "awaited the Pope's judgment" and that "truth has power over the Pope too and he [Luther] no longer awaits any man's judgment where he has clearly recognized the judgment of God."

More important for Luther, because it was of immediate significance for salvation, was the question of the certainty of faith in regard to justification proper as the presupposition for it. He claimed to have maintained against Cajetan that it is "an indispensable condition that man believe with firm conviction that he is justified and not to entertain any doubt that he will obtain grace." Here, he says, has been found a new kind of theology and an error.

To these fundamental viewpoints in the case were added great differences in character and mentality. Cardinal Cajetan, a precise and objective Italian, was soon angered by the obstinate seriousness and presumptuous and passionate manner of this German friar, who fancied himself to be so important with his "curious speculation" and who felt, for his part, that he was not taken seriously and understood. According *to Table Talk* (May 1538), Cajetan shouted at Luther, "Do you think that the Pope cares for Germany?" To Karlstadt Luther wrote from Augsburg:

> Cajetan may be a renowned Thomist, but he is a vague, obscure, and unintelligible theologian or Christian and hence as qualified for judging, understanding, and giving sentence in this matter as an ass is for playing the harp. For that reason my affair is in so much greater danger in that it has such judges who are not only enemies and angered, but also unable to recognize and understand it.

When they separated on the third day, 14 October, Cajetan directed Luther not to come back until he had changed his mind, but at the same time he tried to influence him through Staupitz and Wenceslas Link. They induced Luther to excuse himself to Cajetan in a letter of 17 October for his haughty, biting, and disrespectful conduct and to promise not to treat further of indulgences, provided the others also observed silence. Luther still felt unable to retract, but he asked for a decision from the Pope on the unsettled questions so that the Church could definitely require retraction or faith. In a second letter, on 18 October, Luther announced his departure and also an appeal to the Pope suggested to him by higher authority. This appeal, "from the Pope poorly informed and from his judges to the Most Holy Father to be better informed," he had already registered before a notary and witnesses on 16 October. The doctrine of indulgences, he said, was in many respects unclear. Hence he considered disputation permissible and useful. He had undertaken one and subjected his controversial opinions to the judgment of the Church and of everyone who understood it better, above all, however, to that of the Most Holy Father and Lord, Pope Leo X. On the other hand, he had not been able to give the recantation which the "very learned and amiable Cajetan" demanded, because the points on which he erred had not been pointed out to him.

This appeal was posted at the Augsburg cathedral on 22 October, after Luther had left the city by night through a small gate in the wall. On 19 November a letter from Cajetan, dated 25 October, reached Frederick the Wise; the cardinal demanded the extradition or the expulsion of Luther. The elector should not, because of a miserable friar, stain the renown of his ancestors with dishonor. Luther offered to emigrate for the sake of his prince, who seems for the moment to have agreed to the plan or at least to have given it serious consideration. Spalatin advised against a headlong flight to France. But perhaps he had already thought of hiding Luther somewhere in Saxony.

In the Constitution "Cum Postquam," of 9 November 1518, Leo X rendered the binding doctrinal definition on indulgences which Luther had requested. It was based on a draft composed by Cajetan and its essence was: To render any evasion impossible it is here declared as the doctrine of the Roman Church that the Pope, by virtue of his power of the keys, can remit punishments of sin through an indulgence, by distributing the treasure of the merits of Christ and the saints. This indulgence is conceded to the living as absolution and to the dead by intercession. Cajetan published this bull at Linz an der Donau on 13 December. It was printed several times but had no lasting effect. Public opinion was already too strong against indulgences as a means of satisfying curial avarice, and Luther, despite all protestations of submission to the Holy See, was prepared to retract only if convicted of error on the basis of Holy Scripture as he understood it.

Meanwhile, he had advanced another step. On 28 November, in the chapel of the Holy Body of Christ at Wittenberg, he registered his appeal to the council, soon and legitimately to be summoned in the Holy Spirit. This, he said, was above the Pope in matters of faith. In the text Luther followed the Sorbonne, which on 28 March 1518, in the controversy over the Gallican liberties, had likewise appealed to the council. The printing of his appeal was commissioned by Luther, but it was not intended for distribution; it was merely to be kept ready in the event of his excommunication. But as Luther several times asserts, the edition was almost disposed of by the enterprising printer before the reformer had his hands on a copy.

An action of such great import, then, is supposed to have happened more or less by chance, contrary to Luther's intention. Must we not, then, accuse him of an irresponsible negligence? Or are we dealing with a diplomatic maneuver whereby Luther intended to present the Saxon court with a *fait accompli* without having acted contrary to its clear instructions? The case of the *Acta Augustana* was probably similar. Here, according to Luther, Spalatin's prohibition did not arrive until after the document, except for the last sheet, had already been distributed. But Luther might have tempted fate in the sense that he left the decision in the balance in the secret hope that it would be determined in his favor by other factors. Doubtless he was much more anxious and more inwardly troubled than his often bold and decisive actions and noisy language lead one to suppose. We must allow that Luther perhaps often consciously made any retreat impossible and burned his bridges behind him, while in other cases he carried matters too far but then shrank from the ultimate consequences. When these, nevertheless, occurred, due to the inner or the external dynamics of the facts, he accepted them and even greeted them as God's will. Luther knew in what great demand his books and pamphlets were, and he had enough experience with printers to foresee what would happen in the printing of his appeal. Hence what he wrote to Wenceslas Link — that, to his great displeasure, the printer had distributed the appeal, that he had intended to keep the printed copy for himself but God had disposed otherwise — is only superficially credible. Just as he had assured the Pope that the indulgence theses had been widely circulated against his will but that he could now no longer do away with them, so now he wrote to Spalatin in regard to the publication of his appeal to the council: "What has once happened I cannot undo."

In these weeks Luther again thought of emigrating. He was probably not only concerned not to burden his prince with his affairs but also aimed to obtain liberty of action and to be freed from the network of petty tactical considerations to which his connection with the Saxon court forced him again and again. At this very time (18 December 1518) he thus expressed himself to Wenceslas Link: "I do not know the source of these ideas. In my judgment the case has not yet begun and even less can the lords at Rome yet anticipate its end." And he even entertained misgivings "that the true Antichrist, to whom Paul refers, rules in the Roman Curia. Today I already believe it possible to prove that Rome is worse than the Turk."

The Curia confronted a twofold task: to render the heretic Luther harmless and to gain his prince as an ally on the tax for the campaign against the Turks and especially on the question of the imperial succession. It was still uncertain whether both goals could be pursued with all energy simultaneously, that is, whether Frederick the Wise would drop Luther. To clarify the matter — in other words, to investigate the attitude of the elector — was the commission entrusted to the papal chamberlain, Karl von Miltitz. In mid-November he was finally started on his way to Cajetan at Augsburg, with the Golden Rose, rich indulgences, and a bull excommunicating Luther. But he did not find the legate, by whose instructions he was supposed strictly to be bound. Hence he deposited the Golden Rose and the papal bulls with the Fuggers and in mid-December joined the electoral councillor Degenhard Pfeffinger, who was returning to the court of Frederick the Wise. En route he could not but ascertain how very much German sentiment favored Luther. But this did not cause the conceited, ambitious, and intellectually mediocre courtier to maintain his reserve. On the contrary, he boasted loudly of his alleged commissions and related Roman gossip, according to which the Pope did not think much of Tetzel or of Prierias.

On 28 December Miltitz reached Altenburg, the residence of Frederick the Wise. A short time earlier, on 8 December the elector had finally replied to Cajetan, refusing to surrender or to expel his professor. Luther, he said, had not been convicted of heresy; on the contrary, he was open to correction and ready for a disputation. Thus had Frederick the Wise set himself up as Luther's protector, at the same time leaving the proceedings against him open. With this delaying tactic, the arrival of the pompous chamberlain, who, contrary to his instructions, was posing as mediator, was not unwelcome. Frederick brought about a meeting of Luther and Miltitz on 4 and 5 January 1519 which resulted in the following agreement: both parties were henceforth forbidden "to preach about, write about, or discuss the matter," and Miltitz would induce the Pope to appoint a bishop to designate the erroneous articles for Luther's recantation. Frederick the Wise and Luther did not take the thoughtless officiousness of the "nuncio" very seriously but agreed to the "Miltitziad," because they thereby hoped to achieve their goal of having Luther's case dealt with in Germany, and they at least gained time. In agreement with the elector, Miltitz on 12 June offered the function of arbiter to Richard von Greiffenklau, Archbishop of Trier. In accord with his tactics of putting the blame for the increasing gravity of the situation on the Dominicans, Cajetan and Tetzel, Miltitz reprimanded Tetzel and declared that he would accuse him at Rome of immorality and unlawful personal acquisition of indulgence funds. The indulgence preacher withdrew entirely into the shadows and died on 11 August 1519.

His unprecedented and arbitrary action in bargaining with the friar Martin Luther, who had been declared a heretic by the Pope, ought to have brought down on Miltitz severe criticism from Cajetan and the Curia. But the death of Emperor Maximilian I on 12 January 1519 had created a new situation and was destined to be the prelude to what Kalkoff calls the "greatest diplomatic campaign" of the age, to which everything else, including Luther's trial, had to give way. As early as 23 January 1519 Cajetan received from Leo X instructions to prevent the election of Charles of Spain by any means. Thus the good will of Frederick the Wise must be gained. Hence the intrigues of Miltitz, with no binding force, did not do the Curia any harm; he was at least catered to and temporarily found a willing ear for his frivolous optimism. Cajetan's own role was more difficult: to have to suppress the condemnatory judgment against Luther that was in his hands and to have to offer the imperial crown to the heretic's protector. The highly embellished reports made by Miltitz provided Leo X with a pretext for pretending in a brief of 29 March 1519 that Luther was prepared to recant and for extending to him a fatherly invitation. Before the Pope, the vicar of Christ, he could make the retraction from which he had been deterred at Augsburg only by Cajetan's severity and partisan favoring of Tetzel. If that was the way matters were, then the Pope had no further reason to be annoyed with Frederick the Wise for patronizing the heretic. His wooing of the elector reached its elimination in the message which Miltitz had to deliver eight days before the election. The elector was urgently requested to exert himself for the election of the King of France. If the King's election was impossible, Frederick should himself accept the imperial crown. In return, the Pope would do anything in his power for him and would make one of his friends a cardinal. In Rome at this time Luther was considered the friend of the elector. Thus this could have been a hint that he would be created a cardinal.

Out of concern for the Papal State and the position of the Medici in Italy, then, the Pope behaved as though Luther and his protectors had not been declared heretics. He dropped the proceedings for almost a year and gave the Lutheran movement time to strike deeper roots; he held back the bull of excommunication and instead offered the imperial crown and the red hat.

> If the Roman Court, despite the warnings of Cajetan, forgot, so to speak, the danger which threatened the whole Church from this Martin Luther Eleutherius and put aside the handing of this secular crisis in favor of the momentary exigencies of the papacy's Italian policy, this is perhaps the

greatest proof of all that Luther and the opposition were correct when they reproached the Church of Christ for having degenerated into an institution of legal and worldly authority. (R. Stadelmann)

The Leipzig Disputation

Though political considerations caused the shelving of the proceedings against Luther, the controversy of intellects that he had stirred up was not to be easily appeased. Some theses which Luther's Wittenberg colleague Andreas von Karlstadt had composed against Eck's *Obelisci* afforded Eck the welcome opportunity in August 1518 to issue an invitation for a debate. In October the professor from Ingolstadt had had a relatively amicable conversation with Luther. They agreed to propose Erfurt and Leipzig to Karlstadt as places for the disputation. Karlstadt left the final choice to Eck, who in December asked the Leipzig theological faculty and Duke Georg of Saxony to permit the disputation there. The faculty and the local Ordinary, Bishop Adolf of Merseburg, were opposed, but Duke Georg eagerly favored it and was able to persuade the faculty to agree. That same month Eck had published twelve theses on penance, indulgences, the treasury of the Church, and purgatory. Ostensibly against Karlstadt, in reality they were against Luther and his view of the authority of the Pope and the Church. Thus, for example, Thesis 12 (later 13) stated: "It is false to assert that before the time of Silvester [314–355] the Roman Church did not yet have supremacy over the other churches." Despite his understanding with Miltitz, Luther published opposing theses, and announced that he would participate in the disputation. With reference to Eck's counter-thesis 13, he claimed that the primacy of the Roman Church was demonstrated by forged papal decretals which were only four hundred years old.

Some days later, on 5 March, he assured Spalatin that it had never entered his mind to separate from the Apostolic See in Rome. He was agreed to its being called and being the lord of all. A person must also honor and bear with the Turks because of the power bestowed by God. Hence at that time the papacy was for Luther only a ruling power like any secular authority. But this was not all. On March 13 he whispered to Spalatin that in his study of the decretals for the disputation he had asked himself whether the Pope were not the Antichrist or at least his envoy, since in his decrees he so wretchedly crucified Christ, that is, the truth.

The disputation took place at the Pleissenburg at Leipzig and lasted from 27 June to 16 July 1519. Luther was admitted to it by the Duke of Saxony only at the last moment and through Eck's intervention. First Eck and Karlstadt debated on predestination. Then the controversy between Eck and Luther came to a climax on the problems of divine law, the papal primacy, and the authority of councils. According to Luther, councils could err and had erred; for example, the Council of Constance had been wrong in condemning Hus. Thereby was Scripture set up as the sole source of faith and *sola scriptura* as the formal principle of the Reformation. Luther no longer recognized a supreme ecclesiastical teaching authority which renders a binding interpretation of Scripture. In the disputation Eck's good memory and dialectical skill served him very well. If through his cold precision Eck risked driving his opponent to heretical conclusions and committing him to heresy, still Eck has the merit, granted the absence of dogmatic clarity in his day, of having made it clear that Luther implied, not reform, but an attack on the constitution of the Church.

CHAPTER 66

Luther's Reform Writings of 1520

After the Leipzig Disputation Luther rapidly became the hero and spokesman of the nation. He himself was filled with an apocalyptic spirit and imagined himself called to confront the Antichrist. This outlook gave his words their prophetic solemnity, urgency, and certainty. Knights, townsmen, and peasants, hardly qualified to grasp the reformer's essential religious concern, were carried along by the conviction that Luther would bring about the long-desired reform of Church and Empire. By reform was also understood the realization of one's own social and political aims. From everywhere students flocked to the University of Wittenberg. In 1518, at Luther's urging, the arts faculty had undergone reform in the direction of humanism, and Melanchthon was occupying the chair of Greek. In turn the students were active heralds of Lutheran doctrine to the remotest corner of the Empire.

In addition, printing offered quite new possibilities for propaganda. As early as 1518 the humanist Johannes Froben at Basel had brought out a complete edition of Luther's Latin works in a large number of copies. New, enlarged editions appeared in 1520 at Strasbourg and Basel. At Basel in May 1520 and at Strasbourg in July collections of Luther's German works were made available and sold well. Occasionally Luther employed as many as three printers to make his works available. They were mostly controversial writings, called for by some event of the moment and hastily composed, assailing abuses or parrying an attack. But there were also many works of edification, testimonies to his own religious experiences and at the same time pastoral aids for the many who applied to him. Luther was fully conversant with the language of the people. He was often coarse and full of bitter mockery, never boring and ponderous like the involved disputations of scholastic theology.

The year 1520 brought the first climax in his journalistic activity. Deserving of special mention among his pastoral pieces at the end of 1519 are the sermons on the three Sacraments which alone Luther would henceforth regard as true Sacraments: that on penance, that on baptism, and that on the venerable Sacrament of the Holy and True Body of Christ and on fellowship. Whether Luther still held to the sacramental character of penance in the accepted sense is open to question. From the purely declaratory meaning of absolution, already stressed in the indulgence theses, he deduced that any lay person could grant absolution.

In regard to baptism and the Eucharist, the "two foremost Sacraments in the Church," Luther stresses the subjective acquiring of the grace offered in them and their fruitful effect. The *opus operatum* must become *opus operantis* in faith; otherwise it only produces harm, just as the Cross of Christ became misfortune for the Jews. Luther rejected Spalatin's suggestion that he should write on the other sacraments also, because he said, there is no basis for them in Scripture: "For me there is no other Sacrament. For there only exists a Sacrament where there exists an express divine promise for the exercise of faith."

In the spring of 1520, at Spalatin's request, Luther replied to the charge that, by his teaching on justification by faith alone, he prejudiced works or even rendered them contemptible. In the long sermon "On good works," dealing with the relation of faith and works, he supplied the laity with copious advice for a good Christian life and activity. The most eminent of all works is faith (John 6:28). It is, however, not a good work in addition to others, but the source of all good works. These are fruits of faith which "brings with it charity, peace, joy, and hope." The important thing is not the size of the external work; all that we do can become a good work, if only it has faith as its motivating cause. "For if justice exists in faith, it is clear that faith alone fulfills all commands and makes all their works justified." If we possessed the living faith, "we would not need any law, but each of himself would do good works at all times." But so long as we do not have this liberty of faith for good works, we need laws and admonitions, and, like children, we must be motivated to good works by ceremonies and promises. Faith, however, does not spring from the works, but is a gift of Christ. Faith proves itself in daily life, in obedience to God's command. With that we have our hands full; there is no further need of works which we impose upon ourselves. The works imposed upon me "do not shine and glisten" as do the voluntary works of the "new saints." They are the more sublime and the better the less they "glisten" and "take place so quietly and secretly that no one but God alone is aware of them." In this first and perhaps most important treatise of the decisive year 1520 — a treatise that was not heeded in accord with its significance — Luther was moving among the ideas of German mysticism, especially of Tauler. Through all the polemic it remains clear that he did not reject works as such, but only a piety of works that had become mechanical in many respects.

Not his doctrine of justification but his teaching on the Church led ever more clearly to the break. Luther had been struggling for some time with the idea of the Pope as Antichrist. In February 1520 he became acquainted with Ulrich von Hutten's new edition of Lorenzo Valla's work on the alleged Donation of Constantine (1440). On the strength of this he wrote to Spalatin on 24 February: "I am so afraid that I have almost no doubts now that the pope is really the Antichrist whom the world is expecting according to the general opinion." At the same time there came into Luther's hands the *Epithoma responsionis ad Lutherum* (1519) of Sylvester Prierias, with its strong emphasis on papal primacy and infallibility. In May appeared the Franciscan Augustine Alveldt's *Super apostolica sede,* which was answered by Luther's pupil, Johannes Lonicer. When Alveldt thereupon published in German a revised edition of his work, Luther personally wrote a violent rejoinder: *Von dem Papsttum zu Rome wider den hochberühmten Romanisten zu Leipzig* (1520). In it Luther developed his doctrine of the Church: Christianity, as the congregation of all believers in Christ, is not a "corporal" collection but one "of hearts in one faith." This "spiritual unity" is of itself alone sufficient to constitute Christianity. Baptism and the Gospel are its signs in the world. This Christianity, which alone is the true Church, has no head on earth, "but only Christ in heaven is the head here and alone rules." Bishops are messengers and by divine disposition are all equal. Only by human arrangement is "one above another in the visible Church." Matthew 16:18 must be interpreted by Matthew 18:18. Then it is clear that the keys were given to Saint Peter, not for himself alone, but vicariously for the whole community. Accordingly, the Pope, permitted by God, must be endured in all patience, "as though the Turk were over us."

If Luther was here touching the national resentment against the Curia which had been so often expressed in the *gravamina* of the German nation, he unequivocally made himself the spokesman of these desires and complaints in the first of the three great statements of programs in the summer of 1520, *An den christlichen Adel deutscher Nation von des christlichen Standes Besserung.* On 7 June 1520 he wrote to Spalatin: "I am planning to issue a pamphlet, addressed to the Emperor Charles and the nobility of all Germany, against the tyranny and unworthiness of the Roman Curia." The introductory first part deals with razing the three walls behind which the "Romanists," that is, the Curia, are entrenched in order to avoid any reform. These are: (1) the spiritual power is superior to the secular; (2) only the Pope has the right to interpret Scripture; (3) only he can convoke a legitimate council. In contrast to this, Luther stresses the universal priesthood; he will recognize no other special priesthood. If Pope and bishops have failed, then it is the duty of the so-called secular estates to provide a remedy:

> Therefore, when necessity requires and the pope is vexatious to Christendom, the first person who is able should, as a true member of the entire body, do what he can so that a legitimate and free council may take place. None can do this better than the secular sword, especially since they are now also fellow-Christians, fellow-priests, equally spiritual, equally powerful in all things, and must let their office and work, which they hold from God over everyone, operate freely where there is need and use.

There follows a list of accusations, especially against the "Roman greed and see of robbers." They culminate in the charge that Pope and Curia do not obey their own canon law. In the third part Luther develops in twenty-eight points a reform program, extending from the abolition of annates, reservations, celibacy, and the numerous feast days to the reform of universities and even the closing of brothels. All — nobles, peasants, and the poor in the cities — could here consider the redress of their grievances. What Luther had struggled with in his personal anxieties of conscience became in this treatise the concern of the nation. Accordingly, readers scrambled to obtain it. The sale — 4,000 copies in the first week — was unprecedented.

In the second great statement of program, *De captivitate Babylonica ecclesiae praeludium* (October 1520), one of Luther's few writings on systematic theology, he directed himself to theologians. Its occasion was a work by Alveldt, *Tractatus de communione sub utraque specie* (June 1520), but it went far beyond that and was a discussion of the sacramental doctrine of the Catholic Church. Luther admits only three valid sacraments — baptism, penance, and communion — but they have been "brought by the Roman Court into a wretched prison." The Sacrament of the Eucharist is in a threefold captivity: the refusal of the other species, the doctrine of transubstantiation, and the concept of communion as a sacrifice. Luther does not claim that the second species should be given unconditionally and that the doctrine of transubstantiation is false, but he wants freedom to be preserved. It is Roman tyranny that forbids the chalice to the laity or makes an opinion of Aquinas an article of faith. Luther stresses the true presence of the body of Christ but he wants to leave open the "how." To him the presence of the body of Christ in, with, and under the bread, analogous to the imminence of the divinity in Christ's humanity, is very obvious.

On the other hand, the third prison of the sacrament is a thoroughly impious abuse and a source of further, more deeply rooted evils. Luther here repeats ideas from the "Sermon on the New Covenant, that is, on the Mass" (1520). He demands a return to the "first and simple institution" of Christ, to his word. According to this, the sacrament of the altar is a covenant, in which the remission of sins is granted to us. The words of the narrative of the institution are the essence and the power of the Mass and at the same time the totality and epitome of the whole Gospel. Instead of accepting this bequest in faith, men have, according to Luther, made of it a sacrifice, a work, or, in other words, something which they give to God.

In Christ, the Lord of the Eucharist, Luther sees God simply and not the God-Man, the Mediator. Thus the Eucharist is meant by God for us and not, through Christ the Mediator, for the Father also. Hence Luther likewise sees no inner bond of the community's worship of praise and thanksgiving, the Eucharist, with the sacrament.

> Therefore, these two are not to be confused — the Mass and prayer, the Sacrament and work, the covenant and the sacrifice. For the one comes to us from God through the priest's ministry and requires faith. The other comes from our faith to God through the priests and asks a favorable hearing.

In these years of his attack on the late medieval sacramental practice Luther strongly emphasizes faith, whereby we answer the *verbum sacramenti,* the promise of Christ. In this the real presence, as the seal and pledge of the promise, moves into the background. But Luther holds to the traditional concept of the sacrament, even when he says:

> And as the word is more important than the sign, so also is there more value to the covenant than to the Sacrament. For a man can have the word or the covenant and make use of it without the sign or the Sacrament. "Believe," says Augustine, "and you have eaten."

For by the word is here meant the *verbum sacramenti* and by the sacrament the *sacramentum tantum.* According to the scholastic teaching on the sacraments, only the word transforms the sign into a sacrament and the word is more important than the sign. According to Aquinas, the sacrament produces its sanctifying effect when the sign touches the body and the word is believed (*Summa Theologiae*

III, q. 60, a. 6). Accordingly, scholastic theology is acquainted with a *manducare spiritualiter Christum* in faith, whereas the mere sacramental reception without faith is a sin. Despite his polemic against the concepts *opus operatum* and *opus operantis,* Luther held to what was meant by them. The sacrament is effected independently of the worthiness of the minister, who is an instrument acting in God's stead, and it produces fruit, though of opposite sorts, in the believer and the unbeliever.

This polemic, with its vehement rejection of the sacrifice of the Mass and its denial of four sacraments, not only assailed essential doctrines of faith but also amounted to an elimination of the very heart of the Church's worship and the individual's piety. Thus it provoked scandal and contributed fundamentally to a clarification of positions. Many an old friend, such as Staupitz, recoiled in horror. Erasmus felt that before the appearance of this tract the break could have been healed, and Johann Glapion, the confessor of Emperor Charles V, was of the same opinion. The University of Paris issued a public protest against the polemic, and in 1521 King Henry VIII of England composed his *Assertio septem sacramentorum,* which gained for him the papal designation of *Defensor Fidei.* Thomas Murner, a Franciscan opponent of Luther, expected to turn public opinion against Luther merely by translating the *De Captivitate* into German without comment.

The third statement of program, *Von der Freiheit eines Christenmenschen* (November 1520), was written at the suggestion of Karl von Miltitz after the publication of "Exsurge Domine," the bull threatening excommunication, to convince the Pope of Luther's orthodoxy and good will. Hence in it polemic yields to a warm, popular exposition of the Christian ideal of life. The Christian is a free man, lord over all things and subject to no one, to the extent that he accepts by faith the Gospel, that is, the promises of Christ. But since "on earth there is only a beginning and a progressing," we have received only the first-fruits of the Spirit and thus, in addition, the commandments and laws of God must be observed. But man cannot become pious and saved through observing them, through works. For works do not make a man pious, but a good and pious man makes works good and pious. However, the commandments lead us to a recognition of sin and to contrition. "And so man is justified and lifted up by faith in the divine words, when he is humbled by fear of God's command and has arrived at self-knowledge." The Christian furthermore submits to the law in order to serve his neighbor. Although he is entirely free, he must "willingly again make himself a servant in order to aid his neighbor. . . . Hence from faith flow love and desire for God and from love a free, willing, and joyful life of serving one's neighbor without recompense." Thus the Christian is "a servant of all things and subject to everyone."

CHAPTER 67

The Excommunicated Friar before the Diet of Worms

With the election on 28 June 1519 of the King of Spain as Emperor Charles V, the Curia's consideration toward Frederick the Wise came to an end. But other political worries, financial distress, and above all his private entertainments deterred Leo X from an energetic pursuit of Luther's case. It was not until February 1520 that the Roman proceedings entered a new stage. Under the presidency of two cardinals, the theologian Cajetan and the canonist Accolti, three committees in succession examined Luther's teaching. Johannes Eck played a decisive role in the third, which convened at the end of April. In December 1519 the Cardinal of Tortosa, Adrian of Utrecht, had advised that in the condemnation of Luther not a word should be changed from Luther's own formulation, and this suggestion was to a great extent followed. The opinions handed down by the University of Cologne on 30 August 1519, and by that of Louvain on 7 November, were used as supporting material. The last-named listed the objectionable propositions in Luther's own words, and six of these passed *verbatim* in to the papal bull. The draft submitted by the third committee was discussed in consistory from 21 May to 1 June 1520, and was finally released as the Bull "Exsurge Domine," dated 15 June 1520.

The bull condemned forty-one propositions extracted from Luther's writings as "heretical, scandalous, false, offensive to pious ears, misleading to simple folk, and contrary to Catholic doctrine," without indicating under which category of this very broad gamut of censures the individual propositions fell. Hence it remained unclear where the area of opinions, dangerous but still open to discussion, ceased and heresy began. The condemnation of the latter was thereby deprived of real effect. Johannes Eck himself had to concede this three years later, when in his reform opinion for the Pope he asked for a new bull in which only the most serious errors would be refuted by full recourse to Holy Scripture. In "Exsurge Domine," he said, much remained obscure; some of the condemned propositions were so vague and insignificant that even scholars could not understand why they had been condemned. This inadequacy of the bull was the more consequential in that it was "the sole authoritative papal intervention in the Lutheran affair right up to the Council of Trent."

Luther was given sixty days to recant — the time to be counted from the publication of the bull in the Saxon bishoprics — and his writings that contained the offensive teachings were to be burned. The Italian humanist Girolamo Aleander and Johannes Eck were deputed to publicize the bull and its threat of excommunication in Germany. On 17 July they were appointed nuncios and Eck was also made a protonotary.

In Germany, especially South Germany, the promulgation of the bull ran into difficulties because the bishops were uninterested and feared that it would cause trouble. In Central Germany Eck encountered dangerous opposition. He had to learn at his own peril how very general the resentment against the Curia was. He was able to have the bull posted in Meissen on 21 September and in Merseburg and Brandenburg a few days later. But at Leipzig the university refused publication and the students rioted, while at Erfurt they stormed the printer's and threw the copies they seized into the river. On 3 October Eck sent the bull to the University of Wittenberg, where the matter was pigeonholed. No one wanted to do anything until the attitude of the elector, who was in the west, on his way to Charles V's coronation at Aachen, became known.

At this time Karl von Miltitz was again busy on Luther's behalf. He apparently begrudged Eck the role of papal nuncio and now intended, following Eck's ill luck with the proclamation of the bull, to come forth on his own again as peacemaker and acquire the credit of having achieved reconciliation. On 12 October 1520, at Lichtenburg an der Elbe, Miltitz induced Luther to send Leo X a letter asserting that he had never intended to attack the person of the Pope but had only meant to defend himself against his opponents. Like Tetzel in 1519, Johannes Eck was now to be made the scapegoat. To avoid the impression that Luther's letter had been instigated only by Eck's publication of the bull the letter was to be predated 6 September. With it Luther was to convey to the Pope his homage in the form of a treatise. For this purpose *Von der Freiheit eines Christenmenschen* was composed, in which Luther aimed to offer "the sum total of a Christian life."

Luther's letter to Leo X is a questionable document in so far as Luther, who on other occasions had already termed the Pope the Antichrist, designates him as "Most Holy Father" and "pious Leo" and wants to be regarded as one who has never undertaken anything bad against the person of the Pope and is so well disposed toward him that he desires and wishes the very best for him. But at the same time Luther engaged in wild ravings against the Roman Curia. It is worse than Sodom, Gomorrah, or Babylon; nothing but corruption has proceeded thence for years. Like Saint Bernard, Luther presumes to teach the Pope. A recantation of his teaching, however, is out of the question: "But that I should disavow my teaching — it won't happen."

This distinction between the Pope and the intrigues of the Curia or of Eck was also drawn in the two other writings Luther was composing during the second half of October: a polemic against Eck, *Von den neuen Eckischen Bullen und Lügen,* and the Latin rejoinder to "Exsurge Domine," *Adversus execrabilem Antichrist bullam.* Luther pretended, contrary to his own belief, to doubt the authenticity of the bull. But whoever had composed it, he had no doubt, he said, that it came from Antichrist and hence he meant to treat it as the work of Antichrist:

> I defy you, Leo X, and you too, cardinals, and all other persons who are of importance at the Curia, and say to your face: If this bull really came forth under your name with your knowledge, I admonish you by virtue of the power which I, like all other Christians, have received through baptism: Repent and desist from such satanic blasphemies against God, and do so quickly. Otherwise you must know that I, with all other worshipers of Christ, regard the See of Rome as possessed by Satan and as the throne of Antichrist and will no longer obey or be bound to it, for it is the chief and mortal foe of Christ. If you persevere in this madness, I rather condemn you and hand you over, together with this bull and your decretals, to Satan for the destruction of the flesh that your spirit may be saved with us on the day of the Lord. In the name of him whom you persecute, Jesus Christ our Lord.

In the western part of the Empire, Aleander was more successful in promulgating the bull. On 28 September 1520, at Antwerp, he succeeded in inducing Charles V to issue an edict against heresy for his Burgundian hereditary lands. Lutheran writings were solemnly burned at Louvain on 8 October and at Liège on 15 October. The coronation of Charles V on 23 October brought Aleander into the Rhineland, where he found some opposition. On 29 October he visited Cologne. A number of princes and other personages were staying here after the coronation, including Frederick the Wise, who had remained here because of illness instead of going on to the coronation. At first Frederick declined to receive Aleander, but on 4 November the nuncio succeeded in speaking with the elector, demanding that he surrender Luther and burn his writings. Frederick thereupon consulted with Erasmus, who was also at Cologne. Erasmus expressed himself quite superficially but in a way that amused the elector. Luther, he said, had sinned on two points: he had struck the Pope on his crown and the friars in the belly. On 6 November the elector had his reply sent to Aleander. He had never made common cause with Luther's affair and would be greatly displeased if Luther had written anything improper against the Pope. But without doubt Luther would have been accommodating to the Archbishop of Trier as papal deputy if the latter had summoned him under a safe-conduct, and the same disposition was still to be expected of him. When the report of the elector's position reached Wittenberg, in consequence people were even less eager to heed the bull.

On 12 November Luther's books were burned in Cologne at the instigation of Aleander. However, Luther's adherents seem to have slipped so much waste paper and scholastic codices into the executioner's hands that few of Luther's writings were actually committed to the flames. This too indicates how unpopular the proceedings against Luther were. Just the same it became clear that Rome had begun to take the battle against the Lutheran heresy seriously, and not a few on both sides finally understood its importance.

On 2 or 3 December Spalatin visited Luther in Wittenberg and ascertained that he was determined to burn the papal bull together with some books of canon law if, as at Cologne and Liège, there was any move to burn his books at Leipzig also. Spalatin informed Frederick the Wise, but before the latter replied Luther proceeded to act. On 10 December a Latin notice composed by Melanchthon was posted at the parish church in Wittenberg: Whoever was devoted to seeking the truth of the Gospel should be at the Holy Cross Chapel in front of the Elster Gate at nine o'clock, when the papal decretals and the books of the scholastics would be burned. There was no mention of the bull. The site was the city's knacker's yard, close to the Elbe, the usual place for such undertakings. Several volumes of canon law, a theological *Summa,* and writings of Eck and Emser were burned first. Then Luther approached the pyre and threw a small book into the flames, allegedly saying at the same time: "Quoniam tu turbasti sanctam veritatem Dei, conturbet te hodie Dominus in ignem istum." That the slender volume contained the Bull "Exsurge" was probably not known to all of those present. But even as a burning of the canon law, this spectacle was an impressive challenge to the Curia. It was further underscored by a pamphlet of Luther, *Warum des Papstes und seiner Jünger Bücher verbrannt sind.* The Bull "Decet Romanum Pontificem" of 3 January 1521 now at last carried out the excommunication. On 8 February 1521 Aleander reported to Rome:

> All Germany is in an uproar. For nine-tenths "Luther" is the war-cry; for the rest, if they are indifferent to Luther, it is at least "Death to the Roman Curia," and everyone demands and shouts for a council.

According to the medieval law of Church and state, when Luther was banned by the Church he should have been outlawed: that is, the excommunication should have been carried out by the secular arm. But in fact the Empire negotiated with Luther. This was due only in part to the election capitulation sworn to by Charles V on 3 July 1519, whereby no one might thereafter be outlawed without a previous hearing. In these months Luther had become so truly the voice of the German nation, he had so made himself the advocate of its difficulties and wishes, that no one could have simply ignored him. But for this very reason a further enhancing of his already powerful prestige was to be feared from a public negotiation with the reformer. The papal nuncios sought to avoid this. Moreover, they did not want to let go unchallenged the lay powers' claim to act as judges in a matter of faith already decided by the Pope. In his discourse of 13 February 1521 Aleander stressed that it did not belong to the secular authority "to take cognizance of such matters concerning the faith." Hence the mere fact of Luther's hearing — that the diet should of itself be involved with a question of religion instead of proceeding as a matter of course against the condemned heretic — was a new fact of great import.

But on 28 November 1520 Charles V had promised Frederick the Wise that he would interrogate Luther. The elector was to bring him along to the Diet of Worms. Because of Aleander's intervention this imperial promise was restricted to mean that the elector could bring Luther into the vicinity of Worms only after a recantation had been made. The reply to this was a protest by Frederick the Wise, who maintained it was only fair to give Luther the possibility of defending himself; a condemnation of a German without trial could not but produce profound scandal. At the urging of the elector the diet on 19 February rejected a law for the suppression of Luther's writings, proposed by Aleander in person on 13 February in a three-hour speech, and requested the Emperor to summon Luther to Worms, out of regard for the excitement among the common people, and there to have him questioned by experts. This decision of the diet proved to be a compromise when it finally directed that there should be no discussion with Luther; he was only to be asked whether he was ready to repudiate his writings against the Church and the Christian faith. In the summons, dated 6 March, that was sent to Wittenberg on 16 March with a safe-conduct, there was no further mention of a recantation. In this the heretic formally condemned by the Pope was addressed as follows:

> Honorable, dear, and pious one: After we and the estates of the Holy Empire, now assembled here, have taken up and reached the decision that because of the doctrines and books which for a time have come from you we wish to obtain information from you, and for this we have given you our and the Empire's assurance and safe-conduct so that you may come to us.

Aleander did not admit defeat. He managed the publication on 26 March of an imperial mandate which had been prepared for some time, in which the confiscation of all of Luther's writings was commanded and the summons of Luther to Worms for a recantation was stated. Perhaps Luther was by this means meant to be deterred from appearing at Worms; in any event, this was how he understood it. There was anxiety in the entourage of the Elector of Saxony, but Luther himself was in high spirits, filled with the courage of a martyr, defiance, and a proud self-assurance. En route to Worms he is supposed to have written: "Even though there were as many devils at Worms as tiles on the roofs, I still would go there." He had just published the German version of the great Latin treatise on justification against the Bull "Exsurge Domine," *Grund und Ursach aller Artikel D. M. Luthers so durch römische Bulle unrechtlich verdammt sind.* In the introduction he points out that the prophets and champions of truth have always stood alone. "I do not say that I am a prophet, but I say that they have the more reason to fear that I am one, the more they scorn me and esteem themselves." Just before his departure for Worms he completed the *Antwort* to the *Apologia* of the Italian Dominican Ambrose Catharinus as the second part of *De captivitate.* In it he defined precisely his teaching on the Church and the papacy: The Church is not limited as to place nor bound up with persons. She is where the Gospel is proclaimed and there baptism and communion are celebrated according to it. The papal Church is the demoniacal power described in Scripture as Antichrist, which lasts to the end of days and is to be fought, not with weapons, but with the word and the Spirit.

Full of such ideas and emotions, Luther, accompanied by Kaspar Sturm as imperial herald, began his journey to Worm; on 2 April 1521. From Frankfurt on 14 April he wrote to Spalatin: "We will go to Worms in spite of all the gates of hell and the powers in the air." On 16 April, at ten o'clock in the morning, Luther entered Worms through crowded streets, in his little dray, attended by members of the nobility. The next day, at eight in the evening, he faced the Emperor and the diet in the episcopal palace. The conduct of the hearing was entrusted to Johann von der Ecken, *officialis* of Richard von Greiffenklau, Archbishop of Trier, the prelate whom Frederick the Wise had wanted as arbiter in Luther's case in 1519.

Luther was asked whether he acknowledged as his the twenty books exhibited and published under his name and whether he was prepared "to disavow these books or anything in them." In a low voice, "as though he were frightened and shocked," he acknowledged them as his writings. With regard to recantation he asked for time to reflect, for it would be presumptuous and dangerous were he not to ponder carefully before giving his reply to such a question. This evasive answer need not have been either a tactical move or the result of temporary confusion. Luther, in whose summons there was no mention of a recantation, may have counted on a discussion of faith and may not have been prepared for a simple disavowal without a previous refutation. On the next day, 18 April, he was again asked whether he was prepared to recant. He refused:

> If I do not become convinced by the testimony of Scripture or clear rational grounds — for I believe neither the pope nor councils alone, since it is obvious that they have erred on several occasions — I remain subjugated by the scriptural passages I have cited and my conscience held captive by the word

of God. Therefore, I neither can nor will recant anything. For to act against conscience is difficult, noxious, and dangerous. May God help me. Amen.

Sent back to his lodging, Luther there exclaimed, with outstretched arms and a joyful countenance: "I am through, I am through." The Emperor refused a further hearing but granted a delay of three days during which the estates could try to persuade Luther. Luther appeared before their special committee on 24 April in the lodging of the Archbishop of Trier. These discussions were also fruitless, and von Greiffenklau then made private efforts on Luther's behalf through Johannes Cochläus and the *officialis* Johann von der Ecken. The hopelessness of all these efforts became clear when on the next day Luther again denied the binding force of a conciliar decision. It was not only a question of *gravamina,* not of opposition to an ecclesiastical political view, not even simply of reform, but of fundamentally different concepts of the nature of the Church. On the evening of 25 April Luther received the Emperor's decision: since all admonitions had been without effect, the Emperor, as protector of the Church, would now proceed against him.

The next day the reformer left Worms. Through a hint by his territorial prince he was prepared to be "seized and hidden" somewhere along the way. According to a secret instruction he took a detour via Mohra, where he visited his relatives. Then, on 4 May, in the vicinity of Burg Altenstein, he was kidnapped by prearrangement and taken to Wartburg castle.

The Edict of Worms was prepared by Aleander and on 8 May its draft was approved by the imperial ministers. But it was only on 25 May, when most of the estates had already dispersed, that, with some alterations, it was publicly read at the Emperor's residence. The Elector Joachim of Brandenburg accepted it in the name of the estates, and the Emperor signed it on 26 May. The edict enumerates Luther's erroneous teachings with reference to *De captivitate Babylonica.* It finds fault especially with his attacking the Council of Constance and his causing disturbance.

Luther's adherents and well-wishers were also to be banned. It was forbidden to buy, sell, read, copy, or print his writings, which were to be burned or otherwise destroyed. And to prevent writings hostile to the faith, all books which "touch upon the Christian faith, slightly or to a great degree," must obtain the local Ordinary's authorization for printing.

The edict was valid in law because the estates had allowed the Emperor to proceed against Luther in the event that Luther refused to recant. Nevertheless, the manner of its publication and the fact that it had not been promulgated until after the diet recessed could give rise to doubts as to its authority and provide pretexts to those who lacked the will or the courage to execute it. Immediately after the diet the Emperor journeyed to Spain under the impression that war with France was impending, and he was to remain absent from Germany for nine years. Hence he could not lend personal emphasis to the Edict of Worms, while for his wars in the west, south, and east of the Empire he needed the aid of the pro-Luther estates against which he ought to have taken measures.

CHAPTER 68

Luther at the Wartburg and the Reform Movement in Wittenberg

Luther had just been the center of the Diet of Worms, thus actually of German public life; he had spoken before the Emperor and the imperial estates and had been cheered by the people. Now he was suddenly thrust into solitude. Until his tonsure had grown out and a suitable beard adorned "Junker Jörg," he could not show himself to anyone at the Wartburg except the servant who brought his meals. And in fact these weeks and months — from 4 May 1521 to 6 March 1522 — were for Luther a period of temptations and torment of conscience. He reproached himself for having started the fire and on the other hand for having been too weak before his judges. Furthermore, there were physical sufferings, including constipation, which were certainly not alleviated by immoderate eating and drinking due to emotional unrest. And his anxiety about the friends at Wittenberg who needed his counsel and comfort did not permit peace of mind.

Luther coped with all these difficulties and temptations by means of literary activities that were unusually energetic and prolific, as well as spontaneous and unrestrained. The Wartburg became his "Patmos." He applied himself to the exegesis of Psalm 67 (68), which was followed later by an exposition of Psalms 21 (22) and 36 (37). He also finished his explanation of the "Magnificat," and began to compose a book of sermons as an aid to parish priests and for family prayer. In *Von der Beichte, ob die der Papst Macht habe, zu gebieten* he attacked compulsory confession, which he regarded as a torment of conscience. If a person does not want to confess to a priest, he should open his soul to any man from whom he may expect help.

In *Ein Widerspruch D. Luthers,* Luther continued his controversy with Hieronymus Emser, "the goat of Leipzig." In it he again denied a special priestly state. The *Rationis Latomianae confutatio,* called by Melanchthon *Antilatomus,* was directed against the detailed justification of the Louvain faculty's judgment against Luther by Jacob Latomus. Employing a systematic method not usual with him, Luther here treated a central question of his theology, that of sins persisting: "When all sins have been washed away. there is still a remainder to be washed away." He who has been pardoned is nothing but a "shackled robber."

> [Sins are] entirely remitted but not yet all destroyed. For we believe that the remission of all sins has occurred without any doubt, but every day we have to work and to wait for the blotting out [*abolitio*] of all sins and their complete removal [*evacuatio*]. And those who labor at this do good works. See, this is my faith, for that is the Catholic faith.

Luther's distinction between *gratia* and *donum* corresponds to this twofold process of remission and extirpation of sins, of justification and sanctification. "The law reveals two evils, an inner and an outer: the one, which we have laid upon ourselves, sins or the corruption of nature; the other, which God imposes, wrath, death, and damnation." To these correspond two goods of the Gospel, *gratia et donum.* Grace obliterates wrath and brings God's favor and peace; the gift brings recovery from corruption. Grace is indivisible, "so that the person is really accepted and in him there is no further place for wrath.... Hence it is entirely impious to say that the baptized is still in sins or that not all sins have been entirely remitted."

On the other hand, the inner healing and purification of man, which the gift effects and in which man must cooperate, is a slow process. Even though, according to Luther, we "must separate grace and gift from each other," yet they are oriented toward each other and the one is given for the sake of the other. Man, even as a person, is "not in God's good pleasure and has no grace except because of the gift which is operating in such a manner as to purge out sin." Because sin still has to be purged out, "God does not save imagined but real sinners," and so man must not boast of his purity but "rather of the grace and gift of God, that he has a gracious God who does not impute these sins and in addition has given his gifts in order thereby to purge them out."

If it is borne in mind that Luther is speaking concretely and existentially; that he is employing the concept "sin" analogously, as theology in general does; if, in addition, one does not, like Luther's theological opponents, start with a doctrine of redemption concerned merely with satisfaction and, correspondingly, does not regard the penalties of sin as purely vindictive; then these assertions of Luther are much more reconcilable with Catholic doctrine than is generally held, but in any case they compel the abandonment of the customary scheme of a purely external justification.

The University of Paris, invited to act as arbiter of the Leipzig Disputation, had maintained silence and so could long be counted as a secret partisan of Luther. Not until 15 April 1521 had it condemned as heretical 104 propositions of Luther, one-fourth of them from *De captivitate Babylonica.* Melanchthon came forward with an *Apologia* against the condemnation. Luther translated this and the Paris decree into German and added a foreword and an epilogue in which he specified his attack on the papacy as the decisive point of controversy. For he hurled at the Paris theologians the reproach that in all their articles they had not at all mentioned the most important — indulgences and the papacy. With this allusion to Gallican resentments Luther had skillfully parried the Sorbonne's thrust.

Luther was both violently angry and disdainful when he heard that Albrecht of Mainz, against his better judgment and out of mere avarice, had placed the treasury of relics of Halle on exhibition and was inviting all the faithful to visit it and make an offering, promising rich indulgences. He was even more furious, however, when Spalatin, at the instigation of Capito, who despite his reform sentiments had entered the archbishop's service in 1519, prevented the publication of his tract *Wider den Abgott zu Halle.* The tract did not appear but Luther sent the archbishop an ultimatum on 1 December 1521. In reply the cardinal-elector referred to himself as "stinking filth" and so drew in his horns that the reformer for his part was not certain whether he should praise him as honest or upbraid him for hypocrisy. But to Capito, who wanted to advise him to observe diplomatic caution, Luther wrote pitilessly: "What has a Christian to do with a sycophant?" "You wish to have a Luther who will connive at all your doings if his hide is patted only with nice and endearing notes."

Monastic Vows and Freedom by the Gospel

Luther's absence from Wittenberg enabled others to come more energetically into the foreground and influence the course of the Reformation. To some extent they had an outlook different from his and had in common with him only an attitude of protest against the abuses in the old Church and the demand for reform. Furthermore, they had not suffered nearly so much under the criticized conditions nor struggled with the truth in painful experience as the Wittenberg friar had done. Thus they were more inclined toward a rapid external upheaval; they saw salvation in a change of form and not chiefly in a transformation of attitude. If Luther's critical writings, such as *An den christlichen Adel* and *De captivitate Babylonica,* were convincing, then a series of practical consequences could not but follow, especially in regard to the celebration of Mass, priestly celibacy, and monastic vows.

The Kemberg Provost Bartholomäus Bernhardi, a pupil of Luther's, had married his cook and hence was under indictment. Melanchthon had written in his defense, stressing that everyone may rid himself of a human regulation that endangers his conscience. Would this also be valid if a religious felt he could no longer fulfill the obligations he had assumed? Luther, unlike Karlstadt and Melanchthon, was not ready so quickly to reply in the affirmative. He distinguished between the priests' obligation of celibacy and monastic vows. With regard to vows he looked for a firm basis for the conscience, a "testimonium divinae voluntatis." Karlstadt's arguments had not convinced him, and he was not sure whether by the same token one could also dispense oneself from divine precepts. In his letter to Melanchthon of 9 September 1521 he wrote that he believed he had found the way to a solution in the expression "freedom by the Gospel." At the same time he sent to Wittenberg Latin theses for a disputation on the vows. These begin with the text from Romans 14:23, "Omne quod non est ex fide, peccatum est," henceforth to be quoted again and again.

Gabriel Zwilling, Luther's fellow Augustinian, had fewer scruples. In October he preached violently against the Mass and "monkery." Freedom from the vows was not enough for him. The monk should discard the habit and abandon his state. In November fifteen out of forty Augustinians left the Wittenberg friary. Luther learned of it and feared that not all of them had taken the step with a clear conscience. To help those who had decided to depart he set about composing a treatise on the vows. On 11 November 1521 he wrote to Spalatin: "I have resolved now to take up the question of religious vows also and to free young people from this infernal celibacy." In the same month he had completed *De votis monasticis... iudicium.* Held back by Spalatin, this work did not appear until February 1522.

The dedicatory letter to his father, who had opposed Luther's embracing the monastic life, shows that in this piece he also wanted to settle with his own past. His vows, whereby he had removed himself from the paternal will imposed by God, were worthless, even impious. But now his conscience had become free and that meant freedom in superabundance. "Therefore, I am still a friar and at the same time not a friar; I am a new creature, not the pope's but Christ's." "And so I hope," he wrote to his father, "that the Lord has deprived you of a son in order to counsel through me many others of his sons." On 18 December 1521 he wrote to Wenceslas Link: "I, however, shall continue in this state [*habitu*] and this way of life [*ritu*], unless this world changes."

Decisive for an evaluation of vows is freedom according to the Gospel: "For this freedom is of divine law. God has sanctioned it. Neither will he repudiate it nor can he accept anything against it nor permit man to infringe on it by any, even only a slight, statute." Hence a vow contrary to freedom is null and void — for example, if it were made on the assumption that the religious life is necessary for justification and salvation, which indeed can be obtained only through faith in Christ. Furthermore, vows are to be made only with the provision that there is freedom to abandon religious life again. The vow should accordingly be: "I vow chastity as long as it shall be possible for me, but I can marry if I cannot preserve it." If till now Luther had parried the argument that one may renounce a vow if one is unable to fulfill it with the remark that a complete observance of the commandments is impossible also, he now stressed that the married state makes possible the fulfilling of the precept of chastity. "But if I can observe the precepts of God and not the vow, then the vow must yield in order that the commandments may remain and that vow and precept may not be violated in unchastity."

These ideas could not have been other than alluring to many religious. They made all the more sense to contemporaries because the prevalence of concubinage among the priests of the time made celibacy and the religious state seem to many unworthy of credence. Modern man was less able and ready than man of previous centuries to put up with such tension between ideal and reality. To Luther, however, it was a source of uneasiness that all too many, as a result of his cry of Christian liberty, were abandoning the monastic life.

Regulation of Community Worship

On 1 August 1521 Luther wrote to Melanchthon that, after his return from the Wartburg, he intended first of all to take up a regulating of the Eucharist in keeping with the institution by Christ. However, his followers in Wittenberg, especially Karlstadt and the Augustinian Gabriel Zwilling, would not wait for this. And so on their own responsibility they began to draw the conclusions from Luther's criticism of the Mass in *De captivitate* and other works. They constructed an "evangelical Mass," abolished private Masses, and took steps against the adoration of the sacrament. On Michaelmas of 1521 Melanchthon and his students received the sacrament under both species. Because of Zwilling's sermons the Augustinians ended private Masses on 13 October. These novelties caused a sensation and ran into opposition. The elector was alarmed and appointed an investigating committee. Luther entered the controversy in November with *De abroganda missa privata,* which he then translated as *Vom Missbrauch der Messe.* In it he not only attacks the private Mass, as the title suggests, but the Sacrifice of the Mass in general. In a far more caustic and polemical manner he expounds ideas previously developed on the Mass as a covenant or legacy, as a gift to us, citing as a further argument the "once for all" text of Hebrews against the sacrificial character of the Mass.

Radical though the language of this tract was, powerfully though it called for a correction of the situation, Luther himself still hesitated to introduce a new liturgy. But this does not mean that he rejected the procedure of the Augustinians and the ecclesiastical novelties at Wittenberg as a matter of course. Filled with anxiety and eager to learn about the development at first hand, he secretly left the Wartburg on 2 December 1521 and went to Wittenberg, where he stayed 4–9 December. There on 3 December armed students and townsmen invaded the parish church, drove the priests from the altars, and carried away the missals. The next day a similar scene occurred in the Franciscan friary. The friars were jeered and prevented from offering private Masses. The city council feared there would be an attack on the monastery and had it guarded during the night.

Despite this, Luther wrote to Spalatin: "All that I see and hear gives me special delight. May the Lord strengthen the spirit of those who are motivated by a good intention." But the atmosphere of ferment disturbed him and he intended after his return to the Wartburg to raise a warning voice against it.

At the same time, however, he discovered to his great wrath that Spalatin, from a dread of agitation, had held up his tracts against religious vows and the Mass. Hence he wrote to Spalatin from the Wartburg: "Is one, then, only to dispute unceasingly about the word of God but always to refrain from action?... If nothing more is to be done than what we have done until now, then nothing else ought to have been taught either." But at the same time he sent his friend the proclamation "Eine treue Vermahnung zu allen Christen sich zu hüten vor Aufruhr und Empörung." According to this it is not the business of all ("omnes") to remedy abuses by force. Luther proves the power of the unarmed word of God by pointing to his own fate: "Consider my activity. Have I not done more damage to the pope, bishops, priests, and monks, by my mouth alone, without any wielding of the sword, than all emperors, kings, and princes did previously with their might?" He then warns against making the Gospel a matter of factions and forbids his adherents to call themselves "Lutherans."

The Elector Frederick demanded that the city council punish the authors of the disturbances, but large segments of the townspeople rallied to protesters calling for the free preaching of the Gospel, the abolition of private Masses, the lay chalice, and the closing of public houses — "since they are maintained for excessive drinking" — and of whorehouses. Repeatedly, once more expressly on 19 December, Frederick forbade unauthorized changes. People were to "leave the old customs alone" until greater unanimity should be achieved. Nevertheless, on the fourth Sunday of Advent Karlstadt announced that on New Year's Day he would celebrate Mass with communion under both species, with the words of consecration intelligible and without the other ceremonies and the vestments. Probably to forestall a prohibition by the Elector, he carried out the plan on Christmas. Before a large congregation he celebrated a "German Mass"; that is, he recited the words of institution in German and omitted the rest of the Canon along with the elevation. For the rite he wore secular dress. He pointedly omitted the preparatory confession of sins as unnecessary and administered communion under both species, passing the Host and the chalice into the communicants' hands. On 6 January the chapter of the German Augustinian Congregation declared that the friars were free to abandon the monastery. All who remained were to occupy themselves with preaching or teaching or earn their livelihood by means of a craft. Begging was to be henceforth forbidden. On 11 January Zwilling sounded the call for an attack on images and the elimination of side altars, on the basis that images are forbidden by God's word (Ex. 20:4). On 19 January Karlstadt solemnized his own wedding.

Meanwhile there had appeared in Wittenberg the "Zwickau Prophets," the weavers Nikolaus Storch and Thomas Drechsel, and Mark (Thomas) Stübner, a former pupil of Melanchthon. They prided themselves on being directly guided by the Holy Spirit. For them the "inner word" was decisive, and so they felt less in need of the written word. According to their dreams and visions, the entire order of the world would soon undergo a transformation and through the extermination of priests and the wicked the foundation would be laid for the kingdom of God. If the possession of the Spirit was decisive, then the sacraments were unimportant, and the meaning of infant baptism was questionable. For how could one receive the Spirit as a result of another's faith? Melanchthon, in whose house Stübner had taken up residence, was impressed by these doctrines but also disquieted.

Melanchthon did not venture to give a judgment and turned to Luther, who advised that the criterion of the spirits should be whether their manifestations were connected with frightening phenomena. For God is a consuming fire, and visions of the saints are fearful. "So apply this test and don't let them tell you about Jesus in his glory before you have seen the Crucified." Melanchthon must not let himself be impressed by talk against infant baptism. For no other recourse "is left to any of us except to accept another's faith," the faith whereby Christ believes for us.

The Zwickau Prophets probably did not intervene directly in the situation at Wittenberg, but they supplied a new stimulus to Karlstadt, Zwilling, and the rigoristic elements among the citizenry. Under Karlstadt's influence the city council on 24 January 1522 issued the "Order of the City of Wittenberg." Among other things, this decreed the removal of images, the celebration of Mass according to Karlstadt's liturgy, and the combining of the spiritual revenues into a common social fund, the "common chest." The sequel was resentment and complaints by the orthodox canons to the elector. On the other hand, the "Order" was not radical enough for the fanaticism of the zealots, above all, it was not carried out quickly and decisively enough. In a document dated 27 January, "On abolishing images and that there should be no beggars among Christians," Karlstadt complained that three days after the enactment of the city order the images still had not been removed. People took the law into their own hands and at the beginning of February there was an iconoclastic attack on the Wittenberg parish church.

These radical reform efforts spread to other localities in the electorate. Frederick the Wise was doubly anxious, for in the meantime a decree had been issued by the Imperial Governing Council (*Reichsregiment*) at Nürnberg on 22 January 1522 against the innovations in Electoral Saxony. In this he and the Bishops of Meissen. Merseburg, and Naumburg were obliged "seriously and *ex officio* to proceed against priests who in celebrating Mass deviated from the old usages or who married, and against monks who left their monastery. From 6 February the elector several times intimated to the people of Wittenberg — the last time on 17 February — that they were to observe ancient custom. But the collegiate chapter, the university, and the city council were no longer in control of the situation. In this emergency Melanchthon and the council turned to Luther and asked him to come back to Wittenberg.

Luther, probably on the strength of this, announced his coming in a letter to the elector: "... I have no more time; if God so wills, I intend to be there soon." Luther did not permit the misgivings and remonstrances of his prince to keep him any longer from a public return. He set out on 1 March and, on the way, wrote to Frederick the Wise again, on 5 March:

> In regard to my affair, most gracious Lord, I reply thus: Your gracious Highness knows or, if you don't, then let it be known to you herewith, that I have the Gospel, not from man, but only from heaven through our Lord Jesus.... Such is written to your gracious Highness that Your Highness may know that I am coming to Wittenberg under a far higher protection than that of the elector. And I have no intention of asking protection from your gracious Highness. Indeed, I believe, I wish rather to protect your gracious Highness more than your Highness could protect me.

Filled with this prophetic self-confidence, Luther entered Wittenberg on 6 March 1522. At the elector's request and for his protection against the Imperial Governing Council, Luther stated on 7 March and again on 12 March — in a new draft prepared in accord with an instruction of the Elector — that he had returned to Wittenberg without the elector's "knowledge, will, favor, and permission." His feelings were expressed in letters of the succeeding days:

> Of necessity I have hurled myself alive into the very center of the raging of pope and emperor, to see if I could drive the wolf from the fold. Unprotected, except by heaven, I linger in the midst of my enemies, who according to human law have every right to kill me.

Publicly his anger was directed, not at the Pope and the Emperor but at the fanatics and hotheads. In this he was following the wish of his prince and the latter's regard for the decree of the Imperial Governing Council, but especially his own dislike of tumult and violent revolution. From the first through the second Sunday in Lent 9–16 March he was daily in the pulpit of the parish church, wearing his habit and a newly trimmed tonsure. In these eight Lenten sermons Luther denounced all who made a new law out of the freedom according to the Gospel and demanded regard for weak consciences. Then the Mass vestments and the elevation were resumed and, except for the abolition of private Masses, everything was as before. The directions in *De captivitate,* repeated by Luther in *Von beider Gestalt des Sakraments zu nehmen,* which was completed on 25 March 1522, remained in force. The priest should simply omit in the prayers and the Canon all words referring to sacrifice. Thus he could celebrate Mass according to the Gospel, while the common man would not notice anything to cause scandal. Karlstadt opposed this rescission of the reform and termed Luther and his adherents "neopapists." There ensued a violent scene between him and Luther. A polemic by Karlstadt, containing veiled attacks on Luther, was suppressed by the university.

Likewise in the 1523 liturgical regulations, the *Formula missae et communionis,* Luther still provided a Latin Mass, purified, however, of all allusions to sacrifice. Equally moderate was his German translation of the rites of baptism, also in 1523.

When the German Mass was already being celebrated in many places, not merely in Thomas Müntzer's Allstedt but also in Strasbourg, Nördlingen, Nürnberg,

Basel, Zurich, and elsewhere, the Mass remained in Latin at Wittenberg. The political prudence of Frederick the Wise was surely decisive in this respect. But it was not only regard for his prince that made Luther hesitate to draw the practical consequences from his principles. There were also reasons within him, and they were of several kinds.

For Luther, forms of worship, prayers, rites, vestments, and vessels were "vain and external things," *adiaphora,* neither prescribed nor forbidden. If the Latin liturgy was not to be regarded as necessary for salvation, then neither was the German liturgy. To issue binding prescriptions on this matter meant to restrict the freedom of Christians and to lay unnecessary burdens on "poor consciences." Luther wanted to make it crystal clear that he was concerned for spiritual attitude, not for external conduct or form; for faith, not for works. Of course as a nominalist he underestimated the sign and had too little grasp of the power of images to illuminate or confuse the spirit, and failed to understand that the body aids the spirit into crystallization and even into existence.

Second, Luther demanded regard for "weak consciences." If he aimed first to change man's way of thinking and then to provide this with a suitable expression, he had to exercise patience. Of himself Luther relates that he needed three years of struggling to gain "faith"; *a fortiori* he had to allow time to simple folk and could not lead them into confusion and burdened consciences through precipitate changes not adequately prepared by preaching.

Third, Luther's attachment to tradition and his feeling for form and organization caused him to delay. He was aware that the correct shape of the liturgy cannot be made but must grow. A mere translation of the texts was not enough; melody and text should constitute a unity.

Finally, as a humanist and a teacher, Luther wanted to see the cultural value of the Latin language preserved. The young in particular should be trained in this language through the Latin liturgy. For them the *Formula missae,* or Latin liturgy, should be continued in use, even after the introduction of the German Mass (1526). In fact, if he had his way, he would celebrate Mass on Sundays in German, Latin, Greek, and Hebrew in turn.

Luther's Translation of the Bible

The most important literary product of the Wartburg period was the translation of the New Testament. After his secret visit to Wittenberg in December 1521, Luther, at the request of his friends, prepared it in about eleven weeks. He was intimately acquainted with the Vulgate, and in addition he had the Greek text edited by Erasmus — the second edition of 1519 — with its translation into Latin and its copious exegesis. Considering the brief period of time and Luther's own knowledge of Greek — he had not undertaken serious study of this language until 1518 — it can hardly be called a translation from the original. To what extent he relied on the Greek text is difficult to say, but "in any case this much is certain: he sought to grasp the meaning of the basic text." For the translation of the Old Testament, which was protracted to 1534, he called upon the services of linguistic specialists, and that project may fairly be regarded as teamwork.

There were German versions of the Bible before Luther. Between 1461 and 1522 fourteen High German and four Low German printed editions appeared, not counting German psalters, harmonizations of the Gospels, and books of pericopes. The last named in particular were familiar to Luther from the liturgy and his pastoral duties. It is an exaggeration to say that Luther was the first to give the Bible to the Germans, but in his German Bible he created a work which is unrivaled in accuracy of expression, in feeling for the language, and in literary force. Because Luther himself read the Scriptures "as though they had been written yesterday" (H. Bornkamm), because in fact he saw and heard sacred history as alive, message and German language could be blended into such unity that in its German dress the Bible remained a book to be listened to and the sacred text penetrated remarkably into ear and memory. This was, however, not only the fruit of Luther's power of expression, but also of an encounter, filled equally with painful struggle and joy, with God in his word. For Luther this was not only a testimony of the mighty saving action of God, it was itself the divine power. As no one else could, Luther was able to express by means of speech this living and impetuous power of God's word.

Luther translated the Bible when the process of fusing various German dialects into a uniform literary language was underway. On the fringe of the Empire, in the East German area of colonization, where immigration brought numerous dialects together, the prerequisites for the task were particularly favorable. "It is a Protestant legend that the reformer Luther created the new High German literary language," but he did accelerate the development toward a uniform speech by making use of the idiom of Saxon officialdom.

Certainly the translation of the Bible into a language is of great significance for revelation to the extent that this affects a new group of people. But it is likewise an event for that language, since it is challenged to develop potentialities thus far not realized. This became evident to an outstanding degree in Luther's translation. Even his Catholic opponents did not withhold recognition of his achievement. Johannes Dietenberger (d. 1537) also, in his German Bible of 1534 — which with fifty-eight editions of the complete Bible alone became the most used German Catholic Bible — made use of Luther's text. According to Johannes Cochläus (d. 1527), Luther's German version stirred the religious feeling of the people and awakened in the ordinary man a truly devouring hunger for the word of God.

But the reformer's impulsive nature, directed by experience, poses the question whether he reproduced the meaning of Holy Scripture in pure form. Because of his painful experience in wrestling with the meaning of *iustitia Dei,* he certainly put some of the emphases too strongly, and he occasionally overstepped the bounds of faithful translation. For example, he translated "justice of God" as "justice valid before God," and to Romans 3:26 and 3:28 he added the controversial "alone," which is quite in accord with the meaning but is not in Paul's text.

More serious is the fact that Luther did not accept the Bible throughout as the word of God but for his part determined what was essential and thereby selected and put aside entire books, such as the Epistle of James and the Apocalypse. For him James was a "straw Epistle," which he almost wanted to throw in the stove. But Luke 16 was for Luther a "Gospel right for priests and monks," "one of the quarrelsome Gospels," which "Satan cites as proof." Christ must "be mastered *in suis verbis*"; "he must have himself led by the nose *suis verbis*"; "we must not let ourselves be made fools of by Scripture." In themselves these sentences can be understood as hermeneutical references in which Luther is calling attention to uncritical scriptural expressions or demanding that they be interpreted in their context. Thus he stated in the forty-first promotion thesis of 11 September 1535: "Scripture is not to be interpreted against but for Christ; hence either it must be referred to him or it must not be regarded as true Scripture." But where do we stand if unsuitable doctrines or opponents are thereby driven from the field, as for example according to Thesis 49, "If opponents force Scripture against Christ, we shall force Christ against Scripture"?

With the touchstone of whether the books of Scripture "enhance Christ or not," everyone is in the last analysis left to his own personal judgment. When Luther referred both the fanatics and the orthodox who appealed to Scripture against him to its true meaning, then, ultimately, the reformer's personal experience of Christ decided the meaning of Scripture.

CHAPTER 69

The Reformers in Luther's Circle

Luther's protective custody at the Wartburg had shown that even without him the Reformation was alive; in fact, that without him its growth proceeded more impetuously. Even if Luther had been eliminated, it probably would no longer have been possible to wipe out the reform movement by force. It was not only the fanatics, Karlstadt and Müntzer, who in Luther's absence were trying to determine the form of the movement. In addition, in and outside Wittenberg there were a number of men who were working with Luther and in his spirit. On his return from the Wartburg it was clear that, while he no doubt played a decisive role, he was not the only one who would decide the shape of the new doctrine and of the church into which it was developing. Thus it could be seen at the outset that "Lutheranism" would be both more and less than what was embodied in Luther's person: less, because the sea of forces which he contained and the subjective nature of his prophetic function could not be institutionalized; more, because from the beginning his work was also carried by the formative and preserving force of others. Such helpers in Wittenberg, loyal and dedicated, even though to some extent of a different turn of mind, were Nikolaus von Amsdorf, Justus Jonas, Johannes Bugenhagen, Georg Spalatin, and, most important of all, Philip Melanchthon.

Nikolaus von Amsdorf (1483–1565) had been since 1507 a lecturer at the university and since 1508 a canon of the collegiate church of All Saints at Wittenberg.

He joined Luther as early as 1517, and was thereafter one of his closest collaborators. He accompanied him to the Leipzig Disputation in 1519 and to the Diet of Worms in 1521 and assisted in the translation of the Bible. As a reformer he was active at Goslar, Einbeck, and Meissen, among other places, and especially at Magdeburg, where in 1524 he became senior minister. On 20 January 1542 Luther "ordained" him Protestant bishop of Naumburg, "without any chrism... oil, or incense." In 1547 he had to give way to the Catholic Julius Pflug. He lived as a private scholar at Eisenach and took part in the founding of the University of Jena, which became the stronghold of Lutheran orthodoxy in opposition to "Philippist" Wittenberg. Amsdorf was averse to any compromise in the doctrines of justification and the Eucharist. Hence he was an opponent of the Wittenberg Accord of 1536, resisted the *Interim* of 1547, and came out against Melanchthon in the Synergist Controversy. If Melanchthon, and Georg Major (1502–74) after him, stressed the necessity of good works, if not for justification, at least for the preservation of faith and salvation, Amsdorf established against them the paradoxical opinion of the harmfulness of good works for the salvation of souls. He aimed by means of the Jena edition of Luther's works to transmit the latter's doctrine unadulterated to later generations. Hence he helped to canonize the reformer's theology in the sense of Lutheran orthodoxy and to stamp the latter with an inflexible intolerance.

The jurist Justus Jonas (1493–1555) had studied at Erfurt and Wittenberg and had joined the Erfurt humanist circle. An admirer of Erasmus, he discovered Scripture and the Fathers. From 1518 he was professor of canon law at Erfurt and in this capacity he was called to Wittenberg in 1521 and appointed provost of the castle church. He here changed to the theological faculty and gave exegetical lectures. He became one of Luther's chief collaborators and rendered valuable service in the translation of the Bible. He also put into German important writings of Luther and Melanchthon, including *De servo arbitrio, Loci communes,* and *Apologia Confessionis Augustanae.* His knowledge of law stood the Reformation in good stead on the occasion of church visitations, the setting up of the ecclesiastical organizations in Zerbst, Ducal Saxony, and Halle, and in the Wittenberg consistory. He later established the Reformation at Halle, where he became preacher in 1541 and senior minister in 1544. He accompanied Luther on his last journey in 1546, attended him at the hour of death, and delivered his eulogy at Eisleben.

Johannes Bugenhagen (1485–1558) was from Wollin in Pomerania and hence was known as Pomeranus. From 1504 he was headmaster in Treptow. In 1509, with no theological study, he was ordained a priest and in 1517 became lecturer in Scripture and patrology at the monastery school of Belbuck. Here he became acquainted with Luther's writings. At first shocked by the radicalism of *De captivitate Babylonica,* he was won by this very work, and in 1521 undertook the study of theology at Wittenberg. He was soon lecturing there on the Bible but did not obtain the doctorate in theology until 1533; in 1535 he was made a professor. Disregarding the chapter's right of presentation, the city council in 1523 elected him pastor of the parish church, and Luther announced the election from the pulpit. Bugenhagen had married the previous year. In a sense he created the model of the German Lutheran rectory and energetically stressed its blessings in *De coniugio episcoporum et diaconorum* (1525). As a gifted shepherd of souls, pastor rather than professor, he excelled Luther in his closeness to the people. He displayed more practical sense and did not share Luther's indifference to external forms. At Wittenberg he was even more in Luther's shadow than Melanchthon. His significance was more evident as the trail blazer of the Reformation in North Germany, where through numerous organizations of churches he laid the foundation for the local ecclesiastical structure. In addition to the years of cooperation and friendship, Bugenhagen was intimately bound to Luther as his adviser and confessor. He officiated at Luther's marriage in 1525, comforted him in sicknesses, temptations, and fits of depression, and in 1546 delivered his funeral sermon.

Georg Burckhardt (1484–1545) was from Spalt, near Nürnberg, and for that reason was known from 1502 as Spalatin. He studied the liberal arts at Erfurt, and here came under the spell of the humanist circle. In October 1502 he went with his teacher, Nikolaus Marschalk, to the newly founded University of Wittenberg and there became a master of arts in February 1503. He entered upon the study of law as his special field, but in 1504 he transferred to Erfurt, where Mutianus Rufus in Gotha became decisive for his life. Without completing his legal studies, in the fall of 1505 Spalatin accepted the post of instructor of the novices in the Cistercian monastery of Georgenthal, not far from Gotha. His turning to an ecclesiastical career probably derived chiefly from motives of economic security. As early as 1507, without any real theological preparation, he accepted the pastorate of Hohenkirchen and in 1508 had himself ordained a priest. At the end of that year he was called to Torgau to become tutor of the princes at the court of the Elector Frederick the Wise. From 1511 he was the teacher of the elector's nephews at Wittenberg and took over the direction of the library In addition he worked on a Saxon chronicle and a history of his time.

Spalatin first came into contact with Luther in 1513–14, on the occasion of the Reuchlin controversy. There developed a friendship which found expression in personal communications and in a lively correspondence — more than four hundred of Luther's letters to Spalatin have come down to us — and which reached its climax in 1521 in Luther's reform activity. The sequel to the encounter with Luther was a growing interest in theological problems on the part of the humanist. In September 1516, with his appointment to the Elector's chancery, Spalatin entered the direct service of the court. In particular he had to be concerned with affairs of the university and of the ecclesiastical organization. With Luther, and soon with Melanchthon too, from 1517–18 he promoted the reform of studies in the direction of humanism and of the fostering of the biblical languages.

As private secretary, ecclesiastical adviser, and later court preacher, Spalatin acquired a powerful position in the confidence of the elector, which stood Luther in good stead in the critical years 1518–22. Frederick the Wise did not know the reformer personally; at least he had never spoken with him and for tactical reasons avoided his company. Spalatin acted as intermediary. With an eye for the politically acceptable and the possible, he exerted a moderating influence on Luther. Above all, he knew what could be expected of his prince, who was basically cautious and attached to the medieval Church organization, and how to communicate to him Luther's controversial views and actions. If he was unable to persuade the elector to Luther's views on indulgences and relics, Spalatin at least obtained the assurance that the Wittenberg professor could be certain of the elector's protection. This was decisive for the fate of Luther and of the Reformation. The Curia recognized the importance of Spalatin's influence on Luther's prince when in February 1518 it granted him extensive faculties for confession and the right to concede the indulgences attached to visiting the seven churches of Rome to corresponding exercises of devotion in the castle church. In Rome it was as yet impossible to determine to what extent Spalatin supported Luther. Even in 1521 he still solicited benefices and took care to fulfill conscientiously his duties as the elector's priest and confessor. In keeping with his humanist's reserve, he drew the ultimate consequence of separation from the old Church much later than Luther. On the other hand, the reformer, in many respects insolently pugnacious and pressing his own affairs without regard for circumstances, understood how much he needed his diplomatically experienced friend. After receiving the papal summons he wrote to him on 8 August 1518: "I need your aid now most urgently, my Spalatin." But this did not prevent Luther in succeeding years from interfering time and again by biting statements and writings with the diplomatic activities of the prudent courtier and endangering their success. Just the same, Spalatin was able constantly to afford Luther effective protection. The elector did not need to acknowledge his Wittenberg professor publicly if he tended to his affairs only in a procrastinating manner.

Spalatin embodied a union of humanist culture with reform Christianity. Accordingly, he long sought to mediate between Luther and Erasmus. After the death of Frederick the Wise he accepted the pastorate of Altenburg in 1525 and here established his own household. But he continued to render service to the electoral Saxon court in religious negotiations, as at the diets of Speyer (1526) and Augsburg (1530) and in the compromise negotiations at Schweinfurt and Nürnberg in 1532. In 1527 he was named by the Elector Johann to the visitation commission and thereby obtained a prominent share in the organization of the Church government of the principality. The final years of quiet from 1540 were devoted to historical studies and to his congregation at Altenburg, where he died on 16 January 1545.

The most important of the men around Luther was Philip Melanchthon, originally Schwartzert (1497–1560). If his meeting Luther was the turning point in his life, for his part he had a strong influence on Luther and especially on the course of the Reformation, but he was always in the shadow of the greater and more active man. His relationship with Luther moved between intimate friendship and deep respect for a great achievement and groans over the "shameful servitude" of Luther's irritable intolerance. He remained with Luther through all vicissitudes; even in serious crises and despite the allurement of honorable offers he could not bring himself to leave Wittenberg and the reformer's direct sphere of action.

Melanchthon was born at Bretten in Baden on 14 February 1497. The early death of his father served to enhance the influence of his great-uncle, Johann Reuchlin, on the course of his education. Directly or by means of his students, Reuchlin equipped the gifted youth with the ancient languages and introduced him into the world of Christian Platonism. After attending the Latin school at Pforzheim (1508–10) and earning his baccalaureate in the liberal arts at the University of Heidelberg (1511), Melanchthon transferred in 1512 to the University of Tübingen, where he became master of arts as early as January 1514. The great-nephew of the famous Hebraist was soon himself a celebrated teacher of classical literature and almost of necessity involved in the Reuchlin controversy. Reuchlin directed him to the field of theology, recommended the works of Jean Gerson and of Wessel Gansfort, and presented him with a New Testament, possibly Erasmus' Greek-Latin edition of 1516.

Quite early Melanchthon admiringly looked up to Erasmus as the master of linguistic elegance and humanist culture. Through Oecolampadius, whose friendship he gained at Tübingen, he probably came into contact with the great humanist. Beyond the distinction of his literary style, he was also won by Erasmus' ethically oriented humanism. For him Erasmus opened up the sources of Christian tradition, the works of the Fathers and their scriptural exegesis.

Despite some minor successes, the young scholar did not really make any great headway at Tübingen. Recommended by Reuchlin and with his encouragement, he accepted the chair of Greek and Hebrew at Wittenberg. In his inaugural lecture on 29 August 1518, "De corrigendis adulescentiae studiis," he advocated a scripturally oriented humanism:

> If we grasp the letter, we shall also comprehend the meaning of things.... And if we direct the mind to the sources, we shall begin to understand Christ, his commandments will enlighten us, and we shall be permeated by the blessed nectar of divine wisdom.

Luther was won over to this humanism, which aimed by means of the languages of the Bible to unlock its content. He worked together with Melanchthon on the reform of studies, and the two were soon close friends. The friendship became even deeper when as early as 1518–19 the young humanist embraced Luther's reform ideas and devoted himself to theology. In the theses on the occasion of his obtaining the baccalaureate in theology on 9 September 1519 he proceeded further than Luther himself in his assault on the teaching of the Church.

Melanchthon never became a doctor of theology nor did he ever mount the pulpit. He was satisfied with being able to deliver theological lectures as a bachelor, without achieving full membership in the faculty. With great devotion he dedicated himself to exegetical lectures. We know of thirteen from the years 1518–22 alone, and these include three on Romans. He regarded that epistle, along with the psalter, as the most outstanding book of the Bible, a guide to the understanding of the other books. He gave eloquent expression to his enthusiasm for the new theology under the auspices of Saint Paul in his festive discourse of 25 January 1520, "In divi Pauli Doctrinam." The humanist, made rather for the scholar's study, even ventured into polemics.

Melanchthon's most valuable service to the young reform movement was a work he wrote during Luther's stay at the Wartburg, the *Loci communes rerum theologicarum seu hypotyposes theologicae* (1521). Employing his *Theologica institutio in epistolam Pauli ad Romano* — produced in connection with his lectures on Romans in 1519 — and the *Rerum theologicarum capita seu loci* — a discussion of the scholastic exegesis of "sentences" — and in conformity with the method developed in these treatises from the application of the rules of classical rhetoric to Scripture, Melanchthon listed the fundamental ideas or great essential subjects according to which the truths of revelation are to be arranged. This work made him the theologian of the Reformation, though the characterization of the *Loci* as the "first Protestant dogmatic theology" is applicable to the 1521 edition only in regard to its systematic presentation. The completeness expected of dogmatic theology is lacking. The doctrine of the Trinity and the Incarnation is excluded; only soteriology and ethics are treated. Melanchthon's concern is to grasp all of Scripture by means of the leading theological ideas which he acquired in his study of Romans — sin, law, grace, Gospel — to explain them as a unity, and to show their connection in salvation history. Through the *Loci* Melanchthon aims to assist young students to a right understanding of Scripture and to stimulate them to the study of the Bible. The *Loci* are to be signposts or pole stars for "those wandering lost through the divine books" and to present the basic points of Scripture in outline (*hypotyposis*). The student is to be brought by means of a few ideas into direct contact with that "on which depends the totality of Christian doctrine."

Without subjecting his humanism to a fundamental criticism, without even becoming entirely clear on the distinction between humanism and Reformation, as W. Maurer puts it, Melanchthon accepted radical theses of Luther's anthropology, such as man's inability to arrive at a natural knowledge of God and the lack of free will; saw in the law only a death-bringing law in contrast to the Gospel; and regarded only an ethics of faith as possible. But Melanchthon found himself in a serious crisis in 1521–22 because of the Wittenberg disturbances. He saw himself compelled to reexamine his theological ideas and to turn back more strongly to humanism and to the traditions of natural law of the Middle Ages. In the new editions of the *Loci,* from 1522, the door was again opened to a philosophical ethics. Fallen nature can know the *lex naturae,* and free will suffices for its external fulfillment. Thus the unbelieving man of the flesh can produce acts of virtue, which, while they do not lead to the justice of the heart, do make possible a civil justice (*iustitia civilis*). Now, too, the ceremonies of the Church and the enactments by authority are "good creations of God" and their disregard is a sin. If until this point Melanchthon was inclined to adjust everything, spiritual and secular, exclusively according to the Bible, now he begins to speak of a twofold justice, of a "justice of the spirit" and a "civil justice." Reason and tradition supply the norms for this natural ethics. Thus with Melanchthon there ensued a revival of the classical moral philosophy and even a sort of Protestant, humanist neo-Aristotelianism. It is due to him that the Reformation proceeded, not against but with the education of the age, and it was Melanchthon who, in the future, would largely determine the creed, ecclesiology, theology, and pedagogy of Lutheranism.

CHAPTER 70

The Pontificate of Adrian VI

Notwithstanding the Edict of Worms, the Reformation was able to spread without resistance. The German bishops took no steps, and the Pope, in accord with his character, was neither inclined nor fitted to introduce any effective measures of reform beyond the condemnation of Luther's doctrines. The Emperor was to be kept away from Germany for nine years by the wars with France and the necessity of establishing his authority in Spain. Furthermore, in his war on two fronts, against France and the Turks, he was dependent on the help of the very princes against whom he would have had to proceed if he enforced the Edict of Worms. Charles V's relations with Leo X were strained because of the Pope's pro-French policy and his having taken sides in the imperial election. However, it had become evident in the meantime that France was a threat rather than an effective help to the interests of the House of Medici and the Papal State, whereas Spanish Naples was in a position to afford protection against the Muslim menace to the coasts. Indeed, if the Pope's anxiety in regard to the Turkish danger was serious, his place was at the side of the Emperor and not of the "Most Christian King" who was conspiring with the Turks. Finally, who but the Emperor was to master the Lutheran movement in Germany, so alarmingly described by Aleander? He showed himself to be obliging in this regard, and so Leo X inclined more and more to the imperial side. In May 1521 there emerged an alliance whose goal was to reestablish the rule of the Sforza at Milan and to deprive the French of Genoa. The Emperor promised aid against the enemies of the Catholic faith and was in turn promised imperial coronation in Italy together with help against Venice. Hence Italian politics were decisive, and the Pope was involved both as head of the House of Medici and as Prince of the Papal State.

The alliance was a success. As a result of a rising of the Milanese against the French, papal and imperial troops were able to occupy the city on 19 November 1521, and Francesco II Sforza assumed the government. But soon afterward, on 1 December, the Pope succumbed to malaria. This implied a serious upset in Italian politics and jeopardized the successes thus far gained in France.

But the change of pontificate seemed to assure especially favorable circumstances for cooperation between Emperor and Pope. The conclave, in which thirty-nine cardinals participated — only three of them non-Italians — was difficult. The cardinals, for the most part worldly and at enmity with one another, were a reflection of the Church and of Christendom. But on 9 January 1522 there occurred the completely unexpected election of the absent Cardinal Adrian of Utrecht, Bishop of Tortosa, in Spain. The disappointed Romans were enraged at the choice of the unknown "barbarian."

This Dutchman, the son of a carpenter, was born at Utrecht in 1459. Raised in the spirit of the *devotio moderna,* with a love of virtue and learning, he entered the University of Louvain in 1476. He there became a respected professor and dean of Sankt Peter. His commentary on the fourth book of *The Sentences* and his twelve *Quodlibeta* show him to have been a late scholastic deeply interested in canonical and moral and casuistic questions. In 1507 Emperor Maximilian I appointed him tutor of his grandson, the seven-year-old Archduke Charles. Thus Adrian entered the council of Margaret, Regent of the Netherlands, and in 1515 he was sent to Spain to assure Charles' succession lo the throne. Ferdinand the Catholic annulled the will he had made in 1512, which had promised the Spanish crown to Charles' younger brother Ferdinand, raised in Spain and very popular there. After the death of King Ferdinand in 1516, Adrian, together with the great humanist Cardinal Ximenes, conducted the regency for Charles until the new king was able to assume the government in Spain personally in 1517. Meanwhile Adrian had become Bishop of Tortosa in 1516 and Inquisitor for Aragon and Navarre; he later became inquisitor for Castile and León also, and in January 1517 was made a cardinal. King Charles, in whose council Adrian had a seat, was unable to win the Spaniards. They complained of the arrogance of the Burgundians and the greed of the foreigners and they insisted on their liberties. Hence when Charles went to Germany in 1520, he turned over to the Cardinal as his representative a difficult assignment which proved to be too much for him. There was open revolt in Castile, and Adrian contrived to master it only with the aid of two coregents of Spanish blood. The news of the papal election reached him on January 22 at Vitoria, where he was instituting military measures for the defense of Navarre against France.

In a solemn statement on 8 March 1522, Adrian VI accepted the election. In it he emphasized his reliance on Christ, "who would endow him, though unworthy, with the strength necessary to protect the Church against the attacks of the Evil One, and to bring back the erring and deceived to the unity of the Church after the example of the Good Shepherd." For his journey to Rome the Pope chose the sea route, to point up his independence of both France and the Empire. His departure was delayed and it was not until 5 August that he put to sea at Tarragona. He landed at Ostia on 28 August and a day later was in Rome.

In the meantime Belgrade had fallen to Sultan Suleiman, Hungary was defenseless before the threat of a Turkish invasion, and Rhodes, the last Christian outpost in the Mediterranean, was being besieged by superior forces. The Pope would be able to deal with the tasks imposed on him by this situation only if he succeeded in restoring the political and religious unity of Christendom. For this a reform of the Church was necessary and it had to begin with the Curia. Only thus could the Church win back confidence as a prerequisite for carrying out her functions as the regulating authority in the West.

To the Romans Adrian was a barbarian. At the time of the Pope's arrival a pestilence was raging in the Eternal City, and his coronation at Saint Peter's on 31 August was reduced to the simplest form. In his address in the consistory on 1 September Adrian asked the aid of the cardinals in his twofold concern: the uniting of the Christian princes for a war against the Turks and the reform of the Curia. Evil, he said, had become so widespread that, to quote Saint Bernard, those covered with sins no longer noticed the stench of vice. The cardinals should set a good example for the rest of the clergy.

If the Pope's stern asceticism and piety — his daily celebration of Mass, for example, was unusual — impressed many people quite unfavorably, for most it was even more distressing that he was so stingy with favors. In the consistory of 26 March 1523 the Cardinal of Santa Croce requested the confirmation of the indults and privileges granted by Leo X. When on this occasion he recalled the unprecedented pleasure of the cardinals at having elevated him to the height of the papacy, Adrian replied that they had called him to suffering and prison. He had found an exhausted and impoverished Church and hence he owed them little. Actually they were his executioners. The dull Dutch scholar apparently had no sympathy for the Italian way of life and the splendor of Renaissance art. When he set about abolishing superfluous offices and showing the door to the beneficiaries of Leo X's prodigal mode of life, the widespread consternation and aversion became bitter hatred. His predecessors had bequeathed to Adrian debts and empty coffers. In addition it was necessary to redeem valuables and works of art including the Gobelins made after Raphael's designs, which had had to be pawned after the death of Leo X. Drastic economy measures were thus necessary, all the more if the Pope intended to renounce, within the scope of Church reform, the excessive fees which were causing so much bad feeling throughout the world. Adrian's thrift brought upon him the reputation of being a miser. The Romans forgave him this far less than they had pardoned the prodigality of his predecessor.

In addition, Adrian's activities were initially hindered by the plague, which in the fall became worse. Against all warnings the Pope stayed in Rome, whereas the cardinals and most officials sought to get as far away as possible. It was only at the end of 1522 that the Curia could again be activated. Collaborators in the carrying out of reform were lacking. Disillusionment made the Pope even more suspicious of his retinue and even more lonely, and induced him to do much on his own. Pastor sums it up: "A foreigner, surrounded by foreign confidants, the Dutch pope was unable to find his way about in the new world which confronted him in Rome."

The slower the reform of the Curia proceeded, the more difficult became the Pope's position in Germany. During the absence of Charles V the religious question was turned over to the Imperial Governing Council, which met at Nürnberg on 1 October 1521. With such organizational weakness consistent action and continuity were possible only with great difficulty. Despite these unpropitious conditions the Imperial Governing Council accomplished much that was useful and it especially sought to adjust the divergent interests to the "common good." The endeavor to coordinate criminal justice provided the basis for the *Carolina* (1532). For defense against the Turks it aimed to provide the Empire with a permanent revenue by means of an imperial toll, a withholding of annates, and a reform of the "common pfennig," an imperial tax established in 1495.

The commotion in Saxony and the fall of Belgrade to the Turks peremptorily showed the urgency of unifying the Empire and of exorcising the religious unrest by means of reform, and Adrian VI meant to extend a helping hand. To the Diet of Nürnberg, which had been summoned for 1 September 1522 but did not actually meet until 17 November, he sent Francesco Chieregati. The legate made known the Pope's agreement that annates and pallium fees should for the future be retained in Germany and spent on the Turkish war; but he also vigorously demanded German assistance for imperiled Hungary. It was only on 10 December that the legate referred to the religious situation in Germany. The erroneous doctrine of Luther was, he said, more threatening than the Turkish danger, and the Pope demanded the implementation of the Edict of Worms. The estates gave an evasive reply and showed little inclination to occupy themselves with this delicate question. Only Elector Joachim of Brandenburg, who did not arrive until 23 December, energetically urged the matter, with the support of the Archduke Ferdinand and the Archbishop of Salzburg. On 3 January 1523 the legate read aloud the documents forwarded to him, a brief and an instruction, in which the Pope, in view of the Turkish peril, deplored the religious danger produced by Luther. Worse even than his errors, said the Pope, was the fact that, despite papal condemnation and imperial edict, he had found patrons and adherents among the princes. It seemed incredible to the Pope that a

> nation so pious would let itself be led by an insignificant friar [*fraterculum*], who has apostatized from the Catholic faith, away from the path shown by the Saviour and his Apostles . . . almost as though only Luther were wise and possessed the Holy Spirit, whereas the Church . . . had been wandering about in the darkness of folly and on the road to ruin until Luther's new light had enlightened her.

The Pope spoke in a similar vein in the instruction. Here, however, he not only deplored and condemned heresy and the schism in the Church produced by the Lutheran movement, but he also laid bare the deeper causes and with an unprecedented candor admitted the guilt of Curia and Church. At the same time he asked patience, since abuses so deeply rooted could not be eradicated at one stroke.

> You are to say also that we frankly confess that God has allowed this punishment to overtake his Church because of the sins of men, and especially those of priests and prelates. . . . Holy Scripture loudly proclaims that the sins of the people have their source in the sins of the priesthood. . . . We are well aware that even in this Holy See much that is detestable has appeared for some years already — abuses in spiritual things, violation of the commandments — and that everything has been changed for the worst. Hence it is not to be wondered at that the sickness has been transmitted from the head to the members, from the popes to the prelates. All of us, prelates and clergy, have turned aside from the road of righteousness and for a long time now there has been not even one who did good [Psalm 13 (14), 3]. Hence we must all give glory to God and humble ourselves before him. Everyone of us must consider why he has fallen and judge himself rather than be condemned by God on the day of his wrath. You must therefore promise in our name that we intend to exert ourselves so that, first of all, the Roman Court, from which perhaps all this evil took its start, may be improved. Then, just as from here the sickness proceeded, so also from here recovery and renewal may begin. We regard ourselves as all the more obliged to carry this out, because the whole world demands such a reform. . . . However, no one should be amazed that we do not liquidate all abuses at one blow. For the disease is deeply entrenched and of many shapes. Therefore, progress must be made step by step, and first of all the most serious and most dangerous evils must be dealt with by proper medicines, lest everything become still more chaotic through a premature reform. Aristotle rightly says that any sudden change in a community is dangerous.

The Pope's confession of guilt, which must be regarded above all as a religious act and the prerequisite of inner reform in the Curia, and his appeal to the estates had no immediate decisive effect. Hans von der Planitz, a councilor of the Elector of Saxony, knew how to postpone the decision by referring it to a committee and at the same time directing attention to the lot of four Lutheran preachers in Nürnberg, whose arrest Chieregati had demanded. Finally, on 5 February 1523, the estates replied to the nuncio. Proceedings against Luther would evoke the most serious disturbances unless first the Roman Curia, from which, admittedly, the corruption had proceeded, was reformed and the *gravamina* of the German nation were remedied. The Pope, in agreement with the Emperor, should, as quickly as possible and at least within a year, convoke a free Christian council in a German city. Meanwhile the Elector of Saxony should see to it that Luther and his adherents neither wrote nor published anything else. The secular and ecclesiastical estates would during the same time guarantee the suppression of any inflammatory preaching and pledge themselves that nothing but the true, pure, authentic, and holy Gospel should be preached, according to the approved interpretation of the Church and the Fathers.

These vague and procrastinating statements were the outcome of a diet at which the ecclesiastical estates predominated. If the discussion of the religious question was irksome to them anyway, they did not regard themselves as obligated by the Pope's cry for penance to reflection and energetic penitence but instead felt themselves offended and exposed.

The reaction of Luther and Melanchthon was equally irreligious. It was published in 1523 in their pamphlet *Deutung der zwei gräulichen Figuren, Papstesels zu Rom und Mönchskalbs zu Freiberg in Meissen gefunden.* Luther considered it not worth the trouble to acknowledge Adrian's good intentions. To him the Pope was "a *magister noster* from Louvain, a university in which such jackasses are crowned." It is Satan who speaks through the Pope.

In his concern for the Church, in which the Curia left him unaided, the Pope looked about for outside help. In December 1522 he asked his countryman Erasmus, whom he had known from his days at Louvain, to employ his scholarship and his stylistic gifts against the "new heretics." He could not render a greater service, the Pope said, to God, the fatherland, and Christendom. He also invited him to Rome, where he would have an ample supply of books at his disposal and would find an opportunity for contacts with scholars and pious men. The prince of humanists had congratulated Adrian on his elevation and had dedicated to him his edition of Arnobius' commentary on the Psalms. In a second letter he had offered his counsel to the Pope. The latter asked the scholar to come to Rome or to make known his suggestions as soon as possible. The proper measures had to be found "in order to expel the dreadful malady from the midst of our nation, while it is still curable." Erasmus warned against recourse to force and advised the Pope to surround himself with a circle of incorruptible and worthy men, free from personal animosity. But he declined for himself, pleading poor health. He could do more at Basel; if he should go to Rome and thus openly take sides, his writings would lose their influence.

Unlike Erasmus, Johannes Eck was ready to do what he could for the Pope's reform work. He came to Rome in March 1523 to represent the interests of the Dukes of Bavaria, but he was able to join to this assignment the welfare of the Church and of Christendom. For the enhancing of the Bavarian Dukes' authority over the Church meant a guarantee against the unreliability of the episcopate. In his memoranda Eck called for the restoration of the conciliar system, whose decay was responsible for both the abuses in the Church and the revolt. A general council would not be achieved so quickly. Besides, for Eck the business of Luther was a German affair. He urgently insisted that a mere attack on error would do no good without a serious undertaking of Church renewal. With regard to reform in Rome, Eck called especially for a limitation of indulgences and the abolition of *commendam.*

The Italian political situation had stabilized before the Pope's entry into Rome. A French countermove had been thwarted on 27 April 1522 by German mercenaries under Jörg von Frundsberg, and the French had lost Genoa. Charles V, convinced that God himself had arranged Adrian's election, wrote to the Pope that, united in harmony, they would accomplish great feats. Naturally he expected Adrian to join the league against Francis I. But the Pope, already under suspicion of being a partisan of his former pupil, had to maintain a strict neutrality if his efforts for peace among the princes of Europe for the sake of defense against the Turks were to be crowned with success. This endeavor to maintain his independence vis-à-vis Charles V and especially his tactless and importunate envoy led to a temporary estrangement from the Emperor, without gaining for the Pope the confidence of the French king.

On 21 December 1522, Rhodes fell to the Turks. The Pope's intensified exertions to unite the Christian princes for resistance or at least to arrange a truce were fruitless. All the more he sought by means of tithes and taxes to raise money himself for the Turkish war. In his distress he made concessions to the princes which contradicted his own principles. The disagreement with Charles V and the more flexible attitude of Francis I enabled Cardinal Soderini, a long-time partisan of France, to gain the Pope's confidence and to draw him into the twilight of partiality. A rising against the Emperor was to be contrived in Sicily, and Francis I intended to exploit it for an attack on North Italy. Soderini was arrested and thereafter Cardinal Giuliano de Medici exercised a decisive influence in the Curia. The Pope still tried to bring about peace. On 30 April 1523 he proclaimed a three-year truce for all of Christendom and stipulated the severest ecclesiastical penalties as its sanction. At the end of July he arranged the Peace of Venice with the Emperor.

This and Soderini's trial caused Francis I to show his true colors. In a very insulting letter he threatened the Pope with the fate of Boniface VIII. He also stopped the transfer of money to Rome and readied troops for an invasion of Lombardy. Thus the Pope witnessed the collapse of his peace efforts. On 3 August 1523 he entered into a defensive alliance with the Emperor, with King Henry VIII of England, with Ferdinand of Austria, and with Milan, Florence, Genoa, Siena, and Lucca. In his disillusionment Adrian VI in a sense collapsed. He died on 14 September 1523, after a pontificate of less than thirteen months.

Section Two

The Struggle over the Concept of Christian Freedom

Chapter 71

The Knights' War

Luther's message *To the Christian Nobility of the German Nation on the Improvement of the Christian Estate* did not die out unheard. While the reformer had at this point taken up the complaints of the humanists and of the Free Knights and made himself the spokesman of national self-assertion against "the shameful and diabolical rule of the Romans," conversely many people had become enthusiastic about Luther's religious message because they assured themselves it would mean the fulfillment of their economic, social, and political expectations. The revolt of the Free Knights in 1522–23 and the Peasants' War of 1524–25 indicated the connection of the religious movement with social and political currents.

The profound changes in the economic, social, and political situation at the beginning of the modern age had pushed the estate of the knights into the background. Its position was based on landed property and the feudal rights derived from it. The more a natural economy was replaced by a money economy, a person-oriented feudalism by the territorial and bureaucratic state, and the feudal levy by mercenaries with firearms and cannon, the more the knights, rendered militarily insignificant, were threatened with being crushed by the aspiring cities and princely power. On the other hand, they were no longer ready to support and represent the Empire. They shunned service and refused to pay the "common pfennig." They further undermined the authority of the Empire by violating the territorial peace. By means of private feuds and local conflicts they aimed to enhance their own power and wealth. They were in no way different from the cities and princes in exploiting the weakness of the central power for their own interests. Any of them who was unwilling to maintain himself in a state befitting his rank by more or less disguised brigandage and plundering expeditions had either to enter the service of a territorial prince or to try to raise himself to the position of a territorial prince. This last was possible almost exclusively at the expense of the ecclesiastical principalities. But their elimination meant a great loss for the nobility, which occupied virtually all the episcopal sees and canonicates in Germany. Hence by no means all the knights could be won for a "war on priests." Among those uninterested were extensive groups of Franconian knights who were variously related to ecclesiastical dignitaries.

Ulrich von Hutten (1488–1523) had publicized the "war on priests" since the end of 1520 from Ebernburg an der Nahe, where he had found asylum with Franz von Sickingen (1481–1523). It was not to end without "murderous struggle and the shedding of blood." From this time on Hutten wrote in German; he had his Latin dialogues published as "conversation booklets." His fiery and inspiring polemics gained him great influence over public opinion. But what continued to be literature to him became for Franz von Sickingen and other knights a disastrous and suicidal act.

Franz von Sickingen was born in 1481 at Ebernburg, the scion of a ministerial family of the Palatinate, which in 1488 became a direct imperial vassal. He claimed to have studied under Reuchlin. In 1504 he entered into his paternal inheritance and was successful in strengthening his position. He exploited mines and maintained a small force in his capacity as an official of the Palatinate and in the service of the Archbishop of Mainz. He distinguished himself from the robber knights of his day only through the style and the degree of his enterprises. Exploiting the situation of the Empire, he was able, in attacks on Worms, Metz, Frankfurt, Lorraine, and Hesse, to make himself a considerable political and financial power on the middle Rhine by means of extortion. Under the guise of the knightly ideals of the struggle for justice and the protection of the weak, he had the lower classes turn over to him their alleged and real legal titles and defended them with modern military means such as artillery and mercenaries.

Outlawed for breach of the territorial peace, he entered the service of France. But he was reconciled with Emperor Maximilian, advocated the election of Charles V, and in 1519 took part in the campaign against Ulrich of Württemberg. In this way he became friendly with Hutten and favored his national humanism. Accordingly he supported Reuchlin and forced the Dominicans of the upper Rhine to give way in the controversy with the great humanist. Von Sickingen's castles, as "inns of justice," became places of refuge for reformers such as Bucer, Oecolampadius, Aquila, and Schwebel. He espoused the cause of the Reformation in pamphlets such as *Sendbrieff zu Unterrichtung etlicher Artickel Christliches glaubens* (1522). But the religious question had little effect on him. He had as meager a grasp of the Lutheran doctrine of justification as Hutten had, much as they declared their desire to open a door to the Gospel. Instead they were influenced by the "struggle for German freedom and justice," as they understood it. At an assembly of knights at Landau on 13 August 1522 a "fraternal alliance" of the knights of the middle and upper Rhine, which also had connections with the Franconian nobility, elected von Sickingen their captain. Thereafter disputes were to be settled only by a special knights' court.

Thus assured, von Sickingen began preparations for a great raid against Richard von Greiffenklau, Archbishop of Trier. The challenge was issued on 27 August 1522, and the matter was at first a private affair. But the chief reason alleged was that the Elector, as a partisan of Francis I of France, had, on the occasion of the imperial election, "acted against God, the imperial majesty, and the order and justice of the Holy Empire." Finally, the declaration of war spoke of the opening of the struggle as a campaign for the honor of Christ against the enemies and destroyers of the truth of the Gospel.

In the final analysis what was afoot was a grand-scale brigandage under the pretext of an appeal to ideals. The secularization of the archbishopric was supposed to enable von Sickingen to advance to princely status. But he was unable to mobilize groups of his own estate for this, and still less to separate the city of Trier from the archbishop. The promise to the archbishop's subjects to rescue them from the harsh anti-Christian law of priests and to conduct them to evangelical freedom did not prove very effective.

As a warrior, Richard von Greiffenklau was the equal of von Sickingen and knew how to make use of artillery at least as well as his opponent did. Von Sickingen captured Blieskastel and on 3 September 1522 the city of Sankt Wendel. His force is said to have consisted at that time of 600 cavalry and 7,000 infantry. But he did not attempt to exploit his initial successes at once. While he was awaiting reinforcements the archbishop had time to put Trier into a state of defense and to mobilize defensive forces. When von Sickingen appeared before the city on 8 September he was unable to accomplish much and had to withdraw after an eight-day siege. The Archbishop of Trier, to whose aid the Landgrave of Hesse and the Elector Palatine came by virtue of the "agreement" of Oberwesel (1519), could now proceed to the offensive. In April 1523 he undertook a punitive expedition against von Sickingen. The latter had to retire to his castle of Landstuhl, where he vainly waited for reinforcements and at length was forced to capitulate on 7 May. The victorious princes found him, mortally wounded, behind the shattered walls of the castle, and a few hours later he died of his injuries. Not real power but a skillful and unscrupulous exploitation of the entangled political situation had conducted von Sickingen to success, but when he ran into determined opposition before Trier, he failed miserably. His cause was thereby stripped of its prestige, and the collapse of the knightly estate became clear.

In the summer of 1523 an army of the Swabian League under Baron Georg Truchsess von Waldburg took the field against the Franconian and Swabian knights to put an end to their brigandage and violations of the territorial peace. A cooperative defense by the knights did not materialize. The still bold and defiant resistance of individuals did not suffice when faced with superiority of numbers. In barely six weeks thirty-two castles were burned in the Odenwald and in Franconian Württemberg, and the knightly class was finished as a political force shaping the Empire. The winners were the territorial princes. Some of these saw in the Reformation a promoter of revolution, and this strengthened their will to fight against it.

CHAPTER 72

The "Fanatics" Karlstadt and Müntzer

Men like Melanchthon were so overshadowed by Luther that we are able only with difficulty to evaluate their personal achievement and their significance in the development and form of the Reformation. But there were others, such as Karlstadt and Müntzer, who so quickly ran afoul of Luther, and hence were isolated by him and turned into sectarians, that they were unable to develop and to make their full personal contribution to the reform movement. Neither of them was granted a long and consistent activity nor any possibility of lasting innovation. Only starting points can be examined and these allow no certain judgment. Furthermore, their image was, even in their lifetime, given a prejudiced stamp by the polemics of their opponents, notably Luther. The latter originated the word *Schwärmer,* "fanatics," for Karlstadt and Müntzer as well as for all factions which did not accord with his views, such as those of Zwingli and the Swiss. Only quite recently, and even today inadequately, has the trouble been taken to understand men such as Müntzer and Karlstadt from the basis of their own world of ideas.

Karlstadt

Andreas Rudolf Bodenstein was born around 1480 at Karlstadt am Main and is known by the name of his birthplace. He matriculated at Erfurt in 1499, but he was chiefly influenced not by Erfurt's nominalism but by the Thomism of Cologne, where he studied till the end of 1504. He then went to Wittenberg as a strict Thomist. He became a doctor of theology there in 1510 and was elected archdeacon of the Chapter of All Saints. He held lectures on Aristotle and Saint Thomas. In these he represented a scholastic position opposed to that of Martin Luther, who became doctor of theology in 1512 while Karlstadt was dean and was soon attracting attention by his lectures on the Psalms and Romans. In 1515 Karlstadt traveled to Italy and after a brief stay in Rome gained a doctorate of laws at Siena in 1516. He had thereby acquired the prerequisites for obtaining the provostship at Wittenberg.

From the beginning of 1517 he was preoccupied with Saint Augustine in preparation for a critical discussion of Luther's interpretation of that Father. Under the spell of Augustine's works, especially the anti-Pelagian writings, he became favorably inclined toward Luther. This is evident from Karlstadt's 151 theses on Augustine's theology of 26 April 1517, which were hailed by Luther as witnesses of the new theology, and from his commentary on Augustine's *De spiritu et litera.* In the dedication to Johann Staupitz of 18 November 1517 Karlstadt relates that he had intended to forge from Augustine's works weapons against Luther, but he had been converted to the new theology.

In Karlstadt's commentary the most important question deals with justice and the fulfilling of the law. Of himself man cannot fulfill the law. Justice based on the law — that is, man's claim to fulfill the law by his own strength — is in the strict sense ungodliness, because man attributes to himself what is God's. It is the function of the law to lay bare man's inability and to testify that man cannot become just by the law or his own free will, but "only through the help of the Spirit and through God's gift." The law thus proves our weakness and indicates him, Christ, from whom we must obtain through faith the ability to do what the law commands.

More so than Luther, Karlstadt sees justification as sanctification. Grace signifies a change affecting the whole man, qualifying him for good actions but for that very reason requiring of him also a strict moral conduct. If for Luther the tension between law and Gospel persisted and the law retained the function of disclosing and denouncing man's sin, Karlstadt did not rest content with the opposition of spirit and world, which he felt deeply, but taught, in conjunction with Augustine, that grace enables us to love and to fulfill the law. Grace turns the hearer into a doer of the law. In grace, which is identified with love, Christ gives himself to us and through the Holy Spirit effects good works in us. "Christ himself makes us act; he himself makes his work our good works." The justice bestowed on us is only a deposit; we must take further pains with it. In this life it does not acquire full perfection, and hence no man is without sin.

Like law and grace, Scripture and the spirit are oriented to each other. If the law without grace is dead, and in fact brings death, then the letter is dead without the life-giving spirit. Christ must enlighten the inner man for a right understanding of the external word. "Thus we direct our ears to the preacher and our eyes to the letters, but our heart only to God, creator of heaven and earth, who from within, as the true word, first breathes life into all works and touches the heart." It is incorrect to see in these Augustinian ideas a "devaluation of the external, the preached word." The nominalist Luther was in more danger of undervaluing the external or of representing it as insignificant than Karlstadt was.

The profound difference between the two men was not apparent at first. Karlstadt's theses of May 1518, a confrontation with Eck's *Obelisci,* maintained the scriptural principle and the fallibility of a general council. They and the Leipzig Disputation, for which the theses were responsible, made the two Wittenberg professors appear in the eyes of the public as fighters for the same cause. Karlstadt was above all concerned about the relationship of divine grace and the human will. How little he undervalued the external word of Holy Scripture is made clear in his *De canonicis scripturis* of August 1520, in which he opposed the rejection of the Epistle of James and insisted that sympathy or antipathy is no criterion for the evaluation of Scripture. He thereby criticized Luther, but not by name. For Karlstadt the authority of the canonical Scripture is absolute, standing above every human authority, papal and episcopal included.

When Johannes Eck added Karlstadt's name in the Bull "Exsurge Domine," threatening excommunication, Karlstadt replied with an "appeal" to the general council.

Karlstadt spent May and June 1521 in Denmark as adviser to King Christian II in the latter's Reformation or, more correctly, in his legislative work against the clergy. But after the Edict of Worms he was no longer welcome at the court of the Dane, who was a brother-in-law of Charles V. When Karlstadt returned to Wittenberg in mid-June, Luther was at the Wartburg. Thus Karlstadt automatically moved more prominently into the foreground. In his treatise on the Eucharist, *Von den Emphahern, Zeichen, und Zusag des heiligen Sakramentes, Fleisch und Blut Christi* he is more moderate than Luther. He does not yet demand the chalice for the laity and quite naturally maintains the real presence. On the other hand, he goes further in the attack on religious vows and celibacy. In dispute at Wittenberg over the conformity of the liturgy with Scripture, he maintains in contrast to Luther that private Masses are permissible in case of need. In any case they are to be preferred to a public Mass without communion under both species. Now Karlstadt held that "one who takes only the bread commits sin" and, unlike Luther, did not allow communion under one species. Luther, however, saw unlawfulness in the Mass celebrated privately and wrote to Melanchthon on 1 August 1521: "I will never again celebrate a private Mass." It was not Karlstadt but Gabriel Zwilling and the Augustinians who took the initiative in introducing the reformed liturgy. Partly out of regard for Frederick the Wise, Karlstadt was more hesitant. He, much more than Luther, pressed for the practical consequences of the reform doctrines and the abolition of everything that in his view was opposed to the Gospel. To him, a realist, it was not possible, as it was to the nominalist Luther, to leave dialectical propositions unreconciled. He urged solutions, syntheses, and consequences, and on this are founded his rationalism as well as his mystical thinking.

Karlstadt intended, however, to realize his concept of a congregational Christianity quietly and with the cooperation of the city council. At a disputation on 17 October 1521, in which Karlstadt rejected transubstantiation while demanding the adoration of the sacramental bread, and allowing private Masses in case of necessity, for the sake of communion under both species, Melanchthon impetuously demanded: "Somebody has to make a start; otherwise nothing will happen." Karlstadt retorted: "Indeed, but without any tumult and without providing opponents with an opportunity for slander."

Toward the close of the year he let himself be more and more driven to a change of liturgy by the turbulent pressure of radical elements in the population. Thus, disregarding the elector's regulations, on Christmas 1521 he celebrated the first "German Mass," a Mass with the account of the institution of the Eucharist in German and with communion under both species. He rejected liturgical vestments and let the laity touch with their hands the Eucharistic bread and the chalice to demonstrate that there was no need of a priestly class and that the laity are ministers of the liturgy. On 19 January 1522, in the presence of a group of professors and of Wittenberg councilors, he solemnized his marriage. He had a decisive influence on the Wittenberg city ordinance of 24 January 1522, and vigorously demanded the removal of images by the city council, thinking thus to forestall an iconoclastic outbreak. But in fact through this pamphlet and his sermons he fostered radicalism in Wittenberg. When the electoral councilor Einsiedel called upon him for moderation, he expressly protested against the accusation of insurrection. "I pride myself on hating and shunning insurrection. God grant that my detractors do not in time stir up revolt, which will accomplish no good. I forbid revolt."

Thinking that he had acted in accord with Luther, Karlstadt was deeply hurt by Luther's harsh criticism of him as a fanatic and author of disturbance. The pulpit was denied him, as was any relationship with the community. A treatise in which he defended those of his reforms that Luther had annulled was censured by the university. This and the measures of restoration taken by Luther, the "neopapist," led to a deeper alienation and hastened Karlstadt's own development, which deviated ever more from the path of the Lutheran Reformation. His unpleasant experiences with his colleagues at the university strengthened his anticultural tendencies, which had been becoming more evident since the beginning of 1523. Condemning the new scriptural scholarship and its dogmatic posturing, he turned more and more to the laity, drawing the ultimate consequences of Luther's teaching on the universal priesthood. He stressed the laity's obligation to read the Bible and their right to interpret it. In *Eine Frage, ob auch jemand möge selig werden ohne die Fürbitte Mariens* he would soon advocate the opinion that many craftsmen were more proficient in theology than priests. Once a prelate of high rank and an intellectually proud professor, thereafter he would live, without academic title or official dress, as "a new layman," like the peasants.

Physically too he took his leave of Wittenberg, taking personal charge in the summer of 1523 of the parish of Orlamünde, the revenues of which he drew as archdeacon of the All Saints collegiate chapter. Here he introduced the changes in the liturgy that had been annulled at Wittenberg, enriched the church singing with German translations of psalms, and preached daily to a great concourse of people.

In contrast to Luther, who attributed no importance to external form and regarded it as *adiaphoron,* Karlstadt felt compelled to press for the changing of what he regarded as wrong practices expressions, ceremonies, images — because they seduced the people. To wait in this matter, as Luther wanted to do, until the inner judgment was sound would be like letting a child play with a sharp knife until he is intelligent enough to put it aside on his own.

In Karlstadt's numerous treatises from this period the attack on infant baptism and on the real presence of Christ in the Eucharist are still in the background. To him it is far more urgent to introduce into his community — through thoughts of mysticism — union with the divine will, the "supreme virtue of composure," inner recollection and sanctification. These are the conditions *sine qua non* for being filled with God, a condition granted to the individual by means of divine illumination in conjunction with the word of Scripture.

Karlstadt became the center of a religious movement that was not confined to Orlamünde. This gave the circles at Wittenberg no rest. In March 1524 the university called upon Karlstadt to fulfill his duties as archdeacon and professor and hence to return to Wittenberg. Luther pressed for a prohibition of his writings if he did not submit to the university's censorship. When the petitions and requests of Karlstadt and of the Orlamünde congregation, which claimed the right to choose its priest, were denied, Karlstadt renounced his office as pastor of Orlamünde and resigned the archdeaconry, because he could nor reconcile any further celebrating of Mass with his conscience.

In spite of this isolation by the Wittenberg circles, however, Karlstadt did not allow himself to be enticed by Müntzer to join the league for the annihilation of the godless. As early as 1522 he had urged moderation on Müntzer, and now he expressly renounced any connection with him. Such alliances, he said, were contrary to the will of God, in whom alone one must place one's hope. Similar ideas were expressed in the open letter sent by the people of Orlamünde to those of Allstedt. But this decisive withdrawal from Müntzer and the latter's efforts to restore the order of the Gospel by force if necessary did not save Karlstadt from the accusation of sedition. Luther denied to the people of Orlamünde the right of free election of their priest, a right which he himself had proclaimed. He saw them infected by the fanaticism of Allstedt. Hence the *Letter to the Princes of Saxony* of July 1524, in which Luther asked them to take steps and to forestall insurrection, although directed expressly against Müntzer also included Karlstadt by implication.

On 22 August 1524 Luther preached at Jena against the "Karlstadt fanaticism." Karlstadt was present and in the afternoon in a conference with Luther, he explicitly protested against being identified with the "Allstedt spirit": "You do me violence and injustice in putting me with that murderous spirit. I solemnly declare before all these brethren that I have nothing to do with the spirit of revolt." But he was unable to dissipate Luther's distrust. Even less suited to his purpose was the heated dispute which the people of Orlamünde had with the reformer two days later. Luther convinced the princes of the danger of mob spirit, and on 18 September 1524, Karlstadt, with his family, was expelled from electoral Saxony.

He sought refuge in South Germany, but more than once had to move again. He went, among other places, to Strasbourg and Basel and finally, toward the end of December 1527, to Rothenburg ob der Tauber. In these troubled weeks and despite severe privations, he published eight works, including five treatises on communion. They had probably been partly written, or at least begun, in Orlamünde, but Karlstadt did not publish them until after his expulsion from Saxony. Hence they could not have been used as the alleged reason for his banishment.

Notwithstanding his numerous works on this subject, Karlstadt provides us with no coherent exposition of his teaching on the Eucharist. The reason for this is probably to be found in his restless ways and the adverse circumstances under which the treatises originated. In them he clearly and definitely denies the real presence, but the point of departure in this is not his understanding of the account of the institution of the Eucharist. His curious explanation of "this is my body" is secondary and does not play in his writings the role that could be expected, according to the literature. If for Luther the Mass is a derogation from the Cross of Christ, so for Karlstadt the bodily presence in the Sacrament is also. The Lord's promise to give us his body is a reference to his sufferings and death on the Cross. Here, and not in the Sacrament, occurs the remission of sins. If this were to refer to Christ in his glorified body, the clear relationship with his sacrificial death would disappear. In Karlstadt's view, there are only two modes of Christ's presence — the historical bloody form on the Cross and the glorified form in the splendors of heaven. Karlstadt cannot accept a mysterious descent into the bread: "There are no more than two advents — one in the form of the Cross and Passion here on earth, the other in glory. You must not invent a third, and you cannot add either of the two others to the Host."

Because Karlstadt does not accept a sacramental presence and can understand the real presence of Christ's body only locally, he has to deny the real presence unless he is willing to admit that Christ abandons heaven or is omnipresent in the sense of Luther's doctrine of ubiquity. It now remained to bring this conviction of his — a sort of theological *a priori* — into harmony with the testimony of Scripture. This led to the contrived explanation, greatly ridiculed by Luther, that with the *touto* of the words of institution Christ pointed to the body in which he was present to the disciples.

> Christ's body is not in the bread and his blood is not in the chalice. But we must eat the Lord's body in the remembrance or acknowledgment of his body, which he gave into the hands of the unjust for our sake, and drink from the chalice in the recognition of his blood, which Christ shed for us — in other words, we eat and drink in acknowledgment of Christ's death.

Karlstadt's writings produced loud reverberations and were widely accepted. It was learned with alarm at Wittenberg that the banishment of the fanatic from Saxony had in no way silenced him; in fact, in southwestern Germany and in Switzerland he was now even better known and esteemed.

Luther took a position against Karlstadt in his *Brief an die Christen zu Strassburg wider den Schwärmergeist* of December 1524. In it he admits how difficult a struggle it was for him to accept belief in the real presence.

> I confess that if Doctor Karlstadt or anyone else had said to me five years ago that there is nothing but bread and wine in the Sacrament, he would have done me a great service. I have truly endured such severe temptations in this question, struggled and wrestled with myself, that I would have been glad to be out of it, for I realized that thereby I could have given the papacy the greatest blow.... But I am held captive, I cannot escape. The text is too powerfully present and cannot be driven from the mind by words.

In *Wider die himmlischen Propheten, von den Bildern und Sakrament* he provided a detailed refutation. The first part was in print in December 1524. It attacks the new law of Karlstadt, his iconoclasm, his attitude toward authority, and his disregard of the external word. Luther castigates the spirit which can do nothing but "create more and more law, misery, conscience, and sin." Karlstadt "makes for himself his own Moses" and "his own Christ," just like the Pope, except that "the pope does so by precept, Doctor Karlstadt by prohibition." The Pope "compels and constrains one to do what is not commanded nor forced by God." Karlstadt "prevents and hinders one from allowing what is not forbidden nor hindered by God." "But Christian freedom perishes just as readily when it must give up what is not forbidden as when it is forced to do what it is not obliged to do."

Luther furthermore attacks the disparagement of the external word as opposed to the "spirit," of which one becomes aware in an "inner experience" and to which Scripture is only a confirmation. In the second part of *Wider die himmlischen Propheten,* which appeared at the end of January 1525, Luther discusses the doctrine of the Eucharist in detail. He first of all stresses that, according to God's arrangement, the "external details," the "word of the Gospel given by the tongue" and the "material signs, such as baptism and the Eucharist," precede the imparting of the inner spirit. God "will give to no one either spirit or faith without the external word and sign." Karlstadt, the mob agitator, casts it scornfully and mockingly to the winds and "wishes first to enter into the Spirit." Luther wishes "to take the words simply as they are... and let the bread be the body of Christ." Despite all his attempts at interpreting the words of institution, especially in regard to *touto,* Karlstadt is unable to quote a single scriptural text supporting his theory, but all the more he indulges reason, the "arch-whore and bride of the devil." When he quotes Scripture, he wishes "not to honor the word of God with faith or to accept it according to the plain manner of speech, but to measure and master it with sophistical reasoning and pointed subtlety." He shifts the center of gravity from word and Sacrament to the subject — to the remembering and proclaiming of Christ's death on the Cross. He thereby makes "what Christ promised a command and sets up a work in place of faith." "But it is still worse and more insane that he attributes to such a memorial the power to justify as faith does," whereas "they who preach and proclaim must first be justified."

Luther's words were unusually cutting. Throughout, Karlstadt is called an agitator who "stirs up the crazy mob," a fool or a lying spirit, even a prophet of the devil.

When the Peasants' War broke out in March 1525, Karlstadt was living at Rothenburg. Now, as before, he did not take part in the social-political disputes, but this did not prevent his being branded even more a fanatic, an iconoclast, an agitator, a murderer of souls, a sinful spirit. This extraordinary acidity in Luther's polemic; greatly shocked many contemporaries, including Melanchthon, but especially all who had hitherto regarded Karlstadt as a partisan of the Wittenberg circle. People sided with Karlstadt at Strasbourg and in Switzerland, and he defended himself in three works. In these he sought to shore up his idea of the Eucharist, but otherwise he stressed a practical Christianity which had to produce the fruits of freedom and justice in good works. Caught between the two sides in the Peasants' War — "the ecclesiastical lords hunted me as game, the peasants . . . would have devoured me" — Karlstadt had to leave Rothenburg on 30 or 31 May. He went to his mother in Karlstadt am Main but found no peace there and at last, crushed in spirit, he asked Luther from Frankfurt on 12 June 1525 to obtain from the elector permission for him to return to Saxony. He intended "for the future not to write, preach, or teach any more." In his *Entschuldigung des falschen Namens des Aufruhrs* he again protested against the accusation of being an agitator. "In brief, I know that I am innocent of any share in Müntzer's revolt." And in the *Erklärung wie Karlstadt seine Lehre von dem hochwürdigen . . . achtet und geachtet haben will* he maintained that in his writings on the Eucharist he aimed to question rather than to assert and that he was open to further correction.

Luther was satisfied with this virtual recantation and, happy "to purchase his silence by such a favor and mercy so that he might not cause more distress elsewhere through vengeance or final despair," he recommended that the elector allow Karlstadt to take up residence at Kemberg or in a nearby village. Thus Karlstadt managed to support himself as farmer and shopkeeper, wretchedly and under supervision, first at Segrehna, then at Bergwitz, and finally at Kemberg, until in the spring of 1529 he escaped the increasing spiritual constraint by flight to further misery. Via Holstein, East Friesland, Strasbourg, and Basel he went in May 1530 to Zwingli in Zurich. Here he supported himself as a proofreader in a print shop and then as deacon at the hospital. At the end of 1531 he obtained a pastorate at Altstätten in the Rheintal, but after Zwingli's death he had to give it up. He again sought refuge in Zurich until in June 1534 he at last found his final field of activity as preacher and professor in Basel. On 14 April 1534, Bullinger, preacher at the Grossmünster in Zurich, wrote to his friend Myconius at Basel; "You need have no fear that that man is such as Luther has described him. He is very good-natured, modest, humble, and in every respect irreproachable." In contrast to his earlier hostility to scholarship and titles, at Basel Karlstadt again fostered the traditional disputations and obtaining of degrees. In other ways also, happy to have found an asylum after so much persecution and privation, in the service of the Swiss Reformed Church he seems to have given up "trying to impose his own earlier personal convictions." He died of the plague at Basel on 24 December 1541.

Karlstadt was among the first who had to experience how severely Luther and the reformers, who appealed to their own consciences and their own understanding of Scripture, would proceed against those who made the same claim for themselves. With direct reference to Karlstadt and Müntzer, Luther had said that they should be confidently allowed to preach, for there had to be sects and the word of God had to be on the battlefield and fight there.

Thomas Müntzer

Luther's opposition to Thomas Müntzer was even more bitter and more fundamental. Müntzer was from Stolberg in the Harz Mountains, but details of his youth are lacking. If, with H. Boehmer, we assume that ordinarily young men who were not well off matriculated only when they had reached the minimum age of about seventeen, required for the baccalaureate, then Müntzer's birth must be assigned to 1488 or 1489. For a Thomas Müntzer from Quedlinburg was enrolled at Leipzig on 16 October 1506, and we know that Müntzer's family lived in Quedlinburg. As late as 1512 we find him a student at Frankfurt an der Oder. Obviously his studies were unusually prolonged, but the reasons are unknown. In any event, Müntzer acquired an education that was superior to the ordinary student's. He was well read in the Church Fathers, the mystics, Joachim of Fiore, and above all, Holy Scripture, for the sake of which he studied Greek and Hebrew. In letters he is addressed as master of arts and bachelor of theology. He was a priest of the diocese of Halberstadt and before 1513 an assistant in Aschersleben and Halle; as such he took part in an "alliance" against Archbishop Ernst (1476–1513) of Magdeburg and Halberstadt, a brother of Frederick the Wise. Later (in 1516) he was a prior at the convent in Forse. He was staying at Leipzig in 1519 and perhaps met Luther on the occasion of the disputation. From the end of that year he was confessor at the convent of Beuditz, east of Naumburg. Here he had a slender income but much leisure for study. He occupied himself with Augustine, Tauler, Suso, Eusebius, and other writers and provided himself with the acts of the Councils of Constance and Basel.

In May 1520, on Luther's recommendation, Müntzer became vicar of the pastor Johann Sylvius Egranus at Sankt-Marien in Zwickau, and, when the pastor returned, he accepted the small Katharinenkirche in the same town, with a congregation of craftsmen and miners. A zealous and vehement preacher, filled with prophetic self-assurance and a mysticism of the Cross, he came into conflict with the Franciscans. In the autumn he began to be influenced by Nikolaus Storch and the Zwickau prophets. His language became even more radical in his dealings with these spiritualist and Taborite circles, and he did not shrink from personal attacks, above all on the Erasmian Egranus, pastor of the main parish church.

Müntzer disregarded a summons to appear before the bishop's *officialis* at Zeitz. Eventually the elector's local agent and the council intervened and deposed him on 16 April 1521. Müntzer fled the same night. His subsequent wanderings brought him several times to Bohemia. He preached at Prague and tried to gain adherents by means of a proclamation, the Prague Manifesto of 1 November 1521. This document provides our first concrete hold on his views. It is extant in four versions — two in German, one in Czech, one in Latin. The vernacular versions are especially oriented to the needs and desires of the common people. Müntzer emphasizes the necessity of the sevenfold Holy Spirit, especially the Spirit of the fear of the Lord, for the exercise of faith. Without the Spirit we can neither hear nor recognize God. He fits the parts to the whole. Preachers who offer only the "cold" and the "naked" Scripture are thieves and robbers. They "steal the word of God from their neighbor's mouth" (140; 155). The priests give the people only the "dead words of Scripture" and "the sheep do not know that they should hear the living voice of God, that they should all have revelations" (147). The true preacher should, according to First Corinthians 14, "have revelations, for otherwise he cannot preach the word" (141). God has not ceased to speak. Man must hear the word as now uttered by God and not as a historical report.

If the Church has been made a whore by scholars and priests, now, since God is separating the wheat from the weeds and has appointed Müntzer over the harvest, the "new, apostolic Church" is to begin, first in Bohemia and then everywhere else (150), a church, not of "priests and apes" (*Pfaffen und Affen*), but "of the elect friends of God," who learn to prophesy and thus "truly experience how friendly, in fact cordially, God delights to speak with all his elect" (142). The stressing of the gifts of the Holy Spirit, of the "living Spirit," the tension between the dead letter and the living and timely word of God, the summons to the carrying out of his demanding will, the doctrine of the Church of the elect, which is separated from the godless, and, finally, Müntzer's conviction of being the instrument of God's judgment — such are the special marks of this Prague Manifesto.

Müntzer did not find the anticipated reaction in Bohemia, and the ensuing difficult period up to the spring of 1523 is obscure. Müntzer stayed in his native Central Germany and seems, as can be inferred from a remark by Luther and one of Müntzer's letters of 9 March 1523, to have been in the service of a convent at Halle. He interpreted his sufferings and bitter poverty as a sign of election. The mystical self-annihilation leads to communion with God, which will in turn transform man's cause into God's cause.

At Easter of 1523 Müntzer was tentatively made pastor of the Johanniskirche at Allstedt, a small town of craftsmen and farmers. Here at Allstedt, where he gained the confidence of Johann Zeys, the official agent of the elector, and of the former pastor, he was able for the first time to carry out his ideas. His peaceful outlook and his pressing pastoral concern are evident in his letter to the "brethren at Stolberg," in which he represents suffering and poverty in the Spirit as the prerequisite of the rule of Christ, as well as in his regulation of worship. In the "Deutsch Kirchenamt" — Matins, Lauds, and Vesper — and in the "Deutsch Evangelisch Messe" he created the first completely German liturgy, and in the "Ordnung und Berechnung des Deutschen Amtes zu Allstedt" he provided its theoretical justification. Müntzer intended to foster an intelligible liturgy in keeping with Scripture and thereby to serve the "deliverance of the poor, wretched, blind consciences of men." As the subject of the liturgy, the congregation must actively participate in it. With this emphatically pastoral attitude the "fanatic" Müntzer, like Karlstadt, was much more concerned about formal worship than Luther was. Luther was inspired by him to compose his hymns. Rendered self-sufficient as pastor at Allstedt, Müntzer ceased to court Wittenberg and even sharply criticized Luther and his friends for their hesitation about translating the liturgy into German.

In two doctrinal treatises at the end of 1523, *Von dem getichten Glauben* and *Protestation . . . Von dem rechtem Christenglauben und der Taufe,* Müntzer publicly declared war on Luther. In the *Protestation* he took up the problem of baptism for the first time, warning against overestimating the "external baptism." Nowhere, he said, do we read that Mary or the disciples of Christ were baptized with water. In John 3:5 and throughout the fourth Gospel, water is to be understood as the "movement of the Spirit," which effects the inner, true, and absolutely necessary baptism. The demand for adult baptism is not contained in this train of thought, and Luther and Melanchthon were wrong in making Müntzer the author of Anabaptism. He never practiced rebaptism, which came into use in Zurich only in 1525. Next to Tauler's mysticism of suffering, the spiritualism and chiliastic doctrines of Joachim of Fiore were Müntzer's sources.

Müntzer was profoundly convinced that faith must prove itself in testimony before the world and that the Christian bears an active responsibility for the world and the fate of his neighbor. For him there was no division into two sides as there was for Luther. The will of God demanded an immediate and absolute realization in all spheres. But Müntzer still thought that the goal could be achieved by peaceful means, especially by the preaching of the word of God. His first conflict with the political authorities did not originate in sociopolitical misunderstandings but because the Count of Mansfeld forbade his subjects to attend Müntzer's "heretical" Mass. From the pulpit Müntzer denounced him as a scoundrel and bloodsucker and in a statement of 22 September 1523, which he signed as "destroyer of unbelievers," he reaffirmed his stand. The count was presuming to forbid the holy Gospel. "You should know that in such mighty and righteous matters I do not fear even the whole world." Even if Müntzer threatened, "do not snap, for otherwise the old garment will tear," he was still in no way presenting the picture of a rebel against the social order but that of a zealous man of God concerned about the irrevocable claims of the Gospel.

His "Sermon to the Princes," delivered at the Castle of Allstedt on 13 July 1524 in the presence of Frederick the Wise's brother, Duke Johann of Saxony, and the latter's son and heir, Prince Johann Friedrich, shows how unrevolutionary Müntzer was at the outset and how much he still hoped to achieve his goal along with the princes. In it the kingdom of God is no purely eschatological thing and the princes are not "heathen folk" with merely secular duties; rather, the kingdom of God is to be realized in this world and time, if necessary by the sword of princes. The proved, unlettered faith of the elect cannot be established alongside the order of the world; it must create a new reality in human society. This is true especially of princes. The sword bestowed by God upon authority has no mere function of warding off or punishing evildoers but a positive, constructive task. The true ruler must take hold of authority by the roots. Like the simple believer, the prince who supports the Gospel must also endure a "great cross and great tribulation." For the cross is the mark of the Christian and the pledge of victory. But if princes refuse to use their sword on behalf of the pious elect against the evil, then "the sword will be taken from them and given to the fervent people for the destruction of the godless."

Even after this sermon, when Müntzer was still uncertain of the princes' reaction to his words, he sought to achieve his aims with them. He invited them to join the divine covenant with the people: "A contractual league, that is, regulated by agreed terms, must be made in such a form that the common man may join himself to the pious rulers for the sake of the Gospel alone." Müntzer decried a social misconception of the sins of the league, as though there were a question of material relief.

Meanwhile, at the end of July Luther wrote his *Brief an die Fürsten zu Sachsen von dem aufrührerischen Geist,* in which he branded Müntzer as Satan and asked the princes "to check disorder and forestall revolution." He accused Müntzer of cowardice for having declined a hearing "in the corner," that is, before Luther at Wittenberg. Even after Müntzer had been questioned at Weimar on 1 August after the Allstedt council had abandoned him and his league and his printing press had been forbidden, he still thought at that time of a legal course with the princes, as is evident from his letter of 3 August 1524 to Frederick the Wise. But it soon became clear to him that the territorial authority had rejected him. He was unwilling to accept the fate of sitting down and awaiting their judgment like a dumb animal. And so, on the night of 7–8 August, he secretly left the city and went to Mühlhausen.

But even the *Ausgedrückte Entblössung des falschen Glaubens,* printed at Nürnberg in October, which was a more radical version of the interpretation of the first chapter of Luke submitted to the prince at Weimar on 1 August, shows that for Müntzer not the social question but the religious quest for the true faith was absolutely predominant. Faith implies power to do the impossible. Before it can be achieved, the godless must be hurled from the seat of judgment and man must be made empty by suffering and the cross. Only then can the "power of the Most High" come upon him and the Holy Spirit overshadow him. Holy Scripture confirms faith and from it the road to faith is learned.

Thus for Müntzer the proud who must be toppled from the throne were, before the princes, the scriptural scholars, or rather the "scriptural thieves" with their "monkish idol," Luther. They deceived the people, claiming that the study of Scripture is necessary for salvation and at the same time preaching to the common man that he should permit himself to be oppressed and exploited by tyrants, so that from mere anxiety about his daily bread he has no time for the study of Scripture.

Complaints about material needs are merely incidental. According to Müntzer's mysticism of the cross, man attains to the true faith only through external and inner suffering. If God despises the "bigwigs, the "big heads with fine titles, such as the Church of godless now has, and takes the humble into his service, still the people are not yet ready. They "must first be quite severely punished." They need the right leader, "a servant of God, filled with his grace, in the spirit of Elias." "Many must be awakened in order that, with a sublime zeal and in fervent seriousness, they may purge Christendom of godless rulers." The new John must "by means of a tried and proved life, make known to others the Cross, understood since his youth, and shout into the wretched, desolate, confused hearts of the God-fearing, who are now beginning to be on the watch for the truth."

At stake is religious renewal, the "movement of the Spirit, that man may resemble Christ" in his sufferings and life through the overshadowing of the Holy Spirit, whom the world mocks but who is given only to the poor in the Spirit. Of course, if the genuine Christian government is to be realized in this world and against the mighty, then a regrouping of political and social conditions cannot be avoided.

Even in Allstedt Müntzer had intended to reply to Luther's *Brief an die Fürsten zu Sachsen von dem aufrührerischen Geist,* for on 3 August he wrote to Frederick the Wise that, because of the scandal given to many pious persons, Luther's slanderous letter should not remain unanswered. But it is not known whether it was at Allstedt that he undertook the *Hochverursachte Schutzrede und Antwort wider das geistlose, sanftlebende Fleisch zu Wittenberg.* In any event it was finished only at Mühlhausen—and presumably before 19 September, for in it no mention is made of the revolutionary events there, which ended on 27 September with Müntzer's banishment and flight to Nürnberg.

In this *Schutzrede* Müntzer rejects the charge of having incited "insurrection." He has shown the princes from Scripture that they should use the sword to prevent rebellion, though the princes are not the masters but the servants of the sword. They also are bound by the law. Luther, "father of obsequiousness," "flatterer," "Doctor Liar," attempts "to cover up for them with Christ in concocted validity." For Müntzer law and grace are one: "Christ in the Gospel has made known the Father's righteousness through his kindness." It is not right that Luther should practice the "patience of Christ" toward the great and demand the observance of the law by the little folk. "If the great wish to possess grace, they must also fulfill the law, and the little folk do not need merely to exercise patience but can compel the fulfilling of the law." Thus Müntzer in the most decisive manner rejects the annulling of the law in favor of grace, that is, Luther s doctrine of justification. In fact he insinuates that this doctrine one-sidedly operates in favor of the class interests of the great.

In Mühlhausen, Heinrich Pfeiffer had been active since the beginning of 1523, delivering sermons at the Nikolaikirche which were acquiring an increasingly strong political and social character. The townspeople's dissatisfaction with the council had blazed up again at the time of Müntzer's arrival, and Müntzer and Pfeiffer summarized the demands of the citizens in eleven articles drawn from Scripture. On 19 September open insurrection broke out, with the aim of establishing a new order of city regulations in accord with God's word. With the aid of the peasants the council contrived to put down the rising and on 29 September 1524 Pfeiffer and Müntzer were expelled. In October Müntzer was at Nürnberg, where he succeeded in getting his *Ausgedrückte Entblössung* and *Hochverursachte Schutzrede* printed. But both works were confiscated and he was banished. He went south and was in touch with the rebellious peasants in South Germany, with Oecolampadius at Basel, and with Hubmaier. As a result of an appeal by his followers, he returned to Mühlhausen in February 1525 and was made preacher at the Marienkirche. He now more and more assumed the traits of a social revolutionary, not only in regard to active opposition to a godless authority but also in the reorganization of the total order of life in Christendom to bring it into accord with divine justice.

In March 1525 Mühlhausen elected a new "perpetual council, which was supposed to introduce a new Christian government based only on the word of God:

a Christian democracy under the decisive influence of the preachers. In it Pfeiffer, with his more practical social aims, seems to have had a greater appeal than Müntzer, who remained fundamentally foreign to the people with his preaching of the kingdom of God. In the meantime the Thuringian peasants had rebelled, less because of Müntzer's agitation than as a result of the example set in South Germany. But Müntzer now urged his followers, as "God's servant against the impious," to join the Peasants' War "with the sword of Gideon." He interpreted the war theologically as a struggle for God's rule against every usurped authority. Müntzer accompanied the hordes of peasants in this struggle of the Lord, not as a military leader but as a preacher who spurred their will to resist and sought assistance.

Müntzer's personal participation in the Peasants' War was limited to three weeks and connected with only one episode — the Thuringian rising which was crushed in a massacre at Frankenhausen on 15 May 1525. In this he had, however, an important part, in so far as he had swept the masses along in his optimism, counting on divine intervention and frustrating all negotiations. He was arrested in an attic and after cruel torture was executed outside Mühlhausen on 27 May. According to his farewell letter he felt that he had "not been correctly understood" by the people. They had "sought their self-interest more than the vindication of Christianity's and had picked what suited them out of Müntzer's preaching on the realization of the divine will. Thus "a last token was given publicly that the revolutionary in the name and service of God was neither a 'peasant leader' nor a social agitator, that to him the truly important thing was not human rights and social progress but God's law and a Christianity subject to God in faith and life and mighty in spirit, which then, in obedience to God, cannot but give the right shape and order to the things of this world also" (W. Elliger).

Müntzer's liturgical work survived his fall. His church offices and hymns continued to be sung and were revived in the Erfurt church office of 1525 and 1526. The Müntzer church order at Allstedt was maintained until the visitation of March 1533. According to what Bugenhagen reported in 1543, it was then being used in Wolfenbüttel along with others.

If Christianity exists in tension between the preparatory historical realization of the kingship of God and its final completion in other ages, then Luther with a purely eschatological understanding and Müntzer with a narrow "now-and-here" identification represent the farthest extremes. It is thus not to be wondered at that each felt himself to be closer to "papistry" than to the other.

Posterity regarded Müntzer solely in the light of his connection with the Peasants' War, and overrated his influence on it. This can be traced back, not least of all, to the *Histori Thome Muntzers des anfengers der Döringischen uffrur* of 1526, attributed to Melanchthon, and to Luther himself. Luther defamed Müntzer as a "murderous and bloodthirsty prophet" and represented him as the "archdevil," "who rules at Mühlhausen and causes nothing but robbery, murder, and bloodshed" or as the murderous spirit who, "using God's name, has spoken through the devil." This image was constructed in detail by Melanchthon in his account of the teachings and deeds of the "madman" and was believed by future generations.

Confronted with the essential dissimilarity of men such as Luther on the one side and Karlstadt or Müntzer on the other — a difference not merely in methods but in intellectual and theological content, and also in the harshness with which they fought each other from the start — the question arises: What, then, are the characteristics of the "reform"? What did these men have in common, apart from their attack on the traditional ecclesiastical order?

CHAPTER 73

The Peasants' War

Not only the knights but the people thought that Luther and Zwingli meant the fulfillment of their social and political desires. The reformers had questioned spiritual authority and urged the common man to criticize and to express his opinion. The Bible had been handed to the peasant, who eagerly read it or had it read to him. Zwingli reported: "The house of every peasant is a school in which the New and the Old Testament, the sovereign art, can be read."

The Bible should even be the guide of daily life. In this way the common man was trained to ponder over much that he had hitherto accepted as a matter of course, to form his own ideas. To use an expression of Eberlin von Günzburg, the peasant had become "smart." He looked to Luther for the long-desired reform in which lay liberation from his political difficulties and the fulfilment of his social desires.

Luther himself, in works such as *An den christlichen Adel,* had encouraged such a "sensual" understanding of the Gospel, even if he had always warned that the Gospel would conquer, not through fist and sword but through its inherent divine strength. But why should the struggle against unbiblical human laws deal only with the hierarchy and the monasteries and not be directed also against the territorial lords, who were, besides, often identical with the bishops and abbots? In *Von weltlicher Obrigkeit, wieweit man ihr Gehorsam schuldig sei* (1523) Luther had resisted interferences on the part of the secular power in the ecclesiastical sphere, but at the same time he had directed heavy criticism at its worldly rule and had expressed his concern about an imminent judgment.

In contrast to Luther, Zwingli approved active resistance to an ungodly authority. "If the eye is evil, it must be torn out and thrown away; the hand or foot must be cut off." Accordingly, with the introduction of the Reformation at Zurich he had begun a reorganization of the political situation.

The sixteenth century brought a general amelioration of the peasants' economic status. It is incorrect to speak of a distress of the peasantry, of a special economic oppression. Rather one should speak of a new self-assurance, which was demanding a corresponding status in society and was more than ever resisting the limitation of peasant autonomy and of common holdings in pasture, forests, and water by the developing territorial states. Thus the leaders in the Peasants' War were not the poor of the village, the proletariat, but precisely the prosperous and respected farmers. They demanded their "ancient right" and, in addition, an incorporation on equal terms into civic life, as was their due according to divine justice.

At the same moment many cities were the scene of violent social conflicts, in which the socially inferior strata rose up against the governing bourgeoisie, journeymen and other craftsmen against patricians and masters. Not only peasants but all the poor common folk in city and country fought for their Christian, fraternal liberty and for their social and political status in society. The term "Peasants' War" does not do justice to this frequent cooperation of urban people and peasants.

For some decades before the peasant rising in much of Germany under the influence of the reform movement, local peasant insurrections had occurred again and again.

The Peasants' War affected extensive areas of Germany and penetrated deep into Thuringia and Saxony. But it was not a uniform and centrally directed undertaking. Rather, it was a group of individual movements, all of which caught fire on the same combustible material, made the same demands, and obtained their dangerous fundamental dynamic from the universal unrest or, better, fever of the age. The insurrection began in May–June 1524 with the rising of the peasants of Stühlingen in the southern part of the Black Forest. Here people did not appeal at first to the law of God and the Bible, but defended their old written law against the territorial authority of Count Sigmund.

In the former mercenary soldier Hans Müller the peasants found a leader who had experience in war and in speaking. His aim was a violent confrontation, and he looked around for allies, whom he expected to find in neighboring Waldshut. The municipality had refused to surrender to the Austrian governor their Zwinglian preacher, Balthasar Hubmaier; had again elected him as their pastor; and had expelled the Catholic priests from the city. Thus townspeople and peasants stood together against authority, and the affair of the peasants was connected with that of the Gospel.

The political situation prevented Archduke Ferdinand from resorting to energetic measures. The Turkish peril tied his hands in the East, while war with Francis I made it necessary to have consideration for Switzerland. Furthermore, Ulrich of Württemberg wanted to profit by Austria's embarrassment to recover his principality by means of French money, Swiss mercenaries, and the aid of the peasants. Hence there could be no thought of a quick, forcible suppression of the revolt. The unrest spread, but nothing decisive occurred during the winter. But the defeat of Francis I at Pavia on 24 February 1525 caused Ulrich's fighting force, consisting overwhelmingly of Swiss, to melt away before Stuttgart, just when victory seemed certain. His failure was also a defeat for the peasants.

Meanwhile the movement had spread to Swabia, Alsace, Franconia, Thuringia, Saxony, Tirol, and Carinthia. The Memmingen furrier Sebastian Lotzer drew up the platform in Swabia, the twelve "Chief Articles of the Whole Peasantry." These demands of the peasants were presented by the Zwinglian preacher Christoph Schappeler as the Gospel. On the basis of numerous biblical passages the following points were demanded: free election of pastors; pure preaching; use of the great tithe as salary for pastors; abolition of the lesser tithe; an end of serfdom, since Christ redeemed all men and so they should be free; annulling of privileges connected with hunting and fishing. Demands made previously on the basis of old German law were now deduced from the Gospel. These articles were everywhere seized upon as a weapon.

At first the disturbances were not of a warlike character. The peasants did indeed band together, not for a war with arms but to back up their demands with demonstrations. Negotiations were arranged. It was precisely the fusing of social and economic demands with religious motives that led in many cases to the use of force, to the sacking of castles and monasteries. Nonpeasant elements also joined in. Since a single, strict leadership was lacking and the maintaining of a rather large number of men presented formidable problems, the revolt progressively deteriorated into general plundering.

The peasants' eyes were fixed on Luther, from whom they expected moral support. He sought at first to mediate. In April he wrote the *Ermahnung zum Frieden auf die zwölf Artikel der Bauernschaft in Schwaben,* in which he admonished the peasants not to misuse God's name: "... do not drag in the Christian name, I say, and do not make it a means of concealing your impatient, quarrelsome, unchristian projects." The Christian, he said should suffer injustice and not rise against authority. But he also admonished the lords not to misuse their secular power and to stop "oppressing and taxing" the peasants. "It is not the peasants who oppose you. God himself opposes you in order to punish your madness."

But before this work appeared in print in May, Luther, affected by the war, which was being waged with an almost unbelievable harshness, and by what he regarded as Thomas Müntzer's abuse of the Gospel, called upon the princes to intervene pitilessly. In his *Wider die räuberischen und mörderischen Rotten der Bauern* Luther saw the devil at work in the peasants; their overthrow was a service to God.

The princes carried this out, striking, stabbing, and staying with pitiless cruelty. They would probably not have needed Luther's appeal. After initial successes — the Electors of Mainz and the Palatinate were compelled to accept the twelve articles — the peasant armies were soon overcome by the organized resistance of the princes because they lacked firm leadership and long-range planning. The commander of the Swabian League, Georg Truchsess von Waldburg, defeated the Upper Swabian peasants near Wurzach on 14 April, those of Württemberg near Böblingen on 12 May, and those of Franconia near Königshofen on 2 June and Ingolstadt on 4 June. After overwhelming the Hessian peasants, Philip of Hesse marched to Thuringia and, with Duke Georg of Saxony and the Duke of Braunschweig, annihilated a large army of some eight thousand peasants and townsmen near Frankenhausen. As their chaplain, Thomas Müntzer had fanned their spirit of resistance, leading them into battle with the Pentecost hymn, "Veni, Creator Spiritus." But the battle soon turned into a disorderly rout and a wild killing spree. Müntzer himself was found in an attic and executed. The Alsatian peasants were defeated by Duke Anton of Lorraine near Zabern on 17 May; those of the Palatinate near Pfeddersheim on 24 June. The capture of Salzburg by the Swabian League on 30 July marked the end of the peasants' revolt. All told, some one hundred thousand peasants had perished in battle or been cruelly slain; many were beheaded, run through, burned, or blinded. Settlements agreed upon with the peasants came to an end. All arrangements made with them by lords and princes had to be declared null and void at the demand of the Swabian League or of its general, Georg Truchsess von Waldburg.

The victors were the princes. Even more than the weakened petty nobility, peasants and townsmen were subjected to the power of their prince. Furthermore, the princes confiscated the property of destroyed or abandoned monasteries. To a great extent the Peasants' War meant the end of the Reformation as a popular movement. Luther was often regarded as sharing the responsibility for its attendant ferocity. He accepted these reproaches, even though in quite a different meaning, when in January 1533 he stated in one of his *Table Talks:*

> Preachers are the greatest of all slayers. For they urge the authorities to execute their office strictly and punish the wicked. In the revolt I slew all the peasants; all their blood is on my head. But I pass it on to our Lord God, who commanded me to speak thus.

People took it amiss that on 13 June 1525, in the middle of these dreadful days, Luther married the former Cistercian nun Katharina von Bora. Even Melanchthon was exasperated. No wonder Catholic controversialists, such as Johannes Cochläus, exploited it against the reformer. The common people, disillusioned, abandoned Luther in many cases and joined the Anabaptists and the sects or, indifferent, held themselves aloof. The Reformation had ceased to be a popular movement; or at least the Peasants' War greatly damaged Luther's popularity. His "heroic" period was over. The authorities more and more took charge of the Reformation and exploited it to incorporate their subjects into the modern state. Hereafter we can speak of the age of the Princes' Reformation. The Christian congregation, enjoying free elections of pastors, was succeeded by the territorial Church.

Chapter 74

Luther's Rejection of Humanism— Erasmus' Later Years

The relations between humanism and the Reformation were varied and close. Many of Luther's friends and collaborators — among them Melanchthon, Spalatin, and Justus Jonas — were humanists. Luther himself was in the grip of humanism and favorably disposed toward it, especially as a teacher and lover of the biblical languages. Ulrich Zwingli was a pupil of Erasmus and a humanist, and the other Swiss reformers bore a strong humanist stamp. Humanism had prepared the ground for the Reformation through its criticism of the Church and its urging of reform. Luther found his first response and enthusiastic followers in the sodalities, the humanist circles. Still, humanists such as Johannes Reuchlin rejected the Reformation. Others, including Willibald Pirckheimer, Conrad Peutinger, Ulrich Zasius, Mutianus Rufus, Christoph Scheurl, and Crotus Rubeanus, at first were favorably inclined toward it because they anticipated from it the long-demanded reform. But they backed away when it became clear that the Lutheran movement amounted to a revolutionary innovation which could only shatter the unity of the Church, and when in its sometimes tumultuous course it ran counter to the ideas of this cultural aristocracy. The outstanding men of the older generation, especially, turned completely away from Luther again. If humanism, in its concern with and efforts for the text of the Bible and in its criticism of the Church, formally had much in common with the Reformation, still in its ethical optimism or moralism it was further away from the Reformation's basic principle — *sola fide* or *sola gratia* — than most contemporaries were aware.

This was especially true of Desiderius Erasmus. At the outbreak of the Reformation he had achieved the zenith of his influence, and everyone awaited his decision for or against Luther. But he held back. As late as May 1519 he wrote: "Luther is entirely unknown to me; I have still had no time to read his books." He wanted "to stay away from all controversy, if possible, in order to be the more useful for the revival of scholarship." Even after the publication of the Bull "Exsurge Domine" he saw the war against Luther as a case of "hatred of scholarship." Monks wanted to suppress it "so that they can rule with impunity with their barbarism." As regards Luther, it was only his loudness and pugnacity that Erasmus disliked. "Would that Luther had followed my advice and kept away from these subjects which cause hatred and insurrection!" "His edge is so sharp that, even if all he had written were the purest truth, this business could not have a happy outcome." To the Pope Erasmus wrote in September 1520 that he must not be regarded as a Lutheran just because he had not written against Luther. He declared that he had not the leisure for a thorough perusal of Luther's writings, and this task was beyond his talents and his education. In addition he was unwilling to challenge the position of the universities, which were already preoccupied with this, and, besides, he dreaded calling down the hatred of so many powerful men.

From the desire to remain a spectator and perhaps to act as mediator at the opportune time, he avoided a decision, which he could no longer dodge in Louvain, by "fleeing" to Basel in the fall of 1521. From there he wrote to W. Pirckheimer: "The Lutherans threaten me publicly with invective, and the emperor is almost convinced that I am the source and the head of the whole Lutheran disturbance. And so I am in bad danger from both sides, whereas I have actually, deserved well of all."

When at the end of 1522 Ulrich von Hutten tried to induce Erasmus to come out clearly for the Reformation and at the same time sought support from him in his own difficult situation, Erasmus refused to see him for days. To the bitter reproaches of the mortally ill knight in his *Expostulatio cum Erasmo* (1523), that Erasmus did not dare to draw the consequences because, in his insatiable ambition, he feared for his reputation among the great lords, Erasmus replied, "I remain on the outside. . . . I am not a party to any side. . . . By taking sides I mean total adherence to all that Luther has written. . . . But I love complete freedom and will nor and cannot ever serve one side."

Luther esteemed Erasmus for his services in regard to the biblical languages, without knowledge of which he could not conceive of any genuine theology. He extravagantly glorified the humanist, greeted him as "our adornment and hope," and referred to himself as Erasmus' "little brother in Christ." In *De servo arbitrio* Luther still emphasized the great service that Erasmus had rendered him in the field of linguistics: "I confess that I am much indebted to you and hence I sincerely honor and admire you." But even so the reformer sensed early how incompatible he and Erasmus were spiritually, and he suspected in Erasmus the pagan of intellectual snobbery, to whom "human things are of greater importance than divine things." But Luther was aware of what it would mean for his cause if Erasmus came out against him. If he was unable to gain him for his side, he hoped at least for his silence. Accordingly he wrote in April 1524: "If you are unwilling to contribute further, then at least be a mere spectator of our tragedy. But do not make common cause with our adversaries. Above all, do not publish anything against me, just as I will publish nothing against you.

But by then Erasmus was already working on his *De libero arbitrio diatribe sive collatio.* Of course he took his time, but in September 1524 he informed King Henry VIII: "The die is cast: the book on free will has seen the light of day." Clearly Erasmus had been hard pressed and had been reluctant to take a stand publicly. The choice of topic indicates what to the great humanist seemed especially imperiled — the dignity of man, who despite all dependence on grace is God's partner. In his reply Luther himself acknowledged that Erasmus had grasped the decisive point.

Erasmus had been drawn into the dispute over free will some time earlier. In February 1523 he had to defend himself against the charge of Pelagianism, which had been made by the Lutheran side as a result of his teaching on free will in the explication of Romans (1517). In it he marshaled arguments which he pursued in greater detail in *De libero arbitrio,* seeing man between the Scylla and Charybdis of trust in his own works and an unbridled fatalism. He gathered Luther's teaching from the *Assertio* of 1520, the detailed rejoinder to the Bull "Exsurge Domine." In this the reformer had defended the thesis that "after sin free will is a mere word, and, when man acts according to what is inside him, he sins mortally." In the dispute between Luther and Erasmus the point at issue was not moral freedom in general but the role of the human will in effecting salvation. Can man achieve salvation by himself, that is, can he freely accept or reject the grace offered? In Erasmus' view, Holy Scripture, the philosophers, and common sense testify that the will is free. Otherwise why would Scripture need to blame and to admonish or to praise obedience? God's justice and mercy make no sense unless there is some vestige of freedom of choice in man.

With Augustine, Erasmus would prefer not to rate the role of free will too high: "To my taste is the opinion of those who attribute something to free will but most to the grace of God." Man needs prevenient and concurring grace. It is the source and not the mere accompaniment of the work, which it effects with free will. Against Karlstadt and Luther, Erasmus expounded a third view, which, while leaving room for free will, left no doubt that ultimately everything depends on the grace of God. Scriptural passages which speak of an absolute predestination and of a deliberate hardening of men's hearts by God are, according to Erasmus, to be interpreted prudently. In general he would prefer to make as few apodictic claims as possible.

> I take no delight in rigid claims and prefer to take the part of the skeptics where this is allowed by the sacrosanct authority of Scripture and the decisions of the Church, to which I gladly submit my judgment in all matters, regardless of whether I understand her regulations or not.

But quite apart from man's personal, intellectual, and spiritual make-up, the matter itself calls for a prudent restraint. In any event, the subjective appeal to the "evangelical spirit" affords no certainty. "What am I to do if various interpretations are adduced by several persons and each one swears that he has the Holy Spirit?" The self-assurance with which the reformers came forward and shoved aside the biblical exegesis of the Church Fathers was for Erasmus in striking contrast to the disagreements in their own camp. Consequently the meaning of Scripture could not be as clear as had been asserted. It was not in his nature to make over clear-cut claims. He knew too much about the ambiguity of life, he saw too clearly the false in the true and the true in the false, to commit himself unequivocally. He felt disturbed in an age which pressed so relentlessly for decision. What had previously been freely discussed was now not even to be yawned over. Actually out of love of truth he would prefer to remain undecided. "As a matter of fact, there are in Holy Scripture certain inaccessible passages which, in accord with God's will, we should not fathom more deeply and in which, if we nonetheless do seek to penetrate, increasing darkness encompasses us." Many questions, "instead of being postponed till an ecumenical council, as is often demanded today, should be left for the time when mirror and mystery have been eliminated and we behold God face to face." Above all, obscure and uncertain doctrines and even some passages of the Bible do not bear it well when they are held up to unlettered folk. Erasmus cannot conceive a Christian ethic without the freedom to choose the good and reject the evil, without man's being at least released to this freedom by grace. If the proof of this cannot be unambiguously demonstrated, then a pastoral and theological concern for the uneducated masses compels one to postulate this truth and forbids one to call it in question outside the discussions of scholars.

Luther did not reply to Erasmus at once. He was preoccupied with his fight "against the heavenly prophets" and with the peasant risings. But despite serious setbacks and so many disappointments he seems to have lost none of his certainty in his counterwork, *De servo arbitrio,* which finally appeared in December 1525. It is, he says, necessary to witness to the truth in God's word, without human and pedagogical considerations, even against the Church and her tradition as well as against the seemingly unquestionable judgment of human reason. Erasmus, he writes, seems to have missed the point that Holy Scripture contains only one doctrine — that God is God, that is, absolute and unlimited, and that man is man, that is, limited and dependent on God.

> He is God, for whose will neither cause nor reason has any importance that can be prescribed for him as rule or measure. He has nothing above or

> beyond himself, but his will is the rule for everything. If any rule or measure or cause or reason were to have any importance for his will, it could no longer be the will of God. For it is not because he has to will or has had to will thus that what he wills is right; on the contrary, because he himself wills it, therefore what happens must be right. Cause and reason are prescribed for the will of the creature but not for the will of the Creator.

Correspondingly, in things subordinated to him man is free and acts according to his own law. Differing from the *Assertio,* in *De servo arbitrio* Luther acknowledges a freedom of choice in the civil sphere.

Whereas Erasmus took pains with nuances, Luther overemphasized to make as clear as possible his undoubtedly serious religious concern. In so doing he did not lack a consciousness of mission and self-assurance. Unfortunately he did not hesitate to revile his adversary and to reproduce the latter's views inaccurately when such a procedure facilitated his own argument. In his view Erasmus was an atheist, a scorner of Scripture and destroyer of Christianity, a hypocrite, blasphemer, and skeptic. "A Christian must love assertions, however, or he is not a Christian."

For Luther Holy Scripture is clear in this matter; at the most it offers philological difficulties. Of course the inner clarity in the heart is the prerequisite for understanding. "Man needs the Spirit of God in order to understand Scripture or even only a part of it." It is by no means irreligious and impertinent, as Erasmus claims, "but, on the contrary, salutary and necessary for a Christian to know whether his will can accomplish anything or nothing for his salvation." "If we do not know this" — and revelation alone assists us in this — "then we know absolutely nothing about Christianity and are worse than all pagans." In this matter one should not be afraid of disturbance. "If God and antigod are struggling with each other, must there not be a disturbance throughout the world? To wish to calm this uproar is to wish to annul God's word and to forbid it." It is a question of "humiliating our arrogance and recognizing the grace of God."

> But man is unable to humble himself completely until he knows that his salvation is totally beyond his resources, resolves, and exertions, beyond his will and his works, and depends entirely on the free judgment, the resolve, will, and work of another — namely, God.... But he who in no way doubts that everything depends upon the will of God, gives up all hope in himself, makes no choice but waits for the operation of God — he is closest to the grace of being saved.

Only those thus humbled and annihilated can be saved — those who believe not only in the unseen but in that which is most deeply concealed, "in contrast to the objective, to perception, and to experience." God, revealing himself, remains the hidden one; he even veils himself in the opposite. Luther wants the doctrine of the servile will understood in the context of this mystery of the *Deus absconditus* — that man is possessed either by evil or by the Spirit of God. Man always acts according to necessity, which is not the same as "forced." For external compulsion is not needed; one's desire or inclination, which cannot be changed by one's own strength, makes one act. If the will is changed by the Holy Spirit,

> it is in no sense free even then. It cannot do otherwise, so long as it is animated by the Spirit of God and grace. Thus the human will is placed in the middle, like a beast of burden. If God sits on it, it wills and goes where God wills.... If Satan sits on it, it wills and goes where Satan wills. And it is not within its free choice to run to one of the two riders or to seek him; rather, the riders themselves vie to hold on to him and to take possession of him.

When Erasmus cited the tradition of the Church and the testimony of the saints against this unheard-of view, Luther countered with: "The Church is concealed and the saints are unknown. Whom are we to believe?" Only "Holy Scripture decides who is right" It is all the more true that "whoever denies that the Holy Scripture grants a clear insight deprives men of all light, of every possibility of enlightenment."

On this basis Luther set to work to refute Erasmus' arguments and to defend his own position. He ended with a eulogy of freely operating grace. The unfreedom of the will is a mark not only of fallen man but in general of man as a creature; even man reborn is unfree. At stake is the "powerless free will inherent in all men, which is nothing but clay, nothing but untilled land, precisely because it cannot will the good." But Luther is not depressed by this truth; it is for him the reason for a glad assurance of salvation. Because salvation is not subject to his will, and is promised as a result not of his work but of God's grace, Luther is sure that no devil can overcome him and snatch him away from God.

In view of the overwhelming majesty of God, who is pure will in the Ockhamist sense, there is no place for man's free action. If he is not to pine away out of dread, then he needs assurance at any cost. But where does he obtain the assurance of belonging to the few who cannot fail to be saved?

Erasmus was deeply hurt by Luther's violent and personally insulting manner. In his view Luther had "written in such a manner that no further place for friendship remained." In his *Hyperaspistes diatribae* (1526–27) the great humanist again defended his standpoint. He once more showed that Scripture contains obscure passages and should by no means be discussed in all its parts in front of everyone at all times.

After a struggle Erasmus had come out against the Reformation and had adhered to the teaching of the ancient Church in a question especially close to his humanist heart. His anger and indignation at Luther's reply were strong, but he continued to strive not to appear as belonging to one side. Even such an admission still demonstrates intellectual restraint, a fear about taking sides and maintaining a stand. Skepticism, even a great amount of dogmatism, also characterized the aging Erasmus. He was concerned, not about theology, but about the piety of the heart and about education. Just as he kept aloof from Luther's religious rigorism, so in the *Ciceronianus* (1528) he divorced himself from a pagan humanism which smacked more of Cicero than of Christianity. The more the religious factions fought among themselves, the more he wanted to bring them back to unity by means of a simple, practical, and scripturally inspired Christianity and by deemphasizing dogma and religious creed. In 1526 he wrote to Bishop Fabri of Vienna that partisans should be excluded from the schools and replaced by men "who do not deal with dogmatic controversies but impart to their students only that which contributes, without controversy, to piety and good morals ... who, free from the study of details, teach the useful to the children." He confronts the primacy of truth with the primacy of peace. In a letter to Jacob Sadoleto as late as 1530 he maintained that "If people had paid no attention to Luther in the beginning, this conflagration would not have occurred or certainly it would not have spread." Ultimately guilty, he held, were the friars who first shamelessly preached the indulgence and then attacked Luther when he came forward against it.

It was Erasmus' fate to be born into a time which relentlessly posed the question of truth and pressed for an answer, but to be himself cut out for anything but the role of a martyr. His great friend Thomas More proved that partisanship could be combined with liberal thought, tolerance, and broadmindedness. But nothing better characterizes Erasmus' own failure than his inability to understand the martyrdom of the English chancellor: "If only he had never become involved in that dangerous business and had left the theological matter to theologians."

If the aging Erasmus rejected the Reformation with a growing decisiveness and severity, this was not because of error and heresy but because it was *fatalis tumultus* — it led to unrest, immorality, intolerance, and the ruin of humanistic pursuits. When, under Oecolampadius, the Reformation was forcibly introduced at Basel and the Mass was abolished, Erasmus left for Freiburg im Breisgau in 1529 to find quiet for his literary work. He aimed to restore the unity of the Church (*Liber de sarcienda ecclesiae concordia,* 1533) by a contemplation of the simplicity of the Apostolic Church. A return to Holy Scripture and a confinement to the basic truths of the Apostle's Creed (*Explanatio symboli,* 1533) would put an end to all controversies and enable the Church to rediscover her original spiritual purity (*De puritate ecclesiae christianae,* 1536). These ideas met with the approval of princes — those of the Lower Rhine for example and found adherents among theologians such as G. Witzel, M. Bucer, and G. Cassander. But Erasmus' unwillingness for a decision and for a confession probably hurt rather than helped the unity of the Church he claimed to serve. "For nothing so fostered the ecclesiastical schism," says H. Jedin, "as the illusion that there was none." The budding starts of reform, present in the work of Erasmus and with roots in the Christian humanism of John Colet (1466–1519) and others, were not equal to the tempest of the Reformation and were rapidly destroyed by it.

It is especially as a teacher and catechist that Erasmus became significant in the inner reform of the Church. As early as 1512, at the request of John Colet, he composed in his *Christiani Hominis Institutum* an elementary instruction, a sort of children's catechism in verse. In at least seventy printings this little work obtained a wide circulation. Once more at the request of an Englishman, the father of Queen Anne Boleyn, there came into print in 1533 a larger catechetical work, the *Explanatio Symboli ... Decalogi praeceptorum et Dominicae precationis,* which in later editions was called the *Catechismus.* In its literary form the *Explanatio* is a dialogue between catechist and pupil. The first five of the six lessons deal with the Creed; the last with the commandments and the Lord's Prayer.

The Sacraments are explained only briefly, or, as he himself notes, "in passing." In proportion to the size of the work the section on the Sacraments is briefer than in the *Institutum,* although it was the Sacraments that were so hotly disputed because of the Reformation and it was here precisely that the laity would have had need of a clear answer. There is no more unequivocal indication of how foreign to Erasmus were worship and Sacraments and how very much he dodged not merely theological controversy but also the necessary religious avowal. This appears especially in his treatment of the Eucharist. In the *Institutum* he had still spoken of the mystical food which under the image of bread and wine truly offers us the real presence of Christ. In the *Explanatio,* on the other hand, we find:

> The Eucharist provides strength for the real combat. By it the power of faith is roused in us and we are filled with abundant grace by recalling the holy death, since in some mysterious way we renew that unique Sacrifice to which we owe our salvation.

Not a word about the real presence. This is astonishing in view of the sharp denial of it by Oecolampadius at Basel, but at the same time understandable if we reflect that Erasmus inclined toward the ideas of this reformer because they "are simpler and more intelligible and raise less complicated questions." He had, it is true, emphatically clung to the teaching of the ancient Church, but preferred that the "how" of the bodily presence should be undiscussed and so far as possible not doctrinally established. As a "return to the proclamation of the Bible and the Fathers," the fact here under consideration has not been sufficiently characterized. The effort to limit as far as possible the area of obligatory doctrine remained, therefore, a chief characteristic of the theology of Erasmus even at a time when in the Church it was finally realized that, in view of dogmatic vagueness, it was necessary to establish her doctrine and to apply the brake in the face of error.

In the *Institutum* the author had expressly declared his desire to receive the Sacraments of the Church at the hour of death. But the prohibition of celebrating Mass and the risk of dying without the Sacraments did not restrain the priest Erasmus from returning in May 1535 to Protestant Basel when external calm had been restored there. In the treatise *De praeparatione ad mortem* (1534) he appears to have come to grips with the thought of dying in a non-Catholic environment. According to it, a sincere confession at the close of life is, certainly beneficial, but if a priest cannot be had, one need not tremble in superstitious dread, for prayer and inner sorrow can also bring salvation. A year later, on 11 July 1536, Erasmus died at Basel without priestly support. He was solemnly buried as a Protestant. To the end of his days he had thus given preference over truth to that peace which proved useful, not least for his own well-being and for *bonae litterae.*

CHAPTER 75

Zwingli and the Beginnings of the Reformation in German Switzerland

The reform movement was not uniform in doctrine and ecclesiastical organization because in southwestern Germany, and above all in Switzerland, the Reformation was from the start essentially independent of Martin Luther and, under the influence of such important and individualistic men as Ulrich (Huldrych) Zwingli (1484–1531), Johannes Oecolampadius (1482–1531), Joachim Vadian (1483–1551), and Berchtold Haller (1492–1536), acquired a form of its own. And the Reformation was not uniform even in Switzerland. Every canton has its own Reformation history, although this did not prevent Zurich from acquiring a leading position because of its political importance and the surpassing figure of its reformer, Ulrich Zwingli. If the Wittenberg Reformation was under the auspices of the territorial principality, the stage of the Swiss Reformation was the republican urban and rural communities.

The Swiss Confederates, unconcerned for Emperor and Empire, had long been accustomed to regulate their own affairs at diets — *Tagsatzungen* — of their own. Following the Swabian War they had obtained their *de facto* independence of the Empire in the Peace of Basel (1499). Both as mercenaries in the papal service and in their own they had a great share in the struggle between France, Emperor, and Pope for Lombardy. The dream of obtaining for themselves a place among the great powers by acquiring northern Italy after the victory over the French at Novara came to a sudden end with the overwhelming defeat at Marignano in 1515.

The frequent military assistance given to the Pope had brought the Swiss a number of privileges and had led to a state church that was further developed than was elsewhere customary in the cities. The introduction of the Reformation by the authorities was thereby facilitated. The Reformation first established itself at Zurich, where it was the accomplishment of Ulrich Zwingli. The third son in a family of ten children, he was born at Wildhaus in the county of Toggenburg on New Year's Day 1484. His father was the local cantonal president. Zwingli stressed his rustic origin — "I am a peasant, all peasant" — which stood him in good stead in his graphic, folksy speech. At the age of six he received his first instruction from his uncle, the pastor at Walensee. When he was ten he attended the Latin school at Basel and completed his early schooling with the humanist Wölfflin at Berne in 1497. He did his university studies at Vienna in 1498 and Basel in 1502. Humanism was flourishing in both places, but especially at Basel, with its circle of outspoken scholars.

At the university the *via antiqua* was decisive for Zwingli. Its combining of Thomistic scholasticism and humanism, of rationality and ethics, characterized him throughout life. He claims to have been shown the questionable nature of indulgences by his teacher, Thomas Wyttenbach. However, he did not take his formal study of theology very far. Scarcely had he begun it, after obtaining the degree of master of arts in the spring of 1506, when he was elected pastor of Glarus. Having received priestly ordination, he took charge of his parish on 19 September

1506. Zealous, he organized a pilgrimage and built a chapel for it. The care of souls, in which, aided by three or four chaplains, he had to attend to not many more than a thousand people, left him ample time for the study of the ancient authors, the Fathers, and the Vulgate. From 1513 he learned Greek on his own. At the same time he developed a passion for politics. His first literary works were patriotic fables in verse, in which he warned against the French King's recruiting of mercenaries. He often accompanied the Swiss to Lombardy as an army chaplain and was proud that his countrymen were honored by the Pope with the title of "Deliverers of the Church." For his services he received a pension from the Curia.

Zwingli's solemn appeal to the Confederates at Monza for unity and loyalty to the Pope was unable to prevent the catastrophe of Marignano. Because the "Frenchies" now established themselves in Glarus, he had to resign as army chaplain. On 1 November 1516 he obtained leave to go to Einsiedeln for three years and there was active as a priest in the management of the pilgrimage in the customary manner, and in the summer of 1517 he himself made a pilgrimage to the shrines at Aachen. At the same time he studied Erasmus' Greek New Testament and made his own copy of Paul's Epistles. In Zwingli's case there is no question of a struggle for the Gospel, as there was with Luther, or even of a reform understanding that deeply stirred him. If in 1523 he maintained in retrospect: "Before anyone in our area knew anything of Luther's name, I began to preach the Gospel of Christ in 1516,... " he was referring to reform preaching and criticism of abuses — something that was not new in Erasmus' circle. Zwingli did not take his obligation of celibacy very seriously. When in 1518 he was about to receive a call to become the priest of the cathedral at Zurich, it was urged against him that in Einsiedeln he had seduced the daughter of an official. In a "letter of confession," which in tone did not do justice to the matter and bears very little trace of a theology of the cross, Zwingli stated that she had been the easygoing daughter of a barber and that he had never dishonored a chaste maiden. If he had offended in this regard in Glarus, his sense of shame had caused him to do so in all secrecy. This previous history did not keep seventeen of the twenty-four canons from voting for him.

At his installation he explained to the canons his plan to preach on the text of the Gospel without regard to the order of pericopes. Despite opposition he began on 2 January 1519 with the first chapter of Saint Matthew. In this way he had preached through the entire New Testament by 1525. He did not write out his sermons; at most his thoughts are sketched in one or another later essay.

Zwingli's keeping the indulgence preacher Samson out of Zurich cannot be taken as a reform activity, for the Pope had forbidden this Franciscan to appear again in Switzerland. Likewise, the manner in which in the spring of 1519 he dealt with the veneration of the saints did not go beyond the reform efforts customary among humanists. At that time he wrote, "I have forbidden the worship of the saints; I did not intend to root out entirely the invocation of the saints." He merely attacked the addressing of the "Our Father" to the saints.

A closer acquaintance by Zwingli with Luther's works can be established from 1519. He circulated Luther's writings and saw in them a confirmation of the concept of the Gospel that he had independently gained since 1516. Luther's attitude on the occasion of the Leipzig Disputation deeply impressed him. The treatise *Von der Gewalt des Papstes,* which was printed by Froben at Basel in September, met with his approval. According to this work, Christ rules his kingdom from heaven. The papacy is not of divine law, and councils can err. Scripture alone can be the basis of faith. But when in the middle of 1520 Luther was threatened with excommunication Zwingli found fault with his inconsiderate and extravagant manner. Unwilling to jeopardize his own affairs by a relationship with the Wittenberg professor, the shrewd Swiss peasant kept aloof from him. He stressed that he was not Lutheran and that he had discovered the Gospel on his own. In fact, as late as 1523 he claimed he had read little of Luther's books: "I do not wish to bear Luther's name. I have read very little of his teaching and have often intentionally maintained reserve in regard to his books just in order to satisfy the papists."

At the end of 1519 Zwingli fell seriously ill of the plague. This experience contributed to his inner maturation but not to his conversion or even to his awakening as a reformer. He himself transferred the beginning of his preaching of the Gospel to 1516 and assigned his break with the papacy to the end of 1520. To ascribe the break to a religious shock or to a decisive theological understanding in these months is an invention. Walther Köhler calls the preparatory notes made in the summer of 1520 for a lecture series on the Psalms for the coming winter "the oldest confession of faith of the reformer Ulrich Zwingli." With selected citations from Augustine he expressed what was then in the air and what he himself had expressed earlier in marginal glosses to Augustine's writings. Forgiveness of sins and justification by faith received central significance, but at the same time the stressing of human cooperation and of the good will made free in grace showed full respect for the humanist legacy.

The Break with the Church

Zwingli himself saw his break with the papacy in his refusal of the papal pension: "I rejected it in 1520 in a special letter." This was entirely in harmony with the policy of neutrality which he always clearly professed. An intimate connection of political and reform activity was indeed to become altogether characteristic of his life's work.

At the beginning of his Zurich period he was still devoted to Cardinal Schiner and his anti-French policy, but he even more zealously put forward the idea of peace as held by Erasmus. He encouraged Christoph Froschauer to inaugurate his printery at Zurich with a German translation of the *Querela Pacis.* In May 1521 Zurich alone, of thirteen confederated cantons, rejected an alliance with France, and on 11 January Zurich issued a mandate whereby enlistment was threatened with prison. It is uncertain whether these measures were directly due to Zwingli. In any event he supported independence from foreign powers as well as peace. He sought, with strong words but to no avail, to prevent the city council from allowing the cardinal to raise a levy of fifteen hundred men for the Pope's protection in July 1521. The fact that Schiner tried to lead the troops in the campaign against Milan and France, contrary to the agreement, and that the men, when recalled, had to wait for their wages greatly prejudiced the city against the Pope and contributed to the separation from the Roman Church. Zwingli's renunciation of the papal pension was demanded when he was unwilling to allow his right to take a stand against military support of the Pope to be questioned. The loss of fifty florins, painful in his indigent situation, was somewhat compensated by his admission to the ranks of the canons at the cathedral on 29 April 1521. He continued to perform his priestly duties until October 1522.

An apparently superficial occasion brought about Zwingli's major conflict with the Church. In the Lent of 1522 the printer Froschauer, with a group of citizens, had a dinner of sausages as a demonstration on behalf of the freedom of the Gospel. Zwingli was present but did not eat the sausage. This did not save him from an investigation instituted by the council and the episcopal authorities, for it was evident that offenses against the law of fasting, also seen on previous occasions, were connected with Zwingli's preaching. The matter seemed to proceed without difficulty. A conciliar report of 9 April was accepted, whereby until further notice no one was to eat meat in Lent without a special reason and permission. All malicious conversation regarding the eating of meat and preaching was also forbidden. Zwingli was able to interpret this in his own favor. On 16 April he published as his first reform writing the Lenten sermon that he had preached on 23 March. It was entitled *Von Auswahl und Freiheit der Speisen.* In this he defended the freedom of the Christian: "If you like to fast, then fast. If you do not like to eat meat, then do not eat it, but let the Christian enjoy freedom."

The Bishop of Constance and, even more so, his zealous vicar general, Doctor Johann Fabri of Leutkirch, were further alarmed. In letters to the council of Zurich and to the chapter of the cathedral they warned of the danger to the unity of the Church and of the destruction of her discipline. On 27 May 1522 complaint was made at the *Tagsatzung* at Lucerne that "now priests everywhere in the Confederation are preaching various things whereby indignation, dissension, and error in the Christian faith are springing up among the common people." This probably induced Zwingli to direct to the Confederation in German the petition which on 2 July 1522 he had sent to the bishop in Latin. Ten other priests by their signatures supported the request for the freedom of preaching in accord with Scripture and for the abolition of the obligation of celibacy. All of them were probably already secretly married; in the spring of 1522 Zwingli had entered a secret marriage with Anna Reinhardt, a widow living in his neighborhood. This was not sanctioned until April 1524, shortly before the birth of their first child, by a public procession. Until then ample opportunity was provided for malicious talk.

In the 1522 petition to the Confederat the unhappy consequences of the widespread concubinage were described in detail and the results for the children were amply represented.

The question of Church reform was focused more and more on that of preaching in accord with Scripture and of the principle of Scripture. On the occasion of conflicts between Zwingli and the religious of Zurich, the city council decided that for the future only the Gospel, Saint Paul, and the prophets should be preached. Hence the mandate of the Bishop of Constance of 10 August 1522 — which complained that, despite the condemnation of Luther's heresy by Pope and Emperor, opinions were expressed in pulpits to the detriment of the Church and her organization and the secular authority was asked to assist the bishop in averting the danger — lagged behind current developments. On 19 August the clergy of the Zurich chapter recognized the principle of Scripture and decreed that for the future only that should be preached which could be demonstrated by the word of God. Zwingli now published his written defense, *Apologeticus Archeteles,* the "first and last" word. It signified the break with the bishop. In sixty-nine controverted points the bishop's admonition was opposed with all the resources of scholarly argument, but basically it was the principle of Scripture that was involved.

In September 1522 Zwingli issued in print an expanded version of a sermon against the argument that Scripture requires interpretation by means of the teaching authority and tradition. This was entitled *Von Klarheit und Gewissheit des Wortes Gottes.* The word of God does not need human supports; it imposes itself by its own impact. "The word of God cannot err... it is clear, does not get lost in darkness, teaches itself, reveals itself." Later, in view of the scriptural exegesis of the Anabaptists and on the occasion of the Marburg discussion with Luther, it would become evident how little Scripture by itself was able to maintain the unity of the Church. But Zwingli himself did not rely on the "pure Gospel." He called upon the arm of authority to impose it and, later, to curb the independence of the Anabaptists.

Until now, as a parish priest, he had to provide Mass and administer the Sacraments. On 10 October 1522, in a pulpit declaration, he resigned his office. The council then instituted a preaching position for him. Thus with no great stir he changed from Catholic priest into reform preacher.

Aided by the city council, Zwingli resolutely carried the Reformation further. He induced the city officials to send invitations to a religious colloquy at Zurich on 29 January 1523. The council, not the bishop, summoned the clergy of the territory. A "notification" was sent to "His Lordship of Constance" and his presence was suggested. A delegation named by the bishop and consisting of four gentlemen, headed by the vicar general, Johann Fabri, appeared. Fabri regarded himself as sent by his Gracious Lord, not to dispute "as a fencer, but to be a spectator or even an arbiter of peace." The other cantons of the Confederation had refused to participate. The basis of the disputation was Zwingli's sixty-seven theses, for which he later gave more detailed reasons in his extensive work, *Auslegen und Gründe der Schlussreden,* a "collection of all opinions now in dispute." Differing from Luther in his indulgence theses, Zwingli offered in the epilogue the comprehensive program of his Reformation. He could do so because he knew that, with the council, the ruling circles of the population were behind him. At issue on 29 January was not a disputation and even less a clarification of controversial questions, but the publication of a new order, whose validity was presupposed. In it Christ alone is presented as authoritative for the individual and for all aspects of society. He is "the leader and captain promised and sent by God for all mankind" (6). The Church is "Christ's wife" (8). He who obeys Christ is "drawn to him by his Spirit and transformed into him" (13). What is strictly of a reform nature is expressed in the emphasis on "only the Gospel of Christ" (14), which is self-explanatory. Not by chance does the first article state that "whoever maintains that the Gospel is nothing without the ratification of the Church errs and blasphemes God" and the concluding proposition declare that "here no one should venture to dispute with sophistry and human trifles, but one should come to have Scripture for a judge." According to this principle the papacy, the Mass, the intercession of the saints, regulations concerning food, holy seasons and places, religious orders, celibacy, misuse of excommunication, and other things were repudiated (17–33). Also according to it Zwingli developed his doctrine of the state and justified in practice the ecclesiastical policy of the Zurich council. "The so-called spiritual power in its arrogated pomp is not based on Christ's teaching" (34). "On the other hand, the secular power has its authority and basis in Christ's teachings and practice." Christians must obey it, so long as it commands nothing that is opposed to God (37–38). It alone wields the sword and has the right to kill (40). The other articles deal with correct praying and singing, the forgiveness of sins, penitential works, indulgences, purgatory, the priestly office, and the manner of eradicating abuses. To those who are lacking in judgment one should "offer no physical violence, unless they behave so contumaciously that one could not otherwise deal with them" (65).

There took part in the disputation in the Zurich city hall on 29 January 1523 not only the 212 men of the small and the great council but some four hundred other persons, in particular the clergy of the territory of Zurich. When at the beginning Johann Fabri referred to the council contemplated by the Diet of Nürnberg as the competent tribunal for questions of faith, Zwingli successfully exploited Swiss self-assertion against both the Empire and Rome by stressing: "Here in this chamber is, without any doubt, a Christian gathering." Persons cannot wait for a council. It is a utopia. "For Pope, bishops, prelates, and big Johnnies will not put up with a council at which the divine Scripture is declared purely and clearly." In the explanation of article 64 Zwingli entirely rejected a council.

After a debate on the veneration of the saints the discussion returned to the subject that was decisive for the Zurich Reformation — that of the relations between Scripture and tradition, or the binding force of ecclesiastical laws. In the afternoon the council announced that Master Ulrich Zwingli should continue as before to proclaim the Holy Gospel and the orthodox divine Scripture according to the Spirit of God. "All other parish priests, persons entrusted with the care of souls, and preachers should preach nothing which they cannot justify by recourse to the Holy Gospels and the rest of the divine Scripture." Thus was the principle of Scripture officially declared to be the basic law for all pastors, and the conclusions Zwingli deduced from it were fundamentally recognized. Moved and joyful, the reformer exclaimed; "Glory and thanksgiving to God, who wants his holy word to prevail in heaven and on earth."

But people at Zurich still shrank from the practical consequences. In September 1523, probably because of an address by Zwingli, the chapter of the cathedral was reformed. The posts of canon and chaplain were limited to the number necessary for the "word of God and other Christian uses," and the ecclesiastical property was destined "for the common profit" — that is, the hiring of teachers and the care of the poor. For the overdue reform of the school system Zwingli outlined his pedagogical program in the *Lehrbüchlein,* which, dedicated to his fifteen-year-old stepson, Gerald Meyer, is less a catechism than a mirror of the Christian citizen. The youth should be introduced to his duties in regard to God, self, and the community and learn to serve "the glory of God, the fatherland, and the good of all." A patriotic spirit, motivated by Christianity and humanism, is the goal of education.

Clear encroachments into the sphere of worship, such as the abolition of images and of the Mass, had not yet been attempted. But as at Wittenberg two years earlier, radical elements now pushed to the fore at Zurich and in the neighboring areas. On 10 August 1523, perhaps on the initiative of Leo Jud, the first child was "baptized in the German language" in the cathedral. At the same time Zwingli undertook work on the liturgical practice. He proceeded vary cautiously in his *Versuch über den Messkanon* of 29 August 1523. Except for the readings the service continued to be in Latin, and rites such as the sign of the cross and the Mass vestments were retained. He changed only the Canon and wanted to eliminate whatever referred to the Mass as a sacrifice. When this was not possible because of regard for the "weak," people should stick with the old and be satisfied with a mental restriction. But this was not enough for the radical forces, headed by Konrad Grebel, and in October Zwingli directed against them his *Verteidigung des Büchleins von Messkanon.* Similarly, in regard to images the adherents of the Reformation intended to effect both preaching in accord with Scripture and the elimination of idols. And when on 1 September 1523 Leo Jud preached expressly that, according to Holy Scripture, it was "right that idols should be removed from the churches," restraint was no longer possible. Altar images, statues, and crucifixes were wrecked, the lamps for the perpetual light were shattered, and holy water was ridiculed. But the council had to intervene because of the painful impression created and out of regard for the episcopal officials. Even Zwingli came out for punishment of the iconoclasts. Though he was basically in agreement with them — they were for the most part eventually to become Anabaptists — he was more prudent in his method of procedure.

The council called for a Second Disputation of Zurich to meet 26–28 October 1523 for a clarification of the controverted questions. The bishops were not represented, and the other Swiss cantons, except Sankt Gallen and Schaffhausen, held aloof. On the first day Leo Jud spoke before some nine hundred participants against "images and idols." The next day Zwingli attacked the Mass as a sacrifice. A participant declared that "the measuring and the butchering" had already given him anxiety of conscience. For the future he would dispense the Sacrament under both species. In opposition to delaying tactics, Konrad Grebel demanded that an unequivocal stand be taken against the Sacrifice of the Mass and purgatory and called for the abolition of hosts, of the mingling of water with the wine, of the placing of the bread in the communicant's mouth, and of the communicating of themselves on the part of priests. There was virtual unanimity in regard to the rejection of the Sacrifice of the Mass, but many felt that the time had not yet come for thoroughgoing changes. The secular authority had the final word. The council issued a mandate at the end of October. According to this, matters were to be left as they were for the moment. Images must not be removed, the Mass must not be abolished. And so seven months were to pass before the disappearance of images and a good eighteen months before an Evangelical Last Supper replaced the Mass. This yielding to the authority of the state procured for Zwingli the opposition of the radical groups and soon led to the founding of Anabaptist congregations. Meanwhile, on behalf of the authorities Zwingli wrote *Eine kurze und christliche Einleitung,* a primer intended to prepare the clergy and congregations for the changes about to take place. According to this, representations of God are forbidden and the Mass is contrary to Scripture because Christ was sacrificed on the cross, once for all time. The Christian is free with regard to ceremonies but bound by the law emanating from the magistrates. Even when chaplains at the cathedral emphasized in December 1523 that they were tired of being upbraided as butchers of God and refused to celebrate Mass any more, the hesitant regulation remained in force. "Although it is clear from Holy Scripture that the Mass is not a sacrifice, still there are so many weak and ignorant persons that one cannot suddenly abolish the Mass without giving scandal to the weak." However, the attitude of the council was determined not only by regard for the "weak" but even more by the critical political situation. A powerful movement in defense of the ancient faith was stirring in the rest of the Confederation. At the Lucerne *Tagsatzung* of January 1524 a united front against Zurich was formed and a mandate was issued forbidding any change of faith until the decision of a council. Zurich was to be invited to give up its doctrine. The city declined to do so, calling the extravagant outbursts and the abuses of the Mass a result of misunderstanding of preaching in conformity with Scripture, and sought to shield itself by referring to the needed reform of the Church.

The attitude of the confederated cantons was, to be sure, not so uniform as the mandate of January 1524 made it seem. Bern, Basel, and Schaffhausen did not take a clear stand. Together with Fribourg the five interior cantons especially adopted a position of compromise in regard to the reform movement, which at that time meant that they rejected the principle of Scripture. In April 1524 they joined together for the unconditional defense of the ancient faith and in the Confederate Concordat of Faith of January 1525 they drew up an extensive reform program.

Despite all the official reserve, the Reformation moved forward in Zurich. Like Zwingli in April 1524, the priests married. Processions and pilgrimages were abolished. On 15 June 1524 a conciliar mandate decreed "that images and idols should be removed with all propriety so that a place can be found for the word of God." Images and relics disappeared from the churches without any spectacular iconoclasm. But the council opposed Zwingli's suggestion that now was the time to give up the Mass and celebrate a biblical Lord's Supper. The Latin Mass in the customary vestments continued until 1525, except that all sacrificial prayers were omitted. Zwingli proceeded all the more relentlessly against the Mass in his writings. Between December 1524 and March 1525 he composed his *Commentary on True and False Religion,* the epilogue of a comprehensive exposition of his theology. In the section "On the Eucharist" he subjected the Mass and the worship of the Sacrament to the severest criticism.

> Why do we not bid all Mass priests to refrain from so horrible an affront to Christ? For if Christ must again be sacrificed every day, it follows that the sacrifice which he once offered on the cross does not suffice for all eternity. Is there a greater insult than this? All Masses must be immediately discontinued, and the Lord's Supper must be made use of in accord with Christ's institution.

On 11 April 1525, Zwingli felt that the time had finally come for the decisive attack. With Leo Jud, Oswald Myconius, and two other priests he complained to the council, demanding the abolition of the Mass as idolatry. By means of his *Aktion oder Brauch des Nachtmahls,* which he had just finished, he was able to demonstrate how he understood the celebration of the evangelical Lord's Supper. On the next day, Wednesday of Holy Week, the council, by a bare majority, decreed the abolition of the Mass. The last Mass was celebrated before a great crowd of people, "who wanted to have the Holy Sacrament administered to them according to the old custom, as before." Therefore something that was still entirely alive was abolished by official decree. Even Zwingli had to be lectured by the secular authority in regard to his order of the Eucharistic liturgy. He wanted the *Gloria,* the *Credo,* and Psalm 113 to be alternated by the men and the women, but the council forbade it. It likewise did not concede to the Church the right of excommunication, which Zwingli wanted exercised by the congregation as an exclusion from the Eucharist. The Lord's Supper was first celebrated on Holy Thursday 1525 as a "thanksgiving and memorial of Christ's Passion." Provision was made for only four feasts: Easter, Pentecost, the Dedication, and Christmas. On Sundays only a service of the word of God, similar to the late medieval preaching service, the *pronaus,* was to take place.

> There was no community singing. Quite otherwise than Luther, the musically gifted Zwingli gave no psalms and hymns to those of his church. The organs remained silent. With the singsong of the Latin choral chant, which no one understood, what pertained to music entirely disappeared.

With the elimination of the Mass the Reformation finally achieved its breakthrough in Zurich. At the same time the creation of other institutions was necessitated by the destruction of the ancient ecclesiastical system. Zwingli had commissioned Leo Jud to prepare German rituals for baptism, marriage, and burial. The city council had issued a "Regulation for the Poor" on 15 January 1525 which to a great extent disposed of ecclesiastical and monastic property. A substitute for the canon law on marriage and for the ecclesiastical matrimonial tribunals was urgently needed. Zwingli also left this important innovation in the hands of the council. On 10 May 1525 it announced the Zurich Order of the Matrimonial Tribunal, which had been worked out by a commission in which Zwingli had played a decisive role. This was the first reform. Judicial power was entrusted to six matrimonial judges, two pastors as people acquainted with Scripture and two members each of the great and the small council. The only court of appeals was the city council. In the following year, 1526, the matrimonial tribunal was expanded into a tribunal of morals, which controlled the lives of the citizens by penal and preventive powers and kept watch over them by means of spies. The authority to punish lay with the council, to which a denunciation had to be made after three warnings. With the introduction in 1529 of the obligation of attending worship and the prohibition of attendance at Catholic Masses outside the territory, the city congregation completely controlled the lives of the citizens. In opposition to Zwingli's spiritualism and to his thesis of the inherent power of the Gospel, but at the same time also in consequence of it, the secular authority had seized control of ecclesiastical government. The church congregation had been absorbed into the civic community.

The founding of a theological school, decided on in 1523, could also move nearer to realization in 1525. To provide payment for the teaching personnel, the canonries at the cathedral were reduced from twenty-four to eighteen. Reuchlin's pupil Jakob Ceporinus was appointed professor of Hebrew in January 1525; after his early death he was succeeded by the former Franciscan, Konrad Pellikan. In place of the morning choral office, Zwingli, in association with Ceporinus, gave daily lectures on the Old Testament from 19 June in the cathedral at 8:00 A.M. "All pastors, preachers, canons, and chaplains and the older students" had to attend. Zwingli himself gave to this hour of philological and theological exegesis of Scripture the name of prophecy. It served for the elementary and more advanced education of preachers and at the same time hastened the appearance of the "Zurich Bible." Until then Luther's translation of the New Testament had been reprinted in an adaptation using the Swiss dialect. Similarly the Pentateuch appeared in 1527 and soon afterward came the other historical books and the sapiential books of the Old Testament. People qualified to put the prophetic books, still lacking in Luther's translation, into German were sought in Zurich itself. Zwingli and Leo Jud played the chief roles in this, and Jud also translated the so-called apocrypha. And so in March 1529, five years before Luther's Bible was finished, the complete "Zurich Bible" existed in six volumes.

The Reformation in the Other Cantons of German Switzerland

From Zurich the reform movement was stimulated and fostered in northern and eastern Switzerland. Two laymen, the humanist-educated city physician Joachim Vadian (1483–1551) and the former theological student and later master saddler Johannes Kessler (1502–74), aided in the breakthrough in Sankt Gallen. At first both were under the influence of Erasmus. Vadian was gained for the Reformation by Zwingli. His helper, Kessler, had studied theology at Wittenberg and had then decided to earn his bread as an artisan. They recruited for the Reformation by means of their *Lesinen*, or lay Bible lessons. In 1524 the council put the city church at their disposal and ordered preaching in accord with Scripture. Vadian's election as mayor in 1526 assured the victory of the Reformation. Images, "idols," and altars were removed at night without disturbance and in 1527 an evangelical celebration of the Lord's Supper was introduced.

In Basel humanism and the struggle of the city congregation against the episcopal government had prepared the ground for the Reformation, but on the other side the traditional forces thwarted a quick victory for it. Here the Reformation was under Luther's auspices rather than Zwingli's. The Alsatian Wolfgang Capito (1478–1541), from 1515 preacher at the cathedral, and the Franciscan Konrad Pellikan, *custos* at Basel from 1519, were already spreading Lutheran ideas. Luther's writings were zealously reprinted by the Basel publishers Johannes Froben and Adam Petri. Ostentatious violations of the fasting law and sermons against Church laws led to complaints to the council, which sought to bring calm by a mandate in May 1523. Preachers were urged to adhere to Holy Scripture but not to mention the teachings of Luther and other doctors.

Six months earlier Johannes Oecolampadius (1482–1531) had come to Basel for the second time. As early as 1520 he had come out for the Wittenberg reformer in the *Iudicium de Luthero.* Then in *Quod non sit onerosa christianis confessio paradoxon* (1521) he defended as an escape from his own scruples the view that one need confess only external sins. Thereafter he could no longer stay at the Birgittine monastery of Altomünster. He went to Basel in November 1522 in order to have his translations of Chrysostom printed. After Easter 1523 he began lectures on Isaiah and in the summer was appointed professor of Scripture. Around him gathered the groups of citizens who were inclined toward the Reformation, especially since, in addition to giving his lectures, he preached zealously in Sankt Martin, of which he was named pastor in February 1525. At first he restricted himself to preaching, but before the end of the year he instituted an evangelical celebration of the Lord's Supper. In the late autumn of 1524 he had had a detailed discussion of the question of the Eucharist with Zwingli. In the *Elleboron* (1525), an attack on J. Latomus' *De confessione secreta,* he developed a spiritualist concept of the Church and the Sacraments. Faith, not the sacraments, bestows salvation. In the Eucharist the bread remains what it was. He developed this idea of a purely spiritual reception of the body of Christ in faith, for which the Sacrament is the sign, in *De genuina verborum Domini expositione liber* (1525) and in *Antisyngramma* (1526). He thereby set himself in opposition to Pirckheimer, Luther, and Brenz. He had several contacts with the Anabaptists in 1525–27, but came out against them in favor of infant baptism. He took a leading part in the disputations at Baden in 1526 and Bern in 1528. But at first he was unable to establish the Reformation at Basel against the council and the clergy of the city and the influence of Erasmus. In spite of the proclaiming of religious freedom on 29 February — "everyone is to allow the others to continue in his faith without any hatred" — at Easter 1528 there occurred iconoclast outbreaks and protests against the tithe. The guilds opposed the chapter clergy and the council. In a petition to the council on 23 December 1528 they demanded "the abolishing of conflicting preaching and of the Mass." The council tried to mediate and appointed a disputation for May. But the mob, once mobilized, could no longer be restrained. The cathedral was forced on 9 February and, as in other churches, crucifixes, images, and altars were destroyed. The council yielded to the terror. It excluded its Catholic members, had the iconoclasm carried to its completion by urban craftsmen, and in a mandate of 10 February 1529 forbade images and the Mass in the city and its territory. The cathedral chapter fled to Neuenburg and in May established itself at Freiburg im Breisgau. Erasmus, professors of the university, the Carthusian and Dominican communities and some others also left the city.

Oecolampadius, who was connected with the disturbances and was in fact regarded as their chief instigator, advised the council in the drawing up of the Reformation ordinance of 1 April. In it the council, advised by the clergy in accord with Scripture, dealt with the proclaiming of the word of God, the celebrating of baptism and of the Lord's Supper, the problem of images, and the norms of public morality. In May 1529 Oecolampadius was chosen *antistos* (overseer) of the Church and pastor of the cathedral. He exerted himself at five synods in 1529–31 on behalf of Church doctrine and discipline. He wanted the synods to be controlled by *a presbyterium* of laymen and pastors in a certain independence of the city government, but he had as little success as Zwingli. The city council claimed the right to excommunicate and permitted no central excommunicating authority that would be competent for the entire city but only one for individual parish communities.

Bern was long undecided between the religious factions. The city had to have regard for the conservative rural congregations in its territory. And an outstanding personality was lacking.

Thomas Wyttenbach had done the preliminary work here, but his assistant and successor as canon at the cathedral, Berchtold Haller (1492–1536), is regarded as Bern's reformer. From 1521 Haller was in contact with Zwingli. The Franciscan Doctor Sebastian Meyer and Jörg Brunner, chaplain at the pilgrimage center of Kleinhöchstetten, worked for the Reformation at his side, but with more alacrity. The council sought by means of a mandate of 15 June 1523 to deal with the disturbances caused by their preaching against pilgrimages and the Mass. The spread of Lutheran teaching was forbidden, but at the same time the arranging of scripturally oriented preaching was fostered. Bern adhered to the mandate of January 1524, issued by the Lucerne *Tagsatzung* for the unconditional defense of the Catholic faith but rejected the Concordat of Faith of January 1525. In a mandate of 2 April the council expressly decreed the defense of the seven sacraments, of the veneration of saints, of ceremonies, and of the religious life, out of regard for the frame of mind of the rural folk. Steps were taken against the marriage of priests, but on the other hand the nuns of Königsfelden were allowed to leave their convent. At the beginning of 1526 the situation in Bern was even more unfavorable for the Reformation. On 28 March the great council agreed to participate in the Disputation of Baden, called for 6 May and ordered Berchtold Haller to attend.

Johannes Eck had suggested to the Swiss such a disputation against Zwingli after the Regensburg meeting in June and July 1524. At that time the sacrificial character of the Mass was to be the special topic of discussion, and in 1525 the real presence was added as a controverted point. In a letter of 28 October 1525 Eck again offered his services for a disputation and noted that thus far Zwingli, with Luther, had rejected the Mass, but now he was breaking with him and, together with Oecolampadius, was seducing "many thousands into the detestable heresy... that they should not believe that in the venerable Sacrament are the true body and blood of Christ." Thus the real presence was brought to the fore and related to the doctrinal opposition between Luther and Zwingli. It was shown that Zwingli surpassed in heresy the Wittenberg teacher who had already been outlawed and excommunicated. Zwingli declined to appear at the Disputation of Baden, which was dominated by the Catholic localities. Berchtold Haller held himself entirely aloof. Oecolampadius was the spokesman; he was pitted against Eck, Fabri, and Murner. The first two of the seven theses posted by Eck on the church doors read as follows: (1) Christ's true body and blood are present in the Sacrament of the altar; (2) they are really offered up in the Mass for the living and the dead.

The religious discussion was protracted from 21 May to 8 June 1526. The Catholic side claimed the victory, but the goal of this last effort to preserve the religious unity of the Swiss was thwarted. Even the reference to the doctrinal opposition between Luther and Zwingli did not convince the representatives of Basel and Bern that Holy Scripture did not suffice as a norm of faith and to move them to suppress the new teachings. The "Verdict of Basel" was signed only by the nine Catholic cantons — Lucerne, Uri, Schwyz, Unterwalden, Zug, Glarus, Fribourg, Solothurn, and Appenzell — but not by Basel, Bern, and Schaffhausen. In it Zwingli was declared to have incurred excommunication. Preachers were solemnly bound to the Church's doctrine and worship, and the books of Luther and Zwingli were forbidden. An authority was to be instituted to see to it that persons expelled from one canton were not admitted to another. "The Baden Disputation was the Swiss parallel to the Diet of Worms and the Regensburg Assembly" (L. von Muralt).

On 21 May 1526, the very day on which the Baden Disputation began, the great council of Bern had bound itself under oath to make no change of faith without the consent of the officials. Haller, returning from Baden, was faced with the alternative of offering Mass again or of leaving Bern. He appealed to the council. When the citizenry took to the streets and demonstrated in his favor, he was relieved of his function as canon and hence of his obligation to a sacramental worship and installed as preacher. The elections of Easter 1527 finally brought victory to the new believers. They gained a majority in the great council and were able to prevail also in the small council. The Reformation mandate was renewed. Free preaching was allowed but all high-handed changes were forbidden. This increased the confusion, so it was decided to hold a religious colloquy on 15 November 1527. It was planned to form public opinion and to make an impression on the rural congregations by a pointed display. Eck refused to take part in a "sham disputation" to which the Confederation had not issued the invitation. The Catholic side was not officially represented, and so the disputation of 5–26 January 1528 acquired the character of a display which was to consolidate the decision already basically arrived at. Zwingli set out with about forty Zurich pastors and others from eastern Switzerland under an escort of three hundred armed men. Representatives arrived from the South German cities of Strasbourg, Augsburg, Memmingen, Lindau, Ulm, Constance, and so forth.

The ten theses drawn up by Berchtold Haller and his assistant Franz Kolb were largely a copy of the epilogue of the Ilanz Colloquy of 1526. The first was as follows: "The Holy Christian Church, whose only head is Christ, was born of the word of God; she continues in it and does not listen to the voice of a stranger." According to the fourth thesis it cannot be proved by Holy Scripture "that the body and blood of Christ are substantially and physically received in the bread of the Eucharist." The Mass is contrary to Scripture, as are also the invocation of saints, purgatory, office of the dead, lamps, candles, images, and celibacy. Not many of the clergy refused to sign at the end; a larger number added that they acquiesced in the decision of the council. A few days after the disputation, on 7 February 1528, the council issued a religious mandate. In it the Mass was abolished and a liturgy was introduced according to the Zurich model. The jurisdiction of the Bishop of Lausanne was repudiated and the direction of the Church was transferred to the council. The accession of Bern gave the reform movement in Switzerland a great boost. In 1536 Bern introduced the Reformation in Vaud, which it had conquered.

The expansion of the evangelical movement increased the tensions in the Confederation. Differing from Luther, Zwingli was willing to defend and propagate the faith by political means and even by arms. "Alive in Zwingli was the complete statesman, who understood the struggle for the faith as a power-struggle and was disposed to carry it out as such" (W. Köhler).

Zurich pushed forward an expansion of the existing agreements in regard to citizenship. Bern entered into a treaty with Constance, and Sankt Gallen and Mühlhausen in Alsace soon followed. Basel joined in February 1529, and from there the connections continued on to Strasbourg. Such alliances took place in the first place, so Zwingli felt, "for the honor of God and the unlocking of his holy word." They were aimed directly against the Catholic cantons but no less against Austria. The answer to them was the "Christian Union," formed in April 1529. Incidents, such as the attack on the monastery of Sankt Gallen in the spring of 1529, undertaken under the protection of Zurich and the abbey's secularization, or the execution of an evangelical preacher in Schwyz, intensified the mood for war on both sides. Finally a war for the faith was decided on. When Zurich declared war on 8 June it disposed of imposing forces, estimated at more than twelve thousand in April. The addition of the troops of the allies raised this figure to a total of about thirty thousand, to which the Catholic side could oppose only nine thousand. It was desired to spare the reformer and "not allow him to fight.... But he refused to stay at home. He sat on a charger and had a fine halberd over his shoulder. And so they moved on Kappel." The advance came to a halt there on 10 June. Zurich's allies urged negotiations. Zwingli advised: "Be firm and do not fear war." But Bern in particular refused to take part. The community consciousness of the Confederates asserted itself and on 26 June the First Territorial Peace of Kappel was concluded. The Catholic cantons had to give up their alliance with Ferdinand. Otherwise the terms were not clear and became the source of further conflict. Zwingli had demanded free, that is, Protestant preaching in the Catholic territories. In the peace it was stated "that, since no one is to be forced on account of the word of God, the cantons and their people are likewise not to be coerced." As the people of Zurich had no intention of allowing Catholic preaching and the Mass in their territory, the five cantons saw no reason to permit evangelical preaching. They understood the peace in the sense that each was allowed to persevere in its own faith.

Chapter 76

Anabaptists and Spiritualists

Even as early as the sixteenth century Anabaptism was often traced back to the Zwickau prophets, Karlstadt and Müntzer, or at least they are supposed to have influenced and substantially promoted it. Today it is known that, apart from an occasional contact with these Central German fanatics, the Anabaptists were an independent movement originating in the immediate circle of Zwingli at Zurich. Attempts have also been made to establish connections with medieval sects, such as the Cathari, the Waldensians, the Bohemian Brethren, and others, but Leonhard von Muralt and Walther Köhler have convincingly shown that Anabaptism was a "separate growth of the Reformation period," a religious and not a social revolutionary movement.

Anabaptists are distinguished from the fanatics by the conviction that the kingdom of God is to be realized in this world only in a small circle and must not be established by force. They are distinguished from the Spiritualists by the firm determination to form a visible community of the reborn, which is recognized by the covenant sign of baptism, the celebration of the Lord's Supper, and a penitential life and which is kept pure by a stern community discipline.

The Swiss Brethren and the South German Anabaptists

In 1523 the Zurich city council had introduced the Reformation. Above all, this meant preaching only "in accord with Scripture"; the liturgy should still remain unchanged. When Zwingli agreed to this prohibition of the evangelical Lord's Supper, zealous collaborators broke with him in order to form their own congregation, independent of any hierarchical authority and unencumbered by the mass of customary Christians. The leaders of this movement were Konrad Grebel (c. 1498–1526), son of a councilor, and Felix Mantz (c. 1500–1527), whose father was a canon of the Zurich Cathedral. Both had received a humanist education. As Konrad Grebel wrote to Thomas Müntzer in September 1524, the decisive factor for them was the realization that the Church of the New Testament is not a church of everybody, but a community of the few, who have the right faith and lead a proper life. It is based on voluntary membership and stands as an antithesis to the people's church, which has surrendered itself to dependence on authority. "In human respect and all sorts of seductions there is a more serious and more pernicious error than there has ever been since the beginning of the world." From this concept of the congregation arose the criticism of infant baptism. Only he who has experienced a penitential change of mind and believes personally can testify to this experience of salvation in baptism and be incorporated by it into the community. The question of correct baptism, the baptism of adults, thus became the distinguishing factor, and "rebaptizers" became the name given to the brethren by opponents. They themselves repudiated it, for they regarded infant baptism as no baptism at all.

This new congregation wanted to make itself visible. Its members not only kept aloof from the state Church; they also took no part in civic life. Authority was recognized in accord with Romans 13:14. But the disciple of Christ was not to assume any military duty, for such would lead to a conflict of conscience. When in the fall of 1524 Grebel did not have his newly born son baptized, a conflict with the Zurich council resulted. Following a public disputation of 17 January 1525, the council decreed expulsion from the city and canton for everyone who did not have his child baptized within eight days. Grebel and Mantz were forbidden to speak and their close friends, Wilhelm Reublin (Röubli), Ludwig Hätzer, Johannes Brotli, and Andreas Castelberger, were banished. Ready "to obey God rather than man" (Acts 5:29), those condemned met secretly on 21 January 1525, and on this occasion Grebel administered the baptism of faith to a former priest from the Grisons, Jörg of the House of Jacob, called Blaurock ("Blue Coat"). The latter then did the same for the brethren. Thereupon, they retired to the peasant village of Zollikon, celebrated the Lord's Supper as a memorial and love feast, according to the apostolic model, and thus called into being the first Anabaptist congregation.

The Zurich council intervened here too. In the formation of a free Church of the Brethren it saw insurrection and it quelled it. This led to the spread of the Anabaptist movement into the rest of Switzerland and to South Germany. On 7 March 1526, when even torture was of no avail, the Zurich council decreed death by drowning for anyone who rebaptized. The Anabaptists displayed a great readiness to suffer. Konrad Grebel, who succumbed to the plague in the summer of 1526, had written in May 1525 to Vadian, the reformer, at Sankt Gallen: "I will bear witness to the truth by the loss of my property, even of my home, and that is all I have. I will bear witness to the truth by imprisonment, by outlawry, by death."

On 5 January 1527 Felix Mantz was put to death by drowning and thus became the first martyr of Anabaptism. On the same day Jörg Blaurock was whipped on the exposed upper part of his body and driven from the city. He preached with great success in Tirol, but on 6 September 1527 he was burned after cruel torture. The indictment against him had mentioned abandonment of the priesthood and denial of infant baptism, of the Mass, of confession, and of prayer to Mary. The Anabaptist movement was almost completely wiped out in the canton of Zurich by ca. 1530.

But meanwhile it had obtained a foothold in South Germany, especially in Alsace, Baden, the Palatinate, Württemberg, and Tirol. Augsburg and Strasbourg became the chief centers. In November 1525 Michael Sattler, from Staufen im Breisgau, former prior of the monastery of Sankt Peter in the Black Forest, had been expelled from Zurich. He had gone to Württemberg, where he displayed a brisk activity. He presided at a meeting of Anabaptists on 24 February 1527, at Schleitheim near Schaffhausen, at which his Anabaptist profession of faith, the seven "Articles of Schleitheim," was adopted. This profession contained only the points of doctrine in which Anabaptism differed from the Reformation — baptism of faith, excommunication, common Lord's Supper, separation from the abominations of the world, pastoral office, nonresistance, and rejection of oaths. Soon after the Schleitheim meeting Sattler was arraigned at Rottenburg am Neckar as a heretic and executed on 21 May 1527.

Wilhelm Reublin (ca. 1480–after 1559), expelled from Zurich in 1525, went to Waldshut, where he converted the pastor, Balthasar Hubmaier (1485–1528), and with him almost the entire city to Anabaptism; it had earlier been won for Zwingli's Reformation. Hubmaier wrote a pamphlet against Zwingli, *Vom christlichen Tauf der Gläubigen* (*On the Christian Baptism of the Faithful*), which was very highly esteemed in Anabaptist circles. Because of his connection with the rebellious peasants he had to escape to Zurich at the end of 1525. He was imprisoned here but was able to obtain his release by abjuring Anabaptism. Later he again espoused the cause of Anabaptism; at Augsburg he baptized, among others, Hans Denck. In July 1526 he settled at Nikolsburg in Moravia, where various professions of faith were tolerated side by side. For a time Nikolsburg, because of Hubmaier's zeal, became the center of those sympathetic toward Anabaptism — within a year he published eighteen treatises on the true baptism, Church order, excommunication, the Lord's Supper, and so forth. He strongly emphasized congregational discipline. "Where it does not exist, there is surely also no Church, even though baptism with water and the Eucharist itself are preserved," he states in an inscription of his pamphlet *Von der brüderlichen Strafe* (*On Fraternal Punishment*). Contrary to Hans Hut (c. 1490–1527) and the rest of the Anabaptists, Hubmaier did not advocate complete nonresistance. He allowed the authority and the individual Christians to wield the sword and supported the Moravian nobles in their war against the attacking Turks. He justified this idea of his in the work *Vom Schwert* (*The Sword,* 1527). As Anabaptism gained an ever stronger hold in the Austrian lands, Ferdinand I applied energetic measures against it and demanded the surrender of Hubmaier. The latter's trial was less concerned with his reform and rebaptizing activities than with his seductive teaching at Waldshut, whereby he was accused of having caused insurrection and revolt among the common folk. He tried in vain to justify himself in his *Rechenschaft seines Glaubens* (*Accounting of His Faith*). On 10 March 1528 he was burned at the stake.

Hans Denck (c. 1500–1527) worked a short while at Augsburg, following his baptism in May 1526. Here he baptized Hans Hut, a former adherent of Thomas Müntzer. Both introduced strongly spiritualistic and mystical elements into the Anabaptist movement. Difficulties with the leading Lutheran preacher, Urban Rhegius, over his doctrine of justification, predestination, and the ultimate sharing of all in salvation (the *apokatastasis panton* of Origenism), drove Denck from Augsburg. He went to Strasbourg in November 1526, where he met Michael Sattler and Ludwig Hätzer and, through disputations with Capito and Bucer, attracted attention. He had to leave Strasbourg too at Christmas 1526. He went to the Palatinate and worked successfully by word and writing in the Anabaptist congregations of Landau and Worms. Here he collaborated with Ludwig Hätzer and they gained the Lutheran preachers Kautz and Hilarius for their cause. But Kautz caused disturbances by posting theses and distributing pamphlets and was therefore expelled. Hätzer and Denck went to Worms but had to leave there also. In August 1527 Denck was at the "martyrs' synod" at Augsburg where Hans Hut and his theology of the imminent Parousia were at the center of the discussion. In view of the impending end of the world there was a desire to undertake a large-scale missionary activity, and Denck was dispatched to carry it out in the territory of Basel. Meanwhile there was a strong resurgence of persecution against the Anabaptists. Denck arrived at Basel in October 1527 but in mid-November he died of the plague in the house of a friendly humanist. Broken by persecution and setbacks, he seems to have regarded his work as an Anabaptist as ruined and to have turned to an individualistic spiritualism.

By virtue of an imperial decree of 4 January 1528 and of the recesses of the Imperial Diets of Speyer (1529) and Augsburg (1530), the Anabaptists fell under the law on heresy. They were persecuted on the charge of heresy and sedition by Catholic and often even more relentlessly by Protestant authorities and were put to death or banished. Nevertheless they could not be entirely suppressed.

The ideas common to Anabaptists can be noted as follows. They desired to reestablish the primitive community of Jerusalem. Only the elect, who were determined to lead a new life in the strictest imitation of the Lord and to testify to their conversion by the baptism of faith could belong to it. The life of the individual and of the congregation must be oriented to Scripture, preferably the New Testament. The Spirit of God, which one knows with certainty, guarantees the correct understanding of its content. The real presence was denied, but great significance for the inner stability of the congregation was attached to the Lord's Supper as a memorial and love feast. As the "congregation of the saints" the community must be kept pure by strict application of excommunication, which is the sign of a legitimate Church. A well-developed awareness of their apostolate led to bustling missionary activity, which was powerfully influenced by the idea of the Second Coming. Only he who belongs to the covenant can expect grace at the time of judgment. While private property was everywhere retained, persons wanted to share goods and chattels with their brothers in voluntary charity. If community of property was required, this referred to common use, not acquisition. The brethren were basically prepared to render obedience to authority, even though real Christians need no authority as such. But, by appealing to the Sermon on the Mount, military service, oaths, and the death penalty were rejected. For the same reason an Anabaptist was not to assume any office of authority. Even when the brethren behaved peaceably and submissively, the authorities saw in them a threat to public order and safety. The Anabaptists met persecution with a great readiness for suffering, this being a mark of their election.

The Moravian Brethren

In addition to the Swiss Brethren, who spread from Zurich throughout southwestern Germany as far as Hesse and Thuringia, the Hutterites (or Hutterian Brethren) are to be mentioned as a second group. The Hutterites of Moravia derived their name from Jakob Hutter (d. 1536). Born at Pustertal, he became leader and organizer of Tirolese Anabaptism after the death of Jörg Blaurock. To escape persecution in Tirol, he and his followers sought refuge in Moravia in 1529. There he came upon Anabaptist congregations which practiced a strict community of goods, following the ideal of the Apostolic congregation at Jerusalem. On this foundation Hutter in 1533–1535 built his consumption and production communes. Ulrich Stadler (d. 1540), director of the Hutterite Brethren at Bucovice in Moravia, wrote in his treatise on community property: "Therefore, where there is property, where persons have it and seek it, . . . there persons are outside of Christ and his congregation and have also no 'Father in heaven.' " On the other hand, it is "true calm to place and surrender oneself thus to the service of the saints with all one's possessions and belongings." One of the Moravian Hutterite Brethren was the Silesian Kaspar Braitmichel (d. 1573), chronicler of the Anabaptist movement. The *Geschichtsbuch* that he began is an important source for the Zurich beginnings for the history and self-evaluation of the Hutterite Brethren.

The Anabaptists in the Netherlands and North Germany

The third group, the Anabaptists of the Netherlands and North Germany, goes back to Melchior Hofmann. In the Münster Anabaptist area the movement acquired a radical and even fantastic expression, which was especially prejudicial to the reputation of Anabaptists. However, Menno Simons succeeded in bringing Anabaptism in North Germany back to its originally peaceable character.

The furrier Melchior Hofmann (c. 1500–1543), born at Schwäbisch Hall, had worked from 1523 as a Lutheran lay preacher in the Baltic provinces, Sweden, and North Germany. There he came into opposition to Luther and the Lutheran Reformation because of his fantastic scriptural exegesis, his ideas about the end of the world, and his spiritualistic doctrine of the Lord's Supper. Hofmann became acquainted with the Anabaptists at Strasbourg in 1529 and joined them in 1530. Like them, he demanded toleration and freedom of belief, strict sanctification of life, baptism of adults as the seal of the covenant with God, and nonviolence. But he differed from them in extravagant apocalyptic teaching and his Monophysite concept of the Incarnation. According to this, Christ received his flesh, not from, but out of Mary. For Hofmann the Bible was a secret revelation, which only he who was endowed with the Spirit, as with the key of David, knew how to interpret correctly. As a person so endowed, Hofmann believed he recognized the signs of the end of the world and that he was called to collect from Scripture the divine intentions and demands. He regarded himself as one of the two final witnesses announced, in Apocalypse 11:3 and on several occasions proclaimed the end of the world. He had to leave Strasbourg repeatedly and worked in East Friesland (Emden) and Holland. Through his impassioned eloquence he succeeded in gaining recognition of Anabaptism in Holland and in winning many adherents for the new "community of the covenant." They were later called "Melchiorites" or "Bontgenooten," (Members of the Covenant). The authorities at Amsterdam took measures against them, however, and Hofmann had to flee. His deputy, Volkertszoon, and eight other followers were beheaded at The Hague on 5 December 1531. After this the community operated as quietly as possible. Hofmann himself had given the directive not to baptize for two years and to limit activity to preaching and admonishing until the Lord set the hour. The Swiss Brethren regarded this as cowardice and disobedience to Christ's missionary command.

Jan Matthijs of Haarlem, a neophyte of Hofmann's, also rejected his prohibition to baptize and at the end of 1533 sent out twelve "apostles" to preach and baptize. Two of them, Bartel Boeckbinder and Willem Cuper, baptized in Friesland; among their neophytes was Obbe Philips, whom they appointed as elder. He in turn, some two years later (1536), baptized the former Catholic priest Menno Simons (d. 1567) who was to become the head of the group named for him, the Mennonites.

Hofmann, meanwhile, had been led once again to Strasbourg by his awareness of mission — that, as the new Elias, he had to cooperate in the second coming of Christ. An Anabaptist prophet from Friesland had prophesied to him that he would go to Strasbourg and, after an imprisonment of six months, would, at the Lord's return lead a victorious Anabaptist procession through the whole world. Finding himself left in peace for two months, he presented himself to the Strasbourg council to be arrested. The council complied with his wish in May 1533 and discussed his case on the occasion of the General Synod of Strasbourg, in which Martin Bucer participated. The "new Elias" was subsequently kept in prison until his death ten years later, under conditions that were at times downright shameful. Despite his experience, he clung to his apocalyptic hopes. For lack of paper he wrote his visions on linen cloths. Like many others of his numerous writings — more than thirty-five merely in the decade 1523–33 — these were lost.

Melchior Hofmann, called by Samuel Cramer the "father of Dutch Anabaptism," belonged to the "peaceful, quiet Anabaptism," which renounced any recourse to force and demanded discipline and sanctification. But through his extravagant apocalyptic teaching and his warning of the imminence of the Last Judgment, and above all through his adherents, the Melchiorites — who emigrated from Holland to Westphalia in large numbers — he shared responsibility for the bloody tragedy of Anabaptism in Münster.

Bernhard Rothmann, a chaplain, born at Stadtlohn (c. 1495), had preached Lutheran doctrine at Münster since 1529. In 1531 he had visited Wittenberg and Strasbourg and in the latter city had met Anabaptists and the spiritualist, Kasper von Schwenckfeld. On his return he had established the Reformation at Münster. His church order and Eucharistic doctrine were influenced by Zwingli. From 1533 he was under the influence of the so-called "Wassenberg Preachers," who rejected the baptism of infants, leading to difficulties with the city council.

But, along with the Melchiorites, who had been pouring in since the summer of 1533, even more radical circles gained a footing in Münster. The Dutchmen Bartel Boeckbinder and Willem Cuper arrived on 5 January 1534 and administered rebaptism to Rothmann and other preachers. Rothmann continued the baptizing. At first the city council resisted and the prince-bishop arranged proceedings against the Anabaptists as rebels and agitators. But they succeeded in getting control of the city government and on 23 February 1534 brought about the election of an Anabaptist council. The internal government was, however, exercised by the Haarlem baker, Jan Matthijs, who wanted to do away with all opponents of Anabaptism. But the Münster cloth merchant Knipperdolling simply had them expelled.

Meanwhile, Bishop Franz von Waldeck had the city blockaded. The Anabaptists mobilized the entire population for defense of the city and to a great extent annulled the right of private property. When Jan Matthijs perished in a sortie, the tailor Jan Beuckelsz of Leiden (Jan van Leiden) came forward as his successor. He dissolved the Anabaptist council and instituted twelve elders as rulers of the tribes of Israel. In reality he did the ruling. After a military success on 31 May he had himself proclaimed king, not only of Münster but of the world. Bernhard Rothmann placed himself at the service of the Kingdom of Münster as court preacher and writer. Of the five works from the years 1533–35, the pamphlet *Von der Rache und Strafe des babylonischen Greuels* (*On the Vengeance and Punishment of the Abomination of Babylon*) aimed to induce the Anabaptists in the Netherlands to come to Münster and relieve the besieged city.

Communism was not so thoroughly established as among the Moravian Brethren. Production communism among the crafts resulted rather from military necessity, and the family remained together. Still, in June 1534, polygamy in the sense of the simultaneous marriage of one husband with several wives was introduced and all women without husbands were ordered to marry. Those of the banished "godless" who remained behind were obliged to contract a new marriage. The ability and ruthlessness of Jan van Leiden and the stubbornness of the Anabaptists succeeded in holding the city for a year and four months, though famine appeared by the end of 1534. Even as treachery was opening up a way into the city for the besiegers, the Anabaptists were defending themselves so effectively with the courage of despair that they came near to inflicting defeat on the bishop's troops. Münster fell on 25 June 1535, and the bloodbath was frightful.

Jan van Leiden, his representative Knipperdolling, and the royal councilor Bernhard Krechting were examined under torture for seven months, the king himself being conducted around the country on exhibition, until on 22 January 1536 they were tortured to death at Münster with glowing tongs and their corpses were exhibited in iron cages on the tower of the Lambert church. Thus did the kingdom of Münster, a repulsive "mixture of piety, hedonism, and thirst for blood," as von Ranke styles it, meet a dreadful end. In their striving to establish the kingdom of God visibly in this world and to subject world and society forcibly to its dominion, the rebaptizers of Münster must be counted as belonging to the fanatics and not to the Anabaptists. For nonviolence and withdrawal into communities of brethren are the distinguishing characteristics of the latter.

But the kingdom of Münster seriously and enduringly injured their reputation. It remained for Menno Simons and the Philips brothers to restore Low German Anabaptism to its original character. The Philips brothers were illegitimate sons of a Catholic priest. In 1533 they were baptized by emissaries of Jan Matthijs at Leeuwarden in Friesland. Obbe (d. 1568), barber and surgeon by profession, and Dirk (1504–68), an ex-Franciscan, opposed the revolutionary Anabaptism of Münster and assumed the leadership of the peaceful wing of the Melchiorites, who were for a time called "Obbenites."

Obbe, appointed an Anabaptist preacher through the imposition of hands, ordained his brother Dirk as elder in the Dutch Anabaptist brotherhood. He did the same at Groningen in 1537 with Menno Simons, whom he had baptized a year earlier. But around 1540 Obbe withdrew from the Anabaptist movement. He accused it of falling into the visible and the external, doubted his own vocation or "mission," and advocated an individualistic spiritualism. His "confession" is an important source for the history of the Melchiorites and of Münster Anabaptism.

In contrast to the spiritualism of his brother and of Sebastian Franck — he had come to a parting of the ways with the latter in the *Verantwortung und Reputation auf zwei Briefe* — Dirk Philips concentrated on the congregation and wanted to set up in it a community of truly converted persons. For the sake of its purity and sanctity he required excommunication and a consequent avoidance of the excommunicated. He labored tirelessly in the Netherlands and North Germany. From 1550 his chief residence was at Danzig. He spread his ideas in numerous works, which he collected and published before his death in the *Enchiridion oder Handbüchlein christlicher Lehre.* He thereby became the theologian and dogmatist of North German and Dutch Anabaptism. Clearer and more systematic than Menno Simons, with whom he collaborated for a long time, he in no sense achieved the latter's depth and breadth of influence because of his sharp, one-sided, and obstinate manner.

Menno Simons (1496–1561) worked for seven years in Friesland and North Holland after his ordination as an elder. He simultaneously displayed a prolific literary activity. His chief work, *Das Fundament der christlichen Lehre* (1539) deals with penance, faith, baptism, the Lord's Supper, the avoidance of the godless, and the mission, life, and teaching of preachers. At Emden in January 1544 Menno had a disputation with Johannes à Lasco who was working there as a reformer. They did not agree in regard to the Incarnation of Christ, infant baptism, and the vocation of preachers. Like Melchior Hofmann, Menno defended the opinion that

Christ was born, not of, but in Mary, that he received his flesh, not through Mary, but through the Holy Spirit by virtue of a special creative act of God. After two years' activity at Cologne, his chief residence was in Holstein, and from there he toured the Baltic coast from Lübeck to Livonia.

In various controversies and in regard to rigorists Menno played a reconciling role; he was more and more concerned with peace and unity. Hotly disputed points among the Dutch Anabaptists were excommunication, mixed marriages with those who were not Anabaptists, and the avoidance of an apostate or infidel spouse, which in practice meant divorce. In *Eine wehmütige und christliche Entschuldigung und Verantwortung* (1552) Menno strongly protested against being identified with the Münster insurgents. He and his brethren, he said, were against tumult and did not require community of goods. The charge of polygamy was a wicked calumny. People should not call them rebaptizers or destroyers or souls, for they rejected infant baptism as not a genuine Christian baptism, nor were they blasphemers of the Sacrament, when they did not believe that bread and wine are flesh and blood in substance. Menno repeatedly succeeded in escaping persecution. He died in 1561 at Wüstenfeld near Bad Oldesloe in Holstein. His importance lies in his having gathered together the peaceful Anabaptists of Holland and North Germany and, through his work and his writings, to have gradually brought men to distinguish between those of the Anabaptist persuasion and rebaptizers of the Münster movement. His teaching did not contain much sublime theological speculation. At the center of his doctrine stood rebirth, as the most basic demand of the Christian life. It is the work of God and grows from the seed of the divine word, but it has to show itself in a penitential life, in obedience to God's word and command. Only those truly reborn may belong to the congregation of Christ. Excommunication and the rejection of mixed marriages thus played a big role.

Although Menno Simons was not the founder of the Anabaptist community, which was already ten years old when he joined it, the name Mennonites became popular in the course of the sixteenth century to designate the Anabaptists of the Netherlands and Germany. In Germany it indeed served as a protective designation to distinguish Anabaptists from the "rebaptizers," whom imperial law threatened with death. In the seventeenth century Mennonite became the usual name for all groups of Anabaptists, except the Hutterites. In the independent Netherlands the Mennonites obtained a limited toleration. Persecutions and the idea of isolation led to migration throughout the world and made the Mennonites pioneers in sparsely populated areas. Through their serious and simple way of life and their community solidarity they acquired great importance for the economic development of their localities. In turn this led to the point that, at least in Germany and the Netherlands, they abandoned the principle of separation more and more in favor of an active participation in social and cultural life.

Spiritualism

A striving toward spiritualization runs through all the reform movements of the fifteenth and sixteenth centuries. In opposition to the venality and materialism of piety, there was a demand for inwardness, for a more inward justice. But spiritualism obtains only where the external is absolutely regarded as unworthy or at least as unimportant. Proceeding from Neoplatonic assumptions, people adopted a dualism and set spirit in opposition to body, letter, and the visible Church with externals such as Sacrament, liturgy, and ecclesiastical discipline. Spiritualist traits are found in Erasmus and Zwingli and to a lesser degree in Luther; but in Luther in some respects these traits are more pronounced than in the fanatics, Karlstadt and Müntzer. Of the Anabaptists, Hans Denck was especially influenced by spiritualism and seems to have embraced it entirely at the end of his life.

The most important representatives of spiritualism in the sixteenth century were Kaspar von Schwenckfeld (1489–1561) and Sebastian Franck (1499–1542). Schwenckfeld, a Silesian noble was at first an adherent of Luther. As privy councilor for Frederick II of Liegnitz, he gained the latter for the Reformation and contributed powerfully to its spread in Silesia. He called for the life of the primitive Apostolic community. Hence the moral fruits of Christian life were decisive for him. Because of his spiritualist concept of the Lord's Supper and the suspicion of being an Anabaptist, he had to leave Silesia in 1529. He went to Strasbourg until 1533. During his stay there his doctrine acquired its peculiar form in the exchange of views and in disputes with reformers such as Capito and Bucer and with the various groups of Anabaptists, spiritualists, and fanatics. Bucer banished him to Augsburg, and from there he went to Ulm in 1535. Having run afoul of the Swiss also because of his Christology and having been condemned by the Lutheran assembly of theologians at Schmalkalden as a Sacramentarian and Anabaptist, he led a restless life for the next two decades, seeking shelter on the estates of noble families or in the houses of his adherents. Through his numerous writings, of which more than a hundred were printed while others were circulated in manuscript, he created for himself a large circle of readers, the members of which gave mutual edification and strengthened one another in their faith as they individually understood it. They had to separate themselves from the "Church of creatures." The true Church lives in dispersion; only God knows its members.

Human nature itself is a sin, which it is all-important to overcome, just as Christ made his human nature divine. His glorified flesh is the only everlasting food of believers. Matter cannot communicate spirit. Hence there is only the way from within to the external, and God cannot bind himself to external rites, sacraments, or the written word, but only to man's inwardness. It is not the Scripture that brings the Spirit, but the man filled with the Spirit who brings it to the Scripture. He "must bring the divine light to Scripture, the Spirit to the letter, the truth to the image, and the master to his work."

Sebastian Franck (1499–1542) of Donauwörth was a priest. From 1526 to 1528 he functioned in evangelical congregations near Nürnberg. Then he relinquished his ecclesiastical position and busied himself as a writer in Nürnberg and Strasbourg. He was expelled from Strasbourg on a complaint by Erasmus, whom he had labeled a heretic. For a time he earned his living as a soap-boiler at Esslingen. From 1533 on he managed a printing press at Ulm, but he had to have most of his voluminous works printed elsewhere. They consisted of chronicles (*Türkenchronik*, 1531; *Chronika, Zeitbuch, und Geschichtsbibel*, 1531; *Germaniae Chronicon*, 1538), a cosmography, *Weltbuch* (1534), biblical exegesis, collections of proverbs, and translations. In 1539 he was expelled from Ulm and in 1540 he was condemned by the assembly of theologians at Schmalkalden because of withdrawal from the Church and contempt for the Bible and the office of preacher. He died at Basel in 1542.

In his view "the visible Church of Christ was ruined and destroyed right after the Apostles." Because external doctrine and sacraments were defiled from that time on, God now allows everything to occur through the Spirit in his invisible Church which is dispersed among the pagans. Besides, God only intended the sacraments for the Church for the time of her youth, as a doll for a child. Now one must "seek more serious things, such as faith, penance, self-denial." Pagans and Turks also must be considered as brothers, even though they have never heard a letter of the story of Christ. What is important is that through the inner word they have experienced his power. Christ is the invisible word. His story is as meaningless as the external word of Holy Scripture, the "paper pope." The letter conceals the mystery. God must "awaken the dead and death-dealing letter to spirit and life in us." Franck studied Church history as the history of heretics, in which the latter have to be regarded as the true Christians. "For Christians have been heretics to the whole world everywhere and always." Franck accused the reformers of having given up the principle of the inwardness and freedom of faith, which had been present at the beginning of Protestantism. And, like Schwenckfeld, he fought with all the more vigor for toleration.

Spiritualists and Anabaptists, "the Reformation's left wing," became, because of their basic principles and in consequence of persecution, protagonists of such modern ideas as religious freedom, free Church membership, and separation of Church and state, ideas which of course acquired wider recognition only through the English Free Churchmanship and the French Revolution.

CHAPTER 77

The Catholic Literary Opponents of Luther and the Reformation

In view of Luther's extensive literary activity and of the many broadsides and pamphlets which he and his friends circulated widely among the people, thanks to the printing press, the question arises: What was done on the part of the ancient Church to counteract this? Did the defense likewise avail itself of the new means of publicity for forming public opinion and exert itself to keep in the Church or to win back for her the masses going over to Luther? And how successful was this? The number of theological writers who undertook the defense of the old Church was amazingly high, especially if it is borne in mind how unpopular and burdensome this assignment was. It is only in recent decades that greater attention has been given to the Catholic controversialists and a beginning has been made of rendering their writings accessible in the *Corpus Catholicorum.* These throw much light on the question of the religious and theological force with which Luther was met. Furthermore, for a better understanding of the reformers, their partners in the discussion must be known. And, lastly, the writings of the pre-Tridentine controversialists are important as preparations for the Council of Trent and for a correct evaluation of its theological achievement.

In order not to underestimate the works of the early opponents of Luther it is necessary to delineate the difficulties of their task and the unfavorable conditions under which they had to accomplish it. It was necessary to recognize both the extent and the far-reaching importance of error and to fight it by presenting the truth. The first of these aims was not easy because of the extensive theological vagueness. Many regarded Luther as the one who would effect the long overdue reform and felt it was a question merely of the elimination of wrongs, abuses, and grievances that had permeated ecclesiastical life. As late as 1530 Melanchthon sought to have this view accepted at the Diet of Augsburg. In comparison, men who, like Johannes Eck, pinpointed heresy clearly, logically, and inexorably, could not but appear as zealots and disturbers of the peace.

Once heresy had been established, it was necessary to counteract it. Mere refutation was not enough, for the reform movement was not just the sum of individual errors. Like every heresy, it drew its life from the truth, from the partial truth which had hitherto been overlooked or belied in ecclesiastical practice. It had to be shown how the justified concern of the reformers had its place in the doctrine of the Church and that one was prepared to make it respected. All this demanded religious strength and theological vitality on the part of the Catholic writer. He had to sense the basic coherence of the truth and recognize the center which gives life to everything else and to which the peripheral has to be related time and again. Hence it was of decisive importance whether they were able to be detached enough from the opponent in order to achieve an independent presentation of Catholic doctrine. This, invariably, was not the case. For the most part they were mere counterwritings, and frequently these were not only limited in their direction against one specific reform pamphlet, but also they undertook to expound and refute these sentence by sentence. As late as 1524 Hieronymus Emser was disputing Luther and Zwingli in his writings in this medieval and rather cumbersome manner, even though he was convinced that they could "not be cured of their deeply rooted illness by either arguments of reason or skills." Luther had on his side the verve and the appeal of the new and the pathos of the criticism of abuses. He had the advantage of the offensive as Johannes Cochläus once stated, inasmuch as he "struck the first blow and was able to circulate his booklets in great numbers before a reply could be made by the opposition."

It was all the more unfortunate, then, that the Catholic writers often did not get beyond a purely defensive method and permitted their adversary to dictate to them the course of action. Instead of taking up his fundamental points and refuting them from their center, attention was often concentrated on quite superficial details. Successes thus gained proved to be worthless, because the opponent had long since taken up new positions. In *De captivitate Babylonica* (1520) Luther described this situation to the point: "I am always ahead of them, and hence, while they, like illustrious victors, are celebrating triumphs over one of my alleged heresies, I meanwhile usher in a new one." In addition, the defenders of the ancient Church were confronting a public opinion which had been heavy with anti-Roman sentiments for decades and was filled with a deep-rooted distrust of the Curia, feelings which Luther, with his great flair for publicity and even demagoguery, was able to utilize skillfully. On the other hand, his opponents operated in a tedious, clumsy, and pedantic fashion and found it doubly difficult to deal with a Reformation that had become a popular movement and was carried along by the appeal of the new.

Beyond the propitiousness of the moment and the greater talent for publicity, in the final analysis it was a question of a different method in theology. With Luther proclamation took the place of the systematic analysis of revelation by philosophical means, which was greatly removed from religious and liturgical life. The "for me," the personal experience of salvation, moved him and urged him to confess his knowledge-become-experience before men. As opposed to this, the prosaic and complicated method of scholasticism could only appear pale or faded. It took time before Catholic writers arrived at a theology which was primarily a proclamation and directly answered the needs of the hour.

Frequently the men who felt called upon to defend the Church and who did not refuse their service were not theologians but humanists — men of letters or schoolmen and practical spiritual directors. Johannes Cochläus, for example, "was by calling a school master and philologist interested in editing ancient works, and a theologian only out of a sense of duty" (M. Spahn). It was a sacrifice for him to engage in the conflict. He participated in it because, according to his own statement at the time of the Diet of Worms, the Catholic faith was more important to him than *belles lettres*. Similarly, Hieronymus Emser saw himself faced with the task of leading a theological battle without being a theologian.

Scholastic theology had done little by way of preparation. How was the Mass to be defended, when the theology of the fourteenth and fifteenth centuries had not concerned itself with it practically at all and in regard to the Eucharist had been interested only in transubstantiation or in the cosmological questions connected with it? The unscriptural theology of nominalism, predominantly bogged down in problems of form, on which the criticism of Luther and of the Reformation had caught fire, provided a poor basis for defense. What was the very cause of the Reformation — the dogmatic vagueness and lack of religious depth and force in late scholastic theology — naturally also hamstrung any defense against it.

The principle of Scripture, relentlessly championed by Luther, placed the Catholic controversialists in the presence of a serious problem of methodology. Were they to abandon any appeal to tradition, to the Fathers, councils, and popes and be content with scriptural proof? Were they not to do so at least in practice in order to lend more force to their line of argument vis-à-vis the adherents of the Reformation? In principle they adhered to the view that "not only that which is expressly contained in the divine Scriptures and can be proved from them is to be believed and preserved," and considered tradition as the "living Gospel." The more the Protestants contended among themselves over such central truths as the Eucharist, the Catholics pointed out that Scripture does not adequately interpret itself but needs a living *magisterium* for that purpose. In practice only a few theologians were satisfied with scriptural proofs. This did not stem merely from an embrace of dogmatic conviction or even less from inability to adjust to one's opponent and to follow him to the field of battle; it had its basis in the works of the Protestants themselves. Luther's contention that the idea of the Mass as a sacrifice had developed out of the ancient Christian offering of gifts, that before Gregory the Great private Masses were unknown, or that for twelve centuries the Church had known nothing about transubstantiation could not but stimulate his Catholic opponents to seek proof to the contrary in history. Even more than Luther, the other reformers, such as Melanchthon and Zwingli, appealed to the usage of the early Church and quoted the Church Fathers for this purpose. This not only justified the patristic argumentation of the Catholics but practically promoted it. But it also meant that it more and more acquired the character of an historical proof.

Though at first the more peripheral questions of indulgences, vows, the veneration of saints, and the like formed the object of controversy, soon the basic problems — the doctrine of the Church, of authority, of the papal primacy, of justification, and of the Mass — preempted the stage. In the years 1522–26 there appeared a number of works in defense of the Mass. With its abolition, as idolatry, the reformers interfered the most profoundly and the most noticeably in the religious life of the people. Here the far-reaching effect of their teaching revealed itself most clearly.

The first, most indefatigable, best known, and also most hated adversary of the Reformation was Johannes Eck (1486–1543), diocesan priest and professor at Ingolstadt. At the Leipzig Disputation (1519) he had made plain Luther's abandonment of the idea of the Church. The same end was served by *De primatu Petri adversus Ludderum* (1520), which he submitted in Rome while working there from March until July of 1520 for the condemnation of Luther. Following several work; on justification and penance — among others, *De poenitentia et confessione* (1522); *De purgatorio* (1523); *De satisfactione et aliis poenitentiae annexis* (1523) — he produced a "manual" in 1525, *Enchiridion locorum communium adversus Ludderanos,* as a counterpart of Melanchthon's *Loci communes* of 1521. In this he applies the scriptural and patristic proof to the questions in controversy and then seeks to refute the objections of his adversaries. More than ninety editions and translations prove the importance of the *Enchiridion.* When it turned out that, due to a dearth of Catholic sermon manuals, priests were using those of Protestants, Eck wrote five volumes of sermons in German on the liturgical cycles, the feasts of saints, the sacraments, and the commandments. At the request of his prince, Duke Wilhelm II, he published a German Bible in 1537. He himself translated the Old Testament, with great accuracy, into "High German," that is, the South German dialect. For the New Testament he adopted Emser's translation. Eck endeavored to comply with the trend of the age — "to the sources" — by a careful regard for Scripture and the Fathers. But despite an abundance of citations his encounter with them was not creative. He was unable to make them sufficiently fruitful in a religious and theological sense. Keeping in mind the lack of dogmatic clarity in this period, it was to Eck's merit to have shown clearly and even caustically that Luther stood, not for reform, but for revolution and to have spurned any compromise at the expense of truth. At the same time, however, the question arises whether Eck sufficiently felt the responsibility for unity and was correspondingly concerned about his opponent, or whether in his zeal for the disputation he pushed him to heretical conclusions and committed him to error.

A tireless champion of the Catholic Church at the court of Duke Georg of Saxony was the latter's secretary and chaplain, Hieronymus Emser (1478–1527). Following the Leipzig Disputation he had criticized Luther's position regarding the Bohemians. Alluding to Emser's coat of arms, which displayed an ibex, Luther replied in an extremely harsh polemic, *Ad aegocerotem Emserianum* (1519), the prelude to a series of polemical exchanges between the "goat of Leipzig" and the "bull of Wittenberg." Emser's later writings also, which were directed against Karlstadt and Zwingli as well as Luther and were concerned with the defense of images, the Mass, and the priesthood, did not amount to more than a mere "refutation" of his adversary. In 1523 after Emser had attributed 1400 "heretical errors and lies" to Luther's New Testament, he himself, at the instigation of his duke, published his own translation of the New Testament in 1527, which closely followed Luther's text. Emser had been summoned from the carefree life of a humanist to defend the Church. He had not declined the task but had accepted it zealously. Still, he was not enough of a theologian and commanded too little religious respect to do full justice to it.

Emser's successor as Duke Georg's chaplain was Johannes Cochläus (1479–1552). Like many other adversaries of Luther, he had originally held a positive opinion of the reformer. But as of Luther's treatises of 1520, he became his decided opponent. With more than two hundred writings he sought to serve his Church over a thirty-year span in a tireless and selfless literary activity. He was not a theologian and never became one of any significance. He was too much the humanist to become a writer for the people, and his works were burdened with an excess of scholarship. Devoid of a sense of humor and thus all the more fierce in his wrath, he proved to the "many-headed Luther" his real and alleged contradictions. His *Commentaria de actis et scriptis Martini Lutheri* (Mainz 1549) had a powerful effect later on. As the first extensive biography of Luther, this work yielded important source material for the history of the Reformation, but it also carried a great deal of mud, which the malicious polemics on both sides had stirred up. The distortions presented in Cochläus' commentary on Luther determined the Catholic image of Luther into the twentieth century.

Johann Fabri (1478–1541) and Friedrich Nausea (c. 1490–1552) were able to work effectively against the Reformation and for the inner reform of the Church not only as authors but directly as successive bishops of Vienna. Fabri, humanist and jurist, came into the open against Luther only in 1521 as vicar general of Constance. In 1522 appeared his *Opus,* composed according to the scholastic method, a "work against some new doctrines of Martin Luther, which in every way contradict Christian teaching." In 1524 a Cologne Dominican published it under the new title, *Malleus in haeresim Lutheranam.* As coadjutor of Wiener Neustadt (from 1524), Fabri composed a number of works in German, the most important being the *Summarium* (1526), which had far more popular appeal. In picturesque language and with abundant references to Scripture he defended the teaching of the Church and pointed out the pernicious results of the Lutheran innovation, which had become especially clear in the Peasants' War. In the *Christliche underrichtung*

(1528) he examined the "report of the visitors," and showed how much Luther had "improved." Had he always taught in that manner, said Fabri, this great misfortune would not have fallen on Germany and the Church. This work shows that the Catholic controversialists still did not draw the full consequences from the break and in a sense were still running after their opponent instead of engaging in positive propaganda for their own cause. This is also the case when Fabri proves how Luther was actually dissenting from Hus and other heretics to whom he appealed, and even contradicted himself. As Bishop of Vienna (from 1530), Fabri published a series of sermons and writings in defense of the Mass and the priesthood, and *über den Glauben und die guten Werke.* They were worthwhile works but they give little indication of the heated atmosphere of the age.

Fabri's coadjutor and successor, Friedrich Nausea, had been cathedral preacher and writer at Mainz since 1526. His *Centuriae IV homiliarum* appeared in Cologne in 1532. Following his summons to Vienna by Ferdinand I, he opposed the spread of the Reformation in sermons and in his writings. In his works on parish visitations (*Pastoralium inquisitionum elenchi tres,* 1547), and on the education of candidates for the priesthood (*Isagogicon de Clericis ordinandis,* 1548), and in his *Catechismus catholicus* (1543), he left behind him polemics and can be regarded as a representative of the incipient inner reform of the Church.

Berthold Pürstinger of Chiemsee (1465–1543) had already resigned his episcopal see when in 1528 he wrote his *Tewtsche Theologey,* based on Scripture and closely related to Saint Thomas. It is considered the first work in German on dogmatic theology. His treatises on the Eucharist, the *Tewtsche Rational über das Ambt heiliger Mess* and the *Keligpuechl,* were directly concerned with defense against the Reformation. Whether he wrote the pamphlet *Onus ecclesiae* (1519; printed in 1524 and 1531) is disputed. It came out against the abuses of the age and called for Church reform in head and members.

Cologne and Louvain were the first universities to take a stand against Luther. On 7 November 1519 Louvain issued a *Condemnatio doctrinalis librorum Lutheri.* In 1521 the Louvain professor Jakob Latomus (c. 1475–1544), published *Articulorum doctrinae fratris Martini Lutheri... damnatio* against Luther. Luther later paid him the compliment that he was the "most distinguished writer against me." Later works dealt with auricular confession (1525), the papal primacy (1526), and faith, good works, and religious vows (1530).

The Louvain professor and Dominican friar Eustachius van Zichem (d. 1538) brought out in 1521 a "brief refutation of Martin Luther's errors" and in 1523 a defense of the sacraments and of the ecclesiastical hierarchy. Johannes Driedo (c. 1480–1535), the third among the professors at Louvain, was one of the few contemporary controversialists who knew how to take up new questions and to seek new solutions without rancor and in loyalty to tradition. Hence his writings were still influential at Trent and in the grace controversy. In *De ecclesiasticis scripturis et dogmatibus libri IV* (1533) he discussed the methods and sources of theology; in *De captivitate et redemptione humani generis* (1534), the original state and the redemption of man. Important also for theological anthropology are his *über die Vereinbarkeit von freiem Willen und Predestination* (1537), *über Gnade und freien Willen* (1537), and *über die christliche Freiheit* (1546). These three were published posthumously, the last only in the complete edition prepared by

Ruard Tapper (1487–1559) in 1546. Tapper and his colleague at Louvain, Josse Ravesteyn (1506–70), extend into the era of the Council of Trent. In 1544 Louvain University committed its professors to fifty-nine theses. In them it provided, in a carefully thought-out outline of the controverted teachings, a summary of the work thus far accomplished and essentially anticipated the constructing of the Tridentine decrees.

From the University of Louvain came the influential controversialist Albert Pigge (1490–1542). With the doctrine of papal infallibility, expounded in *Hierarchiae ecclesiasticae assertio* (1538), he exerted influence up to modern times. The Council of Trent adopted his views on tradition but not those on justification. His writings *über den freien Willen des Menschen* (1541) and on original sin in *Controversiarum praecipuarum... explicatio* (1541) were even put on the Index at Lisbon in 1624. In England the first to take up the pen in reply to Luther's *De captivitate Babylonica* was King Henry VIII himself, probably assisted by Thomas More (1478–1535). For, in the face of such heresies, no one could "refrain from opposing them with all one's diligence and resources." In content and method his *Assertio septem sacramentorum* (1521) excelled the other early works of controversy. In 1522 it came out in two German translations, by H. Emser and T. Murner. Luther reacted angrily in his *Antwort deutsch auf König Heinrichs Buch* (1522). Ironically the royal "defender of the faith" had his own collaborators Thomas More and Bishop John Fisher (1469–1535) executed for their opposition to his headship of the Church in 1535. As humanists, both of them had profitably used the new interest in the Bible and the Fathers for the defense of the Church.

Zealous literary adversaries of Luther were found in the several Orders, especially in the ranks of the Dominicans and the Franciscans. The Dominicans had managed the trial against Luther and supplied the first writers against him. Silvester Prierias (1456–1523) was concerned, as *Magister sacri palatii* and censor, with Luther's indulgence theses and "quickly strode into the arena" with his *Dialogus* of June 1518. His polemic was frivolous and clumsy. He showed little readiness to take up Luther's concern but clearly grasped and stressed that the Church, in both its ecclesiastical and papal authority, was in question. To Luther's *Responsio* Prierias gave a preliminary answer in his *Replica.* Then, in the *Epitoma responsionis ad Lutherum* (1519) he announced a detailed discussion with Luther on the authority of the pope and the power of faith indulgences. It appeared at Rome in 1520 under the title *Errata et argumenta Martini Lutheri recitata, detecta, repulsa....* In it he expounded the monarchical constitution of the Church in a quite one-sided fashion. As vicar of Christ, the pope has not only the highest but the only ordinary power. He is *virtualiter* the Catholic Church and the source of all jurisdiction. A council has power only as assigned to it by the pope. This chief polemic of Prierias gained little notice and Luther deigned it as unworthy of an answer.

Cardinal Thomas de Vio (1469–1534), commonly known as Cajetan, the most important theologian of the day, had already composed a treatise on indulgences (*De indulgentiis* of 8 December 1517) before obtaining a copy of Luther's theses and meeting him in person at Augsburg. In that city he wrote a number of essays on indulgences and penance, which he completed, after his return to Rome, with *De indulgentia plenaria concessa defunctis* of 20 November 1519. In this he strove for an objective solution to the difficulties, which he did not deny, and just as he denounced Luther's errors, so also did he blame the indulgence preachers, who talked too big and gave out their private opinions as the Church's teaching. On the cardinal point of the controversy Cajetan in 1521 wrote *De divina institutione Pontificatus Romani* in reply to Luther's *Resolutio... de potestate Papae.* He did not, however, mention his adversary by name nor did he lapse into a violently polemical tone so common at the time. His *opuscula* on the Eucharist (*De coena Domini,* 1525; *De sacrificio Missae,* 1531; *De communione,* 1531) stand out among the contemporary writings of others. Not only does he assert the unity of the Mass and the sacrifice of the cross; he is also able to establish it theologically. Christ is present "immolatitio modo," in the manner of sacrifice. The sacrifice is not repeated, but the unique sacrifice, offered once, continues to endure, and in repeated celebrations the everlasting sacrifice is rendered present. Hence, in the Mass Christ is the real priest and intrinsically the Mass is of infinite value. The faith and devotion of the participants are decisive for its fruitfulness. Here was an answer to Luther's objections to the Mass. But it was not heard in Germany and had little effect even on the Council of Trent.

In *De fide et operibus* (1532) Cajetan took up again the chief controversial point discussed with Luther as Augsburg in 1518 — the certainty of faith versus reflexive faith. He attacked the confusing of a justifying faith with a subjective *credulitas;* he fought against the idea that it is supposedly not enough to receive the Sacrament with confidence in the merits of Christ, but rather that a person has to be certain of being justified, and that this certainty, only in a sense, establishes justification.

Exceptionally noisy and pugnacious was Ambrosius Catharinus (c. 1484–1553), who assailed not only Luther but even his own confreres, Cajetan, Soto, and Spina. This "third of the Thomists," as Luther styled him, composed in 1520, at the command of his superiors, the comprehensive *Apologia pro veritate catholicae et apostolicae fidei* against Luther, and followed it up with the *Excusatio disputationis contra Martinum* even before being in possession of the reformer's vexed reply. The *Apologia* is basically concerned with Luther's *Resolutio Lutheriana... de potestate Papae* and, apart from the authority of the Church and the papal primacy, treats in some detail only penance and purgatory. The author's line of argument does not substantially go beyond Prierias; it is merely much more eloquent and clever, without being any less biting and polemical. He tried to establish that Luther was a heretic. After the *Excusatio* Ambrosius Catharinus took no further part in the dispute over faith until 1540, when his *Speculum haereticorum* appeared. In this he tried to unmask the true aims of the reformers, show the evil results of their doctrines, and call for the extirpation of the heresy.

In Germany the Dominican Jakob van Hoogstraeten (1460–1527) came forward against Luther. Ever since the Reuchlin controversy public opinion had been strongly prejudiced against him. When in the dedicatory epistle to his *Zerstörung der Kabala* in April 1519 he suggested that Leo X take energetic action against the disturbers of the Christian faith, without at all mentioning Luther, the latter reacted sharply against the "grand inquisitor" who lusted after the blood of his brothers but was himself the worst heretic. Hoogstraeten did not go in for cheap polemics. He traced Luther's sources and tried to refute him by Augustine in *Cum Divo Augustino colloquia contra enormes et perversos Lutheri errores* (1521–1522). In this he noted the doctrine of original sin and concupiscence as the stumbling block on which Luther had been shattered. Later works of controversy dealt with the veneration of saints, faith and works, and the liberty of the Christian.

As court preacher at Dessau, the Dominican Johannes Mensing (d. c. 1541) published three treatises on the Mass in 1526, two sermons on the Catholic priesthood in 1527, and in 1529 an essay on the Blessed Sacrament, in particular on the doctrine of concomitance. He also produced an essay on the authority of the Church. He tried to show that the sacrifice of the cross was not confined to the restrictions of history. The very sacrifices of the Old Covenant obtained their efficacy from the Cross and in them Christ was already sacrificed. In the New Covenant the sacrifice on the cross remains present before the heavenly Father and hence the priesthood of Christ is eternal. But Mensing does not explicitly draw the obvious conclusion — that the Mass is the representation before the heavenly Father of the ever present sacrifice of the cross. His *Antapologie* (1533–35) is the most important reply to the *Confessio Augustana* and its defense of the teaching of justification.

Johannes Faber (c. 1470–1530), long-time prior at Augsburg, was a close friend of Erasmus and, like him, opposed any strong action against Luther. He expressed this view in the brief *Iudicium in causa Lutheri* (1527) and even more clearly in a "Ratschlag," which appeared anonymously at Cologne at the end of 1520 and was attributed to Erasmus. It was only after the Diet of Worms of 1521 that Faber changed his mind and came out determinedly against the innovation.

More effective as a writer was Johann Fabri (1504–58), also active at Augsburg. But his works, including a *Katechismus* (1551), *Christlichkatholischer Unterricht* (1556), and a much read work on the Mass (1555), belong to the later phase of the controversy in connection with the Council of Trent. The same holds true of the work of Ambrosius Pelagus (1493–1561), except for his treatises of 1528–1529 on the Mass, directed against Oecolampadius.

The Dominican Johannes Dietenberger (c. 1475–1537) was recruited by Johannes Cochläus for the literary war against Luther. As prior at Frankfurt and Koblenz and as professor at Mainz, he composed some twenty polemical works based on the Bible. In 1534 he published a German Bible, which took over extensive parts of Emser's New Testament. For the Old Testament he used the Vulgate as basis. He tried to avoid the linguistic harshness of the pre-Luther translations and had frequent, if critical, recourse to Luther's Bible. His was the most popular Catholic translation of the Bible into German. It saw fifty-eight editions of the complete Bible, and in addition fourteen of the New Testament and twenty of the Psalter alone. In his last work, the German catechism of 1537, polemics disappear and Dietenberger's popular and deeply religious style attained its full expression.

The controversialist writings of the Franciscans were in general more appealing to the people than the often overly scholastic counterparts composed by Dominicans. Augustin von Alveldt (c. 1480–after 1532), lecturer in theology at Leipzig, published in 1520 eight other works in addition to his *Super apostolica sede* to which Luther reacted violently with his *Von dem Papsttum zu Rom wider den hochberühmten Romanisten zu Leipzig.*

"Of all Luther's literary opponents, without any question the most quick-witted, the cleverest, and the most popular" was the Strasbourg Franciscan Thomas Murner (1475–1537). He was already one of the favorite and most influential authors when he took up his pen against the religious novelties. Among his four works of 1520 against Luther, most deserving of mention is his *Christliche und brüderliche Ermahnung.* It defends the Mass against the *Sermon von dem Neuen Testament.* Genuinely fraternal in tone, it is both popular and deeply religious. Calumnies such as *Murnarr* and defamations later provoked Murner to give in further to his bent for satire and polemics. His satirical epic, *Vom Lutherischen Narren* (1522), is one of the very few Catholic writings of these years which to some extent equalled Luther in journalistic skill and even in poetic vigor. Expelled from Strasbourg, Murner went in 1525 to Lucerne. He took part in the Baden Disputation of 1526 and wrote against the Swiss reformers, among other works, *Kirchendieb und Ketzerkalender* (1527) and *Die gots heylige mess* (1528).

With his *Scrutinium divinae Scripturae* Kaspar Schalzgeyer (1463–1527), provincial of the South German Franciscan Observants, began a productive career in controversial theology that was to yield twenty-nine works in print and sixteen in manuscript. In a truly irenic spirit he tried to write "pro conciliatione dissidentium dogmatum" and did not become bogged down in mere polemics. Through arguments based on Scripture he approached the reformers on the plane of method. Better than anyone else he was able to present the Catholic teaching, especially on the Church and the Mass, in a way that not only refuted the error of the reformers but at the same time pointed out what was legitimate in their concern in the whole context of truth. Unfortunately, his voice could not make itself heard due to the noisy polemics and his premature death.

His confrere at Marburg, Nikolas (Ferber) Herborn (c. 1480–1535), had vainly fought in several polemics against the Reformation that was being carried out by the ex-Franciscan Francis Lambert of Avignon, acting on the orders of Philip of Hesse. Having fled to Cologne in 1527, Herborn wrote a manual against contemporary errors, dealing in popular form with almost all the truths of faith and demonstrating them from Scripture. Without attacking specific persons or books, he called attention to the points in controversy, extolled the Church, and depicted the sad consequences of the revolt.

In the effort to prove one's adversary wrong and to triumph over him instead of winning him back lay the danger of controversial theology. This biased polemical attitude was very plainly characterized by the Dutchman, Johann van Kampen, when in 1536 he wrote from Rome that the "four evangelists" — Fabri, Eck, Cochläus, and Nausea — would, he was convinced, "rather that three new Luthers should arise than that the one Luther should be converted." The writer had been summoned to the service of Cardinal Contarini in Rome. Contarini, with Johannes Gropper, Julius Pflug, Michael Helding, Georg Witzel, and others, belonged to a group of theologians who displayed understanding for the religious aims of the Reformation and at first worked for both unity and reform. As so-called theologians of mediation, they were, of course, often exposed to the charge of making compromises at the expense of the truth.

Gasparo Contarini (1483–1542), in his *Confutatio articulorum seu quaestionum Lutheranorum,* a refutation of the main points in the *Confessio Augustana,* complains that the Christians of his day, instead of confessing the faith and, with it, preserving love and humility, were dazzled by disputatiousness and were concerned with nothing but "defending their own viewpoint and refuting that of the opponent." He himself took pains to be open-minded in regard to his opponent's motives and to do justice to him. Even before his elevation to the purple while still a layman in 1535, he defended the divine right of the papacy in *De potestate Pontificis.* In a comprehensive treatise on the Sacraments he refers to the reform position merely in brief remarks. At the Religious Colloquy of Regensburg both sides accepted the doctrine of twofold justice — the one inherent in us and imperfect; the other the justice of Christ imputed to us. The cardinal explained this in more detail in the *Epistola de iustificatione* of 25 May 1541. But this concept was rejected in a consistory at Rome on 27 May 1541 and later at Trent.

As a student of Albert Pigge (Pighius), Johann Gropper (1503–1559) of Cologne had already maintained the doctrine of a twofold justice in 1538 in his *Enchiridion Christianae Institutionis* and he later worked out the subject in full detail in his *Antididagma* (1544). If this "protagonist of the ancient faith," who preserved Cologne and hence Northwest Germany for the Church, could, like Contarini, be suspected of heresy, and if his *Enchiridion* was consigned to the Index under Clement VIII, then it is easy to see what external and inner danger those persons were courting who did not yet regard the doctrinal split as irreconcilable.

Julius Pflug (1499–1564) likewise fell under the reproach of doctrinal unreliability in a letter from Johannes Eck to Contarini. As Bishop of Naumburg-Zeitz, he was already forced by circumstances, instead of attacking the reformers, to devote himself rather to the instruction of his poorly educated faithful and to gaining back Protestants who had for the most part been only superficially won to the new faith. Especially in *his Institutio Christiani Hominis* (1562), a "catechism in the service of unity of faith," Pflug displays himself as a pastor and a herald of the Gospel far more than as an apologist and controversialist.

Also primarily a preaching theologian was Michael Helding (1506–1561), Auxiliary Bishop of Mainz. Concern for catechetical instruction is the dominant motive in his series of sermons on several books of the Bible and in his sermons on the Mass (1548). His catechetical sermons, delivered in the Mainz cathedral from 1542 to 1544, were printed as *Catechismus, das ist Christliche Underweissung,* in 1551 and later, as a manual for parish priests.

Thus, during the years up to 1540, occurred the development of the literature of controversy from polemics to a positive presentation of the faith, from the *enchiridion,* a brief apologetically oriented compendium of dogma, expanding into a proclamation of the faith in great homiletic works, such as those of Eck (1530–39), Nausea (1542), and Hoffmeister (1547), and into catechisms.

The first German catechism before that of Dietenberger was composed in 1535 by Georg Witzel (1501–73). He had studied for a short time at Wittenberg under Luther and Melanchthon, but, nevertheless, in 1520 he was ordained a priest. In 1523 he married without a dispensation and became a Protestant. According to his own account he was led to this by the allurement of the new, the sad condition of the Church, but especially by "the great hope that everything might become much more Christian." It was precisely on this last point that he was disillusioned. Soon "much in the evangelical Church, above all in regard to morals, began to offend him. In addition, an intensive study of the Church Fathers assured him that the Reformation was not in harmony with the apostolic tradition. He resigned as a pastor in 1531 and in his *Apologie* of 1533 publicly abandoned Luther. Therefore he and his family led an insecure life filled with privations, persecuted by Protestants and often treated with distrust by Catholics. But Witzel labored indefatigably for the reform and unity of the Church at religious conferences and at diets, with memoranda for the Emperors Ferdinand I and Maximilian II, the "Via regia," and in almost 150 writings.

His literary work served primarily for preaching, for the liturgy, and for catechetical instruction. Numerous and frequently printed were his lectures and sermons. His works on the history of the Church and of the liturgy sought to point out the usages of the ancient Church (*Typus ecclesiae,* 1540; Parts I–V, 1559) or aimed to defend the Mass (*Von der hl. Eucharisty odder Mess,* 1534 and later) and the liturgy (*Defensio Ecclesiasticae Liturgiae,* 1564, and other works). By means of translations of the missal, ritual, and breviary he tried to arouse an understanding of the liturgy and to make possible an active participation by the laity. He warmly advocated German hymns. He probably worked on the *New Gesangbüchlein* (1537) of Michael Vehe (d. 1539), but he himself also published German hymnals (*Odae Christianae,* 1541). His *Catechismus Ecclesiae* (1535 and later) was the first in the German language and noteworthy as the first to provide a summary of biblical history. It was followed by other catechisms and catechetical works. Witzel's attempts at mediation were Erasmian in spirit. By means of a serious moral reform and with the aid of a few concessions in dogmatically unimportant points, such as the lay chalice and clerical marriage, he hoped to overcome the religious split on the basis of the doctrine of the Fathers. Witzel's efforts were destined to have no penetrating success, and his rich literary legacy to have only a slight effect.

History followed other paths. It agreed that the Bishop of Ermland and papal legate at Trent, Cardinal Stanislaus Hosius (1504–1579), was right when he prevented the invitation of Witzel to Trent because of the latter's readiness to make concessions. Hosius accepted the separation in faith as a melancholy fact and clearly pinpointed the doctrinal differences By putting decisive emphasis on the divine authority of the Church, indivisible in essence, and on the truth entrusted to her and by pointing at the split within Protestantism he sought closely to tie the wavering to the Church and hoped in time to win back the schismatics. His *Confessio catholicae fidei* (15520–53) brought to a close the Catholic handbook literature. During its author's lifetime it saw thirty editions and translations.

Section Three

The Reform in the German Principalities

CHAPTER 78

The Confessional Leagues—The Imperial Diets of Nürnberg (1524) and Speyer (1526)

The reform movement was able to grow unhindered because the chief representatives of the old order, Emperor and Pope, were consuming their energies in war against each other. The Pope feared Habsburg power in Lombardy and Naples and supported France against the Emperor. The French King conspired with the Turks and urged them, after the fall of Belgrade, to invade Hungary, which, through the marriage of Ferdinand of Austria with Queen Anna, had become the outpost of Habsburg power. Hence Charles V was prevented from energetically tackling the internal problems of Germany. He and his brother Ferdinand, who had remained in the Empire, were not able to take measures against princes whose help they needed in the war against the Turks. Neither the Imperial Governing Council nor the Imperial Diets were able or even willing to implement the Edict of Worms. The Third Diet of Nürnberg, opening in January 1524, continued the policy of procrastination, declaring that the estates should, "as far as possible," act in accordance with the Edict of Worms. At the same time there was a new demand for a free general council on German territory, which should carry out Church reform and clarify the questions in dispute, "so that the good would not be suppressed with the evil and it would finally be discussed how each should behave in the future." It was, however, fully understood that the summoning of the council would take time and that any delay would give further aid to the innovations. This induced especially the staunchly Catholic Bavarian Dukes to demand "a synod of the German nation."

This idea of a national council for settling the religious question and redressing the grievances pointed out in the *gravamina* already had been broached in November 1523 at a conference in Salzburg of the representatives of the bishops of the Salzburg province. The papal legate Lorenzo Campeggio saw in a national council the danger of the apostasy of the entire nation and determinedly rejected it. Just the same, the estates clung to their project and decided that, until the convoking of the general council, an assembly of the German nation should be held. It was to meet at Speyer on Martinmas on 11 November. In Rome there was dismay over the attempt to reach a national ecclesiastical solution and a protest was lodged with the Emperor, who on 15 July forbade the Speyer assembly. A national council had about as little place in the universalism of Charles V as it had in the views of the Pope, and through the imperial veto it was temporarily shelved as a means of solving the Church problem.

But at the diet the legate Campeggio had realized that no implementation of the Edict of Worms could be expected from the Empire and that princes as strongly anti-Lutheran as the Bavarian Dukes had demanded a German ecclesiastical assembly in order to make possible a quick and thorough improvement of Church conditions. He endeavored to do justice to this concern by means of provincial councils or of similar particular boards appointed by the Church. He urged the founding of a league of the South German princes and the Rhenish bishops. In March–April 1524 he had requested permission from Clement VII for a special reform conference. And so on 8 May invitations were issued by the legate and the Archduke Ferdinand to the Bavarian Dukes Wilhelm and Ludwig and to twelve bishops of the Austrian and Bavarian territories to meet at Regensburg in order to discuss an anti-Lutheran front. In addition, the reform of the Church and the mutual grievances of the spiritual and the secular princes were to be the themes of the conference.

In the complaints the secular lords demanded that steps be taken not only in the struggle against Lutheranism but also that the reform and inner renewal of the Church should be seriously faced. The bishops, on the other hand, called for the full restoration of their rights of immunity and of jurisdiction. The princes, especially the Bavarian Dukes, sought to exercise, by means of prelates belonging to their territories, criminal justice against heretical or otherwise culpable clerics in the territories of those bishops who failed to take action. The bishops, seeing in this a threat to their jurisdiction, demanded its complete restoration as a sine qua non of effective reform work.

The Regensburg Conference lasted from 27 June to 7 July. The negotiations were dominated by the secular princes, Archduke Ferdinand and the Bavarian Dukes. The bishops and their proxies had no other choice than to accept the decision of the Big Two and to declare their approval. The resulting resentments naturally impaired the effectiveness of the conference results. These were contained in two decrees. In the Regensburg Agreement of 6 July 1524, the implementation of the Edict of Worms was called for. Furthermore, attention was to be devoted to the preaching of the true Gospel by certified preachers and to the reform of the clergy. As to the celebration of Mass, the administration of the sacraments, and the carrying out of other usages, persons should "adhere to what has laudably come down to us from the holy Fathers and our ancestors." Hence stern measures were to be taken against the reception of the Eucharist without previous confession and against disregard of the laws of abstinence and fasting. Runaway religious and those living in concubinage were to be punished, and the circulation of heretical books was to be stopped by censorship and authorization to print, to be granted expressly. Study at Wittenberg was to be forbidden, and students were to be recalled from there within three months under the threat of confiscation of their benefices. Whoever had studied there should not be admitted to any offices or benefices. Penalties and banishments decreed in one territory should be enforced also in all others. In the event of uprisings the parties would assist one another. These regulations were concerned mainly with measures against Lutheranism, while the Regensburg Reform Order of 7 July 1524, proposed by Campeggio and issued by him, dealt especially with eliminating abuses within the Church and improving the conduct of priests. "If the Regensburg formula had been given effect throughout Germany, as had been planned, the term 'reformation' would no longer have stood for something exclusively Lutheran and a national council would have been superfluous" (H. Jedin).

But even the South German bishops represented at the conference were, from indolence and from concern about their jurisdiction, not overly inclined to put the Regensburg Reform Order into effect. It was, therefore, all the more difficult to move to action other bishops who had not been participants in it. Hence Campeggio's effort to make the Reform Order binding on the entire German Church by means of a decree was a failure, for the Rhenish ecclesiastical princes would not comply with an enactment in which they had not participated. Thus any decisive effectiveness was denied the Regensburg Conference, since one can speak of a league only in a very limited sense. Nevertheless, here the first official step toward Church reform was taken, which served also as the preliminary to forming confessional alliances.

In the succeeding year, on 19 July 1525, a union of princes of North Germany was established at Dessau, corresponding to the Regensburg Union. Influenced by the Peasants' War and convinced that its source was the new preaching, the Electors Joachim I of Brandenburg and Albrecht of Mainz and the Dukes Georg of Saxony and Eric I and Heinz II of Braunschweig-Wolfenbüttel formed an agreement, the League of Dessau, for resisting any peasant risings and for exterminating the Lutheran sect as the "root of this disturbance."

Philip of Hesse (1504–67) had put down the Peasants War, together with his father-in-law, Georg of Saxony. They had the same aim — to strengthen their territorial authority following the unrest. But their differing attitudes toward the reform movement would not allow them to pursue the aim together. Converted by Melanchthon, Philip of Hesse was in 1524 the first German prince to embrace the Reformation. Luther's own prince, Frederick the Wise, on the other hand, did not receive communion according to the Lutheran rite until he lay on his death bed. At his death on 5 May 1525 he was succeeded by his brother, Johann the Steadfast, who came forward more openly and more energetically for the Reformation. On 6 May 1526 Philip of Hesse formed with him the League of Gotha-Thorgau, which was joined at Magdeburg on 12 June by the Princes Ernst and Franz of Braunschweig-Lüneburg, Philip of Braunschweig-Grubenhagen, Heinz of Mecklenburg, Wolfgang of Anhalt, and Albrecht of Mansfeld, and by the city of Magdeburg. Albrecht of Prussia, who had transformed the territory of the Teutonic Order into a secular principality which he held as a fief of Poland, also allied himself with Johann of Saxony. Thus in Germany, not only did differing religious views confront each other; they now had as their counterparts political power alignments, thereby deepening the split and bringing in their wake the danger of religious wars.

After the Peace of Madrid (14 January 1526), Charles V felt he was free to arrange the religious affairs of Germany according to his own views and to enforce the Edict of Worms. Accordingly, he issued instructions to the Archduke Ferdinand for a diet which was summoned to Speyer for 1 May but did not actually begin its deliberations until 25 June 1526. Charles decreed that in matters of faith nothing should be changed; everything should continue as before "until the council should take up and establish a unanimous, Christian, constant, and needed reformation, regulation, and order." In view of the change that had meanwhile occurred in the political situation — on 22 May 1526 the Pope had formed the League of Cognac with the Emperor's enemies, while the Turks were increasing their pressure on Ferdinand's lands — such an edict could only cripple the not very energetic efforts for reform on the Catholic side.

The evangelical estates, notably the cities, showed a high degree of self-assurance. On the cloaks and in the lodgings of the Saxons and Hessians was to be seen the slogan, "Verbum Dei manet in aeternum." In the courtyards of their inns their preachers recruited publicly for the new faith. According to one report, it was evident to all the people that they no longer belonged to the old faith, "for they no longer went to Mass, they observed no fast days, they made no distinction of foods." Thus the ineffectiveness of the Edict of Worms became clear to everyone. A committee of secular and ecclesiastical princes, including Philip of Hesse, submitted an opinion relevant to the traditional ceremonies and the correcting of abuses. According to this, the seven Sacraments and the Mass should be retained; but fees and Masses offered for money alone were to be abolished. To make it possible for the people to participate in a lively faith and an inner union with the Passion of Christ, the texts of the liturgy should be recited in German and explained. The lay chalice should be tolerated until a general council could give a decision and it would be better to allow priests to marry than to watch how they cohabited with persons of evil reputation to the general scandal and with injury to their souls.

The Archduke Ferdinand rejected the suggestions, appealing to the imperial instructions, according to which no break was to be made with the tradition of the Church until the council. But under the pressure of the political situation and the necessity of obtaining help from the estates against the Turks, he gave his consent to the Recess of the Diet of 27 August, just two days before the defeat of the Hungarians by the Turks at Mohacs. According to this, no innovations were to be undertaken in matters of the Christian faith and religion, in conformity with the imperial instruction. It was felt that the best means of establishing peace and unity was to hold, within a year or eighteen months, a free general council or at least a German national council. *Apropos* of the Edict of Worms, the estates were in agreement that, until the holding of the council, they, with their subjects, "should live, rule, and act in such a way as each expects and trusts to be justifiable before God and the imperial majesty.

Such procrastinating decrees could not but have a catastrophic effect on the old faith, the slighter the prospects became for an early convoking of the council. In itself the Recess of the Diet contained no acknowledgment of territorial churches or of a *ius reformandi* and gave no pretext for the suppression of Catholic worship and the confiscation of Church property. But *de facto* it abetted such measures and in the course of time was quoted as their justification.

CHAPTER 79

Luther's Concept of the Church and Doctrine of the Two Kingdoms

In the mid-1520s the first German territorial princes and city governments adhered openly to the Reformation. Thereby the question was raised of what position they should occupy in the new ecclesiastical system and whether they should directly participate in constructing it. This construction proceeded slowly. Many of the old institutions had indeed ended, but Luther hesitated to create new ones. He long did without an order of worship and of Church organization, partly because he regarded all externals as indifferent and hence optional — for him rites and institutions were *adiaphora* — partly because he felt that, like himself, everyone had to find justifying faith by a free decision of conscience; and could be led to this only by the preaching of the Gospel. One must not encroach upon this personal decision of faith by means of external reforms, and no one must be induced or compelled to take part in ceremonies whose inner meaning he does not grasp or again he would be legally mistaken.

Concept of the Church

Luther did not offer a new concept of the Church in the sense of determining a system. In the struggle against the Church of his day, which, as a self-sufficient and even a tyrannical institution, in his view took the place of salvation based on faith in Christ's Gospel, and against the Anabaptists, who based the Gospel only on the subjectivity of man, Luther wanted to destroy what seemed to him to contradict the "true Church" and to stress what seemed hitherto dim. For him the Church was a self-evident precondition, without which the Christian would be nothing. Christ "wishes to hear the multitude, not me, not you, not a Pharisee running around by himself."

But for Luther the Church was not the external authority that threatened him with excommunication, not the hierarchical organization and sacral institution, but the community of the true believers in Christ. Luther did not esteem the word "church," because he incorrectly derived it from "Curia." He preferred "common of all Christians," "Christian community or assembly, "nation of believers," "community of the saints," that is, of the *fideles,* who in faith are certain of forgiveness for Christ's sake. But this community in faith is not to be understood in the sense of congregationalism. It is not produced by the voluntary amalgamation of believers, but "convened by the Holy Spirit in one faith." The Gospel transmitted in word and Sacrament constitutes the Church. She is "creatura verbi." Wherever the Gospel is proclaimed in accord with Scripture, the true Church (*ecclesia spiritualis*) lives in the external church (*ecclesia manifesta*) as the soul in the body.

Word and Sacrament are external signs for the existence of the true Church, which herself remains hidden.

> The signs whereby one can note externally where the same Church is in the world are baptism, Sacrament, and the Gospel. A sign is actually necessary, and we have it — baptism, bread, and, the most important of all, the Gospel. These three are Christians sign of recognition, voucher, and criterion. For, where you see baptism, bread, and Gospel, no matter where, no matter by whom directed, there you must not doubt is the Church.

In this regard the word has precedence over the Sacrament.

> The Gospel is, even before the bread and baptism, the real, surest, and most excellent sign of the Church. For only the Gospel and through the Gospel is the Church received, formed, nourished, attested, fashioned, fed, clothed, adorned, strengthened, armed, equipped, maintained. In brief, the entire life and being of the Church consists in the word of God. In this must one certainly recognize the Christian community: where the true Gospel is preached.

Luther's concern was not for the written but for the proclaimed word, and in that context about the word in the Church. But no special office is required for the proclamation, "for whatever comes forth from baptism may boast that it is already ordained priest, bishop, and pope." Every baptized person has the right and duty "of teaching and spreading" the word of God. Of course, "in order to avoid serious confusion in the people of God," not everyone should discharge this duty. Hence the community calls ministers, who act in its name. Then

> ordination is nothing other than . . . taking one out of the crowd — they all have the same power — and commanding him to carry out the same power for the others, just as when ten brothers, sons of the king and his heirs, selected one to administer the inheritance for them.

The promise in Matthew 16:18 refers "to no person but only to the Church, which is built in the Spirit on the rock, Christ, and not on the pope and not on the Roman Church." For the rock foundation of Christianity must be holy and sinless. Since one cannot know this in regard to Peter,

> Christ alone must necessarily be the rock, since he alone is sinless and will certainly so continue, and with him his holy Church in the Spirit. Just as now the rock [Christ] is sinless, invisible, and spiritual and tangible only in faith, so also of necessity is the Church sinless, invisible, and spiritual, and tangible only in faith.

In regard to its head and its true members the Church is invisible or, as Luther preferred to say, hidden. "The Church is hidden, the saints are unknown." She has no earthly head and Christ has no vicar, "but only Christ in heaven is her head here and alone rules." Of course, in carrying out the ruling of the Church in word and sacrament he makes use of human ministers as mere tubes. However, he alone knows his own, knows in whom his means of salvation are really effective and who really belongs to the Church. For us men there is only the standard of fraternal love. We have to consider every baptized person as a member of the Church of Christ who has not excluded himself. Thus there are many baptized unbelievers, who are outwardly "in the Church," but not "of the Church." The Church indeed lives in the flesh, but

> just as the Church is not without food and drink in this life, and yet, according to Paul, the kingdom of God does not consist in eating and drinking, so also the Church is not without place and body and yet body and place are not the Church nor do they pertain to her.
>
> All this is without importance and optional. Every place is suitable for the Christian, and no place is necessary to the Christian.

Therefore, Luther would like "to abolish or change nothing which cannot be abolished or changed with a clear scriptural warrant," and no one was more hateful to him than he who forcibly abolished voluntary and harmless ceremonies and made necessity out of freedom. On the other hand, he was confident that, with the preaching of the word of God, the necessary external form would grow "of itself."

Luther developed his teaching on the Church in the struggle against the hierarchically established papal Church. In connection with an abbot's right of patronage he defended the fundamental principle: "That a Christian assembly or community has the right and power to review all doctrine and to summon, install, and depose teachers." But this congregational Christianity soon proved to be impracticable. Luther denied the right of free election of its pastor to Karlstadt's congregation at Orlamünde. The Peasants' War and the disturbances produced in the community by the fanatics, together with the various types of disorder in morality and discipline, showed that nothing could be accomplished without ecclesiastical discipline, Church organization, and especially tribunals above the local level. The practice of the late medieval territorial Church, with extensive control of churches, monasteries, and hospitals by territorial lords or city governments, and the theory of the state of emergency as developed by William of Ockham suggested the entrusting of the external direction of the Church to the authority that had become Lutheran. Luther had impeded this development, however, by his teaching on the hidden Church and the competence assigned by him to the congregation, and especially by his rigorous distinction or even separation of the secular and the spiritual power.

Doctrine of the Two Kingdoms

Luther elaborated his teaching on the two governments in view of the steps taken by Catholic princes against the Reformation *Von weltlicher Oberkeit, wie weit man ihr Gehorsam schuldig sei,* 1523), in the struggle against the fanatics (*Wider die himmlischen Propheten,* 1525), and on the occasion of the Turkish war (*Vom Kriege wider die Türken,* 1529). This polemical situation resulted in exaggerations and one-sidedness which not even Luther could maintain to the end. This led in turn to contradictions, which make Luther's doctrine of the two kingdoms seem even today to be a "maze." The doctrine must be understood in relation to Luther's teaching on justification or his idea of law and Gospel. Just as the Christian is at the same time sinner and just, just as he is subject to the claim and jurisdiction of the law and at the same time has been acquitted by the Gospel, so too he belongs to the secular and to the spiritual government.

Luther felt obliged to stress the distinction between, or the separation of, the two governments on two counts. On the one side was the theocracy of the old Church, which, in his view, made the Gospel a law, that is, a political juridical order to be enforced by the sword; on the other was the anarchy of the fanatics, who denied the secular government in the name of the spiritual or understood evangelical freedom as freedom from any juridical order. The two governments must not be understood as the kingdom of God and the kingdom of the Devil. Instead, both come from God's love; they are two different ways in which God rules the world, even though in the secular government he acts only as *deus absconditus.* The secular government wields the sword. It is under the standard of power and the possibility of compulsion and has to maintain external order against the ceaseless anarchical threat from the world, against disruptive tendencies from within and without, the consequences of sin. Sin would have as its result the self-annihilation of creation, if God did not keep destructive forces in check by means of the state and other authorities. The Christian contends against even the Turks, not with weapons, but with God's word, penance, and prayer. He enters the Turkish war because "in his body and his property he is subject to the secular authority," which summons him to the struggle against the Turks. If he falls under Turkish rule, then he is subject to it as to his superior, just as to a papal government, "for the Pope... is much worse than the Turk." But under no circumstances must the Christian permit himself to be misused for war against the Gospel or for persecution of Christians. "The emperor is not the head of Christendom nor the shield of the Gospel and of the faith." As a secular master, he must wage war for the protection of his subjects.

The secular government is indeed from God, but it has no special relationship to salvation. It is not in the order of redemption but pertains to the order of preservation. The Christian does not actually need it, he is "extricated" by Christ. "The Christian, to the extent that he is really a Christian, is free from all laws, is subject to no law, within or without." Even Christ rules him "with the mere word." From this it follows that "if all the world were really Christian, no prince, king, lord, sword, or law would be necessary or useful." But "the world and the multitude is and continues to be non-Christian, even though all are baptized and are called Christians." Therefore, to prevent the triumph of evil, law and compulsory order are necessary. The secular government assures the area in which the proclamation of the word and the administration of the sacraments can take place. These are the tasks of the spiritual government, "by means of which men should become pious and just, so that by the same justice they may attain to eternal life." Whether the

Church of experience, *ecclesia large dicta* or *manifesta,* pertains to the secular government is not clear in Luther and is still controverted.

Because, though justified, he is still a sinner, the Christian is subject to the secular government, or to the "Kingdom on the left," to which, in addition to *politia, oeconomia* pertains, that is, marriage, parenthood, and vocation. However, he is subject to it voluntarily, and out of love, consents to the arrangements prevailing there, and in them serves his brother. In the Christian who takes an interest in the world, Christ's Kingdom is present in the world, even though the world's institutions, such as the state, do not thereby become Christian.

With regard to unjust authority there is, according to Luther, the right of non-violent active resistance by means of public instruction or rebuke, and then of passive resistance and flight; otherwise, the Christian must endure injustice for God's sake. With regard to his equals and his subjects, in accord with Matthew 5:39 he should not resist evil for himself, and so he does not need the secular power and law; but for others, for example, as prince, father, and soldier, he should "seek revenge, right, protection, and aid." Although one may wield the secular sword, one must not have thoughts of vengeance, "for where the heart is pure, there everything is made right and well." Thus was the Sermon on the Mount removed from the sphere of the heart and a dangerous distinction made between "Christian person" and "secular person" or between personal morality and official morality. Only too easily was support provided for a worldly-wise recognition of an emancipated political reality.

Church Government

If Christ alone governs his Church by faith, charity, and the other gifts of the Holy Spirit and she is therefore hidden, but if she is, on the other hand, no *civitas Platonica,* but has a visible side, the question arises: in what does this visible side find its order? Luther gave no systematic answer to this question. We have only scattered remarks of the reformer, occasioned by different polemical situations. It is certain that the constitution of the visible Church is not divine but is based on human regulations. But, is the external aspect of the Church to be attributed for this reason to the secular government, as P. Althaus maintains, or is it constructed according to proper ecclesiastical, even if human, law, which is itself based on principles arising from the spiritual government of Christ, as J. Heckel holds? Have the princes, as the secular authority, any competence in constructing the ecclesiastical system or are they only called to a special ministry as outstanding members of the Church?

As early as 1520 Luther had summoned the secular power, along with all the baptized, to the reform of the Church and of Christendom in his "Sermon von den guten Werken" and in *An den christlichen Adel deutscher Nation.* Because the spiritual authority had refused a thorough-going reform and in particular had opposed the convoking of a council, the secular power should carry out its function. It must protect its subjects from every iniquity, including the corruption of the spiritual power and its interference in the secular sphere. It must punish exploitation, brigandage, and adultery and, in so doing, not stop before Pope and bishops. As Christian authorities, "because now they are also fellow Christians, fellow priests, fellow ecclesiastics, fellow masters in all things," they should be concerned with the convoking of a council. In view of the refusal of the spiritual power, no one can do this "as well as the secular sword." The more Luther had to do with Protestant authorities, the more he stressed their obligation of crushing resistance to the Gospel and of forbidding the celebration of Mass, just as sacrilege and blasphemy were forbidden. "The secular power does not coerce belief but only defends it externally." It should not overcome heresy: "Bishops should do this,... not princes,... for heresy is something spiritual. If heresy exists, let it be overcome by God's word, as is proper." The secular authority must intervene if there is a breakdown of order and in cases of public blasphemy. "Our princes do not coerce to faith and the Gospel, but they prevent external outrages," wrote Luther to Spalatin on 11 November 1525. But "assault, theft, murder, and adultery are not so pernicious as this abomination of the papist Mass." Hence "authority is bound to prevent such a public blasphemy." If this is true of authority in general, then, in addition, the prince, as a "brother in Christ" or "as a Christian member," must cooperate in tasks within the Church, for example, in the appointing of a preacher.

Until 1525 Luther rarely called upon his territorial prince, though the latter was very well-disposed toward his affairs. The order of worship was not the prince's business. "What are we to ask of him? He can do no more than in secular matters." The renewal of the Church should be accomplished in the power of the word on the basis of the congregation. Luther expected the congregation to create an order at the proper time, that is, the institutions necessary for worship and for community life. Luther also thought of bishops, who governed several communities or were over several pastors. They too should be appointed by the congregations. However, such an ordination begins only in the regulated public ministry of word and sacrament. It is merely a ratification by the congregation. Of themselves, all have the same power, but for this very reason no one should on his own "call attention to himself, but rather he should let himself be summoned and brought forward in order that he may preach and teach in the place and at the command of the others." If the papal bishops are not ready for such a call to office, then the leading members of the congregation, should, as Luther wrote to the Bohemians, "lay hands on suitable persons in the presence of the congregation, confirm them, and recommend them to the people and the Church." Thus would they be "bishops, ministers, or shepherds."

The question is whether this call of individuals to the ministry of the word arises only from a practical need when the members of the congregation transfer their rights, so to speak, to an attorney, as Luther more or less consistently maintained in the 1520s, or whether ordination must follow for the sake of the commission and hence is of divine law, which is the view of the *Confessio Augustana* (XXVIII, 20–22), of the *Apologia* (XIII, 7–13), and probably also of Luther himself later.

Luther gave no further thought to other organs of the community. He agreed to ecclesiastical discipline and more than once inflicted excommunication as a shepherd of souls. But he created no office for this. Organizing was not his forte. He preferred to let things grow. Above all, for him a Church order must never become a "necessary law." For Christian congregations can be formed only by the preaching of the Gospel, through faith and charity, not through a reform of rites. It is absolutely unnecessary that the same order be maintained everywhere. No doubt it is good that the liturgy be celebrated uniformly in one lordship or one city with its environs. But a decreed Church order does not have the binding force of laws which oblige because of the obedience commanded by God toward superiors. For authorization to issue such laws is contained neither in the power of the keys nor in the pastoral office of bishops. Human order in the Church is thus not a juridical order in the strict sense, binding in conscience and to be enforced under compulsion.

But this freedom from law should be a freedom for order and for fraternal service; it "is the servant of love and of neighbor." Because of one's brothers, especially the weak, one should hold on to such "worldly and indifferent things" as ceremonies. Luther repeatedly designates the order of the visible Church as "worldly," even as "lying outside the Church." It was natural, therefore to regard the secular government as competent in this regard. The reformer himself was probably not of this view but of the opinion that the Church had to take herself in hand in the ordering of her worldly affairs. Therefore, he even referred to the territorial lords as "emergency bishops," who were to render "first aid" in acute distress. But the development went astray in the direction of even greater secular authority of the prince, although nothing further in the way of an emergency was to be noticed. In the twenty-three Nürnberg visitation articles which were accepted at Schwabach on 14 June 1528, we find:

> The Church is empowered only to choose ministers and to employ Christian excommunication and to arrange that the needy be provided with alms. . . . All other power belongs either to Christ in heaven or to the secular authority on earth.

Melanchthon decisively fostered the development into the princely Church government. He attributed to the authority the "custodia primae tabulae" and hence the supervision of the worship of God. To it belonged also the prohibition of false doctrine and ungodly worship. According to Melanchthon, knowledge of the true doctrine pertains to the whole Church, priests and laity, and, among the latter, especially to princes. They have to make the Gospel respected in public life and carry out the judgments of synods. Hence the secular power is "minister and executive organ of the Church." Its supervision of the ecclesiastical order no longer appears here as an emergency measure. The prince's special position and obligation in the Church result from his character as "foremost member" of the new visible Church. Just as in civil life princes lead the way for their subjects, so also in the service of the Church and of her reform:

> With their authority they are to support the true Church, remove blasphemous teachers, and install pious preachers.
>
> Before all others, the outstanding members of the Church, kings and princes, should aid and care for the Church, in order that errors may be eliminated and consciences may be rightly instructed.

Thus did he write in the treatise *De potestate papae,* which was accepted at Schmalkalden in 1537 as a statement of creed.

As members of the Church, then, the territorial lords took charge of the nomination to office, summoned synods, ordered visitations, and issued Church ordinances. Considering the strong tendency toward the territorial Church — already in existence since the late Middle Ages — it was natural soon to attribute to the secular authority as such what princes or the *pius magistratus* should do as a matter of first aid and out of love, because of their membership in the Church.

CHAPTER 80

The Completion of the Lutheran Community

Luther was disappointed in his hope that the constructing of congregations of real Christians would be effected solely by the preaching of the Gospel. His ideal proved to be impracticable. His expectations were ruined more than ever in the storm of the year 1525. His complaints about the "unspeakable scorn for the word and the dreadful ingratitude of men in regard to the benefit of the Gospel" became ever more serious and bitter. The preaching of justification by faith and of the freedom of the Christian had not produced the anticipated results in the moral life of his followers. On the contrary, according to Luther's own expressions, a moral deterioration and a disregard of the sacrament and of Sunday worship seem to have crept in. His sermons bitterly complained of these developments. Evangelical freedom was abused, and even preachers and pastors retained "of the Gospel only such a lazy, pernicious, shameful, carnal freedom."

Not only disillusionments of this sort, but also the spread of the Reformation and the related destruction of the old Church urgently called for new institutions. In the course of time and with the expansion of the area affected by the new doctrine it became obvious that the reconstruction must not be left to free development and that at least the broad mass were in need of the aid of ceremonies and could not manage without ecclesiastical discipline and the preaching of the law. At stake were the regulation of ecclesiastical property, the liturgy, visitations, and Church order.

Regulation of Church Property

The suppression of the monasteries, the secularization of Church property, and the cessation of foundation Masses and other ecclesiastical rites endowed with stipends caused a series of difficulties. The secular lords — high and low — and the cities were very much inclined to appropriate Church property. Whoever had obligations to monasteries and other spiritual institutions was happy to be freed of them so easily. Foundation Masses and stole fees disappeared, but the Church's ministers had to live as before, except that now they also had to support wife and children. Hardly any of those who benefitted by Church property were ready to assume the expenses of the liturgy, the support of the preachers, the care of the poor and the sick. According to Luther it was important to take care that "the goods of such vacant foundations did not disappear into *Rappuse* that is, did not become spoil for everybody, and that everyone did not struggle for something to snatch." Therefore, like Karlstadt's Church order for Wittenberg of 1521, Luther demanded that the property be gathered into a "common chest." According to the "Order of a Common Chest" for Leisnig (1523), for which Luther wrote the preface and which was regarded as a model for other congregations, all Church revenues should go into a common chest, from which should be drawn the expenditures for the clergy, sexton, and plant, for schools and teachers, and for the needy of every sort. Administration should be taken care of by a board of trustees, consisting of two nobles, two councilors, three townsmen and three peasants from the surrounding villages. All the townsmen and peasants should meet three times a year to receive a report and to pass resolutions. Luther had feared that few would follow his suggestion, because "avarice is a disobedient and unbelieving scoundrel." As a matter of fact, the order did not attain its goal because the city council was unwilling to turn over to the "chest" the foundations under its control, and the elector shrank from forcible intervention. Thus the "chest" lacked means for the intended purposes.

Luther complained vigorously and repeatedly over the congregations' lack of a spirit of sacrifice.

> Once upon a time we gave much money and property to the papists. But now that we should help the ministers of the Church and the Gospel with a few pennies, we have nothing. Where formerly 300 monks were supported, today not one preacher can find bread. It will come to this, that teachers, pastors, and preachers devote themselves to a craft and let the word go. Almost all congregations...want to call their pastors...and give nothing and support no one. Whoever wants to have the power and the right to call should be obliged and bound to support.

This situation called for a tribunal superior to the local congregations, and, since the Church had none, for regulation by the territorial prince. Since all the monasteries and foundations so Luther argued,

> fell into the hands [of the elector] as their supreme head, there also devolved upon him the duty and burden of ordering such things, since otherwise no one takes charge or can or should take charge of them. Because now such goods...are instituted for the divine service, it is only right that they should first of all serve for this.

The visitation of 1529 resulted in the elector's ratifying of the common chest for Leisnig. Later articles of visitation and Church orders adopted this institution, but its character as an autonomous ecclesiastical institution was long in jeopardy, in so far as the city councils sought to take over its administration or even to treat the chest as common property.

Liturgy

The liberty which Luther had allowed to the individual congregations and his dread of binding forms led to a rank growth and an ever greater fragmentation of liturgical forms. As late as 1524 Luther had rejected suggestions for the convoking of a council of his followers for the creation of a uniform liturgy. However, the events of 1525 — the impulses of the "mobsters" and the Peasants' War — convinced him of the necessity of establishing uniform ceremonies. Together with councilors and choir directors of the principality, he put together a "Mass for the Laity in the Vernacular." Thus finally, on 29 October 1525, a completely German Mass could be celebrated for the first time in the Wittenberg parish church. After it had been tested in practice, the "German Mass and Order of Divine Service" appeared in print at the beginning of 1526 and thus could be introduced elsewhere also.

However, according to Luther's preface, the German Mass was not to be the only form of the Evangelical liturgy in Wittenberg, but rather only one of three. Apart from those "who are already Christian" and need no order, because they have "their worship in spirit," Luther envisages the community, that is, "those who are so far becoming Christian or should become stronger," as divided into three groups. The first comprises the young: for them the Latin "Formula Missae" of 1523 should remain binding. The second are "the simple lay folk."

> Among these are many who do not yet believe or are not yet Christian; the greater number among them just stand there and gape... just as though we were celebrating the liturgy in a public square or field among Turks and pagans.

Here it is not at all a question of an ordered "gathering in which one can rule Christians according to the Gospel, but there is an open inducement to the faith and to Christianity."

The third group consists of those "who seriously with to be Christians and profess the Gospel with hand and mouth." For them a simple order is enough; "there is no need for much and long singing." They are a confessional community; they meet in one house expressly for prayer, scriptural reading, reception of the sacrament, and other Christian work. Whoever "does not behave as a Christian" is punished or excommunicated. Luther did not want to establish any order for this narrow circle, for as yet people for it were lacking. If this *elite* community had only been formed, "the orders and methods would soon have followed."

Accordingly, Luther also saw the possibility of finding a place for the circle of the resolute, the confessional Church, "in the common heap," in the people's Church. But in actuality this "Christian gathering" did not materialize and Luther remained content with the liturgy for the "people" who are not yet seized by the spirit of the Gospel and must still be led to the seriousness of justification by faith. But if there is question "for this reason of enlightening and leading the people," then an instruction in worship is inevitable. Accordingly, the Eucharistic Preface became an "exhortation" to the participants in the sacrament, the "Our Father" became an explication, the "Sanctus," an historical report. No longer was there a realization by the community that it was progressing "to the city of the living God to the heavenly Jerusalem, to countless hosts of angels." Rather, the community was instructed in regard to what "happened to Isaiah the Prophet."

Actually the German Mass followed the Roman. But the Roman psalmody was replaced by popular hymns. Most important of all, it was reduced from the viewpoint of the doctrine of justification or the rejection of sacrifice. The Roman Mass adopted by Luther was the private form of celebration, itself only a curtailed form. A creative liturgical achievement could hardly be expected in that period, with its deficient grasp of worship as a representation of salvation history, even from Luther himself, if we abstract from his linguistic power of expression. And so it is not to be wondered at that the German Mass, with its pedagogical tendency, was in some respects only a torso and left "parts of the old liturgy... side by side, quite unexpectedly,... as unconnected rubble" (F. Rendtorff)

Criticism from outside and his own new knowledge induced Luther to revise and make more rigid the baptismal liturgy, already published in 1523. It appeared in the autumn of 1526 under the title of *Das Taufbüchlein verdeutscht, aufs neue zugerichtet* and was widely circulated as a supplement to the small catechism of 1529. Because the pastors proved incapable on their own of preparing a nuptial rite corresponding to the reformed views, Luther composed a *Traubüchlein für die einfältigen Pfarrherren,* which appeared in April 1529 and was also added to the small catechism, which was published in book form soon after. In the remarks with which it was preceded Luther briefly explained his idea of marriage. Already in *De captivitate* 1520) he had refused to regard it as a Sacrament. Consequently, in the *Traubüchlein* it is concluded that, because "matrimony and the married state are a worldly matter, it in no way pertains to us priests and ministers to order or regulate them." However, "though it is a worldly state," it is still a "divine work and command," and so it is right to ask the blessing of the priest or bishop. Hence only prayers and blessing belong to the Church. Marriage itself is a civil act. If the Church officiates at marriage, she does so in the name of the secular authority. In conformity with Luther's *Traubüchlein,* the marriage ceremony took place outside the church, the proclamation of the word and blessing at the altar. This separation of the marriage ceremony, which took place at home or outside the church building, from the ecclesiastical celebration — in the pre-Reformation situation this was especially the nuptial Mass — was not unusual at that time. In the pre-Tridentine Church it was legitimate because the bride and bridegroom administered the sacrament to each other; to Luther, on the other hand, it was legitimate because marriage was not properly a religious act.

Completion of the Ecclesiastical Constitution

Matters did not end with the mere publishing of liturgical books and catechisms. A tribunal was needed to introduce them as an obligation and thereby, as with other disciplinary measures, to put an end to the anarchy in the ecclesiastical system.

In the absence of an ecclesiastical office beyond the local congregation, only the secular power was qualified for this.

The Recess of the Diet of Speyer of 1526 had left the execution of the Edit of Worms to the judgment of the territorial princes. Even though no *ius reformandi* was thereby given them, they claimed it in practice. To the extent that they inclined to the Reformation, they proceeded to enforce the uniform practice of religion in their territories, that is, to liquidate what was left of the Catholic organization and to set up or consolidate the new by the arranging and implementing of visitations.

Meanwhile, Luther had been forced to the recognition that the word alone did not suffice; human authority had to create at least the external preconditions and remove opposition.

Luther thereupon proposed an ecclesiastical visitation. It was started at the beginning of 1526 in a few areas by two officials and the priests Spalatin and Myconius, but soon came to a stop. Luther, however insisted. The visitation was resumed in the spring of 1527, this time with Melanchthon participating. On 16 June 1527 the elector issued an instruction for it. In this he prescribed the visitation as prince and had it conducted by officials and theologians, who had "power and command" from him. The visitation was concerned not only with Church property and the salary of the clergy and with public morality, but first of all with the true doctrine. No pastor should dare to teach, to preach, and to administer the sacraments except according to God's word, "as this has been accepted by us and ours at the time when God has done and given his grace." The elector intends, indeed, compels no one to the faith, but he will forestall "dangerous sedition" and tolerate no sectarianism or schism in his territory. Anyone who is unwilling to accept such a "Christian instruction" offered by the authority should sell all his property "and move out of our territory." Here there is no question that the elector is acting in spiritual matters differently from the way he acts as territorial prince. In other words, "with this instruction the territorial Church government was present" (K. Holl).

Melanchthon took part in the visitation especially as a theologian. Luther played no role, but the reports of the visitation were sent to him for his examination. Adequate instructions for the visitors were lacking and so the implementation of a uniform Church order was not realized.

For this reason Melanchthon worked out an order of visitation, to which Luther contributed a number of improvements. In September 1527 it was discussed by the visitors — to whose number Spalatin had been added — with recourse to Luther and Bugenhagen. Meanwhile, the visitations and a preliminary work of Melanchthon's that had appeared without his knowledge, the *Articuli de quibus egerunt per visitatores* (1527), had caused a stir, and "visitationis rumores" had spread. On the Catholic side it was thought that in the visitation a *rapprochement* with the doctrine and practice of the "old faith" could be established, while in the Protestant camp the Saalfeld pastor, Kaspar Aquila, accused Melanchthon of returning to "papism." In particular, the director of the school at Eisleben, Johannes Agricola, was the spokesman for those who felt that the Wittenberg theologians "were creeping back," that is, reverting to the old Church system. In his view an excessive scope was given to the preaching of the law at the expense of the freedom of the Gospel. Penance must begin, not with servile fear, but with faith and love for justice. Melanchthon, on the other hand, had concluded his *Articuli* with the sentence that the people would be lulled into security without the preaching of the law and that they imagined they had justice from faith, although "faith can exist only in those whose hearts have been made contrite by the law."

For this reason the elector again issued invitations to conferences on the order of visitation at Torgau on 25 November 1527. Here a compromise was discovered. "In order that adversaries might not be able to say that there had been a disavowal" of the doctrine thus far defended, there was added to the first chapter, "On the Doctrine," the following sentence: Nothing should be taught previous to faith, except that "penance follows from and according to faith." Besides the necessity of preaching the law was insisted on. It would be a curtailing of the Gospel to speak one-sidedly of the remission of sins but to say nothing or only little of penance. "Without penance, however, there would be no remission of sins" and it could not be understood. The result would be that people would think they had already obtained remission of their sins and hence they would be secure and without fear. This would be a greater error and a greater sin than ever before. For the sake of the "common, uneducated man such articles of faith should be left alone under the name of penance, commandment, prayer, fear, and so forth, for otherwise the common man could be in error in regard to the word 'faith' and raise useless questions." The frequent reference to the "common man" makes clear the danger of pedagogism or moralism in regard to the Gospel in the Lutheran national Church as it was then developing.

The printing of the "Instruction of the Visitors to the Pastors" was protracted till the end of March 1528. The text is mainly Melanchthon's. Luther wrote the preface, in which he stressed that it was the function of the bishop to be overseer and visitor and that he had "been glad to see it restored again, as something very badly needed." Where the bishops had failed, he said, it would have been natural that the reformers should have taken their place. "However," he reported, "because none of ours had been called to this or had any positive command," he had applied to the elector with the request that several qualified men should be called and appointed to this office. Luther made his request to the territorial prince, but not as a secular authority, which had "not been commanded to teach and to rule spiritually," but for the sake of the "office of charity, which is common and necessary to all Christians." It is the business of the secular authority to break malicious opposition, for it must "see to it that discord, mobs, and sedition not be stirred up among the subjects." With this distinction between what the elector was to do as authority and what he was to do "out of Christian charity" as a member of the Church, on the occasion of visitations, Luther was apparently seeking to maintain the autonomy of the Church. Hence the preface has "the meaning of a certain correcting or of a tacit protest" (K. Holl) against the elector's instruction of 1527 and the princely ecclesiastical government claimed by it. A protest, to be sure, which was ineffective.

In accord with the instruction of 1527, suitable pastors were named as "superintendents" to carry out the visitation. They were to exercise supervision over their fellow officials in a district, and these fellow officials could have recourse to them in difficult cases. Contrary to Luther's expectation, marriage cases especially soon turned out to be such. Pastors whose conduct, discipline, and teaching gave ground for objections and in regard to whom the admonitions of the superintendents were of no avail were, according to the "Instruction of the Visitors," to be reported to the magistrate for denunciation to the elector. There was no higher ecclesiastical office. If one could apply temporarily to the visitation commissions or to Luther, this was still no solution in the long run. And so there ensued the forming of consistories. In this matter also Electoral Saxony gave the example. The need for matrimonial courts provided the first impulse. In 1538, by order of the elector Johann Frederick, Justus Jonas elaborated an expert opinion, together with Bugenhagen, Melanchthon, and jurists, in 1538: "Der Theologen Bedenken von wegen der Konsistorien, so aufgerichtet werden sollen." When the discussions on the subject were protracted, the consistory was set up on an experimental basis and undertook operations at the beginning of 1539. A consistorial order was not drawn up until 1542.

If the superintendents can be regarded as holders of an ecclesiastical office, then the consistory took the place of the bishop, though in reality it was an institution of the territorial prince. He summoned it, nominated its members, determined its order of business, and in all things had the final decision. The consistory was composed of electoral advisers who were experts in law and of theologians. The theologians were often only of secondary importance and were only called upon from case to case. In the course of time the consistory became competent for the administering of ecclesiastical discipline and excommunication, for the total administration of the territorial Church, and for decisions in marriage cases and other ecclesiastical disputes, such as patronage and tithes. The princely ecclesiastical government found in this body its corresponding organ and its definitive establishment.

Schools and Religious Instruction

The destruction of the old ecclesiastical system also had involved schools and universities. "The first effects of the Reformation on the educational system were of a destructive character" (F. Paulsen). Church and school were too intimately connected, not merely in theory but also in actuality, for one to be able to destroy the structure of the former without also striking at the latter. Furthermore, teaching and scholarship needed quiet and peace, which were impossible in the heat of polemics and in the convulsions of the Peasants' War. And finally, there were circles like Karlstadt, which justified by the Bible a rejection of education and schools. All this led to a decay of the schools and a strong falling off in the number of students. In 1528 Erasmus complained to Pirckheimer: "Wherever Lutheran teaching prevails, there is the collapse of scholarship." For Luther, as for Melanchthon, teaching was basically secular in character; it was spiritual only in so far as it was in the service of the word. It was the duty and right of the secular power to set up and maintain the school system.

The treatise *An die Ratsherren aller Städte deutschen Lands, dass sie christliche Schulen aufrichten und halten sollen* (1524) had its origin in the fact that "everywhere schools have been allowed to disappear." It was a summons to the city government to establish Latin schools and not to excuse themselves with subterfuges such as: "If we are only able to teach the Bible and the word of God in German, this is sufficient for salvation." Luther regarded schools as necessary for service to the Gospel as well as to the world. Hence schools constituted a vital question for real Christianity. But the secular government also needed "good schools and scholars" and care had to be taken that "cultured and capable persons' should take an interest in the world.

Here the parents have the most pressing obligations, but this task goes beyond their strength. Nothing is to be expected from the princes. "And so, dear councillors, I want it to continue in your hands alone. You have the capacity for it, better than princes and lords.".

While Luther specified the several fields of instruction, he did not lay down a curriculum. Rather, this was Melanchthon's job. He had already cooperated in the establishing of the school at Eisleben in 1525. In the last section of the "Instruction of the Visitors" (1528) he submitted his ideas on the carrying out of educational instruction in more detail. In this he had in mind the modest circumstances in Saxony and hence he renounced the teaching of Greek and Hebrew from the outset. In fact, in the interests of concentration, "in order [not] to burden the poor children with so much variety," no German should be taught either. With Melanchthon and with the contemporary schools there was concern only for the Latin language. The primer was already Latin; German did not appear at all.

The school was to be organized in three stages. In the first the children learned to read and write; in the second, grammar; in the third, also prosody, dialectics, and rhetoric. One day, Saturday or Wednesday, was devoted to "Christian instruction." "To learn nothing but Scripture" was to be tolerated as little as "to learn nothing from Scripture." The Our Father, the Creed, the Ten Commandments, and a group of psalms should be learned and explained. From the New Testament, the Gospel according to Matthew should be "grammatically explained." Otherwise, at most the explanation of the Epistles to Timothy, of the First Epistle of John, and of Proverbs was envisaged for the older youths. Pedagogical considerations prevented the treating of other books of the Bible, "for it is not profitable to burden the young with difficult and sublime books," such as Isaiah, the Epistles to the Romans, and the Gospel according to John. Contemporary school regulations, such as those of Wittenberg of 1533, of Braunschweig and Hamburg of 1528, and of Schleswig-Holstein of 1542, show that the basic principles of the "Instruction of the Visitors" were established in Electoral Saxony and became models for other districts. New was the admitting of religious instruction into the school curriculum. But this was so only in the cities and even there not for a long time in all of them. Hence the religious education of youth could not be turned over to the visitors alone. Consequently, on Sunday afternoon, because then "the farmhands and young folk come to church... the Ten Commandments, the articles of faith, and the Our Father should be preached and explained in order." In this connection there should "also be sermons intentionally on the sacraments of baptism and of the altar." "For the sake of the children and of other simple and unlettered folks, [the texts should] be recited word for word."

The visitations had revealed a great ignorance in the congregations and among the preachers. Melanchthon encountered a pastor who did not even know the Ten Commandments. Suitable textbooks were urgently needed. Luther had already emphasized in the German Mass: "Now then, in God's name, what is needed first in the German liturgy is a thick, plain, simple, good catechism." Here he meant a catechism in the broad sense, oral instruction in the five chief points — commandments, faith, Lord's prayer, baptism, Lord's Supper. But no less imperative was a book in which this instruction should be set down for pastors and fathers of families, who should "present" the truth to their children and workers. Luther set to work to supply this urgent need.

Others before him had already shown an interest in this task. "Between 1522 and 1529 about thirty such efforts at composing a catechism had been published, some of which were printed in many editions" (J. M. Reu). In addition to Melanchthon and Bugenhagen, Johannes Brenz especially had compiled such a booklet for the religious instruction of the young at Schwäbisch Hall. From 1516 Luther had often delivered catechetical sermons. From this practical activity there came several explanations of the Ten Commandments and the Our Father which had a powerful impact. After the disturbances at Wittenberg the catechetical sermon became a fixed institution in the local parish church. As the substitute for Johannes Bugenhagen, Luther himself in 1528 once again delivered these series of sermons on the five principal points in three cycles during the Ember weeks in May, September, and December. Before the third he had taken part in the visitation, and his experiences in this connection determined him to compose a catechism. The catechetical sermons provided the material. It was to be a book "for the barbarous pagans," that is, for the common uneducated people. But it became too bulky, and so Luther seems to have decided, while he was still composing it, to write another quite brief catechism. This small catechism appeared early in 1529, at first, following the late medieval usage, on tablets which could be hung up in church, school, and home, so that the text could more easily be committed to memory. The large catechism was published in April 1529 as *Deutsch Katechismus Martin Luther.* Then on 26 May appeared *Der kleine Katechismus für die gemeine Pfarrherr und Predigen.* Whereas the large catechism presents the individual items in detail, in the form of a sermon or lecture, the small catechism is drawn up in the form of question and answer. Through it and through his hymns Luther became the great religious moulder of the people. His two catechisms acquired the status of norms quite early. In 1580 they were accepted into the *Book of Concord* and described in the "epitome" of the formula of concord as "the Bible of the laity," "in which everything is included which is dealt with in scattered parts of Scripture and must be known by a Christian as necessary for salvation."

CHAPTER 81

Clement VII and Charles V

Cardinal Giulio de Medici, a firm partisan of the Emperor and candidate of the imperial faction, emerged from the two-months-long conclave on 19 November 1523 as Clement VII, but as Pope he was soon to pursue entirely different paths. He declined to renew the defensive alliance concluded by Adrian VI: with the Emperor and soon established secret contacts with France. His mind was concerned solely with freeing the Papal State from its encirclement by the Habsburg world power which was ruling Naples and Milan. If his own resources did not suffice to expel all "barbarians" from Italy, then at least a political balance should be established by assisting King Francis I of France to gain Milan. In this way Clement VII intended also to profit the interests of his family and to assure the rule of the Medici in Florence. His ideas were first of all political, not, however, in the sense of a universal papacy but as the ruler of an Italian dynasty. But this was too weak an ambition to exert decisive weight in the conflict of the great powers. Furthermore, Clement VII did not possess the character and stability of a great politician. He was, it is true, intellectually alert and conscientious in carrying out his official duties and in regard to his life style he was an improvement over his thoughtless and prodigal cousin, Leo X. "To this were added a dreadful indecision, vacillation and timidity, so that amid endless negotiations and half-measures he let slip his best opportunities and ended by earning for himself from friend and foe alike a reputation for unreliability" (H. Jedin).

Vis-à-vis this Pope Emperor Charles V was a ruler who was filled with the notion of a universal emperor, on whose awareness it had been impressed in 1523 by his great political mentor and chancellor, Gattinara, in a memorandum: "Your affairs are those of the whole of Christendom and, in a sense, of the whole world."

Initially the Pope exerted himself for peace among the Christian powers, rendered urgent by the Turkish threat. But his intervention failed. After a series of defeats Francis I succeeded on 26 October 1524 in again acquiring Milan. Impressed by this success, the Pope on 12 December allowed himself to be won to an alliance with France and Venice which granted the French troops passage through the Papal State and promised the Pope the possession of Parma and Piacenza and the assurance of Medici rule in Florence. To the Emperor, angered at his treachery, Clement VII wrote on 25 January 1575, that he had had to yield to the French "unwillingly and under compulsion." But with the overwhelming defeat of the French at Pavia on 24 February 1525 and the captivity of Francis I, the Pope's cleverly intended calculations were ruined. He saw himself constrained to seek again the protection of Emperor Charles V, who was able to dictate to France the Peace of Madrid (14 January 1526) and apparently to attain the fulfillment of all his desires. Francis renounced, among other areas, Naples, Milan, and Genoa, and also his rights in Flanders and Artois. He promised to cede Burgundy and its dependencies and, as a token of enduring friendship, to marry Charles' sister, Eleonor. And his two older sons became hostages to guarantee the execution of the treaty.

Francis I had, however, in a notarial protest declared the peace null because it had been extorted by means of imprisonment and he did not intend to abide by it. And so, in the last analysis, the Emperor had succeeded only in bringing his old opponents closer together out of fear of Habsburg predominance in a new alliance. England, previously on his side, concluded a separate peace with France and promoted the League of Cognac, formed on 22 May 1526 by Francis I, Venice, Florence, Francesco Sforza, and the Pope. In his letter of 23 June 1526 to the Emperor, the Pope claimed to have been determined to this step by his solicitude for peace in Christendom, the freedom of Italy, and the security of the Holy See, while Charles V was disturbing the peace and repaying with ingratitude a vast number of acts of kindness. The Emperor, on the other hand, uttered a very strong protest in a state paper of 17 September 1526. He maintained that in Germany he had made himself the protector of the Apostolic See. He still desired peace; if the Pope were to lay down his arms, all others would follow his example, and the strength of Christendom could be directed against heretics and Turks. Otherwise, he was no father but an enemy, no shepherd but a wolf. The memorandum concluded with the threat of a council.

The Emperor urged the cardinals for their part to summon a general council if the Pope refused to do so. Clement VII abhorred and dreaded a council for many different reasons. The conciliarism of the fifteenth century had not been really overcome; it had merely been crippled by means of the papal policy of concordats. At the moment a council could not fail to effect a strengthening of the Emperor's central authority, which the Pope feared as much as did France. Finally, the illegitimate scion of the Medici could expect a reform council to be critical of his person or even to call into question his legitimacy as Pope.

The threat of a council did indeed impress the Pope but not to the extent of making him give up his alliance with France and England. This would result only from the military occurrences that overtook Rome and the Pope in the next months. The Colonna family, led by Cardinal Pompeo Colonna, made a surprise attack on Rome and plundered the Leonine City. However, this was only the prelude to worse. Jörg von Frundsberg had crossed the Alps in the late autumn and reinforced the Spanish troops with his mercenaries. In February 1527 he joined Charles of Bourbon. But there was no money with which to pay the soldiers. Fatigue and hunger led to mutinies, with which Frundsberg was unable to deal. Then he suffered a stroke. The insubordinate troops headed for the Eternal City, where they assured themselves they would acquire rich booty and revenge themselves on the Pope, the Emperor's enemy. In addition, the old and deep-seated anti-Roman sentiment of the Germans and the new talk about the Antichrist in the Roman Babel stirred the desire of punishing rich and wicked Rome. Charles of Bourbon fell at the very start of the attack on the Eternal City on 6 May 1527, with the result that the murder and pillage on the part of the leaderless soldiery became all the more unrestrained.

The *Sacco di Roma* became a judgment on Renaissance Rome. The Pope had taken refuge in Castle Sant'Angelo but had to surrender on 5 June and for the next six months he was the prisoner of the imperial troops. By agreeing to the occupation of important cities in the Papal State, paying a considerable indemnity, and promising neutrality, he was able to purchase his freedom on 6 December. Until October 1528 he stayed away from ruined and depopulated Rome. Meanwhile, the Emperor's troops were successful in North Italy and in the Kingdom of Naples.

The Pope saw that his interest lay on the Emperor's side. When he was assured absolutely that the Emperor would not insist on a council and that there were other ways of dealing with the Protestants, such as a court of arbitration made up of scholars or a religious colloquy, he was ready for peace, which was signed at Barcelona on 29 June 1529. The Emperor promised the restoration of Medici rule in Florence and the retrocession of cities such as Ravenna, Modena, and Reggio to the Papal State. In return he was again invested with Naples and obtained the disposal of benefices in the kingdom. Pope and Emperor made a defensive alliance against the Turks, then advancing on Vienna, and bound themselves to common action against heretics. Since peace with France was also being negotiated — it became a reality on 3 August 1529, in the Ladies' Peace of Cambrai between Margaret of Parma and Louise of Savoy, mother of Francis I — Charles V was able to undertake the long announced journey to Italy.

He met the Pope at Bologna on 5 November 1529. For four months he lived next door to the Pope, seeking in private conversations to win him over to a council. He was unable to overcome Clement's misgivings and obtained only a conditional assent. The Pope wanted guarantees that peace was assured and schisms — here he had France especially in mind — were out of the question.

On 24 February 1530, his birthday and the anniversary of the Battle of Pavia, Charles V received the imperial crown from the Pope at San Petronio in Bologna. The old unity of Emperor and Pope seemed restored, the precondition for the peace of Christendom reestablished. This coronation, the last that a Pope was to perform, was, however, rather a conclusion than a new start. A real understanding between Emperor and Pope, that would have been so necessary for defense against the Turkish peril and for overcoming the religious split in Germany, failed to materialize. His dynastic concerns and dread of the Emperor's predominance in Italy brought Clement VII to a new *rapprochement* with France. In October 1533 he went to Marseilles to marry his great-niece, Catherine de Medici, to Henry of Orleans, the second son of the French King. The conversations with Francis I on this occasion remained secret, and so they could only feed the Emperor's suspicions all the more. In the last years of Clement VII's pontificate occurred also the decisive phase of the divorce of Henry VIII and thus the withdrawal of England from the Church. On 24 March 1534 the Pope issued the judgment which declared the validity of Henry's marriage with Catherine of Aragon. Clement did not live to see the final break — the Act of Supremacy of 3 November 1534. He died on 25 September 1534, called by von Ranke "probably the most calamity-ridden of all the popes who ever occupied the Roman See." It was especially mischievous that he took no decisive step toward renewal of the Church, but rather refused the overdue council and felt that the unity of the Church could be assured by political means, by a subtle diplomacy.

CHAPTER 82

The Speyer Protest and the Marburg Religious Colloquy

The Edict of Worms had been suspended *de facto* at the Diet of Speyer in 1526. The Emperor was fully occupied with the war in Italy, while King Ferdinand had to devote himself to the Turkish danger and the struggle for Hungary, that is, for what was left of the kingdom, claimed by him in the name of his brother-in-law, Louis II, who had perished at the battle of Mohacs in 1526. The princes who inclined to the Reformation, Electoral Saxony and Hesse at their head, were able to utilize the opportunity to construct and consolidate the new ecclesiastical organization in their lands. Just the same, there was a growing feeling of insecurity, and the mutual distrust became deeper. Hence people began to look for allies. Especially active was Philip of Hesse, who was little troubled by scruples in political matters. His efforts were directed toward restoring Duke Ulrich of Württemberg to his territory and, by destroying the Swabian League, to gain the South German cities for an evangelical alliance. Both aims were intended to weaken the Habsburgs and to place the adherents of the Reformation in a position to defend themselves against future unfavorable decrees of a diet.

These far-reaching plans of Philip the Magnanimous very nearly led to war because of the "Pack Affair." In February 1528, Otto Pack, a secretary of Duke Georg of Saxony, made known to Philip that King Ferdinand, Duke Georg of Saxony, the Elector Joachim of Brandenburg, and other Catholic princes had concluded an offensive alliance with the Bishops of Mainz, Salzburg, Würzburg, and Bamberg in Breslau in order to extirpate heresy and to deprive the princes of Electoral Saxony and Hesse of their authority. Philip thereupon united with the Elector Johann of Saxony for a preventive war and allied with France, Denmark, and Zapolya, Ferdinand's rival in Hungary. First of all, the bishoprics of Würzburg and Bamberg were to be occupied. Luther and the Wittenberg theologians had scruples about an offensive war for the Gospel and stressed the duty of obedience by the estates to the Emperor. Moreover, the Pack documents turned out to be forgeries, and so the military expedition collapsed at its start. Nevertheless, Philip obtained from the Franconian bishops compensation for the costs of mobilization and from the Archbishop of Mainz the renunciation of spiritual jurisdiction in Hesse.

The Diet of Speyer in 1529

The plans in regard to an alliance acquired a fresh stimulus by means of the Diet of Speyer, which began on 15 March 1529. Charles V had become reconciled with the Pope and peace was about to be concluded with France. Hence the Emperor could think about a regulation of the situation in the Empire. At the beginning of the discussions his proposal was not yet ready. The suggestions submitted by Ferdinand were more rigorous and far-reaching. Aid against the Turks preempted the stage. Nevertheless, the religious question was energetically discussed. Under penalty of outlawry it was to be forbidden to deprive anyone of his authority and property "because of his faith" or to force him to embrace another faith. The Recess of the Diet of 1526 was declared null because it had given occasion to misunderstandings and caprice.

The advisory committee made the proposal stricter. Nevertheless, the innovations were permitted to continue; but the Mass had to be tolerated everywhere, and the Sacramentarians and Anabaptists were proscribed. The evangelical estates, however, issued on 19 and 20 April the solemn protest that gave them the name "Protestants." Without regard for this, the Recess of the Diet was signed on 22 April. In it the Emperor was requested to propose to the Pope the convoking of a "free general council in Germany." It should be summoned within one year to meet at Metz, Cologne, Mainz, Strasbourg, or some other German locality and, at the latest, begin its work after another year, "so that the German nation can be united in the holy Christian faith and the impending schism can be discussed." Otherwise, "a general gathering of all the estates of the German nation," a sort of national council then, should take place. The Edict of Worms should remain in force where it was hitherto observed. Where the new doctrine had been introduced and could not be eliminated without tumult henceforth any further innovation should be prevented until the future council could be convened. Above all, teachings and sects which attacked the Sacrament of Christ's body and blood — Zwinglians and Anabaptists — must not be allowed, and the Mass must not be abolished. "Even in places where the other doctrine has taken root and is maintained, it must not be forbidden to hear Mass nor must anyone be hindered from doing so." All "Anabaptists and the rebaptized, men and women of the age of reason, are to be put to death by fire, the sword, or the like . . . without any previous inquiry by the spiritual judges." Finally, it was stated:

> We, electors, princes, prelates, counts, and estates, have unanimously agreed and loyally promised one another that no one of a spiritual or a secular estate is to offer violence to another or compel or attack him because of faith or deprive him of rents, taxes, tithes, or goods.

No notice was taken officially of the protest of the evangelical estates. Hence they presented it, in an expanded form, as an appeal to the Emperor on 25 April. Now fourteen cities with Sankt Gallen, including the Free Cities of Strasbourg, Nürnberg, Ulm, and Constance, declared their adherence to the protest of the princes. In addition to the Elector of Saxony and the Landgrave of Hesse, Duke Ernst of Lüneburg, Margrave Georg of Brandenburg, and Prince Wolfgang of Anhalt had signed. The dilemma facing the religious question became clear in the protest. People demanded toleration but were not prepared to grant it. They resisted majority decrees in questions of conscience — "in matters relevant to God's honor and the soul's salvation everyone must stand alone before God and give an account" — but appeared to recognize the authority of a general council. They were convinced that they "had the word of God without any doubt, pure, undefiled, clean, and right." Therefore, to grant that the evangelical doctrine would only be tolerated where it had thus far been introduced would amount to "denying . . . our Lord and Saviour Christ and his holy word [not only] tacitly but publicly." On the other hand, only to tolerate the Mass would mean to give the lie to the doctrine of evangelical "preachers which we regard as Christian and reliable." In fact, if "the papal Mass were not against God and his holy word, it must still no longer be retained," because two kinds of worship in one locality is intolerable and must lead "to disagreeableness, tumult, revolt, and misfortune of every sort" among the common people, particularly when they are serious about God's glory.

Even if neither the Emperor nor King Ferdinand were in a position to implement the Recess of the Diet, the Protestants felt impelled to be concerned for their own protection and to look around for allies. On the very day of the Recess, Electoral Saxony, Hesse, Nürnberg, Strasbourg, and Ulm entered into a secret defensive alliance against eventual attacks. But the plans of Philip of Hesse went still further, envisaging a widespread war alliance against the Habsburg. It was promoted by Zwingli's efforts to expand the "Christian citizenship" into an anti-Habsburg coalition, but the controversies over the Eucharist presented an obstacle. These were taken very seriously by the Wittenberg theologians, to whom a confession of faith was more important than a league. Luther had made clear the chasm between him and Zwingli in his solemn *Grosses Bekenntnis vom Abendmahl Christi,* and he had rendered an understanding difficult by his violent polemics and even his defamatory tactics. Philip of Hesse endeavored to mediate. At the Diet of Speyer he had successfully prevented the Lutherans from cutting themselves off from the South German cities which inclined to Zwingli's doctrine. Hence the cities had been able to agree to the protest. On 22 April when the league of Protestants came into existence at Speyer and the "Christian Union" between the Catholic cantons of Switzerland and Austria was ratified at Waldshut, the Landgrave wrote to Zwingli that he should attend a meeting with Luther and Melanchthon in order "to reach an agreement [in regard to the Eucharist] on the basis of Holy Scripture." For at the Diet the papists had profited by the lack of union among those "who adhered to the pure word of God" to promote their "villainy." The discussion did not take place until October, for while Zwingli enthusiastically accepted the plan, people at Wittenberg had political and theological hesitations.

Zwingli's Eucharistic Doctrine

In the epitome of the First Disputation of Zurich (29 January 1523) Zwingli had rejected the Sacrifice of the Mass in a lengthy explanation, in which he referred to the "once for all" of Hebrews 7:27. The Mass implied a "diminution and defamation" of the one perfect Sacrifice of Christ. It was merely a "memorial" of it and an "assurance of the redemption which Christ achieved for us." While Zwingli attacked the refusal of communion under the species of wine, he ascribed no decisive importance to it. Anyone who, from ignorance or compulsion, is content with the species of bread receives Christ. Lastly, one does not need the sacrament at all, for one finds salvation in faith in Christ, even if both species should be denied. The doctrine of transubstantiation was, for Zwingli, a speculation of theologians. "What theologians have concocted in regard to the transubstantiation of wine and bread does not bother me."

He wanted John 6:53–56 understood in faith with reference to John 6:63: "It is the Spirit that gives life; the flesh profits nothing." If we believe that Christ's body was done to death and his blood was shed for us in order to redeem us and to reconcile us with God, "our soul is given food and drink with the flesh and blood of Christ."

Zwingli did not yet question the real presence. But it was only an aid to the faith of the uneducated. In order that "the covenant might be more easily grasped" in its essence, Christ gave his body the appearance of food, and hence they should be "assured in faith by a visible action." But just as immersion in baptism is of no use without faith, so too the body of Christ is of no use if we do not entirely abandon ourselves to him as our salvation.

For Zwingli the words of institution were as yet no problem.

Two years later, in the *Commentary on the True and False Religion* (1525), the reformer formally retracted his profession of faith in the real presence. If the progress of the Reformation outside Zurich had contributed to this change and if Zwingli had obtained the theological arguments for his new view from outside, nevertheless it was entirely in keeping with his thought. In his humanist-oriented spiritualism he understood *spiritualis* not as "spiritual," as a reality given in the Holy *Pneuma,* but as "intellectual" in contrast to "bodily and material." And so he saw no possibility of a spiritual sacramental presence of the Sacrifice of the Cross — historically unique — in the Mass, but only that of a "memorial," that is, of a making present in thought, in the awareness of the congregation. The intellectual and the material are mutually exclusive. God is a spirit, and he who wants to rise to him must leave behind all that is visible. Ceremonies have their meaning at most as incentives for the unlettered, as pedagogical means on the perimeter of the "true religion." Only spirit can attain to spirit. Worship is accomplished in "spirit and in truth" (John 4:24). It is unworthy of God when we seek to get into contact with him by material means or even to influence him, and, conversely, assume that he wants to communicate himself to us in material signs. Thus our achieving an understanding of the Incarnation, of the Sacrament, and even of the word to which the Spirit of God is bound is greatly obstructed.

Zwingli says that he had made up his mind on the metaphorical nature of the words of institution even before the appearance of Karlstadt, except that he did not know "which word was the metaphor." This did not dawn on him until two "pious and learned men" — Heine Rhode and Georg Saganus — had brought him the letter from the Netherlander, Cornelis Hoen. "In it I found the precious pearl: that the 'is' is to be understood as 'signifies.' "

The connection, gained in conjunction with the treatise on the Eucharist by his fellow countryman, Wessel Gansfort (d. 1489), that the copula "is" in the words of institution must be understood as "signifies," had been communicated by the lawyer, Cornelis Hoen of The Hague, in a letter to rector Heine Rhode at Utrecht. Rhode had taken it to Luther at Wittenberg in 1521 but had been repulsed. It was accepted by Oecolampadius and Zwingli, whom he and Georg Saganus sought out in 1523–24. In Hoen's letter Zwingli found a clarification of his notion of the Eucharist and in 1525 he published this work, so significant for him, anonymously. Meanwhile Karlstadt had published five treatises on the Eucharist at Basel at the end of October or the beginning of November 1524. Their crude form made them repulsive. When their content was connected with Zwingli, he had to fear for his reputation. Hence he sought to enlighten his friends by writing a detailed letter on the Lord's Supper in November 1524 to the pastor of Reutlingen, Matthäus

Alber, who favored Luther. It was a first circulated in manuscript with a request for secrecy and did not appear in print until March 1525, when "more than 500 of the brethren" had become acquainted with it. Thus Zwingli's alienation from Karlstadt had become known in the circle of his adherents months before the position he had taken in it against Luther caused disturbances at Wittenberg. But Luther's judgment on Zwingli was clearly made on the basis of oral information. To him Zwingli, like Karlstadt, was a fanatic and a Sacramentarian. Luther wrote on 17 November 1524: "Zwingli of Zurich, together with Leo Jud, in Switzerland holds the same views as Karlstadt." While Zwingli is not named in *Wider die himmlischen Propheten,* he is certainly meant.

Simultaneously with the printing of the letter to Alber appeared Zwingli's great systematic work, *De vera et falsa religione commentarius,* which, like Calvin's later *Institutio,* was dedicated to King Francis I. What is by far the longest of the twenty-nine chapters deals with the Eucharist. Here again Zwingli proceeds, not from the words of institution, but from the sixth chapter of Saint John. "Faith is the food that Christ discusses so forcibly in this entire chapter." He satiates the soul with food and drink so that nothing is ever lacking to it. He who believes in Christ remains in God. "Hence it is a spiritual food" of which Christ is speaking. "If he says, 'The flesh profits nothing' [John 6:63], then human audacity should not dispute about an eating of his flesh." To the objection that we are redeemed from death by Christ's flesh Zwingli replies: "Christ's flesh profits everywhere very much, yes, enormously, but... as put to death, not as eaten. Put to death, it saves us from death; eaten, it profits absolutely nothing." The flesh that brings salvation is enthroned in heaven at the Father's right hand since the Ascension and cannot at the same time be in the bread.

As already stated, Zwingli did not understand the reference to the special, sacramental, and nonhistorical manner of Christ's presence and of the eating of his flesh and blood. He was able to grasp "spiritual" only as "intellectual" in his body-spirit pattern. For him it made no sense to say: "We indeed eat the true and physical flesh of Christ but in a spiritual manner." Faith "does not move in the realm of the material and physical; it has nothing in common with this."

The "insipid," "silly," and "dreadful" opinion of a physical eating, proper only "to cannibals," cannot be supported by the words of institution. They too must be understood in the light of "the flesh profits nothing." "This means: 'This is my body' must not or cannot possibly be understood of bodily flesh or of the physically perceptible body." But the "symbolic sense" is not to be found in the "this," as Karlstadt thought. He did "not take hold of the matter in the passage where the victory was to be achieved." The "hoc" can refer also to a masculine word, to *panis,* and it does not thereby exclude the Catholic interpretation. At stake is the meaning of "est." "For in more than one passage in Scripture this word stands for *significat.* The words of the Last Supper are hence to be understood thus: " 'This, namely, what I present to you for eating, is the symbol of my body, given for you, and this that I now do you should do for the future in memory of me.' "

Like the Jewish Passover, the Lord's Supper is the great memorial feast of the Redemption. The Eucharist is not a real memorial in the sense that Christ by the action of the Church makes his sacrifice present. It is a recalling of the Sacrifice of the Cross, which continues to belong to the past, and a sacrament, or "oath of allegiance," a binding testimony to membership in Christ and profession of faith by the community.

Johannes Bugenhagen in August 1525 took a narrow and strict position against Zwingli's Eucharistic doctrine. He was the first member of the Wittenberg circle to express himself. Luther did not make known his reaction until the middle of 1526 in the preface to a translation of the *Syngramma* of Swabian preachers. Luther and Zwingli then exchanged a series of polemics. Their opposition became deeper in the course of this controversy. Mutual insults further envenomed the atmosphere. Thus it was no easy undertaking when Philip of Hesse tried to bring the two reformers to the discussion table; it could only be even more difficult to move them to a common profession, which was regarded by the Wittenberg theologians as the preliminary to forming a league.

The Marburg Religious Colloquy

On 1 July Philip of Hesse sent the official invitation to Luther and Melanchthon, Zwingli, Oecolampadius, Andreas Osiander at Nürnberg, and Jakob Sturm to convene at Marburg on 30 September 1529. Sturm was to bring along Bucer and another preacher from Strasbourg, but only as observers. Only the two Swiss and the two from Wittenberg were to engage in the disputation.

Luther and Melanchthon came armed with a confession in seventeen articles, comprising their entire faith. Persons had met at Torgau at the middle of September by command of the Elector of Saxony to draw up this creed. From the use later made of them, they were called the "Articles of Schwabach."

After a friendly greeting on 30 September, on Friday, 1 October, Luther and Oecolampadius and Zwingli and Melanchthon received a mandate for a discussion, each group in private. The next day at six in the morning the decisive discussion began in a private room next to the Landgrave Philip of Hesse's bedroom in the presence of a select group of at most fifty to sixty persons. Luther wanted to start from the beginning and submitted seven points in which the Swiss differed from him: the Trinity, the doctrine of the two natures, original sin, baptism, justification, the doctrine of the function of the word, and purgatory. So long as they were not agreed on these, he said, "they would discuss in vain the true value of the Eucharist." The Swiss objected that they had met because of the Eucharist. Luther gave in and at the outset wrote with chalk the words "This is my body" on the table and covered them with the velvet table cloth. He thereby defined the thesis of the disputation but at the same time he stressed that he "rejected carnal proofs and geometrical arguments entirely" and demanded submission to the word of Scripture. On Saturday and Sunday, 2 and 3 October, the debate went on from morning to evening. Melanchthon intervened only once in the conversation. Oecolampadius submitted arguments from Scripture and the Fathers, whereas Zwingli discussed the dogmatic questions. The presence of the Landgrave served to temper the tone of the dispute. Nevertheless, sharp outbreaks were not lacking.

Luther admitted that in Scripture there were figures of speech and metaphors but said that the presence of such had to be proved for each particular case.

In referring to the Spirit that gives life, he said, Christ did not intend to exclude physical eating but only to enlighten the people of Capharnaum "that he was not eaten, like bread and flesh, in a dish, or like roast pork."

Luther referred again and again to Holy Scripture. "Those words, 'this is my body,' hold me captive." "Do away with the text for me and I am satisfied."

The humanist Zwingli, on the other hand, stressed that antitheses are for the "flesh and spirit." Luther, on the contrary, would even eat "rotten apples" spiritually, if God offered them to him. "For wherever the word of God is, there is spiritual use." But it does not exclude the material. "The mouth receives Christ's body, the soul believes the words while it is eating the body."

At issue was not only the Eucharist but the means of grace in general. According to Zwingli, the material cannot communicate salvation. God operates directly. He must not be removed to external things. This is as true of the sacrament as of the word, but it does not stop before the humanity of Christ. Oecolampadius urged Luther: "Do not hang so much to Christ's humanity and flesh, but raise your mind to Christ's divinity!" Luther retorted: "I know no God except him who became man, and I do not want any other."

Not a single truth of faith was disputed, but the basic structure was different. Luther perceived this and expressed it to Bucer: "Our mind and your mind do not make sense to each other, but it is obvious that we do not have the same mind."

It was all the more amazing that a far-reaching agreement was arrived at in the end. At the urging of Philip of Hesse, Luther on 4 October assembled fifteen articles for a concord. The "Articles of Schwabach" served as his model. However, he treated the Eucharist last. Zwingli and Oecolampadius obtained several changes in form. Agreement was reached on the first fourteen of these basically Lutheran articles and on five points of the fifteenth. There was unanimity against the Catholic doctrine and practice in the demand for the Eucharist under both species, in the rejection of the Sacrifice of the Mass, and in the statements that "the Sacrament of the altar is a Sacrament of the true body and blood of Jesus Christ," that there is question "chiefly" of a spiritual nourishment and that the Eucharist was instituted in order to move weak consciences to faith.

At the conclusion they say: "Although we are not in agreement this time whether the true body and blood of Christ are physically in the bread and wine, still each should show Christian charity to the other in so far as each conscience can permit, and both parties diligently ask Almighty God to give us the right understanding through his Spirit." Zwingli's signing the essentially Lutheran Articles of Marburg has been presented as a concession from political considerations. Each side probably interpreted the articles in its own sense and was mistaken as to the unanimity. In the expression "Sacrament of the true body and blood" the Lutherans emphasized "true body," whereas Zwingli stressed "Sacrament," understanding Sacrament as a mere sign. Thus the Articles of Marburg would be "an apparent concord in the sense that each of the partners in the colloquy only signed what he had already known until then and erroneously assumed that the other signed the same as he did." And hence disillusion did not fail to appear. Each side quickly charged the other with breach of faith, and the polemics flared up again. On 16 October, scarcely two weeks after the colloquy at Marburg, Electoral Saxony and Brandenburg again tried at Schwabach to gain the South German cities and Hesse for the "Schwabach Articles," and to separate them from the Swiss. They were again unsuccessful.

Zwingli's Death and Succession

Zwingli and Philip of Hesse pursued further their anti-Habsburg league policy in Europe. Strasbourg entered the citizenship on 12 January 1530. The Landgrave allied with Zurich on 30 July. On 18 November there came into being a "Christian understanding" between him, Zurich, Basel, and Strasbourg, "only for defense and safety" in the event of an attack "because of God's word." The Protestant inclinations of Margaret of Navarre, sister of the French King, awakened in Zwingli the hope of winning France, not only for his political plans, but also for his faith. In the early summer of 1531 he composed a second statement of belief, *Fidei expositio,* for Francis I.

The reformer's fate was decided, however, not by his worldwide coalition policy, but by the domestic confrontation in Switzerland. The conflict was due to the "common governments" of Protestant and Catholic cantons, whose officials rotated after agreed terms and while in power tried to impose their creed, while the other party complained of moral constraint. "Zwingli saw a violation of the Peace of Kappel in every proceeding of the five cantons against an evangelical canton, but was unwilling to concede freedom of conscience to the Catholics in his sphere" (W. Köhler). He urged war, and this time the religious split was to win out over the ties of nationality. True, Zurich was still alone when it demanded war at the *Tagsatzung* on 24 April 1531. When the city continued to demand, it was constrained to be content with a blockade instead of war. On 28 May an embargo on provisions was laid on the five Catholic cantons, which depended on the importing of corn from Alsace and South Germany. They mobilized for defense in order to break the oppressive ring and on 9 October declared war. In Zurich leadership was lacking. Not until the five cantons assumed the offensive on 11 October did mobilization get under way, and then only seven hundred men, instead of twelve thousand, took the field. Finally, two thousand five hundred men of Zurich faced an enemy eight thousand men strong. On 11 October 1531 Zwingli fell as a soldier at Kappel in a war he had passionately wanted. In the Second Peace of Kappel Zurich had to renounce its policy of foreign alliance. Thereby the progress of the Reformation in German Switzerland was slowed down.

On 9 December 1531, the Zurich city council named Heinrich Bullinger (1504–75) as Zwingli's successor. The new *antistes* and all pastors were for the future to confine themselves to the proclaiming of the word of God and not mix in "worldly matters." Bullinger, born on 18 July 1504 at Bremgarten, the son of the local dean and pastor, was twenty-seven when he took up Zwingli's legacy. He succeeded in mastering the crisis relatively quickly and in stabilizing the Church organization in Zurich. In 1532 he created the Zurich Synodal Order. In 1536 he composed the first Swiss Confession for union discussions with the Germans, which collapsed. However, he did achieve agreement with Calvin on the Eucharistic question in the

Consensus Tigurinus of 1549. He thereby put Zwinglianism, which he could not bring to worldwide recognition, at least into intimate connection with powerfully rising Calvinism.

CHAPTER 83

The Imperial Diet of Augsburg

When, after he had made peace with France and with Pope Clement VII, Italy had become somewhat calm, Emperor Charles V was able to think of devoting himself to German affairs. It was important to restore unity in faith and to assemble the political forces for defense against the Turkish peril in the East. Influenced by the Erasmians, his chancellor Gattinara at their head, the Emperor was optimistic in regard to an agreement with the Protestant estates. He counted especially on the effect of the personal impression of his imperial dignity and power. Accordingly, the proclamation of the Diet for 8 April 1530, which went out even before the imperial coronation at Bologna on 21 January, was drawn up in very conciliatory and friendly language. It did proceed from the Edict of Worms but sought a new start of discussion. The Diet was to take measures for defense against the danger from the Turks. Furthermore, it was to discuss the method of proceeding in regard to "the differences and schism . . . in the holy faith and the Christian religion." For the sake of unity people should refrain from all discord, leave "past errors" to God, and try hard to listen to the opinion of the other side and to understand it. Whatever "on both sides has not been correctly explained and done" should be ignored. It is important for "all to accept and hold one single and true religion." and as "all are and fight under one Christ," so also should "all live in one community of the Church and unity."

Among the Protestant estates Luther's prince, the Elector Johann of Saxony, took the religious question very seriously but was not prepared, without more ado, to go along with Protestants "of another mind," that is, the Zwinglians. On the other hand, he was intent upon reconciliation with the Emperor, from whom he awaited investiture with the electoral dignity. From this point of view he strove to present the religious differences of opinion as unessential and was inclined to regard an understanding in the question of religion as possible through the Emperor.

The Landgrave Philip, on the other hand, was much more political in his thinking. He feared that a successful Diet would mean a weakening of his anti-Habsburg policy. Consequently, he subordinated the Protestant movement and in its interest he worked for an adjustment of the doctrinal differences within Protestantism and for a coalition against the Emperor. He would have preferred most of all to remain away from the Diet, for he feared a condemnation of the Swiss. He therefore denied the competence of Emperor and Diet in the religious question and hoped, by recourse to a council, to gain time for his plans.

Like the Emperor, the Papal Legate Lorenzo Campeggio underestimated the intransigence of the Protestant estates. While holding basically to the Edict of Worms, he held out hopes for the effort to gain the princes by concessions or to intimidate the cities. He alone counted seriously on the use of force, even if as the *ultima ratio.*

The Diet met much later than planned. The Wittenberg theologians exploited the time thus allowed them in order to formulate their own religious standpoint, both to be ready for a discussion and to arm themselves against blame. Thus originated the *Confessio Augustana.*

Construction of the Creed

The drawing up of creeds within Protestantism was motivated by confrontations of Lutherans with the fanatics and the Zwinglians and also by the self-assurance vis-à-vis the Imperial Governing Council, which was pressing for an implementation of the Edict of Worms. As early as 1528 Luther had added a "confession" to his great work, *Vom Abendmahl Christi* against Zwingli. In this "confession" Luther further expounded the doctrine of sin, redemption, justification, and Christian perfection (Article 2). In Article 3 he discussed in detail the doctrine of the Church and the Sacraments and sharply rejected the abuses of fanatics and papists.

The seventeen "Articles of Schwabach" go back to this document. They were the first confession to which a group of Lutherans — Electoral Saxony, Brandenburg-Ansbach, and Nürnberg — adhered at Schwabach in Franconia on 16 October 1529 and which they submitted to the envoys of the South German cities. On them the league with the South German "Sacramentarians" was wrecked. The Wittenberg theologians and Electoral Saxony regarded these Schwabach Articles as their confession. Shortly after the opening of the Diet of Augsburg they appeared in print in that city and, together with those of Torgau, served as model in topics and construction for the Augsburg Confession. They were directed, not least of all, against the Zwinglians, who understood them thus.

To prepare for the Diet of Augsburg on 14 March 1530, the Elector Johann of Saxony summoned the Wittenberg theologians to Torgau. Here on 27 March they discussed an opinion which has gone into history as the "Articles of Torgau" and which was taken along to Augsburg as working material. In an effort to demonstrate to the Emperor the purity of ecclesiastical usages in Electoral Saxony, doctrines were less discussed in the articles than were the controverted ceremonies. For "now dissension springs especially from several abuses, which were introduced by men into doctrine and laws."

At Augsburg the Lutherans saw themselves facing two fronts and hence in the presence of a twofold task. On the one side they had to repulse the fanatics and Zwingli or keep aloof from them; on the other side they had to convince the Emperor that nothing else was represented by them than the old, pure doctrine of the Catholic Church, as handed down by the Fathers and that they had nothing in common with Anabaptists and Sacramentarians and recognized authority. These two tendencies lay at the basis of the Augsburg Confession. The Catholics had also prepared for the confrontation at the Diet. Probably because of a request by the Bavarian Dukes to the University of Ingolstadt, Johannes Eck had set to work to compile for the Emperor a list of the errors of the Protestants — Lutherans, Zwinglians, and fanatics. Without further elaboration he added up "404 Articles for the Diet of Augsburg."

In these he presented the Bull "Exsurge Domine" (Articles 1–41), the conclusions of the Disputations of Leipzig (Articles 42–54) and Baden (Articles 55–64), and heresies compiled expressly for the Diet. These, Eck said, were only a selection from three thousand heretical statements in his possession. What mattered to Eck was to unmask the Protestants as heretics. The question arises to what extent he was concerned for the clarity that was necessary and, in the final analysis, salutary in view of the far-reaching doctrinal confusion or whether he did not commit the Protestants to error and obstruct the road to an understanding. In any event, the method by which he split up the truth into single sentences and used these without regard for the context and the concerns of the other side, like arguments in a criminal trial, was inadequate for the situation.

On his arrival at Augsburg Melanchthon encountered Eck's 404 Articles and sensed the necessity of formulating as one harmonious confession the doctrinal and ritual material that he had brought along. Hence he drew the doctrinal Articles of Schwabach and the ceremonial Articles of Torgau into an *apologia,* first conceived only in the name of Electoral Saxony. In the version of the end of May the first article began: "In the Electoral Principality of Saxony it is unanimously taught."

The draft was sent to Luther on 11 May for his objections. As an outlaw he could not appear at the Diet and remained behind at the castle of Coburg. On 15 May he declared his agreement with the draft. He said he was unable to improve on anything in it. He wrote to Johann of Saxony that that "would not be fitting, since I cannot step so easily and lightly." The question arises whether Luther on this basis of "stepping lightly" was criticizing a falsification or watering down of the reform problem by Melanchthon or whether he only intended, as on numerous other occasions, to call attention to Melanchthon's pleasing and courteous style. In any event, he would have been unable, in view of his prince's hopes for agreement at Augsburg, to allow himself any language that was too sharp. At first he expressed himself in regard to the *Confessio Augustana* in a thoroughly positive sense. His later criticism was, to be sure, not related to the doctrine of justification and other central articles of faith. But Luther gave the lie to Melanchthon's "untrue sentence." At the conclusion of the first part, "Tota dissensio est de paucis quibusdam abusibus," when on 21 July 1530 he wrote to Justus Jonas that the *Confessio Augustana* conceals the articles on purgatory, the veneration of saints, and, above all, the Pope as anti-Christ. At the same time he again spoke of "stepping lightly."

The *Confessio Augustana* includes twenty-eight articles and is divided into two parts. Part I (Articles 1–21) deals with the "Articuli fidei praecipui." Part II treats of abuses that later crept in but had now been abolished or replaced by other institutions, such as communion under both species (22), marriage of priests (23), the Mass (24), confession (25), regulations in regard to foods (26), religious vows (27), and episcopal power (28). Other "abuses," such as indulgences, pilgrimages, and the abuse of excommunication, are only mentioned at the end. For ecclesiastical unity, it is stressed, it suffices to agree on the central points of the teaching of the Gospel, as these are professed in Part I. Variety can prevail in the ecclesiastical usages discussed in Part II. From diplomatic motives and genuine concern for the unity of the Church Melanchthon had enjoined great discretion vis-à-vis the Catholic side. But he set the limits all the more strictly "toward the left," the Swiss and the fanatics.

Consequently the South German cities — Strasbourg, Constance, Lindau, and Memmingen... saw themselves forced, because of the controverted doctrine of the Eucharist, to submit a confession of their own, the *Tetrapolitana,* on 9 July. Zwingli had not come to Augsburg but had sent there his confessional work, the *Fidei ratio ad Carolum imperatorem.* It was handed to the Emperor on 8 July.

The Course of the Diet

The Emperor did not reach Augsburg until 15 June. Before this Johann of Saxony had exerted himself to arrive at an agreement with the Emperor on the religious question by means of private negotiations without Philip of Hesse. He had sent several embassies to him at Innsbruck and had declared that he would visit him there but was met with a refusal and with disapproval that he had allowed his pastors to preach Lutheranism at Augsburg.

The Emperor's negative attitude moved the Elector to exert himself all the more for a common confession of Protestants.

On the very day of the solemn entry into Augsburg tension occurred because the Emperor wanted the Protestant princes to take part on the next day in the Corpus Christi procession and forbade Lutheran preaching. The princes stayed away from the procession. A compromise was reached in the question of preaching in so far as it was entirely forbidden to disturb the discussions by polemics from the pulpit. On both sides there was a readiness for an understanding. Melanchthon defended the view that the Lutheran affair was not so misguided as the Emperor had been made to believe; the split, he said, had to do merely with communion under both species, the marriage of priests, and private Masses.

The Papal Legate Campeggio did not avoid the efforts for an arrangement. In his report of 26 June he apparently granted the prospect of union negotiations. On the lay chalice, the marriage of priests, and the changing of the Canon of the Mass he referred to a council as the demand of the Protestants. In return, he said, they were prepared to yield in the question of purgatory, episcopal jurisdiction, and much else.

The readiness for peace found expression in the Protestants' participation in the opening Mass on 20 June. In regard to the order of business they obtained a change in the agenda whereby the discussion of the religious question should precede that of aid against the Turks. But they did not succeed in getting the Catholics to submit their viewpoint in writing since they were unwilling to be pushed into the role of a religious faction and to cooperate in turning the Diet into something of a national council. The Catholics called for a committee of twelve spiritual and secular princes which should receive the Protestants' confession and report to the Emperor. To him, as *advocatus* and supreme protector of the Christian faith, should be left the final decision. From anxiety that the clear Catholic majority would carry its confession in the voting there arose among the Protestants the plan to have the *Confessio* read publicly.

Meanwhile, other Protestant estates had adhered to the *Confessio.* In addition to Johann of Saxony, it was signed by the Margrave Georg of Brandenburg-Ansbach, Dukes Ernst and Francis of Braunschweig-Lüneburg, Prince Wolfgang of Anhalt, the Free Cities of Nürnberg and Reutlingen, and finally the Landgrave Philip of Hesse. The last named failed to carry the modification of the article on the Eucharist in the Zwinglian sense, but he did succeed in substituting for the foreword, drawn up by Melanchthon as an appeal to the Emperor's good will, one written by Chancellor Bruck of Electoral Saxony. In this the legal standpoint was more strongly emphasized and the appeal to a council, expressed at Speyer in 1519 in the event of the failure of agreement, was renewed. The German text was read on 25 June by the Saxon chancellor, Christian Beyer.

While the Catholic theologians were working on a refutation of the *Confessio Augustana,* Melanchthon proceeded further along the path of negotiation. On 4 July he implored Campeggio to accord peace to the Protestants. In his "infamous letter" has been seen "a denial of the Gospel." Be that as it may, it proves Melanchthon's far-reaching desire for peace. In retrospect it can be said that he made the dogmatic differences unimportant. In any event, the legate Campeggio agreed to the intervention and on 5 July sent for Melanchthon. In a testimonial requested from him, Melanchthon asked only for the lay chalice and the marriage of priests; he was willing to retain public Masses and hoped that, after the restoration of episcopal authority, the remaining questions could be regulated. Meanwhile the legate had probably got a glimpse of the first draft of the *Confutatio,* in which the profound doctrinal differences were made clear. He now declined any further private negotiations, for, he said, the questions affect the whole nation and, in fact, all of Christendom.

The *Confutatio*

In view of the tendency of the *Confessio Augustana* to push doctrinal differences into the background, there loomed for the Catholic reply the question whether only the questions posed by the Protestants' confession should be discussed or whether other reform writings should be considered and the controverted points should be mentioned and proved heretical by a substantiated exposition of Catholic doctrine. The legate Campeggio defended this second opinion against the Emperor. Charles V appointed a commission of twenty theologians, including Eck, Cochläus, and Fabri, but it worked too ponderously. Hence the task of composing a Catholic reply was turned over to Eck, who could have recourse to his *Enchiridion,* his "404 Articles," and other works. The quickly finished first version was debated in the commission of theologians, approved by the legate, and submitted to the Emperor on 12 July as *Catholica et quasi extemporalis Responsio.* He rejected it as too long and too polemical. Cochläus and Arnold Haldrein of Cologne sought to comply with his intentions in their *Brevis ad singula puncta Confessionis... responsio.* But on 22 July the Emperor commissioned the drawing up of a *Confutatio* which was to be issued in his name. The *Catholica Responsio* was thereupon reduced to one-third its size by Eck, its tone was softened, and its content was restricted to what appeared in the *Confessio Augustana.* After repeated examination, reduction, completion, and correction it was read in German to the imperial estates on 3 August, but was not handed to the Protestants. That this was a testimonial of theologians had become a viewpoint of the Emperor, which was shared by electors, princes, and cities. The label *Responsio Pontificia* is thus misleading. The *Confutatio* sought to argue on the basis of Scripture and provided for justified criticism. In itself it is an important witness of the confessional discussion but not a complete reply to the controverted questions, because the *Confessio Augustana* was not a full statement of the Protestant idea. Its effect was jeopardized from the outset because the willingness for an understanding, especially on the part of the princes, was not so great as it seemed to be in the assertions and the real possibility of peace was less than the Emperor assumed. He held that the *Confutatio* had refuted the *Augustana* and expected submission without further discussion. Thus, when the Protestants declared that they did not feel convinced by the *Confutatio,* the effort to clarify the doctrinal questions by means of an imperial award collapsed. The Emperor could hardly implement his threat at the end of the *Confutatio* to do his duty as *advocatus* and protector of the Church in the event that the Protestants rejected it, for the Turkish peril did not permit the use of force.

The prospect of settling the religious quarrel by a council was now worse than ever. The letter in which Charles V on 14 July, with reference to the talks at Bologna, had asked the Pope for an immediate announcement of a general council was answered by Clement VII on 31 July with a "yes" that was so involved in conditions that it amounted to a "no." The Curia seemed more prepared to make concessions to the Protestants than to convoke the so greatly feared council. In the circumstances the Emperor again approved negotiations for a compromise. These took place from 16 to 21 August in a Committee of Fourteen, to which each of the parties sent two princes, two canonists, and three theologians. The negotiations foundered on the very question of the lay chalice on which till now an arrangement had been regarded as attainable. The Protestants were unwilling to be content with a mere toleration of the lay chalice and of the marriage of priests. Furthermore, the theological arguments had not been decisive for a long time, even if they were still in the foreground. Nontheological factors, especially political interests, became very prominent. Thus the Protestant estates were often less ready for an understanding than were the theologians. They, and in particular the Free Cities, were decidedly opposed to a restoring of episcopal jurisdiction, which for them was intimately bound up with the restoration of Church property. The committee broke up on 30 August without having come to an agreement in regard to the lay chalice, the Canon of the Mass, the marriage of priests, Church property, and religious vows. And so the negotiations were wrecked on "abuses." More profound differences, especially in the doctrine of the Church, certainly underlay these. But this does not alter the fact that agreement was achieved concerning the doctrinal articles. It is all the more tragic for in the confrontations in the succeeding years it was not the agreement arrived at that was the starting point for discussion. Instead, both sides again had recourse to the polemics of 1517–1525.

On 22 September the draft of the Recess of the Diet, in so far as it touched the religious questions, was submitted to the estates. The Protestants rejected it and sought to present to the Emperor the *Apologia* which Melanchthon had meanwhile composed against the assertion that the *Confessio Augustana* was refuted by Scripture. The Emperor declined to accept it. The Elector of Saxony left Augsburg the next day, and many Protestant estates gradually followed his example. Thus, as at Worms, the Recess of the Diet was issued on 19 November in the absence of most of the Lutheran estates. In order to maintain peace and unity for the good of the Empire the adherents of the *Confessio Augustana* were given time for reflection in regard to the "unsettled articles" until 15 April 1531 (para. 1). Until then they must not introduce other novelties or hinder the practice of the old religion (para. 3). They were to cooperate in prosecuting Sacramentarians and Anabaptists (para 4). Within six months "a common Christian council" was to be proclaimed "for Christian reformation" and to be held within a year thereafter (para. 5). Monastic and ecclesiastical property that had been taken by force was to be restored. The Emperor, as supreme *advocatus* of Christendom, and the "obedient electors, princes, and estates" had decided on the implementation of the Edict of Worms and desired "to allow no change [before] a decision of the next general council" (para. 10). The old ecclesiastical organization was placed under the protection of the territorial peace (para. 65), and the Imperial Supreme Court, then reorganized at Augsburg, was to proceed against the disobedient (para. 67). Thereby the Protestants incurred the danger of being prosecuted as breakers of the peace. But the very concession of a half-year's moratorium showed how impracticable were the terms of the Recess, severe though they might be.

The *Apologia*

The *Confutatio* had been read to the Protestants on 3 August but not given to them. Hence when, in view of the collapse of the negotiations for a compromise, Melanchthon set about composing a rejoinder, he could rely only on his memory and notes. The Saxon chancellor, Bruck, tried without success to present to the Emperor at Augsburg the resulting *Defense of the Augsburg Confession.* This refusal gave Melanchthon the opportunity to revise his work thoroughly and to expand it. Indirectly, by way of Nürnberg, he finally came into possession of a copy of the *Confutatio* and could use it for the expanded version of the *Apologia,* which appeared in print in April–May 1531. In the fall of that year Justus Jonas prepared a German translation, or, more exactly, a free rendition in German. The *Apologia* was at first the private work of Melanchthon. It was only by virtue of its being signed at Schmalkalden in 1537 that it became a confession alongside the *Augustana.* It stressed the doctrinal differences more sharply than did the *Augustana.* Article 4 on justification occupies almost one-third of the entire work. This "important monograph of the reform doctrine of justification," as H. Bornkamm calls it, furthered the one-sided forensic understanding of justification as a mere judgment. It is also said that justification signifies rebirth and new life and gives us the Holy Spirit, and that we become God's children and coheirs of Christ. But what was decisive for the further development and the doctrine of justification of Lutheran orthodoxy were not these statements, but others, which speak of a forensic, merely putative declaration of righteousness. The

> expression of Melanchthon in the *Apologia,* that justification also means making righteous, is too singular; it has had only inadequate consequences in the totality of the reform message. We may understand psychologically and in view of the situation of struggle that the Catholic doctrine of works was rejected. But it should not have been rejected without professing the notion of reward, which is biblical, and attributing to this the proper space. (H. Asmussen)

The *Confutatio* had expressly condemned the teaching that man can merit eternal life by his own powers without grace and emphasized that "every good gift and every perfect gift comes from above" (James 1:17) and that "all our sufficiency [is] from God" (2 Cor. 3:5). But the *Apologia* did not start with this or with the far-reaching agreement in regard to the doctrine of justification that had been established at Augsburg.

CHAPTER 84

The Politicizing of the Reform Movement to the Collapse of the Religious Colloquies

The Diet of Augsburg had exposed the disunity of the Protestants since three different confessions had been laid before the Emperor. In this connection the adherents of the *Confessio Augustana* had striven to hold clearly aloof from the Swiss and the South German cities. But the Recess of the Diet also threatened them with the Supreme Court as breakers of the peace, and so a league for common military resistance suggested itself. In this way the reform movement was further politicized. As early as 23 September, the day after the reading of the draft of the Recess, the Elector Johann of Saxony brought before the representatives of the South German cities at Augsburg his plan for a league "of all Protestant princes and Free Cities."

Right of Resistance

With the coming together for armed defense the question of the right of resistance became acute. Discussions on the subject took place at Torgau in October 1530 between the theologians, led by Luther, and the Elector's legal advisers. Till now Luther had conceded to the princes as individuals only passive disobedience. They might, in fact they had to, deny the Emperor their military service in a religious war against the Lutheran estates. Now the reformer was receptive to the argument of the jurists, who allowed the Imperial Estates a right of armed defense against a violation of the constitution by the Emperor. It was not the business of theologians, he said, to lecture the jurists in regard to their interpretation of the law of the Empire, "for the Gospel does not teach contrary to secular law." The Elector Johann was acting as a political person and not as a Christian, he wrote in January 1531 to Nürnberg, where, under the leadership of Lazarus Spengler, people were further questioning a right of resistance to the Emperor. His being a Christian gave the prince no title to armed action but could at most induce him to renounce his right. These reflections did not have as their point of departure the Emperor's position as superior of the princes also. In the course of further developments Luther was to adhere to the jurists, who held the viewpoint that, in accord with the corporate structure of the Empire, the electors were not to be regarded as subjects of the Emperor. They were called to govern the Empire together with the Emperor, just as, in Luther's version of the conciliar idea, the bishops ruled the Church with the Pope and under his guidance as equal members, *iure divino,* of the hierarchy. But if Emperor and princes were on an equal footing in law, then an armed action against them was not an official executive act but war. Since now in the matter of religion the secular authority had no power of command, a war by the Emperor against the Lutheran estates would be an ordinary raid against their possessions. Lastly, so Luther argued in 1539, in this the Pope was the commander-in-chief and the Emperor was his flunkey.

The League of Schmalkalden

Because of his frequent absence from the Empire, Charles V wanted to provide his lieutenant and brother, Ferdinand, Archduke of Austria and King of Bohemia and Hungary, with greater authority and to have him elected as King of the Romans. He won a majority of the princes over to this plan at Augsburg. But Johann of Saxony aligned himself against it with the anti-Habsburg Catholic Dukes of Bavaria. He replied to the Emperor's invitation to the meeting of electors at Cologne on 29 December, by inviting the Protestant estates to a Diet at Schmalkalden on 22 December to discuss the threatened action by the Supreme Court in the matter of the Reformation and the election of a King of the Romans. Representatives of the South German cities appeared at the Diet, headed by Jakob Sturm of Strasbourg, in addition to the signatories of the *Confessio Augustana.*

Apart from Brandenburg-Ansbach and Nürnberg, which had conscientious scruples about the right of armed resistance, the participants agreed on 31 December to provide common assistance if the Supreme Court should proceed against one of them on the basis of the Augsburg Recess. The formal treaty of alliance was dated 27 February 1531. Entering it were the Elector Johann of Saxony, Duke Philip of Braunschweig-Grubenhagen, Duke Ernst of Braunschweig-Lüneburg, the Landgrave Philip of Hesse, Prince Wolfgang of Anhalt-Bernburg, Counts Gebhard and Albrecht of Mansfeld, and eleven cities — Strasbourg, Ulm, Constance, Reutlingen,

Memmingen, Lindau, Biberach, Isny, Lübeck, Magdeburg, and Bremen. Still other cities — Braunschweig, Göttingen, Esslingen, Goslar, and Einbeck — joined by the beginning of 1532. Membership had been offered to the Zwinglian cities of Zurich, Bern, and Basel with the stipulation of the recognition of Bucer's *Tetrapolitana,* but Zwingli managed to thwart this. The treaty of alliance itself made no declaration of the condition. With Zwingli's death in the battle of Kappel on 11 October 1531, the South German cities ceased to be concerned for Switzerland. Nothing now prevented their seeking support from the adherents of the League of Schmalkalden. The treaty of alliance was signed for six years and in 1537 was extended for ten years. Lengthy negotiations were needed before the twenty-three members of the league agreed on a constitution. This was decided only on 2 July 1533 at Schmalkalden and was not finally accepted by all members until 23 December 1535. As early as the autumn of 1536 it was replaced by a second constitution of the League. According to the "Constitution for Urgent Safety and Defense," the League was directed by two League Captains, the Elector of Saxony and the Landgrave of Hesse, who alternated every six months in the conduct of business. At the Diet the decrees were made by nine spokesmen, of whom two each were named by Electoral Saxony, Hesse, the North German and the South German allied cities, and one by the other princes and counts. The new war councilors, who had the decision in case of war, were determined according to the same ratio. The League army was to be recruited in case of need; however, two months' pay for two thousand horsemen and ten thousand troopers was to be kept in readiness. The Elector of Saxony was to have the supreme command in campaigns in North Germany; the Landgrave of Hesse, in West and South Germany. The League of Schmalkalden became the center of the anti-Habsburg forces. How little it was a question only of the "pure word of God" was made obvious by diplomatic relations with France and England and an understanding with Bavaria not to recognize the election of the Archduke Ferdinand as King of the Romans in October 1531 and to provide assistance if one of them was attacked for this reason.

The Nürnberg Armistice

The Emperor could not even think of proceeding with force and of carrying out the Augsburg decrees. The Turks swarmed into Hungary, and to repulse them the Emperor had once again to purchase the assistance of the Protestants by an armistice. In the Nürnberg Armistice, or religious peace, of 23 July 1532, the members of the League were promised the suspension of all processes by the Supreme Court in religious affairs until the council or, if it did not meet within a year, until the next Diet, and all use of force because of religion and faith was forbidden. The Emperor went in person to Vienna to lead the great army that had been assembled from all his states in the Turkish campaign. But meanwhile the danger had been eliminated. The small West Hungarian fortress of Güns on the frontier of the Burgenland had heroically withstood the onset of the Sultan's troops from 7 to 29 August. This resistance and the reported strength of the imperial army induced Suleiman II to withdraw, with frightful devastation, through Styria, where the German troops were successful in a battle at Graz. The troops of the Empire could not be induced to pursue the Turks more deeply into Hungary and to procure victory for King Ferdinand's cause against the Hungarian claimant, Zapolya. Again the Turkish peril had been exorcised only temporarily; the paralyzing threat to the Empire persisted. The Emperor hurried via Italy to his Spanish kingdoms and was to be away from the Empire for almost ten years.

Introduction of the Reformation in Württemberg and Other Territories

The Protestants had not only held their ground, but they had gained powerfully in self-confidence. Encouraged by the League of Schmalkalden and under cover of the Nürnberg Armistice, which was *de facto* extended also to new members, a group of cities, including Augsburg, Hanover, Frankfurt an der Oder, and Hamburg, and principalities such as Pomerania, Anhalt-Dessau, and Liegnitz and Brieg in Silesia went over to the Reformation.

The fusion of politics and religion became especially clear in connection with the introduction of the new ecclesiastical system in Württemberg. Since the expulsion of Duke Ulrich (1487–1550) by the Swabian League in 1519, the Duchy had been under Austrian administration and at the Diet of Augsburg it had been conferred on the Archduke Ferdinand as an imperial fief. While activating the anti-Habsburg powers France and Bavaria, Philip of Hesse urged the restoration of the Duke, who had found refuge with him. The Landgrave first managed to prevent the renewal of the Swabian League, the prop of the Habsburg policy. In January 1534 he met the French King and obtained a promise of the necessary subsidies in exchange for a mortgage on the County of Mömpelgard near Belfort in Württemberg. Ferdinand was far too preoccupied elsewhere to take serious measures for the possession of Württemberg when the attack from Hesse occurred. The Austrian army was defeated without difficulty at Lauffen on the Neckar on 12–13 May 1534. In the Peace of Kaaden near Eger on 29 June Ferdinand granted Württemberg to Duke Ulrich as an Austrian rear-fief and conceded to him directly the right to introduce the new ecclesiastical system. In return he obtained the recognition of his royal title and the promise of aid against the Turks.

The Reformation, which was introduced immediately, was under the auspices of a liaison of Zwinglianism and Lutheranism. The people of Strasbourg proposed the Zwinglian Ambrosius Blaurer of Constance as reformer; Philip of Hesse, the Lutheran Erhard Schnepf. An effort was made to eliminate the difficulties in the doctrine of the Eucharist by the so-called Stuttgart Accord. The formula of union proposed by the Lutherans at Marburg was taken as its basis. Despite the division of the territory into two areas of the Reformation, the situation remained tense. The pastors were obliged to the *Confessio Augustana.* The Duke ruthlessly confiscated Church property to cover his debts. In 1537 he established the Tübingen *Stift* for the training of spiritual and secular officials. The University of Tübingen did not become Protestant until Johannes Brenz (1499–1570), the reformer of the Free City of Schwäbisch Hall (1522), was summoned there as professor from 1537 to 1538. In 1535 his small catechism was attached to Duke Ulrich's Church order. If the Protestant Church in Württemberg and in South Germany in general obtained a Lutheran stamp, it was due to the influence of Brenz. Under Duke Christoph (1550–

68), as provost in Stuttgart, he became the director of the Württemberg Church and composed the *Confessio Virtembergica* and the *Grosse Kirchenordnung* of 1559.

The Wittenberg Accord

The Württemberg Reformation had again displayed the split among the Protestants and at the same time had indicated the way to union. It had been shown that the *Confessio Augustana* and the Stuttgart Accord did not suffice as the basis for unity. The theologians sought to arrive at negotiations for an accord and approached Philip of Hesse as mediator. After a compromise between Bucer and Melanchthon at Kassel in December 1534 and an arrangement between Luther and the city of Augsburg, which in April 1536 was admitted to the League of Schmalkalden, the negotiations for the accord took place at Wittenberg from 22 to 29 May 1536. Meanwhile the Swiss and the city of Constance had declined and did not appear. Bucer acknowledged that the bread is truly the body of Christ and is given by the minister to all recipients, if the words of institution are not adulterated. Because, in his opinion, such adulteration takes place by means of the lack of faith in the recipient, there resulted the old problem of *manducatio impiorum*. Here Bugenhagen suggested that it may be "said that the unworthy, as Paul says, receive the body of the Lord." Luther was satisfied with this. The text drawn up by Melanchthon reads thus:

> Accordingly, they hold and teach that, with the bread and wine, the body and blood of Christ are truly and substantially present, administered, and received. And although they do not hold transubstantiation, neither do they hold that the body and blood of Christ are enclosed in the bread *localiter* or are otherwise permanently united with it, apart from the use of the Sacrament. However, they admit that, by sacramental unity, the bread is the body of Christ; that is, they hold, the bread is so administered that then the body of Christ is at the same time present and truly administered, and so forth. For, apart from the use, . . . they do not hold that the body of Christ is present.

In addition to the formula *manducatio indignorum* instead of *impiorum*, the expression *unio sacramentalis* involved an intentional ambiguity. Nevertheless, the Wittenberg Accord had importance as a bridge to Lutheranism for the South German cities making possible their adherence to the League of Schmalkalden. It was later accepted into the *Solida Declaratio* of the Formula of Concord (VII, 12–16) and thereby again recognized as Lutheran.

Protestant Refusal to Participate in the Council

Until this time the Emperor and the Catholic Protestant estates had demanded a council in a united front, and the postponing of the question of faith till its convocation had been again and again a welcome way out of the difficulties. It had not become clear that the ideas on the nature, summoning, and place of the council were very divergent also. But this situation changed decisively when on 2 June 1536, Pope Paul III called for a general council to meet at Mantua in May 1537.

The Elector of Saxony objected that nothing was said about the freedom, Christian character, and impartiality of the council and that it was to take place at Mantua. A council, he said, was a court of arbitration; if a person accepted the invitation, he was bound by the award. He demanded a pretext for refusing to participate from his councilors and theologians, he even considered a plan for a Lutheran countercouncil. Luther was to set down on which articles of his current teaching he intended "to stand and to persevere and... not yield." The reformer complied and on 28 December 1536 submitted to a conference of theologians his *Articles of Christian Teaching,* known as the *Articles of Schmalkalden.* To Melanchthon their statements in regard to the Pope were too severe. "For the sake of peace and unity" he was prepared to recognize the Pope's superiority over the bishops *iure humano.* Nevertheless he, with the other Wittenberg theologians, signed the articles, which were sent to the Elector on 3 January 1537 and accepted by him. The three parts of unequal length comprise: articles in which there was no need to yield because they were uncontested, such as the doctrine of the Trinity and of the two natures; articles in which there could be no yielding — atonement and justification by Jesus Christ, the Sacrifice of the Mass and the papacy as divine institutions; and articles which could be discussed with scholars and wise men, such as sin, penance, confession, baptism, ordination and marriage of priests, religious vows, and so forth. Luther expressed himself in particular fullness and with alarming severity on the Mass as the "greatest and most horrible abomination" in the papacy, as though in the meantime there had been no clarifying statement uttered or written on the Catholic teaching of the Mass.

In other respects too Luther, who repeatedly denounced "enthusiasm," the source of all heresy and even of the devilry of the fanatics and of the Pope, did not exactly use a language restrained by God's word. With regard to the imminent council he wrote: There "will we stand not before the Emperor or the secular authority,... but before the Pope and the devil himself, who does not intend to listen but to damn abruptly, to murder, and to force to superstition." At the *Bundestag* at Schmalkalden in February 1537, which was attended by numerous princes, envoys of the cities, and some forty theologians, Luther became ill and could not personally defend his "articles." From dread of a new quarrel over the Eucharist and probably also because of Luther's intransigent language, Melanchthon prevented the articles from being officially submitted to the gathering. The theologians were commissioned to examine the *Confessio Augustana* and to supplement it with articles on the power of the Pope. The formulation was left to Melanchthon. His *Tractatus de potestate papae* received the approval of all and became the official statement of the League by being accepted into the Recess. Luther's "articles," on the other hand, were published as a private work. But they soon enjoyed great esteem and were eventually adopted in the *Book of Concord* of 1580, thus becoming a confessional document of the Lutheran Church.

The gathering at Schmalkalden strictly declined to take part in the council. Acceptance of the invitation would mean to consent to their own condemnation and to accept the Pope as judge in his own case. The bull of invitation to the council was not even taken from the papal legate. Melanchthon, however, was of the opinion that the invitation should not be bluntly rejected. The Pope, he said, did not indeed have a right to act as judge but he did have the right to summon the council. Melanchthon clearly saw as "the most sad thing of all" the fact "that such discord would continue down to posterity." This did not prevent him from composing, by official mandate, the *piece justificative: Weshalb die Fürsten sich dem vom Römischen Papst Paul III. angekündigten Konzil verweigert hoben.*

The Emperor's representative at Schmalkalden was the vice-chancellor, Matthias Held. In accord with his mandate he sought to recruit for the council and rejected the complaints against the Supreme Court but came out more sharply than the Emperor had intended. He faced the harsh reality that the princes insisted on the rejection of the council that had been so vehemently demanded much more than did the theologians. Instead of seeking new paths to an understanding and sounding out the possibilities in the event that no council took place, he pressed for the establishing of a Catholic league. Without this, so he reported to the Emperor in the fall of 1537, everything would collapse, since the heretics were firmly determined to attack the Catholics from the rear, as they did in Württemberg. He found support in King Ferdinand. Consequently, on 10 June 1538 the League of Nürnberg, a defensive alliance between Charles V, Ferdinand, the Dukes of Saxony, Bavaria, and Braunschweig, and the Archbishops of Salzburg and Magdeburg came into existence and lasted for eleven years. With so slight a membership — no elector and scarcely any bishop was involved — and in view of the unclear attitude of Bavaria, the League was in itself not strong. It was soon further weakened by the death of Duke Georg of Saxony in 1539 and the subsequent reformation of his territory.

The Frankfurt Armistice

Even if the League of Nürnberg was not a serious threat to the members of the League of Schmalkalden, the latter felt themselves threatened. This motivated them to bind themselves more closely together. Because of a defeat near Esseg on 9 October 1538 in the Turkish war and the risk of again jeopardizing the ten-years' armistice just concluded at Nice on 18 June 1538 between a league of the Protestants and France, the Emperor could not seriously consider the use of force. In addition, the renewed postponement of the convoking of the council caused him and his contemporaries to doubt the Pope's sincere determination to take hold of the inner problems of the Church. In his effort to restore the unity of faith and of the Empire, Charles V was thus again thrown back upon German resources. He had no choice but to seek peace and aid against the Turks by means of negotiations and to hope to free the way for inner German religious colloquies. At the end of 1538 he appointed as the suitable agent for this the exiled Archbishop of Lund, Johann of Weeze. Prolonged negotiations led on 19 April 1539 to the Frankfurt Armistice. It granted, over and above the Nürnberg peace, an interval of six months to all current adherents of the *Confessio Augustana.* During that time the trials of the Supreme Court were to be suspended and no one was to be attacked because of religion. Peace for fifteen months was offered in the event that the members of the League of Schmalkalden were ready to accept no new members and to renounce any further secularizations. But they could not come to a decision. The Protestants promised to attend the Diet of Princes at Worms to determine the amount of aid needed against the Turks and to implement it. In particular the peace was to facilitate the religious colloquies. These were to take place independently of the council and without the participation of a papal legate in order "to treat of an honorable Christian union." The Elector Joachim II of Brandenburg especially advocated such colloquies. He was in the process of setting up in his own territory a church which occupied a remarkable middle position between the old and the new ecclesiastical system. Since the council was long in coming, he proceeded to introduce the reform as he waited for the council. In August 1539 he ordered debate on a Church order on which Georg Witzel (1501–1573) collaborated and which was decreed in March 1540. It adopted the Lutheran catechism but retained much of the old forms of worship. Luther thought that he could acquiesce in it because the articles on justification and orthodox preaching were guaranteed. Joachim II stressed that he wanted to be neither "Roman" nor "Wittenberger" but "Catholic." A violation of the Frankfurt Armistice occurred with the introduction of the Reformation in the Duchy of Saxony during the summer of 1539, following Duke Georg's death on 14 April. The members of the League of Schmalkalden kept their troops armed that they had recruited before the Frankfurt Armistice until Georg's brother, Duke Heinrich (d. 1541), had taken possession of his inheritance and introduced the Reformation. On Pentecost a Protestant service was held at Leipzig at which Luther himself preached.

The Religious Colloquies of 1540–41

The colloquy arranged for August 1539 at Nürnberg was postponed by imperial order and did not take place. The agreement that no papal legate should take part in the negotiations for a compromise could not but confirm the Curia's distrust of the imperial policy of union. What was here under way was scarcely different from a national council, so dreaded by Rome. The Protestants were hoping in this way to get a recognition of their confession in imperial law — a recognition which would do away with the need to submit the confession to the future council. Intensive papal diplomacy, however, could not deter the Emperor from his union policy. He promised that the Pope should take part in the projected religious colloquy, and people were invited to come to Speyer for it on 6 June. An epidemic forced its transfer to Hagenau. The chiefs of the League of Schmalkalden — the Elector of Saxony and the Landgrave of Hesse — refused to appear, and attendance by other princes and bishops was very meager. Not only King Ferdinand but also the adviser of the Catholics, the nuncio Morone, who was present, complained of the tardiness of the bishops. An exception was the Bishop of Vienna, Johann Fabri, who, together with Johannes Cochläus, Friedrich Nausea, Julius von Pflug, Johann Gropper, and especially Johannes Eck, acted as the Catholic spokesman. Melanchthon was taken sick en route and hence Wittenberg was represented only by Kaspar Cruciger, Friedrich Myconius, and Justus Menius. Other Protestant theologians present were Martin Bucer, Wolfgang Capito, Andreas Osiander, Johannes Brenz, U. Rieger, and Jean Calvin. King Ferdinand, who was in charge, wanted to take the Augsburg discussions for a compromise as the basis and to allow discussion only of the articles not agreed upon at Augsburg. The Protestants refused and demanded the *Confessio Augustana* as the basis. The fact that they were unwilling to be pinned down by concessions possibly made earlier, and indeed their mere presence, made clear the changed situation since 1530. They now represented a strongly consolidated Church organization, behind which stood the League of Schmalkalden, then the only close-knit political power in the Empire.

The colloquy, engaged in by Eck and Melanchthon, began on 14 January with the *Confessio Augustana* as its basis. At the start Eck referred to the not inconsiderable deviations in the text of the *Augustana* the *Variata,* that had been submitted, from that of 1530; these concerned especially the Eucharist. For three days they discussed original sin, especially to what extent the "penalty" remaining after baptism can itself be called sin. In Granvella's residence on 17 January a compromise formula came into existence, worked out by Mensing, Auxiliary Bishop of Halberstadt, Eck, Melanchthon, and Bucer. It was approved by both sides. At the same time an imperial instruction arrived whereby the colloquy was to be transferred to the Imperial Diet appointed for Regensburg. The Emperor was hoping to promote the faltering discussions by his personal presence. Furthermore, during the not very promising discussions at Worms, Granvella had been concerned for a basis of negotiations in the form of a compromise draft. At his urging Gropper and the imperial councilor, Gerhard Veltwyk, had had secret talks with Capito and Bucer at Worms independently of the main discussion. Bucer was encouraged in this by Philip of Hesse. The Landgrave was eager for an arrangement with the Emperor, since he was in a state of bigamy which was threatening to become an embarrassing matter. The basis of these secret talks were Gropper's *Artikall, vor Christlich und der gesunden katholisohen Lehr gemäss erkannt,* as completed and corrected by Bucer. There was quick agreement on original sin and justification. Difficulties arose out of the compromise between the principle of Scripture and the recognition of ecclesiastical tradition, including the Mass and the veneration of saints. Bucer himself, however, took a positive view of the usages of the ancient Church because there had "been one Christendom from the Apostles down to the age of the holy Fathers." Hence he felt he could make concessions in regard to ceremonies and the Mass itself, if only the preaching of the Gospel were allowed. He was able to take much of the formulation that he suggested from the draft for the Leipzig colloquy of 1539, which he had elaborated with Witzel. The compromise draft that thus appeared was accepted on 31 December. It represented the original form of the *Regensburg Book.* Even before the start of the Diet Granvella tried to gain as many of the princes as possible for it. Philip of Hesse was in agreement and Joachim II of Brandenburg enthusiastically sent it on to the Elector of Saxony. But skepticism was expressed by Luther.

At Regensburg the Worms compromise draft, after a few modifications approved by Contarini, Morone, and the Catholic cospeakers, Pflug, Gropper, and Eck, was approved as the basis of negotiations, submitted at the opening of the colloquy on 27 April 1541 and accepted also by the Protestant spokesmen, Melanchthon, Bucer, and Pistorius. Important for the conciliatory mood of the Regensburg religious colloquy was the participation of Cardinal Contarini as papal legate. On the basis of his own religious experience and relying on Paul and Augustine, he was "convinced that the religious starting point of Luther's doctrine of salvation, but not its theological formation and the consequences drawn from it, was primitively Catholic" (H. Jedin) He felt that, with good will on both sides, with charity and humility, the split could be healed. "Now he was to learn that they alone were not enough" (H. Jedin). There was surprisingly rapid agreement on the first four articles of the *Regensburg Book:* the original state of man, free will, the cause of sin, and original sin. On the second day, 28 April, the participants turned to Article 5, on justification. Melanchthon and Eck rejected the version at hand. After a discussion of several days, however, they again had recourse to it but in a considerably abbreviated form, and on 3 May it was possible to declare that there was agreement on this article. All were filled with joy and hope. Contarini sent the formula of union to Rome, and the Emperor was confident that now "an understanding would be reached also in the other questions." The conflict had blazed forth on justification, which was thus felt to be the "articulus stantis et cadentis ecclesiae." According to the formula of union, the sinner is "justified by a living and effective faith." This faith is a "movement of the Holy Spirit," whereby the penitent is oriented to God and attains the mercy, forgiveness of sins, and reconciliation promised in Christ. With him is "simultaneously infused charity, which heals the will,"so that he can begin to fulfill the law. The article seeks to take into account the fact that, on the one hand, we are justified for Christ's sake, his righteousness becomes ours, and we are reconciled with God, and, on the other hand, the new righteousness does not yet have full power over us, "the renewal is still imperfect, and a tremendous weakness still clings to the reborn." "Because of the righteousness inherent in us we are called righteous, for we indeed do what is right and, according to John, he is righteous who does righteousness." We will not, however, place our confidence in this activity of ours, but only in the justice of Christ, just as, on the other hand, we do not doubt our weakness. For this reason no one is excluded from the grace of Christ. There is no question of a "twofold righteousness," but of the one righteousness of Christ the Mediator, which produces full grace, favor, and reconciliation with the Father and renews and sanctifies man but has not yet come here fully into effect.

In the further course of the religious colloquy, however, it was to appear that not justification, but the Church and her office in the interpretation of Scripture and in the administration of the sacraments constituted the articles that were really at the basis of the split. Contarini managed, in opposition to Eck, to have Articles 6 and 9, on the Church and her full authority in interpreting Scripture, postponed. Otherwise, the discussions would have foundered. There was agreement on Articles 10 to 13, the teaching on the sacraments in general, orders, baptism, and confirmation. There were crucial difficulties with regard to Article 14, on the Eucharist. The question of transubstantiation was struggled with for almost eight days. No understanding was reached on it nor on Article 15, on penance, but there was agreement on matrimony (Article 16) and the anointing of the sick (Article 17). With Article 19, on the hierarchical order of the Church, and Article 20, on the Mass and the veneration of the saints, it finally became plain to all that the colloquy had broken down. On 31 May the Protestants submitted a summary of their divergent views relevant to the Church, the Eucharist, and penance. The Emperor's policy of union failed utterly when he did not even obtain an understanding that the articles on which there was agreement should be recognized as settled and that patience should be exercised in regard to the others until the council convened.

Meanwhile, it had turned out that the unity over justification was only superficial. On 10 or 11 May Luther had labeled the article a "botched job," "a new piece of cloth patched on to an old coat, so that the rent becomes worse." On the Catholic side the union formula was charged with being ambiguous. The Curia refused its approval. However, when its rejection reached Regensburg on 8 June, the union was already in ruins and it had become clear for the future how complicated an agreement was. Inner Church reform was thus all the more urgent. To the assembled bishops Contarini directed a pressing admonition to fulfill their pastoral duties, to see especially to preaching and the education of the young, and to avoid all scandal in their own persons and in their retinue. For their part the bishops implored the legate to labor without delay for the convoking of the council; otherwise, all Germany would soon be Lutheran. The council seemed about to become a reality. The Pope had had the Emperor informed that he was determined to lift the suspension of the council and to convoke it at once. Of course, this had come too late to prevent the schism in the Church, as is proved by the repeated rejection of a papal council as a binding tribunal by the Protestants.

In the Recess of the Diet on 29 July 1541, the Nürnberg peace was extended for eighteen months. Within that time a general council or, if necessary, a national council should take place. For the sake of aid against the Turks the Emperor, in a secret declaration, assured the Protestants the possession of the secularized Church property, allowed them to hold the explanation of their theologians in the adjusted articles, and promised them equality in the Supreme Court.

CHAPTER 85

The Breakdown of Universalism and the Religious Peace of Augsburg

The Emperor and the Protestants on the Brink of War

The religious colloquies had failed, and once again the Emperor had had to give in to the Protestants. He familiarized himself even more with the idea of a forcible solution. On the other hand it must be counted as a success when, during the Diet of Regensburg in 1541, he managed to weaken the impact of the League of Schmalkalden by paralyzing the activity of Philip of Hesse. While his lawful wife, the mother of his nine children, was still alive, the Landgrave had married a lady-in-waiting. In a *Beichtrat* Luther, Melanchthon, and Bucer had given their approval and they were even present at the wedding in March 1540. The bigamy could not be kept secret and because of it the reformers suffered a painful embarrassment.

According to the *Carolina*, the imperial law that he himself had proclaimed, Philip had incurred the death penalty. He tried to evade it by a *rapprochement* with the Emperor. In a treaty of 13 June 1541 he bound himself to prevent an alliance of the League of Schmalkalden with France and England and the admission of the Duke of Cleves to the League and to support the Emperor's claims to Gelderland. The Emperor promised not to attack him on religious grounds unless he had to wage war against all the Protestants. Thus a restoration of religious unity by armed force was envisaged by the Emperor as in the realm of the politically possible, but out of the question for the moment due to external political pressures. Charles V went to Italy and at Lucca on 12 to 18 September 1541 he met Pope Paul III, whom he hoped to gain for a council on German soil, effective aid against the Turks, and support against France. The result was disheartening.

Meanwhile, the peril from the Turks was again great. Zapolya, the King of Hungary, had died in 1540. But, on account of the opposition of the Magyar nobles, King Ferdinand was unable to take up the succession promised him in the Treaty of Grosswardein in 1538. The national Magyar circles invited the Sultan Suleiman II into the country but were not a little astonished when, after occupying Buda on 2 September 1541, he installed a pasha as governor and thus made Hungary a Turkish province. The Emperor's desperate diversionary measure against the Muslim danger through an attack on Algiers in October 1541 failed completely because of stormy weather. At the same time the already critical situation with regard to France became worse, making the ten-years' armistice of 1538 illusory. And so, once again ecclesiastical problems had to yield to political cares. The Diet opened at Speyer by King Ferdinand on 9 February 1542 was overshadowed by the Turkish question. The Protestants made their assistance dependent on their recognition in imperial law by means of the adoption of the Regensburg Declaration in the Recess of the Diet and demanded a visitation of and new personnel on the Supreme Court. This time too the King had recourse to an additional declaration. A visitation of the Supreme Court was indeed introduced but as early as June it was again suspended by the Emperor. Thus the Nürnberg Diets of July–August 1542 and January–April 1543 faced the same problems, to which was added in the second the military confrontation with France and Cleves. If the Emperor could not expect any help here either, at least it was a success that the League of Schmalkalden did not come to the aid of the Duke of Jülich-Cleves-Berg, who was beaten in September 1543. He had to annul the Reformation and turn over Gelderland to the Emperor. This meant a strengthening of the northwestern German sees of Münster, Paderborn, and Osnabrück, which, like Cologne, were then in danger of going over to the Reformation.

Progress of the Reformation

The Reformation continued to make great advances. After several years' strife the chiefs of the League of Schmalkalden, the Elector of Saxony and the Landgrave of Hesse, occupied the territory of the Catholic Duke Heinrich of Braunschweig-Wolfenbüttel in July–August 1542, gave it a provisional government, and had the Reformation introduced by Bugenhagen and Corvinus. The Wittenberg theologians had spoken in favor of these proceedings and against the return of the territory to its legitimate ruler on the ground that one "cannot acquiesce in the restoration of unorthodox doctrine, superstition, and persecution in the country." When the Duke managed to gain back his territory, but only to be taken captive by Philip of Hesse in 1545, Luther felt that he should be kept in prison: To prevent him from further exercising his "tyranny, blasphemy, and impiety" was to practice mercy to him.

The obliging of a Lutheran prince to hinder idolatry or the abomination of papal "abuses" served territorial interests in a no less questionable manner in the new choice of an occupant of the see of Naumburg. Following the death of the bishop on 6 January 1541 the cathedral chapter, without consulting the Elector of Saxony, had elected the provost of the Zeitz chapter, Julius von Pflug. The Elector, who for some time had been trying to end the political autonomy of the bishopric, in September entrusted the secular administration to an official of the diocese whom he appointed. Since Pflug did not yield and the chapter declined to elect a creature of the Elector, the last named brought about the election of Nikolaus von Amsdorf by the Lutheran estates of the diocese. Contrary to their original conviction, the Wittenberg theologians had assented to these proceedings. Luther wrote to the diocesan estates that a cathedral chapter which did not make a proper election or clung to a persecutor of the Gospel forfeited its rights. "For the command to teach the right doctrine and to celebrate correct worship takes precedence over all other commands." The control of the worldly property, he said, disappeared with the spiritual power. "Its superstition and its secular power and property" were inseparably united. Luther personally performed the "consecration" of Nikolaus von Amsdorf by the imposition of hands and prayer, "without any chrism . . . and whatever else of the same great sacredness there is," and the enthronement. The next day the council and citizenry of Naumburg did homage to the new bishop at the town hall. But Amsdorf was not to find much joy in his office of Lutheran bishop. He was himself in a "miserable situation" — left to the caprices of the Elector's official in secular matters and in full dependence on the electoral government in the spiritual sphere, without obtaining from the government the necessary support. In addition, the legitimacy of his episcopacy was still disputed. Pflug did not renounce his claims and in March 1542 complained to the Diet of Speyer. The Emperor took his part but was unable formally to invest him with the bishopric until 8 August 1545, after much hesitation. The investiture thus represented the Elector's procedure as robbery. War alone brought a decision favorable to Pflug.

In the Electoral Palatinate the Elector Frederick II (1544–56), who was only superficially religious, inclined to the Reformation. In April 1546 he went over to it publicly and had the Mass abolished. The Catholic majority in the Electoral College was thereby imperiled, for at the same time the Electorate of Cologne was in danger of embracing the Reformation.

The Archbishop of Cologne, Hermann von Wied (1515–17), whose grasp of theology was far too inadequate to enable him to evaluate the import of the differences between the Catholic notion of the Church and Protestantism, had in February 1542 invited Bucer to have religious discussions with him and Johann Gropper. The provincial Diet encouraged the archbishop and on 10 March 1542 gave him extensive powers. When, toward the end of the year, Bucer was invited again and preached in the Bonn Minster, there were lively protests at Cologne from the cathedral chapter, the university, the lower clergy, and the city council, and Bucer's departure was demanded. Gropper broke off his connection with Bucer and on 27 January 1543 transmitted to the archbishop a Catholic reform program. Hermann von Wied rejected it and authorized Bucer to draw up an order of Reformation. With the support of other reformers, who, headed by Melanchthon, had meanwhile been enlisted, Bucer put together the "Cologne Reformation." Simultaneously there began the implementation of the Reformation in the archbishopric. By a brief issued in June 1543 the Pope called upon the Elector to return to the Church.

The intervention of Charles V in connection with the War of the Gelderland Succession in August and September 1543 retarded the reform exertions for a while. In a counterreport Gropper attacked the "Cologne Reformation" as not Catholic. Even Luther opposed it and stigmatized its doctrine of the Eucharist as "fanatical." The Archbishop's declaration of January 1544 that he would be satisfied with the preaching of the Gospel, the lay chalice, and baptism and hymns in German did not suffice to overcome the Cologne opposition. The Catholic circles obtained an effective strengthening from the Jesuits, who settled at Cologne in 1544. In the autumn of that year they energetically demanded that the Archbishop annul the innovations and appealed to both Emperor and Pope. A series of polemics, testimonials, and replies testifies to the passionately fought struggle. Hermann von Wied was excommunicated on 16 April 1546 and soon after deposed by the Pope. But it was only in February 1547 that his successor, the former coadjutor Adolf von Schaumburg, could, with imperial support, force him to yield.

The Schmalkaldic War

The successful Gelderland-Cleves campaign of 1543 confirmed Charles V's conviction that power, employed at a given time and properly, is an entirely fit means for mastering "arrogance."

This applied to the Protestants as well as to the French. Hence it was by no means agreeable to him when the Cardinal Legate, Alessandro Farnese, sought at Kreuznach in January 1544 to gain him to peace or at least to an armistice for the sake of the council — in other words to induce him to renounce Milan and Savoy. The Pope favored France and was silent in regard to France's offer of an alliance with the League of Schmalkalden — so ran the bitter words of reproach. At the Diet of Speyer Charles V obtained military help against the Turks and France from the Protestants, who were themselves not united and impressed by the Emperor's success against Cleves. Of course, he had to be quite accommodating in regard to their ecclesiastical demands. He held out to them the prospect of a diet in the coming fall or winter. It was to produce a "Christian reform" because of the religious dispute. Until then no one was allowed to resort to power and force in religious matters. The processes in the Supreme Court and the Recesses of Diets against the Lutherans were to be suspended. Ecclesiastical property was to remain in the hands of those who held it at the moment. For the sake of a momentary success the Emperor here, for the first time, publicly abandoned important positions. As

Jedin says, "He offered his hand for a future arbitrary, total regulation of the ecclesiastical situation" by a German diet, a regulation "which, in the situation, could and perhaps had to lead to the complete Protestantization of Germany." The Curia reacted with an admonition of 24 August 1544 to the effect that, by his promise to regulate Church affairs at a diet and by his disposal of Church property, the Emperor had become guilty of a serious invasion of canon law. He should revoke the concessions to the Protestants and, by arranging peace, facilitate the way for the council. In Jedin's words, the brief meant "the taking of a position in principle against the Emperor's religious and conciliar policy. But it was neither officially presented nor published. This did not stop its circulation. Calvin published it and was not sparing in his cutting scorn. Luther lost control of himself in one of his last and most extravagant polemics, *Wider das Papsttum zu Rom, vom Teufel gestiftet* (1545). The Emperor did not react but created new facts by a rapid and successful campaign against France. In the Peace of Crépy the French King had to promise aid against the Turks and, in addition, he had to oblige himself in a secret treaty of 19 September 1544 to cooperate in the elimination of abuses and the return of apostates and to participate in the council that was to meet at a time specified by the Emperor at Trent, Cambrai, or Metz. He also declared that he agreed the aid promised against the Turks could be used against heretics also in case it should be necessary to proceed forcibly against them.

When the Pope finally summoned the Council to meet at Trent on 15 March 1545, in the Bull "Laetare Jerusalem," published on 30 November 1544, the Emperor acquiesced. But he did not desist from his plan of first overcoming the League of Schmalkalden by military might and then of forcing the Protestants to recognize and attend the Council. To this he directed all his strength. Besides, he reckoned on a delay, if not on further obstruction to the opening of the Council. For the present he continued along the route of compromise that had been traveled at Speyer in order to lull his opponents into security. At first this was still the situation at the Diet of Worms, which, because of the Emperor's illness, did not meet on 1 October 1544, but at the end of March 1545 under King Ferdinand. According to the Emperor's wish the aid against the Turks and other political questions were to be urgently dealt with and the religious problems left chiefly to the Council. But the Protestants, who were not ready to recognize the Council, demanded the implementation of the assurances given at Speyer in 1544.

On 17 May, one day after the Emperor, Cardinal Farnese arrived at Worms as papal legate. Discussion of a procedure against the Protestants prepared the way at the end of June for an alliance between Emperor and Pope. The latter promised for the war against the League of Schmalkalden 200,000 ducats, 12,500 auxiliary troops for four months, one-half the revenues of the Spanish Church, and permission to convert up to a half-million ducats into ready cash by alienation of Spanish ecclesiastical property. The opening of the Council was to be delayed. The Emperor continued the Diet in order to gain time and to prevent the Protestants from preparing for war. In the Recess of the Diet on 4 August a religious colloquy was even called for at Regensburg. In order to safeguard his rear for the war against the Protestants, King Ferdinand in October 1545 concluded an eighteen-months' armistice with the Turks, ceded the lost parts of Hungary to them, and bound himself to pay tribute. Delegates arrived at Regensburg for the religious colloquy on 27 January 1546, even though the Council of Trent had already begun its work on 13 December 1545. In order not to give rise to any rivalry the Emperor assigned the colloquy a purely informational task for the sake of the Diet that had also been summoned to Regensburg. Out of an understandable mistrust the Protestant side demanded that all talks be recorded in the minutes. This troublesome procedure did not allow any free exchange of views, and the Emperor rejected it. The Protestants broke off the discussions on justification, which had scarcely begun, on 10 March and ten days later they secretly left the city. The Diet, for which the Emperor arrived on 10 April, could only be opened on 5 June. The leading Protestant princes did not attend in person. Religion, peace, and law were to be the subjects of discussion, but in reality everyone counted on war. The Catholics recognized the Council of Trent, while the Protestants demanded a free, Christian council in Germany. In the background the Emperor was diligently trying to isolate the members of the League of Schmalkalden. Bavaria bound itself to a benevolent neutrality. The marriage of the heir to the Duchy with Ferdinand's oldest daughter, Anna, was to end the old Habsburg-Wittelsbach rivalry. Maurice of Saxony entertained hopes of obtaining the Saxon Electoral dignity and let himself be gained to a treaty on 19 June 1546. In it he was promised the protectorate of the bishoprics of Magdeburg and Halberstadt. For his part, he promised to recognize the Council and send representatives to it. On 7 June the Emperor signed a treaty alliance with the Pope. Charles gave the sign for war when, responding to an inquiry by the Protestants about the aim of his warlike preparations, he said that he had taken action against disobedient princes according to law and by virtue of his authority.

Accordingly, the Emperor wanted to avoid the impression of a religious war and to have the war viewed in the framework of imperial law. The declaration of outlawry against Electoral Saxony and Hesse contributed to this. Charles intended to wage the war in these principalities, but before he obtained control of the troops from the Netherlands and of the papal auxiliary corps his opponents seized the initiative. Thus the territory south of the Danube became the first arena. The field commander of the League of Schmalkalden, Sebastian Schertlin von Burtenbach, moved against the Ehrenberger Klause on the upper Lech with the intention of obstructing the Emperor's principal force from Innsbruck and the approach of the papal troops. But the League's war council called him back to the Danube. There was also no determined attack by the still preponderant League on Regensburg. The "greatest military confrontation which Germany had hitherto experienced" (E. Hassinger) was at first an endless maneuvering in the area around Ingolstadt, a cautious probing of the opponent without risking a decisive blow. This was to the Emperor's advantage. He was able to assemble his forces and strengthen his at first weaker position. But in time the ineffectual moving about exhausted the financial resources on both sides and desire for a fight seized the troops. In the late fall the Italians especially had to endure rain and cold. There was not even any decisive action on the Emperor's part when the intervention of Maurice of Saxony of itself brought a change. Together with King Ferdinand and the latter's Bohemian troops, he invaded Electoral Saxony, forcing the Schmalkaldic chiefs to leave the South German theater of operations. The Emperor rejected a request made by Philip of Hesse on 14 November for a truce and he was soon master of South Germany. Charles demanded contributions but left the Count Palatine his electoral dignity and Ulrich of Württemberg his principality and, above all, did not interfere with the religious situation so long as the important outcome had not been decided. And now it was the Pope himself who jeopardized that. He feared that the Emperor's complete success would mean his strong preponderance and, influenced by antiimperial forces, he recalled his troops at the end of January 1547, thereby greatly embittering Charles V. This was all the more dangerous when hitherto neutral North German Protestantism came to the aid of the Elector of Saxony. Maurice of Saxony fell into serious trouble. Severely tormented by gout and bladder trouble, the Emperor hurried to Saxony and there, relentlessly unsparing of himself, at Mühlberg on the Elbe on 24 April 1547, he won the single battle that he ever took part in. The Elector Johann Friedrich was taken prisoner and condemned to death for *lèse majesté* and heresy. There was no intention of carrying out this judgment; it was intended rather to lend force to the subsequent negotiations. In the Wittenberg Capitulation of 19 May Johann Friedrich had to renounce his principality and the electoral dignity. He firmly refused to recognize the decrees of the Council and remained in prison. The same fate befell Philip of Hesse when on 19 June he asked the Emperor's pardon at Halle.

Henry VIII of England had died on 28 January 1547, and Francis I of France on 31 March. Martin Luther had preceded them to the grave a year earlier, on 18 February 1546. Charles V seemed left alone as victor on the stage of history. What could now stop him from setting about establishing the new order of Europe in the sense of his own universal imperial idea and of restoring the unity of faith? But this was denied him especially by the one person whose help he had most need of — the Pope. "The dissension that now broke out between the Pope and the Emperor was the salvation of the German Protestants in their extreme distress" (H. Jedin).

The Violent Diet and the *Interim*

According to the Emperor's plan the Protestants were to be mastered in the field and then brought to participate in the Council at Trent. The first item had succeeded but in the meantime the second had been made impossible by the Council itself with the consent of the Pope. On 11 March it had decreed its transfer to Bologna. The Protestants were certainly not to be induced to attend a council in a city of the Papal State and to accept the decrees issued there. At the Curia, however, the Catholic Church in Germany had already been written off and the Council's task was seen as predominantly the preservation and reform of the Church in lands that were still Catholic.

After the Emperor's victory at Mühlberg Paul III was all the more fearful of the Spanish-Habsburg pincer movement and of the Emperor's universal power. The bitterness produced by the murder of his son, Pierluigi Farnese, on 10 September 1547, at Piacenza and the occupation of that city by imperial troops quickly envenomed the Pope's relations with Charles V.

The "imperialist" Council Fathers had not gone to Bologna but had stayed on at Trent. The Pope could not be induced to transfer the Council back there, but eventually, not wanting to risk a schism, he had to order a cessation of conciliar activity on 3 February 1548.

In view of this development there remained to the Emperor no other possibility than to try to lead the religious affair to a solution within the German framework and without the Pope. This was the central problem of the "Violent Diet" that opened at Augsburg on 1 September 1547. It was the more urgent when the Emperor's other concern, the reorganization of the Empire — a consolidation of the imperial central power — encountered massive resistance. The Emperor envisaged an Imperial League on the model of the Swabian League that, despite everything, had functioned for almost fifty years, from 1487 to 1533, for the management of South Germany and as an instrument of Habsburg policy. Such a league would have offered the possibility of incorporating the Netherlands, Milan, and Savoy and tying the Empire more closely together with the other lands of the Habsburgs. But the days of an imperial reform in the direction of monarchy were past. The princes had become far too powerful through their victories over the knights and the peasants and through the reform movement. As the Elector of Brandenburg had declared, they were not inclined to reduce the Empire "to servitude" to the Emperor by means of a league.

The Emperor was likewise unable completely to regulate ecclesiastical affairs according to his own view, that is, through the return of the Protestants to the ancient Church. He had to content himself with a temporary solution, the *Interim*. At the Emperor's request Julius von Pflug had composed a *Formula sacrorum emendandorum* for the Diet. When a committee on religion at the Diet proved to be unsuited for the task, the *Formula* was, at the Emperor's command, debated and revised by Julius von Pflug, Michael Helding, the Spaniards Pedro de Soto and Pedro Malvenda, and others, together with Johannes Agricola, the only Protestant theologian appointed. The outcome of the two-weeks' work of the theologians was a "compromise" confession, to which the Emperor tried to win the Lutheran and the Catholic estates. But Bavaria and the spiritual princes rejected it. In their view the Catholics should simply be ordered to hold to the ancient faith. After much uncertainty the text was published on 15 May 1548 as *Der römisch-kaiserlichen Majestät Erklärung, wie es der Religion halben im Heiligen Reich bis zum Austrag des gemeinen Concilii gehalten werden soll.* It was imposed on the Protestants in the Recess of the Diet on 30 June.

In the foreword it was asserted that "His Imperial Majesty [was] industriously working to effect a reformation" (paragraph 11), and the conclusion stressed the necessity "of removing the scandals from the Church which have given great cause for the disorder of this time." Hence no one will refuse his encouragement and aid to the Emperor in his efforts "to bring about the useful reform of the Church" (Article XXVI, para. 25).

In the twenty-six articles the fundamental truths of faith were treated: the original state, fall, and redemption of man (I–III), his justification (IV–VIII), the doctrine of the Church (IX–XIII), that of the Sacraments (XIV–XXI), and in particular detail that of the Mass (XXII–XXV). The last article (XXVI) dealt with ceremonies and customs.

Justification takes place on the basis of the merit of Christ's passion and means the forgiveness of sins and renewal in the Holy Spirit. The love of God, which is poured into our heart, brings it about that man "desires what is good and right and accomplishes in deed what he desires." But carnal lusts still fight against the Spirit even in those who "have obtained such righteousness from grace." On this earth man cannot achieve the perfection of this "infused righteousness." Christ must always come to the aid of the weakness of the righteous with his own perfection. Much as justification is God's work and not man's still "the merciful God does not deal with a man as with a dead log but draws him with his will" (Article VI, para. 1). "Prevenient grace... moves the heart to God through Jesus Christ, and this movement is faith" in Holy Scripture and the divine promises. Faith leads to trust and hope and "hope in the promised mercy glorifies God and hence is led to love" (VI, para. 3). Love is fruitful in good works (VII). The Church is the "community and assembly of believers in Christ, in which the Holy Spirit... thus unites the reborn so that they may be one house and one body from one baptism and one faith" (IX). It is invisible and yet also visible (IX, para. 5). The canon of Scripture is established by it (XI, para. 1). It decides doubtful questions by a legitimate council summoned in the Holy Spirit (XI, para. 6). It exercises teaching and the priesthood in special offices. "Although it has many bishops, who rule by divine right the people whom Christ has gained by his precious blood, it still has one supreme bishop who is set over all others in order to avert schisms and dissension" (XIII, para. 1). The theology and practice of the sacraments and Mass are treated in detail. Christ's sacrifice on the Cross is "by itself sufficient... to redeem the whole human race" (XXII, para. 7). The relevant question in the Mass is that "all men will participate in this mighty sacrifice, which has perfectly, sufficiently, and superabundantly achieved salvation for all men, and take advantage of it" (para. 8). The sacrifices of pagans and Jews had meaning in so far as the one sacrifice of Christ was announced and expected in them (para. 10). In the Mass we celebrate without interruption the memorial of this sacrifice and share in its benefits (para. 19). The sacrifice of the cross and that of the Eucharist are "one in substance but different in the manner of offering" (para. 30). The traditional ceremonies are to be retained (XXVI). But they should be explained to the people and all that could "give cause for superstition" should be eliminated (para. 6). The marriage of priests (para. 20) and the lay chalice (para. 21) should be allowed where they are already the custom until a decision by the Council. In the *Interim* nothing is said about the restitution of the property taken from the Church. As a confessional formula it presents the doctrine of the Church with no watering down, but it exerts itself to take up the concerns of the Protestants in both content and language and to do justice to them. Hence it was all the more to be regretted that it did not obtain the assent of the Catholic estates. For the Protestants could only gain the impression that they were to be enticed back to a completely pre-Reformation Church system by means of concessions that were basically not seriously meant, but that would later be required of them. The intransigent, including the otherwise conciliatory Martin Bucer, had no great difficulty in mobilizing resistance to this last effort to save religious unity and in presenting all cooperation as cowardice and betrayal. If the *Interim* did not affect the Catholic estates, still they were not for that reason to be freed of the claims of reform. For them the Emperor on 9 July 1548, issued a *Formula Reformationis per Caesaream Maiestatem statibus ecclesiasticis... proposita et ab eisdem probata et recepta.*

In it the reform of the clergy is presented as urgent. Accordingly, Article I deals with the formation and trial of candidates for the priesthood and the episcopacy.

The pastoral duties of priests and bishops are strongly emphasized. The latter should make it clear by their conduct that they are bishops rather than princes and that their thoughts are directed to heaven rather than to the world (II). The obligation to preach and, as preparation for this, to study Holy Scripture is given special attention. The sacraments must not become spectacles which are merely watched ("otiosa spectacula"); they should again and again be made clear to the faithful in talks (IX). For example, the texts in the administration of baptism and matrimony may be spoken in the vernacular. All rites and every religious usage must promote genuine piety. The people should be warned about superstitious abuses (XVI). Accumulation of benefices is forbidden (XVIII). Visitations and diocesan and provincial synods are especially mentioned among the methods of reform. "In order that the pious zeal for reformation may not cool through long delays," diocesan synods were to be held by Martinmas and provincial synods by the following Lent. As a matter of fact such reform synods did take place for most German sees and for the provinces of Mainz, Trier, Cologne, and Salzburg. Here an effort was made to apply the imperial reform decree to local circumstances and to make them operative. The decrees enacted in this connection gave the episcopal visitors goals and means in their exertions in regard to doctrine and discipline. Even though a complete success was certainly not achieved, still a new spirit was discernible and a start toward inner reform of the German Church became visible. The ground was thereby made ready to some extent for the reception of the Tridentine decrees.

Both the *Interim* and the *Formula Reformationis* suffered from the fact that they were not issued by the proper ecclesiastical authority and represented a problematic intervention by the Emperor into the inner ecclesiastical sphere. To be sure, the papal bull of indult of 18 August 1548 can be interpreted as a certain sanction of these religious-political measures. In this, after protracted negotiations, the Pope granted the dispensations requested by Charles V for promoting reunion. They had the same orientation as the *Interim* and the *Formula Reformationis.* The rehabilitation of repentant concubinaries, the ordination of preachers who had not so far received that sacrament, and the employment of apostate religious in the parochial care of souls were made possible by it. The lay chalice was conceded under definite cautions, and an adjustment with the holders of revenues and wealth from former ecclesiastical property was facilitated.

The *Interim* was difficult to enforce. It was compromised by being the dictate of the victorious power in war and provoked resistance. Also the convictions necessary for realizing its positive potentialities were wanting. There were not enough priests and religious who could have replaced the opposing Protestant preachers. The Jesuits were just beginning to come to Germany. Only in South Germany, in cities such as Augsburg, Ulm, and Constance and in Württemberg did the Emperor have the power to make the *Interim* respected to some extent. In Saxony an attenuated form of it was provided. The Wittenberg theologians, headed by Melanchthon, who was personally ready for an understanding, had laid their hesitations before a Diet at Meissen in July 1548. In the article on justification, they maintained, "much that was good was said," in particular "that we are freely justified by grace without merit," but also much "pharisaical leaven was intermixed." After further discussions at Pegau and Torgau a new formula was produced at

Altzelle. In this were listed the intermediate things (*adiaphora*) on which there could be agreement. This led on 28 December 1548 to the passing of the Leipzig *Interim.* Confirmation and the anointing of the sick were reintroduced, ordination was committed to the bishops, and ceremonies and vestments at Mass and even the feast of Corpus Christi were ordered. The intention was to cling to doctrine and yield in the *adiaphora.* Only an excerpt, the "little Interim," was published, together with a mandate of the Elector Maurice of 4 July 1549. It obtained no very great importance but evoked among the Wittenberg theologians the momentous quarrel over *adiaphora.* Luther's disciple, Matthias Flacius, came out against it, left Wittenberg, and from Magdeburg, "our Lord God's chancery," together with Nikolaus von Amsdorf, led a severe struggle against the *Interim,* which meant for him the *interitus* of the Reformation. In it he heaped mockery and scorn on Johannes Agricola and the dastardly Melanchthon.

Charles V outlawed Magdeburg and commissioned Maurice of Saxony to execute the sentence. This city's effective resistance confirmed the other Protestant cities of North Germany in their rejection of the *Interim.*

The Revolt of the Princes

The Imperial Diet of Augsburg in 1550–51 was influenced by the Council, whose reopening at Trent had been held out by the new Pope Julius III. The Lutheran estates declared their readiness to send delegates but refused to aid in the implementation of the *Interim* and the imperial *Formula Reformationis.* A growing opposition to Charles V was spreading. In the Peace of Passau, which Charles ratified on 10 August, he again allowed only a truce until the next Diet, at which the religious question and the *gravamina* should be settled.

The Religious Peace of Augsburg

Following the failure of an undertaking against France in the late fall of 1552 and the raising of the siege of Metz in January 1553, Charles V left Germany forever and turned over the Empire to his brother Ferdinand. He saw himself unable to restore religious unity in the Empire and had "scruples" about cooperating in another solution. While he actually summoned the long overdue Diet to Augsburg, he did not intend to appear there in person. The meagerly attended Diet was finally opened on 5 February 1555. At the outset the Emperor lodged a protest against everything whereby "our true, ancient, Christian, and Catholic religion would be in the least injured, insulted, weakened, or encumbered. Since the death of Maurice of Saxony in 1553 the Protestants lacked a leader, but they had asserted their determination to work for an unconditional and perpetual religious peace. Of the Protestant princes only the Duke of Württemberg came to Augsburg in person. The negotiations were conducted by princely councilors, professional jurists, and diplomats. There was a great longing for peace and a general conviction of the need for a compromise. To be sure, the time was not yet ripe for a real religious peace. Even though the Protestants demanded the unlimited exercise of religion for themselves, they were not ready to concede it to Catholics or fanatics in their own territories.

Of the Catholic estates only the Bishop of Augsburg, Cardinal Otto von Waldburg, defended a consistent, though impracticable idea. He explained that it was impossible for him to approve a division of the one Catholic Church and to acknowledge in the Diet competence for such a decision. But at the news of the death of Pope Julius III on 23 March, he left the Diet with the legate, Cardinal Morone, in order to take part in the conclave. The fact that he did not return and had himself represented by his chancellor was probably clue to his insight that he stood alone in his unwillingness for concessions.

Theological arguments played scarcely a role in the discussions at Augsburg. The princes or jurists decided the fate of the confessions. There was no further thought of a compromise in dogma and liturgy. What was sought was a lasting ecclesiastical peace between imperial estates that differed in religion. In addition to the question of the ownership and usufruct of Church property, difficulties arose from the demand that the bishops should abandon jurisdiction over the subjects of Protestant princes. There was a severe struggle for the recognition of the "ecclesiastical reservation," whereby a spiritual prince who passed over to the Reformation should lose his office and his rule. The Protestants were unwilling to approve it. When King Ferdinand insisted, stressing that "he had sworn by his honor not to give it up," they made the counterdemand that the ecclesiastical estates should grant "freedom of religion" to the Lutheran knights, cities, and congregations. Ferdinand agreed. He obtained from the Catholics, not its acceptance in the Recess, but only its admission as a subsidiary *Declaratio Ferdinandea.* The "ecclesiastical reservation," on the other hand, was included with the postscript that the Protestants had not approved it.

The Religious Peace of Augsburg was published with the Recess of the Diet on 25 September 1555. It provided that, following so many fruitless efforts for peace, it had been agreed, in an effort to save the fatherland from dissension and ruin, that none of the imperial estates should be attacked by the Emperor or a prince because of its adherence to the *Confessio Augustana* nor suffer any other disadvantage (para. 3). Conversely, the princes of the *Confessio Augustana* were not to inflict any sort of harm on the secular or spiritual estates that clung to the old religion (para. 4). However, all the others which did not belong to the two confessions were to be excluded from this peace (para. 5). The free choice of confession applied only to the imperial estates, not to their subjects, who, in accord with the fundamental principle, "Ubi unus dominus, ibi una sit religio" [later as *cuius regio, eius et religio*], had to accept the confession of the authority. If they could not bring themselves to do so, they should have the right to emigrate after selling their property (para. 11). Because the religious factions could not agree in the case of the conversion of an ecclesiastic to the *Confessio Augustana,* the King, by virtue of the imperial authority, decreed that archbishops, bishops, prelates, or other spiritual estates who abandoned the old religion lost their offices and property, and the chapters could elect a successor who held all the property according to old custom (para. 6). Hence spiritual princes should be able to become Protestants only as private persons, without any right to force their subjects to conform, and with the loss of their authority. In regard to ecclesiastical property, the situation at the time of the Peace of Passau was taken as decisive (para. 7). Until the definitive religious settlement, spiritual jurisdiction should not be exercised over the estates of the *Confessio Augustana* (para. 8). Knights who were immediate imperial vassals were to be included in the peace (para. 13). Where both confessions existed side by side in the Free Cities, matters should remain thus, and each should leave the other in the peaceful possession of its creed, rites, and property (para. 14). The peace should remain valid until the achieving of a peaceful and definitive settlement of religion. If such a union should not come into existence at a general or national council or at a diet, then it should continue in force as "a steadfast, firm, unconditional peace, lasting for ever (para. 12).

The Religious Peace, therefore, was understood as only temporary, until the restoration of unity of faith by a council or another authority competent for religion. It was to be permanent only if no better arrangement could be arrived at. In actuality it introduced a period of peace of a duration otherwise unknown in Germany.

The religious cleavage was definitive and the juxtaposition in law of two confessions was created. The principle of equality was established, but only for the Empire as an equilibrium between confessionally complete parts; hence it was an equality based on inequality in the several territories. Thus there could be no question of toleration and freedom of conscience. Quite the contrary: the territorial prince decided the religion of his territory and of his subjects. By recognition of the right of emigration, he merely renounced the implementation of the medieval law on heresy with its consequences for body, honor, and possessions. The arrangement was based on the notion of the modern territorial state, to the consolidation of which confessional unity contributed substantially. The annulling of episcopal jurisdiction in Protestant areas completed the development of the territorial Church and called for the episcopacy of the prince, who, while unable to direct his Church spiritually, had it administered by his jurists. The politicization of religion and the isolation of the confessions intensified their mutual hostility.

The obscurities in the Religious Peace offered much material for conflict. The Protestant estates did not feel bound by the ecclesiastical reservation. They tried in vain to abolish it at later diets. As a matter of fact, the secularization of the sees and chapters in northern and central Germany reached its climax only after 1555. The *Declaratio Ferdinandea* in regard to the protection of Protestants in the spiritual principalities had, of course, no formal validity in law, but at first it frequently prevented the already insecure Catholic bishops from claiming the right to decide the confessional adherence of their subjects. On the other hand, many Free Cities did not observe the decree for the protection of confessional minorities. The provisional congregations were for the most part again suppressed. Nevertheless, the article on the cities made possible the continued existence of monasteries and chapters in Free Cities with a Lutheran majority. While the peace originally applied only to the adherents of the *Confessio Augustana,* in actuality the Reformed also were soon able to enjoy it, though not without resistance and, until 1648, without any binding force in law. The conversion of the Count Palatine Friedrich III to Calvinism in 1563 contributed decisively to this. Accordingly, the Religious Peace of Augsburg was unable to prevent the split in German Protestantism.

With the abandoning of the exclusive validity of the one Catholic faith the concept of the Empire was fundamentally affected. The Empire had been degraded to a mere federation of territorial states. Hence it was more than a coincidence in time that on 12 September 1556 Charles V renounced the imperial throne. The attitude of the Curia, with whose standards the Religious Peace was irreconcilable, can be understood only if one takes into account that under Julius III an interference in the German situation had been avoided because Germany was already regarded as lost and under Paul IV political differences with the House of Habsburg so predominated that "the Religious Peace was not a determining factor" (H. Lutz). There was no formal protest and no objection through legal process against the Religious Peace of Augsburg, and, we may say, this was advantageous for the consolidating of the Catholic position in Germany. The Catholic estates, Ferdinand I at their head, were convinced that at the moment no better solution was possible if one did not want to suffer further losses or put up with further military confrontations.

Section Four

Europe under the Sign of Confessional Pluralism

CHAPTER 86

The Reformation in Scandinavia

At the end of the Middle Ages the Scandinavian lands were divided among three ecclesiastical provinces. The Danish, under the Archbishop of Lund, Sweden and Finland constituted the province of Uppsala and the Norwegian province of Trondheim (Nidaros).

Denmark

In Denmark King Christian II (1513–23), gifted but unbalanced and ruled by his passions, wanted to break the power of nobles and prelates and make the crown hereditary. He managed to gain the middle class and peasantry by progressive measures such as the improving of popular education and of the administration of justice and the promoting of industry and commerce. In 1520 he was able to impose his rule briefly on Sweden. In the "Stockholm Blood Bath" he tried to get rid of his opponents among the Swedish nobility but thereby incurred such hatred that it was easy for the youthful Gustavus Vasa to win over the people, including leaders among the nobles and churchmen, and to be himself elected administrator in 1521. In the autumn of that year the Danish government had to withdraw and Christian's authority was confined to Denmark, Norway, and Iceland.

In October 1520 Christian had asked Luther's prince, the Elector Frederick the Wise, to send him a preacher of the pure word of God. Thus in June 1521 Karlstadt came to Denmark. But he was unable to realize his radical ideas, for the King, from political motives, including consideration for his brother-in-law, Charles V, was unwilling to go as far as to break with the old Church. Christian II first completed his territorial Church government. He curtailed the rights of bishops and forbade appeal to Rome. He permitted priests to marry. But at the beginning of 1523 he was to fail because of the opposition of the nobles, including a group of bishops. They renounced their fealty to him and raised Duke Frederick of Holstein to the Danish throne. They obliged Frederick to proceed against Luther's disciples and all others who preached against "God, the faith of Holy Church, the Holy Father at Rome, or the Roman Church." But Frederick I (1523–33) came out more openly in favor of Lutheranism as he saw his position consolidated. In June 1526 he gave his daughter in marriage to Albrecht of Prussia, who had been the first spiritual prince to become a Protestant and had transformed the territory of the Teutonic Order into a secular duchy. Frederick favored Hans Tausen (1494–1561), the "Danish Luther," a former Hospitaler, who had been gained to the new doctrine as a student at Wittenberg in 1523, and in 1526 made him his court chaplain, even though a charge of heresy had been made against him.

Especially harmful was the Curia's practice of disposing capriciously of the benefices of the Scandinavian Church. In 1526 Frederick named Aage Sparre as Archbishop, but papal confirmation was refused. Hence Sparre was unable to receive episcopal consecration and governed as archbishop-elect. In 1526 the King obtained from the *Herredag* at Odense a law to the effect that henceforth no cleric might ask confirmation or provision from the Pope.

At the *Herredag* at Odense in 1527 the bishops demanded that steps be taken against "the new government and the new teaching," but the King got his way and obtained protection in law for the Lutherans. They won most cities. Only the episcopal cities and the rural folk, with the majority of the nobility, remained Catholic. Twenty-one Lutheran preachers, under the leadership of Hans Tausen, had submitted to the *Confessio Hafneinsis* to the *Herredag* at Copenhagen in July 1530, and a *Confutatio Lutheranismi Danici.* King Frederick continued consistently his policy of favoring Lutheranism. After his death in 1533 the bishops wanted to thwart the election of his Lutheran-minded oldest son Christian in favor of the latter's younger brother, still a minor. The younger prince had been raised in reform Catholic circles and gave hopes of a Catholic restoration. At the *Herredag* at Copenhagen it was possible to postpone the election. But a civil war forced the election of Christian III (1534–59). This meant the victory of the Lutheran Reformation in Denmark, together with Norway and Iceland. Johannes Bugenhagen was called to Copenhagen to construct the new Church organization. He crowned the King, drew up the *Ordinantia Ecclesiastica* on the model of the Saxon Church Order, and ordained seven superintendents. These later assumed the episcopal title, without bothering about apostolic succession. The *Ordinantia Ecclesiastica* was accepted by the *Rigsraad* in 1539 as a provisional solution until the settlement of the religious question by a general council. But, as a matter of fact, it continued in force until 1683 and created a Lutheran national Church under the King's direction. When in 1538 Christian III joined the League of Schmalkalden, the *Confessio Augustana* became the creed of the Danish Church. In 1550 appeared "Christian's Bible," a translation of the entire Scripture into Danish. Resistance to the Reformation was crushed by prison and banishment. King Christian IV (1588–1648) forbade Catholic priests to set foot in Denmark under threat of death. Exile and loss of property remained for centuries the punishment for conversion to Catholicism. Religious liberty was not granted until 1844.

Norway

Christian III introduced the Reformation in Norway at the same time as he did in Denmark. Without popular support, the Reformation was imposed in Norway on the Danish model. The bishops were deposed, and ecclesiastical and monastic property was confiscated for the Danish crown.

Assemblies of nobles at Bergen and Oslo, powerfully reinforced by Danish vassals, approved the Danish *Ordinantia Ecclesiastica* in 1539. But out of regard for the people, who were unprepared for Lutheran doctrine, the implementation was carried out with prudence. The Catholic faith continued for decades among the rural folk. An obstacle to bringing the people into a close attachment to Lutheranism was the fact that, in addition to the Danish Bible, the liturgy, hymns, and Luther's *Small Catechism* were available only in Danish, and the Norwegian language survived only as the popular dialect. However, the Lutheran Church Order of 1607 brought the Reformation to a definite conclusion.

Iceland

In Iceland too a living Catholic Church succumbed to the Danish King's desire for power. Lutheranism came there, as it came to Denmark and Sweden, through merchants and young clerics educated in Germany. At first Bishops Ogmundur Palsson of Skalholt (1521–40) and Jon Arason of Holar (1520–50) contrived to keep these influences out. On the accession of Christian III Iceland obtained a new governor in Klaus of Merwitz, who demanded that the bishops accept the Danish Church Order. They refused, with their clergy, and in two doctrinal letters warned the people against Luther and his errors. Meanwhile, Gissur Einarsson (1515–48), who had returned as a Lutheran from his academic career in Germany, had dispelled the hesitations of Bishop Ogmundur and secured the blind old man's confidence. When the bishop resigned in 1540 he recommended that young Einarsson, who in the previous years had made himself indispensable, should be his successor. He was elected and at Copenhagen was confirmed by the King as superintendent. When the old bishop recognized his mistake, he became active, despite his feebleness, in defense of the ancient faith. The Danes resorted to force and in 1541 dragged the old man aboard ship, on which he died shortly after putting out to sea. The Bishop of Holar in northern Iceland, Jon Arason, ecclesiastical prince, poet, statesman, and warrior all in one, was determined to defend the Catholic faith along with Iceland's freedom. He had become a bishop, even though he had four sons, of whom two were priests, and two daughters. In 1550 he proceeded, as a true descendant of Vikings, against the south of the island, captured the Protestant Bishop of Skalholt, and expelled the Danish governor and his adherents. Iceland seemed to be under his control, but on his return to the north he fell by treachery into the hands of his enemies. He was executed along with his two priest-sons. Now Christian III had an easy time in introducing the Reformation. This meant at the same time the despoiling of the island and the end of its freedom. It was only in 1584 that there appeared a complete Bible in Icelandic; this was followed by a hymnal in 1589 and a book of family devotions in 1594.

Sweden

In Sweden Gustavus Trolle, Archbishop of Uppsala, had joined the Danes against the Swedish nationalist movement. He was deposed in 1517. In 1520 Christian II of Denmark in his campaign for the subjugation of Sweden posed as the defender of the Church's freedom and protector of the Archbishop. He had the leaders of the Swedish opposition put to death in the "Stockholm Blood Bath" of November 1520. The union of the two Kingdoms was thereby gravely weakened and Archbishop Trolle was compromised. The struggle for freedom was thus directed against him and the Church that he embodied. In 1521 Gustavus Erikson Vasa (1496–1560) was elected administrator of the Kingdom at Vadstena and before long he controlled the whole country except for a few strongholds. The Danish government had to yield. With the dethronement of Christian II in Denmark Sweden was to achieve its definite independence. At Pentecost 1523 Gustavus Vasa was elected King at Strängnäs. The local archdeacon, Lars Andersson (1470–1552), became his secretary and chancellor. He guided the royal policy in the direction of the Reformation and managed to make Gustavus Vasa understand the advantages offered by a Lutheran ecclesiastical organization for the royal power and the public treasury. Religion was not a particularly profound concern of the King. What mattered to him was to secure his power by means of a state Church and to take care of the financial needs of his political organization by means of ecclesiastical property without imposing further burdens on the people and the nobility.

In Sweden the Lutheran movement had also become known through merchants who were Germans or had German connections and through theologians who had studied in the land of the Reformation. The most important among them and the real reformer of Sweden, Olav Pedersson (1493–1552), came directly from Luther's school. He had studied from the late summer of 1516, at Wittenberg. He returned to Sweden in the fall of 1518, full of enthusiasm for Scripture as the supreme authority. He entered the service of the Bishop of Strängnäs and became deacon (1520), master of the cathedral school, and cathedral preacher. When his sermons were challenged, the King created for him in 1524 the position of city secretary and preacher at the main church in Stockholm. He labored zealously there for the Reformation until 1531. He inaugurated his series of numerous, predominantly pastoral writings with *A Useful Instruction* (1526). This first reform treatise in Sweden is a medley of separate sections with translations of passages from Luther, Bucer, and others. Olav composed hymns, translated the New Testament (1526), and in the *Swedish Chronicle* created the first great work of national history.

Hans Brask, Bishop of Linköping, was the steadfast and methodical champion of the Catholic faith. In 1521 Gustavus Vasa had solemnly promised him that he would protect all the rights and possessions of the Church. He distributed religious writings by means of his own printing press. He pressed for a translation of the New Testament and in pastoral essays came out very sharply against Lutheranism. Gustavus Vasa had applied for the papal confirmation with a demand for a dispensation from the customary fees, threatening that otherwise he would confirm, without the Pope, those elected "a solo et summo pontifice Christo" and have them consecrated. The Curia refused. The Pope confirmed only Peder Mansson (d. 1534), superior of the monastery of Saint Birgitta at Rome, as Bishop of Västeras and had him consecrated. Bishop Brask saw the danger of schism and advocated the King's speedy coronation as well as the confirmation and consecration of the bishops. Gustavus Vasa was not to be hurried; in fact, he was more interested in delay. He aimed to eliminate "episcopal rule" in the country, but the royal coronation involved an oath to respect the privileges of the Church and the position of the bishops, and he wanted to evade this. The external organization of the Church remained, but the King could appoint and depose priests. They had to preach the pure word of God.

Gustavus Vasa had achieved his goal at Västeras. Now his coronation and the consecration of the bishops could bring him only advantages and consolidate his position vis-à-vis the outside and the opposition in the country. He made known to the bishops-elect that the people no longer wanted to be without "consecrated bishops." They had to receive consecration or give up their positions. But they should be bishops "in accord with the word of the Lord, not of the Pope." Consequently they had to take an oath to preach the Gospel, to be content with the revenues necessary for their function, and to be loyal to the King. The Pope was not mentioned. A week later, on 12 January 1528 Gustavus Vasa had himself anointed and crowned King by the bishops in the Uppsala cathedral according to the old Catholic rite. But in the coronation oath there was no mention of the protection of Holy Church and of the privileges of bishops.

In February 1529 the synod of Örebro denied to the Pope authority higher than that of bishops but was otherwise reform Catholic rather than Protestant. The break with the papacy became complete when in 1531 the brother of the reformer Olav, Lars Pedersson, who had just finished his studies at Wittenberg, was made Archbishop of Uppsala with no concurrence by Rome. In the same year appeared Olav's *Ordo Missae Sueticae,* a translation and revision of the old order of the Mass in the spirit of the reform. Gustavus Vasa sought the advice of two Germans, the theologian Georg Norman and the jurist Georg von Pyhy, to strengthen his influence over the Church. He placed it under the supervision of a superintendent and to this office he appointed Norman, his sons' tutor, in 1539. From 1543 Olav Pedersson again worked as chief pastor in Stockholm, where he died in 1552.

Gustavus Vasa's attitude on the religious question was subject to change according to the political situation in the succeeding years. On the whole the construction of the Lutheran Church proceeded quietly but methodically. The external institutions were preserved more than they were elsewhere. Of course, much time was needed to gain the people, especially the rural folk.

John III (1568–92), gave the Swedish state Church its present form in the Church Order of 1571. It had been composed by Lars Pedersson in 1561 but suppressed by Erik XIV. The revised edition of 1571 was more intimately related to old Swedish tradition, introduced a richer liturgy, and gave the episcopal office more importance and prestige. The episcopal constitution of the Church was completely restored.

John III was himself interested in theology. His marriage with the sister of King Sigismund II of Poland, Catherine, who remained true to her Catholic faith, his own humanist education, and an encounter with the Anglican Church and its liturgy caused him to think of mediating between the Catholic and the Protestant Churches. He was fascinated by the idea of a Church unity based on the common tradition of the patristic age. Union seemed to him to be possible if the marriage of priests, the lay chalice, and the vernacular liturgy were conceded. His "catholicizing" efforts found their expression in the new Church Order of 1575 and in the *Liturgy of the Swedish Church* of 1576, the so-called *Red Book.* Regardless of the opposition, the King held discussions with the learned Jesuit Anton Possevino (d. 1611) on reconciliation with Rome.

The forces that offered resistance to reconciliation were organized by the third son of Gustavus Vasa, Duke Charles of Södermanland. On the death of John III, Charles felt that the time was especially favorable for energetic measures against a return to Catholicism. John's son Sigismund (1592–99), who had been King of Poland since 1587, and had labored zealously there for the Catholic faith, intended to do likewise as King of Sweden. Duke Charles made use of the time before the King's assumption of the throne to confront him with a *fait accompli.* The national Synod of Uppsala in March 1593 formally ascribed to the *Confessio Augustana* of 1530. The coronation of the new King was made contingent upon his agreeing to these decrees. Disillusioned, he returned to Poland and committed the government to his uncle, Duke Charles. Only when the latter by his autocratic conduct had run afoul of the higher nobility in the *Riksrad* did King Sigismund try to seize power again by armed force. But Charles retained the ascendancy, and in 1604 mounted the Swedish throne as Charles IX (1604–11).

In 1595 the Diet of Söderköping had decreed the expulsion of all Catholics from the country and the suppression of the last monastery, Saint Birgitta's foundation at Vadstena.

Finland

The fate of the Church in Finland was totally determined by the country's dependence on Sweden. The decrees of the Diet of Västeras in 1527 and of the Synod of Örebro in 1529 were authoritative here also. But Canon Peter Sarkilathi (d. 1529) of Abo (Turku), who had studied in Germany, had already spread Lutheran teachings. The most important of these, Mikael Agricola (1508–57), returned to Finland with a letter of recommendation from Luther after a period of study at Wittenberg (1536–39). He became the director of the cathedral school, then coadjutor and in 1554 successor of Bishop Skytte of Abo. Agricola not only became the reformer of Finland; at the same time he laid the foundations of the Finnish written language and literature. His chief work was the translation of the New Testament in 1548. In addition, he produced parts of the Old Testament (1551–52) and a liturgy modeled on the "Swedish Mass."

In the same year as Agricola (1544), Paul Juusten, who had also studied at Wittenberg (1543–46), became bishop of the newly erected see of Viborg (Viipuri). He died in 1576 as Bishop of Abo. The efforts of John III for recatholicization found a receptive soil in Finland, but here too they were cancelled by the Uppsala Synod of 1593. Significant for the attaching of the people to the Reformation were the Finnish hymnal of 1605, an improved edition of that of 1580, a catechism in questions and answers (1618), and a two-volume book of sermons (1621).

CHAPTER 87

The Reformation in Eastern Europe

At the beginning of modern times the countries of Eastern Europe were characterized by a plurality of nationalities, social orders, and constitutional forms. The sequel was that the Reformation made its appearance relatively early and easily but, except in Prussia and Livonia, was nowhere established fully nor exclusively in its Lutheran form. The plurality of forces produced an altogether milder religious climate and a juxtaposition of several confessions in one territory. Often the authority did not impose a uniform confession, and the consequence was not only the toleration of Protestantism but its fragmentation. In addition to Lutherans and Calvinists, the Antitrinitarians — Unitarians and Socinians — and the Anabaptists and Bohemian Brethren, expelled from the lands of their origin, had a chance to develop.

Religion and nationality were closely connected. The Germans were Lutherans and remained such until the time of the Counter Reformation. Poles and Magyars, in so far as they did not remain Catholics, turned chiefly to Calvinism.

For the smaller nations and national groups the reform movement meant a cultural event to a far greater degree than elsewhere. The exertions in regard to Scripture and to a vernacular liturgy and preaching led to translations of the Bible and the publishing of hymnals, catechisms, collections of sermons, and a devotional literature. In this way dialects often became literary languages, and literary monuments arose which supplied both expression and support to the national consciousness.

The German population in the cities and the nobility and great proprietors in the country played an important role in the introduction of the Reformation. Because of their endeavors to secure and expand their jurisdiction vis-à-vis the King and the episcopal tribunals they were all open to a confession not held by the monarchy or the authority. As a result, frequently only a small upper stratum was affected by the reform movement, and a later recatholicization made easy progress.

The Duchy of Prussia

By the Second Peace of Torun in 1466 the western part of the lands of the Teutonic Order — Pomerellen and Kulmerland — together with the bishopric of Ermland was incorporated into Poland. East Prussia with Königsberg was left to the grand master of the Teutonic Knights, who, however, had to take an oath of personal fealty to the Polish King. When Albrecht of Brandenburg-Ansbach (1490–1568) was elected grand master of the order in 1511, he, like his predecessor, tried to evade the taking of the oath and to recover the West Prussian territories of the order. The sequel was war with Poland in January 1520. In the truce of Torun the solution of the controverted question was referred to a commission of arbitration. In the matter of the reform of the order and of the administration of its territory, Albrecht's adviser, Dietrich von Schönberg, as early as 1521 wanted to submit the order's rules to Luther for revision. But this was not done until June 1523, after

Albrecht had meanwhile been gained for the reform movement by Osiander's preaching at Nürnberg in 1522. In December 1523 Luther replied to Albrecht's questions: whether Christ had founded his Church on Peter and on the Popes as Peter's successors, whether the Pope had the power, with or without a council, to issue a law over and above the commandments of God, a law whose observance would be important for salvation, and whether Pope and councils could change God's commandments. In an effort to obstruct the progress of the Reformation in his diocese, the new bishop of the neighboring see of Ermland, Mauritius Ferber, issued an edict against the Lutheran heresy on 20 January 1524. Polentz thereupon decreed the introduction of the vernacular in the administration of baptism in a reform mandate for his diocese, issued on 28 January, and recommended the reading of the following works of Luther: the translation of the New Testament, *Von der Freiheit des Christenmenschen, Von guten Werken,* the *Kirchenpostille,* the exegesis of the "Magnificat," and of the psalms. Instructive of his understanding of Reformation is the fact that he does not mention Luther's polemics.

Luther's German brochure on baptism was printed at Königsberg in 1524 as an aid for pastors and in Lent an explication of the "Our Father" was introduced. In the "Salve Regina" "advocate" and "King Jesus" replaced "Mary." In the two principal churches of Königsberg the images of the saints were removed during Lent, and on Easter Monday and Tuesday Johannes Amandus urged the people in sermons to plunder and destroy the Franciscan monastery. The resistance of citizens with Catholic sympathies to the innovations was officially and forcibly suppressed by Polentz, who at this time was still in charge of government business for Albrecht. In order to push the further spread of the Reformation, Polentz sent Lutheran preachers into the cities and village parishes of the territory confided to him and then carried out their installation by recourse to his office as regent even when the people of a city were unanimously opposed to the measure.

Albrecht had decided to follow Luther's advice and transform the territory of the Teutonic Order into a secular duchy. On 9 April 1525, one day before the armistice agreed to in 1521 expired, he signed the Peace of Cracow, which provided for the suppression of the Teutonic Order in Prussia and the enfeoffment of Albrecht with the order's Prussian lands as an hereditary secular duchy. On 10 April Albrecht solemnly took the oath of fealty to the Polish King. In August Bishop Polentz relinquished all secular authority in his bishopric to Albrecht. "But Polentz remained officially what he was — Bishop of Samland — with all the ecclesiastical rights that he had exercised up to now; he retained the right of ordaining the clergy, the right of visitation of all churches in his territory, and jurisdiction over matrimonial cases, just as he had done as Bishop." Erhard of Queis surrendered his secular authority to Albrecht in October 1527. In the summer of 1525 Polentz, Briesmann, and most religious and priests in Prussia married. Albrecht, who had earlier admitted Briesmann and Johannes Poliander, newly arrived from Wittenberg, into his cabinet as ducal councilors, summoned a Diet for December 1525. At this a territorial ordinance and a Church Order issued by Polentz and Queis were adopted. The annual visitation provided in the latter was first carried out in the spring of 1526. Thereby the Reformation was firmly consolidated in the Duchy of Prussia.

Livonia

The Baltic territories of Kurland, Livonia, and Estonia were under their own master of the Teutonic Order, who was then Wolter von Plettenberg (1499–1535). But he shared the government with the bishops and allowed the cities extensive autonomy. Early on the Reformation got a foothold at Riga, Reval, and Dorpat. In the winter of 1524–25 there were riots directed against the churches and monasteries. The city authorities used these as an opportunity for reorganizing the Church and disposing of much Church property, and not merely for the care of the poor and the preachers.

In the summer of 1524 Riga renounced its oath of homage to the archbishop, Johannes Blankenfeld, who energetically championed the old faith, and offered to the master of the Teutonic Order, Wolter von Plettenberg, the suzerainty of the city, to be exercised alone instead of with the archbishop. Otherwise, the city would look for another lord. This was an allusion to Albrecht of Prussia, whose secularizing notions were well known. Thus the master was in a difficult position. On the one hand, he did not want to infringe on the archbishop's rights; on the other, he had to allow Albrecht no pretext for interfering. But when the archbishop, in an effort to maintain himself, allied with the Grand Prince of Moscow, Wolter von Plettenberg had a reason for arresting him for treason and assuming the undivided suzerainty.

In 1527 the city of Riga summoned the Königsberg reformer, Johannes Briesmann, to become cathedral preacher and also gave him a post corresponding to that of superintendent. He stayed until 1531, elaborating a Lutheran Church Order with Andreas Kopken in 1529. This *Kurtz Ordnung des Kirchendienst,* printed in 1530, contained a liturgy in High German and a hymnal in Low German and was made obligatory by Riga, Reval, and Dorpat in 1533. The efforts of Albrecht of Prussia to make Livonia a secular duchy by means of his brother Wilhelm, who became coadjutor in 1530 and Archbishop of Riga in 1539, and to eliminate the Teutonic Order foundered on the resistance of the order and of its victorious master, Wilhelm of Fürstenberg. But when in 1558 the order, without allies, faced an invasion by the Russians and succumbed to their superiority, Livonia broke up. Ösel fell to Denmark, Estonia to Sweden, while the rest of the order's territory, with the archbishopric of Riga, came under Polish rule in 1561. But King Sigismund II Augustus granted the German cities extensive autonomy and assured them the free exercise of religion according to the *Confessio Augustana.*

Poland

Pre-Reformation currents, the ideas of conciliarism, the impact of Hussitism, and the spirit of humanism also prepared the soil for the Reformation in Poland.

The influence of the royal court, above all that of the Renaissance Queen, Bona Sforza, was harmful to the Catholic Church, especially in the matter of nominations to bishoprics. In this country of a predominantly agricultural economy and an aristocratic society the nobility played a great role. Its struggle against episcopal jurisdiction and for extensive autonomy favored the spread of Protestantism.

The reform movement was introduced and propagated by students who had studied abroad, by merchants' sons who were sent to Nürnberg, Augsburg, or Leipzig for training, and by Luther's writings. As early as 1520 King Sigismund I (1506–48) saw himself compelled to issue an edict, which was made more strict in 1523, against the introduction of Luther's writings. In 1534 and 1540 attendance at heretical universities was forbidden, but the effect of this decree was not too great.

Luther's treatise on the Ten Commandments had already been printed at Danzig in 1520. As almost everywhere else, enthusiasm for the new teaching was connected with social demands, such as that for a reduction of taxes and for a public statement of the household accounts. In January 1525 five preachers of the new doctrine were appointed and in the *Articles of the Community* of 23 January poor laws that had been demanded were provided. Meanwhile, the overthrown mayor, Eberhard Ferber, appealed for help to King Sigismund I. After the Diet, which had been summoned to Piotrkov, and the provincial Diet, convoked at Marienburg for Polish Prussia, had promised the King support, he restored the old order at Danzig, thus stopping for the moment the progress of the Reformation.

Under Sigismund I there were as yet no reform congregations established, but the Reformation gained many adherents among the nobility.

Before the middle of the sixteenth century Cracow and Königsberg were the most important centers for the spread of the Reformation. A Polish translation of Luther's small catechism was printed at Königsberg as early as 1530. The Church Order of the Duchy of Prussia of 1544 appeared not only in German and Latin but also in Polish. Seklucian composed revisions of the catechism in Polish in 1545 and 1547 and published a Polish hymnal at Königsberg in 1547. In 1552 he also published a New Testament at Königsberg, and in 1556 a Polish prayerbook, a free rendering of that of Melanchthon and Spangenberg. The University of Königsberg, founded in 1544, contributed significantly to the spread of the Reformation.

Protestantism reached its greatest development in Poland under King Sigismund II Augustus (1548–72). In 1562–63 some six hundred out of thirty-six hundred parishes were in Protestant hands. In 1569 the Senate counted fifty-eight Protestant members as opposed to fifty-five Catholics, but the latter figure does not include the fifteen bishops. From 1552 to 1565 only Protestants were elected as marshals of the Diet.

The Protestants had great hopes in the King, who corresponded with Melanchthon and Calvin. Calvin dedicated his commentary on Hebrews to him in 1549. Prince Mikolaj Radziwill of Lithuania, a zealous champion of Protestantism, was on friendly terms with the King and as grand chancellor occupied an influential position. But on 12 December 1550 Sigismund II publicly professed the Catholic faith, while at the same time continuing to tolerate the advance of Protestantism.

Sigismund approved the acceptance of the *Confessio Augustana* by the *Landtag* Diet of Polish Prussia in 1559. He likewise assured Livonia, when it came under Polish rule in 1561, the recognition of the *Confessio Augustana*. The Warsaw Confederation of 28 January 1573 guaranteed freedom of religion to every noble.

Despite these successes the impact of Protestantism was weakened by its fragmentation among Lutherans, Calvinists, Bohemian Brethren, and Antitrinitarians. Lutheranism was represented chiefly by the German middle class. About half the congregations in Greater Poland joined in a synodal union. The main body of the

Bohemian "Fraternal Unity" consisted of brethren who emigrated to Poznan after the Schmalkaldic War. They found a great response both among the nobility and among the common people. Their centers were Poznan, Kozminek, and Lissa.

Calvinism made great strides after 1550. Its main centers were Lesser Poland (Cracow) and Lithuania; its adherents came chiefly from the Polish population and the nobility. Jan Laski (1499–1560), a highly educated aristocrat, was its most important figure. After his travels had led him throughout the West, he returned to his Polish homeland in 1556 to act as reformer in Calvin's spirit. Prince Mikolaj Radziwill used his own great influence for Calvinism. Wherever he could, he established a Calvinist worship. He brought about a translation of the entire Bible and founded a press specifically for the printing of this "Brest Bible" (1563). Even the center of the Protestantizing Cracow circle of humanists, Francesco Lismanini, devoted himself to the Calvinist confession after a visit to Geneva at the beginning of the 1550s. With Jan Laski he worked to unite all the Protestants in Poland and to create a strict ecclesiastical system on the Geneva model. But they were unable to overcome the fragmentation and, after Laski's death, Lismanini himself went over to the sect of the Antitrinitarians.

In 1565, under the leadership of the Cracow pastor, Gregor Pauli (Pawel), the Antitrinitarians separated from the Calvinist Church as the "Ecclesia minor." They had taken over the rejection of the dogma of the Trinity from Italian refugees for their faith. Faustus Sozzini (c. 1537–1604) became their leading theologian. They were later called Socinians after him, though he himself did not join their community. After 1600 Rakow became their intellectual and organizational center, and in that city in 1605 appeared the *Rakow Catechism,* based on preliminary studies by Sozzini. In addition to the fragmentation and the lack of educational institutions, the weakness of Polish Protestantism lay especially in its failure to win the broad masses of the people. It remained the affair of a thin upper stratum and of the nobility.

Hungary

At the close of the Middle Ages Hungary was engaged in a close cultural interchange with its western neighbors. And so Luther's writings were circulated in Hungary too, especially among the German population. At the royal court in Buda the Reformation found a promoter in the Margrave Georg of Brandenburg-Ansbach-Kulmbach (1484–1543). He represented German interests in opposition to the Magyar faction under John Zapolya.

The young Queen, Mary of Habsburg, sister of Charles V, read Luther's writings enthusiastically and maintained close contact with the humanists, Simon Grynaeus (1493–1541), and Vitus of Windsheim. Conrad Cordatus (1476–1546) labored for the Reformation as court preacher in 1521–22; he later planned the first collection of Luther's *Table Talk.* Johannes Henckel, his successor, served the same cause. And Paul Speratus also received a call to Buda.

As early as 1521 the Archbishop of Esztergom was moved to have the bull excommunicating Luther read in the churches of the kingdom. The Diet of Buda in 1523 decided to apply the paragraph on heretics to the Lutherans also.

Decisive importance attaches to the battle of Mohécs, where on 29 August 1526, in addition to King Louis II, two archbishops and five bishops fell in the struggle against the Turks. Following the Turkish victory Hungary was divided into three parts: the "Kingdom of Hungary," comprising the northern and western parts, came under Habsburg rule; the Turkish province, which included the Pusta, the low plain in the area of the Danube and the Theiss; and the "Principality of Transylvania," where Zapolya (1526–40) maintained himself as vassal of the Sultan and which, after his death, fell, despite the Peace of Grosswardein (1538), not to King Ferdinand but to Zapolya II.

The ecclesiastical property in the widowed bishoprics was seized by the higher nobility.

The sequel was that in the following years both Ferdinand and Zapolya each named a bishop for the same see, so that some of them, for example Csanad, Weissenburg, Eger, and Grosswardein, at times had two claimants. There was no nomination by the Curia until 1539.

The school of Bartfeld acquired a special importance for the further spread of the Reformation in the German part of the population. The majority of the future statesmen of Hungary went through the humanist-oriented school of Bartfeld, from which proceeded nearby schools and printeries. The five royal Free Cities of Bartfeld, Eperies, Kaschau, Klein-Zeben, and Leutschau joined the Reformation in 1549 by adopting the *Confessio Pentapolitana.* This confession, stamped with a humanist spirit and recognized even by Ferdinand because of its dogmatic moderation, became the basis of the confession of the seven hill towns of Lower Hungary as well as of the fraternity of the twenty-four towns in the Zips.

Johannes Honter (1498–1549), who had studied at Vienna, is regarded as the reformer of the Germans in Transylvania. He was called back home in his native Kronstadt in 1533 and there he conducted a private school and established the first printery in the country. The prefaces to two works of Augustine that he printed in 1539 were early testimonies to his reform outlook. After his friend Johannes Fuchs had assumed the government of Kronstadt in 1541 and even the clergy had been gained for the Reformation, Valentin Wagner was sent to Wittenberg to establish closer relations with Melanchthon. The liturgy was reformed at Kronstadt in the autumn of 1542. The approval by the city of the Reformation brochure that Honter published in 1543 meant the introduction of the Reformation. To defend it, Honter wrote an Apologia for the Diet at Weissenburg. He was intrigued by the idea of a Reformation within the Catholic Church. The word of God, he held, had to be the supreme guideline of every reform. Hence the Mass as a sacrifice should be abolished and the Eucharist under both species introduced. On this point Honter appealed to discussions at Regensburg in 1541 for a compromise. In the doctrine of justification Honter, following Melanchthon and Major, stressed the necessity of good works against the perils of a justification by faith alone.

The *Reformatio ecclesiarum Saxonicarum in Transsylvania,* a Church Order based on Honter's Reformation brochure and valid for the entire Saxon area of settlement, appeared in 1547; it was commissioned by the *Universitas Saxorum,* the political organ of the Saxon element in the population. Its aim was to maintain order against fanatics. The power of the keys and excommunication were again more closely linked with the spiritual function. James 2:17 was cited as the chief proof in the doctrine of justification. Even a censorship of books was provided. The Eucharistic teaching was oriented to Wittenberg. This Church Order was made a law in 1550, a year after Honter's death. During the vacancy of the see of Weissenburg Paul Wiener was elected bishop in 1553. His successor, Matthias Hebler (1556–71), had to defend the Lutheran character of the Church against Calvinists and Antitrinitarians. In 1557 the Diet of Torda conceded to the three confessions equality with the Catholic confession, which was itself forbidden by law in 1566.

The Magyars were won to the Reformation, partly by Germans, for example in Transylvania or by a few itinerant preachers, most of whom had studied at Wittenberg. Melanchthon's pupil, Johannes Sylvester (c. 1504–52), directed the school near Sarvar at the end of the 1530s. After a printery had been opened there in 1537–38, Sylvester published a grammar of the Magyar language and in 1541 the first complete Magyar translation of the New Testament.

Imre Ozorai composed the first printed treatise in the Magyar tongue, a work on Christ and Antichrist (Cracow 1535). Stephan Galszecsi and Stephan Bencedi Szekely each had hymnals printed in 1536 and 1538 respectively. Two important centers of the Reformation arose through the favor of the noble family of Torok in Papa and Debrecen.

By 1560 the greatest part of the nobility and, since the manorial lord could appoint Lutheran pastors by virtue of the right of patronage, of the rural folk had been gained for the Reformation.

In the Slovene and Croatian border areas the noble families of Zrinyi, Erdeody, and especially Ungnad supported the Reformation. Johann Ungnad, Baron of Sonneck (1493–1564), the leading official in Styria, after embracing Protestantism went to Württemberg and on his estate at Urach arranged the printing of Bibles, catechisms, primers, and prayerbooks in Slovene and Croatian.

The leaders in cultivating the Slovene language for the sake of the Reformation were: Primoz Trubar (1508–86), who published, among other things, a catechism and a speller in 1550 and between 1555 and 1577 the entire New Testament and writings of Melanchthon and Luther; Sebastian Krelj (1538–67), with his children's Bible of 1566 and prayerbook of 1567; Jurij Dalmatin (1547–89), who translated the Old Testament; and Adam Bohoric (c. 1520–c. 1600), who published the psalter, hymns, some school texts, and in 1584 a Slovene grammar.

On the Catholic side there appeared at Graz in 1574 the Slovene catechism of Leonhard Pacherneker. But real literary activity only began early in the seventeenth century with the publishing of a catechism, the Gospels, a prayerbook, and a hymnal by Bishop Thomas Hren (1560–1630).

While the German portion of the population remained Lutheran, the Magyar element, especially in the 1550s and 1560s, adhered to Calvinism.

At the end of 1559 appeared the first written Hungarian confession, the *Eucharistic Confession of Neumarkt,* in which the Magyar part of Hungary agreed on the Calvinist view of the Last Supper. Antitrinitarianism became a great danger for Calvinism. A synod met in 1567 at Debrecen, the intellectual center of the Calvinists, for defense against the Antitrinitarian currents. It accepted, in addition to two confessions drawn up by Melius (ca. 1536–72), Bullinger's *Confessio Helvetica Posterior* and a Church Order.

On behalf of the Catholics, Matthias Zabardy, from 1553 Bishop of Wardein, managed to push back Calvinism temporarily. After his death in 1557, however, monasteries were destroyed in Grosswardein and the Franciscans were expelled. The estates of Transylvania prevented the filling of the see, which thus remained vacant until 1716. There were no bishops in the Turkish-occupied areas. In 1543 the Metropolitan of Esztergom transferred his residence to Tyrnau. From 1554 the Archbishop was Nikolaus Olahus (1493–1568), friend of Erasmus and former secretary of Queen Mary of Hungary. He worked for the restoration of Church property, called the Jesuits to Tyrnau in 1561, and in 1566 opened there the first seminary in the country. When he insisted on the observance of celibacy, many married priests went over to Lutheranism.

Whereas Maximilian II (1564–76) sympathized with the Reformation and in 1564 forbade the publication of the Tridentine decrees, Stephen Bathory, Prince of Transylvania from 1571, promoted the Catholic faith and fought the radical wing of the Antitrinitarians, led by Ferenc Dávid. He confided the direction of the Klausenburg Academy to the Jesuits in 1579, but they were expelled in 1595.

It was especially through the work of the Jesuits and of Archbishop Peter Pázmány (1570–1637) of Esztergom, himself from a noble Calvinist family, that Hungary eventually became once again a predominantly Catholic land.

CHAPTER 88

Schism and Reformation in England

As in the Scandinavian countries, so in England the reformation was introduced and carried out "from above" — under the decisive influence of the government. It began as schism under Henry VIII. Under Edward VI Protestantism forced its way into worship and doctrine. And, following the collapse of the Catholic restoration under Mary I, the Anglican Church acquired its definitive form in the reign of Elizabeth I.

Under Henry VII (1485–1509) the Church in England had notably recovered from the devastating effects of the Wars of the Roses. Without possessing a formal right of nomination, the King saw to it that his candidates, usually jurists who had proved themselves in the royal service, obtained the bishoprics in both ecclesiastical provinces: Canterbury, with twenty suffragans, and York, with three. Thomas Wolsey, Archbishop of York (1514–30) and Cardinal since 1515, as Lord Chancellor, was director of domestic and foreign policy, and as Papal Legate from 1518 he also ruled the English Church in virtual independence. By suppressing the smaller monasteries he procured the means for richly endowing his Oxford foundation, Cardinal College, now called Christ Church College. He adopted strict measures to prevent the entry of Lutheranism. The morals of the parish clergy seem, so far as we can learn from pre-Reformation visitations, to have provided fewer occasions for censure than was the average on the continent. But the humanist permeation of Oxford under John Colet and of lay circles especially under Thomas More did not take the place of the missing theological education. Only one out of 349 books printed in England between 1468 and 1530 had a strictly theological content. Popular devotion was zealous but not really healthy — Parker terms it "fervent rather than solid piety." A certain anticlericalism found an outlet in the House of Commons, but because of the protection set up by *Praemunire* against the fee system of the Curia there could scarcely be any question of anti-Romanism. During the Western Schism England had adhered to the Roman obedience; during the conflict between Eugene IV and the Council of Basel, it had upheld the Pope. But the serious danger which the Church in England concealed within itself became visible in the second half of the reign of Henry VIII.

The Marriage Case of Henry VIII

Henry VIII's education, unusual for a prince in that period and including theology, had enabled him to come forward in the *Assertio septem sacramentorum* (1521) in refutation of Luther's *De captivitate Babylonica.* In return Leo X had honored him with the title of "Defender of the Faith." It was the sensuality of the crafty and brutal monarch that occasioned his break with the papacy. Appealing to Leviticus 18:16 and 20:21, he claimed that his marriage with Catherine of Aragon was invalid because she had previously been married to his older brother Arthur, who had died at the age of fourteen. He said that the dispensation granted by Julius II on 26 December 1503 violated the divine law; that a brief of dispensation of the same date, which was drawn up more clearly in several points, had been falsified; and, finally, that before contracting marriage with Catherine he had declared that the marriage was against his will. Despite this, he had consummated the marriage and had had seven children by Catherine, but only Mary, the future queen, survived. Conscientious scruples in regard to the validity of his marriage did not actually occur to the King until Anne Boleyn, a maid-of-honor with whom he was in love, declined to belong to him except as his wife. Catherine denied the consummation of her first marriage with Arthur and the nullity of her second marriage with Henry. At first probably in ignorance of the King's ultimate intentions, Wolsey was prepared to seek from the Pope a declaration of nullity of Henry's marriage by a court of special competence for this case. Emissaries sent by him to Clement VII succeeded in having Wolsey and the highly esteemed jurist Cardinal Lorenzo Campeggio, who had already lived in England as legate in 1518–19, authorized on 8 June 1528 to conduct the canonical trial in England. The Pope promised to confirm their judgment and granted in advance a dispensation for a new marriage in the event that the declaration of nullity should materialize.

But the process, conducted in London, did not result in the judgment desired by the King. At its very opening on 18 June 1529, Catherine appealed to the Pope. The Bishops of Rochester and Saint Asaph upheld the validity of the marriage, but Campeggio observed in regard to the prejudiced conduct of the case: "In another's house one cannot do all that one would like." Hence the Pope, who had meanwhile been set free again by the conclusion of the Peace of Barcelona and who had come under pressure from Catherine's nephew, Charles V, transferred the case to Rome on 19 July 1529. Wolsey had promised too much and had played a double game. He fell from power and died on 29 November 1530, en route to London to be tried for high treason.

In order to influence the Roman proceedings according to his wishes, Henry VIII, upon the advice of Thomas Cranmer, the next Archbishop of Canterbury, gathered legal opinions from universities and individual professors of law, for which he paid handsomely. Favoring the nullity of the King's marriage with Catherine, in addition to the English universities Oxford and Cambridge, were also those of Paris, Orléans, Angers, Bourges, Toulouse, Bologna, Siena, Padua, Pavia, and others. The opposite opinion was held by those of Louvain, Naples, Salamanca, Alcalá, Granada, and others.

The Act of Supremacy

While Clement VII was postponing his decision, Henry VIII was arranging another sort of solution — one without the Pope. On 11 February 1531 the Convocation of the Clergy, under strong royal pressure, voted to hand over 100,000 pounds to the king as "Protector and Supreme Head of the English Church and Clergy," but with the addition, at the suggestion of John Fisher, Bishop of Rochester, of "in quantum per Christi legem licet." All the bishops and likewise Thomas More, who was then still Lord Chancellor, assented to the ambiguous formula. It was the first step toward separation. Parliament forbade any appeal to Rome. On 23 May 1533 the complaisant Archbishop of Canterbury declared Henry's marriage with Catherine null; this was a belated and shabby justification of Henry's marriage to Anne Boleyn, which had already taken place secretly in January.

It was only now that Clement VII intervened. In the consistory of 11 July 1533, he announced that the King would incur excommunication if he did not dismiss Anne by the end of September and take back Catherine as his lawful wife. The decision issued in the canonical trial on 23 May 1534 confirmed the validity of Henry's marriage with Catherine. It upheld the sanctity and indissolubility of marriage. But it can hardly be questioned that the Pope's original effort to be accommodating, determined by political considerations, aroused in Henry hopes impossible to realize, and that the long delay of the final decision made it easier for the King to prepare for the schism.

Already in June 1533 an antipapal pamphlet, *The Glasse of the Truthe,* composed by order of the King, had conditioned public opinion for the coming measures. In the *Articles,* circulated at the end of the year, "the Bishop of Rome, whom some call pope," was branded as "usurper of God's law and infringer of general councils," and, in addition, an enemy of England. In the spring of 1534 Parliament passed five laws which made ready the break with Rome. These laws gave to the King the nomination of bishops; forbade the obtaining of dispensations at Rome and the paying of fees there and subjected all exempt monasteries to the King; made the clergy subject to the civil laws; required the acceptance under oath of the royal succession of the children born of the marriage of Henry with Anne Boleyn (first Succession Act); and, in the Heresy Act, declared that no statement against the primacy of the Bishop of Rome was to be regarded as heresy.

In sermons and pamphlets the content of these laws was made clear to the people and thereby the way was prepared for the final event — the Act of Supremacy of 3 November 1534. By it the title of "the only supreme head on earth of the Church of England" was conferred on the King, and his power was also extended to maintaining the purity of doctrine. A second Act of Succession required of all officials and ecclesiastics an oath to uphold the succession of Anne's children, while the Treason Act branded as high treason the refusal or questioning of the new royal title.

The break with the papacy had thereby been definitively accomplished.

The first victims of the Act of Supremacy were three Carthusian priors. Together with the learned Richard Reynolds, they were hanged at Tyburn on 4 May 1535. On 22 June 1535 followed Bishop John Fisher of Rochester. Before being beheaded he addressed the spectators: "Christian people, I die for the faith of the holy Catholic Church of Christ." Almost identical was the profession of the former Lord Chancellor, Thomas More, before his execution on 6 July 1535. In the legal proceedings he had characterized the Act of Supremacy as "directly repugnant to the laws of God and his holy Church." The nonjurors, however, constituted a decreasing minority. Except for Fisher, all functioning bishops took the oath, surrendered their papal bulls of nomination, and asked and obtained the *licentia regia ad exercendam iurisdictionem episcopalem.* Earlier the overwhelming majority of the diocesan and regular clergy had signed the declaration: "The Bishop of Rome has by divine law in this Kingdom of England no greater jurisdiction than any other foreign bishop." The question arises: How was it possible that the clergy of an entire country submitted almost unanimously to the King's will and denied the doctrine of the papal primacy?

In replying to this depressing question it must be remembered that the episcopate, standing in complete dependence on the crown, led the way and the rest of the clergy followed. Neither group possessed the theological insight that the papal primacy, far from being a theory of curial canonists, was firmly rooted in the Church's awareness of the faith. What were seriously discussed, even by Church-minded theologians and canonists, were merely its extent and its relations to the Church and the episcopate. Significantly, the *Defensor Pacis,* the most radical denial of the divine right of the primacy to date, was now printed in English at the expense of the King, with the omission, to be sure, of the passages on the so-called sovereignty of the people. On the other hand, a book *On the Defense of the Unity of the Church,* printed at Rome in 1538, exercised no influence in England, but gained for its author, Reginald Pole, a relative of the King and a resident in Italy, Henry's hatred.

The Suppression of the Monasteries

Resistance on the part of the people did not show itself until the king, following the advice of the Lord Chancellor Cromwell had a general visitation of the monasteries made in 1535–36 by a commission named by him. Its chief aim was to get control of the extensive monastic property in order to assure the King of defense against any eventual attacks, to fill his privy purse, and to gain support among the nobility. At the same time the religious life was to be defamed by disclosing moral failings. Relying on the reports of the visitors, which were full of accusations against the conduct of the religious, the King, with the consent of the accommodating Parliament, decreed on 4 April 1536 the suppression of 291 lesser monasteries — 191 of men and 100 of women — which had an annual income of less than 200 pounds, and confiscated their real estate and moveable property. However, since the confiscation, and to some extent the squandering, of the monastic properties was a severe financial blow not only to their peasants and servants but also to the inhabitants of the adjoining areas, and the procedure of the visitors stirred up popular indignation, risings occurred, first in Lincolnshire and then in North England. In the latter area Robert Aske, leader of the "Pilgrimage of Grace," declared that the suppression of the monasteries meant the ruin of religion in England and that the royal supremacy was contrary to the law of God. With 9000 men he marched on York and brought expelled monks and nuns back to their monasteries. Since he was willing to negotiate and gave credence to a promise of amnesty, the King gained time for a countermove. The rising was suppressed in blood and Aske was executed.

The first tide of suppression had involved only the lesser monasteries. Between 1537 and 1540 the larger monasteries of the monastic orders were also dissolved, mostly by means of "voluntary" surrender to the King, frequently accompanied by and based on the members' acknowledgment of guilt. The houses of the mendicant orders were suppressed at the same time. "Thus, without noise or outcry, almost without a whimper, a familiar class of men disappeared from English life" (Knowles). The account reported at the end of the reign of Henry VIII by the royal treasurer in regard to the sale of monastic property or the revenue realized from it amounted to the then immense sum of 1.3 million pounds

Alliances and Creeds

Apart from the doctrine of the papal primacy, the Schism of 1534 had not yet attacked the substance of the Catholic faith. This occurred only when the King, in agreement with the docile episcopate, accommodated the faith of his subjects to his foreign policy and the question of a council. Between 1534 and 1547 he prescribed no fewer than four norms of faith — the Ten Articles of 1536, the Bishops' Book of 1537 the Six Articles of 1539, and the King's Book of 1543. In them the Protestant ideas which had meanwhile spread in England came to the surface more or less, in adjustment to the political situation of the moment.

Despite the existing book banning, reform writings had come to England as early as the 1520s from the Netherlands and Germany through active commercial relations. William Tyndale, who in 1524 had left the circle of theologians sympathetic with Luther at Cambridge, had his English translation of the New Testament printed on the continent in 1524. From here it returned secretly to the island along with other works from his pen, anticlerical rather than strictly Lutheran pamphlets.

In *The Obedience of a Christian Man* he championed unconditional subordination to the King, who "may at his lust do right or wrong." During his stay at Wittenberg Robert Barnes accepted the Lutheran doctrine of justification. Recalled by Cromwell, he acted as agent in the King's matrimonial case and in arranging his marriage with Anne of Cleves, but then he lost the royal favor and was burned in 1540. A circle of theologians favorable to innovation, which had been formed at Cardinal College, Oxford, was broken up by Wolsey in 1528. Its most important member, John Frith, fled to Marburg and published at Antwerp, under the title of *De Antichristo,* an English revision of Luther's reply to Ambrosius Catharinus. On 24 May 1530 a list of 251 erroneous propositions which were said to be in the writings of English authors was submitted to the King, who warned against propagating them. When Frith, relying on the imminent break with Rome, returned to England in 1533, he was executed for his teaching on purgatory and the Eucharist. The literary war against Lutheranism proceeded along a parallel line. Fisher's *Confutatio* (1523) belongs with the best examples of pre-Tridentine Catholic controversial writings.

The text of the bull of the major excommunication against Henry VIII was ready on 30 August 1535. But the new Pope, Paul III, hesitated to publish it, because he wanted to assure himself of the cooperation of the great powers in putting the ecclesiastical censures into effect, and for this a projected general council seemed to be the most appropriate means. To prevent its realization became the unchanging goal of Henry's policy. For this reason he joined in discussions with German Protestants. An agreement was arrived at, in the event that the Council, contrary to expectations, should actually meet, for a common protest, but an alliance with the League of Schmalkalden did not materialize, since the discussions of theologians on fundamental questions, held at Wittenberg at the beginning of 1536, did not result in union. The Wittenberg theologians refused to recognize divorce, while Henry would not accept the *Confessio Augustana.*

These fruitless discussions, the convoking of the Council to Mantua, and the disturbances provoked by the suppression of the monasteries constitute the background of the Ten Articles of Faith, prescribed by the King on 12 July 1536. Though ambiguous in many places, they betray the effort to meet the Wittenberg theologians halfway. The principle of Scripture as the sole rule of faith was admitted, justification was described according to Melanchthon's *Loci,* only three Sacraments — baptism, Eucharist, and penance — were expressly named, the veneration of saints and images, though not forbidden, was viewed as the cause of many abuses, and prayer for the dead was permitted, though it was denied that purgatory has a scriptural basis.

The *Institution of a Christian Man,* published in 1537 and referred to as the *Bishops' Book* because it was signed by twenty bishops, was a compromise between the Protestant-minded and the conservative wings of the episcopate. After the manner of a large catechism it treated the traditional points of doctrine, the Creed, the Sacraments, the Commandments, the Our Father, and also the Hail Mary. It mentioned the four Sacraments that had been omitted in the Ten Articles, but did not refer to the Mass as a sacrifice. At the same time the King saw to it that the general Council that had been summoned by the Pope was attacked in several pamphlets.

A new approach to the German Protestants seemed to be under way at the beginning of 1539 when Charles V and Francis I allied against Henry VIII. The English King sent an envoy to Electoral Saxony and arranged to marry Anne of Cleves. Lutheran theologians appeared in London. They became witnesses, however, not of a doctrinal *rapprochement* but of a Catholic reaction. The Six Articles, submitted in the House of Lords by the bishops and assented to by the King on 28 June 1539 commanded under severe penalties the doctrine of transubstantiation, communion under one species, clerical celibacy, monastic vows, the lawfulness of private Masses, and the necessity of auricular confession. This surprising turn was occasioned by a renewal of ties between France and England. Henry no longer needed the Protestant allies against a threatening coalition of the great powers and wished to be regarded as a "Catholic prince." The Lord Chancellor Cromwell fell out of favor and was beheaded, Barnes was burned, and two Protestant-minded bishops, Latimer and Shaxton, resigned. Cranmer, however, maintained his position. A Catholic restoration according to the teaching of the Six Articles did not occur.

The equilibrium between old and new doctrine continued to be the norm governing religious policy even in the last years of the reign, when Henry was allied with the Emperor against France. The *King's Book* of 1543, regarded as a catechism for the laity, showed in its teaching on justification a relationship to the Wittenberg Articles of 1536, but stressed the necessity of good works, and the freedom of the will was maintained, while absolute predestination was denied. The ecclesiology continued to be Anglican. The papal primacy was branded as a human invention. The guardian of the orthodox faith was the King, who was bound "to conserve and maintain the true doctrine of Christ," which is found in Scripture, the three ancient creeds, the first four councils, and the exegesis of the Fathers. In his preface the King spoke of the period preceding the Schism as "the time of darkness and ignorance."

Nevertheless, the change in the substance of faith as a matter of fact already went deeper than the two last-mentioned norms of faith indicate. Hitherto Tyndale's translation of the Bible had been strictly forbidden. But in the revision by John Rogers, who hid behind the pseudonym of Thomas Matthew, the prohibition was removed on Cranmer's urging in 1537 and, as "Matthew's Bible," it was ordered purchased by every parish church the following year. A homiliary composed by Cranmer provided a suitable explanation.

The Upsurge of Protestantism under Edward VI (1547–53)

Protestant ideology invaded the life of the Church of England on a broad front during the regency. The practical sense of the English was taken into account in that the new doctrines were not so much prescribed as formulations of faith but rather were introduced under the guise of a new liturgy, which, however, retained some traditional forms. Just as on the continent, so too in England the abolition of the Mass struck at the center of the Catholic concept of the Church. The process moved forward step by step. At the end of 1547 communion under both species was allowed and Mass endowments were confiscated by the crown. The Catholic doctrine of the Eucharist and of the Mass was attacked in pamphlets and sermons. An English Communion rite, composed by Cranmer and prescribed on 8 March 1548 was modeled on the "Cologne Reformation," composed chiefly by Bucer. A year later (1549) appeared the *Book of Common Prayer.* This not only altered forms, such as the introduction of English as the liturgical language, it also changed the doctrinal content of the liturgy in specific points. Only two Sacraments, baptism and the Lord's Supper, were instituted by Christ. In the rite of the Lord's Supper the sacrificial character was suppressed and any clear acknowledgment of the real presence was lacking. The place of daily Mass was taken by a liturgy of the word; the entire psalter was prayed or sung within a month. The ordination rite introduced in 1550 was based on the texts of Bucer's *De ordinatione legitima ministrorum ecclesiae revocanda* (1549). Contrary to Bucer, the ordinations of bishops, priests, and deacons were distinct, but the consecrating prayers accompanying the imposition of hands were changed. At the same time the prohibition of marriage for priests was abolished. In the revised form of the Prayer Book, which went into effect on All Saints' Day of 1552, the rite, maintained till now, of the anointing of the sick, the anointings at baptism, and prayers for the dead at their burial disappeared. Participation in the new liturgy was obligatory. Whoever took part in another rite was punished with six months in prison for the first offense, a year for the second, and life imprisonment for the third. Only at the end of the reign of Edward VI was the new statement of faith, summarized in the Forty-two Articles drawn up by Cranmer, prescribed.

Neither the fall of Somerset in 1549 nor the opposition of individual bishops, particularly to the new rite of ordination, nor the passive attitude of a great part of the parochial clergy was able to stop this evolution. The confiscation of Church treasures, such as chalices and monstrances, which had begun under Henry VIII but was only now completed, was endured, even though with bitterness. People lamented the disappearance of works of charity, which had earlier been provided by ecclesiastical foundations, and the loss of many parish schools. Nevertheless, the essence of the faith, as hitherto maintained, faded irresistibly with the liturgical forms that had protected it. The loss was so serious that the restoration under Mary I and Cardinal Pole was unable to make it good again. The clergy, high and low, who had submitted to the Church laws of Henry VIII and Edward VI, headed by Gardiner, as Lord Chancellor, were in no position to gain confidence and above all were not zealous executors of the new laws. The strictness with which Queen Mary proceeded against Cranmer, executed on 21 March 1556, and other opponents of her regime gained it no sympathy. The *Book of Martyrs* by John Fox, published soon after Mary's death — in Latin in 1559 and in English in 1563 — glorified them. Emigrants returning from Frankfurt, Strasbourg, and Zurich became the instruments for expanding the Anglican Church under Elizabeth I.

Ecclesia Anglicana under Elizabeth I (1558–1603)

Elizabeth I (1558–1603), the well-educated and clever daughter of Anne Boleyn, first made sure of her throne by an extremely cautious foreign policy. From the start there was no doubt about the direction of her Church policy at home. A new Act of Supremacy and Uniformity in 1559 again put into effect ten Church laws of Henry VIII and Edward VI that had been annulled under Mary and, in addition, the Prayer Book of 1552. The bishops, appointed under Mary and opposed to these measures, were deposed and replaced by new prelates, who were ready to take the Oath of Supremacy. At their head was Matthew Parker, new Archbishop of Canterbury. The penalties decreed for refusing the oath were, however, mitigated — loss of office and, in the event of a relapse into the crime of defending the papal primacy, death. Attendance at the liturgy on Sundays and feasts was prescribed under a fine of twelve pence for each absence. The few monasteries that had been restored under Mary were suppressed. The dividing line was thus clearly drawn against the defenders of the old faith. But a relentless persecution of them did not begin until Pius V had pronounced the major excommunication and deposition of the Queen. On the other hand, the still numerous members of clergy and laity who rejected the new order or were indifferent to it were consciously spared. The Thirty-nine Articles, drawn up by the Convocation of 1563, were a revision of Cranmer's Forty-two Articles of 1552. They breathed a Calvinist rather than a Lutheran spirit. *The Apologia ecclesiae Anglicanae* by the Bishop of Salisbury, John Jewel, which appeared in Latin in 1562 and in English in 1564, justified the new faith and the new order. The *Book of Homilies* (1562) was prescribed for the use of parish priests. The episcopal structure, the cathedral chapters, and the office of archdeacon continued under the shelter of the royal supremacy. In 1583 Whitgift became Archbishop of Canterbury. Toward the close of the Elizabethan Age Richard Hooker in his *Laws of Ecclesiastical Polity* (1593) summarized the doctrine and constitution of the now firmly established Anglican Church. The formation of a new type among the Reformation Churches was thereby achieved. An official translation of the Bible, however, was published only under James I.

Chapter 89

The Struggle over Lutheran Orthodoxy

When, following Luther's passionate protest within the One Church, there gradually developed a particular ecclesiastical system outside and in opposition to the ancient Church, there arose the question of what was distinctive, of what was "reformed." There loomed the task of providing a special, positive profession of the right doctrine for the new reformed congregations. It no longer sufficed to apply corrections and protests to the tradition; now one had to admit into the profession the presuppositions that had, of course, hitherto been accepted as the basis. On the other hand, it appeared that the original outline, alluring in its one-sided emphasis on the reform preoccupation, had to be safeguarded against misunderstandings and extended and corrected.

Luther's struggle against the Pope for the freedom of the Gospel was often understood as a license for revolt, the plundering of monasteries, and laxity of morals. "Now no fear of God is any longer a means of discipline, because the Pope's authority has become obsolete. And everyone does what he wants to," and that "on the pretext of the Gospel."

Melanchthon was often charged with pusillanimity and cowardice for his moderation. Melanchthon did not understand reformation as a merely negative criticism. His anxiety was for the unity of the Church.

Melanchthon did not merely rebuke the excessive zeal of some complainants. He also had the courage and the sense of responsibility to apply essential corrections to his own theology. In 1530 he would no longer recommend to his pupils his *Loci* of 1521, which Luther had then declared to be worthy of canonization. Instead, he referred to his exegesis of the Epistle to the Colossians of 1527. The various versions of his *Loci* were the expression of this change in his theology. The several "Philippist" controversies are to be viewed against this background.

The Antinomian Controversy

As early as 1524 Lutheran preachers had defended at Tetschen the thesis that "The Law was given to the Jews, not to the heathens. And so the Law or the Ten Commandments do not apply to us." Vis-à-vis such preachers, who "speak presumptuously about Christian freedom." Melanchthon stressed that:

> All who teach in the churches may cautiously communicate the doctrine on the Law. If the doctrine of faith without Law is handed on, countless scandals will result. The people become assured and imagine that they have the righteousness of faith, because they do not know that faith can be only in those who have contrite hearts by means of the Law. Now it is customary to speak about faith, and yet what faith is cannot be understood unless penance is first preached. This security is worse than all the errors previously under the Pope.

This notion that preaching about the Law must first produce penance and contrition before faith scandalized Johannes Agricola of Eisleben (1499–1566). He drew up a condemnation of Melanchthon's articles of visitation. Agricola saw in the Law merely an expression of God's anger. It was abolished for Christians by the revelation of God's grace in the Gospel. Christ, he held, preached the Ten Commandments only to the Jews. Thus, penance must begin, not with the preaching of the Law, but with love for righteousness. At the end of November 1527 the electoral court convened a theological meeting to Torgau. Through Luther's mediation there was effected a temporary agreement between Melanchthon and Agricola.

Agricola came out against Luther himself in the second Antinomian Controversy. At Christmas of 1536 the Elector had held out to him the prospect of a position at the University of Wittenberg, and Agricola immediately moved there. With his family he was taken into Luther's house and was frequently asked to represent him. But soon the old controversy, which had seemed to be forgotten, was to blaze forth again. In a collection of sermons, published in June, Agricola defended the thesis of a "twofold revelation: a first one of grace, a second of wrath."

God as Judge, if he has any place as such in Agricola's thought, is first made known through the Gospel. Here God's anger is revealed, not indeed for all who are guilty before God, but only toward all those who, out of false security, deride and ridicule the first revelation of grace. At the same time Agricola circulated a collection of theses in which he sought to play off the young Luther against the later Luther.

While Luther had not taken the quarrel of 1527 too seriously, now he was dismayed by Agricola's stand: "This should not be begun in our lifetime by our people!" In a sermon of 30 September 1537 he stated his own idea of Law and Gospel in opposition to Agricola.

Together with his opposing theses he published Agricola's above-mentioned collection of Antinomian theses and had the first Antinomian disputation take place on 18 December 1537.

The mediation of Agricola's wife brought about another reconciliation between him and Luther. In order to make it public, persons arranged a second public disputation on 12 January. But the real points of controversy were not settled there, and so the conflict broke out again in a third Antinomian disputation on 6 September. Luther now demanded of Agricola a definite recantation, and the court threatened to cut off his salary. Agricola thereupon composed a "form of revocation," which he submitted to Melanchthon as arbiter and which the latter revised. At the same time Agricola turned to Luther himself: "the doctor should himself present him with a form." Luther agreed and wrote the treatise *Wider die Antinomer* in the form of an open letter to the Eisleben preacher, Caspar Güttel. From Agricola Luther demanded in January 1539 theses for another disputation, which he appointed for 1 February. In this way there arose further dissension. Agricola complained of Luther to the Elector and during the very discussions he fled to Berlin, where he accepted a post as court preacher to the Elector Joachim II.

At stake in the Antinomian Controversy was the correct understanding of Luther. Agricola thought that Luther in his writings taught two different ways of justification: "the one way is through Law and Gospel; the other, only through the Gospel, without the Law." Hence he desired a decision as to which way is correct. He tried to solve the problem by extracting expressions of the young Luther for a uniform system. Luther was distressed by the controversy which flared up over his legacy in his own lifetime. His struggle was so harsh and pitiless because he dreaded laxity and caprice as the consequences of Agricola's doctrine.

The Synergist Controversy

In the doctrine of the sole operation of grace in the awakening of justifying grace and of the will's lack of freedom in regard to salvation Melanchthon was accused of deviating from Luther.

Luther, like Melanchthon, had represented a strict determinism in 1520–21:

> Everything happens of absolute necessity. This is what the poet meant when he said: "Everything exists according to a definite law." God even performs bad works in the godless.

Concerning faith, Luther had said that it was the "work of God in us without us." But in practice Luther had appealed to man's personal activity, and consequently he had probably taught that God is all-effective while not consistently teaching that he is uniquely effective.

From 1527 Melanchthon tried to free himself from determinism. If God, according to 1 Timothy 2:4, wills that all men be saved, then the reason why some are saved and others are lost must lie with man. Melanchthon was unable to escape the force of the passage. "Since we must proceed from the [revealed] word and since the promise is universal, we conclude that a cause of the election lies in us: an instrumental cause to lay hold of the promise." If Melanchthon also represents the human will which assents to the promise as a real factor, there is question here not of an autonomous human will, but of a will which, supported by the Holy Spirit, accompanies prevenient grace. Accordingly, three causes cooperate in conversion: God's word, the Holy Spirit, and the human will, which assents to the word and does not resist it.

Borrowing from the *Interim* of Augsburg (VI, para. 1), the *Interim* of Leipzig stated:

> Although God does not justify man through the merit of the special works which man does . . . , nevertheless the merciful God does nor operate with man as with a log but he draws him so that his will also cooperates, if he is of an age to understand.

Matthias Flacius (1520–75) and Nikolaus Gallus (1516–70) had seen in the formulation of the Leipzig *Interim* the "burying of a papist *meritum de congruo*" (O. Ritschl). Melanchthon's pupils, Georg Major (1502–74), Victorin Strigel (1524–69), and later Johannes Pfeffinger (1493–1573), expressly taught the necessity of the cooperation of free will in justification. Pfeffinger was a professor at Leipzig from 1544. In two disputations in 1555 he defended, in dependence on Melanchthon, the thesis that, in conversion, the consent of our will is required. In this connection he spoke of a certain *synergia* of the will. Although, according to him as well as to Melanchthon, the will is here dependent on the help of the Holy Spirit, Nikolaus von Amsdorf accused Pfeffinger of teaching, together with his "gang," that man can fit himself for grace and prepare for it by the natural powers of his free will. For his part Amsdorf maintained that "man's will is, before God, nothing but clay, stone, or wood." Flacius and Gallus wrote in a similar vein.

In the *Weimar Confutation Book,* which, inspired by Flacius, appeared in 1559, Pfeffinger's so-called Synergism was condemned in Article 6. Victorin Strigel, professor at Jena and until now a friend of Flacius and opponent of the Philippists, opposed the introducing of the *Confutation Book* and hence was imprisoned for several months. After his liberation there took place at Weimar a public disputation between him and Flacius from 2 to 8 August 1560 on the freedom of the will. Here the question found its theological precision. After this disputation Flacius in 1566 defended the notion that original sin is man's *forma substantialis.* The

Religious Colloquy of Altenburg, held from 21 October 1568 to March 1569 was fruitless. What made the acceptance of the Catholic idea impossible also prevented an agreement among the Lutherans. The "and" in "grace and free will" was understood as an additive and not as something conclusive, while the divine activity in grace and the releasing of man's will for freedom were envisaged as two self-sufficient causes, moving concurrently on the same plane.

The Majorist Controversy

A similarly embittered struggle blazed up over the relationship between justification and good works. From the Wittenberg professor Georg Major (1502–74), who stirred up the quarrel after Luther's death, it is referred to as the Majorist Controversy. It too was based on a problem left unsettled by Luther, that of the inner relation of justification and sanctification, of grace and gift, and the significance or necessity of love in regard to salvation. Luther had laid emphasis on faith and felt that from it good works proceeded naturally. He loved to stress that the good tree produces good fruit. But he shrank from continuing, in accord with Matthew 7:19, that "Every tree that does not bear fruit is cut down and thrown into the fire." The more narrowly Luther's pupils presented justification in their public utterances and the more the concept of inner renewal for good works was pushed into the background or even denied, the more difficult it became to establish the necessity of good works, which were to follow justification.

Melanchthon came more and more to stress the biblical imperative, but without adequately showing its basis in the indicative, in the new being of the one justified. He was moved by pastoral and pedagogical viewpoints: "In all men there is such a natural weakness that, when we hear the doctrine of the account that will freely follow, we become more careless about good deeds, and our carnal security is consolidated." Hence, Melanchthon, following the Gospels and Paul, speaks of God's command and of the necessity of good works:

> Nevertheless, the righteousness of works must necessarily follow. For it is God's command that we render this obedience, because Christ clearly enjoins, "Do penance"... I do not see why I should shrink from the word "command," since Christ also says [John 15:2], "This is my command," and Paul [Romans 8:12], "We are debtors."

Nikolaus von Amsdorf reported to Luther in a letter of 14 September 1536 from Magdeburg:

> It is said here that the contrary is taught at Wittenberg. That man [Melanchthon] is urging powerfully and to excess in the school that works are necessary for eternal life.

Already on 20 August and 8 September 1536, Konrad Cordatus, then pastor at Niemegk, had turned on Caspar Cruciger (1504–48), who had been professor at Wittenberg since 1528, and attacked him because, he alleged, in his lectures he was presenting a "sophistical and papist" faith and deviating from Luther, "the only man through whom we believe in Christ." The quarrel concerned whether repentance is a *causa sine qua non* of justification and whether the new obedience is necessary for salvation. Melanchthon backed Cruciger.

When Justus Jonas, rector of the University of Wittenberg, dismissed his complaint, Cordatus on 17 April 1537 turned to the Electoral Chancellor, Brück, and complained that there was at "Wittenberg opposition to the dear doctrine of that pious man Luther." Philip, he said, had written to him yesterday: "On my own I have bettered much in my books, and I rejoice that I have done so."

For his part Luther urged Cordatus to be calm and utilized the promotion disputation of 1 June 1537 to clarify the question. He concurred with Melanchthon in the matter to the extent of quoting Augustine: "He who created you without your cooperation will not save you without your cooperation." But he expressed himself against "necessary for salvation," because, he said, it implied something merited.

Thus did this point of controversy come to rest for the time being. But Flacius and Gallus again took umbrage at the formulation of the Leipzig *Interim* of 1548 to the effect "that these virtues, faith, charity, hope, and others must be in us and are necessary for salvation" since it was designed "for the benefit of the papists." Open controversy ensued when Melanchthon's pupil and friend, Georg Major, wrote against Amsdorf in 1552:

> I admit that I have hitherto taught and still teach and will hereafter teach, throughout my life, that good works are necessary for salvation. I say publicly, clearly, and unambiguously that no one becomes holy through evil works and also that no one becomes holy without good works, and I say further that if anyone teaches otherwise, even an angel from heaven, let him be anathema.

Nikolaus von Amsdorf thereupon declared Major to be a "Pelagian, Mameluke, apostate Christian, and twice papist." Against the written attacks of Amsdorf, Flacius, and Gallus, Major defended himself in the sense that he in no way intended to belittle justification by grace alone through Christ and that salvation is not merited by good works. But, he asserted, these are necessary so that salvation can be maintained and not lost again. Melanchthon had taught something similar in his *apologia* in accord with 2 Peter 1:10.

Agricola, with whom Amsdorf was closely allied, had rejected 2 Peter 1:10 in the Antinomian theses: "Peter did not know Christian liberty." In the wider Majorist Controversy between the "Gnesiolutherans," Amsdorf, Flacius, and Gallus, and the "Philippists," namely, Melanchthon's adherents, Major and Justus Menius (1499–1558), the last named tried to be conciliatory and, to avoid the misunderstanding of being thought of as papists, they declared themselves ready to drop the addition: necessary "for salvation or for eternal life." However, no real compromise ensued Flacius and his friends were not satisfied with a mere dropping of the proposition; they wanted it to be condemned as false. Melanchthon, for his part, declared:

> In sum, . . . we say clearly that we cannot abandon this proposition: new obedience is necessary in all the converted. If anyone will not endure this, we regard him as an Antinomian and an enemy of God.

In order to justify his position Melanchthon appealed, in addition to Romans 8:12 and 10:10, 1 Corinthians 6:9, 2 Corinthians 7:10, 1 Timothy 1:18, and other places, also to Philippians 2:12: "Work out your salvation with fear and trembling." As opposed to this the Gnesiolutherans wanted to maintain the full assurance of salvation and security of conscience. If works were somehow necessary, then salvation depended on man, who could not even be sure of himself. From this viewpoint follows the claim of Nikolaus von Amsdorf that good works are prejudicial to salvation, for they seduce man into placing his confidence of salvation in something in himself rather than exclusively in the grace of God. In this way the Gnesiolutherans — in their theology became ideology, their bias, and their "endless revolving around the I, its temptations, and its consolations" — were absolutely not qualified to advance in love beyond themselves to God and neighbor. "If the chief interest of the new man in ethics, as Flacius describes it, proceeds to the point of acquiring feelings of comfort, then there is not much time left for the business whose center is the neighbor" (L. Haikola).

The Adiaphora Controversy

If behind the outward form of Melanchthon's doctrine of justification, which involved the Antinomian, Synergist, and Majorist Controversies, there lay the problem of protecting men from a false security and from carelessness, Melanchthon's attitude in the Adiaphora Controversy must be understood from the viewpoint of his concern for the right order and the unity of the Church. In a testimonial on the *Interim* he wrote on 1 April 1548:

> I sincerely wanted to advise peace and unity, and many years ago I proposed several serious articles on unity in my teaching, as many wise persons know, and I have never taken pleasure in quarreling about unnecessary and unimportant matters. I am now so old that I well know that great division and destruction follow useless squabbling.

Melanchthon and the other theologians who had assembled at Torgau to discuss the *Interim* stated in 1549 that it was "criminal obstinacy and confusion" to brand as papist whatever one does not wish to retain. Many would quarrel "more about their own freedom than about high and necessary articles of Christian doctrine and about right and false appeal and good discipline." Answering the charge of idolatry in the Mass they insisted: "And even this form which we retain in the Mass was observed one thousand years ago, as Dionysius clearly testifies."

Apart from political grounds, a developed confessionalism was also important to Flacius, who rejected any community with the opposing side and for whom there were no *adiaphora,* because Church customs under the papacy were the "seat of godlessness and superstition."

The Osiander Controversy

Philippists and Gnesiolutherans stood together in a common front in the controversy with Andreas Osiander (1498–1552) concerning justification. In cooperation with Lazarus Spengler, Osiander had won Nürnberg for the Reformation. He had been lector at the Augustinian monastery there in 1520 and in 1522 had become preacher at Sankt Lorenz. He had compiled a list of twenty-three questions and doctrinal articles for the Nürnberg ecclesiastical visitation. On behalf of the city he had taken part in the Marburg Religious Colloquy of 1529 and in 1530 he had composed a work on justification for the Diet of Augsburg. Together with Johannes Brenz he had drawn up the Brandenburg-Nürnberg Church Order of 1533. In this connection there had been difficulties with the people of Nürnberg, because in their model Osiander and Brenz had expunged public guilt (general confession) and the general absolution following the admonition to the Lord's Supper in order to restore private confession to prominence. Osiander was opposed in principle to general absolution. For it is to be understood either conditionally ("if you do penance") and then it is neither a Sacrament nor absolution, or unconditionally, and then it is the most ridiculous sacrilege thus to cast pearls before swine. Osiander argued further:

> If this is really absolution, no excommunication can maintain a place in the Church, for every excommunicated person can immediately have absolution, since no one can forbid him to listen to preaching.

In November 1548 he had abandoned Nürnberg as a protest against the *Interim* and in 1549 he had accepted a professorship at the University of Königsberg.

He began his teaching activity on 5 April 1549, with a disputation on the Law and the Gospel and then lectured on the first chapters of Genesis. There soon ensued controversies over penance, the meaning of Christ's Incarnation, and the attitude to the *Interim,* which Osiander had sharply criticized. A public quarrel broke out over Osiander's "Disputation on Justification by Faith" of 24 October 1550. As he had already done in regard to the doctrine of justification in the *Interim,* he now publicly attacked that of Melanchthon as one-sided: "They are teaching something colder than ice who teach that we are to be regarded as justified only for the forgiveness of sins and not also because of the righteousness of Christ, who dwells in us through faith." Osiander wanted to bring into prominence that man is really justified and to stress against a one-sided emphasis on Christ's vicarious atonement his life-renewing activity in man. Christ alone is righteous, but not so much because he fulfilled the Law as because

> he was born from all eternity, a righteous Son, from the righteous Father [John 17:25]. Hence it is this righteousness of the Father and the Son and the Holy Spirit whereby he who is himself righteous justifies the godless, that is, the righteousness of God, which is precisely the righteousness of faith.

He explained the creation of Adam as the image of God thus:

> Hence there dwelt in Adam through grace the Word, the Son of God, and consequently also the Father and the Holy Spirit. Thus, as our Lord Jesus Christ was by nature God and man, Adam was man by nature but by grace he was a sharer in the divine nature and participated in it.

Christ's righteousness consisted in his divine nature. The original righteousness of the justified consists in his participation in the divine nature. Proceeding from this notion Osiander explained 1 John 4:2, the coming of Christ in the flesh, simply as the indwelling of the Lord in us. It is said of the justified that both natures are in them, just as in Christ. Accordingly, justification is the reproducing of the Incarnation of the essentially divine righteousness in the individual man: "The ontological 'indwelling' of the essential 'righteousness' of Christ in the believer is what is primary, and only on the basis of this does God declare him to be righteous" (E. Kinder). In his emphasis on the essential righteousness of God in us, in contradistinction to righteousness *extra nos,* Osiander appealed to Luther. Melanchthon, whose doctrine of justification Osiander attacked, tried at first to mediate, but finally was induced in 1552 to publish a *Reply.*

In this he first alluded to the distinction between grace and gift and then insisted:

> And so we clearly profess and have always taught, as all the churches can testify, that it is true that a change must occur in us and that certainly God, Father, Son, and Holy Spirit, effect consolation and life in us in conversion and hence are in us and dwell in us to the extent that the Gospel is accepted with faith, whereby the Eternal Word, the Son of God, operates and gathers to himself one Church.

He said there was no quarrel over this presence of God in us. However, it is not the basis of our confidence. Faith is based on the God-Man Jesus Christ, on his merits and his intercession. Even after rebirth man is still in need of the forgiveness of sins. He obtains it through the Mediator, Jesus Christ, who is to be distinguished from the Father and the Holy Spirit. If Osiander had censured the superficiality of Melanchthon's doctrine of justification and felt that "this teaching makes people secure," Melanchthon referred to the salvific function of Christ's humanity and to his historical work of redemption, which came off badly in Osiander's mystical doctrine of justification.

Flacius, Menius, Amsdorf, and Mörlin (1514–71) at Königsberg also wrote against Osiander. And Franciscus Stancarus, opposing him, went the other extreme, teaching that Christ justifies man only by virtue of his human nature. The *Formula of Concord* rejected both the doctrine of Osiander and that of Stancarus.

The Second Eucharistic Controversy

While the Lutherans were fighting among themselves over the *Interim,* Calvin and Bullinger reached agreement on the Eucharist at Zurich in the *Consensus Tigurinus.* Calvin had made concessions for the sake of unity. Bread and wine are still only signs of the spiritual community (actual communion) with Christ's flesh and blood. In this way was jeopardized the common understanding with Lutheranism, which had been declared at least in form by the signing of the *Confessio Augustana Variata* in 1541. The Zurich agreement was first sent to the other Swiss churches for their acceptance, and hence its publication in print was delayed until 1551. German Lutheranism then saw itself faced with a growing influence of Calvin's theology and an encroachment by Calvinism in German soil. Thus the quarrel now erupting over the real presence of Christ in the Eucharist acquired a special violence and a more strongly confessional tone, which injected controversy into the congregation; to a far greater extent than earlier. The division did not run clearly between the Calvinists and the Lutherans. Instead, many in the ranks of the latter, especially the educated, showed themselves to be accessible to the Calvinist teaching on the Eucharist. They opposed the then incipient Lutheran orthodoxy and the dogma of ubiquity which it represented. For this reason, following Melanchthon's death in 1560, they were labeled Cryptocalvinists and attacked.

The Hamburg pastor Joachim Westphal (1510–74) began the struggle in 1552 with a work entitled *Farrago.* It was a summons to the Lutherans in view of the menacing danger. The extent of the chasm separating the Protestant confessions became clear when in 1553 in flight from England with his Calvinist congregation, Jan Laski sought refuge in Germany. They met rejection and even hatred from the North German Lutherans. Westphal called them martyrs of the devil, and Bugenhagen had them told that he would sooner support papists than them. They were finally received at Danzig and Emden. Laski composed a catechism at Emden in 1554. Thereupon strife broke out at Bremen between Melanchthon's pupil Albert Rizaeus Hardenberg (1510–47), whom Laski had gained for the Reformation in 1542 and who had been cathedral preacher at Bremen since 1547, and Johannes Timann, called Amsterodamus (d. 1557). Timann's polemic was answered by Laski. Westphal denied to the Calvinists the right to appeal to Augustine. Calvin himself did not intervene in the quarrel until January 1555, with a *Defense of the Doctrine of the Sacraments.*

Westphal refuted this in his *Legitimate Defense against the False Accusation of a Certain Sacramentarian* (1555). To Calvin's annoyance it was printed at Frankfurt-am-Main. Laski had gone there with his fugitive Calvinist congregation. Referring to the Religious Peace of Augsburg, the Lutheran clergy demanded agreement with the *Confessio Augustana,* which Laski tried hard to demonstrate. Calvin dedicated his *Second Defense of the Devout and Right Faith,* of the beginning of 1556, to the pastors of Saxony and Lower Germany, stressing that he was not fighting against them, but was only defending himself against Westphal's attacks. He represented Westphal as a disturber of the peace and an outsider.

The key figure in this dispute, conducted with great bitterness by both sides, was Melanchthon. Lutherans and Calvinists appealed to him. Westphal sought to prove that Melanchthon did not agree with Calvin. Calvin, on the other hand, claimed him for himself but accused him of favoring, by this silence, "unlearned, restless characters," who had again started the dispute over the Sacrament. "For," he wrote on 23 August 1554, "however insolent their stupidity may be, no one doubts that if you decided to admit publicly your opinion, it would be easy for you to calm their rage, at least to some extent."

Here, as in the other controverted questions, Melanchthon was not the one to assume leadership. In the effort to avoid a dispute he had only made it worse through his reserve.

The Eucharistic doctrine which he represented was from the outset more different from Luther's than both of them realized. From the start Melanchthon stressed the sacramental action: it, the eating and drinking, was the sign to a greater degree than were the elements. Instead of the presence of Christ's body "in" the bread, he spoke of its presence "with" the bread in the course of his controversy with the Swiss. This allowed him to cling to the real presence without attaching it to the bread and giving occasion to spatial notions. In the *Confessio Augustana Variata* he had contributed the diluting formula: "that with bread and wine Christ's body and blood are truly administered to those who eat of the Lord's Supper." In this Melanchthon had far greater possibilities of a connection with Bucer, Bullinger, and Calvin than with Luther. He did not expressly deny the reception of the body of Christ by the unworthy, but probably out of regard for Luther he did not mention the subject. At first he also passed over in silence the doctrine of ubiquity, but from about 1531 he attacked it as a false understanding of the *communicatio idiomatum.* "We must take care not to stress the divinity of Christ's humanity so much that we destroy his true corporeality." The ancient Church rejected "this thesis that Christ is everywhere in his body," and we must not introduce any new dogma. For Melanchthon Christ, by his ascension, has occupied a place he did not previously have. But this did not mean, as Zwingli thought, that Christ could be only in heaven in his body; rather it meant that Christ is present where he wished to be. Melanchthon emphasized the mystery. In relation to his notion of the "intended presence" of Christ Melanchthon also rejected a presence apart from the action instituted by Christ ("extra usum institutum") and an adoration of the elements (artolatry): "What is left after the celebration is not a Sacrament." Melanchthon did not undertake a careful exegesis of the scriptural passages that speak of the Eucharist. He referred to 1 Corinthians 10:16, in which he saw the best formula of union. He understood it to mean: the bread is the distributing of the body of Christ. Paul, he held, did not say "the bread is God," but "it is that by which arises communion with the body of Christ." Melanchthon was profoundly distressed by the many theological quarrels which were destroying the unity of the Church and especially by the fact that they flared up over the Eucharist.

But Luther had already denied the doctrine of transubstantiation as an inadmissible speculation and wanted to leave the "how" of the presence uninvestigated. However, the very necessity of a confrontation with adherents of the Reformation had caused him to seize upon the *theologoumenon* of the ubiquity of Christ's humanity, which brought with it far greater difficulties. Despite all his protestations of being satisfied with the fact of the presence as the pledge of the divine promise, Melanchthon could not do otherwise.

The quarrels continued after his death. If the educated then subscribed to a Cryptocalvinism, this was because the particular formulas offered were open to a humanistic spiritual understanding. Toleration was again demanded for the Swiss on the basis of the *Consensus Tigurinus,* until an international synod should have formulated a common Protestant doctrine. The strictly Lutheran Elector August I (1553–86) felt that he had been imposed upon by his theologians. Strict Lutheranism was restored in Electoral Saxony by the ecclesiastical power of the prince. The route back to the Lutheran position was found in the Torgau Eucharistic Confession of 1574 and at the same time the way was prepared for the doctrinal consensus of the adherents of the *Confessio Augustana* in the *Formula of Concord* of 1577. Article 7 of the *Concord* states: "Nevertheless they hold and teach that, with the bread and wine, the body and the blood of Christ are truly and essentially present, given, and received."

CHAPTER 90

Jean Calvin: Personality and Work

Youth, Studies, and Early Writings (1509–36)

The Reformed Church of Western Europe bears the stamp of the personality and work of Jean Calvin, born on 10 July 1509, at Noyon in Picardie.

A benefice at Noyon opened up for young Calvin the way into the clerical state, but first of all it provided him especially with the means to commence his studies. He obtained his earliest education with the sons of a friendly noble family, and with them he went to Paris in 1523, at the age of fourteen. Calvin was admitted to the College de la Marche and in 1524 into the College Montaigu, which was steeped in tradition. There nominalism was the prevailing approach. In 1528 Calvin obtained the licentiate in the liberal arts. But he did not continue his studies in theology. Apart from the fact that, during his arts courses, he became acquainted with the Fathers and with theological problems — his teacher in this faculty was the Scotsman John Mair (Major) — he never studied theology as such and earned no degree in it. His impressive later knowledge of it was due to private study.

At the wish of his father, he studied law at Orléans under Peter de l'Estoile and later (1529) at Bourges under Andreas Alciati, and in 1532 obtained the licentiate. During his studies at Orléans and Bourges he was in contact with the Swabian Melchior Volmar, a reform-minded humanist (born at Rottweil in 1496, died at Tübingen in 1556). Volmar introduced him to Greek. After his father's death in 1531, Calvin went to Paris, where he concentrated especially on the humanities. The fruit of this interest was a commentary on Seneca's *De clementia* (1532), which shows a familiarity with the classical authors and the Church Fathers. It also has a strong political and ethical tone and exhibits its author as a humanist reformer of a juristic stamp. Calvin was still under the spell of biblical reform humanism, whose chief at Paris was Lefèvre d'Etaples (ca. 1450–1536). But the young reformer was too much a man of clarity, of precise commitment, and of ecclesiastical order to be satisfied with the humanist "Nicodemitism." It cannot be exactly determined when he turned to Protestantism. If we follow the late testimony of Calvin and accept a sudden change, it must have occurred at the end of 1533. But in that case it is still doubtful whether Calvin, who always defended himself most fiercely against the charge of having split the Church, at that time regarded his conversion as a break with Rome or instead as a summons to "reestablish prostrate religion" or to the "honorable function of preacher and minister of the Gospel." For Calvin the reform of the Church was prominent. He was concerned for *vera religio* against the idolatry of the contemporary Church and, as a layman, he intended to aid *pietas* against the *impii.* The decisive turning points of his life were determined by experiencing that God had laid his hand upon him and destined him for the service of the Church. He was unable to withhold himself.

Thereafter, Calvin led a wandering life. Among other places, he stayed at Angoulême, and perhaps it was here that he began the preliminary work on his chief literary production, *Institutio Christianae Religionis.* In May 1534 Calvin's benefices in Noyon were distributed to others, and this is generally seen as his final separation from the old Church. At the end of that year or early in 1535 he went via Strasbourg to Basel. Here he met not only the Basel reformers Simon Grynaeus (1493–1541) and Oswald Myconius (1488–1552), but also Heinrich Bullinger (1504–75) of Zurich, who was continuing Zwingli's life work, and Martin Bucer (1491–1551) and Wolfgang Capito (c. 1480–1541) of Strasbourg.

In the summer of 1535 he finished the *Institutio,* which was printed in 1536. This first edition contained a brief compendium of the teachings of the Gospel and at the same time an *apologia* for the French Protestants with a dedicatory note to King Francis I. The King had taken measures against the Protestants when lampoons attacking the Mass had been posted in several parts of Paris and even in the royal Chateau Amboise on the Loire. In a letter to the German Protestant princes he had represented his action as directed against Anabaptists and anarchists. Against this, Calvin intended to plead "the common cause of all the pious, the very cause of Christ himself." For, according to him, the godless have achieved their purpose in that the truth of Christ, if it is not dying scattered and banished, at least remains buried and neglected, and the *paupercula ecclesia* is either carried off by horrible murders or is driven into exile, or, discouraged by threats and terrors, no longer dares to open its mouth. This "poor little" persecuted Church is the one Church of Jesus Christ, which cannot be "seen with bodily eyes" and cannot be "circumscribed by borders." For Calvin, who sharply defended himself against the reproach of schism and sectarianism, the dispute arose because his opponents "claimed, first, that the Church was constantly present and was visible in her external form, and, second, that they fixed the form of the Church in the Roman See and the hierarchy of their bishops." "The Church can also exist without a visible form," or at least her essence does not depend on it. Her marks are "the pure preaching of the word and the legitimate dispensing of the Sacraments." The *gloria Dei,* Calvin's main concern, is often stressed in this letter. It is a question of "how God's glory is to be inviolate on earth, how God's truth is to maintain its dignity, how Christ's kingdom is to be well established and supported among us."

The *Institutio* of 1536 shows how in Basel Calvin's theological thought acquired its definitive form. Probably decisive were his status as a fugitive, life in the reform congregation of this city, and the profound study here possible to him. His studies comprised especially the Bible and Luther's writings, chiefly his catechisms, the *Freiheit eines Christenmenschen,* and *De captivitate Babylonica.* The locally prevailing theology — Zwingli's — seems to have been less influential on him. Whereas the 1536 edition of the *Institutio* offered only a brief summary of Christian doctrine in six chapters, Calvin constantly enlarged the work, and the edition of 1559–60 finally became a comprehensive treatise on dogma in four books and eighty chapters.

First Activity in Geneva (1536–38)

After a short stay at Ferrara and at his old home, Calvin prevented by the war from going to Strasbourg, went to Geneva in July–August of 1536. The Reformation had been established here a short time before. In October 1533 the citizens had expelled Bishop Pierre de la Baume (d. 1544), who was merely the puppet of the Duke of Savoy. Thereafter the bishop and the cathedral canons had resided at Annecy.

Guillaume Farel had appeared in Geneva as a preacher as early as 1532. The opposition of the canons, however, had forced him to leave the city, but at the end of 1533 he was back. The reform currents found powerful support in Geneva's ally, Bern. Following a disputation between Catholic and reformed theologians, lasting from 30 May to 24 June 1535, the struggle was decided in favor of the latter, and in May 1536 the city council and the people solemnly resolved "to live according to the Gospel." When Calvin arrived there in the summer of that year, everything was, as he expressed it, topsy-turvy. Farel needed his help, especially his talent for organization, and hence urged him to stay. Calvin wrote later: "It was as though God had stretched out his hand from above and laid it on me in order to stop me." He first ministered not as preacher or pastor but under the title of a "lecturer on Holy Scripture." He interpreted the Epistle to the Romans and preached only occasionally. It was only at the end of 1536 that he was appointed preacher and pastor of the Church of Geneva.

The *Articles concernant l'organisation de l'Eglise,* submitted to the city council "by Master Guillaume Farel and other preachers" on 16 January 1537 were largely Calvin's work. As was stressed from the outset, governing laws for the congregation and ecclesiastical discipline were necessary for the dignified celebration of the Lord's Supper. Exclusion from the Sacrament — excommunication — is needed in order to keep out the unworthy and preserve the Church spotless. Because of the profit to believers, who thereby "really share in the body and blood of Christ, in his death, his life, his spirit, and all his gifts," communion should be celebrated every Sunday as a praiseworthy demonstration of the divine wonders and gifts of grace and as an encouragement to a Christian life in peace and in the unity of the body of Christ. For "Jesus did not institute this Sacrament so that we might celebrate it two or three times a year as a memorial meal, but that we might strengthen and exercise our faith and love through a frequent celebration." However, because of the ignorance of the people, Calvin would agree to a monthly celebration. The city council would not accept even that and decreed that the celebration of Communion be held only four times a year. This became the rule, contrary to the reformer's intention.

In all sections of the city expressly appointed men of strong and incorruptible character were to keep a watchful eye on the behavior of their fellow citizens. If they ascertained improper conduct or vice in anyone, they were to discuss this with a pastor so that he might admonish the guilty and urge them fraternally to mend their ways. Here were the origins of the later *presbyterium.* In the second section of the "articles" directions are given for the congregational psalmody. The third deals with the instruction of children. With the aid of a catechism they should be made capable of confessing the faith.

As soon as the articles had been adopted by the council, Calvin brought out a catechism in French,. In brief chapters it deals with the commandments, the Creed, the Lord's Prayer, the Sacraments, and spiritual and secular authority. To this catechism is added a Creed, "which all the citizens and inhabitants of Geneva and all subjects of the region were to bind themselves on oath to observe and uphold." Comprising twenty-three articles, it begins: "We confess that, as the rule of our faith and of our religion, we will follow only the Holy Scripture, without the addition of any human ideas whatsoever." Whoever refused to accept this Creed was to lose his citizenship and "go elsewhere to live." The ecclesiastical officials were to see to it that everyone lived according to the Creed, and the council was to punish those who refused. The council had prevented the forming of a court independent of the civil authorities, with the result that the Church government was to a great extent dependent on the secular power. This should be kept in mind in speaking of a theocracy at Geneva. At most, at that time, a theocracy existed only in so far as public affairs were to be regulated according to the word of God and the authorities had to supervise religion.

Even in this mitigated form the implementation of the articles encountered opposition. Nevertheless, on 13 March 1537 the "small council" decided that the Church organization was to be obeyed in full. On 29 July the council secretary Michael Roset mounted the pulpit and read aloud the Creed and the city ordinance. The "presidents of the tenths," or heads of the city districts, were to bring the inhabitants of their territories to the cathedral of Saint-Pierre, where all would bind themselves under oath to the Creed. But many stayed away or refused, and on 12 November the order was renewed. Whoever did not take the oath was to incur the loss of all rights in Geneva. But this was easier said than done. Opposition to the council grew, and the animosity against the French pastors increased.

Calvin did not budge. At the beginning of January the reformers told the council that they would exclude from communion everyone who had not taken the oath to the Creed. But the council, viewing developments with some alarm, decreed that admittance to the Lord's Supper was to be denied to no one. When, in February 1538, men hostile to Calvin and Farel were elected to the council and the opposition obtained a majority, the council forbade the reformers to mix in political affairs. The reformers, on the other hand, tried to preserve the independence of religion when Bern urged that the customs it had retained — the baptismal font, unleavened bread, and holy days apart from Sunday, such as Christmas, New Year's, and the Ascension — should be reintroduced at Geneva. On 11 March 1538 the Council of Two Hundred voted its acceptance of ceremonial agreement with Bern and ordered the pastors to comply. They declined to do so. Calvin and Farel refused to administer communion on Easter 1538, on the ground that, with so much unrest, mockery, and mob activity, it would be a sacrilege. Despite a prohibition, they mounted the pulpit. On Easter Tuesday, 23 April the council decreed the banishment of Calvin and Farel, who had to leave the city within three days. At the news Calvin said: "If we had served men, this would be a poor recompense. But we serve a great Lord, who will not withhold his reward from us." His bitterness over the wrong did not keep him from admitting that he himself had made a few wrong turns, as he wrote to Farel in September 1538.

Strasbourg (1538–41)

On 25 April 1538 Calvin left Geneva and went to Basel, intending to live there as a private scholar and to revise his *Institutio.* At the time he seems to have entertained doubts as to his pastoral calling. But Bucer, Capito, and Sturm asked him to come to Strasbourg. When Calvin hesitated to undertake again a pastoral office, Bucer threatened him with the anger of God, with reference to the Prophet Jonah. Calvin went to Strasbourg in September 1538. He assumed the function of preacher in the French refugee community and at the same time was made lecturer in Scripture at the secondary school conducted by the humanist Johannes Sturm. Here he composed the second, much enlarged and revised, edition of the *Institutio,* which appeared in Latin in 1539 and in French in 1541. But the Strasbourg period was more decisive for his development by providing him with an apprenticeship in practical theology. Now he learned from cooperating with Bucer and Capito how to build up a community and its order of worship and thus found his complete formation as a reformer.

A "German Mass" had been celebrated in Strasbourg as early as 1524. Bucer had further elaborated it. Calvin was able to utilize these works in a liturgy for his French congregation at Strasbourg; in 1540 issuing a formulary for the liturgy of the word, communion, and baptism. Already in 1539 he had compiled in French a psaltery, containing eighteen psalms, the Apostles' Creed, the canticle of Simeon, and the Ten Commandments in hymn form. He had himself put five psalms in poetic form; the others were done by the French court poet, Clement Marot. For these texts the reformer adopted Strasbourg melodies. Bucer had also done the spade work in Church discipline. In Strasbourg Calvin did not have to fear difficulties similar to those in Geneva because his little refugee congregation was under the scrutiny of the city council to a lesser degree. In Idelette de Bure, widow of an Anabaptist, he found a wife who became also a helper in his life's work.

By participating in religious discussions at Frankfurt (1539), Hagenau (1540), Worms (1540–41), and Regensburg (1541), Calvin became acquainted with religious conditions in Germany and came into contact with leaders of German Protestantism, especially Melanchthon. Luther and Calvin never met; they knew each other only through their respective Latin writings. On 25 November 1544 the latter wrote to Heinrich Bullinger of Zurich:

> I hear that Luther recently made a fearful verbal attack, not only on you, but on all of us.... I do not know whether Luther was provoked by any of your writings; but even if a nature such as his, which is not only irritable but downright soured, goes into a rage for a trivial reason, he certainly could have no adequate grounds for such a storm and uproar. I now hardly dare to ask you to keep silent; for it would not be right to let the innocent be treated so shamefully and to deny them the opportunity to justify themselves; it would also be hard to say whether it would be good to keep silent. But this is my desire: that you keep in mind how great a man Luther is, with what extraordinary spiritual gifts he is endowed, how bravely and unshakeably, how skillfully, how learnedly and effectively he has always hitherto labored for the destruction of the rule of Antichrist and for the spread of the doctrine of salvation. I have already often said: if he were to call me the devil, I would still do him the honor of regarding him as a most outstanding servant of God, who, it is true, suffers from great defects, just as he is rich in brilliant virtues. If only he had exerted himself to control better his impetuous nature, which explodes everywhere! If only he had constantly turned his innate passion

against the enemies of truth instead of letting it flare up against the Lord's servants!

Calvin participated in the Regensburg Colloquy of 1541 as delegate of Strasbourg. He had several reservations in regard to Bucer's conciliating method and the unclear formulae of the *Regensburg Book.* Still, he accepted the concept of twofold justice and defended it against Farel. But he would not be satisfied "with half a Christ" for the sake of union. He expressed himself very critically in regard to the negotiations on the doctrine of the Eucharist: "Philip Melanchthon and Bucer drew up ambiguous and fine sounding theses on transubstantiation in an attempt to satisfy their opponents without really yielding anything. The plan does not please me." Calvin firmly opposed the treatment of the Mass and departed before the colloquy foundered on this subject. Soon after, on 13 September 1541, Calvin returned to Geneva.

There was a prelude to his return. In Geneva the situation had become ever more confused, and pastors and mayors were in no position to reestablish orderly life. In this situation Cardinal Jacob Sadoleto, Bishop of Carpentras, at the suggestion of an episcopal conference at Lyons, published an open letter to the city of Geneva, inviting it to come back to the bosom of the Church, which "for now fifteen centuries has found unanimous acceptance and approval." After treating of justification by faith alone, of the Sacraments, and of the invocation of the saints, he concluded:

> Return to the unity which is guaranteed only in the venerable, ancient, Catholic Church. For she is guided always and everywhere by the Spirit of Christ. Only thus can we appeal with confidence before the judgment seat of God. But he who separates himself from this Church has no champion at the Last Judgment, and the outer darkness awaits him. Therefore, attach yourselves again to the Catholic Church and its spiritual leaders, for Scripture says, "Do what they say." We have only your salvation in view.

This letter made an impression, and the Geneva pastors were at a loss what to do. A request for a rejoinder was sent to Calvin at Strasbourg. The *Reply to Sadoleto* was composed in six days and is signed: Strasbourg, 1 September 1539. It deals mainly with the Church, justification, and the sacraments. The Church is based, not on the approval of the centuries, but on the word of God. She proves that she is the true Church by her doctrine, organization, sacraments, and correct worship. Calvin solemnly calls God to witness that he did not split the Church nor withdraw from her.

The letter again won Geneva for the Reformation. The people became all the more aware of the inability of their pastors, and the desire to have Calvin back grew. Furthermore, in February 1539 mayors had come into office who were sympathetic to radical reforms. Calvin was called back, but he declined. In October 1540 an official petition from the "small council" reached him. It was seconded by friends such as Farel. But for Calvin the will of man was not the determining factor. He consulted his conscience and tried to determine the will of God. When Calvin finally left Strasbourg on 4 September 1541 he was probably thinking only of a temporary stay in Geneva, for he did not take his family.

The Organization of Church Authority in Geneva (1541–64)

Calvin went to Geneva in the spirit of his motto, *prompte et sincere.* On 13 September 1541 he entered the council hall and was treated with the greatest politeness and was told he would be well provided for materially. He avoided acting harshly and in any way taking his opponents to task. All the same, serious struggles over the independence of the spiritual power from the city government were still in store for him. He immediately set about organizing the congregation, and already on 20 November 1541, *Les ordonnances ecclésiastiques,* modeled on those of Strasbourg, were accepted by the councillors. There soon followed a liturgy (*Forme des prières et chants ecclésiastiques,* 1542) and the catechism (1542–45). From Bucer at Strasbourg Calvin adopted the system of four ecclesiastical offices — pastors, doctors, elders, and deacons.

Pastors were to preach the word of God and administer the Sacraments. Those of the three city churches and of the surrounding villages constituted the *Vénérable compagnie des pasteurs.* Every week it was to meet for the study of Scripture and consultation on pastoral matters. In differences of opinion as to correct doctrine it was to decide according to God's word what was to be believed. Every three months the mutual, fraternal "censorship," a criticism of conduct was to take place. The *compagnie* was to nominate new pastors, but the sole power of selection rested with the council. It presented them to the congregation, which could only assent to the choice of the council after the event. Calvin wanted to retain the imposition of hands in ordination as an apostolic custom, but he was only too ready to accommodate himself to the city council on the grounds that, out of consideration for the current superstition, it was perhaps better to give up the imposition of hands. Hence there was preserved the remark that pastors should be inducted into office without any superstitious ceremonies, with only instruction on the office and prayer.

Doctors, as teachers of theology, were to deliver lectures on the Old and New Testaments. They also had to supervise candidates for the office of pastor. In the secondary school they were to teach the biblical languages and impart a general education. The council named them after consulting the pastors.

The elders, or presbyters, had to supervise the behavior of the members of the congregation. Together with the five to ten pastors they formed the Church council or consistory. In Geneva the "elder" was an agent of the city council. The twelve elders were selected by the "small council," in agreement with the pastors, from among the membership of the council and confirmed by the "great council." A mayor was chairman of the consistory. Calvin was unable to achieve the full independence of the Church. As preaching and the administration of the sacraments were the duty of the pastor, so the direction of the Church pertained to the consistory. The elders had to supervise the conduct of the congregation by means of, among other things, regular visits to homes. Whoever was guilty of gossiping, drunkenness, usury, immorality, brawling, card playing, and so forth, was brought before the consistory each Thursday by a city official. In criminal cases the city council had competence. Stubborn contemners of the Church order had to be excommunicated after three warnings and denounced to the council. Thus ecclesiastical justice was largely subject to the civil law. Calvin had to fight a prolonged battle in order to reserve at least the admission to communion to the spiritual tribunal. In the definitive version of *Les ordonnances ecclésiastiques* of 1561 he was, it is true, able to gain more prominence for his idea of the congregation.

Deacons were stewards of ecclesiastical institutions or took direct charge of the poor and the sick.

Following the organization of the Church, Calvin compiled a catechism in November 1541. This "Geneva Catechism" of 1542 consisted of questions and answers. It abandoned the arrangement of Luther's small catechism. Whereas the latter treated the law before the Creed, the order in the Geneva catechism of 1542 was: faith, law, prayer, sacraments. In this is expressed a new concept of the law and the Gospel. The law is not only a "disciplinarian," its meaning lies not merely in convicting man of sin; but as the regulation of the covenant it gives the baptized the rule of Christian life.

The community organization at Geneva could be realized only after drawn out struggles. When a start was made of imposing a strict Christian manner of life, many again regarded this as an unpleasant limitation of personal freedom. The opponents of Calvin called themselves patriots, but his friends called them "libertines," because they stood for a more liberal concept of morals and for the right to a pleasanter life. The question arose as to the limits of the consistory's power. For years Calvin had to put up with various restrictions and affronts. But in the elections of January 1555 the "libertines" suffered a decisive defeat. The new mayors and a majority of the council were on Calvin's side.

Calvin was now able to give the congregational idea greater importance. The ecclesiastical council obtained more freedom from the secular government.

When, after 1555, Calvin was certain of the support of council and citizenry, he turned to the realization of his old plan, the founding of a university. The academy finally opened in 1559 with two departments. In addition to elementary instruction, Latin, Greek, and philosophy were taught in the "Schola privata," a continuation of the earlier Latin school. On this was based the "Schola publica," in which lectures were given in Greek, Hebrew, the branches of the liberal arts — that is, philosophy and literature — and in theology, especially exegesis and dogma. Calvin found a rector for the academy in Theodore Beza (1519–1605). Beza and Peter Viret (1511–71) had come from Lausanne. The new university exercised a very strong attraction on students far beyond the boundaries of Switzerland and contributed decisively to the transplanting or the consolidating of the Reformed Church in other European countries including Kaspar Olevianus (1536–87), the Trier reformer and later professor at Heidelberg; Philip Marnix de Sainte-Aldegonde (1540–98), organizer of the reform in Holland; and John Knox (c. 1515–72), the reformer of Scotland; all of whom studied there.

Until December 1559 Calvin was not even a citizen of Geneva, and hence could act in political commissions at the most as an adviser. But then the council spontaneously offered him citizenship as a "recognition of the many valuable services that Calvin [had] rendered since the Christian Reformation of the republic." By an extensive correspondence Calvin exercised influence beyond the walls of Geneva on the organization of the churches of France, Belgium, the Palatinate, Poland, Hungary, and many other countries. He forced an enormous amount of work on his weak and almost always ailing body until his death on 27 May 1564.

Basic Outline of Calvin's Theology

As a second generation reformer and because of his own intellectual make-up and his education, Calvin was much more a systematizer than Luther was. In the *Institutio* he has left us a compact treatment of dogma, but we must not forget that in it he intended only "to introduce the theology candidate to the reading of the divine word" and to equip him "to establish what he should principally seek in Scripture and to what goal he should relate its content." Calvin wished above all to be an exegete, and hence his numerous exegetical works must be related to the exposition of his theology.

What the theologian was able by himself to say about God and man was "vain folly." He must let himself be instructed by God himself in Scripture. "No one acquires even the slightest understanding of the correct and salutary doctrine unless he first becomes a student of Scripture" (*Institutio* I, 6, 2). Scripture "bears its proof within itself"; by virtue of the illumination of the Holy Spirit it is recognized by us as the word of God. The Holy Spirit alone is the proper interpreter of Scripture. He "who spoke by the mouth of the prophets must penetrate our heart" (I, 7, 4) and open it up to the Word which lies hidden in the words of Scripture. The determining idea in Calvinist theology is the glory of the sovereign God — *soli Deo gloria.* The glory of God is the meaning of creation and of the redemption of the elect as well as of the punishment of the damned. Calvin's strongly developed doctrine of the Trinity has a soteriological character. He staunchly defended the truth of the Trinity against the heresy of Servetus and others because he wanted to assure the true divinity of Jesus Christ. Calvin strongly emphasized divine providence against the fatalism of the Renaissance and against deistic currents (I, 16–18). The course of things is determined, not by any fate, but by God, Lord of the world. God maintains the creature in existence, gives it its sphere of activity, and guides everything to its goal.

God's special concern is for man, his noblest creature. But in the human realm the greatest importance belongs to the Church. God's providence does not take away man's responsibility. On the other hand, the active government of the world by God will not allow us to speak, in regard to evil, of his merely permitting it. Here we confront the mystery which we must not seek to unravel and which is especially impenetrable in the Cross. "And indeed if Christ had not been crucified by the will of God — from where would our redemption come?" (I, 18, 3). God does not force man to evil. "He guides all of man's acts in so marvelous and incomprehensible a way that man's will is left unhampered." Here "our wisdom [can] consist in nothing else than in this — that we accept, humbly but eagerly, everything without exception that is proclaimed to us in Scripture" (I, 18, 4).

Even more impenetrable to Calvin is the mystery of predestination, "the eternal choice whereby God has destined one for salvation, another for damnation" (III, 21, 1). Prying curiosity has as little place here as does a fearful concealing of God's word. To keep silent about the mystery of predestination was "to lessen God's glory." For only when "God's eternal election has been made known" to us do we become aware that our salvation issues from the spring of the unmerited mercy of God. Calvin's definition is as follows:

> By predestination we understand God's eternal order by virtue of which he decrees in himself what, according to his will, is to happen to every individual human being. For men are not all created with the same destiny. To some eternal life is assigned; to others, eternal damnation. Accordingly then, as the individual is created for the one or the other goal, he is, we say, predestined to life or to death. [III, 21, 5]

To look for a reason over and above the divine good pleasure, such as the foreknowledge of man's merits, would be to make God's will dependent on external causes.

The basis of our predestination to salvation and at the same time of our assurance of salvation is Jesus Christ. In him God has sealed the covenant of life with us. The sign of our election is acceptance of the preaching about Christ and fellowship with him in faith and in communion. Even works, as "fruits of the calling," can have a certain significance for this recognition of our salvation, but only by inference. The stronger he stresses that grace is irresistible in the elect and that they are unable to lose salvation, the darker becomes the mystery of reprobation. How is it that Christ is not active in all? Should he be so powerless that he is unable to win to himself all who resist him? Here Calvin sees himself, like Paul, before the unfathomable secret of the will of God.

In his doctrine of justification and sanctification Calvin starts with Jesus Christ. He asks: "In what way do we now participate in the grace of Christ? ... How do the treasures which the Father has confided to his only-begotten Son reach us?" (III, 1, 1). The answer — that we attain to them by faith — does not satisfy Calvin. It is necessary "to seek more deeply" and to confess that "the Holy Spirit is the bond whereby Christ effectively joins us to himself" (III, 1, 1). In him Christ takes hold of us and he effects in us the "yes of faith, which is the orientation to Christ brought about by the Holy Spirit.

We distinguish justification and sanctification. Although sanctification is the result of justification, in the *Institutio* Calvin treats it first in order from the start to dispose of the misconception that faith, through which alone we are justified by grace, is sterile and without works. By sharing in Christ's death and resurrection we die and rise "to a new life which corresponds to the justice of God" (III, 3, 9). This rebirth has as its goal the restoration of our being the image of God, which by Adam's sin "was as good as effaced." However, renewal does not occur "in a moment," and we are not at once in full possession of freedom; but we must "spend our entire life in penance" (III, 3, 9). Hence, sanctification is a slow process; the believer remains a sinner, but sin must not prevail in him (III, 3, 13). Accordingly, if sanctification can be partially realized and if it can be increased, justification on the contrary must come to us as a whole. "A fragment of justification would not soothe the conscience until it had been determined that we are pleasing to God, because without reservation we are justified in his sight." But, on the other hand, justice does not become essentially imminent in us, but is imputed to us. Justification meant for Calvin "the acceptance whereby God receives us in grace and has us pass for justified ... it is based on the remission of sins and the imputing of the justice of Christ" (III, 11, 2). Calvin emphasizes the "spiritual relationship" with Christ (III, 11, 10). Through the power of the Holy Spirit we grow together with

Christ, our head (III, 11, 5). Thus our justification is outside us, that is in Christ, and at the same time it is our own. Because of this union with Christ, not only are we ourselves justified, but our works too are regarded by God as justified, "because all the infirmities in them are buried by the purity of Christ and hence are not imputed" (III, 17, 10).

Doctrinal Trials

"Christ's spiritual kingdom and the civil order" were, for Calvin, "two entirely different things" (IV, 20, 1). But this does not imply that Church and state stand side by side and unrelated. In Christ both have the same Lord, and for his earthly life the Christian needs the state. For Calvin the state was reckoned among the "external means" whereby "God summons us to fellowship with Christ and preserves us in it" (IV, 1, 1). The secular authority has to protect the preaching of the Gospel and to take care "that idolatry, blasphemy against God's name, calumny against his truth, and other scandals relating to religion may not flaunt themselves publicly" (IV, 20, 3). The rulers are also bound by the word of God, since there is no sphere which stands outside God's claims. Accordingly, throughout his life Calvin worked to place ecclesiastical discipline in the hands of spiritual officials and to guarantee the independence of the consistory vis-á-vis the power of the state. But he did not hesitate to urge the city council to proceed against his theological opponents.

Sebastian Castellio (1515–63), to whom the Geneva school system was greatly indebted, was disqualified from the office of pastor because of his biblical criticism and his concept of Christ's descent into hell and had to give up his position as rector of the Latin school. He went to Lausanne in 1544 and to Basel in 1545. At Basel he became professor of Greek, translated the Bible, and appealed for freedom of conscience.

The former Carmelite friar, Jérôme Bolsec (d. 1584), practiced as a physician after embracing the Reformation. But he retained his interest in theological questions and took part in the weekly meeting of the *Compagnie des pasteurs.* He opposed Calvin's doctrine af predestination and charged that he was not a true interpreter of the Bible. Following the meeting of the *Compagnie* in which he had engaged in a violent dispute with Calvin, Bolsec was arrested. Whoever corrupted the soul was more guilty than one who injured the body, and, like the second, the first crime could be punished by the secular court. It was of no avail to Bolsec that he based his claim on Melanchthon and that the congregations of Bern and Zurich, when asked for an opinion, called for moderation in so difficult a question. On 23 December 1551 Bolsec was banished from Geneva by a judgment of the court. He later returned to Catholicism and avenged himself on Calvin by a very polemical biography of the reformer.

The trial for heresy of the physician Michael Servetus caused a great sensation and severe criticism of Calvin. He was burned on 27 October 1553, in compliance with the sentence of the Geneva city council. Born at Villanueva in Aragon on 29 September 1511, he was the son of a Spanish father and a French mother. He studied law, theology, and medicine and discovered, among other things, the pulmonary circulation of the blood. As early as 1531 he attacked the doctrine of the

Trinity in a brief work, *De erroribus trinitatis.* For him it was a question, not of three Persons in God, but of three forces or manners of operation. The title *Christianismi Restitutio* already discloses his polemic against Calvin. The attention of the Lyons Inquisition was directed to Servetus by Guillaume de Trie, a French refugee living in Geneva. Calvin himself contributed original letters whereby Servetus could be unmasked as author of the *Restitutio.* But he escaped from prison and, *in absentia,* was condemned to death by burning. Fleeing, he came to Geneva, where he was accused before the city council by Calvin's secretary, and then arrested.

The trial began on 15 August and was dragged out for weeks. In many respects it took the form of theological discussions between Calvin and Servetus. The Swiss cities whose opinion was sought — Bern, Basel, Zurich, Schaffhausen — all declared Servetus guilty. On 26 October 1553 the council decided that Servetus should be burned alive and his books consigned also to the flames. Calvin had demanded the death penalty. But he and other pastors sought to have the sentence mitigated by asking for decapitation instead of the pyre. His intervention, however, was fruitless. The sentence was in keeping with the convictions and practice of the time.

Calvin's Doctrine of the Eucharist and His Efforts for Ecclesiastical and Sacramental Fellowship among the Protestants

In his proceedings against "heretics" — Castellio, Bolsec, Servetus — Calvin is clearly a man of intolerance, determined to preserve the unity of the Church at any cost and to assure it with all the means provided by Church discipline, including recourse to the power of the state. Calvin's thinking was more decidedly ecclesiological than was Luther's. His basic question is not, "How do I find a merciful God?" but "How does one arrive at the power of God over mankind?" God's universal rule becomes concrete in the visibly constituted Church. Calvin treats this in detail in the fourth book of his *Institutio,* according to which the Church is one of the "external means whereby God invites us to fellowship with Christ." In Chapter I, "On the true Church with which we must maintain unity, because she is the mother of all the devout," he discusses in nineteen out of twenty-nine sections the unity which the Christian must maintain with the Church. Powerfully as Calvin stresses the congregational idea, still, for him, the Church does not grow out of an amalgamation of believers, but she is an institution planted from above. He often quotes Cyprian's saying that no one can have God for his father who does not have the Church for his mother (IV, 1, 1; 1, 4). His concept of the Church is organic, conceived according to the Pauline image of the body of Christ. Corresponding to this, the Church is visible and necessarily one, as he had written already in the first edition of the *Institutio* (1536).

According to Calvin the Holy Scripture speaks of the Church in a twofold manner. First, she is the community of all the elect since the very beginning of the world. I must believe this "Church, visible only to God's eyes." In the second meaning the Church comprises the flock scattered throughout the world, consisting of those who confess Christ, who "are equipped by baptism for faith in him, and by partaking of the Eucharist testify to their unity in the true doctrine and charity" (IV, 1, 7).

There is no genuine faith in the Church without esteem for this visible Church and without readiness for fellowship with her (IV, 1, 7). She becomes visible "where God's word is truly preached and heard and the sacraments are administered according to Christ's institution" (IV, 1, 9).

For Calvin Reformation means restoration of the original Church, shattered by the papacy, and of her real unity. Calvin admits *vestiga* or *reliquiae* of the true Church even in the papal Church, especially in baptism (IV, 2, 11), but this Church lacks "the true and legitimate organization which is found on the one hand in the fellowship of the sacraments as signs of confession, but on the other hand especially in the fellowship of doctrine" (IV, 2, 12). He is chiefly concerned with the Universal Church. Absolute unity in regard to doctrine and sacraments must be preserved in her. But, apart from specified central points of doctrine, "differences of opinion" among the individual churches can prevail without any injury to unity in faith.

This especially appears in the controversy among the reformers over the Sacrament of unity and peace, the Eucharist. Theologically, Calvin had derived his views from Luther, but before 1536 he had already become acquainted also with Zwingli's *Commentarius de vera et falsa religione.* On 22 September 1537 he took part on behalf of Geneva in a synod at Bern. It had been called at the urging of Martin Bucer to settle the controversy between Zwinglians and Lutherans in regard to the Eucharist. The Swiss charged that Bucer, by consenting to the Wittenberg agreement of May 1536 with its vague notion of the "unio sacramentalis" of the bread and the body of Christ, had sacrificed the Bern Disputation of 1528 and was seeking the union of Lutherans and Swiss at the cost of truth. At the Bern synod of 1537 Bucer intended to clear himself of this suspicion and put an end to distrust. When the violent discussions between him and the Bern preacher and teacher Kaspar Megander (1495–1545) led to no result, Calvin, Farel, and Viret were asked to draw up *a Confessio fidei de Eucharistia.* It was composed by Calvin and signed by the Strasbourg theologians as a sign of their consensus with the Swiss.

According to this confession, Christ offers us in the signs of bread and wine a real participation in his flesh and blood. But this does not mean local presence, which we are deprived of through Christ's ascension. His spirit, however, is in no way limited in its activity. It is the bond of sharing and nourishes us with the substance of Christ's body and blood. Thus Calvin occupies a position between Luther and Zwingli. Against Luther he rejects local and historical and bodily presence. Against Zwingli he so emphasizes the reality of the fellowship in Christ's body and blood that he does not even shy away from the word "substance."

Calvin made a special gesture of good will by signing the *Confessio Augustana* at the Regensburg Religious Colloquy of 1541. This was not the *Confessio* of 1530, but the *Confessio Augustana Variata,* a version drawn up by Melanchthon in 1540 with a view to an understanding with the Swiss. At first the *Variata* encountered no opposition from Lutherans and was actually tacitly tolerated by Luther himself. The difference had to do especially with the doctrine of the Eucharist. Whereas the version of 1530 met the Catholics half-way and seemed to teach even transubstantiation, the *Variata* showed consideration to the Swiss. Article 10 reads: "Concerning the Lord's Supper they teach that, with bread and wine, the body and blood of Christ are really given to those who partake." Instead of "under the appearances of bread and wine" it has now "with bread and wine;" instead of "is present," "are given to those who partake." This admitted an interpretation in Calvin's sense. And in later controversies he could refer to his having signed the *Confessio Augustana* without having disavowed his view.

As a result of Luther's *Kurzes Bekenntis vom heiligen Sakrament* (1544), the dispute with the Swiss over the sacraments had flared up again. The next year Heinrich Bullinger defended his predecessor Zwingli and the Zurich Eucharistic doctrine in the rejoinder, *Wahrhafte Bekenntnis der Diener der Kirche zu Zürich . . . insbesondere über das Nachtmahl.* Earlier, on 25 November 1544, Calvin had asked Bullinger not to let himself be provoked by Luther's harshness and to keep silent. On this occasion he had expressed the desire to treat orally some time with Bullinger their differences in regard to the Eucharist.

Though harmony was not destined to be achieved so quickly, still Calvin succeeded, in his serious efforts for unity over a period of three years, in gaining Bullinger's confidence. Then in April 1549 Bullinger surprised Calvin with the report that now very little stood in the way of a general Swiss confession. Calvin journeyed happily to Zurich, although Bullinger stated rather reservedly that the matter could be arranged by writing. From all this it becomes clear "that it was not Bullinger and the people of Zurich who pressed for the agreement, but Calvin, who for this purpose traveled several times to Zurich." The accord, in twenty-six articles, was drawn up at the end of May 1549. It was, however, not printed until 1551, because the consent of the other Swiss congregations was awaited.

The twenty-six articles deal almost exclusively with the doctrine of the sacraments in general and with the Eucharist. The sacraments are to be understood only in relation to Christ, Priest and King (1–4). This Christ communicates himself to us, makes us one with himself, through his Spirit. The Gospel and the sacraments testify this (5–6). Through the Sacrament God makes present and seals his grace. This happens also through the word. But it is a great thing that living images are represented to our eyes and thus our senses are more strongly impressed (7). A distinction must be made between sign and thing signified, and still sign and reality must not be separated. All who, in faith, take hold of the promises held out in the sign receive Christ spiritually with all his spiritual graces. If union with him already exists, then it is continued and renewed (9). Hence more attention should be paid to the promise than to the sign. For it is not water, bread, and wine that are able to make us sharers in spiritual gifts, but only faith in Christ's promise (10). Of themselves the sacraments effect nothing. God alone acts through his Spirit. If, in so doing, he makes use of the sacraments, this does not mean that he, as it were, infuses his power into them and they operate independently of him (12–15). Hence not all who receive the sacraments share in their grace, but only the elect. Accordingly, it cannot be said that all those receive grace who do not present the obstacle of mortal sin. God does indeed offer grace to all, but only believers are capable of laying hold of it. The sacraments give nothing which faith would not already have received, but they strengthen and increase faith (19).

Articles 21 to 26 deal specially with the Eucharist. Any notion of bodily presence must be eliminated. Christ as man is to be sought only in heaven and indeed only in spirit and in the knowledge of faith (21). To enclose him within the elements of this world is a wicked and infamous superstition. The words of institution, "this is my body," are to be understood figuratively. The thing signified is transferred to the sign. Bread and wine are termed that for which they are signs (22).

This formulation was subsequently too weak for Calvin. He was especially concerned that there was no mention of the eating of the flesh. And so he asked Bullinger to agree to the insertion of the following Article 23, "De manducatione carnis Christi." The eating of his flesh and the drinking of his blood, represented in the sign, mean that Christ nourishes our souls in faith in the power of his Spirit, but any "intermingling or interpenetration of substance" must be excluded. Article 24 even more strongly attacks "transubstantiation and other absurdities." In it are to be rejected, along with this papal invention, all "crass fancies and idle sophistries" which "either detract from his heavenly glory or are not in full harmony with the truth of his human nature." It is indeed regarded as no less absurd to localize Christ in the bread or to confine him to bread than to change the bread into his body. According to Article 25, Christ's body is in heaven as in a place and as such it is to be sought only there. In this way the distance in space is to be expressed and emphasized. If our imagination, then, must not confine Christ in bread and wine, it is also "even less permitted to adore him in the bread" (26). Bread and wine are signs of union with Christ. As signs they are not the thing itself nor do they contain this within themselves nor unite it with themselves.

The *Consensus* can be regarded as his view. He himself so declared when he was reproached because of it. The development of the Calvinist doctrine of the Eucharist from the first edition of the *Institutio* in 1536 to the *Consensus Tigurinus* of 1549 or the *Institutio* of 1559 is characterized by a steadily decreasing mention of an inner connection between the signs of bread and wine and union with Christ's body and blood. If in 1536 and 1543 it is still said that bread and wine are sanctified, in the *Consensus Tigurinus* and in the 1559 *Institutio* they are only signs of partaking of the body and blood, which takes place, by the power of the Holy Spirit, on the occasion of celebrating communion. With Calvin there can be no question of the real presence, but of real communion with the body and blood of Christ. The believer to whom bread and wine are given at communion really shares in the fellowship of Christ's body and blood. But they are not tied to bread and wine — to say nothing of being inclosed in them. This is impossible because of Christ's true humanity which, locally circumscribed, is enthroned in heaven and will not come to us until the *parousia.* The divine Word "is united with the nature of man in one person but is not confined in it," so that it still has reality outside it (II, 13, 4; *Extra calvinisticum*). On the other hand, the true humanity of Christ forbids our attributing to it properties such as ubiquity, which belong to the divinity alone. Calvin regards this as assumed in both the Lutheran and the scholastic doctrine of the real presence. The Holy Spirit effects communion with the life-giving flesh of Christ.

> The Lord grants us through his Spirit the favor of becoming one with him in body, mind, and soul. The bond of this union is, accordingly, the Spirit of Christ. [IV, 17, 12; 17, 33]

The local presence of Christ in heaven prevents his descending to us and being present on the altar. Calvin's idea becomes fully clear in its practical consequences. Since the body and blood of Christ are in no way united to the bread and wine, the veneration of the Sacrament is forbidden. We must direct our mind, not to the sign, but to the signified, to Christ in heaven. The sacrament is offered to all, but unbelievers receive only the sign, while the union with the life-giving flesh of Christ, affected by the Holy Spirit, does not take place.

The *Consensus Tigurinus* saved the unity of the Swiss and Reformed Protestantism while making definitive the break with Lutheranism. This became evident in the disputes of Calvin and the Calvinists with Joachim Westphal (1510–74) and Tilemann Hesshusen (1527–88) in the so-called Second Eucharistic Controversy.

CHAPTER 91

The Spread of Calvinism in Western Europe

In contradistinction to Luther, who was concerned about the "merciful God" and personal justification, Calvin's question was: "How does one arrive at God's dominion over mankind?" If he saw the Reformation as the establishing of the kingdom of God, then he could not limit himself to Geneva. The community there was in his view only the cornerstone of a worldwide Church. In his extensive correspondence Calvin maintained contact with the decisive personalities of Europe. He intervened wherever he saw a door opened for his movement and acted with a sound political sense and great tenacity. Like Calvin, Calvinism showed itself to be active, militant, and at times ruthless. The reformer demanded that his adherents translate their faith into action and realize it, not only in private, but also in public life. They were to carry their confession into the world and set up Reformed congregations wherever they went. To this goal of realizing the kingdom of God on earth they had to subordinate even political exertions. It goes without saying that Calvin claimed the authority of the state for his aims, and, wherever it was denied him, he turned on the opposing forces. For a prince who attacked the Church that had been reformed in accord with God's word — in other words, the only valid form of Christianity, prescribed by God — was failing in his duty and thereby ceased to be a prince. Orderly "resistance" to him was permitted. Differing from the Lutheran, a Calvinist who was not in agreement with the religious policy of his ruling authority had in his very religion a legal basis for resistance, if necessary by armed force. The religious wars in the West, which aroused Frenchmen, Dutchmen, Englishmen, and Scotsmen against their monarchs, were thus partly inspired by Calvin's spirit.

France

Calvin's relations with France, his native land, were especially close. Many French refugees found a home at Geneva and from there preachers were sent to French cities in order to foster the establishing of congregations.

King Henry II (1547–59) continued the anti-Protestant religious policy of his father, Francis I. In October 1547 Henry obtained from the *parlement* the establishing of a special court for heresy cases, the *Chambre ardente.* There were then throughout the country groups of adherents of the Reformation, who were referred to as Lutherans, though they were really oriented to Strasbourg and at first sought their preachers there. They recruited from all strata of the population, including the higher nobility, but practiced their faith secretly, had their children baptized in the old Church, and often even participated in the Mass in order to escape persecution.

Calvin was to mould congregations out of these groups of people who regarded themselves as converts to the Gospel, congregations which were prepared, for their part, to convert their environment. He sharply attacked "Nicodemitism." Anyone who could not hold himself aloof from the "defilements of the papacy" should emigrate. If he cannot belong to the number of the elect to whom God grants the strength and the honor of martyrdom, then he should at least withdraw to where he can find God's word, a genuine Church, and the pure sacraments. The administration of baptism and the celebration of the Lord's Supper, Calvin advises, should wait until a stable community has been founded on the basis of the assembly for prayer and preaching. Despite persecution congregations were formed in many places from 1555 based on the Geneva model. At first the gatherings took place in secret, but in 1558 Calvinists dared to sing psalms publicly in Paris. From 1555 to 1562 the Geneva *Compagnie* sent eighty-eight pastors to France. They often exchanged places in order to evade persecution. At an assembly in Poitiers in 1558 it was decided to hold a synod at Paris the next year in order to define the confession of faith and the Church Order. Representatives from fifty congregations met in this first Calvinist National Synod on 25 May 1559. Calvin sent envoys, to whom he gave a confession of faith. The synod added several articles to it. The definitive version, the *Confessio Gallicana,* had, like the appended Church Order, the *Disciplina,* forty articles. The first treated of the authority of Scripture. It alone is authoritative. The real, though spiritual, community with the body and blood of Christ in the Lord's Supper is clearly stressed. But it is shared only by believers and a real presence in the bread and wine is not accepted. The secular authority has to punish by the sword crime against the first panel of the Ten Commandments, and hence heresy and the like (39). One must be subject, "with a good and free will," even to an unbelieving authority, "provided that God's dominion remains intact (Acts 4:17ff.)" (40). A right of resistance is here formulated only cautiously and *ad casum,* if indeed it is actually formulated at all.

Calvinism found adherents, or at least sympathizers even in circles in the higher nobility and in the royal house itself. Jeanne d'Albret, Queen of Navarre, her husband, Anthony of Bourbon, his brother, Prince Louis de Condé, the Coligny brothers — Admiral Gaspard, infantry general François d'Andelot, and Cardinal Odet de Coligny — and other influential persons were among Calvin's adherents.

Henry II died in 1559, just as he was beginning to act still more energetically in the struggle to maintain religious unity in his country. In the reign of his sickly fifteen-year-old son, Francis II (1559–60), the Guise brothers took control. The *coup de main,* attempted at Chateau Amboise with the aim of removing the King from the influence of these advisers, failed and cost many Protestants their lives. From that time they were known as Huguenots (*hugenauds*), a word probably derived from *Eidgenossen* or *aiguenots,* the term for the adherents of the Reformation in Geneva, who were rebels against Savoy.

The Queen-Mother, Catherine de Médicis, now took the business of state into her own hands. She pushed aside the Guise brothers and summoned their protégé, Michel de L'Hôpital (1503–73), to the chancellorship. As an Erasmian, he was opposed to force in religious matters, just as Catherine, for political reasons, was intent upon *détente.* She assumed the regency for Charles IX (1560–74), brother of the deceased Francis II. She intended to effect a compromise by means of a religious colloquy, which she arranged at Poissy. Such a synod could, better than a general council, provide a remedy in France's difficulties by reform of morals and doctrine. The assembly turned into a religious colloquy, in which Theodore Beza from Geneva confronted the Cardinal of Lorraine and the Jesuit general, Lainez. The question of the Eucharist showed how profound the division was.

The number of Calvinists grew. Coligny offered the Queen the assistance of more than two thousand congregations. In January 1562 the Edict of Saint-Germain-en-Laye allowed the Huguenots to hold synods and to celebrate their liturgy outside of cities and private devotions inside them. A triumvirate, consisting of the Duke of Guise, the Connétable Montmorency, and the Marshal Saint-André, was formed to save the Catholic faith; it actively opposed the government's policy of toleration. On the other hand, the concessions did not satisfy the Huguenots. Coligny tried to induce the Queen to an anti-Spanish policy; the Catholic party sought in turn to involve Spain and the Pope. *The parlement* of Paris refused to register the Edict of Saint-Germain.

The overture to the eight Wars of Religion, which were to devastate France until 1598, was sounded by the Massacre at Vassy on 1 March 1562. Francis of Guise caused the breaking up of a service of worship, which was taking place in the city, contrary to the edict. In the skirmish seventy-four participants were killed and around a hundred wounded. The Huguenots, led by the Prince de Condé and Coligny, flew to arms. Massacres, profanation of churches, and acts of retaliation convulsed the country. Catherine de Médicis turned for help to the Duke of Savoy, the Pope, and King Philip II, while the Huguenots asked aid from Queen Elizabeth of England. The Edict of Amboise in 1563 put an end to the first war. It conceded the free exercise of religion to the nobility; in addition, Calvinist worship was to be permitted in one city of each *bailliage,* except Paris. Since neither side was satisfied, the implementation of the edict led to new difficulties. Condé brought on the second war (1567–68), allegedly to free the King from his mother's control. Catherine de Médicis saw the collapse of her policy of reconciliation. Condé was killed in the third war (1568–70) and Coligny became the sole leader of the Huguenots. Fearful of the power of the Guises and of Spain, Catherine again showed herself accommodating to the Huguenots and granted them liberty of conscience in the Peace of Saint-Germain (8 August 1570). Calvinist worship could be held. And four fortified towns were granted to the Huguenots for two years.

The engagement of the King's sister, Margaret of Valois, to Henry of Navarre, the future Henry IV, who had fought on the Huguenot side, appeared to strengthen the compromise. In 1571 the Huguenots were able to hold a national synod at La Rochelle, where the confession and Church Order of 1559 were revised to strengthen the position of the pastors.

Catherine de Médicis sought to exploit the situation to reestablish her influence and exclude Coligny. Four days after the marriage of her daughter Margaret with Henry of Navarre, at which the Huguenot nobility was strongly represented, she arranged an attempt to assassinate the admiral, who, however, was only wounded. An investigation ordered by the King in search of the guilty threatened to expose Catherine. She convinced her son of the necessity of getting rid of Coligny and the other Huguenot leaders. From three to four thousand men in Paris alone are said to have fallen victim in the subsequent massacre of Saint Bartholomew's Day, 23–24 August 1572, that was thereupon perpetrated by agents of the Guises. The carnage was continued for weeks in the provinces, with the cooperation of the mob. Not religion but an alleged conspiracy against the King and his court was the pretext for the slaughter. This was the explanation sent to the Curia. The Huguenots were now without leaders but they did not give up and successfully defended themselves in La Rochelle. Under Henry III (1574–89) they again obtained religious liberty throughout the kingdom, apart from Paris, in the Peace of Beaulieu (6 May 1576). The Catholic League was established to oppose them with the aim of maintaining the interests and liberties of the estates against royal absolutism as well as of defending the Catholic faith.

With the death of the Duke of Alençon, the youngest brother of the childless Henry III, in 1584, Henry of Navarre, leader of the Huguenots, became heir presumptive. In view of the danger thereby presented of a Protestant succession to the throne, Henry of Guise assumed the direction of the League. An alliance was concluded with Philip II of Spain and, by means of a popular tumult, the King was compelled in the Edict of Nemours in 1585 to repudiate all concessions to the Protestants and to forbid their liturgy under penalty of death. The Eighth War of Religion was initiated by the League in the autumn of 1585 and before long it became an open opposition to Henry III. A popular rising in May 1588 compelled him to leave Paris, which favored the League. King Henry III tried to ward off the threatening might of the Guises by having Duke Henry assassinated on 2 December 1588 and the Duke's brother, Cardinal Louis, on the following day. The League's opposition was thereby strengthened and on 7 January 1589 the Sorbonne declared that the King's subjects were released from their oaths of loyalty. Henry III sought to ally with Henry of Bourbon-Navarre but this only intensified the hatred against him and led to the assassination of the "tyrant" by a fanatical adherent of the League, the Dominican Jacques Clement, on 1 August 1589.

The mortally wounded King had designated Henry of Navarre as his successor. The latter, as Henry IV (1589–1610), proclaimed on 4 August that he would not injure the Catholic religion and that he wished to submit to the decision of a free general or national council. This did not satisfy the League. On 17 May 1593 the King declared to the Archbishop of Bourges his willingness to become a Catholic and on 25 July he repudiated Calvinism. After being anointed at Chartres he was able to enter Paris in March 1594. The remaining Catholic opposition in the country gradually disappeared. Peace with Spain was finally granted to the exhausted land in May 1598 through the Pope's mediation.

A few weeks earlier, on 13 April 1598, Henry IV in the Edict of Nantes had given his former coreligionists a position in the state, which, while not complying with all their demands, certainly far exceeded what people were then inclined to concede to a minority in the way of religious and political rights. At the time the number of Huguenots was about 1.2 million, so that they constituted a good twelfth of the population.

The Catholic religion was recognized as the prevailing faith in the state. Catholic worship had to be reinstituted where it had been suppressed, and buildings and property that had been withdrawn from it had to be given back. The adherents of what was called the "religion prétendu réformée" obtained liberty of conscience in the entire country and freedom of worship in places where they had actually exercised it in 1596–97 and, in addition, in the country seats of the nobility and in one place in each *bailliage,* with the exception of Paris. They were permitted to hold consistories and synods, to lay out cemeteries, to institute schools and printeries in the places where they had the right of free worship. In regard to admittance to the universities, schools, and hospitals, Calvinists were not to be discriminated against. Even more far-reaching were the concessions in civil law and in politics. The Huguenots were competent in law without restriction and had access to all offices. Mixed tribunals, made up of Catholics and Calvinists on an equal footing, were to be established to decide their dispute. As guarantee they received more than a hundred fortified towns for eight years. Their commandants were to be Calvinists and the garrisons were to be supported by the state.

When the Pope expressed his consternation the King maintained the political necessity of the edict for the restoration of the Kingdom. The *parlements,* the supreme courts, procrastinated about registering the edict and thereby giving it force.

The Netherlands

Due to its clear dogmatic line, its strict organization, and its political theory, Calvinism made rapid progress in the Netherlands, answering as it did to the efforts for independence in the area. It soon counted adherents in all classes and even the nobles professed it in great numbers. Thus Calvinism became the confession of the national revolution.

The political situation proved to be especially favorable to its spread. Emperor Charles V, it is true, was concerned for a good administration in Flanders and Holland and thus had the Netherlands governed by regents beloved by the *bourgeoisie.*

Influenced by the current theory that the peace and strength of a nation were based on unanimity of religion among all its members and fearful that the Protestant-inclined Netherlands could expose his flank to France and the

Lutheran imperial estates, Charles proceeded along with the Church against heresy. (W. Durant)

A decree of 25 September 1550 stated that: "No one was to print, transcribe, reproduce, keep, conceal, sell, buy, or give any book or writing of Martin Luther, Johannes Oecolampadius, Ulrich Zwingli, Martin Bucer, Jean Calvin, or any other heretic condemned by Holy Church" (L. Motley). Further the Emperor forbade private and public gatherings, in which adherents of the above-mentioned heretic" spoke. Anyone under even a general suspicion of heresy must not be lodged and aided by the citizenry.

This edict was intended, among other things, to destroy the Calvinists in the Netherlands, but as a matter of fact the activity of the Calvinist preachers and congregations was intensified. Thus the religious was fused with the political and national. In addition there existed a special sympathy for Calvin, who always displayed a great understanding for the religious situation in the Netherlands. He came from neighboring Picardie, and his mother was from Cambrai. He thus called himself a Belgian. He had come into contact with Anabaptists at Strasbourg and had married one of them, the widow Idelette de Bure. Soon afterward (from Geneva) he had made contact with Belgian reformers.

The most important representatives of the new teachings in the Netherlands were the teacher Johannes Sturm (1507–89); the historian Johannes Sleidan (1506–56); the noble Jacques de Bourgogne; the ex-Dominican Pierre Brully (d. 1545); and Guy de Bray (1522–67). The Protestant congregation at Strasbourg exercised a great influence on the development of Calvinism in the Netherlands, especially in the French-speaking parts. In 1544, the first Flemish translations of Calvin's writings were published and his name appeared on the Liège *Index*.

Calvinism gained strength in the Netherlands in spite of severe persecution by the Inquisition, and many Netherlanders went to Geneva to learn there the pure doctrine. The new teaching spread more and more in the Flemish area through the activity of French congregations.

The most important Calvinist in the Netherlands and the best preacher was Guy de Bray. Born at Bergen in Hainault, he is regarded as the "Reformer of the Netherlands." Following his conversion to Calvinism, he spent some time in England and at Lille and Frankfurt. He studied at Geneva and Lausanne and preached at Doornik, Sedan, and Antwerp. Finally he was preacher at Valenciennes; with the capture of this city he was executed on 31 May 1567. He was the author of the *Confessio Belgica* of 1561; in composing it he adhered strictly to the Huguenot confession, "but in an entirely independent spirit." "The special character of the Netherlands confession" lies, "on the one hand, in the detailed recourse to the doctrinal forms of the ancient Church in an effort to renew orthodoxy, and, on the other hand, in the telling use of scriptural passages in the text itself" (P. Jacobs). Especially informative is the definition of the true and the false Church in Article 29. Against the "false Church" de Bray launched the charge that it attributed greater validity to its institutions than to the word of God. "It is based on men rather than on Jesus Christ and persecutes those who live a holy life according to God's word and who reproach its vices, such as avarice and idolatry." The organization of the Netherlands Church is explained in Articles 30 to 32. Elders and deacons constituted, with the pastors, the council of the congregation, by which the "ministers of the word of God" were to be chosen. Calvin exercised a direct influence on the numerous writings of de Bray, the "minister of the word of God in the Netherlands."

When Guy de Bray was at the height of his activity, Philip II (1556–98) assumed the government of the Netherlands. Despite his stern exertions against the Reformation, he was unable to stop the expansion and consolidation of Calvinism. Philip was soon confronted by a powerful opposition, headed by the Prince of Nassau-Orange, governor of the provinces of Holland, Zeeland, and Utrecht. Philip II's conflict with the Calvinists split the Netherlands in two. There was formed at Brussels in 1565 a league of the lesser nobility for the struggle against the Inquisition. These nobles were termed *Gueux*, beggars, by their opponents. The revolt by the Gueux and the constant progress of Calvinism induced Philip to send the Spanish Duke of Alba to Brussels with full powers. Immediately after his arrival, Alba established the "Council of Troubles," which passed many death sentences. Many Calvinists sought religious freedom in London, Wesel, Emden, Geneva, Strasbourg, and Frankfurt. These congregations of emigrants, "the Church under the cross," provided themselves with a definite order at the Assembly of Wesel (1568) and the Synod of Emden (1571). At Emden an effort was made to realize a "Church reformed in accord with the word of God," which should be united with the state but not dependent on it. The synod worked out a plan for the government of all the churches in the Netherlands and thus united them into a national Church. The *Confessio Belgica* was adopted, and the Geneva Catechism was made obligatory for the French-speaking districts, the Heidelberg Catechism for the Flemish-speaking.

Alba's measures brought about a struggle for freedom; the Prince of Nassau-Orange emerged as its leader. During his contest with Spain Calvinism consolidated itself especially in the provinces of Holland and Zeeland. In 1575 the University of Leiden was founded and soon became the scholarly center of Calvinism. In the "Pacification of Ghent" in November 1576 all the provinces united for the expulsion of the Spanish. The more the political struggle contributed to the spread of Calvinism, the more the Catholic provinces — Walloon, Flanders, Artois, and Hainault — feared for their existence. They joined for the defense of the Catholic faith in the Union of Arras on 6 January 1579 and recognized Philip II as their lord. Spain honored this by withdrawing its troops from the provinces of the Union.

The Calvinists' reply to the Union of Arras was the federation of the provinces of Holland, Zeeland, and Utrecht and of the "Ommelanden" around Groningen, together with John of Nassau, governor of Gelderland, in the Union of Utrecht. Of itself it was supposed to have no confessional features, and it expressly guaranteed religious liberty.

Calvinism had conquered the northern Netherlands, but the southern provinces, thanks not least of all to the skill of Alessandro Farnese (1578–92), remained in the Catholic Church. By agreement with Spain the establishing of a Dutch Republic was effected in 1609. Once external peace had been achieved for the Calvinist Church of the Netherlands, serious inner theological conflicts erupted over predestination. "Supralapsarianism" defended a predestination independent of the commission of sin, whereas "Infralapsarianism" saw it as sin's consequence.

The national Synod of Dordrecht (1617–18), attended by representatives of almost all the Calvinist churches of Europe, meant the definitive consolidation of the Reformed Church in the Netherlands.

Germany

Calvinist communities appeared on the lower Rhine when, around the turn of the years 1544–45, Walloons and Flemings moved there for economic reasons and as a consequence of Charles V's more rigorous religious policy in the Netherlands. They met with a good reception especially at Wesel, which from 1540 was regarded abroad as a city of the *Confessio Augustana.*

On the accession of Mary the Catholic to the English throne in 1553 many Protestants who had emigrated there left the country again and sought a new shelter, among other places, at Emden, Frankfurt-am-Main, and on the lower Rhine. A rather large group came again to Wesel. The denial of their own celebration of the Last Supper and the demand to accept the *Confessio Augustana* led, in the case of this relatively closed group, to a much greater resistance than was earlier true of the Walloons. They wanted to maintain their confessional standing in congregations of their own. The question was discussed in 1556 with Calvin and Jan Laski at Frankfurt, where similar problems had arisen. Calvin now advised that ceremonies should be overlooked for the sake of the unity of the Church. But the quarrel extended to the doctrine of the Eucharist. They were expelled in 1557. The victorious Lutheran faction, inspired by Tilemann Hesshusen, in its zeal for the pure doctrine, went to such extremes that it antagonized the city council; the result was a reaction at Wesel. This encouraged the willingness to receive the stream of refugees from the Netherlands, pouring into German territory from 1567, when the Duke of Alba became Spanish governor at Brussels. These, migrants were decided Calvinists. At that time Wesel became a Calvinist city. The number of Calvinists on the lower Rhine had increased to such a degree by 1568 that it was possible to consider giving them an organization. Thus on 3 November numerous pastors and elders and some nobles gathered in synod, the "Wesel Assembly." The synodal organization in use in France and the Netherlands was applied to the new situation. Three years later the guidelines of the Wesel Assembly were declared binding at the general Synod of Emden (4–14 October 1571). This synod was the affair of the scattered Dutch congregations. The local church council played no role. It was only under Menso Alting (1541–1612) that Emden became the "Geneva of the North."

Nevertheless, beyond the Netherlands and the lower Rhine "the congregations of the continent" were united through the Emden Synod "into a Church with a common confession and common order" (W. Niesel). The laity were much used in the service of the Church. Together with the preachers (*ministri*), the elders and deacons constituted the consistory, which was to meet weekly (Article 6). "In places where the service of the word could not be carried out" lecturers, elders, and deacons were to be instituted so that congregations could be assembled (41). Hence, in times of persecution, the congregations could, if necessary, get along without preachers. Several congregations formed a "class" (7). Thus the individual congregation found support in the larger unity. The Calvinism of the lower Rhine felt itself bound to the Church of the Netherlands and long remained closely united with it. It was not until 1610 that the congregations of Cleves, Mark, Jülich-Berg, and Ravensberg established in Duisburg their own general synodal union. In 1655 the founding of a Calvinist university for Brandenburg-Cleves finally took place in Duisburg, the chief center of the Calvinist confession.

On the lower Rhine and in East Friesland Calvinism had arisen from below by the founding of congregations and had built itself into a synodal union on the French and Netherlands model. The situation was different where it was introduced from above, by the decision of a prince or of a city government. In these cases the authority sought to retain control of Church administration and hence the congregational organization, created by Calvin, was subject to some restriction. The first German prince to accept the Calvinist creed and introduce it in his territory was Friedrich III of the Palatinate (1559–76). His most important assistants in introducing Calvinism were Melanchthon's Silesian pupil, Zacharias Ursinus (1534–83), and Kaspar Olevianus of Trier (1536–87).

The Elector Friedrich III had, shortly before, succeeded the childless Otto Heinrich (1556–59). His wife, Mary of Hohenzollern, had gained him for Lutheranism. In his religious and ethical seriousness he inclined to rigorism and was intolerant of Catholics, Jews, and, later, of Lutherans. Concerned for the unity of Protestantism, he was personally involved in the Eucharistic quarrel between the pugnacious Lutheran, Tilemann Hesshusen, and university circles. The Elector was indignant at the strife of theologians, especially at Hesshusen's fanaticism and, for his own part, intended to arrive at a solution through prayer and the study of Holy Scripture. He declared the Eucharistic formula of the *Confessio Augustana Variata* to be obligatory. According to this version, "the body and the blood of Christ are really administered," not in or under, but "with the bread and wine." In this way one could profess Calvin's view and at the same time be included in the protection afforded by the Religious Peace of 1555 as an adherent of the *Confessio Augustana.* Hesshusen was dismissed, and his His place was taken by a church council of three theologians and three laymen. The Elector Palatine inclined more than ever to the Calvinist viewpoint. On 12 August 1560 he issued an edict whereby ministers who were unwilling to accept Melanchthon's Eucharistic formula had to leave the principality. At the same time Calvinists driven from their homelands, such as Kaspar Olevianus from Trier, Zacharias Ursinus from Breslau, and Wenceslaus Zuleger from Bohemia, acquired great influence at the Electoral court. When his efforts to assure the unity of Protestantism by again acquiring signatures for the *Confessio Augustana Variata* failed at the Naumburg Diet of Princes in 1561, Friedrich III went over definitively to Calvinism. But he hesitated to adopt the Geneva Catechism, which would have signified an open break with the *Confessio Augustana,* so he commissioned the drawing up of a special catechism. The resulting Heidelberg Catechism of 1563 was essentially the work of Ursinus. In 129 questions the catechism provides a systematic and carefully composed theology. Following the Introduction — "What is your single consolation in life and in death? That one is the property of Christ his Saviour" — come three parts: I. 'On Man's Misery" (sin, which is recognized by virtue of Christ's two-fold commandment of love of God and neighbor); II. "On Man's Redemption" (questions 12 to 85: the Creed, baptism, the Lord's Supper); III. "On Gratitude" (questions 86 to 129: works the decalog, the Lord's Prayer). The Calvinist doctrine of predestination and any polemic against the Lutheran teaching on the Eucharist are abandoned. The fourth and definitive edition of the catechism was published, along with the Church Order, in November 1563 for the dominions of Friedrich III of the Palatinate. Beyond this area it won, among other places, Nassau-Orange, the lower Rhineland, the County of Mark, and especially the Netherlands. It was translated into Dutch as early as 1563 and at the Dordrecht Synod of 1618–19 it was declared to be the symbolic book whereby the way into the entire Calvinist world was opened up.

The Church Order dealt with preaching and the administration of the sacraments. Exclusion from the sacraments was provided for. Eventually the Church Order regulated the eleemosynary system, dress, marriage cases, the care of the sick and of prisoners, and burial. The Church council acquired a new order in 1564. It had to exercise authority over the territorial Church as one of the prince's administrative offices. Olevianus instituted Church discipline on the Geneva model, whereby it was entrusted rather to the congregation or to a court selected by it. He was able to see his plans realized at least partially when in 1570 the Elector issued a disciplinary order for the Church council. According to this the council had the means of calling to account every deviation in doctrine or too outspoken notion.

The appearance of the Heidelberg Catechism brought Friedrich III into new difficulties with imperial law. In a letter of 13 July 1563 the Emperor stated that the Calvinist Lord's Supper was not in accord with the *Confessio Augustana* and hence the Electoral Palatinate was excluded from the Religious Peace of 1555. Then and in 1566 at the Diet of Augsburg, when the accusations were repeated, it was argued by the champions of the Palatinate that they were in agreement with the *Confessio Augustana* as properly understood and in accord with the teaching of great foreign Protestant churches. These difficulties led to the printing and approving of a profession of faith which Bullinger, for personal reasons, had put in writing in 1562 in the expectation of his death. It was printed in 1566 as the *Confessio Helvetica Posterior* and sent to Heidelberg.

This temporarily threatening situation did not keep Friedrich III from again proceeding forcibly against Lutheranism and especially from suppressing Catholic worship and faith.

After his death Lutheranism was restored for five years by his son and successor, Ludwig VI (1578–83), who had recourse to the same state-police methods.

In Nassau, Count John VI (1559–1606), a brother of William of Orange, favored Calvinism; he was confirmed in this by his close connections with the Netherlands. When the Calvinist theologians were expelled from the Palatinate and the Cryptocalvinists from Wittenberg, they obtained a public reception in Nassau in 1577. On 8–9 July 1578 the Synod of Dillenburg adopted the Nassau Confession. A *presbyterium* was instituted in the same year. The General Assembly of 1531 adopted the Palatinate Church Order and the Heidelberg Confession. The Johannes University, established at Herborn in 1584 on the model of the Geneva Academy, acquired a great reputation through its important teachers, Kaspar Olevianus, and others, and became, after Geneva and Leiden, a center of Calvinist theology. The Herborn Order, an effort to unite the Geneva presbyterial-synodal system with the territorial institution of superintendents, continued to operate until the Rhenish-Westphalian Church Order of 1835.

In Bremen Philippism had gained influence through Hardenberg. In 1572, an "Agreement on the Chief Points of Christian Doctrine" was accepted. The influence of Calvinism also grew at Bremen. A confession that Christoph Pezel composed, the Consensus Bremensis, was signed on 2 May 1595, by all members of the Church officialdom and in 1644 it was declared by the council to be the valid creed. In comparison with the Nassau Confession, it was enlarged by, among other points, a section on predestination and it represented a strict Calvinism.

Prince Joachim Ernst of Anhalt (1546–86) brought all parts of the principality under his rule from 1570. While inclined to Lutheranism, he could not be induced to sign the *Formula of Concord.* Wolfgang Amling (1542–1606) called by him to Zerbst in 1578 to become superintendent, opposed to the *Formula of Concord* a *Confessio Anhaltina* and an *Apologia Anhaltina.* Some clerics who had been driven from Saxony under the suspicion of Cryptocalvinism were welcomed in Anhalt. In 1585 Prince Joachim Ernst had his theologians draw up a "Brief and True Profession of the Lord's Holy Supper," which all clergymen of his territory had to sign. His successor, Johann Georg I, through his marriage was in close connection with the Electoral Palatinate. In 1596 they both decreed that the tablets and wooden crucifixes on and over altars, the candles, and the vestments were abolished. Altars were to resemble tables, and the clergy were to break bread behind the table and facing the congregation. The confessional basis of the territorial Church consisted of the *Confessio Augustana Variata,* the Palatinate liturgy, and the Heidelberg Catechism.

Thus around 1600 the formation of the Calvinist territorial Church in Germany was completed. A leading role in this had been played by pupils of Melanchthon, some of whom had had to give way to Lutheran orthodoxy at Wittenberg. They proclaimed their passage to Calvinism as a "second Reformation." In their eyes, Lutheranism, with its "papist" relics, was a preliminary step; Melanchthon, with his theology of mediation, was the transition; Calvinism, on the other hand, with its liturgy, its ecclesiastical discipline, and its idea of Christian authority, was the consistent completion of the Reformation. In contradistinction to the "Reformation of doctrine" that was carried out by Luther, in Calvinism was seen the "Reformation of life."

Scotland and England

In 1549 the Scottish National Synod stressed two reasons for the deterioration of the Church in Scotland: the immorality and the defective formation of the clergy. An improvement in the manner of life of the clergy was everywhere called for, so that "those who show others the way might not themselves be at fault" (W. C. Dickinson). From a report made by Cardinal Sermoneta to Pope Paul IV in 1556, it appears that none of these demands of the synod was carried out. This climate created a good soil for the reception of the new teaching, and even the political situation was favorable. James V of Scotland died in 1542, when his successor, Mary, Queen of Scots, was only a week old. The struggle over the regency between the Archbishop of Saint Andrews, Cardinal David Beaton (1539–46), and the Earl of Arran, heir presumptive to the throne, ended in the victory of the latter. The outcome was an encouragement of Protestantism. For, like many other nobles, the Earl favored the Reformation in the expectation of thereby acquiring a part of the property of the Church.

John Knox (c. 1505–72) was the chief figure in the Scottish Reformation. He carried on the work much more decisively and even more fanatically and thus became the "Reformer of Scotland." When, following a two-years' absence abroad — from 1547 to 1549 he was in detention on a French galley — he returned to Scotland, the Scottish court was under the domination of Mary Stuart's mother, Mary of Guise, Francophile and Catholic. Knox was able to stir up the Protestants, who had been forced into the background, to new activity. At the Scottish provincial synod in 1552 it was decided to publish a catechism in the Scottish tongue as an aid for the clergy in explaining the Bible. This "Hamilton's Catechism" accepted a Protestant ideology, especially in the teaching on predestination.

The Covenant of 1557 constitutes a climax in the development of the Scottish Reformation. In this the Scottish nobility swore to defend the "congregation of Christ" and to annihilate the "congregation of Satan." From now on the Catholics were confronted by a compact array of influential men. Meanwhile, Knox had spent a year (1554–55) at Geneva, where he became a definite follower of Calvin. He preached, with Calvinist severity, resistance to "unrighteous authority," as well as the destruction of images, churches, and monasteries. He knew how to captivate the masses. As an example may be cited his *Against the Monstrous Regiment of Women,* composed in 1558. The persecution of Protestants in England by Queen Mary I was attributed to this work, which thus understandably aroused resentment in the persecuted against Knox. This example makes clear how the more radical bent of John Knox, stamped by Calvinism, differed from the more moderate English Protestants and what course Scotland would hereafter follow. The marriage of Queen Mary Stuart with the future Francis II of France in 1558 was unfortunate for the Catholics of Scotland. Because of the marriage distrust and discontent between Catholics and Protestants grew to such an extent that finally civil war broke out in 1559. The immediate reason was the support given to the Ancient Church by Mary of Guise. The Protestants managed to maintain themselves with the help of English troops.

In 1560, after the death of Mary of Guise, an assembly of spiritual and secular lords met in Edinburgh, at the urging of John Knox. Three important decisions were taken, almost unanimously, by this meeting of the estates: the authority and jurisdiction of the Pope were abolished, the Mass and all else that was opposed to the Protestant confession were forbidden, and the *Confessio Scotica* was declared in force. This *Scottish Confession* was composed by a committee of six on the initiative of Parliament. The leading spirit was here again John Knox. The assembly which enacted the *Confessio Scotica* is called the "Reformation Parliament." It was attended by a large number of members of the lesser nobility, all of whom were enthusiastic Protestants. Mary Stuart, who, following the death of her husband, assumed the government of Scotland in 1561, never signed this *Confession of Faith and of Doctrine.* Under her, a convinced Catholic, the religious question remained unsolved. Vis-à-vis the Calvinists she adopted a very liberal position, but she was nevertheless regarded by them as a danger for their faith. She had to promise by proclamation to maintain the status quo, that is, to accept Protestantism as the state religion, as it had been since 1560. The Queen's privy councilors even promised to support the Calvinist Church; this meant that one-third of the Church property was confiscated. The Calvinists obtained one part of this; the remainder went to the Queen. In view of the activity of Knox's adherents, Mary could not dare to uphold those of her own faith, especially since Knox more and more emphasized that the Calvinists must not be forced to concur with the "idolatrous Queen."

Mary's second marriage, to Henry Darnley, in 1565 did nothing to improve her position. On the contrary: when this incompetent man was murdered on 10 February 1567, the Queen was accused of complicity, since three months later she married the Protestant Earl of Bothwell who had taken part in the crime. Knox ranted against the Queen and demanded her execution. In July 1567 there was nothing left for her except to abdicate in favor of her infant son, James VI, who was later to become James I of England. He was educated as a Calvinist.

More so than elsewhere, in Scotland the Reformation was a lay movement, lacking so theologically distinctive a leader as Luther, Calvin, Zwingli, or Cranmer. John Knox is in a different category from the reformers just mentioned; he was a fanatical Church leader rather than a theologian. But he did not succeed in fully realizing the plans and hopes which he had set forth in his *First Book of Discipline* in 1560. For the Scottish Lords regarded the Church Order advocated by him, the proposal of an earthly republic which was to prepare for heaven, from quite another viewpoint than his own and "refused to consider an independent system of canon law, in which the Church ruled the state, took over the schools, and provided for the sick and weak" (A. Zimmermann). Knox envisaged an intimate cooperation between Church and state. In his *Book of Discipline* he protested, in agreement with Calvin, against Church festivals; they were human institutions and hence to be abolished. A further section had to do with church buildings. Worship was permitted only in parish churches or schools not in monasteries or in abbeys. The place of worship had to be properly equipped. Knox devoted himself in great detail to the "admission of ministers." Every congregation had the right to elect its own clergy. The prerequisite was a definite educational level; ordination and imposition of hands were repudiated. A comprehensive support of the families of ministers in which there was a definite need was demanded; attention to the education of the children and the maintenance of the widows was especially stressed. Knox required that the poor in general be supported, not those "who followed the profession of begging." These demands and proposals point to the modern welfare state.

Knox's remarks on the use of superintendents give an insight into the organization of the Church. The entire country was to be divided into ten or twelve provinces, and each province was to receive a superintendent. Their duties were to establish congregations and institute clergymen. They were responsible for the order and morals of the congregations and their ministers. The Church was also responsible for the education of the people. Every congregation in the city had to appoint a schoolmaster who was able to teach grammar and Latin. In the country instruction in the catechism, in accord with the *Book of Common Order*, had to be provided for children and adolescents. "Colleges" were to be founded in the larger cities, in particular in the superintendent's seat, and in these the arts and languages were to be taught. In addition, three universities — St. Andrews, Glasgow, and Aberdeen — were demanded for all of Scotland. It was made possible for pupils and university students to obtain scholarships; the deciding factors here were the intellectual ability of the candidate and the financial situation of his parents.

The "Kirk Session" — a tribunal of laymen and ministers — was to be of great importance for the ecclesiastical organization of the Church. At its annual session took place the election of deacons and elders. It was the duty of the elders to assist and supervise the pastor. Unworthy pastors were to be deposed by the elders with the approval of the Church and the superintendent; here the presbyterial system was already making its appearance.

As far as possible, baptism was to be administered only on Sunday, following the sermon; the Lord's Supper was to be celebrated four times a year — on the first Sunday of March, June, September, and December. The requirement for reception was to be a knowledge of the "Our Father," of the Creed, and of the ten commandments. Every church had to possess an English Bible. The faithful were to be obliged to listen to the Bible and its explanation. Every head of a family had to instruct the members of his household in Christian doctrine. All the faithful were to learn psalms and practice so as to be able "to sing along mightily" at worship.

If, with the deposition of Mary Stuart in 1567, Protestantism flourished again and the *Confession of Faith* and the *Book of Discipline* were recognized, no practical consequences really resulted from this approval. The Catholic bishops and priests were at first left undisturbed in their positions, but they no longer had any influence on the faithful. There thus existed, side by side, two Churches; the one was reduced to silence, but wealthy, while the other was active, but poor. Meanwhile, the Calvinist Church was completing its institutions at synods. When positions became vacant, they were given to Calvinist preachers. The bishops were treated in the same way. From 1572, on the basis of the Concordat of Leith, they were no longer nominated by the crown but were examined and accepted by Calvinist preachers, and they were subject only to the General Assembly, the general synod of the Scottish Church.

Andrew Melville found this "tolerant" attitude of the Scottish Calvinists when in 1574 he returned from Geneva to become Knox's successor. He thus felt called upon for a *Second Book of Discipline*. Like the *First Book*, he claimed to be merely going back to the word of God. Like Knox, he wanted all the possessions of the Church to be turned over to Calvinist ministers, schools, the poor, and other ecclesiastical institutions. But the demand for the equality of ministers was a departure from the *First Book*. The episcopal organization was superseded by the presbyterian. Church discipline was to be guaranteed not only by clerics but by tribunals of laymen and ministers. These were called the "Kirk Session," "Presbyter Synod," and "General Assembly," and had authority to give decisions in regard to laymen and clerics in ecclesiastical matters. If the secular power offends in matters of conscience and religion, it is subject to Church law. It is the Church's duty to prescribe to the secular power how it is to bring its activities into harmony with the word of God. Here was the initial step toward a Church that could determine the policy of the state.

King James VI (1567–1625) was intelligent enough to recognize the danger in this development. It was to be feared that the General Assembly would soon control every aspect of royal authority. Melville, in fact, maintained that the authority of the Church stood, not merely alongside, but above that of the state. In 1584 he made it known to the King's secret council that it was a usurpation to control the ambassadors and envoys of a King who was far above him, the earthly King. James wanted an episcopal system; he wanted bishops who would be named by the crown. In this he saw the sole possibility of being master in his country. Melville, on the contrary, worked for a presbyterial system, independent of the state and actually over it.

With the arrival of Erné Stuart, Lord d'Aubigny, came new difficulties. He was suspected of being a papist agent. In an effort to end this suspicion James VI, Lord d'Aubigny, who had meanwhile become Earl of Lennox, and the entire royal family signed the "King's Confession" in 1581. It was also called the "Negative Confession," because in it every religion and doctrine that was not in harmony with the *Confessio Scotica* of 1566 was rejected. Two months later all Scotland had to subscribe to this document.

In August 1582 the King, by whose orders the "Confessio Negativa" had been drafted, was imprisoned because he was still regarded as a danger to true religion. After James' escape Melville was charged with treason against the country, but he fled to England. The King, embittered by his imprisonment, now turned against everything that Melville had demanded for the Church. The so-called "Black Acts" were enacted in May 1584 as measures of retaliation. They stated that Parliament and Council were above all spiritual and temporal estates and sanctioned them as such. It was declared that this decree was directed especially against Presbyterianism. This was unacceptable to the Calvinists. The "Magna Charta of the Church of Scotland" meant the repudiation of the "Black Acts" by the King. In it he confirmed all privileges of the Calvinist Church and again promised it the right to convoke general assemblies, synods, and presbyterial meetings. He even declared that the "Black Acts" were not to oppose the "privilege which God has given to spiritual officials in the Church" (Dickinson). Despite these concessions the equality of all clergymen was for the King the cause of all evil, or "mother of confusion"; hence his change was a purely external one. His diplomatic skill soon enabled him to give the episcopal form the predominance again over the presbyterian form.

In sum, it can be said of the development in Scotland. In organization and doctrine the Scottish Church was Calvinist. It was not yet Presbyterian under Knox, who never called for the equality of all clerics. It was only his successor, Melville, who pushed the development further in this direction and realized a full Presbyterianism. In James VI it discovered a great opponent. An so in the period that followed there was a continual struggle between King and Presbyterianism for the leadership of the Church.

In England Calvinists were long unable to establish themselves. For the most part they were refugees from France or Englishmen who had become acquainted with Knox's ideas in Scotland. Having become used to the simplicity of the Calvinist worship, they regarded as too much to approve the "Romish" rite of the Anglican Church. Thus the Calvinists were in conflict with the Anglican Church. They had no possibility of developing an ecclesiastical system of their own, however, for the

Act of Uniformity, issued under Queen Elizabeth I in 1559, prescribed a uniform Anglican liturgy. The Calvinists did not stop demanding a "pure" Church, "in accord with Scripture," thereby acquiring the name "Puritans' around 1566. The middle class especially favored them. At first they represented a group with a particular intellectual outlook within the Anglican Church. When the state Church would not go along with their demand, they separated from it and instituted their own congregations in 1567. They gave themselves a democratic Church organization and thus became Presbyterians. Following this their opposition to the Anglican High Church became notorious and severe persecutions ensued. Many "Dissenters" went to prison, but they could not be exterminated. Many left England. In 1620 one group, the "Pilgrim Fathers," sailed for North America on the *Mayflower* and established a new home for themselves in Massachusetts. Their idea of the autonomous congregation under Christ as its unique head contributed substantially to the American notion of democracy as the political form of government most in accord with God's will.

Puritans were also persecuted in England under Charles I (1625–49). In particular Archbishop Laud of Canterbury (d. 1645) tried to restore unity of worship and proceeded sternly against Puritanism and Presbyterianism in Scotland. This led to civil war. The King's defeat in 1645–46 and execution in 1649 meant the temporary end of the Anglican Episcopal Church and the victory of Presbyterianism.

CHAPTER 92

The Development of Denominations in the Sixteenth and Seventeenth Centuries

When the division of the Western Church had long been a sad reality and there was already a multiplicity of religious communities which differed substantially in doctrine, worship, and law, people were still in no sense aware of the full import of these facts. Only relatively late were there denominations in the sense of ecclesiastical communities, whose members knew they were united in professing clearly defined truths of faith and by means of a common worship and common norms of moral conduct and that they were separated from other groups. Denominational formation took place in a slow process of more than a century and in a manner quite different according to countries and even localities. In Catholic territories it was ordinarily much more rotracted than in Protestant lands. Acceptance of the Reformation by a state or a city did not mean, of course, that the masses also took this step from their own convictions. If the reformers did not intend to found a new Church, *a fortiori* their adherents were not thinking of any schism in faith and Church. People wanted "preaching according to Scripture," they professed the "pure doctrine," and, in short, intended to take reform seriously. When Christendom was actually split into denominations, each of them thought of itself as universal, as the true Church, and accordingly considered all others as heretical. People clung to the traditional notion of the unity of the Church and of its teaching, which could be formulated in obligatory dogmas. To deviate from them was to become guilty of wicked heresy.

The situation was complicated but also mitigated by the fact that not only Catholics and Protestants were in opposition. For Protestants soon split into various groups, and again had to defend themselves, together with the Catholics, against Anabaptists, fanatics, and Spiritualists. Then all groups, more or less, found it necessary to be more firmly united. This process of clarifying and acquiring awareness from within and of stabilization and differentiation from without, which we call denominational formation, was not only and not even most powerfully urged and supported by religious forces but also by cultural and social and especially by political strength. Undoubtedly, Lutheran preaching was only in its beginnings from 1520 in broad areas of Germany and Switzerland. But the destruction and rebuilding of the ecclesiastical organization that it had called for could as yet be regarded only as the long overdue and longed-for reform of the Church.

At Augsburg the Protestants were invited by the Emperor to present their viewpoint. The result was the *Confessio Augustana* and its *Apologia.* But these were intended as a confession of the "Catholic Church" and endeavored to show that what was sought was not a new Church but only the abolition of abuses. The unity of religion with a particular political sphere was still taken for granted by all concerned. According to Luther, no contrary preaching should be tolerated in a principality or city, for the sake of peace.

When religious unity could no longer be preserved for the Empire, it was assured for the individual territories by awarding to the princes the right to decide the confession of their subjects. The princes made a powerful contribution to the formation of denominations after the 1555 Religious Peace of Augsburg by striving to create in their territories a distinct and uniform religious situation. They tried to eliminate other creeds and to consolidate their own by various means. Where authority made no use of its right to determine the religion of its subjects the process of denominational formation was longest drawn up.

Consequently, the relationship of the political authority to the Church in its territory was in no sense everywhere the same. "Cuius regio eius et religio" was, of course, universally in force as a principle, but it was not everywhere made use of in the same way. Partly the political power of the princes did not suffice to impose their religion. Resistance came, not from the masses of the people, but from the leading circles of the cities and from the rural nobility, which asserted its independence from state authority by means of a religion different from that of the prince. In the Swiss Confederation and in some Imperial Free Cities political necessity produced a juxtaposition of confessions. Economic viewpoints could also motivate the tolerating and even the granting of privileges to denominational minorities. Difficulties easily occurred in areas of condominium, when lords belonging to different religions held the territorial sovereignty.

The manner and degree in which the secular power influenced the religious situation differed according to denomination. Lutheranism allowed the greatest amount of influence to the state. Calvinism sought to gain the authority of the state for itself but at the same time to preserve its independence in the sphere of dogma, worship, and ecclesiastical discipline. The Catholic Church also claimed the secular arm for the organizing of Church life and in return had to permit some interference in the spiritual sphere. In principle she made decisions independently in matters of doctrine, worship, and canon law, and she did so from central headquarters without regard for political boundaries. This was felt as irksome by some governments and led to conflicts between the spiritual and the secular power.

How did the population react? How did it accept the control of its religious confession by its lord? It is difficult to find a universally valid answer. The response would differ according to particular areas and decades. At the beginning of the seventeenth century people were no longer as ready as they had been at the middle of the sixteenth century to change their religion along with their prince. This was the result of a better religious formation and of the increased denominational awareness. The rural folk especially clung to traditional customs. Monasteries and collegiate chapters often resisted the introduction of the Reformation by the authority and yielded only to force. On the whole, however, change of religion as decided by the political power was effected rather smoothly.

The masses were mostly uneducated and often unaware of the change of faith. This was possible especially in the sphere of Lutheranism, where the retention of ceremonies was allowed. The elevation of the Host, for example, was retained at Wittenberg until 1542. The fact that great portions of the Canon, which was in any event prayed silently, had been dropped did not necessarily attract the notice of those in attendance. In northern and eastern Germany the retaining of the Catholic organization and usages went especially far. How should the common folk have noticed the distinction? The ease with which entire populations of subjects were led to the Reformation or back to Catholicism is all the more understandable.

In addition to legitimate Catholic traditions that had been accepted in Church Orders, some practices were maintained which were irreconcilable with a Protestant ideology but which the people, especially the rural folk, were unwilling to give up. Denominational uncertainty, frequent change, and the circumstance that pastors suitable for the religion decreed from above were not available fostered indifference and increased the number of those who no longer went at all to church and the sacraments. Complaints were heard.

Crass ignorance in matters of faith, neglect of religion, and immorality characterized the situation in the second half of the sixteenth century cutting across all denominations. Massive superstition, curiosity for marvels, astrology, and the witchcraft delusion also flourished where people boasted of the pure Gospel. They especially spread in the now Protestant northeast of Europe, where Christianity had up to then scarcely established itself against paganism and the gloomy forces of blood and earth. And so, together with the clarifying and deepening of the awareness of the particular denomination, it was important for Christianity in general to send new roots into the masses as doctrine and life. In this what routes were traveled? What help was at hand?

First of all, by means of formulated "confessions," catechisms, and textbooks an effort was made to end the uncertainty about what the doctrine was and the arbitrary way it was proclaimed. Assent to the true teaching became the distinctive mark of belonging to a denomination.

In the *Confessio Augustana* Lutheranism had started the practice of defining a particular standpoint by means of a denominational book. But it had turned out to be inadequate in the doctrinal strife within Lutheranism, and meanwhile a differentiation in regard to Calvinism had become necessary. After years of struggle, the result was the *Formula Concordiae* of 1577. On 25 June 1580, the *Book of Concord* — the collection of Lutheran confessional documents ending with the *Formula of Concord* — was published at Dresden. The Concord was signed by fifty-one princes, thirty-five cities, and more than eight thousand theologians.

From the outset Calvinism had followed the path of clear creedal formulae and of systematic exposition of doctrine. Jean Calvin had set the example with the Geneva Catechism of 1542–45 and the *Institutio Religionis Christianae* (1536; 4th edition 1559). There followed official formulae of faith on a national basis: the *Confessio Gallicana* (1559), *Scotica* (1560), *Belgica* (1561), *Helvetica posterior* (1566), and the Heidelberg Catechism of 1563. In accord with the Calvinist ideas of the Church, these confessions also contained instructions in regard to congregational organization and discipline.

In the Catholic Church an end was put to what Jedin calls the "doctrinal confusion" by the decrees of the Council of Trent. The *Catechismus Romanus* of 1566, based on them, provided clergy and people with a compendium of Christian doctrine. The *Professio fidei Tridentina* had to be sworn to by all bishops and also by professors of theology. King Ferdinand I fostered the work of Canisius on the catechism, prescribed it for his territories, and issued detailed instructions on the manner of using it. The formulae of faith and the catechisms put an end to the dogmatic uncertainty but at the same time necessarily restricted the area of free discussion and produced a polemical discrimination vis-à-vis other ideas.

Second, in addition to the clear formulation of doctrine, a Church Order was of great importance for the introduction and consolidation of a denomination. This regulated worship, law, education, salaries of pastors and teachers, administration, and the care of the poor for the Church in a territory, a city, a lordship, and, in certain circumstances, in a mere district. In the period 1550–1600 the number of such Church Orders increased to the hundreds.

To enforce the Church Orders and to see to it that the territorial religion was also practiced by the subjects was the business of the periodic visitations. The records of visitations gave a picture of the religious situation and were the reason and the motive for further political and pastoral measures. On the Catholic side, visitations, following diocesan or provincial synods, were the means of assembling forces that had become uncertain and disoriented and of implementing the Tridentine reform.

Third, if the defective formation of clergy and people was the chief reason for the uncertainty and confusion in matters of faith, the establishing of educational institutions and the care for the formation and social security of pastors was the best means of creating a clear denominational situation. The concern for a better formation of the clergy had tangible success from 1600, but of course the situation still differed from one locality to another. These efforts to educate the clergy and for the development of schools were to be observed in all denominations toward the close of the sixteenth century. On the Catholic side the profession of teacher and tutor in secondary schools, universities, and seminaries was the chief activity of the Jesuits. "All of pedagogy was geared to the practice of Christianity in the sense of denominations" (E. W. Zeeden).

Fourth, the appearance of Calvinism at the end of the 1550s eventually contributed powerfully to the formation of denominations and the defining of fronts. Its very consciousness of election, its organizational strength, and its aggressiveness had as their consequence a well developed denominational awareness.

The effort to distinguish itself denominationally from Calvinism led in Lutheranism to an emphatic love of ceremonies and to the restoration of Catholic institutions, such as Mass vestments and the elevation of Host and chalice. If denominational differentiation here produced a certain degree of enrichment, the contrary was normal. As soon as definite usages and ceremonies became characteristic of one denomination, they were thereby forbidden to the others, even if, in themselves, they were *adiaphora* and had nothing or only remotely to do with differences of doctrine. If the sign of the cross or the "Angelus" was "Catholic," then it was for that reason no longer to be practiced by Lutherans. While at the middle of the sixteenth century it still seemed possible by the concession of the lay chalice to preserve for the Catholic Church large groups in Bavaria, Austria, and the lower Rhineland, who desired Communion under both species, the form of administering Communion soon became so much a question of denominational distinction that the granting of the chalice merely caused confusion. Similarly, the reform demand for the vernacular in the liturgy brought it about that in the minds of Catholics the Latin language acquired the special character of orthodoxy and the initial steps taken in the Middle Ages toward a more careful regard for the vernacular were not followed up. In view of the Protestant denial of an official priesthood, this was pushed so powerfully to the foreground by the post-Tridentine Church that the priesthood of all Christians, based on baptism and confirmation, was almost forgotten. In view of Luther's doctrine of the hidden Church, the Church as a visible community and institute of salvation was so greatly stressed that her inner mystery as the mystical Body of Christ was hardly seen any more. On the one hand, the Church, as the bride of Christ, as the mother of the faithful, as the protector of the truth and minister of the life of grace, became herself the object of devotion; on the other hand she risked succumbing to the appeal of a superficial triumphalism. Compared with the Protestant communities as churches of the Word, the Catholic Church became a narrow Church of the Sacrament.

Thus the form and rise of the denominations were greatly influenced by the "anti" to the other. People were in danger of overlooking the common inheritance because of the emphasis on differences and even of becoming impoverished and narrow. Controversy and polemics took up much room in theology. A popular song of the Lutheran Cyriacus Spangenberg (1528–1604) began: "Keep us, Lord, in your word and arrange the murder of Pope and Turk." The poet and theologian Paul Gerhardt (1606–76), by whose hymns all denominations today feel themselves enriched, in his strict Lutheran orthodoxy said in the pulpit: "I cannot regard the Calvinists, *quatenus tales,* as Christians." All this constituted the negative side, weighing heavily on the future of the formation of denominations, a process that, as such, was necessary for clarifying and solidifying, after the Reformation had finally led to a split in, instead of to the reform of, the one Church.

Part Two

Catholic Reform and Counter Reformation

Hubert Jedin

Section Four: Josef Glazik

The Historical Concepts

Both concepts, "Catholic Reform" and "Counter Reformation," presuppose the term "Reformation" as an historical definition of the Protestant separation from the body of Catholic believers. We prefer the designation "Catholic Reform," because it avoids the term "Reformation" in the sense of "Protestant Reformation" — an expression that is subject to certain misgivings but is in general use — while on the other hand it indicates the continuity of the efforts for the reinvigoration of the Church from the fifteenth to the sixteenth centuries, without excluding, as does the term "Restoration," the new elements and the influence of the schism on the progress of the movement. However, it requires the additional concept "Counter Reformation," for the Church, inwardly renewed and strengthened, did actually proceed after the Council of Trent to a counterattack and recovered lost territory, in association, to be sure, with confessional absolutism. Hence both concepts are justified, as signifying not separate but intimately correlated movements. Also, Catholic authors, such as Paschini and Villoslada, hold that the term "Counter Reformation" is permissible for the entire movement of renewal and counteraction. Only when the terms "Catholic Reform" and "Counter Reformation" are used in conjunction can they be considered epoch-making in Church History.

Section One

Origin and Breakthrough of the Catholic Reform to 1563

CHAPTER 93

Preliminary Steps in Italy and Spain

The Catholic Reform drew its strength from the large medieval endeavors for religious renewal, which were able to maintain themselves in Italy and Spain without being interrupted by schism. Its further development became possible only when, under Paul III, the reform movement gained a footing in Rome, when it began to eliminate obstacles inherent in the practices of the Curia, and when it finally affected the whole Church through the Council of Trent. Its growth and its breakthrough to Rome, which became apparent in the papal elections of 1555, occurred under the pressure and influence of the defections in northern Europe, which showed that an interior renewal of the Church was absolutely necessary. In substance Catholic Reform meant an orientation toward the apostolate and active *Caritas*, an orientation which came about through Christian self-realization. Not only did the religious points of departure vary, but the emphasis which the individual proponents of this reform assigned to these elements also differed. In several instances, laymen and secular powers participated in the beginnings, but it was of decisive importance that the episcopate and the papacy initiated the necessary steps for the reform of the diocesan and the regular clergy.

Reform Efforts in Italy

The amply developed system of religious confraternities in Italy produced, apart from numerous "Compagnie," which were run like ordinary clubs, a tendency in the fifteenth century toward a more profound inwardness and an uncommon devotion to charitable goals.

In the "Fraternitas divini amoris sub divi Hieronymi protectione," established at Genoa in 1497, the layman Ettore Vernazza (ca. 1470–1524), influenced by Saint Catherine of Genoa, effected a combination of self-sanctification and apostolate. According to its statutes, it admitted no more than thirty-six laymen and four priests. Its aim was "to implant in hearts the love of God, that is, Caritas." "Whoever wishes to join it must be humble of heart and center all his thought and hope on God." Striving for perfection, common religious exercises, and serving the sick were closely bound together. The brotherhood maintained a hospital, started by Vernazza, for the incurable sick, the prototype of similar institutions established from the turn of the century at Savona, Bologna, Rome, and Naples.

All of these were surpassed in importance by the Roman brotherhood, usually called the "Oratory of Divine Love." Founded before 1515 under the patronage of Saint Jerome, it bound its sixty members, lay and clerical, to daily attendance at Mass, at least monthly confession and communion, assiduous prayer, visiting the sick, and service in the hospital of the incurable, entrusted to them by Leo X in 1515. Once a week they gathered for Mass and community prayers in the parish church of Santa Dorothea in Trastevere. The statutes and activity of the brotherhood were to be kept secret. A list of members compiled in 1524 includes, among fifty-six members, fourteen "laymen," so expressly termed, and also six bishops and several high curial officials. Among them are the founders of the Theatine Order, but not, as was formerly assumed, Sadoleto, Aleander, Giberti, and Contarini. After 1527 the Oratory ceased to exist. Though short-lived and inconspicuous, it was a deeply earnest cell of Christian renewal in Medicean Rome.

In 1521 a member, the curialist Bartolomeo Stella, left Rome and founded a hospital for the incurable in Brescia and in 1525 an Oratory, which obtained the approval of Clement VII and was patterned after the one in Rome. The members designated themselves as an "amicitia."

Independent of and uninfluenced by these brotherhoods, the young Venetian patrician, Paolo Giustiniani (1476–1528), gathered around himself in Venice a circle of like-minded men who had become acquainted at the University of Padua. In a house of his on the island of Murano they studied together the Bible and the Fathers of the Church, not out of a purely humanistic interest but as a means to Christian perfection. The only priest was the humanist Egnazio. The others were laymen: Vincenzo Quirini (1479–1514), for a time Venetian ambassador at the courts of Philip the Fair of Burgundy and the Emperor Maximilian I; Gasparo Contarini and Nicolò Tiepolo. Contarini was Venetian ambassador at the Diet of Worms in 1521; Tiepolo, at that of Augsburg in 1530. After a visit to the Holy Land, Giustiniani determined to renounce the world completely and entered the hermitage of Camaldoli near Arezzo. He was soon followed by Quirini and Sebastian Giorgi but not by Contarini, who, after a hard inner struggle, deliberately sought a Christian way in the world. The experience of justification, which he describes in a letter of 24 April 1511 to Giustiniani, resembles Luther's tower experience and explains his later appreciation of Luther's religious concern.

The importance of these reform circles becomes clear when one considers their cross-connections, in both personnel and ideas, with the founding of new religious institutes and with the Tridentine reform.

New Orders

The founding of the Theatine Order was the work of two members of the Roman Oratory. Both Saint Cajetan of Thiene (c. 1480–1547) and Gian Pietro Carafa (d. 1559 as Paul IV) sought the spiritual renewal of the clergy. The Neapolitan Carafa, had been Archbishop of Chieti (*Theate*) in the Abruzzi since 1505 and had been entrusted with several diplomatic missions. Together with the priests Boniface di Colle and Paolo di Siglieri, he founded in 1524 a society of clerics on the basis of the so-called Augustinian Rule. Carafa joined them. The society was to have neither real estate nor fixed income but neither was it to live by begging, as the mendicant Orders did. Its support was to be left to divine providence. It was approved by Clement VII on 24 June 1524, with Carafa as its first superior. Pride of place was assigned to the careful fulfillment of all priestly duties: the praying of the Office, the worthy celebration of Mass, preaching, and every sort of pastoral activity. Their recovery began with Carafa's election as Pope. He called upon them for the reform of the breviary and promoted one of them, Bernardino Scotti, to the College of Cardinals.

A native of Cremona, Saint Antonio Maria Zaccaria (1502–37) was ordained a priest in 1528 after the completion of his medical studies at Padua and, with the jurist Ferrari and the mathematician Morigia, established at Milan in 1533 a society of priests, the Clerics Regular of Saint Paul, who were to imitate the Apostle of the Gentiles. They were known as Barnabites after the monastery of San Barnabà had been given to them. For them the apostolate held the first importance. They especially stressed missions among the people, in which they were assisted by a community of women, the Angelicals, established in 1530 by Luisa Torelli, and the deepening of devotion to the Eucharist through the introduction of the Forty Hours' Prayer. Their rule was approved by Gregory XIII in 1579 after it had been examined by Saint Charles Borromeo, who made use of it in the reform of his diocese.

Works of charity held the first place among the Somaschi. Their founder, Saint Jerome Aemiliani, shortened to Miani (1481–1537), had undertaken the education of orphans in Venice, and had established orphanages, partly with the active assistance of the members of the Oratory. The society, approved in 1540, was responsible for its support. It was confirmed as an Order by Pius IV in 1568.

Closely associated with the pious circles of Brescia was Saint Angela Merici (1474–1540); she founded there, with twenty-eight companions, the "Company of the Servants of Saint Ursula," a society for the education of neglected girls. The common life and simple vows were introduced by Saint Charles Borromeo in 1572 on the authority of Gregory XIII. The Ursulines became an Order with strict inclosure and solemn vows after their establishment in France (1612), where they were especially strong until the French Revolution. Individual convents were at times combined into a union, but they were never centrally administered.

Reform of the Mendicant Orders

Parallel to the rise of these new institutes ran efforts for the renewal of the mendicant Orders. From the end of the fifteenth century their generals were frequently drawn from the Observant branches, which had gained the right to exist in the canonical form of congregations alongside the provinces in all the mendicant Orders, though in the course of time they had lost something of their original austerity. Their aims were essentially the same: suppression of all private ownership, restoration of the common life, more careful training of novices, and improvement of theological studies. For those in dread of reform it was easy to obtain, by approaching the Sacred Penitentiary, authorization to live outside the monasteries (*licentia standi extra*) and thereby to escape the claustral discipline.

In the Order of Preachers success attended the reform work of the generals, Thomas de Vio of Baetá (1506–18), together with his general procurator, Nikolaus von Schönberg, and García de Loaysa (1518–24). All three were later made cardinals. In Aegidius of Viterbo (1506–18) the Hermits of Saint Augustine acquired a general of outstanding spirituality and a zealot for reform, whose instructions constituted the basis for the renewal of the Order. Between 1523 and 1562 the reform of the Carmelites was in the hands of the Cypriot Nicholas Audet, who continued the work of the most zealous promoter of the observance in the fifteenth century, John Soreth. However, during the first years of his office he was hampered by a schism that occurred in France. Among the Franciscans the General Chapter of 1517 had consummated the separation of the two branches, Conventuals and Observants, without providing a solution to the centuries-long dispute over the Order's ideal. Although the Observants obtained a scholarly general in Francesco Lichetto (1518–20) and earnest reforming superiors in Francisco Quiñones (1523–27) and Vincenzo Lunelli (1535–41), the Capuchin Order was founded as a third branch of the Franciscan religious family.

Matteo da Bascio and Ludovico da Fossombrone, ascetics belonging to the Observance but dissatisfied with it, obtained from Clement VII in 1528, authorization to follow the Franciscan Rule in its original austerity and to wear a habit of coarse material with an angular capuche. The movement established for itself a preliminary constitution envisaging the eremitical ideal and lay activities, such as manual labor and the care of the sick. Despite powerful opposition the number of members grew — there were thirty-five houses in 1535. It was the Vicar General Bernardino d'Asti who, through the constitutions which he drew up in 1536, prescribing the care of souls and preaching, gave to the originally ascetic movement the character of an Order dedicated to pastoral work and thereby became its real founder. Vittoria Colonna had exerted her influence to obtain it. When the most renowned preacher of the new Order, Bernardino Ochino of Siena, accused in Rome of teaching Lutheran ideas, fled to Geneva in 1542, the Capuchins were for a time forbidden to preach. The restriction of the Order to Italy lasted until 1574.

Cardinals and Bishops

Although the College of Cardinals had received a thoroughly secular tone as a result of the creations of Sixtus IV, there sat in the Senate of the Church a few outstanding individuals, even under Julius II and the two Medici Popes. Oliviero Carafa (d. 1511) had a share in the reform gesture of Alexander VI. Included in the great creation of 1517 were the generals of the Dominicans and the Augustinian

Hermits, Thomas de Vio and Aegidius of Viterbo, who had been prominent at the Fifth Lateran Council. The former was an unsurpassed commentator on Saint Thomas and an original exegete; the other, a Platonist and humanist, who in a "keynote" sermon at the opening session of the Council had formulated the guiding principle of the Catholic Reform: "Men must be transformed by the holy, not the holy by men." Adrian VI found an expert adviser for his reform undertakings in Lorenzo Campeggio (d. 1539), who did not enter the clerical state until after more than ten years of married life.

Not only in the College of Cardinals but also in the Italian episcopate there were at hand individuals favorable to a Catholic Reform, though not very many. All the great sees belonged to absentee cardinals or, through resignation, to their relatives or intimates, so that they have been labeled by Tacchi Venturi "fiefs of the great noble families." Bishops of a really spiritual life and of genuinely pastoral activity were rare.

Although the opening up of the archival sources is as yet only in its beginnings, it may be held that good bishops were not entirely lacking.

The model of the future Tridentine reform on the diocesan level was Giovanni Matteo Giberti, Bishop of Verona (1524–43). From 1527, when he left Rome for his diocese, he systematically improved the care of souls despite numerous obstacles. He began by assuring a higher quality among the clergy through an association of priests and the providing of lectures for their further education, the development of an existing boarding school into a seminary, the drawing up of registers of households in the parishes, the organization of preaching and of the instruction of adults and children, and the establishing of a charitable society (*Societas Caritatis*) in which the bishop and the pastor cooperated with the laity. The entire work of reform was in 1542 condensed in printed constitutions. Soon after, Giberti's secretary, Zini, sketched the bishop's life under the title *Example of a Good Shepherd.* A new episcopal ideal was forming and was being described in writing. Absenteeism, hitherto so lightly regarded, was more and more understood to be incompatible with it.

A stimulus toward religious renewal made itself felt in the domain of the Eucharist itself from the close of the fifteenth century. In almost all the larger cities of Italy arose confraternities devoted to promoting the cult of the Eucharist. Out of their own means the members saw to the worthy reservation of the sacred species and the maintenance of the perpetual light. They provided an escort when the Sacrament was carried to the sick. The founding of an archconfraternity of the Eucharist at Santa Maria sopra Minerva in Rome by Paul III gave these confraternities a center.

The Fifth Lateran Council

On the eve of the schism the single attempt at a general reform of the Church, the Fifth Lateran Council, had, it is true, produced salutary results in the mendicant Orders, which were forced to defend themselves against the attacks of the bishops by means of self-reform, but otherwise its success was meager. No abuse was really eradicated, no reform decree was consistently carried out.

Lacking consistency, the feeble gesture of reform grew even weaker. In order to cut the ground from under the legitimate complaint that at Rome ordinations were conferred on clerics of foreign dioceses without the necessary examination of the candidates, without the consent of the proper Ordinarios, and, secretly or publicly, in a manner smacking of simony. Definite improvement did not occur until the appointment of Filippo Archinto as Vicar of Rome (1542) and the examination of candidates by the Jesuits. The colleges established by Cardinals Capranica (1475) and Nardini (1484) for future priests touched only a slight fraction of the candidates and can be regarded only in a very restricted sense as forerunners of the Tridentine seminaries. The reform decrees of Clement VII for the Jubilee of 1525 likewise brought very little change in the situation. Only the catastrophe of the *Sacco di Roma,* which was almost universally considered to be a judgment on Renaissance Rome, produced in the papacy a change of heart or at least an awareness that things could no longer go on as they had.

France and Germany

North of the Alps, in France and Germany, were there no efforts for a Catholic Reform? There too, on the eve of the schism, were bishops who were concerned for improving the quality of the clergy and for the care of souls. Parochial pastoral activity was in general superior to that in Italy, and the duty of residence was less neglected. But neither the plan of the Fleming Standonck for the reform of the French diocesan clergy (1493) nor the initial efforts for a synodal self-reform, notably in the province of Salzburg — the Provincial Council of 1512 and the Mühldorf Reform Council of 1522 — nor the encouragement proceeding from the northern version of the current Christian humanism was of immediate advantage to the Catholic Reform. They were all overwhelmed by the schism before sustaining support came from the Church's center, from the papacy. A decisive impulse for reform flourished only in the Iberian Peninsula. It differed from all the other movements thus far mentioned.

Spain

Whereas in Italy the sources of the Catholic Reform were found in small communities of clerics and lay persons, from which proceeded several new religious institutes and eventually some strong personalities, in Spain even before the turn of the century the episcopate and the monastic and mendicant Orders became, with the active encouragement of the Catholic Kings, the representatives of religious and ecclesiastical renewal. While in the rest of Europe the crusading idea had long since lost its force, in the Iberian Peninsula the *Reconquista* — the total expulsion of the Muslims — remained a political and religious goal. It was achieved when in 1492, under Ferdinand and Isabella, the united kingdoms of Castile and Aragón succeeded in taking Granada, the last Islamic stronghold.

Earlier, at the national Council of Seville (1478), an agreement had been reached between the Catholic Kings and the bishops, under the presidency of the "Great Cardinal," Pedro González de Mendoza, that crown and episcopate should promote the reform of the Spanish Church together and ward off any possible interference from outside. The close cooperation between the spiritual and the secular powers promoted the reform in that the pious and energetic Queen Isabella, influenced by her director, the Hieronymite Hernando Talavera, named efficient prelates, zealous for reform, to several Castilian sees.

Far-reaching was the activity of Cardinal Ximenes de Cisneros, Archbishop of Toledo (1495–1517). Originally a jurist and vicar general of Cardinal Mendoza in Sigüenza, in 1484 he had joined the Observant Franciscans and as provincial worked for the reform. Finally he was promoted to the primatial dignity by his spiritual daughter, Queen Isabella. He enforced the reform of the diocesan and regular clergy with a firm and at times hard hand and in the University of Alcalá, which he founded, created a center for humanism and positive theology; its supreme achievement was the Complutensian Polyglot (1514–17). At his suggestion the *Imitation of Christ* was translated into Spanish.

The typically Spanish cooperation of crown and episcopate was confirmed again when on 17 December 1511 Ferdinand the Catholic summoned several prelates to Burgos for consultation in preparation for the Fifth Lateran Council. In the advice which they gave to the King, as well as in his instructions for the delegates to the Council, ideas emanating from the days of the reform councils were evident. Almost all the abuses which were later discussed at the Council of Trent were enumerated, but the positive program of reform was not so fully developed. Deza advocated the introduction of the concursus for nomination to parishes, following the model of the diocese of Palencia, thanks to which that see had more properly educated clerics (*clérigos letrados*) than all the other bishoprics of Castile combined. In his instruction for the delegates to the Council the King called for Church reform expressed along with national reform; it was agreed that the current reform of the Spanish Church could not achieve its goal without a general Church reform.

In the Spanish branches of the mendicant Orders the Observants experienced progress unequaled elsewhere. The Franciscan Recollects were greatly aided by Ximenes, who was one of them. The reformed provinces of the Augustinian Hermits were as distinguished for fidelity to the rule as were the Observants, but frequently caused difficulties for the central authority in the Order on account of their highhandedness. The Spanish Dominican provinces were united with the Observants at the Chapter of Burgos (1506). The ascetical and reform ideas of Savonarola entered Spain through Dominico de Mendoza and greatly stimulated the spiritual life. The assignment of the Dominican Francisco de Vitoria to Salamanca made this university the starting point of the renewal of scholastic theology. Vitoria made the *Summa theologiae* of Saint Thomas the basis of his enthusiastically attended lectures and treated also the pressing questions of colonial ethics and international law, reform and council, according to Thomas' concepts. Without making concessions to the conciliar theory, he called for assurances against papal disregard of the decrees of ecumenical councils. From his school proceeded the great Spanish theologians of the Council of Trent — Dominico Soto and Andrés de Vega — and outstanding bishops of the reform era.

Spanish Church reform suffered a setback during the first years of the reign of Emperor Charles V because of the political disturbances then current — the Comunero Revolt. At the same time Spain was invaded by the ideas of Erasmus, for which the University of Alcalá had become the port of entry ever since the Conference of Valladolid took place. Their chief proponents were the brothers Juan and Alfonso Valdéz, both in the service of Charles V. Spain's contribution to Catholic Reform lay in its episcopate, desirous of and experienced with reform, and in the theology of the Salmanticenses. These had a vital share in determining the image of the Council of Trent because behind them stood the Spanish world power. Finally, Spain also gave birth to the most effective reform Order, the Society of Jesus.

CHAPTER 94

Ignatius Loyola and His Order to 1556

The Society of Jesus became the most effective agent of the Catholic recovery. In the person and the work of its founder the fundamental principles of the Catholic Reform clearly emerge, obtain a new character, valid for centuries, and become of the greatest historical significance.

The Founder

Iñigo López de Loyola, born in 1491 in the ancestral castle (province of Guipúzcoa) of one of the ten great families of the Basque country, received the tonsure and a family benefice when still a boy, but was trained as a knight at court, where he not only learned courtly manners but was also deeply impressed with the moral worth of loyalty to the ancestral dynasty. Heeding his impulses for adventure, he was seriously wounded at the siege of Pamplona by the French on 20 May 1521. While the healing of his shattered leg long confined him to his sick bed, he read the Franciscan Ambrose Montesa's Spanish translation of the *Life of Christ* by Ludolf of Saxony and a Spanish translation of the *Lives of the Saints* (*Flos Sanctorum*) of Jacobus à Voragine. When he found that this literature produced in him an inner peace, whereas the courtly romances were disquieting, he longed "to do great things in God's service" instead of seeking the warlike deeds of heroism that were denied him, and above all "to accomplish great external works of the sort mentioned [works of penance], because the saints had accomplished such for the honor of God." After a general confession in the monastery of Montserrat upon his recovery, he hung up his dagger and sword before the miraculous image of the Mother of God, put aside his clothes, assumed the dress of a pilgrim, and kept a night vigil at the altar. Then he went to nearby Manresa, where, preoccupied with reading the *Imitation of Christ,* between March 1522 and February 1523 he experienced a mystical transformation and put into writing the first part of his *Exercises.* After a period of despair, during which he sought forcibly to acquire peace of soul by extravagant penitential practices and long hours of prayer, he received in new visions, principally in one at the chapel of Saint Paul on the Cardoner River, such an illumination in regard to the reality and the relationship of the mysteries of faith that later, whenever he was approached for decisions by his companions, he would refer to the insights acquired at that time. To dedicate himself entirely to the service of God and the salvation of souls was henceforth his life's goal: "In the mystical transformation of Manresa," says H. Rahner, "from Iñigo, the pilgrim and penitent, emerged Ignatius the churchman."

A pilgrimage took him in 1523 *via* Rome to Jerusalem, but his plan of settling permanently in Palestine was vetoed by the Custos. On his return home he applied himself at Barcelona to a study of the rudiments of Latin and at Alcalá (1526–27) began the Arts course. Since, assisted by like-minded people, he began to engage in the spiritual direction of ladies, he came under suspicion as an *alumbrado,* was questioned three times by the Inquisition and the episcopal court respectively, and was imprisoned for forty-two days. After a similar experience while continuing his studies at Salamanca, he departed for Paris in 1528, and there he lived in the College of Saint Barbara. He earned his livelihood by begging on journeys as far away as Flanders and England. Once again he fell under suspicion for having conducted spiritual exercises for his fellow-students. He took the degree of master of arts and at Montmartre on 15 August 1534, with six companions — Lainez, Salmerón, Bobadilla, Francis Xavier, Rodrigues, and Faber — vowed poverty, chastity, and a pilgrimage to Jerusalem, as well as work for the care of souls. At the renewal of vows in 1536 Lejay, Broët, and Condure joined the group. In order to carry out the planned pilgrimage to Jerusalem the companions met in Venice on 8 January 1537. Prevented from sailing, they engaged in pastoral work and in hospital service there and in the vicinity, and on 24 June 1537, Ignatius received the priesthood.

After a year they decided to offer their services to the Pope. With Lainez and Faber, Ignatius proceeded to Rome in November 1538, encouraged shortly before arrival by Christ's promise, made during prayer in a chapel at La Storta: "I will be gracious to you." Because of the good impression made by the apostolic activity of the small community, the atmosphere became favorable, and Ignatius then definitely decided in the spring of 1539 to found an Order.

A petition, presented to the Pope on 3 September 1539 through the good offices of Cardinal Contarini, contained the *Formula Instituti,* that is, the fundamental idea of the foundation. What was new in it was that, in addition to the vows of poverty and chastity, a vow of obedience to the Pope was to be taken. Once the hesitations of especially Cardinal Guidiccioni, who was very close to Pope Paul III, and of the conservative Cardinal Ghinucci had been overcome, the Society of Jesus was confirmed on 27 September 1540 by the Bull "Regimini Militantis Ecclesiae." Its aim was "to fight for God under the standard of the Cross and to serve only the Lord and the Roman Pontiff, his Vicar on earth," by preaching, teaching, and works of

Caritas. The members took the three customary vows and also a fourth — to obey without hesitation ("sine ulla tergiversatione aut excusatione") every command given by the Pope for the salvation of souls and the spread of the faith. Their number was limited to sixty. Ignatius was elected superior (*Praepositus*) on 8 April 1541 and a solemn profession followed at San Paolo on 22 April.

The founder lived thereafter in Rome, from 1544 in the house of the professed near the little church of Santa Maria della Strada, preoccupied with composing the constitutions and consolidating the Society. The *Formula Instituti* of 1539 was the basis of the constitutions, in the formulation of which Ignatius consulted not only Lainez but also his most intimate coworker, Nadal, and his secretary, Polanco. Repeatedly altered in the succeeding years, the constitutions were essentially in final form at Ignatius' death and were put in force by the General Congregation of 1558. They devote special attention to the reception and the studies of the members. Simple vows are made only after a two-years' novitiate. The study of philosophy and theology, lasting at least seven years, is interrupted by practical activity as teacher and tutor; during this period the "scholastic" is a member of the Society but he can be dismissed at any time. After being ordained, he completes a third year of novitiate (tertianship). Then, depending on aptitude, he is admitted to perpetual simple profession of the three vows as a "spiritual coadjutor" or, after additional years of trial, to the solemn profession of the four vows — the fourth being that of obedience to the Pope — as a "professed" in the strict sense. The "professed" constitute the real heart of the Order; they alone occupy the higher offices.

The constitution of the Order is strongly monarchical. The general (*Praepositus generalis*) is elected for life by the General Congregation and has virtually unlimited authority. He names all superiors, and they are required to make regular reports to him. In the government of the Order he is aided by the assistants, to whom several provinces are assigned at a time. The General Congregation meeting after the general's death is composed of the vicar general elected for the interregnum, the assistants, the provincials, and two elected delegates of each province. It exercises the supreme legislative authority. The strong centralization promotes the Society's goal of acting in military uniformity and strict obedience for the cause of Christ and the Church. In Ignatius' eyes obedience is the concrete realization of the surrender to the will of God and self-renunciation. In his last will he lays down the rule: "In all that is not sinful I must follow the superior's will and not my own," for "God speaks through every superior." Defense against Protestantism soon became more and more the center of Loyola's attention, because the crisis in the Church required the effort on this front. But Ignatius' primary goal continued always to be inner renewal, promoted by the *Exercises*, and a worldwide apostolate.

The forgoing of a special religious habit and of choir service, customary until then in all Orders, and above all the election of the general for life encountered strong criticism from Pope Paul IV, who, since his conflict with Ignatius at Venice, had been hostile to him and characterized him as a "tyrant." He forced the Order to make appropriate changes in the constitutions, but after his death they were annulled by Pope Pius IV.

When Ignatius died on 31 July 1556 the Order was in a serious external crisis, brought about by the hostility of Paul IV toward Spain and Spaniards, which led to the Carafa War against Spain. Just as soon as he had received news of the election of the Carafa Pope, Ignatius, according to his own admission, trembled in his whole body. On the outbreak of the war the Roman house of the professed was searched for weapons; none was found. There was further suspicion when the Spanish fathers suggested that the General Congregation be held outside Rome. The Vicar General Lainez won his point that it should take place in Rome (August–September 1558). It was due to his good sense and prudent tactics that the Order came safely through the difficult period of the Carafa pontificate.

We are relatively well informed in regard to Ignatius' external appearance. He was short (5′2″) and of a delicate rather than a strong constitution. His head, with its high forehead and aquiline nose, was dominated by piercing eyes; the serene facial expression was that of a man united to God. Ignatius combined cold reason with mystical devotion to Christ, the military rigor of his idea of obedience with great liberty in the shaping of the interior life, imperturbable foresight in regard to the worldwide tasks of the Society with a tender sympathy for the individual person, the courtesy of a man of the world with the practical good sense of the Basque peasant. Constantly maintaining an aristocratic reserve, he was never on familiar terms with even his closest associates. He made a point of considering his decisions long and carefully, of listening to others' advice, of seeking divine guidance in prayer, and then, when the decision had been reached, of enforcing it without respect for people and even with severity. In his *Exercitia Spiritualia* he shows himself to be one of the great teachers of the spiritual life, thoroughly familiar with human nature, and a master in the handling of men.

In content and construction the *Exercises* are undeniably Ignatius' work, the fruit of his own searching for God. After being examined by the Cardinal of Burgos, the vicar general of Rome, Archinto, and the Master of the Sacred Palace, Egidio Foscarari, they received papal approval on 31 July 1548 "It has long been established by history that the spirit and thought of Ignatius Loyola acquired their clearest expression in the book of *The Spiritual Exercises* and that his Order emanated from the deliberations of this book and continues to come forth from it." "With the help of the two most important meditations of this book — 'On the Kingdom of Christ' and 'On the Two Standards' — we can summarize in a single sentence the basic organization of the perfect life: Man has been created to wage war in the Church Militant against Satan in loyal service to the majesty of the Triune God through assimilation to the crucified Man Jesus and thus to arrive at the glory of the Father." What was peculiar to this ideal of perfection and made it appropriate to its age was its intimate relationship to the visible Church: "From the union of love that bursts everything open with his being tightly compressed into the body of the Church is released that vast power which we can establish as historically certain in his work" (H. Rahner). Though eminently personal traits are not wanting, such as the explanation of the Kingdom of Christ in terms of a worldly kingdom in whose service Ignatius had grown up, the book of *Exercises* is full of the basic thought of traditional theology. When on the fourth day of the second week of the *Exercises* he poses the question under which of the two standards (*banderas*), Christ's or the devil's, one desires henceforth to fight, he is taking his stand on the Augustinian theology of the two Cities. The older characteristics of the Christian ideal of perfection, which he had seen at first only in the opaque light of medieval legends, he later grasped more exactly through study of the great religious rules and fused them into his new ideal, which was different from them but was filled nevertheless with the spirit of the tradition. The blending of ascetical tradition and personal experience made the *Exercises,* in the words of H. Böhmer, a "book of destiny for mankind." "The work of Ignatius is unequalled in its ability to transform, in the spirit of its author, the men who came upon it" (K. Holl).

Spread of the Society

The two great books, *Constitutions* and *Exercises,* radiate the strength of Ignatius' personality and constitute the basis of the astonishing expansion of the Order in the very first decades after its establishment. Until about 1550 the individual effort of the members in the care of souls and in teaching was in the foreground, but thereafter the Order was consolidated by the erection of an increasing number of foundations — houses of the professed, colleges, residences — and the development of the organization. The limitation of the number of members to sixty was abandoned as early as 1544. Already in 1539 Father Araoz had gone to Spain. In 1540 the Order was established in Paris. In the same year Father Faber set out for Germany in the company of the imperial diplomat Ortiz, who had earlier made a retreat under Ignatius, and, soon after, Peter Canisius was won for the Society. Fathers Lejay and Bobadilla went in 1542 to Regensburg to strengthen Catholicism there. At the request of King John III of Portugal, Francis Xavier and three companions sailed to the East Indies in April 1541. Lainez and Salmerón took part, as papal theologians, in the first period of the Council of Trent. At the beginning of 1548 Jesuits were entrusted at Rome with the examining of candidates for the priesthood. The requests by bishops and other highly placed people to the general to put Fathers at their disposal became so numerous that all of them could by no means be satisfied. But there was also opposition.

In the Spanish realm, from which the majority of the first members came, neither Charles V nor his successor Philip II was well disposed toward the Society, and the Dominican Melchior Cano, highly esteemed as a theologian and at court, was its bitter enemy. It found strong support, though, in Francis Borgia, Duke of Gandía and Viceroy of Catalonia, who received seven Jesuits at Gandía in 1545 and in 1546 entered the Society. The excessive asceticism of Borgia and other Spanish members, however, endangered the uniform development of the Spanish branch for a time. In Granada Archbishop Guerrero, a good friend of the Society, made possible the founding of a college, and about the same time colleges were established in Zaragoza, Seville, and Medina del Campo. In Portugal the Society experienced a downright spectacular growth because of Rodrigues, who was highly esteemed by King John III. The first foundation arose at Lisbon in 1541.

In Italy the founding of colleges at Messina (1548) and Palermo (1549) was followed by the establishment of the Roman College (1551), which developed as the Order's principal educational institute. In 1556 colleges had already been founded or were coming into existence in twenty Italian cities, including Naples, Florence, Bologna, Modena, Ferrara, Venice, and Genoa. On the other hand, in

France the Order encountered the opposition of the *Parlement* of Paris and the Sorbonne. Although a French province had been established in 1552, it was not until 1556 that, thanks to the assistance af the Bishop of Clermont, the first college could be opened at Billom. After the successful appearance of Lainez at the Religious Colloquy of Poissy (1561), the *Parlement* of Paris gave its consent for further foundations, whereupon there followed at close intervals those in Tournon, Rodez, and Paris. The establishment of colleges in the Low Countries was at first delayed by the refusal of the States General to grant the Order legal recognition as a corporation; not until 1562 were colleges founded at Brussels and Tournai.

Nadal's saying, "Vae nobis, si non iuvemus Germaniam," expresses the importance attributed by Ignatius to the crisis in Germany. The Order's chief promoters were Cardinal Otto of Augsburg, the Dukes of Bavaria, and King Ferdinand I. But the soul of the movement was Peter Canisius, who from 1549 was active at the University of Ingolstadt as professor and spiritual director. He began the erection of colleges at Vienna (1552) and Ingolstadt (1556) and in 1556 became provincial of the Upper German Province, from which a Lower German Province branched off. The colleges at Munich (1559), Trier (1560), and Dillingen (1563) — the last named grew to be a university — developed into strongholds of the gravely threatened Catholicism of Germany.

The ever increasing number of colleges founded from the mid-1550s was the sequel to an expansion of the Order's activity which was to be of the greatest importance. While not ceasing to be pastorally oriented, it became increasingly a teaching Order, because the formation of a new generation was recognized as the most urgent task. The colleges, which were originally intended for the training of the Order's recruits at existing universities and hence were permitted to possess fixed revenues and real estate, proceeded to accept externs who did not plan to join the Order. In the definitive edition of the constitutions the emphasis had already shifted: the colleges were "rather for externs" and served also for the education of recruits.

Lainez may be regarded as the chief promoter of the new role of the colleges. Probably the Order's keenest theological mind, during his generalship (1558–65) he fostered the move toward a teaching Order and obtained from Pius IV the right to confer academic degrees. In 1563 there originated at the Roman College the first Marian Congregation, which aimed to further religiously and ascetically the pick of the best. The Order grew at an ever faster tempo. At the founder's death (1556) it had had about 1000 members in twelve provinces; when Lainez died on 19 January 1565, it counted 3500 members in eighteen provinces.

CHAPTER 95

The Beginnings of the Catholic Reform in Rome under Paul III

The self-reform of the members, as realized in the Italian reform groups and the new Orders proceeding from them, in the Spain of the Catholic Kings, and above all in the Society of Jesus, could not extend throughout the Body of the Church until it had first gained the Church's Head. Its advance on Rome made strides in the pontificate of Paul III, not only because of its inherent strength but because of the pressure of the seemingly irresistible progress of the schism, which at that very moment was consolidating itself in Germany as a distinct Church and was beginning to spread throughout Europe. While Paul III (1534–49) cannot be regarded as the first Pope of the Catholic Reform, he was its forerunner.

From a conclave lasting only two days (11–13 October) came forth as Pope the oldest and most intellectual of the cardinals, the Dean of the College, Alessandro Farnese. A product of the Renaissance and formed by it, he not only owed the red hat, conferred by Alexander VI in 1493, to the depravity of that era, but in his own personal life he had paid tribute to it. His children, Pierluigi and Costanda, born out of wedlock before his promotion to higher Orders, and his grandsons, Alessandro the Younger and Ottavio, seriously compromised his pontificate. The exaltation of his family and its admission among the dynasties of Italy had a disastrous influence on both the political and the ecclesiastical decisions of the Pope. His policy of neutrality between the two great powers, the Habsburgs and France, at times served his dynastic interests no less than those of the Church. Nevertheless, his pontificate marks a new start. Paul III had understood that the policy of Clement VII, opportunistic and almost exclusively diplomatic, could only founder, because it failed to recognize the predominant forces of that era and that the papacy had to extend its hand to the agencies of renewal, if it wanted to halt the progress of the schism. A Catholic Reform had to confront the Protestant Reformation.

The establishment of the Roman Inquisition served the purpose of defense rather than of reconstruction. The points of entry of the new doctrine into Italy were Milan and Venice, which were closely bound to southern Germany and Switzerland through commercial relations; but communities of dissidents were found also in Central Italy (Modena and Lucca) and at Naples. Lay persons interested in religion crowded into lectures on the Pauline Epistles and argued about problems of justification, grace and freedom, and predestination.

Hence, through a brief of 14 January 1542, the Pope annulled for Italy every exemption in matters within the competence of the Inquisition and by the Bull "Licet ab initio" of 21 July 1542 he entrusted responsibility for maintaining the purity of the faith and investigating and punishing all doctrinal errors on both sides of the Alps to a commission of six cardinals — Carafa, Toledo, Parisio, Guidiccioni, Laurerio, and Badia — whose powers included the infliction of the death penalty on "obstinate heretics"; judgment on those willing to recant was reserved to the pope. In keeping with the Pope's attitude, the procedure of the new institution was relatively mild during his pontificate. It became stricter as the influence of

Carafa, the spiritual father of the new foundation, grew. As early as 1543 the Roman Inquisition forbade any introduction of Protestant books into Italy; the enforcement of the prohibition naturally depended on the secular arm. The significance of the press for the spread of Protestantism and for the Catholic Reform was not sufficiently appreciated until later.

More important than these defensive measures was the strengthening of the reform element at the Curia through the nomination of strongly Church-minded cardinals and the fostering of reform in the Orders. Even in the High Renaissance the Senate of the Church had not been entirely lacking in men zealous for reform. Oliviero Carafa, Francesco Piccolomini, Aegidio of Viterbo, and Cajetan had maintained the great tradition of the fifteenth century, but they could not prevail against the powerful *nepoti,* the worldly minded scions of Italian princely families, and the crown cardinals of the great powers. And yet only a purified College of Cardinals could elect a reform Pope. Paul III began by creating two youthful *nepoti,* Alessandro Farnese and Guido Ascanio Sforza, but the next creation (21 May 1535) included, in addition to the martyr-bishop John Fisher, the future leader of the reform party at the Curia, Gasparo Contarini (1483–1542). Deeply imbued with the spirit of Giustiniani's circle, as Venetian ambassador at the imperial court (1521–25) Contarini had witnessed the beginnings of the schism and, though a layman, had exerted himself as a theologian. He became the soul of the Catholic Reform in Rome and of contact with the Lutherans. In the following years the purple was bestowed upon Carafa, cofounder of the Theatines; the humanist Sadoleto; Aleander, well informed on the events in Germany; and the Englishman Pole, highly esteemed for his deep piety. If one takes into account that even among the new cardinals selected from curial posts and among the crown cardinals, especially the Spanish, there were men who were convinced of the need of Church reform, then it does not seem to be an exaggeration to speak of a renewal of the College of Cardinals.

Of course, the reform cardinals did not constitute a homogeneously oriented group; they were agreed on the goal but not on the choice of means. Contarini and Carafa were convinced that profound and radical interventions in the organization of the curial offices, the Orders, and the diocesan clergy were necessary; the conservatives, mainly consisting of curial canonists, felt that reform of the Church could be effected through a return to the "old law," that is, the observance of the canonical rules. Opposed to any change in the status quo was the organized curial bureaucracy, whose revenues were threatened by reforms.

The renewal of the College of Cardinals was not without effect on the reform of the mendicant Orders, in whose charge lay, at least in Italy, theology, preaching, and urban pastoral work. As their protectors, the reform cardinals were able to promote the reform element in this important field. Far-reaching plans for the unification of the various kinds of Orders, such as had been suggested from the time of the reform councils, were put aside — Benedictines and Cistercians as the only monastic Orders, Dominicans and Franciscans as the only mendicant Orders, and, in addition, one military Order, and also Carafa's proposal to suppress the Conventual branches of the mendicant Orders.

Following the retirement of the excellent general Cajetan and Loaysa, the Dominican Order suffered at first from frequent change in administration and the weakness of the generals and its protectors, were indifferent to reform. In the Franciscan religious family, whose two branches had been separate since 1517, the Conventuals at first continued to suffer from the decay of discipline, though they still produced capable theologians, such as Giovanni Antonio Delfino. The Observants acquired distinguished minister generals, who were seconded by the protectors. The Augustinian Hermits, especially imperiled by Luther's apostasy, elected Seripando as general at the General Chapter of Naples (1539), on the personal initiative of the Pope, and commissioned him to restore morals and orthodoxy. When he resigned in 1551 after an excellent administration, he saw to it that the reform would be continued under his successor. As regards the Carmelites, out of thirty provinces, six in northern Europe were destroyed, while the others had either been already reformed or had at least been persuaded to reform.

Without prejudice to the diversity of constitutions, these reformers pursued essentially the same goals: restoration of the common life, abolition of private ownership, and greater attention to the admission and training of recruits. They used the same means: extended journeys of visitation for the enforcement of the decrees of general chapters and designation of energetic provincials. The authority of the generals was strengthened, and in the mendicant Orders there was a definite tendency toward centralization, as realized in the Society of Jesus. As the progress of the reform became more evident, the special position of the Observant branches seemed less justified. The Pope encouraged this development in the interest of reform, but could not bring himself to eliminate the influence that was especially harmful to religious discipline — that of dispensations and privileges all too easily issued by the Curia, and chiefly by the Sacred Penitentiary, and, particularly, the flagrantly abused permission to live outside the community and to receive benefices, whereby those dreading reform escaped being reformed.

"Purga Romam, purgatur mundus" — this challenge directed to Adrian VI was still valid. Beginnings of a reform of the curial offices had been made since the days of the reform councils, but none was carried through. On the contrary, the number of salable official posts had been constantly increased for financial reasons. They were made lucrative by raising and multiplying the fees, many of which were not fixed but were determined by the *Datarius* in an arrangement with the parties. Every reform curtailed the income of the officials and the Pope.

At first Paul III did not go beyond the reform gestures that had by now become almost routine. Soon after his election he set up a commission of cardinals for a "reform of morals," and on 23 August 1535, the commission, activated and expanded, was operating in the traditional manner. It was only the impending Council that moved the Pope to summon to Rome in the fall of 1536 eight independent and uncommitted men, from whose deliberations emanated a reform statement, the "Consilium de emendanda Ecclesia." On 9 March 1537 this was submitted to the Pope and commented on by Contarini. With admirable candor it designated as the root of all evils the exaggerated growth of the papal theory and avarice; it called for a ruthless correction of the curial procedures in regard to dispensations, a restriction of exemptions, a greater care in the conferring of ordinations, a new and sincerely Christian countenance for the city of Rome.

The memorandum did not remain secret. It was printed, first in Italy and then in Germany, and misused as an alleged confirmation of the charges raised earlier by the opponents of the papacy. Symptomatic of the fate of the bold attack was the struggle fought in 1537–38 in regard to the *Dataria.* Contarini and Carafa did not prevail against the canonists Ghinucci and Simonetta; the "compositions" of the *Dataria,* openly branded as simony in the memorandum, found defenders among theologians, and the Pope shrank from putting up with the threatened loss of a considerable part of his income. At the end of 1537 an observer reported: "The reform of the *Datarius* has gone up in smoke." In the succeeding years, a similar fate befell efforts to reform the Chancery, the *Camera,* the Penitentiary, and the Rota, chiefly because the corporations of functionaries utilized the opportunity to defend their alleged "legitimate rights."

Of all the abuses in the pre-Tridentine Church the worst was the neglect of the duty of residence on the part of those responsible for the proper care of souls — bishops and parish priests. Absenteeism sprang from the view that the right to a benefice and its revenues was distinct from the personal fulfillment of the official duties connected with it. Cardinals possessed bishoprics which they had never seen; dozens of bishops lived permanently in Rome and Venice who scarcely ever visited their dioceses and had them administered by vicars. Neglect of residence by parish priests is less easy to ascertain by statistics. On 13 December 1540 Paul III called upon eighty bishops present in Rome to go to their dioceses. They defended themselves by pointing to the manifold hindrances to episcopal activity from above, from below, from outside. They cited the numerous exemptions of individual person, Orders, and corporations, their own scant influence on the nominations to benefices, the abetting of reform-shy elements by appeals to the Roman tribunals, and the many interferences on the part of the secular power with the exercise of jurisdiction and the administration of ecclesiastical property. The demands of the bishops were at least partially met in a reform bull, drafted early in 1542 but not enforced.

Convocations of the Council

Undeniably, the greatest service of Paul III to the Catholic Reform was convoking the Council of Trent. Long convinced that the delaying tactics of his predecessor were ill-advised, he fixed his eyes from the start on the organizing of a general council. He was aware, and became increasingly more conscious, of the risk connected with it for the papacy since the emergence of conciliarism and in the face of the widespread anti-Romanism. The difficulties had increased with the long delays in the calling of a council. Papal promises of a council were regarded by Protestants as altogether insincere and were not taken at face value even by many Catholics. A council that was supposed to be attended by representatives from all parts of Christendom required the concurrence of the Christian princes and kingdoms, for whom it was at the same time a political event of the first importance. In regard to the rival great powers, the Habsburg Emperors and France, the Pope was determined to remain neutral, but how was this compatible with the fight against the apostasy?

In the spring of 1535 the Pope announced the imminent summoning of the Council through his nuncios, and proposed as the meeting place Mantua, his first choice, and then Turin, Piacenza, and Bologna. France declined, fearing from the council a weakening of the Protestant opposition to the Emperor and a corresponding increase in the power of its chief foe. It relented when the Pope in a personal meeting with Emperor Charles V had obtained his consent to Mantua without yielding his own fundamental neutrality in the impending war with France. The Bull "Ad Dominici Gregis Curam," of 2 June 1536, summoned the council to Mantua and listed as its tasks the condemnation of heresies, the reform of the Church, and the restoration of peace among Christian princes for defense against the Turkish threat.

Three causes conspired to frustrate this first summons. On 24 February 1537, the League of Schmalkalden firmly declined the invitation; Francis I announced that Mantua, situated within the Emperor's sphere of influence, was unacceptable; and the Duke of Mantua demanded that the Pope maintain a force of from five thousand to six thousand to protect the council. After the announced opening date, 23 May 1537, had passed, Paul III saw himself compelled to substitute Vicenza for Mantua. The three legates went there, but the bishops did not appear, and so the opening had to be postponed a second time. On 21 May 1539 it was prorogued to an unspecified date.

Although the war between Charles V and Francis I had in the meantime been ended by the armistice of Nice, the plan for a council was for a time laid aside, since the negotiations initiated by the Emperor for reunion with the German Protestants seemed to indicate that another solution of the religious crisis was within the realm of possibility. Its dramatic climax, the Religious Colloquy of Regensburg in 1541, proved the impossibility of bridging the gap.

During a meeting with the Pope at Lucca (September 1541) the Emperor proposed Trent as the place of the council, for, situated in imperial territory, it satisfied the demand for a council "on German soil." The Pope finally approved the agreement of the Nuncio Morone with the Imperial Estates in regard to Trent and by the Bull "Initio Nostri Huius Pontificatus" of 22 May 1542 summoned the council to meet there on 1 November 1542. This second summons was also fruitless. Since the unsettled situation in Trent could not continue without of loss of prestige, the Pope on 29 September 1543 ordered the suspension of the council.

The tension between him and the Emperor increased when the latter, in order to obtain the assistance of the estates against France at the Diet of Speyer (1544), made considerable concessions to the Protestants and proposed for the next diet a reform of the Church without the Pope's participation. In a brief of reprimand the Pope lodged a solemn protest and renewed his offer of a council. This again became a possibility unexpectedly fast by the conclusion of the Peace of Crépy. Not only did it eliminate the principal obstacle which had obstructed the success of this first convocation of the Council to Trent, but it also contained a secret clause whereby Francis I dropped his opposition to Trent and declared his willingness to participate in a council to be held there. Thus the Emperor had seized the initiative in the matter of settling the question of the council. He carefully explored his great plan of forcibly crushing the religious and political opposition of the League of Schmalkalden and of then inducing the Protestants to accept the hitherto rejected invitation to the council, where the existing doctrinal differences were to be authoritatively decided and a general reform of the Church resolved.

Without entering upon further negotiations with the powers, the Pope, in the Bull "Laetare Jerusalem" (30 November 1544), thereupon annulled the suspension of the Council and appointed Laetare Sunday, 15 March 1545, as the opening date. On 22 February Cardinals Del Monte, Cervini, and Pole were named as legates.

When, on 13 March, they arrived at Trent and were welcomed by the local bishop, Cardinal Christoforo Madruzzo, not a single other bishop was there except the papal deputy Sanfelice. Because the viceroy of Naples had designated four bishops of the kingdom to represent the entire Neapolitan episcopate and had directed the others to grant them full powers of attorney, the Pope on 17 April 1545 forbade the naming of proxies without sufficient reason. While the bishops who had meanwhile arrived in Trent were impatiently awaiting the signal for the opening, an understanding between Pope and Emperor was reached in regard to concerted action together with the Council against the German Protestants. It had been prepared through dispatch of Alessandro Farnese to Charles V at Worms. The Pope bound himself to furnish an auxiliary corps and to contribute a subsidy; the Emperor, to promote attendance at the council after victory had been achieved. The beginning of the war had to be deferred to the following year, for the Emperor was not yet prepared for the attack, and a new colloquy with Protestants, organized at Regensburg, stirred new misgivings at Trent. The Pope, however, disregarded all misgivings and appointed the third Sunday of Advent, 13 December, for the opening in Trent. In addition to the three legates and Madruzzo, four archbishops, twenty-one bishops, and five generals of Orders took part in the first session.

CHAPTER 96

The Council of Trent under Paul III and Julius III

"Now the gate is open," the Augustinian general Seripando wrote happily in his diary. But the deliberations got under way slowly, the delay arising from three causes. The number of participants was meager. There was as yet no order of business nor clearly drawn up program. And, whereas the Emperor, seeing the Council in the framework of his great plan and looking forward to the eventual participation of the German Protestants, favored postponing questions of doctrine until Church reform had been achieved, the Pope insisted that priority belonged to matters of faith.

Due to the constantly repeated admonitions addressed by the Pope to the bishops of Upper Italy and to those staying in Rome and Venice, the number of the voting members rose by 17 June to sixty-six; it dropped to about fifty in the autumn, and at the beginning of 1547 again reached almost seventy. In addition to the Italians, who constituted approximately three-fourths, only the Spaniards were present in any number. They were represented by outstanding bishops and, led by Cardinal Pacheco of Jaén, formed with the bishops of Naples, Sicily, and Sardinia, a compact group in political questions. France was represented by three bishops; Germany, only by the proxies of the Archbishops of Mainz and Trier.

Agreement as to the right to vote in the general congregations was reached at the end of December: Entitled to vote were all bishops, including auxiliaries, the generals of the mendicant Orders, and two abbots from each of the monastic congregations. All plural voting was excluded. The indult granted to the German bishops and abbots on 5 December 1545, whereby they could be represented by voting proxies, was modified by the legates to mean only a consultative vote. The conciliar officials were named by the Pope. In its second session (7 January 1546) the Council prescribed its regimen. The decision of 22 January, which called for the considering of dogma and reform at the same time, was actually observed throughout the duration of the Council.

In order to acquaint the Fathers with the theological problems proposed for discussion, the plenary sessions of the Fathers entitled to a vote (general congregations) were, from 20 February 1546, preceded by particular congregations, in which the theologians delegated by the Pope (the Jesuits Lainez and Salmerón) and the theological advisers of the participants, mostly mendicant friars, discussed questions formulated by the legates or propositions from the writings of the Reformers and their confessional books. These were followed by full debate in the general congregations, in which each qualified member cast his vote. The proposed rough drafts of decrees were drawn up either by selected committees or by the legates, with the assistance of expert prelates and theologians. They were debated in the general congregations, often in several readings, and correspondingly revised until acceptance in the solemn session was secured. Dread of conciliarism induced the legates not to admit into the decrees the designation of the Council as "universalem Ecclesiam repraesentans, which was again and again called for by the Spaniards and some Italians.

Although the Emperor repeatedly (2 May and 16 June) besought the legates through his ambassador, to postpone dogmatic decisions for the present, namely, until the end of the war, the Council, during the period from February to June 1546, issued dogmatic as well as reform decrees, in conformity with the decision of 22 January. Fundamental for all later doctrinal definitions was the decree of the fourth session on the sources of revelation. The Canon of Holy Scripture includes also the deuterocanonical books; the books of both Testaments, having for their author the one God, and the apostolic traditions concerning faith and morals, insofar as they have been preserved through the uninterrupted succession in the Catholic Church, are accepted with the same, and not merely "similar," respect. The opinion that revelation is in its entirety contained in Holy Scripture and that "tradition" is only the interpretation of it as given authoritatively by the official teaching office, led to a slight change in the original draft of the decree (substitution of "et... et" for "partim... partim"), but there is hardly any doubt that the overwhelming majority of the Fathers understood the apostolic traditions as a stream of revelation complementing Scripture. The adoption of the decree on the Vulgate was preceded by a spirited debate on the lawfulness and appropriateness of translating the Bible into the vernacular. The "vetus et vulgata editio" of the Bible was declared "authentic," that is, free from doctrinal error, and suitable for scholarly and practical use. The correction of the Vulgate text, acknowledged as necessary, was carefully considered; study of the original languages of the Bible and versions in the vernacular were not forbidden. Just the same, the decree occasioned hesitations in Rome, but without resulting in an alteration of its text.

Canon 5 specified the remission of sin in every respect ("totum id, quod veram et propriam peccati rationem habet"); concupiscence, it states, is at times labeled sin in Saint Paul because it issues from it and lures to it. The Council declared that it did not intend to include the Mother of God in the decree on Original Sin; the constitutions of Sixtus IV concerning the dispute between Dominicans and Franciscans over the Immaculate Conception were to remain in force.

A reform decree dealing with the establishing of prebends of lectorships in cathedral and collegiate churches sought in this traditional manner to improve the defective instruction of the clergy. The bishop was personally obliged to the preaching of the faith; parish priests, to vernacular sermons on all Sundays and holy days.

The Decree on Justification

With the simultaneous publication of the two reform decrees and the decree on Original Sin in the fifth session (17 June), the Council was confronted with its most difficult assignment: the definition of the doctrine of justification. The opinions propounded by the thirty-four conciliar theologians on six proposed questions — nature of justification, faith and works, grace and freedom — reflected the views of the three great theological schools represented at the Council — Dominican, Franciscan, and Augustinian. The proposal on which the general debate was based distinguished three stages (*status*) of justification: the conversion of the sinner; the increase of justification; its recovery following the loss of grace. The first draft was so severely criticized that it had to be withdrawn. The simultaneous outbreak of the Schmalkaldic War and the advance of the Protestant army against the Ehrenberger Klause having occasioned a panic in Trent, the legates considered the transfer of the Council to Bologna, which, situated within the Papal State, conformed to the Pope's original plan as to the place of the Council. Though they had received full authority from the Pope in this regard, they lost precious time by making an inquiry at Rome and missed a favorable opportunity, since the military situation soon stabilized itself. At Cervini's suggestion, they submitted a new draft composed by Seripando, which complemented the "canones" by a positively stated "doctrina."

The Emperor's faction, now firmly held together, sought to delay the conclusion. In order to meet them halfway and to gain time in which to arrange the contemplated suspension of the Council, the legates called for particular congregations (15–26 October) on two problems which had come to the foreground in the course of the debate: the question, open since the Regensburg Religious Colloquy of 1541, of twofold justification (justification by the justice of Christ and that by grace immanent in man); and the possibility of attaining certainty on the state of grace (Luther's certainty of faith and the Scotist view on the efficacy of the Sacraments). Both questions were argued in the general congregations together with the "November draft" of the decree, with the result that the doctrine of a twofold justification was rejected but not formally condemned. As for the certainty of grace, the Council confined itself to striking out against Luther's certainty of faith. Here, as in other matters, the Council adhered to the principle of not deciding differences of opinion within Catholic theology. Throughout December the form of the decree was polished by a committee (*Praelati theologi*); the definitive wording (the fifth) was approved on 11 January 1547, and two days later unanimously accepted in the sixth session. In sixteen dogmatic chapters and thirty-three canons, it defined the responsibility of grace for justification in all its stages, its nature as sanctification and renewal of the inner man, the necessity of a preparation, and the importance of faith in the process of justification; the increase of justification, its restoration, and the possibility of merit; and eternal life as grace and reward.

The length of the debate on justification was due not only to the subject but also to political considerations. In an agreement on 16 November between Cardinal Farnese and the first imperial ambassador, Mendoza, it was proposed to suspend the Council for six months and to complete the debate on justification, but not to publish the decree. But when the Emperor refused to ratify this agreement of Trent, the legates proceeded to promulgate the decree.

Whereas the acceptance of the decree on justification was unanimous, the reception of that on the duty of residence of bishops and parish priests, promulgated in the same sixth session of 13 January 1547, was greatly divided. Members of both factions qualified their *placet* in the session with so many stipulations that the approval of the decree appeared doubtful. The legates were obliged to broach once more the problem of residence.

A reform proposal of 3 February 1547, prepared by the commission of canonists, already contained the basic features of a new law dealing with ordination and appointments to office. It gave to the bishop concerned the responsibility for ordination, including control of dimissorial letters issued by the Curia, and recognized the principle that office and benefice were inseparable by forbidding pluralism and requiring definite personal qualifications in those designated to become bishops and parish priests. In an effort to meet the demands of the opposition halfway, the Pope had at the beginning of the year transmitted to the legates the sketch of a reform bull in which the position of the bishops was strengthened. By a consistorial decree of 18 February he forbade the cardinals to hold more than one see. Hence in the general congregation of 25 February 1547, after careful examination of the votes cast in the session, the acceptance of the decree on residence could be proclaimed. Bishops of every rank, including cardinals, who failed to fulfill the duty of residence for six successive months were deprived of one-fourth of their revenues; if the absence continued for a year, they lost another fourth. The climate of the reform discussions had so greatly improved that the new reform proposal, which had meanwhile been extended to include statements opposing the union of benefices and dealing with the bishops' right of visitation, was accepted in the seventh session on 3 March 1547 by a large majority.

The preparation of the thirty canons on the sacraments in general, baptism, and confirmation, promulgated in the same session, had begun on 17 January when a collection of thirty-five erroneous propositions, extracted from the writings of the reformers, was submitted for evaluation by the theologians of the Council. The current rivalries among the schools in regard to the causality of the sacraments and a certain insecurity as to the nature of the sacramental character did not prevent complete unanimity with reference to the nature and sevenfold number of the sacraments. In the general debate (8–21 February) the Council decided to limit its definition strictly to the condemnation of the concepts of the reformers and not to draw up a doctrinal decree of a positive nature, modeled on the *Decretum pro Armenis* of 1439, nor to condemn the reformers by name along with their writings. The last-mentioned decision was in accord with the policy suggested by Cardinal Farnese at the beginning of the Council: that doctrines and not persons be condemned. On 25 February he again impressed this policy on the Council and added as a reason that otherwise the reformers ought to be summoned to the Council and heard by it. The canons accepted in the seventh session defined the sevenfold number of the sacraments and their institution by Christ. The Council described their nature as efficacious signs by having recourse to the scholastic terms added only during the concluding debate on 1 March: *gratiam non ponentibus obicem conferre* or *ex opere operato conferre.* The importance of faith was only negatively stated: The sacraments were instituted not only for the strengthening of faith and operate not only through faith in the word of promise. Rebaptism was condemned and the bishop was designated as the ordinary minister of confirmation.

Transfer to Bologna

During February the theologians had discussed the doctrine of the Eucharist. It had just been referred to the full Council when several cases of typhus fever, presumably brought to Trent from the German theater of operations in the war, provided the grounds for the decision reached on 11 March in the eighth session, by a vote of thirty-nine to fourteen (with five doubtful), to transfer the Council to Bologna. However, it is equally certain that the legates and the Italian majority had long aimed at the transfer and felt that they were thereby complying with the Pope's desire, but a direct charge to the legates is not demonstrable. The imperial minority regarded the decree of transfer as not binding and remained at Trent. The long-existing tension led to a rupture just at the moment when the Council seemed to have assumed the function of restoring Church unity.

For, since the turn of the year 1546–47, a victory of the Emperor over the Schmalkaldic League was in prospect. The army of the League had had to evacuate South Germany, and several Free Cities, the Duke of Württemberg, and the Count Palatine had submitted to the Emperor. However, instead of now negotiating, as Paul III desired, with the still unconquered leaders of the League, the Elector Johann Friedrich of Saxony and the Landgrave Philip of Hesse, and their secret patron, France, Charles V aimed at total victory, which he obtained at Mühlberg on 24 April. In a brief of 22 January the Pope had ended his alliance with the Emperor and had recalled his troops. His aim in the war was the subjugation of the Protestants, not the revival of the imperial power in Germany and the consolidation of Charles V's universal monarchy. Considering the Spanish supremacy in Italy, it was not without reason that he feared becoming dependent upon Charles V. Incensed by this change in papal politics, the Emperor showered the Nuncio Verallo with reproaches. The transfer of the Council to Bologna frustrated his great plan completely and wrecked the understanding laboriously established two years earlier between the two leaders on whom the plan depended. Charles demanded that the Pope annul the transfer of the Council, but the Pope refused on the ground that it was the business of the Council alone. However, the gathering in Bologna stipulated as a condition to any discussion of a return to Trent that first the minority that had remained there must submit to the decree of transfer and move to the new place of meeting. Nevertheless both parties made serious efforts to avoid a complete break. The Pope allowed the Council at Bologna to discuss but not to publish any decree; the Emperor established a provisional ecclesiastical settlement for the Empire without the direct participation of the Pope but with his tacit toleration.

In the ninth session (21 April 1547) the Council had constituted itself officially at Bologna and during May the debate begun at Trent on the Eucharist had been resumed. But the eight canons on the Real Presence, already completed, were not published in the tenth session (2 June) for the reason just mentioned. The same fate befell the canons discussed in June on the sacrament of penance and those on the anointing of the sick, holy orders, and matrimony, which engaged the general congregations and the then very prominent theological commission (*Praelati theologi*) during July, August, and September. The Council theologians, whose number rose at times to eighty and never fell below fifty, were preoccupied with the doctrine of purgatory and indulgences in June and July, with the Sacrifice of the Mass in August. The reform commission appointed on 6 June drew up as a program for the discussion of reform the abuses in the administration of the sacraments, and, after preparatory work in the commission of canonists, these abuses were debated in the plenary sessions during the autumn and winter. A new commission was formed to codify abuses in the celebration of Mass, in indulgences, and in religious Orders.

Though in its sessions at Bologna the Council did not issue a single reform decree, this period was important for almost all the subsequent decrees in that their topics were now for the first time thoroughly discussed. The view previously put forward at Trent, that the improvement of pastoral activity was the Council's central concern, was brought into clearer focus; once again the need to strengthen the position of the bishops was affirmed, and consideration was given to the arrangement of provincial and diocesan synods, the preparation of a catechism, and the liturgy.

After the Emperor's final move, through the dispatch of Cardinal Madruzzo to Rome to induce the Pope to restore the Council to Trent, had failed, he lodged a formal protest against the transfer in Bologna on 15 January 1548 and in Rome on 23 January. Imperial circles were already weighing the continuation of the Council by means of the minority that had remained in Trent. To avoid the threatened schism, the Pope on 1 February decreed the suspension of discussions at Bologna and requested the Council to defend the legality of the transfer before a tribunal set up at Rome; the minority in Trent also received the invitation to send a deputation to Rome. It declined. The deputies from Bologna were heard by the tribunal in the summer of 1548, but no verdict was reached.

Meanwhile, the Emperor had undertaken to settle the religious affairs of Germany, regardless of the Council, by means of the *Interim* of Augsburg and the "reform" simultaneously published for the Catholic estates. These were not authorized by the Pope, but their realization was indirectly furthered by him when he sent two reform nuncios to the Empire, Pighino and Lippomani, with extensive faculties for the reconciliation of Protestants. The *Interim* foundered on Protestant resistance. The Augsburg "reform" led to a series of provincial and diocesan synods but could effect no thorough Church renewal because the forces of regeneration were still too weak. The death of Paul III on 10 November 1549, however, opened up the prospect of reactivating the Council of Trent and hence of resuming the original "Great Plan."

Second Period of Sessions

Though the new Pope, Julius III, had, as Council president, brought about the transfer to Bologna, he conceded to the Emperor the return of the Council to Trent on the assumption that the Protestant estates, in conformity with the Recess of the Diet of 30 June 1548, would submit to it. The assumption proved to be wrong, for their submission, given under pressure of military defeat, was bound up with two conditions: that the Council should not be under the Pope's direction and that it should reopen for discussion the doctrinal decrees promulgated during the first period of sessions, taking as a starting point the Protestant principle of Scripture. The Emperor and even the Pope, who was at first inadequately informed of this state of affairs, acted as though an unconditional surrender were at hand. The Bull "Cum ad Tollenda" of November 1550, reconvoking the Council to Trent, maintained the view held by the Curia that the transfer had been legitimate by speaking of "resuming" (*reductio*), but at the same time it met the Emperor halfway by designating the new meeting at Trent as a "continuation" of the earlier. France, having recognized the transfer, declined to participate.

The Legate Marcellus Crescenzio, in association with co-presidents Pighino and Lippomani, who were previously active in Germany as reform nuncios, opened the meeting on the appointed day, 1 May 1551, but discussions did not get under way until September. The character of the gathering differed from the earlier one, for the imperial minority, which had held out in Trent after the transfer, had been increased during the fall and winter by thirteen bishops from Germany and Switzerland, including the three Ecclesiastical Electors, and the previous predominance of the Italians had been broken. Among the Council theologians there were now present, in addition to the great Spaniards, representatives of the University of Louvain and the German theologians Johann Gropper, Eberhard Billick, and Ambrosius Pelargus. And, above all, there appeared for the first and only time ambassadors of the Protestant imperial estates: Brandenburg, Württemberg, Strasbourg, and Electoral Saxony, among them the historian Johannes Sleidanus.

The ten articles on the Eucharist which were submitted on 2 September were related to the articles of Trent, but, thanks to the preliminary work accomplished in Bologna and to the complete agreement on this article of faith, the debate was relatively brief. It defined the Real Presence and the notion of transubstantiation as suitable (*aptissime*) for designating the substantial change and condemned the teaching that Christ is present only at the moment of reception. A decision in regard to communion under both species was deferred.

Likewise, the twelve articles on the sacrament of penance and the four on the anointing of the sick were not identical with the Bologna canons. Contrary to Luther's teaching that penance consists in a recalling of baptism and is essentially a penitential attitude, the Council defined Penance as a Sacrament, consisting of three elements: contrition, confession, and satisfaction. Confession of all serious sins committed after baptism is required by divine law, and priestly absolution is a judicial act. The anointing of the sick is no mere ceremony adapted for the relief of those who are ill, but a sacrament instituted by Christ and promulgated by the Apostle James.

Less satisfactory was the progress of the discussions on reform. Spaniards and Germans agreed that reform was not being adequately pursued. In December and January, during the debates on the Mass and holy orders, the negotiations with the ambassadors of the Protestant imperial estates, which were conducted by means of the imperial representatives, Count Montfort and Francisco de Toledo, made no progress. The envoys of Württemberg and Electoral Saxony were received in the general congregation of 24 January 1552, and on the next day, in the fifteenth session, obtained the amended safe-conduct that they had demanded. But a theological discussion failed to materialize, for the Protestants insisted on their earlier stipulations relative to recognizing the Council. "For both sides," said Bizer, "it is clearly a question of principle, in which to yield would have meant to surrender."

At the same moment there arrived alarming reports concerning the military activity of the Elector Maurice of Saxony, who was allied to France. The German archbishops took their departure, the Legate Crescenzio fell gravely ill, and the suspension of the Council seemed inevitable. But the Emperor, strenuously resisted any admission that his great plan had definitely collapsed and commanded that the suspension be opposed. When the rebel princes took the initiative in April and compelled the Emperor to flee from Innsbruck, no alternative remained. On 28 April 1552, in the sixteenth session, the Council decided to adjourn indefinitely. After the dissolution a Spaniard wrote, with resignation: The suspension has revealed the futility of the Council; neither have the heresies that arose in Germany and elsewhere been liquidated, nor has the Church been reformed, nor has peace been restored among Christian princes. Disappointment obstructed the view of what had really been achieved, but it was incontestable that the Council presented itself as a torso: Its doctrinal decrees embraced only a part of the disputed teachings, the reform decrees eliminated some but in no sense the most crying abuses, and they had no binding force, because they had not yet been confirmed by the Pope.

CHAPTER 97

The Breakthrough of the Catholic Reform (1551–59)

The decade 1549–59 witnessed the breakthrough of the Catholic Reform in Rome. In 1555 two of its leaders mounted the Throne of Peter in rapid succession.

Julius III, as nephew of Cardinal Antonio Del Monte, who was much esteemed under Leo X and Clement VII, had risen high in the curial career and was an outstanding canonist. After a long conclave (November 1549 to 7 February 1550) he was elected as a result of an understanding between Cardinals Guise and Alessandro Farnese, after the zealous reformer Pole, one of the Emperor's candidates, had failed by one vote to obtain the required two-thirds majority. Julius declared his official neutrality in the struggle for Siena, which broke out in the summer of 1552 on the expulsion of its Spanish garrison. But the two peace envoys, sent in the spring of 1553 — Dandino to the Emperor, Capodiferro to Henry II — accomplished nothing. The Sienese, supported by France, lost their freedom to Cosimo I of Florence, and Spanish predominance in Italy was finally consolidated. The Pope came to terms with it, on the advice of Dandino, favorable to France, and of Ricci, inclined to the imperial side. Ricci had undertaken the virtually impossible task of rescuing the finances from the chaos produced by the *nepoti* policy of Paul III. The costly Parma War and the preparations for the defense of the Papal State, rendered necessary by the Siena War, deepened the financial distress.

The most important event of his pontificate, the Catholic Restoration in England, fell into Julius III's lap without his participation. On 19 July 1553, Mary, daughter of Catherine of Aragon, was proclaimed Queen of England. Resolved from the start to lead the nation back to the Roman obedience, she proceeded cautiously in the question of religion, advised by her cousin, Charles V, and mindful of the strong opposition she had to overcome even after her accession. The religious laws of Edward VI were repealed, Catholic worship was restored, and on 1 April 1554 Bishop Gardiner, whom she had appointed Lord Chancellor, consecrated six bishops to replace those deposed. The Queen herself applied to the Pope for their confirmation.

But Cardinal Pole, named as Papal Legate, was not permitted to set foot in England until the end of November 1554, after the marriage arranged by the Emperor of Charles V's son Philip to Mary had taken place. On 30 November 1554, the legate solemnly pronounced the absolution from schism in the presence of the Queen and Parliament. Demands for the return of alienated Church property were dispensed with and the current holders were confirmed in possession on 24 December. The Provincial Council of Canterbury, presided over by Pole (4 November 1555 to 10 February 1556), was to institute the rebuilding of the Church in England and was in accord with the spirit of the Catholic Reform in its concern for obliging bishops to reside in their dioceses and to preach, the organizing of groups of preachers to take the place of the mendicants, and the decree on the founding of seminaries for boys, which became the direct model of the Tridentine decree on seminaries.

The task of reconstruction was hampered by the fact that half the bishops in office had been compromised by the schism that there were not enough priests on hand, and above all that after twenty years of schism a great part of the faithful were estranged from the papacy and Catholic worship. The judicial proceedings against schismatics and Protestants, normally instituted by the secular judge, frequently aroused popular resentment, because a number of the ecclesiastical judges themselves had cooperated with the earlier system. Among the 273 persons put to death were, it seems very likely, many Anabaptists, who had been persecuted by the Anglican Church as well as by the Catholic Church. The flight of Protestant-minded preachers to the continent, from fear of the Queen, prepared the collapse of the restoration.

The most pressing, but so far deferred, task of the papacy continued to be the reform of the Roman Curia. In the autumn of 1550 Julius III had summoned to Rome three resolute members of the reform party, Cervini, Pole, and Morone, and through them, and a little later through still other cardinals, he expanded the reform commission which had been formed soon after his election. But, like Paul III, he had not carried out his original purpose of anticipating the impending reconstitution of the Council by a papal reform of the Curia. During the winter of 1552–53, Cervini and Maffei pushed so zealously the reform of the conclave, the consistory, the *signatura,* and the Sacred Penitentiary, taking into consideration old and new opinions, that Andreas Masius, agent of the Duke of Cleves, expected the "reformation of the Roman Court in a few days." The Tridentine reform decrees, completed by a "reform of the princes" and modified in several points, were to be put in force by a great reform bull.

The driving force sprang out of events in Spain and Portugal, where many bishops, supported by the secular powers, were beginning to carry out certain reform decrees of the Council, notably Chapter 4 of Session VI concerning the visitation of exempt capitulars, though these still lacked papal confirmation and hence were without the force of law. The Pope reacted with great firmness. On 15 January 1554 he referred the King of Portugal to the forthcoming reform bull; in Spain he intervened in favor of the exempt cathedral canons of León, Astorga, Segovia, and Calahorra and categorically demanded that the bishops withdraw the orders issued against them. He thereby rejected the view that conciliar decrees possessed validity as "directives of the Holy Spirit for the good of souls" without papal confirmation and at the same time squarely faced the Erastian tendency to play them off against the papacy. In the introduction to the projected reform bull (spring of 1554) was expressed the intention of conferring the force of law through it on the conciliar decrees together with the newly drafted reform chapter. The bull was submitted to the cardinals for their consideration at the beginning of December 1554, but before it could be given a final polishing Julius III died on 23 March 1555.

Seripando's judgment, that Julius neither promised nor achieved Church reform ("nec dixit nec fecit"), sprang from the disappointment of a reform zealot, but it is too severe. Numerous notes in the acts of reform, in the Pope's own hand, testify to his personal interest. Among the twenty cardinals he created were such splendid men as Puteo, Dandino, Bertano, and the Pope's nephew, Nobili, but there was also the totally unworthy adopted son of his brother Baldovino, Innocenzo Del Monte. Julius had encouraged reform bishops by grants of full apostolic authority. At the beginning of 1554 he issued a list of only fourteen bishops who, needed for service in the Curia, were permitted to remain in Rome; the others were to go to their dioceses. But to reform circles these measures seemed inadequate; they expected more.

On the death of Julius III the reform party proved to be strong enough to secure the tiara for one of their own. Neither the imperialists nor the French could expect to rally the two-thirds majority for one of their candidates. Furthermore, the leading candidate of the French, Ippolito d'Este, who was wholly a Renaissance figure, damaged rather than promoted his own candidacy through his intrigues. Hence the imperialist faction, led by Sforza, contrived to carry the election, after a four days' conclave (6–10 April 1555), of the most ardent of all the reform cardinals, Cervini, who was all along acceptable to the French.

Marcellus Cervini, born at Montepulciano near Siena in 1501, was a Christian humanist and patristic scholar, and as tutor of Paul III's nephews had been raised to the purple as early as 1539. Though not in continuous residence, he had conscientiously cared for his sees (first Nicastro, then Reggio-Emilia, and finally Gubbio). As legate at the Council he had retained the Pope's confidence, even after he had fallen out with Alessandro Farnese over the latter's unscrupulous family politics. In his decision not to change his name and to be known as Marcellus II is discerned his wish to remain as Pope what he had been before. In a suggestion for his administration, which he had solicited, appeared the deeply moving sentence: "For twenty years people have talked about reform and openly admitted that it is necessary, but nothing has resulted." Marcellus II was resolved to take vigorous action; hence he is the first Pope of the Catholic Reform. But he died on 30 April, "shown rather than given" to the Church. However, the breakthrough had been achieved.

In the next conclave (14–23 May 1555) the same constellation within the College of Cardinals produced a similar result. The election of Puteo, pushed by the imperialists, misfired and in his place was chosen a declared enemy of the Spaniards, the dean of the College, Gian Pietro Carafa, a man of irreproachable life but dreaded for his severity. Paul IV, born in 1476, belonged to one of the great baronial houses of the Kingdom of Naples. Having renounced his benefices, he had founded the Theatine Order with Cajetan of Thiene. A judgment drawn up in Venice in 1532 on defense against Protestantism in Italy and certain proposals of the "Consilium de emendanda Ecclesia," notably with regard to the establishment of the Roman Inquisition, presented his radical views, wholly different from the thought of the humanistic reform movement.

Despite his advanced age the tall, ascetic, but passionate Neapolitan was in full possession of his physical and mental powers. Profoundly conscious of the majesty of his office and an adherent of the papal theory in its most extreme form, an autocrat by character and conviction, he abandoned the political neutrality maintained by his predecessors and sought, without regard to the changed situation, to rule Christendom after the manner of a Pope of the High Middle Ages.

By family tradition and his own observations a violent opponent of Spanish rule in Naples and of Spanish ascendancy in Italy, he permitted himself to be led into an alliance with France and a war against Spain by Carlo Carafa, his energetic and ambitious, but morally worthless nephew. The war laid bare the military and political impotence of the Papal State, led to defeat near Paliano, and ended with the Peace of Cave on 12 September 1557.

The death on 17 November 1558 of Pole and of Mary the Catholic and the accession of Elizabeth I brought a sudden end to the Catholic Restoration in England. Though long since determined to renew the schism, the new Queen deferred the break with Rome until her throne was firm. In February 1559 she recalled her ambassador from Rome, on 23 March the bill concerning the royal supremacy — with "head" replaced by "governor of the Church of England" — was accepted against the opposition of the bishops, and in the summer of 1559 the Anglican liturgy was reintroduced. All the bishops, except the Bishop of Llandaff, refused to recognize the new establishment and were deposed. But still Paul IV pronounced no ecclesiastical censure on Elizabeth.

The situation of the Church in Poland was likewise threatened. The Nuncio Luigi Lippomani found the existence of Catholicism in great danger, for a part of the higher nobility, headed by Prince Radziwill, were Protestant-minded, the greater number of the bishops were compliant or even suspected of leaning toward Protestantism, and King Sigismund Augustus was powerless. The royal demands for the marriage of priests, the lay chalice, Mass in the vernacular, and a national council were flatly rejected by the Pope. At the Diet of Petrikow (1558) Lippomani's successor, Mentuato, in whose retinue was Peter Canisius, managed to prevent the issuing of resolutions directed against the Catholic religion but not to stop the continuation of Protestant propaganda.

In Germany the Protestant estates of the Augsburg Confession gained recognition by imperial law through the Religious Peace of Augsburg of 25 September 1555. The Pope had sent Lippomani to Augsburg with instructions to do all in his power to prevent the ratification of the Peace of Passau. The Emperor was known to be opposed to the Passau concessions. These measures were inadequate. The Pope's exasperation with the Habsburg brothers was so intense already in 1556 that their deposition was discussed in all seriousness. Before Ferdinand I was able to refer the quarrel to the Diet of Augsburg and thereby introduce into a totally changed world the medieval struggle between *Sacerdotium* and *Regnum,* the Pope died.

As in politics, so also in the ecclesiastical sphere Paul IV followed paths different from those of his predecessors. For him the resumption of the Council of Trent was out of the question.

The Theatines Scotti and Isacchino and the papal librarian Sirleto busied themselves at the Pope's orders with the reform of the breviary and the missal, an old concern of Paul IV and the Theatines. In time the Pope proceeded ever more exclusively to extirpate with Draconian severity the grievances against which he had earlier inveighed in vain, above all to check the advance of Protestantism through stern measures of repression.

The presenting of monasteries to secular clerics *in commendam* was forbidden. Severe penalties were visited on "apostates,' religious who had abandoned the common life without authorization or with a surreptitiously obtained indult. Any who were apprehended in Rome were taken into custody. Public immorality and acts of violence, once an everyday occurrence, were suppressed by excessively severe decrees of the governor of the city. Renaissance Rome changed its image. In an effort to impose a halt to the spread of Protestantism, at least where the Church's arm reached, Paul created and sharpened two weapons: the Index of Forbidden Books and the Inquisition.

State as well as ecclesiastical authorities began, in view of the annually swelling flood of publications of the religious innovators, to forbid books that had already appeared, individually or by drawing up lists. On 21 December 1558, Paul IV withdrew all previously granted licenses for the reading of forbidden books, commanded that they be surrendered, and the next year published the first Papal Index of Forbidden Books. In arrangement and content it was modeled on the Louvain catalog, but in severity it far surpassed it. In addition to the writings of the reformers, all the works of Erasmus, whatever their content, were forbidden, all works on occult sciences (palmistry, geomancy, etc.), all publications issued in the preceding forty years without the name of the author or publisher, and finally, regardless of content, all products of sixty-one printers specified by name, fourteen of whom were from Basel alone. The great majority of editions of the Bible and of the Fathers fell under the prohibition, and many scholars saw themselves deprived of their scientific tools.

Almost passionately the Pope addressed himself to the improvement of the Roman Inquisition. It acquired precedence over all other offices and its general delegate had the same powers as the cardinals of the Inquisition. Its jurisdiction was extended to embrace moral lapses of the greatest variety. The doctrinal tribunal became a bureau of morals. Death sentences were passed more frequently than before, and no one was safe.

The Pope was rudely aroused from the most serious self-deception when, early in 1559, the Theatine Isacchino apprised him of the scandalous doings of his nephews. Paul IV banished them from Rome, but the moral damage could not be repaired. He had refused to pay any heed to the wishes of the great powers in his creations of cardinals. But the more he had enriched the college with such distinguished men as Ghislieri, the Theatines Rebiba and Reumano, and his great-nephew Alfonso Carafa, so much the more flagrant appeared the crimes of his nephews.

The Pope was lacking in moderation. He took such pains with the nomination of bishops that in October 1558 no fewer than fifty-eight sees were vacant. The undeniable tightening of all ecclesiastical standards was a great forward step on the road of Catholic Reform, but the narrow-mindedness and harshness of his measures and his prolonged blindness in regard to his nephews made his pontificate a great disappointment. After his death (18 August 1559) the repressed hatred for the Pope and his family exploded in the destruction of the headquarters of the Inquisition and the abuse of his statue on the Capitol.

The success of the reform movement in the papal elections of 1555 did not yet mean definitive victory over the crisis. The apostasy was making apparently irresistible progress. England was about to be lost to the papacy once more. The Religious Peace of Augsburg had been concluded in the Empire. In France and Poland the position of the Church was shaky. She still held her own, unchallenged, only in the two southern peninsulas, thanks to the support furnished by the secular arm. But the very relations of the papacy with Spain, which became the leading European power in the Peace of Câteau-Cambrésis in 1559 between Spain, England, and France and regarded itself as the protector of the Church, were almost ruptured. The Catholic Reform had now reached the head; the resumption and conclusion of the Council of Trent enabled it to embrace the members.

CHAPTER 98

Pius IV and the Conclusion of the Council of Trent

The first two periods of the Council of Trent were occasioned by the German religious split and were oriented to it. Their dogmatic decrees were the reply of the Church's teaching authority to the doctrinal concepts of Luther and Zwingli and the ecclesiastical communities based on them. Their reform decrees were an as yet inadequate endeavor to meet the Protestant Reformation with a Catholic Reform. The third and final period of the Council was motivated by ecclesiastical events in France, where Calvinism seemed about to gain for itself the most heavily populated country of the West, the one that had been the intellectual leader into the late Middle Ages. Had this goal been achieved, the Catholic Church would have been definitely confined to the two southern peninsulas of Europe.

After a dramatically developing conclave of over three months (5 September to 26 December 1559), in which the three about evenly matched factions of Spanish, French, and Carafa cardinals confronted one another, the Milanese Gianangelo Medici, was elected. Pius IV, who had been employed mostly in the administration of the Papal State and made a cardinal by Paul III in 1549, was not an outstanding politician, and in his entire previous career he had not belonged to the reform party. His closest adviser was Cardinal Morone, just liberated from Sant'Angelo, and in matters of high politics he usually followed the counsels of the crafty Duke Cosimo, who had come to terms with the Spanish power in Italy. The Pope's "new course" implied a break with the Carafa regime and a return to the Church policies of Paul III and Julius III. Not a reform assembly at Rome but the continuation of the still suspended Council of Trent lay in the administrative program of the new Pope.

His very first contacts with the great powers made it clear that two basically different views confronted each other. Philip II of Spain, undeniably the mightiest monarch in Europe since the Peace of Câteau-Cambrésis, regarded the envisaged Council as the continuation of the two earlier sittings, whose decrees, even though they had not yet been ratified by the Pope, might not be changed. The Emperor and France, on the other hand, wanted a new council: Ferdinand I, out of regard for the German Protestants, who feared a continuation of Trent would endanger the permanence of the Religious Peace of Augsburg; France, in the hope of finding in a new council, in default of other means, a settlement with the rising Huguenot faction. The Bull of Convocation, "Ad ecclesiae regimen," of 29 November 1560, favored the first view by referring to the lifting of the suspension, without excluding the second in using the expression "announcement" (*indictio*). None of the parties was satisfied and all hesitated in accepting the bull.

The Protestant estates, meeting at Naumburg, gave the Nuncio Commendone another flat refusal. Ferdinand I replied ambiguously to the Nuncio Delfino, who had been sent to him and to South Germany, and in this he was supported by France, where the Queen Mother, Catherine de Médicis, was acting as regent for her second son, Charles IX. This niece of Clement VII, to maintain herself in power, was playing off the two religious factions and their political exponents against each other and, advised by the Chancellor Michel de l'Hôpital, was seeking an accommodation. While as yet no definitive acceptance had been given by the powers, the Pope in February and March 1561 named five legates for the Council: the highly cultured and politically experienced Ercole Gonzaga, who in the last conclave had come close to gaining the tiara; the canonist Puteo; the one-time general of the Augustinians, Seripando, now Archbishop of Salerno; Stanislaus Hosius, expert in controversial theology, Bishop of Warmia, and nuncio to the Emperor; and the curial canonist Ludovico Simonetta, who possessed the Pope's full confidence. Later the papal nephew Sittich von Hohenems was substituted for the ailing Puteo.

Though Gonzaga and Seripando were in Trent from 16 April 1561, it was not certain that the Council would actually meet until the autumn. To be sure, Philip II, once he had obtained the Pope's assurance in a secret brief of 17 July that the Council was to be regarded as the continuation of the earlier sittings, had commanded the Spanish bishops to prepare for the journey. And Ferdinand I had finally promised to appoint envoys. But events in France decided the issue. The assembly of the clergy at Poissy in August–September 1561 — really a national council — and the religious discussion there with the Calvinists under the leadership of Theodore Beza made clear the danger of the country's gradually drifting toward Calvinism. The first Spaniards made their appearance at the end of the year. It was possible to have the opening on 18 January 1562, in the presence of 109 cardinals and bishops, four abbots, and four generals of Orders.

The legates endeavored to put aside the continuing controversy concerning the relationship to the earlier sittings by submitting on 11 March twelve reform articles which were inspired by a memorandum of some of the Italian bishops. Article 1 took up the still unsettled problem of the duty of residence. In the course of the debate, which began on 7 April a minority, consisting of Spaniards and reform-zealous Italians, declared that the obligation of residence on the part of the bishops is of divine law and hence not an object of the Pope's dispensing power. The other side vigorously attacked this *ius divinum* argument as prejudicial to the papal primacy. When the legates brought this main point to a vote in the general congregation of 20 April, sixty-seven Fathers expressed themselves in favor of the *ius divinum*, thirty-five against it, and thirty-four left the decision to the Pope. Alarmed, the Pope on 11 May forbade the continuation of the debate on residence. In the nineteenth session on 14 May the Council received the "orators" of the King of Spain, the Republic of Venice, and Duke Cosimo; in the twentieth session on 4 June, the ambassadors of France and of the Catholic Swiss cantons. Those of the Emperor had been in Trent since spring. On 6 July these last presented to the legates the Emperor's carefully prepared reform project, which, among other things, asked for the grant of the chalice to the laity and the marriage of priests.

The decision for the continuation, which the Spanish Ambassador Pescara had again demanded, was actually made through the decree of the twenty-first session, 16 July 1562, on, Communion under both species; it reflected the Eucharistic decree of 1551. The petition for the grant of the lay chalice, was referred to the Pope after a long debate and over the strong opposition of the Imperial Ambassador.

In the succeeding debate on the sacrificial character of the Mass, its relationship to the Sacrifice of the Cross was worked out. The chief point of controversy was whether the Last Supper was a propitiatory sacrifice. The "August draft," submitted on 6 August, suppressed the passage on the subject in the schema of 1552. But as the opponents of this doctrine continued to constitute a minority in the debate, it was restored in the "September draft" and passed into the definitive wording of the decree on the Mass. The Mass is the reenacting and recalling of the Sacrifice of the Cross and the applying of its fruits, a propitiatory offering for the living and the dead, offered by the same Christ who offered the Sacrifice of the Cross (*una eademque hostia, idem nunc offerens*) but by means of priests and performed in a different manner. The Canon of the Mass is free of error. It is allowed to celebrate Mass in honor of the saints, though of course the Sacrifice is offered to God alone. Private Masses are lawful, and the use of the vernacular in the Mass is not practicable (*non expedire*). A corresponding reform decree abolished some of the many abuses listed by a conciliar commission.

The lingering crisis of the Council became acute when on 13 November Charles de Guise, the "Cardinal of Lorraine," arrived in Trent with thirteen French bishops. After a briefing on the position of the conciliar business he espoused the side of the opposition and became its leader. The discussions initiated on the sacrament of holy orders in the general congregation of 13 October and the new decree on residence, submitted on 6 November, converged on the problem of primacy-episcopacy. The institution of the episcopal office *de iure divino,* contained in the schema of 21 January 1552, had been suppressed in the proposal given to the theologians on 18 September, and the new decree on residence traced the obligation to divine *and* human law. The French and Spanish opposition, supported by a part of the Italians, urged "episcopalism" to solve the problem, while the *zelanti,* encouraged by Rome and supported in the body of legates by Simonetta, aimed at a strictly curialist decision. Though Gonzaga and Seripando exerted themselves from December 1562 to February 1563 to discover compromise formulas, the opposing camps became so adamant that the Council was disabled, the Catholic powers began to intervene, and the collapse of the Council seemed a distinct possibility. To keep the Council busy, the legates inaugurated particular congregations on the sacrament of matrimony. Cardinal Guise, extremely bitter over the obstinacy of the *zelanti,* obtained from the Emperor, during a visit to Innsbruck, a serious letter of admonition to the Pope not to resist reform by the Council and to impose restraint on the *zelanti.* The conflict, hitherto constantly avoided, over the relation of the Pope to the Council, seemed at hand.

The great crisis in the Council was not overcome until a new president was acquired in Morone, who enjoyed the Pope's full confidence.

Now, after an interruption of almost ten months, it was possible on 14 July 1563 to hold the twenty-third session, which became the turning point of the Council. The compromise proposed by Cardinal Morone and accepted by the opposition amounted to this, that the Council limited itself to rejecting, in canons 6 to 8 on holy orders, the Protestant teaching on the episcopal office while avoiding a definition of the papal primacy. In the remaining canons and in the appended doctrinal chapters were defined the institution of the priesthood of the New Law by Christ and the distinction of major and minor orders. The new decree on residence increased the penalties for neglect of the obligation and left the *ius divinum* unmentioned. No less important was the final chapter (chap. 18) of the reform decree: the bishops were obliged to establish seminaries for the training of future priests.

On 30 July 1563 Morone handed to the orators of the powers for their comments a reform proposal in forty-two articles. It took into account numerous postulates from the reform memoranda under consideration by the Council, but so constructed that none of the current claims of the Curia was abandoned in principle. In the general congregations from 11 September to 2 October twenty-one articles, taken from this schema but slightly revised, were debated. Previously, during July and August, in the debate on matrimony, the declaration of the nullity of clandestine marriages and the question, relevant to the practice of the Greeks, of divorce by reason of adultery had evoked spirited arguments. The fourteenth session on 11 November 1563, embraced three decrees, the significance of which cannot be too highly esteemed. A dogmatic decree affirmed the sacramental nature of matrimony, its indissolubility, and the Church's right to establish matrimonial impediments. The reform decree "Tametsi" made the validity of future marriages dependent upon the observance of the *forma tridentina,* the exchange of the marriage promises before the authorized parish priest and two or three witnesses; it also ordered priests to keep registers of baptisms and marriages. The general reform decree, in twenty-one chapters, contained norms for the method of nominating bishops, including the conducting of processes for obtaining information, for the holding of triennial provincial councils and annual diocesan synods and for episcopal visitations, and finally for cathedral canons and appointments to parishes. Throughout, where pastoral considerations required, the rights of bishops were extended at the expense of exempt Orders and corporations by grant of apostolic authority.

Even after Cardinal Guise, most of the Spaniards, and the imperialists had been won to Morone's policy of reconciliation, an increasingly dwindling minority of Spaniards, notably the Bishop of Segovia, held firm in their opposition and were supported by Count Luna, who had been introduced on 21 May 1563 as ambassador of Philip II. Luna was against the legates' exclusive right of proposition and Morone's exertions for a quick conclusion of the Council; the reform project introduced by the president, he said, neither satisfied the Spanish postulates of reform nor took sufficient consideration of the German situation. Cardinal Morone overcame these and other obstacles adduced by the powers against a speedy closing of the Council when he threatened the consideration of a proposed "reform of the princes," that is, the complaints of the bishops against the interference of the secular powers in the ecclesiastical domain. During November the rest of the great reform schema was discussed.

The final session was set for the middle of December, but at the news that the Pope was ill it was advanced to 3 December and continued on 4 December (the twenty-fifth session). It included decrees on controverted doctrines not so far considered: purgatory, the veneration of saints and their relics, images, and indulgences, all of which could be debated only briefly on 2 and 4 December. The reform of the Orders, sketched under Julius III, preserved the character of a skeleton law which did not annul their existing constitutions but merely modified them in specific points. It contained norms for the acceptance of new members and on the novitiate, poverty, and the inclosure of nuns. Despite the bristling opposition of Alessandro Farnese and other cardinals, the cardinals too were included in this session's second reform decree, which in chapter 1 sketched the duties of bishops. In addition, it contained directions for the conducting of the visitation (chap. 6) and the administration of the Church's hospitals, a reorganization of the *ius patronatus* (chap. 9) and of the proceedings against concubinaries (chap. 14). The revision of the Index of Paul IV, for which a conciliar commission had been appointed early in 1562, the reform of the missal and the breviary, also dealt with, and the drawing up of a catechism for parish priests could not be brought to completion. The Council decided to turn over to the Pope the preliminary work "so that it can be finished and put into effect by his authority."

After all the decrees of the two earlier periods under Paul III and Julius III had been once more read aloud, all the bishops present confirmed their acceptance over their own signatures. The decrees were signed by six cardinals, three patriarchs, twenty-five archbishops, 169 bishops, seven abbots, and several generals of Orders.

The importance of the Council of Trent in ecclesiastical and secular history is based on two achievements. First, it precisely defined the Catholic deposit of faith against the reform doctrines, though not in every controverted point, for the definition of the papal primacy and of the concept of the Church, the most violently challenged teachings, was prevented by episcopalism and Gallicanism. The Council did not aspire to settle theological differences of opinion within the Church. Second, to confront the Protestant Reformation the Council set up a Catholic Reform. Not a *reformatio in capite et membris* in the late medieval sense, it admittedly disregarded many postulates of the reform movement — it bypassed the reform of the Curia — but it did eliminate the most crying abuses on the diocesan and parochial levels and in the orders, effectively strengthened the authority of the bishops, and gave priority to the demands of pastoral care.

However, the Council's reform achievement could become operative only if the papacy took charge of the execution of the decrees. In accord with the resolution contained in the last session, Morone sought papal confirmation of the conciliar decrees. This was given orally on 26 January 1564, and, after strong curial resistance had been overcome, in writing on 30 June by the Bull "Benedictus Deus," antedated 26 January. To prevent the exploitation of the Council against the Pope, Pius IV reserved to himself the interpretation of the decrees and on 2 August 1564 instituted a congregation of cardinals for their authentic interpretation and enforcement. They were made of obligation outside Rome from 1 May 1564. By the end of March they were available in print in the official version but the plan of also publishing the conciliar acts was dropped. Peter Canisius delivered texts of the decrees with accompanying papal briefs to the German bishops. In Italy the enforcement began when on 1 March 1564 the Pope urged the bishops present in Rome to take up residence in their dioceses. At the same time the first diocesan synods and episcopal visitations were held, as prescribed by the Council, and the mendicant Orders brought their constitutions into conformity with the regulations of Session XXIV. In the Bull "Dominici gregis," of 24 March 1564, the Index of forbidden books, prepared at the Council, was published. The Pope complied with the petition for the lay chalice by allowing it, with certain reservations, to the bishops of the six provinces of Germany, the provinces of Esztergom and Prague, and several exempt dioceses on 16 April 1564. A brief summary of the dogmatic results of the Council, the "Professio Fidei Tridentinae," was prescribed on 13 November 1564, to be taken by bishops, religious superiors, and doctors. Thereby the Council made a distinct impression in the domain of belief.

Paul III had begun but not pushed the reform of the Curia as a result of the Council, but with the breakthrough of 1555 a longer reprieve was clearly impossible. Since Pius IV insisted that the reform of the administration was not within the competence of the Council, he had to take up the task himself. In 1561 and 1562 appeared in rapid sequence decrees on the reform of the Rota, the Sacred Penitentiary, the Chancery, and the Camera, and thus on 29 June 1562, the Pope could assert: "We have announced and accomplished a strict reform of Our court." A bull of 9 October 1562 was directed against abuses that had occurred in the last conclave. The chief representative of the new spirit was the Cardinal-Nephew Borromeo, concerning whom Soranzo, the Venetian ambassador, reported: "He in his own person does more good at the Roman Court than all the decrees of the Council together." In actuality, the renewal of the papacy formed the basis for the enforcement of the Tridentine decrees, which in turn led to the successful self-assertion of the Church in the Counter Reformation. The forces of renewal now began to operate, but the crisis had by no means been surmounted.

Section Two

The Papacy and the Implementation of the Council of Trent (1565–1605)

CHAPTER 99

Personality and Work of the Reform Popes from Pius V to Clement VIII

A glance at the contemporary religious map of Europe makes clear the gravity of the crisis in which the Church found herself as the conclusion of the Council of Trent. Only the inhabitants of the Italian and Iberian peninsulas had remained positively Catholic. In Western Europe the Calvinist offensive threatened to sever France from Rome, as it had already succeeded in doing with Scotland. In Rome there was still reluctance to admit that England, by renewing the schism, had definitely entered the ranks of the Protestant powers. The Scandinavian North was gone; in Poland kingship and Catholicism were wavering. In the Empire the Religious Peace of Augsburg had not stopped the progress of Protestantism: in North Germany the last footholds of the ancient Church were lost, in the South and West she was asserting herself with difficulty in the ecclesiastical states and under the protection of the houses of Wittelsbach and Habsburg, but Austria, Bohemia, and Hungary remained exposed, and the Swiss Confederation continued to be split on the question of religion.

That the Church overcame the crisis and at the end of the century stood forth renewed and strengthened is due to the carrying out of the Council of Trent by the papacy. Because of the efforts of three outstanding Popes its decrees did not remain a dead letter but permeated the life of the Church. The methods employed by them were as different as their personalities, but the goal was identical: the regeneration of the Church in the spirit of the Catholic Reform.

Pius V

In the conclave following the death of Pius IV which was, according to Pastor, "freer from external influences than any other in the memory of man," Cardinal Borromeo prevented the election of Ricci, skillful in business and favored by Duke Cosimo, and of Alessandro Farnese, and, after the rejection of the candidates whom he promoted (Morone and Sirleto), succeeded, in an understanding with Farnese, in having the Dominican Michael Ghislieri elected, who was, in the judgment of the Spanish Ambassador Requesens, "the pope demanded by the times." But it was an accurate appraisal, for he differed from his patron by thinking and acting in all spheres from the religious viewpoint. His court was as austere and frugal as was the Pope himself. In the severity of his measures against blasphemy, immorality, and the profanation of holy days and in his zeal for the Inquisition he did not yield place to the Carafa Pope. It was said of him that he sought to turn Rome into a monastery. The sentences of the Inquisition were made known and carried out in public *autos-da-fe.* The number of Inquisition processes soared.

These repressive measures, in comparison with the work of positive reconstruction, are of meager importance in the total picture. The catechism for parish priests, begun by the Council of Trent, was brought to completion. The reformed Roman breviary (1568) and the Roman missal (1570), were prescribed for use in all dioceses and Orders which had not had breviaries and missals of their own for the preceding 200 years.

But far more decisive than these supplements to the Council was the Pope's will of steel to enforce the Trent reform decrees and to tolerate no return to the former lax procedure in regard to dispensations, which would have detracted from their validity. A reform of the Sacred Penitentiary, restricting its competence to the internal forum, definitely sealed off this source of limitless abuses. Observing the Tridentine regulation, the Pope visited the Roman patriarchal basilicas in person; he entrusted the visitation of the parishes to a commission to which Borromeo's vicar, Ormaneto, belonged. The "Confraternity of Christian Doctrine," transplanted from Milan to Rome, received such a powerful impetus from Philip Neri and his companion Pietra that people designated "the Roman Reform as the daughter of the Milanese" (Pastor). Convinced that the Tridentine reform decrees were the instrument of Church renewal throughout the world, he took pains to have them published also in mission lands, as far as Mexico, Goa, and the Congo.

The pattern of a vigorous and effective application permeating all aspects of Church life was furnished by Charles Borromeo through his activity at Milan (1565–84). By his personal efforts, his visitations, and his legislation at eleven diocesan and six provincial synods, he became, in Pastor's words, "the paragon of a Tridentine bishop." The regulations he issued for the daily routine and manner of life of his household were evidence of the new spirit: a *praefectus spiritualis* took charge of the spiritual life of the group. A seminary was established in Milan for the training of priests with several minor seminaries attached, among them one for late vocations. He intensified and improved the care of souls by dividing the extensive diocese into twelve districts, each under a trusted deputy. The Jesuits and the Theatines obtained colleges; the schools of Christian Doctrine counted more than twenty thousand pupils in 1595. Borromeo visited in person even the most remote Alpine valleys of his diocese and still found time to travel from place to place in his suffragan sees, such as Bergamo, in his capacity as apostolic visitor. His presence in Rome, where the measures of the "zealot" of Milan had many opponents, restored the situation. The acts of the fourth provincial council were ratified and a papal brief vindicated the archbishop before the Milanese who chafed under his strictness.

Pius V blazed a new trail in the nomination of bishops by instituting a commission of his own for examining candidates. But what was decisive was that Pius V excluded the slightest vacillation in affirming the Tridentine Reform. The Pope's death on 1 May 1572 was suffused with the glory of the victory over the Turks at Lepanto on 7 October 1571, achieved by the fleet of the Holy League with Spain and Venice which he had laboriously brought into being in 1570. He was beatified in 1672 and canonized in 1712.

Gregory XIII

His successor, the canonist Ugo Buoncompagni, originally a curial official, did not possess the ascetical severity and unflinching consistency of his predecessor, but his long pontificate (1572–85) was no less significant for the carrying out of the Council of Trent, in which he had taken part, and the consolidating of the Catholic Reform. Gregory XIII owed his unusually speedy election on 13 May 1572 to the intervention of Philip II. But his frank recognition of Spanish hegemony did not prevent him from defending, with moderation, ecclesiastical jurisdiction in Milan and Naples and even in Spain against the Spanish state Church. In 1576 he concluded, with a mild verdict, the trial of Archbishop Carranza of Toledo, indicted by the Spanish Inquisition whom Pius V already had summoned to Rome. Jealously concerned for his independence, he allowed only a restricted influence on his decisions to even his most intimate adviser. In the application of the Tridentine norms he was more open than his predecessor to considerations of ecclesiastical politics.

Gregory's chief merit was to have transformed the nunciatures into instruments of Church reform. They had in the past never been exclusively diplomatic agencies, but now their ecclesiastical duties moved so far into the foreground that a generation later it could be claimed: "On them depends to a great extent the restoration of religion, worship, and ecclesiastical government" (Pastor). To the existing permanent nunciatures at the Catholic courts — the Emperor, Spain, France, Portugal, Poland, Venice, Florence, Savoy — were added nunciatures, expressly for reform, in Upper Germany, Switzerland, and Lower Germany, which carried out duties like those of the apostolic visitors in Italy and were the origin of the permanent nunciatures in Lucerne (1579), Graz (1580), and Cologne (1584). The view, widespread under Paul III and his successors, that Germany was lost to the Church, was now abandoned. The "German Congregation," formed by Pius V and comprising experts on German affairs, acquired a clear picture of conditions and from 1573 coordinated relevant measures.

Since the enforcing of the Tridentine decree on seminaries encountered serious difficulties in the imperiled lands, Gregory XIII encouraged the expanding of existing Roman colleges to care for the training of clerics and founded new ones. By virtue of these educational foundations Gregory XIII inaugurated a development of incalculable significance: Rome, long a center of ecclesiastical administration, became likewise a center of theological scholarship and of the training of clerics for the Universal Church.

Finally, identified with the name of Gregory XIII is the reform of the Julian Calendar, projected long before. Now, after the views of numerous scholars had been obtained, agreement was reached on February 1582. The synchronization of the astronomical with the calendar year was assured by dropping ten days (5–14 October 1582) and introducing a new rule for leap years.

Sixtus V

Like that of 1565–66, the conclave after the death of Gregory XIII (4 April 1585) was virtually free from the influence of the great powers. Cardinal Medici, supported by the French against Farnese, succeeded in having the Friar Minor Felice Peretti of Montalto elected on 24 April 1585, and thereby brought a towering personality to the highest office in the Church. Sixtus V (1585–90) combined in himself the strictly ecclesiastical outlook of Pius V, who had raised him to the purple in 1570, with the statesmanlike gifts of a Paul III, which the papacy needed even more than in Paul's day if it was to maintain its independence. His inflexible sovereign will impressed its features on the Roman Curia and on the City of the Popes for centuries. His most important contribution to the Catholic Reform was the reorganization of the Roman Curia.

Yielding to the firm wishes of the Popes, the Council of Trent had waived the *reformatio capitis.* But the existing organs of government — the plenary meeting of the cardinals (Consistory) and the central administrative offices handed down from the Middle Ages (Chancery and *Camera*) — though meanwhile purged of the grossest abuses, were no longer adequate for the mounting tasks of the reform Popes. Ever since the Catholic Reform had gained a foothold in Rome, the Popes had proceeded to depute the weightiest tasks to commissions of cardinals, several of which had, because they were permanent, already acquired administrative authority. By a bull issued on 22 January 1588, Sixtus V created fifteen permanent congregations of cardinals with carefully circumscribed competence and administrative character. Six directed the government of the Papal State. The others tended to the business of the Universal Church — Inquisition, Index, the Council, Bishops, Regulars, the Consistory, the *Signatura Gratiae,* Rites, and Vatican Printing Press. From 1588 on the participation of the cardinals in the government of the Church was discharged in the congregations. At the same time the number of cardinals, limited to twenty-four by the Council of Constance, was fixed at seventy — six cardinal bishops, fifty cardinal priests, fourteen cardinal deacons — and a new list of titular churches and deaconries was drawn up. The Pope filled the vacancies by creating thirty-three new cardinals.

The closer union of the members with the head was promoted by the new arrangement of the visit to Rome on the part of bishops (*visitatio liminum*), dated 20 December 1585. On the occasion of the visit a report on the state of ecclesiastical life (*Relatio status diocesis*) was to be submitted in a definitely prescribed form. At that time they frequently constituted the point of departure for papal reform instructions. In this way the steps taken by the Pope became a "turning point and permanent factor of the Catholic Reformation" (Schmidlin).

Obsessed with a passion for building, Sixtus V undertook to make Rome, by means of imposing buildings and of a carefully supervised city planning, the most beautiful city in Europe and at the same time the center of the world. The cupola of Saint Peter's was completed by Giaconio della Porta; together with the obelisk set up in the Piazza San Pietro and the palace designed by Domenico Fontana, it is still for every Roman pilgrim the distinctive landmark of the Eternal City. The tortuous complex of buildings at the Lateran Basilica, though sacred because of a millennium of history, had to make way for a new construction. The principal church of the Jesuits, the Gesù, begun in 1568 and erected according to the plans of Vignola and Giaconio della Porta, was consecrated on 25 November 1584, the first great monument of Roman Baroque architecture. The Chiesa Nuova of the Oratorians was under construction. The medieval city, hitherto confined to the bend of the Tiber, reached out again to the hills which had been built up in Roman imperial days but now lay desolate. On the Quirinal Gregory XIII had begun to construct in a more healthy location a new residence, which was finished by Paul V a generation later. Other newly laid out streets facilitated the pilgrimage to the seven principal churches, a custom revived by Philip Neri. The crowning of the columns of Trajan and Marcus Aurelius with the statues of the Apostles Peter and Paul symbolized the Pope's aims for the construction of a new Baroque Rome. Rome had become a "new city," whose progress in the epoch of the Catholic Reform left far behind all other cities of Europe.

The limits to the creative aims of this great Pope, to whom are due also the new construction of the Vatican Library and the establishment of the Vatican Press, became apparent in his solution of a scholarly task which the Council of Trent had planned but had not achieved — the revision of the Vulgate Bible. For decades the learned Sirleto had been doing preliminary work for the revision of both the Greek and the Latin texts of the Bible. The commission set up by Sixtus V for the revision of the Vulgate, to which, among others, Cardinal Carafa belonged, took great pains but proceeded too slowly to suit the impatient Pope. He had them turn over the data to him and through arbitrary manipulations so altered the sacred text that the edition, which appeared in print on 2 May 1590, had to be recalled after the Pope's death on 27 August 1590, though it had already been sent to twenty-five princes and the accompanying bull of introduction had been published. A new commission, set up by Gregory XIV and headed by Cardinal Colonna, eliminated the crudest blunders. At Robert Bellarmine's suggestion the edition thus rectified was published by Clement VIII in 1592 as the *Sixto-Clementina.*

The Tridentine generation died out with three popes who followed one another in rapid succession; all of them had personally taken part in the Council. Urban VII (15–27 September 1590), Gregory XIV (5 December 1590–16 October 1591), and Innocent IX (29 October–30 December 1591) had cooperated actively, as bishops or nuncios, in the carrying out of the Council decrees. The pious but ailing Gregory XIV continued the Council's reform work by regulating the procedure for determining the qualifications of candidates for the episcopacy.

Clement VIII

Like the three preceding ones, the conclave of 10–30 January 1592 was strongly influenced by Spain. It did elect Ippolito Aldobrandini, who was equally acceptable though far weaker. Clement VIII (1592–1605) disappointed Spanish hopes, however, when, after much hesitation, he granted absolution to Henry IV of France despite the powerful opposition of Philip II. Thereby the papacy recovered its political freedom of movement, was enabled to act as mediator in the arranging of the Franco-Spanish Peace of Vervins (1598).

In his person Clement VIII embodied the episcopal ideal of the Catholic Reform. He led the austere life of a devoted priest and zealous bishop, made a monthly pilgrimage on foot to the seven principal churches, heard confessions in Saint Peter's for hours at a time during the Jubilee Year, made the visitation of the patriarchal basilicas and of several monasteries and hospitals. He chose Baronius as his confessor and honored Philip Neri as a father. The reform movement nevertheless lost ground under Clement. The quarrel which had erupted between Dominicans and Jesuits on the question of grace Clement left undecided, and he was unable to make up his mind in regard to promulgating the new collection of decretals, which was completed and was supposed to bear his name. Though as a former nuncio in Poland he was in no sense politically inexperienced, the conscientious but indecisive Pope abandoned the conduct of affairs almost entirely to his nephews, Cincius and Peter Aldobrandini, and threw the papal finances into disorder by excessive gifts to his family.

Despite these weaknesses of the Aldobrandini Pope the Jubilee Year of 1600 turned out to be a triumph for the regenerated papacy. When, on 31 December 1599, Clement VIII opened the Holy Door, 80,000 persons were present. The total number of pilgrims was estimated at 1.2 million. In order to accommodate at least a portion of the teeming masses, the Hospice of Santa Trinita dei Pellegrini, founded by Philip Neri, was enlarged. In order to gain the indulgence fifteen churches had to be visited by the foreign pilgrims, thirty by the Romans.

A generation had sufficed to change the face of the Church. Following the close of the Council of Trent the Popes had carried its decrees like a banner and had gathered and encouraged the religious forces at hand. The papacy's authority was restored, if not throughout the medieval *Respublica Christiana,* at least within the peoples that had remained Roman Catholic. The restoration of papal power by means of the Council of Trent was not a sly trick of power-hungry curialists, but the natural result of the Catholic Reform, sought sincerely though not always with strict consistency and complete success. The new centralization, replacing the fiscally oriented late medieval centralization, was based on religious and spiritual foundations. The papacy had given the norms of Trent validity. One Bible, the Vulgate; one liturgy, the Roman; one Law Code guaranteed unity and effected a far greater uniformity of Church life than the pre-Tridentine Church had known. But the Tridentine Reform was no mere restoration of the Middle Ages. In almost all its manifestations it displayed anti-Reformation characteristics. From the affirmation of its own special nature it drew the strength for self-renewal and self-assertion.

CHAPTER 100

Self-Assertion of the Church in Western and Eastern Europe

From the close of the Council of Trent the Catholic Reform had been canalized and coordinated — it was virtually identical with the enforcement of the Tridentine decrees under papal leadership. Proceeding from the medieval view that the secular arm must cooperate, the Popes exerted themselves, though not always to the same degree, to secure the acceptance of the Council by the state, successfully in Spain, the Spanish Netherlands, and Poland, unsuccessfully in France. The two "religious wars" of the period, in which political as well as religious power struggles were decided — the Huguenot Wars and the Revolt of the Netherlands ended at the turn of the century. The French monarchy and the southern Netherlands were saved for the Roman Church; the northern Netherlands were lost. The Anglican state Church was consolidated in England, Calvinism in Scotland; only in Ireland did the majority of the people remain Catholic. The return of the Swedish King John III and his son Sigismund to the Church cost the latter his throne. In Poland, recently recovered, Catholic Reform made progress and raised hopes of a union with the Russian Orthodox Church.

Spain and the Netherlands

Under Philip II (1556–98), sincerely religious and conscientious but indecisive and aloof, Spain was the Church's strongest support and the leading European power. It was only after detailed consideration that he decided to accept the Council's decrees, with the restrictive clause "without prejudice to the rights of the crown." These included the *placet* for papal dispensations, the *recursus ab abusu* — the right to appeal to the secular power against abuses of the spiritual power — the autonomy of the Spanish Inquisition, and the *patronato* in the colonies. It would, however, be unfair to condemn the "ecclesiastical establishment" of Philip II for its numerous interventions in the sphere of Church jurisdiction and to disregard entirely the King's zeal in effecting the Catholic Reform when this work encountered resistance, chiefly from exempt canons and Orders, and sought support in Rome. The papal nuncios were in a difficult position whenever they had to champion papal complaints about state interference with the Church.

Even though the Tridentine reform decrees by no means complied with all the desires of the Spanish episcopate, the bishops, at the royal command, set a good example to all other countries by promulgating them in provincial and diocesan synods. Several Tridentine seminaries, the founding of which started early in Spain, could not be maintained because whose liable for contributions opposed giving them. The unreformed Orders had to put up with serious interference based on Pius V's briefs of 2 December 1566 and 16 April 1567.

Long before the ecclesiastical organization of the mother country had been carried further, three new ecclesiastical provinces had been established in the Spanish Netherlands on 12 May 1559, at the request of Philip II: Cambrai, Mechlin,

Utrecht. The imperial bishopric of Liege remained in the province of Cologne. Of the eighteen sees fourteen were new.

The national opposition to Spanish rule was bound up with religious opposition, chiefly Calvinist. While Margaret of Parma was governor, the "Geusen" (so called from *gueux,* the beggars) had demanded the mitigation of Charles V's edicts on religion (the "placards"), the abolition of the Inquisition, and the convocation of the States General. An iconoclasm in 1566 destroyed irreplaceable works of Christian art. The "Council of Troubles," set up by the Duke of Alba, could not suppress the revolt, but the statesmanship of the governor Alessandro Farnese, Margaret's son, succeeded in having the almost wholly Catholic southern provinces break away from the Pacification of Ghent (1576). The mostly Protestant northern provinces, allied in the Union of Utrecht (1579), proclaimed their independence in 1581 and, at first under William of Orange (assassinated in 1584) and then under his son Maurice (1585–1625), carried on the war against Spain until the truce of 1609. In the States General all Catholic worship had been forbidden since 1574. The care of the still numerous Catholics was provided in an insufficient manner under the direction of a vicar apostolic in Utrecht.

The Council of Trent had been accepted by the governor, Margaret of Parma, on 11 July 1565, with the same reservations as in Spain, but the political confusion, together with the not infrequent resistance of the clergy, delayed enforcement. Definite progress came only in the governorship of the Archdukes Albrecht and Isabella.

France

In France, too, the Church was engaged in a struggle for existence which was not conducive to the progress of the Catholic Reform. Like the revolt of the Netherlands, the Huguenot Wars (1562–98) were never purely a religious conflict. They became more and more a power struggle between the Houses of Bourbon and Guise, with Spain intervening on the side of the Catholics, England and the States General of the Netherlands on the side of the Calvinists. Correspondingly, the papal policy was straightforward when the preservation of Catholicism and the suppression of Calvinism was or seemed to be in question, but cautious vis-à-vis the political power groups, especially the League of Henry of Guise, Charles of Bourbon, and Philip II, established in 1576 and revived in 1584.

The Edict of Amboise (1563), which ended the First Huguenot War, granted Calvinists the right of worship in one town of each *bailliage.* When, not satisfied with this success and supported by English money and German troops, they again took up arms, Pius V sent subsidies and a military force, only to be disillusioned when the Huguenots, several times defeated, were accorded freedom of religion in the Peace of Saint-Germain (1570). In an effort to shield her son, Charles IX, from the influence of the Huguenot leader, Admiral De Coligny, Catherine de Médicis sought to remove the latter by assassination. When this proved unsuccessful, she tried to conceal the crime by a still greater one, the Massacre of Saint Bartholomew's Day, 24 August 1572. Misled by euphemistic and misleading reports, Gregory XIII saw in this damnable act, proceeding from an unscrupulous greed for power, the thwarting of a treasonable attempt against the King and a victory over Calvinism. He prescribed a Te Deum and personally attended a thanksgiving service in the French national church of San Luigi. He played no part in the preparation and execution of the crime, which claimed between five thousand and ten thousand victims.

The opposition of the Huguenots became even more bitter. In the Fifth Religious War they obtained from the weak Henry III in the Peace of Beaulieu (1576) almost complete religious freedom, but in the following year it was again restricted by the Edict of Poitiers. The danger that the French crown would devolve on a Calvinist became acute when, on the death of the younger brother of the childless Henry III, the Bourbon Henry of Navarre was recognized as his successor by the King and also by many Catholics. Though Sixtus V did not actually join the Catholic League formed against Henry of Navarre, he forever excluded him from the succession in 1585 as a relapsed heretic. The League gained military ascendancy and in 1588 forced Henry III to issue the Edict of Rouen, which envisaged the suppression of Calvinism. To rid himself of pressure from the League, the King a half year later procured the murder of its leaders, Henry and Louis of Guise, at Blois and allied himself with Henry of Navarre, only to be himself stabbed to death by the Dominican Jacques Clément on 1 August 1589. Henry of Navarre, who as Henry IV had very quickly promised to protect the rights of the Catholic Church and who also had a strong Catholic following, found a steadily increasing recognition, particularly after he had returned to the Church on 25 July 1593. Henry IV maintained the upper hand and, when, though remaining indifferent to religion ("Paris is worth a Mass"), he approached the Pope, Clement VIII condescended to absolve him under specific conditions. By the Edict of Nantes (30 April 1598) Henry IV granted to the Calvinists unrestricted freedom of conscience, access to political office, the right to worship publicly in all places where this was allowed in 1596–97 and in two places in every *bailliage,* and finally possession of 200 strongholds for eight years. These were quite extraordinary rights, but the crown and the vast majority of the people remained Catholic and once again France was a Catholic power. In politics Sixtus V had felt that in regard to Spain he was impotent, "like a fly facing an elephant." But now the papacy had again achieved a limited political independence.

The reception of the Council of Trent in France ran into strong opposition from the partly Huguenot, partly Gallican-minded, jurists of the highest tribunals, the *parlement,* in which every law valid in France had to be registered. The Calvinists Du Moulin and Gentillet denied the binding force of both the dogmatic and the reform decrees; the Gallicans Ranchin and Thou rejected only the reform measures. To what extent the publication of the Council by order of the state was a sign of the King's religious conviction is evident from the advice given to Henry IV by Cardinal Gondi, Archbishop of Paris: "Publish the Council of Trent!" Although the clergy again presented a petition, the King, influenced by the Gallicans Harlay and Thou, did not in 1600 live up to the promise he had given through his proxies before his absolution. Gallican anti-Trent journalism was strong enough to bring about the definite denial of acceptance by the state at the Estates General of 1614.

Meanwhile, the bishops, left to themselves, had begun to carry out the Council. The reform will of bishops and clergy finally proved sufficiently strong to proceed without regard to the state. At the assembly of the clergy in Paris on 7 July 1615, three cardinals, forty-seven archbishops and bishops, and thirty deputies of the rest of the clergy swore to accept (*recevoir*) and to carry out (*observer*) the Council of Trent. This decision produced a powerful reform wave and formed the prelude to the steep ascent of the French Church in the next generation. Until this moment there had been, despite isolated and usually short-lived foundations, "a search for a solution of the seminary problem" (Broutin) It was not only the known opposition to financing it that had delayed the realization of the Tridentine decree on seminaries, but also the rivalry of the universities and the Jesuit colleges and the absence of a clearly formulated ideal. In the course of the seventeenth century France finally became the leader in this field through its development of various types of priestly formation — Bourdoise, the Sulpicians, the Eudists.

England

By means of the Act of Uniformity of 1559 — slightly mitigated by substituting "Supreme Governor" for "Supreme Head" — Elizabeth I of England had effectively renewed the Anglican Schism; the reintroduction of the *Book of Common Prayer* and the Thirty-Nine Articles of 1563 had restored the creed and liturgy of Edward VI in the English state Church. Of the sixteen bishops who had functioned under Mary the Catholic, fifteen were deposed for rejecting the Oath of Supremacy and for the most part replaced by clerics who had taken refuge on the continent during the Catholic Restoration. The overwhelming majority of the parish clergy took the oath, and the laity were encouraged by the threat of considerable fines to frequent the Anglican worship. Just the same, the Queen, who was well versed in all diplomatic tricks and was supported at Rome by Spanish efforts of pacification, knew how to ward off the menacing blow until such time as her throne was secured against every assault from within.

It was not until 25 February 1570 that Pius V pronounced the major excommunication against Elizabeth I and her deposition. The bull of excommunication aggravated the situation of the English Catholics all the more in that Mary Stuart, a prisoner in England since 1568, was regarded as the Catholics' claimant to the throne, and hence, on the outbreak of war with Spain, they came under suspicion of high treason. From 1581 death was the penalty for celebrating Mass, administering the Sacraments, and sheltering priests. One hundred and twenty-four priests and sixty-one lay persons were executed, including the Jesuit Campion. A college was established at Douai (1568) by William Allen (cardinal in 1587, died 1594) to train priests for the extremely dangerous ministry to the English Catholics, who continued to exist despite all measures of suppression. The Jesuit Persons founded similar institutes at Valladolid and at Eu and Saint-Omer, and there were English colleges in Rome and Reims.

The Anglican Church was consolidated under the Archbishops of Canterbury, Parker (1559–76) and Whitgift (1583–1604). The Elizabethan establishment, attacked by the Presbyterian Cartwright, was justified and defended in the eight books of Richard Hooker's *Laws of Ecclesiastical Polity.*

The ruin of the Catholic Church in Scotland was sealed in the enactments of the Parliament of Edinburgh in 1560. The religious discussions of Aberdeen and Edinburgh and Ninian Winzet's literary defense (1562) could do nothing to alter the *fait accompli.* Following the Queen's forced but not undeserved abdication in 1567, the suppression of Catholics gained in intensity. Four priests were condemned to death for having celebrated Mass. The care of the few remaining Catholics was exercised mostly by priests who had fled from England. James' cleverly feigned inclination toward Catholicism and his wife's conversion did not keep him from further increasing the penal laws against Catholics after his accession to the English throne as James I (1603–25).

Only the Irish successfully resisted the introduction of the Anglican Church in the Emerald Isle. Their attachment to the ancestral faith, kept alive by native priests and by missionaries sent from Rome, was identified with the struggle against England.

Poland, Sweden, and Russia

King Sigismund II Augustus of Poland (1548–72), whose wavering attitude had made possible the progress of Lutheranism and later of Calvinism and the anti-Trinitarians, accepted the Tridentine decrees in 1564, but the "Warsaw Confederation" of the mainly Protestant nobility interceded in favor of the equality of the dissidents with the Catholics (1573). The Catholic renewal got under way with King Stephen Bathory (1575–86). Deeply Catholic, yet tolerant, and inspired by bold projects, he had the cooperation of the Nuncios. The Provincial Council of Piotrkov (1577) repudiated the Warsaw Confederation and accepted the Council of Trent. Bishop Karnkowski of Wloctawek founded the first Tridentine seminary. The Jesuit College at Vilna became an academy. The Jesuit Skarga made many conversions, including Prince George Radziwill, who became Bishop of Vilna and a cardinal. Jesuit colleges in Riga and Dorpat worked to recover Livonia for the Roman Church.

The prospect of the restoration of Catholicism in Sweden seemed to be favorable when King John III (1586–92) became a Catholic in 1578 hoping to win the Polish throne. John's son Sigismund, raised a Catholic, had to confirm on oath before his coronation (1594) the exceptional laws demanded by the assembly of the clergy at Uppsala in 1593 against Catholics, including the prohibition of public worship and exclusion from offices of state. After his departure for Poland the last traces of Catholic ritual disappeared, such as the elevation after the consecration. The nuns of the Birgittine convent of Vadstena were expelled. When Sigismund had tried without success to put down the revolt led by his uncle Charles, he was deposed (1599) and the profession of the Catholic faith was severely penalized. The great hopes connected with the conversion of the House of Vasa crumbled.

The same fate befell an approach directed toward Russia. Hard pressed by the victorious Polish King, Czar Ivan the Terrible in 1581 sent an embassy to Rome to ask mediation for peace and promised to participate in the war against the Turks. Possevino did indeed negotiate a truce between Poland and Russia but in talks with him he discovered no leaning toward union. Disappointed by this failure, Sixtus V now supported Bathory's far-reaching plans: the conquest of Russia, which, after Ivan's death (1584), was weakened by internal dissensions, and then a concentrated assault on the Turkish Empire. They became pointless when Bathory died at the age of only fifty-four and Sigismund Vasa established himself as King against the Curia's candidate, Archduke Maximilian of Austria.

During the long reign of Sigismund III (1587–1632) Polish Catholicism grew progressively stronger. About half the lost churches became Catholic again. A new elite of clergy and laity was formed in the Jesuit colleges of Poznan, Braunsberg, Vilna, Polock, and Lublin, and at the same time popular missions extended the field. The Jesuit Wujek produced a Polish translation of the Bible and a *Catholic Prayer Book* which was used for three centuries. Two synods, which the Ecumenical Patriarch Jeremias II held in connection with his journey to Moscow for the consecration of the patriarch (1589), were unable to settle the disputes among the Orthodox bishops. This situation is the key to the origin and fortune of the Union of Brest (1596).

As early as 1590 the four Orthodox bishops of Tuck, Chelmno, Lwow, and Przemysl had declared their readiness, under specific conditions, to break with the Metropolitan of Kiev and attach themselves to Rome. But the declaration had no sequel. A new statement of Bishops Terlecki of Tuck and Pociej of Vladimir, in Torczyn at the end of 1594, was followed by discussions with the representative of the nuncio in Cracow. Even before a settlement had been reached, Prince Ostrogski's violent opposition decided the King to send Terlecki and Pociej to Rome, where on 23 December 1595 they returned to the Union of Florence. The Bull of Union allowed the Ruthenians to retain their rite; bishops were to be named by the metropolitan, who was himself to be elected by the bishops. The Synod of Brest (6–10 October 1596) accepted the union; a countersynod, held at the same time excommunicated the Uniates. In addition to Ostrogski, the union was resisted by a group of theologians, notably the future Ecumenical Patriarch Kyrill Lukaris, who was under Calvinist influence, and the lay brotherhoods, which had been ignored during discussions of the Synod.

Recognized as such by the King alone, but not, like the Latin bishops, admitted into the Senate, the Uniates held their own. But they were unable to prevent persons from going over to the Latin Rite, favored by the Polish side, though this had been forbidden by the Congregation of Propaganda since 1624. Alongside the constantly expanding Church of the Latin Rite, the Uniate Church declined more and more in importance. Its status found no improvement until the accession of the Orthodox bishops of Galicia to the union in 1681.

CHAPTER 101

Crisis and Turning Point in Central Europe

As the Council of Trent was finishing its work, the Catholic Church in Germany seemed to be on the point of total dissolution. The Religious Peace of Augsburg had not halted the Protestant movement. The majority of the secular princes and the great Free Cities had joined it; a large part of the nobility and of the cities in the Catholic territories had done the same. Episcopate and clergy had by no means overcome their defeatism; slight was their concern for self-reform, and their will for self-defense was weak. The more precise doctrinal clarification effected at Trent was the first step toward recovery and the prerequisite for taking the second step, which was much more difficult, namely, the implementation of the Council's reform measures, enacted virtually without the cooperation of the German episcopate and hence not adapted to the German situation.

The determining of confessional allegiance was settled by the Religious Peace of Augsburg; it was definitively and by law taken away from Emperor and Empire and transferred to the states; thus making acceptance of the Council of Trent by the Empire an impossibility. Nothing of the sort could be expected from the Protestant-minded, "enigmatic emperor," Maximilian II (1564–76). However, at the Regensburg Diet of 1576, to which Cardinal Morone had been sent as legate, it was possible to prevent ratification of the *Declaratio Ferdinandea,* which would have undermined both the principle contained, but not expressly formulated, in the Religious Peace — "Cuius regio, eius et religio" — and the Ecclesiastical Reservation. The significance of these for the preservation of Catholicism revealed itself even more clearly. To avoid the appearance of violating the Religious Peace, the Catholic estates maintained a cool reserve in regard to the Council.

Furthermore, even public opinion was unfavorable to Trent. A new kind of leadership, which would in itself embody the Tridentine ideal of the shepherd of souls, had to develop and implant the ideal in others. Hence, apart from a few starts, the Tridentine Reform made general progress only from the turn of the century. This process took place amid the formation of denominations and the struggle for self-assertion.

The delimitation of the "confessions" was much slower and required much more time than was formerly thought. Only by having people make the Tridentine Profession of Faith, "will it be possible to ascertain who is of the Catholic Religion and who is opposed to it." declared the Würzburg Cathedral Chapter in a resolution to this effect of 3 March 1570. The determining factor, in accord with the Religious Peace, was the right of the territorial state to determine religious adherence, but in practice there were barriers of different kinds, such as consideration for neighboring princes of another creed and the opposition of the estates.

Nevertheless, the territorial state first fixed the clearly changing ecclesiastical map of the Empire. Where there existed an impossibility or an unwillingness to adopt a definite viewpoint, odd mixtures resulted, as on the Lower Rhine. Into the seventeenth century it is at times impossible exactly to determine from reports of visitations to which denomination the pastors belonged. Because the indult granting the chalice to the laity obliterated the frontier between denominations, it fell into disuse. The attitude of the laity toward the officially imposed religion differed from place to place. But on both sides there were convinced and loyal believers, who remained steadfast in the midst of an alien religious environment or emigrated elsewhere. Repeated shifts of religious allegiance on the part of the government, led not infrequently, of course, to insecurity of faith and to indifference.

The Tridentine Reform took hold first of all in the ecclesiastical province of Salzburg, where, since the beginning of the religious cleavage, the reform efforts of the bishops had never been entirely broken off. All clerics were obliged to make the Tridentine Profession of Faith and to observe celibacy. These measures and the diocesan synods had only meager success. The "definitive victory of the Tridentine renewal" (Oswald) was not achieved until after the turn of the century, when shepherds of souls in the spirit of the new episcopal ideal assumed leadership — Hausen in Regensburg (1600–1613), Gebeck in Freising (1618–51), Lodron in Salzburg (1619–53). Passau, from 1598 to 1664 dominated by Habsburg archdukes, obtained capable administrators. In the Austrian part of this extensive bishopric the dynasty decided the issue anyway.

The strength of Protestantism in Austria was gradually broken after the suppression of a peasant uprising by the "General Reformation" (1597–1602) decreed by Emperor Rudolf II; from 1600 Jesuits were active in Linz.

In Franconia leadership was assumed by the city of Würzburg under Julius Echter von Mespelbrunn (1574–1617), equally outstanding as bishop and statesman. A Jesuit college, with a seminary attached, had already been founded by his predecessor, Bishop Wirsberg (1558–73). Without binding himself strictly to the letter of the Tridentine decrees and always maintaining a certain independence even toward Rome, von Mespelbrunn combined the internal renewal of the diocese, through visitations and by establishing the university, with the reconversion of the, since 1585, mostly Protestant subjects of his see. His activity is the classical example of combining the Catholic Reform with Counter Reformation.

In Constance, a new era dawned with Bishop Jakob von Fugger (1604–26) in the diocesan synod of 1609. The statutes of the synod were printed and later repeatedly renewed and reprinted, and a visitation was made by the bishop.

Of the Rhenish archbishoprics only Trier under Jakob von Eltz (1567–81), energetic both as a bishop and as a territorial prince, was exposed relatively early to the reform, which was actually carried out by Archbishop Johann von Schönenberg (1581–99). Under Schweikard von Cronberg, another alumnus of the Germanicum, the Rhenish part of the see was brought back to Catholicism; his "Order of Reformation" (1615) could be regarded as a substitute for a Tridentine diocesan synod. The realization of the Tridentine Reform, "for which efforts had been made in Mainz for a century without real success" (Brück), fell to the lot of the great Johann Philip von Schönborn after the Thirty Years' War.

That the most serious danger to the stability of the prince-bishoprics was internal is indicated by events in Strasbourg and Cologne. In Johann von Manderscheid (1569–92) the see of Strasbourg had had a zealous reform prelate. Nevertheless, after his death a Protestant-minded minority in the cathedral chapter elected Johann Georg von Brandenburg. The Catholics chose the Cardinal Charles II of Guise, who established himself with French aid and obtained imperial investiture with the see after he had accepted as his coadjutor the Archduke Leopold. In Cologne under the successors of Adolf von Schaumburg, who was well disposed toward reform, Protestant infiltration made great progress, and the cathedral chapter entered into negotiations with the rebel Dutch for the secularization of the see. With Cologne the remnants of Catholicism in North Germany, in fact the very continuance of the Catholic Empire, were in danger; the loss of Cologne would have meant the loss of the remaining archiepiscopal sees of North Germany and would have assured the Protestants a majority in the Electoral College. Ferdinand of Bavaria (1612–50), accepted as coadjutor in 1595, can be regarded as the first Tridentine reform bishop in the Rhenish metropolis. He personally visited the see, at least in part, held five diocesan synods, obliged the pastors to make the Tridentine Profession of Faith, and out of his own resources founded a modest seminary (1615), which lasted only thirty years.

In Münster, where Bishop Hoya (1566–74) and the zealous dean of the chapter, Raestel, had prepared the ground, Ferdinand of Bavaria created "an environment in which Trent could enjoy free operation" (Schroer).

Definitely lost in North Germany through the chapter election of Protestant administrators were the archbishoprics of Magdeburg and Bremen and the prince-bishoprics of Minden, Halberstadt, Verden, and Lübeck.

Not until the struggle over the Religious Peace of Augsburg and the carrying out of the Tridentine Reform in the last third of the sixteenth century was it decided that the South and West of Germany would remain mostly Catholic. To be sure, one can speak of a "carrying out of the Tridentine Reform" only within limits; it was indeed attempted, but until the turn of the century it was realized only to a very slight degree. None of the three distinguishing marks by which the reform is usually measured is ascertainable in all places — reform synods on the basis of Trent, episcopal visitations according to its norms, and the founding of Tridentine seminaries.

Not until toward the end of the century did a new class of ecclesiastical leadership appear. The cathedral chapters, which decided the choice of the bishops and which regarded themselves as coowners and corulers of the sees, were, partly through papal provision, interspersed with elements zealous for reform, especially from the Collegium Germanicum. While the bourgeois were not excluded, preference was shown to students of noble birth, out of regard for the current capitular statutes, with the result that, of the 800 students who had entered the college by 1600, six became bishops and eight auxiliary bishops. Mainz, the highest ranking bishopric in the Empire, had from 1604 to 1647 three archbishops who had come from the Germanicum.

The Tridentine ideal of the bishop as shepherd of souls was found in only a few individuals, and in none of these to a very high degree. The prince-bishop had to prove himself as a prince. Only with the prestige stemming from his status of territorial lord could he maintain the Catholic character at least of his own see. The struggle forced upon the Church for her very existence led to a flagrant violation of the Tridentine prohibition of pluralism. In order to preserve Cologne for the Church, and the even more seriously exposed North German sees of Paderborn and Hildesheim, as well as Liège, threatened by its Dutch neighbors, these bishoprics were given to Bavarian princes; thereby ecclesiastical interests were joined to dynastic, so that for almost two hundred years there existed on the Lower Rhine a sort of Bavarian secundogeniture. In these cases of pluralism, tolerated rather than encouraged by the Popes, was revealed the importance of the Wittelsbach and Habsburg dynasties in maintaining Catholicism and the Tridentine Reform. Wherever re-Catholicization of territories almost or completely lost was undertaken, it was done upon the initiative of the territorial lord, that is, the estate.

Inner renewal in the spirit of Trent came to the German Church not from its own strength but through the use of existing political means and through help from abroad. Not bishops but secular princes, the Bavarian Wittelsbachs, led the way with the strict implementation of the right to determine religious allegiance as guaranteed to, the territorial prince by the Religious Peace. In all Germany there was no succession of princes so resolutely Catholic as Albrecht V, Wilhelm I, and Maximilian I of Bavaria. The Habsburgs followed them only a generation later, after overcoming strong opposition from their estates.

It is difficult to imagine how the Tridentine Reform could have made progress if the Popes had not kept the episcopate under unrelenting pressure through nuncios. The lack of suitable personnel for education and the care of souls was somewhat remedied by the introduction of the Orders, especially of those originating in the course of Catholic Reform — the Society of Jesus and the Capuchins.

The network of Jesuit colleges, in which the future Catholic elite was formed, became ever more widespread between 1564 and 1618, particularly in the Habsburg territories, but also in the West and North, where they proved to be the strongest centers of the renewal.

No oil was poured on troubled waters by the court confessors, such as Blyssem and Viller in Graz and Mengin in Munich, whose presence was at first resented by their superiors, but who were in a position to contribute to the direction of the ecclesiastical policies of the courts. However, their influence has often been overestimated. Far more effective and influential were others: Peter Canisius, as organizer of his Order in Germany, as agent of the Popes in matters of ecclesiastical policies, as teacher, preacher, and writer, et al. The undeniable success of the Jesuits explains the hate they inspired in Protestants.

Shortly before the turn of the century the Capuchins entered the lists on the side of the Jesuits as popular preachers, confessors, and missionaries in Tirol (Innsbruck, 1593), Salzburg (1596), and Bavaria (Munich, 1600).

As in the Empire, in Switzerland also Tridentine Reform and self-assertion in the face of Protestantism went hand in hand; and the forces and counterforces in action were similar. The implementing of the Council began in the Catholic central parts of Switzerland and was supported by the lay authorities when the bishops of Constance, whose responsibility it was, failed to act.

The Abbots of Einsiedeln and Sankt Gallen, Joachim Eichhorn and Othmar Kunz, were able to boast at the diocesan synod of Constance in 1560 that they had "fully observed and carried out" the Council. Internally regenerated, the two great abbeys fortified a consciousness of the faith in all of Catholic Switzerland.

The self-assertion of the Church in Central Europe and the progress of the Tridentine Reform, together with the ending of the Huguenot Wars, the continuing union of the southern Netherlands with Spain, and the consolidation of Catholicism in Poland, made it possible after the turn of the century to regard the crisis of the religious cleavage, if not as overcome, at least as definitely checked. Contributing not a little to this outcome was the weakening of the Protestant front resulting from the conflict between Calvinists and Lutherans. The deepest cause, however, lay in the reinvigoration of the spiritual and intellectual substance of ecclesiastical life, which was manifested in the flowering of theology, of religious life, and of piety.

Section Three

Religious Forces and Intellectual Content of the Catholic Renewal

Chapter 102

The Revival of Scholasticism—Michael Baius and the Controversy over Grace

Just as in the Middle Ages the flowering of scholasticism was intimately connected with the rise of the universities, so now its revival was associated with the formation of new centers in the development of the European universities. Now, as before, the University of Paris maintained its great authority in doctrinal decisions; this was impaired only by the university's Gallicanism and its opposition to the aspiring Society of Jesus. Alongside Paris new centers of theological activity sprang up from the second third of the sixteenth century. In Louvain, which through Latomus, Driedo, and Tapper had very early joined Cologne in opposing Luther and had strengthened its reputation through the presence of its professors at Trent in 1551–52, Augustinianism received a new stimulus at the hands of Baius, Hessels, and the older Jansenius. The revival of scholasticism, which stamped its character on the era, did not, however, proceed from these universities situated on the very battlefield of religious innovation, but from Spain, whose universities at the time of the Council of Trent and until the turn of the century exercised a leadership similar to that of the Spain of Philip II in politics.

At Salamanca the Dominican Francisco de Vitoria, as holder of the first theological chair at the university, the *Catedra de prima,* founded a theological school which spread not only in Spain and Portugal but even to Rome and Germany. Of the seven chairs of theology, six were reserved for speculative theology, and for these the Dominicans of the Colegio San Esteban competed with members of the other mendicant Orders. In addition, there were four chairs of Greek and two of Hebrew. Even more keenly was positive theology pursued at Alcalá, in keeping with the aim of Ximenes, the founder.

In the last third of the century Rome overtook the Spanish universities through the brilliance at the Jesuits' Roman College of stars of the first magnitude, all of them Spaniards, except Bellarmine: Francisco de Toledo, Maldonado, Suárez, Vázquez, Ruiz. They made Rome what it had never been in the Middle Ages or in the Renaissance — a stronghold of theological study. Theologians of the rising Society of Jesus carried the revitalized scholasticism to the German universities of Ingolstadt and Dillingen, the "citadels of the Catholic counter-offensive in the Empire" (Willaerts).

How did the spirit and method of this reinvigorated scholasticism differ from the content and teaching method of the late medieval theological schools?

Whatever the answer to the question of Luther's nominalism, the fact is that this school of thought had scarcely any champions left at the Council of Trent. There the Franciscans had numerically the strongest representation, but the Dominicans were best able to undertake the defense of the Church against Protestantism. Neither of these schools was entirely able to free itself from the influence of Humanism, which was strongest in the Augustinian School led by Seripando. Above all, the fact that the Protestants asserted the sufficiency of Scripture and invoked the authority of the Fathers on behalf of the new doctrines forced upon Catholics an intensive preoccupation with the Bible and the witness of Tradition, which were not only given more weight than formerly and consulted at first hand in systematic theology but also led to the establishment of an autonomous domain of positive theology. Both revived scholasticism and controversial theology were committed to positive theology. Four new approaches resulted from this return to the positive data of revelation contained in Scripture and Tradition.

First, the new scholasticism proceeding from Salamanca sought, like the medieval, to reconcile *fides* and *ratio* but dispensed with the ballast, amassed in the late Middle Ages, of oversubtle questions amounting to dialectical acrobatics and took as its standard the classical period of scholasticism and especially Thomas Aquinas. Thus the reproof of the *humanists — Perdunt nugis tempora* — was no longer applicable and once more theology became simpler, clearer, and more relevant to life. Second, attacked by humanist and reformer alike, it reexamined the method of theological proof. Third, as controversial theology, it grappled with the theological problems raised by the religious cleavage, but also sought answers to the ethical and juridical questions which became acute with the colonizing activity of the Iberian peoples in the New World. Fourth, in the pastoral spirit of the Council of Trent, it was much concerned with popular religious instruction and preaching. All five Doctors of the Church who lived at this period were eminently practical theologians: Canisius and Bellarmine as compilers of catechisms, John of the Cross as a mystic, Francis de Sales as a teacher of the spiritual life, Lorenzo of Brindisi as a preacher.

Revival of Scholasticism

The "Golden Age of Scholasticism" was inaugurated by the Dominican Francisco de Vitoria (d. 1546). He was introduced to the study of Saint Thomas by another Dominican, Petrus Crockaert, at the University of Paris, but he was also familiar with the investigation of the sources that was going on at Louvain. After his change in 1526 to Salamanca as holder of the first theological chair he based his teaching very largely on the *Summa* of Aquinas. His dynamic lectures, above all on questions of moral theology, and his celebrated conferences (*Relectiones*) had an extraordinary effect on his large audiences, sometimes numbering as many as one thousand people, even though not one of his books was printed in his own lifetime. The *Summa sacramentorum,* compiled by one of his pupils and first printed in 1560, went through more than thirty-three editions and became "the manual of pastoral theology most used by the Spanish clergy in the sixteenth century" (Stegmüller). Thomistic in his basic approach, Vitoria was not narrow-minded. His moderate views on the relationship between Pope and Council determined the attitude of many Spanish bishops at the Council of Trent. His analysis of the ethical and juridical problems of the Spanish Colonial Empire entitles him to be considered the founder of modern international law. Hugo Grotius is heavily indebted to him.

Among the sixty-six doctors of Salamanca who attended the Council of Trent were many bishops and theologians who had sat at Vitoria's feet. His pupil and successor in the chair, the Dominican Melchior Cano (d. 1560), became, through his *De locis theologicis* (1563), the founder of theological methodology. Following the Humanist Rudolf Agricola instead of the Topics of Aristotle in the definition of *loci* (sources), Cano distinguished ten such *loci* (or *domicilia,* as he also called them) from which theological arguments are drawn: Holy Scripture, Apostolic Tradition, the *magisterium* of the Universal Church, the councils, the *magisterium* of the Roman Church, the Fathers, the scholastics and canonists, natural reason, the philosophers, and history. This work made Cano the "father of theological methodology" (Lang).

Though the groundwork for this revival had been laid at the very beginning of the sixteenth century by the great commentators Cajetan and Koellin, Thomism received a powerful stimulus and a wide dissemination from the Salamanca School. In 1567 Pius V proclaimed Aquinas a Doctor of the Church. His *Summa theologiae* gradually supplanted the *Sentences* of Peter Lombard as a textbook. But in the last third of the century a differentiation was beginning to show. The Spanish Dominicans were developing the "classical Thomistic School" (Grabmann), that is, strict Thomism; while the Jesuit School, increasingly prominent, went its own way in both method and doctrine.

Jesuit Theology

The general congregation of 1593 prescribed Thomas as the guide of the Society's theologians, allowing them to depart from him only in exceptional cases and for good reasons (*gravate admodum et rarissime).* The voluntarist and activist tendency of the Society, however, soon made itself felt in theology, both in Spain (Molina) and in Rome and Germany.

Gregorius of Valencia (d. 1603), who had been educated at Salamanca, combined a sound grasp of scholasticism with a humanist attitude and remarkable talent for exposition. As professor at Ingolstadt (1575–97), he contributed to a large degree through the training of numerous pupils — hence his title of *Doctor Doctorum* — to restoring the good name of scholasticism in Germany, where it had been most exposed to contempt by the criticism of humanists and reformers.

Clearly decisive for the further growth of the new scholasticism were its spread to Rome and its development by the great Jesuit theologians, Francisco de Toledo, Bellarmine, Suárez, and Vázquez. Important also as an exegete, Francisco de Toledo (d. 1596), taught from 1559 at the Society's Roman College; in 1593 he became the first Jesuit cardinal. The most profound and most prolific of these men, both in philosophy and in theology, was the *Doctor Eximius,* Francisco Suárez (d. 1617). He produced his works on grace and law — "summing up the achievements of sixteenth-century Spanish theology in natural law, international law, and political philosophy" (Stegmüller) — as well as a large-scale defense of religious Orders and of the Society of Jesus. On several occasions he intervened in the dispute concerning grace to contribute his expert opinion, and Protestant universities also paid attention to his philosophy. Like Suárez, Gabriel Vázquez (d. 1604) was active only briefly (1586–91) at Rome and then returned to Spain. His relationship to Suárez has been compared to that of Scotus to Thomas. An extremely keen-sighted theologian, dreaded as a fiery debater, Vázquez became famed among his contemporaries as a "second Augustine" because of his knowledge of the Fathers of the Church; he entered the dispute over grace as a strict Molinist.

The brightest star of the Jesuit School and the systematizer of controversial theology was Robert Bellarmine (1542–1621). A nephew of Pope Marcellus II, he had already occupied himself with the Protestant concepts as a teacher at Louvain (1570–76), where he distinguished himself as a preacher. Appointed professor of controversial theology at the Roman College (1576–88) and in 1592 its rector, then consultor of the Holy Office and theological adviser to Clement VIII, he won such esteem that the Pope in 1599 made him a cardinal. Because of differences with the Pope over the controversy on grace, he was removed from Rome by his appointment as Archbishop of Capua in 1602, but returned after the death of his former patron and under Paul V took part in all the great disputes in which the papacy was involved: the quarrels with Venice and James I of England and the Galileo case. His *De potestate Pontificis in rebus temporalibus,* composed at this time (1610), which enlarged on the teaching he had already championed in the *Controversies* in regard to the merely indirect power of the Pope in the temporal sphere, met with violent opposition from the advocates of the *potestas directa,* as well as from the Protestants. At the peak of his scholarly activity and finally as a cardinal, Bellarmine remained as devoted to pastoral activity as he had always been. His cause was introduced in 1627 but was suspended by Benedict XIV. He was beatified in 1923 and canonized in 1930; the next year he was declared a Doctor of the Church.

Bellarmine's chief work, the *Disputationes de controversiis fidei* usually called *The Controversies,* is a synthesis of the Catholic controversial theology of the sixteenth century. Though by no means original, it is inspired by a consistent fundamental concept and enriched by an astonishing command of literature. Whereas the Council, because of the opposition of Gallicans and "episcopalists," had avoided a declaration on the concept of the Church, Bellarmine, after a discussion of the sources of revelation — Scripture and Tradition — placed the doctrine of the Church at the beginning (Book I) and only then passed on to the Sacraments (II) and to the doctrine of grace and justification (III).

Michael Baius

At the Council of Trent the moderate Augustinian School led by Seripando had been unable to carry the day. Even before the Council was finished Augustinianism in its strictest form found scholarly and stubborn representatives in the Louvain professors Michael Baius (d. 1589) and Johannes Hessels (d. 1566). When one of their pupils, the Franciscan Sablons at Nivelles, defined the freedom of the will as freedom from external compulsion and expressly declared that Calvin's teaching on the subject was correct, twenty of his propositions were censured by the University of Louvain at the beginning of 1560; both professors concurred with the judgment on eighteen of them. In the summer of the same year the Sorbonne likewise censured eighteen theses of the Franciscan. Baius and Hessels traveled to Trent in 1563; but the Council, then at its worst crisis, did not take up the matter. Baius himself explained his teaching on man's original state, justification, freedom of the will, merit, and also on Sacrifice and sacraments in a collection of treatises (1563–64). Numerous propositions extracted from this work were, at the request of Philip II, censured by the University of Alcalá, and by the University of Salamanca. The University of Louvain then asked Rome for a judgment. After the expanded new edition of the offending book had been censured once more by the University of Alcalá, Pius V in the Bull "Ex omnibus afflictionibus" of 1 October 1567, condemned seventy-nine of the 120 propositions rejected by the Spanish censors in the sense intended by the author, although some of them could have been interpreted in an acceptable sense. Baius submitted to the bull, which had not been made public, later (1569) formally repudiated the errors attributed to him, and in 1575, under oath, professed the faith of the Council of Trent.

Nevertheless, the dispute grew in intensity. A case brought before the Holy Office ended in 1580 with a new condemnation by Gregory XIII. Baius accepted this too in the presence of Francisco de Toledo, who had been dispatched to Louvain, and the Louvain Faculty committed itself to an anti-Baian formulary. As the unquestionably sincere submission of Baius to the several papal judgments shows, his basic attitude was Catholic, but the difficulty of reconciling the decisions of the *magisterium* with the conclusions to which his studies had led him created a genuine conflict of conscience. The Louvain disputes were, however, soon eclipsed by the great Molinist conflict over grace though they did break out again with full force in the Jansenist quarrel of the seventeenth century.

Controversy over Grace

In 1588 there appeared in Lisbon, with the approval of the censor of the Inquisition, the Jesuit Luis de Molina's book, *Liberi arbitrii cum gratiae donis, divina praescientia, providentia, praedestinatione et reprobatione concordia,* which undertook to explain the compatibility of the universal efficacy of grace with the free will of man by virtue of God's foreknowledge, and which was expressly directed against the Thomistic teaching presented in the commentary on Saint Thomas published just previously (1584) by the Dominican Báñez. Molina's *Concordia* was, for this reason, suppressed for three months by the Portuguese Inquisition, but after its release it was at once reprinted by leading publishers in Lyons, Antwerp, and Venice.

In the same spring of 1598 the case, which had meanwhile been brought to Rome, took a turn which seemed to bring victory within the grasp of the Dominicans. The theological commission appointed by the Pope had been directed to examine, not the disputed point as such, namely, the teaching of both parties, but only Molina's teaching. It decided on 13 March 1598 that the book and the doctrine were to be forbidden and renewed this decision after weighing the exhaustive expositions of both schools, in which the most eminent theologians on both sides took part, the opinions of the Universities of Salamanca, Alcalá, and Sigüenza, and the views of five Spanish bishops and four Spanish theologians. A report was presented to the Pope, proposed that sixty theses of Molina be condemned. Thus far Molina himself had not been directly heard, although he had requested a hearing in a petition to the Pope. In order to permit the Jesuits to have a better opportunity to speak, Clement VIII, at the intercession of Philip III of Spain and other highly placed patrons of the Society, had the two generals, Beccaria and Acquaviva, each assisted by eminent theologians — among others, the Dominican Diego Alvarez and the Jesuit Michael Vázquez — define orally and in writing their viewpoint in the controversy. The Dominicans resisted any side-tracking of the real issue, which in their opinion concerned only the teaching of Molina. The Jesuits insisted on discussion of the entire problem, including Báñez's teaching on the *praemotio physica;* in any case, they said, Molina's teaching was not that of the Society. They won their point, despite the protests of the Dominicans.

The success was only a brief one. When the Theological Commission, enlarged by three members, resumed its activity at the Pope's command, it again decided against Molina, by a majority of nine to two, and rejected twenty propositions contained in his works. On 5 December 1601 it submitted all its documents to the Pope. Clement VIII decided to hear both parties himself and to pass sentence personally. The Pope felt unable to reach a decision. Bellarmine had clearly been right in warning him not to try to settle so weighty a question himself but to refer it to a council or to trained theologians. At the Pope's death nothing had been settled.

Paul V had both sides present their views to him concisely and in writing. Pope Paul V ordered that only the fundamental question should be considered: how the efficacy of grace on the free will is to be understood. Thus the doctrine of Molina, which had been generally fixed as the point at issue under Clement VIII, was put aside and the Pope now yielded to the original demand of the Jesuits. These endeavored to refute the Thomistic doctrine of the *praemotio physica* and to prove that it was akin to the Calvinist theory of grace.

After the conclusion of the disputations the consultors were directed to answer four questions: 1. Which propositions on grace should be defined; 2. Which should be condemned; 3. Where lay the difference between the Catholic and the heretical views; 4. Whether a bull should be issued on the subject. The opinion of the consultors, rendered at the end of November 1606, was that forty-two propositions of Molina were to be censured. The Pope refrained from a decision, saying that the teaching of the Dominicans was quite different from that of Calvin, the teaching of the Jesuits, different from Pelagianism; so that no definition was necessary. The *Congregatio de Auxiliis* was dissolved and silence concerning the discussions was enjoined on all participants. The Inquisition, on 11 December 1611, decreed that, for the future, writings published on the subject of grace would require its previous approbation.

Molina barely had escaped condemnation, but the Society of Jesus, accused with him, had held its own. No definition concluded the greatest dogmatic controversy which had ever broken out within Catholic Theology, over what is, in the final analysis, an almost insoluble problem, and which had kept in suspense not only the Catholic but also the Protestant world. The issue remained officially undecided and probably had to, because the mystery of the collaboration between divine grace and man's free will defies ultimate clarification by human reason. The antagonism between the two schools, Thomists and Molinists, has begun to diminish only quite recently.

CHAPTER 103

The Rise of Positive Theology

Humanism's slogan, "To the sources," had riveted attention on the Bible and the Fathers. Now the confrontation with the Protestant doctrinal system on the basis of Scripture and Tradition, defined at Trent as the sources of revelation, together with the defense of the Church institutions that were under attack, led to the construction of historical theology. While at first Spaniards and Italians played the leading role in the Catholic Reform, the French joined them with distinguished achievements.

The Tridentine decree on the Vulgate did not prevent work on the Hebrew and Greek texts of the Bible. Despite Trent's contrary attitude, the Bible was translated into the vernacular, especially in countries threatened by Protestantism. The German translations begun in 1614 by Caspar Ulenberg, but not completed until after his death by Heinrich Francken-Sierstorff (1630), continued in use into the eighteenth century as the "Mainz Catholic Bible," so called because of revisions by theologians of Mainz. The French Bible going back to Jacques Lefèvre d'Etaples was placed on the Index in 1546, but after being revised by Louvain theologians it was reprinted at least two hundred times.

Biblical exegesis was not outdistanced by textual criticism. In the extent of exegetical accomplishment all were surpassed by Cornelius a Lapide (van Steen, d. 1637), who commented on almost all the books of the Bible during his long teaching career at Louvain. Sixtus of Siena (d. 1569) established the "introduction" to Scripture on a scientific basis. His *Bibliotheca Sancta* contained not only the most complete introduction to Scripture up to that time but also a critical history of biblical interpretation.

Church Fathers and Councils

The Fathers of the Church, the knowledge of whom had been so greatly promoted by Erasmus' complete editions, became the arsenal of controversial theology. It was necessary to produce witnesses for the antiquity of the Mass and the Real Presence, for the official priesthood and the papal primacy, for ceremonies and the veneration of saints. John Fisher and Hieronymus Emser had already had recourse to them. For purposes of controversial theology Cochläus published writings of Cyprian, Optatus of Milevis, Gregory Nazianzen, and Chrysostom. Guglielmo Sirleto submitted evidence to the Council of Trent from the Vatican manuscripts, especially those of the Greek Fathers. Although he published little, he was a pioneer of Greek patrology. Athanasius, Basil the Great, Gregory Nazianzen, and Chrysostom were first termed Doctors of the Church in the breviary of Pius V. The early complete editions had provided their works only in Latin translation; after the turn of the century editions in both Greek and Latin appeared in rapid succession. The most prominent scholar active in this work was the French Jesuit Fronton du Duc (d. 1624). The Basel complete editions of Augustine (by Amerbach in 1506, by Erasmus in 1528f.) were replaced by the Louvain editions (1577); the Basel editions of Erasmus' texts of Jerome (1516–20) and Ambrose (1527), by the Roman editions (Jerome in 1565–72 and Ambrose in 1579–87). About the same time the Sorbonne professor Marguerin de la Bigne (d. 1589), in his *Bibliotheca Sanctorum Patrum,* published writings of more than 200 ancient and medieval authors in order to provide material for refuting the Magdeburg Centuriators. The authenticity of the *Apostolic Canons* and of the pseudo-Isidorean decretals was disproved by the *Pseudo-Isidorus et Turrianus Vapulantes* (1628) of the Calvinist Blondel. The *Apostolic Constitutions,* first published in 1563, also by Torres, and to an even greater degree the researches of the Augustinian Hermit Onofrio Panvinio (d. 1564) on the Roman stational churches, titular churches, and deaconries, the origin of the College of Cardinals, and the iconography of the Popes "lighted the fire of the science of Christian antiquity" (De Rossi), which culminated in the rediscovery of the catacombs.

Individual catacombs had indeed been accessible during the Middle Ages and had been visited by pilgrims, for example, San Sebastiano, San Pancrazio, San Callisto. But the way was really paved for their exploration by the devotion to the Church of the Martyrs enkindled by Philip Neri. The systematic exploration of the old and the recently discovered catacombs began in 1593 with Antonio Bosio (d. 1629), of whose grand-scale *Roma sotteranea* only a part was published, posthumously, in 1632. The reawakened interest in Christian antiquity was further stimulated by fortunate discoveries.

The conflict over the Council had brought forth the first complete editions of the ancient councils. All were far surpassed by the Roman edition in four volumes

(1608–12), ordered by Sixtus V but not completed until the pontificate of Paul V. It not only gave better texts; it was the first to give the Greek.

To facilitate a general survey of Christian literature, which in the course of the sixteenth century had increased enormously, most of all through the abundant publication of sources, the Augustinian Hermit Angelus Rocca (d. 1620) composed an *Epitome,* at first for his own convenience but published in 1594 with a dedication to Clement VIII. It contained, though not yet in chronological order, a summary of editions of the Bible and exegetes, the works of the great Latin and Greek Fathers, of the great scholastics, and of selected modern writers. Of a similar origin but far more satisfactorily arranged in chronological order was Bellarmine's brochure of 1613 on ecclesiastical authors. Much more detailed than both was Possevino's alphabetically arranged *Apparatus sacer,* with an attached guide to ecclesiastical libraries. The old catalogues of authors by Jerome, Gennadius, Sigebert of Gembloux, and others had been reedited in 1580 by the Frisian Suffridus Petri (d. 1597).

Church History

Even more important than these advances in Christian literary history were those in Church history, which, literally refounded at this time, at once displayed a monumental achievement. The *Catalogus testium veritatis* (1556) and to a much greater extent the Church history by Matthias Flacius Illyricus and his associates, known as the *Centuries,* which set for itself the goal of establishing the "integram ecclesiae Christi ideam"; in reality it was an historical defense of orthodox Lutheranism drawn up with great scholarship. A satisfactory reply had to wait for the *Annales ecclesiastici* of the Oratorian Caesar Baronius (1538–1607). Neri induced him "to make for that immensely broad sea" and undertake the composition of a Church history based on the sources, which, in spite of its annalistic arrangement and its fundamentally apologetic tendency, is outstanding as a sincere searching for truth. Tirelessly the always unassuming but strong-principled scholar, who was raised to the purple in 1596, continued his work through twelve volumes to 1198.

As the Magdeburg *Centuries* unintentionally contributed to the development of general Church history, so did the biased history of the Council of Trent by the Servite Paolo Sarpi stimulate research into this fundamental event of the entire era. Sforza Pallavicino (d. 1667), succeeded in producing a history of the Council that would be the standard Catholic work into the nineteenth century. He availed himself of the rich source materials amassed by his predecessors and considerably augmented by himself. By his own avowal, he intended it as an historical defense, and that is what it was.

The Protestant rejection of the cult of the saints was met by the hagiographers Lippomani and Surius with their collections of lives of saints. The *Vitae sanctorum priscorum Patrum* of Luigi Lippomani (d. 1559) contained, among other items, the first translation of the lives of Byzantine saints by Simon Metaphrastes and John Moschus. The Carthusian Laurentius Surius (d. 1578), meritorious as editor of the councils and also for a contemporary history and his translations of the works of Suso, Tauler, and Ruysbroeck, received from Lippomania a third of his material, chiefly Metaphrastes, but often had recourse to the original sources, including those in manuscript. The reproach hurled at him, that he arbitrarily altered various *vitae,* or rather the critical texts, can be verified in only a few cases, but he frequently changed expressions and suppressed passages that might have offended Catholic readers. These defects were to some extent rectified in the third edition (1618). Surius' work was the chief forerunner of the *Acta Sanctorum,* which, first projected by the Jesuit Heribert Rosweyde in 1607, appeared in its initial volumes in 1643. The *Martyrologium Romanum,* compiled by Cardinal Sirleto with the assistance of Baronius at the order of Gregory XIII, was prescribed for liturgical use in 1584.

The apologetic tone of not only hagiography but of other aspects of historical theology gradually lessened and the historico-critical method asserted itself. The Jesuit Dionysius Petavius (1593–1652) main work, *Dogmata theologica,* is regarded as the foundation of the history of dogma.

Canon Law

A trend toward the positive historical method is seen, finally, in canon law. Of the Spanish triple constellation, Martin de Azpilcueta (d. 1586) and his pupil Diego de Covarruvias (d. 1577) were systematizers. The first named, the "Doctor Navarrus," moved to Rome and from the time of Pius V was looked upon as an oracle even in difficult questions of moral theology. On the other hand, Antonio Agustin (d. 1586), who had been educated at Alcalá and Salamanca, applied the historico-critical method during his stay in Italy first to Roman and then to canon law under the influence of the jurist Andrea Alciati. His textual criticism of the Decree of Gratian indicated numerous errors in the new edition of 1582, ordered by Gregory XIII.

The progress of historical theology did not yet include, on the Catholic side, the introduction of Church history into the theological curriculum. Whereas at most Protestant universities universal history — still treated from the viewpoint of salvation history — and Church history became fields of study, the perceptible trend at some Catholic universities toward academic instruction in history disappeared.

Printing Houses and Libraries

Connected with the rise of positive theology was the growth of efficient printing presses and of well-equipped ecclesiastical libraries. Of the printing centers, Basel, where Erasmus' editions of the New Testament and of many Church Fathers had appeared, had become Protestant, while Paris and Lyons were severely handicapped by the Huguenot Wars. Now, alongside Venice, reformed Rome became the place where excellent works were published. Catholic works were published also at Cologne, Ingolstadt, and Dillingen. A survey of new publications was rendered easier after 1564 by the Frankfurt book catalogues, which on the eve of the Thirty Years' War recorded more than fifteen hundred titles a year. Occasionally they were accompanied by indexes of Catholic books, compiled at the instigation of the Jesuits, as counterparts of the Index of Forbidden Books.

The *Ratio Studiorum* ordered for each college the preparation of a library budget, because the Fathers would otherwise be "unarmed soldiers." The importance of libraries was also clearly grasped at Rome. The Vatican Library grew enormously. Its manuscript and book collections were enriched by the gift of the Heidelberg Palatina, made to the Pope by the Elector Maximilian of Bavaria. By 1669 Italy had eighty libraries, the Netherlands fifty, France twenty-seven, Germany twenty-three, and England eleven."

CHAPTER 104

Spiritual Life, Popular Devotion, and Art

Ascetical and mystical literature leads to the sources of the Church's renewal. The connection of this literature, in regard to both its content and the persons involved, with the reinvigorated theology makes apparent its relevance to life. Luis de León stated as its aim "to explain the sound doctrine which rouses souls and conducts them to the way of virtue." It proceeded from Spain and in Spain culminated in the Carmelite mystics. Until about the mid-century people were content with guides to the interior life and prayer and to a virtuous life. The influence of Savonarola, predominant in the Spanish Dominican reform, is evident in the *Guia del cielo* (1527) of the Dominican Pablo de León and in the most popular ascetical works of the Catholic Reform, the *Libro de la oración y meditación* and the *Guia de precadores* of Luis of Granada (d. 1588). The latter's real model was his director, Juan de Avila (d. 1569), the "Apostle of Andalusia." In the last years of his life, when physically broken as a consequence of overexertion in preaching and pastoral activity, Juan had his *Audifilia* printed (1557) — a guide to the spiritual life intended for Doña Sancha Carillo — and thereafter devoted himself to the direction of souls. His spiritual letters are the fruit of this preoccupation.

The Augustinians' "most read, most often translated, and most often commented" author was Luis de León (d. 1591), who received from Domingo Soto the position of professor of Scripture at Salamanca. His exposition of the fourteen biblical names of Christ *(De los nombres de Cristo,* 1583) and his *La perfecta casada* (1583), intended for his cousin, Maria Varela, showed him to be a poet of real inspiration (K. Vossler) and a master of language, who fused theological depth with practical sense. Not his least merit is to have made possible the printing of the works of Teresa of Avila by his judgment "de muy sana y católica doctrina."

Carmelite Mysticism

After the mid-century the cultivation of contemplative prayer brought forth the flower of mysticism in Carmel. Teresa of Avila, actually de Ahumada y Cépeda (1515–82, canonized in 1622), surpassed the late medieval German mystics in blending the most refined psychological observation and mystical experience with a truly Spanish practicality and tireless activity for the reform of her Order. The story of her interior life to the beginning of her reform activity (1562) is contained in her autobiography, recorded at the command of the Toledo Inquisitor and completed in 1565. The exquisitely refreshing *Libro de las fundaciónes* narrates the establishing of eighteen reformed houses between 1567 and 1582, accomplished after overcoming strong opposition. Intended for her nuns was the *Camino de perfección,* composed about 1565 at the request of her confessor, the Dominican Báñez. The most complete of her mystical writings is *El castillo interior* (1577), in which she describes her progress to mystical union with God in seven stages. A knowledge of her truly great personality is provided by her less mystical writings, by her 440 letters, while the constitutions approved by the chapter of 1581 show her activity in the Order. She profited by her careful reading of spiritual works — Augustine's *Confessions,* the German mystics, Osuna — to describe correctly her own mystical experiences concerning whose divine origin she was long troubled, and to express them without affectation in classical Spanish.

Associated with Teresa from 1568 was John of the Cross (1542–91, canonized in 1726, declared a Doctor of the Church in 1926), who had made his theological studies at Salamanca. As spiritual director of the convent of the Incarnation (1572–77), of which Teresa was superior, he seconded her endeavors, only to be thrown into prison himself by the opponents of reform. When the autonomy of the reformed branch of the Order had been achieved, he occupied posts in the Order at Baeza and Segovia and died in Ubeda, misunderstood and shamefully treated but purified by suffering. In his chief works, *Subida del Monto Carmelo* (1579) and *Noche oscura del alma* (1579), he describes the active and passive purification of the soul and outlines a system of mystical theology: The night of the senses and the night of the spirit must be overcome in order to mount "far above all limitations of knowledge" to union with God in the essence of the soul. The *Cántico espiritual* and the *Llama de amor viva,* composed during his imprisonment in Toledo, are genuinely poetic, expressing a never surpassed exclamation of the soul, cleansed by suffering and united with God.

Italy and France

Italy too produced mystics. The most influential ascetical work, after and alongside the *Exercises* of Saint Ignatius, was the *Combattimento spirituale* (single and unrevised edition: Venice 1589) of the Theatine Lorenzo Scupoli (d. 1610). The Jesuit school of spirituality, after some hesitation while Borgia was general, adhered to the sober and psychologically sound asceticism of the founder. Luis de la Puente (d. 1624), a pupil of Francisco Suárez and Balthasar Alvarez, in his *Meditaciónes de los misterios de nuestra Santa fé* (1605) and even more in his commentary on the Canticle of Canticles (1622) and the *Sentimientos* (published posthumously in 1670), makes it clear that he "was blessed with the gift of mystical prayer" (Guibert).

From the turn of the century the French school became increasingly prominent. Francis de Sales (1567–1622, canonized in 1665, proclaimed a Doctor of the Church in 1877), very successful as a missionary and as Bishop of Geneva, promoted a realistic asceticism in his *Introduction à la vie dévote* 1608, usually known as *Philothea)* and his *Traité de l'amour de Dieu* (1616, also called *Theotimus).* His correspondence with Jane Frances de Chantal (d. 1641, canonized in 1767) is a monument of understanding and firm spiritual direction. His *Humanisme dévote* is much indebted to the mystic Barbe Acarie (d. 1618), who, married and the mother of six, established the Discalced Carmelites in France and, after her husband's death, joined them. It owes even more to the Oratorian Pierre de Bérulle (1575–1629, a cardinal in 1627), founder of the French Oratory (1611) and influential in Church politics, who is to be considered the real founder of the French school of spirituality. Educated in the Jesuit College de Clermont, in his youth Bérulle was influenced by the German and then by the Spanish mystics. Beginning in 1601 with his *Discours de l'état et de la grandeur de Jésus* there was formed in him a strictly Christocentric piety, which he spread as director of souls.

Preaching of the Faith

The stream of spiritual literature was indeed broad, but not broad enough to touch the uneducated classes. This duty was fulfilled by means of preaching and popular catechetical instruction, which the Council of Trent made obligatory for parish priests on all Sundays and holy days. In the Latin countries, as earlier, the Advent and Lent series, given mostly by preachers of the mendicant Orders, continued in practice. But the mission and apologetic sermons favored by the Jesuits and Capuchins were a new development.

The clergy had at hand far more and far better tools for catechetical instruction than had been the case before Trent. In addition to the *Roman Catechism,* Peter Canisius' *Summa doctrinae christianae* (1554) for catechists and Bellarmine's *Dichiarazione* (1598) and the corresponding popular catechisms — Canisius' *Parvus catechismus* (1558) and *Catechismus minimus* (1556) and Bellarmine's *Dottrina cristiana breve* (1597) — found a wide circulation. The Confraternity of Christian Doctrine, introduced in Milan by Borromeo, spread in and beyond Italy. The catechist César de Bus founded at Aix the Congregation of Priests of Christian Doctrine. The Piarists of Joseph Calasanctius acquired an importance in elementary education analogous to that of the Jesuit colleges in higher education.

Like the acceptance and implementation of the Tridentine reform decrees, the introduction of the reformed breviary and missal of Pius V made very slow progress outside Italy.

Administration of Sacraments

The rite of administering the Sacraments and the frequency of reception still differed greatly from region to region. At the beginning of the sixteenth century annual Easter Communion was the almost invariable rule. Reception three or four times a year, prescribed in the Third Orders and the confraternities, was interpreted as a sign of religious zeal in the laity. But from the middle of the sixteenth century reception became much more frequent, especially under the influence of the new Orders — Theatines, Barnabites, Jesuits, and Capuchins — and in consequence of the general rise of devotion to the Eucharist.

As a rule Communion was preceded by confession. The confessional, hitherto usually open and moveable and in most churches close to the altar or the choir inclosure, was gradually replaced from the turn of the century under the influence of the *Rituale Romanum* by one that was stationary and provided with a wooden screen. The anointing of the sick was seldom requested in Germany, according to the records of visitations. Confirmation slowly became more common in connection with visitations. The rite of contracting marriage exhibited, as previously, very great differences, but, due to the decree "Tametsi," there was a tendency to specify the reception of the Sacrament in the exchange of consent before the parish priest or in the blessing given by him.

Popular Devotion

Popular devotions, processions, and pilgrimages, frequently arranged by the again flourishing confraternities, became genuine expressions of popular piety. What was new in this post-Tridentine piety was its emphasis on specifically Catholic doctrines and forms of worship; it became anti-Protestant and hence a confessional piety. The Eucharistic confraternities, going back to the fifteenth century and having as their model the *Confraternita del SS. Sacramento* at Santa Maria sopra Minerva promoted devotion to the Eucharist in addition to communion, in particular the maintenance of the perpetual light and the providing of an escort for the taking of communion to the sick. The Corpus Christi procession, recommended by Trent, was celebrated with great solemnity in several Catholic districts of Germany (Munich Processionals, 1582–1611). In Spain the *Fiesta del Corpus* became during the second half of the sixteenth century the "highest of all Church feasts" and was enhanced by special performances, the *autos sacramentales.*

Devotion to Mary was intensified. The Marian Congregation, established by the Fleming Johannes Leunis in 1563 for the students of the Roman Jesuit College, made it the starting point of self-education and the fostering of an apostolic attitude. Introduced into almost all Jesuit colleges, by 1576 it numbered 30,000 members. The Marian place of pilgrimage, Loreto, was visited by many Romans, and the Litany of Loreto, was traceable there back to 1531. The rosary acquired its present form and was promoted by rosary confraternities.

The book of family devotions, the private prayerbook, and the devotional picture became popular. The example given by the courts of the Catholic Habsburg and Wittelsbach dynasties was imitated in popular devotion. Spanish and Italian forms of piety and the saints popular in those countries were especially made known by religious Orders — Ignatius and Francis Xavier by the Jesuits, Anthony of Padua by the Franciscans, devotion to Saint Joseph by Teresa of Avila. Religious folklore increased in the course of the seventeenth century, and so did superstition.

Arts and Literature

The Tridentine decree on images had as its aim to defend the lawfulness of sacred images and their veneration against the Calvinist iconoclasm in France and to eliminate abuses, but not to determine the canons of artistic production. The first large church buildings of the Jesuits, the *Gesù* in Rome and St. Michael in Munich, in which the style of the Renaissance is little changed, coincide in time with the climax of the Catholic Reform; along the Rhine and in the Low Countries the Jesuits at first built in the Gothic style. The history of the construction of the new Saint Peter's reflects the gradual turning away from Renaissance concepts and the return to the traditional plan, but at the same time it represented the breakthrough of the Baroque style by the architects Maderna and Bernini. The beginning of Baroque art in Rome corresponds to the papal assumption of leadership in the implementation of the Council of Trent and of Church renewal. The zenith of German Baroque proceeded side by side with the reestablishment of the Church and the carrying out of the Tridentine Reform after the Thirty Years' War. The effect of Trent on iconography is unequivocal. Painting and sculpture favored the controverted subjects defined at Trent. They aspired to strengthen Catholic awareness of the faith and to stir up devotion.

The legend started by Agazzari (1609) that the Council of Trent's contemplated prohibition of polyphonic music was dropped because of Palestrina's "Missa Papae Marcelli" is historically true to the extent that this Mass, presumably produced during the Council (1562), and the conciliar prayers composed by the Dutchman Otto Kerle realized the demands of the reformers — textual integrity and moral purity. As Palestrina (d. 1594) in his choral compositions combined classical proportions and deep feeling, so too did the extremely productive Orlando di Lasso (d. 1594), court composer for the Duke of Bavaria at Munich. The compositions of the Spaniard Thomas de Vitoria (d. 1613) were also in the spirit of Palestrina. The Medicean edition of the *Graduale Romanum,* was published in 1614–15 at the command of Paul V. It altered the Gregorian melodies in accord with humanist principles.

If the Spanish national literature of the *Siglo de Oro* is unthinkable apart from Spain's leading role in the ecclesiastical sphere, the relationships are more complicated in Italy and France and even more so in Germany, where antibourgeois, courtly, and absolutist tendencies are bound up with the anti-Reformation trends. Certainly from the religious background came the Jesuit theater, which culminated in the dramas of Jakob Bidermann (d. 1639), the "Cenodoxus" and the martyr plays "Adrianus" and "Philemon Martyr." According to Kindermann, "it is one of the chief glories of the European stage in the seventeenth century."

CHAPTER 105

The New and the Old Orders

The fundamental motives of the Catholic Reform — first, self-sanctification, then the apostolate and works of charity — which had been basic to the new pre-Tridentine foundations, continued to operate in the religious life of the post-Tridentine period. The most powerful impulses came from Spain and Italy and, with the turn of the century, from France.

The idea of the apostolate is found in probably its purest form in the Oratory of Philip Neri (1515–95, canonized in 1622). After being ordained in 1551, this affable and humorous "Apostle of Rome," beloved by high and low, began to gather young men, chiefly students, at San Girolamo della Carita for spiritual conferences, often with musical interludes. The society of diocesan priests, founded in 1564 and soon joined by the future Cardinals Baronius and Tarugi, was formally established in 1575. Other houses arose in Naples, Palermo, Lucca, and elsewhere in Italy. In 1611 Pierre de Bérulle transplanted the Oratory to France, where it received a fresh impetus.

The Oblates of Saint Ambrose were a society of diocesan priests, founded at Milan by Borromeo in 1578. Their single vow obliged the members to be at the disposal of the Archbishop of Milan in the care of souls and instruction. The Regular Clerics of the Mother of God, living according to the Augustinian Rule, were founded at Lucca in 1574 by Giovanni Leonardi (d. 1609, canonized in 1938) and later moved to Rome. Among them the education of poor children gradually assumed primary importance, and it became the real aim of the Piarists, called in Italy the *Scolopi,* an abbreviation of *scuole pie.* The Aragonese Joseph Calasanctius (1556–1648, canonized in 1767), who, on settling in Rome in 1592, had first been active in the Confraternity of Christian Doctrine, opened there in 1597 the first free elementary school and gathered his coworkers into a community with simple vows (1617). Its field of activity continued to be elementary education.

The Society of Jesus was, and became even more so, the most influential Order in education. Following its tempestuous growth at the beginning, it experienced under the generals Borgia (1565–73) and Mercurian (1573–80) a period of internal consolidation, which was completed by the intellectually distinguished Claudius Acquaviva (1581–1615). The order of the day and manner of life of the members was fixed, a *directorium* for the conducting of the Exercises was drawn up, and, after long preparation, the *Ratio Studiorum* was put in force (1599). Their ultimate goal in education was "to stimulate the knowledge and love of our Creator and Redeemer." Following the "Paris Method,"a mastery of written and spoken Latin (to a lesser extent, of Greek) was systematically aimed at; on it was built the philosophical and finally the theological training. The pupils' ambition was incited by competition, and plays and dramatic presentations open to the public forged a bond between students and parents. Following the uniform instructional plan of the *Ratio Studiorum,* the 372 colleges which the Society maintained in 1616 were training an ecclesiastical and secular elite which shaped Church and world more effectively than any other factor.

The Society found and maintained its definitive frame and reached the height of its influence during the late sixteenth and early seventeenth centuries. Popes Pius V and Sixtus V, both from mendicant Orders, sought without success to remodel it along mendicant lines by introducing the choral office and having solemn profession precede ordination and even to change its name. Gregory XIII, favorably disposed, curtailed the hitherto predominant Spanish influence on the government of the Society by procuring in 1573 the election of the Belgian Mercurian in place of Polanco, who had long been the Society's secretary. Acquaviva publicly disavowed the intervention in politics of such prominent members as Auger in France and Skarga in Poland. In conflicts with his critics he demonstrated both firmness and moderation. The number of members, about 3500 in 1563, rose to more than 13,000. Under Acquivava's mild and sensible successor, Mutius Vitelleschi (1615–45), the Order obtained in 1622 the canonization of its founder and greatest missionary, Francis Xavier, and in 1640 celebrated the first century of its existence with great pageantry. The magnificent *Imago primi saeculi Societatis lesu* documented its achievement.

Though the Jesuits, in the spirit of their founder, rendered great service as preachers and confessors in the pastoral care of all classes through their conducting of the Exercises and of popular missions, still, in works for the masses, they were at least equalled by the Capuchins from the close of the sixteenth century. Once Gregory XIII had removed the restriction of this new branch of the Franciscans to Italy in 1574, it spread extraordinarily fast in France, Spain, the Low Countries, and the German-speaking world. When in 1621 Paul V freed it from dependence on the general of the Conventuals, it already numbered 15,000 members. The greater the number of preachers trained in higher institutions — Saint Bonaventure became the Order's Doctor in 1578 — the more attention they devoted to itinerant preaching and popular missions, in addition to the customary sermons of the Advent and Lent cycles, and they became the favorite guides and confessors of the people.

Jesuits and Capuchins, their apostolic zeal and their new pastoral methods, are as integral to the picture of the sixteenth-century Catholic renewal as were the then new mendicant Orders to that of the thirteenth century. And once again the mendicants showed their vitality. They now adapted their constitutions to the Tridentine decree on Regulars. The effort for a strict observance of the rule led in some Orders to the founding of houses of Recollects within the provinces, in others to the formation of new branches with a "stricter" and a "most strict" observance. Among the Franciscans, the Alcantarines, also known as Discalced, and widespread in the Spanish empire, surpassed, because of their penitential strictness and their extreme poverty, the "Riformati," who had originated at Fonte Colombo near Rieti and were very popular in Italy and South Germany; they also surpassed the French Recollects, who first united at Nevers after the Huguenot Wars. This was also true of the Spanish Discalced Augustinians, who from 1601 constituted a separate province of the Augustinian Hermits. In 1621 this was divided into four provinces and even obtained its own vicar general. Several reform congregations of the Dominicans were changed into provinces.

On the other hand, the Carmelite general Rossi did not succeed in leading back the reformed houses of friars and nuns that had been established in Spain by Teresa of Avila and John of the Cross "to a less austere observance and to obedience to the superiors of the Order," in accord with the decree of the general chapter of Piacenza in 1575. In 1580 the reformed set up a province of their own with statutes which stressed strict observance of the rule and the cultivation of interior prayer. When in 1593 they obtained the right to elect their own general, they became an independent Order, the Discalced Carmelites. In 1631 Urban VIII approved their revised constitutions, which brought them close to the penitential monastic Orders of Carthusians and Camaldolese through the extremely strict manner of life they prescribed — prohibition of meat, fasting from 14 September to Easter, two hours of meditation a day, and perpetual silence in the convents of hermits. The *Collegium Complutense Philosophicum* (Alcalá, 1624) and the *Cursus Theologicus* of the Order's theologians at Salamanca (1631) gave them a great reputation for scholarship.

Whereas the enforcing of the regular observance in the centralized mendicant Orders frequently produced centrifugal tendencies, the concern of the Benedictine reforms continued to be to protect the individual monastery from isolation and decay by organization in a larger union. The Council of Trent in its reform of regulars had prescribed the federation of exempt monasteries either in provincial chapters or in congregations. Italy and Spain already had the great congregations of Montecassino and Valladolid. The Congregation of Flanders, founded in 1564, and the "Great Gallican" Congregation in France, from which that of Saint-Denis split in 1617, satisfied the letter of the Tridentine requirement but did little for reform because many monasteries were still, as earlier, the property of commendatory abbots and had only a few monks. A new flowering of Benedictine monasticism was first effected by the Congregation of Saint-Vanne, to which abbeys of Lorraine and Burgundy belonged, from 1604 to 1670; also important were the Belgian Congregation, formed by Abbot Fanson of Saint-Hubert in 1629 after violent struggles with the episcopate, and especially the Maurist Congregation, confirmed in 1621. The Maurists, finally comprising 178 monasteries, gave themselves, on the model of the Montecassino Congregation, a strict organization under a triennial general, residing at Saint-Germain-des-Prés, with a general chapter, a strictly regulated visitation, and a common novitiate in each of the six provinces. In it there came to maturity in the succeeding epoch the great works on the history of the Benedictine Order and patristic editions. The Maurists also perfected the historico-critical method in these provinces.

Despite great losses, the Union of Bursfeld in northern and western Germany had weathered the storms of the Reformation. In South Germany the Swabian Congregation was formed in 1603; the Swiss Congregation had originated in 1602. Success crowned the effort of the German Benedictines to create a center of scholarship in the University of Salzburg, founded in 1617 by Archbishop Mark Sittich and incorporated into the Order.

Among the Cistercians too the pre-Tridentine trend toward merging reformed monasteries into congregations continued. The Cistercians of the Strict Observance were separated as the Trappist Order in the following period.

The strengthening of the episcopal control of the hospital institutions by Trent could not impede their progressive secularization. However, the physical and the spiritual needs of the sick, especially during epidemics, were attended to, sometimes with heroic risks, and two new Orders dedicated themselves exclusively to this work. John of God (1495–1550, canonized in 1690), having been converted as a result of a sermon delivered by Juan de Avila, in 1540 founded at Granada a hospital, which, provided with new accommodations with the help of Archbishop Guerrero, also received the insane. The community, consisting of helpers whom John of God had attracted, received the Augustinian rule from Pius V in 1572. Under Urban VIII the Brothers Hospitallers had seventy-nine hospitals in the Spanish Empire under a general resident at Granada. Shortly before, in 1584, Camillus of Lellis (1550–1614, canonized in 1746) had founded in Rome the Clerics Regular for the Aid of the Sick, especially the dying. Also called "Camillians," they distinguished themselves during plagues in Rome and Naples and from the time of Gregory XV bound themselves to this ministry by a fourth vow. At the founder's death the Order had sixteen houses in Italy.

Although Trent's strict regulations on inclosure at first constituted an impediment, communities of religious women began to engage in the Church's works of social charity. In addition to the Ursulines, the Visitandines and the English Ladies devoted themselves to the education of young girls. The Visitandines, founded at the suggestion of Saint Francis de Sales by the widow Jane Frances Fremiot de Chantal (1572–1641, canonized in 1767), were at first occupied in the service of the poor and the sick. But after they had become an Order with the Augustinian rule in 1618, they took up the training and instruction of young girls in boarding schools, out of regard for the Tridentine prescription of inclosure. At the death of de Chantal the Order had eighty-six independent convents, all in French-speaking countries. The Institute of the Blessed Virgin Mary, whose members were popularly known as the English Ladies, was established at Munich in 1626–27 for teaching in girls' schools and became the source of many new foundations in South Germany. Only Vincent de Paul succeeded in founding a female Order for the care of the sick. The Daughters of Charity, took the place of the associations of women organized by Vincent for the care of the poor and the sick. Together with the Borromeans of Nancy (1652), they blazed the trail for the grand-scale development of the modern congregations of women, without which the Church's social work in the nineteenth century could not be imagined.

Section Four

The Springtime of the Missions in the Early Modern Period

CHAPTER 106

The Missions under Spanish Patronage

The discovery of the Canary Islands (1312–41) may be considered the prelude to the great discoveries of the fifteenth and sixteenth centuries. What followed set the example for all missionary activity in the so-called Age of Discovery. As early as 1351 Pope Clement VI appointed the Carmelite Bernard as Bishop of the "Happy Islands," and in 1368 Urban V directed the Bishops of Barcelona and Tortosa to send missionaries there. But these early endeavors were unsuccessful. Thirteen missionaries are said to have been slain by the inhabitants in 1391. Only the conquest of the islands by the Spaniards created more favorable conditions. In 1404 the bishopric of the Canary Islands was established as the new diocese of Rubicon, and in 1424 Fuertaventura became the second see. Besides Dominicans and Augustinians, it was especially Franciscans who labored for the conversion of the presumably Berber islanders. Their work was seriously hampered by the encroachments of the Spanish conquerors and merchants, and Pope Eugene IV had to protect the neophytes from exploitation and enslavement and defend their human rights. By 1476 the majority of the islanders were Catholics, and in 1483 Las Palmas became the episcopal see for the entire archipelago.

The marriage of Isabella of Castile to Ferdinand of Aragon paved the way for Spanish national unity, and the victory at Granada in 1492 completed the *reconquista.* In the same year Spain entered into competition with Portugal in the field of exploration. The Genoese Christopher Columbus (1451–1506), in the service of Spain, discovered America, which he thought to be a part of Asia and hence called the "West Indies." To counter Portuguese claims, the Spanish royal pair secured from Pope Alexander VI the recognition of their right to the newly discovered regions and the drawing of a line of demarcation 100 leagues west of the Azores and the Cape Verde Islands: All lands discovered on the far side of the line were to belong to Spain, all lying on the other side of the line were to belong to Portugal. In 1494 this imaginary line was advanced some 270 leagues farther to the west, at the request of Portugal, in the Treaty of Tordesillas. In any case, on the basis of this revision, Portugal could legally claim possession of Brazil, occupied by Cabral in 1500. Following the first circumnavigation of the globe and the discovery of the Philippines by Ferdinand Magellan (1480–1521) there broke out a protracted struggle for a corresponding line of demarcation in the Pacific. This quarrel was to be of great importance in the missionary history of the Far East. It concerned not only the Philippines but eventually Japan and China. And the fact that the Spanish missionaries had to go to Asia via America (Mexico) is noteworthy.

Passions have been frequently aroused by Pope Alexander VI's award, referred to as the "partition of the world" and the "Donatio Alexandrina." It seems clear that it granted a national monopoly of the missionary work in specified regions, for, in return for the "donation," the Spanish King assumed the obligation of promoting the spread of Christianity in the new lands, thereby laying the basis for the royal *patronato*. Responsibility for missionary work implied corresponding rights in the ecclesiastical sphere and these were given to the Spanish crown in 1508 by Julius II's Bull "Universalis Ecclesiae." To the duty of supporting the clergy, churches, and dioceses was added the right to found dioceses and to name all benefice-holders, even bishops.

From its mission mandate Spain deduced the right of conquest and annexation. The *conquista* became a war against paganism, as the *reconquista* had been a war against Islam — it was waged for the faith. "The sword in one hand, they held out the Gospel with the other" (Baluffi, cited in Schmidlin). The force taking possession of an area sometimes issued a *requerimiento* whereby, under threat of the most severe penalties, the inhabitants were called upon to accept Christianity and to recognize the dominion of the Spanish King. Whoever refused lost his freedom or was killed. The missionaries who accompanied the troops, being men of that era. They were not prepared for their missionary work and had absolutely no knowledge of peoples of a strange culture. They felt that exotic peoples could become genuine Christians only if their views, customs, and worship were first destroyed ("method of *tabula rasa*"). To this end, recourse to force was at times necessary.

The overall view of the age contained a theological bias which did not keep pace with the problems raised by the widening of the world horizon. Thus, the unsolved question concerning the salvation of pagans and the nature and extent of the faith necessary for salvation led to the too speedy conferring of baptism, producing many new Christians but only a superficial christianization. How little people were aware of the new situation is revealed by the fact that at Trent the Fathers hardly mentioned the overseas lands, let alone seriously discussed them. Hence Church life in the missions retained its pre-Tridentine stamp long after 1561. The home situation was transferred just as it was to areas of very different culture where closed and exclusively Latin-European dominions were established under the rule of the "Catholic" King of Spain.

Spanish discoverers made rapid strides in the sixteenth century. In 1513 Vasco Nuñez de Balboa, having crossed the isthmus of Panama, reached the Pacific, which he called the "South Sea." By 1519 the northern coast of the Gulf of Mexico was traversed; by 1526 the southern outlines of South America had been determined. Discovery was followed by conquest, and in a little more than a half-century America from Chile to Oregon was claimed to be under Spanish rule.

The Antilles

It can be regarded as almost certain that Columbus was not accompanied by any priest on his first voyage. Missionary work in America really began with the departure of a group of Franciscans in 1500. Already in their first letter they were able to report 3000 baptisms. The erection of an archdiocese and two suffragan sees for the Antilles, decreed in 1504 by Julius II, foundered on King Ferdinand's objection that his rights had been disregarded. Only when these had been assured (1508) could the sees of Santo Domingo and Concepción de la Vega on Hispaniola (Haiti) and San Juan on Puerto Rico be established in 1511. The first diocese on the American continent, Santa Maria Antigua del Darién (Panama), followed in 1513.

In the meantime Dominicans also had come to America in 1509–10, inaugurating a new epoch in the scarcely opened missionary history of America. As early as 1501 the import of Negro slaves from Africa was allowed. Scarcely more than twenty years of colonization sufficed to reduce the population of the Antilles from millions to 14,000 and finally to a few hundred. From 1517 Negroes were systematically settled on Haiti, and very soon they constituted two-thirds of the island's population.

The abuses induced the Dominicans to intervene. Antonio de Montesino was the first to make a violent protest. To his aid came Bartolomé de las Casas (1474–1566), who was a diocesan priest at that time but became a Dominican in 1522. Las Casas crossed the ocean seven times to implore the king to protect the Indians deprived of their rights. He obtained the righting of the worst abuses and exercised a decisive influence on Spanish legislation in favor of the Indians. He forced the theologians and lawyers of his time to face squarely the still unsettled questions as to the human rights of the Indians, the lawfulness of war against infidels, and Spain's claim to have a legitimate title to the occupation of America. In a certain sense, Las Casas is the source of the *leyenda negra,* which discredited the whole colonizing and christianizing activity of the Spaniards abroad and contributed to the judgment, hardened by tradition, on the Spanish methods. In this he was, in the final analysis, neither more nor less than one of the authentic representatives of the Christian conscience of Spain in the New World.

Mexico

By arbitrarily changing his mandate to explore, Hernando Cortés (1485–1546) quickly put an end to the Aztec empire in Central America (1519–1521). Montezuma II (1502–20) was killed, the capital, Tenochtitlán, was razed, and in its stead Mexico City was founded. The complete pacification of the country, however, was not achieved until about 1550.

Cortés was typical of the *conquistadores*. Violent and excessively cruel, at the same time he was zealous for the spread of the Christian faith. Everywhere he set up crosses, forbade human sacrifice, and destroyed idols. The reports he constantly sent to Charles V testify to his zeal. He always had priests in his army to preach the faith. Franciscans were joined by Dominicans in 1526 and Augustinians in 1533. The Spanish religious houses were emptied in behalf of the new overseas provinces of the Orders. In 1559 in Mexico alone the Franciscans numbered 380 members in eighty houses, the Dominicans 210 and the Augustinians 212 in forty houses each.

From Mexico proper the missionaries spread over the areas to the north and the south of New Spain subject to the Viceroy of Mexico. The success of conversion corresponded to the supply of missionaries. The sources speak of millions of neophytes and extol their faith. Many a conversion may have been merely external. The mass baptisms — as many as 14,000 a day! — betray a hurried and superficial procedure and the numerical data in regard to destruction of temples and idols refer to the use of force. Still, the Indians' conversion must have been genuine and sincere on the whole. The rapid establishment of the hierarchy testifies to the development of Christian life. In 1546 Mexico City became the metropolitan see of New Spain, with all the other dioceses as its suffragans.

It is, then, understandable if the Franciscans quickly exerted themselves for the education of the Indians. The Jesuits, who did not arrive until 1572, created nothing new in this regard. They devoted themselves at first chiefly to the care of souls and instruction of the Spanish city dwellers. From 1584 they too turned to missionary work, and in 1609 forty-four of them were tending four missions of their own. The Carmelites and the Mercedarians followed the Jesuits. All together, there were about 400 religious houses in New Spain at the turn of the century. Mexico had become a Catholic country, and the stage of direct missionary work was over.

The essence of missionary work was regarded as the conferring of baptism. Of the other sacraments only confession and matrimony were stressed. For decades serious hesitations existed in regard to allowing the Indians to receive communion and even more so in regard to ordaining them. Into the nineteenth century the Church maintained the appearance of a foreign institution.

Peru

Between 1532 and 1536, starting with a force of only 180, Francisco Pizarro (1475–1540) undertook to conquer the Inca empire, extending from southern Colombia to northern Chile and northwest Argentina, which had already been weakened by the rivalry between the cities of Cuzco and Quito. The Inca Acahualpa received the Spaniards in a friendly manner but was made prisoner and, despite the surrender of his treasury gold and the reception of baptism, was executed. The collapse of the Inca empire was thereby sealed, though the conquest of the vast territory was not completed until 1572. Power-struggles among the *conquistadores*, strong protests against the laws aimed at protecting the Indians (*nuevas leyes*), and the elimination of the "Pizarro Dynasty" by the royal government long disturbed the peace of the largest viceroyalty in Latin America. Lima, the "City of Kings," founded by Pizarro in 1535 and made a diocese in 1541 and an archdiocese in 1546, was so much the political and ecclesiastical center that the history of all of South America, except Brazil, can be read in its story.

Missionary work in Peru was begun by the Dominicans, whose first representative, Vincent Valverde, came in 1531. The Franciscans came next and spread across the land. They were joined by Augustinians and Mercedarians and in 1568 by the first Jesuits. The early Jesuits worked almost exclusively in the larger cities.

The religious Orders determined the history of the missions and of the Church in the viceroyalty. In their presence the diocesan clergy, predominantly Spaniards and Creoles, could maintain themselves only with difficulty. However, along with the Dominicans, Franciscans, and Augustinians, they also provided prelates for the numerous sees which were suffragans of Lima.

The internal development of the Church kept pace with its expansion. The Archbishops of Lima exerted themselves to lay a firm foundation at the numerous provincial councils. Though the conciliar acts betray the prevailing defects in methods of evangelization, they also certify a clear insight into the necessity of thorough reforms. Thus the Council of 1567 warned against hasty baptism and insisted on the obligation of systematic instruction of catechumens and neophytes. The establishing of the so-called *doctrinas,* meaning both "instruction" and "community," was intended to meet this need. Not only the parish priests (*doctrineros*) but also the *encomenderos* were responsible for this work twice a week.

The same council made obligatory the study of the native languages and strictly forbade the hearing of confessions through an interpreter. The Church festivals were celebrated in great splendor, if not with pomp, but it was soon discovered that pagan customs often were concealed by ecclesiastical ceremonies. Hence the method of eradication (*tabula rasa*) was advocated, the too ready admission of Indians to the reception of communion was disapproved, and their very ability to become priests was flatly denied. It was not until the Tridentine decrees on the qualifications for the priesthood had become known overseas that a more conciliatory view became evident in theory. In practice, however, the admission of Indians, *mestizos,* and mulattoes to the priesthood was closed into the seventeenth century, even though in 1576 Gregory XIII had allowed ordination to persons of illegitimate birth in order to obtain priests conversant with the vernaculars.

The implementation of the conciliar decrees was seriously impeded by the vast extent of the province of Lima. Other obstructions were the inadequate means of communication, the difficult geographical and climatic conditions in the widely varying altitudes, and the sparse and widely scattered Indian settlements. Saint Toribio needed six years for his first missionary journey, four for his second.

From Peru proper Christianity spread through all the neighboring areas. In Chile, in spite of the strong and centuries-long resistance of the Araucanians to the Spanish colonists, cities, churches, and monasteries could be erected and many conversions could be realized. In the La Plata districts christianization made evident progress when in 1547 the connection with Peru was established by means of El Gran Chaco. At the close of the sixteenth century Paraguay and Uruguay were also included in the missionary zone and the whole region was divided into dioceses.

New Granada

Colombia, conquered for Spain by Quesada in 1536 and united with Venezuela in 1549 to form the Audiencia of New Granada, was evangelized chiefly by Dominicans. Contrary to what had occurred in Mexico and Peru, here the Dominicans did not establish any monasteries at first, but merely isolated missions and schools. It was not until 1551 that the individual enterprises were gathered into a congregation, which in 1569 included eighteen priories, forty *doctrinas,* and 100 Indian villages. The Dominican province of New Granada was canonically erected in 1577. The Franciscans had to defend their neophytes against the *conquistadores.* Around the mid-century the Augustinians also joined the ranks of the missionaries. Due to the efforts of all of these Orders, the population became Christian within a few decades.

Venezuela, also belonging to the viceroyalty of New Granada, had been evangelized at the beginning of the sixteenth century from the Antilles. But success on the continent was more and more frustrated by the outrages of the licentious Spanish soldiers, for whose misdeeds the missionaries had to pay with their lives in various places. And the attempt of Bartolomé de Las Casas to make a settlement in this region (Cumaná in 1521) foundered as a result of atrocities committed by a punitive expedition against the Indians. When in 1528 Venezuela was assigned by Charles V to the Augsburg business house of Weiser as holder of the monopoly for the importation of Negro slaves, matters hardly changed.

The first great theorist of the missions in modern times, the Jesuit José de Acosta (1540–1600), in his *De procuranda Indorum salute* (Salamanca 1588), gives a detailed report on the success of the South American missions and on the shortcomings of the methods employed. Here the lack of qualifications in the clergy is presented as the reason for the symptoms of decay. However, de Acosta expresses himself as opposed to admitting Indians and colonists' sons to the priesthood.

The Jesuit Reductions in Paraguay

An especially characteristic undertaking of the Latin American missionary endeavor is provided by the so-called Reductions, villages where Christian Indians, segregated from the Spanish immigrants, lived under the more or less patriarchal authority of the missionaries. Best known are the Jesuit Reductions in Paraguay, but they were neither peculiar to this country nor to the Society of Jesus. In fact, such Christian villages were begun in the very first years of South American mission history. As early as 1503 an instruction laid down regulations for Indian settlements of this sort, and Las Casas experimented with this method of colonization and evangelization. In a sense, the *doctrinas* (like the *aldeas* in Portuguese missionary territory) were forerunners or variations of the reductions. But the system existed on the largest scale and in its most typical fashion in the Jesuit missions of Paraguay.

Invited into the country in 1585 by the Dominican Bishop Vittoria of Tucumán to evangelize the Indians who had retreated before the Spaniards into the inaccessible forests of the Pampas and the Gran Chaco, the first Jesuits conformed to the then prevailing methods of the itinerant mission. But the conversions thus made were not lasting, and the Jesuits were considering abandoning the work as a failure when their general Claudius Acquaviva ordered the erection of permanent settlements in which the Indians should live shielded as far as possible from outside influences. The mere spreading of the word, he said, was not enough; the seeds must also be tended. This project of isolation and concentration met with the approval of the Spanish crown, despite the colonists' opposition. The still unoccupied Paraná territory was turned over to the Jesuits with the full authority to gather all Christian Indians, independently of any other supervision and far from contact with the outside world. The execution of the mandate began in 1610. In four decades of assiduous work the missionaries pushed forward to the Brazilian province of Tape and united the Indians of the Guaraní and Chaco peoples into a Christian Indian state. There was no lack of resistance on the part of Church and state. Finally, the Indians had to be equipped with firearms in order to repulse raids made by *mestizo* kidnappers from Brazil. In the wars with the so-called *Paulistas* or "Mamelukes," thousands of neophytes were carried off and several reductions destroyed, but some thirty reductions, with about 150,000 Christian Indians, were victorious in 1641.

Problems of evangelization and of colonization, as they presented themselves, were on the whole brilliantly solved.

The Mission in the Philippines

With the Portuguese Ferdinand Magellan, who in Spanish service discovered the Philippines in 1521, there also landed Spanish Augustinian Hermits, who together with the crew proclaimed the Gospel to the natives. On Easter Magellan had Mass celebrated and a cross set up, to which the island Kings had to do reverence and homage. A village which refused was reduced to ashes. This act of violence caused a rising in which Magellan was murdered, and the crew and missionaries only escaped with difficulty.

In 1569 Spain formally took possession of the islands, regarding them as an extension of her American holdings and as outposts of the continent of Asia. The road from Madrid to Asia went via Mexico and the Philippines. Attention was directed almost exclusively at China, and this is the reason why missionary work on the islands was taken up only reluctantly.

Here too there began a downright migration of Spanish friars. Twenty-four Augustinian Hermits landed on Luzón in 1575 and were followed by the first Franciscans in 1577. Manila was made a see in 1579, and the first bishop, the Dominican Dominic de Salazar, wanted his confreres to play a role in the evangelization. His exertions in this regard make clear the dangers a journey overseas involved at the time. Of the twenty friars whom the bishop brought along, eighteen died en route, while only fifteen of thirty-two Dominicans who sailed from Spain in 1586 reached Manila. Still, the influx of new missionaries did not cease. Into the beginning of the seventeenth century 450 religious are said to have embarked for the Philippines.

From the islanders, who practiced a primitive animism, the evangelists encountered almost no resistance. Only in the Islamic principalities on Jolo and

Mindanao in the south of the archipelago was a barrier raised against their endeavors. On the other islands they could find gratification in abundant success. The number of Christians was 400,000 as early as 1585, and it increased to more than 2 million in 1620. In scarcely more than a half-century the mass of the inhabitants had become Christian.

From the viewpoint of method, the Philippine missions occupy an exceptional position within the history of the Spanish missions and *patronato,* the reason being the special status of the Philippines in the Spanish Colonial Empire. The islands could be reached only by way of Mexico. This so impeded commerce with the mother country that, in comparison with missionary work, it withdrew completely into the background. The missionaries seem to have recognized this exceptional situation, and they profited by it to avoid and prevent the mistakes that had been made in America. What had been impossible to a Las Casas could be realized here. There was no slavery and no forced labor. The missionaries had themselves named as protectors of the "Indians" and were able to shield them from all excesses of the whites. The consideration and gentleness shown to the natives did not fail to produce an effect. The Filipinos remained loyal to Spain and to their missionaries, with whom they maintained the colonial empire during 150 years against all attacks by Moros, Chinese, and Dutch.

The success of the undertaking meant a new Catholic nation, the only one in the Far East. The educational system flourished, with schools and colleges everywhere. In 1611 the Dominicans established the Colegio Santo Tomás, which became a university in 1645. A direct result of this intensive educational activity was that soon there were native priests, who in the course of time took charge of almost half the parishes. It was only the decline of the Spanish world power that was to make the first change in this favorable picture.

CHAPTER 107

The Missions under Portuguese Patronage

The transfer to the Portuguese kings of the rights of the *Militia Christi* and Alexander VI's award to Portugal of all territories to the east of the line of demarcation constituted the basis of Portuguese *padronado.* In the lands recently discovered and still to be discovered the Portuguese Crown had not only the duty of spreading the Christian faith but the right to nominate suitable incumbents to sees, churches, and benefices. "By this fact the Church in the Portuguese colonies was for all time delivered over to the state" and "thus the dignity of grand master of the *Militia*

Christi became the source of state absolutism in Portuguese missionary areas" (Jann)

When Columbus discovered the "West Indies" for Spain in 1492, Portuguese caravels in search of the Indies had already occupied the key positions of the African coast and under Bartolomeo Diaz in 1486–87 they had sailed around the "Cape of Storms," which John II (1481–95), overjoyed to be so near his goal, renamed the "Cape of Good Hope." In 1498 Vasco da Gama pushed up the East African coast and from there, aided by Arab pilots, reached India. In 1500 Pedro Alvares Cabral discovered Brazil; from there he sailed around the southern tip of Africa to India and brought the first cargo of Indian spices to Lisbon. The Arab spice monopoly had been broken. The approaches to the "Spice Islands" proper, or Moluccas, were in Portuguese possession by 1511. The taking of Malacca was celebrated in Lisbon as a victory for Christianity over Islam. And not entirely without justification: in the same year the Kings of Sumatra and Java, of Siam and Pegu (Burma) entered into friendly relations with Portugal, and in 1512 the Negus of Ethiopia sent an embassy to arrange peace and friendship with King Manuel I (1495–1521) of Portugal.

King Manuel at once took up the question of Portuguese missions. He had informed Alexander VI of his decision to send diocesan and regular priests as missionaries to the lands discovered since 1499 and had obtained by the Bull "Cum sicut maiestas" of 26 March 1500 the right to subject the region from the Cape of Good Hope to India inclusively to an apostolic delegate, who, like the grand prior of the *Militia Christi,* was to be given quasi-episcopal jurisdiction. Julius II encouraged these missionary endeavors by granting Portugal spiritual advantages and all of Manuel's missionaries a plenary indulgence. In the interests of a more efficient direction of the regions, which could be hardly supervised from Portugal, the urgency of erecting an overseas bishopric more and more imposed itself. For this purpose Manuel suggested to the Pope the capital of Madeira, Funchal. Leo X thereupon suppressed the jurisdiction of the *Militia Christi* and by the Bull "Pro excellenti praeeminentia" (12 June 1514) erected the diocese of Funchal, to comprise all conquered islands and lands from the southern border of Mauretania to the Indies in the East and Brazil in the West. Simultaneously King Manuel had all lands conquered and to be conquered adjudged as his inalienable possession.

It was not until 1534, at a time when Spain already had seven missionary jurisdictions in her overseas territories, that, in the interests of a further division of the vast diocese, Funchal was raised to metropolitan rank and given as suffragans Santiago de Cabo Verde, São Tomé, São Salvador de Angra (Azores), and Goa. But even this new arrangement was inadequate, for Goa embraced the entire area from the Cape of Good Hope as far as the Japanese islands, limited of course to the boundaries of the Portuguese colonial holdings, a restriction that was later to become extraordinarily significant. Just the same, the elevation of Goa to diocesan status made possible a development in keeping with local circumstances.

Portugal made absolutely no effort to penetrate beyond a more or less extensive coastal strip into the interior of the continent of Africa. And even here she possessed mere bases serving and protecting trade. The names given to the various coastal strips — Pepper Coast, Ivory Coast, Gold Coast, Slave Coast indicate what Portugal expected from Africa. Most lucrative was the commerce in "black ivory," or slaves, who were annually exported by the tens of thousands to the West Indies. Even priests, biased in favor of the opinions of the day, took part in this commerce.

When Portugal, toward the close of the sixteenth century and in the course of the seventeenth, ceased to be a world power and was losing one colonial area after another to the Dutch and the English, she was no longer able to fulfill the duties of her patronage completely. The personal union with Spain (1580–1640), resulting from the extinction of the Dynasty of Aviz, eventually affected missionary work. Prolonged vacancies in the overseas dioceses resulted and hence led to the decay of what had been so laboriously built up in the missionary lands.

Africa

West Africa to the mouth of the Congo, included under the name "Guinea" in contemporary reports, was entrusted by Pius II in 1462 to the Franciscans. Dominicans were also active in West Africa from 1486. But there were no enduring successes to be recorded except in the neighborhood of the Portuguese strongholds.

In the *Congo* (1482) the victory of the Infante Afonso over the pagan opposition led by his brother inaugurated a period which held out hope of the Christianization of the entire Congo. King Afonso himself preached to his subjects and, when his requests for missionaries went unanswered, sent his own son with several companions to Lisbon to be educated there as priests. It seems that Afonso's letters were falsified by interpreters or were suppressed by the local Portuguese authorities. Finally, "since he could no longer trust any Portuguese," Afonso had a Congolese student write to entreat Manuel I "by the Saviour's Passion" to help him; in the letter he likens the whites in Africa, including the priests, to the Jews who crucified Christ. Finally, he had the consolation of receiving back his son Henry as titular Bishop of Utica (1521). Afonso expected great things of him for the Christianization of his Empire. There is no news of Henry after 1534, and a letter written by his father in 1539 speaks of him as dead. King Afonso himself died in 1541.

King Afonso of the Congo is one of the most tragic figures in the history of Europe's encounter with lands beyond the seas. He asked for bread and received stones. Manuel I of Portugal thus instructed his envoys to him: "Although our efforts are directed first of all to the greater glory of God and the satisfaction of the King, still you must explain to the King of the Congo, as if you were speaking in my name, what he has to do in order to fill our ships with slaves, copper, and ivory."

Under Afonso's grandson Diogo the first Jesuits came to the Congo in 1548. They found a greatly decayed Christianity. Their remonstrances, which did not spare even the King, so enraged him that he ordered all whites to quit his Empire. All attempts to begin again were failures.

Angola, explored by the Portuguese as early as 1520, did not establish contacts with Portugal until 1558. In a letter announcing the departure of the first missionaries it is expressly noted that the Gospel had not hitherto been preached in Angola. It was not till 1581 that the Portuguese won a victory and the missionaries their first converts.

East Africa. Authenticated information on missionary activity on the east coast of Africa does not antedate 1559. The priests in the fortified port cities labored exclusively among the Portuguese soldiers and traders. Even Saint Francis Xavier, passing through Mozambique, had to be content with preaching to Portuguese Christians.

In 1559 a report reached the Jesuits in Goa that a son of the King of Inhambane (Zambesi) had had himself baptized and in his father's name was asking for missionaries. The Jesuits accepted the mission, since Inhambane had not yet been touched by Islam. Furthermore, from there they hoped to find access to the Gold Emperor of Monomotapa. In Inhambane Father Gonçalo da Silveira he achieved initial success, baptizing the King and 400 of his people. And in 1561 he was able to baptize the Emperor of Monomotapa, thereby arousing a strong movement toward Christianity. This alerted the Muslims, who feared for their trade and influence. In Inhambane, too, things became so difficult that the missionary who had remained there decided to return to India. The East Africa mission had collapsed, and the Portuguese traders in Mozambique, with an eye to their trade, opposed its continuance. At length Dominicans resumed their missionary work in 1577 and Jesuits in 1607.

Asia

India. The early missionary age in India was inaugurated by diocesan priests and the older Orders, chiefly Franciscans and Dominicans. Coming with the explorers and conquerors, they built monasteries and churches or destroyed temples and replaced them with churches. But their activity among the natives was limited by their ignorance of the languages and their faulty methods. Baptism was the goal of their preaching; once it was achieved, the missionaries moved on, without taking sufficient care for the absorption of Christian doctrine. There was no dearth of successes so far as numbers go. Many conversions to Christianity were obtained by the sword, others were purchased by worldly benefits. Successes could be obtained even among the schismatic "Saint Thomas Christians" of South India. However, missionary efforts were seriously hindered by the wicked lives of the Portuguese and by the Hindu caste system. Christians came almost exclusively from the lowest strata of the population.

The second period of India's missionary history began with the entrance of the Jesuits into evangelization. Ignatius Loyola, approached by John III for some members of the Society, which had just obtained papal confirmation, selected Francis Xavier (1506–52) for India. Paul III named him legate in 1541 and provided him with the fullest authority. Francis Xavier became the Apostle of India and of the entire Far East and is the greatest missionary of modern times.

Francis waived his legatine authority and placed himself at the disposal of the Bishop of Goa. At the beginning of his career he differed from the other missionaries only in his extraordinary zeal. His method, like theirs, was determined by tradition. His first care was for the Portuguese colonists, whose moral and religious life had hopelessly deteriorated. Only then did he turn to the conversion of the pagans. He visited the existing congregations on the Paravas and Malabar coasts, worked to organize them, preached, and baptized. In 1545 he undertook a missionary exploration of the Portuguese colonial area. His journey carried him beyond Cochin and Malacca to the Moluccas (Amboina, Ternate) and then back to Malacca, where his attention was directed to Japan. In Japan (1549–51) he conceived the plan of extending his activity to China; but entry was denied him. Alone and forsaken, he died on the night of 2–3 December 1552 on the rocky island of Sanch'uan near Canton.

Francis Xavier's merit does not lie in his having shown the methods of the modern mission in the Far East. Far more important for the missions among the highly cultured peoples of Asia was the realization that, if the missionaries wanted to gain foreign and unfamiliar peoples for Christianity, they must adapt themselves to them. Questions about the successes of the saint, who was canonized by Gregory XV in 1622, about his miracles and the gift of tongues attributed to him, should therefore pale before the appraisal of his understanding of method. The number of those he baptized, including many children of Christian parents, may have amounted to 30,000 people. Reports of miracles appeared only after his death, and in his letters he complained of the difficulties in communication because of language. What made him a great missionary was the saint's power to attract.

In 1557–58 Goa became the metropolitan see of all of East Asia. This early granting of autonomy to the Church in India was of great importance for missionary procedure. At numerous provincial councils in Goa steps were taken against the use of force and against state interference and a more convincing method of conversion was recommended.

Jurisdiction over the St. Thomas Christians on the Malabar Coast, was disputed among the Nestorian Patriarch of Mosul, the Chaldean Patriarch of Amida, and the Archbishop of Goa. Matters were aggravated by the fact that both patriarchs sought to install in the sees of the Saint Thomas Christian men of their respective obediences, while the Portuguese Franciscans, active in Malabar for a half-century, wanted a Latin bishop at Angamale. The attendant scandalous political intrigues only confused the situation.

Elsewhere in India Christianity spread very slowly. A promising endeavor was undertaken by the Italian Jesuit, Roberto de Nobili (1577–1656). He realized that the transfer of Western usages and institutions deprived Christianity of any prospect of lasting success. Hence he decided to adapt himself to the Hindus' manner of life and viewpoints. He studied Tamil, Telugu, and Sanskrit and dressed and lived as a penitential monk. His neophytes were allowed to retain Hindu customs in so far as these were not pagan in character. This method proved to be very effective with the Brahmins, who had hitherto rejected Christianity. In 1609 he had to build a church for them. De Nobili did not escape opposition, but his method was finally approved by Gregory XV. At de Nobili's death the Madura mission counted 40,000 faithful.

Malay Archipelago. The goal of the Portuguese seafarers' commercial policy was the "Spice Islands," the source of the cloves so much desired by Europe. In 1511 they were discovered in the Moluccas. In accordance with the attitude of the age, the merchants felt obliged to spread the faith in the islands they had discovered. They sought to win the chiefs, and, if successful, left there the religious who had made the voyage with them. However, since most of the inhabitants were Muslims, the Christians and their missionaries were persecuted. As early as 1521 the Portuguese had erected a fortress on Ternate for the protection of their commerce. The island had to be reconquered and "reconverted" after 1534. Francis Xavier visited the Moluccas in 1546–47. Eventually the Dutch gained possession of the islands and the missions fell into ruin.

The first missionary efforts on Celebes (1525) were fruitless. But in 1548 the Franciscans arrived and their preaching of hell-fire converted whole princedoms in South Celebes; elsewhere too the concept of hell is said to have impressed the Muslims far more than tidings of paradise. Christianity was unable to penetrate North Celebes until Jesuits arrived there in 1563. They are supposed to have baptized a quarter of the population.

The small Sunda Islands, discovered by Spaniards in 1522 during the first circumnavigation of the globe, were, however, successfully evangelized by the Dominicans. Their chief center was the island of Solor, from which Christianity spread to the other islands, and before long more than fifty thousand believers were counted. But Muslim opposition and Portuguese blunders almost wiped out the successes. In spite of the Dutch conquest of the islands, the Dominicans continued their work and were even able to induce a new flowering of Christianity. The Solor missions managed to survive into the eighteenth century.

Japan was accidentally discovered by the Portuguese in 1542–43, when a vessel, driven off course by a typhoon, landed there instead of in Siam. In 1548–49 the Portuguese undertook the first expedition to establish commercial relations with Japan. Francis Xavier had become interested in the island empire of the Far East and went there with them in 1549. His aim was to win the Emperor to the faith and through him and the Buddhist monasteries to convert the people. But he soon had to acknowledge that the Mikado was only the nominal ruler of the country. In fact, Japan was in a state of anarchy; the island empire had dissolved into some fifty petty states and the territorial princes, or Daimyos, did as they pleased. To gain access to them, Francis decided henceforth to proceed as papal legate in great splendor and he directed that future missionaries should seek to win the people by their public appearance, among other things by observing the Japanese rules of etiquette. The encounter with the high culture of the Japanese induced the saint to abandon the traditional Europeanizing method and to urge a far-reaching accommodation. In his religious discussions with Buddhist monks he unhesitatingly accepted their religious concepts, for example the term *Dainichi* for God. But when he discovered that *Dainichi* denoted, not a personal being, but the original substance of all things, he resumed the Latin *Deus.*

Francis Xavier returned to Goa in 1551, entrusting to his companion, Father Cosmas de Torres, three Christian communities with approximately 1000 neophytes, all of them from the lower classes. The first Daimyo was not baptized until 1563, but so many others soon followed that their conversion became the special mark of the early Japanese mission. Their example attracted many Samurai and Bonzes and finally the people. In certain parts of Japan regular mass conversions occurred. Since in Japan the mission could not, as was the case elsewhere, claim the assistance of the Portuguese state, these successes cannot be overestimated.

Of course, the missionaries had to support themselves. This unfortunately induced them to participate in the Portuguese silk trade and to lease houses which they had received as gifts. This would have been permitted if disagreements in regard to procedures had not arisen among the missionaries. De Torres' successor, Francisco Cabral, was opposed to any accommodation and insisted on the Europeanizing missionary method traditional among the Portuguese. This produced tension within the Christian communities, especially among Christians of the higher classes. Still, the number of Christians grew and reached 150,000 while Cabral was in charge (c. 1580). In 1576 Japan was detached from the diocese of Malacca and placed under the new see of Macao.

The internal crisis was exorcised by the arrival as visitor of Father Alessandro Valignano (1539–1606). This farsighted and intelligent man quickly carried out a reform of the mission in accord with Xavier's principles of accommodation, prescribed a thorough study of the language by the missionaries, and, with the construction of two seminaries, laid the foundation for a native diocesan and regular clergy. On his departure he took along a Japanese embassy to the Pope and the King of Spain. The embassy not only caused a sensation in Europe (1582–90) but aroused a keen interest in the Japanese mission.

Meanwhile a reaction had taken place in Japan's internal politics. Following the restricting of the arbitrariness of the Daimyos by the Commander-in-Chief Nobunaga between 1564 and 1568, Hideyoshi acquired as regent of the Mikado an almost unlimited authority in the early 1580s. Originally friendly to the Christians, he became suspicious because of the indiscretions of the mission superior Coelho and was turned into a foe of Christianity. In 1587 he issued an order for the expulsion of all missionaries. Though the order was not carried out, the work had to be done much more circumspectly. Still, between 1587 and 1597 the Jesuits gained 65,000 additional converts. In 1588 Japan became a separate diocese, with Funai as the episcopal residence.

In the missionary sphere too an entirely new situation had arisen in Japan. After the union of the Portuguese and Spanish crowns in 1580 Spanish missionaries from the Philippines sought to enter the Portuguese missionary area, though in 1585 Gregory XIII had granted the Society of Jesus the exclusive right to evangelize the Far East. In 1593 Franciscans began missionary work in Japan. Having gained the good will of Hideyoshi, they displayed great zeal and, though adhering to the traditional Spanish method, had considerable success. But the national antipathies of Portuguese and Spanish were more fundamental than the differences in method and the rivalry of the Orders. Hideyoshi skillfully exploited these by subtle trickery and finally discovered a pretext for striking at Christianity, the celebrated and still sharply debated remark of the pilot of the *San Felipe,* that the Spaniards sent merchants and missionaries in order to conquer foreign lands with their assistance. The sequel was the first mass martyrdom of Nagasaki, where the six Spanish Franciscans, three Japanese Jesuits, and seventeen other Japanese Christians suffered death on 5 February 1597. Despite this, the Franciscans resumed the work in Japan in 1598 and, following the annulment of the Jesuits' privilege, Spanish Dominicans and Augustinians also arrived. The number of Christians continued to grow in spite of the persecution and in 1614 amounted to about three hundred thousand. The first Japanese priests were ordained in 1601.

On Hideyoshi's death in 1598, wars raged again between rival army commanders. The victor, Tokugawa Ieyasu, established a military dynasty that lasted until 1868. That the Christians among the Daimyos might, perhaps with outside aid, unite against the central government was sufficient cause for Ieyasu to declare war on Christianity. The commercial intrigues of the European powers, aggravated by the denominational opposition of Portuguese and Spaniards on the one hand and Dutch and English on the other, made him see in the religion of the West a national danger for Japan. From 1603 one after another apostatized. In 1613 Ieyasu issued an edict against Christians, which was followed in 1614 by a decree of banishment. Only eighteen Jesuits, seven Dominicans, six Franciscans, five diocesan priests, and one Augustinian remained. Every year many Christians died as martyrs. In the second mass martyrdom 100 died together, including eighteen missionaries from the four Orders. The persecution grew in intensity. After 1623 every Japanese had to declare publicly his religious adherence every year. From 1627 the so-called *efumi,* or "image-trampling," prevailed, for the persecutors desired to make apostates rather than martyrs. By 1630 the number of those who had died for their faith amounted to 4,045. The persecution found its final climax in the Shimabara Revolt of 1637–38, in which 30,000 Christians were put to death. Japan shut itself off more and more from the outside world. The Dutch alone were able to conduct a modest trade on the island of Deshima until 1854. To achieve this, they had cooperated in putting down the Shimabara Revolt. Christianity had thereafter to lead a catacomb existence in Japan but did maintain itself into the nineteenth century.

China, Francis Xavier's death at the very gates of China was the reason prompting the Jesuits to seek admission to the sealed off Middle Empire, which had been known to the Portuguese since 1514–15. But the Portuguese did not succeed in establishing relations with China until 1554. They acquired the Gozan peninsula and there founded the city of Macao, which was to be the focal point of European interests in the Far East for 300 years. The city soon became also the base and refuge of missionaries, but all efforts from 1555 on to set foot in China failed. Macao became an episcopal see in 1576, and, to satisfy the Spaniards, Manila had to be given the same honor in 1581. Thus in the Far East there were two centers from which efforts were made to obtain access to China. Many difficulties of the China mission derived from the fact that missionaries of different nationalities took up their activities in the Middle Empire from different starting points. Here too the personal union of the two Iberian empires made itself felt.

Finally in 1583 two Jesuits, Michele Ruggieri and Matteo Ricci (1552–1610), succeeded in obtaining authorization to reside in China. They settled at Chao-ch'ing near Canton and began their work dressed as Buddhist monks. They eagerly learned Chinese and studied the writings of Confucius and other Chinese sages. Compared with the statistics then in use, their success was slight. By 1586 they had gathered no more than forty converts. An effort to extend their sphere of activity brought forth a prohibition of remaining longer in Chao-ch'ing, but they were permitted to settle in another place in the same province. There they changed their dress, for they had discovered that the Buddhist monks were not highly regarded. From then on they appeared in the robes of scholars and were able to use their knowledge of the profane sciences for the spread of the faith. From Ricci's discussions with Chinese scholars came his *The True Doctrine of God,* a brochure later admitted among the Chinese classics.

The missionaries had quickly learned that everything depended on gaining the good will of the Emperor. Ricci sought in every way to be admitted to the

Court at Beijing. His efforts led to the founding of settlements at Nan-ch'ing and Nanking, where Ricci himself took up residence in 1598. Here he produced the famous "Map of Ten Thousand Empires," a map of the world on which Ricci, to avoid hurting the feelings of the Chinese, made China literally the "Middle Empire" in the very center of the map. It was here that Ricci gained his most important convert, the scholar Hsu Kuang-ch'i, who, as Paul Hsu, was to play a notable role in China's mission history.

In 1601 Ricci was able to settle in Beijing. The Emperor himself presented the Jesuits with a house and allowed them to erect a church. Ricci developed an extensive teaching and gained influential members of the imperial court and the learned world for the faith. When Ricci died in 1610 at the age of fifty-eight, exhausted by his tireless activity, he left his confreres, in his own words, "before a gate that can be opened to the advantage of all but not without toil and danger."

Soon after Ricci's death his liberal accommodations — that the Chinese Christians might continue after baptism to honor their ancestors and Confucius — caused scandal and later gave rise to the so-called Dispute over Rites and Accommodation. About one thing there is no room for doubt: Ricci was a man of apostolic outlook and a capable missionary, who destroyed prejudices against the Christian religion and won important scholars for the faith. His converts endured heroically the persecutions that soon overtook them. In spite of all difficulties, Christianity in China rose from 5,000 in 1615 to 38,200 in 1636.

Johann Adam Schall von Bell (c. 1591–1666) of Cologne was Ricci's real and effective successor for the period from 1630 to 1666. He skillfully brought the mission through the troubles of his day.

Political confusion was aggravated by the tension among the Christians, which had been produced by missionaries from the Spanish Philippines.

The appearance of the Spanish missionaries, who showed very little consideration for the missionaries already active in the country, caused much perplexity among the faithful. They went about in their habits, preached publicly, cross in hand, and made clear to the faithful their opposition to the worship of ancestors and of Confucius. The conflict in method was to grow into the disastrous Disputes over Rites. Around the middle of the seventeenth century the China mission experienced a new flowering in spite of all the internal and external confusion. In 1651 the Congregation of Propaganda was already considering a plan to erect a patriarchate in Beijing and to subject to it two or three archbishoprics and twelve bishoprics. But matters were to take an entirely different course.

Indochina. From 1511 Malacca served as the point of departure for mission work in Indochina. It was an almost fruitless effort because of the deplorable example of the Portuguese, although Franciscans, Dominicans, Jesuits, and Augustinians had monasteries and churches in the city and in 1557–58 Malacca had been made a diocese.

Toward the close of the sixteenth century missionaries were admitted to Burma, the ancient Pegu, as chaplains for the Portuguese mercenaries and Goan prisoners of war, who, having married Burmese wives, established Catholic village communities.

The Church's most promising mission field lay to the east, in the empires of Annam, Cochin-China, and Tongking. But here too the work of the Portuguese

Franciscans was made more difficult by their Spanish confreres from Manila. The Jesuits were the first to succeed in establishing stable communities (from 1615). In spite of a royal prohibition (1630), the number of Christians continued to mount, thanks to native lay catechists. In 1639 there were 82,000 Tonkinese Christians.

Brazil

From the time of its discovery by Europeans in 1500 Brazil saw numerous but isolated missionary endeavors, made by Portuguese, Spanish, and Italian Franciscans of the various branches of the Order. As a consequence of the cruelty of Portuguese soldiers, traders, and colonists, these undertakings had little permanent success. Enduring missionary activity had to await the arrival of the Jesuits, who came in 1549 with the governor, Tomé de Souza. The first bishop, Pedro Fernandes Sardinha, could not cope with the situation. The insubordination of his own priests threatened to cancel out their labors as missionaries. In 1556 the bishop fell into the hands of pagan Indians, who ate him.

In 1506 there arose in Bahia the Colegio de Jesus, which was destined to become the famous center for the training of the Brazilian clergy and a model for all similar institutions in the larger cities of Brazil. Its importance becomes clear from the curious fact that in the Portuguese colonial sphere of influence in America there was not a single university or printing press.

The Jesuits' educational activity was entirely geared to the service of the missions among the Indian population. The missionaries, who within a few years pushed forward to the extreme south of the country and began their Guarani mission, along the Portuguese-Spanish border, sought to acquire the local languages, instructed the children in reading and writing, and translated prayers and catechisms. In regard to missionary methods it is significant that the Jesuits were very cautious about conferring baptism. They required a long period of preparation and carefully selected the neophytes from the number of catechumens. They were even slower in allowing the new Christians to receive communion. The first ones were not admitted to Easter Communion until 1573 and they had to prepare for it by fasting and mortification. This procedure explains why the Jesuits did not accept a single Indian into the Society or let any be ordained.

The work of the missionaries was obstructed by the colonists, above all by the mulattoes known as "Mamelukes." Before long the Jesuits in Brazil were filling a role analogous to that of Las Casas in Spanish America. To protect the Indians, they gathered them into communities called *aldeas* or *doutrinas* or into reductions. In 1609 they succeeded in doing away with Indian slavery, but the Portuguese colonists were able to render the law inoperative by introducing forced labor.

Toward the end of the sixteenth century other Orders also entered the field. Carmelites came in 1580, Benedictines in 1581, and a bit later Augustinians and Oratorians. When the competing French broke into Latin America at the beginning of the seventeenth century and founded a colony of their own at Maranhão in North Brazil, they obtained Capuchin missionaries for their district. France was preparing to enter the contest with the Iberian colonial powers.

Entry of France into the Mission Field

North America. Francis I of France (1515–47) was not inclined to stand aloof from the partition of the world. He assisted Giovanni de Verrazzano, a Venetian in French service, who sighted the Hudson in 1523, and Jacques Cartier, who in 1534 took possession of Canada for France. Francis also, either from conviction or from political considerations, looked upon discovery and conquest as a means for the conversion of the "savages." But possession of Canada remained unexploited. French failure in Brazil — in 1557 they were driven from the Bay of Rio de Janeiro which they had occupied two years before — made them recognize *de facto* the division of the world by Alexander VI. Later Henry IV (1589–1610) managed to secure in the Treaty of Vervins of 1598 the right to annex territory north of an east-west line which intersected the Canary Islands.

The Near East. France was chiefly interested in gaining influence in the Near East, and to this end Louis XIII (1610–43) and his minister, Cardinal Richelieu (1585–1642), made special use of the Capuchins. Their most eager assistant was Father Joseph of Paris, born François Le Clerc du Tremblay, Baron de Maffliers (1577–1638), in whom was a strange blend of crusading ardor and diplomatic finesse. Within a short time he managed to have 100 of his confreres sent to the Near East under a French protectorate.

Hence France's entry into the mission field took place despite the Portuguese and Spanish rights of patronage. And from the beginning it was clear how deeply national interests were involved. Thus was the ground prepared for the French protectorate of the missions that was destined to play a fateful role in their future history.

Chapter 108

The Sacred Congregation for the Propagation of the Faith

Into the seventeenth century the history of the missions was determined almost exclusively by the partition of the world into Portuguese and Spanish spheres of influence and the related rights of patronage. But it became increasingly more apparent that the two powers were far more concerned for their rights than for their duties. The view was even expounded that the Pope in granting the right of patronage had renounced his own rights over the missions. His instructions and decisions were subjected to a royal *placet,* without which they were not valid. In mission affairs the Kings were no longer regarded as merely the Pope's vicars but as the direct representatives of God.

This development and the resulting abuses in mission lands called for the taking of decisive action by Rome, especially since the reform Popes had just taken the first steps to recover leadership in missionary work. It was not until Clement VIII that a specific Congregation of the Missions was constituted.

The view that a congregation of this sort must form part of the permanent set-up of the Curia made steady progress and found literary expression in the *De procuranda salute omnium genitum* of the theorist of the missions, the Carmelite Thomas of Jesus (1564–1627). In Book III the institution of a Roman Congregation for the Propagation of the Faith was urged. Gregory XV took up the suggestion and before the end of the first year of his pontificate established the *Sacra Congregatio de Propaganda Fide* on Epiphany 1622. The Pope claimed in the fullest degree the duty and right to spread the faith as the chief task of the papal role of shepherd of souls. In this way the new congregation was to prepare for the change "from the colonial mission to the purely Church mission" (Kilger). Hence the entire mission system was to be subordinated to the Roman central authority; all missionaries were to depend on it in the most direct manner possible and be sent out by it, missionary methods were to be regulated, and mission fields to be assigned by it.

To carry out this task it was important first of all to clarify the status of the missions. For this purpose the earth was divided into twelve provinces, which were allotted to the respective nuncios in Europe and to the patriarchal vicars in the Near East. The nuncios were to compile information from their districts and then to report to Propaganda. In actual fact, the first reports came in from the missionary Orders. Relying on them, the first secretary of the congregation, Francesco Ingoli (1622–49), composed three important memoranda in which he exposed the shortcomings and hindrances in missionary work and indicated remedies that would eliminate them. Almost everywhere missionary activity was the victim both of jurisdictional quarrels between the local bishops and the religious and of the opposition between the older Orders and the Jesuits. Similarly, nationalist rivalries among missionaries and a mania to feather their own nest during residence overseas contributed to making their work ineffectual. Hence Ingoli felt that a clear distinction of missionary areas according to membership in the Orders and nationality was the first achievement to be sought. In addition, the sees were to be increased in number and assigned as far as possible to members of the diocesan clergy. An on the spot supervision of missionary work should be realized by the dispatching of papal legates or nuncios. In order to stop the mercantile activities of the missionaries, all departing missionaries had to be checked in regard to their pure intentions, and to guarantee this Ingoli wanted branches of Propaganda to be set up in Seville and Lisbon. He regarded as particularly urgent the formation of a native clergy, which should share in the work and in the direction of the missions on an equality with the foreign missionaries.

A cursory glance at the *Collectanea S. Congregationis de Propaganda Fide* is sufficient to show that these guidelines had existence not only on paper. The first care was for the training of missionaries, and as early as 15 April 1622 a special committee for the Roman seminaries and national colleges was set up. The various generals of Orders were admonished to establish schools for teaching languages to future missionaries (no. 7), and Propaganda itself erected seven schools of apologetics for the education of missionaries destined for work among heretics. On missionary bishops was imposed the obligation of admitting qualified youths to the priesthood. Before long Propaganda was in a position to carry out its principles.

Many things which are today taken for granted in missionary efforts were first proposed at that time, even though they could not be immediately realized. Such are: the duty of submitting an annual report (no. 22); the prohibition of giving up the mission without authorization (no. 41); the determining of the conditions in which missionaries may act as physicians (no. 42); the distinction between religious superiors and mission superiors (no. 46); the granting of special faculties to missionaries (nos. 88f.); and regulations on Church music (no. 107).

Not unexpectedly, this activity of the Propaganda Congregation encountered lively opposition from the powers enjoying patronage. Portugal especially, which had suffered painful losses of power in its East Indian possessions because of the union with Spain, defended its patronage in order thereby to retain influence overseas at least in the spiritual domain. But in the final analysis, the Congregation of Propaganda was concerned less with power than with an entirely new concept of the missions. The patronage powers had after all proved that it was their aim to assimilate the newly gained Christians to themselves in every respect, that in fact they were transplanting European Christianity overseas. But the Propaganda represented more than ever before the contrary idea. By means of a clergy recruited from the mission countries an indigenous Christianity was to be developed and a Church in complete harmony with it was to be founded.

The Spanish patronage power also resisted the claims made by Propaganda in regard to the papacy's exclusive right over the missions. The Catholic powers stubbornly refused to accept Propaganda's claim to the exclusive right to issue orders in regard to the missions.

It should cause no surprise that Propaganda sought to deal in another way with the difficulties arising from the patronage powers and the Orders by establishing missions outside the patronage lands and entrusting them to religious communities which had hitherto done little or hardly any missionary work, such as the Carmelites and the Capuchins. Since France had long sought, for reasons easy to understand, to open up overseas colonial areas of its own and to maintain missions in them, Propaganda obtained the opportunity it wanted. For soon almost all the dioceses in the Portuguese patronage area were vacant. In 1649 Brazil and Africa were without bishops, as were the East Indian sees of Cochin, Mailapur, Macao, and Funai. The course adopted by Rome in an effort to liquidate this state of affairs introduced a new period in the history of Catholic missions.

Section Five

European Counter Reformation and Confessional Absolutism (1605–55)

CHAPTER 109

Paul V, Gregory XV, and the Beginnings of the Central European Counter Reformation

Sustained by the religious and intellectual forces of the Tridentine Reform, the papacy under Paul V and Gregory XV attained a position which can be compared only with that of the High Middle Ages. Its neutrality between the rival Catholic great powers, Spain and France, did not as yet work against Catholic interests, because France's relations with the rising Protestant powers of the North, the rebel Netherlands, England, and Sweden, had not yet been solidified into alliances for war. Hence the active Catholic faction in the Empire, the League, and Emperor Ferdinand II succeeded in defeating the disunited Protestants and in pushing the restoration of lost lands to the Catholic Church. But since Urban VIII was unwilling and perhaps not in a position to thwart Cardinal Richelieu's policy of alliance with Protestants, the defeat of the Catholics in the Empire sealed the end of the Counter Reformation and of the papacy's position of political leadership. From the Peace of Westphalia in 1648 its influence subsided irresistibly and the spirit of the Catholic Reform weakened. Religious and intellectual leadership within the Church passed from Italy and Spain to France, but also the secularization of European thought announced itself.

The French Cardinal Joyeuse succeeded in carrying the election of Cardinals de Medici. As ambassador of Cosimo I in Rome, Leo XI had become the favorite disciple of Saint Philip Neri and was highly esteemed for his piety and integrity. But on 27 April 1605 he died as a result of a chili which he had caught when taking possession of the Lateran.

In the next conclave (8–16 May 1605), after vehement confrontations, the disputing parties agreed on the fifty-two-year-old Camillus Borghese, hardly noticed until now. Paul V came from a family of lawyers. At first lacking in political experience, he conscientiously familiarized himself with matters of state.

Paul V's policy was based on the principle of neutrality vis-à-vis the tension between Spain and France. In an effort to prevent the threatened war from breaking out, Cardinals Millini and Barberini were dispatched as peace envoys to Spain and France, but before they were able to carry out their commission Henry IV was assassinated on 14 May 1610 by a fanatic. The impending European war was averted, but the pernicious rivalry of the two great powers continued even though the dynastic alliance desired by the Curia was effected by the marriage in 1616 of the Bourbon Louis XIII to Anne of Austria, daughter of the Habsburg Philip III.

Conflict with Venice

The conflict of Paul V with the Republic of Venice very nearly led to a European war, which would necessarily have acquired the character of a religious war. Even before the Pope's accession the Venetian *Signoria* had forbidden the erecting of churches, monasteries, and hospitals and the acquiring of real estate by the Church without the permission of the state and, without regard to the *privilegium fori*, had brought two unworthy clerics to trial and had imprisoned them. In briefs of 10 December 1605 and 26 March 1606, Paul V condemned these procedures and, on the republic's declining to cancel its measures, sent an ultimatum threatening excommunication and interdict on 17 April 1606. On the advice of its official theologian, the shrewd and fluent Servite Paul Sarpi (1552–1623), the *Signoria*, protesting its divine right, forbade the publication of the papal censures under pain of death. After the expiration of the four weeks' respite allowed, the censures became effective but were ignored by the republic as invalid. A majority of the clergy obeyed the state and disregarded the interdict. All diocesan and regular priests who observed it, headed by the Jesuits, were banished. In his *Treatise on the Interdict* and numerous other polemics Sarpi denied its validity on the ground that the Pope was abusing his authority and whoever obeyed him was guilty of sin. The conflict over Church policy was escalated to a conflict of principle over the relations of the spiritual to the secular power. The apostasy of Venice from the Church and even a European war were distinct possibilities, especially when England, through its ambassador, Wotton, held out to the *Signoria* the prospect of support by the Protestant powers.

It was only after Cardinal Joyeuse, acting on instructions from Henry IV, had ascertained in the spring of 1607 how far the *Signoria* was prepared to yield that the Pope also gave in. The two imprisoned ecclesiastics were surrendered to Joyeuse. The *Signoria* promised not to repeal the laws in dispute, but not to enforce them, and the Kings of France and Spain vouched for this. On 21 April 1607 Joyeuse absolved the *Signoria* from the ecclesiastical censures it had incurred; thus the *Signoria* tacitly acknowledged their existence. The Pope's defeat was only thinly veiled. The demanded surrender of Sarpi and of his partisans, Micanzio and Marsiglio, was refused and for almost fifty years the Jesuits were excluded from Venetian territory. Sarpi's *History of the Council of Trent*, printed in London in 1619, was inspired by hatred of the papacy and greatly damaged its prestige.

Paul V's death was followed by a brief conclave on 8 and 9 February 1621. The choice fell on Allessandro Ludovisi, beloved for his kindness, esteemed for his knowledge of law, but in poor health. In memory of Gregory XIII, his fellow Bolognese, he styled himself Gregory XV. His right arm was the Cardinal Nephew, Ludovico Ludovisi, very much like him in character and a gifted statesman, whose many-faceted intellectual interests are demonstrated by the construction of Sant'Ignazio, the layout of the Villa Ludovisi on the Pincio, and his collections of antiques. "Let the fear and love of God be your political wisdom," was the Pope's admonition to his nephew. According to Pastor, "Probably never has a short pontificate left such deep traces in history."

In the bull on the papal election, 15 November 1621, the so called election by adoration which had taken place in several recent elections, was not excluded, but the secret written vote was prescribed as the rule. Subsequent "accession" was for the future to be allowed only in writing and only once after each of the two daily scrutinies. The greatness of the Ludovisi pontificate was revealed most clearly in the establishment of the Congregation for the Propagation of the Faith in 1622. Financially well endowed and furnished with exceptional authority, it was conceived as the organ for the coordination of the missions in America, Asia, and Africa and as the counterpoise of the patronage exercised by the Spanish and Portuguese crowns. But since relations with the Eastern Churches and the spread of the Catholic faith in the parts of North Europe that had become entirely or mostly Protestant were assigned to it, it developed into the headquarters of the Counter Reformation. Its presupposition was the continuance of the Catholic Reform, in which were concentrated the forces for the self-assertion of the Church in the struggle against Protestantism, and no less the political and military successes of the Catholic powers at the beginning of the Thirty Years' War.

Successes and Failures

The implementation of the reform decrees of the Council of Trent was the chief concern of both Paul V and Gregory XV. The duty of residence was again enjoined on the bishops, and titular rather than residential bishops began to be appointed nuncios. The exertions of the Nuncios Barberini and Ubaldini to achieve the acceptance of Trent by France finally collapsed at the Estates General of 1614–15 because of the resistance of the Third Estate and of the *Parlement* of Paris, but on 7 July 1615 the clergy voted the publication of the reform decrees in provincial councils. In the Spanish Netherlands the decrees of the Provincial Council of Mechlin (1607) and of the diocesan synods following were declared binding by the government. In 1621 the Cologne Nuncio Albergati wrote that "the salvation of Germany depends" on the publication and observance of Trent. In the conviction that the Catholic renewal was based not merely on the enforcement of laws but equally on the strength of ideals, the great sixteenth-century champions of renewal were raised to the honors of the altar. Charles Borromeo was canonized in 1610. Paul V had beatified Ignatius Loyola in 1609, Teresa of Avila in 1614, Philip Neri in 1615, and Francis Xavier in 1619; on 12 March 1622 the four of them were canonized in a single ceremony which in brilliance surpassed all previous celebrations.

But setbacks were not lacking. When on 5 November 1605 it was discovered that a group of English Catholics planned to blow up Parliament in order to kill King James I, suspicion of complicity fell on the Jesuit Garnet, who had acquired knowledge of the "Gunpowder Plot" under the seal of confession but had sought to stop the crime. New laws aggravated the situation of the English Catholics. An oath was required of them to the effect that James I was the lawful King of England and that the Pope had no power to depose him. The attitude to the oath of loyalty split the English Catholics into two factions.

In the Habsburg hereditary states the dissension between the incompetent Emperor Rudolf II and his brothers resulted in far-reaching concessions to the Protestants, which raised apprehension of serious losses to the Church. The Calvinist estates of Hungary obtained religious liberty in the Peace of Vienna (1606), as did the adherents of the Bohemian Confession in the "Letter of Majesty" of 9 July 1609. King Matthias extended the rights of the Hungarian Calvinists and in 1609 granted religious liberty to the Protestant estates of Upper Austria, a move synonymous with the suppression of Catholicism in their lands.

Despite these reverses the Catholics' self-assurance was so strengthened that they ceased to be satisfied with merely preserving what they held and considered the pushing back of Protestantism and the reconquest of lost areas. Thus the Counter Reformation sought the aid of Poland, where the political disunion of the Catholics had been surmounted through the establishing of the League, while in Emperor Ferdinand II the House of Habsburg acquired a leader for whom the defense and propagation of the Catholic religion was a matter of conscience.

Start of the Thirty Years' War

The execution by Duke Maximilian I of Bavaria of the ban against the Free City of Donauwörth, which had violated the Religious Peace, and the unlawful imposition of Catholicism on the city led to the bolting of the Diet of Regensburg by the Protestant estates and to the forming of a league, the Union (16 May 1608), led by the Calvinist Elector Palatine. The reply to this was the concluding a year later of a Catholic defensive alliance, the League, at the prompting of Maximilian I. At first it comprised, besides Bavaria, only the most seriously menaced spiritual princes — Würzburg, Constance, Augsburg, and Regensburg — and after 30 August 1609, the three spiritual electors, but not the Habsburgs, who were quarreling among themselves. The Pope hesitated to enter into a formal treaty with the League and made his financial support contingent upon proof that there existed a general Protestant Union directed against the Catholics; legalist that he was, he did not wish to be suspected of violating the Religious Peace. It was not until 1610 that he promised subsidies, while at the same time he urged the inclusion of the Emperor in the League. For its part, the Union acquired powerful support through alliances with England (1612) and Holland (1613).

While Emperor Matthias was inclined to yield to Protestant demands in the Empire, such as permitting the Protestant administrator of Magdeburg to sit in the

Diet, his successor, Ferdinand II, elected King of Bohemia in 1617 and King of Hungary in 1618, was opposed to any compromise. The revolt of the Protestant nobles in Bohemia and the election as anti-King of the Count Palatine Friedrich V set off the long-threatening religious war. Both Ferdinand II and the reinvigorated League obtained considerable subsidies from the Pope from 1620 onward. The "Winter King," left in the lurch by his allies, was defeated in the Battle of the White Mountain on 8 November 1620. To enable Ferdinand II and the League to make the most of their victory, Gregory XV in just two and one-half years contributed subsidies in the amount of about 1,239,000 florins in sound money and of about 700,000 florins in bad money, depreciated through inflation. The transfer of the dignity of Elector Palatine to Bavaria was energetically pushed by the Pope. These military and political successes formed the basis for the Counter Reformation now getting under way, first of all only in the Habsburg states.

At the instigation of the energetic and circumspect nuncio, Carlo Carafa, Protestant ministers and teachers were expelled from Bohemia. At the start only those who had taken part in the revolt were affected, but later all were included on the basis of the King's right of reformation. Mixed commissions under military protection restored the churches and introduced Catholic pastors. Resistance, especially from the urban middle class and from the peasants, who were unwilling to forego the lay chalice, was quashed by military force. In order to avoid oppressive billeting, expected to force conversions, many Protestants emigrated. Recourse to these measures of force was not mitigated until 1626 and then without abandoning the fundamental requirement of return to the Catholic Church.

The soul of the rebuilding of Catholicism was Cardinal Harrach, Archbishop of Prague (1624–67), advised by the Capuchin Valerian Magni. At his urging, the role of the state's means of pressure gradually yielded to pastoral action. The chief source of difficulty was the lack of diocesan priests, and thus the lion's share of the immensely heavy burden fell to the Orders, most of all to the Jesuits and the Capuchins, but also to the older institutes. The University of Prague was entrusted to the Jesuits. Corresponding to Harrach in Prague was Cardinal Dietrichstein in his bishopric of Olmütz. In Silesia, where the "Letter of Majesty" continued in force, the Counter Reformation was carried out only in the principalities directly under the King and in the territory of the see of Breslau, which was held by Habsburg archdukes from 1608 to 1665. In Upper Austria on 12 October 1624 the Protestants were given until Easter of 1626 to return to the Church. In Lower Austria, where Ferdinand II had assured religious liberty to the nobles adhering to the Augsburg Confession, the authorities were content with expelling the Calvinist preachers. In Styria, Carinthia, and Carniola the Protestant nobles too were banished (1628). The restoration of Catholicism in Hungary was almost entirely the work of Cardinal Pázmány, Archbishop of Esztergom (1616–37).

As early as 1621, opinions concerning the anti-Reformation measures to be adopted recognized both the urgency and the questionable character of the Church's use of secular means of compulsion. Success, it was felt, depended on the intensification of the care of souls. The political postulate of denominational unity continued to be admitted. The extending of the Counter Reformation to the Empire belongs in the pontificate of Urban VIII.

CHAPTER 110

Urban VIII, Innocent X, and the End of the Counter Reformation

In the conclave of 19 July to 6 August 1623, the small Ludovisi faction was so reinforced by the adherents of Aldobrandini, the German Cardinals Zollern and Klesl, and the Princes Farnese and Medici that it was almost equal to the followers of Borghese and was able to prevent the election of Millini, which Borghese was urging. The illness of a number of the cardinals hastened an agreement by the two party leaders on the person of the Florentine Maffeo Barberini, who, to the delight of the Romans, called himself Urban VIII. Only fifty-five years of age, he had acquired valuable political experience that qualified him to participate personally in the conduct of affairs. He did so, at least in the first third of his pontificate, proving his skill in dealing with diplomats and his keen self-assurance. He had a dislike of Spain and a partiality for France that went back to the period of his nunciature in the latter kingdom (1604–7). More given to nepotism than any other Pope of the century, he bestowed the purple on his brother Antonio and his nephews Francesco and Antonio the Younger and enriched his family so prodigally that on his death bed he felt remorse of conscience. His extravagance toward the Barberini family presented a painful contrast to his niggardly contributions for the support of the Catholic side in the Thirty Years' War. But since Duke Olardo Farnese, whom the pope was trying to punish, found support in France and formed a league with Venice, Tuscany, and Modena against the Pope, the "Castro War" ended with the Pope's defeat. The Papal State, enlarged by the territory of Urbino following the renunciation of claims by the last duke, della Rovere, suffered severely from the devastation of large areas and disordered finances.

A connoisseur of both ancient and modern literature, owner of a large library, and himself an accomplished stylist, the Pope personally took part in the reform of the breviary of 1631, rewriting a number of the hymns. The reform commission contented itself with trifling changes in the lives of saints and the homilies. Liturgical centralization found its culmination in the constitution of 5 July 1643, in which beatification and canonization were reserved to the Pope and every liturgical cult of a saint was forbidden which had not been in effect for at least a century with proper ecclesiastical approval. In 1630 Urban VIII granted cardinals the title of "Eminence." In nine promotions he bestowed the purple on seventy-eight men.

Church Policy during the Thirty Years' War

Following the principle, correct in itself, that the papacy must stand above the rivalry of the great powers and intervene for the preservation of peace, Urban VIII was unable and perhaps not really willing to thwart Richelieu's superior and crafty diplomacy, which, without regard for the interests of the Church, aimed at the destruction of the power of the Habsburg lands and at French hegemony in Europe. He failed to grasp that the defeat of the Emperor and of the League involved the ruin of the Counter Reformation which his predecessors had promoted.

It was the interlacing of political and religious interests that made Urban's position so difficult. In Spain there was talk of convoking a general council, while Richelieu threatened schism. But when France's open entry into the war in 1635 compelled Ferdinand II to make concessions to the Protestants in the Peace of Prague, the Emperor was severely blamed, whereas Richelieu received merely an admonition to peace. The peace congress convoked to Cologne was sabotaged by Richelieu, but the Pope drew no conclusion from this attitude. It is hard to avoid the impression that Urban VIII's policy of neutrality actually amounted to a patronage of France. Its inescapable sequel was the cessation of the Counter Reformation in the Empire and heavy damage to Catholic interests.

Counter Reformation in the Empire

From the beginning of the seventeenth century the Catholics had held the initiative in the Empire. The legal basis for a large-scale operation was to be furnished by the Imperial Edict of Restitution of 6 March 1629. The Edict of Restitution decreed: (1) the return of the two archbishoprics, twelve bishoprics, and numerous monasteries, direct imperial fiefs, that had been alienated since the Treaty of Passau; (2) the return of mediatized sees and monasteries and their property, alienated in the same period; (3) by means of the abrogation of the *Declaratio Ferdinandea,* the equalizing of the Catholic estates with the Protestant in the "right of reformation." Defensible in law, the edict was a serious political mistake, for it united German Protestantism by threatening its very existence.

Imperial delegates were appointed to carry it out. But before the execution of the edict was completed and the interior permeation of the newly won lands had passed beyond the initial stage, the preconditions for distribution of power for the counteroffensive were offset. Wallenstein was toppled, and the victories of Gustavus Adolphus and his advance into South Germany involved the loss of all gains in the North and of most of the South, especially in Württemberg. In the Peace of Prague with Saxony (1635) the Emperor was forced to renounce the Edict of Restitution and concede for forty years to those adherents of the Augsburg Confession who assented to the peace the ecclesiastical lands they had occupied from the Treaty of Passau until 12 November 1627.

The Peace of Westphalia

The peace signed on 24 October 1648, contained three provisions which solidified the religious cleavage in the Empire, defined the property of the denominations, and brought the Counter Reformation to an end: (1) The Religious Peace of Augsburg was extended to include the Calvinists; (2) Except in the Austrian hereditary states, the standard year for deciding the practice of religion and the ownership of Church property was computed as 1 January 1624; (3) The "right of reformation" of the estates and the Ecclesiastical Reservation, which had hitherto been assailed by the Protestants, were both recognized. In the Peace of Westphalia a new age proclaimed itself; the system of European states freed itself from papal controls. Urban VIII's successor, by whom the protest was made, could do nothing to arrest this development.

In the conclave of 1644, the factions united to elect Gianbattista Pamfili, though he was not acceptable to the French. More to the point than any other characterization of Innocent X is the portrait by Diego Velazquez from 1650: a majestic appearance, intelligent, reserved, even distrustful, hence slow, sometimes vacillating in reaching decisions, intent on right and order. His pontificate was overshadowed by his tyrannical and venal sister-in-law, Olimpia Maidalchini, to whom he allowed far too much influence in secular matters and in personal politics.

England's Hegemony among Protestant Powers

In England the marriage of Charles I to Henrietta Maria, daughter of Louis XIII of France, did not bring the expected alleviation of persecution to the Catholics. The promises made when the dispensation was obtained were not honored when Parliament raised opposition. To replace the archpriest hitherto functioning there, a vicar of episcopal rank was named in 1623. But strife with the Jesuits induced the second holder of the office to leave England, and thus the approximately one hundred fifty thousand Catholics were without a head. Catholic worship continued to be proscribed, while absence from the Anglican service was punishable by a fine. Under the influence of the King, who inclined personally to the Catholic Church, and of the Queen the persecuting laws were more mildly enforced and even the possibility of reunion was discussed, but Charles' absolute rule and, in the ecclesiastical sphere, the greater emphasis on the episcopalian constitution, which his father had gradually reintroduced in Scotland, and the communion rite, closer to the Catholic tradition, which he himself had prescribed there in 1637, encountered powerful opposition in Parliament and among the Presbyterians and Independents respectively. Although on the outbreak of the Civil War in 1642 he was supported by the Catholic nobility and eventually by the Irish, he was defeated and executed (1649). The fanatically anti-Catholic Lord Protector, Oliver Cromwell, abolished the fine for non-attendance at Anglican worship (1650), but the religious toleration granted by him was of slight benefit to Catholics as "idolators." Anyone who rejected the oath of abjuration, demanded of laity and clergy from 1655 — repudiation of the papal primacy, of transubstantiation, and of the veneration of saints and images — lost two-thirds of his property and almost all his civil rights, and priests had to leave the country under pain of death.

The English revolution annihilated also the hope of an alleviation of the lot of the harshly suppressed Irish Catholics. Their at first victorious rising against English rule had been supported by Urban VIII through money and the sending of nuncios. The Treaty of Kilkenny (1645), in which the royal agent Glamorgan had guaranteed them religious liberty, was not ratified by Charles I and it was not until shortly before his fall that he granted it to them in return for an assurance of armed assistance in the struggle with Parliament. The concession came too late. With severity Cromwell subjected the country to his control and by means of an act of settlement expropriated a great part of the property of Catholic landowners. A decree of 6 January 1653 prescribed that all Catholic priests had to leave the country under penalty of high treason. The Catholics were decimated, partly through deportation to the West Indies, partly through emigration and famine.

Cromwell made England the greatest Protestant power in Europe. The Netherlands obtained the definitive recognition of their sovereignty in the peace with Spain. Sweden, though unable long to maintain the position of a great power gained by Gustavus Adolphus, still dominated the Baltic Sea through its bridgeheads on imperial soil and forced Poland to make peace. The Protestant powers, in which the Catholic faith was virtually exterminated, were in the ascendancy. Spain, the former Catholic power, was defeated by the France of Richelieu who was unwilling to accept Philip II's role of protector of Catholic interests. The Counter Reformation had come to a stop in Central Europe, but the Tridentine reform had not. Like his predecessors, Innocent X worked for it and, soon after the conclusion of peace, set in motion in the Empire a wave of Church renewal.

In condemning five propositions from the *Augustinus* of Cornelius Jansenius (d. 1638 as Bishop of Ypres) on 31 May 1653, Innocent X delivered the most momentous official doctrinal decision of the century. It can be appreciated only in connection with the quarrel over the Augustinian doctrine of grace, which had broken out again under Urban VIII. This controversy continued the quarrel over Baius and Molinism but, in contrast to them, it affected almost all facets of Church life far into the eighteenth century.

Under Innocent X occurred a change still operative in regard to the highest political office in the Holy See: the respective Cardinal Nephew was supplanted as chief minister by the secretary of state. In the pontificate of his predecessor the Cardinal Nephew Francesco Barberini, who at first had been overshadowed by the secretaries of state Magalotti and Azzolini, had contrived to secure a predominant influence at the side of and in fact ahead of the secretary of state, Ceva, whom the Pope regarded as a counterpoise, and finally (1643) obtained this post for his creature, Spada. But this enhancement of the political importance of the cardinal nephew was no more than an episode. The leading rule went instead to the secretaries of state, Panciroli and after 1651, Chigi, with whom begins the series of cardinal secretaries of state. "For the first time in the history of the secretariate of state the nuncios and legates sent their correspondence directly to the secretary of state; for the first time the secretary of state alone signed letters and instructions" (Hammermayer). And Chigi became the first secretary of state to ascend the Throne of Peter.

The paralysis of the Catholic counteroffensive did not involve that of artistic powers. On 18 November 1626, Urban VIII had consecrated the new Saint Peter's, for which his architect, Bernini, executed the bronze baldachin over the *confessio* and the tomb of the Barberini Pope. Numerous churches of martyrs, such as Santa Bibiana and Santi Cosma e Damiano, were restored by him, his nephews, and other cardinals. The rebuilding of the Seven Hills, started by Sixtus V, was continued with the laying out of new streets and the erection of a splendid family palace, and the appearance of the city was enhanced by the installation of numerous fountains. The guides to Rome were no longer pilgrims' guides to the sanctuaries and relics but experts on the artistic monuments of pagan and Christian Rome from antiquity to the present. Under the prosaic and thrifty Innocent X Bernini was for a time out of favor. The belfrey of Saint Peter's that he had erected was again torn down but the interior decorations were completed and thus the estimated seven hundred thousand pilgrims of the Jubilee Year 1650 viewed the church in essentially its present form. The same holds for the Lateran Basilica, restored by Borromini, and the Baroque churches of Sant' Ignazio and Sant' Andrea della Valle, finished after a long period of construction. The jewel of all the Roman squares, the Piazza Navona, where arose the Pamfili family palace, received its final form with Bernini's Fontana dei Fiumi. Baroque Rome was now completed. In the march of the Catholic Reform its universities and colleges had made it a center of ecclesiastical scholarship. Now it became the goal of cultural journeys.

CHAPTER 111

Denominationalism and Secularization

The strict doctrinal and territorial separation between Catholics, Lutherans, and Calvinists, "confessionalization," and the resulting doctrinal quarrels are the outstanding characteristics of the century between the Council of Trent and the Peace of Westphalia. But the very violence of the opposing polemics and the blood-letting of the wars of religion gave rise to a new longing for religious peace and Church unity. While it is true that the ever more numerous conversions around the turn of the century and a series of religious colloquies led to renewed strife, nevertheless the hazards of irenicism were embraced, though only by individualists. When it became clear that religious unity within the state could no longer be enforced, the idea of toleration made progress, but, except in the France of Henry IV, it was unable to carry the day.

Strictly speaking, conversions to the Catholic Church presupposed the strict differentiation of the Catholic doctrine from the Protestant by the Council of Trent. In Germany converts of princely rank began in 1590. It is obvious that in some of these conversions political and opportunistic motives played a part. For the conversion of scholars the disunity of the Protestants and the diversity of their doctrinal concepts were frequently given as motives, while the uniformity of the Catholic doctrinal system and the beauty of its worship exercised a powerful attraction.

The religious conversations of the age varied from place to place. The Religious Colloquy of Baden (1589) had been summoned by the Margrave Jakob of Baden-Hachberg, the future convert. Its chief topic was the doctrine of justification. The prospect of conversion was also the basis of the Regensburg Religious Colloquy of 1601, jointly convoked, after careful preparation, by Maximilian I of Bavaria and the strongly Lutheran Philip Ludwig of Palatinate-Neuburg. The topic was the relationship of Scripture and Tradition. No fewer than fifty-five controversial works came out of this discussion. King Ladislaus of Poland summoned the Religious Colloquy of Torun in 1645 in the hope of ending the altercations going on within his country. Effective incentives for mutually drawing closer did not emanate from any one of these meetings, but came from elsewhere.

The humanist irenicists around the middle of the sixteenth century always started from the Erasmian distinction between the fundamental articles of faith, concerning which there was or at least could be agreement, and theological doctrinal opinions, which were to be left to free discussion; in them the traditional consciousness of the one Christianity lived on.

The Dutchman Hugo Grotius (d. 1645), while he was imprisoned for having attacked the dominant strictly Calvinist line and for high treason (1619–21), developed the theological principles of his later efforts to bring closer especially the Protestant denominations, the Anglicans, and the Orthodox. Though as a boy he had sought to induce his Catholic mother to apostatize, because she "was too intelligent to remain a papist," toward the close of his life he drew nearer the Catholic Church by championing the apostolic succession, the hierarchy, and the Catholic concept of the sacraments. He declared that the solution of the religious split, which with Erasmus he regarded as unnecessary and pernicious, was possible on the basis of the *Confessio Augustana* and, in the midst of the Thirty Years' War, outlined the ideal of a reconciled *Magna Universitas Christianorum,* headed by the supreme priest, the Pope.

Whereas, on the side of the Reformed — partly from ecclesiastico-political motives, since Calvinism was not yet recognized in imperial law — exertions for the union of Protestants were never broken off, the principle of tradition, which at first Georg Calixt (d. 1656) had sought to exploit against the Catholic Church, became the basis of his irenicism, which consciously made use of Cassander. Apostolicity and the universal consensus of the ancient Church on the fundamental articles of Christian faith constituted for him the only possible basis for reunion. The efforts of Johann Philip von Schönborn, Elector of Mainz, to achieve a *rapprochement* of the denominations, sought a reunion of the Lutherans, not of the Calvinists, with the Catholic Church on the basis of the *Confessio Augustana,* the marriage of priests, the lay chalice, and certain dogmatic and disciplinary concessions. As "reformed Catholics" they were to return to the obedience of the Pope. The Elector remained aloof, and in Rome the project was presumably never given serious consideration.

Different in principle from the efforts of the irenicists, though resembling them in their results, were the discussions on the lawfulness of toleration by the state. While the postulate that only one religion or denomination should prevail within a state remained essentially undisputed, it could not be maintained in practice. During the Huguenot Wars the *politiques* advocated cooperation with and toleration of the Calvinists. According to Bodin (d. 1596), the monarch is obliged to preserve the religious unity of his country if it exists, but it must not be restored by force. Later Bodin inclined to the view that it is best to allow to each his own personal religion. After Henry IV had granted religious liberty to the Huguenots in the Edict of Nantes, the English and the Dutch Catholics asked in vain for the same concession. In Germany the Jena theologian Johann Gerhard (d. 1637) characterized unity of faith within a state as a desirable but scarcely realizable ideal. In the denominationally mixed state the prince might tolerate individuals of other faiths but not public worship for fear of serious disorders; excepted from toleration were Anabaptists and Unitarians.

Theories of State and Absolutism

In these theological exchanges over the permissibility of toleration by the state is reflected the power shift in the relations of state and Church since the religious cleavage. Earlier, during the Great Schism and the struggle against conciliarism, the papacy had had to court the secular powers. Now it was the princes first of all, and individuals only in the second place, who determined adherence to religion and creed. The Council of Trent took place in agreement with the princes, and only with their cooperation could it be enforced and implemented. To an even higher degree the Counter Reformation was their work. The power shift proceeded hand in hand with a change in the structure of the state, from a feudal to a modern bureaucratic state, with the development of princely absolutism and modern theories of government in which the way was prepared for its secularization.

Machiavelli's idea of the autonomous power state, subject to its proper law, the reason of state, slowly gained ground. In his *apologia* against Henry VIII, Cardinal Pole had clearly recognized the threatening danger. Later writers, such as Giovanni Botero, for a time in Borromeo's service, believed it possible to transform Machiavelli's idea into a Christian one and thereby to neutralize it. Bodin did not question the religious obligations of the prince, but subordinated the form and laws of the state to the concept of the sovereignty and the natural conditions of nations and individuals, in the final analysis, to the welfare of the state. Friends and enemies of Machiavelli derived arguments from Tacitus. Justus Lipsius, who revived him openly championed Machiavelli and his *Politica* (1589) was translated into five languages.

The roots of princely absolutism reach back into the late Middle Ages, but its refinements, differing widely according to countries and people, were incontestably furthered, in both the Protestant and the Catholic areas, by the religious split and its consequences. Considerable power accrued to the Protestant territorial princes through the formation of the territorial Church and the secularization of Church property. The Catholic princes not only made use of their right to determine the religion of their subjects; while protecting the Church and promoting reform and even reconquering lost territory for her, they extended their own authority in the ecclesiastical sphere, frequently with the consent or at least the toleration of the papacy. Roles were reversed: the state no longer afforded help to an imperiled Church, but the Church, even unconsciously and often unwillingly, aided a state that was becoming absolute.

The intrusion of the modern state into the ecclesiastical field is essentially different from the ascendancy of the lay power in the early medieval Western Christian family of nations. Now for the first time there arose a genuine Church establishment. The papacy defended the freedom and independence of the Church particularly against the claims of the dominant Catholic powers, Spain and France, but in most cases without any outstanding success. Papal decrees were subject to the royal *placet;* clerical privileges, such as the *privilegium fori* and the right of asylum, were curtailed; Church property was taxed, with or without papal authorization and in France by means of clerical contributions voted by the national assembly; the Inquisition and ecclesiastical censure of books were impeded or, as in Spain, nationalized. The Church was forced into a defensive position.

The doctrine of the right of resistance and of tyrannicide is to be explained by the increasing pressure of princely absolutism. In the last third of the sixteenth century assassinations of princes increased in number, and Bodin declared tyrannicide lawful. Nevertheless it created a sensation when the Spanish Jesuit Juan Mariana in his *De rege et regis institutione* (1599), dedicated to King Philip III, expounded the theory that a usurper may be killed by anyone, but a legitimate prince only if, in the general opinion (*si vox populi adsit*), he is destroying the state, despising religion and laws, and there is no other way of inducing him to cease from tyranny. These rules, unobjectionable in regard to content, were intended as a warning to princes who ruled in an absolutist manner, but since they were related to a thinly veiled approval of the assassination of Henry III of France the Sorbonne condemned Mariana's book, and the Society's general, Acquaviva, disavowed it and forbade further debate.

Secularization of Thought

Even more portentous than absolutism and Church establishment, or than the rising secularization of the concept of the state, were the beginnings of the secularization of European thought in both the arts and the sciences. It must not only be assessed negatively as a natural process of maturation. It must also be regarded as a reaction to the extreme claims of theologians and their quarrels, to the recourse to ecclesiastical and political means of power in the religious sphere, and to the luxuriant growth of superstition. Skepticism and incredulity became a problem. A growing number of religious individualists, abandoning the central doctrines of the Christian faith, were rejected by the Catholic Church as well as by the Protestant denominations. And religious splintering proceeded noticeably. Unrelated to theology, there arose the "natural system of intellectual knowledge" (W. Dilthey). The natural sciences, with no regard for authority, based themselves on empirical observation and mathematical computation, but in the "Galileo Case" they encountered the Church's opposition.

In the "century that wanted to believe" superstition proliferated. The most frightful aberration of superstition, the witch trials, claimed thousands of innocent victims in both Catholic and Protestant Germany. Denunciations and the ruthless resort to torture to extort confessions released the basest instincts; not infrequently piety led to the suspicion of witchcraft.

The resort to ecclesiastical and political means of compulsion for the preservation of orthodoxy had already led, with Sebastian Castellio (d. 1563) and Jacobus Acontius (d. 1566–67), to the repudiation of any external force in the religious sphere. Religious individualists and groups, repelled and suppressed by the prevailing denominations, demanded freedom of conscience and of teaching; for example, the Arminians in Holland. Some even attacked the central dogma of the Trinity, especially Italians who had broken with the Christian faith and had fled from the Inquisition, usually into Switzerland. They had taken refuge, some in western, some in eastern Europe. Celio Secundo Curione lived in Basel until his death in 1569; Bernardino Ochino died in Moravia in 1565; Lelio Sozzini, who had attacked the dogma of the Trinity in his commentary on the prologue of the

Fourth Gospel, closed his turbulent wandering life at Zurich in 1562. Whereas the earlier anti-Trinitarians, such as Adam Pastoris, had drawn their objections from the Bible, the later ones were more rationalistic in their approach.

Unitarianism established itself between 1560 and 1568 — Peter Gonesius constitutes a transitional stage. The "Polish Brethren" were partly inclined to Anabaptism, and hence the leader of the anti-Trinitarians, Fausto Sozzini (d. 1604), Lelio's nephew, prevailed only slowly. His catechism appeared in Polish in 1605. In 1638 and in 1658 the adherents of the sect were expelled from the country. Part of them took refuge in Holland; the historian of the Unitarians found them in Hamburg, also.

In France François de Rabelais (d. 1553) had already posed the problem of unbelief. The skeptical outlook of Montaigne (d. 1592) was directed especially at the existing authorities and was compensated by a fideism. For René Descartes (d. 1650) methodical doubt was the beginning of philosophizing. His awareness of the sovereignty of constructive thought places him at the head of modern philosophy, emancipated from theology.

Though dependent on modern scholasticism in his doctrine of rights, and in particular on Francisco de Vitoria and Suárez, Hugo Grotius had preceded Descartes in understanding law as "an effective function of life, based on natural law and reason" (E. Wolf). The ethical foundation of law lies in man's social nature. Hence law is spiritually autonomous; its connection with theological and philosophical assumptions is not entirely broken but it is loosened. To this extent Grotius is the founder of modern natural and international law.

The rising independence of the arts, including history, was in itself a natural maturing of the European mind. It did not necessarily have to lead to conflict with the faith and with theology, any more than the constructing of a natural science on empirical observation and mathematical computation had to. The reason why the systems of natural philosophy, suspected of Pantheism, of Tommaso Campanella (d. 1639) and Giordano Bruno were, together with their creators, condemned by the Church lay in the attitudes of their representatives.

Far more momentous was Galileo's encounter with the Inquisition. Nicholas Copernicus (d. 1543) had dedicated to Paul III his *De revolutionibus orbium coelestinum*, which had endeavored to prove by mathematical arguments the motion of the earth around the sun. Since that time the "Copernican World System" had, like its preliminary steps in the Parisian natural philosophy of the fourteenth century, encountered no hostility from the Church. After 1594 the University of Salamanca made the text of Copernicus the basis of instruction. Luther, Melanchthon, Osiander, and the University of Tübingen attacked the Copernican system as contradicting Scripture. Nevertheless, it was further developed around the turn of the century. Johannes Kepler discovered the laws of planetary motion. Galileo Galilei (1564–1642), active in Florence from 1610, found confirmation of the Copernican system by observing the heavenly bodies, such as the moons of Jupiter. With the help of a telescope he constructed and defended it against objections drawn from Scripture (Josh. 10:12f., Ps. 103:5). Following denunciation by the Dominican court preacher Lorini, Galileo was summoned before the Roman Inquisition. Until then he had enjoyed the greatest esteem in Rome's ecclesiastical circles and in 1611 had been admitted to the Papal Academy. But by his vehement efforts to demonstrate the compatibility of his system with a correct interpretation of Scripture, he so provoked the consultors of the Inquisition that on 24 February 1616 it declared his propositions on the standing of the sun and the movement of the earth as heretical or erroneous and forbade him to defend them in the future. He was not obliged to abjure them or to cease his investigations, and Pope Paul V granted him an audience and assured him of his protection. Just the same, on 5 March 1616 the work of Copernicus and all books that defended his system were placed on the Index. After the accession of Urban VIII Galileo, relying on the Pope's benevolence, dedicated to him his reply to a criticism by the Jesuit Grassi and, following a visit to Rome, was extolled "as the man whose fame shines forth in the sky and permeates the world." But when, confident of the Pope's favor, he published, with the *Imprimatur* of Riccardi, Master of the Sacred Palace, his *Dialogues on the two most important World Systems* in 1632, the Inquisition again summoned him on 23 September 1632, for having violated the earlier prohibition of 1616. Though during the second trial he declared that interiorly he did not adhere to the Copernican system, he was condemned on 22 June 1633 to abjuration and to life-imprisonment. He recanted and the imprisonment was commuted to a mild detention on his estate of Alcetri near Florence. The sequel to the Galileo trial was that his mathematico-physical concept of the world was not accepted by the Church and his chief work, *Discorsi e dimostrazioni matematiche intorno a due nuove scienze* (1638), the "first text in physics" (Von Laue), had to be printed in Leiden. Galileo's personal fate was determined by his taking into his own hands the resolving of the apparent contradiction between his conclusions from his study of natural science and scriptural revelation, instead of leaving it to theologians.

A new epoch in Church history begins in the mid-seventeenth century. The Peace of Westphalia definitely settled denominational rights in the Empire and put a stop to the Counter Reformation as an ecclesiastico-political activity. It brought to a close the age of the Wars of Religion and at the same time shifted political powers. The Peace of the Pyrenees (1659) decided the struggle for European hegemony in favor of France, and a decade later the recognition of the English Navigation Acts by the States General of the Netherlands put the seal on England's maritime supremacy. However, the Church had been interiorly renewed since the Council of Trent and had overcome the crisis of the religious schism. She was asserting herself and was even able to recover lost ground, but to restore the unity of the Church had proven clearly impossible. Confessionalization divided the Christian peoples of the West into three sharply defined and quarrelling bodies Catholics, Lutherans, and Calvinists — and lessened the convincing force of Christian thought. Forced into a defensive position, the Church was unable to master the religious and intellectual forces pressing to the surface, some of them released by the split, others having their roots deep in the late Middle Ages. She lost command, and a new crisis, the supreme crisis of the European mind, announced itself.

Parallel to, and often intertwined with, this changing relationship to the "world" were structural changes within the Church. Defense against Protestantism and inner renewal of the Church from the time of the Council of Trent were possible only because the papacy sharply tightened the reins of the central authority and, in a new centralization, very different from the medieval, strengthened the threatened members who were themselves too weak, by means of nuncios, controlled the bishops through the *visitatio liminum,* and in the congregations that were becoming stabilized and being organized as offices created an effective instrument, which, unlike the chancery and *camera* of the late Middle Ages, did not pursue a mainly financial end. The "Episcopalist" currents, which, becoming ever stronger in the course of the seventeenth and eighteenth centuries, resisted this tendency, left themselves open to suspicion because in part they attenuated or denied the Pope's primacy of jurisdiction, in part they relied on the protection of the national estate, as in France and Spain, or on secular means of power, as in the Holy Roman Empire. From the time of Bellarmine ecclesiology put the doctrine of the papal primacy in the center and caused the function of the college of bishops to withdraw into the background. After Trent no general council was summoned for more than three centuries.

The Tridentine doctrinal system and reform work, to which the Church owed her renewal and self-assertion, impressed their stamp on the Church's life and well-nigh became its unique form. The post-Tridentine Church was anti-Protestant and became anti-reform. Theological schools which had been unattacked in the Middle Ages, such as Augustinianism, were hard put to maintain themselves. Gratian and the older canon law lost their importance. And the historical picture of the Church which could have been obtained from the flourishing study of patrology and Church history became ineffectual. Just as liturgy in its post-Tridentine form hardened into rubricism, so canon law became formalistic and remained so for three whole centuries. Is one justified, then, in extending the "Tridentine epoch" of Church history or the "Counter Reformation" into the nineteenth century or even to the present?

It is not to be denied that certain characteristics of the post-Tridentine Church — her anti-Protestant orientation in doctrine and piety, her centralization and formalism — remained active after the time limit here treated, the middle of the seventeenth century. Nevertheless, it is misleading and ruinous to any effort to obtain an insight into the real historical process if the centuries that have elapsed since Trent are studied from the one viewpoint of the present, of ecumenism and the openness to the world as displayed by the Second Vatican Council, while the influence of the Enlightenment and of the great upheavals since the French Revolution — to cite only these examples — are treated as of little significance. It is no less one-sided to regard the schism in the Church as a tragedy only, while overlooking the deepening and activating of the religious life which it had as a consequence, the wealth of values which came to light in the Catholic Reform, in new and old Orders, in asceticism and mysticism, in piety and art, in missionary expansion on three continents. In the hard crust that was forming there lay hidden a precious kernel, a specific, not to be mistaken kernel, encountered only in this epoch. To throw it away as worthless, not to recall that every period of Church history stands directly before God, is unhistorical and presumptuous: unhistorical, because one cannot see the limits and possibilities of the pilgrim Church; presumptuous, because it means forgetting that even we are not in possession of the perfect. Instead we are awaiting it — and only then will we dispose of the standards for judging fairly.

Book Six

THE CHURCH IN THE AGE OF ABSOLUTISM AND ENLIGHTENMENT

Translated by Gunther J. Holst

Part One

The Leadership Position of France

Section One

Ecclesiastical Life in France

Louis Cognet

CHAPTER 112

Christian Renewal after 1615

French Catholicism under Louis XIII

When Henry IV was assassinated on May 14, 1610, France had again become a great Catholic nation which was not only tied closely to the Roman Catholic religion, but had even begun to put religious sentiment above national considerations. Proof of this can be perceived in the unpopularity of the war against Spain prepared by Henry IV at the time of his assassination. However obscure the background of the regicide may be, religion was a definite motivating factor in Ravaillac's crime. Spain — hitherto an obstacle in the path of French expansionism — was at this time already on the decline. Under these conditions, waging war to confirm the hegemony of France would have been politically justified. Public opinion in France was nonetheless opposed to it since the most pressing obligation of the Catholic states was considered to be an alliance against the Protestant Reformation.

Although Protestantism still occupied a powerful position, it was evident that in France the Reformation had to end in failure. The conversion of Henry IV had no doubt been a mere gesture of political opportunism by a ruler indifferent to the faith. But it became obvious that no Huguenot ruler could be forced upon the kingdom. Calvinism had reached its pinnacle about the year 1571. Although its outward manifestations seemed unimpaired, it was in a process of irreversible retrogression. It became a minority party and was conscious of that fact. After the religious wars the real basis for the appeal of Protestantism was the intensive religious life of many of its members, which hardly found a counterpart in the politicized Catholicism of the Holy League. Toward the end of the reign of Henry IV, however, the Reformation had lost this advantage. Endeavors by the great Catholic spiritual leaders — Francis de Sales, Benedict of Canfield, Father Coton, Bérulle, and many others — had brought about a Catholic climate whose piety and inward orientation was equal to that of the Reformed Churches. At this time, this *milieu dévot* or *parti dévot,* as it was also called, was still a compact group firmly united by common ideals revolving around the triumph of Catholicism and the defeat of Protestantism. On the other hand, the Protestants found themselves more and more hampered by becoming socially disadvantaged. Following the king's example, other conversions had taken place among the aristocracy and the upper bourgeosie — with equal lack of sincerity. Now it was obvious that being Catholic would henceforth be an indispensable prerequisite for achieving high positions. For a long time Sully was to be the last Protestant minister of France and the death of Henry IV forced him to resign. For quite some time France, along with the rest of Europe, was far from reaching the maturity needed for a tolerant attitude. The attitude of public opinion toward the Edict of Nantes was symptomatic in this regard. No one perceived in it a laudable attempt at achieving religious peace. The Catholics considered it a concession required by necessity, a despicable and offensive infringement on the immutable rights of the true religion, while the Protestants saw it as something fundamentally too unjust and precarious to be permanent. Although the two blocs had for the time being abandoned the violence of the religious wars, beneath the surface the antagonism remained unchanged. Given another opportunity, it could break out into open warfare once again.

Materially speaking, the situation of the Church steadily improved under the reign of Henry IV. Of course not all the devastation caused by the religious wars could be repaired. Even today more than a few abbeys and parish churches are still in ruins. The possessions of the Church however had regenerated very quickly and — since their parts by definition cannot be lost — increased steadily. In a memorandum written around 1625 Richelieu estimated that one-third of the national property was in the hands of the clergy. This financial aspect was preeminent in the eyes of many Catholics. This was true especially for members of high society who felt and advocated quite openly that the possessions of the Church should be used to make up for the insufficiencies of family fortune. The same view was held by the lower class, for whom the priesthood represented the only possibility for social advancement. As a matter of fact, the sees continued to be the appanage of the aristocracy. A cleric unknown at the court had no chance to rise to the bishopric. Many great families moreover acted as if an episcopate once possessed were a kind of inheritance which was to be retained at any price by means of a royal warrant authorizing it to be handed on from uncle to nephew. The nominations of bishops were made by the King and were generally decided by the *Conseil de Conscience,* but even Vincent de Paul, a member of this council from 1643 to 1652, could not prevent some scandalous appointments. There were indeed very distinct differences in the quality of individual appointees. Numerous bishops remained in the service of the court or pursued literature, warfare or diplomacy and never actually set foot in their respective dioceses.

The condition of the parish clergy as well had hardly improved since the religious wars. The root cause for this stagnation lay in the almost total lack of education of the clergymen. The deplorable consequences of such a practice are not surprising. In 1643 an archdeacon of Bourges ascertained that many priests did not know Latin, several could hardly read and some were incapable of administering the Holy Sacraments validly and did not even know the words of absolution.

Concubinage and drunkenness among the clergy were widespread and in some dioceses were looked upon as common practice. Besides their clerical duties many priests held common jobs and frequented taverns. In certain areas they frequently practiced exorcism. Most of them never preached a sermon, no longer taught catechism and abandoned their churches to a state of scandalous neglect and squalor. But these shortcomings were rarely ever remedied. Intervention was very difficult because bishops could make appointments in only a few parishes of their diocese since most of them were controlled by abbeys or by lay patronage. Another impediment was the canonical regulation requiring three corresponding verdicts against an accused priest before he could be prosecuted, a situation that could be indefinitely extended.

Conditions among the members of religious orders were hardly better, although here sporadic attempts at reform had been introduced since the end of the sixteenth century and especially under Henry IV. In fact, all orders were in need of reform, with the exception of the Carthusians, who at this time were relatively numerous and had their establishments in close proximity to the towns. They had retained their traditional obligations; their austerity impressed the masses and even led to conversions. And yet the image of the other orders should not be painted entirely black. To be sure, even now there were frequent and blatant scandals. The court, influenced by the *parti dévot,* began to deal with these matters and civil authorities intervened in order to eliminate the most flagrant abuses. But this happened only in exceptional cases. On the whole the monasteries deteriorated into physical and moral mediocrity; they hardly even kept up the appearance of monastic seclusion, which was to them merely a distant memory, for now outsiders came and went freely and casually. Often the vow of poverty existed in theory only; monks and nuns usually established their own financial resources aiming thereby to alleviate the deficiencies of a life which all too often was characterized by a distressing degree of penury.

This decadence which had become more and more noticeable since the end of the Middle Ages had its foremost cause — common to both men and women — in the quality of the vocation or rather in the lack of a true vocation. The number of those entering of their own accord was very small. The family commonly made the decision to enter their children in a monastery — and usually for financial considerations. Excess children who for lack of necessary family means could not be put into suitable positions, the later-born left without an inheritance, those unable to bear arms, girls who could not be given a dowry, all of them were simply pushed off on the Church. Girls especially were sent into convents at an irresponsibly young age.

Another practice, but one that affected monasteries only, contributed to the mediocrity of the monastic environment. This was the fairly common custom of the commendam, which originated in France in the thirteenth century and was generally applied after the Concordat of 1516. The procedure consisted of separating the clerical functions of an ecclesiastical office from the secular income connected with it. The office was granted to a titular who was barred by canon law from executing its office and who was therefore dependent upon another person who had the necessary authority. The holder of the benefice, however, kept the greater part of the income and only gave the substitute and his subordinates a barely sufficient part, the *portio congrua.* In time, the beneficiary became accustomed to curtailing it even more so that the designation ultimately came to mean a "restricted and insufficient part." This practice had rendered the enormous properties of the Church back into the hands of the monarchy. The kings used them unscrupulously for the purpose of rewarding loyal servants and supporting artists and literati: Sully, although a Protestant, was titular of four abbeys. When Louis XIII began his reign, some of the abuses of the commendam had disappeared; the system was no longer applied to bishoprics, but only to monasteries. And yet virtually all monasteries and priories were benefices and many of their titulars were mere tonsured people less than twenty years of age. Indeed, up until the Revolution most bishops supplemented the income of their bishoprics by the proceeds from one or more abbeys. In most cases the titulars kept at least two-thirds of their incomes for themselves and many attempted to increase their portion by reducing the number of monks. They were therefore not at all inclined toward initiating any sort of reform or even to tolerating one that would have resulted in lowering their income.

Overall the situation was further impaired by unpleasant differences of opinion between the secular clergy and the orders. The latter enjoyed the privilege of exemption and therefore could a most completely evade the jurisdiction of the bishops. This had a twofold disadvantage. For one, it caused reform bishops who were becoming more numerous in the course of the century to encounter insurmountable obstacles, which frustrated their attempts at abolishing certain scandalous conditions and enabled the large abbeys, including those of nuns, brazenly to defy those bishops. In addition, some ardent and influential congregations used their status of exemption to establish a sort of parallel clergy. They did this by attracting to their chapels a great number of visitors who — frequently members of aristocratic families — deserted their own parish churches. This held true especially for the Jesuits and Capuchins. The diocesan and provincial synods attempted to alleviate this problem by obliging the faithful to attend Mass at their parish churches on a certain number of Sundays. But these measures had virtually no success and, worse, they often led to violent incidents. So it is not surprising that even the best representatives of the episcopate were somewhat reluctant to oppose the orders whose good qualities they otherwise valued. In 1632, Saint-Cyran joined the fray. Under the pseudonym Petrus Aurelius he emphatically defended the rights of the hierarchy in a number of pamphlets which received official character, so to speak, by being approved by the *Assemblées du Clergé.* To be sure, the situation subsequently calmed down a bit, but difficulties of this sort nonetheless surfaced throughout the *ancien régime.*

Negative aspects notwithstanding, French Catholicism had embarked on its renewal with the beginning of the reign of Louis XIII. The *milieu dévot* which had originated with the Holy League was an extremely eager and active Catholic group. Its central figure was a mystic from the highest level of society, Mme Acarie. In her circle one could at times encounter a bishop in the person of Francis de Sales, more frequently such secular priests as Bérulle and Gallement, or professors at the Sorbonne such as Duval, Jesuits like P. Coton, father confessor to the King, Capuchin monks such as Bene dict of Canfield, Carthusians such as Dom Beaucousin, and ladies of high society including Mme de Sainte-Beuve or Mme de Maignelay, sister of Gondi. At first this group was primarily concerned with monastic reforms which had actually had definite results in only two convents, the Benedictine convent of Montmartre (1598) and that of the Cistercians of Port-Royal (1608). The movement subsequently encompassed other convents as well. Another effort concerned the introduction of orders from other countries, where they had already been reformed. Considerable success was achieved with the Carmelites who had been reformed in Spain by Saint Teresa. In 1610, the Ursuline order was established in Paris. The male congregations fared less well with the exception of the two large orders, the Jesuits (1552) and the Capuchins (1573), introduced into France in the sixteenth century; they flourished and were able to maintain their influence in spite of all the attacks upon them. Although the barefoot Carmelites managed to extend their order from Spain to France in 1611, they were opposed in this by the *milieu dévot,* who were afraid of their competition in directing the affairs of the Carmelites. One of the most significant was the Order of the Visitation of Holy Mary in 1610 by Francis de Sales and Jane Frances de Chantal. It was initially conceived as a partially active congregation without complete claustration, but in 1618, impelled by Marquemont, archbishop of Lyon, it had to change into a contemplative order with ceremonious public vows. But this did not impede its expansion in any way. Soon the sisters of the Visitation, as had many other claustrated convents (e.g., Port-Royal), took over educational tasks.

After 1610 the *milieu dévot,* despite its vitality, began to dissolve. It was gradually weakened by internal dissention.

Richelieu and the *Milieu Dévot*

At the beginning of the regency of Marie de Médicis the *milieu dévot* was highly respected. It could easily impress the not so intelligent queen, who valued the piety, probity and unselfishness of its representatives. Bérulle was an important figure in this group. The queen's favorite, Concini, maréchal d'Ancre, willingly left all religious affairs to the *parti dévot.* He did not consider himself to have sufficient authority nor was he particularly interested in them. Because of these circumstances, Bérulle contributed considerably to advancing the career of a young cleric who had become bishop of Luçon in 1606; Armand du Plessis du Richelieu, ten years his junior and from a less distinguished family, but in whom he had discovered brilliant abilities. Ambitious and clear-sighted, Richelieu did not hesitate to seek contact with the queen mother and the *parti dévot* although later he was to turn against it. He began by flattering Bérulle and in 1612 he was one of the first to introduce the Oratory in his diocese. His widely noticed speech to the Estates-General in 1615 contained skillful encomia for Marie de Médicis, which gained him entrée to the affairs of state. In November 1616 he became minister of foreign affairs to Concini, whose assassination almost caused him to fall out of favor. That Richelieu was able to rehabilitate himself in 1619 was primarily due to the support of a member of the *parti dévot,* Sébastian Bouthilliers. Not until 1624 was he actually appointed to a first-rate position, but by that time his political ideas had fully matured and increasingly he conflicted with Bérulle and the latter's friends. In 1619, after Richelieu's brother Henry died a tragic death in a duel, Bérulle, moreover, made the somewhat naive mistake of taking Richelieu's protestations that he wanted to withdraw from politics seriously. Aggravating the relationship further was the fact that in 1621 Bérulle had a hand in Richelieu's being denied the cardinalship, which he subsequently did not receive until September 1622.

Bérulle and Richelieu indeed developed their respective political positions in totally opposite directions. Bérulle and the *parti dévot* subordinated politics to the concerns of religion while Richelieu's position was the exact opposite. A clash between these contradictory tendencies could not be avoided for long. Gradually the supremacy of the state became Richelieu's basic argument. The *parti dévot* on the other hand, reinforced by Port-Royal, demanded priority for the rights of religion over the claims of individual conscience. Richelieu's views, taking up, as they did, political ideas dating back to the Middle Ages, were without doubt reactionary, whereas those of the *parti dévot* showed the way into the eighteenth century and into the mentality of the modern era.

Before Richelieu had firmly secured his position, the contradiction between the two positions became manifest as a result of several incidents. In the conflict between the new Emperor, Ferdinand, and the Protestant Elector Palatine Friedrich V, which broke out toward the end of 1619, President Jeannin, through mediation by Bérulle and Minister Luynes, succeeded in gaining the support of the Royal Council for the Catholic faction. But the victory of the Catholics at the end of 1620 had radicalized the claims of Austria and Spain, putting France into a difficult situation. As a consequence, Richelieu was moved to criticize the policies of Luynes and of the *parti dévot* by means of several anonymous pamphlets. The controversy became even more evident on the occasion of the marriage of Henriette de France, sister of Louis XIII, to Charles I of England. Bérulle favored this marriage because through it he hoped to save what was left of Catholicism in England. Richelieu wanted it as well, but hoped to secure through it the alliance with England against Spain. But both were soon disappointed. Bérulle — even at the price of war — wanted to realize those clauses in the marriage contract which would have favored the Catholics. But Richelieu, who had scant concern for the English Catholics and was governed by ruthless realism, dropped the contractual clauses without regrets and turned toward Protestant Germany. But Bérulle, who in 1627 had also become a cardinal, continued to exert a powerful influence on the queen mother, who had remained well-disposed toward the *parti dévot.* But in 1629 Bérulle irrevocably fell out of favor when Richelieu succeeded against Bérulle's recommendation in inducing the Royal Council to come to the aid of Charles de Nevers, Duke of Mantua, who was under siege by the Spanish at Casal. On the following 21 November Richelieu was appointed first minister of the state.

The death of Bérulle was a heavy blow to the *parti dévot.* A final crisis which momentarily threatened Richelieu's power ended in the *Journée des Dupes* (Day of Dupes, 12 November 1630) and the queen mother's being exiled. After this, Richelieu was in a position methodically to eliminate his opponents. But Richelieu found himself confronted by yet another opponent who was all the less vulnerable in as much as he rarely involved himself in affairs of state. He was Jean Duvergier de Hauranne (1581–1643), of Basque origin, abbot of Saint-Cyran since 1620. He had been a brilliant university student, friend and fellow student of Cornelius Jansen from Flanders. After finishing his studies, Saint-Cyran had embarked on a career as secular cleric which had led to ties of friendship with Richelieu. In 1618, on the occasion of his ordination, Saint-Cyran had undergone a moral crisis, from which he emerged a changed person, converted to an inner life. A chance meeting around 1620 soon led to a close friendship and occasional collaboration with Bérulle. After the death of Bérulle the Oratory, for fear of the cardinal-minister, hardly dared eulogize their founder. Yet Saint-Cyran on 5 October circulated an impressive letter to Fr. Bourgoing, the subsequent second successor to Bérulle in the generalship of the congregation, which contained unreserved praise of the deceased. Without wanting to, Saint-Cyran quickly occupied an exposed position with the *parti dévot* and became an opponent of Richelieu. During the brief period in which the party held decisive power, immediately prior to the *Journée des Dupes,* the queen mother had even designated him bishop of Bayonne. Initially, Richelieu did not dare proceed against his former friend, because he either lacked sufficient grounds or was still hoping to win him back over to his side.

Saint-Cyran, knowing himself to be in a dangerous situation, behaved most cautiously while the cardinal's anti-Spanish policies intensified and in May 1635 culminated in a declaration of war. Yet the public was aware that Saint-Cyran condemned the hostility toward a great Catholic nation as well as Richelieu's alliance with the Protestants of Germany. In the course of the summer of 1635 Jansen, whose connection with Saint-Cyran was well-known, published his *Mars gallicus, seu de justitia armorum et foederum regis Galliae,* a blunt and cutting pamphlet against Richelieu's foreign policy. Saint-Cyran did not approve of this far too partisan comment. But Richelieu was offended; he reacted sharply and marked Saint-Cyran the victim of his revenge. At the same time, he was afraid that his opponent might openly resist him in a delicate matter of extreme importance to him. It involved the marriage of Gaston d'Orléans, brother of the King, who on 3 January 1632 had married Marguerite of Lorraine without the crown's consent. This union interfered with Richelieu's policies because he was speculating on the properties of Marguerite's brother, the duke of Lorraine. By an edict of parliament (1634), the minister had the marriage dissolved on the strange pretext that Gaston had been the victim of an abduction. To buttress his case and to soothe the King's conscience Richelieu obtained — though not without difficulty — expert opinions from the Assembly of the Clergy, from fourteen Parisian congregations, and from sixty doctoral academicians, all of whom attested to the marriage's being invalid. But the Holy See continued to consider it valid. This was also Saint-Cyran's opinion and in spite of using the utmost discretion he could not conceal it, particularly because he was a friend of Condren, general of the Oratory and Gaston's confessor. Richelieu, aware of this, was at once resentful and uneasy. Richelieu, with newspaper writers in his paid employ, knew very well of the power of the press and of public opinion, which could have been reversed by an active intervention on the part of Saint-Cyran. At this time, moreover, the minister was making public his plan to establish a French patriarchate relatively independent of the Holy See. It was obvious from the beginning that Saint-Cyran would oppose with all his force this schismatical design in which Richelieu, as he was well aware, had most of the nation against him. So Saint-Cyran unintentionally became the cardinal's foremost antagonist. Once more Richelieu attempted to win him over by arranging to have the bishopric of Bayonne offered to him in the spring of 1637. The abbot refused because he did not want to relinquish his independence, but knowing full well that this refusal would expose him to greater danger. At this point Richelieu actually thought of using force. But the intellectual authority of the abbot, his reputation for piety and integrity, and the seclusion in which he dwelt made him a difficult target. It took the incidents at Port-Royal, to provide the cardinal with the seemingly religious pretext he was seeking. In any event, Richelieu could now assume that the arrest of Saint-Cyran would seal the disintegration of the already weakened *parti dévot.* He could not foresee that Port-Royal would endure as the strongest bastion of resistance against absolutism.

The Reform of the Clergy

During the few years under the regency of Marie de Médicis in which the *parti dévot* enjoyed a full measure of power, its foremost aim was the reform of the secular clergy and that of the orders. This endeavor was supported and continued by Richelieu. After 1610 the efforts in behalf of monastic reform were not only sustained by the *milieu dévot,* but were indeed frequently pursued by civil authorities as well. It must be pointed out that the idea of monastic reform had a twofold significance. In some cases an outstanding religious personality at the head of a community was able to restore strict observance and to turn it into a center of spirituality simply by persuasive power and by setting an example. In other cases, the authorities intervened from the outside and when necessary applied force in order to do away with the most flagrant excesses and to bring about at least a minimum of observance of the rules. The religious significance of the reform is of course basically different in the two cases.

A decisive position in the movement for monastic reform was occupied by Cardinal François de la Rochefoucauld (1558–1645). He had met Saint Charles Borromeo in Italy; now he was consumed with the idea of emulating Borromeo's reformatory zeal. La Rochefoucauld had close ties to the *parti dévot* and it was probably Henri de Gondi, bishop of Paris, who had recommended him to Louis XIII in about 1620 to work on monastic reform. La Rochefoucauld, who by the way was unscrupulous in his accumulation of church benefices, had among his acquisitions of abbeys that of Sainte-Geneviève in Paris, a monastery of the Canons Regular, which made him primarily interested in the reform of this particular branch. For this purpose he collaborated in establishing the *Congrégation de France,* which was to integrate all the abbeys of the Canons Regular. Dom Étienne Maugier, abbot of La Charmoye, took over the leadership of the reform movement. With the support of La Rochefoucauld he initiated a movement claiming independence for the reformed chapters. The ensuing dissension split the order until the end of the century. Even the constitution *In suprema* by Alexander VII, prescribing slightly more moderate statutes, could not restore harmony, but on the contrary evoked spirited resistance. Among the disputants was Armand-Jean le Bouthillier de Rancé (1626–1700). After a checkered career as a worldly abbot he converted and in 1664 became titular abbot of his commendam La Trappe in Normandy, where he embarked upon a reform of his abbey. While far exceeding the Cistercian ideal in its scope and severity, his reforms nonetheless caused an immense awareness because Rancé was known widely. But within the order it was greatly resisted by, among others, Dom Eustache de Beaufort, who had initiated the reform of his abbey of Sept-Fons in Bourbonnais in 1663. The Cistercian nuns also joined the reform movement, which had been initiated in Port-Royal in 1608; by the end of the century several congregations of reformed Bernardine nuns had been founded.

The Benedictines as well benefited from several attempts at reform emanating from Lorraine where the congregations of Saint-Vanne and Saint-Hydulphe had been formed in 1604. The reform of Saint-Vanne was transferred to France in 1613. Several cloisters joined in, but since Lorraine at this time was part of the Empire, they had to form an autonomous congregation in 1618, the *Congrégation de Saint-Maur;* this was encouraged by Louis XIII and canonically sanctioned in 1621. Gradually most of the important Benedictine abbeys joined the congregation with the exception of Cluny and its chapters. In 1631 the renowned abbey of Saint-Germain des Prés in Paris emerged as the center of the Maurists. Simultaneously, instances of reforms in the Benedictine convents also increased. Some of these reforms adapted the Benedictine traditions to contemporary forms of piety, as was the case with the Benedictine nuns of Calvary, founded in 1617 in Poitiers. The change was even more marked in the case of the Benedictine nuns of the Holy Sacrament founded in 1653 by Mother Mechtilde in Paris.

During the first half of the seventeenth century almost all the old established orders in fact had to submit to reform for internal reasons. For the Dominicans, Sebastian Michaelis had managed in 1608 to establish a reformed congregation for the Toulouse region; in 1613 it expanded to Paris, where it assumed the name *Congrégation de Saint-Louis.* The reform of the Premonstratensians started in 1617 in Lorraine and spread to France in 1623. First indications of a Carmelite reform of Touraine appeared in 1604. Reform of the clergy of the orders on the whole resulted from individual and private efforts, rather than from initiatives by the state. Later on Richelieu had the abbeys of Cluny, Cîteaux and Prémontré conveyed to himself in order to be in a position to intercede effectively. Yet he used them primarily for the income he derived from them. In reality, the leadership was making too much profit from the existing abuses to want to remedy them. But for all the difficulties they faced, the efforts by the reformers were not in vain. Many cloisters not only turned into places of sincere spiritual life, but also had a profound effect on the laity. Even in houses at the periphery of reforms the most scandalous excesses were stopped; transgressions were no longer overt. Eventually the religious orders regained their dignity.

Reform of the secular clergy posed a completely different problem. From the outset, the whole *milieu dévot* agreed that it would be useless to undertake a reform of the present clergy, that it was necessary to start all over again by bringing up a new clergy. But from this point on, the proposed solutions diverged. One feasible idea was the creation of an organism whose sole function was to be the education of a clergy worthy of its duties. This had actually been prescribed by the Council of Trent when it ordered the establishment of seminaries. Yet in spite of efforts in this direction by many clerics including La Rochefoucauld, the council's decrees never became state law; implementation was left instead to private initiative. So the bishops were quite late when they began to establish seminaries, which, moreover, were frequently forced to operate under very difficult conditions.

In fact, there appeared to be another solution to the reform of the parish priests: the creation of a secular clergy to be both example and complement to the existing clergy. Bérulle approved on 10 November 1611 when he founded the Oratory of Jesus, an unpretentious congregation of secular clerics without special vows. His model was the foundation of Saint Philip Neri in Rome. Neri had designed the Oratories in the various towns as autonomous houses without an organic connection. In contrast, Bérulle had planned his French Oratory from the beginning to be a single congregation structured under the authority of a superior general whose members could change houses if required by circumstances. In this respect, Bérulle's design was better adapted to the requirements of France, which had the kind of political unity lacking in Italy. The members of the Oratory immediately took over the various forms of parish apostleship, to which they soon added educational duties. The Oratory developed swiftly. By the time of its first plenary session in August 1631 it already had seventy-one houses. This quantitative as well as qualitative achievement proved that the Oratory fulfilled the needs of a large segment of the religious public. In spite of its liberal attitude, expansion and centralization actually gave the Oratory the posture of a large national congregation, comparable in France to the Society of Jesus.

The role and influence of the Oratory and the priestly spirituality promoted by Bérulle and his successors, contributed significantly to raising the level of the secular clergy. Meanwhile the Oratory and its followers were occupied to create institutions which were to insure the proper education of the clergy. While Bérulle was alive, the Oratory already took over seminaries, many of which were attached to secondary schools such as the seminary of Saint-Magloire, founded for the Paris diocese. But these institutions met with limited success in counteracting the problems within the secular clergy. Bérulle's successor at the head of the Oratory, Charles de Condren (1588–1641), an indecisive person who shunned responsibility, did not make an effort to continue the task of establishing seminaries within the Oratory although he recognized the need for them and recommended them to his students. One of them, Jean-Jacques Olier (1608–57), realized a work of fundamental significance. Having become pastor of Saint-Sulpice in 1642, he established a seminary in his parsonage which soon brought forth the *Compagnie de Saint-Sulpice,* an association of secular priests. Following the model of the Oratory, it was dedicated to teaching at diocesan seminaries and directing them. Before long the Sulpician seminaries were considered exemplary and their education became the prototype of clerical training. Educated in accordance with the spiritual principles of Bérulle regarding the eminence of the priesthood and its place in the hierarchy, a certain type of priest emerged from these seminaries. Pious, well educated and charitable, leading a dignified and retired life, they all came from a certain social stratum, which was to endure through the upheavals of the Revolution to the threshold of our century. However, the education and training was limited by the quality of the candidates. This improved, although a decision for the priesthood was not always in response to a true calling. The aristocracy continued to provide the recruits for the episcopate, but usually had its candidates, too, go through the seminaries. Talleyrand's *Mémoires* indicate that these clerical youths on the eve of revolution were prepared to upset the strict order of the seminaries. Among the lower levels of society, the priesthood remained as always the simplest means for social mobility. Parents would simply enter their most gifted children into the priesthood — whether the children wanted it or not.

The reform movement also brought about other foundations which were concerned with clerical education. One of the most significant emanated from Vincent de Paul (1581–1660). As a farmer's son from the area of Landes, Vincent's youth had been wanting in material things. Although his reputed stay in Tunisia must be considered a legend, he nevertheless had to undergo a number of adventures before he settled in Paris at the end of 1608. After 1610 his life led him on the path to an even more demanding holiness under the influence of Bérulle. Yet he took many more years to discover his true destination. In 1618 he started to devote himself to the rural missions, but not until 1625, supported by one of the most powerful families of the *milieu dévot,* the Gondi, did he establish the *Congrégation des Prêtres de la Mission.* The new congregation, which initially occupied itself with the rural apostolate and later on with several foreign missions, developed so rapidly that by 1641 Vincent de Paul was able to use his priests in establishing some diocesan seminaries. At the time of his death there was a total of about a dozen houses. At the request of the archbishop, Vincent de Paul five or six times a year offered a week's contemplation at Saint-Lazare for candidates for ordination. These retreats were highly frequented and very successful. In July 1633 — also at Saint-Lazare — the renowned Tuesday conferences were initiated (*Conférences du Mardi),* at which gathered the foremost representatives of the Parisian clergy to instruct one another and to discuss the problems of the apostolate. The following years, the Vincentians established similar organizations in the large provincial towns. All of these institutions were objects of Vincent de Paul's constant occupation. This was true especially for the seminaries where the candidates for the priesthood unfortunately spent no more than a few months. This was too short a time to enable them to receive a solid education. Even at that, the results were positive as Vincent himself stated at the end of his life.

Vincent de Paul quickly freed himself from Bérulle's initial influence; this even led to some differences of opinion between the two. In addition to them, the Oratory brought forth another great founder in the area of rural mission and seminary work: Saint John Eudes (1611–80), a member of the Oratory from 1623 to 1643. The sole reason for his leaving the Oratory in 1643 was the fact that he was opposed by the superior general, François Bourgoing, when he established a seminary in Caen. He founded the *Congrégation de Jésus et Marie,* which assumed the direction of numerous seminaries and remained dominated by a spirituality inspired by Bérulle. At the same time there were other experiments and foundings. And yet these efforts did lead to a genuine, gradually expanding reform of the prevailing mentality. After 1650 most of the dioceses established seminaries; the conditions for ordination began more and more to conform with canonical norms with the result of raising standards among the parish clergy rapidly without, however, going beyond the above-mentioned limitations.

CHAPTER 113

Origin and Development of Jansenism to 1653

Augustinianism in Louvain and Jansen

The congregations *De Auxiliis* had not resulted in a condemnation of Molina's *Concordia.* While Paul V did not want to diminish the esteem enjoyed by the Jesuits, who had rendered to him inestimable political services, he was nonetheless determined to maintain the fundamental position of the Augustinian-Thomist system of grace. This is why he allowed the Dominican Diego Álvarez (d. 1635) to publish his monumental treatise *De auxiliis divinae gratiae* (1611) as a work of quasi-official character. In order to prevent words on the same topic by the Jesuits Lessius and Suárez to be published, he had the Holy Office issue a decision (not a decree!), which was communicated to those involved and forbade them to publish anything involving the subject of grace. Numerous works proclaiming to be commentaries on the *Summa* of Saint Thomas circumvented the prohibition of 1611; the Jesuits on the whole continued to defend Molina.

The Louvain group then remained identified with Augustinianism; Baius, whose condemnation was considered unfair, enjoyed continued sympathy. It was in this atmosphere that Cornelius Jansen (Jansenius) (1585–1638) developed. He was a student in Louvain under the tutelage of Jansson. From 1609 to 1616 he resided for the main in France, where he met and for some time shared a domicile with Jean Duvergier de Hauranne, who later was to become abbot of Saint-Cyran. After his return to Flanders he dedicated himself to a peaceful and honorable university career. From 1617 until 1624 he was president of the Sainte-Pulchérie Seminary and was then appointed representative of the university at the court of Spain. In March 1630 he was rewarded with the Regius chair of Sacred Scripture and wrote commentaries on numerous books of the Bible, which avoided the touchy issue of grace. In the meantime his ideas about this problem had taken on very definite form. Only after his return to Louvain — under the influence of Jansson — did he undertake a systematic study of Augustine's works, excerpting the essential theses and compiling them into a system of thought. At this point Jansen began to secure various political connections — in France with the help of Saint-Cyran — who were to aid him in his intention to bring about a triumph of Augustinianism over Molinism. Since 1621 he had also been planning to write a comprehensive synthesis of the Augustinian doctrine of grace. After 1627 it advanced with remarkable speed; his letters to Saint-Cyran offer insight into the various stages of progress. On 27 March 1630 he was able to send him the table of contents for the first volume. In spite of interruptions by his professorial duties and the anti-Protestant polemics in 1630–31, he started on the third volume in February 1635, hoping to finish it within a year. But in August 1635 he was appointed rector of the university; on 28 October 1636, he became bishop of Ypres and was occupied intensively with his episcopal duties. Under these circumstances he was unable to complete his great treatise. With a caution understandable in a time that was aggravated by polemics, he had gone about his work with the utmost discretion. But he was not to see its publication. He died from the plague in God's peace on 6 May 1638, having placed his manuscript into the hands of his pupils Henri Calenus and Liber Froidmont.

In spite of Jansen's precautions, the Jesuits of Flanders had some knowledge of his undertaking. Since the Jesuits looked upon a resumption of the polemics on this topic as a potential disaster, they had mobilized support for themselves especially in France and Spain and had also kept the Jesuits of Rome informed. Soon they knew that Jansen had left behind a completed work and so did their utmost to prevent its publication. Through an internuncio in Brussels, they reminded Calenus and Froidmont of the prohibition of 1611 and the decree of 1625, which forbade publications on the subject of grace. But since these decisions were never officially communicated to the University of Louvain the latter considered them of no consequence. The treatise was made public in September 1640. This huge folio of more than thirteen hundred pages in small print of two columns per page was entitled simply *Cornelii Jansenii Episcopi Yprensis Augustinus.*

This extensive book, the work of a lifetime, was indeed in itself a remarkable synthesis of the Augustinian concepts on grace and predestination. But in it Jansen proceeded from the most extreme positions advocated by Saint Augustine in his fight against the Pelagians without taking into consideration the long history of their development. What evolved was a rigid system often sharply formulated. The first volume treats the positions of the Pelagians or Semi-Pelagians. In a "Liber proemialis" introducing the second volume, Jansen investigates the correlations between philosophy and theology; he opposes the methods of Scholasticism as being too rationalistic and claims Augustine's authority in regard to the issue of grace. He then talks about the state of fallen nature from a perspective characterized by Augustinian pessimism with special emphasis on the basic depravity which emanated from sin and about the power of concupiscence, which grants man no more than the freedom of evil. In the process he also addresses the classical problem of the state of pure nature, which he solves in a negative fashion. He concludes that by creation man was elevated to a supernatural calling. The third volume, by far the most significant, examines the healing of human nature and its restitution to true freedom by virtue of the redeeming grace in Christ. Jansen stresses emphatically that grace becomes unfailingly effective without however destroying man's freedom and that this grace is accorded to him by God totally unowned by virtue of a decree of predestination. He rejects the notion of freedom which consists of the ability to posit opposite actions. In his view, freedom is identical with the unfathomable spontaneity of nature, which he calls will. Thus he disregards the Scholastic distinction between will as instinct and will as free choice. His will seeks fulfillment and pleasure spontaneously. But a fallen nature can find its fulfillment only in the creature, in egotistical self-love and therefore turns away from God perforce. It takes the intercession of grace in order to heal it, to breathe into it an inspiration of divine love which resurrects the will in this love and inclines it to a spiritual and holy pleasure through which he puts his whole happiness in God and in the fulfillment of His demand. This is his theory of victorious pleasure through which the will unfailingly enters into harmony with God. In all this, Jansen supposedly reflected the thoughts of Saint Augustine, but actually it is evident that he was influenced by the Baianistic atmosphere of his training. The work as such obviously avoids any and all polemics, but an appendix entitled

Parallèle vigorously attacks the Molinists and compares their teachings with those of the Pelagians. Jansen strove strictly to maintain the language of Augustinianism and, like Baius, rejected the concepts of the Thomists, which otherwise would have given strong impulses to his undertaking.

Augustinianism in France: Saint-Cyran and Port-Royal

While it was torn by the religious wars, France paid scant attention to the controversy concerning divine grace. With peace restored, the universities, above all the Sorbonne, regained their former luster; the most famous professors lectured with great clarity concerning grace, openly adhered to Thomism and revered Augustine as their teacher; Molinism was either completely or almost unknown to them. From the beginning of his career, Bérulle appeared dominated by Augustinianism, but not exclusively. Duvergier de Hauranne, formerly a Jesuit pupil, too, did not at first oppose the new ideas. But just about the time when Jansen in Louvain discovered Augustinianism, a similar range of perception opened up to the future abbot of Saint-Cyran under the influence of Bérulle. Yet the strictly intellectual mode of Augustinianism, which Jansson had disclosed to his pupil Jansen, was not identical to the Augustinianism provided to Saint-Cyran by Bérulle. The latter was not very much interested in abstracting a coherent theory of grace and predestination from the works of the bishop of Hippo. Involved in the practice of Christian spirituality, he sought to derive from Augustine a method that would make the souls realize their total dependence on God and their personal wretchedness. Saint-Cyran moved along the same lines. Yet, disregarding the difference in their individual outlook, Jansen and Saint-Cyran united in a common defense of Augustinianism. In the autumn of 1621 Saint-Cyran spent some time with Jansen in Louvain. At this meeting they decided to enlist political support in order to effect a breakthrough of Augustinianism against the Jesuits. But these political initiatives were unsuccessful: given Richelieu's attitude, the two friends realized that they could not hope for anything from him. On 10 May 1623, they met again in Péronne and decided to start waging the battle in the universities and on the intellectual level. After 1621 they had made use of a secret code, a common practice at a time when the postal service was still very uncertain. This enabled them to carry on a regular and sufficiently secure correspondence until 1635, when it was interrupted by the war. Until this time, Saint-Cyran was thus in a position to follow the progress of this great treatise, to give data and advice to his friend and even to send him a first draft of the "Liber proemialis." Only Jansen's letters were preserved, but they show clearly that he and Saint-Cyran developed in two different intellectual worlds and that Augustinianism never meant the same to the two of them.

Jansen's pamphlet against Richelieu, *Mars Gallicus,* was a sore point with the cardinal, yet Richelieu did not draw upon this pamphlet for his main argument against Saint-Cyran, who was at the pinnacle of his fame by 1634. Generally considered the indisputable head of the *parti dévot,* he maintained excellent connections through his friendship with the elite of French Catholicism. But by then another event involving him was unsettling his life. Since 1620 he had been a close friend of Robert Arnauld d'Andilly, a diplomat, active at the court. The eldest child of a family whose nobility derived from being in the King's service, he was a brother of the famous Mother Angélique, abbess and reformer of the Cistercian abbey of Port-Royal, which had formerly been located in the Chevreuse Valley and in 1625 transferred to Paris. Saint-Cyran had only had occasional slight connections with Mother Angélique and her sister Mother Agnès. Meanwhile Mother Angélique had left Port-Royal for a few years. Together with the bishop of Langres, Sébastien Zamet, she had founded a new order, the *Institut du Saint-Sacrement.* But Zamet, a strange and uneven personality, soon incurred the enmity especially of the archbishop of Sens, Octave de Bellegarde. The latter, intending to damage the *Institut,* provided himself with a devotional text by Mother Agnès entitled *Chapelet secret du Saint-Sacrement.* He represented it as the spiritual charter of the new foundation and managed to have it critically examined by eight professors of the Sorbonne on 18 June 1633. Upon Zamet's request, Saint-Cyran agreed to defend the text, in which he recognized Bérulle's influence. He won out totally and incurred Mother Angélique's deep gratitude. Mother Angélique came to admire Saint-Cyran not only as a pure intellectual, but also as a great spiritual leader.

Yet in this area Saint-Cyran had some very personal convictions inspired in part by Francis de Sales and Bérulle. He rejected the idea that Christian life could alternate constantly between a state of grace and a state of sin. So he endeavored to lead his charges to a truly new life by a method designed to trigger a psychological shock. It consisted of going through the intermediate stage of penitence, yet during this period the penitent would deny himself Communion and delay receiving absolution. Only after this delay, generally lasting a few weeks, did he receive absolution and Communion. Following this he had to live in as much seclusion as possible in order to preserve the grace he had received. This method had been worked out prior to 1627. But he made the mistake of telling the nuns of Port-Royal and Saint-Sacrement about it. They were filled with enthusiasm for it, indeed all of them wanted to set out on this journey to self-renewal. But they also talked about it outside their monastic environs without considering that they were exposing Saint-Cyran to accusations of indulging in dangerous innovations and were providing Richelieu with weapons against him. Plagued by severe scruples, Mother Angélique remained without Holy Communion from Easter to Ascension Day 1635. That she did so in spite of reprimands by Saint-Cyran did not lessen his responsibility for it in the eyes of the public. But soon this affair concerning the recluses of Port-Royal took on a completely different significance. Mother Angélique had a nephew, Antoine Lemaistre, a brilliant young lawyer in who high hopes were placed for a future in the Paris court of law. In 1634, following a sentimental disappointment, he wanted to commit suicide, but was stopped by Saint-Cyran. The sudden death of one of his aunts on 24 August 1637 brought about an enthusiastic wish for conversion. After a long probationary period, Saint-Cyran, on about 15 December 1637, permitted him to write an open letter to Chancellor Séguier in which he announced his decision henceforth to live in seclusion and penitence, but without wanting to become a priest or joining an order. It was common knowledge that Saint-Cyran was his spiritual guide and so he was accused of wanting to establish a new order, especially since other pupils of his began to join Lemaistre in his seclusion. Richelieu took this to be a budding resistance and decided to intervene severely. But before he did, he tried once again — and failed — to buy the benevolence of his erstwhile friend by offering him a bishopric in February 1637. In March 1638 Claude Séguenot, a member of the Oratory, published a translation of Saint Augustine's *De Sancta Virginitate* together with a commentary in which he violently attacked the religious orders and espoused a rigid uncompromising Augustinianism. Journalists in the pay of Richelieu designated Saint-Cyran as the actual author of the book, since his connection with the Oratory was well known. The arrest of Séguenot on 7 May was followed on 14 May by the incarceration of Saint-Cyran at the palace of Vincennes.

Public opinion initially considered Saint-Cyran guilty of aggravated heresy and Richelieu intended to compromise him by putting him on trial. But when his papers were scrutinized and his friends and pupils interrogated, the accused turned out to be completely innocent. For a while, Richelieu hoped to use the issue of attritionism against him since Saint-Cyran had always defended the need in the Sacrament of Penance for a *contritio* based on the love of God. Richelieu held this concept to be in contradiction to the decisions of the Council of Trent. But on 14 May 1640 Saint-Cyran, for whom this problem was actually of little practical importance, announced that he was prepared to draft a letter relatively favorable to attritionism. By doing so, he deprived Richelieu of his main charge. Nevertheless Saint-Cyran remained in custody without a trial. His only hope was that the unhealthy conditions of his jail at Vincennes would soon destroy his fragile health. By now the Catholic circles among the public knew what was going on and public opinion turned against the cardinal. Saint-Cyran, on the other hand, having acquired an aura of martyrdom was able to initiate from his jail a voluminous correspondence which influenced an ever more significant group of pupils. Seriously ill and threatened by blindness he was repeatedly near death. Yet he was destined to outlive Richelieu, who passed away on 4 November 1642. Saint-Cyran was able to leave his jail on 6 February 1643. But he remained in ill health and died of apoplexy on 11 October, without having resumed his activities. Yet he left a number of pupils who continued his work.

The Beginnings of the Jansenist Conflict— The Bull *In eminenti*

It was foreseeable that the publication of Jansen's *Augustinus* would ultimately result in a renewed controversy regarding the question of grace. So no one, least of all the Louvain group, was caught unprepared; in fact, everyone had carefully prepared his position ahead of time. The Jesuits started the campaign by disregarding the prohibitions (1611 and 1625) of publications on the topic of grace, in which they had originally concurred without reservations. On 22 March 1641 lectures were read at the Jesuit college of Louvain in which Jansen was accused of renewing the errors of Calvin and Baius, of reducing human freedom to nothing and of limiting salvation to the chosen few. These theses met with spirited rejoinders and innumerable polemics. Henceforth the faculties were split into Jansenists and anti-Jansenists.

France, too, was a ready battlefield for renewed strife. Saint-Cyran's spiritual heir turned out to be the youngest brother of Mother Angélique, Antoine Arnauld

(1612–94), whom posterity accorded the sobriquet Le Grand Arnauld. For a long time Saint-Cyran was disappointed by the young man's exclusively intellectual and all too worldly ambitions although he demonstrated remarkable abilities all along. At that time the short works by Augustine against the Pelagians were hardly available, but through Jansen's good offices Saint-Cyran had gotten about twenty copies of the Louvain edition of 1555. He gave one of them to young Arnauld and was amazed at the quickness and depth with which the latter grasped the main points of the treatise. For the baccalaureate in theology on 14 November 1635, Saint-Cyran had him defend some clearly Augustinian theses whose content was close to that of *Augustinus.* The defense proved quite successful; it demonstrated that Augustinianism continued to have enthusiastic adherents at the Sorbonne and provoked no polemics of any kind. In December 1638 Arnauld received the subdiaconate; shortly thereafter he converted to an intensive and challenging life of the spirit under the exclusive guidance of Saint-Cyran. The latter had him continue his studies at the Sorbonne, where he was awarded his doctorate on 18 December 1641. By that time Saint-Cyran had already called on him to defend his ideas in several publications.

Since Augustinians as well as Molinists had correspondents in Louvain, several copies of *Augustinus* were sent to France when it appeared in September 1640. The following November and December six Parisian professors gave their approval for a reprint which appeared in 1641 in Paris, followed by another one in Rouen in 1643. There were groups whose defense of Augustinianism had by then become a tradition: Oratorians, Dominicans, Carmelites and numerous professors at the Sorbonne. But several professors joined the fray on the side of the anti-Jansenists, among whom the Jesuits played an especially significant role. Foremost among Jansen's opponents was Richelieu, who had never forgiven him for his *Mars Gallicus.* Richelieu was inclined toward Molinism; in his *Instruction du Chrétien* of 1619 he had supported attritionism, whereas *Augustinus* represented a lively defense of contritionism. Yet he did want to spare the Jesuits, several of whom were rendering him great political service at the time. Although he showed his sympathies openly, he was very late in giving the signal for the start of the battle.

By the end of 1640 Saint-Cyran, too, had in his jail a copy of *Augustinus.* But weakened by illness and in danger of going blind, he was unable to analyze the large folio systematically. Apparently he read only the table of contents and a few chapters. No doubt he derived his knowledge of the work primarily from analyses given him by Arnauld. He had had no connection with Jansen since 1635, so he was not familiar with the final projections of the work, especially of the third volume, in which he was astonished to find an attack on attritionism. He had been unable to keep his original agreement with Jansen, namely, to go over the work before it was published. Now he found it dry, harsh, incongruous with its subject matter and out of touch with the spiritual aspects of the problem. Nevertheless he acknowledged it as a well-founded presentation of the fundamentals of Augustinianism. A short time later, for the benefit of informing Arnauld d'Andilly, he expressed his own ideas about it in a small treatise *De la grâce de Jésus Christ.* At any rate, he desired no hasty polemics and impressed this upon his pupils. He confined himself to promoting other Augustinian writings which complemented the works of Jansen. The Paris edition of *Augustinus* contained an appendix with a treatise by Conrius in which he maintained that children who die without the benefit of baptism were condemned to hell. At the same time a small treatise by Jansen, *Oratorio de interioris hominis reformatione* (1627) was printed and translated into French by Arnauld d'Andilly in 1642. This prompted the Jesuits to have the anti-Jansenist theses, presented at the University of Louvain in March 1641, reprinted. Shortly before his death Richelieu initiated the altercation by ordering Isaac Habert, canon and professor at the Sorbonne, to attack Jansen in his sermons. This last attack was especially vehement. Thereupon the prisoner of Vincennes decided to let Jansen's defenders break their silence and charged Arnauld with a reply to Habert. Arnauld, under the direction of Saint-Cyran, then composed his extensive *Apologie pour M. Jansénius,* but the intervention by President Molés and the archbishop of Paris, François de Gondi, who preferred continued silence, delayed its publication until September 1644. They could not prevent the appearance meanwhile of numerous polemics

It is improbable that this affair has a strong effect on Urban VIII. He was an old man consumed by illness and scruples who occupied himself mainly with poetry and politics, concentrating his efforts on the glory of his family, the Barberini, and leaving the government to his nephew, Cardinal Francesco Barberini. The latter — since he had been unable to prevent the publication of *Augustinus* — at the very least wanted to silence those involved in the controversy. The Jesuits started a comprehensive campaign aimed at having the teaching of *Augustinus* explicitly condemned. Several lists of anathematizeable theses were sent to Cardinal Barberini, but the Holy Office refused to condemn them before studying the work itself. However, Barberini superseded this decision and condemned the work on the grounds that it reiterated sentences condemned by Pius V and Gregory XIII. A corresponding bull dated 6 March was proposed. It was probably authored by Francesco Albizzi, an assessor in the Holy Office who took an especially active part in this affair. But additional negotiations ensued in which the nuncio of Cologne, Fabio Chigi, took a significant part because he expected to gain from them a reputation as a peacemaker. These negotiations delayed the publication in Rome of the bull *In eminenti* until 19 June 1643. The Belgian Jesuits had received copies of the bull from their Roman brothers and published it on their own responsibility even before the nuncios had been appraised of it. Antonio Bichi, internuncio in Brussels, who had succeeded Stravius in that office in July 1642 and his uncle, Fabio Chigi, nuncio in Cologne, were officially informed of the bull shortly thereafter and published it, but they amended their own text and dated it 1643. Other editions were circulated, again offering different variations. When it was finally recognized, the text contained so many doctrinal and juridical difficulties that in Flanders it was not effectively published until 1651.

In Louvain the dean of theology, Schickelius, who had been won over to anti-Jansenism, tried to have the bull accepted before its publication. But he failed because most of his colleagues considered its motives erroneous, especially the assertion that *Augustinus* had stirred up trouble in the Church. Sinnich received an audience with Urban VIII in the course of which the venerable Pope acknowledged that it was his intention not to have Jansen named in the bull. This indirectly implicated Albizzi as being responsible for the actual authorship of the bull. Taken aback by this development, Albizzi had the bull confirmed by a decree of the Holy Office on 16 June 1644. Urban VIII died on 29 July 1644 and was succeeded by Innocent X (Pamfili). In several briefs he demanded execution of he bull, but in reality he would have preferred to have things drag on. Sinnich returned to Louvain empty-handed in September 1645. The situation in the Netherlands gradually calmed down. It was in France that this matter was to take a decisive turn.

For some obscure reasons, the nuncio of Paris, Cardinal Hieronymus Grimaldi, did not receive his copy of the bull *In eminenti* which had been dispatched on 10 June 1643; the official documents regarding this problem did not reach him until September. Arnauld, advised by Saint-Cyran, now gathered all possible arguments against the authenticity of the bull. These appeared in his *Premières* and *Secondes observations sur la bulle* in August 1643 and made a strong impression on public opinion. In the fall, after the authenticity of the bull had been acknowledged conclusively, the delegates from Louvain arrived in Paris on their way to Rome and coordinated their moves with the French Jansenists. With the help of efficacious parliamentary support Jansen's followers succeeded in preventing the adoption in France both of the bull and the decree of 16 June 1644. This was at the beginning of the regency of Anne of Austria and the unsettled state of the country marked by Mazarin's rise to power provided the Jansenists with opportunities for wide-ranging action. At the same time Arnauld replied to a Jesuit polemic against Saint-Cyran in his *Apologie pour M. de Saint-Cyran.* It touches upon several problems of the doctrine of grace. But the basic problems of doctrine in *Augustinus* were hardly referred to at that time.

This unstable period was above all affected by conflicts kindled by Arnauld's *De la Fréquente communion.* This voluminous quarto had originally been nothing more than a very brief refutation of an essay published in 1641 by the Jesuit Sesmaisons, who presented ideas regarding penance and the Eucharist which were diametrically opposed to those of Saint-Cyran. With the aid of Saint-Cyran, Arnauld's work had grown into a comprehensive defense of Saint-Cyran's theses concerning the practice of "renewals," which later were represented as a return to the discipline of the early Church. This in turn had to please the representatives of the *milieu dévot* and of the Counter-Reformation. In August 1643 the work appeared with an approbation by fifteen bishops and twenty-one professors. It triggered a spirited exchange of charge and countercharge. Arnauld countered in 1644 by publishing a copious collection of texts translated by Lemaistre, *La tradition de l'Eglise sur le sujet de la pénitence et de la communion.* But governmental circles where Mazarin's anti-Jansenism was gaining ground were not well-disposed toward Arnauld. Mazarin considered himself to be in a position to initiate rapport with the Holy Sea by ordering Arnauld personally to defend the work in Rome. Arnauld preferred to withdraw from Mazarin's immediate sphere of influence, but the Gallican circles protested against the decision, which in the last instance remained inconsequential. Those bishops who had given their approval felt involved by the controversy and brought the matter before the Holy See through a letter of 5 April 1644. A professor of the Sorbonne who had been one of those who had given their approval also was dispatched to Rome. By the time he returned in 1646, the Holy Office had examined the book thoroughly and declined to censure it. Parallel to this quarrel, which actually was a mere diversion, the first attacks against the laxism of the Jesuit theory of morality in the *Théologie morale de jésuites* began.

The Five Theses and the Bull *Cum occasione*

By 1645 it became obvious that Mazarin was exercising complete control over the queen regent and was continuing Richelieu's policies, including the latter's anti-Jansenist orientation. At court several of the friends of Port-Royal grasped the situation and changed their position. Those who remained loyal to Port-Royal were considered part of the opposition and were excluded. Arnauld d'Andilly himself ended his secular career and in 1646 withdrew from court. Vincent de Paul, a member of the *Conseil de Conscience* since 1643 and formerly a friend of Saint-Cyran, to whom he was indebted for many services, no longer dared oppose his fellow councilors; in 1648 he came out against Jansenism. Finally Port-Royal remained the last bastion of resistance, which first Mazarin and then Louis XIV sought to reduce. For several years there were mere superficial quarrels in which the Jansenists were prominently represented by Arnauld, Barcos, and the Oratorian P. Desmares, and the anti-Jansenists by Habert and the Jesuits Deschamps and Pinthereau. The latter managed to procure some of the papers confiscated in Saint-Cyran's apartments and from 1646 to 1655 he published skillfully chosen excerpts from them, supplemented by an exceedingly dishonest commentary. In this manner he provided posterity with a wealth of valuable documents. By 1649 the stage was set for a massive attack on Jansen. At a meeting of the Sorbonne on 1 July 1649 the syndic Nicolas Cornet, without reference to a particular work, submitted the following seven propositions to be examined:

1. Some of God's commandments cannot be followed by the righteous with the help of those powers available to them in the present state even if they want to follow them. Neither do they have the grace which would make it possible for them to be followed.
2. In the state of fallen nature inner grace never meets resistance.
3. In the state of fallen nature merit or demerit does not require man's freedom from inner compulsion; freedom from outer constraint is sufficient.
4. The Semi-Pelagians admitted the necessity of antecedent inner grace for the individual acts, also for the beginning of faith. Their error was to maintain that human will could resist or obey this grace.
5. It is Semi-Pelagian to assert that Christ has died or shed his blood for all men.
6. The acts of disbelievers are sins.
7. The Church earlier believed that the Sacrament of Penance was not sufficient for secret sins.

Immediately a stormy and chaotic discussion ensued, in the course of which several professors asserted that the present intention was to condemn the teachings of Augustine under the name of Jansen. A short time later Arnauld made public his *Considérations sur l'enterprise faite par Maître Nicolas Cornet,* in which he declared the formulation of the propositions to be deliberately ambiguous. In as much as a superficial reading could make them appear to have a heretical meaning, they could — from the Augustinian viewpoint — be taken in a completely orthodox sense. The situation at the Sorbonne was further complicated by the act that professors belonging to a religious order were each given a vote, whereas the old rules limited this right to only two representatives of each order so that block voting in accordance with instructions by the order could be avoided. Under these conditions it was impossible to compose and publish a censure of the propositions. Recourse to the Holy See, suggested earlier by the Roman Jesuits, now appeared unavoidable. This coincided with Rome's desire not to have such an important issue left up to the Sorbonne.

Toward the end of 1650, Isaac Habert, by now bishop of Vabres, wrote to Innocent X, submitting to him the first five propositions and vaguely ascribing them to Jansen. For this letter the anti-Jansenists collected the signatures of bishops and when it was sent to Rome early in 1651 there were seventy-eight, another fifteen signatures were added later. At that time the French episcopate totaled about one hundred and thirty bishops. Arnauld countered the letter by arguments similar to those used in his reply to Nicolas Cornet. The episcopate also had supporters of Jansen, among them Henri Arnauld, bishop of Angers and brother of the Great Arnauld. At the meeting of clergy from February to March 1651 several bishops protested to the nuncio against Habert's action. A little later eleven participants wrote a letter to Innocent X, an action which later gained the support of two more bishops. In the following months other Jansenist delegates came to Rome. The anti-Jansenists, too, initially represented there by the Franciscan Mulard, sent three more emissaries in April 1652. All signs pointed to a long wait for a decision. Meanwhile the conflict again turned to less important matters.

From the start, the Jansenist delegation in Rome made the mistake of demanding convocations with public discussions similar to the congregations *De Auxiliis,* while Innocent X wanted to be the sole judge in this issue. There was only one Jesuit member and the commission of cardinals was distinguished by the remarkable manner in which the Franciscan Luke Wadding defended Jansen. The two delegations were empowered to send briefs to the commission, but were not allowed official meetings with each other. They were received in audience very rarely and even then only separately. Several extremely interesting polemical writings originated at that time, especially the *Écrit a trois colonnes* which was handed to the commission by Jansen's supporters on the occasion of their last audience on 19 May 1653. It is extremely significant if one is to understand Jansenist thought. For each of the five propositions it distinguishes between orthodox and heretical meaning and also lists the opposing Molinist position. In reality political factors had a decisive part in the negotiations. On the one hand, Rome did not want to change its mind and retract the bull *In eminenti.* On the other hand, the Holy See — very sensitive on the issue of Gallicanism — had been well disposed to the appeal by the anti-Jansenist bishops and was prepared to allow them to emerge victorious especially since they represented a large majority of the episcopate. After all, Mazarin, with whom good contacts were desired, had come out openly against Jansenism and in 1651 had even sent to Rome a letter signed by the young

King Louis XIV. Given these conditions, another condemnation of Jansen was unavoidable and indeed it seems as though the responsible circles in Rome never thought of an alternative. The bull *Cum occasione*, published on 3 June 1653, condemned without reservations the five propositions which it ascribed to Jansen, the first four as heretical, the fifth one as erroneous. This bull was a complete victory for the anti-Jansenists. In Flanders it was accepted without difficulties. The Jansenists, hit hard by the recent censures of the archbishop of Mechelen and the bishop of Ghent and much weakened by the deaths in quick succession of Calenus and Froidmont (February, October 1653, respectively), resisted but feebly. Indeed Louvain was no longer the home of the Jansenist party; it was now Paris.

CHAPTER 114

The Jansenist Conflict to 1713

The *quaestio juris* and the *quaestio facti* — The *Provinciales*

The bull *Cum occasione* no doubt represented a victory for the anti-Jansenists, since Mazarin exerted his own efforts at having the bull accepted throughout France. An order to this effect was addressed to parliament and the clergy by means of a royal declaration dated 4 July 1653. Mazarin had the bull acknowledged in the name of the whole clergy by the twenty-eight bishops present in Paris at that time and shortly thereafter the Sorbonne was also forced to accept it. But a few bishops published it with certain reservations by means of which they sought to save orthodox Augustinianism. Port-Royal found itself in an especially difficult situation. The *Fronde* had become weaker and weaker. In the most recent disturbances the people of Port-Royal, while proving their absolute loyalty to the crown, had clearly shown their antipathy toward Mazarin, the real victor. In addition, there is no doubt that several pamphlets by the coadjutor of Paris, the future Cardinal Retz, had been edited by the men of Port-Royal. It is therefore understandable that the Jansenists at first took refuge in silence. But the clumsy triumph of their adversaries enabled them to come out into the open again. First they responded to a tasteless cartoon in an almanac which appeared in 1654. In it Jansen and his pupils are depicted throwing themselves into the arms of Calvin. Sacy replied in a long satirical poem *Enluminures du fameux almanach des jésuites*. In February 1654 the Jesuit Father François Annat, the King's father confessor, published a polemic with the title *Chicanes des Jansénistes* asserting that the Pope in his last bull had intended not even to spare the teachings of Saint Augustine. He also maintained that the five propositions had been taken literally from the *Augustinus.* In March Arnauld responded with three essays which represented a manifesto of the new Jansenist point of view. First he cleared up the question of the so-called *quaestio facti.* he proved that only the first proposition is contained in the *Augustinus* but in a context proving it to be orthodox. He goes on to prove that the rest of the propositions might have summarized other passages of the work, but that these, too, are de facto orthodox and reflect only Augustinian thinking. Finally, he cites propositions from the *Augustinus* which pronounce the opposite of those that were condemned. Arnauld concludes that while the propositions with a heretical meaning were justifiably condemned by Innocent X, they were in their heterodox meaning not ascribable to Jansen.

But Arnauld could not actually reach public opinion. In a conference of thirty-eight bishops of 9 March 1654, Mazarin prevailed with a text which acknowledged the condemnation of the propositions as reflecting Jansen's ideas. In a rejoinder of 29 September Innocent X issued a brief with the same objective. On 15 January 1655 Mazarin forced a conference of 15 bishops to have all the clergy and female branches of orders sign a formulary condemning Jansen. But in order not to aggravate the situation, this measure was not immediately implemented. Once again the actual doctrinal issue was not resolved. The Jesuit Étienne Deschamps revived it in his voluminous treatise *De l'hérésie jansénienne* (1654).

Another incident soon heated up the conflict again. On 1 February 1655 the vicar of Saint-Sulpice, Picoté, refused absolution to the Duke of Liancourt because of the duke's well-known relations with Port-Royal. This incident attracted much attention and even the intercession by Vincent de Paul came to nought. Three weeks later Arnauld made the issue public through his *Lettre a une personne de condition,* which his adversaries countered with about ten pamphlets. It took Arnauld four months, until 10 July 1655, to reply to them in his *Seconde lettre à un duc et pair,* which is actually an extensive work summarizing the position of French Jansenism with a remarkable degree of clarity. He accepts without reservation the condemnation of the heresy contained in the five propositions, but he considers it preferable not to comment as to whether or not they should be attributed to Jansen. He adds that he had not discovered them in a close reading of *Augustinus.* Then he vigorously attacks the Molinist concept of *gratia sufficiens* citing Peter and his denial of the Lord as an example of a righteous person who sinned because he was lacking in grace. Arnauld's opponents immediately sought to have him condemned because of the last two propositions concerning the *Augustinus* and Peter. Arnauld wanted to anticipate them by bringing the issue before the Holy See by a letter of 27 August. Nonetheless it was placed on the agenda of a meeting of the Sorbonne on 4 November. It took place in spite of protests by Arnauld, who asked in vain for a hearing and just as unsuccessfully multiplied his written justifications to the assembly. An initial censure was pronounced on 14 January 1655 under circumstances so contrary to the rules that sixty professors withdrew from the Sorbonne. Nevertheless Arnauld was expelled from the Sorbonne on 15 February. In his defense he was supported by a young theologian from Chartres, Pierre Nicole (1625–95), who from then on played a significant role in the quarrel over Jansenism. Unfortunately Arnauld and Nicole only spoke the language of theologians. Whereas their extraordinary level of erudition in this field assured them of a hearing among their kind, their works hardly met with a response from the general public. At this time, however, as Mazarin's position was gradually weakening, the actual problem was on the level of public opinion. Then, even before the final condemnation of Arnauld, Port-Royal found a man who was uniquely suited to help them out: Blaise Pascal (1623–62).

Up to this time the recluses of Port-Royal had considered Blaise Pascal a young man of the world, occupied with the sciences, a recent convert who was friendly toward the convent in which his younger sister Jacqueline had lived as a nun since January 1652. When Arnauld, Nicole, and he were in Port-Royal des Champs in January 1656, a casual invitation by Arnauld prompted him to lend his literary ability to a polemic which was intended for society at large and not for specialists. On 23 January 1656 the *Provinciales* came into being. This first letter to a friend in the country was an enormous success and initiated a new episode in the conflict. The collaborators quickly found that they were on the right path and so another seventeen *Provinciales* were issued in the course of a little more than a year, the last one dated 24 March 1657. This campaign, being rather dangerous, forced Arnauld, Nicole, and Pascal to go into hiding in order to evade a *lettre de cachet* which would have sent them to the Bastille. The printing, too, was done in hiding and successfully evaded every police investigation. In spite of the dangerous conditions the *Provinciales,* starting with the fifth letter, were printed in 6,000 copies, at that time an unusually large circulation. Attesting to the lasting nature of their success is the fact that three editions in one volume appeared between 1657 and 1659. For a long time the public was left to guess about the author; not until 1659 did the fact of Pascal's authorship gradually become known.

Pascal collaborated closely with Arnauld and Nicole; he lent the magic of his incomparable style to the documentation and arguments of the two specialists. He also made use of numerous polemic writings which had appeared earlier and whose contents were now made known to the broad public. Yet he did not meet with complete agreement at Port-Royal; Mother Angélique and Singlin considered this campaign to be irreconcilable with Christian love. With the fifth *Provinciale* — after Arnauld was defeated at the Sorbonne — Pascal counterattacked. Taking up an old polemic, he assailed the laxist morality of the Jesuit casuists. With this topic he found himself on favorable terrain. Rigorism in morality was indeed not only inherited by Port-Royal, but widespread as well among the best representatives of the clergy and among the faithful. By identifying the Jesuits with laxism, Pascal discredited the Society of Jesus to such an extent that they could never quite overcome it. The conflict thus introduced was to continue far beyond the *Provinciales.* The secular clergy took up the fight again by means of the *Écrits des Curés de Paris,* in which Pascal also collaborated. This led to a number of decrees by the Holy Office under Alexander VII (1665, 1666) and Innocent XI (1679), which condemned 110 laxist propositions; 50 of them were indirectly from the *Provinciales.* Unfortunately Pascal had no congenial adversary in the opposite camp. Aside from several replies by individual anti-Jansenists, the Jesuits after the sixth letter published collaborative retorts whose main authors were probably Fathers Annat and Nouet, the latter an excellent writer in the field of spirituality, but merely an average polemicist. These retorts, discussing a boundless wealth of details from the casuist texts quoted by Pascal, were indeed mediocre. But they benefitted Pascal since they gave the impression to the public that the Jesuits were actually identifying themselves with these controversial casuistic positions. The tone of the *Provinciales* became increasingly sharper and more vehement. But this did not prevent a Parisian Jesuit, Georges Pirot, from publishing a clumsy *Apologie des casuistes* in December 1657, which by provoking spirited disapproval further weakened the Jesuit position.

The *Provinciales* indeed had great influence on the public. Public opinion was also agitated by the famous miracle of the holy thorn which occurred on 24 March at Port-Royal, where Pascal's niece, Marguerite Périer, was healed from a lachrymal fistula by means of a thorn from the Holy Crown. In spite of objections by the Jesuits this was generally seen as a sign in favor of Port-Royal. But none of this changed the attitude of the prominent circles. Mazarin, as well as Chancellor Séguier, irritated more than ever by the *Provinciales,* made increasing attempts to eliminate Jansenism. Innocent X, of a rather more indifferent nature, never wanted to get seriously involved in this fight. When he died on 7 January 1655 he was succeeded by the former nuncio of Cologne, Fabio Chigi, a decided anti-Jansenist who acceded to the papal throne as Alexander VII. As of the end of 1655, a new bull concerning Jansen was being prepared, but initially kept secret in order to be issued ar some advantageous point in time. In the summer of 1654 the French assembly of the clergy pressured by Mazarin again ordered signing of the formulary against Jansen and by an official letter to Alexander VII, dated 2 September, requested a definitive decision in the *quaestio facti.* The Holy See considered this a favorable moment: on 16 October 1656 the bull *Ad sacram* was officially signed.

The Formulary

The bull *Ad sacram* caused a violent outbreak of emotion in France. For the Jansenists it represented another defeat and forced them into formulating a new position. Arnauld and Nicole dealt with this problem in various writings published between April and August 1657. In the *quaestio juris,* that is concerning the heresy contained in the five propositions, Arnauld came out in full agreement with the papal condemnation. But in the *quaestio facti,* that is concerning the actual presence of the five propositions in the *Augustinus,* he presented the view that the Pope was simply in error. He maintained that this was entirely possible since the Church was not infallible in nonrevealed facts. On this point he thus refused his inner concurrence and obliged himself to a mere "reverential silence." But this attitude on the part of Arnauld and Nicole did not meet with complete agreement by Port-Royal. Several thought that in the last analysis the condemnation of the five propositions redounded upon Augustinianism as such and that it should therefore be opposed without reservation, even at the price of a schism. Yet others held Arnauld's tactical comments to be absurd. Proceeding from the concept of an unalterably evil world in which it is impossible to defend the truth, they thought it better to submit to the papal condemnations and to leave to God's care the victory of His cause. Barcos, the nephew of Saint-Cyran, was a central figure of this group. But by virtue of his theological authority, Arnauld's ideas were clearly given preeminence.

For Mazarin, anti-Jansenism had actually been above all an argument intended to secure papal neutrality in the conflict with Spain. Having reached this goal he was no longer intent upon a crisis. But after his death (9 March 1661) Louis XIV personally took charge of the battle. Pursued by the specter of the *Fronde* he was determined to do away with all the sources of opposition which endangered national unity. His determination had a bearing upon both Jansenism and Protestantism. Yet on this point the King, who was not very intelligent and indeed very ignorant in religious matters, was totally in the hands of his Jesuit confessors. On 20 February 1661 the bishops of the Assembly of the Clergy had again taken up the issue of the formulary and had asked Alexander VII for his approbation. On 23 April a decree by the Council of State relentlessly demanded the signing of the formulary and in doing so forced the Jansenists to take a stand. Arnauld declared himself ready to sign the formulary, but only if his distinction between the *quaestio juris* and the *quaestio facti* were appended to it. The two vicars general who were administering the Paris diocese in the absence of their archbishop, the famous Cardinal Retz, who had fled, accepted Arnauld's condition. On 8 June 1661 a pastoral letter probably edited by Pascal himself prescribed the signing with the added distinction, which satisfied the group around Arnauld. But faced with opposition by official circles they had to retract the pastoral letter on 31 October and instead to demand the signing without any reservation. Thus Port-Royal was driven to refusal.

At this point the convent and its friends had already suffered severe agitation against them. By 23 April the postulants and pupils had been removed. The spiritual leaders and confessors as well as the most prominent recluses were to be exiled by *lettres de cachet* or imprisoned, but they managed to flee, pursued by the authorities. Later, in May 1666, the police with the aid of an informant succeeded in arresting the nephew of Mother Angélique, Isaac Lemaistre de Sacy, who was subsequently jailed in the Bastille till October 1668. The nuns were prohibited from flight by their monastic confinement and were therefore in the midst of the situation. But their reverence for Saint-Cyran absolutely convinced them of Jansen's orthodoxy. So a majority of them rejected any signing of the formulary, even a conditional one, and on this point stood in opposition to Arnauld. Mother Angélique died in August 1661; in the course of the summer passionate internal disagreements erupted at Port-Royal. The resistance was led by Angélique de Saint-Jean and Jacqueline Pascal. But when the pastoral letter by the vicars general was retracted Arnauld and the nuns again agreed in their unqualified refusal to sign. A short time later the archbishop of Paris, Retz, resigned; his successor, Pierre de Marca, died four months later without having occupied the bishopric. Thereupon Louis XIV appointed his former teacher Hardouin de Péréfixe. But in July 1662 some difficulties arose between France and the Holy See. As a result Péréfixe had to wait one and a half years for his bull of investiture and the events centered upon Port-Royal were left in abeyance. There were some who understood that compromise was preferable to the continued conflict.

In April 1664 Péréfixe finally became archbishop of Paris. At once irascible and good natured, an average theologian, he was convinced that he could easily overcome the Jansenist resistance. On 8 June 1664 he issued a pastoral letter which acknowledged the distinction between de jure and de facto by demanding the divine faith for the *quaestio juris* and a simple "human faith" for the *quaestio facti.* But this could only half satisfy the theologians of Port-Royal, who were unwilling to go beyond the "reverential silence" in the *quaestio facti.* Nicole was entrusted with the reply and in his *Lettres sur l'hérésie imaginaire* and other pamphlets he sharply rejected the archbishop's view. Péréfixe, beside himself, took his revenge on the nuns. On 21 and 26 August, after two dramatic visits at the convent of Paris, he had twelve of them deported to other convents. Among them were Angélique de Saint-Jean and the aged Mother Agnès. In Paris and at the convent of des Champs the nuns were refused the sacraments and were placed under police supervision. The incredible moral torture brought about by such coercion on the part of the archbishop and his people finally made twelve of the nuns sign the formulary, but some of them renounced it later. Reports about these events written by the nuns immediately afterward and smuggled outside were published. They created a great stir, for the archbishop had frequently been compromised by his intemperate disposition. Furthermore the *Apologie pour les religieuses de Port-Royal,* composed at the beginning of 1665 by Arnauld and Nicole, brought all the events before the public. The small number of signatures he had gotten from the nuns was a serious defeat for the archbishop. In an attempt to stabilize the situation, those nuns who refused to sign were gathered at Port-Royal des Champs and guarded by a police unit, while those who, had signed stayed in Paris with a special abbess. But neither of these measures solved the problem.

In the meantime Alexander VII had responded to the wishes of the French clergy by issuing in February 1665 the bull *Regiminis apostolici,* which also ordered the signing of a formulary. But the bull only made matters worse because four bishops published it together with a clear distinction between the *quaestio juris* and the *quaestio facti* and in doing so openly took the side of Port-Royal. The Courts of France and Rome were equally annoyed. In January 1667 the Holy See appointed a commission to initiate a trial against the dissidents. This prompted an immediate declaration of solidarity by nineteen bishops; twenty more entered a protest against the papal action. But Clement IX, a peaceful man, who had succeeded Alexander VII as Pope, desired reconciliation. Louis XIV, having also recognized that war with Holland was unavoidable, wanted to settle the religious quarrels and reunite the kingdom. In 1668 Nuncio Bargellini was charged with the task of seeking ways to reach an agreement. The Jesuits were excluded from the negotiations in which Gondrin, archbishop of Sens, Ligny, bishop of Meaux, and Vialart, bishop of Châons, played a decisive role. In the summer of 1668 there was reason for hope. It was agreed that the four bishops in question were to write to the Pope pledging to publish the bull *Regiminis apostolici* again and to have it signed in their dioceses. The Pope on his part was to tolerate tacitly that the signing would be performed through protocols which — theoretically secret, but in reality generally known — would make the distinction between de facto and de jure. The group of people around Arnauld and Nicole who tended more toward the status of a moderate third party was completely satisfied with this agreement, but not so the extremists of the two opposing parties. A council decree of 23 October 1668 and a brief by Clement IX of 14 January 1669 gave the Clementine Peace official sanction. But the nuns of Port-Royal, still tortured by the same doubts as before, could not decide in favor. Urged by Sacy, they finally signed on 15 February 1669 and were ceremoniously admitted to receive the sacraments.

The Clementine Peace

For almost thirty years the Clementine Peace, imperfect though it was, brought to an end the doctrinal controversies and accorded Port-Royal its last quiet decade. During this period the old convent had loyal and highly placed friends; it was cared for and protected by the former heroine of the *Fronde,* the duchess de Longueville, cousin to the King. But all this could not but displease Louis XIV, who continued to see in this circle a source of opposition against his absolutism. Yet he was intent on letting nothing happen that could reignite the conflicts.

The people of Port-Royal were now in a position to turn their intellectual endeavors to peaceful areas, in which they had excelled earlier, among them the subject of spirituality. A decision was made to research the documents left by the great deceased, to emend them and make them available to the public. At the beginning of 1670, Pascal's *Pensées* appeared, followed in 1671 by two volumes of the *Considérations sur les dimanches et les fêtes,* excerpts from the notes of Saint-Cyran, whose *Lettres chrétiennes et spirituelles* was reissued in Louvain in 1679. Port-Royal strove to make biblical texts accessible to the faithful. During the last crisis in 1667 the group had published a translation from the Greek of the New Testament. Called the *Nouveau Testament de Mons* after its place of origin, it owes its existence primarily to Arnauld, Nicole and Sacy. Although it was a precise and elegant translation, it provoked a violent polemic and was put on the Index in 1668. Sacy — while jailed at the Bastille — had started work on a translation of the Vulgate which he began publishing together with commentaries from the church Fathers. After his death in 1684 his pupils concluded the work. The liturgical translations of Port-Royal — *Heures de Port-Royal* and *Office de Saint-Sacrement* (1659) had several revised reprints. Finally the group also turned to polemicizing against the Calvinists, Arnauld and Nicole collaborating with Bossuet. Nicole — although collaborating with Arnauld — was the main author of *Perpétuité de la foi de l'Église catholique touchant l'Eucharistie,* an imposing work whose first volume appeared in 1669.

In reality both sides knew that the peace thus maintained was very fragile and several incidents clearly demonstrated the true sentiments of the court. In 1675 Henri Arnauld was accused of not permitting the unqualified signing of the formulary in his diocese of Angers. For this Louis XIV reprimanded him through the Edict of Camp de Ninove (30 May 1676). The King was very annoyed in the beginning of 1677 when a memorandum authored by Nicole and signed by two bishops submitted several laxist propositions to the new Pope Innocent XI. But most of all it was the unpleasant regalia quarrel between Louis XIV and the Holy See going on since 1675, in which Arnauld unequivocally sided with the Holy See against the King. When the Treaty of Nijmegen had ended the war and the duchess of Longueville died on 15 April 1679 Louis XIV decided to liquidate Port-Royal without, however, causing the doctrinal quarrels to be rekindled. On 16 May the confessors, pupils, and novices were removed from the convent, an action which condemned it to die out. Arnauld, fearing for his freedom, left the country in June 1679. Although Innocent XI had a retirement home and probably also a cardinalate offered to him, he rejected this solution because it would make it impossible for him to return to France. After a long period of indecision he took up residence in Brussels, where he died on 8 August 1694, having continued polemics against the Jesuits and later on against Malebranche and his ideas of grace. Nicole, who had gone into exile with Arnauld, received the support of the new archbishop of Paris, Harlay de Champvallon, which enabled him to return to France in 1683. But he no longer participated in the conflicts with the Jesuits and because of this the party looked upon him to some extent as a turncoat.

In 1685 Arnauld received two Oratorians in Brussels who had been forced to leave France because of their Augustinian convictions. The younger of the two, Jacques-Joseph du Guet (1649–1733), was soon forced by ill health to return home, where he began a career as a religious writer. The other, Pasquier Quesnel (1634–1719), remained till the end a loyal companion to Arnauld. Before his arrival, Quesnel had distinguished himself by scholarly works, among them an excellent edition of the writings of Leo the Great. His personal views were determined by an Augustinianism strongly influenced by Bérulle. He was also strongly affected by the thoughts of Saint Thomas Aquinas, whose work he knew extremely well. Given these conditions, the rigid, archaizing Augustinianism of Jansen did not appeal very much to him and so it was understandable that he had earlier signed the formulary four times. Quesnel, moreover, tended toward Gallicanism and was influenced by ideas advocated by Edmond Richer at the beginning of the seventeenth century. He shared Richer's belief that within the Church the blessing of truth is not entrusted to the Pope and the bishops alone, but to the totality of the faithful who share the responsibility for it and therefore have the same right as the hierarchy to judge the doctrine. A dogmatic truth then could only become binding if the host of the faithful accepted it. Intellectually Quesnel clearly influenced Arnauld in a Thomist direction. This is apparent most of all in the last great works of the aged theologian. Quesnel was also much more the politician than Arnauld. A determined opponent of Jesuits and Molinists, he perceived that the presence of Jansenism among the leading ranks of those advocating parliamentarianism, which was traditionally opposed to royal absolutism, created a set of favorable circumstances to be used to good advantage. For this purpose Jansenism had to be changed into a firmly structured party and this was Quesnel's achievement. Clear-sighted and persistent, endowed with leadership qualities, he soon established an expansive network of Jansenist agencies all across Europe and so perfected the work started by some of his predecessors, mainly by Du Vaucel and Pontchâteau. But even though Quesnel wanted the Augustinian party to be victorious, he was not willing to side with Jansenism, which he did not esteem very highly. Through his *Tradition de l'Église romaine sur la prédestination des saints et sur la grâce efficace*, which connected incarnation and grace completely from the perspective of Bérulle and thereby at great remove from Jansen, he tried to remain aloof from the latter (1687–90).

But there still were supporters of Jansen who considered him the authentic interpreter of Saint Augustine. This view was shared by Barcos (whose manuscripts Quesnel at one time even ordered destroyed), by a significant group of theologians in Louvain who put up a desperate fight, and by a French Benedictine, Dom Gabriel Gerberon (1628–1711), whose intransigent Jansenism forced him into Dutch exile. From there he liberally criticized Arnauld and Quesnel, who on their part held him to be a dangerous muddlehead. To counter Quesnel's ideas, Gerberon had an earlier essay by Barcos, in which the latter had advocated an aggressive but awkward Augustinianism, *Exposition de la foi catholique touchant la grâce et la prédestination,* published in 1690. This untimely publication led to excited protests in Paris even by moderate Jansenists. But at the same time it offered the intransigents a point of reference. The new archbishop of Paris, Noailles, outwardly manifested Augustinianism. He felt obliged to condemn the *Exposition,* and did so in an order of 20 August 1696, whose doctrinal part, composed by Bossuet, emphatically laid a foundation for Augustinianism. Of course he distrusted everyone. Quesnel thereupon advised silence, but Gerberon and the intransigents in Paris circulated several pamphlets against the archbishop, among them the especially malicious *Histoire abrégée du jansénisme* (1697).

In 1695 when he was still bishop of Chalons, Noailles had given his approbation to Quesnel's *Le Nouveau Testament en français avec des réflexions morales sur chaque verset,* a revised edition of a much shorter work of the year 1671. On the spiritual level much of the commentary was excellent, but Quesnel's Augustinianism was often expressed in very categorical formulas and his sympathies for Richer's system were clearly discernible. Noailles was quite dismayed when a brochure entitled *Probléme ecclésiastique* appeared toward the end of 1698 which posed the question of whether the Noailles who had approbated Quesnel or the Noailles who had condemned Barcos was to be believed. He found himself in a position of having contradicted himself. For a long time this piece was attributed to the Jesuits; the real author was not identified until modern times: he was Dom Hilarion Monnier, a Benedictine from Saint-Vanne who was an extreme Jansenist, but had had nothing to do with its publication. The pamphlet was condemned by parliament on 10 January 1699 — a reply was imperative. Noailles turned to Bossuet, who composed an *Avertissement* to appear at the beginning of a new, revised edition of the *Réflexions morales.* But meanwhile the prelates got into a squabble over the issue of quietism. Bossuet's text was not published until 1710, but Noailles made use of it in the four *Lettres d'un théologien* (1700). Although he was not immediately involved in this matter, Quesnel again played the part of a mediator. At this point the whole affair came to a halt and no one could foresee that it was destined to become the starting point for eighteenth-century Jansenism.

The Way to the Bull *Unigenitus*

Another incident soon renewed the conflict. At the beginning of 1701 the priest of Notre-Dame du Port at Clermont, Fréhel, submitted to the Sorbonne a question of conscience. It was soon common knowledge that it concerned Pascal's nephew, Louis Plérier. The question: can a penitent be granted absolution when he asserts that he cannot go beyond the reverential silence in the *quaestio facti?* A well-known Jansenist, Nicolas Petitpied, drafted a positive answer which — after various negotiations — was approved by forty professors on 20 July 1701, but rejected by Bossuet. It was not published right away. But in July 1702 the *Cas de Conscience* and the answer were printed and promptly generated a flood of pamphlets. The Holy Office condemned the *Cas* on 12 February 1703. Noailles, who had initially been on the positive side, joined in the condemnation on 22 February.

But this did not end the polemic, for not until 4 September 1704 did the Sorbonne issue the condemnation. Petitpied refused to recant and withdrew to Holland.

By that time Fénelon had decided to enter the fray. Sympathetic to the Jesuits, who for the most part had defended him loyally on the issue of *L'Explication des Maximes des Saints sur la vie intérieure,* he had opposed Jansenism for the past ten years. So when Gerberon offered to defend his ideas concerning Pure Love, he did not have to change his convictions at all. On 15 February 1704 he made public a pastoral instruction in which he developed ideas which placed him in the center of the conflict without being able to satisfy anybody at all. As he saw it, the condemnation of Jansen could have a bearing only on the *sensus obvius* of his book, but not on the personal intentions of its author. But concerning this *sensus obvius,* the Church could make a decision and indeed an infallible one. In fact he asserted that the Church could be infallible in such dogmatic facts as were not revealed; that included Jansen's *quaestio facti* as well. This theory encountered opposition by almost all the specialists in France and by many theologians in Rome. But Fénelon defended and further defined his ideas in three more pastoral instructions in March and April 1705. At the same time he made use of his good relations with Pope Clement XI in order to achieve an unequivocal opinion from the Holy See in favor of his thesis of infallibility in nonrevealed facts. But the Holy See was not so inclined and would have preferred for Fénelon to support the thesis of the personal infallibility of the Pope defended by a majority of the Roman theologians. This led to a misunderstanding and cooled the relations between the prelate and Rome, whereupon Fénelon — sorely disappointed — no longer demanded the formulary to be signed in his diocese.

In the meantime the pamphleteering of Quesnel and Gerberon had made the authorities of the Netherlands uneasy. On 30 May 1703 the two were arrested in Brussels and incarcerated at the jail of the court at Mechelen. Gerberon was extradited to the French police and never regained his freedom, but Quesnel managed to flee in a most unusual manner on 13 September. He took up residence in Amsterdam and resumed his activities. But the documents confiscated in his apartment demonstrated the power and efficacy of the Jansenist network spread over all of Europe. They led directly to the arrest of a number of party agents, among others Quesnel's correspondent in Paris, Germain Vuillarts. The documents also showed the strange way in which the Jansenists adhered to the respectful silence; it did not keep them from publishing innumerable works. Louis XIV — badly informed until that time — had thought Jansenism almost extinguished; Quesnel's documents made him comprehend how much alive and how dangerous it was and also that his efforts had failed. Mme de Maintenon, who gave herself the appearance of being extremely orthodox so that the issue of quietism would be forgotten, urged him to request another bull from Rome condemning the respectful silence. But Clement XI, who understood that this measure would not be any more efficacious than the past ones, was not very enthusiastic and delayed his decision. Only when the French court kept urging him, did he issue the bull *Vineam Domini Sabaoth.* While it condemned the respectful silence, it did so in such terms as to imply that the silence concerned the *quaestio juris,* but not the *quaestio facti.* Fénelon was disappointed that it did not contain a statement about infallibility regarding the facts. In some points, moreover, the documents contradicted Gallican principle; as a result, parliament — to Rome's chagrin — only accepted it with serious reservations. Of the numerous polemics inspired by the bull, the *Denuntiatio Bullae Clementinae* by a theologian from Louvain, De Witte, is especially important. It contained an appeal to the general council, an idea which would show an effect in the future.

Aside from this revival of the conflict the bull *Vineam Domini* had few actual results if one excepts the last nuns of Port-Royal. Death had gradually decimated their ranks and only about twenty aged nuns occupied the imposing building of Port-Royal des Champs. They were forced to sign the bull, but they added a reservation saying that they were not willing to deviate from the arrangement made for them in the Clementine Peace. Not even threats could make them submit. Finally, at the urging of Mme de Maintenon, Louis XIV in October 1709 had their community dispersed and the nuns deported by the police to several different convents. This act of force was roundly condemned by public opinion, even by people who did not consider themselves Jansenists. To prevent the deserted convent from becoming a place of pilgrimage, Louis XIV had it demolished in 1711 and had the remains of the graves thrown into a mass grave in the cemetery of Saint-Lambert. In spite of this, there were pilgrimages and the stones of the ruins became relics. The abbot Le Sesne Etemare and the Jansenists published the *Gémissements sur la destruction de Port-Royal,* which was well received.

The bull *Vineam Domini* was indeed a disappointment for Louis XIV. The difficulties regarding its acceptance by parliament and also by the Assembly of the Clergy showed him that Jansenism could count on substantial support, even extending into the episcopate, for whom the King had always selected candidates who were above the slightest suspicion. Among these friends of Jansenism, Noailles, who owed his see in Paris to Mme de Maintenon's favor, soon played a prominent role. Quesnel from his shelter in Amsterdam quickly reorganized his network. His arrest had made him the undisputed leader of the party, especially since the disappearance of Gerberon had destroyed integral Jansenism once and for all. Quesnel used his voluminous correspondence to extend his influence far afield. But he was ominously destined to draw future attacks by the anti-Jansenists. After some cooling, Fénelon had reestablished his close relations with Rome. He immediately resumed his polemics against Jansenism. Deviating not a whit from any of his ideas, he warned the Holy See untiringly of the seriousness of the situation. Future events proved him correct. In 1710 he attacked Quesnel. The latter, no mean polemicist himself, vigorously rejected the prelate's ideas in some blunt pamphlets. One of Quesnel's advocates turned out to be Noailles, whom Fénelon resented ever since he had opposed him on the issue of quietism. So Fénelon decided to direct his attack to Quesnel's *Réflexions morales.* This work had already been denounced in Rome by the Capuchin Timothée de la Fleche in 1703 and condemned on 13 July 1708 by the brief *Universi Dominici gregis.* But the brief contained clauses contradictory to Gallican principles and had not been accepted in France. Fénelon, unwilling to be personally involved, used two of his friends, the bishops of Luçon and La Rochelle, as straw men. Those two issued a pastoral letter whose details were furnished by Fénelon. In it they condemned the *Réflexions morales,* accusing them of reiterating the errors of Baius and Jansen. Noailles, having approved the work, thus considered himself indirectly addressed and correctly so. Both bishops had nephews at the seminary of Saint-Sulpice, the diocesan seminary of Paris. Noailles promptly dismissed them without giving a reason. On 28 April 1711 he replied to his adversaries in a sharply worded pastoral instruction. The King thereupon reprimanded Noailles and through Mme de Maintenon demanded that he retract his approbation of Quesnel's book. Noailles of course refused to do so.

Noailles' refusal resulted in a complicated web of intrigue. Gradually Mme de Maintenon turned against the former protégé. At the very least she wanted to scare him into acquiescence. She apparently succeeded in making the new confessor to the King, the Jesuit Le Tellier, go along with her, whereas his predecessor, La Chaize, had consistently thwarted her plans. With her approval, Tellier collected a file of letters by bishops demanding the condemnation of the *Réflexions morales* and then sent a sample letter ultimately intended for the King to several different dioceses. But a letter by Abbot Bochart de Saron to his uncle, the bishop of Clermont, uncovering the scheme was intercepted in the mail and made public by the Jansenists. Noailles was extremely angry and hardened his position. When the King pressed him again to disassociate himself from Quesnel he refused and it became more and more obvious that part of the episcopate was supporting him. Louis XIV, grasping that he was threatened by a schism in the hierarchy, found himself in a quandary. The only way out seemed to be to involve Rome. So on 16 November 1711 he requested a papal bull against Quesnel, assuring the Holy Office that he would be able to force it upon the episcopate and parliament if he were made privy to its contents beforehand. At this point Noailles declared himself willing to submit to the Pope's decision. But when the King's request was transmitted by the French ambassador it encountered less enthusiasm than had been assumed. The Pope was extremely well informed and — unlike the King — had few illusions about the effect such a measure would have in France. He was also anxious to avoid the appearance of following orders by Louis XIV. The commissioners charged with examining the problem quickly recognized moreover that the subtle, unctuous text of the *Réflexions morales* offered less of a basis for attack then the *Augustinus.* But after long hesitation Clement XI gave in on 8 September 1713, he signed the bull *Unigenitus Dei Filius* condemning 101 propositions from the *Réflexions morales*.

CHAPTER 115

Gallicanism and Protestantism

Gallicanism at the Beginning of the Seventeenth Century

In the beginning of the seventeenth century the theses offered by the majority of French theologians and canonists concerning the function and power of the Pope were clearly aimed at decreasing his importance. These "Maxims of the Parisian School," supported by the writings of such medieval luminaries as Jean Gerson, Pierre d'Ailly, Jacques Almain, and John Mair, endorsed the relatively independent authority of the bishops in their respective dioceses, but they refused to consider the Pope a universal bishop. They demanded superiority of the general council over the Pope and maintained that the council could convene even without the Pope. They concluded that the Pope was in no way omnipotent and that natural law, canon law, and even the civil law of Christian nations placed limits upon his authority. Yet the French theologians unanimously acknowledged the true primacy of the Pope, his universal authority, and his position as the center of the unity of Christians.

Of course, none of these ideas was intended to sacrifice a single one of the privileges traditionally called "Liberties of the Gallican Church." On this point their views were clearly political and identical with that of Parliament which saw itself as official guardian of these liberties, which had been codified in 1594 by Pierre Pithou, a lawyer of parliament. While this codification remained authoritative for the whole *ancien régime,* four more treatises on this topic by parliamentary jurists had appeared between 1594 and 1604. These works clearly demonstrate to what extent French parliamentary jurists viewed themselves as heirs to the great medieval jurists whose traditions they were continuing. The eighty-three liberties listed by Pithou were unequivocally aimed at restricting the authority of the Holy See in France, limiting its interference to a minimum and at the same time expanding the King's powers relative to religious matters. Although he had no spiritual authority, the King was responsible for the well-being of the French Church, possessing the requisite authority by virtue of divine right. Yet the crown was free of any and all vassalage or state of dependence vis-à-vis the Pope. Parliamentary jurists and theologians alike appeared sensitive to a high degree on all issues concerning the person of the King, who was regarded as sacrosanct. The theological faculties repeatedly censured writings which sought to justify not only the Pope's authority to depose a ruler guilty of heresy but even theories advocating tyrannicide. So it was not surprising that essays by the Jesuits Mariana (1611) and Santarelli (1625), one an apologia for regicide, the other a demand for papal authority to depose kings, provoked great excitement and censure. All of this contributed toward maintaining a state of latent tension which was skillfully manipulated until the time of the Revolution by kings and ministers intent on expanding the power of the monarchy.

The manifestations of Gallicanism, however, continued to be relatively moderate; its advocates kept a low profile by avoiding extremism. This was shown in the events surrounding the writings of Edmond Richer (1560–1631). Richer, a priest from Langres who was a creative personality with an excellent education, became syndic of the theological faculty of Paris in 1608. In 1606 he had published the writings of Gerson with additional annotations and treatises designed to emphasize the latter's Gallican tendencies. In 1610 Bellarmine published his *Tractatus de potestate Summi Pontificis in rebus temporalibus adversus Gulielmum Barclaeum,* which emphatically reclaimed the rights of the Holy See. Richer replied in 1611 with a small brochure of only thirty pages, *De ecclesiastica et civili potestate libellus,* which summarized in the name of the tradition of the Parisian School his own very extreme ideas. According to him temporal and spiritual authority each in its respective realm — are sovereign and independent. But he goes beyond that in asserting that the Church possesses spiritual authority only and must be subordinate to the King in all temporal matters and requirements. He agrees with Gerson that the Pope is merely the prime minister of the Church, whereas the Church's head is Jesus Christ. But while Gerson meant to say that the Pope is Christ's deputy receiving from him the authority for the commonweal of the Church, Richer interpreted this concept in a way that conceded nothing more than an executive authority to the Pope. The actual legislative authority, the leadership, is constituted in the general council, which alone is infallible because infallibility is a property only of the whole Church, whose representatives comprise the general council. The Pope is responsible only for the *status*, that is for the implementation of the canons issued by the council, but he can not impose anything binding upon the Church without its consent. In Richer's view Christ has entrusted jurisdiction of the Church to the totality of the priestly order within which the bishops represent the Apostles and the pastors the seventy-two disciples. The Church, then, is led by an aristocracy, the bishops, who by divine right are above the priests and whose authority is binding even on the Pope. The episcopate does not constitute an order of its own since the body of the priesthood is already realized in the priests; instead it constitutes simply an office which, derived from divine right, gives them an immediate jurisdiction independent of the Holy See. By stressing the fact that the *Depositum fidei* is indivisibly entrusted to the complete Church, Richer concludes that a dogmatic statement can become obligatory only if agreed to by the total Church and that neither the Pope nor the bishops can force the acceptance of such a statement upon the Church without its agreement. To all practical extent, this makes the faithful into judges of the dogma.

The publication of Richer's *Libellus* created considerable excitement at the universities and in political circles. Rome immediately pronounced condemnations, but they were neither unexpected nor did they have any practical significance, because one of the Gallican Liberties stipulated that the decrees of the Holy Office would not be accepted in France. But the condemnation of the work by a provincial council (March 1612) chaired by the famous Cardinal du Perron in the archbishopric of Sens, to which Paris was subordinated at that time, was quite serious. The theological faculty joined in the condemnation and — for the first time since its existence — dismissed its syndic. Richer took a stand and emphatically defended his ideas in several publications, in turn provoking numerous replies, before he finally admitted defeat. On 30 July 1622 he was prudent enough to sign a declaration submitting to the Holy See. In actuality he persisted in his viewpoints. Richer contiriued to attract followers. While, in 1630, France was not yet ready for his ideas, these were to reemerge in the Jansenism of the eighteenth century and take on great significance.

Richer's most determined opponent in this fight was another professor at the Sorbonne, André Duval (1564–1638). His views demonstrate clearly how far those Frenchmen who — in relative terms — were most dedicated to the idea of ultramontanism were willing to go. Duval, a professor at the Sorbonne since 1597, had opposed Richer ever since the latter had published Gerson's works in 1606. In 1612 he replied to Richer in an elenchus sharply rejecting his adversary's *Libellus.* In addition to several other pamphlets he wrote two rather more significant works relating to this quarrel. The ideas developed in these works are remarkably balanced, moderate and conciliatory. He determines very precisely those points actually stipulated by Christian faith and respects freedom of opinion vis-à-vis others. Regarding the superiority of the general council over the authority of the Pope he remarks that the theological faculty of Paris alone supports this view, but he presents these opposing views objectively and refrains from rendering a qualifying judgment on either position. He openly defends the personal infallibility of the Pope without, however, raising the accusation of heresy against those who deny it. With this presupposition he advocates the view that a doctrinal decision by the Pope can actually be binding on the faithful only after the universal Church has accepted it at least tacitly. While obliging the ruler to respect those privileges which are the Pope's, he upholds the King's independence in the temporal and political realm.

Richelieu and the Holy See

In 1612 Duval said of Richer and his views that the hot-tempered syndic unwittingly paved the way for the schism. As a matter of fact, from this point on some French Catholics considered a more or less total divorce from the Holy See. In the Estates General of 1614 the Third Estate proposed a basic law which was to stipulate France as being immediately dependent only on God. The attitude of numerous clerics during Marie de Médicis' regency provided Rome with a feeling of relief. After the Regent transferred the conduct of foreign affairs to Richelieu in 1617, the latter began concealing his true sentiments, allowing the nuncio to think that he was squarely on the side of the Holy See and Spain. Not until 1621 when he urged the King to resist Spain did he give even a hint of his true position. Spain, as a great Catholic nation, traditionally could count on the support of the Holy See. In his conflict with Spain, which even within France was opposed by the *parti dévot,* Richelieu thus had to ensure himself of Rome's neutrality by any available means. Blackmailing Rome with the issue of Gallicanism was the most effective method toward achieving this aim and the cardinal-minister made use of it unscrupulously.

But Urban VIII saw through it although he, too, made a conciliatory move. At the end of 1628 Richelieu entered the war against Austria and again signed treaties with the Protestants of Germany and England. The Pope now stiffened his attitude against the minister by systematically denying him all favors he requested. After Richelieu declared war on Spain (26 May 1635) the situation was further aggravated. In order to defy Urban VIII, Richelieu appointed Marshal d'Estrées, who was known for his temper and crudity, ambassador to Rome. The marshal occasioned so many incidents that in 1639 his equerry, Rouvray, was murdered. Almost simultaneously the Pope, in a countermove, appointed Scotti, hardly an ideal choice, as the new nuncio to Paris. It is accurate to say that the Pope at this particular time enjoyed considerable sympathy among the French episcopate, which was up in arms about the heavy taxation imposed on the Church's possessions by Richelieu.

This tense situation explains why Urban VIII used all means to prevent Richelieu from assuming any sort of legal or canonical authority over the Church of France. The minister, eager in every way to consolidate his power, had long wanted such authority. In 1627, during a short span in which his relations with Rome were somewhat less aggravated, he let it be known discreetly that he would be glad to accept the title of permanent papal legate to France; ultimately he unequivocally demanded the title. Although Richelieu argued the precedent of Cardinal d'Amboise, Urban VIII, convinced of the cardinal's schismatic intentions, did not relent. It was only with great reluctance that he offered him the title for the limited period of a few months after the birth of the Dauphin, but Richelieu declined.

In 1635 Richelieu began to develop a new plan. The obligation on the part of the French clergy to obtain bulls for the canonical investiture of various church benefices from the Holy See, sanctioned in the Concordat of 1516, was obviously very unpopular and led to a number of protests. What Richelieu had in mind was branding the Concordat as illegal and contradictory to the old church discipline, and returning the privilege of electing bishops to the chapters. Subsequently he planned to call a national council into session where the King was to forego his regalia, which was very oppressive to the dioceses. In return he was to be given the right to hand out benefices directly and without participation by the Holy See. The final stage provided for Richelieu to be appointed patriarch of Gallia or of the Occident, with privileges similar to those of an Eastern patriarch. This would make the French Church almost independent of Rome in all but matters of faith, and the Pope would actually retain no more than an honorary primacy. Richelieu appears to have soon made a few politicians he trusted privy to his plan. Among them Chancellor Séguier, who suggested the royal councilor Pierre de Marca, in his role as a jurist, and several newspaper writers capable of propagating the idea among the public. Richelieu was well aware of the great difficulties he faced in trying to realize his plan. He also knew how difficult it would be to win the French public over to his scheme. He hoped to win public opinion over to his side by personally initiating a mass conversion of Protestants, who would look favorably upon such an undertaking by a French patriarch. This explains his mild treatment of the defeated Calvinists whom he allowed the free exercise of their cult. Polemicists in the minister's pay were ordered to extend concessions to members of the Reformed Churches as far as possible. As a result several pastors were won over. Richelieu even thought of calling a spectacular conference of Protestants with him as their protagonist.

In order to create a basis for his plan, Richelieu again facilitated publications with Gallican tendencies. Public reaction was more negative than positive. Two years later, in 1639, the brothers Dupuy, two well-known scholars, published two works by order of the minister. These works, based on ample documentation, virtually did away with everything, including the special privileges of the Pope and immunity of the clergy. The public was greatly perturbed. On the initiative of Cardinal La Rochefoucauld, who defended Rome, and Nuncio Bolognetti, eighteen bishops present in Paris severely censured the work. The cardinal-minister permitted the censure, but did not in any way suppress the books of the brothers Dupuy.

At that point the project of the Gallican patriarchate was beginning to be talked about, although in cryptic fashion. By January 1646 the public had become so sensitized to the subject that the tiny pamphlet *Optatus gallus de cavendo schismate,* announcing the impending schism, created an enormous emotional response. The author, whom Richelieu could not identify, was Charles Hersent, a former Oratorian. Initially the minister was very annoyed with the pamphlet. But then it probably occurred to him that the *Optatus gallus* incident, given the proper exaggerative embellishment, would alarm Rome sufficiently to form the basis for extensive extortion. So he ordered several of his favorites to reply to the *Optatus gallus.* One of the replies, whose author, the Jesuit Rabardeau, made it appear to be coming officially from Richelieu himself, represented the establishment of the patriarchate as being totally legitimate and in no way schismatic. In fact, several Jesuits openly supported Richelieu's plan. The most significant of the replies was one by Marcas, *De concordia sacerdotii et imperii* (1641), who sought to prove that the Gallican Liberties did not run counter to the rights of the Holy See. Rome appeared to take the apparent schismatic intentions of Richelieu very seriously, especially when he confirmed them by various measures designed to prevent all contact between the nuncio and the episcopate. But Urban VIII was clever enough to exercise extreme restraint. In time Richelieu had to admit to himself that his plan of a patriarchate was not meeting with a favorable response from the public, especially when the war against Spain as well as his domestic policies were becoming more and more unpopular. When Richelieu died on 4 December 1642 the issue was unresolved. Urban VIII manifested his sentiments for the dead prelate by forbidding the solemn mass for the dead, customarily celebrated in Rome at the death of a cardinal.

Mazarin, although a cardinal, was hardly an ecclesiastic personality in the customary sense; he was unable to continue Richelieu's undertakings. And yet he inherited his policies, especially in regard to Spain, and thereby incurred Rome's enmity. Innocent X scorned Mazarin as much as his predecessor Urban VIII had hated Richelieu. But now the Jansenist conflict began to interfere with Gallicanism and slightly to modify the respective positions. The attitude of the French government became unequivocally anti-Jansenist, a position it would maintain for some time to come. It was its anti-Jansenism that forced the French court constantly to appeal to the dogmatic authority of the Holy See. This met with some benevolence on the part of the papal court. Originally Rome had been favorably disposed toward the French *milieu dévot,* the traditional defender of papal rights, and had emphasized this attitude by refusing to condemn Arnauld's *Fréquente Communion* as requested by Mazarin. But when the *milieu dévot* turned into the Jansenist party, Rome was forced to intercede against it. While this created an area of rapprochement with the French court, Rome's reticence nonetheless remained obvious. Mazarin experienced this in the upheavals during the *Fronde* when he found himself in opposition to the famous Cardinal Retz, coadjutor of Paris, who had automatically succeeded his uncle François Gondi as archbishop after the latter's death. Upon his flight Retz sought refuge in Rome in September 1654. Innocent X welcomed him benignly; he treated him according to his station as archbishop and cardinal and denied Mazarin the right to appoint a commission of bishops for the purpose of initiating a trial against Retz.

The Gallicanism of Louis XIV

During the last years of his life Mazarin had been determined to maintain the status quo. But under young Louis XIV this position underwent a fundamental change. Imbued with absolutist ideas, the King strove for religious as well as political unity in his realm. Moreover, he was surrounded by advisers with decidedly Gallican tendencies, among them his confessors Father Annat and Father de la Chaize, who — although they were Jesuits — were shaped by the Gallican tradition. A revival of Gallican ideas can be perceived from the very beginning of the grand monarch's absolute rule. The violent confrontation between the Corsican guards and the French soldiers which took place on 20 August 1662, not far from the Palazzo Farnese, seat of the French ambassador, apparently had no doctrinal significance, but Louis XIV used the occasion to threaten an invasion of the Papal States and to humiliate the Pope, who was ultimately forced to capitulate at the Peace of Pisa (12 February 1664). In January 1663 Gabriel Drouet de Villeneuve had meanwhile presented some theses to the Sorbonne which openly advocated papal authority, calling the Gallican Liberties simple privileges granted by the Holy See. A parliamentary decree censured three of these theses on 22 January. The Sorbonne was very indignant over this incursion into its decision-making area. Bossuet, at that time just embarking on his Parisian career, endangered his advancement by joining the opponents. On 1 March the Sorbonne capitulated. But a month later, on 4 April, another incident occurred regarding the theses of a Cistercian monk, who granted to the Pope total jurisdictional authority in the entire Church *in foro externo* as well as *in foro interno*. The court and parliament vehemently demonstrated their opposition and took repressive steps. On 11 May, upon the intervention of the King's minister, the Sorbonne signed six clauses in favor of the independence of the King and of the Gallican Liberties, rejecting both the Pope's superiority over the council and his infallibility.

Yet Louis XIV continued his efforts toward religious unity in his realm and to insist upon extending the Concordat of 1516 to all the areas subject to him, to bishoprics as well as abbeys. This presupposed a broadening of the right of regalia, the spiritual regalia which enabled the King to fill the benefices of a bishop while the bishopric was vacant, and the secular regalia enabling the King to gain possession of the income of vacant bishoprics. An edict of 10 February 1673 made this extension official and a declaration of 2 April 1675 recognized the measure. It applied to approximately sixty dioceses, for the most part in the southern provinces, which had been exempt from the regalia. Almost all bishops submitted, although in some cases with covert resistance. Only two resisted openly: Nicolas Pavillon, bishop of Alet, and François Étienne Caulet, bishop of Pamiers. Both of them had already demonstrated their independence on the issue of the formulary. Thus Jansenism unequivocally manifested its opposition to Gallicanism. In their instructions Pavillon and Caulet expressly rejected the sovereign rights and submitted the matter to the Assembly of the Clergy of 1675. Not until the middle of 1677 did Louis XIV decide to intervene by having the council of state annul the instructions of the two rebellious bishops, who promptly turned to the Holy See for support. Innocent XI, elected in 1676, had immediately proved his zeal for ecclesiastic reform by abolishing nepotism and by defending his rights against the princes. It could be assumed that he favored the opponents of the regalia, but he had not as yet spoken out on this point. The burden of the fight was on Caulet, who had been condemned by his metropolitan, the archbishop of Toulouse, and had turned to the Pope on 26 October 1677. In a highly laudatory brief of 2 March 1678, Innocent XI sided with the prelate against the King.

But the matter of Pamiers was by no means ended by Caulet's death: the chapter elected a new chapter vicar who continued the resistance and was supported in it by Rome. Next, Louis XIV tried to intimidate Innocent XI by furnishing proof that he had public opinion and the clergy well in hand. On 31 October 1681 he convoked a special plenary assembly, attempting to lend to it the significance of a genuine national council. The deputies were carefully selected and demonstrated total deference to the royal power. On 3 February 1682 the assembly officially accepted the extension of the right of regalia: on 19 March it published the four articles of the famous Declaration of the French Clergy (*Declaratio cleri gallicani*). This document asserted the independence of civil authority in secular matters and the council's superiority over the Pope. His authority was thereby limited to the Church canons; his decisions, even in matters of faith, were to be subject to concurrence by the total Church. Innocent XI openly showed his bitterness, but the Roman commission charged with examining the four articles could not agree upon the qualification to be imposed upon it. Innocent XI therefore chose not to take any official measures. He merely refused to issue the bulls for canonical investiture to those new bishops who had participated in the assembly of 1682.

Around this time the conflict between France and Rome reached another climax. To restore orderly conditions to the city of Rome, Innocent XI had revoked the quartering privileges of houses located in close proximity to the embassies in 1677. But Louis XIV had refused to yield to this measure. So the bull *Cum alias* of 12 May 1687 excommunicated those who acted contrary to the decree. On 16 November 1687 the new French ambassador, Marquis de Lavardin, entered Rome at the head of 100 armed men. In spite of having been excommunicated, he had the sacraments administered to himself in full view of the public at the church of San Luigi dei Francesi. As a result the church was interdicted. At the beginning of January 1688 Innocent XI secretly informed Louis XIV that he and his ministers had been excommunicated. The King immediately took several countermeasures. At the same time Louis XIV openly prepared the occupation of the papal possessions of Avignon and Comtat-Venaissin. On 27 September Louis XIV formally renewed his appeal to the general council and had it recognized by several clerical bodies, among them the various theological faculties. Finally, he not only had the papal nuncio, Ranuzzi, unlawfully jailed, but he also forbade the bishops and Jesuits any and all correspondence with Rome. The general public liked

Innocent XI and was not well inclined toward the King's intransigent position, but through forged documents, skillfully propagated by the King's minister, Colbert de Croissy, in the summer of 1688, public opinion was modified somewhat on this point. But the majority of the Jansenist party remained loyal to the Pope. The situation was now in danger of entering a period of stagnation, when suddenly it was fundamentally altered by an unforeseen event: the conquest of England in November–December 1688 by William of Orange. Faced with this new danger, Louis XIV attempted rapprochement with Rome and recalled Lavardin. But Innocent XI, without even referring to his previous statements, remained silent, made no official decisions, and continued to keep the King's excommunication secret. The Pope died on 12 August 1689.

During the pontificate of the very conciliatory Innocent XII (1692) the aim was mutual pacification. An agreement was achieved in September 1693. The conflict regarding the regalia, which was destined never to be resolved, was simply ignored. A letter from Louis XIV to the Pope said that all possible steps had been taken to prevent the execution of the edict of 1682 concerning the Four Articles. In the future, relations between Rome and France achieved a relatively peaceful "modus vivendi" lasting for the remainder of the *ancien régime*. Yet the ideas involved in the dispute went their own way.

Protestantism in Seventeenth-Century France

After the death of Henry IV, Catholics as well as Protestants considered the regime established by the Edict of Nantes a mere armistice in a continuing state of opposition. Hardly anyone perceived in it the basis for mutual toleration. At this time the Huguenot party knew themselves to be a minority, but they did not give up. The regency of Marie de Médicis was not well disposed toward them, indeed it brought men of the Catholic Counter Reformation to power. The renewal of Catholic spirituality deprived the Huguenots of the esteem they enjoyed because of the deep personal piety of many of them. From this point on, conversions from Protestantism to Catholicism increased while those in the other direction decreased. The Huguenots, were therefore firmly resolved to make full use of the guaranties given them by the Edict of Nantes and indeed even to broaden them. But the Huguenots encountered resistance on the part of Richelieu, who had his own ideas in this matter. He decided to subjugate La Rochelle, the bastion of the Calvinists, which was considered to be impervious to attack. The city surrendered after a terrible siege of eleven months. Although Bérulle and the *parti dévot* tried to talk Richelieu into exterminating all vestiges of heresy, the cardinal refused to follow up his victory. The Peace of Alais (28 June 1629) granted to the Calvinists the free exercise of their religion and equality in the service of the King, but it deprived them of their military guarantees. In this way Richelieu was not only hoping to keep his connections with Germany's Protestants intact, but perhaps even to become the promoter of a general return to the faith by the Protestants. This would have put him in a very strong position with the Holy See. Mazarin, on the other hand, preferred to let the matter rest, especially since the Protestants had been clever enough to render proof of their very deep loyalty during the upheavals of the *Fronde*.

Intolerance was the rule on both sides. Protestants and Catholics lived in a sort of mutual fear of each other which frequently led to indelible hatred. It was only within the educated and moneyed classes that friendly relationships could at times exist.

The beginning of the absolute reign of Louis XIV brought about certain changes. In the very limited intellectual horizon of the King, whose ignorance in religious matters was well known at court, the political unity of the kingdom had to be followed by religious unity as well. The cohesion and power of the Protestant community appeared dangerous to him, especially since this active, diligent, and enterprising minority possessed a significant part of the national wealth. He therefore more or less confessed to a desire to weaken it if not to disband it altogether. Initially he thought that he would reach his goals by means of an intellectual controversy and by withdrawing royal favor from them. After 1660 the learned disputes on Christian dogma gained added intensity. These disputes also led to positive results, the most manifest being the public abjuration by Turenne (23 October 1668), which was the culmination of a long intellectual development. There was in fact no dearth of Reformed who desired reunification and a return to the oneness of the Church. And so there were several common attempts along those lines. After the Peace of Aachen (2 May 1668) Turenne, who by now had converted, conceived a comprehensive plan which envisioned winning over at least fifty absolutely reliable pastors and convening a conference with them. He also planned the revocation of the Edict of Nantes for some point in the future when the conversion of the majority of Protestants would have made the edict academic. Turenne appears actually to have been successful with some of the pastors, but he encountered the firm resistance of the intransigent faction of Calvinists who did their utmost to nip the plan in the bud. The war against Holland and the death of Turenne put a final stop to it. So the "cabal of the mediators between the religions" — as it was called then — proved unavailing.

There were moral and religious, but also material and financial reasons for that failure. Indeed it took money to aid the newly converted and especially the pastors, who were frequently abandoned to misery by their return to the Roman Church. Earlier, the only money available had been in the form of private donations. The King was persuaded to create a cash fund, soon known as the "conversion fund" (November 1677), to which was allotted a part of the income from regalia benefices. The view prevailed, at any rate, that the application of money could make the use of force unnecessary and that at least the children of converts would become good Catholics.

Meanwhile the Catholic public in France was strongly affected by events in England and the resumption of the persecutions of "Papists." The execution of five Jesuits in London on 30 June 1679 triggered violent emotions, and now the attitude began to prevail that the civil authorities in France were much too tolerant of the heretics. It appeared to Louis XIV that the occasion was ripe for violent measures. Actually such measures had been used since the beginning of his reign: a new declaration of 1669 applied a much more restrictive and oppressive interpretation to the Edict of Nantes. The most effective method was one conceived by the provincial governor of Montauban, Foucault: soldiers were forcibly quartered with the Reformed; their actions were equivalent to those in occupied territories. This was the origin of the infamous *dragonnades* which aroused indignation throughout Europe. Of course this method effected many conversions and even now some families started emigrating abroad.

It is certain that the King's motives were religious in only a few of the cases; for the most part they were political in nature. The events in Holland caused him to impute republican sympathies to the Reformed. He was also convinced that his fame would rest on the completion of the work he had initiated: the restoration of the religious unity of the kingdom. Lastly, he hoped that this would make him appear to be the great defender of Catholicism in the eyes of Innocent XI and thus put the latter in a difficult situation regarding Gallicanism. These motives led him to use violent measures which actually did not correspond to his character. Against the advice of some of those around him, he published the Edict of Fontainebleau (1685). It revoked the Edict of Nantes and prohibited the public exercise of the Reformed religion. French and even foreign public opinion generally accepted this act enthusiastically. Innocent XI, who gauged the motives of Louis XIV correctly, was among the most reticent. He waited for a full year before he had a Te Deum celebrated in gratitude. But the revocation also had more serious consequences, both religious and political. The ensuing emigration by the Protestants unbalanced the economy of the realm. The abominable persecution following on the heels of the revocation is a blemish on French Catholicism. The forced conversions prepared the soil for the spread of religious relativism and indifferentism in the eighteenth century.

The King, moreover, was forced to acknowledge that the revocation was for the most part a failure, for in spite of everything a strong Protestant resistance was kept alive, especially in areas with a traditionally Calvinist majority. Painful and dangerous, the condition of the Protestants remained a constant source of unrest for the remainder of the *ancien régime.* It was beyond doubt one of the causes of the Revolution.

Chapter 116

Spirituality in Seventeenth-Century France

Major Trends in Seventeenth-Century Spirituality

The French *milieu dévot,* which made its appearance after the religious wars and brought about a true renewal of Catholicism, exhibited very clear directions within its spirituality. Despite the chaotic conditions, French spiritual literature was abundant during the whole of the sixteenth and the first third of the seventeenth century, but it consisted almost totally of translations. The foremost were the great authors of Rhenish-Flemish mysticism, Tauler, Suso, Harphius, Ruysbroeck, Louis de Blois and the *Perle Evangélique;* Spaniards such as Louis of Granada and above all John of Ávila; later on Saint Teresa and John of the Cross also played a significant role; the Italians are represented by the *Combat spirituel* of Saint Catherine of Genoa. These mystics, who combined Platonic theories with the mysticism of Nordic spirituality, were strongly influenced by the writings of Pseudo-Dionysius, excellently translated into French. The foundations were laid for a spiritual forum characterized by a mysticism whose ultimate fulfillment of the inner life was an immediate union with the divine essence, surpassing all created means and even the humanity of Christ. The growing influence of this "abstract school" was favored by the impassioned predilection of this period for mysticism. The period is rich with mystics who enjoyed great esteem. While some of them, such as Mme Acarie and later the blessed Carmelite Marie de l'Incarnation (1566–1618) belonged to the noblest Parisian society, there were others like Marie Teysonnier (Marie de Valence) (1570–1648) and Marie des Vallées (1590–1656), the Saint of Coutances, who came from the poorer classes. Their mystical experiences were interpreted by those around them in a very abstract sense.

To complete the picture, it should be mentioned that parallel to the mystical trend there was also a propensity for the diabolic. It originated in the Middle Ages and persisted throughout the seventeenth century, at times leading to tragic incidents. The cases of demoniacal possession produced lively curiosity; immense numbers of people hurried to witness these events. Public exorcisms degenerated into horrific mass hysteria. But Richelieu, who was personally interested, encouraged them because he hoped they would provide him with decisive arguments against the Protestants. Only toward the end of the century did persecutions of witches and devil trials abate.

The themes of the abstract school were summarized in the work of a Capuchin friar of English origin, Benedict of Canfield (1562–1610). In 1609, almost at the end of his long career as master of novices and guardian, Canfield published his *Règle de perfection.* Although Platonic mysticism slowly became unfashionable after 1630, it did have advocates even into the time of Fénelon. Between the years 1654 and 1659 the work of a blind Carmelite, John of Saint-Samson (1571–1636), a great mystic, appeared posthumously. His writings took up the most extreme themes of Ruysbroeck and Henry of Herp.

In the reign of Henry IV other spiritual tendencies began to appear which were no less fruitful. In his *Introduction à la vie dévote* (1609) Francis de Sales strove to make Christian perfection attainable for simple Christians all over the world. To this end his *Traité de l'amour de Dieu* (1616) develops an extraordinarily well-balanced concept of Christian mysticism centered around charitable love and a very optimistic view of the possibilities of man, a concept placing him in close proximity to humanism. By leading the soul to a devotion to God in "holy indifference" he points the way for most of the representatives of the classical period of spirituality to follow, each in his own way. Numerous printings of his *Introduction* — almost one a year in the course of the century — were spreading the Salesian view of piety.

The founder of a true school of spirituality is encountered in the person of

Pierre de Bérulle (1575–1629), appointed cardinal in 1627. Proceeding from the abstract school he brought about a truly Copernican change in the field of spirituality by recognizing the preeminent significance for the inner life of the secret of Jesus' incarnation and by subsequently concentrating his piety on the person of the Incarnate Word. It was only when forced to defend his position that he gave definitive shape to his ideas in the twelve volumes of *Discours de l'état et des grandeurs de Jésus* (1623), which he composed with the help of his friend Saint-Cyran. His influence was maintained through the Oratory and the Carmelites and even though his was not the only impulse for the Christological piety of the seventeenth century, it has remained the most significant one. Some of Bérulle's pupils remained loyal to their master's ideas, such as Saint-Cyran and above all the Oratorian François Bourgoing (1585–1662). The many reprints of the latter's *Vérités et excellences de Notre-Seigneur Jésus-Christ* (1636) made Bérulle's system accessible to a wide public in the form of devotionals. Guilleaume Gibieuf (1580–1650), in his *La Vie et grandeurs de la très sainte Vierge Marie* (1637), initiated the Mariological orientation of Bérullism. Other successors gave their own imprint to Bérulle's ideas. Foremost among those was Charles de Condren (1588–1641), Bérulle's successor in the Oratory, an intellectually curious spirit, but hostile to the written word, whose influence was felt above all by way of the spoken word. In Condren's ideas the themes of vanity of the human creature and of sacrifice through destruction gain extraordinary significance and lend strangely pessimistic and negating characteristics to him. Similar perspectives formulated with rare literary talent determine the work of one of Condren's pupils, Jean-Jacques Olier (1608–57), founder of Saint-Sulpice, whose *Journée chrétienne* (1657) enjoyed rare success. Saint John Eudes (1601–80), also an Oratorian until he founded his own *Congrégation de Jésus et Marie* (1643), was at first under the profound influence of Bérulle and later under the more mystically oriented influence of Marie des Vallées. In its simplicity, his first great work, *La Vie et la royaume de Jésus dans les âmes chrétiennes* (1637), is essentially obligated to Bérulle. He was among the initiators of the devotion to the Sacred Heart of Mary and the Sacred Heart of Jesus, which he later developed in a Christocentric atmosphere. Thus, among the authors of the classical period, the efforts of Bérulle's successors gradually led to a theological wealth of piety under the imprint of the devotion to Christ, a piety resting soundly on biblical and patristic foundations.

A special position in this development is occupied by the French Jesuits. But their spirituality was in no way uniform. Especially at the beginning of the century, many of their members arrived at the *humanisme dévot* through their predilection for aesthetic literature. They weakened, at times to a dangerous extent, the traditional demands of Christianity. But in Pierre Coton (1564–1626), the compliant confessor of Henry IV, we encounter a rival of Francis de Sales. His *Intérieure occupation d'une âme dévote* (1608) also attempts to make piety accessible to the members of the court, but with less psychological penetration. In the person of Louis Lallemant (1588–1635) we meet a true mystic who in his capacity as instructor of the tertiaries put his stamp on a whole generation of Jesuits. He wrote nothing himself. Lallemant skillfully combined the most essential themes of Ignatian mysticism with those stemming from Rhenish-Flemish mysticism. The significance he gives to the unity of man with Christ puts him close to Bérulle, whom he admired without, however, being influenced by him.

The Great Christian Works

Although the French *milieu catholique* was characterized by a spirituality rooted in mysticism, it nonetheless grew into a center of practical activities and efficacious undertakings. It developed popular mission work and the reform of the secular clergy and that of the religious orders, but it also initiated numerous other works. Vincent de Paul became a symbol of Christian charity. There was hardly a single sort of distress that escaped his attention. Starting in 1618, he turned his attention to the miserable condition of the galley slaves, touching the imagination of the people to such an extent that legend had him take the place of a manacled galley slave. As we know, abject poverty and begging were two of the great festering sores of the seventeenth century and Vincent de Paul quickly became involved in these problems. In 1624 he found a helper of extraordinary ability in the person of Louise de Marillac (1591–1660). In September 1621 Vincent de Paul had established a *Confrérie de la Charité* in Mâcon to help the poor. With the participation of the aristocracy, similar institutions were founded in other towns. But it was difficult to create close ties between the individual fraternities. In 1628 this task was entrusted to Louise de Marillac. A year later she was asked to organize the charitable fraternities in Paris and in 1634 she was given the very important charge of helping the sick of the Hôtel-Dieu. The most noble ladies of Paris participated in this work, especially the duchess of Aiguillon, a niece of Richelieu. But of equal importance was the formation of a group of helpers of the poor for such tasks as were closed to the ladies of the aristocracy by the conventions of the times. The courageous Louise de Marillac became its focal point in November 1633. This was the beginning of the *Filles de la Charité,* whose formation was promoted vigorously by Vincent de Paul. Soon after, they were practicing the apostolate of charitable love.

In 1638 through the *Dames de Charité* Vincent de Paul was able — initially on a very modest basis — to establish a charity for foundlings. Although it continued to grow, it never reached the level required to solve this painful problem; in the seventeenth century there were three to four hundred foundlings in and around Paris every year who were sold at eight *sols* to one *livre pièce* to beggars and carnival people. Yet another broad field of endeavor for Vincent de Paul's charitable love was to ameliorate the sufferings of war. In the almost total absence of logistics for supplying the troops, they existed at the expense of the populace. In the process, the mercenaries committed wholesale murder, arson, pillage, and plunder, and left in their wake fields which were devastated for a long time to come. In 1639 Vincent de Paul became involved in the sad fate of Lorraine, the Picardie, and the Champagne, which were destroyed by the Thirty Years' War. Even though he had gone over to the anti-Jansenist side — albeit more from opportunism than conviction — he yet dared turn to Charles Maignart de Bernières (1616–62), a friend of Port-Royal. In order to arouse the public to this problem, twenty-nine *Relations* were distributed from 1650 to 1655 describing the plight of the respective provinces. In this way, abundant alms were collected and distributed on the spot to refugees.

In all his charitable works Vincent de Paul frequently received support from a secret association of piety and brotherly love, the *Compagnie du Saint-Sacrement.* It had been founded in 1630 by Henry de Lévis, Duke of Ventadour, with the concurrence of Louis XIV. It developed very rapidly and soon counted some of the most illustrious names of France among its members. Beyond that, Bernières founded a house for spiritual exercises, called *Hermitage,* which radiated its effect through all of Normandy. The *Compagnie du Saint-Sacrement* placed a high value upon maintaining its lay character and its independence; it accepted no members of religious orders and very few priests, one of whom was Bossuet. Spread across France and having at its disposal a far-flung network of connections by virtue of the high social standing of its members, it played an important role on the religious as well as the political level. The *Compagnie du Saint-Sacrement* frequently had large financial resources; it was in a position to support numerous charitable works. The national and foreign missions owe much to the *Compagnie.* Mazarin disliked the *Compagnie's* political perspectives, which were exclusively Catholic-oriented; some of its members, moreover, had repeatedly demanded his dismissal from the Queen. Its virtually omnipresent system of police surveillance, used to prevent the laws of the Church from being violated, was ill-received, as was its intercession to have the most important posts filled with good Christians and to exclude men who were suspected of free thought. And finally the *Compagnie* showed itself to be utterly merciless in the fight against the Protestants. It did not hesitate to use any means at its disposal to close the churches and schools of the Reformed faith. It even went so far as to have Calvinist tradesmen barred from working. But more than anything else it attacked the Jansenists, who in turn swore bitter revenge. In 1660 a well-known Jansenist, Charles du Four, abbot of Annay, published two pamphlets about the *Hermitage* of Caen, which was known to be an affiliate of the *Compagnie,* and mentioned the latter by name. When Mazarin made skillful use of the situation, the *Compagnie du Saint-Sacrement* understood the implications: in the summer of 1660 it announced its disbandment and destroyed the larger part of its archives. On 13 December a decree prohibited all associations which had not been authorized by royal letters patent.

Among the apostles who were supported by the *Compagnie* was the venerable nun Marie of the Incarnation (1599–1672) — not to be mistaken for the Carmelite by the same name. Leading an intensely mystical life, she joined the Ursulines in 1630, became a friend and confidante of Bernières and in 1639 went to Canada, where she completely immersed herself in her apostolic work. In this period she arrived at the most exalted stages of mystical union. Her spiritual experiences are preserved in two admirable autobiographical reports. In her capacity as a religious writer she is without a doubt comparable to the great Carmelite. Moreover she bears witness to the rich development of French mysticism in the middle of the seventeenth century.

The *milieu catholique,* being dedicated above all to the task of education, continued the initiatives of the early sixteenth century. The Society of Jesus, with its long tradition in this form of the apostolate, remained the leader in this field. Their colleges enjoyed continued esteem; they were frequented by the aristocracy and granted royal favor. Since the society concentrated heavily on the teaching of Latin literature, it trained many excellent humanists and some eminent specialists. But then the Jesuits encountered serious competition in the form of the Oratory. Initially Bérulle had not intended the establishment of a college, but in 1616 he changed his mind and founded one in Dieppe, which was soon followed by others. But an experiment in a dual emphasis on Greek and Latin was not entirely successful. Mathematics and physics, on the other hand, were given a prominent position in the curriculum. On the whole the pedagogical methods of the Oratorians were both more liberal and more modern. In the framework of education we should also mention the "schools" of Port-Royal, not for the size of their enrollment but for their historical significance. Of all the Port-Royal "recluses" it was Claude Lancelot who was most consistently involved with them. He created a number of "methods" for these schools, among them the famous *Jardins des Racines grecqes* (1657), which advanced the state of pedagogy considerably. The activities of the Ursulines and the Sisters of the Visitation in the field of girls' education were important. Their education never received the same high level of attention as that of boys. In spite of these lacunae, the education of the higher classes had reached an excellent level by the end of the seventeenth century.

This did not hold true for the lower classes. To be sure, parish schools and charitable schools had been established almost everywhere, but these had encountered great difficulties both in general and in the training of teachers; for these reasons their achievements were not more than mediocre.

Christian Life

The efforts by involved Catholics showed rapid achievements in the realm of religious practices, piety, and Christian life. Along with the increasing renewal of the clergy the parishes were once again turning into genuinely spiritual places. Sermons were given regularly; the clergy had recourse to solid materials in sermon books readily at their disposal. Catechism classes were revived; many dioceses published catechisms, some of which enjoyed great success. This revival made possible a steady increase in devotional literature. As a matter of fact, the production in this area is overwhelming; it includes works designed for a relatively well-educated audience as well as for the more simple readers. In the process there came about a variety of literary genres, of which three were favored: works of meditation, moral treatises concerning the duties of daily life, and the hagiographies. While the saints occupied the first place among the latter, they satisfied a mere part of the demand. The seventeenth century loved religious biographies, and whenever a personality revered in some fashion died, a historian surfaced, so that there was never a dearth of such books.

The seventeenth century was above all a privileged period for devotions. While they were not any more popular than in the Middle Ages, they now found followers among the educated and were propagated by the great representatives of spirituality and by famous theologians. In first place was the worship of Mary. Although theologians repeatedly protested abuses in the worship of Mary, especially toward the end of the century, they received no support among the general populace. There was also the devout worship of the Sacrament of the Altar, with its intention of expiating the insults by the Calvinists. The group around Bérulle now developed a loving worship of Jesus' infancy. This was inspired primarily by a young Carmelite from Beaune, Marguerite Parigot, whose convent name was Marguerite of the Blessed Sacrament (1619–48). In 1636 she founded a devout association called the *Famille du saint Enfant-Jésus.* While devotion to the Sacred Heart has earlier origins, it nonetheless created special forms of expression in the seventeenth century. But this new type of piety encountered strong resistance and did not spread until the following century.

The liturgical efforts of the seventeenth century must be viewed from a threefold perspective. First, new liturgical texts were created. At this time the bishops had extensive authority in this matter. It is certain that numerous dioceses had their own breviaries or missals. There was also an attempt to provide the liturgical books with thorough and accurate theological commentaries. Finally, a third problem had to be solved: the liturgical text had to be made accessible to those of the faithful who did not understand Latin. This presented an obstacle of a very special kind. Many Catholics feared that the translation of liturgical texts into French might favor the Calvinist spirit, since this was precisely one of the main demands of the Reformed Church. On the other hand, there was also the conviction that the use of Latin provided a necessary element of mystery to the ceremonies which would be lost by translating, especially the Canon of the Mass. Yet in the period 1587 to 1660 at least five separate translations of the Ordinary were printed.

Translation of the books of the Bible posed similar problems. Reading the Holy Scriptures in French was one of the chief demands of the Reformed Church and this created among the Catholics a certain emotional prejudice toward any such translations. Consequently the number of French translations available to the Catholics for most of the seventeenth century was very small. Only the New Testament which appeared frequently in separate printings, improved through a few supplementary translations, achieved a broader distribution. The situation changed somewhat after 1660 when several translations reached the general public. The Jansenists played a significant role in this field of endeavor with the so-called Mons New Testament (1667) and, above all, with the Bible annotated by Sacy whose thirty-two volumes appeared from 1672 to 1696. Predictably, the translations of Port-Royal caused several polemics in which Arnauld took an effective part. But these attacks did not make them any less appreciated. Moreover, translations of the Bible and liturgy were frequently needed for use by new converts from Protestantism.

A significant part of Christian life was the development of religious art. Characterized by a profound inwardness in the very sobriety of its form it slipped into a decorative phase after 1668. In the field of architecture the difference in inspiration is to a certain extent obscured by the continuity in planning. At first a strong Roman influence can be perceived: even Bernini was asked for designs. A great religious zeal produced a boom that resulted in more than thirty churches' being built in the first half of the century. Several among them excel by virtue of their truly authentic religious character, such as Port-Royal of Paris, Val-de-Grâce, and the chapel of the Sorbonne. After 1660 church architecture became an instrument to the glory of the

King, as represented by the Hôtel des Invalides and also by the chapel of Versailles, both of which attest in their own way to the change in the artistic climate.

From Cartesianism to Quietism

The far-reaching religious transformation in France after 1660 came from a profound change of mentality in which Cartesian rationalism was able to gain ground. There was a simultaneous development toward psychological and moral analysis and introspection. The tendency in regard to the inner life was toward seeking one's own identity within a clear consciousness, within clearly formulated thoughts; all obscure elements and those that could not be articulated were viewed with distrust. Mystical experience gradually disappeared from the perspective of consciousness; its dynamic and fundamental role in Christian life was being forgotten. In its place a spiritual psychologism and moralism were introduced into devotional literature.

One of the most prominent representatives of this movement was the Jansenist Pierre Nicole (1625–95), the longtime collaborator of Arnauld. In 1672 he began publishing his famous *Essais de morale,* a sequence of small treatises and commentaries on the Bible which enjoyed great popularity until the Revolution. Two other Jansenists were competing with him. One was the Oratorian Pasquier Quesnel (1624–1719). He was also a remarkable religious author. Quesnel's literary abilities almost equaled those of Jacques-Joseph Du Guet (1649–1733), a former Oratorian as well, who was deeply engaged in the disputes over Jansenism. Du Guet was an admirable author who deserves to be counted among the greatest. He advanced the art of psychological analysis farther than did Quesnel and showed rare powers of differentiation. Quesnel and Du Guet followed in Nicole's footsteps and ensured the continuity into the eighteenth century.

The development of psychologism in spirituality gradually led to a distrust of mysticism and created a climate favorable to the outbreak of a crisis. This process crystallized around a woman, Jeanne-Marie Bouvier de la Motte (1648–1717), widowed since 1676. She was a devout person given to a somewhat exaggerated mysticism who used her considerable fortune and the freedom of her widowed state in order to dedicate herself to a spiritual apostolate. Having returned to Paris in 1686, she was embroiled in a financial controversy in 1688. The latter introduced her into the royal residence of Saint-Cyr, where in October 1688 she met Fénelon. After a little hesitation he recognized her spiritual gifts and entered into a close relationship with her. By this time Mme Guyon had already written a lot, but published very little. Only her *Moyen court et très facile pour l'oraison* (1685) had been fairly successful. The rest of her writings were published very much later, between 1712 and 1720. Not very original, but also not without talent and skill, Mme Guyon's writings present the classical teachings of the great tradition of Christian mysticism.

Fénelon, too, had been introduced at Saint-Cyr by Mme de Maintenon. Under his and Mme Guyon's leadership the spirituality there was influenced in a clearly mystical direction. But the trial in Rome against Molinos (1687) had aroused public opinion even in France and resulted in an attitude hostile to mysticism. Given the maliciousness of the court, where Mme de Maintenon was hated, this was enough to accuse her of spreading quietism at Saint-Cyr. Mme de Maintenon tried to counteract the accusation by removing Fénelon and Mme Guyon from Saint-Cyr in the spring of 1693. She also prevailed in having Mme Guyon's writings examined by Bossuet, who was by no means a specialist in matters of mysticism. This did not prevent him from rendering an unequivocally negative judgment in March 1694. Above all he reproached Mme Guyon for her views on the passive state, which in his opinion was incompatible both with the practice of the prayer of supplication and the exercise of Christian virtues. Fénelon, having been appointed archbishop of Cambrai in February 1695, succeeded in having a protocol composed which contained thirty-four paragraphs relating to the inner life. This brought the conferences to a hardly satisfactory conclusion.

Next Bossuet wrote a long pastoral instruction on this topic largely designed to prove Mme Guyon wrong for which he hoped to obtain Fénelon's concurrence and, with it, the latter's disassociation from Mme Guyon. But Fénelon rejected any sort of condemnation of her. He had received significant ideas from her and maintained an unswerving devotion toward her. He perceived that the time had come for him to clarify his own position. In the summer of 1696 he used a stay in Cambrai to compose his *Explication des Maximes des Saints sur la vie intérieure,* a compact systematization of his mystical spirituality centered around his ideas of pure love and completely unselfish Christian charity. Bossuet, having been apprised of the existence of the work, tried to prevent its publication. But Fénelon's friends thereupon hurried the printing along so that the *Maximes* were published at the beginning of February 1697, more than a month before Bossuet's *Instruction sur les états d'oraison,* a work very much lacking in matters of spirituality. Next, Bossuet started agitating public opinion and prejudicing the King against Fénelon, whom he openly accused of quietism. But Fénelon succeeded in securing the King's permission to put the matter before the Holy See.

In France, Fénelon and Bossuet exchanged numerous polemics and the conflict was joined by many other experts. On 15 September 1697 Fénelon defined his ideas extremely well in a remarkable pastoral instruction which received the support of numerous theologians. By April 1698 Bossuet realized that he would not win this fight on the level of doctrine. Urged on by part of those around him and blinded by vengefulness, he then engaged in a contemptible campaign of defamation. In June 1698 he published his *Relation sur le quiétisme* which completely avoided the basic problems and was nothing but a long persiflage. This tactic turned out to be very effective and Fénelon's beautiful *Réponse a la relation* (August 1698) was unable to save the situation.

Innocent XII, who scorned Bossuet because of the latter's Gallicanism, did not conceal his sympathy for Fénelon because of the latter's recognition of papal prerogatives. Convinced of the archbishop's profound orthodoxy and of his loyalty to the authentic mystical tradition, he tried his best, including the use of procrastination, to avoid having to condemn Fénelon. But Bossuet's propagation in Rome of the *Relation sur le quiétisme* was most injurious to Fénelon's reputation. Yet Innocent XII would probably not have given in had it not been for the personal persistent interference on the part of Louis XIV, who was completely on the side of Bossuet. It was well known that, given the Pope's advanced age, a conclave was not far off and that the cardinals feared a negative attitude on the part of France. So they pressured Innocent XII in order to obtain a condemnation in principle and the Pope regretfully gave in. But Cardinal Albano, secretary of briefs and the future Clement XI, succeeded in defying Bossuet even by means of this condemnation. The brief *Cum alias,* dated 12 March 1699, was simply a brief, whereas Bossuet had expected a formal bull. Furthermore, it contained the proviso "motu proprio," which usually caused the French parliament to reject it. Twenty-three sentences from the *Maximes* were condemned as a whole, but without any individual qualifications. The term "heretical" did not occur in the brief. Fénelon accepted the condemnation without reservation in a pastoral letter of 9 April, and on this occasion Innocent XII sent him a letter of unusual praise. A little later, in October, in order to demonstrate his sympathy he announced his intention to elevate Fénelon to a cardinalship, an honor which he persistently refused Bossuet. But Fénelon's friends kept him from it because they feared the wrath of Louis XIV. For the rest of his life Fénelon was banished from the court to his diocese of Cambrai. It was only in March 1703 that Mme Guyon was freed from her incarceration and exiled to Blois. From here she was able secretly to correspond with Fénelon, who in turn sent his nephews and selected pupils to her. Mme Guyon subsequently had a strong influence on the milieu of Protestant Pietism, especially in England. But the foresight of Innocent XII was proved correct: the condemnation of Fénelon damaged Christian mysticism on the whole and caused it to enter a period of regression for more than a century.

CHAPTER 117

Christian Thought in Seventeenth-Century France

Systematic and Scholastic Theology

Catholic renewal, initiated at the beginning of the seventeenth century, was manifested less in the realm of thought than in the area of Christian life and spirituality. The men of the Counter Reformation did not occupy themselves with a renewal of theological methods. Patristics and history became objects of detailed studies only inasmuch as they were forced upon them by the exigency of polemics with the Reformed Churches. But it was not their intention to continue the efforts of the great Christian humanists of the Renaissance in these areas. The famous theological faculties and above all the Sorbonne remained bastions of traditional speculative theology. Here the situation of the prominent Parisian professors was characteristic. Their teachings were almost exclusively Thomistic, their lectures nothing but commentaries on the *Summa theologica.* This does not mean, however, that they were actually based upon a genuine Thomism. Rather they were frequently influenced by the deteriorating Scholasticism of the waning Middle Ages.

Within the same framework were others representing even more independent thoughts. This holds true for André Duval. His commentary on the *prima pars* of the *Summa* is still unpublished in the Bibliothèque Nationale in Paris; that on the *secunda pars* was published by him in 1636. Duval, a follower of the abstract school, approved of Canfield's theses. He had read Ruysbroeck and Henry of Herp and was preoccupied with Platonic ideas. All these influences are reflected in his commentary on Saint Thomas Aquinas as well. He is therefore an informative witness for the Platonic tendencies in spirituality and theology especially up to 1630; of Platonic origin was *De libertate Dei et creaturae* by the Oratorian Guilleaume Gibieuf. Gibieuf's complex system posits the highest idea of freedom in God and its perfect realization in Jesus Christ, the God-Man. Therefore, man's freedom increases the more it approximates that of Christ and becomes incapable of sin. Gibieuf rejects both the Thomist idea of *praedeterminatio physica* as well as the Molinist idea of the *scientia media.* His thoughts are clearly inspired by Ruysbroeck and Henry of Herp. This work provoked a violent controversy in which the Jesuit Theophile Raynaud pointed out the Rhenish-Flemish origins of his opponent. Gibieuf's presentation breaks with Scholastic tradition by virtue of its continuous structure, but his primarily deductive method is absolutely ahistoric. His work was unique in its way, since Platonism in theology as well as in spirituality was retreating after 1630.

After this period the teaching at the theological faculties more and more lost contact with reality, toward an abstract speculation out of step with the spiritual tendencies of the time. The rejection of Cartesianism by official circles may serve as an example. Henceforth the teaching duties at the Sorbonne, instead of being a source of true intellectual education, appeared to even the best of minds as no more than a condition for achieving university degrees. Some minds were aware of this stagnation and, in an attempt to renew the theology from within, strove for a synthesis with spirituality, yet still by traditional methods. Dominican Guillaume de Contenson (1641–74), the author of the *Theologia mentis et cordis* (1668–87) provided a work of importance. Left incomplete, it was concluded by his fellow Dominican Massoulié. The *speculationes,* a presentation of the dogma with a heavy Scholastic imprint, are followed by the *reflexiones,* subtly differentiated spiritual discussions which — while at times going rather far afield — do contain some very beautiful pages. Unfortunately these spiritual reflections are not always connected in a natural fashion with the theological part. Consequently the work does not show the necessary unity; its speculative tendency is weakened by its methodology.

Moral theology was no doubt in a more critical situation. Theologians frequently developed problems of moral theology following the respective *quaestiones* of Saint Thomas' *Summa,* but in a purely speculative and theoretical fashion. No one intended to create the basis for an individual theological moral philosophy. At the same time an ever more distinct predilection for casuistry was developing. Yet the Society of Jesus scarcely produced any famous casuists in France; the most prominent authors in this field were foreigners. Probabilism, without any theoretical justification, is applied as the basic principle. The method of casuistry soon crossed over into the field of controversialism and in so doing became one of the most controversial topics of seventeenth-century religious thought, mainly for political reasons. The major cause lay in the old enmity between the university and the Jesuits. A regulation, issued in 1618 and jealously upheld, obliged the candidates for a baccalaureate degree to study for three years with the professors of the theological faculty and not to have any other teachers of theology. This excluded the Jesuit pupils from the baccalaureate. The Jesuits were most reluctant to submit to this humiliating regulation; toward the end of 1642 they attacked it, causing another round of polemics. In order to discredit the Jesuits, partisans of the university published a pamphlet in August 1643 entitled *Théologie morale des jésuites extraite fidèlement de leurs livres,* a collection of clearly laxist solutions from the pens of Jesuit casuists. Although the controversy was belayed quickly, the public remained sensitive to this issue. Thus the ground remained fertile for the great talent of Pascal, who resumed the battle in 1656 with his fifth *Provinciale.* But it should be noted that no one actually unfolded the problem by starting with its root causes. Neither Pascal nor Nicole in his annotations, added to his Latin translation of the *Provinciales* (1658), nor the Jesuit Georges Pirot (1599–1669) posed the question of the actual value of probabilism in its fundamental principles. Henceforth Jesuits and laxism, and Jansenism and rigorism were firmly identified with each other in the eyes of the general public. The moralism of the spiritual authors of the waning seventeenth century is of a purely psychological and empirical nature.

The Development of Historical Theology

Various causes contributed to the fact that Scholasticism gradually became archaic and unfashionable. The anti-Protestant controversies played a significant role in this development. We should recall that the Reformed, especially the Calvinists, refused to recognize medieval theology, viewing it as the application of totally heathen logic to the realities of the revelation. So their own weapons had to be used against them: the Scriptures and the Fathers. From 1575 on, the *Bibliotheca patrum* of Marguerin de la Bigne (1546–90) offered a valuable source to the controversialists. In 1644 it was reprinted in seventeen folios. After 1600, scientific editions of authors from Christian antiquity multiplied, and numerous formerly unpublished works were made accessible. Work in this field encompassed the entire century and reached a high level of scientific precision, especially in the great editions of the Benedictines of Saint-Maur. Initially this abundant material was used primarily for polemics. But soon the scientific investigation of that period became an independent science, disregarding polemical prejudice and seeking fulfillment in the interest in Christian antiquity, an interest which spread from the Italian Counter Reformation to the French *milieu dévot.*

Some famous specialists excelled in this field: the Jesuit Jacques Sirmond (1559–1651), his fellow Jesuit Théophile Raynaud (1582–1663), François Combéfis (1605–79) (It was also his somewhat dangerous merit to prove that the acts of the

Sixth Ecumenical Council concerning the condemnation of Pope Honorius were in no way a falsification.), and Jérôme Vignier (1606–61).

Among the French scholarly groups the reformed Benedictines of Saint-Maur (Maurists) whose center was the Benedictine abbey of Saint-Germain-des-Prés occupied a special place. The actual organizer of their scholarly work was Dom Luc d'Achéry (1609–85) the founder of the marvelous library of Saint-Germain who placed at the disposal of his fellow monks tools which were unique at that time. The work of the Maurists continued until the Revolution and comprised the majority of the patristic literature. Even today their folios represent a prime example of scholarship. Their untiring efforts extended into all other areas of the holy sciences.

Another product of these editorial activities were the comprehensive syntheses of patristic theology. These endeavors were dominated, however, by the mighty figure of the Jesuit Denis Petau (1583–1652), whose *Dogmata theologica* (1644–50) represented a theretofore unsurpassed monument of patristic work of extraordinary informational and analytical precision. Petau's work quite unintentionally sealed the disrepute into which Scholasticism had fallen even before the century had reached its midpoint. Jansen had already criticized its methods in his *Augustinus* and Saint-Cyran faulted Saint Thomas for having lived in a century in which philosophy and human judgment were overvalued.

An analogous development can be traced in the field of exegesis. The tradition of spiritual, moral, and even allegorical exegesis continued to be widespread. They were used primarily by the people of Port-Royal, and especially in Sacy's Bible and in the *Explications sur le Nouveau Testament* (1683) by his secretary Nicolas Fontaine (1625–1709). A parallel, albeit less significant tradition, was that of scientific exegesis. It originated in the humanistic endeavors of the Renaissance and was represented by the Jesuit Johannes Maldonatus in Paris. In 1645 this form of exegesis had led to the publication of the beautiful polyglot Bible by the lawyer Guillaume Le Jay. But the actual founder of biblical criticism was another Oratorian, Richard Simon (1638–1712), intellectually a genius of comprehensive education. Initially he tried to achieve a clear and satisfactory definition of the infallibility of the Bible and thus to demonstrate that the normal methods of historical criticism could be applied to the Holy Scriptures. In 1678 he attempted to present his ideas in his *Histoire critique du Vieux Testament.* But Bossuet, warned through an indiscretion, managed to get a table of contents of the book and promptly intervened. He had the work confiscated and all copies destroyed. The Oratorians thought their congregation endangered by Simon and expelled him on 21 May 1678. He then became parish priest at Bolleville in the diocese of Rouen. His ideas were indeed too far ahead of his time, and all the world opposed him; Bossuet, the Great Arnauld, and Protestants such as Vossius and Jurieu. In 1689 Simon published a *Histoire critique du texte du Nouveau Testament,* followed by several similar works and finally by a translation of the New Testament in 1702 which led to another incident with Bossuet. The latter continued the fight, but died without having completed his *Défense de la tradition des Saints Pères,* in which he wanted to refute the exegetical methods of Richard Simon and to justify the traditional principles.

The development of scholarship was attended by that of historiography, which now ceased being a literary composition in favor of becoming a genuine science. This movement had already been indicated since the beginning of the century by the historian Eudes de Mézeray, brother of Saint John Eudes, but its actual development did not start until 1630. In the field of church history Baronius had some competitors in France since all the great specialists in historical theology were interested in it as well. Jean Morin, Petau, and Thomassin created significant works in this field, but the true French Baronius was an Oratorian, Charles Lecointe (1611–81), whose *Annales ecclesiastici Francorum* appeared in eight folios from 1665 to 1683. But in this connection the Bollandists served as an example in France inasmuch as numerous specialists now tried to examine the historical truth of the lives of local saints. Others nonetheless followed, mainly the Benedictines of Saint-Maur, who excelled in this sort of research, contributing an extraordinary number of works. By virtue of the quality as well as quantity of his work Mabillon occupied the most prominent position among them. He authored the *Acta sanctorum ordinis sancti Benedicti* (1668–1701; in collaboration with Dom Thierry Ruinart) and the *Annales ordinis sancti Benedicti* (1703–13). In his famous work *De re diplomatica* (1681) he determined the basic rules applying to works in the field of historiography. Many of the successors and pupils of Mabillon gained prominence in the difficult area of local and regional history. These works gained a considerable reputation throughout Europe for their comprehensiveness and quality. Louis XIV expressly requested to have Mabillon introduced to him. Port-Royal, too, contributed one of its finest representatives in this field in the person of one of its last pupils, Sébastien Le Nain de Tillemont (1637–98). While he was not blessed with a long career, his enormous energy enabled him to complete a monumental number of works. All of his work is characterized by a profound scholarship and an unusual scientific rigor. Tillemont, who was very sympathetic to the Maurists, left to them his complete documentation on Augustine, from which the Benedictines compiled a history of the life of Saint Augustine and added it to volume twelve of his works (1700). Additionally, he collaborated on the patristic biographies of the Jansenist Godefroy Hermant (1617–90), who wrote the lives of Saints Athanasius (1671), Basil, Gregory of Nazianzus (1674), and Ambrose (1678).

Cartesianism and Religious Thought

One of the main reasons for the decline of Scholasticism in the seventeenth century was the success of Cartesian philosophy. In order to comprehend its full significance, the presence of a latitudinarian, skeptical, and even at times atheistic current in France has to be taken into consideration. Its origins go back to the sixteenth century and possibly even farther; it invokes Jean Bodin, Montaigne, and Pierre Charron. For the first thirty years of the seventeenth century this intellectual current attracted a large part of high society. In these circles were poets such as Théophile de Viau, Saint-Amant, Tristan, and even Cyrano de Bergerac. They were joined by philosophers as well. Around them gathered the *libertins érudits,* the learned latitudinarians who were also encountered in scholarly circles and even in the famous cabinet of the brothers Dupuy. Latitudinarianism persisted throughout the century.

René Descartes was himself in no way a latitudinarian. His Christian education was profound, his faith serious, and his astonishing ties with Thomism are of greater significance for deciphering his personal thought than generally assumed. It is understandable that he was encouraged by Bérulle at the beginning of his career. When he structured his essay on the rational mastery of all reality by following a method of systematic doubt, Descartes had no anti-Christian intentions. He limited himself to pursuing the old dream of a comprehensive explanation of material as well as intellectual reality by means of a single principle. But the *Discours de la Méthode* (1637) represents in every respect a turning point in Western thought. His search for evidence, aimed for by the application of sharp and clear logic, created a new way of thinking. This gradually crossed over into the religious realm and left behind the cumbersome synthetic dialectics of Scholasticism, but by its systematic application of doubt it also furnished arguments for the skepticism of the latitudinarians. The success of Cartesianism was extraordinary. It is very interesting to see for instance how widespread Cartesianism was even in Port-Royal circles. In Port-Royal as well as in secular circles Cartesianism was of great interest for the sciences, especially mathematics and physics. This interest spread to the intellectuals among the clergy. Philosophic-scientific circles were formed in Paris.

Pascal also owed much to Cartesianism, although he turned against it after his conversion. Pascal's is an interesting case inasmuch as he is at the origin of a new Christian philosophy. But we should not forget that he did not at all aspire to be a philosopher and that his interests were not in this area. He wanted to be an apologist and defend the Christian religion against the latitudinarians, whom he had gotten to know better than anybody else during his secular period. In this regard he joined a long tradition. But these pre-Pascal polemics missed their target because they were too ponderous and inept. On the day after the miracle of the Holy Thorn (24 March 1656) Pascal had jotted down some notes concerning the value of miracles. But not until 1657 did he resolve to oppose the latitudinarians and to collect notes with a view toward an apologia. His project had caused some disquiet at Port-Royal since he was considered a mere amateur in the field of theology. Moreover, Port-Royal, while skilled in controversies with the Protestants, had no experience in polemics against the latitudinarians. So Pascal was asked to give a lecture which was to detail his plan. For this conference Pascal took an initial inventory of his notes. Fortunately this compilation is preserved and provides insight into Pascal's way of thinking at the time of this presentation, probably around June 1658. Pascal's sickness and subsequent early death kept him from completing his work, which, by the way, was not given very great importance by Port-Royal. In honor of his memory, Pascal's sister Gilberte and his friend, the duke of Roannez, insisted on compiling the *Pensées* from the surviving papers. These appeared in 1670, but only in a partial edition whose text was much changed. Not until 1844 was the precise and complete wording of Pascal's manuscripts made accessible to the readers. But the edition of Port-Royal had sufficed to call the public's attention to Pascal's method, his rich view of man and the world, and the profundity of his analysis of the *conditio humana* and *christiana*. But it was merely a limited success: in his manner of humiliating man's intellect vis-à-vis a God unfathomable to the intellect but able to be experienced by the heart, Pascal opposed the rationalism of Descartes, which nonetheless won out. Few people in the eighteenth century understood the *Pensées.*

Only those who attempted a synthesis between Cartesianism and Christianity managed to reach public opinion. They deserve praise because this undertaking was not without danger. This resulted in a fight replete with complex and unpleasant episodes, reaching a climax on 1 September 1671 when, after the Mass of the Holy Ghost, the resolutions against Descartes' philosophy were read at the Sorbonne. The dean, Morel, explained that this condemnation concerned especially those who denied the *materia prima* and the *formae substantiales.* The public derided the Sorbonne's insistence upon this sort of archaic Scholasticism and Boileau mocked it in his *Arrêt burlesque.* But the majority of the congregations thought it wiser to prohibit any and all teaching smacking of Cartesianism in their schools. This prohibition was enforced even with measures insulting to some professors.

Understanding these conditions makes it easier to appreciate what the courage of Nicolas Malebranche (1638–1715), also an Oratorian, meant in such an atmosphere. Fully to comprehend him we need an appreciation of what he really was: an admirable religious author who expressed himself through his metaphysics. He was also an apologist, but one who proceeded from his heart, who wanted to lend to religion a metaphysical and logical coherence able to convince both the intellect and the heart in this century of Enlightenment. His daring identification of *ratio* with the word of God combined Descartes' method with the original Augustinian principles, and that is the meaning of the synthesis for which he strove. A Cartesian by deep conviction, he proceeded to contemplate the religious universe of Augustinianism. In his *Recherche de la Vérité* (1674) Malebranche presented his basic ideas precisely at the time of the incidents at Angers. His opponents immediately gave voice. From this point on, the mild-mannered and peaceable Malebranche showed himself to be the kind of powerful polemicist he was to remain till the end of his life. In subsequent editions of his work he countered every attack. His other works raised the expression of his thought to ever higher levels, probably reaching a climax in the *Méditations chrétiennes et métaphysiques* (1683). But his apologias also embroiled him in lively polemics with the representatives of the old school. The system by means of which Malebranche wanted to synthesize the mechanism of Descartes with the Augustinian concepts of the *praedestinatio* and the *gratia efficax* was daring and new. But it did contain numerous weak points, which was why Malebranche encountered such a dangerous adversary in the person of the Great Arnauld and why this dispute ended in a draw. Malebranche was quite conscious of that. Long after Arnauld's death in 1712 he was still planning a summary of all his responses to Arnauld. Bossuet was quite hostile to Malebranche's views. Fénelon's work was not published. In spite of the resistance from various parties, the reputation of Malebranche grew more and more. In all of Europe those who knew the problems involved — foremost among them Leibniz — considered it an honor to have maintained connections with Malebranche.

Section Two

The Papacy in the Period of French Hegemony

Burkhart Schneider

Introduction

The Peace of Westphalia, which ended the Wars of Religion in Europe (with the exception of England) and determined the configuration of the confessional map of Europe up to the first half of the present century, also meant a turning point in the position of the papacy. It had to resign itself to the factual situation. The protest of Innocent X charging the accords with contravening or injuring the rights of the Church have frequently encumbered the Church by the implication that the Pope, by his protest, wanted to undermine the making of peace in favor of continuing the war. Yet it amounted to nothing more than a formal legal reservation which, furthermore, was published with considerable delay in the brief *Zelus Domus Dei,* antedated by almost two years, so that the protest really had no practical effect.

The outcome of the Thirty Years' War meant a strengthening of the power of the state in ecclesiastical matters as well and led to the gradually expanding principle of the established Church, which, although developing differently in the various countries, had in common the diminution of the influence of Rome. In the following period the papacy increasingly lost esteem and the power to influence events. This can be demonstrated by the diminishing participation of the Holy See in the peace negotiations of the time. In the eighteenth century decisions between the powers were generally made without the Pope and at times even against him.

As far as the Catholic powers were concerned, the papacy became in this period an object of their politics rather than those politics being determined to any degree by the Pope. In any given case he was caught within the existing and continuing field of tension based upon the constant opposition between France and the Habsburgs on the one hand, and between France and England on the other. The only area in which the Pope retained a certain initiative of his own was leadership in repelling the continuing Turkish threat.

For the most part the papal elections turned into political power plays between groups of cardinals in sympathy either with France or the Emperor. It was only in rare cases that the "Third Party" of independents — after the conclave of 1655 they were called the *squadrone volante* because of their political neutrality and their mobility resulting from it — could make a decision. As the result of political pressure on the papal elections it was not altogether rare that a compromise had to be sought and that sometimes there were elections which would have been unthinkable without the massive intervention of the various powers. In general it held true that no candidate could be elected against the express will of the French King. Yet this did not always mean invoking the *ius exclusival,* since the two-thirds' majority required by the rules of papal elections did create the possibility of a blocking minority.

The appointments of cardinals as well were jealously watched by the various governments so that none of the individual powers would in any way be favored. There still remained the unwritten "right" of Catholic sovereigns to suggest to the Pope a number of candidates for the cardinalate in order to have, by virtue of these "Cardinals of the Crown," a special representation of their own interests within the College of Cardinals primarily for the event of a papal election. The nepotism of the previous period was not entirely overcome, even if some Popes kept themselves either partially or totally aloof from this traditional form of governing and family welfare.

The position of the papacy in the field of dogma and church discipline was aggravated and even endangered by tensions that appeared at mid-century which, spreading rapidly, were destined to lead to internal divisions. The ideas of Gallicanism and the Jansenist movement continued to be in opposition to each other into the next century. No doubt the Church lost a good deal of initiative and strength by these continuing dogmatic disputes which no longer were of concern merely to theological experts, but encroached on the life of the Church itself.

The intellectual movement known as the Enlightenment also had its beginnings around this time. Rome was late in recognizing its importance and even then underestimated it because the Holy See's attention was riveted too much upon the negative effects and especially upon the attack on the belief in revealed religion. This necessarily widened the gulf between the leadership of the Church, arrested in traditional ways of thinking, and the new intellectual current emanating from England and France and influencing the whole Western world, a movement that soon went beyond the narrow circle of scholars to lead to a generally accepted new attitude toward life and the intellect even within the bourgeoisie. Its basic concerns, such as the demand for critical examination instead of a mere faith in authority, or its idea of tolerance and a practical humanity were viewed with distrust and rejection even when they were pronounced with the best of intentions by the foremost moderate representatives of the Enlightenment, such as Leibniz. The fact that the Church offered nothing but a rigid rejection of this challenge directed energetically against the traditional forms of church life contributed to both Church and papacy being viewed more and more as outmoded. More so than in other countries, where certain concerns of the new intellectual current were gradually accepted by ecclesiastical circles, resulting in something like a Catholic Enlightenment being formed, the above reaction could not but have its effect in Italy and primarily in the Papal States. It was here that the influence of Rome was most immediate and developments which were possible elsewhere could only take place with great difficulty or not at all.

The simple faithful remained relatively untouched by the Enlightenment; they preserved their faith. A clear indicator of this was the noticeably high participation of the faithful in the popular missions which experienced a new flowering in this period especially in Italy.

CHAPTER 118

The Popes from Alexander VII to Clement X

Alexander VII (1655–67)

After the death of Innocent X, Cardinal Mazarin, who conducted French policies, wanted to push through the election of Giulio Sacchetti. The latter had been considered as far back as 1644 but had been excluded by Spain and since then been called Cardinal Trentatre because of the insufficient thirty-three votes he consistently received over a period of time. But Sacchetti personally intervened with Mazarin in favor of the candidacy of Fabio Chigi, which he had earlier opposed. Because of his actions at the Peace Conference of Münster (Westphalia) he was initially not agreeable to France. But with Mazarin's concurrence Chigi was elected on 7 April 1655 after a conclave of eighty days. He chose his name in memory of his countryman Alexander VII.

After twelve years as nuncio on the Rhine his predecessor appointed him Secretary of State in 1651 and cardinal in the following year. But toward the end of the pontificate of Innocent X he lost influence because of Olympia Maidalchini's intrigues against him. Alexander VII, impressed by his personal experience of the extant abuses, was initially resolved to end the practice of nepotism completely. But later on he gave in to the entreaties of diplomats and even some well-known cardinals who urged him to call his relatives to the papal court and entrust them with governmental positions. The safeguards designed to prevent abuses subsequently proved insufficient.

From the very beginning of Alexander's pontificate, his relationship with France, the supreme Catholic power, was tense. Added to the fact that Chigi was not Mazarin's actual choice, his papal government was also encumbered by problems he inherited from his predecessor. Among them was that of Cardinal de Retz who had been arrested in France as an enemy of Mazarin. In August 1654 he was able to escape and make his way to Rome via Spain by the end of the year. In spite of all the efforts by the Pope to arrive at a satisfactory solution of this case, the presence of de Retz in Rome could not fail to have a deleterious effect on the relationship with France. In addition, the negotiations concerning the appointments of bishops in the newly acquired areas of France, which were not covered by the Concordat of 1516, had stagnated under Innocent X. Lastly, Mazarin did not like the Pope's efforts to promote peace between France and Spain. Therefore Rome was excluded as the site of a peace conference. In March 1656 the French ambassador at the Holy See was recalled. The negotiations, which resulted in the Treaty of the Pyrenees (1659) and the uniting of the dynasties of France and Spain through the marriage of Louis XIV to the infanta Maria Teresa, the daughter of King Philip IV, took place to the deliberate exclusion of the Pope.

After the death of Mazarin (1661), tension between France and Rome increased. The twenty-two-year-old Louis XIV, convinced of his dignity and power and raised in the spirit of Gallican ideas, sought to prevail in his ecclesiastic policies. Sending the duke of Créqui as ambassador to Rome in June 1662, although welcomed by Alexander VII as a sign of support of the papal defensive policy against the Turks, was designed at the same time to demonstrate the hegemony of France. Then problems of ceremony led to displeasure. The new ambassador, moreover, claimed immunity for the buildings bordering on the Palazzo Farnese. The demand of this extended "quartering privilege" was initially rejected. After several fights between the ambassador's retinue and the papal soldiers from Corsica billeted near the Ponte Sisto, the Corsicans got carried away and fired upon the Farnese Palace putting Créqui himself in danger of his life. In spite of immediate measures by the papal administration and an offer by the Pope to make amends, Créqui retired to Florence. The incident offered to French policy makers a good opportunity to exact some special concessions in matters of ecclesiastical policy and so they escalated their demands. Avignon was occupied and military actions against the Papal States were prepared. It was under this kind of pressure that the Treaty of Pisa was concluded on 12 February 1664. Alexander VII was compelled to accept the humiliating conditions. On the issue of bishops' appointments the Pope had to comply fully with the wishes of the French King. Only then did Louis XIV return Avignon (May 1665); in order to give another signal for the decrease of tension he recalled the duke of Créqui in May 1665 and put in his place the duke de Chaulnes.

The Pope's attitude toward France was also conditioned by the Turkish threat. The island of Crete, belonging to Venice, was especially vulnerable. A diversionary attack against the Dardanelles in June 1657, conducted with papal support, failed and resulted in the loss of several islands in the Ionian Sea. In 1660 after the Battle of Clausenburg the Turks conquered Grosswardein. When Emperor Leopold I appealed to him for aid, the Pope attempted to establish a defensive league. But the success of his efforts depended entirely on France. The negotiations conducted by the duke de Créqui were interrupted by the incident involving the Corsican soldiers. It was feared that the Turks would attack Vienna as early as 1664. Surprisingly, Louis XIV sent a contingent of seven thousand men in the summer of 1664 with whose help the Turks were decisively defeated near the Cistercian convent of Sankt Gotthard on the Gyor River (1 August 1664). Yet the victory was not exploited. The Emperor was eager to conclude the Peace of Eisenburg because he could neither be sure of continued aid from the Empire nor of support from France.

The next military objective of the Turks was again Candia. In the last months of his life Alexander VII again sent an urgent appeal to Louis XIV and the other Catholic princes asking for military aid for the Signoria of Venice. The Pope on his own part authorized a great sum of financial aid and had the papal galleys prepared.

In his appointments to cardinalates, Alexander VII kept to the traditional practice of giving primary consideration to Italians. Out of a total of thirty-eight appointments with six promotions, foreigners were appointed only twice — two Spaniards and Germans each and one Frenchman. The conspicuous favoring of Sienese was taken note of even then; the great number of reservations *in petto,* a total of seventeen, is surprising. The reason for that was the lack of adequate remuneration for the appointees. But the appointments were nonetheless pronounced in order to complete the traditional membership of seventy in the College of Cardinals and thereby to forestall the demands by Catholic powers for crown cardinals.

The condemnation of laxist propositions by the Holy Office in 1665 and 1666 are thematically related to the continuing Jansenist disputes. The decrees were triggered by censures on the part of the universities of Louvain and Paris, some of whose wording was included verbatim in the Roman condemnations. Even though probabilism was not rejected as a system, this first detailed condemnation of "laxist" propositions represented a considerable success for the opponents of the Jesuit order, which was accused of lax morality.

A great stir was caused when Queen Christina of Sweden, daughter and successor of Gustavus Adolphus, renounced her throne and converted to Catholicism. After renouncing the throne on 6 June 1654, Christina secretly pronounced the Catholic confession of faith on Christmas Day that year in Brussels. On 2 November 1655 she reiterated it publicly in Innsbruck. Shortly before Christmas she entered Rome with great ceremony. It was characteristic of the situation that the Pope exhorted the cardinals to make sure that the royal convert could not take offense at their behavior. He told them how his own work in Germany had taught him how scrupulously the northerners watched the Romans. Yet Aleander VII was never lacking in benevolence and helpfulness toward the former queen. The tension decreased after Cardinal Azzolini gained influence about 1660 and managed to eliminate the undependable elements from Christina's retinue. Aside from two stays in France and two trips to Sweden in connection with her appanage, the former queen remained in Rome.

Rome's culture was considerably enhanced by the extension of the University of Rome. New chairs were established, among them that of church history, together with an appropriate library called the Biblioteca Alessandrina after its founder. But most prominent were the construction projects in the Vatican initiated by the Pope and executed by Bernini. The *Cathedra Petri,* a simple oaken armchair decorated with small antique tablets of ivory and used in the Middle Ages in the liturgy on Saint Peter's Day (22 February) was to be the focal point in the apse of Saint Peter's, which was empty at that time. Bernini's design of four bronze statues of the great church Fathers carrying the *Cathedra* enclosed in bronze was approved by the Pope, who personally supervised all the work. Construction of Saint Peter's Square was started at the same time, again planned and executed by Bernini. According to the original design as shown on a medallion coined on

28 August 1657 on the occasion of the laying of the cornerstone, the space between the two half-arches of the colonnades was to be closed by a continuation separated only by two relatively narrow entrances. By the end of Alexander VII's pontificate only part of the construction work was finished. The Pope also had Bernini build new stairs to the Scala Regia and to the Sistine Chapel; this Scala Regia was finished in 1666. Four years later the equestrian statue of Constantine the Great, created by Bernini and completed during Alexander's VII lifetime, was placed in the vestibule.

Clement IX (1667–69)

On 20 June 1667 Cardinal Giulio Rospigliosi was elected Pope after a remarkably brief conclave of only eighteen days. As nuncio at Madrid he had obtained Spain's goodwill, but — unknown to Spain — he was also in the favor of Louis XIV. Also active in his behalf were the cardinals of the *squadrone volante,* who were primarily credited with the outcome of the election. The new Pope had been secretary of state under his predecessor and was famous for his humanistic education and poetic talent. His choice of the name Clement was prompted by the meaning of the word rather than its connection with an earlier bearer of the name, as was often the case. A short pontificate was expected from the start because of his frail health.

The pontificate of Clement IX was troubled by two major problem areas. One was the continuing tensions in France caused by the Jansenist movement and the Pope's efforts to allay them. This was to be achieved by the so-called Clementine Peace, but in the last analysis the Pope's efforts remained unsuccessful. The other was the danger posed by the Turks. The island of Crete was again their prime objective. They had already conquered the larger part of the island and were preparing to attack the capital of Candia (Megalo Castro), still in the hands of the Venetians. Just like his predecessor, Clement IX attempted to bring about joint aid by the Western powers. He tried to bring an end to the war between Louis XIV and Spain (War of Devolution) which broke out in May 1667 when France invaded the Spanish Netherlands. But the Pope's suggestions and the entreaties of various nuncios extraordinary sent to all the capitals were hardly successful. But the political constellation resulting from the alliance between Holland, England, and Sweden made the French King condescend to a negotiated peace. He kept his conquests in the Netherlands, but had to return the occupied Franche-Comté. The fact of the papal mediation was emphasized in the peace treaty of Aachen (2 May 1668).

Clement X (1670–76)

A few days before he died on 9 December 1669, Clement IX had appointed seven cardinals, bringing the complement of the college back up to the traditional seventy. The subsequent conclave, lasting more than four months, proved difficult. The French rejected two possible candidates (D'Elce and Odescalchi), while the Spanish opposed two others (Vidoni and Brancaccio), virtually eliminating any chance of those four being elected. The long duration of the conclave provoked great displeasure and gave rise to many satires. The representatives of the Catholic powers probably exerted greater influence on this papal election than on any previous one. Upon mediation by Venice, Spain and France finally agreed that one of the cardinals appointed by Pope Clement IX before his death should be elected. The choice was the oldest of that group, the eighty-year-old Cardinal Altieri. The election took place on 29 April 1670. Resisting for some time, Altieri finally gave in to the urgings of the cardinals and accepted the election as Pope Clement X. The advanced age of the newly elected Pope resulted in the cardinal-nephew Paluzzi-Altieri gaining in importance while the secretary of state lost influence.

The pontificate of Clement X was largely determined by the increasing danger posed by Turkey. In 1672 the objective was Poland, which was weakened by internal disorder. The Pope sought to have the Emperor and the Catholic princes of Germany coalesce into a defensive alliance and even appealed — probably following a suggestion by Queen Christina — to the King of Sweden, Charles IX, who refused, however, to enter into any direct negotiations with the Pope. Conversely, Russia now sought Western support against the Turks and after thirteen years of war concluded an alliance with Poland. With financial support from the Pope and a personal contribution from Cardinal Odescalchi, Jan Sobieski had formed his own army in 1673. He advanced against the Turks and defeated them decisively at the Dniester (11 November). But more dangerous by far were the applicants from the house of Brandenburg. Finally, on 20 May 1674, Jan Sobieski was elected king. The following summer he again succeeded against the Turks in the defense of the city of Lemberg.

While the Pope made every effort to form a defensive alliance against the Turks, Louis XIV prepared for a war of conquest against Holland, which had permitted itself to become politically isolated. This war was propagated by France as a holy war for the restoration of the Catholic religion. Initially the Pope in fact believed this professed goal. Briefs of praise and Te Deums in Rome upon the victories of the French army demonstrate how effective that propaganda was. After about the summer of 1674 Clement X perceived that he had been deceived regarding the actual aims of the war against Holland. In addition, Louis XIV tried to frustrate the Pope's peace negotiations at every turn. At the same time a papal representative was designated for the actual peace conference, although no place or time had been considered yet. The instruction composed for this purpose is important since it clarifies the developments since the time of the Peace of Westphalia. Now the papal representative was permitted to establish communication with the Protestants as well. He was instructed not to offend them by pedantic considerations and to make concessions for the sake of peace in Europe. Yet for the time being these preparations did not lead to anything.

More than his predecessors the aged Pope was hard pressed by the Catholic powers to accede to appointments to the cardinalate. In addition to fifteen Italians, Clement X appointed a mere five cardinals of other nationalities: two French, one German, Spanish, and English. France especially exerted constant pressure. Louis XIV above all wanted to have the bishop of Laon, César D'Estrées, promoted to cardinal. D'Estrées was indeed appointed *in petto* on 24 August 1671, but he was not satisfied with that. Even before the appointment was published the brother of the new cardinal arrived in Rome as the new ambassador of France. By order of Louis XIV, César also remained at the Curia. Now both brothers pursued the appointment of additional favorites of the French King to cardinalates.

CHAPTER 119

Innocent XI

After having met with the determined resistance of France at the previous conclave, Cardinal Odescalchi's election came as a complete surprise. At the beginning of the present conclave his candidacy had been openly promoted by the nephew of the late pope, Cardinal Altieri, with whom Louis XIV and his ambassador to Rome were totally at variance. Furthermore, Altieri acted in concert with the Spanish cardinals, also opponents of France. When D'Estrées threatened to invoke the *ius exclusivae* if the election were to take place before the arrival of the French cardinals, the number of votes for Odescalchi decreased markedly. But in the meantime the French ambassador had asked Louis XIV to approve the election of the candidate originally rejected by him. Cardinals Chigi and Rospigliosi, both in the King's favor, supported this action by emphatically recommending Odescalchi to Louis XIV. The King concurred and he was elected unanimously on 21 September 1676, after having received a mere eight votes on the previous day.

The new Pope chose his name in memory of the one who had appointed him cardinal in 1645 when he was a mere thirty-four years of age. His charity, extreme conscientiousness, and austere piety were widely acknowledged. Before he accepted the election he insisted that all cardinals sign the fourteen articles of reform suggested by him during the conclave. He had never spent any time abroad, so that his knowledge of the political situation was insufficient. While he was an excellent administrator with a special skill in financial matters, he was lacking in knowledge of human nature and even in theological education.

Innocent XI refrained from any kind of nepotism. Frugal by nature, he put the financial affairs of the Papal States in order. But in his strict, sometimes overly pedantic instructions concerning any sort of luxury and the reform of public order he several times went so far as to prohibit all carnivals, consequently becoming the butt of ridicule by the Romans.

The pontificate of Innocent XI bears the stamp of two problem areas. In addition to his efforts in the defense against the Turks, the tense relationship between the Holy See and France was a major problem. It emanated from the unrestricted right of regalia claimed by the French King. Ever since the Middle Ages the King had had the right to make appointments to ecclesiastical livings in certain vacant dioceses (spiritual regalia) and to receive the revenues of bishoprics (temporal regalia). Since Louis XIII, care had been taken not to use these revenues for improper purposes. The second council of Louvain (1274) had forbidden further extension of this right. In so doing it appeared to recognize implicitly or at least to condone it. After several earlier attempts to extend the right of regalia to other dioceses, Louis XIV — considering it a true right of the crown — decreed in 1673 and 1675 that it was to apply to all areas subject to the French crown. Clement X, informed of the decree by his nuncio, did not make any response. Almost all the French bishops, in part influenced by the papal silence which could be construed as acquiescence, submitted to the royal decree. Only Bishop Pavillon of Alet and Bishop Caulet of Pamiers resisted. Not getting any support from their metropolitan they appealed to the Pope. The fact that Innocent XI accepted the bishops' appeal was in accord with his conviction not to permit any encroachment upon the rights of the Church. But under the circumstances it was a somewhat dangerous assertion of principle in a matter of secondary importance. As a consequence the Pope was viewed as a friend of the Jansenist party. This was incorrect yet understandable in view of the personality of the two appellants, who were well known from the Jansenist conflict. A brief, sent in March 1680, was more to the point. It warned the King of the wrath of Heaven which could manifest itself in making him die without a successor. But Louis XIV, having been struck by the idea of a national council, decided upon a noncommittal answer. After a lengthy delay, Cardinal d'Estrées, who was to conduct negotiations, arrived in Rome in the spring of 1681. At that time the so-called "Small Assembly" of the French clergy under the direction of the archbishop of Paris, Harlay, and the archbishop of Reims, Le Tellier, supported the King's position concerning the right of regalia and suggested convening a national council or an extraordinary Assembly of the Clergy. In general they involved efforts genuinely serving the reform and the promotion of church life even though the self-consciousness of the Gallican Church appears always to have been involved, intent on safeguarding its special privileges and position. Depending on the importance of these assemblies, the King and his government increasingly tried to influence their composition, either by means of recommendations or by exerting pressure upon the elective body of the individual church provinces. Such measures were also employed in the preparation of the assembly of October 1681. The assembly agreed with the King that regalia was an exclusive right of the crown. In a general way the assembly noted that the ruler was independent of the authority of the Church in all purely temporal matters. The codification of additional articles designated as "Gallican Liberties" required lengthy discussion. In the end they were formulated by Bossuet, who was trying to avoid a more radical version. The King then decreed that they be included as binding doctrine.

The news of the assembly's conclusions arrived in Rome during the negotiations between the Pope and Cardinal d'Estrées, which were immediately interrupted. Since the threat of Turkey had become more and more acute, Innocent XI was prepared for a moratorium. As an outward sign of détente he was to send a nuncio extraordinary to France upon the birth of the first son of the Dauphin. Although it was not the birth of a crown prince, the nuncio was to present the diapers blessed by the Pope as a special sign of goodwill. But the most important reason for the nuncio's mission was to get the support of Louis XIV for the war against the Turks and to pave the way for a reconciliation between France and the

Emperor. The gravest impediment was the issue of the vacant sees. Innocent XI steadfastly refused to confer canonical investiture upon the new bishops nominated by the King if they had participated in the Assembly of the Clergy of 1681/82 and had not disavowed the four Gallican articles.

During this conflict between the Pope and France another one arose in Rome. It had to do with the quartering privilege claimed by the ambassadors to the Holy See. From the very beginning of his pontificate Innocent XI was determined to put an end to those abuses. Spain declared its willingness to forego the quartering privilege if the other powers would follow suit. But no agreement could be reached. So the Pope let it be known that he would receive no new ambassador unless he would surrender the franchise in advance. Venice was first to give in. After a lengthy period of resistance Spain followed suit in 1682. After the death of the French ambassador d'Estrées (30 January 1687), the Pope informed France that the new ambassador would only be received if he acceded to the conditions laid down by him. Subsequent proposals for settling the issue were rejected by Innocent XI. In November the new ambassador de Lavardin entered Rome at the head of a large retinue. Since he was considered subject to the sanctions of the bull *In Coena Domini,* he was not granted the papal audience he had requested. At the same time the French King was informed by the nuncio that the censure of the bull applied to him as well. The conflict broke into the open on 24 December 1687 when de Lavardin attended midnight Mass at the French national church of San Luigi dei Francesi. He was ushered to the seat of honor according to his rank of ambassador and given the sacrament. The Pope thereupon put the church under the interdict.

The tension was increased by the issue of the appointment of a coadjutor of Cologne. Both candidates, Cardinal Wilhelm von Fürstenberg, Bishop of Strasbourg, nominee of Louis XIV, and the seventeen-year-old Clement of Bavaria, the Emperor's nominee, needed the Pope's dispensation. The Pope appointed the Bavarian. This led to the outbreak of the war between France and the Emperor in September 1688.

The conflict with France had a bearing on simultaneous efforts by the Pope to establish a defense against the Turks.

At about the beginning of Innocent XI's pontificate, Kara Mustafa had become grand vizier and had taken over the direction of the Turkish government. This increased the danger of a renewed offensive. In order to counter this danger and to make sure of an effective defense the Pope engaged in mediation to end the war between France and the Emperor. For this purpose he sent a legate to the peace negotiations at Protestant Nijmegen. This was the first time since the schism that a papal representative set foot on Dutch soil. The peace terms were especially unfavorable for Catholics living in Protestant areas. By doing nothing to advance the cause of the Catholic religion Louis XIV disappointed the Pope's expectations.

The advent of peace did not further the Pope's main goal of bringing about a defensive and offensive alliance against the Turks. Yet Innocent XI did not tire in pursuing his plans of a great offensive. He envisioned French naval operations in support of a land-based attack by the Emperor and Poland. This was basically the same plan suggested fifteen years before to Louis XIV by the young Leibniz. Assurance of France's benevolent neutrality in the eventuality of an attack upon the Emperor coupled with Thököly's revolt in Hungary confirmed Kara Mustafa in his intentions against Austria. But now this direct threat had the effect of reversing Polish policy, leading to a defensive alliance with the Emperor (April 1683). The Pope expended approximately one and a half million guilders in subsidies, about two-thirds of which went to the Emperor. By 14 July Vienna, defended by Rüdiger von Starhemberg, was completely surrounded. At the very last moment a relief force consisting of Austrian, Polish, and Bavarian troops under the nominal command of Sobieski approached and on 12 September 1683 forced the Turks to retreat. Vienna owed its liberation above all to the efforts of Innocent XI.

In spite of the allied victories at Ofen and the conquest of Gran in October of the same year, the alliance was endangered by a renewed rapprochement between Sobieski and the Hungarian rebels and by Louis XIV's attempts at joining Poland to France in a closer relationship. But the Pope managed to maintain the alliance. In 1684 it was joined by Venice after diplomatic relations were reestablished between the Serenissima and the Holy See. The powers of the "Holy League" pledged to use their troops only against the Turks, to update war plans annually, and not to negotiate without the agreement of the other allies. In addition to the significant financial aid it was the untiring efforts of the Pope which had brought about the alliance against the Turks and at least to some extent had kept it together.

Innocent XI was extremely strict in his direction of the Church. He tried to restore church discipline especially among the clergy and the orders, but in the process he sometimes dissipated his energy in details. His conscientiousness, almost bordering on scrupulousness, was also manifest in the promotion of cardinals. During his pontificate he decided on only two appointments.

Innocent XI's position within the Church was marked by his firm opposition against any form of Gallicanism. Opponents of Gallicanism met with ready understanding on the part of the Pope and with support that was not always wise from a tactical viewpoint. This explains why many of the Pope's decisions and actions were viewed as partisanship in favor of the Jansenist movement, since it was precisely the Jansenists who took an especially strong stand against the Gallicanism of the King. In addition, the manifest religious severity of Jansenism and its stress on church discipline corresponded with the Pope's personal views. The moral system of probabilism offered by the Jesuits, who were certainly the most confirmed enemies of Jansenism, nonetheless represented a dangerous move toward laxism. Even at the beginning of his pontificate a small group of French bishops, among them Pavillon of Alet, urged the Pope to condemn certain moral propositions. At the same time, the University of Louvain attempted to effect a similar condemnation. This took place in 1679 by means of a decree of the Holy Office. Within the Jesuit order, Tyrsus González de Santalla tried to push back probabilism; in 1680 he received papal approbation for his system of probabiliorism. The fact that he was elected general of the order in 1689 was a result of the benevolence of Innocent XI, who clearly let it be known to the General Congregation of the order on the occasion of an audience whom he wished to have at the head of the Society of Jesus.

Ever since the middle of the century a quietistic current had spread primarily in Italy. Beginning with an intensification of the religious life of the individual and stressing the practice of contemplative prayer, the movement led to the sole emphasis on the efficacy of grace to the total exclusion of personal deeds, amounting finally to a complete passivity of the individual. The Spanish priest Miguel Molinos became the focal point of a large circle in Rome where he was joined by important laymen as well as by many clerics, among them Cardinal Odescalchi. Jesuits were the first to offer reservations against Molinos and his doctrine. In the meantime more reservations against Molinos' doctrine arose. In 1682 the Holy Office had Cardinal Hieronymus Casanate compose an instruction for confessors whose actual publication can not be ascertained. In 1685 Molinos was arrested by the Inquisition and his writings were confiscated. Innocent XI had earlier had high esteem for Molinos. As late as 1686 he had elevated Pier Matteo Petrucci, who had held similar views, to the cardinalate. So he waited for some time before granting his permission for a formal trial, which was concluded in 1687. Of an original 263 propositions 68 were condemned. Thirteen of these were taken from the defense which Molinos submitted to the Inquisition. Molinos was condemned to life in prison and died in 1696. After an investigation against Cardinal Petrucci the latter had to recant in front of the Pope. But Innocent XI advocated mild treatment. As a consequence Petrucci retained all his rights as a cardinal and as bishop of Jesi.

Soon after the Pope's death the Romans began to venerate Innocent XI as a saint, but not until 1956 was he canonized by Pius XII. The procedure, initiated by Clement XI, was delayed primarily by the opposition of the French government, which was apparently unable to forget the Pope's struggle with Louis XIV which had endured through almost his whole pontificate.

CHAPTER 120

The Popes from Alexander VIII to Clement XI

Alexander VIII (1689–91)

The conclave took place during a war which enveloped the larger part of Europe. But before the monarchs' wishes were made known, the majority of the cardinals had already decided upon Pietro Ottoboni from Venice. France concurred in his candidacy after Ottoboni's nephew had given assurances that canonical investiture would be conferred on the French bishops who had participated in the Assembly of 1681/82 and that Lavardin would be received as ambassador. The new Pope chose his name in memory of Alexander VII, to whom he felt especially obliged. Although he was eighty years of age, he performed his work with unusual energy. His personal life-style was diametrically opposed to that of his predecessor, which ensured him of the immediate goodwill of the Romans. It was disastrous, however, that he permitted the practice of nepotism to be revived.

Alexander VIII also differed from his predecessor Innocent XI in his attitude toward the great powers. Relations with the German Empire cooled off noticeably. Financial aid granted Leopold I for the Turkish Wars was decreased considerably, not in the least because Venice, worried about its own interests in the Levant, looked with a jaundiced eye upon Austria's great military successes. On the other hand, the Pope sought improved relations with France, which had a growing number of uninvested bishops. The consistory of February 1690 was designed as a sign of rapprochement. Disregarding serious reasons to the contrary as well as protests by the Emperor, the Pope fulfilled a longstanding wish of Louis XIV by appointing to the cardinalate the bishop of Beauvais, Toussaint de Forbin-Janson, who had participated in the assembly of 1682. When the third consistory of Alexander VIII passed in November 1690 without the Pope's appointing any of the Emperor's nominees, Vienna threatened to break off diplomatic relations. The ambassador was indeed recalled, but additional resolves were not translated into action because of the Pope's serious illness.

But attempts by the King of France to represent his war as a war in defense of Catholicism and to have it approved as such by the Pope were unsuccessful. Since Louis XIV, largely under the influence of the newly appointed Cardinal Forbin-Janson, who was leading the negotiations in Rome, proved to be unyielding on the issue of the Gallican articles, Alexander VIII, already on his deathbed, decided to publish the decree prepared under Innocent XI which nullified the four Gallican Liberties.

Alexander VIII fell ill in January 1691. On 30 January, in the presence of ten cardinals he ordered the publication of the above-mentioned decree against the Gallican articles and dictated a personal letter to Louis XIV. On 1 February he died at the age of eighty-one.

Innocent XII (1691–1700)

The conclave beginning on 12 February 1691 lasted exactly five months. The front-runner was Gregorio Barbarigo. But Vienna considered him too submissive to France because of his connections with Venice. As a consequence the imperial government sought to prevent his election, yet without making use of a formal *exclusivae.* Since the French group also failed to support Barbarigo's election — which was promoted by the *Zelanti,* the apolitical party of the College of Cardinals — although Barbarigo was personally agreeable to Louis XIV, his candidacy failed. After many futile attempts at a compromise, agreement finally centered on Antonio Pignatelli, who received the votes of various blocks and finally those of the French as well. The seventy-five-year-old aristocratic cardinal from the south of Italy had been nuncio in Poland and Vienna; he had been raised to the cardinalate rather late, in 1681, by Innocent XI. His choice of name was intended to be an expression of gratitude for his predecessor. In his mode of governing, his care for the poor, and the simplicity of his personal life-style, he indeed resembled Innocent XI. The most important reform document of his papacy was the bull against nepotism (22 June 1692). After some initial resistance by a good many cardinals, this bull, which for all practical purposes put an end to the practice of nepotism in papal history, was signed by all cardinals. Innocent XII also restricted the sale of ecclesiastical offices at the Curia. To make up for the resulting financial loss he applied thrift to the running of the papal court, and, most importantly, he enlarged the harbors of Civitavecchia and Netuno in order to promote trade. Yet many of his reform measures were impeded by his excessive attention to details.

A compromise was reached with Louis XIV after the latter was forced to be more conciliatory by the formation of the Grand Alliance. As an initial step, the new bishops, appointed by the King since 1682, who had not participated in the Assembly of the Clergy of that year, were granted papal approbation. In return, Louis XIV promised to revoke the decree prescribing the four articles of 1682 as doctrine. The participants of the assembly signed a declaration of obedience. In return the King kept his promise and revoked the decree concerning the Declaration of the French Clergy. Thereupon the bishops in question were granted canonical institution. By the end of 1693 the French hierarchy was restored. Yet the King's right of regalia remained intact in spite of the Pope s protestations. But this act of rapprochement between Rome and France was viewed with distrust by the Emperor.

The death of Sobieski in 1696 reignited the struggle for the Polish succession. Ostensibly maintaining neutrality, the Holy See nonetheless made efforts to have a Catholic King elected. Friedrich August, elector of Saxony, who had declared his willingness to convert to Catholicism in the event of his election was chosen. Innocent XII was initially somewhat reticent about the new Polish King. Only when the latter had consolidated his rule did the Pope have his letter of recognition and congratulation transmitted.

Innocent XII, having increased his efforts since 1696 toward bringing about an end to the European war of Louis XIV against the Grand Coalition, welcomed the Peace of Rijswijk (1697) although the Holy See had not been officially represented at the congress. He especially liked the so-called Rijswijk Clause, a stipulation keeping the Catholic religion intact in all places made subject to Protestant rule by the terms of the peace. Originally suggested by the Count Palatine Johann Wilhelm von Neuburg, the clause was included in the negotiations and put through at the last minute by the representatives of Louis XIV, to whom it had been expressly recommended by the Pope.

At the end of his pontificate the Pope had to deal with the issue of the Spanish succession. The heir designated by the childless Spanish King, Charles II, died suddenly on 6 February 1699. The Spanish King wanted a successor from the Austrian dynasty, but the Council of State under the direction of Cardinal Portocarrero preferred the French dynasty. Innocent XII, whose advice the Spanish King had requested, approved the decision of a commission of cardinals in favor of the French solution. The demise of the Pope (27 September 1700) preceded that of Charles II by a mere few weeks.

Clement XI (1700–1721)

The death of Charles II led to protracted political manipulations and finally to the election of Cardinal Gian Francesco Albani, nominated by the *Zelanti.* He chose the name Clement XI after the saint of the day (23 November). Appointed by Alexander VIII, he had become probably the most powerful of the cardinals during the pontificates of Alexander and the latter's successor. He had received his ordination late (in September 1700) and was consecrated a week after his election to the papacy. Since he was only fifty-one years old, he could count on a long pontificate.

From the very beginning the new pontificate was affected by the danger of renewed warfare in Europe. King Philip V of the French dynasty was recognized by most of the European powers and the Pope as well. By recognizing the royal title, arbitrarily assumed by the elector of Brandenburg, the Emperor was able to ensure himself of Prussia's support. He also obtained the support of the two naval powers England and Holland, who felt themselves endangered by France's expansionist policies. Clement XI was immediately involved in the conflict by his very proximity to the Kingdom of Naples, which he considered a papal lien. His claim was disputed by both the opposing sides. At first he tried to avoid a decision in order to gain time. The Pope's attempt to keep Italy out of the war and to form a defensive league of the Italian states for the purpose of protecting his own neutrality failed. After Mantua surrendered to the French troops without a battle (5 April 1701), Italy became a theater of war with parts of the Papal States under occupation. Both belligerents violated the neutrality of the Papal States in northern Italy. France's skillful propaganda, representing the Emperor's alliance with the Protestant powers as a danger to the Church and to France and simultaneously picturing Spain as the sole protector of Catholicism, achieved some success with the Pope. When Joseph I succeeded his father Leopold I on 5 May 1705, tensions between the Pope and the Emperor worsened. During the following year the military situation clearly changed in favor of the Emperor. In September French troops had to vacate all of northern Italy. In spite of protests by the Pope the imperial army occupied some of the legations. In May 1707 the Pope was forced to grant free passage to Naples for the imperial troops. Within a few weeks almost all of the kingdom was in their hands. Contrary to papal claims, Parma and Piacenza were taxed as imperial liens. A bull of 27 July 1707 pronouncing excommunication against those abuses achieved nothing. Since Clement XI still adhered to Philip V as the rightful King of Spain, the Austrian pretender, Charles III, ordered a freeze on all revenues of the Church in Lombardy and Naples (April 1708), which caused many members of the Curia to lose considerable parts of their income. Next, the imperial troops invaded the Papal States without a declaration of war and occupied the Comacchio, important for its production of salt (situated between Ravenna and Ferrara on the coast). In autumn 1708, hoping for help from Louis XIV, the Pope decided to oppose the Emperor by force of arms. But left to his own devices, Clement XI was unable to stop the attacking imperial army. On 15 January 1709 he had to accept the Emperor's harsh conditions: disarmament of the papal troops, recognition of Charles III as King of Spain, recognition of the Emperor's precedence over the King of France, a peaceful solution of the territorial issues concerning Parma, Piacenza, and Comacchio. In return he received a promise that the prohibition against the transfer of money would be revoked and compensation would be paid for the damages caused by the occupation of the Papal States.

Although Philip V had encroached on church rights several times, the actual break occurred upon papal recognition of his rival Charles. The defeat of Louis XIV at Malplaquet and Spain's breaking off of diplomatic relations with Rome resulted in a definitive recognition of Charles III on 10 October 1709. Clement XI refused canonical investiture to the bishops appointed by Philip V after the latter had closed the nunciature in Madrid. The unexpected death of the Emperor on 17 April 1711 of smallpox and that of the French Dauphin, who had succumbed to the same disease three days earlier, caused a complete turnabout in the issue of the Spanish succession. In the face of French machinations, the Pope held fast to Charles' candidacy. England was immutably opposed to a union of Spain and the Empire under one monarch: Philip V was to remain King of Spain while Austria was to be compensated by the Spanish possessions in Italy and the Habsburg Netherlands.

At the peace congress starting in Utrecht in January 1712, the papal representative Passionei — since he was devoid of any diplomatic rank he could only act as a common agent of the Pope — had a twofold charge: to prevent the revocation of the Rijswijk Clause and see to it that the feudal rights of the Pope over Parma, Piacenza, and Sicily were upheld. But he could, in fact, achieve very little. The territorial alterations turned out to be damaging to the Church. France recognized the Protestant succession in England and withdrew its support of the pretender James III of the house of Stuart, hitherto staunchly supported by the Pope; Sicily was promised to the duke of Savoy without consultation with the Pope. Personal efforts by the Pope to influence Louis XIV notwithstanding, the Rijswijk Clause — while not formally revoked — was in effect weakened. However, in the parallel peace treaty concluded in Rastatt between the Emperor and the King of France (March 1714) the clause was included. But since the estates of the realm had not participated in the negotiations, a new congress had to be convoked. This took place in Baden, Switzerland, where the Protestant estates again worked toward a revocation of that clause. Passionei, back in his role as papal agent, was again charged with upholding the rights of the Church, with the Rijswijk Clause still being promoted by the Pope. The imperial peace concluded in September 1714 indeed corresponded to that of Rastatt, so that the efforts of the Holy See can be considered partially successful.

Passionei had to protest against those stipulations that were unfavorable to the Catholic Church: the recognition in toto of the Peace of Westphalia, the recognition of the Protestant electoral status of Hanover and of the Prussian royal title, and the ceding of Catholic territories to Protestant princes.

While the Northern War, which lasted beyond the War of the Spanish Succession, did not directly affect the papacy and the Church, the end of the European war renewed the Turkish threat. Initial preparations by the Holy See centered around Venice. Following the example of Pius V, Pope Clement XI tried to bring about a defensive alliance against the Turkish naval threat. Yet the Emperor, distrustful of the French, was unwilling to engage in a military operation on such a large scale. As a consequence the Turkish fleet achieved a series of great successes in the summer of 1715. Venice lost the entire Peloponnesos; an attack upon Italy itself was greatly feared. Urged by the Pope, Philip V of Spain had Clement XI transmit formal guarantees to the Emperor at the end of 1715 that the imperial possessions in Italy would not be endangered for the duration of the Turkish war. With great financial aid and upon constant urging by the Pope, the Emperor concluded an alliance with Venice in April 1716.

In order to interest Spain in taking an active part in the war against Turkey and on the condition of completely restoring the nunciature in Madrid, the ambitious Alberoni, who had created for himself a superlative position of power, was appointed cardinal. The Spanish fleet, largely equipped by means of financial aid from the Pope, was now expected to intervene in the naval war against the Turks so that the continental military operations of the Emperor, which had led to the conquest of Belgrade in August, could be supported. Instead Spain had conceived a plan to attack the Italian possessions of the Empire in order to establish a secundogeniture. Four days after Alberoni found out about his elevation to the cardinalate the Spanish fleet sailed from its harbor and — in violation of the peace — took Sardinia from the Emperor. The Pope, who had given a moral guarantee for the security of the imperial possessions in Italy was assigned part of the blame for this outrageous betrayal and even accused of complicity in it. By invading papal territories and making unacceptable demands Madrid increased the tensions to the point of a complete break of diplomatic relations with Rome. In 1718, while the Spanish fleet was busy conquering Sicily, the Emperor, France, England, and Holland formed a quadruple alliance for the purpose of reordering Italy. When Spain rejected the suggestions of the alliance, the Spanish fleet was destroyed by the English fleet. The Emperor acquired Sicily; Sardinia went to Savoy. Don Carlos, son of Philip V and Elizabeth Farnese, was to assume the succession in Parma and Piacenza. The traditional feudal rights of the Holy See in these territories were disregarded. The trial against Alberoni, initiated by Clement XI and promoted strongly by Philip V for political reasons, was concluded under Clement's successor, Innocent XIII, on the whole in favor of the cardinal, who had even participated in the conclave of 1721. His office and rank were completely restored to him.

In addition to the difficulties caused by the wars, the long pontificate of Clement XI was also troubled by a series of natural catastrophes such as floodings of the Tiber river, epidemics, and earthquakes. The penal institution for juveniles, San Michele in Rome, established in 1703, was a pioneering effort in the modern penal system.

Clement XI has been criticized for his timid and indecisive character and his inability to lend needed emphasis to important decisions. But the lack of success of his pontificate in the area of politics and the Church was surely caused above all by the unfavorable state of affairs confronting the Pope. He died on 19 March 1721 after a pontificate lasting over twenty years.

Section Three

The End of the Denominational Era in Europe: Progress and Stagnation of the World Mission

Chap. 121: Heribert Raab; Chap. 122: Quintín Aldea Vaquero
Chap. 123 Patrick J. Corish; Chaps. 124–25: Bernhard Stasiewski;
Chap. 126: Johannes Beckmann

CHAPTER 121

Reconstruction and Constitution of the Church of the Empire

The Peace of Westphalia had ended the Thirty Years' War, but it had not been able to bring peace to the Empire. Throughout a series of wars lasting into the first third of the eighteenth century and barely interrupted by a few years of peace, the ecclesiastical states within the "constituted anarchy" of the Empire were helpless pawns of the great powers. Again and again afflicted by military campaigns and the aftermath of war, repeatedly threatened by secularization and manipulation at European peace conferences, their reconstruction was also seriously impeded by their own constitution as electoral states, by joint dominion with the cathedral chapters, a lack of continuity, and the dual function of ecclesiastical princes.

In the period of 1500 to 1720, the archbishopric of Trier, for example, had to suffer a total of one hundred years of war, pestilence, and occupation. Only the peace treaties of Utrecht, Rastatt, Baden (1713/14), and Aachen (1748) were preludes to lengthier periods of peace. Lamentations were heard across the land uniformly decrying, in the typical hyperbole of the baroque, the pervasive wretchedness, the misery of the war in the west, the threat of the Turks in the east, joined by woeful tales of pestilence, famine, and the decay of morals. Even if one were inclined to take the tendentiousness and exaggeration of the contemporary accounts into consideration and not view conditions as being totally hopeless, the political and economic reconstruction, beset by constant reverses, was yet an impressive achievement. The same holds true for the renewal and deepening of religion and church life, which were palpably expressed in the sacred art under the rule of the various dynasties, those of Wittelsbach, Habsburg, Pfalz-Neuburg, and Schönborn.

The ecclesiastical territories of the Empire, militarily and politically impotent and reduced to relying on the law, had been afflicted most grievously during the Thirty Years' War. Hardly a prince-bishop was able to do what the zealous Archbishop Paris Lodron of Salzburg (1619–53) had accomplished: preserved his land from war and its aftermath, founded the university, the Collegium Marianum (1645), the Rupertinum (1653), and finished construction of the cathedral. Neutrality had spared neither the prince-bishopric of Liège under Ferdinand of Bavaria nor the bishopric of Basel, although the migration after the war into more depopulated areas of the Empire, as for instance from Liège to Seligenstadt, might have created the opposite impression. Even in those areas of the Catholic Church of the Empire which had never directly suffered pillage and destruction, the war had decreased prewar indebtedness, severed traditional ties, created misery for many refugees, and affected living conditions. By 1659 the bishopric of Brixen was so deeply in debt that the annates and taxes to Tyrol could not be paid and the major portion of its revenues had to be applied to the amortization of interest.

Compared to the bishoprics on the periphery of the Church of the Empire west and south of the Danube, political, economic, religious, and moral conditions around the middle of the seventeenth century were even worse in the so-called "priests' alley" on the Rhine and Main, as well as in those bishoprics of northern Germany which had remained Catholic. In most of the ecclesiastical territories whole regions had to be almost completely recolonized, numerous deserted villages and decayed towns rebuilt, exorbitant debts repaid, monetary confusion and infringements by secular masters on the assets and prerogatives of churches and clerics had to be checked. "Reports received by us of visitations undertaken at war's end show a disconsolate picture of the destruction of churches, of the inferior condition of the sparse number of clerics, of the dissolution and ruin of all church life, of the moral degeneration and the wild superstition of the populace" (I. P. Dengel).

In 1647 upon the accession of Johann Philipp von Schönborn in Mainz, the so-called primary see with its second residence of Aschaffenburg had vacancies in 77 of 105 parishes. The archbishopric on the left bank of the Rhine including Mainz, which was left half-destroyed after the Swedish occupation, remained in French hands until 1650. In the archbishopric of Bamberg "the population was decimated by atrocities, famine, and pestilence. The survivors were quite impoverished as a consequence of repeated tributes" (J. Kist). In the prince-bishopric of Münster, religious and moral conditions were more precarious than the economic ones. Church discipline had deteriorated, strange cults had been introduced, and when Bishop Christoph Bernhard von Galen entered office, a large part of the clergy lived in concubinage. The report to Rome by Bishop Johann Franz Vogt von Altensumerau and Praßberg of Constance, the largest diocese of the Catholic Church of the Empire, counted only six hundred occupied parishes among more than a thousand. In 1654 the bishopric of Regensburg had more than three hundred vacant parishes. Conditions were not much better in most of the remaining prince-bishoprics. In addition to the well-known aftermath of the war,the political, economic, and religious reconstruction was often impeded by foreign occupation troops, raids, and considerable reparation.

Wherever reliable sources are available, they demonstrate that the indebtedness of many prince-bishoprics dating back to the late Middle Ages could not be reduced substantially even in the most affluent archdioceses. Among the reasons were the financial burdens of war, monetary deterioration, wrong financial policies, excessive expenditures for households, construction projects, and maintaining the relatives of the reigning princes. During the seventeenth and eighteenth centuries the following prince-bishoprics were considered either quite poor or highly indebted: Chur, Constance, Regensburg, Paderborn, Hildesheim, in part also Worms, Speyer, Trier, and Freising. The cumulation of bishoprics has to be seen from economic viewpoints as well. Those bishoprics which were economically healthy and therefore relatively rich were desirable political objects for princes and knights of the Empire. In the period mentioned, these included the archbishopric of Mainz with annual revenues of approximately 1.5 to 1.7 million imperial talers (around 1790), the archbishopric of Cologne, the bishoprics of Münster, Strasbourg, Würzburg, Augsburg, and also Bamberg after it was reconstructed by Bishop Philipp Valentin Voit von Rieneck. The revenues of Bishop Wilhelm Egon von Fürstenberg (1740) from the prince-bishopric of Strasbourg, the abbeys of Saint Arnulf in Metz, Saint Michel and other benefices are estimated at 600,000 to 700,000 *livres* annually, those of Elector-Archbishop Max Franz of Cologne at more than one million imperial talers.

Yet the justifiable criticism of the financial policies of many an ecclesiastical prince should not obscure their merits in the promotion of the arts, especially architecture — as by the Schönborns — painting, the music of the baroque and rococo, but also of science, and their charitable efforts, all of which can more than hold their own in comparison with the more powerful secular territories. The absence of standing armies, the primary instrument of power in modern absolutist states, and the close connection between the military and the exchequer tended to hold back the ecclesiastical territories in their public organization and as a political factor. At the same time it provided them with the possibility to solve by means of older forms of governing the basic question of the affairs of any state, to bring about in a faster and simpler way and in correspondence with the natural order a relationship between the individual and society, between man and the state, not least under the aspect of future salvation in the hereafter. The lack of political format, destined to become a fateful issue in the areas governed by crosier and miter, could not but provoke criticism on the part of the Enlightenment; yet it was nonetheless a positive force since it promised relatively more freedom and a certain worldly happiness. On the eve of secularization, Friedrich Carl von Moser wrote: "The often scorned *Pfaffengasse* [priests' alley] constitutes a Pyrenees of sorts of inestimable value to the German people and worthy of their eternal gratitude. Thanks to it the power of monarchs was prevented from enchaining all and everything, as it did in France and Spain, leaving these Alps intact." He continues by saying that only the ecclesiastical princes "deserve the name of public administrators in the true sense of the word because bad and damaging actions are not let pass, as in the case of secular sovereigns, since the eyes of the chapter are on and around them."

The ecclesiastical princes could not expect significant help from Rome or from the nunciatures in Cologne, Vienna, and Lucern for the task of religious reconstruction. There is scant reference to actions by the nunciatures on behalf of reforms, unlike the case in the waning sixteenth century and the first two decades of the seventeenth century. As a matter of fact, some bishops pushed through reforms against the resistance of certain nuncios. In the case of Cologne, hardly more than the central part (the bishoprics of Cologne and Liège) were left of the vast jurisdictional area which the nuncio of Cologne, Sanfelice, casting his eyes toward Metz, Toul, and Verdun, warned against giving up. But even in the part that was left, opposition against the jurisdiction and the existence of the nunciature assumed dangerous proportions.

The latent existential crisis or the threatening "total ruin" of some prince-bishoprics could not be averted by either the nunciatures or by the steadily weakening papacy. They could be averted only by the Emperor and the Empire and by the policies of the Wittelsbachs and the Habsburgs, of the Pfalz-Neuburgs, and the great chapter families such as the Eltz and Schönborns, the von der Leyens, Dalbergs, Stadions, Metternichs, Walderdorffs, and their relatives among he knights of the Empire. After a fashion, these efforts were fairly successful in the first century after the Peace of Westphalia, but less so after the middle of the eighteenth century. Much to their credit was the securing of ecclesiastical properties and the re-Catholization in the Upper Palatinate, Silesia, Jülich and Berg, in the diaspora areas of the Catholic Church of the Empire. But the political results of the conversion of princes have usually been overestimated.

The renewal of church life, initiated in force after 1648, received a late start in comparison with the Romance countries. It can only be fully understood if its special constitutional aspects and the difficulties arising from them are taken into account.

According to the constitution of the Empire, the bishops were not only dignitaries of the hierarchy and successors of the apostles, but as holders of ecclesiastical territories granted as fiefs of the Empire they were also pillars of the Empire, full members with a vote in the imperial diet, princes with the sovereignty granted them by the Peace of Westphalia, albeit a sovereignty which few of them were able to claim for lack of concrete power. This duality of ecclesiastical and secular functions of the prince-bishops and prince-abbots had a positive potential for Church reform. But it also represented a temptation which in a courtly world of absolutism frequently surpassed their strength and permitted the worldly prince in them to win out over the bishop. Forgoing the pomp and circumstance, as was often demanded by contemporary critics, or the demand for a more profound scientific education on the part of prince-bishops only scratched the surface of the problem.

A Church of the Empire in the sense of an association comprising all bishoprics under an ecclesiastical head empowered to lead and direct never existed. As far as its unity was concerned, the Church of the Empire could not be compared with the *Ecclesia Gallicana.* But after the canonical and historical foundation of episcopalism, initially in imitation of Gallicanism, had made some progress, it proudly put its own freedoms — Prince-Abbot Martin Gerbert even spoke of a "national freedom of the German Church" — on a higher footing than those of the Gallican Church, which were considered basically to give expression only to the dominance of the King over the Church. In its legal aspects the Church was initially and exclusively based on the Concordat of Vienna (1448), including, most importantly, its stipulations regarding the filling of bishoprics in the Empire, the granting of benefices, and the financial tribute to the Roman Curia. In the late seventeenth century, following the ambiguous Cologne election of 1688 and the efforts of G. W. Leibniz, there was an attempt to revive the Concordat of Worms and to deduce from it the right of the Emperor to decide conflicting elections. The episcopal church law of the Empire stressed the rediscovered *Concordata Principium* of 1447 and specifically the Mainz Acceptation of 1439 in order to use them in an attempt to modify the Concordat of Vienna. The reform councils of Constance and Basel viewed as foundations of the Church of the Empire the pertinent stipulations of the Peace of Augsburg, the Peace of Westphalia, the Emperor's election capitulation, and the Rijswijk Clause, in addition to the more significant peace treaties of the seventeenth and eighteenth centuries. In neither of these centuries did the Church of the Empire effect a new concordat satisfying the demands of the time.

The church province of Mainz and the idea of a *Primas Germaniae* was brought up as an age-old unifying tie between the bishoprics of the Empire. When Magdeburg joined the Reformation, the archbishops of Salzburg not only claimed the title of *Primas Germaniae,* but were able to maintain their claim with the support of the Emperor and even have it recognized by the Imperial Chancellery in 1750. Yet it had never really amounted to more than an honorary title when the elector-archbishops of Mainz raised their claim to it. This held true even though Mainz, with some justification, was considered the *Metropolis Germaniae* until the fall of the Empire, "increasingly in the sense that involved legal and constitutional aspects of the Empire, decreasingly in the sense of ecclesiastical primacy, and hardly at all in the sense of territorial power" (J. Bärmann). It was in his capacity as elector-archchancellor of the Empire that the archbishop of Mainz occupied the most respected position among the ecclesiastical princes. The prince-bishops of Eichstätt assumed the title of a *Sanctae Moguntinae Sedis Cancellarius* whose task it was to watch over the inviolateness of the Empire and the rights of its Catholic Church. But in spite of the occasional use of the title of primate and some attempts to make themselves the spokesmen representing the interests of the Church of the Empire, their ecclesiastical authority was no greater than that of the other three archbishops.

The extent and borders of the Church of the Empire have never been precisely defined; nor do they correspond to Wessenberg's later definition of the "German Church" under a German primate. They are best determined according to the area affected by the Concordat of Vienna (1448) combined with the basic law of the Empire calling for the free election of bishops. Fluidity and obscurity of its borders, overlapping authority, strange legal conditions, as in the case of the prince-abbeys of Sankt Gallen and Murbach-Luders, the Salzburg bishoprics proper, the abbeys *nullius dioecesis* and the quasi-bishoprics, the alternation of Osnabrück and the denominationally mixed cathedral chapters and benefices all lent a special character to the Church of the Empire and made many a reform difficult. Not counting the elevation of Fulda and Corvey to bishoprics in the second half of the eighteenth century, the number of bishoprics remained constant during the 150 years following the Peace of Westphalia. Neither strength nor will were sufficient to establish Counter Reformation bishoprics, although Joseph II was not the first to perceive the necessity for reordering the organization of the bishoprics, which was almost a thousand years old at that time. Landgrave Ernst von Hessen-Rheinfels (1623–93) demanded that the Empire be restructured into 150 archdioceses and dioceses with each of them having no more than 200 parishes and annual revenues of 4000 talers. Even individual corrections in the administrative structure could not be effected without considerable difficulty. Thus the centuries-old issue between Salzburg and Passau concerning exemption was not decided until 1728, in favor of Passau.

For all practical purposes, the Catholic Church of the Empire ended at the borders of the Emperor's patrimonial dominions, yet it also overlapped the borders of Switzerland and France. In spite of some corresponding details, its situation in the Bavarian sphere of influence cannot simply be compared with that of the Rhenish ecclesiastical electorates. In the Austrian hereditary lands the Church was to a large extent an established Church; despite their extensive property holdings, the bishops were merely members of the provincial diets. With the exception of aristocratic clerics of the Empire who played a significant role in Vienna or Prague (as did the vice-chancellor of the Empire, Walderdorff, and Archbishops Manderscheid and Salm-Salm), and the bishops of Brixen, Trent, Seckau, and Lavant, the clergy of the hereditary lands, unless they simultaneously occupied a seat in the cathedral chapters of Passau, Salzburg, Regensburg or in imperial chapters, simply could not have very strong feelings regarding their ties to the diocesan structure of Germany. Since the turn of the eighteenth century, moreover, the Habsburg emperors started to carve an Austrian monarchy from the Empire and increasingly to consider themselves heads of an established Church.

And yet if one looks for a head of the Church of the Empire, able to exert influence upon it, it would most likely be the Emperor, the *Advocatus ecclesiae.* The seat of German Kings and Emperors in the choir stall of many a cathedral, to be sure, had become a sort of venerable legacy. The office of an archchancellor of the empire, occupied by the prince-abbot of Fulda, or that of the archmarshall, claimed by the prince-abbot of Kempten was endowed with a very modest influence. But these various offices and the artistic aspects of "Imperial Halls," the historiography and architecture of the *Germania sacra* demonstrate its "amphibious constitution." In spite of the denominational split, the Empire remained Catholic, albeit semi-ecclesiastic in its claims and its mission. It was not only political self-preservation that prompted a bond with the Empire, generally stronger than in most of the secular territories. Only within the framework of the Empire were these many Caesaropapal states of varying size able to develop a political and cultural life or eventually realize their lack of political power relative to the rise of the modern absolutist states.

The basic laws of the Empire, especially the stipulations of the Peace of Westphalia and the electoral capitulation obliged the Emperor to secure the status quo of the Church of the Empire, to maintain the *Concordata Nationis Germanicae,* and to stop the complaints against the Roman Curia. Since the thirteenth century the German Kings and Emperors had exercised the privilege of "First Entreaties" (*Jus primariarum precum*) even without a papal indulgence and under Joseph I held fast to it in the face of a violent dispute with Rome. They granted so-called panis letters "which ordered a religious chapter or congregation that upheld or was still upholding the custom of a common table to provide for a certain person's livelihood for life either in agricultural products or money" (W. Wagner).

Although basically respecting the electoral freedom of the cathedral chapters, the Emperor was nonetheless able to influence the filling of bishoprics and through this the policies of ecclesiastical territories by dispatching electoral ambassadors, or by means of recommendations, tokens of favor to Austrian canons or those loyal to the Empire, that is by political and financial means. The presence of imperial election commissioners at the decisive preliminary negotiations, although not at the election itself, was considered legally necessary. But even the right of decision in ambiguous episcopal elections and the *ius exclusivae,* for whose justification the proponents of an established Church in favor of increased advocacy invoked the Concordat of Worms and imperial custom, did not prevail against the resistance of the cathedral chapters and the prebendal aristocracy.

In Trent, where the Compacts of 18 September 1363 and the Note of Speyer of 1571 granted extensive concessions to the Habsburgs, and in Brixen, Passau, Eichstätt and Salzburg, whose "Eternal Statute" (1606) prohibited the election of Bavarian princes and Austrian archdukes and practically excluded all but Tyrolians and Lower Austrians, as a rule candidates from Austrian nobility and those in the service of the Emperor ascended to the see. A position unique in the Church of the Empire and indeed within the Church as a whole was occupied by Salzburg. It had the privilege of appointing, confirming, and consecrating the bishops of its own four small bishoprics of Gurk, Seckau, Chiemsee, and Lavant. Only in the case of Gurk had there been an arrangement made between King Ferdinand I and Archbishop Matthäus Lang (25 October 1535) to the effect that of three successive bishops the first two would always be appointed by the ruler.

The ecclesiastical territories on the Main and middle Rhine were for the most part ruled by prince-bishops who were patriotic and loyal to the Emperor. These cathedral chapters of knights of the Empire repeatedly and successfully demonstrated their independence to candidates nominated by the respective rulers. The knights of the Empire prevailed over proof of ancestry and immediate exclusiveness as well as over the great Catholic dynasties such as the Wittelsbachs, Habsburgs, Pfalz-Neuburgs, and Wettins. But they also prevailed over the mediate nobility who dominated the northwest German cathedral chapters but were in a much more difficult situation in trying to ward off the candidates of their princes. Their resistance was aggravated by the system of coadjutorships, which was expanded in the course of the Counter Reformation and dynastic policies to the extent of a "quasi-hereditability" in a number of states. Thus the prince-bishopric of Freising was referred to as "our parish" by the court of Munich. As a consequence of the Wittelsbach coadjutorships only two elections took place in more than two hundred years in the archbishopric of Cologne (1688 and 1763), although the election of coadjutors was never acknowledged as an actual election or postulation by the Curia, at least in theory. Yet in spite of considerable disadvantages, the coadjutorships at least had the advantage of avoiding interregna and provisional governments by cathedral chapters in the case of vacant sees and the attendant negative consequences.

The ecclesiastical territories were electoral states without any continuity in their foreign and domestic policies or in their attempts at clerical reform. To be sure, they were spared disputes and partitions of inheritance, but were not immune to dynastic rivalries, the ambitions of prebendal families, their nepotism and conflicts of interest. Interregnum and provisional governments during vacancies — not unfairly characterized as "cathedral chapter harvest" — were frequently marked by an express animosity toward the person, the family, and government of the deceased prince-bishop, as well as against his advisers, who at times were not spared personal persecution. This, as well as the considerable cost of an episcopal election and the sums to be raised for annates, services, and pallium contributions, made all reforms exceedingly difficult. Many prince-bishops started their reign without financial means and consequently with little authority. In addition they were tied to the electoral capitulations acknowledged by the Peace of Westphalia, which secured for the cathedral chapters joint government in the bishopric and participation in the clerical administration of it, altogether guaranteeing the estates to be constitutionally embodied in the ecclesiastical territories.

Some wishes for church reforms were reflected in the electoral capitulations, among them the demand to forgo accumulations of bishoprics, a stricter observance of the residence obligation, the settlement of clerical jurisdiction, and the care of elderly and indigent clergy. Those elected were frequently obliged not to take on a coadjutor, not to seek a cardinalate or to do so only if the electoral privilege of the cathedral chapter was assured, not to admit religious orders, which could mean a diminution of episcopal jurisdiction, to root out heresy and to promote the Catholic mission. In the prince-bishoprics of Würzburg, Speyer, and Eichstätt, lengthy lawsuits ensued because of the electoral capitulations. In 1690 Prince-bishop Johann Gottfried II von Guttenberg of Würzburg managed to be absolved from the electoral capitulation by the Pope. The prince-bishops of Eichstätt, Bamberg, and Constance tried to achieve a similar solution In 1692 a particular congregation examined all the German electoral capitulations. Following its suggestions, Innocent XII issued the constitution *Ecclesiae catholicae* (22 September 1695). By threatening dire penalties, it prohibited any and all agreements prior to the election and made all obligations to be contracted after the election subject to concurrence by the Holy See in order to be valid. Emperor Leopold I expressed similar sentiments concerning the invalidity of the electoral capitulations. This *Constitutio Innocentiana* was a decisive blow to the electoral capitulations of several archbishoprics, such as Würzburg, Bamberg, Cologne, and Salzburg, but in those chapters which refused to obey the papal bull and the Emperor's resolution it could not abolish them. In those places a tolerable modus vivendi was obtained which was only occasionally disturbed since the capitulars made the bishops keep to their stipulations and forgo recourse to Rome. Moreover, no prince-bishop who had to consider the consequences for his family could afford deliberately to seek a conflict over the electoral capitulation.

Social differences, reduced during the late Middle Ages, again played a more prominent role in the Church of the seventeenth century. In an unprecedented campaign of securing established positions and in the process of Catholic renewal the hierarchy and leadership of the Church of the Empire consisted exclusively of the few Catholic princely families and the prebendal nobility. Half of the Church of the Empire seems to have been dominated by the Habsburgs and Wittelsbachs. Finally, when the archdynasty of Austria for lack of male descendants could no longer furnish candidates for the bishoprics, the nobility of the hereditary lands and later on the related houses of Pfalz-Neuburg, Wettin, and Lorraine took their place.

To be sure, accumulations of bishoprics as practiced under Leopold Wilhelm of Austria and Ferdinand of Bavaria were rarely equaled after the middle of the seventeenth century. For three generations the history of the ecclesiastical territories on the Rhine and Main was determined by the rule of the Schönborns and their related families.

Dynastic policies within the Church of the Empire undoubtedly contributed to a concentration of power, securing of ecclesiastical properties, and slowing the process of secularization. But as a means of securing a livelihood for younger sons of princes not always suited for the clerical estate they also carried with them grave dangers for the Church. Even taking into account the beneficial influence of the suffragan bishops, the accumulation of bishoprics nonetheless militated against church reform emanating from the hierarchy. Toward the end of the seventeenth century the Church of the Empire had a number of weak and theologically uneducated bishops who were more interested in politics, war, art or entertainment than in their clerical tasks. Yet the number of unconsecrated bishops did decrease. In fact, there were more excellent and truly religious bishops who came close to the ideal than is immediately apparent. Among the exemplary bishops who earned great merit in the implementation of church reforms were the following: Johann Hugo von Orsbeck, archbishop of Trier; Johann Ernst von Thun (1709), archbishop of Salzburg; Sebastian Count von Pöking (1673–88), bishop of Passau; the reformatory Franz Wilhelm von Wartenberg, bishop of Regensburg and Osnabrück (d. 1661), "one of the greatest church politicians of his century" (G. Schwaiger); and J. F. Eckher von Kapfing (d. 1724), bishop of Freising, who was "the type of baroque prince of the Church whose intellect and soul were dedicated to the *Tridentinum*" (B. Hubensteiner).

The capitulars looked on themselves as "hereditary lords" of the archbishoprics, as "condomini et conregnantes" or as "patriae et statuum protectores" (from the 1729 electoral capitulation of the electorate of Trier). These "princes of the Papal State"; (Sartorius) have often enough been harshly judged. They were taken to task for their inept mediocrity, their lack of zeal and theological education, their chasing after prebends, belligerence, and their chronic gambling and drinking (deplored by the papal nuncios almost in terms of a German national vice). They were blamed for a good part of the abuses in the Church and for the fact that they delayed or hesitated in implementing reform. The prebendal nobility was rooted deeply in the courtly world of the baroque. There were lethargic, incompetent prebendaries, talented politicians, sophisticated cavaliers in the cathedral and collegiate chapters, but there were also unobtrusive supplicants and humble pious priests. Greed for fame and money were widespread, but so were preparedness for penitence and expiation. The prebendal nobility were not exclusively engaged in taking care of their families. While they were open to criticism concerning the "aristocratic Church of the Empire," their achievements for Church and Empire, for the arts and sciences deserve recognition. The Schönborns and Eltzes, the Stadions and Dalbergs, the von der Leyens, Breidbach-Bürresheims, Walderdorffs, Fürstenbergs, Thuns, and Firmians, to mention a few, have left their mark on inner and outer aspects of the Church. Their clerical and political decisions, their courts and church architecture, their collections and foundations represent prominent high points in the course of German history.

Efforts to strengthen the principle of exclusiveness had to do with the desire for political, economic and religious security. In the course of the seventeenth century the requirements regarding proof of ancestry were generally augmented. In 1606 the cathedral chapter of Bamberg increased its demands to include eight ancestors. The statutes of the cathedral chapter of Mainz dated 19 December 1654 required of prebendal applicants the witness of eight matriculated knights of the Empire to the effect that the former's ancestors corresponded with the traditions of the Mainz Church. By increasing their demands regarding proof of ancestry in Bamberg, Würzburg, Mainz, and later on in Trier, Worms, and Speyer, the knights achieved exclusive status for their class and to a large extent also for their territories, unaffected by the resistance of the mediate nobility of the Lower Rhine and Westphalia, who were supported by Prussia and Hanover. The bishops of these dioceses — disregarding the special circumstances in Trier — were almost exclusively from families of knights of the Empire from Franconian, electoral Rhenish, and Swabian areas.

In the cathedral chapter of Cologne, where proof of sixteen ancestors had had to be demonstrated since the end of the fifteenth century, the dominance of the nobility was breached by eight pastoral prebends accessible to members of the bourgeoisie. These prebends required both ordination and the doctorate; the equality of rank between the doctoral degree and noble origin thus continued. In the cathedral chapters of Liège, Brixen, and Chur the bourgeois element was not only represented, but actually gained influence in the course of the eighteenth century. Even if one readily admits to cases of reactions against the candidacy of prebendal nobles or princes of the Empire in Stablo-Malmedy or Liège, reactions based on territorial issues or the question of mediate or immediate imperial status, the assumption of a contrast between an aristocratic Church and a rising bourgeoisie can no longer be taken for granted. This is the conclusion to be drawn if one examines the composition of the upper German chapters, the list of their abbots — with Sankt Gallen a case in point — as well as the origin of the various prelates and the suffragan bishops. Entering a monastery in the period of the baroque was more a matter of "social rise than a policy for securing a livelihood" (J. Salzgeber), for the monasteries of that period made tremendous contributions toward reforms and cultural changes, not least in the area of diminishing the differences between social classes.

The Council of Trent had aimed at strengthening the position of the bishops within the diocese, doing away with the separation of the pontificate and the secular-political office characteristic of the development of the Church of the Empire prior to the Reformation. It had also raised a demand for the abolition of the suffragan bishop, this *larva ecclesiae Dei.* To be sure, the bishops had increasingly returned to the center of diocesan life, especially since the middle of the seventeenth century, and there was hardly a diocese within the confines of the Church which could not point to at least one and in most cases several exemplary bishops in the period between the Peace of Westphalia and the Catholic Enlightenment. Yet there was no dearth of complaints concerning the position of the suffragan bishops, that German "bizarrerie, que l'Évêque in partibus n'est que pour les fonctions Épiscopales de l'ordre, et qu'il n'a que voir au gouvernement spirituel, celui qui en est chargé n'étant que Prêtre" (Antoine Arnauld to Landgrave Ernst von Hessen Rheinfels, 30 September 1683), more so if conditions in the Church of the Empire were measured against the Tridentine or early Christian ideal. "A bishop can do everything according to his plans," was the complaint of the learned and profoundly religious suffragan bishop Niels Stensen, who withdrew to his jurisdiction of the "Nordic Missions" as a protest against the controversial election of the Cologne elector Max Heinrich to the prince-bishopric of Münster. He continued: "But I am only permitted pontifical acts; therefore all those other functions, such as visitations, synods, schools, and other things necessary to prepare a candidate for ordination, are out of my hands."

Compared to the aristocratic ecclesiastical princes, not all of whom had been consecrated or were able to fulfill their residence obligation, the suffragan bishops were very much in the background even in the historical representations of the Church, since their work appears to have been limited primarily to pontifical acts and their lives were evidently lacking in prominent events and were too dull and colorless to merit the interest of historians. This one-sided picture of an aristocratic Church of the Empire in modern times must be rectified by an improved assessment of the role and origin of the suffragan bishops. Although the prince-bishops and the cathedral chapters tended to be exclusively members of the high nobility the vast majority of the suffragans were from the bourgeoisie. This was also the case during the seventeenth century, while during the eighteenth century it was the knights of the Empire who predominated, so that in the course of two centuries the two were approximately of equal representation.

The suffragans more or less took care of the ministry in their bishoprics and undertook a great part of the reforms. Their work, insufficiently known even today, characterized an inner aspect of the Church of the Empire, which at times has been seen too much as an "aristocratic Church," as ecclesiastical principalities, as a merger of secular and clerical rule, and as the exclusive domain of Catholic princes and aristocratic families.

The economic condition of the parish clergy and its education immediately after the Thirty Years' War was poor throughout. Even in the following decades, ravaged by war and epidemics, it was rarely better. Abject poverty, hunger, and totally inadequate housing were frequent occurrences. The comment by the deacon of Bingen, Dr. Vogt, regarding the conditions at Niederheimbach pertained to the average income of many priests: "The revenues of the parish priest are such that they do not permit a priestly existence unless he were to sustain himself by means of only bread, milk, and smoked meat, without wine except in autumn, when he may drink cider until the wine is finished and sold."

Greed, gambling, drunkenness, and violation of the law of celibacy in many a place were probably consequences of dire distress. The circumstances explain why many a priest assumed the glebe lands for his own use, disregarding encumbrances and the unavoidable consequences. Patronage rights and incorporation on one hand, surplice fees and oblations on the other, but also economic and spiritual anguish, the difficulties in ministering and trying to lead a pious life can no more than imply the problems of the parish clergy in the second half of the seventeenth century and the early eighteenth century until the reform efforts of the Enlightenment and the parish regulation of Joseph II.

The parish clergy was often hopelessly overburdened. Given the severe lack of priests during the seventeenth century, the restoration of church life would have been impossible without aid not only by the orders, especially the Capuchins, Carmelites, and the Jesuits, but also by the chapter clergy. The number of monastic parishes in Bavaria and Austria was considerable. The prebendary chapter of Sankt Florian near Linz administered thirty-three parishes; Klosterneuburg near Vienna twenty-three, and in the Cologne deaconry of Zülpich thirty parishes were in the care of religious order. But these "expositures" led to many an incompatibility for the *expositi,* their monastic establishments, and the secular clergy. On the whole, the end of the eighteenth century not only saw an increase in the number of priests but also a more profound intellectual and religious life within the clergy.

In the opinion of contemporary sources of the seventeenth century, seminaries appeared to be the best means to restore and improve church discipline. Given the great need for priests, it was tempting to favor exemplary conduct over theological education, thus enabling a less than ideal alternative to have its effect on the rivalries of the ministering regular clergy. The first seminary in Germany was established in 1564 by Bishop Martin von Schaumburg in Eichstätt; the Swedes destroyed it in 1634 and it could not be reopened until 1710. The seminary of Breslau, began to flourish again after the Thirty Years' War under the reign of Archduke Leopold I Wilhelm of Austria (1656–56). The diocese of Ermland had a seminary since 1567; it closed its doors between 1625 and 1637 as a result of the Swedish incursion and was given a new building in 1651. Other seminaries were opened in Würzburg (1570), Salzburg (1577/79), Basel (1606), and Dillingen (1614, for the Augsburg diocese). With the exception of Salzburg these seminaries were unable to develop steadily either because of the vagaries of war or because of financial problems.

After the deluge of the Thirty Years' War and given the total impoverishment of the ecclesiastical territories and their deep indebtedness even from the period before the war — in Constance under Prince-Bishop Jakob Fugger (1604–26) it amounted to 200,000 florins — there could be no thought of establishing new seminaries. It was not "a lack of goodwill on the part of the bishops and not a matter of resistance against the idea of seminaries as such, but primarily the question of finances which created the greatest difficulty" (E. Reckers).

The papal seminaries in Fulda and Dillingen, to be sure, provided some relief and the relatively well educated monastic clergy successfully took part in the ministry. Yet the fact that many bishops had to have their theologians trained in the orders or in foreign and often backward universities was rather disadvantageous for the Church of the Empire. There was a noticeable discrepancy between the meager and sometimes very poor conditions in the training of priests and the background of monumental architecture in the ecclesiastical states; in the mediate chapters, there was a vivid contrast between many a poor village church and splendid monastic libraries.

In Speyer and Trier the training of clerics was insufficient until the turn of the eighteenth century. The boarding seminary of the Speyer cathedral chapter had perished in the tumult of the Thirty Years' War. During the warring seventeenth century there had not been enough money, and so it was not until 1723 that Prince Bishop Damian Hugo von Schönborn was able to establish a pastoral seminary. Trier did indeed have the Bantus Seminary founded in 1586/92 and, after 1667, there was the aristocratic, lavishly endowed Lambertus Seminary established by an endowment of Ferdinand von Buchholtz, but it hardly produced any ministering clergymen. Under the influence of reform-Catholic efforts and a moderate administrative enlightenment, a considerable improvement took place in the condition of the ministering clergy. This included the establishment of houses for retired priests and a better education of recruits for the priesthood.

CHAPTER 122

Spain and Portugal to 1815

The General Intellectual Situation

The structure of the Spanish and Portuguese Church from 1650 to 1815 was determined by the rules and mentality of the *ancien régime.* It was a socially privileged Church with significant agricultural and urban assets, with an unchallenged authority over the faithful. Based on a religious foundation, it also exerted its influence on the bureaucracy of the state. The period falls into two divisions: the century from 1650 to 1750 bears a counterreformational character, while the period from 1750 to 1815 should be considered part of the Enlightenment. However, this concept demands refinement. Was the Spanish Enlightenment Catholic or antireligious? Was it an importation or did it stem from inner dynamics, although characterized by foreign elements? What relationship was there between the Spanish Enlightenment, the Encyclopedists, and the French Revolution? Was it congruent in time with the rest of Europe? These questions contain a number of stimulating problems which cannot be comprehensively or even adequately solved here, but must be mentioned briefly in order to provide a perspective toward a better understanding of this period. The three basic components of the "enlightened Spaniard" as he was represented by a good many clerics of that time were: a Catholic education, European culture and a social and economic reformative zeal.

In its origins, the Spanish Enlightenment was not antireligious. While anticlerics and disbelievers could have joined it, all the typical exponents of the Spanish Enlightenment were Catholic. The clergy especially, being most prominent in the life of the nation, were considered the great representatives of this form of the

Enlightenment. The fact that the most pressing problem was socioeconomic reform, with the state as its most important instrument, was not accompanied by scorn for the supernatural order and even less by opposition to it. And if the authority of the state did usurp the rights of the Church in a pernicious and extremely destructive manner, it was an error on the part of the authority and not of the Enlightenment. Similar to the Renaissance, Enlightenment existed only in its various shadings according to the perception of those who adapted to it.

The representatives of the four generations of the Spanish Enlightenment, referred to by Vicens Vives and adopted here according to their respective generations are Feijóo (1676–1764), Flórez (1702–1783), Campomanes (1723–1802), and Jovellanos (1744–1811). The first two were prominent personalities from religious orders. Jovellanos was tonsured and, although not ordained, remained loyal to the principles of his ecclesiastical office. Campomanes, one of the great regalists of his century, was educated by his uncle, the capitular of Oviedo, and by the Dominicans of Santillana; he steadfastly avowed his Catholicism.

The Geographic, Sociographic, and Economic Situation

At the beginning of the nineteenth century the Spanish Church had 59 bishoprics and, beyond that, 648 dignities, 1,768 prebends, 216 pensions and 200 half-pensions in the cathedral, and collegiate churches. There were 64 collegiate and 115,481 parish churches. The wealth of the Church at that time has been exaggerated just as much as the number of clerics. Yet it must be noted that the economic condition of the Church was good. As in society at large, there existed a significant inequality between the higher and the lower clergy. The most important source of revenue was the *diezmo,* the tenth part of the agrarian gross income. But it fluctuated according to the harvest. In 1592 the annual income of the Church amounted to 10,400,000 ducats; by 1638 it had decreased to 7,000,000. In addition there were the simple benefices and the religious foundations. But these revenues were decreased by a number of contributions to the state or the Roman or national church administration, such as annates, bishops' subsidies, pensions, welfare funds, monthly assessments, etc. There were also the church seigniories, which were dependent on bishoprics, monasteries, or other church bodies. Most of this economic system disappeared in the nineteenth century, together with the *ancien régime.*

The Development of Ecclesiastical Institutions

In the present state of research it is not easy to render a complete picture of the hierarchy, but some general characteristics can be pointed out.

In spite of political decadence, church discipline did not deteriorate. The lateral transfer of prelates was more frequent in the earlier years. From the point of view of the pastoral administration it was possible that this practice was commendable. The question then is whether the motive should be sought in rank or remuneration.

Toward the end of the seventeenth century there was an increase in the appointments of bishops from the ranks of religious orders. We do not know the reasons for this phenomenon. Rome did not have full confidence in the Spanish episcopate; several expressions of distrust were voiced regarding its loyalty to the disciplinary norms of the Curia. The episcopate was assumed to be subservient to the court. It was suspected of standing up more for the fulfillment of its own material interests than for the defense of church jurisdiction and the decisions of the Roman Curia. The latter therefore called the attention of the nuncios to this situation and to the existing tension between the lower clergy, organized in a large association called the *Congregación del clero de Castilla y de León,* and the residing bishops. The nuncios were recommended, whenever justified, to support the demands of the cathedral chapters against the bishops, thereby making them ever more dependent on the will and the protection of the nuncios. Was there a reason for the state secretariat to interpret the situation in this manner? No doubt there was a danger that being dependent on the King for promotion to a better paid or more prestigious position could change into a golden cage. On the other hand, there was criticism in Spain of the Curia and the nepotism of Popes and members of the Curia. The sources do not reveal that the submissiveness of the episcopate to the King or his dynastic concerns was a fundamental disadvantage for the Church. Devotion to the King had its limits; in every case we know of the bishop either accepted the royal decrees in accordance with his conscience or he freely argued his pastoral duties when these did not permit him to obey such decrees. Conversely, opposition of Spanish bishops to the Curia was frequently aimed at the latter's centralism and fiscalism or the anti-Spanish policies of Popes. In the seventeenth century Spain had neither a political and theological episcopacy, as did France, nor did the episcopate form a united front with a more or less uniform mentality for or against Rome or Madrid.

In the middle of the eighteenth century the historian and enlightened reformist Gregorio Mayáns y Siscar (1699–1781) deplored the lack of interest of some bishops in culture and enlightenment and their preoccupation with Scholasticism. Yet most of the bishops made great efforts in the area of charity and material improvement within their dioceses. Since they were generally of modest origins, they stayed in contact with their faithful. The "economically active" bishops promoted public buildings and established schools and houses for the poor.

Within the episcopate a group of Jansenist bishops attained prominence. Though small, it was extremely active and influential: Asensio Salas and José Climent, both of them bishops of Barcelona, Felipe Bertrán of Salamanca, Antonio Tavira, also of Salamanca and later of Osma, as well as others.

At the end of the eighteenth century (19 November 1799) the Austrian ambassador to Madrid, Kageneck, had some disparaging things to say about the bishops of that time. According to him they had no influence on the government, in spite of their wealth, nor did they form a social body within the monarchy. Yet all the while they represented a high level of authority for the pious faithful in the provinces. He continues by saying that it was the custom of the Spanish cabinet of the time not to select highly intelligent people for high offices and none at all who could pose a serious threat to the regime. Kageneck did not reproach the high clergy so much in regard to morality, but referred to the majority of the prelates as insignificant, of low estate, occasionally given to intrigues once they attained positions of leadership, and of being covetous of honor and money. The fact that the bishops were not all submissive as could be assumed was evidenced on the occasion of the regalia decree of Urquijo (5 September 1799). Of sixty-one bishops only ten agreed to it, among them the leaders of the Jansenists, Antonio Tavira, bishop of Salamanca, and Francisco Mateo Aguiriano, bishop of Calahorra. Regardless of all the weakness of the system, this century had great bishops, such as Belluga, Valero, and Lorenzana.

As in other countries and times, the lower clergy, too, was deeply in need of reform and adaptation. To be sure, the demands of the Council of Trent for reforms were theoretically still in force. But a broad spectrum of the clergy — with the exception of some select groups — lagged far behind the priestly ideal. Ignorance, stinginess, and a worldly spirit were the deficiencies castigated by Cardinal Belluga, bishop of Cartagena, in his lengthy pastoral letter of 1705. In order to remove these ills, Innocent XIII, with the help of Belluga, issued the bull *Apostolici ministerii* (13 May 1723) containing twenty-six points for the reform of the clergy. This bull replaced the provincial councils, advocated by the archbishop of Toledo, Francisco Valero, and the national council, demanded by some politicians. From 1650 to 1815, as a consequence, no provincial councils were convened, the only exception being the province of Tarragona, where seventeen meetings were called, the majority of them to deal with economic matters.

Preaching had declined from the classical ideal of the "Golden Era" of Spain, which boasted of so many exemplary teachers. There was a sizeable school of parish missionaries who regularly traversed the peninsula. Dominicans, Franciscans and Capuchins competed in this apostolic task, but the Jesuits were the leaders. One of the most prominent parish missionaries of this period was Father Jerónimo López (1589–1658), who untiringly wandered through Catalonia, Aragon, Valencia, the Balearic Islands, Navarre, and many villages of the two Castiles. He was the author of the well-known *Acto de contrición,* a pious book of devotions with which he went through the streets delivering sermons. These missions were extremely fruitful; above all they revived the practice of the sacrament among the masses.

A typical form of piety in this period was the Sacred Heart devotion. It was propagated by Fathers Cardaveraz (d. 1720), Bernardo de Hoyos (d. 1735), Juan de Loyola (d. 1762), and Pedro de Calatayud. Along with the parish missions, though without the fanfare, went retreats which gradually changed the lives of certain groups of priests and laymen.

In Portugal there were two great figures who deserve special mention, Antonio Vieira (1608–97), called "the Portuguese Demosthenes," and Manuel Bernardes, more esteemed as an author than as an orator.

The persecution of the Jesuits started in Portugal, a country most favored by the society. Under the weak King José I, his minister, the Marquis de Pombal, reigned supreme. Pombal ordered the confiscation of all Jesuit property in 1759 and a few months later their expulsion. Seventeen hundred Jesuits (aside from the nine hundred missionaries) were expelled in a most brutal fashion, deported to the Papal States, or incarcerated in dirty jail cells in their own homeland. Some twenty Jesuit schools were taken over by laymen.

The Jesuits in Spain had great influence and practically a monopoly in the educational system, having a total of 130 colleges. This was one of the causes leading to a tragedy in Spain similar to the one in Portugal. Other reasons for the expulsion were: prejudices on the part of those who had earlier felt themselves disadvantaged by the Jesuits, their assumed wealth, the close connection of the Society of Jesus with the Pope, the suspected opposition to the authority of the King, theological differences of opinion, especially on the issue of probabilism, which many orders and bishops, such as Lorenzana and Armañá, condemned as laxism but without actually knowing it. In addition there was their political and social influence, and finally, the example of Portugal and France. The trial did not take place in the *Consejo* of Castile, as had been the custom, because there the majority favored the Jesuits. For this reason the famous *Consejo extraordinario* was convened, excluding all having any connection with the Jesuits. During the night of 2 and 3 April 1767, all Spanish Jesuits, approximately twenty-seven hundred, with twice that number overseas, were driven from their homeland without having been given a hearing or having been properly convicted. Fear of repression by the King suppressed all protest. The reasons for this decision remained a secret of Charles III. Through his ambassador in Rome, Moñino, he obtained from Clement XIV the brief *Dominus ac Redemptor* (21 July, 1773). When in 1769 the King questioned fifty-six bishops, forty-two of them agreed with the measures against the society, six abstained, and eight opposed them.

The decree *Pro Seminariis* of the Council of Trent, stipulating the establishment of a seminary in every diocese, was at first followed conscientiously. But the difficulties encountered militated against further implementation. Among those were the large number of colleges, which absorbed the elite of the youth, and the high cost of constructing the necessary buildings. But more important than the construction costs were the direction of seminaries, the selection of applicants and the curricula, which were generally antiquated. By the end of the sixteenth century twenty seminaries were founded; in the seventeenth century eight, and in the eighteenth century seventeen, for a total of forty-five by 1816. Of the thirteen seminaries existing in Portugal by that year, five were established in the eighteenth century.

As everywhere in Europe, Scholasticism and above all theological studies at the universities slowly regressed. There was a lack of originality and realism. One was satisfied with composing the no doubt necessary *cursus* or compendium of theological or philosophical knowledge for the use in schools. But in the background of Scholasticism were the new philosophy, the Enlightenment, and the positive sciences. There were significant personalities nonetheless, such as Cardinal Alvaro Cienfuegos (d. 1737), Pedro Manso (1736), Luis de Losada, Francisco Armañá and others.

Historical studies flourished considerably through men such as José Sáenz de Aguirre, Enrique Flórez (author of the *España sagrada*), Andrés Burriel, and Jaime Villanueva. There was a group of literary figures of great quality, such as Benito Feijóo, Francisco Isla, and the group of exiled Italian Jesuits. Among the religious authors who should be mentioned were the venerable Mother Agreda (d. 1665), who was often consulted by Philip IV, and Manuel de Reguera y Álvarez de Paz, and the Portuguese Luis Brandão and Alonso de Andrade.

The authority of the Inquisition decreased considerably, as can be seen by the number of autos-da-fé held at the time: there were 782 under Philip V, 34 under Ferdinand VI and only a dozen under Charles III and Charles IV. The last condemnation by the Inquisition was pronounced in Seville on 7 November 1781.

The royal confessors, who did not limit themselves to the sacraments but freely interfered in the problems of state, enjoyed great esteem. In the council of state they had a voice and a vote just like any other member of the council.

In the course of the sixteenth century and at the beginning of the seventeenth century twenty Spanish saints were canonized, whereas the period we are discussing here lists only two: José Oriol (1650–1702) and José Pignatelli (1737–1811).

Church and State

Relations between Spain and the Holy See rested on the principle of the two authorities: the papal and the royal authority, each supreme in its realm. But the person of the Pope had an additional position: not only was he the successor of Saint Peter, but the prince of the Papal States as well. In cases of doubt the Spanish politicians followed the delimitation formulated by Gabriel Pereira: if there is doubt whether a civil law violates the ecclesiastical weal, the decision of the Pope has to be adhered to. Whenever there is doubt whether it violates the political weal, the decision of the civil authorities prevails. These principles were applied in the theory of the indirect authority of the Pope in Spain under the Habsburgs, and the concepts of the great Spanish writers Vitoria, Molina, Mariana, Suárez and others were followed. Just shortly before the Bourbons took over the reign, Bossuet formulated his views of the divine origin of the monarchs' absolute power on which the Bourbons based their interference in church affairs, especially in the second half of the eighteenth century.

The legal claims of royal intervention were based — over and above his general position as a Christian prince — on the obligation to ensure observation of the decrees of the Council of Trent and, above all, on the royal patronage of Spain, from which the missions patronage over the West Indies is derived as well. The institution of the patronage in Spain was traced to the sixth canon of the twelfth Council of Toledo (681) and formulated by Philip II (1565) in the first law, section six of the first volume of the *Nueva recopilación* as follows: "Legally and on the basis of old custom, just claims as well as apostolic concessions we are patrons of all cathedral churches of these kingdoms and are entitled to appoint the archbishops and bishops, the prelates and abbots of these kingdoms even if they fall vacant in Rome." The following were the decisive steps in the development of the patronage system: The granting of universal and eternal patronage over the Kingdom of Granada, the Canary Islands and Puerto Real (from this was derived in part the royal patronage over the West Indies), which was granted by the bull *Orthodoxae Fidei* (13 December 1486) by Sixtus IV; the granting of presentation in the cathedrals and consistorial benefices for the rest of Spain by a bull of Hadrian VI (6 September 1523); the granting of the royal universal patronage over the entire national territory by virtue of the concordat of 11 January 1753. Benedict XIV reserved for himself no more than the granting of fifty-two benefices. This constituted the climax of the presentation privilege in Spain.

Since the reign of Philip II, Spain and Portugal had been united under the Spanish crown. In 1640 the Portuguese rose up against Philip IV and crowned Juan IV (1640–70) King. This posed great problems for the Holy See, not just because of the diplomatic recognition of the new King, but also regarding the filling of vacant bishoprics in Portugal, which was the King's prerogative. The conflict lasted until the consolidation of Portuguese independence. In 1670 relations between Portugal and Rome were resumed and the bishoprics filled.

A special role was played by the *Gravamina Ecclesiae Hispanae.* In 1632 the parliamentary estates of Castile and León submitted to the King a petition listing the encumbrances of the Spanish Church by the Roman Curia and the nunciature in Madrid. The number of complaints, especially against the dataries, increased until the end of the eighteenth century. Several Spanish cardinals, such as Zapata and Gil de Albornoz, criticized the granting of marriage dispensations, the filling and authentication of church benefices, and the distribution of pensions from them. The complicated fees in the case of marriage dispensations, their high rates, and their arbitrary application led to Cardinal Zapata's comparing the datary with a house of commerce. Complaints against the Apostolic Chamber in connection with the *spolia* and the revenues of vacant bishoprics did not cease until the publication of the Concordat of 1753, whose Article 20 granted these revenues to the church where they originated. The Madrid nunciature was accused of economic and jurisdictional abuses, the latter as well bearing close connection with economic factors. It was accused of charging inordinately high fees, accepting original law suits, making illegal demands for gold and silver money, issuing marriage dispensations contravening the decrees of the Council of Trent and so forth. In 1634 when repeated protests on the part of the ambassadors in Rome, especially by the ambassadors extraordinary Pimentel and Chumacero, were rejected Madrid used the pretext of the death of Nuncio Campeggi to discontinue the activities of the Madrid nunciature for the period of one year. The so-called agreement of Nuncio Facchinetti of 1640 brought about a new table of rates, but until the Concordat of 1753 and essentially until 26 March 1771, when the Spanish *Rota* was established according to the model of the Roman *Signatura iustitiae,* the problem remained unsolved.

"Regalism," that is the abuse of privileges or rights of the King in church matters, is an ambiguous concept. Regarding Spanish regalism one has to differentiate between the reign of the Habsburgs and that of the Bourbons. One must also take into consideration the dialectics of a modern state with its steadily growing administrative autonomy and the intimate ties between Church and state of earlier epochs. The inordinate extent of ecclesiastical immunity of persons as well as properties had created a state within the state and triggered considerable tensions. This explains the origin of recourse to the King, the reticence of papal bulls and the laws of amortization. Yet these events are also a page in the process of secularization of modern society, manifesting itself in the usurpation of spiritual tasks and hostility toward ecclesiastical institutions.

After 1700, when the first Bourbon, Philip V, had ascended the throne of Spain, monarchical absolutism following the French example was intensified by attempts to limit the independence of the Church. Regalism, more radical than ever before, was turned against the papal reservations which had developed into a sort of "regalism of the pope."

Philip V reacted violently against the recognition of Archduke Charles as King of Spain, a step forced upon Clement XI during the War of Succession (1700 until 1715). He founded the *Junta Magna,* which on 25 February 1709 ordered the nuncio expelled and the nunciature closed, the *spolia* and revenues of vacant bishoprics sequestered and all relations of Spanish ecclesiastics with Rome prohibited. These were restored after the Peace of Utrecht (1713) and a provisional concordat concluded in 1717.

When Charles III ascended the throne (1759) the front of the advocates of regalism hardened. The political and ecclesiastical complications brought about by the letter of exhortation of Parma, the expulsion of the Society of Jesus, the Fourth Mexican Provincial Council (1771) and the State Junta (1784), with its famous *Instrucción reservada,* were manifestations of an extreme regalism. Charles IV followed along this path until the publication of the decree of 5 September 1799. It provided that the Spanish bishops in case of a *sedes vacans* of the Holy See "would in accordance with the old church discipline make use of all their faculties for marriage dispensations and other powers," without regard to the papal reservations. This betrayed the extreme philosophy of the royal minister Urquijo, whom a good many people called a schismatic.

After the eradication of the *ancien régime* by the French Revolution the vestiges of Bourbon regalism gradually died out in Spain. The rebellion of Porto in 1820 signaled the beginning of new ideas in Portugal and the start of an epoch of liberalism in both countries.

CHAPTER 123

The Condition of the Catholics in Great Britain and Ireland in the Seventeenth and Eighteenth Centuries

The Early Stuarts

The history of English Catholicism in the first half of the seventeenth century has already been treated briefly. What remains to be added is that English Catholicism at this time had already assumed the social structure which it was to retain until the great Irish immigration during the Industrial Revolution. The faith survived in isolated groups on the estates of individual rural aristocrats who supported the clergy and consequently demanded a certain amount of control over them. The same structure also dominated among the few Catholics of the Scottish Lowlands.

On the Gaelic islands and in the Scottish Highlands, Catholicism maintained itself in stronger groups. They were efficaciously supported by Franciscan missionaries. In Wales Catholicism was almost completely abolished after 1650 when Puritan preachers introduced the nonconformist tradition.

Ireland, on the other hand, had remained predominantly Catholic. Subject to the English crown but with its own parliament, the island had not developed into a homogeneous nation. At the beginning of the seventeenth century three groups can be clearly distinguished: The old Irish of Gaelic origin; the old English from before the Reformation, and the new English who had come to Ireland since the Reformation. The latter group was Protestant, the former two were Catholic. The Tudors had subordinated their desire for religious conformity to political conquest. The old English, strongly represented in the Tudor parliaments, had seen to it that the penal laws in Ireland were never as strict as in England. In addition, the local administration was in the hands of the old English, so that the laws were not as harshly applied as the government might have wished. After about 1570 the Irish — by nature a conservative people who for religious reasons were little susceptible to Protestantism — had at their disposal a growing number of priests who had been educated on the continent according to Tridentine ideals. A considerable number of Irish seminaries had been established on the continent as early as around 1600. To be sure, the seminary priests did not gain immediate access to the old Irish, but these had suffered so deeply during the Tudor conquest that their Catholic faith had become part of their resistance against the new rulers. The old English, on the other hand, continued to keep their wealth and possessions.

In the early seventeenth century the Irish Catholics fought in vain for a political agreement which was to recognize both their loyalty and their Catholicism. Just as in England, James I continued the Elizabethan penal legislation. He also promoted her policies of colonialization. Extensive settlements, especially in Ulster, brought a strong Protestant element into the country for whose economic acumen the conservative Irish Catholics were no match. The King's policies, moreover, excluded the Catholics from public service. The parliament of 1613 clearly manifested that the Catholic influence on legislation had sharply decreased. Political pressure upon them was maintained; around 1640 the old English Catholics had every reason to fear that in the eyes of the administration they were merely "semi-subjects" — as James I had called them — who, like the old Irish, were robbed of their political rights because of their religion and whose right of property was being questioned.

Yet in actual practice there was sufficient tolerance at this time to enable the Catholic Church to carry out a comprehensive reorganization of its mission. From the colleges on the continent Ireland received enough priests who were trained to teach a people whose religious formation had been neglected for a long time. The Catholic episcopate, too, had been renewed. Even during the reign of Elizabeth nominations to the Irish bishoprics had not ceased, although there had at times been lengthy vacancies. From the ranks of the first generation of seminary priests emerged a superior group of bishops who had been appointed around 1620. They were confronted by serious problems, especially on the part of the monastic clergy, who continued to claim the right of extensive missionary authority as it had been granted to them by the Holy See at the time of Elizabeth. But in collaboration with the newly founded Roman Congregation for the Propagation of the Faith the bishops succeeded in establishing a parish system. The monastic clergy calmed down since it now became possible for them to found their own houses. By 1636 the situation had been stabilized by a series of decrees for the Irish mission issued by the Propaganda.

In 1641 the old Irish took up arms in order to reconquer their rights and property. After brief hesitation the old English joined them. United in the Confederation of Kilkenny, they undertook anew an effort to regain their position as "the King's Catholic subjects." Their negotiations with the King were difficult and were further aggravated by the arrival of the papal nuncio, Rinuccini, in 1645, who demanded the restoration of Catholicism on the basis of strict counterreformational principles which did not take into account the complexity of the Irish situation. Several attempts to prevail with his views, even in the face of ecclesiastical censure, finally split the confederation and forced him to leave the country. Thus weakened and divided, Ireland easily fell prey to Oliver Cromwell.

Commonwealth and Restoration

Under Cromwell's rule the two islands had a single administration in the years around 1650. This meant that the more repressive English laws were automatically extended to Ireland as well. Cromwell's concept of "freedom of conscience" condemned the Anglicanism of the High Church of Charles I and Catholicism in like measure. Paradoxically, this meant that the English Catholics were not subject to the bloody persecutions which they had feared because their sympathy had been with the royalists during the civil war. They escaped persecution because they constituted a minority and also because for a time they could successfully claim the principle of freedom of conscience.

The Irish Catholics, on the other hand, suffered a bitter fate. In addition to their being Catholics they were viewed as inferior and uneducated, criminal and politically dangerous. Cromwell had conquered the country in a brutal war of extermination. As a general rule, clergymen captured in the war were executed without a trial. Then followed a large-scale process of confiscation. The propertied Catholics were banished to the province of Connaught. A sharp distinction must be made between the continuity of Catholicism in Ireland and England.

When the war was over, a priest — according to an Elizabethan decree of 1585 — was guilty of treason by his mere presence in Ireland. As a result many clergymen voluntarily went into exile. Those who stayed were persecuted relentlessly, but after 1654 the government preferred to jail the prisoners or to banish instead of executing them. Only a relatively small number of priests were able to follow their vocation — receiving help in numerous ways and assuming various disguises. Mass was usually celebrated in the open, on the "Mass rock." No doubt this was the most severe test ever faced by the Irish Catholics. Fortunately, it lasted but a short time.

The reorganization of the previous generation had been totally destroyed. Again priests exercised their office by virtue of missionary authority if indeed they had such authority at all. But around 1657 the Propaganda in Rome set up new plans for the Irish mission. By the end of 1659, two bishops had returned to Ireland. On 29 May 1660, Charles II reoccupied the throne of his father.

Following the Restoration, England, Scotland, and Ireland again had separate parliaments, which were now much more powerful than under the early Stuarts. The King, striving to safeguard his personal authority, endeavored to secure the support of his royal cousin, Louis XIV of France. The struggle between King and parliament in England was aggravated by distrust on the part of parliament of the King's benevolence toward the Catholics (Charles himself converted to Catholicism on his deathbed and his brother James, duke of York, the heir apparent, converted shortly after 1668).

In 1670 Charles signed the treaty of Dover with Louis XIV, which parliament countered a year later with an act banishing the Catholic clergy. Charles in turn issued the Declaration of Indulgence in 1672, which extended toleration to the dissenters, including Catholics. But parliament proved to be the stronger. The Test Acts of 1673 and 1678 affirmed the exclusion of Catholics from public life. Although the balance of power between King and parliament was sufficient to guarantee the Catholics enough toleration, some of the Catholic gentry and consequently their tenants and vassals left the faith. Church authority was maintained in a much reduced fashion by a canon chapter established in 1623 by Apostolic Vicar William Bishop. It represented a conservative body with Gallican tendencies in which vacancies were filled by election.

In Ireland, Charles had to accept the fact that power was held by those who had profited by the great land confiscations and now increasingly looked on themselves as the "Protestant Interest." In trying to prove their loyalty, Catholic laymen gave considerable support to a movement known as the "Remonstrance," which wanted to obtain from the Irish Church a declaration of Gallican principles. The resistance of the clergy against this demand, which to some extent can be seen as a justification of Rinuccini's ultramontanistic attitude of twenty years before, came to a head in 1666 during a synod in Dublin But at this point it had become clear that a large majority of the dispossessed Catholics would not get their property back.

Again the Church had to rebuild its ministry. There were only two bishops remaining in the country and those who lived in exile were politically compromised by the events of the religious conflicts so that they were not permitted to return. There was indeed a real shortage of priests. For almost a decade no new bishops were appointed, but priests were ordained in considerable numbers often with insufficient or no preparation for their vocation. Both decisions appear to have been made by Rome; no doubt they were the wrong ones.

It was not until 1669 that the first bishops were appointed; by 1671 most of the sees were again occupied. The new bishops were worthy men, some of them even superior. Helped by a greater degree of toleration in the years around 1670, they started the restoration of the parish system by a series of synods and visitations. But toleration was merely relative; congregations continued to be reduced to making use of the "mass rock," although there were some modest chapels or "mass houses" the Catholics were able to establish. But in 1673 a royal proclamation ordered all members of religious orders and clerics with jurisdictional authority to be banished. While this proclamation was not implemented strictly, it did affect an episcopate already in distress. Some of the clerics, ordained in the last decade, now proved themselves unequal to their task. The reconstruction of the parish system led to renewed divergence between the secular and monastic clergy, aggravated by the fact that all the clergy were dependent on gifts by the people, since the Catholic laymen as well as the clergy had lost all their wealth and property.

The Catholics of both islands were exposed to bloody persecutions when Titus Oates instigated a conspiracy in 1678 in order to exclude the duke of York from the royal succession. Oates was an unprincipled adventurer and totally untrustworthy, but because of the political hysteria of the time he was able to have an impact. On 11 October 1678 the archbishop of Dublin was arrested; he died in jail in November 1680. The trials in England began on 15 November 1678. More than twenty-five Catholics were executed and the number of those who were jailed ran into the hundreds. The last and best-known victim was the blessed Oliver Plunkett, archbishop of Armagh, who was executed at Tyburn on 1 July 1681. He was the last victim of the conspiracy as well as the last priest to be executed under the penal laws applying at that time.

The hysteria collapsed as quickly as it had arisen. In February 1685 James II followed his brother to the throne. He was an incompetent politician and ignored the fact that at most 10 percent of his English subjects were ready to accept a Catholic monarchy. The birth of a Catholic heir cost him the throne, which went to his Protestant daughter Mary and her husband William of Orange. James fled to France and later returned to Ireland to lead the resistance there.

The great Catholic majority in Ireland had enough freedom to exercise their religion. The bishops received a maintenance from the government and the congregations were established publicly. When James arrived in Ireland, he convened a parliament which promised freedom of religion and the return of confiscated property to the Catholics. But the further course of events was determined by William's victory over the Irish-Jacobite forces, which enabled the "Protestant Interest" to regain its political power.

The Penal Code of the Eighteenth Century

After William's victory the laws excluding Catholics from public life in England were again noticeably tightened up. On the other hand, several laws concerning property proved to be ineffective and the Catholic landed gentry continued to be accepted on the social level. Yet in the following century there were more and more cases of apostasy among them. During the reign of James II there had been about 300,000 professed Catholics, by 1780 this figure had decreased to 70,000.

An act of parliament of 1700 replaced the death penalty decreed in 1585 with life imprisonment. William tended toward a concept of limited toleration practiced in Holland. Although the English Protestants could not quite accept this, there was, in practice, an increasing extent of toleration; only a few priests were actually jailed. Those who were under the protection of the Catholic gentry were almost completely safe, although the price of this safety may at times have been a humiliating state of dependence. Other clerics, especially in London, had to execute their office in greater secrecy. Bishop Giffard, the vicar apostolic of the London district, was jailed several times.

The jurisdiction of the bishops had been reestablished in England during the reign of James II. In 1685 John Leyburn was appointed vicar apostolic and in 1688 the country was divided into four districts, each headed by a vicar apostolic. All four vicars were jailed during the revolution, but released afterward. Their authority over the clergy had to be exercised very carefully, especially over those who were chaplains with the gentry and even more so with the monastic clergy who were against the restoration of the bishops' authority. In 1753 Benedict XIV made a final decision in favor of the bishops.

The only truly predominant figure among the English bishops of the eighteenth century was Richard Challoner (1691–1781), who was head of the London district for more than forty years. Reticent, strict, and very English, he had a great formative influence on Catholicism not only in England but to some extent also in Ireland. He made his influence felt through numerous written works which he composed over and above a life filled with the work of ministry. His *Garden of the Soul* (1740) *Think well on't* (1728), and *Meditations* (1755) became almost synonymous for his kind of spirituality. Challoner was also influential through his translation of the *Imitatio Christi,* the *Confessiones* of Augustine and the *Introduction á la vie dévote* of Francis de Sales. His revision of the bible translation of Douai-Reims continued to be the Holy Scripture most used in England until recently.

The Scottish Catholics were subjected to penal legislation very similar to that of England, but for them it was frequently even more oppressive, since Jacobite sympathies were more widespread in Scotland. In 1653 a priest had been installed for the purpose of directing the Scottish mission and in 1694 Bishop Thomas Nicholson was appointed vicar apostolic. In 1731 two more vicariates were established, one for the Highlands and one for the Lowlands. From the remote hamlet where each bishop had his residence he directed the education of candidates for the priesthood in order to do his part for the next generation which emerged from the Scottish colleges on the continent. The Catholics of the Highlands suffered profoundly under the repression after 1745, which led to a lasting wave of emigration, particularly to the country which was given the name "New Scotland" (Nova Scotia).

The minority in Ireland, constituting the "Protestant Interest," was faced by some very complex problems. Theoretically it was obliged to work toward the extermination of Catholicism. But for all practical purposes a mass conversion was unthinkable, since this would have meant an immediate threat to the property which the "Protestant Interest" had gained by confiscation. The religious articles of the Treaty of Limerick (1691) had promised the Catholics even better conditions than had prevailed under Charles II. William wanted to respect these agreements, but after the Treaty of Rijswijk (1697) he was more inclined to give in to the Protestant parliament in Dublin.

An act of 1697 ordered all members of religious orders and clerics with jurisdictional authority banished. Those who returned were put under sentence of death. About five hundred monastic clerics were deported and only three bishops managed to stay. The secular clergy had always enjoyed a certain immunity, an outcome of the resistance on the part of the old English in the Elizabethan parliaments. The aim was to put the clergy under surveillance by means of the Registration Act of 1703 and if possible to oppress them. The act provided for the official registration of one priest for each parish; he had to perform his duties under strict control. There were no provisions at all to fill vacancies. In 1704 a total of 1089 priests registered in accordance with the Registration Act, they included three bishops and a number of priests who can be identified as monastic clerics.

The system of controls and possible extermination collapsed with the Act of Renunciation of 1709, which demanded of each priest an oath renouncing the cause of the Stuarts. Only thirty priests swore the oath. Although new laws were passed for another generation, the government had finally given up its goal of religious conformity and instead pledged itself to a policy of social and political humiliation. The Acts of Banishment and Registration were not consistently implemented. No more priests were condemned to death. To be sure, parliament passed laws, but their implementation was in the hands of an executive answerable directly to the crown. The administrative apparatus was weak, especially in remote areas, and even in Dublin it had to proceed with caution to keep the Catholic masses from rioting.

In spite of the Act of Banishment new bishops were appointed in 1707 and almost all the sees were occupied by 1720. Priests were ordained, some on the continent, others within the country, but the latter all too often were given insufficient preparation. The monastic clergy had a large number of recruits and after 1720 were able to resume a certain measure of communal life. But many of its representatives were not personally engaged and were often in unpleasant competition with the parish priests for the alms of the faithful. In spite of great difficulties the bishops wanted to reinstall a parish clergy. But because their mere presence was legally prohibited, they had to act with caution, especially in times of political tension, as for instance in 1715 or 1745. Poverty was a constant problem and sometimes it was very difficult for them to live in their dioceses for any length of time.

By 1730 a more stable parish system emerged. The conflicts between the secular and monastic clergy were lessened by a number of decisions from Rome, which were reaffirmed by Benedict XIV in 1751. They placed limitations upon the monastic clergy which transcended even the rules prescribed by general canon law. On the other hand, they also limited, perhaps too rigorously, the number of priests to be ordained by any one bishop. Yet the papal decisions were motivated by well-founded grievances, based above all on numerous cases of premature ordination. Within a short time there were complaints concerning the shortage of priests to minister to the growing populace, but this situation was never very serious. The continental colleges took care of the recruits needed for the priesthood until they were closed by the French Revolution and Maynooth assumed their role in 1795.

By the middle of the century the "mass rock" was replaced everywhere by the "mass house." Only in Ulster did this process take longer, because the large-scale settlements at the beginning of the seventeenth century had created a Protestant majority there. For the most part, the parish priests had their own houses and the monastic clergy, too, were able to maintain a communal life. Each of the two groups developed its own missionary field. The offerings of the faithful guaranteed both of them a suitable subsistence. In the eighteenth century Ireland finally found peace and gradual economic improvement. Problems reemerged when

England — unlike Ireland — was industrialized. Most of the Catholics remained impoverished. This was the case in all the social classes, even though a small number of the gentry had at least kept some of their estates and a middle class was able to establish a certain affluence from skills and commerce. But it required the first Relief Act of 1782 for new churches to be built. In 1800 a report of the bishops to the government made note that the average annual income of a bishop amounted to 300 pounds sterling and that of a priest to 65 pounds sterling. This constituted a modest but sufficient subsistence.

The long fight for the Mass had inculcated the latter firmly into the center of religious life in Ireland. Veneration of the Most Blessed Virgin and above all the Rosary had also become deeply rooted. Catholic teachers, although outlawed, continued to teach religious instruction in cooperation with the clergy. By the late seventeenth century religious tracts in English were widely distributed; during the eighteenth century a sizeable system of publication and distribution was developed. The inventories of book dealers in the second half of the century show that the works of Richard Challoner were the most popular. Almost nothing was printed in the Irish language, but a good many devotionals were distributed by means of copies, a procedure based on a long tradition. These writings, too, were for the most part translations, occasionally from English, but most of them were translations of European works of counterreformational spirituality.

The traditional devotions also survived. The great pilgrimages especially were kept alive, although the bishops frequently forbade them because of the danger of superstition connected with them. The government also prohibited them because it feared all gatherings of Catholic groups. Modern Irish-Catholic spirituality as it crystallized in the eighteenth century was a mixture of old and new characterized — at least in the English-speaking middle class — by a strict and fearful ethos. This is customarily ascribed to the Jansenist influence, but historically this connection cannot be demonstrated and many other causes can be assumed for it. One of the predominant traits of Irish Catholicism is its traditional severity; even today the popular pilgrimage to Lough Derg is considered a genuine penance. To some extent this attitude is derived from the strict attitude of Challoner, but perhaps more so from the experience of persecution which has been deeply imprinted on Irish Catholic consciousness.

Catholic Emancipation

The Relief Acts canceling the penal laws were prompted primarily by the situation in Ireland, where the consequences of the acts were extremely important. Under the reign of George II (1727–60) suggestions were submitted on numerous occasions which aimed at the approval of a "suitable number" of priests, and even some bishops, provided that they would accept a certain measure of government supervision. But these suggestions were unacceptable to parliament. The succession to the throne by George III (1760), the death of the eldest son of James II (1766), and the American Declaration of Rights (1774) created a changed political climate which made it possible to alleviate the condition of the Catholics.

Derived from English tradition, the Declaration of Rights had been partisan to the politically oppressed. A more urgent problem was England's need to increase its army; to this end the Catholics of Ireland and the Scottish Highlands constituted a promising pool of recruits. To call them to arms without granting them a certain measure of political recognition was impossible. So in 1774 an oath of allegiance, couched primarily in political terms, was accepted by parliament and — after some initial hesitation — by the Catholics as well. In 1782 some concrete concessions were made. These were easier to put through in England, but an attempt to expand them to Scotland had to be given up in the face of the Protestant rebellion.

In 1782 the Gallican laity of England founded the Cisalpine Club, which suggested an oath of allegiance for England very similar to the one decreed by James I in 1607. This oath rejected papal power of removal as being "heretical" and in so doing resurrected an issue which had been largely laid to rest. More importantly, the oath withdrew from the Pope all spiritual authority which was not in accordance with the laws and constitutions of the Kingdom. The vicars apostolic resisted, whereupon parliament decided to replace that suggestion with the Irish oath of 1774.

By 1791 full religious emancipation had been achieved in England; in 1793 it was extended to Scotland. The Irish Catholics, too, obtained similar relief, wrested in a long fight from a resisting parliament by a middle class which was developing the beginnings of a Catholic democracy.

Many political deficiencies continued to exist. Their elimination was difficult as long as Ireland, with its sizeable Catholic majority, retained its own parliament. William Pitt, the English prime minister, therefore suggested a common parliament for the two islands with some governmental control of appointments in the Catholic hierarchy. After the sudden loss of all their continental seminaries the Irish bishops had accepted a subsidy from the government when Maynooth was founded in 1795; four years later, in 1799, they accepted in principle a government veto power over appointments of bishops.

The union of the parliaments took place in 1801, but George III refused to support Catholic emancipation, and for a number of years the issue of the veto dominated public and parliamentary discussion. In 1805 the Holy See approved a limited veto privilege and thereby created acceptable conditions for the leaders of the Catholic laity in England. But in Ireland the budding Catholic democracy rejected this concession; in February 1809 the Irish bishops declared the veto to be unacceptable. An opinion from Rome of 1813 and another from Pope Pius VII two years later favored the veto, yet neither of the two opinions appeared to be acceptable to Ireland. In 1813 the Irish Catholic democracy had found a talented leader in Daniel O'Connell. Political emancipation was finally granted in 1829 without creating any obligations for the Church vis-à-vis the government. In consideration of the annual subsidy the curators of Maynooth were the only ones answerable to parliament until the Irish Church Act of 1869.

CHAPTER 124

The Russian Orthodox Church

The rise of the duchy, or rather grand duchy, of Moscow to the tsardom and the close connection of the Orthodox Church of Russia with the rulers in Moscow led to the relocation of the metropolitan see of Kiev and all of Russia to the north. The dependence of the Russian branch Church upon the patriarchate of Constantinople was weakening as was attested to in a letter dated 1393 from Patriarch Antonios to Grand Duke Vasili I (1389–1425). As a result of the election at the Moscow synod (1448) of Bishop Ioanna of Riazan as metropolitan (1448–61), desired by Grand Duke Vasili II (1425–62) and certified in the synod of 1459, the Church for all practical purposes obtained its ecclesiastical independence, even though it was not released from the jurisdictional ties with Constantinople until its elevation to a patriarchate.

Moscow the Third Rome

After the fall of the imperial city on the Bosporus in 1453, the metropolitans, in concert with the rulers of Moscow, expanded their independence and gradually took over the central position, which had been occupied by Byzantium, the New, the Second Rome, for almost a millennium. The formulation of a "Third Rome" represented an easily remembered symbol for the symbiosis between the Moscow tsars and the metropolitans. In 1472 Ivan III (1462–1505) married as his second wife Sophia (Zoë), niece of the last of the Palaeologoi emperors, Constantinos XI (1448–53). He included the Byzantine double eagle in his coat of arms, assumed the Greek imperial title of autocrat and the Byzantine court ceremonial. In 1492 Metropolitan Zosima (1490–95) designated: "Ivan Vasilevich, chosen by God, loyal to faith, as tsar and autocrat of all of Russia, a new Emperor Constantine for the new Constantinople-Moscow."

Intellectual-historical, political and religious motives, ideas of Rome, New Rome, and Jerusalem, Byzantine heritage, a messianic sense of mission and eschatology mingled with each other and formed a concept which was to prove historically powerful. The theory of Moscow as the Third Rome lent to the Orthodox faithful and to the tsar a strong sense of mission, which continued its effect in the Russian ideology of state and empire and was evidenced even in the first decades of the twentieth century in the newly established Moscow patriarchate.

The First Moscow Patriarchate

The ecclesiastical independence existing since the middle of the fifteenth century was under the direction of the metropolitans of Moscow, who — given the symbiosis of Church and state in the grand duchy of Moscow and the growing power of the Moscow tsardom — grew ever more dependent on the state. A new ritual was published by Metropolitan Makari (1542–63) and Tsar Ivan IV (1533–84). The Synod of the Hundred Chapters (1551) solved the conflict between the "Altruistic" and the "Propertied" by compromise. The former were composed of followers of starets Nil Sorski (d. 1508), who advocated a complete separation of Church and state. The latter, called "Josephites" after their founder Iosif of Volokalamsk (d. 1515), were in favor of close collaboration of Church and state and wanted to put at the state's disposal an elite troop to permeate society in the form of a tightly organized monasticism. The rule of terror by Ivan IV (starting in 1560) which gave him the sobriquet "the Terrible," rigorously interfered in the affairs of the Church. Makari's successors tried in vain to put a stop to his ruthless frenzy. Metropolitan Afanasi (1564–66) resigned; Metropolitan German (1566) was driven out; Metropolitan Philip (1566–68) was banished to a monastery and strangled in 1569. Their successors Cyril III (1570–77), Antoni (1577–80), and Dionisi (1581–86) were helpless in the face of Ivan's fury; he traced his autocracy back to God and used church property for purposes of the state. The Church's dependence on the state persisted under Ivan's mentally retarded son Fedor I (1584–98) and the latter's brother-in-law, Boris Godunov, who reigned in his place and followed him as tsar (1598–1605). When Metropolitan Dionisi attempted to limit Godunov's influence, he was removed from office and replaced by Archbishop Job of Rostov (metropolitan: 1586–89, patriarch: 1589–1605). The "dismissals and appointments of hierarchs by the ruler" can be called with some justification "Russian Gallicanism" (K. Onasch). These actions did not prevent the Patriarchs of the East who suffered under the supreme rule of the sultan requesting and receive gifts from the Moscow tsar. Negotiations and visits made the tsar's authority within the total Orthodoxy grow. In 1585, for instance, Silvester, patriarch of Alexandria, communicated to the tsar "not to let the Holy Places be lacking in his protection." At the same time he prophesied for him the inheritance of Emperor Constantine. These and other utterances prompted the government to aspire to have the autocephalic Russian Church elevated to a patriarchate in order to strengthen its position in the sense of the Orthodox symphony of state and Church. When Patriarch Joachim V of Antioch visited Moscow as a petitioner in 1586, he received — along with generous gifts of money for the other patriarchs as well — the charge to enlist their sympathies for a Moscow patriarchate. When the Serbs had obtained the restoration of their patriarchate of Peć at the insistence of Grand Vizir Mohammed Sokolović, the ecumenically minded patriarch was faced by the decision to recognize yet another autonomous patriarchate.

When Patriarch Jeremias II of Constantinople arrived in Moscow in 1588, he was forced to agree to the establishment of an independent patriarchate of Moscow and of the entire Russian tsardom. The synod meeting in January 1589 nominated three candidates for the new office, of whom the tsar selected Metropolitan Job of Moscow, who was anointed and enthroned by Jeremias II on 26 January 1589 as the first Russian patriarch. At another synod the eparchies of Novgorod, Kazan, Sarai (Kruticy), and Rostov were elevated to metropolitanates. The ecclesiastical arrangement also included six archbishoprics and eight bishoprics whose borders were determined.

Tsar Fedor I and Boris Godunov forced Jeremias II to recognize the patriarchate by a synodal resolution of the other patriarchs. The synod in May 1590 in Constantinople — in the absence of the patriarch of Alexandria, Silvester, who had died and whose successor had not yet been elected — approved the actions of

Jeremias II and assigned to the Moscow patriarchate the fifth place in the ranks of the patriarchates (Constantinople, Alexandria, Antioch, Jerusalem, Moscow). The tsar was not satisfied with this order; he claimed the third place. He further insisted that Meletios Pigas, the new patriarch of Alexandria, who had not entered his office until June 1590 and had protested the resolution, agree to this. Fedor I sent messengers to the four patriarchs with letters and gifts of money to persuade them to agree. In 1593 a synod in Constantinople finally announced the approval of all the patriarchs, without, however, changing the ranking.

The establishment of the Moscow patriarchate in 1589 and its recognition by the whole of Orthodoxy did away with the special position usurped by the Russian Church since the middle of the fifteenth century and concluded its Slavonicization. The diarchy of ecclesiastical and secular rule, considered agreeable, was now represented by a tsar and patriarch who were dependent upon each other. According to the theory of the Third Rome, they stood side by side to act in concert for the salvation of the faithful entrusted to them. In point of fact, the patriarchs remained just as dependent on the tsars as had been the case with the Russian grand dukes and the Moscow metropolitans. Only under special circumstances did some of the eleven patriarchs (1589–1700) succeed in asserting themselves in the face of the tsarist autocracy and to strengthen the authority of the Church by dint of their powerful personalities.

Patriarch Job (1589–1605) was completely overshadowed by Fedor I and Boris Godunov. Following the extinction of the Riurik dynasty, there occurred the "Time of Troubles," during which the false Dmitri pretended to be a son of Ivan IV. With Polish help he conquered Moscow in 1605, deposed Job and elected Ignati, until then archbishop of Riazan, in his stead (1605/06). After The assassination of Dmitri under the rule of Tsar Vasili IV Shuski (1606–10), Ignati had to make way for the metropolitan of Kazan, Germogen, who became patriarch from 1606 to 1612. When the Poles again advanced to Moscow in 1610, they threw Germogen into jail and reinstated Ignati as patriarch. Germogen on his part stirred up nationwide resistance against the Poles until the exterior threats and upheavals of Russia could be overcome by the election of Tsar Michail Romanov (1613–45).

The tsar's father, Fedor Romanov, who had assumed the name Filaret after he entered the monastery and who, as metropolitan of Rostov had been imprisoned by the Poles until 1618, had been designated for the office of patriarch. When he regained his freedom, he took over the highest church office in Russia (1619–33) whose affairs had been conducted by an administrator for seven years (1612–19). Until his death a constellation unique in Russian church history prevailed: father and son — both had the title of "Sublime Ruler" — reigned together as patriarch and tsar. The Orthodox symphony of spiritual and secular power became a reality in this rule of two tsars in which the two forces strengthened each other and gave a strange imprint to the idea of the Third Rome. The Moscow patriarchate was stabilized by the establishment of the archbishopric of Tobolsk in Siberia (1620), the reordering of the patriarchal administration within the structure of the state (1625), and the rejection of all Western infiltrations by the Roman Catholic Church, the Uniates, and the Protestants.

The next patriarchs Ioasaf (1634–40) and Iosif (1642–52) benefited from the heritage of their predecessor Filaret, even though the reign of Tsar Alexei (1645–

76), who codified extant law in 1649, brought about a noticeable tendency toward subordination of the Church under the authority of the state. The establishment of a central government office for church affairs and the prohibition of acquisition of property by the Church initiated the deterioration of church privileges Patriarch Nikon (1652–66) attempted once again to achieve a status of priority of the Church over the state. In an appendix to the *Epanagoge,* a Byzantine book of laws written between 879 and 886 in which Patriarch Photios opposed the hegemony of the Emperor in the Eastern Church, Nikon developed an ideal of church autonomy: "To the tsar are entrusted the affairs of the body, to the clergy those of the souls... therefore the priesthood is far higher than the tsardom." His recourse to Greek models is demonstrated as well by his re-edition of the collection of canon law of the *Nomokanon* and in the improvement of liturgical texts in adherence to the Greek originals by correcting the deviations which had become custom in Russia. With this work he continued the views of Grecophile Russian hierarchs who expected to raise the cultural level of the clergy and ministry by contacts with the Eastern patriarchs. Nikon, who had met the patriarch of Jerusalem, Paisios, in Moscow received texts, among others "a ritual for the execution of the liturgy in the East by a bishop." They were transmitted to him by the former ecumenical patriarch Athanasios III Patellaros, who had been in Moscow in 1653–54. In 1653 the ecumenical patriarch of Constantinople, Paisios I, sent him a large volume containing the precise rules of the Greek Orthodox liturgy and descriptions of the holy implements and vestments.

With the help of these and other documents Nikon initiated his reforms. In an admonition to the Moscow clergy in 1653 he ordered the seventeen genuflections at certain prayers reduced to four and decreed the use of three instead of two fingers for making the sign of the cross. Even these first few reforms on the Greek model created confusion in Moscow. The Moscow protopopes Avvakum (1621–82) and Ivan Neronov protested against the innovations and appealed to the tsar as the protector of Orthodoxy. At the Moscow synod of 1653 Nikon had Neronov condemned, demoted, and banished to a remote monastery; Avvakum was sent to Siberia. At the Moscow synods of 1654, 1655, and 1656 the patriarch pushed through the adaptation of the liturgy to the Byzantine liturgy. Tsar Alexei acknowledged the reform resolutions, made them law, and recognized the penalties against protesting clerics, simultaneously trying to have them ameliorated. The close ties between the Moscow and Constantinople patriarchs opened political perspectives. Because the Treaty of Pereiaslaw of 1654 united the larger part of the Ukraine with Russia — since then Nikon had called himself patriarch of Greater Russia, Russia Proper, and Byelorussia — the avenue to Constantinople appeared open. At the occasion of his stay in Moscow the former ecumenical patriarch, Athanasios III Patellaros, had implied that the orthodox subjects of the sultan could place themselves under the protection of the tsar and encouraged him to "conquer Constantinople and to install his patriarch there as ecumenical patriarch" (A. M. Ammann). There were distinct possibilities of the Third Rome uniting with the Second.

Nikon, allowed since 1654 to bear the title of *velikii gosudar,* like his predecessor Filaret, was administrator of the realm during the Russo-Polish War of 1654/55. His exaggerated self-assurance, the overemphasis of his position, above all the growing movement of the Old Believers, who considered the reforms as interference with the blessed Russian tradition and consequently took up a fight against the state and the Church causing a schism within the Russian Orthodox Church unsolved to the present day, all these contributed to a break between him and the tsar in 1658. Nikon threatened his resignation, whereupon Alexei took away his title of *velikii gosudar* and convoked a bishops' synod in 1660 which was to issue a declaration that the patriarch had resigned his office voluntarily. When his attempt failed, Greek theologians were called in and expert opinions were requested from the four former patriarchs. At the great Moscow synod of 1666/67, in which the patriarchs Paisios of Alexandria and Makarios of Antioch as well as numerous monks and Greek princes of the Church participated, Nikon was dismissed for refusing the opinion of the united Orthodox patriarchs, for restructuring valid canon law, and resigning unjustifiably. He had to retreat to a monastery as a simple monk and spend the last fifteen years of his life there (d. 1682). Nikon's attempt to upgrade the office of the patriarch had failed; the tsar had had his way. At the end of January 1667 the synod submitted a list of three possible candidates for a successor, of whom Alexei chose Ioasaf, the aged abbot of the Monastery of the Trinity near Moscow, to be the next patriarch. The fall of Nikon affirmed the priority of the secular ruler in church matters.

The last four patriarchs who were more or less appointed directly by the government could not stop this development. Ioasaf II (1667–72) followed the tsar's wishes in every way. To be sure, at the end of the great synod he advocated the rights of the Church and obtained an amelioration of the limitations put upon the ecclesiastical court jurisdiction in 1649, but had to recognize that the reform of the liturgy implemented by Nikon had actually been advised by the tsar. According to the records of Paisios Ligarides, a member of the Jerusalem patriarchate, the position of the tsar within the Church was solved by a compromise according to which "neither of the two powers were to interfere in the affairs of the other. In secular matters the tsar was to prevail, the patriarch was to have priority in spiritual ones." The resolutions of the synod honored the tsar as a new Constantine, Zealot of the faith, Defender of the true faith, Judge and Avenger for the Old Believers and the disobedient. The Old Believers rejected their being condemned as a partisan and uncanonical act. The brotherhood of the Solovecki monastery on the Caspian Sea reasoned for their views in several petitions: it was convinced that the end of the world was immediately impending, since tsar and hierarchs had fallen from the old faith and had betrayed the charge of the Third Rome, while the members of the synod had interpreted the idea of the Third Rome according to their own opinions. The brotherhood did not accept the Archimandrite Iosif appointed by Patriarch Ioasaf II and elected its own superiors. The monks defended themselves passionately and resisted the troops called out against them from 1670 to 1676, when their monastery was finally stormed.

After only seven months in office Patriarch Pitirim (1672–73) was followed by Ioakim (1674–90). Next to promoting strict monastic and Church discipline and rejecting all Western influences, he considered the implementation of the decisions of the 1666/67 synod one of his main tasks. This was shown at the bishops synod of 1675 and even more so at the synod of 1682, which continued the development of liturgical reform and declared anew that the punishment of the Old

Believers was a duty of the state. One of the first victims was the Protopope Avvakum, who ended at the stake in 1682. A religious conference at the beginning of the reign of Tsarina Sophia (1682–89) who took over the regency for her minor brothers Ivan V and Peter I after the death of Tsar Fedor II (1676–82), ended with draconic measures and the execution of the main speakers for the Old Believers. A ukase of 7 April 1685 ordered their prosecution and conviction as rebels and enemies of the state. In the following years thousands of them were executed; many evaded their persecutors by self-immolation. They rejected the actions of the state and the Church as being dictated by the Anti-Christ, idealized the past of the Russian Church, and as itinerant priests proselytized for their views. Two groups were now formed, those with priests and those without. The suppression of the *raskol* had serious consequences for Russian monkdom. Many monasteries which had hitherto been centers of religious life and literary production, now ceased to fulfill that function. Most of the monks, because they had joined the Old Believers and rejected the reforms decreed by the patriarchal Church and later on also by the government, were suspected of being enemies of the state.

The synod of 1682 was also occupied with the moral and educational reform of the secular and monastic clergy. New bishoprics were established and the organization of the metropolitanates was tightened. In 1685 the metropolitanate of Kiev was incorporated in the patriarchate in 1686 Patriarch Dionysios of Constantinople released it from his jurisdiction. This incorporation aggravated the tensions within the Russian Church because the academy founded by the Ukrainian metropolitan Peter Mogila (1633–47) in Kiev was prepared to engage in a discourse with Catholicism and the Counter Reformation. It also required a knowledge of Latin in addition to Greek and gained influence beyond its borders of the Ukraine in the second half of the seventeenth century. One of its pupils, Simeon of Polock (1629–80), who had been tutor of the princes in Moscow and had opened a Latin school, and his friend, the monastic priest Silvester Medvedev, spread the many-faceted intellectualism cultivated in Kiev to Moscow. The fight between the conservative forces and those of the "Latinists" who were supported by the government came to a head during negotiations concerning the establishment of a university in Moscow. Although a slavic-Greek-Latin academy was founded in Moscow in 1687, Patriarch Ioakim prevailed at the Moscow Synod of 1689/90: the followers of the Ukrainian movement were demoted; Medvedev was convicted, laicized, and executed.

The relative uniformity of Russian church life at the beginning of the patriarchate gave way to noticeable differentiations at the end of the seventeenth century. Although publications on canon law, liturgy, and hagiography predominated, the revision of the liturgical books represented a new scientific contribution. The interior disputes with Ukrainian and Greek theologians led to a loosening of traditional ties. Baroque culture flowing from the Ukraine to Russia enriched church literature, architecture, painting, and music. The icon painter Simeon Ushakov (1626–86) made use of typically baroque emblematics, the icons show traces of individual portraiture. In architecture the traditional elements combined with Greek ideas and influences of the baroque. Polyphony was added to the customary homophonous singing. The Russian Church, then, received many impulses during the time of the first patriarchate, but these were rejected by the influential conservative circles that determined matters.

One of them was Patriarch Adrian (1690–1700). He tried once again to protect the privileges of the Church, but did not have the strength to prevail against Tsar Peter I, who, together with his debilitated half-brother Ivan V (1689–96) and after the latter's death, ruled and restructured the realm as autocrat (1696–1725). Just as his predecessor Ioakim, Adrian was so steeped in tradition that the tsar's predilection for foreigners and his European trip (1697–98) were totally inconceivable to him. When Peter I returned from abroad in 1698 and ruthlessly proceeded against the revolt of the Streltsi, Adrian, paralyzed since 1696, asked him in vain to apply mercy; henceforth tsar and patriarch communicated only in writing. The patriarchal Church and the Old Believers were united in rejecting the new customs introduced by the tsar, as for instance the wearing of European clothes and shaving of beards. Peter I did not refrain from parodying and scorning church ceremonies. His church policies were an integrated part of his desire, shaped by rationalism and the philosophy of early Enlightenment, to reform the realm. His reforms were aimed at the commonweal — albeit interpreted by him in an arbitrary fashion — and for this he made use of the Church as well. While he took into account the ties of his people with the Orthodox faith, he nonetheless considered the Church no more than an institution for moral education, which he wanted to implement by legal norms instead of religious commandments. During his travels through Catholic and Protestant countries he had become familiar with the dependence of the Churches upon secular authority. He was determined to subordinate the Church to the state in Russia as well.

The Dissolution of the Patriarchate and the Establishment of the Holy Synod

The death of Patriarch Adrian on 16 October 1700 meant the end of the autonomous patriarchal administration. Peter I arbitrarily interfered in church affairs. He did not allow the election of a new patriarch. Two months later he simply appointed Stefan Javorski (1658–1722), metropolitan of Riazan, to the position of administrator and regent of the patriarchate. He was given the supervision of ecclesiastical matters, the right of nomination to fill vacant bishoprics — they amounted to a total of twenty-three — and the surveillance of opponents of the Church, especially the Old Believers, whereas the overseeing of church properties was handed to the Office of Monasteries (1701–20; church judicature was considerably curtailed. The tsar thought that Stefan Javorski, a former professor of the Kiev academy who had occupied himself with polemical theology and had lectured at the Moscow Academy in 1697/98, would be open to his plans.

Initially they collaborated in the mission to the pagans and Mohammedans and in the struggle against the Old Believers. In 1703 Stefan Javorski had dealt with them in an essay, "The Signs of the Appearance of the Antichrist and the End of the World." But he was soon chagrinned by several significant measures of the tsar's. The latter confiscated monastic revenues to finance his army; he practiced tolerance toward the Protestants, granting them freedom of conscience and autonomous rights when he annexed the Baltic provinces; he appointed Pastor Barthold Vagetius superintendent of the Lutheran congregations in Russia, and, finally, he subordinated the Office of Monasteries to the "Reigning Senate" created in 1711, which became the supreme supervisory office, usurping all administrative and judicial functions. In 1712 Javorski used a sermon to take a stand against the church policies of Peter I and his marriage to Katharina (Catherine) Skravronka, later Tsarina Catherine I: "You stormy sea of man's transgressions of the law, why do you break and devastate the shores? The shores are God's law; since its creation it has consisted in not coveting the wife of one's neighbor and in not leaving one's own. . . ." In 1689 the tsar had separated from Evdoxia Lopuxina, mother of Tsarevich Alexei, and decreed that she enter a convent. In the same sermon, Stefan Javorski also expressed his sympathies for the heir to the throne who did not agree with his father's methods of governing. As a consequence Javorski was prohibited from giving sermons for the period of three years. His polemics against the Protestant circles of Moscow and the army surgeon Dimitri Tverentinov, who represented Calvinistic views, led to a summons before the Senate. When the physician Foma Ivanov, a follower of the surgeon, hacked apart some icons, the patriarchal regent had a bishops' synod in 1714 sentence him to death at the stake. The tsar, outraged by this action, forced Stefan Javorski into humiliating apologies. Henceforth the latter did not dare express his opinions freely. But he put them down in his "Rock of Faith, Dedicated to the Sons of the Holy Orthodox-Catholic Eastern Church for their Strengthening and Spiritual Edification, but as Support and Betterment for Those who Perceive it as a Stumbling Block." In this manuscript dedicated to Tsarevich Alexei he maintained that the Church was superposed over the state: "Tsars are the guardians of the laws of God and of the Church, but they are not legislators; it is not theirs to determine what should be part of the faith."

When the conflict between the tsar and his son caused a trial in 1718 against Alexei and his followers, the investigation extended to ecclesiastic dignitaries, who were made answerable for the widespread opposition and an alleged conspiracy. Stefan Javorski advocated a pardon, but was unable to avert the death penalty. The opposition between the patriarchal regent and Peter I, whose founding of Saint Petersburg (1703) had created a symbol for the Russia changed by him, had become unbridgeable. Church life was paralyzed more and more each year by the incursions of the autocrat. In 1714 he prohibited the building of new churches for ten years in favor of the construction of Saint Petersburg, elevated in 1712 to be the capital. In 1716 the Senate ordered the bishops to bind themselves by oath to deal mildly with the opponents of the Church, to employ clerics and sacristans only when needed, and not to interfere in secular affairs. In 1717 the tsar demanded of all confessors that they tell him personally all news of attempts directed against the state. In 1718 he ordered Feofan Prokopovich (1681–1736) to draft a "Description and Evaluation of an Ecclesiastical College," intending to direct the central authority of the Church according to his ideas and to incorporate it in the total administration of the state.

Feofan Prokopovich was one of the most important Russian theologians of the first half of the eighteenth century. Although he referred to certain basic ideas of Protestantism and tenets of the Enlightenment, he tried to combine the Byzantine heritage and Moscow tradition with the demands of his time. After his studies at the Kiev Academy he had temporarily become a Basilian monk and successfully passed a course in Catholic Scholastic philosophy at the Greek College of Saint Athanasius (1698–1701). On his way back through Switzerland and Germany he had met Calvinist and Lutheran theologians. In 1704 he became an Orthodox monastic priest and soon rose to the position of professor (1706) and then rector (1711) in the academy. In 1716 the tsar, who had known him personally since 1706, called him to Saint Petersburg as his adviser and in spite of reservations on the part of the patriarchal regent succeeded in having him appointed bishop of Pskov in 1718. After his sermon concerning the power and honor of the tsar on 6 April 1718, the basic ideas of which he deepened in 1722 in his essay "The Right of the Monarchic Will," the collaboration between him and the tsar became closer. Its product was the *Spiritual Regulations,* which made the Russian Church a part of the order of the state and placed at its head the Holy Synod as a state institution. The text drafted by Feofan Prokopovich in 1720 was corrected by Peter I and submitted to the Senate for its information and for all bishops to sign. It regulated church supervision, church education, the order of Mass, appointment to church offices, the ecclesiastical court and the administration of church property. The tsar's manifesto of 25 January 1721 made the council form of government of the Church stipulated in the regulations its basic law and decreed that the Ecclesiastical College could not do anything without his approval. In the first meeting of 14 February 1721 Feofan Prokopovich gave the opening speech based on John 15:16, stressing the decisive role of the monarchic will. At this meeting the designation "Ecclesiastical College" was changed into "Most Holy Governing Synod." It was composed of eleven members who received princely salaries. Saint Petersburg was designated as the seat of this office. Peter I appointed Archbishop Stefan Javorski first president and Bishop Feofan Prokopovich second president. When Javorski, who could not stop this development and whose protests were disregarded, died in 1722, the tsar did not appoint another president but transferred the authority to Prokopovich as vice-president. In April 1722 the Holy Synod issued supplements to the regulations concerning the monastic system. Men could not be vested as monks anymore until the age of thirty; women were prohibited from being vested until the age of fifty to sixty.

On 11 May 1722, Peter I — to whom the Senate had given the title of Emperor and the sobriquet "the Great" in 1721 — installed within the Holy Synod the office of a chief procurator corresponding to the procurator general in the Senate. Subordinate to the will of the tsar, who simultaneously made him head of the chancery of the synod, he was to have full supervision of the synod "as Our eyes and administrator of the business of the state." J. V. Boltin, colonel of the dragoons, was the first chief procurator (1722–25). His successors were elevated to the rank of ministers in the nineteenth century and became key figures of the Russian established Church. Under the direction of its vice-president, the Holy Synod attempted to return the Old Believers to the Church by means of words of exhortation; it took steps to reform the monastic system and to make it useful to the state, to improve the education of the people, and to raise the level of knowledge of the clergy. Feofan Prokopovich composed a "First Instruction for Boys," a catechism for children which had to be read to all the congregations four times a year. He also expanded the Alexander Nevski Monastery in Saint Petersburg into a model seminary.

It was not easy for the members of the Holy Synod to explain to the Orthodox clergy within and without Russia its role as a bishops' synod, able to invoke Orthodox traditions, and its functions as an organ of the state. The Holy Synod had the legislative, executive, and judicial power within the church government which had earlier rested with the Moscow patriarchate. It tried to calm the bishops with the following message: "The synod has the honor, authority, and power of the patriarchs, if not more so, because it is a council." The petitions of the liturgy henceforth mentioned the Holy Synod instead of the patriarchs. The commemoration of the other patriarchs was to cease, lest it create the impression that the Holy Synod was below them. The tsar took it upon himself to inform Patriarch Jeremias III of Constantinople of the new church order in Russia and asked him in turn to communicate it to the other three patriarchs of the East. But in his devoutly phrased letter of 30 September 1721 he did not mention the content of the regulations, which he designated merely as "Instruction." He also kept silent concerning the incorporation of the Holy Synod into the collegiate system of state administration and the subordination of the Church to the supervision of the state. Furthermore, he changed the text of the manifesto of 25 January 1721 in several places. In 1723 the patriarchs of Constantinople, Alexandria, and Antioch recognized the "Most Holy Governing Synod" as "Holy Brother in Christ," only Patriarch Chrysanthos Notara of Jerusalem refused his approval. Aside from the one-sided information they had received, the decisive factor in obtaining their recognition was the patriarchs' dependence on Russian subsidies because they were under Turkish domination.

The uncanonical installment of the Holy Synod meant the complete dissolution of the Moscow patriarchate. The Russian Orthodox Church became the Orthodox Church in Russia. To be sure, it continued to be connected with the other Eastern Churches in its teachings, the celebration of its liturgy and sacraments, but received a new structure in its relation between Church and state by virtue of the abolition of the earlier dual rule of tsar and patriarch and its subordination to the state. The decrees of the Holy Synod were published in the name of the tsar, by order of His Imperial Majesty. The harmonious collaboration between state and Church aligned for centuries according to the symphonious Byzantine model was part of history. Dostoevski's acerbic judgment that "the Church has been in a state of paralysis since Peter the Great," is exaggerated. But in the history of the Russian Church the establishment of the Holy Synod meant the beginning of the dictatorship of the established Church.

The Russian Established Church under the Holy Synod

The Holy Synod was the instrument by which the state subjugated the Church in the eighteenth century. Its members, reduced to four in 1730 and fluctuating between three and eight in the following decades, possessed the legislative, administrative and judicial power. The administrative offices of the Holy Synod prepared all decisions for the conferences usually taking place twice a year. The directives of the ruler were decisive in everything; the chief procurators appointed by them merely received orders.

Under Catherine I (1725–27) the Holy Synod was placed under the "Supreme

Secret Council" established in 1726. Archbishop Feodosi Janovski of Novgorod, having shortly before criticized the tsarina's church policies, was demoted and banished to a monastery on the Caspian Sea as an ordinary monk. Feofan Prokopovich, promoted to archbishop of Novgorod in 1725, had to fight for his leadership position in the Holy Synod during the reign of Peter II (1727–30), the son of Tsarevich Alexei, because the great families protecting the young tsar again declared Moscow the capital of Russia and permitted discussion of a possible restoration of the patriarchate stimulated by some princes of the Church. In 1728 Archbishop Lopatinski of Tver published the "Rock of Faith" written by Stefan Javorski, in which the basic attitude of Feofan Prokopovich was suspected as Lutheranism. The first edition was quickly out of print; the second was sent to all bishops and abbots in 1729.

After the death of Peter II, under the reign of Anna Ivanovna (1730–40), a niece of Peter the Great, Archbishop Prokopovich again obtained dictatorial powers. He removed from the Holy Synod three members who had been supporters of the nun Evdoxia Lopuxina, the first wife of Peter I, for the succession to the throne. He also proceeded against all people who had favored the dissemination of the "Rock of Faith." The Metropolitans Georgi Dashkov and Ignati Smola were stripped of their ecclesiastical office and dispatched to separate monasteries as ordinary monks; Archbishop Lopatinski was divested of his bishopric after a three-year pretrial arrest (1738) and taken to the fortress of Vyborg. Feofan Prokopovich cast suspicion on his adversaries as enemies of the state; he packed the Holy Synod, by now subordinated to the cabinet of ministers, with men whom he trusted and intensified the dependence of the Church upon the state. He punished bishops and abbots if they resisted government regulations, such as total obedience to monastic legislation. When he died in 1736, the arbitrary rule of the tsarina and her favorite, Duke Ernst Johann von Biron, interfered even more in church matters. In 1737 all church officers between the ages of fifteen and forty with the exception of priests and deacons were drafted into the army. Conscription even reached into the monasteries. These and other measures, making it problematical to enter a monastery, reduced the number of monks and nuns from approximately twenty-five thousand to hardly fourteen thousand. In 1738 the Holy Synod had to hand the College of Economics over to the jurisdiction of the Senate, with the result that all church property revenues flowed into the state exchequer. The tsarina ostensibly represented herself as a benefactress of the total Orthodox Church. In 1732 she established a budget for gifts of charity, granting the patriarch of Constantinople an annual 1000 and the other patriarchs 100 rubles each. Other beneficiaries were the Balkan Slavs, the Athos Monasteries, and the Georgians.

After the short interregnum of the minor Prince Ivan VI and the regent Anna Leopoldovna (1740–41) the oppressed situation of the Church improved temporarily at the beginning of the reign of Tsarina Elizabeth (1741–61), a daughter of Peter the Great. She granted freedom to several bishops and returned the administration of the properties of the Church and monasteries to the Holy Synod. Basically she continued the church policies of her father. The chief procurator, Prince Shakovskoi (1742–53), and his successors made sure that the interests of the state were safeguarded; they prepared for the secularization of all church property. The mission among the Mohammedans of the Volga region, suppressed under

Anna Ivanovna, was now promoted by the state. Mosques in places cohabited by Christians and Mohammedans were destroyed. The increase in the number of souls by almost a half million may have strengthened the self-assurance of some bishops, to be sure, but the necessary expansion of the church organization — in 1753 there were thirty bishoprics with about 18,000 parishes — was limited to mere outward appearances. The edition of the Holy Scripture, a revision of the 1581 edition in Church Slavonic of the Ostrog Bible after the Greek original text, which was published by the Holy Synod in 1751, and the exhortations of some princes of the Church against the incursions of ideas of the Enlightenment were unable to stop the process of the Church's being pushed more and more from public life. Moscow University and its branches, founded in 1755, did not include a theological faculty.

Over the following decades the Church lost the last vestiges of its autonomy. The infantile Peter III and his ambitious wife Catherine II (née princess of Anhalt-Zerbst), who pushed him aside and usurped the throne, continued the subjugation of the Church under the yoke of the state. Peter III, the son of Tsarina Anna and Duke Karl-Friedrich of Holstein-Gottorp, reigned for only half a year (1761–62). He did not have the slightest understanding of the special character of the Orthodox Church. The president of the Holy Synod, Archbishop Dimitri Seshchenov of Novgorod, was expected to remove all icons except those of the Redeemer and the Blessed Virgin, to abolish the monasteries, and make the clergy adopt the dress of Protestant ministers. Complete control by the state over all church property was introduced by the reinstatement of the governmental College of Economics and the inventorying of all monastic estates.

To be sure, Catherine II (1762–96) designated herself "Orthodox Empress," but was guided mainly by the spirit of the French Encyclopedists, with whom she corresponded. She deliberately and stubbornly completed the church policies of Peter I. Even prior to her coming to power she had jotted down the following maxim: "Respecter la religion, mais ne la faire entrer pour rien dans les affaires d'État." Once empress she called herself "chef de l'église grecque" or "chef de son église." At times she referred to the bishops as "people being part of the administration of the state, subject to the will of the monarch as well as to the Gospel." Chief procurators, such as J. J. Melessino (1763–68), who suggested the abolition of fasting, abbreviation of the Mass, and facilitation of divorces, and P. P. Shehebyshchev (1768–74), an avowed atheist, gradually made the Holy Synod comply with the wishes and demands of the tsarina.

At the very beginning of her reign Catherine II appointed a commission to deliberate the problem of the Church properties The result was the secularization law of 26 February 1764, which ordered all properties to be transferred to the Office of Economics. Four hundred eighteen monasteries were dissolved; the budget for all bishoprics, churches, and monasteries, whose number was further decreased in the following years, provided for three different income scales. At first the process of secularization included only the monastic institutions of Greater Russia; after the special status of the Ukraine was phased out in 1786 and 1788, it was extended to the southwestern territories as well. Aside from a very few other clerics only one prince of the Church, Metropolitan Arseni Masejevich of Rostov (1742–63), who had earlier proved his courage by a paper opposing the wrongs done to Stefan Javorski, dared protest publicly against the nationalization of church property. When he prophesied the destruction of Church and piety in two petitions to the Holy Synod, whose members he characterized as "mute dogs" who look on without barking," he was tried by a synodal court in 1763, stripped of his consecration as bishop and priest, and banished to a remote monastery. Shortly thereafter he also lost his monastic status and was condemned to life in prison at the fortress of Reval, where he died in 1772.

The established Orthodox Church bowed to the will of the Tsarina in all matters. This was manifest in the preparation of a new legal code and the expansion of the system of higher education. The religious academy in Moscow, being refused any connection with the university, and the seminaries were so meagerly supported that the Church was reduced more and more to the liturgical realm. All the while Catherine II represented herself as guardian of the Orthodox faith. In the peace treaty with Turkey in 1774 she obtained protectionary rights over the Orthodox faithful in the principalities of Moldavia and Walachia. The "Greek Project," a plan to restore the Byzantine Empire under a Russian secundogeniture, pursued visions of even greater scope, which could not, however, be realized.

In the second half of the eighteenth century the Church — in a condition of total dependence on the state since Peter I — was endangered from within by the advances of rationalism, the Enlightenment and Freemasonry. Some princes of the Church sought to avert the infiltration by means of compromise, such as the Moscow metropolitan Platon Levshin (1773–1812). He went back to the works of Feofan Prokopovich, whose views were prevailing at the Moscow Academy, and himself published sermons and catechetical works. The number of bishops and monks who deliberately concentrated on the religious core of their tasks was small. Personalities of high profile were exceptions in the Orthodox Church of Russia at the time of Catherine II. The condition of the Church was characterized by the process of secularization, through which it had lost the major part of its self-support for its charitable and social tasks. The schism of the Old Believers continued. The government tried to move those who followed official church dogma to recognize the established Church and was prepared to tolerate separate customs for its concession. But it also took harsh measures when it deported twenty thousand Old Believers who had settled on the Dnepr island of Vjatka to Siberia. The "priestless" Old Believers split up in numerous groups. New sects were formed, such as the Chilysty, Skoptsy, Milk-Drinkers and Dukobors, who separated from the established Church and — although they were small in numbers — were troublesome to the Holy Synod.

Paul I (1796–1801) considered the Church an ally in his fight against the consequences of the French Revolution. He called the welfare of its servants "one of the main duties of the imperial rule" and made the expansion of church schools possible so that four Church academies and forty-six seminaries were in existence at the end of the eighteenth century, but he considered the clerics civil servants, as had his mother Catherine II. He was the first to award medals to the bishops, thereby tying the already pliant ecclesiastic princes even more firmly to the state. Even as heir apparent he had a religiously embellished concept of an autocrat feared and honored by his subjects "because he is the image of the Most High." In the law of succession drafted in 1797 he had himself designated "Head of the Church."

He chaired the Holy Synod and claimed supreme supervision of the established Church; he appointed and transferred bishops according to whim. The designation of the tsar as "Head of the Church" was the culmination of the development of centuries and sealed the state's domination of the Orthodox Church of Russia.

Protestants and Catholics in Russia

The population of Russia at the time of Peter the Great is estimated at approximately 14 million, most of whom were of the Orthodox faith. The attitude of the patriarchal Church toward the Lutheran congregations which had formed in the course of the seventeenth century was negative. When the number of Protestant immigrants grew considerably at the beginning of the eighteenth century, especially after the Edict of Solicitation and Toleration by Peter I (16 April 1702) and the annexation of the Baltic provinces, the state issued special regulations for them. In 1721 the Holy Synod was given control over all congregations. In addition to ministering to the Orthodox it became responsible for the administrative and judicial problems of the Lutherans, Calvinists, Catholics, and Jews as well. The individual Protestant congregations were dependent upon themselves and had no higher administrative office. Only the church organizations in Livonia, Estonia, and Finland had their own central administration which represented their interests to the state. The congregations had to announce the election of their clergy and the prepositors to the Holy Synod for confirmation. The prepositors had to affirm their loyalty to the tsar by oath. In turn they took the oath from all pastors and submitted pertinent documentation with their signatures. The Holy Synod had to give its approval for the opening of new churches and the establishment of church schools. The College of the Judiciary, founded in 1718, and its department for Livonian and Estonian affairs extended its authority to include supervisory power over the Protestant Church. In spite of ostensible recognition the Protestants had to obey the repeated prohibition against proselytizing (1702, 1723, and 1735). Special advantages were promised to those who converted to the Orthodox faith. In her manifesto of 22 July 1763, Catherine II solicited new settlers from Germany and western Europe for the Volga regions. She promised them free exercise their religion, but prohibited clerics of non-Orthodox Christian faiths from attempting to convert Russian subjects to their faith.

While the Protestants in Russia — in spite of subordination to the Holy Synod and subsequent limitations — were tolerated by the government and in part furthered, the situation of the Catholics of the Latin and Uniate Rite was oppressive. Following the split between the Western and Eastern half of Christianity in the Middle Ages, and anti-Catholic prejudice had developed in Russia; it became even more pronounced after the Unions of Florence and Brest, which rejected the papacy and condemned Roman efforts at union as interference in the rights of the Orthodox Church. The repeated conquests of Moscow at the beginning of the seventeenth century were connected with the Catholic Counter Reformation and strengthened the distrust of everything Catholic. The Jesuits who had come to Moscow in the retinue of foreign legations in 1684 were expelled in 1689. Although they returned after a few years as legation priests of Emperor Leopold I, their ministry was severely limited to Catholic immigrants; they were again expelled in 1719. Their place was taken by Capuchins and Reformists, who were given scant possibilities to function and were, moreover, suspected of espionage.

Peter I, who — after his visit to the Sorbonne in 1717 — had ordered an opinion from Feofan Prokopovich and Stefan Javorski regarding prospects of a union between the Russian and Catholic Churches, kept up a good personal relationship with several Catholics in his service. But he showed a clear dislike for the Uniate Catholics whom he encountered during his campaigns in White Russia and Lithuania. He was angered by the fact that of the four Orthodox bishops in the southeast of Poland-Lithuania three (of Przemyśl, Lemberg, and Tuck) had joined the Union of Brest (1691 and 1702).

When the Catholics, along with all other non-Orthodox Christians, were placed under the authority of the Holy Synod in 1721, there were mainly German, French, Italian, and Polish immigrants involved. The suppression of the Orthodox in Poland-Lithuania in the first half of the eighteenth century increased anti-Catholic sentiment in Russia. In 1746 and 1760 Tsarina Elizabeth allowed the Austrian auxiliary troops freedom of their religion only because she had to. As a result of the settlement manifesto of 1763 about six thousand German Catholics came to the Volga region of Saratov. They were permitted to build churches, but monasteries and conversion among members of other Christian faiths were forbidden to them.

After the Counter Reformation had prevailed in Poland-Lithuania and Catholicism as the national religion had relegated the other Christian faiths to a minor role, Catherine II contrived to have her favorite, August Poniatowski, placed on the Polish throne (1764–95). Through her ambassador Nikolai Vasilevich Count Repnin she repeatedly interfered in the ecclesiastic affairs of her neighbor to prevent reforms initiated by prominent clerics. In 1767 she had the Bishops Kajetan Sołtyk of Cracow and Józef Andrzej Załuski of Kiev arrested and deported to Russia because they resisted her demands. The Polish partitions (1772, 1793, and 1795) caused large segments of the Catholic population to come under Russian rule. The tsarina found a willing helper in the person of the former Calvinist Stanisław Siestrencewicz-Bohusz (1731–1826), who through her protection rose from suffragan bishop in Vilna to metropolitan of Mogilev, an archbishopric created by her. The new archbishopric to which all Catholic parishes were attached had to follow the *Regulations* of 1769. Only the Jesuits were able to preserve a certain amount of independence after their order was officially dissolved by Clement XIV (1773), because they willingly placed themselves at the disposal of the new rule in the capacity of teachers. The protest by Nuncios Giovanni Andrea Archetti and Lorenzo Litta notwithstanding, all Catholic church property in the areas occupied by Russia were secularized.

Catherine II proceeded ruthlessly against the Uniate Catholics. With the exception of the archbishopric of Polock all Uniate bishoprics were dissolved. Moral force and police measures recombined the Uniates with the Orthodox. Those who dared protest were convicted as rebels. When the Uniate metropolitan of Kiev, Feodosi Rostovski, traveled to Saint Petersburg in order to protest, he was not allowed to return. The bishops of Chelm and Vladimir and the coadjutor of Łuck tried in vain to obtain help from the Curia. The Basilian order was secularized, its monasteries and property confiscated. the church policies of Catherine II cost the

Uniate Church 8 million faithful, 9,316 parishes, and 145 Basilian monasteries from 1773 to 1796. In the region of Polock, too, government pressure became unmistakable. In a pastoral letter of 3 November 1795, Archbishop Heraklius Lisowsky had to announce that no one was allowed to put obstacles in the path of those who wished to convert to the Orthodox faith.

Under Paul I there was at first some amelioration. The former Warsaw nuncio, Lorenzo Litta, participating as papal legate in the crowning of the tsar in 1797, submitted a memorandum concerning the desperate situation of the Uniate Catholics and the wishes of the Pope for improving the relationship between the two rites in Russia. The tsar did not accede to any negotiations, but he did revoke the dependence of the Catholics on the Department of Livonian and Estonian Affairs, decreed at the beginning of his reign, and instead subordinated them to a special department of the College of the Judiciary. Of his own accord he ordered six suffragan bishoprics to be incorporated in the archbishopric of Mogilev, recognized the Uniate archbishopric of Polock, and reestablished the dissolved Uniate bishoprics of Łuck and Brest in order to calm the unrest that had broken out in Wolhynia and White Russia. In November 1798 he issued a *reglament* for the Catholic Church of the Latin and Uniate Rites. After expelling Lorenzo Litta he appointed Archbishop Stanisław Siestrencewicz-Bohusz as head of the Catholic Church in Russia. A ministerial instruction explained the decree by saying that the complete "outward aspect" of the Church was claimed by the state and only the "religious aspect" was part of the Pope's supremacy.

Parallel to the development in western, central, and southern Europe, where the system of established Churches had to a large extent prevailed, the absolute claim of the state's leadership over the Church had become a reality in eastern Europe as well. Neither the Orthodox Church nor other Christian faiths could avoid this development.

CHAPTER 125

The Autonomous and the Uniate Churches in the East

After the conquest of Constantinople by the Turks in 1453 the Ottoman Empire reached the zenith of its power under Selim I (1512–20) with its expansion to Syria and Egypt and under Suleiman I (1522–66) with advances into southeastern Europe, the Mediterranean, and Asia, which made its sphere extend from Algeria and Tunisia to the Persian Gulf. In the seventeenth century a gradual decline set in brought about by interior crises as well as pressure from the Republic of Venice, the Habsburgs, Poland-Lithuania and the rise of Russia. The Sultans succeeded in spreading the Islamic faith to the Balkans and in consolidating it in their empire, which spanned three continents. The Koran was considered binding not only as a religious code but it also shaped the empire's political and cultural life. The "infidels" who did not embrace the faith of Mohammed were *reaya* ("grazing herd") and had to pay a head and property tax to the sultan. They had limited rights and were merely tolerated. The Moslems as representatives of the ruling religion designated the heretical religious communities as *millet.* This concept goes back to the Koran designating the Jews (Abraham's *millet*). In Turkish the word underwent a secular change coming to mean "nation." Thus the Orthodox Christians were combined in the *rum millet,* the Monophysite Christians in the *ermeti milleti,* which also included the Armenians, Copts, and Jacobites. A religious head (*millet bashi*) was responsible for the independent administration of these various bodies; he was directly under the sultan. The ecumenical patriarch, whose title the Greeks freely translated as "Ethnarch," was the most prominent. He could stabilize his ecclesiastical power by adaptation to the sultanate. The interests of the small groups of Catholics of the different Uniate rites and the even smaller ones of the Latin Rite, especially in the Holy Land, were represented by the Pope, French diplomats, and after the seventeenth century also by the German Emperor. Some Orthodox Churches were financially and politically supported by the Russian government. These factors contributed to the fact that the Ottoman Empire, imbued with the Islamic faith, guaranteed certain rights to individual Christian communities. But to a large extent the Eastern Churches, whether separated from or connected with Rome, were exposed to the caprice of the sultans and their officials. Consequently there were a great many defections from Christianity to Islam.

The Uniate Churches

The union of Rome with the Greeks, signed at the Council of Florence in 1439 and in 1442–45 joined by the Armenians, Copts, Syrian Jacobites, and groups of Nestorians and Maronites living on Cyprus, was but of short duration. The further the Ottomans advanced west and south, the more quickly the ties between the Apostolic See and the Uniate Churches in the Near East, the islands of the eastern Mediterranean and the Balkan peninsula were cut. The Popes had no means by which to counter these reverses. Their expectation that military victory over the Turks fighting under the banner of their prophet might pave the way for reunification of the separated halves of Eastern and Western Christendom proved illusory. They tried in the sixteenth and seventeenth century to bring about coalitions against the Turks, and at times were successful, as evidenced by the defense of Vienna in 1689. But their becoming part of the development of the Western world was manifested in the modern-day unions organized by them. To be sure, these unions bore a different stamp from the *communio* of all partial Churches in existence during the first millennium. In the West a uniformly and well-organized Church had been developed under the direction of Popes who had scant understanding of the autonomous administration of the Eastern Churches which had developed since Christian antiquity. In addition, many members of religious orders urged Latin spirituality upon the Uniate Churches and, further, the Greek (1576) and Maronite Colleges (1584) founded in Rome for the education of Uniate clerics were based (among other things) upon Scholastic theology. The Congregation for the Propagation of the Faith gave orders initially to win individual believers over to the Catholic Church but at first to have them remain in their mother Church. The intention was to gain influence slowly and — given a vacancy — to get a patriarch or catholicos appointed who would embrace Catholicism.

For several reasons the unions — with the exception of the one concluded with the Maronites in 1515 — lasted but a short time or proved to be durable only after several tries. The Popes paid close attention to keeping the privileges granted the Uniate Churches and safeguarding their Armenian, Byzantine, Chaldaic, Coptic, Maronite, and Syrian rites. But several Western rulers formulated plans to effect a union while pursuing their own motives, as for instance the Kings of France in the Near East, the German Emperors in Siebenbürgen (Hungary), and the Kings of Poland-Lithuania with their magnates in the Ukraine.

The unions were generally considered an intermediate step between Latin Christendom and an Eastern Christendom which was to be eschewed. In the course of the centuries the influences of Latin liturgy and Roman canon law became more and more noticeable in the life of the Uniate Churches. The blend of Eastern features and Latin traditions sharply criticized as "Uniatism" by Eastern theologians, militated against the development of many unions in eastern and southern Europe, in the Near East, in northeastern Africa, and the Indies.

The union with the Ruthenians and Ukrainians in Poland-Lithuania, concluded in Rome (1595) and accepted at the synod in Brest (1596), was slow to permeate all segments of the population. It lacked the support of the authoritative circle of the magnates, who were either Orthodox or Roman Catholic. Polish theologians considered union as a transitional phenomenon and therefore extended their efforts toward a reduction in the separate customs granted to the Uniate rites and toward a gradual Latinization of their cult. In 1620 when the Orthodox Church reestablished its metropolitanate of Kiev, which flourished quickly under the leadership of Archbishop Petrus Mogilas (1633–45), several Uniate bishops returned to it. The piecemeal defections from the union could not be stopped until the reign of King Jan III Sobieski (1674–96), when the Uniate Basilians formed a new congregation and several Orthodox eparchs switched to the union. The Synod of Samosc (1720) convened by Archbishop Leo II Kiszka (1714–28), was presided over by the papal nuncio Girolamo Grimaldi. Its significance for the Uniate Ukrainians has been compared to that of the Council of Trent for the Latin Church. It wanted to eliminate abuses, elevate education and discipline among the clergy and populace and harmonize the Orthodox tradition with the demands of the time. Its decisions — in contrast to those of the Synod of Brest — demonstrated a certain amount of adaptation to the Latin Rite and the customs of the Roman Church. This synod gave to the Byzantine-Ukrainian Rite its special form, which has remained the most widespread non-Latin Rite of the Catholic Church to the present day. After just a few decades of undisturbed development, witnessed by the church architecture of Lemberg, Polock, and other towns, the Polish partitions and the westward expansion of Russia initiated strong political pressure against the Uniate rites within the Russian sphere of influence, forcing them to return to the Orthodox Church. Only in Galicia, which had come under Austria, could they continue to develop their Churches.

In 1646, in accordance with the example of the Union of Brest, the Union of Užhorod was concluded with the Ruthenians who had settled in Podcarpathia (Carpathian Ukrainians) who belonged to the Orthodox bishopric of Mukačevo, established in the second half of the sixteenth century. From 1633 to 1711 that area was the domain of the Princes Rakoczy, who enlisted sympathies for the spread of Calvinism. This prompted the bishops of Mukačevo to seek ties with the Catholic Church. Bishop Basilios Tarasovič (1633–51) negotiated union with the Latin bishop of Erlau, George Lippay (1637–42), who rose to become bishop of Gran and primate of Hungary (1642–66), as well as with Emperor Ferdinand III and the apostolic nuncio Gasparo Mattei. In 1642 he embraced the Catholic faith in Vienna, but was prevented by Prince George I Rakoczy (1633–48) from returning to his see. Although he reverted to the Orthodox Church, he did recommend shortly before his death (1651) the election of a successor who would be sympathetic to the union. In 1646, meanwhile, the union had been announced by the bishop of Erlau, George Jakušič. It was embraced by 63 of 650 priests and spread further by Bishop Petrus Partheneus Petrovič (1651–66). Upon his death a serious crisis set in when — in addition to the successor elected by the Uniate Church — the Emperor and Princess Sophie Rakoczy each appointed another successor. This confusion was not ended until the appointment of the vicar apostolic of Mukačevo, John Joseph Camillis (1689–1706), a Greek born in Chios and educated at the Greek college in Rome. He convened several synods, published a catechism and consolidated the union, which had 420 member parishes by 1693. During the first several decades of the eighteenth century the Latin bishops of Erlau managed to have the Uniate bishops of Mukačevo made subordinate to them. The Uniate clergy protested in vain against the restrictions placed upon their bishops. Not until 1771 did Pope Clement XIV alleviate the tense situation by issuing his bull *Eximia regalium* and granting personal jurisdictional rights to their bishops. The Uniate bishopric was comprised of 839 churches and 675 parishes; in 1776 it became a suffragan bishopric of the archbishopric of Gran.

Similar to Podcarpathia, Calvinist rulers also had great influence in Siebenbürgen. When the region came under imperial supremacy and was placed under the Hungarian crown, the danger of domination by both Magyars and Calvinists was a growing threat. The Orthodox Bishop Theophilos Szeremy of Alba Julia detailed a plan for union on the occasion of a Rumanian synod in 1697. The members of the synod were favorably inclined, but demanded complete safeguards of their Orthodox rites and customs as well as equality with the Catholic clergy. The union was accepted under Bishop Atanas Anghel (1697–1713) at the Synods of Alba in 1698 and 1700 after the Emperor granted to the Uniate Church the same rights as were enjoyed by the Catholics. In 1701 the imperial court named Atanas bishop of the Rumanian nation in Siebenbürgen. Cardinal Leopold Karl Kollonics, archbishop of Gran conditionally reconsecrated him, an action which was sharply protested by the Orthodox theologians and bishops. Yet the Uniate Bishop Atanas was joined by almost all the Orthodox Rumarians, about half a million. In 1721 Pope Innocent XIII established the bishopric of Fagaras for the Uniates, which was joined with the archbishopric of Gran by Emperor Charles VI. In spite of the difficulties created by the Calvinists and the emissaries of the Orthodox patriarch of Ipek the Uniate bishops were able to consolidate the union. In the town of Blaj the Uniate Bishop Peter Paul Aron (1752–64) founded a college led by Basilian monks and a press which published liturgical books and brochures for religious instruction. The union was further promulgated by his successors, such as Athanasios Rednik (1764–72) and Gregor Major (1773–82), with support by Empress Maria Theresa and many clerics who had studied in Rome.

The families who had emigrated from Bosnia to Croatia in 1573 were served by the Orthodox bishop who resided at the monastery of Saint Michael in Marca. In 1611 Bishop Simeon Vratanja embraced Catholicism before Cardinal Robert Bellarmine, but was able to persuade only a part of the monks of the Marca monastery and of the Orthodox Serbians to join the Union. Subsequent tensions with the Latin archbishop of Zagreb (who considered the Uniate bishop a subordinate auxiliary bishop), efforts by the patriarch of Ipek to rejoin the Uniates with the Orthodox Church, the existence of a Uniate vicariate for Syrmia (1688–1706), whose ordinary resided at the Monastery of Hopovo, and the sacking and destruction of the monastery of Marca by members of the Orthodox Rite (1739) prompted Bishop Gabriel Palkovič (1751–59), who saw his bishopric endangered from within and without, to relocate it to Pribic. In 1777 Pope Pius VI issued the bull *Charitas illa,* creating the diocese of Kreutz for the Uniate Church of Byzantine Rite as part of the archbishopric of Gran.

The majority of Greeks who had fled from Albania to southern Italy and Sicily, the so-called Italo-Albanians (Italo-Greeks) succumbed to a process of Latinization. After they had achieved the opening of seminaries for the education of their own priests at Piana in Sicily (1716), at Ullano in Calabria (1732), and at Palermo (1736), Pope Benedict XIV acknowledged in his constitution *Etsi pastoralis* (1742) the validity of the Greco-Albanian customs, but he stressed the *praestantia* of the Latin Rite. The Italo-Greeks were given an auxiliary bishop in Calabria (1735) and in Sicily (1784). Of the numerous Greek monasteries in Italy only Grottaferrata near Rome and Piana in Sicily preserved the Byzantine Rite although there, too, mixed forms of the liturgy were practiced along with the Latin liturgy.

In addition to the unions of different national groups of Orthodox Christians in eastern Europe, southern Europe, and Italy, there were the Monophysites who had emigrated from Greater Armenia to Poland-Lithuania and had an Armenian bishopric in Lemberg. Bishop Nikolaus Torosowič (1627–81) joined Rome in 1630. While he did become archbishop of the Uniate Armenians for Poland and Walachia with his residence in Lemberg (in 1635), it was his coadjutor and successor Vatan Hunanian (1686–1715) who definitively broke with the catholicate of Etchmiadzin and stabilized the union. The Polish partitions caused the archbishopric to be split into a Russian and an Austrian part.

Efforts by zealous religious prompted some individual Armenian bishops in Constantinople, Etchmiadzin, and Sis to agree to the union. But the Dominicans in Transcaucasia, the Mechiharists called into existence in 1701 by Mechithar of Sebaste (1676–1749), and the missionary order of the Armenian Antonites founded in Lebanon during the eighteenth century, had only limited success. In Syria the Catholics attempted to fill the vacant patriarchal see of Sis with one of their own in 1737. The Monophysite Armenians elected Michael, the Catholics elected Archbishop Abraham Ardzivian of Aleppo as successor. The latter received recognition of his office and the pallium as Catholicos Abraham Peter I (1740–69) by Pope Benedict XII in 1742. But his intention to relocate his residence to Constantinople was thwarted by the protest of the Monophysite Armenians. So he resided at the monastery of Krim in Lebanon and his successors in nearby Bzommar. They were responsible for the Uniate Armenians in Cilicia, Palestine, Mesopotamia, and Egypt. The members of the Uniate rites in the north and west of Asia Minor, in Constantinople, and the European part of Turkey were given their own vicar-bishop, who was subordinate to the Latin vicar apostolic of Constantinople.

While efforts toward union were initially unsuccessful among the Orthodox Georgians, they showed promise among the Orthodox Melchites, but could not come to fruition because of the rivalry among Uniate dignitaries during the eighteenth century. Although Capuchins, Carmelites, and Jesuits in Syria enlisted some bishops and patriarchs for the union, a widespread movement did not occur until the appointment of Archbishop Euthymios of Sidon and Tyre (1683–1723), administrator of all Catholic Melchites in the patriarchate of Antioch since 1701, and the engagement of the missionary congregation of the Most Holy Redeemer, founded by him in accordance with the rules followed by the Basilian order. After the death of the Melchite Patriarch Athanasios (1724), who embraced Catholicism on his deathbed, the Catholic minority elected as his successor Seraphim Tanas, a nephew of Euthymios, who assumed the name of Cyril VI (1724–59). At the same time the opponents of the union elected a nephew of Athanasios as Patriarch Jeremias III. The latter had Cyril and his followers excommunicated at a synod in Alexandria in 1728. Having been forced to leave Damascus, Cyril VI took up residence in Sidon. He initiated the line of Uniate Melchite patriarchs of Antioch whose jurisdiction was broadened in 1772 to include all Catholics of the Byzantine Rite within the confines of the patriarchates of Jerusalem and Alexandria.

After Capuchins and Jesuits had enlisted some individual Jacobites for the Church, Bishop Andreas Akidjian of Aleppo was elevated to the vacant Monophysite patriarchate (1662–77). As a result of mediation by the French consul he was recognized as patriarch of the Syrian nation by the sultan. His successor Ignatius Petrus IV (1677–1702) was repeatedly persecuted for his adherence to the union, alleged to be an agent of France, and finally driven out. Many Uniate western Syrians left Monophysitism, part of them going over to the Maronites. Their number diminished in the course of the eighteenth century so that by 1768 no more than 150 Uniate families were counted in Aleppo and 50 in Damascus. Not until 1783 were they given a new patriarch in the person of Ignatius Michael Garweh (1783–1800). His election in Mardin in 1781 by four of the six Jacobite bishops was recognized neither by his opponents nor by the Turks. He was forced to make way for the Jacobite Patriarch Matthias and withdrew to the monastery of Scharfeh in Lebanon. In 1783 the Pope recognized him as the Syrian patriarch of Antioch whose line can be traced up to the present.

Since the Nestorians of eastern Syria had been split into several jurisdictional areas, the Chaldeans who had joined the union also formed several centers. The patriarchate of the Chaldeans in Diarbekr, created in the middle of the sixteenth century under John Sulaqa came to an end by the return to Nestorianism of Simon XIII (1662–1700). Archbishop Joseph of Amida (Diarbekr), who had become Catholic in 1672, was elevated to the patriarchate as Joseph I (1681–96). He ministered to about one thousand faithful. His successor Joseph II (1696–1713) called himself patriarch of Babylon and the nation of the Chaldeans. The Dominicans succeeded in recruiting for the union the nephew of the Nestorian patriarch, Elias XII Denha (d. 1778), who resided in the monastery of Rabban Hurmuz near Mosul. He was elected patriarch and then appointed metropolitan of Mosul and administrator of the patriarchate of Babylon. The rivalry between the two Chaldean patriarchates of Diarbekr and Mosul, which latter was comprised of a mere few thousand faithful, ended in 1834 with the enthronement of John Hormez as patriarch of Babylon.

The Maronite Church of Lebanon had been firmly tied to Rome since the Fifth Lateran Council. The embassy of the Jesuit Giambattista Eliano (1578 and 1580) introduced an increased Latinization of the Antioch Rite which was protested in vain by several monks and bishops. In 1584 Pope Gregory XIII created the Maronite college in Rome which produced a number of important priests and scholars, the members of the Assemani family (as-Simani) being especially prominent among the latter. In 1606 the Gregorian calendar was introduced among the Maronites. Patriarch Stephanus Ad-Duwaihi (1670–1704), who had been educated in Rome, had valuable help from the order of Saint Anthony of Saint Isaias in developing his Church. The disputes created by the elections of dual patriarchs and the rejection of increasing Latinization were to be resolved in 1736 at the Synod of Kesrowan. In the presence of the papal legate Joseph Simon Assemani, the decisions of the Council of Trent and the *Catechismus Romanus,* which appeared in Arabic in 1786, were accepted. Latin vestments were prescribed for celebrating the Eucharist. In 1741 Pope Benedict XIV accepted the decisions of the synod. The following year he divided the patriarchate into eight dioceses, giving them the titles of old Syrian metropolitanates. Five Maronite monks were in sharp disagreement with the negotiations of the synod and the papal utterances. Not until the second half of the eighteenth century under Patriarch Joseph Estephan (1766–92) could unity be reestablished in the Maronite Church. The seminary founded by Estephan in Ain-Warka (1789) continued the activities of the Armenian college in Rome after it was dissolved in the tumult of the French Revolution. The Synod of Bkerke in 1790 contributed significantly to consolidating the Maronite Church.

Among the Monophysite Copts the contacts with Patriarch John XVI (1676–1718), initiated by Jesuits and reformed Franciscans, were unsuccessful. The assistant to the patriarch of Cairo, the Coptic Bishop Athanasios of Jerusalem, who had embraced Catholicism in 1739, was given the leadership of the approximately two thousand Uniate Copts by Pope Benedict XIV in 1741. But since he was unwilling to terminate his connection with the Coptic Church, the Propaganda named Justus Maraghi vicar general (1744–49). He was followed in that office by prefects of the reformed Franciscans. In 1761 the former Coptic Archbishop Antonius Fulaifil became the first vicar apostolic in Cairo. He was unable to achieve much progress because the bishops and priests who were prepared to join the union insisted on conditional reconsecration.

After the initial successes in Ethiopia achieved by Portuguese missionaries in the seventeenth century collapsed, the union was unable to establish firm roots.

Capuchins and Franciscans who dared enter the country of the negus were either driven out or died a martyr's death.

The successful union concluded in the sixteenth century with the Christians of Saint Thomas in India was weakened by the creation of the Jacobite Church under Mar Thomas I in the middle of the seventeenth century. Those Thomas Christians who had remained Catholic were under a vicar apostolic directly subordinate to the Propaganda; at the same time they were under the Portuguese *padroado,* which in turn was under the influence of the Jesuits. The vicar apostolic, Mar Alexander Parampil (1663–94), was successfully supported by Carmelites who became his successors. The partition into two jurisdictional areas brought with it all sorts of difficulties which were overcome only when the Jesuit order was dissolved in 1773 and the Carmelite order started furnishing the majority of apostolic administrators.

In spite of the tensions from without and within to which the unions, concluded from the sixteenth to the eighteenth century, were exposed, the Apostolic See was able to unite both large and small religious communities with Rome. Reverses were inevitable and many unions were limited to small numbers of faithful. Yet the eastern border of the Catholic Church, rigid since the Middle Ages, became fluid. Several ethnic groups of eastern and southern Slavs, of Maronites, Thomas Christians, and others were joined to the Roman center of the Church.

CHAPTER 126

The Propagation of the Faith in America

The Waning of the Missionary Spirit and the Decline of the Missions

The manifest diminution of the missionary spirit in the seventeenth and eighteenth century contrasted with manifold, often heroic incidents of missionary activity. This fact alone shows clearly that the history of the propagation of faith in America did not follow a simple and transparent line of development, but was instead of a rather complex nature. The gradual flagging of the missionary spirit with its logical consequences goes back to events of the sixteenth century, which must be described briefly if one is to understand and judge fairly the course of the seventeenth and eighteenth century.

A decisive factor was the long struggle between Pius V (d. 1572) and Philip II (d. 1598) for the growing and potentially immense Church in the New World. Philip II demanded the establishment of an "Indian Patriarchate" which was to exist and be considered as a more or less autonomous Church parallel to the Roman Church. The patriarch was to be appointed by the King and reside in Madrid. This demand was emphatically rejected by Pius V, as was the moderated form of a "royal vicariate" for the overseas territories, which was also opposed in 1634 and 1643 by the newly founded Congregation for the Propagation of the Faith. Pius V, on his part, sought ways in which to realize the papal claims and the papal influence in Spanish America. Upon the suggestion and with the collaboration of the Jesuit general Francis Borgia, he formed a congregation of cardinals in 1568 for the ecclesiastic and religious affairs in the overseas territories which — while its structure and goals already corresponded to those of the Congregation of Propaganda to be organized in 1622 — could neither be an effective instrument nor a permanent one. Subsequently Pius V strove in vain to foil the machinations of the Spanish crown, first by dispatching a nuncio and then, with the help of papal visitors composed in the main of Spanish or Hispanophile Jesuits, by at least providing himself with precise knowledge concerning the situation in the American lands.

After the Pope had exhausted all means of subordinating the American Church to papal supremacy, he tried to make the powerful personalities of the New World responsive to the interests of the Church by means of personal letters and briefs. But Pius V could hardly foresee that as of the end of 1568 all his efforts would be in vain. That year an event took place which — as we know today — assumed an essential, indeed decisive significance for the development of the Church in America: the Great Junta of Madrid in 1568.

The *Junta Magna,* which in addition to selected members of the Council of Castile included all the members of the Council of the Indies and other prominent personalities, was to reach two goals which Philip II had in mind: (1) to expand the right of patronage to such an extent that any influence of Rome would be excluded for all titles (Up to that point the patronage had been restricted more or less to the outer organization of the Church, the establishment and borders of the dioceses, the appointment of the bishops and other ecclesiastical dignitaries. From now on the system was to be extended to include not only every representative of the clergy, secular and regular, but also the internal affairs of the Church.); (2) to supplant the Indian Church coming into existence by achieving a breakthrough for a Church which would bear the Spanish imprint.

The implementation of the decisions of the *Junta Magna* was entrusted to the newly appointed viceroy of Peru, Francisco de Toledo, who not only participated in several of the junta's meetings, but was also furnished a set of secret instructions. It was quite certainly a skillful move by Philip II that he selected a personal friend of the Jesuit general Francis Borgia to execute his plans while simultaneously acceding to the latter's repeated requests to permit the first large-scale expedition of twenty-four Jesuits to South America, a prelude to the missionary activities in Spanish America by that order. It can be assumed that Philip II gave his viceroy some valuable instructions regarding missionary work, but most probably of such nature that he, i.e., the government, became the actual guarantor of the conversion of the Indians; the previous secular and regular missionaries turned into mere executive organs.

As was the case for all Spanish laws overseas, it took some considerable time of compromises and transitional solutions until the patronage right was implemented down to its very last ramifications. In the course of the seventeenth and eighteenth century the King and the Council of the Indies received crucial help from theologians as well as jurists. As early as 1600 the Franciscan Miguel Agia, missionary in Guatemala, published his fundamental work on the necessity and importance of the secular arm for missionary work. This work was concretely applied in three expert opinions on the forced labor of the Indians (1604). Among the Augustinians it was the bishop of Santiago de Chile, Gaspar de Villaroel, who traced the line from the right of patronage to regalism in his comprehensive *Govierno Eclesiástico Pacífico,* which first appeared in 1656 and was reprinted in 1738. Actually his work was intended to reduce the tensions between Church and state in America. An extreme partisan of regalism toward the end of the eighteenth century was the Carmelite José Antonio de San Alberto, bishop of Tucumún (Córdoba) and later archbishop of La Plata. With his legalistically oriented pastoral letter of 1786 he published a *Catecismo real,* as the work was called. The scholarly Jesuit Pedro Murillo Velarde compiled the regalist canon law in the more than one thousand pages of his two-volume work *Cursus Juris Canonici Hispani et Indici* in 1743. His fellow Jesuit Diego de Avedaño had taken a more reticent stance in his *Encyclopädie für die Missionspastoral und für das Mission- und Kolonialrecht Thesaurus Indicus* (Antwerp 1668).

But in the final analysis neither theologians nor canonists exerted the decisive influence regarding the extension of the right of patronage; the most prominent part was played by the counsels for the crown. Among them was most prominently, Juan de Solórzano Pereira (1575–1655). He was professor in Salamanca, official of the Curia in Lima, and after his return to Spain a member of the Council of the Indies. The first volume of his *De Indiarum Jure* appeared in 1629, the second in 1639. They are a consistent continuation and development of the basic ideas of Ginés de Sepúlveda, the great adversary of Bartolomé de las Casas. For more than two centuries this work determined the relations between the state and the Church in accordance with Spanish state law. To be sure, it was condemned and put on the Index by Rome in 1642. But since the Council of the Indies did not recognize Rome's decision, it had no validity in Spain and America.

Theory and practice gradually led to extensive legislation which more and more constricted the activities of the Church. The final codification (1791) in the *Recopilación de Leyes de los Reynos de las Indias* represented the finishing touch, predetermined as early as 1771 by the fourth provincial council of Mexico in accordance with the precise instructions of the Council of the Indies.

Regalism or state absolutism proved to be one of the most serious obstacles to the missionary development of the American Church in the seventeenth and eighteenth century. Except for the papal bulls of investiture and some few privileges, all the influence of Rome was practically eliminated. This had a paralyzing and demoralizing effect on the total missionary effort. Just how negative its effect on individual missions was can be gleaned from unpublished documents — unpublished because mention of such matters was not allowed in print — concerning the life of the Apostle of California, Junípero Serra. For this reason his biography, written by his long-time companion and successor Francesco Palou (1787), speaks only of the positive aspects concerning the cooperation of Church and state and of the necessity for military protection of the missions in Mexico as well as California.

Not only was the application of the principle of regalism most injurious to the interests of the Church, but the brutal prevention of establishing an Indian Church turned an already bad situation into a catastrophe, because it was an Indian Church and not one after the Spanish model that was envisioned by the missionaries, especially the Franciscans, soon after the beginning of evangelization, even if neither the goal nor the means were as yet fully recognized.

That the *Junta Magna* of 1568 prevented the Indian Church from coming into being can be shown by several negative features which were clearly recognizable as the result of its decisions. Principal among them is the suppression of all publications relative to the propagation of the faith which stressed the great abilities and good qualities of the Indians. Of the Franciscan writings we mention *Motolinia* (Toribio de Benavente), *Historia de los Indios de la Nueva España,* a basic source, first published 1858 by its discoverer, the Mexican historian J. García Icazbalceta, the *Historia Eclesiástica Indiana* by Gerónimo de Mendieta (also discovered by Icazbalceta; published in 1870), and last but not least the life's work of the scholar Bernardino de Sahagún. Only one of his many works was published during his lifetime, the *Psalmodia christiana* (Mexico 1583). The manuscripts of his other works, his comprehensive *Historia general de las cosas de Nueva España* included, were confiscated and sent to Spain for examination only to disappear in government archives, where they were newly discovered in the nineteenth century.

Whereas Bartolomé de las Casas was able to have a number of his writings printed in 1552, among them the virulent *Brevísima Relación de la destrucción de las Indias,* his other works, especially the lengthy *Historia General de las Indias,* were not published until the nineteenth and twentieth century. His fellow religious, Diego Durán, did not fare any better with his *Historia de las Indias de la Nueva España,* which was completed in 1581. Conditions in other countries, especially Peru and Colombia, were no different from those in Mexico.

The lifework of the Franciscan Pedro Aguado, the first chronicler of Colombia, which did not become well known until the twentieth century, was illuminated by the Colombian historian Juan Friede by means of a comparison of handwritings. In the process he sifted out the principles of government censorship (those of the Church had to be obtained beforehand in each case). They were: (1) everything that diminished the good reputation of the *conquista* or the *conquistadores* had to be suppressed; (2) in treating the missions, all mention of conflicts, especially those with government offices, had to be left out; (3) the Indians had to be represented as a low human race without culture. Authors, including chroniclers of the religious orders, who wanted to obtain the requisite imprimature had to follow these unwritten yet painstakingly enforced rules.

The discrimination against the Indians carried out according to J. Friede by government censorship, shows clearly that it was aimed against an essential element in the creation of an Indian Church: the education of indigenous clergy. Indeed the Council of Mexico had already prohibited the ordination of Indians in 1555, but in a more general context (in connection with the Muslims [*moros*], mestizos, and mulattos), but at the Third Council of Lima in 1567/68 the prohibition already referred exclusively to the newly converted Indians.

Judging from the text of the council, precluding priesthood for the Indians appeared to have been a temporary measure (*hoc tempore*). In point of fact it was to last until the eighteenth century. The Franciscans found this out in their college of Tlaltelolco (Mexico), which had been established by Bishop Zumárraga in 1536 primarily for the education of a native clergy. The various parties, those among the laity, the secular and the regular clergy — even among the Franciscans — who were hostile to the Indians continued to hold the upper hand and after the 1560s the formerly flourishing school was merely vegetating. The same experience was had by the Jesuits working in the country since 1572. Under the spiritual leadership of Juan de Tobar, who was born in Mexico, they tried to get permission from the Jesuit general to establish a college for the education of Indian priests. After fifteen years of trying, their plan was categorically rejected. The final decision by General Claudius Acquaviva had been indicated earlier by the guideline of the junta of 1568.

In this connection the efforts of the Propaganda, i.e., of its first secretary Francesco Ingoli, are deeply moving. In letters and petitions to popes, cardinals, and generals of the orders he gave the most cogent arguments for the ordination of Indian priests in America, but the power of the Council of the Indies could not be broken even by the Popes.

In his ideas of regalism Philip II was by no means guided by anti-Church sentiments. He was deeply convinced of the divine mission which he thought to have been given especially for the formation of the American Church. The bishops nominated by him were all well educated, pious and apostolic men, as were the visitors of the orders. The building of churches and monasteries, of hospitals and schools was supported. Beyond that he tried to promote everywhere the veneration and reverence for the Holy See and the Popes. Thus we witness the paradox that reverence for the Pope was nowhere greater than in the American territories, where practically all papal influence was eliminated. It was well known that his opponent, Pius V, had the implementation of the Council of Trent close to his heart. So in order to keep him from making demands regarding the American Church, Philip II in a letter of 12 July 1564 had ordered the implementation of the Tridentine rules. Consequently, Archbishop Alonso de Montúfar as early as 1565 convened the Second Council of Mexico, which was to promulgate, adapt, and reacknowledge the Council of Trent. The Third Council of Lima in 1567/68 served the same purpose for South America.

While the Council of Trent was a blessing for the European Church, it was a double-edged sword for the budding Indian Church. Quite aside from the fact that — as a result of the actions of Charles V and Philip II — America, in spite of the efforts by individual bishops, was not represented in Trent and its problems were nowhere discussed, the centralist tendencies beginning at this point could not but have an impeding and in the long run seriously damaging effect. The greatest damage was probably in discontinuing the already initiated organic growth of an Indian Church; the original main ideas concerning missionary work were discarded with noticeable haste. The first generation of missionaries had in mind the example of the original Church; the dogma of the Church as the mystical body of Christ was impressed very quickly on their Christians. The message was deeply rooted in the Holy Scripture and the doctrines of the Fathers. That the dogma was adapted especially to the intellectual capacity of the Indians, is supported by the expression Theologia Indiana. In the sixteenth century this referred to the instructional books and tracts in the native languages. After the sixteenth century this intellectual attitude receded more and more, making way for a purely European-Spanish direction, for instance by translating European catechisms (like the one by Bellarmine) and relegating the Holy Scripture and the Fathers to a position of lesser importance.

In the exterior realm it was primarily the execution of the Tridentine rules concerning the ministry of regulars and their relationship to the bishops which had appalling consequences, especially since both sides, bishops as well as the orders, were somehow right. On the side of the bishops were the regulations of the Council of Trent, at whose inception, however, no one had thought of missionary conditions. On the side of the mendicant orders were experience in missionary practice and the immense distances of the sees. It was self-evident that the increase in the number of secular clerics would place the regular Spanish ministry in their hands. But the conditions were different in the often remote and extensive *doctrinas* (missionary stations) of the Indians. Their creation and expansion throughout was the work of the mendicant orders, who were executing their priestly functions on the basis of a papal bull of Hadrian VI (1522) known by its abbreviation *Omnimoda.* These privileges were reaffirmed again and again by successive Popes, such as Pius V in 1567.

When efforts by the bishops resulted in an increase in the number of secular clerics in the second half of the sixteenth century, and the positions in the cathedral chapters and parishes heretofore administered by missionaries were occupied by them, the secular clergy pushed more and more into the well-established *doctrinas* of the Indians. The transfer of the *doctrinas* had already begun in the sixteenth century. In spite of resistance by some orders the change initially took place without resulting in great damage, especially since knowledge of the native language and suitability for serving in the *doctrinas* were required of the secular clerics as well. Only after the great councils of Lima and Mexico was the extent of the transfer of *doctrinas* to the secular clergy increased and the earlier missionaries with all their experience and linguistic ability were shunted into the large religious houses in the cities. The great disadvantages of this practice began to have a real effect in the seventeenth century. The most fatal actions in this connection were probably those of Bishop Juan de Palafox y Mendoza (1600–1659), bishop of Puebla and visitor general of Mexico since 1639 (in 1612 he was viceroy of Mexico until the arrival of the newly appointed viceroy; he ejected the archbishopric of Mexico and returned to Spain in 1646, where he died as bishop of Osma). Barely having arrived in Mexico, he already submitted to the King an indictment against the Franciscans charging them with usurpation of jurisdiction. The same year he issued his first pastoral letter to the clergy of Puebla, in which he stressed the right of ministry on the part of the secular clergy for the total ministry. In 1642 the Dominican Luis de Orduna sent a defense to the King. But because of the bishop's authority all the *doctrinas* of the Franciscans were soon transferred to secular clerics. Other bishops in Mexico, and South America followed this example. By these actions Palafox had inflicted upon the American Church what was perhaps the worst possible irreparable damage. This becomes clear if one takes into account the fact that the mendicant orders, especially the Franciscans, maintained in their *doctrinas,* frequently serving more than twenty thousand Indians, relatively small religious houses with only three to five priests. Only one of these, the *doctrinero,* was paid from government funds, while the others, as auxiliary staff, depended upon the Indians for their livelihood. While the secular priests did use the religious houses as their parish houses, they had no auxiliary staff available to them.

The conflicts between the bishops and the Jesuits, resounding worldwide, were concerned with jurisdictional issues, but were primarily centered around the issue of the tithe which the bishop demanded from the missions' property.

In view of the Tridentine reforms and state absolutism, Palafox acted correctly. Privately he had great respect for the Indians and their abilities; he provided a thorough education for the clergy by establishing the first Tridentine seminary in the New World, combining with it the first public library in Mexico. But Palafox overestimated his secular clergy, to whom he respectfully referred in his first pastoral letter as "Venerable Congregación de San Pedro" they could not take the place of the missionaries of the mendicant orders in the *doctrinas,* especially in the barely accessible ones. Many a parish was soon dissolved as such or rarely visited by a priest, and the unadorned but attractive religious and parish houses fell into ruin.

The problem can be illustrated by the following figures: in the sixteenth century 63.16 percent of the appointed bishops were from religious orders, in the seventeenth century it was still 50. 81 percent, but in the eighteenth century it was only 24.25 percent. The development reached a climax of sorts under Bishop Palafox even though it did not actually prevail in the more remote areas. Yet as late as 1722 the nuncio in Madrid received an instruction from Rome for the archbishop of Mexico concerning the transfer of Indian parishes to secular clerics.

The above figures are not intended to represent a value judgment. Among both types of clerics there were superior missionaries. Among the bishops of the secular clergy we should mention the contemporary of Bishop Palafox, Alonso de la Peña Montenegro (1596–1687, bishop of Quito). He, too, looked after his rights vis-à-vis the regulars, the Franciscans and the Jesuits, but without onesidedness and imprudence. His *Itinerario para parochos de Indios* (Madrid 1668) had an enduring influence throughout the Spanish colonial period. Its tenor is a sense of missionary responsibility and great respect for the Indians, although a strong canonistic-casuistic direction and a narrow application of the Tridentine regulations for the Indian mission are also noticeable.

In the initial stages of missionary work by the secular clergy the lack of linguistic knowledge had an important negative effect. But this was improved by the establishment of teaching chairs for the study of native languages at the large universities of Mexico and Lima and later on in Guatemala and other places; missionaries of the secular clergy produced some outstanding linguistic experts. It was precisely their knowledge of languages and their solidarity with the people which enabled them to participate in extraordinary measure in missionary work and to serve the bishops as visitors or interpreters. Some also fought paganism in their role as writers.

The displacement of the regular clergy gave rise to many a quarrel, especially on the issue of language. The Hispanicizing decrees of the Council of the Indies, applied to the Indian settlements as well, were for the most part without effect because no financial means were allocated for their execution, but especially because the priests in the Indian parishes, both the regular and the secular priests, but above all the mestizos, resisted the decrees most strenuously. Most deleterious was the decision by the archbishop of Mexico, Antonio de Lorenzana (d. 1804 as cardinal-archbishop of Toledo), in a pastoral letter to require the acquisition of Spanish for the benefit of the Indians and the elevation of religious life in Mexico.

The character of Portuguese Brazil was completely different from that of the Spanish territories. The Spanish had occupied and settled whole countries, whereas the Portuguese for a long time limited themselves to individual coastal areas. They did not advance into the interior of the country until the seventeenth century and then only did so gradually. The establishment of bishoprics reflects both the colonial and the ecclesiastical expansion. After 1551 Bahia was the only bishopric for over a century. In 1676 it was joined by Rio de Janeiro, Olinda-Recife, and Maranhão; in 1745 by São Paulo and Marianna (Minas Gerais); in 1781 by Goiaz and Cuiabá. Missionary work, too, had initially limited itself to the coastal areas, there Franciscans and Dominicans, Jesuits and Capuchins, but also Benedictines and Carmelites were active in the seventeenth and eighteenth century. In order to ameliorate the conflicts between the individual orders there was a rough jurisdictional division of certain areas between the Jesuits, Franciscans, Capuchins, and Carmelites. In the larger monasteries and colleges of the coastal areas the orders also educated native priests, sons of Portuguese settlers, mestizos, and some few Negroes (but no Indians), all of whom demonstrated a higher degree of adaptability and linguistic ability than the European missionaries.

Aside from the effects of patronage, injurious in Brazil as well, missionary work there was hampered in the seventeenth century by the Dutch occupation in the north and the French occupation in the south. But the greatest disaster was slavery. The Dutch occupation (with its center in Pernambuco) united all forces in the country, governmental and ecclesiastical, Portuguese and native, in a common defense. Yet the prevailing attitude toward slavery became a significantly divisive element in missionary work. The Franciscans sought to protect the Indian villages (*Aldeias*) which they served against the Portuguese slaveholders, whereas the Jesuits under the leadership of the most eloquent Antonio Vieira (d. 1697) pursued their fight against slavery in Brazil as well as in Portugal primarily in the public forum. Neither order achieved any lasting success. In 1640 the Jesuits were even driven out of São Paulo. They were not allowed to return until 1653, and then only after they promised not to oppose the slave expeditions of the Paulists or *Bandeirantes* inasmuch as the latter were concentrating on the Indians in the reductions of Guairá, which belonged to the Jesuit province of Paraguay. A royal edict of 1758 tried to put a definitive end to Indian slavery although the enslavement of Negroes continued until the end of the nineteenth century.

Under these conditions it is not surprising that the first synod in Brazil was not convened until 1707. On this occasion Archbishop Sebastian da Vida published the first constitutions of the archdiocese of Bahia after he had become personally familiar with the church situation in the country through laborious visitations. The second synod of Brazil did not take place until 1888. The great significance of the *Constitutiones* of 1707 lies in the fact that for the first time the total religious life of Brazil, down to the last details, was dealt with and regulated in 1,318 paragraphs, giving thought to the Indians and Negroes in the appropriate places with the intention of securing their religious life. The constitutions were printed in Lisbon (1719) and Coimbra (1720), but in 1750 Marquis de Pombal began his activities, which were to be equally disastrous for Brazil.

The Revival of the Missionary Spirit and the Expansion of the Missions

The extant religious missions in America again and again produced prominent men in the course of the seventeenth and eighteenth centuries, so that the orders cannot be said to have been decaying. The original missionary spirit was revived by new foundations and orientations.

The Franciscans

The rejection of an Indian Church by Philip II and the Council of the Indies damaged the Franciscan mission more than others, as did the gradual transfer of the already established *doctrinas* to the secular clergy. To be sure, the Franciscans retained a number of *doctrinas,* even in Mexico, after the actions of such prelates as Bishop Palafox. Propagation of the faith among the remaining pagan Indians was both started and continued, albeit with great sacrifices. But it took Antonio Llinás to bring about a true reorientation. Born in Mallorca in 1635, he joined the Franciscan order of strict observance and went to Mexico in 1664. After he worked as a lecturer in philosophy and theology for ten years, he became guardian in Valladolid in 1674. He did his duty and pursued music as a hobby. But the stricter observance of the rules of the order and devotion to apostolic work (popular missions) led to his being elected in 1679 as representative to the upcoming chapter general. At the beginning of 1680 he arrived in Spain and used his time until the chapter of Toledo to prepare his lifework, the foundation of mission colleges. For soon after he began his apostolic work, Llinás recognized that the required apostolic manpower could no longer be obtained from the large monasteries in the cities of Mexico, most of which had been in existence for more than one hundred years. In 1682 the general of his order agreed to the statutes of these mission colleges and designated the monastery of the Holy Cross in Querétaro, Mexico, for the planned new foundation; he allowed Llinás to recruit twenty-four missionaries in the Spanish provinces. Innocent XI approved the statutes through a brief of 8 May 1682, the Congregation for the Propagation of the Faith did so by decree of 15 June 1682. The Holy Office also assigned the necessary faculties for the apostolic work.

The constitutions of the mission colleges, probably authored by the general of the order, José Ximénez Samaniego, but derived from Llinás' experiences, were based on the perception that true apostolic work is only possible in conjunction with the strictest observance. The monastery of the Holy Cross in Querétaro, the cradle of the mission colleges, was already a monastery of recollection (*recolección*) and strict observance. As were later mission colleges, it was released from the provincial structure and placed directly under the commissioners of the order in Mexico. The college was to be an institution for training in the missionary parish work and in the languages of the natives. It was planned to enable the missionaries to retreat there for longer or shorter periods of time for the purpose of contemplation. The rule for the new Indian missions was that the missionaries would only work there until the Indians were truly converted and could be left to the care of the secular clerics. Because of the disputes between the native Spanish regulars and the Creoles, the mission colleges sought to refill their ranks with new recruits from Spain, although in principle Creoles and members of other provinces in the country were not excluded. This attitude with its attendant consequences prompted the founder of the college of Querétaro to return to Spain at the end of 1684 in order to save the endangered foundation. The superiors both of the order and the Church renewed their approbation. But Llinás did not go back to Mexico because he was entrusted with a new challenge in Spain which he had not foreseen, but nonetheless accepted with pleasure: the founding of similar mission colleges in Spain, which were to secure a rising generation, grown up and already schooled in the missionary spirit of the overseas colleges. The colleges in Spain were also to take over the task of popular mission there. Their title, *Colegios de Propaganda Fide,* is surprising and can be traced to the recognition of the foundation in Querétaro by the Propaganda. They were accorded great esteem but no more. The mission colleges were also subject to the Spanish right of patronage. When Llinás was negotiating in Rome in 1685/86, the Spanish ambassador received a letter from the Council of the Indies requesting him to make sure that no patronage rights were violated. It stipulated that Llinás was not to confer about the conversion of the Indians because the King himself, contrary to opinion, in Rome, had manifested the greatest concern for the missionary work. All documents written in Rome prior to and at this time were to be submitted again to the Council of the Indies for their appraisal.

The most important mission colleges were founded in Mexico. The monastery of the Holy Cross continued to be the parent monastery, as it were. The missionaries initially worked in the pagan enclaves of the country, among the Otomis near Querétaro, the Tlaxcaltecs near Puebla, the Coles and Lacandones in the Verapaz, and among the Licques Indians of Honduras. To these were soon added the Talamanca mission in the southeast of Costa Rica and missionary work in what is now Texas. The mission in the Verapaz and among other Indian tribes of Guatemala prompted the establishment of the second mission college of the "Crucified Christ" in the city of Guatemala. Another foundation, "Our Dear Lady of Guadelupe" in Zacatecas, received royal acknowledgment in 1704. Emanating from Zacatecas, the southern stretch of land in the Gulf of Mexico known as Nuevo Santander was successfully missionized. In 1733 the college of San Fernando was founded in the capital; it was confirmed by the King in 1733. Since the Discalced also opened a similar mission college (1733), designed to take over the mission in the barely accessible mountains of Zimapán. Mexico now had five colleges for the propagation of the faith.

Mexico also became the point of departure for the establishment of other colleges in South America. In Ocopa in the south of the archbishopric of Lima the Colegio di Santa Rosa was founded (1724). From 1779 to 1783 it was charged with the mission on the island of Chiloé and later on some additional ones, among them those of the expelled Jesuits. In Colombia the colleges of Popayán (founded 1747 in Quito and relocated 1749 in Popayán) and Cali (1756) were set up. In

Tarija (Bolivia) the local college took over the mission among the Chiriguanos in the Chaco, stagnant for over two hundred years. Their apostle was the venerable Franciscus del Pilar, who, living among them as helper and servant of all from 1765 until his death in 1803, gradually overcame their resistance. By 1810 the mission comprised twenty-two stations with 16,425 Christians. In 1756 the college of Chilláin (Chile) was founded; after 1767 it was in a position to take over the majority of the missions of the expelled Jesuits. The last college to be founded in the eighteenth century was San Carlos on the Paraná (1784); it was designed especially for the conversion of the Indians in the southern Chaco and in Paraguay. The historian of the Franciscan order justifiably speaks of "that glorious new epoch of the eighteenth century which begins with the entrance of the apostolic colleges into the vineyard of the Lord" (L. Lemmens). The new missionary spirituality is especially well reflected in the life of two men.

One of the founders of the Mexican colleges was Antonio Margil (1657–1726). He spent forty-three years in Central America and not only founded the colleges of Guatemala and Zacatecas, but to a large extent put his stamp on the spirit of the colleges. He worked as a missionary in all the areas of Central America, to Talamancas in Costa Rica, and on the other side up to Texas, where he spent the period from 1716 to 1722. After his sermons got him a firm foothold somewhere, he hurried on, leaving his successors to consolidate his achievements. The apostle of California, Junípero Serra (1713–84), belonged to the mission college of San Fernando in Mexico. In 1750 he left the professorship of his native university (Palma de Mallorca) and at first worked among the Indians of the Sierra Gorda and after 1767 as superior of the Franciscan mission in California, initially in Baja California, where the Franciscans of the colleges took over the missions of the expelled Jesuits. Finally, he pioneered the mission in present-day California, where even now a number of Franciscan names are a reminder of the modest beginnings of Indian missions. In a constant fight with regalism, dominant even in California, Serra succeeded in establishing a chain of missionary stations all the way to San Francisco. The state of California has placed a statue of its actual colonizer in the capital in Washington.

By the middle of the eighteenth century and the expulsion of the Spanish by the Americans the mission colleges had — with few exceptions — taken the place of the earlier missionaries of the Franciscan provinces in the newly opened missions in the north, and in the states of New Mexico, Texas, Arizona, and California (later annexed by the United States). The spirit of these colleges could only be broken by force, in Mexico by their abolition in 1827, somewhat later in other countries. Just a few of them continued on into modern days, incorporated in the reorganized Franciscan provinces.

The Jesuits

A new impetus to the missionary spirit was expected from the Society of Jesus, which arrived in America relatively late. But government and Church alike wanted the Jesuits above all to serve the Spaniards, or rather the Creoles, especially in the field of education, where they indeed earned their greatest merits, indirectly of benefit to the Indian mission as well. Subaltern officials and the secular clergy were educated in their schools. The dispatch of the Jesuits to America met with great opposition in Spain and indeed even within their own order. Thus the Jesuits only gradually grew into their role as Indian missionaries. Even in the vice-kingdom of Peru, where they had arrived in 1568 and where the propagation of the faith had developed most intensively, it was not until 1576 that the provincial chapter of Cuzco took over the large missionary center of Juli on Lake Titicaca, sending the first missionaries there in the same year. Yet at the colleges of Lima and Cuzco the Jesuits had already worked successfully among the Indians in those areas. The refusal to take over their own *doctrinas* or Indian parishes was probably based on the fear that this would tie them too closely to the civil and ecclesiastic authorities.

In the following period Juli not only became a model of Jesuit missionary work on Lake Titicaca, but a universal center of Peru. The missions of the Maynas (on the upper Amazon in eastern Ecuador), among the Moxos (in present-day Bolivia), and especially in Paraguay had their roots there. The Chiquitos mission in Bolivia, too, was indirectly connected with Juli.

This expansion of the Jesuit colleges and missions in South America resulted in the formation of more and more provinces. What gave these areas, especially the missions among the Indians during the seventeenth and eighteenth century, their very own character was the steady increase of non-Spanish missionaries. Jesuits from countries under Spanish dominion, such as Italians, Flemish, and Walloons were the first to be admitted. Then, toward the end of the seventeenth century, subjects of the Habsburg lands received permission to travel abroad (1678), and finally others as well, such as Germans and Swiss. The major portion of the non-Spanish missionaries went to the reductions in Paraguay. According to A. Huonder, the province of Paraguay, separated from Peru in 1606, included about one hundred twenty-five German-speaking missionaries, most of them in the reductions. The reason for this was not only the fact that the foreign Jesuits in faraway Paraguay were at greater remove from supervision of Spanish officials, but also that their labor and skills were highly esteemed. They excelled as prominent architects and musicians, as ethnologists; very much in demand were the German and Flemish brothers who were highly skilled in the trades but were also working as artists and apothecaries. All of this was of great use to the reductions, but caused growing antipathy among the Spanish population in the surrounding countryside. Immense herds of mules and cows provoked the envy of the urban Spaniards. The major export articles were Paraguay tea, the production rights of which was granted to the Indians by a royal cedula on 1645, and woven goods. The tragic outcome of the courageous fight against the slave hunters of São Paulo, leading, in the end, to Portugal's claiming a number of reductions in the present Brazilian state of Paraná contributed significantly to the decline of the large-scale "Indian State" of the Jesuits. The order by the Jesuit general to obey in every way the regulations of the Portuguese and finally the cession to Portugal of seven reductions, together with all their territory (stipulated by the Treaty of Madrid in 1750), had a disastrous effect. The missionaries were forced to abandon their Indians when the latter, deprived of help from the fathers and the other reductions, were defeated in battle by a Portuguese-Spanish alliance. This completely undermined the Indians' confidence in their missionaries. The Jesuits, frequently with great ceremony, had assumed the legal protection over the Indians because they knew all too well that their Christians were sold without mercy on the slave markets of Brazil, especially since they were more valuable to the sellers than other Indians by virtue of their skills in agriculture and the crafts. In 1768, when the Jesuits, together with about one hundred thousand Indians, were driven out of their remaining thirty reductions, there was no resistance on the part of the Indians.

Closely connected with these events was probably the downfall of the social utopias which had initially been nurtured by older Jesuits and then taken root among the Indians, leading to some syncretistic movements among them. In the end, this undermined the vitality of the Indians of Paraguay and the surrounding reductions. Adding the totally paternalistic attitude of the missionaries, which had after all prevailed for 150 years, one can understand in historical terms the extent of the tragedy inherent in the downfall of such an idealistic undertaking. But one must also know that the missionaries of other orders, especially the Franciscans, were no more successful. By 1802 the thirty former Jesuit reductions contained a mere 30,116 inhabitants. A large number had retreated into the forests.

The arrival of the Jesuits in the vast areas of New Granada (Colombia) and Venezuela occurred relatively late and they had few missions there. But early on they built a large college in the port city of Cartagena, the point of entry for vast areas of South America and at the same time the largest place of reshipment in the slave trade. At least two names should be mentioned among the missionaries of this college as an example of the apostolate among the black slaves. Alonso de Sandoval (1571–1652) was not only the actual organizer of this ministry, but also the first and only theoretician of the Negro mission in America. In 1627 a Spanish-language version of his work appeared in Seville. The thirty-two chapters of the first part of his *De Instauranda Aethiopum salute* dealt with Africa and its cultures, primarily those between the islands of Cape Verde and Angola, from where most of the slaves were coming. The second part describes the miserable conditions of the Negro slaves; the third part treats the qualities and methods required for this special kind of ministry; the fourth part gives the reasons which call for Jesuits above all to dedicate themselves to this task. Sandoval's pupil and successor, the Catalan Pedro Claver (1581–1659), sought to ameliorate the social conditions of his charges as much as possible. He secured the privilege for Negroes of attending Mass in the college church of the Jesuits. He defended them before the courts and the Inquisition. By taking on the role of "slave of the slaves" day after day he was protesting the practice of slavery.

The Jesuits did not come to the vice-kingdom of Mexico until 1572. Here, too, their principal service was initially to the white population. By and by colleges were built in Mexico, Puebla, Oaxaca, and Valladolid, the great novitiate of Tapozotlán, the seminary of San Ildofonso in Mexico, and the residences in Guadalajara, Pátzcuaro and Vera Cruz. For some time there was no actual Indian mission, a fact which was deplored in contemporary documents by those Jesuits who were eager to missionize. An order by the Jesuit General Acquaviva was required to initiate Indian missionary work of more sizeable proportions; this started in 1584 in the northwestern part of the country. The work not only comprised the Tarahumara Indians, but also the tribes of Sonora and the Pimeria Alta and spread from there across the area of present-day Arizona to Southern California. The most prominent figure among these Jesuit missionaries was a native of Trent, Eusebio

Francisco Kino (1645–1711), trained in that southern German province not only to become one of the greatest missionaries, but also a superior explorer and cartographer. The world owes him the first precise knowledge of California. But Father Kino was foremost a missionary and organizer of the far-flung northeastern missions, architect and builder of mission stations and churches. He was so modest about his mission theory that it was not discovered until very recently; it has yet to be evaluated. His greatest worry was the dearth of suitable missionaries; his requests for additional missionaries, especially from German-speaking countries, were fulfilled. Yet the shortage persisted. In his annual report to the general of 1 December 1751 the Swiss provincial Johann Anton Balthasar mentioned that of the 624 members of the Mexican province there were only 111 missionaries available for the territories of the northwest and California.

Contrary to Hispanic America, the Jesuit mission in Brazil (after 1503) and Maranhão (after 1627) was more limited in its development, though not for lack of manpower. The Portuguese homeland allowed neither the establishment of a university nor of a press. Industries whose development the Jesuits had aided were restricted or prohibited altogether lest the colonies become too strong. The predominant Jesuit of the seventeenth century was Antonio Vieira (1608–97). His parents had brought him to Brazil as a little boy; in 1623 he joined the Society of Jesus. Having worked as Portuguese legate in various countries, he returned to Brazil as a missionary in 1652. Because of his fair and humane partisanship for the Indians he and the other Jesuits of the college of Belem were deported to Portugal by the colonists. Some individual doctrines in his prophetic, utopian works primarily in his *Esperanças de Portugal, Quinto Imperio do Mundo* and the *Historio de futuro,* resulted in his being jailed by the Inquisition after a trial lasting four years. A change of government brought about his release in 1669. Vieira viewed the widely expanded system of patronage as the instrument willed by God for the final realm of the Messiah, the fifth realm of the eschatology coinciding with the universal rule of Portugal. While he was in Rome to justify himself from 1669 to 1675, he was removed from the jurisdiction of the Portuguese Inquisition, but he rejected all ecclesiastical offices offered to him. After twenty years of banishment he returned to the Maranhão mission, where he died at the age of eighty-nine at the college of Bahia. The strength of the Society of Jesus in Brazil now seemed to be spent. The discovery of the gold mines of Minas Gerais and the coffee plantations of São Paulo no longer offered the same possibilities for missionizing as before. In 1759 the Jesuits were expelled by Pombal.

After an auspicious start, the wars between the Iroquois and Hurons and the killing of the Jesuits working among them (1642–49) brought an end to the mission in the French colonies. Only after 1665, when Carignan secured Canada for the French, was missionary work able to be resumed in earnest. The Jesuits joined in it until the Peace of Paris in 1763, which relinquished Canada to England. During these 100 years they furnished 320 missionaries, most of them for the five Indian villages built after the fashion of Paraguay. As a result of an agreement between the Jesuits and the French Capuchins (1632), the latter worked in Nova Scotia while the Sulpicians, the Paris Missionaries, and the Recollect Franciscans supported the work of the Jesuits in Canada proper.

During the Indian Wars a number of Catholic Indians had been pushed south and southeast. This occasioned the great explorations of the Jesuits, foremost the ones by Jacques Marquette (1637–75), who reached the Mississippi in 1673 and worked among the Illinois and Miami Indians. Other Frenchmen, such as de la Salle, among whose companions was the Franciscan Louis Hennepin (d. 1701), succeeded in exploring the entire stream to its estuary. The Jesuits restricted their mission work to the Indian tribes in the northern areas with whom they were familiar, while others, especially those of the Foreign Missions of Paris, were active farther in the south. None of these groups was truly successful. In spite of all efforts Louisiana was not given its own church organization; it was under the jurisdiction of Quebec until the eighteenth century.

Other Orders

The Dominicans were the first missionaries of Peru; from there they spread all over South America. The two saints of this order in Peru can be considered as programmatic symbols: Rosa of Lima (1586–1617), a Creole, member of the Third Order and example of a contemplative, mystical life, and Martín de Porras (or Porres, 1569–1639), a mulatto from Lima trained in the art of healing, a Dominican brother who gave himself in charitable love to all, regardless of class or race.

The Dominicans also maintained the Indian missions established in the sixteenth century and further expanded them during the next two centuries. They achieved special merit in the promotion of higher education. In addition to the state universities in Lima and Mexico City, founded in the sixteenth century, they operated the University of Santo Domingo from 1538 into the eighteenth century. In 1620 they initiated a *studium generale* in Guatemala which was expanded into a full-fledged university as the Real y Pontificia Universidad de San Carlos, recognized in 1676. Following this, two more universities were founded: the Universities of Santiago de Chile (1685) and Quito (1683). The seventeenth century also marked the beginning of a most quarrelsome competition with the Jesuits, who were able to base their claim on papal briefs similar to those of the Dominicans. As a result, places such as Bogotá, Quito, and Santiago de Chile soon had a Dominican and a Jesuit university. The Dominican monastery of San Juan de Letrán in Cuba was expanded into a university in the eighteenth century, as was their Colegio Seminario of Caracas. In some fashion all these institutions were in the service of the Indian mission because the secular as well as the regular clergy received their education and their training in the native languages there.

The humanistic aspect of missionary work in the sixteenth century was primarily represented by the Augustinian Hermits. Alonso de la Vera Cruz was the first professor of theology in the New World (University of Mexico); even his first lectures in 1553/54 dealt with the Indian problem in the spirit of Las Casas and with the weapons of a theologian schooled in Salamanca. The fact that succeeding generations of Augustinian Hermits of the seventeenth century were filled by his spirit is demonstrated by the chronicles of Fray Antonio de la Calanchal and Francisco Romero. The latter, a Creole Augustinian from Peru and itinerant missionary of South America, wrote the very moving *Llanto Sagrado de la América Meridional,* printed in Milan in 1693. It was a fearless indictment of the Spanish policy of exploitation of the Indians and was immediately confiscated by the Inquisition. In spite of their efforts Romero and the missionaries recruited by him did not succeed in converting the Tames Indians in the province of Popayán in present-day Colombia. At the beginning of the seventeenth century the wilderness of Raquira became the site of the first hermitage, Our Lady de la Candelaria, founded by the reform movement of the Barefoot Augustinians (Recollects). It became the focus of renewed missionary zeal and religious renewal for Colombia, Venezuela, Central America, and later on for Peru and Mexico. But the Philippines ultimately were to become the most fertile missionary field for them.

The last Spanish missionaries in the Americas of the seventeenth century, the Capuchins, initially went to what is now Venezuela. The Council of the Indies had been unwilling to admit yet another order to America. But the lay brother Francisco de Pamplona, formerly General Don Tiburcio de Redín (with excellent connections to Philip IV), prevailed in having missionary work initiated first in Darien and then in Venezuela proper (1650). The first Capuchins did not establish large monasteries nor did they accept novices from the ranks of the Creoles. Thus they maintained closer ties with their Spanish homeland provinces than the other orders. They also sought to implement a new method of missionary style. From the north they advanced to the yet unconverted Indians, establishing small houses and gradually moving farther and farther south and southeast. Thanks to their unobtrusive method they were able to survive the tumult of the times.

It is a striking fact that the participation of the nuns in the task of conversion in America has either been omitted or at best just cursorily described. Remarks by early writers permit us to conclude that the problem of women's education was indeed tackled, since Bishop Juan de Zumárraga, to whom Queen Isabella had sent help in the persons of tertiaries (*Beatas*) in 1531 and 1535. Toward the end of the seventeenth century there were twenty-two convents in Mexico City alone and ten in Puebla. All of these convents counted among their pupils Spanish, Creole, and Indian girls. Such convents were also founded exclusively for Indian girls, daughters of caciques, among them the convent of Corpus Christi in Mexico (1724). Emanating from here, the Indian convents of Cosamalsapán (1737) and Oaxaca (1782) were established with the particular aim of avoiding tensions among the races. Indian women had never been denied admittance to the orders. The provincial synod of Charcas (Sucre, Bolivia) of 1629 indeed stressed that all sisters would enjoy equal rights in the convents. It emphasized that half-castes were to be accepted among the officiating nuns, "cum apud Deum fides non genus in pretio sit." In the more distant provinces missionaries probably followed the example of the *Beatas* of the sixteenth century, founding *Beaterios* with the daughters of Indians. Only a thorough study will be able to show the extent of the contribution to the cultural life of the individual countries made by the convents.

The alleviation of misery and disease was the goal not only of all the religious orders but also of the native societies, such as the numerous brotherhoods, founded for Spaniards, Indians, and Negroes. Social aid in all of Brazil was taken over primarily by the brotherhood of the *Misericordia,* whose model dates back to 1498 in Lisbon. The Hospitalers of Saint John of God, active in Mexico since 1603, especially excelled in the nursing of the sick. From Mexico they spread out to the Central and South American countries, establishing their hospitals and gaining the recognition of all levels of the populace in the service of lepers and those sick with the plague. In Mexico alone sixteen of their number died during the plague of 1736. Long before this, in 1594, Clement VIII had granted the privileges of hospitalers to a society in Mexico founded by Bernardino Alvarez. They were named Hippolites, after the first hospital they built in Mexico dedicated to Saint Hippolyte. After the first vow dedicating themselves to the care of all the sick, they also took the vow of obedience and after 1700 also that of celibacy.

The order of the Bethlemites, originated in Guatemala, maintained its own character. It went back to Pedro de San José Betancur (1616–67), who initially undertook the education of children but then included the care of convalescents, especially of strangers and transients. After Betancur's early death his helpers continued his work. They founded an order of lay brothers which was recognized by the Pope in 1672 and spread surprisingly fast to Mexico and South America. Toward the end of the eighteenth century the order deteriorated and was dissolved in 1820. At this time it still operated ten hospitals in the Mexican and twenty-two in the Peruvian provinces. A similar foundation for women, started by Maria Anna del Galdo in Guatemala (1688), did not grow very much and was also discontinued in 1820.

Every one of these hospitaler orders had physicians trained in the native country. The fact that racial discrimination had no place in the treatment of the sick constitutes a great part of its missionary importance.

The Enlightenment and Its Consequences

A fair evaluation of the Enlightenment in Latin America is a difficult undertaking even now. The intellectual history of Spain and Portugal of the eighteenth century as a period of obscurantism and Scholastic rigidity has received scant attention up to the most recent past. This holds true even more so in regard to America, little of whose intellectual life in the colonial period is known in Europe. As a consequence, historical research has shown little interest in the cultural phenomena in which the missionaries had a significant part. The first generation of missionaries in Mexico, such as the Bishops Juan de Zumárraga and Vasco de Quiroga, were guided by contemporary humanists: Zumárraga by Erasmus, Quiroga by Thomas More. This intellectual attitude continued to be the determinant, especially for the missionary work. Two institutions were always connected with European intellectual life: the libraries, especially those of the monasteries, and the universities.

Although there are only a few monographs and precious few particulars or even inventories of books from the earliest times, references in letters, chronicles, and books relating to libraries manifest two facts: 1. their collections were comprehensive; theological works most surely predominated, but there was no dearth of works from classical and modern literature; 2. new European publications, even from distant or Protestant cities, reached the Spanish American countries relatively quickly.

The universities were decisive elements of intellectual life. Toward the end of the colonial period there were twenty-three universities in Spanish America. Seven of them were comprehensive state universities, probably with a faculty of theology, but — just as in Spain — operated by secular and regular priests. In addition to the state universities there were sixteen other ones, recognized by the state, with only faculties of philosophy and theology. Fourteen of these were led by the various orders, two of them by bishops. The preponderance of higher education was undeniably in the hands of the state universities, in which laymen had the major influence.

Libraries and universities prepared the way for the advance of new ideas and the advance of the Enlightenment with its positive and negative elements. The Jesuit college of Saint Paul in Lima contained the collected works of Isaac Newton, as well as histories and publications of the Académie des sciences and the Prussian Academy in Berlin. The major works of one of the most important forerunners of positive Enlightenment, the Benedictine Benito Gerónimo Feijóo y Montenegro (d. 1764), the *Teatro crítico universal* in eight volumes and the *Cartas Eruditas* in six volumes were to be found not only in the college libraries but also in the private libraries of the professors. Even works by the English deists were widely represented in the libraries. The Latin works of the German philosopher Christian Wolff could be found in several libraries of Latin America.

These books were eagerly studied everywhere and used in lectures at the universities and colleges. Wherever the well-educated Creoles, even missionaries at remote stations, manifested familiarity with the intellectual currents of Europe, they owed it to the education they had received at the universities or at their monasteries. The two examples of the Jesuit universities of Quito and Córdoba demonstrate the reception of modern European intellectualism. The Swiss Jesuit Jean Magnin in Quito was probably the first to deal systematically with René Descartes after 1746. The English Jesuit Falkner, a pupil of Newton, introduced experiments in the natural sciences in Córdoba and closely followed Christian Wolff in his philosophy lectures. His fellow Jesuit Domingo Muriel before him had incorporated modern philosophy in his lectures. In 1749 one of his students wrote about him: "In order to further the understanding of the old scholastic philosophy he added a precise knowledge of the modern." Richard Konetzke justifiably countered the wrong impressions by saying "that rationalism and the Enlightenment were propagated early and quickly in Spanish America, where contemporary European currents were almost immediately experienced... it was precisely the priests, monks, and prebendaries who were the forerunners of the Enlightenment in Spanish America..., modern ideas were promulgated especially by the Jesuits...." Thus the ideas of the Enlightenment were able to be promulgated on all the cultural levels of the individual American countries through the universities, colleges, and seminaries. Initially they had a positive effect. The level of studies was raised everywhere and expanded; a fresh wind blew through the institutions of learning, which had become somewhat rigid. Research centers in the natural sciences were established, as were associations of scholars. There was a first wave of periodicals, but it died out after a few years even in the large countries such as Mexico and Peru. In all these movements the clergy furnished the initial contributors; the episcopate promoted participation or at least did not oppose it. The Inquisition generously granted permission for the reading of proscribed books or overlooked violations of the Index. Overall, the Enlightenment in Latin America was able to develop more freely than was initially the case in Europe.

Initially the intellectual elements of the Enlightenment had less of a negative impact than the abuses of regalism, whose anti-Roman tendencies were strengthened by the skillful promotion of Gallican and Febronian ideas. Most fatal especially overseas — was the implicit acceptance of decisions by the state in religious matters, which became more and more a matter of course. Two events had far-reaching consequences. The expulsion of the Jesuits, initiated in 1759/60 by the Marquis de Pombal both in Portugal and the colonies, was followed by the Spanish colonies in 1767. It was executed smoothly but mercilessly, ending in 1768 in the deportation of the missionaries from the reductions of Paraguay. In regard to Brazil and the Spanish colonies various reasons were advanced to justify the expulsion of the Jesuits. The main one was that the Jesuits because of their inner structure could not be made an integral part of the regalist framework of enlightened absolutism. The other equally portentous event was the provincial synods of 1771 invoked by the Spanish King. A detailed list of points to be negotiated, the *tomo regio,* had been given beforehand to the members of the synods by the Council of the Indies. Archbishop Francesco Antonio de Loranzana presided over the synod of Mexico; those of Lima and La Plata took place in 1772. Loranzana submitted decrees drafted by him and the bishop of Puebla, Fabián y Fuero, and then simply called for a vote, precluding any discussion. In order to prove their loyalty to the representative of the viceroy they added two provisions which threatened the penalty of excommunication for any form of resistance to a royal decree or any insult to the King. When the bishop of Durango, José Vicente Díz Bravo, called this procedure tyrannical, he was put on trial, deprived of his bishopric, and sent to Madrid to defend himself. He died on the journey to Spain. Loranzana and his colleague from Puebla, on the other hand, were promoted, the former to the office of archbishop of Toledo (1789) and to the cardinalate, the latter was elevated to the bishopric of Valencia. These regalist synods were never recognized by Rome and even Loranzana did not dare submit the *acta* to Rome.

The negative elements of the Enlightenment as an intellectual movement were noticeably slow to develop in America. They were, moreover, of a different nature from those in Europe. Eighteenth-century America appeared not at all to be a carbon copy of European mentality. Even in the transition to the nineteenth century, America represented the most diverse views encompassing the entire spectrum from strict spirituality to rationalistic thought. G. Furlong has called this period in Argentina that of "Eclecticismo." An actually anticlerical, radically nationalistic current appeared later when the university chairs were occupied by Creoles who had received their education in Coimbra (dominated by Pombal), or at French universities, and to a lesser extent in Spain. Yet at the turn of the nineteenth century political freedom was the one element which unified all the different currents.

The paradoxical aspect of the Spanish movement of liberty and independence lies in the fact that it was triggered primarily by the enlightened absolutism of the mother country and especially by the often farsighted and just rules for reform. Although many a utopian concept may have been connected with them, the improvement of conditions, especially for the Indians, and the elimination of the vestiges of slavery and forced labor were based precisely on these rules. The above-mentioned role of the Creoles in the context of the Enlightenment is very ambivalent, for the ideals of freedom valid for all mankind contradicted their traditional economic and political world. While they did claim these freedoms for themselves, they denied them to the Indians. From this Creole element emerged the Spanish-speaking clergy who were in the front lines in the wars of independence.

The victims of these conflicts were the Indians. The Spanish had oppressed and exploited them, but for all that they had at least created a paternalistic relationship which was sought to be further improved by the enlightened monarchs and their ministers. Although the Indians for the most part had fought on the side of the Creoles against the Spaniards, they were soon ignored by the victors and indeed considered as nonexistent. Their particular problems have remained unsolved even today, as have those of the mestizos, Negroes, and mulattos. From this point of view, Richard Konetzke has characterized the movement for independence as a "reaction against historical progress. In this regard the era of the waning Spanish colonial rule was at any rate more modern than the subsequent epoch of independent states during the nineteenth century."

Part Two

The Established Church and the Enlightenment

Section One

Concepts

Oskar Köhler

Chapter 127

Foundations and Forms of the Established Church in the Bourbon States of the Seventeenth and Eighteenth Centuries

The decline of papal power from the middle of the seventeenth century, contrasted with the intellectual and spiritual flowering of baroque Catholicism and the development of royal absolutism, is manifested not only by the European peace congresses, the unsuccessful protests against the Prussian demand for the royal title (1701), and the establishment of the house of Hanover as the ninth electorate (1707). The papal elections and the use of the *ius exclusivae* by Catholic powers demonstrate even more clearly the deterioration of the international esteem in which the papacy had been held previously and the growing strength of the concept of the established Church. To be sure, the papal elections during the seventeenth and eighteenth century almost invariably fell on deserving candidates. Yet they were aged and in many cases because of age and illness they were unable to respond to the demands of their office.

The interests of the state and the ambitions of absolutist rule over the Church turned almost every conclave into a battleground mainly between France on one side and Spain and Austria on the other, with all parties seeking preliminary decisions reflecting their ambitions for an established and national Church. Until the middle of the eighteenth century each succeeding pontificate endured growing pressure from Spain, France, Austria, and the Bourbon secundogenitures of Italy. In addition, the militarily helpless, irreparably indebted Papal States, which could no longer fulfill their original purpose of ensuring freedom of action for the head of the Church, inescapably enmeshed the Popes in the tumult of the Italian policies of the great powers. Rigid adherence to outdated legal claims, such as feudal supremacy over the Kingdom of the Two Sicilies and the duchy of Parma-Piacenza challenged those states which were in the process of integrating to take ever harsher countermeasures against papal church supremacy, *pirateria beneficiale*, nunciatures, and ecclesiastical jurisdiction.

The desire to influence the papal elections had grown in proportion to Italy's having become the battleground of the European powers and the growing conviction that the inviolability of the Papal States appeared better safeguarded by an Italian prince than by the head of Christianity. The *ius exclusivae* of the Kings of Spain, France, and the German Emperor, applied more and more frequently since the middle of the seventeenth century and based on legalities of the established Church, was "in reality a demand of the voters not to give their vote to a certain candidate in the interest of peace between the state and the Church" (Wahrmund) and to exclude that candidate legally.

At the very beginning of the conclave following the death of Urban VIII (d. 29 July 1644) Spain eliminated the candidate of the Barberini party, Cardinal Giulio Sacchetti, by means of the *ius exclusivae*. It repeated this action against the same candidate in the conclave of 1655. In 1644, however, Mazarin's veto against Cardinal Giambattista Pamfili arrived too late to forestall his election (Innocent X, 1644–55). At the next election in 1655 Mazarin also failed in his opposition to Fabio Chigi (Alexander VII, 1655–67). The election of Giulio Rospigliosi was by no means owing to the protection of Louis XIV alone, even though it was later represented in this manner by the French. The Spanish, not knowing of France's sympathy for him, had also supported Rospigliosi. Finally, the latter had also impressed the *Squadrone volante* as the most suitable candidate. Clement IX, whose election, then, had not been clouded by any exclusion, was granted the privilege of having a part in ending the war between Spain and France and bringing about the Peace of Aachen (2 May 1668). By doing so, he was able to attenuate the humiliation of the papacy by the Peace of Pisa (1664) and to weaken the French concept of an established Church.

The conclave upon his death was again characterized by opposition between Spain and France and a heretofore unprecedented influence by the ambassadors. The French ambassador Chaulnes formally applied the *ius exclusivae* to Cardinal d'Elce, whereas the Spanish ambassador Astorga presented the reservations of his queen-regent against Cardinal Vidoni and caused the candidacy of Cardinal Brancaccio to run aground on the *ius exclusivae*. The mediation of Venice finally steered the election to the eighty-year-old, kind, but insignificant Emilio Altieri (29 April 1670, Clement X, 1670–76). His successor, Innocent XI (Benedetto Odescalchi) was not elected until the approval of Louis XIV had been delivered to the entrance of the conclave on 20 September 1676. Although the War of the Spanish Succession prompted great efforts in connection with the election of Alexander VIII (1639–91), neither Louis XIV nor Leopold I was able to exert any decisive influence this time. The next lengthy conclave (12 February–12 July 1691) was again dominated by opposition between the French and the Spanish-Austrian parties. The promising candidacy of Gregorio Barbarigo, who was later canonized, failed by virtue of the fact that Emperor Leopold I, while forgoing formal exclusion, called his election undesirable, the Spanish ambassador conspired against it, and Louis XIV resisted it out of consideration for his allies. Cardinal Antonio Pignatelli (Innocent XII, 1691–1700), who was elected in the end, was a compromise candidate already seventy-five years of age.

The Spanish succession — Charles II, the last of the Habsburgs on the Spanish throne had died little more than a month after Innocent XII (d. 27 September 1700) — and the prospect that because of the dead Pope's partisanship for the French succession, the feudal claim over the Kingdom of the two Sicilies, and the helpless military condition of the Papal States the Apostolic See would be involved in that European conflict overshadowed the conclave (9 October to 20 November 1700). In this conclave the *Zelanti* were finally able to prevail with their candidate, Gian Francesco Albani (Clement XI, 1700–1721). On 2 April 1721 during the scrutiny prior to reaching a two-third's majority, Cardinal Althan announced the imperial exclusion preventing the election of the candidate of the nepotist party, Fabrizio Paolucci. After the Emperor and France had reached an understanding, Cardinal Conti (Innocent XIII, 1721–24) was elected. Nine years later the candidate of the *Zelanti,* Lorenzo Imperiali, foundered on the protest of the Bourbon courts and Paolucci on the exclusion of the previous conclave. The papal election of 1730 also marked the first appearance of the Savoy Party. The last public exclusion was issued by France on 24 June 1758 against Cardinal Cavalchini because of his position in the canonization of Bellarmine and on the issue of the constitution *Unigenitus.*

The *ius exclusivae* was to serve the fulfillment of aims regarding the established Church and the attainment of other long-range goals. For the common disputes with the Church either the already existing institutions of the pre-Tridentine established Church were further developed or new means created. The confinement of the nunciatures to a position of mere diplomatic representation of the Papal States, put into effect by the established Churches in an alliance with episcopalism, was complemented by the institution of the *Agenzie,* developed in Spain and France and taken over in 1714–17 by Charles VI first for his Dutch and Italian possessions and then for the hereditary lands and the Empire as well. In 1759 the ordinariates of the Habsburg monarchy were ordered to make use of the Roman *Agenzie* after 1767 all business with Rome, with the exception of the *forum internum,* had to go exclusively through this state institution. More than anything else the established Church made use of the *Appellatio tanquam ab abusu* and of the *placet* in its disputes with the hierarchy.

The *Appellatio ab abusu,* also called *Recursus ab abusu, Recursus ad principem, Appel comme d'abus,* or *Recurso de fuerza,* is the appeal to state authority against an alleged misuse of church authority, especially in connection with jurisprudence and administration. Even in its initial stages this institution, which grew from various roots in Spain, France, and in the medieval communities and principalities of Italy, signaled the claim of absolute rule over the Church. If possible all jurisdiction competing with that of the state was to be eliminated. In conjunction with the Pragmatic Sanction of Bourges (1438), the *Appel comme d'abus* had been expanded, acknowledged by Leo X in the Concordat of 1516, and legalized in the *Ordonnance* of Villers Cotterêts of 1539. In the course of the seventeenth and eighteenth century the *Recursus ab abusu* although condemned since 1581 by the bull *In Coena Domini* and censured by the Church, was developed in all Catholic states "as a weapon of territorialism against the hierocratic system" (E. Eichmann). In Lorraine, where the conflict regarding the Code Léopold (1701–10) was almost exclusively focused on the *Recursus ab abusu,* it represented a means of defense on the part of national autonomy. The *Recursus ab abusu* was intended to express the territorial sovereignty of the state and to complete the development initiated by the *Privilegium de nonevocando* with state control of church jurisdiction. But it was also intended to delineate the respective competencies of the state and the Church. While it was primarily an instrument of the established Church, it also contributed toward putting into disuse the Pope's recourse to a general council.

The sharpest weapon of the established Church, "the main guarantee of the rights of the state," (E. Friedberg) was the *placet* (also called the *Placetum regium, Exequatur Jus retentionis,* and, in Lorraine, *Pareatis*). It was first formulated in England; after the tumult of obedience ensuing from the Great Western Schism it was used as a prescriptive right by the sovereign princes. It represents the right on the part of the sovereign or those offices charged by him — as the Inquisition tribunal in Spain — to examine with a view toward the interests of the state certain church decrees, especially by foreign superiors, to permit their publication and execution or to prohibit them under certain penalties, of which those ordered by Philip II in 1569 were especially harsh (they included banishment and even the death penalty). Within the concept of the established Church the *placet* was part of the *Jura circa sacra* and of the sovereignty of the state. It was based on council resolutions, the Catholic view of the state, the responsibilities of the sovereign prince, and, during the eighteenth century, increasingly on natural law. The state has the *placet* vis-à-vis the Church, but not the other way around because the Church is in the state, whereas the state is not within the Church. In the seventeenth and eighteenth century the *placet* was applied against papal and episcopal decrees of disciplinary as well as dogmatic content, even though Philip IV (10 June 1659), emphasizing that it was unnecessary in connection with instructional announcements, at that time prohibited such innovative application in the Netherlands. The greater duchy of Tuscany, as well as Spain, France, Venice, Naples, and Vienna, denied the *Exequatur* for the bull *Auctorem Fidei* (28 August 1794) of Pius VI condemning the Synod of Pistoia.

The *placet* had the purpose of maintaining law and order in the state, preventing intervention or abuse by the Roman Curia in the affairs either of the state or the competent bishops. Ever since Innocent VIII and his Bull *In Coena Domini* the *placet* was censured, but not until the middle of the nineteenth century was the *ius, quod vocant* "exequatur" actually condemned. An ordinance of 1475 by Louis XI had ordered the *placet* for papal edicts as part of the Gallican Liberties. An inspection *placet* had existed in Lorraine since 1484. Recommended by Cardinal Ximenes and emphatically prescribed for all Catholics by Ferdinand (1509), it was one of the fundaments of the Spanish concept of the established Church. It became a model via the Netherlands and Northern Italy for the Habsburg established Church, which increased its application even under Leopold I.

A treatise published in 1712 by the well-known Louvain canonist van Espen took on special importance for the theoretical justification of the *placet.* Van Espen viewed the *placet* not as a means of limiting the independence of the Church, but rather as a means of the authorities who were instituted by God, of maintaining both ecclesiastical and political order. Van Espen's views were of enduring influence on the Josephinist study of canon law. During the last few years of Charles VI the glare of public attention focused on the discussion regarding the appointment to the chair of canon law at the University of Innsbruck, which was to be taken away from the Jesuits and conferred on Paul Josef Rieger. As admitted by the government, the crux of the matter was to protect the students from the very injurious principles aimed at the predominance of the clergy and instead to teach them "the true doctrine as reflected in Covarruvias, Van Espen *et similibus.*"

In an unsuccessful effort Innocent X and Clement XI tried to counter the *placet* by the bull *Nova semper* of 9 November 1714. The fight with the established Church, which had grown in strength since the Counter Reformation and had displayed ever stronger aspirations in the course of the seventeenth and eighteenth centuries, is reflected in the history of *In Coena Domini,* in the form of its text as well as in the measures by the various sovereign princes. Its publication in Spain had led to serious conflicts even under Charles V and Philip II. In 1763 a new prohibition was issued in Spain. In retaliation to the papal monitory, *In Coena Domini* was suppressed in 1768 in Parma, Venice, Naples, Spain, Austrian Lombardy, and Bohemia. After 1770 it was no longer announced. The established Church also ignored the Roman *Index librorum prohibitorum.* Under the principle of advocation the *Ius proscribendi libros perniciosos* was claimed for the state, which then could refuse the request of the Church for intervention and could even act against the wishes of the Church. The Church was forced to suffer its most infamous defeats of the eighteenth century in this arena in the form of repeated failure to proscribe Hontheim's ("Febronius") *De statu ecclesiae* and Osterwald's *Wider die geistliche Immunität in zeitlichen Dingen,* and, finally, it had to tolerate the abolition of the Apostolic Book Commissariat in Frankfurt am Main.

The established church system, promoted by the Church during the Counter Reformation for the sake of self-preservation and reform, differed in the structure attained during the seventeenth and eighteenth century from the pre-Tridentine form by its consistent systematism and doctrinarianism. It flourished in the absolutist Catholic states, in Spain and France, the Bourbon states of Italy, in the Spanish Netherlands, Lorraine, the Republic of Venice, several Catholic cantons of Switzerland, in the Electorate of Bavaria, and in Austria. In regard to canon law the established Church was a complex system whose bent for episcopacy, national Church, and opposition to the Curia differed from one state to the other. Gallicanism, deeply rooted in French history and closely related to the growing strength of a national kingdom, the weakness of the papacy during the Avignon exile and the Great Western Schism, was firmly placed on a course of maintaining the national unity of the Church in the time following the Reformation. Its goal in counteraction to papalism was the reform of the church constitution in the episcopal or Richerian sense, but above all it aimed at the predominance of the state over the Church. Its claim was based on the Pragmatic Sanction of Bourges (1438) and, after its abolition by the Concordat of 1516, on the latter's stipulations which granted the King the right of appointment to almost all bishoprics and abbeys and, with it, factual dominance over the Church of France. The introduction of the *placet* for papal decrees (1475), the *Appel comme d'abus* (1539), and the writings of Pierre Pithou, Dupuy, de Marca, and Richer around the turn of the sixteenth century strengthened the system of the established Church and the concept of the so-called Gallican Liberties, which according to Pithou's authoritative interpretation merely paraphrased the rule of the King over the Church in France.

Following the quarrel over the quartering privilege and the Peace of Pisa (1664), which humiliated the papacy, the issue of Gallicanism reached its climax in the regalia dispute and the *Declaratio cleri gallicani* of 19 March 1682. Next, Louis XIV treated the regalia right as an essential right to the crown. He extended the right of nomination according to the Concordat of 1516 to all the bishoprics and abbeys; he also claimed the ecclesiastical regalia, which enabled him to fill all the benefices of a bishopric while the latter was vacant. When Innocent XI demanded the revocation of the edict, the Assembly of the Clergy under the influence of the King and with decisive participation by Bossuet who had been appointed bishop of Meaux, decided to accept the expanded regalia right and the *Declaratio cleri gallicani de potestate ecclesiastica.* According to these four Gallican articles (19 March 1682), which constituted a revival of the Pragmatic Sanction of Bourges, the authority of the Pope did not extend to civic and temporal matters (John 18:36; Luke 20:25, Rom. 13:1f.). According to divine order, kings and princes are not subject to ecclesiastical authority in temporal matters. Thus they can neither be directly deposed by it, nor indirectly by releasing their subjects from their oath of loyalty. In spiritual matters as well the authority of the Apostolic See was limited in France by the decrees of the Council of Constance concerning the superiority of the council. These decrees had been approved by the Apostolic Sees, acknowledged by their application throughout the Church, and most scrupulously observed, especially by the Gallican Church. The exercise of papal power was regulated by the *canones,* the statutes of the church Fathers, tradition, and the prescriptive law of France and the Gallican Church. In matters of faith the Pope was most favored, but his judgment was subject to change unless the total Church agreed to it.

The four articles were published as state law and taught at the universities. Not until 1690 was a declaration of nullification pronounced by Alexander VIII. The tensions with Rome concerning the regalia right and the *Declaratio* were aggravated by the quarrel about the quartering privilege, but a schism was avoided. Innocent XII reached a compromise (1693) by which Louis XIV forwent the implementation of the four articles in exchange for toleration of his regalia right and recognition of the bishops appointed by him. But well into the nineteenth century the established church law continued to be determined largely by the *Declaratio cleri gallicani.* In 1749 an amortization law against the acquisition of property by the Church was passed; in 1762 the Society of Jesus in the French province was dissolved by application of the *Appel comme d'abus.*

The Spanish established Church was tightly structured. Owning a disproportionate part of the real property and national income, it was totally in the hands of the state. Its rise and fall proceeded in tandem with the political development. The King had nomination right for all bishoprics and — as under the weak Habsburgs in the seventeenth century and the Bourbons of the eighteenth century — many an unworthy person was appointed. The princely income of many bishops was in glaring disproportion to the condition of the ministering clergy, to the poverty of the lower classes, and the meager theological education among large segments of the regular and secular clergy. Attempts at reform by the Jesuit Eberhard Nidhard (d. 1681 as a cardinal), whom Queen-Regent Anna Maria had appointed grand inquisitor and member of the Secret Council of State, were doomed to failure. The consolidation of absolutism under Philip V also began to have its effects on the relationship with the Church. When Clement XI recognized the Habsburg pretender to the crown, Charles III (1709), the results were the cessation of diplomatic relations with Rome, the closing of the nunciature in Madrid, the suspension of the temporalities, and — as a countermeasure — refusal by the Pope to confirm the bishops appointed by Philip V. In 1713 Melchior Raphael de Macanaz, treasurer of the Council of Castile, summarized the doctrines and demands of the regalists: abolition of the bull *In Coena Domini,* abolition of the Pope's supremacy over the kings, and universal patronage over all church benefices. The concordats of 1717 and 1732 could not allay all the disputes; they actually pleased neither party. The concordat, concluded in dire straights by Benedict XIV, gave to the Spanish King the universal patronage he demanded, with the exception of fifty-two benefices, besides "creating an almost total change in the discipline of the Spanish Church" (A. Kirsch). And yet new conflicts were created under Charles III when P. R. Conde de Campomanes (1723–1792) intensified the *placet* (1761) and expelled the Jesuits.

On the basis of the privilege *Quia propter prudentiam tuam,* granted Count Roger by Urban II (5 July 1098), the kings of the Two Sicilies ever since the end of the Middle Ages had claimed the title and rights of a *legatus natus papae* or a *legatus a latere* and with them all those rights not expressly reserved for the Pope. Ever since the sixteenth century this legatine power was characteristically called *Monarchia Sicula.* Ferdinand I, "the Catholic" (d. 1516), possessing the ecclesiastical jurisdiction as well, had himself called *Monarca.* The *Monarchia Sicula* involved the claim of the right of visitation of dioceses and monasteries, the right of decision in the election of church superiors, the right of excommunication and absolution even of cases in the papal reserve, the penal right for bishops, nuncios, and cardinals, and the right of demoting secular and regular clerics. When Philipp II failed to obtain a confirmation of the *Monarchia Sicula* from Rome, he appointed Nicolaus Stizzia to the position of the first permanent judge of the "monarchy" (*Judex Monarchiae Siculae*) on 13 July 1579. In so doing he created "a central authority which systematically combined the highest ecclesiastical jurisdiction in one hand" (F. J. Sentis). The trials before the tribunal of the "Monarchy" were not permitted to be advocated by the Pope nor brought to Rome by way of recourse.

The constant conflicts with the *Monarchia Sicula,* the latter being motivated by rigorous principles of an established Church and extreme "schismatic principles," reached a climax under Pope Clement XI during the Spanish War of Succession and the disputes connected with the efforts by Joseph I and Charles VI toward an established Church. The cause, insignificant on the surface, was the filling of the episcopal see of the Lipari Islands, on which occasion a small tax was levied. This appeared to Bishop Tedeschi, the secretary of the Congregation of Rites, a violation of ecclesiastical immunity in the sense of the bull *Coena Domini.* So he reacted by excommunicating the responsible civil servants, whereupon the judge of the "Monarchy" pronounced absolution. When the dispute went to the Congregatio of Immunities in Rome by way of recourse, it quickly became part of the fierce quarrel between Clement XI and Philip V.

By recognizing the Habsburg pretender Charles III as "Catholic King of Spain" (10 October 1709) Clement XI had gained some concessions in the Emperor's

Italian policy, but at the same time he had to suffer harsh retaliatory measures by Philip V: Nuncio Zondadari was expelled from Madrid, all relations with Rome were prohibited, all revenues of the Holy See in Spain were frozen, ecclesiastical immunity and jurisdiction came under attack. On 11 October 1711, Clement XI declared all decrees directed against church immunity and jurisdiction null and void, and their originators to be subject to church censure. In addition he refused to confirm the bishops nominated by Philip V.

This immediate quarrel intensified the conflict over the *Monarchia Sicula.* A decree by the Congregation of Immunities (26 January 1712) and a brief by Clement XI (12 June 1712) declared the absolution by the judge of the "Monarchy" of those involved in the excommunication as being invalid and reconfirmed their excommunication. The response was given in the form of an edict by the viceroy: all papal decrees and edicts were null and void because they violated municipal laws, privileges, customs, and the regalia of the realm. The battle was then propelled to its climax by excommunications and local interdicts by one side, countered on the other side by absolution from Church censure by delegates of the "Judge of the Monarchy," suspension of temporalities, and the expulsion of the bishops of Catania, Girgenti, and the archbishop of Messina.

Disregarding the feudal claims of the Pope, the Peace of Utrecht (1713) demanded the transfer of Sicily from Spain to Duke Victor Amadeus II of Savoy. Additionally, the already tense relations between the Curia and Piedmont were aggravated to the extreme by exceedingly harsh measures in Sicily. As a consequence Clement XI on 20 February 1715 annulled the *Monarchia Sicula* by his bull *Romanus Pontifex,* predated by exactly one year.

The annulment received attention only because of an appeal by the procurator of the treasury prompting Philip V of Spain to insist on his rights by means of a formal protest. Less than three years later the establishment of the Quadruple Alliance (2 August 1718) gave Sicily to Austria in exchange for Sardinia. After difficult negotiations Emperor Charles VI agreed to return Comacchio to the Papal States (1725), a process in which Prosper Lambertini, the future Pope Benedict XIV, collaborated. This opened the door to a compromise regarding the *Monarchia Sicula.* Benedict XIII — while not expressly revoking the absolution bull — insisted in his bull *Fideli* (ratified 30 August 1728; in Vienna: 10 November 1728) that the *causae vere maiores* remain in the province of the Roman Curia or a special papal delegation in Sicily, that, furthermore, the title "Judge of the Royal Monarchy" be changed to *iudex ecclesiasticus delegatus.* The King received the privilege to appoint as the highest juridical office a *Iudex delegatus in partibus.*

The Vienna Treaty (3 October 1735) — again in complete disregard of the papal feudal rights — gave Naples and Sicily to Don Carlos as a Spanish-Bourbon secundogeniture. Under his rule (which he assumed after the death of his half-brother), but even more so under his minor son Ferdinand IV, the minister of state and chairman of the council of regents, Bernardo Tanucci, articulated the claims of dominance of an enlightened absolutist state by means of passionate attacks on the Church, harsh reforms, and endless harassment. The excommunication of the duke of Parma by Clement XIII (30 January 1768) furnished the pretense for reprisals by the Bourbon family alliance against the "ridiculous and scandalous pretentiousness" of the Roman Curia. These reprisals included the occupation of the papal enclaves of Benevento and Pontecorvo. Only after the abolition of the Society of Jesus, which Clement XIII was still rejecting at that time, were these territories returned (1774).

In implementing his church reforms, many of which were not without inner justification, Tanucci invoked the *Monarchia Sicula* and the presuppositions created by the unfortunate Pietro Giannone (16760–1748), whose *Istoria civile del Regno di Napoli* (4 vols., 1723) has been called "the bible of anticurialism." He also invoked kindred spirits among Jansenists and enlightened Freemasons. An Italian translation of Mesenguy's *Exposition de la doctrine chrétienne* appeared between 1758 and 1760. The Enlightenment, regalism of the Spanish variety, Jansenist and Freemasonic influences under Tanucci were meshed into a system whose anticlericalism continued well beyond his fall, brought about by Maria Carolina (1776).

Even the enfeoffment of the Kingdom of the Two Sicilies (10 May 1738) granted by Clement XII did not improve the tense relations between Rome and Naples. Nor did the concordat concluded by Benedict XIV after difficult negotiations (2 June 1741) lead to a modus vivendi, but instead to ever new conflicts in spite of the fact that the Pope — much to the chagrin of several cardinals — made substantial concessions. Agreement concerning the controversial "Tribunal of the Monarchy" was reached by which a court consisting of three clerics and two laymen appointed by the King was to execute church jurisdiction on a higher level as well. Rome made concessions in the matter of personal, local, and property immunity; the right of sanctuary was circumscribed; foreigners were excluded from holding benefices in the kingdom and a few smaller bishoprics were abolished. In exchange the *placet* was to be eliminated and the *Recursus ad principem* modified.

But soon the interpretation of the concordat and the unchanged estabishmentarian, anticlerical course set by Tanucci in Naples resulted in endless new disputes. Tanucci, who made the Church responsible for the economic miseries of the kingdom, disregarded the Benedictine concordat; he reduced the number of monasteries, restored the amortization regulations, eliminated the spolia right, and claimed for himself the power of appointment to all bishoprics and the awarding of all benefices. The unscrupulous expansion of the *placet,* which had been founded in "international law and the peaceful spirit of religion," to include even the *forum internum,* the confinement of the Church to the sacraments and liturgy, and, finally, the expulsion of the Jesuits from the realm (1769) were expressions of that harsh establishmentarianism and radical anticlericalism.

Tanucci's fall meant the end of the reforms, but not the end of anticlericalism and vexatious oppression of the Church. In 1778 all connections between the monasteries and Rome were interrupted. The *placet* was refused for all briefs and dispensations if the royal permission for recourse to Rome, the so-called *Liceat scribere,* was not obtained first. In point of fact, this procedure cut off all communication with the head of the Church. The claim of a royal presentation right in all bishoprics led to thirty vacant sees in 1784 in Naples alone; in 1798 there were more than sixty. In 1787 the King of the Two Sicilies formally refused to recognize papal feudal rights by refusing the presentation of the White Horse (*Chinea*) customary sign of vassalage since the time of Charles of Anjou, and payment of the usual seven thousand gold ducats, invoking international law and historical grounds. The papal protest ceremoniously pronounced in Saint Peter's on 29 June 1788 fell on deaf ears.

During the second half of the seventeenth century and in the eighteenth century as well, anticlerical policies and strict establishmentarianism continued to flourish in the Republic of Venice even after the worst of the conflicts over Paolo Sarpi was overcome. In 1754 the republic demanded government permission for all communication of its subjects with Rome, as well as for the execution of papal bulls and decrees. Gifts to the dead hand were forbidden, monasteries were closed, and the religious orders were placed under the authority of the bishops, who were not permitted to leave their dioceses without government permission.

Establishmentarianism assumed even harsher forms in Parma under Guglielmo Du Tillot and after the excommunication of the duke (30 January 1768), but after the fall of the prime minister the latter's successor reverted to a more moderate course (1771). In Sardinia the *Appel comme d'abus* remained in effect even after the concordats of 1727 and 1742; it was further expanded by additional regulations in 1770 and 1771. The right of sanctuary was modified, but the bishop was enabled to invoke the aid of the temporal authorities against the clergy. Establishmentarianism in Tuscany was not developed until the rule of the dukes of Lorraine. Francis I transferred the book censorship to the temporal authorities; he issued an amortization law and closed several monasteries and convents. The canonical reforms of his son Leopold, for which Pompeo Nero and Giulio Rucellai had paved the way, with some few modifications were basically identical to those in Austrian Lombardy, the Kingdom of the Two Sicilies, Parma, and Piacenza, but Leopold's aims went far beyond theirs and the establishmentarianism of Josephinism. The formative development of the Habsburg establishmentarianism, starting with the consolidation of imperial power and the integration of the state under Leopold I, Joseph I — the conflict involving Comacchio and the recuperation policy in Italy — and under Charles VI was influenced by the model of Venice, the Spanish Netherlands. and Lorraine.

CHAPTER 128

The Enlightenment

Concept

The epoch of intellectual history called "La crise de la conscience européenne," "Lumières" (French), "Enlightenment" (English), "Illuminismo" (Italian) indicated not so much a tendency toward crisis but rather its distant origin: the metaphysics of light left to the formative Western world by Augustine. The designation "Aufklärung" (C. W. Wieland), applied since the middle of the eighteenth century to the intellectual progress taking place, corresponds to the older French "éclaircissement." But the Augustinian "illuminatio" of God within man was now conceived to mean man's self-illumination in the light of autonomous reason. This authorization of the human intellect which had its prehistory in the power asserted by Thomism that enables man in the knowledge of creation to rise to an analogous knowledge of God, except that rationality (according to Scholastic philosophy) is to be combined with the belief in revealed religion, now sought its reason within itself. The rationalism of Enlightenment is historically inconceivable without the philosophy of Scholasticism. By the same token, the anti-institutionalism of Enlightenment, initially aimed at the constituted Church and accepting for the time being the absolutist state, which in turn took its ideological foundation from the rational law of nature, but then ended in the Revolution, had its roots, through its ties with the religious inwardness of Pietism, in the Christian concept of the uniqueness and freedom of the individual person. Rationalism and anti-institutionalism, which was in the process of emancipation from its own tradition, furnished the conditions for the universal concept of Enlightenment of the one humanity. But for its part the latter is inconceivable without the Passion and Salvation of Christ, which in its original form was universal ("Jews and Gentiles" in Rom. 11:25; 1:16; 10:12), but then again historically particular *(gesta Dei per Francos).* But even if Enlightenment can be viewed as the result of centuries of "diastasis" of medieval history (Mayer-Pfannholz), the diastasis between the ecclesiastical and political realm, between inwardness and institution, freedom and authority, the world and God, it is precisely because of the result of that diastasis that it constituted a crisis of the European intellect. This crisis is institutionally characterized by the fact that the Church now "lost its position of leadership" and that Christianity, from which Enlightenment stemmed, was "publicly put on trial" — with different degrees of intensity, to be sure, varying in accordance with the people and countries involved — without the accuser being able to be distinguished from the accused even before the end of the epoch had been determined. In looking at the characteristics of this crisis, not only its origin in the tradition of Western thought, but also its complexity, indeed its inner contradictoriness must be taken into account. Skepticism was not only turned on the dogmas of Christian faith; it was the innermost element of man's reason itself and this reason could therefore be celebrated enthusiastically, be subjected to criticism and — although only on the periphery at first — be cynically discredited. Against the certainty of Cartesian consciousness and its "innate ideas" the psychological empiricism of J. Locke was raised, for whom the soul is a blank page. He was to have a profound influence on Montesquieu, Voltaire, Rousseau and others, finally ending in sensualism. Hume attacked Locke's deism as a new dogma and criticized the concept of "natural religion," which was to be the dome over all the revealed religions, as an empty construct. In its place he posited, in terms of psychology, the religious need, rooted in fear and hope, as only one of the many other needs. Theology, more substantially than in the course of the English Enlightenment, continued to be an ever present partner in the dialogue of the German philosophy of Enlightenment from

Leibniz to Kant albeit a partner separated by a critical line of demarcation. This clearly supports for the overall context of Europe the fact that in the aspirations toward Enlightenment "Christianity was the infinite object of toil for the centuries constituting the modern age." And if one is not deceived by the acid quality of the language, this partnership was also felt in French Enlightenment, in the person of Pierre Bayle, son of a pastor whose relationship with Calvinism is controversial, and in the anticlerical hatred of Voltaire's "Ecrasez l'Infame." If one considers the Enlightenment in its totality without arbitrarily separating the great personalities from the multiplicators, who had a profound effect on the broad segment of the educated, including those people who, while they could not read, had themselves read to, then the scope of the Enlightenment reached from an "insipid striving for bliss to the sublime mysticism of Spinoza and Malebranche."

Next to the concept of philosophy as the "universal process of philosophizing," which intended to bring about a new order the natural sciences were a determining element of this epoch. Their observations and experiments provided an ever growing consciousness of man's sovereignty. Although the mathematics and physics of Newton created a lasting understanding, whereas the biology of the seventeenth and eighteenth centuries in the aggregate is no more than historically significant, an epochal turn of events made all of nature including man the object of empirical research. Its results confronted the traditional theory of creation, a confrontation not lightly undertaken by the prominent natural scientists.

This endogenous process of the European Enlightenment corresponds with the criticism prompted by reaction to world exploration, a criticism of Western traditions, of Christianity (or at least its practice in Europe), brought about by comparison with the high cultures of Asia or primitive peoples of America. Its significance — at the time unintended yet innate — lies in the fact that it was above all the reports by missionaries from Asia, especially China, and from America which caused a "cultural crisis," just as Saint Francis Xavier had done before, intending at first to raise up a Tacitean mirror to their native countries. But the result was that precisely those men who had stepped out into the world for the sake of Christian faith and its propagation unintentionally laid the foundation for doubting the complex claim of Christianity's absolute nature through criticism which had actually been intended for only that form of the claim representing an identification of *christianitas* with Western culture. Thus the Christian faith proved to be an "enlightenment" inasmuch as it questioned its own historical embodiment and with it the whole Eurocentric view of the historical world. Just as the doctrine of creation became a problem vis-à-vis empirical knowledge of nature, so did the doctrine of salvation become problematic for the experience of a universal history, notwithstanding the lack of clear factual knowledge.

The "rationalism" of the Enlightenment represents radicalization of Western rationality as well as misunderstanding of the secret which man will always be; "naturalism" is both discovery of the world and the loss of its total dimension in the abbreviation of materialistic interpretation; the detheologization of natural law in a line from Grotius to Pufendorf and Thomasius is at once the foundation of the tolerant state as well as its becoming an absolute concept as the *primum principium* of political and social life; in actuality "indifferentism" is both nihilistic skepticism and the tolerance which was indicated intellectually and politically after the dissolution of medieval universalism (which had its own problems) and was reaching for a new universality of truth. The Enlightenment can only be understood in the light of this ambivalence, which is especially noticeable in its mixed relationship with the idea of progress which had taken the place of the promise represented by the traditional belief in salvation.

The altercation with tradition was reflected also in the system of education. The old institutions, the universities and the ecclesiastic and municipal schools for a long time were averse to the Enlightenment. Its major influence emanated from the academies and scientific associations, followed by the private tutors of the aristocratic families and the salons. Almost all the proponents of the Enlightenment were occupied with pedagogical questions. The most prominent pedagogues of this period were John Amos Comenius (1592–1670 [Amsterdam]) with his *Orbis sensualium pictus* (1654) and his *Didactica magna* (1672) and J.-J. Rousseau. Reaching the broad masses of the people with the spirit of the Enlightenment, however, is a long process which — moved from within by a "second Enlightenment" — has lasted into our century. The communications media played an important part in this.

If the Enlightenment is considered solely in its historical context, it is not easy to determine its beginning. It is different from humanism inasmuch as the latter — in spite of its strong pagan features — is yet part of criticism and reform within the Church; where it initiated secularization, it tended generally to avoid the theological realm. This can be seen most clearly in the development of its attitude toward history. Regional areas are subjects of humanistic historiography; it takes them out of the medieval horizon of Christian salvation, applies its criticism to its proper objects, but — contrary to Voltaire — it leaves the *Historia Divina* unscathed. It can hardly be said that "only a return to life on a Christian basis" after humanism led to overcoming the "static thinking of antiquity" (which was not all that static). This much of it is indeed valid, namely, that the radical argument between the Enlightenment and the Christian faith received both from this argument and from the secular reinterpretation of Christian eschatology those dynamics which characterized the new age. The Enlightenment was by the knowledge of itself distinguished from the Renaissance and humanism. Because of this the dispute between the "Ancients" and the "Moderns" conducted in French literature since the seventeenth century inclined progressively toward the side of emancipation from antiquity (Fontenelle [1657–1757] spoke of the "absurdities" of Greek mythology; Voltaire criticized the "blind adoration of antiquity," although the art of antiquity at the same time remained the absolute model for the Neoplatonism of A. Shaftesbury [1671–1713]). Criticism of antiquity and of the relationship between humanism and antiquity is part of the Enlightenment's criticism of tradition on the whole. Benedetto Croce viewed the intellectual consciousness of the time by saying that it not only emerged from the "darkness" of the Middle Ages, but also from the "dawn" of humanism and the Renaissance into the full light of reason. The changed relationship with the Christian faith is the most essential element of the connection as well as of the difference between humanism and the Enlightenment — not only in the context of church history.

The Enlightenment within the Political and Social Conditions of Individual Countries

The course of the Enlightenment proceeded in several phases, in intellectual climates which differed according to the countries involved. The individual proponents of the Enlightenment also occupied opposing positions; their personal relationship to each other could change from affinity to pronounced hostility. Regardless of the way in which the Enlightenment was a consequence of processes in the history of Western ideas, it was conditioned in the totality of history by the extremely rapid consumption of religious views during the religious wars for the purpose of undergirding positions of political power. This consumption was aggravated by the indifference of purely political acts of tolerance, in the bottleneck of establishmentarian censorship of French absolutism as much as in the abolition of precensorship and the supervision of book imports in England (1695). In the context of social history the consumption took place mainly in the rise of an educated bourgeoisie, which relegated the orthodox clergy to backwardness. Even though it was isolated from the common folk, it yet claimed a monopoly in education.

In England the religious opposition of the Puritans and the parliamentary opposition established an alliance against the Anglican absolutism of James I (1603–25). This was followed by the Holy War of Oliver Cromwell, to which not only Charles I (1649) fell victim but also the Presbyterians of parliament. Yet during the Restoration under Charles II (1660–85) religious engagement of the public had remained so strong that religious statements were among the most important arguments in the fight for seats in parliament. But in this body the "genuine Protestantism was defended by those who unscrupulously fulfilled the Test Act (1673; prescribing the Anglican Communion and the oath of supremacy of the Anglican Church for all occupants of government offices), because they were for the most part free-thinkers" (C. R. Cragg). After the Glorious Revolution the Toleration Act of 1689, while still stipulating the Anglican faith to be that of the realm and at least for the time being not barring nonconformists from holding state office, provided an arena in which the Enlightenment could develop in a more or less unfettered way, especially after the succession of George I (1714) from the Lutheran house of Hanover. The Royal Society had been founded in 1662; ten years later it counted Isaac Newton as its most prominent member among such others as the founder of scientific chemistry, Robert Boyle, the mathematician John Wallis, the physicist, astronomer, and architect Christopher Wren, and others. The Royal Society was a model for the founding of academies everywhere; they were progressive institutions compared to the universities. In 1709 the *Tatler* appeared, followed in 1711 by the *Spectator*, the model for the daily and weekly papers which spread the great intellectual movement for the benefit of the progressively minded reader. Following the *London Gazette*, which appeared at irregular intervals (1665), the *Daily Courant* appeared (1712), on which the leading intellectuals of England were collaborating.

In the *Discourse on Freethinking* (London 1713) Anthony Collins (1676–1729) for the first time generally applied the term "freethinker" to fellow deists (formerly used for John Toland specifically), whereas in France "libres penseurs" primarily denoted atheists such as Helvetius and Holbach. It was also in England that

Freemasonry originated, that "self-demonstration of a European society which was freeing itself from the ties of the estates, from political forms of authority, and from church dogmata" (F. Wagner). In the course of the seventeenth century the associations of church stonemasons that also had technicians and natural scientists as honorary members had grown into intellectual groups, into lodges. The association of the Greater Lodge of England (1717), whose constitution was drafted in 1723 by the Anglican cleric James Anderson at Saint Paul's in London, was a signal for similar foundings in almost all the European countries, albeit with different intellectual tendencies which indeed led to some divisions. English Freemasonry was dedicated to the moralistic ideal of "Men of Honor and Honesty," to be enhanced by deistic piety.

Such was the political and social context which permitted England to be the first country in which the Enlightenment developed, although with a certain degree of dispassionate moderation. The movement was able, moreover, to benefit from the footing of centuries of empiricism as an intellectual trait of the nation. In his *Novum organum scientiarum sive indicia vera de interpretatione naturae* (1620) Francis Bacon (1561–1626) had tried to refute atheism by means of a sharp separation of *theologia naturalis* and *theologia revelata.* He offered a theory of empiric-inductive science founded on philosophy as one who, much like a bee, not only (empirically) gathers, but also (interpretatively) alters. The *Philosophiae naturalis principia mathematica* (1687) of Isaac Newton (1643–1727), insisting on an absolutely inductive method, is as different from Bacon as it is from Cartesianism. In his introduction Newton defined the method according to which the "force of gravity" is deduced from "celestial phenomena" by means of mathematical postulates and maintained that "the other phenomena of nature should be deduced from mathematical principles" as well. As an author of theological works on the Old Testament, the discoverer of calculus was "ever intent on investigating the total intellectual structure of the empirical world, which permitted an inference of the Christian God of creation." From the first to the third edition of his *Principia,* to be sure, he exhibited a tendency toward a theory of an absolute absence of presuppositions in natural science. Around the middle of the seventeenth century the physician William Harvey (1578–1657), who had studied in Padua and become professor of anatomy in London in 1615, gained fame as the discoverer of the circulatory system, for which he was censured by the Sorbonne. In his *Exercitationes de generatione animalium* (London and Amsterdam, 1651) he applied the causal-inductive method. To be sure, he formulated his theory "ovum esse primordium commune omnibus animalibus" without ever having seen a mammalian egg. The turn of the century brought the English form of empirical criticism, systematic empiricism. In his *Essay Concerning Human Understanding* (1690) John Locke (1632–1704), not one of the most profound, yet one of the most successful intellectuals of his time, especially in his political writings, turned the subject of who investigates nature into the object of his concern. This empiricism rather than the "innate ideas" of Descartes henceforth dominated the period (even though George Berkeley [1685–1753], continuing in Locke's footsteps, considered human perceptions as being arranged by God [*Treatise Concerning the Principles of Human Understanding* (1710)]). Locke's substantiation of deism in the *Letters Concerning Toleration* (1689/92) were no less important than his influence on political theory (contract, separation of powers). In the *Letters* Locke attempted to imbed historical revelation and the proof of its reasonableness in the general system of rationality (*The Reasonableness of Christianity* [1695]). The doctrine of "Natural Religion" had already been offered by Herbert of Cherbury (1582–1648) under the title *De veritate, prout distinguitur a revelatione, a verosimili, a possibili et falso* (1624). John Toland (1670–1722), initially raised in the Catholic faith, who influenced such materialists as Holbach, drew more radical conclusions than Locke from the rationalization of revealed religion. In his publicly burned essay *Christianity not mysterious* (1696; reprint 1969) he maintained that faith did not contradict reason, but conversely did not contain anything beyond that either. Matthew Tindal (1656–1733) on the other hand interpreted the Gospel as a restoration of natural religion (Republication of the Religion of Nature) in his *Christianity as old as the Creation* (1730). In addition to his psychological writings (*Enquiry Concerning Human Understanding* [1758]), those on moral philosophy (*Enquiry Concerning the Principles of Morals,* [1751]), and political science (*Political Discourses,* [1752]) David Hume (1711–76), probably the most important figure of the English Enlightenment, was also an incisive critic of natural religion and deism. His *Natural History of Religion* (1755) and *Dialogues Concerning Natural Religion* (posthumously; 1779) influenced Rousseau, J. G. Herder, and especially Kant. According to Hume, man is determined not by his perceptions, part of which is natural religion, but by his behavioral modes (in the case of religion, by fear and hope), which should be analyzed by psychology. The theologians, he maintained, are intent on proving the greatest paradox; instead, man should admit that "the whole of the world is an enigma, an unfathomable mystery" (*History of Religion,* sec. XV). In his important early work *A Treatise of Human Nature* Hume prophetically related all sciences to the doctrine of man, from which a "complete system" was to be developed (Introduction). A work by the Socinian J. Priestley (1733–1804), *A Comparison of the Institutes of Moses with those of the Hindoos and other Ancient Nations* (1799), is characterized by one of the most important elements of the Enlightenment: the knowledge of non-Christian religions, promoted most of all by Christian missionaries. His *History of the Corruption of Christianity* (1782), a theme also of the pietist J. G. Arnold, is an example of the kind of criticism to which Christian morality, too, was subjected. Sociological and political theories — although characteristic for all of the Enlightenment and its rationalization of natural law — are yet a special feature of the English variant. Whereas an individual and social catalogue of virtues could be derived from the psychology of the liberal David Hume, H. Bolingbroke (1678–1751), politically a Tory (in 1714 he was forced to flee to France), but intellectually an extreme freethinker, replaced the moral idea with his sensualism, of influence also on Voltaire. His ideas were followed by Bernard de Mandeville (1670–1733), born the son of French parents in Holland, who developed the thesis that egoism is the only real social principle (*The Table of the Bees* [1714]). Next Adam Ferguson (1723–1816) attempted to elevate sensualism into a sociohistorical concept. In it, history, brought about by the human species, becomes the essential differentiation from the animal world (*Essay on the History of Civil Society* [1767]). Egoism was viewed as the central principle of social life regardless of the fact that T. Hobbes (1588–1679) developed a theory of absolutism (*Leviathan sive de materia, forma et potestate civitatis ecclesiasticae et civilis* [1651]; *De homine* [1658]) from the formula "Homo homini lupus" or that Adam Smith (1723–1790) a century later offered a theory of liberalism (*Inquiry into the Nature and Cases of the Wealth of Nations* [1776]).

In France the politically motivated confessional toleration under Henry IV (Edict of Nantes [1598]) had created a climate in which, parallel to Catholic renewal in the first half of the seventeenth century, an attitude ranging from indifference in matters of Church and religion all the way to atheism was able to flourish as well. Indifference was indirectly promoted by the conflict with Jansenism, whose political persecution (aside from that by the Church) finally led to its own politicization, just as its religious spiritualism gradually converged with the Enlightenment. But the most important element was the radical move initiated by Richelieu to make the Church into a function of the state whether it be an antipapal move (Declaration of the Gallican Liberties [1682]) or — following an understanding with the Curia — consisted of granting the bishops special privileges vis-à-vis parliament and the lower clergy (Edict of 1695). The revocation of the Edict of Nantes (1685), an outgrowth of establishmentarianism and the authoritative attitude of Louis XIV, had a considerable impact within France when it prompted the emigration of about half a million Huguenots. It was especially important within the European intellectual context, for in addition to the lodges of the Freemasons these refugees represented an "adhesive of European consciousness." Furthermore, their younger, elitist generation, outgrowing their church ties, "replaced the parish congregation with an international republic of letters" (F. Wagner). Aside from the religious nonconformists of France, the Calvinists and Jansenists, who were fighting among themselves, the rationalists as well became increasingly suspect to the absolutist state. While the state had founded the Académie des Sciences in Paris (Colbert in 1666), it also maintained the strictest control over the system of publication and the press within the framework of its mercantile policies. On the other hand, the bourgeoisie, experiencing a powerful rise under Louis XIV, was both bearer and audience of the intellectual movement. During the political and economic decline and in spite of continuing censorship after the death of Louis XIV the Enlightenment was able to develop strongly and even to deviate into extremes. The literary circles and salons, whose members had equal rights of membership after the middle of the century, were the centers of the movement. But the most significant propagator was the *Encyclopedia,* initiated by Jean-Lérond d'Alembert (1717–83); he was named Jean le Pond after the church where he had been abandoned as an illegitimate baby; his intellectual guide was Denis Diderot (1713–84) who was the son of a smith and had studied with the Jesuits. His *Pensées philosophiques* (Paris 1746), publicly burned as anti-Christian, was crowned by the *Promenade d'un sceptique* and a materialistic philosophy of nature. The *Encyclopedia* documented the second half of the century of France by the different positions of its authors, the predominance of empirical sciences, and in its history (1751–72: twenty-four volumes, by 1780: seven supplementary volumes); it was initially granted imprimatur by the Sorbonne, prohibited in vain in 1752, and indexed by Clement XIII. About a decade before the Revolution, almost a century after England, the censorship laws were practically overcome. In 1771 the *Journal de Paris* began to appear. Together with the literary salons the lodges of the Freemasons were the social foundation of the Enlightenment; the Scottish current was conservative, the merger of many lodges forming the *Grand Orient de France* (1773) was a radical and emphatically anticlerical move. In 1738 and 1751 papal prohibitions were issued against it.

Twenty years after the death of René Descartes (1596–1650), his philosophy was banned in France. Its method of doubt was considered as absolute skepticism; there was fear that it was dissolving the authority of the state and society. The Jesuit pupil Descartes (1606–14 at the college of La Flèche), who all his life considered himself to be a devout Catholic, but for the most part was forced to live outside of France, had questioned daily experience as well as general concepts. In this process of critical thinking he had found "clear and explicit" certainty only in the *res cognitans* itself. Equally clear to him was the concept of God: as He is perfection, human *cognatio* possesses but one aspect of Him (his major works: *Meditationes de prima philosophia* [1641]; *Principia philosophiae* [1644]). To speak of Descartes' emancipation of philosophy from theology is valid only in a limited sense by virtue of the fact that only by means of the theological implication of the truth of God can the *res extensa* of divisible matter of physical things by called certain, representing of course a single geometric mechanism. Yet within this mechanism Descartes' *Discours de la méthode* (1637) qualitatively equates the universal saving nature of God's help in the execution of the natural laws, initially created for the chaos, with the act of creation itself. Here is a profound difference from the physicist Pierre Gassendi (1592–1655), who, contrary to both Aristotelian and Cartesian philosophy, viewed all processes in nature as being caused by forces contained in the atoms. The philosophy of Descartes can be interpreted as an endeavor to overtake the emancipation — triggered by Galileo's interpretation of the Copernican view of the world — not only from theology but also from traditional philosophy in an attempt to "trace mathematics back to philosophy" and to do so by means of logic and its direction from the general to the specific. This led to the anti-Cartesian reaction of the empirically oriented eighteenth century. Based on Descartes, the Oratorian Nicole Malebranche (1638–1715) attempted to go back to Augustinian metaphysics of light. In his concept of "Vision en Dieu," merely stimulated by sensual experience, in which all ideas are directly seen (as distinguished from Descartes' "innate ideas") he sees in God the sole *causa activa seu efficiens,* which makes use of human action as the *causes occasionelles* (*Recherche de la vérité* [1674]). This was of great influence on Leibniz. But these attempts to obtain in an era of autonomous reason and mathematical-scientific thought a new central position for theology were rejected alike by the Sorbonne, the traditional theologians (especially the Jesuits), and in part by the Jansenists, as well as by the intellectuals of the Enlightenment, whose philosopher was not Descartes but Locke. In the person of Pierre Bayle (1647–1706) — son of a Huguenot pastor, attended the Jesuit school at Toulouse in 1669, a Catholic for a period of seventeen months, and after 1681 professor of philosophy in Rotterdam — France produced the man who largely determined the intellectual climate of the century. He did so by his unsparing and exceedingly effective criticism of tradition, by the categorical separation of faith and knowledge, by his criticism of the moral discrimination of atheists, but also by his skepticism toward reason (which he considered stronger in the discovery of errors than in positive cognition). He was opposed to Leibniz, Descartes, and Spinoza, yet also cognizant enough of the consequences of the "Pyrrhonisme" to hold fast to the natural idea of reasonableness as the basis for an autonomous moral law. His *Dictionnaire historique et critique* (1697) often adds to insignificant keywords lengthy footnotes which contain the actual substance of the work. But while Bayle could unequivocally state that he would rather be godless than an idolator, the aristocratic Montesquieu (1698–1755) in his *Esprit des lois* (1748) considered the various religions from the point of view of their usefulness to the state. In his conservative criticism of absolutism he held religion to function as the only existing limitation upon those who disregard human laws. This work, which first appeared anonymously in Geneva, exercised great influence by its many editions and translations, representing as it does a biological (climate) and sociological comparative constitutional doctrine. But there exists for him an original ground of being to which the laws are connected, since the absurdity of blind fate would not have been able to produce intelligent beings. Montesquieu rendered one of the most characteristic judgments of Voltaire (1694–1778; son of a notary): Just as monks did for the glory of their order, so did Voltaire write history for the glory of "his monastery," but bad history. Voltaire's partisanship for his "monastery" of restless spirits is the pendant of his fanatical hatred of the Catholic Church (*Sermon des Cinqantes* [1761], *Le philosophe ignorant* [1766], *Profession de foi des Théistes* [1768], and *Dieu et les hommes* [1769]). His life and voluminous literary work cannot be reduced to a formula. The deist philosophy he received from England is meager, but the *Eléments de la philosophie de Newton* (1738) were deadlier for Cartesianism in France than its prohibition by the established Church. Like all those in France who called themselves "philosophes" Voltaire is the prototype of the *écrivain* who was equally able to write the cynical epic *La pucelle d'Orléans* (1739) as well as the profoundly moving *Poème sur le désastre de Lisbonne* (1755). Following is a brief biographical sketch: from 1704 to 1710 he was at the Jesuit college Louis-le-Grand; in 1717 he spent eleven months in the Bastille; as an eminent writer he was received into aristocratic society, this permitted his secret return from banishment in England (1726–28). A successful financial speculator, member of the Académie in 1746, intellectual vagabond after 1750, he spent his final twenty years in Fernay near Geneva. From there he exerted his intellectual influence on all of Europe by means of his voluminous correspondence, aside from the *Encyclopedia* the most important factor in the propagation of the thought of the Enlightenment. His *Candide ou l'optimisme* (1759) documented in exemplary fashion the ever-present possibility of a sudden shift into pessimism. The *Essai sur les moeurs et l'esprit de nations* (1756) gained fame through its added introduction entitled "Philosophie de l'histoire." It represents a fundamental attack on the interpretation of world history according to the details of the Christian Gospel. Next to Bayle, Montesquieu, and Voltaire — his life in many respects is comparable to Voltaire's but a complete opposite in the course of his intellect — Jean-Jacques Rousseau (1712–78) the son of a watchmaker from a Huguenot family who had emigrated to Geneva, was the most significant figure of the French Enlightenment. Under the guidance of the convert Mme von Warens in Annecy (Savoy), who later became his lover, he converted to Catholicism in 1728. But neither his conversion nor his return to the Reformed Church in Geneva (1754) was among the essential inner stations of his life to which his literary work corresponds. All self-stylization aside, his "Inspiration of Vincennes" (conceived in 1749 on his way to visit Diderot in jail) described in the *Confessions* ("en remontant aux traces de mon etre sensible," finished in 1770) may be ascribed the significance of a turning point. As it says in the *Confessions,* it is solely the institutions which make man evil. Following the criticism of culture represented by his *Discours sur les sciences et les arts* (1750), criticism of its institutions was also the thesis of the second discourse ("Sur l'origine et les fondements de l'inégalité parmi les hommes") in 1754. It was this radical inwardness, this resolute anti-institutionalism with its pietistic extension in J. G. Arnold which — aside from determining Rousseau's pedagogy of self-development (*Émile ou sur l'éducation* [1762]; burned as atheistic) — produced the immediate revolutionary impact of Rousseau. The *Contrat sociale* (1762) in one of its possible interpretations did not become truly significant until the French Revolution. There were individual reasons for Rousseau's disassociating himself in 1758 from Diderot, who had influenced him so strongly, for opposing Voltaire, and becoming alienated from D. Hume, with whom he had gone to England in 1765. What these actions demonstrate is the transition from an Enlightenment of reason to an Enlightenment of the "heart," which loses none of its explosive power in the course of nineteenth century intellectual and social history. Rousseau's temporary intellectual companion Diderot, at least initially, had moral reservations against atheism, as did Voltaire. These were not shared by the physician Julien Offroy de la Mettrie (1709–51), who viewed human intellectual powers as pure bodily functions (*Histoire naturelle de l'âme* [1745]). In the Netherlands, where he went after the condemnation of this work, he published the radically materialist atheist essay *L'homme machine* (Leiden 1748), in which he transferred the mechanism of the physical world, asserted by Descartes, to man as an intellectual being. Many of the writers of the Enlightenment worried about securing the moral bases of society. The extreme representative of materialist atheism in France was P. H. D. von Holbach (1723–89). Raised in France as the son of a wealthy upstart from the Palatinate, his vulgarly materialist *Système de la nature* (1770) also appeared in a German translation (1783). His pamphlet *Les Prêtres démasqués* (1768) was rejected even by the likes of Diderot as tasteless. Voltaire, Rousseau, and Georges-Louis de Buffon (1707–88), the famous author of the *Histoire naturelle* (1749–88), withdrew from the circle which Holbach attracted around himself. In contrast to the materialism of the literary figures the important natural scientists of the eighteenth century for the most part were reluctant to accept generalizations — regardless of the radical manner by which they delimited their empirical methods from theology and metaphysics. This was also true of G.-L. de Buffon, intendant of the royal gardens in Paris since 1739, to whom Louis XIV dedicated a bust with the inscription "Majestati naturae par ingenium." He held fast to the "infinite distinction" between man and "the most perfect animal"; for him the "unnoticeable degrees" of gradation in nature were "suddenly rendered invalid" by virtue of the difference between the thinking and the material being. His original theory of the constancy of species, which — it was long felt — could not be abandoned in view of the doctrine of creation, was corrected by de Buffon after 1753. This theory was even more decisively polemicized against by de Buffon's friend and protégé Jean-Baptiste de Lamarck (1744–1829), who offered an initial theory of evolution (*Philosophie zoologique,* 2 vols. [Paris 1809]; *Histoire naturelle des Animaux sans vertebres,* 7 vols. [1815–22]). But avowed atheism is encountered more among the literati than the truly scholarly natural scientists. The idea of progress, just as atheism, was, in its enthusiastic form of expression, mainly a phenomenon of the French Enlightenment. But it was also a case where the French Enlightenment retained an amount of skepticism toward that faith, as was nowhere more clearly expressed than with Voltaire. Robert-Jacques Turgot (1727–81) who initially studied theology and then turned to economics — he was finance minister from 1774 to 1776 — in 1750 read two essays at the Sorbonne entitled "Sur les progrès successifs de l'esprit humain" (not published until 1809). In them he established a correspondence between the historical development of production stages and global commerce on the one hand, and the development of moral forces toward a moderation of customs and habits and a peaceful rapprochement of nations on the other, which includes the influence of Christianity. A friend of Turgot's was the Girondist Antoine de Condorcet (1743–94). His *Esquisse d'un tableau historique des progrès de l'esprit humain,* written in 1794 when he faced death at the hands of the Revolution, in such a situation could not fail to go beyond the question of perfectivizing the satisfaction of basic needs, posing the question which fundamentally contradicts the belief in progress, the question of individual death, which cannot be extinguished by any collective perfectibility of mankind. The answer lies in the hope for a time in which individual life expectancy has been expanded far enough so that man slowly looses his energies and desire for life and, while not becoming immortal, dies satiated by life. To be sure, in such a meditation, eye to eye with one's own violent death, the possibility of the "unusual coincidence" cannot be excluded.

In 1621 after the Synod of Dordrecht (1619) the Remonstrant Hugo Grotius was forced to flee to France and was banished again upon his return in 1632 from the Republic of the United Netherlands, which had been founded in 1588 following the battle against religious and political oppression. In his Dutch refuge Descartes had met with the opposition of the Calvinists, just as he had met with the opposition of the Sorbonne and the Jesuits in France. But in 1638 Galilei's main work, the *Discorsi e dimonstrazioni,* was able to appear in Leiden. For the Trinitarians, expelled from Poland in 1658, the federation became the same refuge which it later became for the Huguenots. It was celebrated by Pierre Bayle, who had been in Rotterdam since 1681, where he met with John Locke as "l'arche des fugitifs." There Bayle founded the *Nouvelles de la République des Lettres,* a journal read by modern intellectuals all over Europe (Amsterdam 1684–89 in six volumes; edited by Bayle himself until February 1687). But in 1693 he was forced to relinquish his chair of philosophy. Yet the Netherlands, led by an urban bourgeoisie with their avant-garde gazettes in Leiden and Utrecht, their presses, whose names appear in the best-known works of the Enlightenment, and with its book trade became an intellectual market place.

The philosopher Baruch (Benedictus in his own Latinization) de Spinoza (1632–77), of Portuguese Jewish parentage, is only geographically Dutch. Ceremoniously expelled from the synagogue in 1656, he lived in lonely poverty in The Hague from 1670 on as a grinder of optical instruments. In his philosophy — the main work being his *Ethica ordine geometrico demonstrata,* published posthumously in 1677 — he takes up the basic problem of Cartesian dualism, asserting the *res cogitans* and the *res extensa* as being the two recognizable ones under the attributes of the *deus omnium rerum causa immanens, non transiens* of the *natura naturans.* This philosophy was rejected by Leibniz and did not have a full impact until the post-Kantian philosophy of monism in Germany, even though it had had some influence on G. E. Lessing and J. G. Herder.

In the German Empire and its countries the principles of the Religious Peace of Augsburg concerning the determination of 1624 as the fixed year had been modified in 1648 inasmuch as a change of denominations occurring between 1624 and 1648 was tolerated, although with some exceptions. The formation of larger territories had resulted in a mixing of denominations (the Reformed Churches were also recognized); in individual cases the immigration of new elements of population had been promoted (especially through the admittance of Huguenots); the "enlightened absolutism," theoretically based on Pufendorf's and Thomasius' doctrine of natural law, had developed (although at different times) in the various countries. But in spite of some modern features in government, conditions had on the whole remained conservative in comparison to western Europe. A primary reason for this is the fact that even under the enlightened regimes the bourgeoisie did not play as prominent a role by far as it did in England and France. Additionally the Reformation had continued to constitute a much more serious religious and theological problem in the Empire than in western Europe. This also contributed to the fact that church historiography was a specific medium for the process of Enlightenment in western Europe. Corresponding in its mathematical spirit to the Enlightenment, the worldly age of the baroque, in addition to its music and architecture, also created religious monuments of exceptional splendor in the German countries and Italy. Because of the chronological lag of the German Enlightenment compared with that of western Europe, arising from historical conditions, the intellectual movement in Germany was confronted with the extremes of the late Western Enlightenment and especially the terrorist phase of the French Revolution, and thus became susceptible to restorative ideas. Romanticism subsequently created revolutionary elements of its own kind.

Important centers of German Enlightenment were the universities of Halle (1694), part of Brandenburg since 1680, and Göttingen (1737), whose Hanoverian rulers became kings of England in 1714, a factor which influenced the political and historical sciences taught there. Among those founded in Germany on the model of the Berlin Academy (1700) whose establishment was assisted by Leibniz, the Göttingen Academy was one of the most important ones (1751). In 1732 the *Göttingische Zeitungen von Gelehrten Sachen* started to appear; as the *Göttingische Gelehrte Anzeigen* it became the leading voice of liberal science in Germany. Among the numerous "Moralische Wochenschriften" in Germany, appealing especially to women eager for education, *Die vernünftigen Tadlerinnen* (from 1725) by J. C. Gottsched (1700–1766), based on Wolff's philosophy of rationalism, was very successful. Its competition was the *Discourse der Mahlern* (from 1721), edited by the Swiss J. J. Bodmer (16980–1783) and J. J. Breitinger (1701–76), which was critical of Gottsched's rationalistic poetry. In 1773 the *Teutsche Merkur,* edited by C. M. Wieland (1733–1813), appeared as an organ of confirmed Enlightenment. Following the *Lexicon universale* (1697) of J. J. Hofmann of Basel, the *Große Vollständig Universallexikon aller Wissenschaften und Künste* (1732–50) represented the new status of general education and the difference in spirit from the French *Encyclopedia.* But the most prominent propagandist of German Enlightenment was the Berlin publisher Friedrich Nicolai, editor from 1765 of the journal *Allgemeine deutsche Bibliothek* (106 volumes). Starting in 1761 he also edited the *Briefe, die neueste Literatur betreffend,* one of whose contributors was G. E. Lessing. In 1788 Nicolai published his *Öffentliche Erklärung über seine geheime Verbindung mit dem Illuminatenorden.* This order had been established in 1776 by the Ingolstadt professor, A. Weishaupt and suppressed in 1783.

Along with Descartes and Spinoza, Gottfried Wilhelm Leibniz (1646–1716) was the most important philosopher of the pre-Kantian period. After serving the elector of Mainz from 1666 to 1673, he traveled to Paris and London for three years, subsequently serving as librarian and privy councilor at the court of Hanover. A scientist and mathematician, he wrote a criticism of the anti-Cartesian empiricism of Locke (*Nouveaux essais sur l'entendement humain,* posthumously [1765]). In his *Monadologie* (1714) he attempted to overcome both Descartes' dualism and Spinoza's monism by positing the universe as joined in the form of monads in "prästabilierter Harmonie" (predetermined harmony), but independent of each other and immaterial. Since they are nonconstructed units they can only "come about and perish all at once," that is they can only be created by creation and perish by destruction. They are ordered according to Cartesian "distinctness and clarity" — man on an intermediate level is unclear regarding his senses and therefore only conditionally clear regarding his reason — in ascending order to God as the uncreated "central monad." While God is called "inventor and master builder" for the "works of nature," He manifests himself "on the other hand as king and father of substances endowed with intellect whose souls are formed according to His image" (E. Cassirer). In his *Essai de Théodicée sur la bonté de Dieu, la liberté de l'homme et l'origine de mal* (Amsterdam 1710) against Bayle, Leibniz addressed one of the major problems of the whole epoch, the question of the origin of evil in the world, to a greater extent than Shaftesbury, Pope, Rousseau, and, in his own way, Voltaire had done. In it he states that the world is of necessity imperfect because it is necessarily limited. Just as Leibniz's monadology and theodicy at important junctures function theologically, so is his position on history determined by religion. His confidence in the progress of humanity in the sense of an infinite process in the last analysis is founded in his faith in a divine universal design: "It is not in keeping with divine harmony to err frequently in the same manner." Regardless of the rationalism of his philosophical theology, his differentiation of the two kinds of truth, the *vérités de fait* and the *vérités de raison,* prevents a rationalization of faith as that of Toland and Tindal. In contrast to historical pyrrhonism the *vérités de fait* are actual truths, part of which are the doctrinal truths of revelation. Christian Wolff (1679–1754), a protégé of Leibniz's at the University of Halle (1706), did not reach the latter's profundity. As a reaction to psychologism Wolff took up elements of "Scholasticism which had until then been pushed into the background" (M. Wundt). Because of a speech about Chinese moral philosophy he got into a conflict with the orthodox segment; as a result of their agitation he was banished from Halle by Friedrich Wilhelm I in 1723. Friedrich II permitted him to return from Marburg seventeen years later. Because of this conflict, and even more so because of his conciliatory attitude (which fit in with the German intellectual climate) Wolff obtained great influence, which extended even to Russia (*Vernünftige Gedanken von Gott, der Welt und der Seele des Menschen, auch allen Dingen überhaupt* [1719]). Among his colleagues in Halle who had found refuge there was the lawyer Christian Thomasius (1655–1728), whose theory of natural law continued the process of rationalization started by Hugo Grotius by separating the legal duties from the inner moral ones. His teacher, Samuel Pufendorf (1632–94), the first German to be appointed professor of natural and international law in Heidelberg, had already established the separation from theology in his major work *De Jure Naturae et Gentium* (1672). To be sure, he defined the *primum principium* as constituting the divine will, but in practice as the absolute state: it is "the pinnacle of human achievement if one, supported by the totality of the powers of the state, can say that one recognizes none higher." But in his doctrine of duty he demonstrated a conservative attitude. Yet in the German domains theological issues retained their priority. The fact that Leibniz's philosophy, oriented toward theology, continued to dominate that geographic area until the arrival of Kant is manifest even in Gotthold Ephraim Lessing's (1729–81) essay *Das Christentum der Vernunft* (1753). But Lessing, the son of a Lutheran pastor, a considerable part of whose literary work was occupied by the issue of the Christian doctrine of revelation, was at the intersection of differing intellectual currents. He was impressed by P. Bayle, for a time by Voltaire, but also by the philosophy of Spinoza. Although he applied as a criterion the correspondence with "Natural Religion" in his work *Über die Entstehung der geoffenbarten Religionen* (1755), he differed from French deism by adhering to the historic necessity of true and false positive religions. These were ideas which he expanded in a more profound fashion in his *Erziehung des Menschengeschlechts* (1780). It is here — more so than in his polemic with the Hamburg pastor J. M. Göze, caused by Lessing's edition of the radically rationalist *Wolfenbütteler Fragmente eines Ungenannten* (by the orientalist H. S. Reimarus [d. 1768]; 1774–78) — that Lessing's specific relationship with Christianity is expressed. For him it was not a matter of finding an abstract rational concept for the truth of revelation. Instead he traces the education of mankind as an analogy of Christian salvation through the stages of the revelation (warning against its untimely abandonment) to the God-given *ratio* which is a category of the future, the "new eternal Gospel" which Lessing invokes with reference to Joachim of Fiore. Just as Lessing's "Natural Religion" differs from the indifference of late French Enlightenment, so does his concept of tolerance: the model for his drama *Nathan der Weise* was the philosopher Moses Mendelssohn (1728–86), who had remained true to his Jewish faith. Enlightenment as history, as in the *Erziehung des Menschengeschlechts,* was a lifelong topic of Johann Gottfried Herder (1744–1803), a church official in Bückeburg from 1771 to 1776. But he sounds more like a Christian in the *Älteste Urkunde des Menschengeschlechts* (1774), where he investigates the difference between the biblical and the general manifestation of God in nature, and in his *Auch eine Philosophie der Geschichte zur Bildung der Menschheit* (1774), a combination of philosophy and theology (a second part did not come about). But only in his *Ideen zur Philosophie der Geschichte der Menschheit* (1784–91) does the Christian religiosity recede behind a concept of universal nature initiating Romanticism. As F. Meinecke stressed, Jesus is now designated as the teacher of "the most genuine humanitarianism." Yet for Herder's total undertaking the words of Kant in his critique of the *Ideen* apply: "... a sagacity skillful in the finding of analogies... combined with the skill to captivate one through feelings and perceptions for a subject always kept at a mysterious distance." Immanuel Kant (1724–1804), whose critique of metaphysics and the bases of perception was prompted by the Enlightenment, overcame the latter by attempting to fathom it. He raised it to a universal principle with his famous definition: "Enlightenment is the emergence of man from a state of minority of his own making" (1784). In his essay *Mutmaßlicher Anfang der Menschengeschichte* (1786) he applied Lessing's method of interpretation to Genesis 2–4, without Herder's application of feeling, but also without the historical sense with which Lessing lets the revelation pass in his *Erziehung des Menschengeschlechts.* By interpreting the transgression of God's command as the "first attempt at a free choice," which was connected with "the discharge from the maternal womb of nature," Kant defined man in his historical relevance more thoroughly than Voltaire and Herder. By his fall from grace man exits "from the era... of peace into that of work and discord, as the prelude to joining in society"; but the goal, the use of reason — as it is expressed in his essay *Idee zu einer allgemeinen Geschichte in weltbürgerlicher Absicht* (1784) — is not reached within the individual, but rather against the individual of the species, in the "antagonism of unsocial sociability of man," which causes the birth from history of "Enlightenment as a great possession." Here the detheologization of history is radical. But at the same time Kant's *Idee zu einer allgemeinen Geschichte* ... seeks to forestall a concept of history as "a purposeless aggregate of human actions." This is not only an historiographical problem, one that was discussed explicitly by the Göttingen historian August Ludwig Schlözer (1735–1809), who had had a falling out with Herder. More so than the moral work *Die Religion innerhalb der Grenzen der bloßen Vernunft* (1793) — suppressed by order of the Prussian council as a "disparagement of Christianity" — the two above-mentioned works from 1784 and 1786 manifest the critique of religious tradition, whose Western themes nonetheless continued to be the guiding ideas in the great works of Kant: soul, world, God — immortality, freedom, God (G. Söhngen).

If anything, the Enlightenment in Switzerland was even more conservative than in the territories of the Empire. Here the differences in the intellectual climate of the cities played a considerable role; the German-speaking part of Switzerland was more practical than speculative. The first masonic lodges were established in the French part of Switzerland, in Geneva and Lausanne, then in Basel and Zurich, whereas Bern suppressed the order. In all of these cities (except for Berne) academies were founded. The fact that members from both denominations could belong to the *Helvetische Gesellschaft* (1761) was a first step beyond the long-lasting Swiss confessionalism. Among the most important figures of modern science in Switzerland were the brothers Jakob (1654–1705) and Johann Bernoulli (1667–1748), both of them mathematicians in Basel. Jakob Bernoulli, initially a pastor and widely traveled in France, the Netherlands, and England brought up again the suppressed Copernican system, but in the spirit of Newton he considered the mathematical laws a natural manifestation of God. Jean-Alphonse Turretini (1671–1733) can be seen as representative of the French part of Switzerland. He was a theologian and naturalist in Geneva who represented a moderate orthodox Enlightenment based on ethics. The Berne patrician Albrecht von Haller (1709–77), who had studied medicine in Tübingen and Leidell, became a pupil of Johann Bernoulli. He described his naturalist observations as poetic impressions (as in the didactic poem "The Alps"), but got into difficulties with his research in anatomy. In 1738 he became a professor at the University of Göttingen and, having attracted considerable fame, returned to his native city in 1753. He was a preformationist who considered the germ cell to contain the whole animal in miniature (*Elementa physiologiae corporis humani,* 8 vols. [Berne 1757–66]) and polemicized against La Mettrie's "godless opinion" of the soul (*De partibus corporis humani, sensibilibus et irritabilibus*). The Genevan Charles Bonnet 1720–93) was able to combine Locke's empiricism with the theory of preformation. He was widely criticized for his *Palingénésie philosophique* (1769), which attempted to combine the belief in revealed religion with Voltaire's empiricism. For his research concerning the reproduction of plant lice he was appointed a corresponding member of the Paris Academy at the age of twenty. He developed a theory of the stages of nature according to their organizational perfection, excluding not even the angles (*Idée d'une échelle des êtres naturels* [1745]) and believed in the possibility of "constant progress of all species toward a higher state of perfection." The naturalist and historian Isaac Iselin (1728–82) worked in the tradition of Basel humanism; in 1747 he lived in Göttingen, in 1752 in Paris, where he met J.-J. Rousseau, whose criticism of culture he rejected. Raised with the philosophy of Christian Wolff and deeply impressed by the *Esprit des lois,* he advanced a utilitarian ethic. After an illness in his thirties he changed his attitude toward Enlightenment: Voltaire now appeared to him to be "a witty poisoner of the human heart." In 1764 after a long period of preparation his *Geschichte der Menschheit* appeared.

French Enlightenment extended to the southern European countries, but its influence within society was limited, but least so in Portugal under the rule of Pombal (1699–1782; prime minister after 1756). In Spain under Charles III (1759–88) the reading of works by Montesquieu, Voltaire, and Rousseau became proof of a progressive mind; authors of the English Enlightenment were translated. Enlightenment in Italy came from the same sources, but there it was Jansenism which represented the actual critical element. The native modernistic literature in the southern European countries ran the gamut from critical Catholic reform to a moderate Enlightenment (with the exception of Portugal). The Italian physician and physiologist Mariello Malpighi (1628–94, in 1691 appointed as his personal physician by Innocent XII) was epoch-making in the biological developmental theory; he investigated the egg of a chicken and of a silkworm microscopically and advanced the hypothesis of the universal unity of developmental laws in flora and fauna. At the same time he maintained that since "the essence of things is hidden," one would have to "go through the whole range of phenomena" empirically (*Anatome plantarum,* 2 vols. [London 1675–79]). A solitary figure within his century, misunderstood even by many of his late discoverers, was the highly gifted historian Gianbattista Vico (1670–1744), an unappreciated professor of rhetoric in his native Naples. In his *Scienza nuovo* (1725, revised 1744) — contrary to the geometric ideas of Cartesianism, but tying in with Augustine — he attempted to discover the one "ideal, eternal history, in accordance with which the course of all the histories of all peoples passes chronologically." Whereas man cannot recognize the order of nature in which God rules "freely and unimpeded," he can recognize the world of history which he himself made. But since man, "intending the opposite," was led to a just society only by providence, the object of the "New Science" must be a "rational theology of divine providence in history."

The Scandinavian countries reacted to Enlightenment primarily in a receptive manner. Stockholm had the reputation of being a refuge (although not always an auspicious one) for great foreigners or a place where their work would come to fruition, as it was for Descartes and Pufendorf respectively. The son of a Swedish country pastor, the physician Carl von Linné (1707–78), who during his studies in Uppsala was asked to assist the theologian Olaf Celsius in compiling a work about biblical plants, represented his country prominently in the history of natural sciences, although many of his works appeared in the Netherlands, where he had investigated the botanical collections in Leiden. He attempted to discover a natural system of organisms in which their "rational order" would be visible. For purposes of the flora he chose — although not exclusively — the reproductive organs as a principle of classification. Like Buffon before him, Linné later abandoned this theory and considered the generation of new species possible. Characteristic of the enlightened optimism is the transference of absolutistic notions to nature where God has "police supervision" and the animals have the duty "to maintain the balance among the plants... so that the perfection of the creator can shine in its full glory everywhere" (*Politia naturae* [Uppsala 1760]).

The history of the Enlightenment in eastern Europe was similar to that in northern and southern Europe. As a consequence of the political history in Poland, French Enlightenment especially that of Rousseau — did not have a noticeable influence there until the end of the eighteenth century. The Enlightenment was received both sooner and more extensively — yet also in an adapted form — in Russia, where it also became an element in its native literature. In a country without a bourgeoisie this was a process initiated from above. The Academy of Sciences in Petersburg was built in the spirit of Peter the Great (1689–1725), but for a long time it had to rely on a foreign faculty. A significant role was played by the Western doctrine of natural law, which was, however, subject to certain limits because of the Russian concept of sacred rule. Suvalov, minister of state to Elizabeth (1741–62), the daughter of Peter the Great, who founded the first Russian university in Moscow (1755), commissioned Voltaire to write the *Histoire de l'empire de Russie sous Pierre le Grand* (1759–63). Under her rule M. V. Lomonosov (1711–65) was appointed professor of the academy at Petersburg. A follower of the philosophy of Christian Wolff, which had generally spread in Russia, he combined an unorthodox religiosity with an optimistic rationalism. Princess Sophie Auguste von Anhalt-Zerbst, who became Tsarina Catherine II (1762–96), opened her court to the influence of French Enlightenment. Under her rule it was possible to publish the five-volume *History of Russia from its most Ancient Times,* written by V. N. Tatiscev from 1686 to 1705. Its theological and philosophical interspersions represented anti-Church criticism as well as the principles of a "Natural Religion." Catherine read Pierre Bayle and Montesquieu, corresponded with Voltaire, Diderot, d'Alembert, and permitted masonic lodges. To be sure, the effects of this sort of literature were limited. But the elements carried into the educated aristocracy by French tutors by means of the French language — the latter having been made the European educational medium by the Enlightenment — can be traced throughout the modern history of Russia.

Creation and Natural Law — The History of Salvation and the World of History

As far as the Enlightenment was concerned, the objectionable theses of the Christian faith were identical with those to which the classical opponents of Christianity and those involved in present-day theological discussion have objected: original sin, the incarnation, and the resurrection. The deist concept of God cannot be reduced to a simple formula. It was characterized by two elements of intellectual history: the perception of a universal law in the natural world and the experience of plurality in the world of history, either recognizable in its laws (the *ricorso* of Vico or the variously perceived progress) or unrecognizable in its context (as in Pierre Bayle), a world no longer identifiable with the world of Christian salvation. The concept of a *providentia divina,* although often used as an empty moralistic formula — especially during the late Enlightenment — continued to pose a problem, preventing a monistic idea of the world among the significant thinkers such as Descartes, Newton, Leibniz, or Vico. Regardless of the various interpretations of the concept of "soul," the idea of the difference between man and the world was adhered to, except by the representatives of a radical materialism. Although the variations of customs, laws and morality, conditioned by nature or history, were stressed (as by Montesquieu), the uniformity of humanity was not questioned, but was rather to be reconceived beyond the level of historical differences.

The two typical forms which furnished the battleground for the fundamental conflict between tradition and the present were represented within the movement of the Enlightenment: harmonizing the opposites and controversy, both on a high and low level. The Anglican bishop J. Butler gained fame with his conciliatory essay *The Analogy of Religion, Natural and Revealed, to the Constitution and Course of Nature* (1736). A classical representative of a decisive separation of the two realms was Pierre Bayle, whose Calvinist tradition has been underestimated heretofore. He demanded a resolution of the *difficultés de la raison* solely by means of *raison.* But to the Christians he said — and there is no reason to interpret his words as scoffing: "C'est aux Métaphysiciens à examiner s'il y a un Dieu et s'il est infaillible; mais les Chrétiens, en tant que chrétiens, doivent supposer que c'est une chose déja jugée." And, not so far from Pascal's position, he writes about Jesus ("Il a voulu que son Évangile choquât"), religion, and pagan aphorism in Paulinian terms. Bayle's harsh "all or nothing" was for those who wanted to save the Trinitarian faith, but abandon original sin. Yet attempts at reducing the nature of the conflict to a superficial and harmless level should be distinguished from the true intellectual effort in this period to preserve the continuity of tradition while trying to resolve the crisis. These efforts revolved around two main problems.

The laws of mathematics and physics could be conceived as the work of *the factor coeli et terrae,* the master builder of the world. Just as Leibniz emphatically considered himself a "Christian mathematician," so did Newton call the "omnipotent" God the one who "guides all things and knows all things which are or can be created." But the problem — while not in the case of Newton himself — consisted of describing the divine will in mathematical terms, from which resulted in the perception of the eighteenth century the absolutely regular course of the world in accordance with theoretical principles and without the need for the continued presence of God once it was set in motion. The topic is broached when Newton mentions God's "unlimited, uniform sensorium," in which God moves the bodies and in so doing is able "to create and recreate the parts of the universe." He posits his sensorium, namely, absolute space, in terms of physics, whereas Leibniz ascribes the latter to the "seat" of God. From then on the dilemma was created between the laws of the world — open to *ratio* — and the mystery of the world. This was a dilemma which G. Berkeley in his *Analyst* (1734) would only name but not solve when, in his polemic against the astronomer Edmond Halley (1656–1742; discoverer of the autonomous motion of the fixed stars) and in disagreement with the principles of calculus, he posed the question whether such findings were more plausible than the "religious mysteries and the articles of faith." The course of rationalism was indeed unstoppable; it was a distant path to the rediscovery of the mystery. But the issue concerning God had yet another aspect for mathematicians and physical scientists such as Newton and Leibniz. The *factor coeli et terrae* is also a recognition of the *pater omnipotens,* the God of history who led Israel out of Egypt. The importance of Newton's essays on the Bible, long excluded from his biographies as mere eccentricity, is now recognized. Leibniz's writings concerning biblical language and history as well as his fragment on the history of theology are more than the work of a "polyhistor."

Historiographers completely disregarded Newton's theological writings. Other theologically motivated theories on the problems of biology in the course of the seventeenth and eighteenth century take on the appearance merely of burdensome elements retarding the course of research if one regards them solely in the perspective of modern biological insight. But seen in the historical perspective they represent an admirable effort in the conflict between empirical research and religious interpretation. Two main theories were involved, that of the preformation of the living being in the germ cell and that of the constancy of species. Jan Swammerdam (1637–80), cofounder with Malpighi of microscopic anatomy, attempted by means of insects and parts of their bodies to prove the thesis that all parts are preformed in miniature in the germ cell. Except for Caspar Friedrich Wolff (1733–94), who did not accept "the idea which is inherent in the uterus" and whose epigenetic theory had already been implied by W. Harvey, the preformation theory was generally accepted. It was given a religious foundation by A. von Haller and C. Bonnet, whose *Paligenesis* was translated by Lavater with the title *Philosophische Unterschung der Beweise für das Christentum* (Zurich 1771). The thesis of all succeeding generations also being contained in the germ cell was comprised in Leibniz's theory of the preformed germ cells existing continuously since creation. The idea of extreme constancy of the species because their propagation is "vera continuatio," as formulated by the early Linné in his *Philosophia botanica* (1751), is based on the theory of the initial perfection of creation. This was accepted in principle by Descartes, although he added the proviso that it would improve the understanding of this matter if "the gradual genesis from the seed were observed." Linné himself modified the theory of the constancy of the species. His contemporary opponent, G.-L. Buffon, called Linné's classification an invented construct and considered "the nature of the species" to be constant, "just as old and constant as nature," even if there are variabilities resulting from climatic effects, but all of them within the "idea of an initial plan." In opposition to the "rash" classification by Linné, which postulates the "omnipotence of nature, capable of extracting" all organized beings from a single one, he emphatically invokes the Book of Genesis. But Buffon, too, arrived at a point where he modified his thesis. Lamarck considered the constancy of the species for the duration of many generations merely a rare special case. If all organisms are products of nature, their gradual subsequent origin begins with the simplest organizations without a goal being involved — this was in contradiction to Leibniz's image of the world. What appears to us as a goal "is in reality only a necessity." An opponent of his was Erasmus Darwin (1731–1802). In his *Zoonomia* (1794) he combined the change of species with the faith in the creation by the assumption of a "first great cause" which gave to changeability the direction toward perfection. Joseph Gottlieb Koelreuter (1733–1806) represented a caesura inasmuch as he violated the taboo of "unnatural propagation" by attempting crossbreeding.

With all the consequences resulting from the total scientism, progressively applied to the world view (including present-day space travel), the issue of the human being was a decisive one. The fact that much existed in the world prior to the arrival of man, as Descartes emphasized, could be reconciled with the report of the creation. But has the world been created with a view toward man? Leibniz gave an affirmative answer to this question, albeit with some provisos. On his "échelle des êtres naturels," C. Bonnet (1745) placed man at the top because his organization was the highest; above him were the angels. But like most of the natural scientists he too underwent a change in his world view, even though he continued to adhere to the "fins" of creation. Still concealed, but nonetheless efficacious, was the documentation of the sort of masochism which prompted man, who was just then reaching for his godlike humanity, to kick himself from the throne of creation by pronouncing an unreflected evolutionism deriving man from the fishes, as proved by the scales on his skin. For Holbach's materialistic anthropology the question of the origin of man was essentially irrelevant; La Mettrie introduced a temporary parting from philosophy by remarking that "an unlimited number of experiences and observations... can be found in the annals of medical scientists who were philosophers, but nowhere among the philosophers who were not medical scientists."

Perhaps the discussion of Kant's critique of divine proof on the part of New Scholasticism permitted the problem "creation and natural law" to gain inordinate prominence in the development of Enlightenment vis-à-vis the other process, which touches more profoundly on the Christian faith because the latter is essentially a historical faith: the "Enlightenment" of the Christian history of salvation. The exact formulation of that which happened there comes from Voltaire. In his polemic against Bossuet he called it ridiculous "to attempt to prove that the God of all nations of the earth and of all creatures of other stars did not occupy himself with the revolutions of Asia and that only with a view upon the small Jewish nation did he send so many conquerors, one after the other, in order to humiliate that nation and then again to lift it up..., and that this small stubborn and rebellious horde were the center and the object of world revolutions." This points up two aspects: the denial of the specific history of salvation explodes the medieval congruence of world history and the history of salvation; at the same time it poses the question of a universal view of history to include all cultures. We must hasten to add that the same Voltaire for whom "true history is the history of progress of the human intellect" expressed the profound skepticism of his age toward history: "Les temps passés sont comme s'ils n'avaient jamais eté. Il faut toujours partir du point où l'on est. . . . " No matter the point of time in the present, which latter can be celebrated and also scorned: these words by Voltaire mark with brilliant trenchancy what would be called the "loss of history" in the twentieth century, the break with tradition. The words of Pierre Bayle: "A historian as such is like Melchizedek without a father, without a mother, and without parentage," cited most often as testimony for the approaching objectivity of historicism, should rather be viewed as witness of precisely that break. Origin and future designated by Christian salvation has been lost. But all of these and other similar utterances must be kept in mind in order not to have the relationship between the Enlightenment and history (containing the problem of salvation) blocked by the scolding of it by the Romanticists. The latter were first refuted by W. Dilthey when he said: "Enlightenment . . . has brought about a new perception of history. . . . The view of the solidarity and the progress of the human race in these works spread its light across all peoples and eras." In view of the enduring Eurocentricity of the Enlightenment these words cannot be accepted without reservation. B. Croce's remark on the other hand, according to which the Asian cultures had served Enlightenment only for the purpose of "expressing its love of tolerance or rather of religious indifference" without their representatives having taken the "historic realities" seriously, requires an added remark: while Orientalistics in the strict sense belongs to a later time, the idea of viewing all nations and ages from the perspective of the human race is indeed a fruit of the Enlightenment. The fact that the problem of the presentation of universal history was one involving the subject matter itself if it was to be more than a mere aggregate was demonstrated with astonishing farsightedness by August Wilhelm Schlöer of Göttingen in his *Vorstellung einer Universalhistorie* (1772). He obviously refers to Bayle in demanding of a universal history that it should spread "without a fatherland" across all geographic areas. With reference to Voltaire he demands that it not have a predilection for "the people of God, nor Greeks and Romans," but rather be occupied with everything, "be it on the Hwang Ho and Nile, as well as on the Taber and Vistula." The criterion of selection, he maintains, could not be gleaned from "special histories" but only with a view toward its "influence in the whole or in large parts of the world," thence a world history will order the "special histories" into a "lucid whole." In view of the fact that a universal connection of events appears only with the advent of modernity, "the universal history will connect nations who formerly had no connection or no visible one and will create a system by means of which the multiplicity can be comprehended all at once." But, contrary to J. G. Herder, this is not to be a system of philosophers but of historians. What is to be demonstrated is the way in which man, "this mighty sub-God," recreated the earth into his dwelling, this man who, to be sure, "is kept on a long chain" by the highest of beings. Schlözer did not write this world history but — except for the rational-theological concept of Vico — he formulated the problems it entailed as hardly another. In this way he was a creature of the Enlightenment, which, after all, only created the designs for a universal history, but no world history deserving that name. Yet the Enlightenment recognized that such a history could no longer be comprehended in a state of identity with the history of salvation, which was Vico's main problem. No doubt this is also reflected in the Enlightenment's doctrine of the state, in the rationalization of international law from Grotius to Thomasius, in the rationalization of administration and politics. In addition, the question should be brought up as to what distinguishes the sacred foundation of the absolutist kingdom from the sacredness of the medieval ruler to the point when finally "the theocratic charge is viewed in a more and more conventional manner" (F. Wagner).

The causes of this profound change in the relationship to history were contained partly in the endogenous process of Europe in Enlightenment and partly in the concrete experience of the world outside of Europe. In the process the two elements intensified each other. The strongest impression was made by the reports of missionaries since the late sixteenth century, upon which the Augustinian Juan Gonzales de Mendoza relied in his description of China. Foremost among them were the reports of Jesuits, those of Matteo Ricci (1552–1610), followed by the *Nouveaux mémoires sur l'état présent de la Chine* (1696) by Louis le Comte, who reflected on the relativity of traditional customs. They also included the *Description... de la Chine et de la Tartarie, chinoise* (1735) by Father Du Halde. The other authentic and fictional travelogues cannot be explicitly mentioned here. The fact that François de la Mothe Le Vayer (1588–1672; tutor of Louis XIV), in his essay *De la vertu de payens* (1642) was tempted to exclaim "Sancte Confuci, ora pro nobis," not only anticipated Arnold Toynbee's syncretistic litany, but it also demonstrates the profound impression made by this figure who was instrumental in bringing about the China rapture enduring until the end of the eighteenth century, parallel to which criticism of Chinese absolutism also grew stronger and stronger as a vehicle of criticism of European absolutism. The fascinating aspects of China were its sophisticated culture without a religious doctrine of revelation, the moral philosophy on a purely natural, societal fundament, and the high culture based on it. With an astonishing intuition Leibniz in his *Novissima Sinica historiam nostri temporis illustratura* (1697) called China "orientalis quaedam Europa," endorsing in that way the only high culture which had a global opportunity like that of Europe. In accord with his harmonizing way of thinking he expressed the idea that China send missionaries of natural theology to the corrupt Europeans, while the Christians should dispatch missionaries of revealed theology to China. Following the erroneous opinion that Chinese philosophy originated long before Greek philosophy, he condemned as unwise the prejudice that "nous autres nouveaux vénus après eux, et sortis a peine de la barbarie" condemn Chinese philosophy because it does not correspond with Scholastic concepts.

Perhaps more profound yet than the ideas of the high culture of China was the effect of the encounter with the primitives of America on European historical consciousness, primarily because the enduring topic of the "noble savage," originating in the sixteenth century, was a means of cultural criticism. Here, too, missionary reports played a large part. In his *General History of the Antilles* (1654, enlarged in 1667) the Dominican Du Tertre does not tire of contrasting the natural morality and simplicity of the people falsely called "savages" with the evils of European civilization. Programmatic by virtue of their title are the two volumes *Moeurs des Sauvages Amériquains comparées aux Moeurs des Prémiers temps* (1724) by the Jesuit Lafitau, in which the Iroquois and Hurons of Canada are described as witnesses of original manifestation and as counterwitnesses of Bayle's assertion of atheism among the primitives. While the missionary reports only indirectly resulted in criticism of the Christian tradition, it was different in the case of Baron de La Hontan, who had served with the French army in Canada, had gone over to the Indians, and returned in 1715. Protected by the mantle of a fictitious polemic with an Indian, his *Travels, Memories and Dialogues* (1703) attacked the Christian faith head on by awarding victory to the "natural religion" of the primitive. Enlightenment itself attacked the legend of the "noble savage," Voltaire with sarcastic scorn, Kant based on his principle of societal antagonism. Rousseau's "homme naturel" is not the primitive who is already a representative of a developing society, but the ideal construct of man prior to history. This going beyond all history back to the "beginning," from which vantage point one hoped to arrive at a critical judgment of history as a whole and win the future, was the revolutionary element. Whether it was a case of praising the "noble savage" in his heavenly countryside and his "natural religion," which was superior to revelation, or a case of outdoing each other in imagining the beginnings of mankind in animalistic ways, the origins of the history of mankind became a problem which the Bible no longer appeared to solve.

This loss of an answer in terms of salvation history to the question concerning the origin and the future, the latter either pessimistically conceived or optimistically envisioned as progress, constitutes the general historical situation of the Enlightenment. Its attempts to find new answers is only judged fairly if one views this situation not as an unavoidable but as a logical result of Western history and if one reflects upon the reasons why the Church "lost its leadership."

Section Two

Church Life under the Influence of the Established Church and the Enlightenment

Chaps. 129–31: Louis Cognet;
Chaps. 132–33, 135–36: Heribert Raab;
Chap. 134: Bernhard Stasiewski; Chaps. 137–38: Wolfgang Müller

CHAPTER 129

Jansenism in Eighteenth-Century France

The Bull *Unigenitus*

On Friday, 8 September 1713, Clement XI signed the bull *Unigenitus Dei Filius,* which condemned 101 theses from the *Réflexions morales sur le Nouveau Testament* by Pasquier Quesnel. This was the first official condemnation of Quesnel, who was generally considered the head of the Jansenist party after the death of Arnauld; the brief of 1708 had not been accepted, although it could have been assumed that this document, requested by the King, would meet with strong sympathy. In spite of the initiatives undertaken by the Holy See, France was not immediately informed of the text of the bull; on 9 September it was simply handed to Cardinal de La Trémoille and not made public until 11 September. Louis XIV received it on 24 September at Fontainebleau and immediately expressed his extreme satisfaction because with it he believed to have found the argument necessary for the liquidation of Jansenism. According to Gallican prescriptive law the bull, in order to become legal, had to be provided with letters patent, accepted by the bishops and registered by the chambers of parliament. The text was therefore carefully designed not to affect the sensitivities of Gallicanism. But difficulties arose from another side. The 101 articles selected for condemnation from a list of 155 were to be arranged in such a way as to furnish a sort of summary of the Jansenist doctrine. But a number of these articles could be authenticated by means of patristic texts; some of them in fact seemed to be nothing but quotes from the most esteemed of the Fathers. Furthermore. several of them on first perusal appeared to express the traditional Augustinian doctrines, especially those of unmerited predestination and efficacious grace. Obviously an interpretive effort was needed to glean from them a heretical meaning. The fact that Quesnel was the author was beyond doubt: the Latin translation was a faithful rendition of theses from the *Réflexions morales.* In contrast to what had happened in Jansen's case, the *quaestio facti* caused no problems here. But in the eyes of many readers the bull seemed to go beyond Quesnel and actually to condemn Augustinianism, to which many of the theologians and the faithful continued to adhere passionately, considering it one of the cornerstones of Christian thought. For them the bull was totally erroneous regarding the *quaestio facti.* One should also not disregard the fact that at this time the personal infallibility of the Pope was advocated by hardly any of the French theologians and that there was no agreement that this privilege even extended to so simple a bull. Thus the circumstances were quite different from those at the time of the Jansenist conflict.

Louis XIV at first did not conceive of any difficulties in getting the bull accepted. Accustomed for a long time to absolute subservience, he did not take into account that he had aged, that the end of his reign had become predictable, and his opponents now dared act much more openly. It can be assumed as almost certain that he had assured Clement XI that the bull would be accepted without prior discussion. Initial events seemed to prove him right. By means of a pastoral letter dated 28 September the vacillating archbishop of Paris, Noailles, retracted his approbation of the *Réflexions morales,* but without expressly recognizing the bull. On 27 and 28 September it was submitted to a group of parliamentarians, and Procurator General Daguesseau determined the central aspect of the debate by declaring that for him the bull was proof of the fallibility of the Popes. The parliamentarians did recognize that the bull contained nothing contradictory to the Gallican Liberties, yet they demanded provincial synods to be convened which were to accept the bull prior to its registration. At this point Louis XIV and Le Tellier, his confessor and advisor, recognized that their plan was more difficult than they had expected. Since the solution involving the provincial synods appeared to be all too difficult, the court decided to have the bull accepted by a special synod which was to be convened as quickly as possible and include all bishops present in Paris and these who could be summoned without delay. A letter of 5 October convened this synod for the sixteenth of the month. On that day twenty-nine prelates gathered at the episcopal see in Paris under the chairmanship of Noailles; during the following few weeks they were joined by another twenty prelates. The motion for an immediate acceptance of the bull was at once rejected in spite of the efforts of a small minority because the bishops were claiming the right of an examination of the papal decision. A commission of six members under the direction of Cardinal de Rohan was entrusted with an examination of the bull. In the process, Msgr. Bissy, bishop of Meaux, quickly assumed a significant position because of the confidence he enjoyed on the part of the King and Le Tellier. Clement XI predictably felt insulted; through his nuncio he complained about the fact that his decision was not to be subjected to judgment by the bishops.

By the court's request one of the first actions of the commission around 4 November was the dissemination of a French translation of the bull. But this proved to be a mistake since it prompted the formation of a spirited opposition movement within the clergy and the public. The deliberations by the committee were protracted. By the end of December it finally became quite clear that a majority of the assembly were resisting the King's pressure, refusing simple acceptance. As a condition for any acceptance at all they demanded explanations which would preserve the Augustinian doctrine. Arguments for and against the bull were circulated; memoranda composed by Quesnel himself were sent to the commission. In the course of January 1714 Clermont-Tonnerre, bishop of Langres, with the collaboration of Rohan suggested acceptance of an annotated version of the bull by means of an episcopal pastoral instruction. At first Noailles seemed to be agreeable, but then his friends moved him to revert to his earlier decision. On 12 January eight bishops, among them Noailles' brother, gathered about him and declared their intention not to take part in the meeting scheduled for the fifteenth. But the King, informed of their decision, ordered them to attend, so that the assembly finally included all forty-nine prelates present in Paris. The sessions were lengthy and stormy. On 1 February Noailles and the eight opponents declared their unwillingness to take any action until the Pope had been requested to furnish explanations which they considered indispensable for the preservation of the inviolate doctrine. The assembly dissolved on 5 February after forty bishops had accepted the constitution and the nine opponents lad rejected it. Louis XIV denied them permission to send a collective letter to the Pope. On 8 February Noailles was ordered not to appear at court; the other eight were told by secret letter to return to their dioceses. From this point on the split in the episcopate became common knowledge.

Yet the King considered the acceptance by forty bishops sufficient to have the bull registered in parliament. The letters patent were issued without delay despite the heated opposition of numerous members of parliament who rejected the formulation "we are making it the bishops' duty to accept the bull." But the King insisted on precisely this wording because it was intended to enable him to proceed harshly against the opponents. The registration took place during a session of parliament on 15 February where several members refused to take part; Daguesseau and Pucelle especially were marked in their opposition. The resistance in parliament aggravated the King to such an extent that he burst into veritable fits of anger at Versailles in the presence of Daguesseau and the advocate general, Joly de Fleury. In the meantime the declaration of acceptance had been sent to Rome and Clement XI thanked the forty bishops involved in a brief full of praise. But the Gallican public was shocked by the significance which the brief ascribed to this act of submission to the Holy See. On 28 February Noailles reacted by circulating a pastoral instruction dated 25 February in which he forbade the clergy in his diocese to accept the bull, pending further instruction. Several other opponents followed his example. The King thereupon decided to force the Sorbonne into accepting the bull. It was submitted at a regular meeting on 1 March and accepted over the violent opposition of Dr. Witasse in a vote which took place under very dubious circumstances. A number of professors protested; five of them were exiled by secret letter. Shortly thereafter the pastoral instruction, composed by the assembly and edited by Bissy, the bishop of Meaux, was sent to the entire episcopate. During the following months the bull was published in 112 of the 126 dioceses of France. No doubt this constituted a large majority, but not the unanimity which the King desired.

The most grievous problem was that those bishops who had accepted the bull were in fact not supported by any sizeable part of their clergy. A number of priests refused to read the pastoral instruction of their bishop from the pulpit or did so only with reservations. The same split occurred in the orders and monasteries. The opposing bishops, for their part, issued pastoral letters expressing the desire for a papal explanation of the bull. Yet most of them accepted a temporary condemnation of Quesnel's works in their dioceses with the notable exception of Jean Soanen, bishop of Senez, a former Oratorian who was soon to occupy a central position within the Jansenist resistance. At any rate, the debate was now conducted before the public and prompted the appearance of an incredible number of works of any and all format, ranging from brief brochures to voluminous folios: in 1714 alone the contemporary catalogues listed more than 180 titles. This large volume of writing actually made use of only a very limited number of basic arguments. Those favorable to the bull, a small minority by far, stressed that submission was due the King as well as the Pope and strove to demonstrate the identity of Quesnel's Augustinianism with that of Jansenism. This was the basic idea especially of a memoir which was widely circulated in the form of a manuscript. No doubt for good reason it was ascribed to a professor of the Sorbonne, Honoré Tournély (1658–1729), at the time a highly esteemed personality. On the side of the opposition, too, the fight was conducted on two levels. The primary intent was to present the basic orthodoxy of Quesnel, his absolute conformity with the Fathers, and, most of all, with Augustine. The most important of those works is *Les Hexaples ou les six colonnes sur la Constitution Unigenitus* (Amsterdam 1714), in which the 101 condemned theses are juxtaposed with the Holy Gospel and tradition and are justified by other passages from the works of Quesnel and by additional long treatises. All the great theologians of the Jansenist party contributed to it. The work, originally comprising one quarto, was enlarged with each succeeding edition until in 1721 it reached the very respectable extent of six volumes. In addition to these, the same group of collaborators published a four-volume *Histoire du livre des Réflexions morales* which, while partisan, was admirably well documented, thus representing an important source. Beyond this, the opponents had to justify their position vis-à-vis a formal decision by the Pope in a question which no longer, as in the case of Jansen, concerned the *quaestio facti* but the *quaestio juris.* Characteristic in this regard was the treatise by the Oratorian Vivien de la Borde (1680–1748) entitled *Du témoignage de la vérité dans l'église* (1714). Its author wanted to show that within the Church it is the totality of the faithful and clergy and not only the Holy See and the hierarchy who are the custodians of the truth of revelation. It follows from this that the bishops and the Pope can err; it can even happen that the majority of the bishops can be in error. In such a case, it is the reaction of the Christian conscience on the part of the faithful which is the sign of the truth. The author does not hesitate to push his principles to the very extreme by asking all his readers to consider themselves judges of the doctrine by the same right as the hierarchy. By encouraging them into unfettered examination he manifests the motive force of E. Richer. The Jansenist literature of this period generally manifested an increasing receptivity to Richer's ideas, accentuated by the demands of the lower clergy, who were hard put to bear the absolutism of the episcopate. This literature shows the first designs of political Jansenism and its agreement with Gallicanism.

Louis XIV and the people around him did not grasp the seriousness of the problem. The animosity against the bull was to them merely the sort of resistance which had to be broken. Moreover, a brief by Clement XI of 8 May 1714 recalled to the King in a veiled fashion the obligations which he had contracted. But to find the right methods was not easy. Since it was evident that the Holy See would never give the explanations demanded by the opposition, Cardinals d'Estrées and de Polignac attempted to act as mediators in order to induce the King to accept the following solution: In a pastoral instruction Noailles was to give his own explanation and under this condition to accept the bull. In the course of the summer of 1714 a hesitant Noailles appeared to tend toward this suggestion, but then Rohan and Bissy managed to interfere in the negotiations and to insert clauses which Noailles held to be unacceptable. The result was a renewed split by the end of October. Irritated by the delays, the Pope at times seems to have mentioned his inclination to let the French bishops lacerate each other without intervening. But at this point the intervention of Fénelon became decisive. The latter's anti-Jansenist sentiments had become stronger than ever, especially since he now saw an opportunity to take revenge on Noailles. For the purpose of publishing the bull *Unigenitus* in the French part of his diocese of Cambrai he had used — with some modifications — the model of the pastoral instruction stipulated by the February assembly. For the Flemish area he composed a separate pastoral letter, dated 29 June, which represented an emphatic defense of the bull. In the course of the summer he also published his voluminous "Instruction pastorale en forme de dialogue sur le système de Jansénius." As of 1709 the relationship between Fénelon and the Holy See had improved. Fénelon thus was a suitable mediator; it is certain that Le Tellier more than once asked for his advice. After all, it was well known that Fénelon had had a part in the dispatch of the brief of 8 May 1714. In October 1714, after the negotiations had failed to produce an agreement, Louis XIV decided to proceed against Noailles although this was difficult to do without arousing the opposition of his colleagues in the episcopate. Around 25 October a system advocated by Fénelon was adopted: the convocation of a national council which was to condemn the opponents and pronounce their removal from office. This plan was not without a certain amount of danger. On the one hand, even the weight of the King's authority could not ensure the assembled bishops to be prepared to accept such injurious measures against their colleagues in the episcopate. On the other hand, it was certain that Rome — distrustful of national councils, especially in the Gallican Church — could not be particularly eager to agree to the scheme. But Fénelon was not to be deterred by these obstacles. He was more than ever convinced that forcible measures were needed, because any attempts at conciliation with Noailles would be to the advantage of Jansenism. Also he was now mentioned as possible president of the proposed future council, which would give him far-reaching possibilities to proceed against Noailles and the other opponents. In addition, the esteem that he was held in by the Pope and the Curia had reached its high point; shortly before Christmas 1714 Clement XI openly alluded to his intention to appoint Fénelon to the cardinalate in the very near future. At this point Fénelon decided to make use of his influence by sending the Holy See two memoranda concerning the necessity for a national council and for promulgating the bull in every single church. At the same time Louis XIV dispatched his minister of state, Amelot, to Rome, where he was to negotiate this matter. The King had a great deal of confidence that Fénelon's intervention in this undertaking would be crowned by success. The archbishop of Cambrai for his part was quite ready to do everything in his power when his untimely death on 6 January 1715 robbed both the Pope and the King of an irreplaceable mediator.

Given this situation, Amelot's negotiations in Rome took a difficult turn. Renewed attempts in Paris to reach a compromise failed and Bissy, the bishop of Meaux, was appointed cardinal at the request of the King (June 1715). In July 1715 the King announced that the council would be convened even without the agreement of the Pope. Parliament stayed in the background; several memoranda favoring the opponents mentioned the possibility of an appeal to the general council, an idea which soon began to spread. Shortly thereafter the King made known his intention to have parliament pass a formal resolution excluding the opponents from the future council. But this idea encountered resistance on the part of several parliamentary councilors, especially Procurator General Daguesseau and the advocate general Joly de Fleury. In order to have his way the King prepared for a formal trial proceeding in parliament. But neither in Rome nor in Paris had any final decision been made when Louis XIV died on 1 September 1715. The idea of a national council died with him.

In his memoranda to Rome and his correspondence with Le Tellier, Fénelon again and again had stressed the fact that for the most part public opinion, in spite of an outward show of submission prompted by fear of the authorities, in reality adhered to Jansenism. Events following the death of Louis XIV proved him right. The regent, Philipp of Orleans, who was almost wholly without faith in religious matters, initially went against the policies of the deceased King and deliberately favored the Jansenists, especially since there were many personal enemies of his among those who had accepted the bull. After he had the testament of Louis XIV (which only granted him the chairmanship of the council of regents) declared invalid and had himself appointed sole regent of the realm, he rewarded parliament by creating six councils charged with conducting public affairs in which the parliamentary councilors were to occupy an important position. One of them was the *Conseil de Conscience,* whose function had been severely limited under Louis XIV. Now it was enlarged and Noailles was made its president. The archbishop of Paris once again was an important personality at court; Daguesseau and Pucelle, well known for their opposition to the bull, were also invited to court, whereas Bissy and Rohan were excluded. Le Tellier was exiled, first to Amiens and then to La Flèche. At the beginning of October Clement XI expressed his dissatisfaction in a brief. The majority of persons exiled or jailed because of their advocacy of Jansenism regained their freedom. For a while recalling Quesnel to France was even contemplated, but in a communication by Pouillon several of his friends advised him "not to accede to the urgings to relinquish a state which derived to his glory." The old man elected to remain in his seclusion. In his first appointments to bishoprics the regent favored persons who openly showed their Jansenist sympathies, as in the case of Bossuet's nephew, Jacques Bénigne, who was appointed bishop of Troyes, a person of more than dubious morality who used the fame of his uncle as a cover. Clement XI refused his bulls of investiture for the regent's candidates. But an Assembly of the Clergy, convened on 25 May 1715, had not been interrupted by the death of Louis XIV. One of its most marked decisions was the condemnation of the *Hexaples* (15 October) and of the *Témoignage de la vérité* (29 October), which permits the conclusion that these two works were considered the two most important ones in opposition to the bull. The regent promptly forbade publication of these censures. But this did not represent any progress in the issue of the original condemnation either.

During this time, public opinion considered the pro-Jansenist attitude of the regent a veritable liberation. Numerous people and bodies of people now retracted their original acceptance of the bull, pointing to the pressure to which they had submitted. This was the case with the Sorbonne when it elected a syndic in the person of Ravechet, who openly favored Jansenism. The result was a number of stormy sessions, characterized by acrimonious disputes with the acceptants among the bishops. Yet the Sorbonne did not expressly retract its acceptance of the bull. But other theological faculties did so, among them those of Nantes (2 January 1716) and Rheims (1 July 1716). Yet the problem of the opposing bishops was not removed. Initially the regent hoped to solve the issue in a way to which Noailles had agreed in principle: an acceptance of the bull in connection with a pastoral instruction which was to give a more explicit explanation compared to that of 1714. In December 1715, eighteen bishops from among the acceptants signed a letter to the regent asking him to request explanations from the Pope. A second, more satisfactory letter increased the number of signatories to thirty-two. The rest of the original acceptants adhered to their decision in spite of the regent's requests, to whom it would have been useful to have a majority of the episcopate demand an explanation. Shortly thereafter Clement XI let it be known that he would not give any explanation until the bull was accepted unanimously; in May 1716 he sent a brief with threats against the opponents, which was rejected by the regent. At this point a different plan was formulated. Since the fall of 1715 the opposing bishops, with the concurrence of the regent, had gathered around Noailles in Paris. They had agreed to compose a "corps de difficultés" containing their objections to the bull, and a "corps de doctrine" which was to present their opinions regarding the controversial points. Yet agreement on this was also not easily achieved; from this point on four of the bishops seceded from the group as protagonists of extreme resistance against a bull which they considered irreparably bad. The documents were finally published in May 1716, albeit not without difficulties. What remained was to induce Rome to accept this solution. The regent decided to entrust the negotiations to a man whom he trusted completely, the Abbé Chevalier, vicar general of Bissy, who tended somewhat toward Jansenism. The Abbé's sympathies became obvious when he chose de la Borde, author of the *Témoignage de la vérité,* as his traveling companion. This could not have a convincing effect on Clement XI. Provided with instructions by Noailles, Chevalier set out on 14 May.

The negotiations were difficult from the start. Chevalier was not received by the Pope; not until 25 June did he even receive an audience with Secretary of State Paolucci, which was hardly encouraging. On 26 June Clement XI convened a general congregation of cardinals present in Rome, which was extremely unusual. In a speech lasting two and a half hours he presented the background of the bull and announced the dispatch of two briefs which were to demand of Noailles and the opponents to accept the bull within two months. Then he asked the cardinals how they would proceed against the opponents. The Pope did agree to have Chevalier meet separately with the cardinals and since he did not want to receive him in audience he appointed two cardinals who were to hear Chevalier and give him an account. The letters of Chevalier show that he was laboring under some illusions concerning his talks with the cardinals. These submitted their opinions around the middle of July; on the whole they were strongly against Noailles and the opponents. The more moderate cardinals were satisfied to request one more attempt at reconciliation before proceeding harshly. Chevalier meanwhile continued his negotiations until the middle of August. At that point Clement XI told the representative of France, Cardinal de la Trémoille, that he did not intend to give any explanations of the bull *Unigenitus* because he assumed that they would not be any better received than the bull itself. Although Chevalier remained in Rome until the fall of 1717, his mission had actually failed. Rome and Paris agreed on another negotiator, the Jesuit Pierre-François Lafitau, whose service was rewarded with the bishopric of Sisteron in 1719. At the time he was living in Rome and in September 1716 he spent about three weeks in Paris, without an official title. He, too, was to pass on the "corps de difficultés" and the "corps de doctrine" compiled by Noailles and the other opponents and to effect their acceptance. These documents were dispatched to him shortly after his departure for Rome. But Lafitau could achieve no more than Chevalier. He was not received by Clement XI either. The latter, in fact, hardened his position. On 6 December 1716 a courier extraordinary arrived in Paris carrying a letter from the Sacred College to Noailles exhorting him to accept the constitution. He also delivered a papal brief for the regent demanding that he proceed against Jansenism and a brief for the acceptants encouraging them to reject any and all compromises and to announce measures against the opponents, and, lastly, a brief for the Sorbonne canceling its privileges.

The regent and his advisers were disappointed and confused by this renewed opening of hostilities. Noailles, on the other hand, sensing support from the court, had more and more stiffened his resistance. On 17 August 1716 he had announced to the Jesuits of his diocese that he would not renew their right of sermon and confession, with the exception of the five Jesuits active at the court. But before his authority had run out Cardinal de Rohan, grand almoner of France, had appointed a Jesuit, de la Ferté, Advent preacher at the court. Consequently the Jesuit assumed himself to be fully authorized to begin his sermons on All Saints' Day, according to custom and with the concurrence of the regent. But Noailles, incited by part of his clergy, obtained a revision from the regent and then revoked all privileges from the Jesuits. There was growing agitation on the part of the lower clergy manifesting violent opposition to the bull. Noailles felt overwhelmed by the letters and expressions of solidarity heaped upon him by his priests. Publications for and against the bull continued to appear with great rapidity in 1716, although not quite as numerous as in the preceding year. Those concerned with the disputes of the Sorbonne constituted a large number, but all of them evidenced the rise of Richer's ideas. In such an atmosphere it is understandable that new papal statements met with a negative reception. The regent refused to accept the brief addressed to him and forbade the letter by the cardinals to Noailles. On 9 December in a letter written by Maupéou, representative general of the clergy, he forbade the acceptants among the bishops to accept the brief addressed to them. Finally, a decree of parliament dated 16 December, followed by numerous provincial parliaments, prohibited the acceptance of the brief against the Sorbonne. Going back to Gallican positions once again made it possible completely to neutralize the Roman intervention.

Although an Assembly of the Clergy was planned for 20 November, the regent preferred to cancel it in view of the unsettled circumstances and instead to permit only partial conferences conducted on a private level. These again dealt with the issue of a "corps de doctrine" as a precondition for accepting the bull. In spite of conciliatory efforts by the regent the positions of the opposing parties proved to be farther apart than ever, especially since Colbert and Soanen heatedly announced that they were prepared to resist to the utmost. At this time the Sorbonne managed to clarify its position in an extraordinary assembly on 12 January 1717. It declared the bull to be unacceptable and assured Noailles of its alliance. All the while the negotiations were continued. On 1 February 1717 Daguesseau became chancellor and minister of justice. His great authority in this area enabled him to support his regent's efforts at conciliation. Noailles did not cease to vacillate, creating ever more difficulties. In spite of a warning from the papal state secretary Paolucci, Rohan and the other acceptants appeared to be ready for some concessions, which met with some positive inclination by the regent. A final meeting on 26 February 1717, while not reaching a definitive goal, did show some progress. For a while it appeared as if agreement was near, but then one incident was to put everything in doubt again.

The Appellation

With the convening of new conferences in November 1716 an extremist group within the ranks of the opponents gradually had a significant impact. The initiative leading to its formation appears to have come from Jean Soanen (1646–1740). An Oratorian from the Auvergne, he had started his brilliant career as court chaplain Jansenist correspondents accused him of being ambitious and having obtained his modest bishopric of Senez (1695) merely by virtue of his complacency toward de la Chaise. He was pious and charitable and an excellent bishop who did not enter the controversy until the bull *Unigenitus* was published. A solid theologian and confirmed Augustinian, he expressed his opposition from the start. Gradually he became convinced that any attempt at reaching a compromise was dangerous. The death of Louis XIV increased his hopes and prompted him to spend some time in Paris in order to follow further developments there. Noailles' indecisiveness began to irritate him to the point of creating friction between them. In the fall of 1714 he appears to have decided upon a method designed to exclude any possibility of compromise: an appeal to a general council. In his radical opposition to the bull he had found support in the person of Colbert de Croissy (1667–1738), son of the minister to Louis XIV, bishop of Montpellier since 1696. He was a member of a powerful and wealthy family, no doubt accustomed a little too much to pomp and luxury. Yet he was an upright bishop who did his duty faithfully. Early on he had had some problems with the Jesuits in his diocese, but had not involved himself officially in the Jansenist issue until he started to express his opinions in 1713. At that point he did not hesitate to join Soanen in the latter's emphatic opposition.

In November 1716 Soanen and Colbert decided to appeal to the general council. We do not know just what prevented them from going ahead with it at that time. In the course of the following weeks Soanen and Colbert gained two more allies for their appeal: Pierre de Langle (1644–1724), bishop of Boulogne, and Pierre de la Broue (1643–1720), bishop of Mirepoix, both of them virtuous and highly respected prelates. But in this issue they only played a subordinate role. Consultations between these four bishops were kept secret and nothing seems to have been divulged to the general public. It is certain that Noailles was informed and that he encouraged the appellants, but was unwilling to compromise himself. After several corrections demanded by La Broue the appellation document written by the theologian Boursier was signed in the presence of a notary from Paris, Chouvenot, on 1 March 1717. Most of the text had been taken from the "corps de dificultés" of the opponents. What was left was to negotiate the canonical significance of the appellation. The four bishops considered the theological faculty to be the most suitable organ for the implementation of their plan. Ravechet, the syndic, had been won over and the faculty had been alienated by a very recent *lettre de cachet* from the regent which demanded that the act of 12 January containing a pronouncement against the bull be eliminated from the register. Ravechet was taken into confidence, but the vast majority of the public was totally surprised on the morning of 5 March 1717 when the four bishops requested to be admitted to the extraordinary session of the faculty about to begin. La Broue read a preamble and Soanen read the appeals document, which was then deposited in the chancellery of the Sorbonne. Of the 110 professors present 97 immediately voted for the appeal. At the beginning of the session one of the professors left in order to notify Rohan and the regent, who immediately had Noailles informed of the proceedings. On the very next day the archbishop expressed his sympathy for the four bishops by having their appeal registered with his office. After this the matter entered a new phase.

One of the initial effects of the appeal consisted of the regent switching to the anti-Jansenist side. On the evening of 5 March a council of which Rohan and Bissy were members decided to banish the four bishops to their dioceses, to exile the syndic Ravechet by means of a *lettre de cachet,* and to throw the notary Chouvenot into the Bastille, where he remained from 15 to 24 March. Ravechet died on his way into exile in Rennes on 24 April 1717 and was celebrated as a martyr by the entire party. But it was too late to stop the movement. Almost two years of policies sympathetic to Jansenism were bearing fruit and the regent was soon to become aware of it. News of the appeal spread rapidly, causing enthusiasm among many of the clergy. It is very difficult to get a precise idea of the situation because the contemporary literature did not give an objective account of it and we have no accurate statistics. It appears that those priests who favored the appeal were especially numerous around the universities and among the urban clergy. Montempuys, the rector of the University of Paris, on 6 March started to get other universities to join in the appeal, but the regent forbade discussion of the matter, though without success. Shortly thereafter the theological faculties of Nantes and Rheims joined the appeal. After their return to their dioceses the four bishops immediately published pastoral letters containing their appeal. In the course of a few months fourteen colleagues in the episcopate joined them. On 3 April 1717 Noailles also signed the appeals document, but to the chagrin of the other appellants kept the fact secret for a long time. In fact, several among them did not divulge their position until much later. This was especially true for the bishop of Auzerre, Charles de Caylus, who had signed his appellation on 14 May 1717, but did not make it known until 4 October 1718 in a pastoral letter. Later he nonetheless assumed a very important position within the Jansenist party. Among the lower clergy, too, the appellations increased. It is impossible to make a listing; given the present state of documentation even a numerical estimate will perforce be inaccurate since some kept their appellation secret, others retracted it very quickly. On the other hand, the united support of numerous parishes must be qualified by the fact that genuine unanimity was never really achieved. Based on the very well-documented collective work edited by the Jansenist Nivelle, *La Constitution Unigenitus déférrée à l'Église universelle* (Cologne 1757), it can be assumed that the number of appellants ranged between 3,000 and 4,000, while the total number of clerics in France was approximately 100,000. But these numbers again have to be interpreted by taking into account that, on the one hand, there were appellations based on mere favor which — if one is to believe the acceptants — were even bought with money; on the other hand, many of the nonappellants accepted the bull against their will because they did not dare expose themselves; yet in their hearts they were on the side of the appellants. In addition, there were appellants among the nuns and laymen. On the whole the number of appellants formed a relatively small minority, but one that was very active and enjoyed the sympathy of a broad segment of the public. The action by the four bishops was highly effective since it placed the problem on safe ground, given the prevailing Gallican atmosphere.

It could, in fact, invoke a well-known precedent: the appellation by Louis XIV to the council against Innocent XI (January 1688). This appellation, while not having the desired results, had not been condemned by the Pope. On 22 June 1716 in a speech to a general assembly of the university its rector, Montempuys, had recalled that in 1688 Procurator General Harlay had requested only one second to the appellation, namely, that of the university. Thus the precedent had not been forgotten. Parliament on the whole considered the appellation canonically unimpeachable. The regent was of like opinion and in an audience of 10 March 1717 he told Noailles and the opponents so. His only complaint was that the appellation had been undertaken without his knowledge. Several of the acceptants among the bishops confirmed the canonicity of the appellation. Memoranda on this issue were circulated in the form of brochures. The acceptants on their part merely countered that the appellation was null and void and could not be supported because the bull had already been implicitly accepted by the whole Church. Thus the Gallican principles which had formed the clergy for more than thirty years gave the appellants a solid base for their undertaking. Under these conditions the publication of the appeal changed the situation and led the whole issue into a new phase. It is now understandable why there were seven bishops among the appellants who had initially accepted the bull; this was the case, among others, with Caylus, who had published the bull in his diocese on 28 March 1714. Furthermore, it should be stated that all the appellant bishops had been appointed by Louis XIV, who was intent on keeping clerics sympathetic to Jansenism out of the episcopate; further, that all of them had signed the formulary against Jansenism, that almost all of them continued to demand its signing in their dioceses, and that some of them even asserted that Quesnel's book renewed the errors of Jansenism: this fact reveals the extent to which the issue of Jansenism was perceived as being independent from the issue of the bull *Unigenitus.* Lastly, the appellation in its broad spectrum reveals the influence of Richerism, which had gradually permeated the lower clergy and even the faithful, who now frequently considered themselves judges of the doctrine. In this regard a reading of the appeals document is important. Here, too, the events of 1688 represent a precedent because Louis XIV had ordered Harlay to obtain the consent of the Parisian clergy. In the ensuing period of time the theoretical positions had been formulated. Publications openly inspired by Richer were now multiplying, e.g., the *Témoignage de la vérité* by de la Borde. In June 1716 Nicolas Le Gros, canon of Rheims, who had been exiled because of his Jansenist position and returned after the death of Louis XIV, published his treatise *Du renversement des libertés de l'Église gallicane* (1716), which was an immediate success. This work is more moderate than that of de la Borde. But it is based on the principle that within the Church the authority of the body of the faithful is fitting and the members of the hierarchy are only its delegates. He designates the priests as successors of the seventy-two disciples of Christ and demands a special position for them. Lastly, he concedes validity to the judgment of the bishops only inasmuch as it expresses that of their flock and especially that of the body of the priests. Thus a sort of church democracy began to take shape which was destined to develop further throughout the century. As a consequence the Church of France was placed in a state of war, since all its dioceses were divided into appellants and acceptants and the bishop's authority was generally disregarded by the followers of the party opposed to him. For many years French Catholicism was split because of a number of conflicts which had a debilitating effect, although this was not being admitted. The regent recognized it, however, and tried to prevent appellation by priests and laymen, but it was too late for such a reaction.

Pursuant to the desire of the four bishops, the appellation temporarily blocked all attempts at conciliation. The disquiet it had caused in Rome was partly ameliorated by the news that the regent had joined the party of the anti-Jansenists. Yet Rome and Paris alike were unclear about the method to be applied now. On 21 April Clement XI sent a personal letter dated 25 March to Noailles, couched in paternal and imploring terms. It had no effect on Noailles, who — as was known — had signed the appellation on 3 April and confidentially began to talk about it now. By the end of May even Rome was informed. The regent sent the Duke de la Feuillade to Rome in order to renew negotiations. To the bishops he sent an encyclical prohibiting appellations "without need and as long as the negotiations are under way." Around 6 July Noailles answered the letters by the cardinals and the Pope, warning against forcible and severe methods which could not but embitter the people and lead to unrest. These letters reached Rome on 23 July, spreading great disappointment. At about this time the regent made desperate attempts to regain control of the situation. On 7 October he issued a royal decree ordering both parties to be silent on the matter. In fact, he distrusted all parties involved, including Clement XI, who found out about this on 19 October and was injured by the fact that both appellants and acceptants were put on the same level with each other. Next, the regent had an outline of the doctrine, written by one of the acceptants, sent to the Pope in an attempt to obtain approbation by the Holy See and in the hope that this would induce Noailles and his party to accept the bull. But on 9 November Clement sent a severely negative answer. Meantime, in order again to disrupt the search for a compromise, the appellants had printed and circulated Noailles' appeals document, a copy of which had probably been found among the papers of the deceased bishop of Lectoure. Noailles, although angered, emphatically refused to deny his text, ignoring pressure by the court. At the beginning of December the regent pushed through parliament several decrees which suppressed Noailles' appellation and condemned a publication running counter to the royal decree. Some success in Rome gave rise to the hope that an agreement could yet be reached. But again the regent encountered an unbending attitude on the part of the appellants and unwillingness by Nuncio Bentivoglio, who was hostile to any compromise. Once more the regent tried to demonstrate his preparedness to Rome by dismissing Daguesseau and replacing him as chancellor with Voyer d'Argenson, lieutenant general of the police, who was known as a friend of the Jesuits. But even this had no positive results: France ignored the order of silence and Rome initiated forcible measures.

On 8 March an Inquisition decree surfaced condemning the appellation of the four bishops and that of Noailles. Parliament countered by condemning that decree on 28 March. Now the regent tried another way of putting pressure on the Holy See. Since the Pope had stubbornly refused to issue bulls of investiture for the bishops appointed by the regent, the latter convened a commission at the beginning of May which was to find a solution to this problem. Saint Simon, one of the members, solicited pertinent memoranda from experts among them several of the great Jansenist theologians: Du Guet, Petitpied, Boursier, and Le Gros. The majority of answers demanded the right of the chapters in the election of their bishop, some with the proviso that it had to take place upon nomination by the King. The person elected could thus be consecrated independently of any bull from Rome. These recommendations were favorably received in France and discussed publicly. The Holy See was informed about this by the nuncio. In the regency council mention was made of appealing to a general council in the name of the French nation. In an attempt to intimidate Rome the regent mentioned in a letter the possibility of return to the old customs. This time Clement XI gave way; on 15 May 1718 the bulls of investiture arrived in Paris. But the regent seems not to have intended to reintroduce the right to appoint bishops, he merely wanted to scare Rome. But the idea went its own way and was soon to be realized in the Dutch Church. The dispatch of the bulls did not defuse the tense situation in Rome. Clement XI appeared less and less inclined toward a compromise. Correspondence from Rome in the summer of 1718 more and more frequently alluded to new forcible measures. In Paris one bishops' conference was followed by another, all of them gradually running out. But in them a new personality played an ever more significant part. This was Jean-Joseph Languet de Gergy (1677–1753), appointed lo the bishopric of Soissons in 1715. He was consecrated by virtue of the recently arrived bull and was to become archbishop of Sens in 1730. Because the situation continued to stagnate, Clement XI intended to decide the matter by publishing the *Pastoralis officii* (8 September 1718), a letter addressed to all the faithful which excommunicated all those who did not accept the bull, yet did not make mention of the appellation. Predictably, the opponents hardened their position. On 24 November Noailles officially published his appeals document, causing another wave of approval. On 3 October he issued another pastoral letter protesting the *Pastoralis officii.* This met with the approval of the majority of his clergy, while within the dioceses tension and unrest were on the increase. Also on 3 October the parliament in Paris issued an appellation decree against the *Pastoralis officii;* it was immediately followed by the provincial parliaments. In practical terms this deprived the excommunication of any actual effect and consequence.

In the meantime a new personality had come upon the scene on the side of the regent: Abbé Dubois, who fancied himself the Richelieu of his time. The acceptants held a large majority, so he thought it best to bet on them and to influence the regent accordingly. On the other hand he was hoping to be rewarded with a cardinalate, for which Rome made him wait until the following pontificate in July 1721. But Dubois completely failed to master the events. In the course of the summer of 1718 Bissy and the bishop of Nîmes Laparisière, an acceptant, published a collection of pastoral letters by French and foreign bishops favoring the constitution under the title *Témoignage de l'Église universelle en faveur de la bulle Unigenitus.* On 14 January 1719 Noailles countered with a pastoral instruction couched in extremely sharp terms. In Rome, as in Paris, it was recognized more and more that Noailles would never accept the bull. In the course of 1718 Languet de Gergy had become prominent by the publication of his blunt *Avertissements de Msgr. l'évêque de Solssons à ceux qui dans son diocèse se sont déclarés appelants de la Constitution,* which had brought him heated answer, by Guillaume Dagoumer and Nicolas Petitpied. De Gergy was also the one who used a pastoral letter of 2 February and another one of 25 March 1719 to reply both to Noailles and to a pastoral letter by the appellant bishop of Angoulême. Bissy also answered by a pastoral letter of 22 February. In his own pastoral instruction of January, Noailles seemed to make some concessions that were disquieting to the rest of the appellants. The latter clarified the matter on 25 May 1719 in a pastoral letter by Langle, who published the appellation of the four bishops against the *Pastoralis officii.* To complicate matters further, the accepting archbishop of Rheims, the hotheaded Mailly, published a letter dated 14 May to all cardinals, archbishops, and bishops energetically advocating the cause of the bull. This letter was rejected by parliament on 22 June. Shortly before that, on 5 June, another royal decree tried to impose quiet on both parties for one year. Neither in Rome nor in Paris was it received any better than the one before and it had just as little effect. It could also not prevent parliament from proceeding severely against de Gergy in the following few weeks.

While he engaged in intrigues in Rome by means of Lafitau and at the same time tried to secure for himself the archbishopric of Cambrai and the cardinalate, Dubois was also concerned with achieving religious peace. From his retreat in Fresnes, Daguesseau, still out of favor, took an active part in the religious issues but moderated his position. In three memoranda he authored in December 1719 and January 1720 he considered the appellation a failure because the number of appellants was too small. The memoranda indicated that he had returned to the idea of an interpretation of the bull by a "corps de doctrine." A new text, written under the watchful eye of the regent by one of Noailles' theologians, the Abbé Couet, was submitted to Noailles, Rohan, and Bissy in January 1719. The latter two had demanded of Noailles that he retract his appellation and his instruction of January 1719; the prelate seemed ready to give in. In March thirty-eight bishops present in Paris were prepared to sign the "Explications sur la bulle Unigenitus." Mailly, too, accepted the signing after de Gergy had intervened with him. Emissaries of the regent were to obtain the signature of the other bishops in the provinces. By 10 May 1720 a total of ninety-four prelates had approved the agreement. Approval by Noailles, which would have brought around a large number of the opponents, was counted upon. But in the meantime the safeguards to ensure secrecy had been broken and the public had been informed. Among the ranks of the priests and the laity violent opposition was aroused against any compromise at all and the four bishops, joined by Caylus, sharply criticized Noailles' "apostacy." The Pope, on the other hand, appeared little inclined toward a compromise which he viewed as an impairment of the rights of the Holy See. A letter of Noailles to his priests explaining his actions was condemned sharply in his diocese. In a parallel action many of the acceptants accused Languet de Gergy of having weakened. In addition to that, parliament, which had been exiled to Pontoise as a result of the Law affair, refused to register a royal declaration of 4 August sanctioning the agreement, in spite of the fact that Daguesseau, who had returned to the chancellorship a few weeks prior and had changed his position, exerted all his influence. Having delayed his acceptance all summer long, Noailles finally gave in and published a pastoral letter on 19 November containing his acceptance coupled with explanations. At that time parliament also joined a compromise and was recalled to Paris on 16 December. Then the Sorbonne submitted. Dubois and the regent thought they had won the day. La Broue had died on 20 September, but not before he and the three other bishops had signed a reappeal document on 12 September, authored by Laurent Boursier, which sharply admonished Noailles. It was published by the three other bishops almost simultaneously with Noailles' pastoral letter and his acceptance. A decree by the regency council of 31 December prohibited the reappeal document. In the meantime a reappeal document for the lower clergy dated 19 November had appeared. It contained the signatures of a large number of appellants, about fifteen hundred. But this number was far below that of the appellations of 1717, so the court was not visibly moved by it. Shortly thereafter a handwritten list of appellants was circulated and printed in 1721; this put the reappellants within the grasp of the authorities. At the head of this list was Abbé Jacques de Bidal d'Asfeld, a friend of Du Guet, who had to appear before a police lieutenant and was exiled to Villeneuve-le-Roi. At that point the three reappealing bishops wrote to the regent explaining their position. None of their colleagues from the episcopate followed suit. Languet redoubled his polemics. The death of Clement XII caused a moment's confusion, but soon it was clear that his successor, Innocent XIII, would continue somewhat the same policy. The confused polemics which filled his brief pontificate of three years hardly changed the elements of the problem. Initiated on 9 June by a letter to the Pope, signed by seven appealing bishops, these conflicts provoked a large number of publications in which Languet de Gergy was in the forefront of the acceptants, while Colbert and Caylus played an ever more significant role on the side of the appellants. Bissy joined the fray with a sharply worded lengthy pastoral instruction of 17 June 1722 which provoked an answer in much the same tone by the six appellants in February 1723. Dubois and the regent tried to control the situation by reintroducing the signing of the formulary against Jansenism as a condition for obtaining benefices and university titles; this custom had been discontinued in many faculties and dioceses. The result of this measure, implemented on 11 July 1722, was renewed unrest, especially in the university circles. The majority of the appellants obeyed because for them the issue of Jansenism was quite apart from that of the bull. But Colbert signaled the connection by prescribing the signing in conjunction with the distinction between the *quaesto juris* and the *quaesto facti* and the words of Clement IX concerning the keeping of the peace. In doing so he became involved in a long and embarrassing affair. The year 1723 was characterized by profound changes among the main actors on the stage. On 15 February Louis XV was declared of age; Dubois died on 10 August; the regent on 2 December. A little later, on 7 March 1724, Innocent XIII also died. At the same time a new protagonist appeared in the person of André de Fleury, bishop of Fréjus and former teacher of the King, who had enjoyed the latter's complete trust.

The new Pope, Benedict XIII, a former Dominican friar, was very open to the doctrines of Augustine and Thomas, but could not simply cancel the problem caused by the bull. But he issued the brief *Demissa preces* of 6 November 1724, addressed to the Dominican general, which expressed his great sympathy for Augustinianism and Thomism and gave renewed hope to the opponents of the bull. But Noailles, in spite of the Pope's conciliatory stance, persistently refused to retract his appellation. At the beginning of January, following a very disappointing series of correspondence with Rome, he sent to Rome a collection of twelve doctrinal articles, characterized strongly by Augustinianism (which were probably edited by Boursier), and asked for their approbation by the Holy See. Some of these articles openly seemed to favor Jansenism and the Roman authorities were scarcely inclined to accept them. In France, Rohan and Bissy, supported by Fleury, took a position against negotiations which they thought could cause acceptants to leave the fold, and the bishops of Saintes and Marseille condemned the twelve articles by pastoral letter. By an encyclical dated 20 June 1725 Colbert finally let the opponents know that in his opinion the twelve articles would not make the bull any more acceptable. Under these conditions there was no use in continuing the negotiations. A short time later, in June 1726, the duke of Bourbon fell from favor and was replaced by Fleury, who occupied this post until 1743. Smooth and agile, but of steely persistence, Fleury was firmly resolved to weaken the Jansenist opposition. With support by the moderates and those inclined toward reconciliation he did not hesitate to proceed severely against the extremists; more and more he resorted to the weapon of the *lettre de cachet,* a policy that proved effective in the end.

First he had to make an example of one of the appellant bishops in order to frighten the others. The most rebellious among them was without a doubt Colbert, who strove for the signing of the formulary after 1722. On 21 September 1724, a decree of the council of state had even deprived him of his temporal revenues. But Colbert had strong support. The aged Du Guet had a letter printed which he had written to the bishop on 25 July 1724 and which strongly influenced public opinion. On 13 February 1725, by the way, this letter and the publications of Colbert regarding the same topic were condemned by the Holy Office. The Assembly of the Clergy of 1726 demanded the convening of provincial councils to counteract the unrest and, in this regard, joined forces with Fleury. But the latter did not dare attack Colbert, who was protected by the power of his family. On the other hand, the utterly defenseless Soanen, bishop of the tiny diocese of Senez, was a suitable victim. Soanen himself furnished the weapons for his adversaries. Toward the end of 1727 — believing that he had only a short while to live — he made public a pastoral instruction dated 28 August 1726 which was to represent his spiritual testament. In it he emphatically took the part of Colbert and, unraveling the whole background of the bull, he violently attacked its acceptants. This seemed a sufficient pretext. By 24 May 1727, all the bishops of the province of Embrun, to which the diocese of Senez belonged had *lettres de cachet* delivered to them. Their metropolitan was Pierre Guérin de Tencin (1680–1758), formerly a close collaborator of Dubois and the latter's representative in Rome, a prelate of more than dubious morality. Tencin convened a provincial council for 16 August 1727, which Soanen attended. This council was characterized by complex and stormy episodes where irregularities abounded. On 18 August Soanen had rejected the jurisdictional competence of his judges, whose partisanship and hostility were beyond doubt, but an appeal based on misuse of power filed by Soanen on 26 August was ignored. On 27 August he protested against the irregularity of his trial in an encyclical to all the bishops. The judgment was dated 20 September and pronounced two days later. Soanen was dismissed from all his functions as bishop and priest, pending retraction of his pastoral instruction. Shortly thereafter he was exiled by *lettre de cachet* to the abbey of La Chaise-Dieu. He left Embrun on 13 October and arrived at the abbey ten days later. In spite of his advanced age he lived there for another thirteen years; he died on 25 December 1740 at the age of ninety-three, revered by the entire Jansenist party as a saint and martyr. All the while he had conducted a voluminous correspondence and taken an active part in most of the affairs that concerned public opinion. After his death even the smallest objects which he had used were preserved as relics. The council of Embrun, called by the opponents, "the Synod of Robbers," did not have quite the effect hoped for by Fleury. To be sure the Holy See approved it by brief of 17 December 1727, and it induced about ten opponents to switch sides. But the unrest it caused was lasting and violent. On 28 October 1727, twelve bishops, among them Noailles, Colbert, and Caylus, sent a letter of protest to the King authored by Petitpied, which was returned to them on 15 March 1723, together with a legal opinion which was disquieting to some of the signers. Boursier collected and published a *Consultation de 50 avocats* which asserted the invalidity of the council of Embrun. This was protested on the part of the acceptants by a *Lettre de 26 évêques au rois* (4 May 728), which in turn provoked a polemic by the lower clergy calling attention to its rights. Since Soanen had demanded a general council beyond the provincial one, petitions were circulating in the dioceses for his appeal; they contained no fewer than two thousand signatures. Innumerable polemics appeared;

the portrait of Soanen, the "Prisoner of Jesus," was distributed in copper etchings; a number of his followers managed to visit him at La Chaise-Dieu. The conflicts which were tearing the diocese of Senez apart were passionately commented on. In the end the total result was uncertain. The procedure was not repeated even though there was a plan afoot to convene a provincial council at Narbonne for the purpose of condemning Colbert, who had emphatically defended Soanen.

One of Fleury's major goals continued to be the neutralization of Noailles. At the end of 1726 the rumor surfaced that Noailles would give in to pressure by the minister and publish a pastoral letter containing an unqualified acceptance. It prompted a large number of the Parisian clergy to rise up against it. On 3 February 1727, a letter to Noailles, edited by Petitpied, appeared in which thirty parish priests who considered themselves successors of the seventy-two disciples, refused to follow Noailles in any act of submission. Furthermore, they demanded that a general synod of the diocese be convened. The movement was led by Goy, the appellant priest of Sainte-Marguerite, and Feu, appellant priest of Saint-Gervais. A decree of 14 June prohibited this letter, but in the "Très humbles remonstrances des curés de Paris" of 5 September Petitpied again brought up this topic. In the meantime the affair of Embrun had led Noailles back to the opposition. After he signed the letter of the twelve bishops, he also signed (on 7 May 1728) a document opposing the registration of the papal brief which had approved the council of Embrun. But soon the situation changed. By this time Noailles was visibly weakened by age and his ideas became increasingly unclear. Toward the end of February 1718 sickness had deprived him of his most valued adviser, who had always encouraged him to resist: Antoine Dorsanne, official of Paris and author of a *Journal* which was published posthumously in 1753. Fleury, on the other hand, found allies among those around the cardinal in the persons of the chancellor Daguesseau and especially the archbishop's niece, wife of the Maréchal de Grammont. They obtained Noailles' signature on a document revoking his stand against registration of the papal brief of 7 May. On 19 July he also signed a letter to Benedict XIII assuring him of his submission and absolute obedience. At this point several appellants appear to have regained some influence over him inducing him to sign a declaration (22 August; the original version was sent to Soanen) in which Noailles revoked the document of 19 May and in advance repealed any public document accepting the bull which might be wrung from him in the future. On 24 September, furthermore, he signed another document protesting in advance against any forced dismissal from his archbishopric. This did not prevent a pastoral letter by Noailles, dated 11 October and containing an unqualified acceptance of the bull *Unigenitus*, from being posted in Paris on 24 October. As a countermeasure the appellants had the revocation act of 22 August posted as well. The Duke de Noailles, nephew of the archbishop, managed to induce him to write a letter to Fleury in which he revoked this act of the twenty-second. But a few weeks later, on 17 December, he reaffirmed it. In addition he signed another declaration on 26 February 1729 in which he revoked his pastoral letter of 11 October; the manuscript of that declaration was also sent to Soanen. The death of the unfortunate cardinal on 4 May 1729 finally put an end to these embarrassing conflicts revolving around an old man whose weakness and instability had been cruelly exploited.

The Defeat of Jansenism

The death of Noailles represented a turning point in the history of Jansenism. It marked the disappearance of the most important man of the party, whose personal deficiencies had nonetheless been clad with the aura of the cardinalate. More deaths and desertion; from the ranks of the appellants followed, soon leaving a mere four. Aside from Soanen, who was exiled to his faraway mountains and deprived of all his authority, there were Colbert in Montpellier (d. 1738), Bossuet in Troyes (d. 1743), and Caylus in Auxerre, who survived the others until 1754. Although Jansenism, to the extent that it was inspired by Quesnel, developed more and more in the direction of parochialism by according a growing importance to the parish priests and the lower clergy, it found no leader. There was nothing that could make up for the lack of leadership, properly provided by a bishop; none of the three remaining appellant bishops was able to fill that role. Nor did anyone take the place of Quesnel, who died on 2 December 1719 in Amsterdam at the age of eighty-five. In spite of some internal disagreements the Jansenist party did preserve a real cohesion, but in the future it was an army without a general.

Noailles' successor was Charles-Gaspard de Vintimille du Luc, until then archbishop of Aix. He was moderate yet an acceptant by conviction, fully in agreement with Fleury's opinions. Henceforth *Unigenitus* posed no more problems regarding compromise. The French court and the Holy See agreed in their demand of an unreserved acceptance. Vintimille was firmly resolved to break all Jansenist resistance in his diocese of Paris, even though it initially appeared that he underestimated the difficulties of such an undertaking and the impossibility of destroying an opposition which, to some extent, was to endure until the Revolution. Within a few days of taking office, on 6 September 1729, he obtained approval of the bull from twenty-five canons of Notre-Dame, but met with resistance among the lower clergy. This did not keep him from enforcing the signing of the bull by a pastoral instruction of 29 September. At the beginning of November a *lettre de cachet* declared the appellant professors to be dismissed from the Sorbonne, depriving it of a number of famous theologians; the remaining faculty was characterized by Pucelle as a "rump." Other opponents were eliminated post-haste by *lettre de cachet,* especially those among the parish clergy. On 29 October all confessors and priests were ordered to appear within four months at the episcopal see in order to have their ecclesiastical authority renewed. This enabled Vintimille to refuse that authority to about thirty appellants among approximately eleven hundred priests. The others had to accept the bull.

It was probably by request of Vintimille that Fleury initiated even harsher measures. A royal declaration of 24 May 1730 elevated the bull *Unigenitus* to the level of a state law; it again ordered the signing of the formulary of Alexander VII and declared the benefices of those who did not sign it as "vacant and available for reappointment by full legal power." The weight of economic and financial sanctions of this declaration brought about the desired effect. Since church life in the *ancien régime* was founded on the system of benefices, such a measure put the Jansenists outside the pale of the existing order. But the text of the declaration, recognizing a papal act as state law, clearly manifested an ultramontane inspiration. Owing to Fleury's skill, it demonstrated a new posture, through which France and

Rome found a modus vivendi which for a long time eliminated this perilous problem from the relationship between the two courts. It was in the nature of things that the most spirited resistance to this scheme came from parliamentary circles. In fact, the parliaments in their opposition took the place of the clergy, who, due to their very insecure position, could hardly express their opinion anymore. This explains the growing connection between Jansenism and parliamentarianism, a connection which, cannot but seem paradoxical because a growing number of parliamentarians left the faith and turned to the Enlightenment instead. Parliament refused to register the declaration of 24 March. It took a formal trial proceeding to change its mind on 3 April 1730. The declarations of the ecclesiastical councilors concerning this topic were substantially inspired by E. Richer, they strongly advocated the demands of the parish priests. Applying the same principles a short time later, parliament supported three parish priests of the diocese of Orléans against their bishop, Fleuriau d'Armenonville. This explains why the Assembly of the Clergy in 1730 complained about the rebelliousness of the lower clergy and the transgressions by parliament. The growing importance of parliamentarians led to the Jansenist theologians placing more and more stress on an argument taken over from Quesnel and de la Borde: the validity of lay witness. Innumerable polemics continued to develop this argument and defended it against attacks by the proponents of the bull.

When Daguesseau and Joly de Fleury submitted the royal declaration to parliament, they assumed that it would be a surely theoretical matter without any practical application. But in fact this declaration opened the floodgates for persecution of the Jansenists. The *Nouvelles ecclésiastiques,* numerous polemics, and an incredible number of archival documents testify to numerous unpleasant incidents concerning priests, laymen, parishes, and whole congregations. By means of the simple *lettres de cachet,* which dispensed with all due process, a large number of opponents were sent into jail or exile. Since there are no statistics available, it is impossible to list accurate figures, but it can be assumed as certain that practically all dioceses and orders were affected, including the women's congregations, the Benedictines and the Oratorians, the Carmelites and the Sisters of the Visitation, and even the Carthusians. In order to reduce the extent of resistance, the powers that be unscrupulously resorted to forcible measures: several houses were closed and their members either deported or dispersed. It all contributed to the creation of a martyrdom mentality in Jansenist circles. But the measures were effective; by and by the various congregations officially accepted the bull, albeit generally without enthusiasm. The Dominicans had done so in 1728; the Benedictines and Doctrinarians followed suit in 1744, the Genovevians in 1745, and the Oratorians a year later in 1746. But it must be added that the acceptance was never general and that a good many members of religious families more or less admittedly continued to be sympathetic toward Jansenism. The dioceses of the appellant bishops continued to represent a natural refuge for those who managed to escape exile or jail: Montpellier, Troyes, and Auxerre took in many refugees; others sought asylum in Holland. Others were accepted into communities covertly under an assumed name. Numerous laymen placed themselves, their homes, and fortunes in the service of those persecuted.

Vintimille's tenure in office also abounded in parliamentary conflicts. The first dispute ensued when a council decree suppressed a memorandum by forty lawyers from Paris in favor of opposing priests from Orléans. At first the other lawyers reacted heatedly, but calmed down when Daguesseau intervened and ameliorated some of the harshness. But the forty lawyers were called to task by some of the bishops, among them Vintimille. They were about to formulate a reply when another council decree again put them in the wrong. Thereupon they went on strike. In retaliation ten of them were exiled, but the others did not give in and so the ten had to be recalled from exile in November 1731. The highly complex and more or less emotional hostilities continued and parliament had to suffer a *lettre de cachet* forbidding any discussion of matters pertaining to the bull. By publishing a pastoral letter on 27 April 1732, abruptly suppressing the party organ *Nouvelles ecclésiastiques* Vintimille initiated a new phase in the conflict. As many as twenty-one priests in Paris refused to disseminate the pastoral letter, in other parishes some of the faithful left the church while it was read. A royal declaration of 10 May 1732 forbade the parliament from dealing with this affair. The ecclesiastical councilor Pucelle and another by the name of Titon protested loudly and were promptly arrested. A strike suppressed by royal decree provoked new incidents and 158 officials of the magistrate were dismissed on 20 June. When parliament remonstrated, the dismissals were retracted by the court. The remonstrations by parliament were very serious and on 8 August the court replied with a harsh statement which could only be registered after a formal trial on 1 September. This led to renewed protests resulting in 140 parliamentarians being exiled. But now the public was so enraged that the government had to give in, admonish Vintimille, and forgo proceedings against twenty-one protesting priests. This is a good example of the way in which ecclesiastical matters were again taken up by parliament.

Thereafter Vintimille avoided any additional problems. He shunned conflicts with priests who were undeterred and continued in their appeals; he even maintained friendly relations with some of them. He extended authorizations for hearing confession or renewed them in the case of opponents and asked well-known Jansenists for their services. When he died in 1746 he had succeeded relatively well in keeping peace in his immediate environs. The church policy of Fleury has been subject to various kinds of judgment. It could be considered brutal and repressive and it is certain that he did everything he could to diminish the ranks of the appellants. Without doubt he was interested in a peaceful settlement of the problem. His appointments placed moderate bishops at the head of dioceses. He avoided chicanery toward those prelates who were suspected of Jansenist sympathies. Fleury died in 1743; his successor in the Ministry of Culture was the Theatine Jean-François Boyer, who had become Bishop of Mirepoix in 1730 and tutor of the Dauphin in 1736. Boyer proved to be much more unyielding than Fleury, often brutal. Although he was the black sheep of the Jansenists, as explained in the many articles about him in the *Nouvelles ecclésiastiques,* he was not even respected by the enemies of Jansenism. His death in 1755 was generally felt to be a liberation.

Boyer had to undergo the last embarrassing affair of the Jansenist conflict, that of the certificate of confession. A preliminary sign was the fact that some of the acceptants among the bishops were refusing the last rites to notoriously obstinate appellants. This affair reached its climax with the intervention of the archbishop of

Paris, Christophe de Beaumont, the uncompromising successor of Vintimille. He resumed the fight against Jansenism and ordered his priests who were ministering to the dying to demand from them a certificate of confession, written by a regularly approved priest, in which the dying would accept the bull *Unigenitus.* The most astonishing aspect was that this measure was applied without reservation even in the case of poor and totally uneducated people. One of the first incidents (on 17 February 1749) involved the Jansenist theologian Boursier, whom the priest of Saint-Nicolas du Chardonnet, Garnot, gave the last rites and a formal burial with the complete rites of the church without having demanded a recantation. Garnot was exiled to Senlis. On 21 June 1749, the former rector of the university, Charles Coffin, died without the last rites because he refused to show the required certificate of confession, though he did receive a church burial in Saint-Eustache. During the following months several more incidents occurred and the problem spread to other dioceses in the provinces whose bishops had issued similar rules. Parliament, of course, repeatedly intervened in favor of the opponents and its relationship with the court became so critical that it was exiled from May 1753 until September 1754.

At this point Louis XV resolved to put an end to this conflict which weakened royal authority and could even call into question the very institutions themselves. Upon the return of parliament he issued a declaration, written on 2 September and registered on 5 September, which imposed silence on both parties. This important declaration marked the beginning of yet a new phase because the King, especially as of 1756, was bent on having it respected. In order to set an example, several bishops who violated it — among them Beaumont himself — were temporarily exiled. Then, too, the Holy See was at this time occupied by a well-educated and moderate man, Benedict XIV. The divided Assembly of the Clergy of 1755 turned to him and in reply received the brief *Ex omnibus* (16 October 1755), which approved the silencing and treated the matter of the certificate of confession in an acceptable manner. Boyer died in 1755; his successors, Cardinal de La Rochefoucauld and after him Jarente de la Bruyère were intent on pacification and succeeded in having the order of silence respected. More and more bishops concurred in their views. This attitude, combined with the progressive deterioration of the Jansenist patty, altered the elements of the problem.

The scene of events also changed. Although the Society of Jesus had played a relatively subordinate role in the context of political Jansenism, it incurred violent hostility, not only from the Jansenists but also from several acceptants among the bishops. Several incidents occurred in quick succession. In 1738 Isaac-Joseph Berruyer, a Jesuit, published the first part of a voluminous *Histoire du peuple de Dieu* which presented the passion and salvation of Christ in the form of a novel. It was condemned by Colbert, enabling Daguesseau to resist publication of the following volumes. The eight volumes of the second part did not appear until June 1753. They were not approved by the Jesuit superiors, a fact which incurred for them the reproach of duplicity. The ensuing scandal was of considerable proportions. In December 1753 the work was condemned by twenty-seven bishops. But Berruyer defended himself; a condemnation issued by Benedict XIV on 16 February 1758 did not keep him from publishing the remaining five volumes of the third part, which were condemned on 2 December 1758. Numerous polemics against Berruyer appeared, the most significant of which was written by a former theologian of Colbert's, Jean-Baptiste Gaultier. His *Lettres théologiques* also attacked another Jesuit, Jean Hardouin, who — although he had died in 1729 — was considered to be the source of Berruyer's ideas. On 1 August 1759, Fitz-James joined the fray with a pastoral instruction of several thousand pages, composed by a well-known Jansenist theologian, Étienne Gourlin, and containing a severe refutation of Hardouin and Berruyer. It was followed by other censures, including one by the Sorbonne.

All this created an atmosphere favoring further attacks against the Society of Jesus, whose reputation had been declining, even in Rome, since the end of the seventeenth century and which was now coming under attack from almost all sides. At a time when political power was increasingly based on a growing nationalist sentiment, the society was accused of being allied with a foreign power, the temporal power of the papacy. Conversely, contemporary philosophy saw the society as the strongest barrier against the deism of Voltaire. Henceforth even the slightest incidents were pounced upon. In 1756 a regrettable financial affair involving a Jesuit, de la Valette, furnished the desired pretext. The parliaments went on the attack against the Society, a decree of 8 August 1761, the first of several others, declared its constitution irreconcilable with the laws of the realm. After several cases involving promissory notes the King gave in to the pressure exerted by Mme de Pompadour and his minister Choiseul: a decree of 18 November 1764 banned the Society of Jesus in France. A similar campaign had been carried out in a number of European countries and led to the brief *Dominus ac Redemptor* by Clement XIV, by which he abolished the Jesuit order. These measures were celebrated as victories by the Jansenists, who were unable to see that it was a triumph of skepticism and not of Saint Augustine. On both sides of the issue the conflict led to a great number of publications, the most interesting of which is still the *Annales de la Société des soi-disant jésuites,* an ambitious work which was probably financed by Choiseul himself and compiled by the Jansenist Gazaignes. It remained unfinished but its completed five volumes (1764–71) contain a wealth of valuable details.

These polemics involving the Society of Jesus refrained from resuming the Jansenist issue because the court was firmly resolved to enforce the law of silence and to avoid any rekindling of the conflict. Even Rome now understood that it was better not to permit the matter to be revived. The pontificate of Clement XIV was ready to let things rest. Pius VI on the occasion of his trip to Vienna on 20 April 1782 publicly announced to the bishops of Hungary that the bull *Unigenitus* should be spoken of in historical terms and not in dogmatic ones, "historice, non dogmatice." Several years later, with the advent of the French Revolution, the political aspect of the problem was to enter a completely new phase.

In the meantime political Jansenism — as opposed to the religious Jansenism of the seventeenth century, which had been limited to France and Louvain — had gained considerable ground. In the Netherlands, where the Jansenist group enjoyed firm support, the situation quickly came to a head. The eight dioceses had accepted the bull *Unigenitus* almost immediately after it had been issued. Prior to that the faculty of the University of Louvain had accepted it, although not without spirited resistance by part of its members. In 1716 Thomas-Philippe d'Alsace de Bossu, hostile to Jansenism, became archbishop of Mechelen. On 17 October 1718, he issued a pastoral letter which excommunicated the opponents of the bull. The other seven dioceses, as well as the Louvain faculty, followed suit. Supported by officialdom, the archbishop initiated a number of forcible measures against the opponents. Toward the end of 1727 the famous canonist Zeger-Bernard Van Espen (1646–1728) had to flee to Holland, where he died six months later. In the meantime Van Espen's advice had contributed considerably toward the creation of a schism in the Dutch Church. Since the end of the sixteenth century the Church had been governed by vicars apostolic with the title "in partibus infidelium." Jean de Néercassel, vicar apostolic of Utrecht, had been a close friend of Arnauld's and had facilitated the Jansenist infiltration into Holland. His successor in 1688 was Pierre Codde, archbishop of Sebaste, who had flatly refused to sign the formulary. He was cited to Rome, but even there he adhered to his position and was banished for it (May 1702). The chapters of Utrecht and Harlem stood up for him; the latter quickly gave in, but Utrecht, followed by a large number of its faithful, stood fast in its opposition to the Holy See and refused to recognize the vicars apostolic who succeeded Pierre Codde. Several French prelates were willing to ordain priests who had been issued letters dimissory by the chapter acting as administrator of the archbishopric, but the regent prohibited the bishops from continuing this practice. Thereupon the chapter of Utrecht and its faithful who had joined in the appellation of the bull *Unigenitus* consulted several canonists, among them Van Espen, who had always supported the legitimacy of the rights of the chapter. The majority of the replies reaffirmed the chapter's right to elect its bishop and to have him consecrated. A priest of the foreign mission, Dominikus Varlet, consecrated bishop "in partibus" of Babylon, was willing to act as consecrator upon the request of the Dutch chapter but was suspended for so doing (1720). He took up residence in the United Provinces and on 15 October 1724 he consecrated Cornelius Steenoven, the elected candidate of the Utrecht chapter, who in turn consecrated the first three of his successors. Furthermore, the archbishopric of Utrecht created suffragan seats in Harlem (1742) and Deventer (1758), ensuring the continuity of apostolic succession. Although supported by the Dutch government, the Church of Utrecht suffered a rapid decrease in its membership: around 1750 it had less than ten thousand members, contrasted to the total of two hundred thousand Catholics in Holland. Several attempts at rapprochement with Rome were undertaken, but all of them foundered upon the steadfast refusal by the chapter to recognize the bull *Unigenitus.* Throughout the eighteenth century the Church of Holland served as a refuge for numerous appellants; even today their archives, enriched by many documents from France, constitute one of the most important sources regarding the history of Jansenism. The French immigrants, several of whom, such as Leclerc and Le Sesne d'Étemare, were widely acknowledged theologians, contributed to maintaining an undeniable intellectual vitality in the Utrecht schism in spite of its numerical minority. The Jansenist infiltration in Ireland, England, Germany, Austria, and Spain was of minor importance, but not so in Italy. There the problem took on a special aspect.

Jansenism and the Religious Mentality of the Eighteenth Century

When the conflict involving the bull *Unigenitus* broke out, Jansenism included a large number of first-rate theologians in its ranks. Several of them by their age were still part of seventeenth-century Jansenism. Pasquier Quesnel, who, as we have seen, occupied a place of extraordinary importance, possessed an amazing vitality belying his eighty years. The incredible number of memoranda, polemics, and replies which he authored until shortly before his death on 2 December 1719 in Amsterdam is astonishing. But this wealth of literature did not augment his system. He continued to represent a moderate Augustinianism as coined by Bérulle. Richer's ideas, advocated by him, combined with the fact that the army of appellants was composed primarily of priests and faithful, led him to accord increasing value to the rights of the lower clergy and laity without, however, going as far as the almost Protestant exaggerations of de la Borde. While he did, in fact, remain a revered figure within the Jansenist group, he was surpassed by some of the younger of his allies, over whom he no longer had the uncontested authority he did during the period between 1690 and 1710. Not so in the case of Jacques-Joseph du Guet (1649–1733), his younger companion who had accompanied him to his refuge with Arnauld in 1685 but was forced to return to France soon afterward. Although thereafter he lived in cautious seclusion, his voluminous correspondence with numerous friends even outside the Jansenist circle had proved his extraordinary intellectual and literary abilities and had obtained for him a position of high respect expressed by the sobriquet "the Seer," given to him by his friends. Although he had at first shown little inclination for writing, he had two small treatises printed in 1717 (*Traité de la prière publique* and *Traité des saints mystères*) which enjoyed great success and made his name as an author. He also continued his career as a moralist, especially in the ten volumes of his *Lettres de Morale et de piété*, several of which had been printed in 1707 without his permission and which he edited himself after 1718. The last few volumes appeared posthumously. He was a gracious and shy person who eschewed public appearances. For that reason he refused to take on a prominent role of leadership in the controversy involving the bull. But he was frequently asked for advice; he checked and corrected numerous writings of his friends. Himself an appellant and reappellant, he had advised the four bishops at the time of the appellation. But the number of polemics published by him is small, the most important one being his letter to Colbert of 25 July 1724 concerning the signing of the formulary which he had printed the following November. His actual theological work is limited to a small volume entitled *Dissertation théologique* (1727) which deals primarily with baptism and the Eucharist. In addition there are the two volumes published posthumously of the *Conférences ecclésiastiques* (1742), actually a work of his youth. Written around 1678 it demonstrates the influence of Richer's doctrine as advocated by Quesnel. But in general, Du Guet's ideas, dominated by Augustinianism, are sharp, penetrating, very subtle and solid, his morality determined by a relatively moderate rigorism. Innumerable reprints throughout the eighteenth century popularized this admirable, talented author who deserves better than the oblivion which has been his fate.

François-Laurent Boursier (1679–1748), professor at the Sorbonne, was a much stronger and more aggressive personality. Highly respected as a theologian by his peers, he made a name for himself in 1713 by his book *De l'action de Dieu sur les créatures, traité dans lequel on prouve la prémotion physique par le raisonnement,* a powerful defense of Augustinian-Thomistic ideas. Malebranche, who felt himself and his *Traité de la nature et de la grâce* attacked, considered the work worthy of an answer and replied in his *Réflexion sur la prémotion physique* (1715). Unfortunately, the ensuing polemic claimed all of Boursier's strength, so that he did not find time to realize his plan for a comprehensive work concerning the *gratia efficax.* As a confidant of Noailles and the appellants he composed a respectable number of texts for them, including the appeals documents of 1717, 1719, and 1720 and several of Soanen's pastoral instructions. He also achieved merit as the central figure in the negotiations, initiated with Jubé, the priest of Asnières, and eighteen other professors, which were to bring about a rapprochement with the Russian Orthodox Church. His exclusion from the Sorbonne (1730) was predictable and his death in the parish house of Saint-Nicolas du Chardonnet, provoked an incident. An important theologian with a comprehensive patristic as well as Scholastic education, courageous and unselfish, Boursier enjoyed an undisputed authority within the Jansenist party and his intervention was usually decisive. Comparable to him was another professor of the Sorbonne, Nicolas Petitpied (1665–1747), who had expressed his views on the issue of conscience at the beginning of the century and for that reason was forced to flee to Holland. He was a highly respected canonist; in 1718 Saint-Simon had him return to France in order to ask his advice in the matter of the bulls of renewal rejected by Rome. On 1 June 1719, he was readmitted to the Sorbonne. The anti-Jansenist reaction forced him to go into hiding and then again to flee to Utrecht in 1728. As a moderate yet unyielding spirit, he objected to the deviations of the Jansenists and their acts of violence against the hierarchy and because of that was accused of weakness. But his sterling character ensured him of high esteem even on the part of his adversaries and in 1734 the court permitted him to return to France. But his esteem within the party gradually decreased, his intervention against several polemics met with heated criticism. Soanen was the only one who kept him in his confidence and Bossuet of Troyes asked him until the end to write his pastoral instructions for him. His work is considerable: it comprises more than eighty titles, but is submerged totally in his polemics. There are three major works: two volumes entitled *Oboedientiae credulae vana religio* (1708), defending the *silentium respectuosum;* the five volumes of his *Réponses aux avertissements de M. l'évêque de Soissons* (1719–24), a powerful refutation of Languet de Gergy; and the posthumously published *Examen pacifique de l'acceptation de la bulle.* The lucid and prolific intelligence of Petitpied's was able to contribute new and unassailable arguments on a number of ever-recurring problems and many of his writings deserve to be read even today. Along the same lines, albeit of a lesser intellect, the deacon (who also had licentiate from Sorbonne) Jacques Fouillou (1670–1736) deserves mention. He was also prominent in the issue of conscience and joined Quesnel in Holland in 1705. He did not return to France until 1720, where he helped formulate Boursier's *Prémotion physique* and furnished a significant contribution to the famous *Hexaples* concerning the bull *Unigenitus.* But his major work is the three volumes of his *Justification du silence respectueux* (1707). Jean-Baptiste Louail (d. 1724), prior of Auzay, is best known as the author of the first part of the *Histoire du livre de Réflexions morales.* The main author of the remainder of the work is Jean-Baptiste Cadry (1680–1756), former teacher of theology at the cathedral chapter of Laon, who also wrote numerous polemics of lesser interest.

In the person of Nicolas le Gros (1675–1751), doctor of theology and canon of Rheims, forced by his quarrels with Bishop Mailly in 1714 to take refuge with Quesnel, we encounter a personality of a different spirit. He returned from his exile after less than a year to resume the fight. In 1716 he brought out the best known of his works, *Du renversement des libertés de l'Église gallicane dans l'affaire de la Constitution Unigenitus.* In it he advocates a very traditional Gallicanism, modified by a few theses of Richer's concerning the rights of the parish priests, whom he calls shepherds just like the bishops. The latter are therefore obliged to act in concert with their priests and to listen to their advice. But he also upholds the rights of the hierarchy. Although he accords to the Christian people the right to elect their bishops and priests, he nonetheless stipulates that this election does not give them the power of consecration or jurisdiction, which they must receive from God through the mediation of the established hierarchy. This starting point leads him to a very subtle theory combining Gallicanism and the position of Richer with great success. An appellant and reappellant, he barely managed to evade a *lettre de cachet* and, following a sojourn in Rome and England, he once again returned to Holland. He joined the Church of Utrecht, to which he was of great service in the years between 1726 and his death. He was one of the first to create close connections between the French Jansenist faction and the Dutch schism. While in Holland he worked on a comprehensive volume, part of which is dedicated to a commentary on the Holy Gospel applying the mode of allegorical exegesis favored in Jansenist circles. Around 1745 the Utrecht Church had a somewhat more burdensome guest in the person of Pierre Leclerc (1706 until approx. 1781), subdeacon of the diocese of Rouen, a strange and in some respects eccentric figure with an obscure past. In 1756 he published two slim volumes under the title *Renversement de la religion et des lois divine et humaines par toutes les bulles et brefs donnés depuis près de 200 ans contre Baius, Jansénius, les cinq propositions, pour le formulaire et contre le P. Quesnel.* In it he develops an exaggerated presbyterianism by equating priests with bishops and insulting the Pope and the hierarchy. The same ideas are repeated in other works in which he called himself another Gilles de Wittes, former priest of Mechelen who also had strong Presbyterian tendencies. He found followers, in the Church of Utrecht and created disciples for himself, but for the Jansenist faction both of France and Holland he was a disappointment. In September 1763 the archbishop of Utrecht convened a provincial council in which the parish priests had the same vote as the bishops; this council was strongly protested by Leclerc. Although he published a few more tracts marked by extraordinary vehemence, all traces of him were eventually lost.

In spite of his excesses the personality of Pierre Leclerc manifested the problem of the propagation of Richer's ideas within the Jansenist faction. In the meantime a canonist who possessed the requisite erudition which Leclerc was lacking had given voice to the most daring demands of the lower clergy. This was Nicolas Travers, (1674–1750), a prolific writer and local historian. He became known in 1734 by virtue of his work *Consultation sur la juridiction et approbation nécessaires pour confessor,* followed in 1744 by the *Pouvoirs légitimes du second ordre dans l'administration des sacrements et le gouvernement de l'Église.* He denies the bishops any and all priority of *jura divina,* regarding them as of purely human origin; he also denies them any special power of ordination and advocates that all functions reserved for the bishops can also be delegated to simple priests. From this he draws the conclusion that all priests by virtue of their own ordination receive the power of ordination and of jurisdiction and consequently have no need for an authorization by the local ordinary to hear confessions and to grant absolution validly and licitly. Travers' ideas produced mixed reactions among the Jansenists; they were virtually all put on the Index. But it is possible that his ideas spread and were actually practiced by some Jansenist priests; at least they are emphatically accused of this by their opponents. Similar theses, but based on a wealth of extraordinary erudition, are found in the large body of works of a lay canonist, the lawyer Guilleaume-Nicolas Maultrot (1714–1803). A specialist in curial law, he tried to prove in a series of twenty-nine volumes the most daring positions of Richer's and the right of the parish priests to jurisdiction on the basis of their ordination. During the second half of the eighteenth century Maultrot met with a relatively favorable response in Jansenist circles and was supported by another renowned lawyer and canonist, Adrien le Paige.

Among the last great theologians of Jansenism at least three deserve mention. First among them is Jean-Baptiste le Sesne de Ménilles d'Étemare (1682–1770). He became a cleric at the suggestion of Du Guet and was ordained in 1709. He read one of his first Masses at Port-Royal, shortly before the expulsion of the nuns. Part of his superabundant work is as yet unpublished; a significant part, is occupied with allegorical exegesis. He took an active part in all the controversies and maintained an intensive correspondence with the entire Jansenist group. In order to retain his independence, he carefully avoided all official titles and functions. He loved to travel, spent time in Rome, England, and frequently visited Holland, where he took up residence in 1754 and died in 1770. In Rhynwick he founded a sort of French seminary under the auspices of the Church of Utrecht, to which he had close ties, leaving to it an admirable collection of documents. D'Étemare was an important spirit with a profound and comprehensive education whose work, though extremely interesting, is never even marred by his allegorical exegesis. Another theologian worth mentioning was a friend of D'Étemare's, Jean-Baptiste Raymond de Beccarie de Pavie de Fourquevaux (1693–1767), a former officer whose modesty prompted him to remain a mere acolyte. The regular correspondence which he maintained with D'Étemare represents an extremely fertile source of information deserving publication. As a confirmed appellant he published several polemics, the most interesting of which is the *Catéchisme historique et dogmatique.* Its first two volumes appeared in 1729; a new edition of 1758 enlarged the work to five volumes. It is a historic presentation of the controversies surrounding the bull *Unigenitus.* But the horizon of Fourquevaux's presentation is very narrow. Such cannot be said of the third theologian to be mentioned in this context: Pierre-Étienne Gourlin (1695–1775), bachelor of theology, vicar at Saint-Benoît, appellant, and victim of the interdict by Vintimille, which forced him to spend his life in seclusion. He authored several very important polemical works, the best of which is the comprehensive *Mémoire justificatif* (1742; for the appellation of the priests of Sens against Languet de Gergy). He put his pen in the service of several bishops, among others the author of Fitz-James' pastoral instruction against Berruyer. He also left a considerable number of theological treatises in manuscript form; unfortunately, not all of them have been published. But two of the most important ones did appear: *Tractatus theologicus de gratia Christi salvatoris* (1781) and *De Jansenio et de Jansenismo* (1790). At a time when no one was occupied with Jansenism anymore and even Augustinianism had fallen into the background, these two works witness an unusual erudition and a thinking of rare profundity. In the France of this epoch Gourlin is probably the last heir of the great theological tradition. One must acknowledge also that the Jansenist group was at that time the only one in which theological thought remained truly active. Independently of the great controversies, this group was also involved in several other interesting theological disputes. The first of them — concerning the relationships between the *timor servilis* and the *fiducia filialis* — was caused in 1728 by the appearance of Fourquevaux's *Traité de la confiance chrétienne,* attacked by Petitpied in 1734 in nine successive letters but defended by D'Étemare, who in turn was disputed by his fellow member of the Oratory, Mariette. Other controversialists entered the fray until Boursier, in his *Lettre sur l'espérance et la confiance chrétiennes,* finally put an end to the conflict in notable fashion (1739). Petitpied and Boursier also were the protagonists in a controversy concerning the theological virtues (1742–46) in the course of which Boursier wrote a very interesting *Dissertation sur les vertus théologales* (1744) which was primarily directed against a new treatise by his fellow Oratorian Mariette. Unfortunately, all the great minds of Jansenism had already passed away by 1778 when a last great doctrinal controversy broke out involving the *Traité du sacrifice de Jésus-Christ* by Abbé François Plowden, a cleric of English origin who sympathized with the Jansenists. He viewed the essence of the sacrifice of the Mass not in the destructive change of the offering, but in the presentation of a sacrifice made once and for all. The entire Jansenist contingent entered this controversy.

After 1730 the Jansenist party was irrevocably condemned and it was aware of it. A minority from the start, it now watched its substance gradually melt away without a chance to renew itself. Even the diligence of its members could not deceive anyone about the impending fateful end. The mentality of the group changed progressively: it assumed the attitude of a clan withdrawn unto itself, embittered, full of resentment, belligerent, narrow-minded, suspicious; the tenor of Jansenist polemics became more and more unpleasant. The most significant document in this regard was the famous *Nouvelles ecclésiastiques.* During the Council of Embrun (1727) the party had planned establishment of an informational journal which was to replace the hand-copied *Nouvelles ecclésiastiques* which had appeared in the seventeenth century. The editorship was initially entrusted to a deacon, Boucher, and to a chaplain of Bicêtre, de Troya, but the latter was incarcerated a short while later. A few months later Boucher, who continued to collaborate on the journal, handed its direction over to a priest of the diocese of Tours whose Jansenist membership had forced him into exile, Jacques Fontaine de la Roche (1688–1771). The latter quickly demonstrated an extraordinary organizational talent; he built up a network of information and distribution of such perfection that he was able to thwart investigation by the police throughout the century. The first issue of the *Nouvelles* appeared on 23 February 1728. But the authors also published a fascicle reviewing the sequence of events since the issuance of the bull. In the face of all sorts of difficulties Fontaine succeeded in maintaining the weekly appearance of the publication almost without interruption. D'Étemare, the brothers Desessarts, and Fourquevaux were regular contributors, especially noted for the reviews and the doctrinal articles. After the death of Fontaine, his responsibilities were taken over by Marc-Claude Guénin de Saint-Marc, supported by a group which included Gourlin and Maultrot. After 1794 the *Nouvelles* was continued in Utrecht by a refugee priest, Jean-Baptiste-Sylvain Mouton, who reduced it to two issues a month. The last one appeared on 24 May 1803; Mouton died on the following 13 June. The basic tone of the *Nouvelles* is one of incredible vehemence. Everything coming from the appellants is heaped with praise; the slightest utterances by an acceptant or a Jesuit is mercilessly criticized. Reading the journal is simply unpleasant, yet one must acknowledge the extraordinary accuracy of the information used in it. This makes it for us an extremely valuable source. Predictably the *Nouvelles* was subject to repeated condemnations, among them a decree of parliament of February 1731, a pastoral letter by Noailles of April 1732, and a decree by the Holy Office of April 1740. Starting in 1734 the Jesuits tried to counter the *Nouvelles* by their own *Suppléments,* which was by no means any more objective and had to be discontinued in 1748. The *Nouvelles* also reflected the controversies which split the Jansenism milieu. Its vehement tone caused them to be condemned by some of the most famous Jansenist theologians. Du Guet was a case in point: he condemned the *Nouvelles* in a letter (dated 9 February 1732) to a young fellow Oratorian of the College de Juilly, Pinel. At the instigation of a niece of Du Guet's, Mme Mol, who was hostile to the Jansenists, this letter was publicized. This resulted in a long series of polemics between D'Étemare and Le Gros. This was also the case with a letter by Petitpied made public in 1735. As a countermove Fontaine welcomed the touching approbations of Soanen and gave them all the desired publicity he could. In addition to the *Nouvelles* there was a wealth of published material the majority of which were pamphlets of the most regrettable satire, some of which, however, are publications of valuable documents, especially the irreplaceable *Journal* by Dorsanne (1753) and the *Anecdotes ou mémoires secrets sur la Constitution Unigenitus* by a member of the Academy, Joseph Bourgoin de Villefore (1744).

On the whole the spirituality of the Jansenist milieu of the eighteenth century continues to be of the intellectual, psychological, and rational kind. The doctrinal reliability of the works it created could not, however, hide the progressive withering coming about as a consequence of its break with the living sources of inner experience. The literary production is more than abundant. Yet more frequent were reprints or editions of hitherto unpublished works of the seventeenth century. The fourteen volumes of the *Essais de morale* by Nicole came out in incredibly quick succession and were even incorporated in non-Jansenist libraries. In addition, there were the *Instructions chrétienne* by Singlin (1744); about twenty works by the doctor of Port-Royal, Jean Hamon, among them some previously unpublished ones; the interesting *Lettres chrétiennes et spirituelles* by Saint-Cyran, which had also been previously unpublished (1744); the *Exercices de piété* of Port-Royal (1787), and many others. Naturally the Jansenists were emphatically antimystical, manifest in the irony with which the *Nouvelles* announced the publication in 1752 of the admirable *Instructions spirituelles en forme de dialogue* by de Caussade. But the main target of the Jansenists was the devotion to the Sacred Heart of Jesus. Strangely enough, the people of Port-Royal had frequently talked of the Heart of Jesus devotion in their devotional literature. But in 1729 when Languet de Gergy published a voluminous *Vie de la Vénérable Mère Marguerite Alacoque*, the *Nouvelles* published a malicious review in January 1730 in which the Heart of Jesus, however, was hardly mentioned. Not until 1758 did its opposition to this devotion become apparent. It became more virulent in 1765 when a brief by Clement XIII officially recognized the devotion to the Sacred Heart of Jesus. Thereupon the *Nouvelles* increased the number of articles rejecting the devotion. In 1781 the most vehement polemicist in the person of Marc-Antoine Raynaud, the priest of Vaux (1717–96), joined the battle, heaping insults and sarcasm upon those whom he called "cordicoles."

The Jansenist faction, nonetheless, must also have been aware of the fascination of the miraculous and irrational. Ever since the famous Miracle of the Sacred Thorn in 1656 most of their representatives were forced to accept the idea that God manifests himself in favor of His cause by means of miracles. Yet miraculous events within the group of appellants did not occur until relatively late. The appellants, of course, increased the publicity in 1727 when suddenly miracles began to happen at the grave of a well-known appellant, Gérard Rousse, canon of Avenay in the diocese of Rheims. These constant references by the appellants led to a heated polemic between Languet de Gergy and Colbert which at least had one positive result: In a printed letter of 5 February 1727, Colbert published Pascal's thoughts concerning miracles. These were previously unpublished fragments of his unfinished letter about the Miracle of the Sacred Thorn, copies of which were circulating in the Jansenist faction. But the most spectacular events occurred in Paris in the small cemetery surrounding the church of Saint-Médard at the grave of an appellant and reappellant, François de Paris (1680–1727), the eldest son of a rich parliamentary councilor, who had modestly remained a mere deacon. He had lived and worked in seclusion and written a few commentaries on the Holy Gospel and several devotional works. The occasionally frightening asceticism of his way of life and his inexhaustible charity toward the poor had made him famous; his personal holiness cannot be doubted. His funeral on 3 May 1727 was triumphal and there was talk of miracles reputed to have happened at that occasion. Noailles finally ordered an investigation which was interrupted by his death and the unwillingness of his successor to resume it. But the masses continued to come and pray at the grave of François de Paris. Again and again miracles were said to have occurred. But on 3 November 1730, the sensational healing of a certain Anne Lefranc occurred, which was doubted and declared false by a pastoral letter of Vintimille dated 15 July 1731. Additional miracles created great excitement among the public, which now veritably flooded the small cemetery of Saint-Médard.

A short time later another episode began. On 21 July 1731, a poor and almost totally paralyzed servant woman by that name of Aimée Pivert was healed at the deacon's grave and immediately afflicted by violent nervous seizures. During the next few weeks the phenomenon reoccurred with other patients. At the beginning of September a cleric, the Abbé de Bescherand, was seized at each of his visits at the cemetery, his reactions evident to all. This phenomenon proved to be more and more contagious, turning the cemetery into a scene of extraordinary mass hysteria in the course of autumn 1732; soon the discussions of the onlookers degenerated into brawls. Several interventions by the police led to a royal decree on 27 January 1732 ordering the cemetery to be closed and placed under police surveillance. But the convulsions did not cease. They merely assumed a different character. Until then they had been a healing process, but now they turned into a prophetic manifestation. Several people, as a general rule members of the highest society and among them even a brother of Voltaire, had strange meetings at their homes around a crucifix or some Jansenist relic, most often one of Deacon de Paris. Following a period of prayer an individual participant, especially gifted in this manner, fell into a trance and began to prophecy in favor of the appellants while the rest of those present reverently collected and wrote down his words. Among these were some privileged beings, such as the famous Sister Holda, who were given warlike names and considered genuine oracles. The wealth of manuscripts with her prophesies contains, among a lot of verbiage, some beautiful pages. Several participants fulfilled prophetic deeds, others regressed into a childlike state. All of the participants, of course, viewed the phenomenon as a divine sign in favor of the appellation. Then various phenomena of yet another kind occurred. At the end of 1732 several among them in a trance asked the others to beat them or wound them in order to give them relief. This practice spread rapidly and became customary among the convulsionaries. Truly sadistic meetings ensued. A distinction was made between the "small assistance" — beatings with whips, sticks, or wooden trestles — and the "large assistance" or "murderous assistance," for which nails, daggers and sword were used. There were women whose breasts or extremities were pierced, others who were crucified for several hours. What had started as acts of penance became the miraculous manifestation of insensitivity, invulnerability, and sudden healing of injuries. The participants wrote exceedingly accurate reports, many of which were left to us but are hard to judge so long after the events. In many cases fraud or hysteria are easy to distinguish, but in some cases one seems in fact to be confronted by strange and extraordinary phenomena which are hard to understand. In all of this the participants, of course, saw miracles in favor of Jansenism. It is, on the other hand, quite certain that this system of "assistance" which gradually spread over a large part of France made possible a number of moral aberrations and sexual excesses.

The authorities tried to restrict the convulsionaries to their homes. Then a royal decree of 17 February spoke against them and their meetings were prosecuted by the police. From 1732 on there were innumerable arrests; the questionnaires kept in the archives of the Bastille furnish a number of interesting details in this matter. Yet the meetings of the convulsionaries continued into the nineteenth century. Such an unsettling phenomenon predictably led to heated conflicts within the Jansenist party, where the positions differed considerably. There were avowed opponents of both the convulsionaries and their assistance. The best known among them was no doubt Du Guet, who died in 1733 and witnessed only the beginnings of it. But his niece, Mme Mol, continued the fight in his name, followed by a number of the great theologians of the party: Fouillou, Boursier, Petitpied, and Gourlin. The expert opinion against the convulsions signed by thirty doctors on 7 February 1735 includes many Jansenists. The most vehement opponent no doubt was Debonnaire, who thundered against the convulsions in a number of pamphlets. By all accord, the one who showed the most common sense was the physician Pierre Hécquet. In his book *Naturalisme des convulsions* (1733) he characterized them as either fraud or sickness. Most characteristic is the case of the bishop of Auxerre, Caylus, who at first recognized the miracles of the deacon François de Paris, but then emphatically turned against the movement of the convulsionaries. The attitude of the Jansenist opponents in this matter naturally furnished a welcome issue to the defenders of the bull, especially to the Benedictine Dom Lataste. Others, while they approved the convulsions as a prophetic manifestation, condemned the so-called assistance as most immoral. This was the position of Colbert, Soanen, D'Étemare, and the *Nouvelles ecclésiastiques*. But there were also some passionate advocates of the so-called assistance, as well as of the convulsions.

The bull *Unigenitus* posed a difficult problem for the Jansenist party. They considered it totally erroneous in the area of the faith, but were forced to admit that the majority of the Church had recognized it. What then was the state of the promise of infallibility which Christ had given to his Church? The main features of the answer to this question were outlined even prior to 1720, they took on a clear form after 1730: this almost general apostasy of the Church is the sign that the end of time is drawing nigh. This was presaged in the Holy Gospel and the appellants are the small remainder of the steadfast few mentioned by the prophesies. This is the cause for the strange eschatological mentality in the Jansenist faction, the expectation of the impending and victorious return of Jesus Christ. Many theologians of the group sought their justification in the Holy Gospel, interpreting it according to the principles of a very specific allegorical exegesis practiced neither by the great theologians of the seventeenth century nor by Quesnel, but whose initial features can be encountered in Pascal. Du Guet's system, which can be called figurism, consists of viewing everything that has happened to the Jewish people as an allegory, a figure of that which is fated for the Church. By this perspective he arrived at the conviction that the end of time had to be preceded by a general conversion of Israel. It is possible that he even managed to convert Bossuet to his ideas around 1682. The exegetical principles of Du Guet's, however, were not published until later, in his *Régles de l'intelligence des Saintes Écritures* (1716), on which his friend D'Asfeld had collaborated. This slim volume also contains an (important) appendix concerning the conversion of the Jews. In the course of his long career Du Guer applied his method to lengthy commentaries on a part of the Bible. For the most part they were not published until the end of his life or after his death. The entire work comprises about fifty volumes, but the text has been emended several times. These commentaries, whose spiritual aspects often result in some admirable perspectives, enjoyed success even outside of the Jansenist milieu. But in the meantime Du Guet had been passed by his pupils. On 8 April 1722, D'Étemare had been present at a conversation about this topic between Du Guet and Charles de Sévigné, son of the famous Marquise de Sévigné, and this talk which converted him to figurism had opened up broad perspectives for him. He followed Du Guet's system to its outer limits and arrived at a point where he viewed the entire Holy Gospel as a chain of symbols concerning the Church, the future of the Jewish people, and the end of time. In it he thought to have found proof that the apostasy of almost the entire Church had to be followed immediately by the conversion of the Jews. In 1723 he started developing his views in several works, primarily in his *Tradition sur la conversion des Juifs* (1724). Du Guet, who held these ideas to be exaggerated, was irritated and criticized them in his conferences. Yet D'Étemare had become popular and found many followers, among them Le Gros, Fourquevaux, and many others. The expectation of the conversion of the Jews to the Christian faith and that of the arrival of Elijah as a sign of the end of time played a significant role in the Jansenist milieu. The convulsionaries spoke of it in their prophesies and the famous/infamous Vaillant called himself Elijah. The Apocalypse offered the ideal subject matter for such commentaries, but these were generally so audacious that no one dared to publish them. Those of D'Étemare did not appear until the nineteenth century (1866), those of Le Gros have remained unpublished. D'Étemare clearly expressed the idea that the locusts are identical with the Society of Jesus and Le Gros thought that Babylon represents the Christian and corrupt Rome. In addition, D'Étemare advocated the idea of a "millennium," a spiritual reign of Christ on earth prior to the end of the world. Some of the exegetes attempted by means of calculations, whose perspicacity, however, was again and again deceived, to determine the date of the conversion of the Jews.

One last feature characterized the Jansenist faction, one that stemmed from its mentality as a minority: its hero cult. Initially its heroes were essentially the great men of Port-Royal, the nuns and friends of Port-Royal. Then toward the end of the century the famous appellants became objects of veneration. Some Jansenists remembered them during Mass on the same level with the canonized saints. Their relics developed into a veritable cult; even the smallest vestiges of bone or clothing were kept in valuable reliquaries. But this veneration is interesting to us primarily because of the preservation and publication of important documents which fortunately were left to us and represent an irreplaceable source. The Church of Utrecht has a collection of documents of incredible abundance the most important part of which is kept at the seminary of Amersfoort, which has possession of it today. Another collection was compiled by Françoise-Marguerite de Joncoux (1668–1715), a loyal friend of the last nuns of Port-Royal, who managed with the help of a Lieutenant Voyer d'Argenson to save the documents confiscated at the destruction of the convent. She also collected a wealth of other items or had them copied. Mlle de Joncoux, who had received an extraordinarily thorough theological education, took an active part in the controversies and in 1699 originated the idea of publishing the *Provinciales,* in which she translated Nicole's Latin annotations into French. During the eighteenth century her work went through fifteen reprints. At her death her collection was left to the Abbey Saint-Germain-des-Pres and is now in the National Library. Another much larger and more complete collection was compiled by Marie-Scholastique de Ménilles de Thémericourt (1671–1745), who had been a pupil at Port-Royal and had close ties to the nuns and their friends. About 1715 she undertook a systematic listing of all historical documents relating to the dissolved convent. She was supported in her task by some devoted friends, such as Mme de Bourdun, the mother of D'Étemare. She could only collect a few of the original documents, but employed several professional copiers who copied and carefully compared all documents which she was able to borrow. Then she put them together into various methodically arranged collections which she then annotated. She also inspired several publications. Later on she added her manuscripts to the rich collection of documents relating to the controversies which was compiled by Adrien le Paige; the entire collection remained in the possession of the Society of Port-Royal. Several other holdings have been transferred to public libraries without any sizeable losses.

These archives were able to satisfy the needs of Jansenist circles for veneration because they placed at their disposal the works of their heroes and the recollection of the authors of memoirs. According to the custom of the times these publications changed the text to some extent, leaving out what could be troublesome or superfluous; yet they are very informative. A close determination of the conditions under which these editions originated is quite difficult. The production was especially intensive around the middle of the century; thereafter there were hardly any more new editions, proof that interest was gradually lessening. Instead there appeared the *Lettres* of Mother Angélique (1742), the "memoirs" about her written by various nuns, which have become known under the title *Mémoires d'Utrecht* (1742), numerous devotionals by her niece Angélique de Saint-Jean, and the famous *Recueil d'Utrecht,* containing voluminous documentation about Pascal (1740). The great memoirists of Port-Royal were presented to the public: Lancelot and Fontaine in 1738, Thomas du Fosse in 1739. There were several attempts at historical synthesis which, although tendentious in favor of the Jansenists, are nonetheless interesting. The best work is the *Histoire générale de Port-Royal* (1757) by the Benedictine monk Dom Clémencet.

CHAPTER 130

Spirituality and Its Development in Eighteenth-Century France

Christian Life

In eighteenth-century France the religious energies were for the most part consumed by the Jansenist conflict and its aftereffects. This led to impoverishment in other areas as well. Embroiled in daily battles which left room for only the most immediate questions, even the best minds were unable to recognize that the actual danger was lurking in the growing influence of deist philosophy. On 18 November 1751, a collaborator of the *Encyclopedia,* Abbé Jean Martin de Prades (1720–82), submitted to the Sorbonne several theses inspired by philosophic deism which the syndic Dugard naively found to be "full of nice sentiments in favor of religion."

Although parliament reacted soon after, it was only against a contumacious thesis regarding the inequality of the classes. The Jansenist Étienne Gourlin was the only one to attack the problem perspicaciously, making the bull *Unigenitus* responsible for this pervasive blindness. This explains to a great extent the weakness of Catholic apologetics in the century of the Enlightenment.

Spiritual life itself was impoverished because of the crisis of quietism, which for a long time discredited all mystical elements, cutting off Christian piety from its living sources of inner experience. Henceforth psychologizing moralism was to triumph. Several authors who were actually part of the seventeenth century had their widest dissemination in the eighteenth century. As mentioned above, this was the case with the great Jansenist moralists: Nicole, Du Guet, and Quesnel; Jean-Jacques Boileau (1649–1735) who sympathized with the Jansenists but was clever enough never to expose himself unduly, also belongs to this group. He was the author of several very conventional devotional books, but above all he was appreciated as a spiritual guide. After his death two volumes of *Lettres sur différents sujets de morale et de piété* (1737–47) were published which really deserve our interest. They are the source for the famous story of the chasm which Pascal constantly thought he saw on his left side. Lastly, it should be remembered that Bossuet also did not become famous as a religious author until the eighteenth century, since his great works in that field *Élévations sur les mystères* (1727), *Méditations sur l'Évangile* (1731), and the *Lettres et opuscules* (1748) were not published until then.

The Jansenist tradition was continued by numerous authors the majority of whom have deservedly been relegated to oblivion. One of the most interesting authors among them was no doubt Paul Collard (1698–1775), superior of the small seminary of Troyes at the time when Bossuet's nephew was bishop there. He was a keen spiritual guide, dedicated to a rigorism that made no concession, author of the posthumously published *Lettres spirituelles* (1784) in which he developed a severe spirituality raised to extremes. Similar qualities are encountered in the historians Jérôme Besoigne (1686–1763) and René Cerveau (1700–1780), who also wrote devotional literature. Their works are doctrinally sound and their devotion to the incarnate word places them among the successors of Bérulle. But their style is dry and artificial, their psychology insufficient and conventional, which makes them hardly worth reading. Similar qualities can be ascertained in several of their non-Jansenist contemporaries.

This situation attests to an undeniable deterioration of the intellectual level while that of Christian practice was maintained — so it appears — throughout the century. There were villages even in 1788 whose number of inhabitants was determined by attendance at the Easter Communion and where this number was destined to sink almost to zero in 1804, after the concordat. The congregations, especially the contemplative ones, attracted fewer and fewer members; the nadir appears to have been reached around 1765, at the time when the government took up the problem by means of the famous *Commission des Réguliers.* Later on the houses again attracted a greater number of recruits and this increase continued until the Revolution. In this climate new foundations were rare, yet where they were undertaken they were invariably dedicated to teaching or the care of the sick. But the charitable organizations of the laity remained active; the secret

"A.A." associations (*Associatio amicorum*) were formed everywhere. The work of the popular missions was continued, ensuring a periodic renewal of parish life. Religious zeal stayed alive to the extent that it made possible the Catholic resistance during the Revolution and the subsequent renewal.

In addition, we have to call attention to the liturgical efforts in eighteenth-century France. The best example was the initiative by Vintimille, the archbishop of Paris, who provided for his diocese a new missal (1736) and a new breviary (1738), which latter enjoyed a great success. The missal was the work of Mésenguy, an appellant and reappellant; the breviary had been adapted by the Oratorian Vigier, who was sympathetic to the Jansenists. Both books contained admirable Latin poetry in the form of hymns, prose texts, and sequences, among them the older creations of the canon of Saint-Victor, Santeul, and the very beautiful ones by the rector of the university, Charles Coffin (1676–1749), as well as hymns by other authors. The breviary offered a new order of psalter which made its weekly recital possible since the excessively long psalms had been shortened. As we know his was the model for the breviary of Pius X. Although both the missal and the breviary were very controversial, they made their way and were adopted or imitated by many other dioceses.

The Continuance of Mysticism

It would be wrong to assume that the crisis of quietism extinguished mysticism; it merely pushed it to the periphery and almost made it into a secret movement. A detailed examination of the documents shows, for instance, that the number of nuns in the convents who received the grace of mysticism stayed exactly as high as in the preceding century. But whereas it had once been surrounded by an interested environment and almost invariably attracted a biographer, they were now enveloped by silence and secrecy, penetrated only by a few of the initiated. This was true for the Marseille Sister of the Visitation Anne-Madeleine de Rémusat, a champion of the Sacred Heart of Jesus devotion. Her spiritual guide was the Jesuit Claude-François Milley (1668–1720), who died as the result of his caring for the plague-stricken. He did not publish anything during his lifetime, but his very beautiful spiritual correspondence appeared in print not too long ago. To his charges he preached unreserved surrender of the self, disassociation from all temporal ties, the secluded life in God and pure love; thus he continued the great seventeenth-century mystical tradition of the Society.

Other congregations furnished just as interesting a contribution. The *Avis sur différents états de l'oraison mentale* by the Dominican Jean-Baptiste Rousseau (d. 1756), which came out after the quietistic crisis, courageously fights for the legitimacy, indeed the necessity of contemplative prayer, manifesting the influence of the great Rhenish-Flemish mystical tradition down to Saint Theresa and Saint John of the Cross.

The best religious author of the eighteenth century no doubt was the Jesuit Jean-Pierre de Caussade (1675–1751), who seems to have owed much to the Sisters of the Visitation of Nancy, with whom he resided from 1729 to 1731 and again from 1733 to 1739. He published only one work, the *Instruction spirituelle en forme de dialogues sur les divers états d'oraison suivant la doctrine de M. Bossuet* (Perpignan, 1741). In it he undertakes the difficult task of demonstrating that Fénelon and Bossuet concurred in the essential points and that Bossuet was basically a defender of mysticism. To prove his point he referred to a text entitled "Manière courte et facile pour faire l'oraison en foi et de simple présence de Dieu" which had been ascribed to Bossuet by the Sisters of the Visitation of Meaux and which de Caussade published in an appendix. Ironically, it appears that this originally anonymous little work was actually by Mme Guyon. Although de Caussade's argumentation is not totally convincing, his essays on contemplative prayer and the unifying life are most interesting. His correspondents and the Sisters of the Visitation had gathered several collections of his letters on the topic of spiritual guidance. In the nineteenth century Ramière compiled from them the book *L'abandon à la Providence divine* (1861), which gained posthumous fame for Caussade, acknowledged by numerous reprints and a critical edition which appeared quite recently. Caussade shows himself to be heir to the great authentically mystical Ignatian tradition as well as to Salesian influences. It is easily noticeable that he is also indebted to Surin and the Jesuits of the seventeenth century; moreover, Fénelon remains in many aspects his major stimulus. Just like the latter, Caussade wanted to lead man to pure faith and pure love, to guide him in holy indifference to a total devotion to God and to introduce him to contemplation beyond all conceptual and didactic ways. Caussade's remarkable literary talent ranks him among the foremost of the religious authors, a position granted him by our time, whereas in his own time he was scarcely known beyond the circle of his charges.

But toward the end of the century we encounter a truly great author in the Jesuit Jean-Nicolas Grou (1731–1803), who was also influenced by the Sisters of the Visitation. In England, where he was forced to seek refuge in 1792, he composed the major part of his voluminous work, which was not published until the nineteenth century and is read even now. It presents to us in an admirable form a profound mystically oriented doctrine of the inner life.

Popular Devotions

We have already mentioned that devotions continued to be popular among the people in the seventeenth century, but the educated public took a critical stance toward them, demanding moderation and theological distinctions. Some aspects of the devotion to Mary, especially, were questioned. But the spirited controversy provoked in 1673 by Widenfeld's *Monita salutaria* and continued in 1693 by the pamphlet *De la vraie dévotion à la Sainte Vierge et du culte qui lui est dû* by the Jansenist sympathizer Andrien Baillet barely reached into the eighteenth century. It was simply a case of special caution being applied on this point. But it was precisely this epoch that witnessed the work of Saint Louis-Marie Grignion de Montfort (1673–1716), whom posterity has considered one of the great apostles of the devotion to Mary. Yet the question arises of whether (at least to some extent) this might not be a case of optical illusion. His work has been handed down to us under very unsure circumstances. His career, short but checkered, was primarily occupied with his missionary work, in which the devotion to Mary played a significant although not exclusive role. This is the case in the only work he ever published, the *Lettres aux amis de la Croix. L'amour de la Sagesse éternelle,* which he left in manuscript form and the accurate text of which was not published until 1929, is certainly the best of his writings. In it the influence of Suso is combined with that of the Bérulle school, which he received during his education at Saint-Sulpice. But the significance of his *Traité de la vraie dévotion à la Sainte Vierge,* now his best-known work, should not be exaggerated. To be sure, the idea of Marian servitude advocated by him is highly interesting, yet it resumes — in a very personal form — a practice reaching back into the sixteenth century and used by Bérulle. But one must question to what extent Montfort actually disseminated it beyond just a small circle of the initiated. It is certain that the manuscript of the *Vraie devotion* was forgotten after the death of its author. Rediscovered in 1842, it was published a year later and did not find an echo until the nineteenth century. Although the doctrine presented in the pamphlet cannot be faulted, some of its formulations would hardly have permitted its publication in the eighteenth century.

The spread of the Sacred Heart devotion within the framework treated here was in fact one of the most significant elements characterizing the eighteenth century. Although it prevailed in the end, it was preceded by lengthy controversies. At the end of the preceding century this devotion had assumed two forms: that of Saint John Eudes, the more theologically oriented form, and the more emotional one of Saint Margaret Mary Alacoque, whose central idea was penance. This latter form was able to prevail very quickly, propagated by the Sisters of the Visitation and the Society of Jesus, who then accorded a central position to the revelations of Saint Margaret Mary and emphasized the painful and human aspect, as symbolized by the human heart of Jesus. These traits appeared very clearly even in the first of the significant works dedicated to this topic, that of the Jesuit Jean Croiset (1656–1738). Published in Louvain, it was very successful, but it was also resisted to the same extent, especially from within the ranks of the Jesuits. In 1704 it was finally placed on the Index. The decisive work was written by Joseph de Gallifet (1663–1749), who occupied an especially influential position by virtue of his office as assistant to the Jesuit general in Rome. In 1726 he submitted to the Congregation of Rites a very important memorandum "De cultu sacrosancti Cordis," in which he developed the theological reasons for the devotion, perhaps insisting too much on the heart as the seat of the emotions and on the revelations of Margaret Mary. Prosper Lambertini, the future Pope Benedict XIV, took a stand against him and on 12 July 1727 the congregation gave him a negative reply, reiterated in 1729, concerning the introduction of the celebration of this feast. This did not discourage Gallifet; in 1733 he had a French translation of his work published under the title *L'excellence de la dévotion au Coeur adorable de Jésus-Christ* in which the major part of Margaret Mary's autobiography appeared for the first time.

At about this point a rather important episode occurred in this connection. In 1729 Languet de Gergy, bishop of Soissons and late archbishop of Sens, had published his *Vie de la Vénérable Mère Marguerite Alacoque.* Although at this time the work was attributed to the Jesuits, to whom Languet had merely lent his name, the latter does seem to have been the actual author who had edited the documents placed at his disposal by the convent of Paray-le-Monial. By the criteria of his time the work was not bad. But Languet was then one of the celebrities of anti-Jansenism and the book inevitably provoked the opposition of that group which had earlier been indifferent to the Sacred Heart devotion. This hostility became especially virulent after 1765. But in view of the progressive weakening of the Jansenist party at that time its opposition had no more than a limited effect, presenting no obstacle to the continued development of the devotion, which was able to spread almost everywhere.

On 26 January 1765 a brief by Clement XIII finally approved a Mass and an office for the Sacred Heart of Jesus for Poland and the Roman archfraternity. This made possible the liturgical devotion wherever there was a desire to introduce it. In 1748 an altar had been dedicated to the Sacred Heart of Jesus at the church of Saint-Sulpice in Paris. On 22 June 1767 a pastoral letter by the archbishop of Paris, Christophe de Beaumont, ordered the feast of the Sacred Heart to be celebrated in his diocese, and several other dioceses followed suit. The polemic now reached its climax. Disregarding it, Fumel, the bishop of Lodève, published a pamphlet *Le cult de l'amour divin ou la dévotion au Sacré-Coeur de Jésus* which was violently attacked by the Jansenists. Yet the confraternities dedicated to the Sacred Heart multiplied almost everywhere and attracted followers even among that segment of the aristocracy who remained tied to the traditional religion. This astonishing growth explains the fact that devotion to the Sacred Heart continued to flourish unimpaired even during the Revolution.

CHAPTER 131

Anglican Spirituality in the Eighteenth Century

The Anglican spirituality of the seventeenth century produced fruitful and manifold impulses. They reflect the essence of a profound but highly intellectual piety tied strictly to the Gospel, best exemplified by Bishop Lancelot Andrewes (1555–1626). His *Preces privatae* is an admirable collection of poetry compiled from biblical texts and written almost exclusively in Greek. Newman, a great admirer of this work, published its well-known translation in a series of pamphlets by the Oxford movement. Other authors express this sort of piety by poetry of a tender mystical lyricism. This is the case with John Donne (1572–1631), a passionate and complex figure, and more so with the admirable Henry Vaughan (1622–95), some of whose poems, as for example "The Night," remind us of John of the Cross. Yet other poets anticipated pietism, especially the strange Nicholas Ferrar and the Puritan Thomas Goodwin (1600–1680), whose work *The Heart of Christ in Heaven toward Sinners on Earth* (1642) was a precursor to the Sacred Heart devotion. The Platonizing tendency, well developed especially among the educated circles of Oxford, brought forth interesting and curious works, especially those of Henry More. He was under the influence of the esoteric mysticism of Jakob Böhme, who enjoyed great esteem in seventeenth-century England; Charles I had a personal interest in him and had his works translated. One of the most interesting works from the Puritan circles is that of John Bunyan (1628–88), a tinker who became a popular preacher. He achieved lasting fame through his treatise *Grace abounding to the Chief of Sinners* (1666), but even more so through his *Pilgrim's Progress* (1678), expressing a spirituality which — while intellectually meager — is pragmatic and soulful. Even more interesting — by virtue of his position at the periphery of the official Churches — is the case of the founder of the Quaker movement, George Fox (1624–91). His intriguing diary offers a beautiful itinerary of his calling; his numerous spiritual treatises develop an illumination theory sharply opposed to all institutional Churches, but especially to Catholicism. His protégé, William Penn (1644–1719), the founder of the Quaker state of Pennsylvania, was much more tolerant. In his famous treatise *No Cross, no Crown* (1669) he defends the Quaker view of life and does not hesitate to quote an excerpt from the biography of the Baron de Renty by the Jesuit Saint-Jure as proof of his thesis that the soul must concentrate on a point in the sea of destruction.

This quote raises the question of the influence of continental spirituality on Anglicanism. An examination of the total picture shows that this influence was very significant even in the seventeenth century and that it deepened even more during the following centuries. The English public was very much interested in the religious controversies which were stirring up France and frequently interpreted them in an antipapal sense. In general their sympathies were with Port-Royal and the Jansenists, who were viewed as the least corrupted among the Roman Catholics. Numerous texts of Jansenist origin were quickly translated into English, among them the *Provinciales* (1657) and the *Pensées* (1704) by Pascal. In 1669 Theophile Gale published *The True Idea of Jansenism;* based on his stay in France, his work is remarkably well informed and perspicacious. But some other representatives of French spirituality were also highly respected. The Puritan J. Alleine invoked De Renty, just as Penn had. The famous historian G. Burnet (1643–1715), a bishop with latitudinarian tendencies, did likewise. R. Roach, who had at first been a member of the sect of the Philadelphians, inspired by Böhme, and had then become a millenarian, expressed his admiration for the mystics from Francis de Sales to Fénelon (1725).

At the very beginning of the eighteenth century the influence of Fénelon and Mme Guyon in England was indeed very considerable. There was also a noticeable influence of a much less convincing mystic, Antoinette Bourignon (1616–80), who was officially a Catholic but joined a variation of illuminatism, similar to that of the Quakers. While English publicists ironically compared the Quakers with the quietists of the continent, the Quakers themselves devoutly invoked Fénelon, Mme Guyon, and Antoinette Bourignon. Between 1727 and 1738 one of them, Josiah Martin, published translations of Fénelon and Mme Guyon, while Nathanael Hooke, a Catholic sympathizer and friend of Pope's, translated the *Vie de Fénelon* by Ramsay. Personal ties were soon formed. Numerous members of the English aristocracy visited Fénelon at Cambrai, where he had been banished, and Mme Guyon, exiled to Blois after she was set free. Both of them had a profound influence on the Protestant segment of England, especially on the followers of James II in Scotland, where several of their friends were arrested and executed during the rebellion of 1715. The most prominent personality of the Protestant group was André Michel Ramsay (1686–1743) who converted to Catholicism when he was with Fénelon and became secretary to Mme Guyon until her death. A well-known physician from London, John Keith served as a focus for the whole group where all the correspondence converged. Through him Mme Guyon sent a copy of her autobiography to England. This entire group also had great appreciation for Pierre Poiret (1646–1719), a pietist pastor of Calvinist origin, editor of the works of Mme Guyon, Antoinette Bourignon, and of many other mystical texts. Their admiration was, by the way, quite eclectic, extending as it did to Francis de Sales, Pascal, Renty, Olier, Surin, Laurent de la Résurrection, a fellow Carmelite well liked by Fénelon, as well as to a simple Breton servant woman, Armelle Nicolas (1606–71), called the Bonne Armelle.

The Episcopalian milieu of Scotland was in fact strongly influenced by the mysticism of the continent since a command of French was widespread among the educated. Robert Leighton, originally Presbyterian and then Archbishop of Glasgow, had lived on the continent for a long time and maintained close ties with the Jansenists; like them he favored Augustinianism and had a certain preference for the early Church. In regard to spiritualism his most sincere sympathies were reserved for Francis de Sales, in whom he sought the idea of a preeminent inner religion beyond all dogmatic controversies. His pupil Henry Scongal, before his untimely death at a very young age, was able to publish a small volume oriented along those lines, *The Life of God in the Soul of Man,* whose many reprints attested to its success.

Similar influences were at work in the circle of those clerics who had refused to swear the oath of loyalty to William of Orange after the revolution of 1688. Spiritually and liturgically they formed a very interesting group, asserting themselves until the very beginning of the eighteenth century. They had close ties with French Gallicanism and Bossuet. In 1712 and 1718 efforts were made toward reunion. The pious bishop of Bath and Wells, Thomas Ken, who had a reputation for saintliness, sought his ideal in the Jansenist Nicolas Pavillon and was inspired by Pascal and Saint-Cyran. A member of the group, Francis Lee, translated Fénelon's pastoral letter concerning the love of God in 1715. Thus their ritualistic tendency by no means kept them from making the personal inner life the foremost goal of their efforts.

Among those who had refused the oath of loyalty, William Law (1686–1781) was an interesting personality and a great author. His convictions had forced him to leave Cambridge and he withdrew to the house of the historian Gibbon as tutor of the latter's family. As an author of devotional literature he was strongly influenced by Francis de Sales. While God must be the only object of human activity, he asserted that the Christian can arrive at holiness under all conditions. An expert in German religious thought, he was also influenced by Tauler and the *Theologia teutsch.* This concept of Christian perfection, at once challenging and elastic, is expressed in his two best works, *Treatise of Christian Perfection* (1726) and *Serious Call to a Holy Life* (1728), both of which — though especially the latter — are classics of the Anglican spiritual literature. Around 1733 he made the acquaintance of George Cheyne, a fashionable physician who took a passionate interest in mysticism. He was a friend of Pope's and pupil of the brothers Garden, as well as of the French eccentric Saint-Georges de Marsay. Under Cheyne's influence Law discovered Böhme, whom he learned to admire and through whom he arrived at a unique esoteric position. On the other hand, he severely criticized Antoinette Bourignon and Marsay; yet he consistently respected Fénelon and Mme Guyon. Among Law's friends, John Heylin should be mentioned. He was a teacher at the cathedral school of Westminster Abbey and had lived in France for some time. In 1724 Heylin published *Devotional Tracts concerning the Presence of God and other Religious Subjects,* which includes texts by Fénelon, Mme Guyon, and, above all, Laurent de la Résurrection. In 1721 Heylin also published a translation of the homilies of the pseudo-Macarius, which had a strong influence on Wesley, who was one of his friends. Lastly, we cannot leave the topic of the High Church without making mention of Joseph Butler (1692–1752), bishop of Bristol and later of Durham, author of a work entitled *The Analogy of Religion Natural and Revealed* (1736), remarkable by virtue of its view of conscience and the supernatural which greatly influenced Newman during the latter's youth.

John Wesley (1703–91) and Methodism

Of all the religious currents which were shaping England in the eighteenth century Methodism possessed the greatest vitality. Its founder's family was of Puritan origin; his parents, Samuel and Susanna Wesley, however, had staunchly adhered to the High Church and faithfully kept to its principles in their small parish of Epworth. The parents gave their large progeny of nineteen children an example of piety and learning. Samuel was enthusiastic about the early Church and occupied himself with the works of Bossuet and Arnauld; Susanna had memorized almost the entire translation of Pascal's *Pensées* by Kenneth (1704). The example set by his family could not but influence Wesley strongly; he belonged to the High Church until 1737. Later on he reproached himself for indifference in his spiritual life until 1725. At this point he experienced his first conversion, in which he also involved his brother Charles, who appears to have played a prominent role in the subsequent events. This first experience, which prompted Wesley to devote himself entirely to God, was influenced by reading the *Imitation* by Jeremy Taylor and the works of Scongal and Law. As we know, the latter two were very much steeped in the mystics of the continent. Wesley now sought to go back to the sources. Around 1730 he read Francis de Sales, Pascal, Quesnel, and Fénelon. At this time he was also influenced by Heylin in a clearly mystical sense. In 1732 he had the opportunity of making the acquaintance of William Law, but as a person Law disappointed him. On the other hand, he was still fascinated by the vision of the original Church. He now read *Les moeurs des chrétiens* by the confirmed Gallican historian Claude Fleury (1640–1723), who was a friend of Fénelon's and Bossuet's. At about this time he also read Tillemont and in 1733 he even sought the acquaintance of the latter's translator, Thomas Deacon. Together with his brother and some other fellow students he founded a student society in Oxford, the "Holy Club," where he lectured about his ideas. At that time he discovered the work

Vie de Renty by Saint-Jure, who was also revered by his father. Its discovery was followed by that of Tauler, Mme Guyon, and Molinos.

In point of fact, Wesley, during the years 1731–36, underwent a severe inner crisis and sought help from the Catholic mystics. Toward the end of this crisis he took part in a missionary expedition to Georgia. But the meager success of this mission caused him great disappointment and affected him profoundly. In the course of this mission he met the Moravian Brethren, pupils of Zinzendorf, who was a strange mystic of illuminism. After his return to England a short time later Wesley initiated personal ties with Zinzendorf. For a time the Lutheran-inspired Moravian Brethren caused him to give primary importance to the idea of justification solely on the basis of faith and the idea that the justification of man is solely the justice of Christ imputed to him. At the occasion of a conference of the Moravian Brethren on 24 May 1738 Wesley heard a reading of Luther's introduction to the letter to the Romans. This became a decisive element, causing his second, his "evangelical" conversion. He felt his heart "strangely warmed" and received the inner conviction that Christ had forgiven his sins and saved him from the law of sin and death. After a short sojourn in Germany, where he visited the communities of the Moravian Brethren, Wesley, supported by his brother Charles and some of his pupils, began to pronounce his ideas by means of open-air or field preaching. To this task he dedicated himself until his death with a courage and stamina that shrank from nothing. He gave about forty thousand sermons, and we also have a considerable number of hymns composed by his brother Charles for those camp meetings. But John Wesley did not want to be a "dissenter" at all. What he actually wanted was to give people a personal religious life within the framework of the established Church and he consistently refused to give up those ties which connected him with official Anglicanism. He was accused of "enthusiasm," meaning an irrational illuminism, and for that reason he encountered strenuous resistance, especially on the part of Joseph Butler. But Wesley did not change his position. He knew how to organize and sweep along his listeners so that soon he had strong groups of followers. He divided them into classes of twelve faithful each who were under the direction of a leader who was responsible for their spiritual progress. These firm and clearly delineated structures impressed public opinion; hence the name "Methodism," initially given to them somewhat scoffingly. As a matter of fact, the activities of Wesley and his group had the effect generally of raising the social and human level of his followers, having a positive and beneficial influence on English society.

Early on Wesley apparently started to keep a diary whose entries as of 1735 have come down to us, still partly unpublished. Aside from being a fascinating document concerning his travels and sermons, it also offers us a spiritual experience of rare quality, some points of which, however, remain obscure. It is, for example, not easy to find out why Wesley in 1736, toward the end of his crisis, turned against the same mystics from whom he had sought help and solace before. He reproaches them for their excessive desire to isolate the Christian in solitude and for their attempt to reinterpret the inner trials as constituting grace while he saw in it nothing but a sign of God's anger. His brother Charles, although his confidant, did not follow him in this. Wesley later on changed his position without, however, expressly revoking it and included the mystics in his anthologies. At any rate, it is certain that his experience of 24 May 1728 was not the last of his spiritual trials; his state of depression lasted for several months until he regained his inner peace. Several commentators think that this is proof enough for questioning the actual significance of that experience. But the value which Wesley himself gave to it contradicts this interpretation. There can be no doubt that the analysis of his own case led him to put his "evangelical" experience on a much less sentimental level than some of his successors did and to put it manifestly in the area of a moral decision.

Thus Wesley arrived at very complex points of view regarding certain Protestant positions. He had always been an opponent of the Calvinist idea of predestination and on this point he soon contradicted his pupil Whitefield. But to the extent in which he became aware that conversion had to be translated into a challenge within practical life he rejected the Lutheran idea of justification solely through faith and without good works. No doubt he held the opinion that Christ is the sole savior and that man is saved only by believing in Him. On this point he completely shared the Christocentricity of the Moravian Brethren, but without accepting its sentimental and pious aspects. More and more he arrived at the conviction that faith could be given valid expression only through works. Luther's commentary on the letter to the Galatians and his reflection on the letter of James which Luther called an "epistle of straw" seemed blasphemous to him. At the same time he began to reject the idea of imputed justice as absurd. On this point he was contradicted by the Moravian Brethren and Zinzendorf; he conferred with the latter on 3 September 1741, but their talk was disappointing because each persisted in his position. Shortly thereafter Wesley encountered similar resistance from some of the members of his own movement.

Yet his ideas continued to develop in this direction. More and more he arrived at the conviction that justification had to be connected with a progressive sanctification through man, a sanctification achieved through his own efforts under divine grace, leading man to a genuine moral progress. In his eyes, faith acted through love and love was developed through deeds. Factually he drew away farther and farther from the positions of Protestantism while approaching traditional Catholic ethics; from this he unhesitatingly drew the moral consequences necessary for the actual ministry. Once he did this, he encountered the problem of creating the instruments and aids for his faithful which they needed on this path toward perfection. For this purpose he published the fifty volumes of his *Christian Library* (1750–56), a collection of spiritual anthologies to which more volumes of the same genre were added later on. Its very eclectic selection is highly significant. Naturally the English and among them the Anglicans are most prominently represented, but there are also many Puritans whose seriousness and Christocentrism Wesley appreciated. There are some German Pietists, especially Arndt. The Spanish are represented by John of Ávila, Gregor López and Molinos. Because of their exclusively mystical orientation, Wesley did not include Saint Teresa and Saint John of the Cross. The French are heavily represented with Laurent de la Résurrection, Fénelon, Mme Guyon, Antoinette Bourignon, Saint-Cyran, Pascal, Du Guet, De Renty, and Armelle Nicolas. In his selection Wesley seems to have been inspired by similar anthologies of Pierre Poiret, although he limited the proportion of mystics.

In such a perspective the spirituality of John Wesley, without loosing its elasticity, gradually reassumed the moral and even pragmatic shadings which were given a rare communicative value by virtue of his eloquence. Of course he encountered the spirited resistance not only of the Calvinists, who accused him of giving man the possibility of saving himself by his own power, but also that of the established Church, which he stirred from its lethargy by reminding it emphatically of the urgency of its apostolic task. But it must also be admitted that he developed, especially toward the end of his life, a certain indifferentism toward the strictly dogmatic aspects by moderating their severities and lessening their significance. This point of departure, to be sure, enabled him to create an attractive, albeit fragile, synthesis between the Protestant doctrine of grace and the Catholic ethic of sanctification. The respectable spread of Methodism after Wesley's death attests to the vitality of the spiritual enthusiasm he created. But the Calvinist orientation of many of his disciples shows how difficult it was to maintain that doctrinal balance for which Wesley had hoped.

CHAPTER 132

Episcopalism in the Church of the Empire from the Middle of the Seventeenth to the End of the Eighteenth Century

Practical Episcopalism from the End of the Seventeenth to the Beginning of the Eighteenth Century

The roots of the seventeenth and eighteenth-century episcopalism of the Church of the Empire extend back to the late Middle Ages. Spanning the Council of Trent and the Reformation, it tied in with the reaction against papal claims in the late Middle Ages, with the church reform movement of the fourteenth and fifteenth centuries, the Councils of Constance and Basel and the prereformational *gravamina*. As a practical episcopalism it initially based its claims concerning beneficiary rights, episcopal jurisdiction, and payments to the Curia on the Concordat of Vienna of 1448. Using the controversial clause "In aliis autem" (buttressed by historical research) as its point of departure, episcopalism next extended the basis of its claim to the Princes Concordats of 1447, which were acknowledged in the above clause and were much more advantageous to the Church of the Empire. Finally it advanced as a rationale the Mainz Acceptation of 1439, comparable to the Pragmatic Sanction of Bourges, the basic law of the Gallican Church. After 1762 the episcopalism of the Church of the Empire viewed as its basic law and program the Basel Decrees accepted in Mainz. The attempt to reform the Church's constitution in favor of episcopalism, simultaneously changing the ecclesiastical principalities into modern, enlightened absolutist states on a Catholic foundation was shaky from the start. It was to be brought about by reviving the decrees of the Council of Basel; in some places there was even talk of overcoming the religious schism. This attempt, however, was immediately countered by more than three hundred years of ecclesiastical and imperial history; it was full of inner contradictions and doomed to failure by the empiric-historic method it was based on.

The Council of Trent had created decisively positive as well as negative conditions for the revival of episcopalism a century after its last sessions. The less the ecclesiastical territories were threatened in their existence and the more the prince-bishops concentrated on their ecclesiastical and political tasks, the more frequent were the quarrels with the papal nuncios in Cologne, Vienna, Lucerne, and with the Roman Curia about violations of the Vienna Concordat, the archiepiscopal indults for the papal months, quinquennial faculties, the jurisdiction of the nunciatures, annates, confirmation fees, pallium payments, exemptions, and decimations.

In the first decades after the Treaty of Westphalia, leadership of the opposition in the Church of the Empire was represented by the elector-archbishops of Mainz and Cologne, Johann Philipp von Schönborn and Max Heinrich von Bayern. In his capacity as lord chancellor of the Empire, Johann Philipp considered it his foremost task to watch over the liberties and rights of the German nation. As archbishop of the *Metropolis Germaniae,* concerned with the reform of the higher and lower clergy, he complained in 1648 about the diminution of his ordinary rights by the Cologne nunciature. He was confirmed in his hostility to the nunciature by his political and Gallican views as well as by the unionist intentions and anti-Roman sentiments on the part of several of his advisers, especially the convert Johann Christian von Boineburg. For the Cologne elector Max Heinrich, whose heated disputes with Johann Philipp concerning the right of coronation had been resolved in the so-called Coronation Tractate of 1657, there were several causes for the outbreak of tensions with Rome in 1659. Among them were theological and canonical misgivings regarding the direct interference of the nuncios, especially those of Cologne and Liège, with their idea of the special rights of a "born legate of the Holy See"; the influence of his favorite, Franz Egon von Fürstenberg, who was oriented toward the Gallican model; and, most importantly, the Wittelsbach church policy.

In this regard it should be stressed that nine years earlier, in 1650, the election of the very pious, yet weak Max Heinrich in Münster had been rejected by Christoph Bernhard von Galen because Max Heinrich "was too much a cleric to be a good ruler and general as demanded by the times" (W. Kohl). When his brother Albrecht Sigismund planned to resign, he sought to succeed him in the bishopric of Freising, although he already held the Cologne electorate and the prince-bishoprics of Hildesheim and Liège; as far as political power was concerned Freising was insignificant. With some justification it was later designated as "our parish" by the elector Max Emanuel. With only two interruptions, the Wittelsbach dynasty ruled the prince-bishopric from the middle of the sixteenth to the middle of the eighteenth century. But it was an "arcanum" of Freising politics in no case ever to separate from the Emperor and the Empire. One of the goals of the Wittelsbach church policy had always been to unite Freising in a personal union with either the old Bavarian bishopric of Regensburg or the ecclesiastic secundogeniture in the northwest German *Germania Sacra,* founded by Duke Ernst. In addition to Max Heinrich, the other candidates for Freising were Cardinal Friedrich of Hesse, Franz Egon von Fürstenberg, and the prince-bishop of Osnabrück and Regensburg, Franz Wilhelm von Wartenberg, progeny of the marriage of Duke Ferdinand of Bavaria to a commoner.

But Pope Alexander VII refused to accept Albrecht Sigismund's resignation unless the Holy See were granted the unreserved right to the new appointment; he withdrew the election rights from the Freising chapter and ordered the nuncio to thwart the election of the Cologne elector. These differences, stemming from the policies of the Wittelsbach imperial Church were intensified by the failure of Max Heinrich's designs on Paderborn, because of the quarrels covering the quinquennial faculties and the archiepiscopal indults to fill the benefices becoming vacant during the papal months. In the fall of 1660 — probably on the advice of his minister Franz Egon von Fürstenberg, who was hostile to Rome — Max Heinrich suggested the convocation of a national council to counter the presumptiousness of the Holy See and the abuses in the Church of the Empire.

According to the Vienna nuncio, this was to be accompanied by the reunion project, the so-called "Mainz Plan,' propagated in September 1660 by Frankfurt. Its goal was said to be the reunion of the Church into a national Church achieved by means of far-reaching concessions to the Protestants. One year later, in November 1661, the Cologne nuncio, Marco Gallio, declared that he had heard of a plan of an intended union between the three ecclesiastical electors in order to "realize an absolute power of disposition over all church benefices, independent of Rome" (A. Franzen).

At the Imperial Diet in Regensburg violent attacks against Rome were to be expected. According to testimony by the Salzburg archbishop Guidobald von Thun, the elector-archbishop of Cologne intended "di costituire un patriarca in Germania e di costituire o almeno d'introdurre nel clero dell'imperio la prattica e lo stilo della chiesa Gallicana." The compromise, achieved by conciliatory action of the Pope, was of short duration. In 1665 the Diet and the Supreme Court in Speyer unequivocally opposed the practice of appeals to the Pope and the nuncios in trials concerned with temporal matters.

A first climax in the opposition by the Church of the Empire is the *gravamina* of the three Rhenish elector-archbishops in 1673. Max Heinrich, elector-archbishop of Cologne and prince-bishop of Liège and Hildesheim; Lothar Friedrich von Metternich, elector-archbishop of Mainz and prince-bishop of Speyer and Worms; and Karl Kaspar von der Leyen, elector-archbishop of Trier, formally protested the violations of the Vienna Concordat concerning the freedom of episcopal elections, the annates, and the right of appointing beneficiaries. They demanded that the Curia respect the indults granted the archbishops when the Vienna Concordat was accepted and, further, that the German Church not be placed at a disadvantage compared to the French and Spanish Church.

Nor was there any lack of complaints in the future about violations of the concordat and interferences by the nuncios in the ordinary episcopal jurisdiction. When Archduke Joseph was elected Roman King (1690), the electorate of Trier moved to renew the formulation of *gravamina* against the Holy See. The pertinent article of the electoral capitulation, which had bound even Ferdinand III in 1654 to remove jurisdiction in temporal matters from the nunciatures and the Roman Curia and to insist on the observance of the concordat, had been discussed again and again. At the election of Charles VI in 1711 that article was reformulated as Article XIV, remaining valid until the time of Leopold II. A "language quite corresponding" to the Punctation of Ems in 1786 appeared in a complaint by the *Corpus Evangelicorum* as early as 1703, when it intervened in the quarrel that began in 1699 between the Roman Curia and the cathedral chapter of Münster concerning the appointment to the provostship. Similar conflicts ensued between the Curia and the cathedral chapters of Worms and Constance. The episcopal attitude of the Mainz chapter during the waning seventeenth century, was hostile to the nunciatures. Elector-Archbishop Lothar Franz von Schönborn resolutely opposed all attempts on the part of the Cologne nunciature to communicate officially with Mainz or Bamberg, since "neither the archbishopric of Mainz nor the local bishopric (Bamberg) are located within the boundaries of his legation, but are both *ab omni nuntiatura* free and directly subject to the Holy See."

For a time it might have seemed as though Lothar Franz von Schönborn — after his uncle Johann Philipp the second prominent lord chancellor of the Empire from that family which for three generations determined the episcopal history of Germany — would place himself at the head of the aspirations for a national Church. The relationship between the Rhenish archbishops and the Cologne nunciature deteriorated to the outer limits of tolerance" (K. Walf) as a result of the proscription of Elector Joseph Clemens von Bayern, the most recent armed conflict between the Emperor and the Pope involving Comacchio, the execution of the controversial *preces primariae,* and, finally, the *Privilegium illiminatum de non appellando* granted to the electorate of Trier. As the executor of "First Prayers" and uncle of the imperial vice chancellor Friedrich Karl von Schönborn, who with Joseph I was held responsible for the latter's anti-Roman policy (dictated by specific Habsburg interests), Lothar Franz was made to feel Rome's irritation at his coadjutor election in Bamberg and the demanded recantation. He found himself in a very delicate situation between the Emperor and the Pope. Yet in spite of his episcopal antipathy toward Rome and his patriotism for the Empire he did not permit himself to be made a tool of Josephinist church policy. This emerging dilemma of episcopal Germany caught between the Pope and the Emperor, or rather between Rome and Vienna, was at the same time aggravated by differences with the Catholic lay princes, as in the case of Elector Palatine Karl Philipp from (1731 to 1734), who managed — against the resistance of the prince-bishops — to shift their oppressive tax burdens onto the Church, thanks to papal indults. Practical episcopalism, even before it was provided with a sufficient theoretical foundation, was confronted at the beginning of the eighteenth century with the same constellation of forces which had frustrated it earlier in the fifteenth century.

The Canonical and Theological Foundation of Episcopalism in the Church of the Empire

The political-ecclesiastical opposition within the Church of the Empire against Rome, notwithstanding its severity in the first third of the eighteenth century, lacked a real theological and canonical foundation; it was only peripherally touched by the Enlightenment and not at all by theological rationalism. Only occasionally did such opposition arise because of the striving by ecclesiastical principalities for an order corresponding to their dual function within Church and Empire. Since the "evolution of Austria from the Empire" and the strengthening of the established Church within the monarchy the opposition could only occasionally rely on the Emperor as the *Advocatus Ecclesiae,* as the *Vindex canonum.* Aside from such occasions as the rejection of Gregory VII's "Offizium," the false "Hildebrandism," and "ultramontane" principles practiced too openly, an appreciable reaction among the faithful occurred only during the conflict involving the Munich nunciature or the Udligenschwyl dispute. The episcopalism of the Church of the Empire can only vaguely be compared with Gallicanism. Even in its most radical utterances it never put in doubt the unity of the Church; it never strove for a German national Church, but merely for the securing of its rights and liberties.

Efforts toward a justification of practical episcopalism based upon canon law and theology did not start until the end of the seventeenth century under the impact of the conflicts between Louis XIV and Innocent XI, the growing particular differences with the nuncios and Rome and with the acceptance of Gallican and Jansenist ideas and those concerning an enlightened established Church. One of the pioneers of German church freedoms, the Protestant canonist Johannes Schilter, was indebted to Petrus de Marca in his work *De libertate ecclesiarum Germaniae,* written one year after the *Declaratio Cleri Gallicani.* It contains the germ of Febronianism, intending to prepare the way for a reunification of the denominations by means of a reduction of the papal primacy of jurisdiction and the abandonment of the doctrine of papal infallibility. By its glorification of the medieval imperial power it reinforced the anti-Roman tendencies in the Church of the Empire. Episcopal, established Church, and Jansenist ideas were assimilated into the Church of the Empire from the theories of Zeger-Bernard Van Espen, who published his pioneering *Jus ecclesiasticum* in 1700. The decisive stimuli for the canon law of the Empire and the theoretical justification of German episcopalism in the second third of the eighteenth century emanated from the Schönborn sphere of influence, even though the later Mainz suffragan bishop Schnernauer, during the years of feud between Cardinal Damian Hugo von Schönborn and his metropolitan, developed ideas which almost anticipated the Koblenz and Ems Punctations.

Among the professors at the seminary and university at Würzburg, where the former vice-chancellor Friedrich Karl von Schönborn had been rector since 1734, was a former pupil of Lambertini's, Johann Kaspar Barthel. He was celebrated by his contemporaries as the prince of canonists and oracle of his century. In accordance with the charge by his bishop and ruler he taught a canon law which, adapted to the special German conditions, was at variance from what was taught in Rome. As the future Würzburg suffragan bishop Gregor Zirkel wrote in 1794, Barthel taught "the German Church to feel its rights and independence" (A. F. Ludwig). He contradicted the Jesuits and the Roman Curia with German frankness, transplanted principles of French canonists to Germany, exposed Roman policies from history and thus created as many opponents to Rome as he had listeners. Barthel rejected an absolute form of governance by the Church for theological, historical and ecclesiopolitical reasons. According to him the doctrine of papal primacy should distinguish between *essentialia,* based on divine right, and *accessoria,* acquired by prescriptive right and historical development ("Olim non erat sic"). Papal primacy has not been granted "in destructionem sed in aedificationem ecclesiae" and could be limited in the interest of harmony between *imperium* and *sacerdotium.* The independence, coexistence, and orientation of ecclesiastical and temporal power toward a common goal makes it difficult, says Barthel, to delimit the authority and rights of the two since from the fulfillment of a common divine mandate grows the "quasi confusio" of ecclesiastical and temporal laws; from necessary mutual subordination arises the obligation to create harmony between Church and state.

The episcopalism of the Barthel school, following the lines of the Schönborn sphere of influence, spread from Würzburg to the ecclesiastical states on the Main and Middle Rhine and from there to Bonn, Cologne, Salzburg, and to almost all the Catholic universities. Georg Christoph Neller, the most prominent pupil of Barthel, was called to the chair for canon law at the University of Trier by Franz Georg von Schönborn. His appointment, opposed by the Jesuits, had important consequences. It established the connection between the Franconian Enlightenment and the political and canonical views of the Church arising from the border situation of the archdiocese and from the differences with the Austrian Netherlands and France promoted by the spread of Jansenist ideas and those of the established Church. Such views were represented at the court of Ehrenbreitstein by the convert Jakob Georg von Spangenberg and his friend, the former officialis and later suffragan bishop Johann Nikolaus von Hontheim, especially after the negotiations involving the election stipulations of Emperor Charles VII (1742). Neller's tenure in Trier, his friendship and collaboration with Hontheim marked the turning point from episcopalism to Febronianism. His *Principia juris ecclesiastici ad statum Germaniae accommodata,* compiled substantially from Gallican authors and published anonymously in Frankfurt in 1746, made his name as a scholar. In it he sharply attacked the traditional constitutional doctrine of the Jesuit canonical position and intensified the episcopal theses. Spangenberg's wish — it is probable that Neller had already made Hontheim's acquaintance at that time — for a canonist who could differentiate between the original power of the Pope in church matters and the mere presumptions of the Curia appeared to be fulfilled by Neller's appointment. In his more than thirty years of teaching, in numerous publications Neller was largely responsible for the breakthrough of episcopal canon law in the Empire. As a friend and collaborator of Hontheim he occupies a superior place in the history of Febronianism.

Febronius and Febronianism

According to corresponding testimony by Hontheim and Spangenberg, the immediate impetus for the genesis of Febronianism was furnished during the negotiations for the election of Emperor Charles VII by the discussion of Article XIV of the imperial electoral capitulation concerning the German concordats, the *Gravamina contra Curiam Romanam,* and the demand by the electorate of Trier to abolish the jurisdiction of the nunciatures in Germany. Based on his study of the *gravamina* and the reform councils, Spangenberg suggested that a future work summarize the rights and liberties of the Church of the Empire after the model of the Gallicans Pithou, Dupuy, de Marca, as well as the Protestant canonist Johannes Schilter and that it create better conditions for surmounting the "Calamitas Imperii," for the reunification of the denominations, by a far-reaching reduction of papal claims. The erudite, personally irreproachable suffragan bishop Hontheim, who followed in the tradition of Van Espen's school, encountered these problems in the course of his two decades of ministry in a large diocese. Through historical research, efforts to reform both the Church and the universities, but above all through scholarly collaboration with his friend Neller he hit upon possible solutions. Considerations for the Dutch and French part of the archbishopric of Trier required a modus vivendi with those governments which were oriented toward an established Church. Schönborn episcopalism had to be defended against Roman claims based upon ecclesiastical and political considerations. Religious and ecclesiastical reforms and political practice in the Church began to orient themselves after the ideal of the *Ecclesia primitiva* — the ex-Jesuit F. X. Feller called it "a whim of souls with a mania for innovation" — and to demand the restoration of a historically transfigured church constitution which had been spoiled by pseudo-Isidorianism and "Hildebrandism." Their demands were addressed one-sidedly to Rome, so that the transformation of ecclesiastical territories into enlightened absolutist states was not made impossible. These aims and a delimitation of the rights of the prince-bishops and the Pope, better corresponding to the interests of the Church of the Empire, were to be achieved, at least in part, by a work written under the pseudonym Justinus Febronius, *De statu ecclesiase et legitima potestate Romani Pontificis liber singularis ad reuniendos dissidentes in religione christianos compositus* (Frankfurt 1763; reprints and supplements 1765–70; expanded to five volumes in 1770–74). The means to the goal were to be the revival of the *Concordata Nationis Germanica integra,* of the Mainz Acceptation of 1439, and the decrees of the reform Council of Basel. Reviving an idealized pre-Hildebrandian or pseudo-Isidorian church constitution was to provide the stimulus for a religious and ecclesiastical reform in connection with a moderate Enlightenment. By means of the empirical-historical method, based on the Gallicans, Van Espen, and the Würzburg school of canonists, Febronius used the well-known distinction between the *jura essentialia, quae tendeunt ad unitatis ecclesiae conservationem* and the *jura accessoria* in order to relegate the papal primacy to a preeminence of honor after the model of the first eight Christian centuries. According to him, the Pope is not entitled to a jurisdiction competing with that of the bishops since the latter are not his *vicarii* but are reigning as successors of the apostles by the authority of divine right. With the help of the Holy Spirit only the Church and the

General Council as representation of the *Corpus ecclesiasticum* are infallible. The Pope is the *centrum unitatis* only insofar as the representation of a federalist system permits. As is evident by the title Febronius borrowed from Pufendorf, the *Analogia Ecclesiae cum Imperio* was the godfather of his doctrine of the *status mixtus* of the Church constitution. Febronius also considers a reduction of papal rights and supervision of all undertakings of the Roman Curia necessary in the interest of the state. In spite of a basic recognition of independence, coexistence, and submission to a common final goal his ideas of the relationship between Church and state amount to a superiority of the state. It passes into Josephinism by virtue of concessions to the temporal princes — according to divine right they are the born defenders of the Church — and in view of the doctrine of the *Jus circa sacra* (*jus advocatiae, jus cavendi*). The corresponding theory of a *Jus circa civilia* is characteristically lacking.

In spite of the fact that his work was a compilation and contained innate contradictions, Febronius exercised a very strong influence on the ecclesiastical and intellectual history of the eighteenth and early nineteenth centuries. Beginning in 1774, under the influence of undercurrents of Enlightenment and Jansenism, Febronianism was either increasingly opposed by elements of an established Church, or accepted in a radicalized form, but it was also rejected by many moderate episcopalists, such as Abbot Martin II Gerbert.

An intense battle involving countless attacks and counterattacks by such as the brothers Ballerini, Johann Gottfried Kauffmann, Tomaso Maria Mamachi, Ladislaus Sappel, and Francesco Antonio Zaccaria was waged against Febronius. It took place on the literary and scholarly level, but beginning around 1770 it was also conducted for and against a revocation by the aged author. Not until April 1764 did the elective nuncio Niccolò Oddi with the help of the Frankfurt canon Damian Friedrich Dumeiz manage to identify Suffragan Bishop Hontheim as the author. Prior to that several others had been suspected of the authorship, among them Barthel, Neller, the enlightened Mainz lawyer Johann Baptist Horix, the future suffragan bishop Ludwig Philipp Behlen, and the canonist Benedikt Oberhauser from Fulda. Hontheim's persistent denial of his authorship was facilitated by the compiled nature of the work of Febronius, the fact that his collaborator Neller was also suspected, and the benevolent attitude of the imperial court and a considerable segment of the episcopate. This denial cannot be explained sufficiently by weakness of character, being of two minds, or Jansenist insincerity. Finally, in 1778 a heavy-hearted Hontheim, upon the urging of his elector-archbishop Clemens Wenzeslaus and the "Counsel of Conscience" of the Alsatian Franz Heinrich Beck, agreed to a formal revocation. On the advice of his friends and under the pressure of the discussions provoked by his revocation, and especially the press campaign involving the voluntary nature and sincerity of his utterances, Hontheim substantially attenuated his retraction by his *Commentarius in suam retractationem*, (based on the Gallican theses of 1682) and by his correspondence. His ambiguous and somewhat insincere conduct, whose motives have not been clarified yet, but even more so the clumsy steps taken by the Roman Curia abetted the efforts to make him into a martyr for the freedom of the German Church against "ultramontane" positions, intrigues by the Curia, and ecclesiastical obscurantism. The assumption that Hontheim "revoked his revocation prior to his death (2 September 1790)" was countered even by his contemporaries by means of his correspondence with Prince-Abbot Martin Gerbert of Sankt Blasien and the testimony of the Luxemburg ex-Jesuit Jardin, who called attention to Hontheim's true Catholic and apostolic-Roman faith. Yet the history of his revocation remains obscure on many points and requires additional clarification and complement.

Although the traditional constitutional doctrine was defended skillfully by Joseph Kleiner, Johann Mathias Carrich, Hartzheim, Eusebius Amort, Kauffmann, and others, the progression of the "Catholic revolution of ideas" led to an ever-growing spread of episcopalism-Febronianism at the German universities and prince-episcopal sees. Even in 1758 Johann Baptist Horix in Mainz had called attention to the acceptance of the Basel Decrees of 1439. The interest he aroused gave a new impetus to the opposition of the Church against Rome. In 1763 the document of acceptation appeared in print for the first time and immediately became the charter of German episcopalism. The future suffragan bishops Behlen and Würdtwein supported the Mainz policies with their historical and canonical writings. In Salzburg the famous canonist Gregorius Zallwein advocated a quasi-monarchical church constitution; he called for the liberties of the Church of the Empire, which he called preferable by far to the *Libertés de l'Église Gallicane,* and the special privileges of the Salzburg archbishop. The legal proceedings between the disputatious dean August von Limburg-Styrum and his cathedral chapter of Speyer (1763–64) threatened to escalate into a frontal attack of German episcopalism on the appellations, the nunciatures, and all interferences into episcopal jurisdiction, especially after the Palatinate and the archbishop of Mainz joined tho action. Yet the Palatine monition during the negotiations for the electoral capitulation of Joseph II failed, as did the Trier petition of 1742 requesting limitation of the jurisdiction of the nunciatures. Febronian positions and those of the established Church merged in a work by Joseph Anton Felix Balthasar, *De Helvetiorum juribus circa sacra,* which had grown from a decimation conflict of the Republic of Lucerne with the Curia. The book was fought by the bishop of Constance and put on the Index by Rome on 1 February 1769. It nonetheless formed the basis for "the entire system of the modern-day established Church of Lucerne, starting with the monastic reform at the end of the eighteenth century to the articles of the Baden Conference" (J. Schwendimann), indeed, all the way to the battle against the Vatican decrees of 1870/72.

The Coblenz *Gravamina* of 1769

Among the high points of episcopal aspirations in the Church of the Empire was the compilation of the Coblenz *gravamina.* It came about under the influence of publications concerning the concordats, the canonical works of the episcopalists of Würzburg, Trier, Mainz, and Cologne, and the influence of the enlightened ministers of state in the ecclesiastical electorates. On the one hand, these *gravamina* were the result of enlightened-absolutist concepts which were making an advance at the ecclesiastical courts in the years of peace after Hubertusburg. These concepts were aimed at reordering the relationship between Church and state primarily for political and economic reasons. On the other hand, these *gravam-*

ina represented a reaction on the part of episcopalism within the Empire to the constant disputes with the nunciatures and the papal refusal for the retention of the prince-bishoprics of Regensburg and Freising by Clemens Wenzeslaus of Saxony, who had been elected elector-archbishop in Trier and had succeeded the deceased prince-bishop Joseph von Hessen-Darmstadt as coadjutor in Augsburg. In this connection the Apostolic See had claimed the right to fill the two vacant Bavarian bishoprics, ignoring their right to an election as guaranteed by canon, concordat, and the law of the Empire. When Clement XIII, under pressure of the Church of the Empire, finally granted an election to the two cathedral chapters, it was interpreted as an attack on the freedom of the German Church. In March 1769 it was countered by the electorate of Mainz with a request to all ecclesiastical princes for a confidential exchange of ideas directed against the ultramontane claims of rulership. In Mainz, during the disputes of the Speyer cathedral dean Damian August Philipp von Limburg-Styrum with his chapter and because of the exemption of the new bishopric of Fulda, the position, by tradition scarcely friendly to Rome and definitely hostile to the nunciature, had hardened. The reformative, moderately enlightened elector-archbishop Emmerich Joseph von Breidbach-Bürresheim, embroiled in a violent fight with Rome over the annates, taxes, and confirmation fees for Worms and Mainz, on the advice of his minister Groschlag and his official and later suffragan bishop Ludwig Philipp Behlen, strove to unite the ecclesiastical princes in a concerted action against Roman presumptions and to become the "Patriarca in Germania."

Two other canonical conflicts drove the Cologne elector-archbishop Max Friedrich von Königsegg-Rothenfels to the side of Mainz. Max Friedrich, whose vicar general Johann Philipp von Horn-Goldschmidt and the latter's adviser Franz C. J. von Hillesheim held Febronian views, was enmeshed in an argument with the Cologne nunciature over the visitation of the Augustinian house of Saint Michael at Weidenbach and with the Curia in Rome because of the intended closing of the Benedictine seminary of Überwasser in favor of a university in Münster. In spite of a basic agreement, Cologne and even more so Münster, where Fürstenberg emphasized that he was not a Febronian, were not terribly enthused about the far-reaching plans by Mainz and caused the pertinent suggestions to be attenuated. The Mainz initiative also met with misgivings on the part of the prince-bishops of Hildesheim, Paderborn, and Würzburg-Bamberg. They were worried that a realization of the Febronian program would bring no advantages to the bishops but would merely expand the metropolitan rights and, in the end, exchange dependence on Rome for an increased dependence on the German archbishops. The initiative for a union and concerted action by the ecclesiastical princes, initially the Rhenish electors, was clearly started in Mainz. It raised the threat of a national council, an assembly of the Catholic princes and dignitaries of the Imperial Diet after the model of 1523, and a new concordat. For the extreme case it toyed with the idea "that perhaps even a separation of the harmony and concurrence between Church and state might have to ensue and the rights granted to the sovereigns immediately by the grace of God prevail."

On 27 January 1769, after toilsome negotiations an eight-point preliminary convention between Mainz and Cologne was signed, obligating the two parties to list the "old original" episcopal rights, not to withdraw unilaterally from the concerted action, and to induce the Emperor and the elector-archbishop of Trier to join them. To be sure, considerable efforts and the diplomatic skill of the Mainz minister C. W. von Groschlag were initially required to obtain the support of Suffragan Bishop Hontheim for the plans of Mainz and, toward the end of 1769, with his help to overcome the reservations of Elector-Archbishop Clemens Wenzeslaus, which had been caused by political considerations and his innate caution. Clemens Wenzeslaus appears to have borne a grudge against the Mainz group around Emmerich Joseph, who had opposed him at the election of Trier by nominating the brother of Elector Ernst von Breidbach-Bürresheim and had thwarted his designs on the bishopric of Worms. But above all it had been his persistent designs on the foremost electoral bishopric of the Empire and for the establishment of a Wettin episcopal realm extending from Trier via Liège, Cologne, and Münster to Paderborn and Hildesheim which prompted him to use extreme caution toward Rome, the Cologne nunciature, and the Imperial court. Neither in Rome nor in Vienna did he want to see the Wettin church policy damaged by Febronian-metropolitan actions.

A firm union of the three ecclesiastical princes had not yet been effective and the misgivings of the suffragans of Cologne and Mainz concerning the archiepiscopal enterprise not yet overcome when the Mainz lawyer Deel, the Cologne ecclesiastical councilor Hillesheim, and the sixty-eight-year-old Trier suffragan bishop Hontheim met in conference to put the finishing touches on the complaints against Rome and to agree on the manner of asking the emperor, the *defensor ecclesiae,* to support their plan. In the opinion of Mainz the aid of the Emperor and a firm union of the three ecclesiastical electors were indispensable conditions for the realization of their Febronian ideas.

Within a short time, on 13 December 1769, Deel, Hillesheim, and Hontheim, who had already been agreed on the most important issues as a result of lengthy preliminary negotiations, concurred in thirty-one *gravamina* and the text of a letter which was to submit the complaints to the Emperor. Under "Imperial protection" the German Churches were to regain "their hereditary freedom so that they would not be behind the churches of other countries" in order that the German church system could be reordered according to the requirements of a modern state. The frailties of the church constitution and the disregard of the *gravamina* by Rome were generally considered as "one of the main causes of the weakness and debility of the Catholic lands of the Empire." The Coblenz desiderata invoked the Councils of Constance and Basel, the Mainz Acceptation of 1439, the *Concordata Nationis Germanicae,* and especially the concordats with Eugene IV (1447). All of the accepted Basel decrees "in favorem atque utilitatem Ecclesiarum Germaniae promanare possunt" would have to be executed. Episcopal authority, "the freedom of the German Church," was to be restored to its original extent, the reforms executed in a manner corresponding to the demands of the time. The initial *gravamina* were concerned with the abuses in awarding benefices. Henceforth the archiepiscopal indult to fill the benefices of the papal months was no longer to be limited to five years but extended to life or abolished. The higher nonpontifical dignities at the cathedral and collegiate churches were no longer to be subject to papal reservation but to be bestowed by the ordinary collators. The reservations of the extravagants, *execrabilis* and *ad regimen* were to cease and all chancery rules, with the exception of *de idiomate, de viginti, de triennali possessione,* were to become invalid within the Church of the Empire. The annates and monastic exemptions were to be abolished. The episcopal informatory process was to be followed according to the Tridentine decrees and the "vassal oath" of the bishops, customary since Gregory VII, was to be replaced by its original form. Papal orders and decrees by Roman congregations were not to be published without prior knowledge and concurrence of the ordinaries. The power "to bind and loose" of the bishops in their sees was to be unrestricted. In legal proceedings the successive appeals were to be strictly observed; the nunciatures were to be abolished. The accepted Basel Decrees, acknowledged by the *Concordata Nationis Germanicae,* were to be the basic laws of the Church of the Empire.

Attempts to strengthen the union of the Rhenish archbishops by electing participation by the archbishop of Salzburg, Cardinal-Bishop Franz Konrad Kasimir von Rodt of Constance and Cardinal-Bishop Franz Christoph von Hutten in Speyer failed. In Vienna, where the Coblenz *gravamina* were not submitted until July 1770, the desired support did not materialize, just as the Mainz ambassador J. G. von Brée had correctly predicted; "to the immense detriment of the German Church and the German Nation," as Hontheim's friend and biographer Krufft thought. Joseph II let the archiepiscopal initiative come to nothing, not because a "movement away from Rome" would have meant at the same time "a movement away from the Empire," but — this is evidently the motivation of Vice-Chancellor Colloredo — because a realization of the episcopal reform program would have strengthened those forces which were resisting the territorial established Churches and would have consolidated the position of the ecclesiastical princes in the Empire vis-à-vis the Emperor as well. In order not to endanger his own plans for an established Church, Joseph II did not want to burden himself with the complaints of the German archbishops against Rome. No doubt his delaying tactics, dictated by long-range political goals and the negative attitude of the Mainz ambassador to Vienna, Friedrich Karl von Erthal, toward the action of the Rhenish archbishops contributed to its failure. The reaction in Vienna had the effect of causing Clemens Wenzeslaus to distance himself from the three ecclesiastical electors out of consideration for the Wettin church policies. Suggestions by the Mainz archbishop concerning a second meeting in Coblenz and a congress in Frankfurt for the end of August 1771 or for the dispatch of a common negotiator to Vienna floundered on the conflicts of interest between the Rhenish electoral courts. The large-scale attempt to turn episcopal ideas and concepts into reality came to naught. The enlightened episcopal movement steadily gained ground as a result of the monastic regulations (30 July 1771), the amortization law (6 June 1772), the school and university reforms, and, lastly, the substantial elimination of the cathedral chapter from participation in the government until the death of Emmerich Joseph (1774). During the interregnum and the first few years of the reign of Friedrich Karl von Erthal this prompted a countermovement.

The Nunciature Dispute and the Congress of Ems

It was not long before an anti-Roman current regained the upper hand. Stephan Alexander Würdtwein, Franz Anton Dürr, Johann Georg Schör, and Johann Jung broadcast their episcopal views in numerous theses and in most of the journals. Not only the elector-archbishop of Mainz, but also the ecclesiastical electors in Coblenz and Bonn persistently tried to apply Febronian principles in cases of marriage dispensations, disputes concerning benefices, visitations, on the issue of the archiepiscopal "first prayers," and ecclesiastical jurisdiction. The number of conflicts between the Church and Rome increased steadily and some of the south German prince-bishops had to wage hard-fought defensive battles against the Bavarian established church system. The last great conflict of the Church of the Empire with Rome and the movement representing an established Church broke out when the Palatine-Bavarian Elector Karl Theodor tried to bring about an adaptation of the church organization of southern Germany to political borders and the replacement of prince-bishoprics by provincial ones. Eighteen nonresident bishops and archbishops were responsible for the Palatine-Bavarian territories, combined since 1777. Each of them resided outside the borders of these territories and, by means of his own territory, which was subject to the Emperor only, possessed a last independent ecclesiastical and political sphere vis-à-vis the absolutist claims of powerful temporal neighbors.

For a period of about two hundred years, the aspiration for the establishment of Bavarian provincial bishoprics had to some extent been compensated by the Wittelsbach secundogenitures, especially in the old Bavarian bishoprics of Freising and Regensburg. When Cardinal Johann Theodor died in 1763 the dynasty was no longer able to present proper candidates for the episcopal see and the rule over the prince-bishoprics and the Church in Bavaria had to be put on a different basis, corresponding more to the enlightened absolutist political concept of the state. An added reason was the fact that the elections were getting very hard to arrange for eligible aristocrats who could be assumed to put up little or no resistance against the Bavarian established Church. This was clearly shown by the example of the related Clemens Wenzeslaus of the Wettin dynasty in Freising, Regensburg (1763, 1768), and Augsburg (1765). To be sure, the plan for a Munich provincial bishopric (1780–83), aimed against the aristocratic liberties of the Church of the Empire, failed. But an alliance of expedience against the common enemy represented by episcopalism, strengthened by personal meetings between Elector Karl Theodor and Pope Pius VI, produced the compromise of establishing a nunciature in Munich (7 June 1784). The new nunciature, consistent neither with the constitution of the Empire nor with tradition, was obviously intended to strengthen papal authority in the *Germania Sacra,* to meet the Bavarian established Church halfway, and to form a counterweight against Josephinism. The new nuncio Cesare Zoglio, who also was to occupy the see of a provincial archdiocese, was equipped with extraordinary powers. This would enable the forces of the established Church to encompass the far-flung Palatine-Bavarian territories like a pincer and push back the episcopal movement. On the other hand it inevitably challenged the episcopate of the Empire to ward off the "curial pretensions" and the territorial established Church.

The battle of the nunciatures, smouldering for a long time with varying intensity, broke into the open even before the new nuncio arrived in Munich when the immediately affected metropolitans of Salzburg and Mainz and the Freising prince-bishop Ludwig Joseph von Welden raised formal complaints. The major participant in the second phase was Elector-Archbishop Max Franz of Cologne, the brother of Joseph II, whose request for the installation of *Judices in partibus* had been rejected by Rome. He now found his episcopal rights transgressed not only by the Cologne nunciature, but in addition by the Munich nunciature, responsible for the Palatine-Bavarian territories of his see. But the main defense by the Church of the Empire had to be directed against the territorial established Church. If Karl Theodor were emulated by others, "the day would come when the prince-bishops and their dioceses would be limited to their territories and lose the reason for their existence" (K. O. v. Aretin). In their fight against the two fronts of Rome and the established Church, conducted against the background of the growing threat of secularization, the German archbishops, while basically encouraged by Emperor Joseph II, were only insufficiently supported by him. The change in the endangered *Nunziatura ad tractum Rheni* by the transfer of the moderate titular Archbishop Carlo Bellisomi to Lisbon and the subsequent appointment of the merely twenty-eight-year-old Bartolomeo Pacca, who was unfamiliar with the German situation, increased the tensions.

At a conference of the representatives of the four German archbishops in Bad Ems (July–August 1786), convened after lengthy preliminary negotiations and characterized by considerable differences of opinions, a twenty-two-point reform program for the Church of the Empire was formulated which constituted a declaration of war against the nunciatures. The Ems Punctation (25 August 1786) took up where the *gravamina* of 1673 of the Rhenish archbishops, the Coblenz desiderata of 1769, Febronius and the *Massime moguntine,* going beyond Febronius, left off. The independence of the episcopal from the Roman authority was most strenuously emphasized in Ems. Additional demands included: the cancellation of the exemptions and the quinquennial faculties, the complete abolition of the nunciatures, but at least of their competing jurisdiction, the right of the bishops to dispose of charitable contributions, the episcopal *placet* for Roman bulls and briefs, and the conduct of ecclesiastical legal proceedings by native judges. The prereformational demand to reduce the annates and pallia was renewed. No longer was the Vienna Concordat (1448), but rather the Mainz Acceptation (1439) and the *Concordata Principium* (1447) to be the basis for the constitution of the Church of the Empire. Lastly, the Emperor was asked to restore the archiepiscopal rights and "to bring about the council at least on a national level which had been promised [in the German concordats] by His most high intercession to take place within two years at the most for the purpose of definitively removing all of these complaints" and in the case of insurmountable obstacles to effect redress by constitutional means.

The difficulties militating against the Ems program, in spite of the positive consent of a part of the educated public, and the weakness of the archiepiscopal position in its fight against the alliance of expedience between Rome and Munich were soon evident. Emperor Joseph II had indeed declared inadmissible "the exercise of jurisdiction in ecclesiastical matters" by the nunciatures and had also annulled an encyclical by Pacca. Yet he could not make up his mind about the far-reaching political plans for his Church which his brother Leopold had advised. These called for "throwing off the selfish and despotic yoke of the Roman court in Germany forever by encouraging and supporting with all one's might the German bishops, by abolishing the nunciatures in Germany forever, and convincing the bishops and ecclesiastical princes to convene and to form a national council." The distrust and, finally, the resistance of the suffragan bishops against an expansion of the metropolitan authority and the power of the ecclesiastical electors assumed the character of an anti-Ems movement, especially when Prince-Bishop August von Limburg-Styrum of Speyer began to exert his efforts and when an assembly in Waghäusel or Bruchsal was suggested. The union of the four archbishops dissolved rather quickly. The Mainz electorate was pried from the ranks of the opponents of the nunciatures through Prussia, with which it was joined in the Alliance of Princes and in connection with the election of Karl Theodor von Dalberg to the position of coadjutor of Elector-Archbishop Friedrich Karl. In view of its desire for a special ecclesiastical position for its northwest German possessions, Prussia was not interested in strengthening the metropolitans' power. Consequently, it recognized the jurisdiction of the Cologne nunciature. Theological, canonical, and personal doubts, but especially considerations of his second bishopric of Augsburg (which extended onto Bavarian territory), as well as growing difficulties in the French parts of his archbishopric of Trier induced Clemens Wenzeslaus, to disavow the Ems program. The early death of Joseph II prevented a hearing of the nunciature dispute in the Imperial Diet. Max Franz of Cologne almost single-handedly continued the fight against the nunciatures and the established Church. The only concrete result of all the efforts was the inclusion in Article XIV of the Imperial Electoral Capitulation of 1790 of a stipulation aimed at abolishing the jurisdiction of the nunciatures in ecclesiastical courts. The Ems Punctation thus remained "the mere declaration of a feud against Rome, not followed by the feud itself" (Werminghoff). Under the threat of the impending French Revolution, the events in the Netherlands and their impact in western Germany the archbishops' opposition to Rome and the modern established Church collapsed. But far into the nineteenth century, when the established Church had long turned against its erstwhile ally, the papal central authority, and when the Church prepared to fight the late absolutist state for a modicum of freedom, the ideas of Ems stayed alive, to be called up again by many a government in their conflicts with Rome, even though they misunderstood the historical connections.

CHAPTER 133

The Established Church and the Enlightenment in the Temporal Territories of the Empire—Theresianism and Josephinism

The eighteenth-century upheaval regarding the respective rights within the system of the established Church is inadequately described as a usurpation of the ecclesiastical realm or as an absolutist abuse by the ruling princes with the goal of making the state omnipotent. Neither is it sufficiently characterized as an outgrowth of enlightened absolutism, dominated by the concept of the "welfare state." As the reductions in the number of monastic establishments and the case of Josephinist charity demonstrate, the induced participation of the Church in the service of the enlightened welfare state had a special importance for the realization of the rationalistic postulate of "the greatest possible happiness of all." But this also involved the fulfillment of partly neglected yet genuine demands of Christian morality, the state as the guardian of public morality, and the creation of a Church, reformed in the Jansenist-enlightened sense, eliminating baroque abuses in the interest of a better order in this world and salvation in the hereafter.

In the Empire the problem of "state versus Church" emerged to a lesser extent as one between the Pope as the supreme head of the totality of the Church and the Emperor as the protector of the Church of the Empire. Instead it was a dispute between the larger territories rising to the status of modern states on one side and the bishops, nunciatures, and the Roman Curia on the other. As a consequence of ecclesiastical and temporal rule being combined in one person, the fact that in these cases there could be no integration into a modern state, and, lastly, because of a lack in self-reform, the ecclesiastical principalities experienced the problem more as an "internal affair," as an episcopal opposition to the nunciatures and the Roman Curia or as moderate administrative enlightenment on the well-known battlefields of monastic reform, reduction on the religious feast days, amortization laws, matrimonial legislation, and the field of education.

In the Catholic temporal territories the relationship between Church and state in the matter of their respective rights hardly differed from that of the Protestant states. The necessity for reforms in many areas was widely recognized here too. The realization that if the nascent enlightened welfare state wanted to fulfill its comprehensive tasks it needed an enlarged material basis and therefore had to break with the traditional preferences and privileges of the Church was not limited to enlightened enemies of the Church. The amalgamation of the ecclesiastical and the temporal had reached a highpoint in the late seventeenth century. The rise to absolutist principalities had taken place thanks to extensive support to the Church inspired by the Counter Reformation. But even in the period of the Enlightenment, especially in the years of economic distress and reconstruction following the Austrian War of Succession and the Seven Years' War, the Church with its possessions and revenues continued to represent a potential reservoir of state power. By way of ecclesiastical secundogenitures it offered the Catholic dynasties a possibility of providing for their sons, of increasing their prestige and power, and promoting their foreign and domestic policies. By means of cathedral chapters and religious establishments it secured for the feudal aristocracy and the knights of the Empire a sphere of freedom against the absolutist principalities. To the chagrin of the enlightened and the reform-minded, the territory, the rise to statehood, the jurisdictions, finances, and the economy everywhere were permeated by the Church. This made it advisable for the Catholic princes who at the time of the Enlightenment were still considering themselves as protectors of both tables of law to find better ways to control the Church, both in the interest of the state and for the sake of needed reforms in the Church. The respective limits were to be redetermined based on rational law and a deepened understanding of each other's nature and tasks.

When the Catholic states began to consolidate and to take on new tasks it was but a small step from protection of the Church (*ius advocatiae sive protectionis*) to protectorate or tutelage by means of Enlightenment. In many respects this step could appear to be almost one of self-defense by the princes against exaggerated ideas and oppressive power of the Church. Dispensation from taxes and local immunity were issues well suited to promote the idea of the Church as a state within the state. The assets of the mortmain, the great number of mendicant houses, the many feast days, processionals, and pilgrimages could be represented as weakening the economic and financial strength of the territory, this in turn being responsible for the political weakness of the Catholic states. Furthermore, it could be attacked as being inconsistent with genuine piety.

There is no doubt that the growth of the established Church — especially since the middle of the eighteenth century — and its distinct Austrian variety inadequately called Josephinism intended to reduce ecclesiastical power and ultimately achieve state supremacy over the Church. Yet this movement was neither inimical to the Church, nor was it innately synonymous with Enlightenment. Max III Joseph of Bavaria went relatively far in his sympathy with the Enlightenment; Joseph II wanted to assign it no more than a certain precisely limited sphere; and Karl Theodor, who implemented his system of an established Church in league with Rome, fought against Enlightenment in a variety of ways. A good many regulations of the established Church in the second half of the eighteenth century in ecclesiastical as well as temporal states were intended to remove abuses in the Church and to effect a church reform whose aim, dictated by the selfish interests of the state, by Jansenist, episcopal, and reform Catholic currents, was an approximation of the ideal of the *Ecclesia primitiva.*

Josephinism differs sharply from the old established church movement which reaches back into the late Middle Ages and reassumes a more prominent role as of the sixteenth century. It is "a 'harmonizing' of disparate elements of tension disharmonious within itself" — and came about "through the mutual permeation of all movements and tendencies at work during the reign of Maria Theresa which did not unreservedly support baroque Catholicism" (P. F. Barton).

Theresianism and Josephinism

A fairly accurate conceptual determination of Josephinism encounters considerable difficulties because of the variety of the Habsburg territories, their rulers, and most influential personalities, and because of the interaction of disparate phases of its development. E. Winter, restricting himself to Bohemia and Moravia with their Protestant tendencies, provokingly calls Josephinism a reform Catholicism and the result of bourgeois ideas in the nascent national state. Making the unyielding established church system seem less offensive, he interprets Josephinism as "an attempt of a basic reform of the Roman Catholic Church in favor of the original Church" (E. Winter). In a narrow jurisdictional approach, F. Maaß calls it an enlightened Austrian established Church. Not church reform, he continues, but omnipotence of the state was the ultimate goal of Josephinism. Valjavec, on the other hand, views it in its totality as an intellectual, spiritual, political, and economic phenomenon, determining Austria's history less in the eighteenth century than in the nineteenth century, whose mode of expression during the reign of Joseph II was not even its most typical. Josephinism, he maintains, was the result of attempts to harmonize the political, ecclesiastical, and cultural perceptions of the prior period and the spirit of the Enlightenment. Kann minimizes the significance of the church reforms, but stresses the totalitarian features and the national component of Josephinism. According to Rieser "the liquidation of the sphere of power of the Church within the state" represented the means of achieving the ultimate goal, "the omnipotence of the state." Josephinism is also interpreted as a "latent decline from a revealed religion to a natural religion." Reinhardt avers that Josephinism was not pointed in the direction of the future but instead represented "a reactionary force." It strove for dominance over a Church which had long before been emancipated, at least in its claims and doctrine. According to Reinhardt it attempted to glue together certain areas which had fallen apart.

The immediate prior history of Josephinism, among whose pioneers the "ultra-Catholic" Ferdinand II is also included, was the established church system of Maria Theresa. She was the impulsive, ambitious daughter of the pious, intolerant Charles VI, who had promoted re-Catholization in Silesia, warded off renascent heresy in Carinthia and Styria, but steered the hard Bourbon course of an established Church against the Roman Curia. Maria Theresa was part of the tradition of a crumbling Habsburg baroque piety and anticurial concepts of which even Jesuits at the Vienna court of the seventeenth century were not entirely free. There were hardly any typical features of that baroque piety present in her husband, Franz Stephan of Lorraine, who appears to have been the religiously and intellectually dominant part of that marriage. During her widowhood after 1765 Maria Theresa herself was not closed to the ascetic way of Jansenism nor to reform Catholic tendencies. Privy Councilor Heinke, one of the most prominent representatives of Josephinism, showed the way toward harmonizing orthodox piety with the new, enlightened established Church: "God alone entrusted the prince with his power; with it the right to protect religion and Church is inseparably connected, to the extent that he may never divest himself of this responsibility, for not without cause has God given him that right. But he protects the sanctuary of the Lord best if he redresses that which in itself can cause incurable wounds to be inflicted on the saving faith and in fact has done so."

The intensified consolidation of the Austrian established Church, which under Maria Theresa and Joseph II professed to be as ecclesiastical as before, can be attributed in part to the economic and political distress following the Austrian

War of Succession and the Silesian Wars. Their contemporaries considered the cofounders of Theresianism to be the "Great Four" in Vienna: the impetuous personal physician to the Empress, Gerard von Swieten, moved by Jansenist ideas and hatred for the Jesuits, although a very religious man who in his capacity as censor released the book of Febronius and initiated university reforms; the Jansenist-leaning confessor of the Empress, Ignaz Müller, provost of the Augustinian prebendaries of Sankt Dorothea; the jurist Karl Anton von Martini, who made a name for himself as an opponent of torture; and, lastly, Ambros von Stock, prebendary of Sankt Stephan and future suffragan bishop. But the actual driving force behind the Theresian reforms and creator of the established church system based on the tenets of rationalistic law was Count Wenzel Anton von Kaunitz-Tietberg, prince of the Empire after 1764, who was a free thinker like Voltaire and a dispassionate proponent of power politics. He was supported by Privy Councilor Franz Joseph von Heinke. Kaunitz's program to transform the territories of the Habsburg monarchy into an absolutist modern state with the Church in its service contained the basic features of Theresianism and Josephinism, whose most radical manifestations he nonetheless eschewed. But the suggestion to replace the designation "Josephinism" by "Kaunitzianism" is prompted by an overestimation of his influence and the erroneous assumption that this established church system can be reduced to one great personality.

As a field of experimentation for the new system Kaunitz chose the Austrian Lombardy. In 1765 the *Giunta Economale* was established in Milan as the highest authority in ecclesiastical matters. The Milan governor Count Karl von Firmian was already familiar with Catholic reform concepts through his sojourn at the knights' academy of Ettal and his connections with the Salzburg Muratori circle. When difficulties with Clement XIII ensued over the appointments to the sees of Como and Mantua, the *placet* was introduced in Lombardy after the Spanish, Venetian, and Sicilian model. Next to be solved were the issues of church property, the taxation of the clergy, ecclesiastical censorship, and limiting the authority of monastic superiors. The suppression of small orders, which had been variously desired by the monks themselves, began in 1769 after compromises with the Pope. The excommunication on 30 January 1768 of Duke Ferdinand of Parma, the future son-in-law of the Empress, gave impetus to the Habsburg aspirations for an established Church. Having charged an imperial commission with the supervision of all ecclesiastical institutions in 1750, Maria Theresa radically restricted the assets of the mortmain by means of an amortization law in 1771. Regulations forbidding the taking of solemn vows before the age of twenty-four and others regarding termination, the presence of regulars outside their monastic institutions, and the abolition of monastic jails were to serve the reform of the regular clergy. Under the influence of reform Catholic and enlightened ideas, Maria Theresa then proceeded against the use of exorcism and processions. According to the canonist P. J. von Riegger, who was highly esteemed by the Empress, the reduction of church holidays, executed with the concurrence of the Pope, was an excellent means of promoting religiosity, reducing idleness, and creating due respect for useful activities and deserved scorn for useless ones.

Maria Theresa basically claimed all *Iura circa sacra,* so that the Theresian established Church differed from Josephinism merely in subtle distinctions and a stronger influence of the Enlightenment. We can no longer call Maria Theresa's attitude consistent with the traditional Catholicism of the Church; we should rather consider her the "mother of Josephinism" (F. Maaß). As supreme protector and guardian of the Church, supported by Kaunitz, Joseph von Sonnenfels, Marc Anton Wittola, and Abbot Rautenstrauch (who submitted a curriculum for philosophical and theological studies), Joseph II — even during his coregency — had demanded complete subjugation of the Church under his enlightened system of an established Church. During his own reign he tried to effect this by measures which were frequently despotic and petty. In the course of one decade more than six thousand decrees were issued in order to eliminate any voice by the Church in mixed matters, to restrict the Church to the administration of the sacraments, to intrachurch matters, and a service function in the enlightened welfare state. According to Sonnenfels the Church was a police institution, obliged to serve the aims of the state to the point where enlightenment of the people permits its replacement by the temporal police. The suppression of the Society of Jesus, pronounced by Clement XIII under pressure from the Bourbon courts (21 July 1773), was celebrated as a triumph of Enlightenment. "General seminaries" (1783) under the direction of Abbot Rautenstrauch were to educate a new sort of parish priest corresponding to the ideal of the "pastor bonus." The entire church assets were considered by Joseph II as "a patrimony for the benefit of spiritual welfare and human nature of which the clerical individuals and establishments are beneficiaries only to the extent of their needs appropriate to their station, while the secure disposition of the surplus for the above designation is a matter for the ruler as supreme guardian of the Church and the *canones*."

The evaluation of Josephinism has often been decisively influenced by its hostility to monasticism and the orders; even today this is one of the determining factors. But a one-sided picture must perforce emerge if the antimonastic attitude of the baroque is contrasted with the promonastic tendency of the Enlightenment. This is also the case if the monastic reductions are justified only by the abuses which were certainly present but tendentiously exaggerated by the contemporary printed media. The decree of 29 November 1781 initiated the abolition of all houses of contemplative orders which did not fulfill charitable, pedagogical, or ministerial tasks because — according to the influential opinion of Kaunitz — they "were incapable of promoting the best in their fellow men and were consequently useless for bourgeois society." The reductions were subsequently extended to noncontemplative orders as well. This resulted in immeasurable loss of cultural assets, considerable damage to learning, and a rather large financial loss. The confiscated assets were to be transferred to a "religious fund" for ecclesiastical, charitable, and educational purposes. But this did not always happen. Monastic reductions and parish regulation were closely connected with the financial aspects involved. But it is debatable whether the injurious effects of the reductions on the ministry and religious life could be made up for by the establishment of new parishes from the religious fund and the intensification of parish ministry as demanded by Jansenists and reform Catholics since the parish priests had to assume an increasing number of administrative tasks including the role of "health and veterinary police." In regard to fiscal policy, which was one of the main motives for the abolition of the monastic houses, the profit does not seem to have fulfilled expectations. Also abolished in 1783 were the numerous brotherhoods, closely connected with the system of guilds, whose customs and personal religiosity were called "superstitious and fanatical" and not consistent with Catholic reform concepts. They were to be merged into a single charitable association with "all ecclesiastical privileges, indulgences, and favors" whose task it was to ameliorate existing social miseries.

The diocesan regulation by Joseph II stemmed from an old demand by the established Church to make the diocesan borders coincide with those of the territories; it was also prompted by economic and religious motives. The organization of the bishoprics in the hereditary lands, no doubt in need of reform, was to be made independent of nonresident foreign ordinaries; Austria was to be lifted out of the Empire in this regard with a concomitant practical reorganization of the indigenous sees. The new delineation of their borders was another step toward the subjugation of the Church, yet also a reform measure which held out the promise — at least to the native episcopate — of an intensification of the ministry and "the greatest possible independence from Rome and in some individual cases an expansion of the diocese." To the affected prince-bishops the reordering of the dioceses could not but represent an attack on the constitution of the Church of the Empire, a violation of their "liberty"; it called for political consequences. The restructuring ran counter to the law of the Empire, all tradition, and amounted to toppling the constitution of the Church. It met with resistance in Rome. The reaction of the affected bishops ran the gamut from weak remonstrances to energetic protests (which were echoed in the Imperial Diet) to entreaties to the League of German Princes. The Mainz metropolitan and archchancellor Friedrich Karl von Erthal, in his capacity as "first archbishop and primate of the German Church," was considering joint action by the episcopate of the Empire "in order to maintain the constitutions of the Empire and the Church, so intimately interwoven in their time-honored state."

Right after the beginning of his independent reign Joseph II initiated the reordering of the dioceses in Tyrol and Upper and Lower Austria. Following the death of Bishop Leopold Ernst Cardinal von Firmian (13 February 1783), he separated the Austrian part from the diocese of Passau, dividing it between the newly created bishopric of Linz and the former bishopric of Wiener Neustadt, which latter was transferred to Sankt Pölten. The issue was not brought up in the Imperial Diet because the cathedral chapter, consisting mainly of members of the Austrian nobility, shrank from such a step and the new prince-bishop, Count von Auersperg, was satisfied with the return of his confiscated Passau properties. In 1786 the archbishop of Salzburg, Colloredo, was forced by Joseph II to forego his diocesan rights in Styria and Carinthia, but Salzburg did retain its diocesan rights in Tyrol and the metropolitan, confirmation, and consecration rights for the enlarged sees of Seckau, Lavant, Gurk and the newly established but short-lived bishopric of Leoben. It retained the nomination right for only the three first-named bishoprics; the right of appointment was reserved for the Emperor, who was endowing Leoben. The death of the Regensburg prince-bishop Anton Ignaz von Fugger in 1787 was exploited by Joseph II "according to the old recipe" (Aretin); during the *sedes vacans* he separated the district of Eger from the archdiocese of Regensburg and incorporated it into the archbishopric of Prague (1787). The newly elected prince-bishop of Regensburg, Max Prokop von Törring-Tettenbach, solicited the help of the archchancellor in Mainz and of Rome protesting the separation of the Eger district, since it was a pledged imperial fief and had never belonged to the crown of Bohemia. In 1789 Joseph II finally acquiesced to the appointment of an episcopal commissioner for that district. His death in 1790 delayed the final separation of Eger until after the decline of the Empire (1807–18). Hardly a stir was caused by the separation of the districts of Freising located in Styria, and of those diocesan parts of Liège which extended into the Austrian Netherlands. A realignment of the borders of Trier did not occur for political considerations, although here, too, Joseph II severely curtailed the rights of his relative, Archbishop Clemens Wenzeslaus. The strange suggestion of adapting the Silesian bishopric to the territorial borders — the Austrian part of the Breslau diocese was to be separated in exchange for Prague and Olmütz foregoing their Prussian parts — foundered on the refusal of Prussia. Efforts to realign the diocesan borders of Augsburg, Chur, and Constance also failed. Nor were plans realized to create a territorial bishopric of Bregenz or to elevate the prince-abbey of Sankt Blasien to the status of a bishopric for Lower Austria. But the Austrian parts of the Venetian dioceses of Udine and Pola were separated and the diocesan borders in Bohemia, Moravia, and Galicia were realigned.

The bishops of the newly established dioceses were "in a certain sense civil servants and closely tied to the Josephinist concept of the state and the established Church" (Hugo Hantsch). Even today the cross on the chest of the vestment of the prebendaries of Linz and Sankt Pölten recalls the origin of these dioceses in the established Church. The diocesan realignment by Joseph II severed the last ties between Austria and the Empire. The reputation of the Emperor in the ecclesiastical territories, indeed in all of Catholic Europe, was damaged to such an extent that King Peter III of Portugal instituted in his realm "public hours of prayer for the Emperor blinded by the devil."

Maria Theresa rejected the free exercise of religion for religious and political reasons, viewing the Catholic Church as a unifying element in the *Monarchia Austriaca.* In the second half of the century, under the influence of the Enlightenment, as well as for political and economic considerations, various German territories developed religious toleration on a legal basis which no longer took into account the existing law of the Empire.

The Patent of Toleration (13 October 1781) by Joseph II, shaped by the ideas of the constitutional expert Martini and Privy Councilor Beck, granted to the Augsburg and Helvetian Lutherans and members of the Reformed Churches as well as to the non-Uniate Greeks the right to private exercise of their religion and certain civil rights which amounted to a limited equality with the Catholics. To the extent that non-Catholics already had the right of public exercise of their religion, they were not affected. The preferential position of the Roman Catholic Church — which in principle was the only one permitted to have public religious exercise — was also not to be affected by the patent. Non-Catholic churches were not to have spires, bell ringing, or access from the main street; surplice fees were to be reserved for the appropriate parish priest. Beyond the sanctioned denominations, no sects or deists were tolerated, but the emancipation of the Jews was initiated in spite of the Emperor's antipathy to them.

Over the objections of the Curia and the nunciatures, the toleration patent of Joseph II was soon emulated in the ecclesiastical territories of the Empire: in the archbishopric of Salzburg under the enlightened Hieronymus Colloredo, in Cologne under the youngest brother of the Emperor, Max Franz, and in Trier under Clemens Wenzeslaus of Saxony. These initiatives did not restrict the dominant position of the Catholic Church nor did they pave the way for religious indifference.

In the end, the hectic, often ruthless reforms, the petty interventions in the life of the Church and popular religious customs, the "intolerable tutelage" (H. Tüchle) of the Church by the state discredited Josephinism as a reform movement. While it stopped many an abuse and introduced welcome innovations, it also shook the fundaments of the living faith in a manner which threatened the state as well.

The objections by the Curia and the Vienna nuncios Giuseppe Garampi and G. B. Caprara against the Josephinist established church system were ineffective. The "apostolic" trip by Pius VI to Vienna (1782) brought about insignificant concessions, made out of courtesy rather than as a result of having come to an understanding about the essential problems. Emperor and Pope at first talked in a conciliatory but nonbinding fashion about the Patent of Toleration, the cancellation of the bulls *In coena Domini* and *Unigenitus,* and, finally, accompanied by growing alienation, about almost all the political issues concerning the Church. An open break was avoided only by the Emperor's sudden but precisely calculated return visit to Rome in December 1783. One other result of this visit was the concordat of 20 January 1784 concerning the right of appointment for the duchies of Milan and Mantua, which had hitherto been exercised by the Holy See.

The archbishop of Vienna, Cardinal Christoph Anton Migazzi, headed the generally weak opposition against Josephinism in the hereditary lands. In Hungary, where "the desire was for an aristocratic monarchy instead of an enlightened despotism" (A. Wandruszka), the primate, Cardinal Joseph Batthyány, was a consistent opponent of the established Church. The rather inglorious campaign against the Turks was followed by open resistance in that kingdom and Joseph II, except for the Patent of Toleration, revoked his reform measures. From within the Empire the archbishops of Cologne and Trier registered their misgivings concerning a good many of the reforms. But the most vehement opposition to Josephinism and the centralist bureaucratic system was encountered among the clergy of the Austrian Netherlands, at their head the archbishop of Mechelen, Count Johann Heinrich Ferdinand von Frackenberg, and among the cities and estates of that province. When Joseph II revoked the *Joyeuse Entrée,* the Austrian rule, except for the area around Luxemburg, collapsed in the Brabant revolution.

The "deterioration in the psyche, body, and morale of the solitary and embittered Emperor" (H. L. Mikoletzky) and the accession of his more deliberate brother Leopold II initiated an amelioration of the Josephinist system, although Leopold was no less in favor of the established Church. The alleviation signaled by the restoration of some bishoprics and monastic establishments and the change of the order of worship, however, should not be taken as a dismantling of the established Church but rather as a contribution toward making peace. After all, Leopold's program regarding the established Church in the end went far beyond that of his brother. Because of the resistance by the bureaucracy, which continued to be dominated by the Josephinist spirit, there could be no retrenchment for some time yet. Even after 1815 when the Vienna Romanticism and ecclesiastical restoration around Friedrich Schlegel, Adam Müller, Zacharias Werner, and Clemens Maria Hofbauer signaled a movement against the Enlightenment and Josephinism, it never went beyond the starting point. Ideologically and politically radicalized after the July Revolution and then becoming gradually weaker and weaker, Josephinism represented a decisive force in the history of Austria until 1859. Its aftereffects are still present in many areas.

The Established Church in Electoral Bavaria

The transition from the firmly traditional church sovereignty of the *Bavaria Sacra,* often rigorously maintained at the time of the Counter Reformation and denominational absolutism, to an enlightened established Church was initiated around the middle of the eighteenth century. Elector Max III Joseph (1745–77), to be sure, went "before his public as its Catholic ruler on many days of the year" (Rall) just as his predecessors had done, adhering to the exclusivity of Catholicism in his land. Yet in theory and practice the established church system became stricter under his rule and more irritating to the orthodox believers. Enlightenment enveloped the Catholic territories of the Empire somewhat later than the Protestant ones; rationalism did so to a lesser degree. The older aspirations concerning the rights of the established Church were not completely transformed by the Enlightenment. They were merely given a new direction and a justification, misunderstood as a loss of religious substance, but instead derived from rationalistic law, to a lesser extent from history, but foremost from the concept of the all-encompassing enlightened welfare state.

At the core of Bavarian church policies from the sixteenth to the nineteenth century was the issue of separating the Bavarian lands from the old diocesan and metropolitan arrangement guaranteed by the constitution of the Empire. The secularization project under Charles VII, which could have decided the issue all at once and opened the road to a rearrangement, could not be realized. All attempts to establish indigenous territorial bishoprics also failed.

A measured sort of Enlightenment fashioned by Barthel's Würzburg school of canonists and the concepts of Christian Wolff (1679–1754) and Christian Thomasius (1655–1728) was started under the influence of Johann Adam von Ickstatt (1702–66). He was called to Munich as tutor to the future elector Max III Joseph in 1741 and five years later took over the first chair for jurisprudence and the office of director of the Bavarian university of Ingolstadt. Ickstatt's pupil Johann Georg von Lori, like his teacher a firm opponent of the Jesuits, continued the development and laid the foundation for the "Churbayerische Akademie." The reform, aimed at a consolidation of the established Church and a new foundation for the *Tura circa sacra,* whose urgency was caused largely by the economic and political distress after the Austrian War of Succession and during the Seven Years' War, goes back less to Ickstatt's teacher Wolff than to Pufendorf, Thomasius, and the church law of the Würzburg school of canonists, getting support also from the older laws of the Bavarian established Church. In 1750, the privy council regulation, along the lines of the territorial Church policies of the eighteenth century which viewed the Church as a state institution, called it the duty of the sovereign "to undertake to augment the glory of God, to propagate the true Catholic religion, and to prevent all superstition, heresy, and injurious error."

The actual initiator of pertinent measures which began in 1761 and no longer were based on privileges and concordats but on local law was Peter von Osterwald (1717–77), a convert from Weilburg, pupil of Wolff, and temporal director of the Ecclesiastical Council as of 1761. His programmatic work *Veremund von Lochsteins Gründe sowohl für als wider die geistliche Immunität in zeitlichen Dingen* (Strasbourg 1766) emanated from the disputes with the Bavarian monasteries about the decimations and was built on the writings of Van Espen, Giannone, Grotius, and Pufendorf. In it he rejects as presumptions not only the principle of immunity, hitherto claimed by the ecclesiastical authorities, but also the curialist theory of the relationship between Church and state as a "monstrous doctrine" and as "the language of all violators of royal sovereignty." Contradicting the existing view of the personal and real immunity of the clergy, which lifts it from the subject structure of the state, Osterwald points out that such immunity and the clergy's subordination under another sovereign power contradicts the sovereignty of the state. Ecclesiastical immunity in temporal matters, he continues, is a state privilege and therefore subject to immediate restriction or recall. Local immunity (the right of asylum) must be abolished. All mixed matters, merely annexed to the *spiritualia,* such as weddings, charitable bequests, exemptions of the clergy, and *spiritualia* not directly required for the blessedness of man (for instance, pilgrimages, processions, etc.) are by their nature essentially within the province of the state.

Osterwald's goal was the replacement of the numerous arrangements — often unclear in their stipulations and varying in their basic tenor — made with the prince-bishops in the last 150 years by a single uniform concordat. He strove for the extension of state sovereignty over the Church and the realization of a moderately enlightened welfare state. Osterwald's theses offered the state possibilities for far-reaching interventions even in the actual ecclesiastical realm, but on the other hand rejected any interference by the Church in temporal affairs. As a result, the Bavarian government taxed the clergy "for the needs of the land" on the basis of sovereign right (1769, 1770), creating difficulties with its own clergy. This problem as well as financial considerations soon prompted the government to seek papal decimation approvals which were quickly granted on 21 September 1771.

The amortization law of 13 October 1764 was a result of economic considerations. After previous amortization laws proved ineffective, (1672, 1704, 1730), the fight against the mortmain (with its origins in the late Middle Ages) was to be pursued more energetically in Bavaria. The reorganization of the Ecclesiastical Council (1768) which restored the influence of the laity to its status prior to the concordat of 1583 improved the possibilities for putting the territorialist ideas into practice. The first monastic mandate (29 September 1768) demanded precise numerical details about the houses and submission of the letters of endowment. The founding of brotherhoods was made subject to government approval on 9 December 1768; those already in existence had to submit painstaking reports concerning their origin and founder, statutes, activities, and assets (1769). The mandate of indigenousness of 20 December 1768 excluded foreigners and nonnatives from all benefices.

The reform mandates of the next few years invoked the protectionary power over Church and religion entrusted by God to the elector. On 16 February 1769, a governmental book censorship, independent of ecclesiastical censorship, was installed. "The especially urgent need for a reform of the ecclesiastical right of betrothal" (Pfeilschifer-Baumeister) led to the sponsalia mandate of 1769, which contained strict regulations: betrothals were henceforth to be made only in the presence of two witnesses and, in the case of young or indigent persons, only with the permission of parents, guardians, or the state; disputes involving betrothals were to be subject to temporal justice. The mandates in monastic matters, partly justified and aimed at the condition of "first investiture" were hastened by discovery and disclosures of abuses and the monachal tendency of Enlightenment. A mandate for the reform of religious orders in 1769 prohibited the taking of solemn vows before the age of twenty-one, largely limited the penal authority of the superiors, and abolished monastic incarceration. For certain cases it permitted the *Recursus ad principem,* applied since the end of the sixteenth century against excesses of ecclesiastical authority, and generally forbade collections by religious. In 1763 after the prohibition of visitations and election supervision by nonresident prelates in Bavaria, a law of 30 December 1769 aimed at a total separation of the Bavarian monasteries and convents from foreign superiors and provinces. If there were more than three institutions of the same order within Bavaria, an independent Bavarian province was to be established. The number of foreigners in monastic communities was to be no more than one sixth of the regulars; only natives were to be entitled to the passive franchise. The episcopal elections in Freising, Regensburg, Passau, and Chiemsee were to include the presence of Bavarian election commissioners in addition to the imperial ones and the rights of the former at the elections were to be substantially expanded. On 3 April 1770, the occasionally practiced *placet* was prescribed for all ecclesiastical regulations and the practice of recourse was expanded. The congress of delegates of the Bavarian bishops in Salzburg (1770–71) represented an episcopal-Febronian reaction to this enlightened-territorial church program which culminated in the establishment of one of several territorial bishoprics. The suggestions, formulated in the main by the dean of the Salzburg cathedral chapter and later bishop of Chiemsee, Count Ferdinand Christoph zu Zeil, floundered on the difficult legal situation, the lack of unanimity among the Bavarian episcopate, and on the fact that the Bavarian government came to an understanding with the Curia. Zeil managed to bring about a conciliatory agreement concerning the election of prelates (1774), but the negotiations for a uniform concordat were at an impasse when the elector died in 1777. As could be ascertained a year earlier at the talks regarding the establishment of a nunciature in Munich, the goals of an established Church in Bavaria were intended to be achieved in concert with Rome and in the face of the imperial episcopate.

Elector Max III Joseph was succeeded by the sensitive Karl Theodor (1742/77–99), who united the Palatine Electorate and Bavaria under his rule after the Wilhelminian line of the Wittelsbachs became extinct. While he vacillated "between the Enlightenment and its opposite and in 1790 once again from one pole to the other" (Rall), the Bavarian established Church was not only basically maintained but further developed by means of individual regulations which extended the sovereign protection of the Church into a sort of church administration and ended in the "complete muzzling of the Church" (Schwaiger). When the Ecclesiastical Council was reconstituted, the *Recursus ab abusu* was expanded, regulated by law, and the *placet* was again enjoined. In 1781 the court ordered the founding of an independent Bavarian branch of the Knights of Malta; its partial secularization was designed to provide for the court's protégés. This course was abandoned in favor of tapping the considerable assets of the suppressed Society of Jesus. The initial plan triggered a quickly collapsing reaction by the Bavarian prelates but no objection by Rome. In spite of his measures toward an established Church, Karl Theodor remained on good terms with the Curia. These were consolidated by his personal meeting with Pius VI in Munich and stood the test of opposition by the imperial Church on the occasion of the Munich nunciature conflict. Karl Theodor did not achieve his ultimate goal, the separation of Bavaria from the Church of the Empire and the establishment of one or more territorial bishoprics, a goal inherited from the Wittelsbach political tradition. But he was able to obtain from Pius VI the compromise solution of a permanent nunciature in Munich (1785) and, in an alliance of expedience with Rome, substantially to subjugate the *Bavaria Sacra.* By the brief *Convenit provide* (1789) Rome agreed to the founding of a court diocese after the model of Sardinia and Naples, restricted to the newly organized collegiate see of Our Lady and the court churches, but exempt from ties with the Freising diocese and the Salzburg metropolitanate. The connection between the court diocese and the presidium of the Ecclesiastical Council confirmed the political intentions of the Bavarian government in relation to the episcopate. It was — as the most immediately affected bishop of Freising had already been forced to realize when the electoral capitulation was changed by the cathedral chapter — a revolutionary intervention in the thousand-year-old German church constitution and an initial, albeit modest, beginning in the reorganization of the Bavarian episcopate.

The tensions between the Munich court bishopric and the Freising ordinariate partly explain the intervention by Karl Theodor in the Freising episcopal election, conducted during the interregnum of 1790 and vehemently attacked by the episcopal media. In contradiction to the statutes of the cathedral chapter, by applying his rights as the Palatine imperial vicar and by effectively setting aside the right of free election Karl Theodor prevailed with his candidate, the prince-provost of Berchtesgaden, Joseph Conrad von Schroffenberg, known as an opponent of episcopalism. Against the protests of the cathedral chapters and the Mainz elector Friedrich Karl von Erthal (in the latter's capacity as lord chancellor and "first bishop of the German Church"), he dispatched vicariate commissioners to the episcopal elections in Regensburg and Eichstätt. Although his candidate prevailed only in Regensburg — again it was Schroffenberg, who agreed in 1795 to the annexation of his chapter of Berchtesgaden by Bavaria, which was the equivalent of secularization — and he failed to obtain the right to first prayers during the imperial vicariate, Karl Theodor had nonetheless; succeeded in these episcopal elections "to prevail with a principle which opened new possibilities for the Bavarian established Church in future interregnums" (Aretin).

The rights of Bavarian election commissioners regarding elections in native monasteries, consolidated under Max III Joseph, were again expanded by a decree dated 5 February 1791 for the purpose of "maintaining canonical freedom." The attacks against the monasteries came to a head in 1793 with the regulation regarding investiture and profession examinations. A reform-Catholic tendency for stopping abuses appears to have determined the reduction of processions and pilgrimages, the prohibition of passion plays, and the attenuated application of regulations concerning holidays. The decimations, approved by Pius VI in 1787 and 1798 for the purpose of alleviating the state of emergency, can be taken as a result of the alliance between Rome and the Bavarian established church system. Their implementation, prepared with the help of the nuncio Ziucci for the latter's personal advantage, demonstrate the absolute sovereignty of the state in taxation. It consolidated the state's dominance over a Church already under the shadow of secularization and raised the specter of an even more oppressive established church system for a future already threatened by political unrest and wars. The secularization of 1803 eliminated the ecclesiastical states, which — as irritating foreign bodies in the Bavarian territory — had been the actual opponents of the established Church and opened the way for the reorganization of the Church, an object of aspirations since the sixteenth century.

CHAPTER 134

State and Church in Poland-Lithuania to the End of the Republic of the Aristocracy

After the Counter Reformation in Poland-Lithuania had prevailed under Sigismund III (1587–1632) and Ladislas IV (1632–48), the Roman Curia expected the Polish kings to support its diplomacy in eastern Europe and consequently involved them in the coalition against the Turks and its efforts to persuade the Orthodox into union with Rome. In 1648 when the Jesuit John Casimir was elected king, Pope Innocent X granted him dispensation from his vows and laicized him. The King temporarily succeeded in pacifying his country, which had been ravaged by Swedish, Russian, and Turkish invasions, and by Cossack rebellions. The heroic defense of the Pauline monastery on the Jasna Góra near Częstochowa in 1655 turned this place of pilgrimage to Mary into a Polish national shrine. In 1656 the King declared the Virgin Mary Queen of Poland (*Regina Poloniae*). The contest by the French and Habsburg courts for influence in Poland, as well as domestic and foreign difficulties prompted him to abdicate. Successes against the Turks could not be achieved until the reign of Jan Siobieski (1674–96), who was instrumental in lifting the siege of Vienna by the Turks in 1683 regaining for Poland the designation of "The Outer Wall of the Occident" (*antemurale christianitatis*). But Sobieski was unable to prevail when the nobles continued to insist on their privileges. As a consequence the Polish-Lithuanian state suffered greatly under the unrestrained liberties exercised by the nobility and the disastrous veto right of any delegate to the Sejm (diet) (*liberum veto*).

During the interregnum Primate Cardinal Radziejowski solicited votes for the French candidate, Prince François Louis Conti, while the nobility were in favor of the Wettin elector Friedrich August the Strong. Prior to the election the latter secretly converted to Catholicism and when elected called himself Augustus II (1697–1733). The rival King Stanislas Leszczyński, supported by Sweden and later on by his father-in-law Louis XIV, was able to maintain himself only during the Northern War (1704–9) and the Polish War of Succession (1733–35). After the death of Augustus II, Emperor Charles VI and Tsarina Anna Ivanovna made sure that the son of the dead King succeeded him to the throne as Augustus III.

The Counter Reformation had excessively enlarged the power of Catholicism. The Protestants were oppressed; they were not allowed to build any new churches after 1717; in 1724 after the Protestant population stormed the Jesuit school in Thorn, the mayor and nine other Protestants were executed. The Uniates, treated as second-class Catholics even in the seventeenth century, were forced to accept certain rites and customs of the Roman Catholic established Church. The rights of the Orthodox were also restricted. The kings of Prussia and the tsars gave protection to the Protestants and Orthodox respectively. As early as the reign of the Saxon kings the Russians intervened repeatedly in Polish affairs; their troops were stationed on Polish soil after 1717 in order to break any opposition to Russian interests. After the death of Augustus III, Catherine II helped her favorite, Stanislas Augustus Poniatowski, to ascend to the Polish throne (1764–95). Aside from the supremacy and discord of the Polish nobility it was the expansionist tendencies of the neighboring great powers that brought about the disintegration of Poland at the end of the eighteenth century.

The Catholic patriotic opposition, founded in 1768 by Bishop Adam Stanisłas Krašinski of Kamieniec as the Confederation of Bar, was unable to stem the tide of Russian power; the rebels were crushed by the Russians after four years of fighting. The first partition, decreed by Russia, Austria, and Prussia in 1772, cost Poland about 30 percent of its territory and almost half its population. Well-known clerics participated in attempts to stabilize the domestic conditions by means of reforms. They included the Piarist Stanisłas Konarski (1700–1773), famous as a preacher and politician, Bishop Adam Stanisłas Naruszevicz of Łuck (1733–96), recognized as the founder of modern Polish historiography, and the prebend Hugo Kołłatej (1750–1812), who reestablished the Cracow academy. They also participated in formulating the constitution of 3 May 1791, which recognized Catholicism as the state religion but also guaranteed the free exercise of religion for all dissidents. The efforts of inner renewal came to an abrupt end through the second partition of Poland by Russia and Prussia and through the third partition, wherein the three neighboring countries occupied the remainder of the country. The name of Poland was removed from all maps. Nuncio Lorenzo Litta (1793–95) protested in vain against the dismemberment of Poland-Lithuania, of which Russia had seized 465,000. Prussia 145,000, and Austria 115,000 square kilometers.

The Church was substantially weakened by confiscations and secularization. Its organization with its two church provinces of Gnesen and Lemberg was enmeshed in political disputes. The religious orders which had shaped Polish

Catholicism under the successive influence of Spain and France lost many of their establishments. In spite of the threat represented by Orthodox Russia, the Josephinist established Church of Austria, and Protestant Prussia during the following decades, membership in the Catholic Church was a factor which united the majority of Poles across the borders of their partitioned country.

CHAPTER 135

The Decline of the Church of the Empire in the Great Secularization

The suspension of the Restitution Edict, the imperial offer to Brandenburg of 1 February 1647 to satisfy its compensatory claims by means of secularizations meant the beginning of the end for the ecclesiastical states and thereby the initiation of the dissolution of the Empire, concluded a century and a half later with the total secularization of 1803. Secularization, the deterioration of the Empire, and the rise of modern, absolutist German principalities in the seventeenth and eighteenth centuries were intertwined in a very complex process. This is demonstrated by the printed media, the political theory of the state, the peace negotiations of Osnabrück and Münster, Nijmegen, Rijswijk, and Baden, and by the secularization projects between 1648 and 1789. The Peace of Westphalia acknowledged the secularizations as a means of restitution after the standard year of 1624, as compensation and reparation. In assigning ecclesiastical principalities to temporal territories it took into account the actual denominational status and the political necessities, even to the extent of the compromise of a partial secularization of the prince-bishopric of Osnabrück by means of an alternation principle between a Catholic bishop and a prince of the Guelfs ("pseudobishop"). While the surviving ecclesiastical dignitaries of the Imperial Diet and holders of benefices did have certain guaranties by virtue of the standard year and day as well as the Imperial electoral capitulation, there were a number of secularization projects and actual secularizations of church assets by the various principalities during the seventeenth and eighteenth centuries. According to Pufendorf the most serious political omission by the Empire was not to go ahead with a total secularization at the Peace of Westphalia after the Swedish or Danish model. The course of church history in the period between that peace treaty and the imperial delegates final recess was decisively determined by a number of elements: aspirations for secularization initially on the part of Protestant princes, the fear of secularization, the desire by the Church of the Empire to secure its existence by deferring to the dynastic church policies of the Habsburgs, Wittelsbachs, Lorrainers, and Wettins, and, finally, the accumulation of benefices by the eligible nobility.

In the seventeenth and eighteenth centuries the secularizations in their various stages of development have to be considered as a fight for the continued existence or the dissolution of the Empire, for Catholic or Protestant hegemony, and as preliminaries of the total secularization of 1803. They emanated from those territories and dynasties who thought themselves disadvantaged in the great give-and-take of administrative realignment and compensation of the Peace of Westphalia and who felt they could raise claims for ecclesiastical properties either on the basis of their being intermingled with ecclesiastical states of because of certain stipulations of the peace agreements. Among the prime objects for secularization were the archbishopric of Hildesheim, a Catholic island in the midst of the Protestant territory of the Guelfs and rendered helpless by the Quedlinburg Recession; the archbishopric of Osnabrück, partially secularized by the disastrous alternation principle; and, lastly, the small archbishopric of Worms, situated as it was in the tense area between the electorates of Mainz and the Palatinate. These ecclesiastical states were saved from secularization in the seventeenth and eighteenth centuries only by personal union with more powerful imperial bishoprics (such as the electorates of Cologne, Mainz, and Trier) and by the church policies of the great Catholic dynasties, who exploited the territorial and political disputes between the Protestant princes.

The plans for secularization in the seventeenth century are permeated with vaguely formulated intentions of conversion and negotiations for church reunion, especially in the cases of Ernst August von Braunschweig-Lüneburg, first in his capacity as "pseudobishop" of Osnabrück and then as duke of Hanover, and the elector Karl Ludwig of the Palatinate. The dynastic policies vis-à-vis the Church of the Empire with the expectation of consolidating ecclesiastical secundogenitures in general delayed plans for secularization in the Catholic part of the Empire. On the other hand, there were reformers of the Church and the Empire, such as Antoine Arnauld or the learned Landgrave Ernst von Hessen-Rheinfels, a convert to Catholicism who intended to establish a total of sixty new German bishoprics from secularized properties of the Church of the Empire, create an electorate reserved for the Emperor, and make an offer to the Protestant princes for a reunion with a reformed Catholic Church.

None of the revolutionary plans for reform amounting to a complete secularization — probably at the expense of the Church — was realized. A greater danger for the ecclesiastical states was the desire for expansion and administrative realignment of the temporal territories combined with inner reforms. According to the well-known words of Ranke, Prussia was not the only state founded on the principle of secularization since the time of the Great Elector. As the ecclesiastical states were gradually reduced to the status of a political sop, as manifested in the negotiations of the Nijmegen Peace, in the Austrian War of Succession, and the third Silesian War, the will on the part of the Catholic Emperor and that of the papacy as well to defend "God's inheritance" in the Empire steadily slackened. Plans to revoke the secularizations in connection with a territorial reorganization of the Empire as proffered by Nuncio Bevilacqua at the peace negotiations of Nijmegen and by Passionei at Baden came to nought because of the weak position of the Catholic powers relative to the prevailing interests and alliances.

Fears of secularization of the *Germania Sacra* were repeatedly used in the eighteenth century as weapons of Wittelsbach and Hapsburg politics in the context of the Church of the Empire, especially so by Maria Theresa in her fight against the Wittelsbach Emperor Charles VII, at the episcopal elections around the middle of the century, and during the Seven Years' War against Frederick the Great for Silesia and hegemony in the Empire. At the time of the Austrian War of Succession and during the crisis of the Empire when there was a possibility of a Swabian kingdom for Charles VII and a southern German buffer state between Austria and France, Berlin promoted a secularization project. It intended to use the southern German archbishoprics of Freising, Regensburg, Salzburg, and Eichstätt as imperial reserves for the formation of a household force for the Wittelsbach Emperor Charles VII, to expand Prussia by the addition of the ecclesiastical territories of Breslau-Neiße and Münster, and, lastly, to compensate Austria with the prince-bishopric of Passau. A weak Charles VII, who had not given a clear negative reply to that tempting secularization project advocated by his Prussian ally, tried the traditional path of imperial church politics. He had in mind securing for his brother Johann Theodor — in addition to the archbishoprics of Regensburg and Freising — the prince-bishoprics of Eichstätt, Speyer, Worms, Liège, Trier, and the prince-diocese of Ellwangen. Such a second Wittelsbach episcopal realm would have created the required additional power for his dynasty by a partial, "Catholic" secularization.

Maria Theresa, at odds with Prussia and Bavaria, employed all the means at her disposal to oppose this secularization project and to discredit the powerless and landless Wittelsbach Emperor in the Catholic part of the Empire. That part of the country was dissatisfied not only with the church policies of the *Defensor ecclesiae,* but also with the attitude toward the ecclesiastical princes of the Francophile Pope Benedict XIV, who distrusted the pragmatic powers. Episcopal Germany felt the growing discomfort of Rome over the consolidation of crosier and sword, of bishopric and sovereign power. But in the interest of the Church it was unwilling to give up this consolidation, since the will and the power to protect the ecclesiastical states seemed to decrease in direct proportion to the growing authoritarian demeanor of the prince-bishops toward the nunciatures and the Roman church offices, and the more they tried to realize episcopal concepts regarding the church constitution and to execute the transition from a late medieval territory to a modern absolutist state.

By the end of 1743 the most acute danger to the ecclesiastical states had passed, even though the following year Wilhelm VIII of Hesse-Kassel staked his claim to the secularization of the prince-bishopric of Paderborn and the abbeys of Fulda and Corvey and although there was a possibility that the secularization project of the Westphalian ecclesiastical territories in favor of a new electorate of Hesse-Kassel might surface again. Plans for secularization entered a new phase with the beginning of the Seven Years' War, which Ranke thought had been a religious war, "not explicitly so, but by its nature and perceived as such by everyone." An end to the alternation principle in the archdiocese of Osnabrück, the secularization of Paderborn, Hildesheim, and Münster in favor of England-Hanover, of Erfurt and Eichsfeld (at that time part of the Mainz electorate) in favor of Hesse-Kassel, Hanover, or other Protestant states played a very prominent role in the projects of Frederick the Great until 1759. Combined with other intended changes they would have enabled Prussia and Hanover "to tear Northern Germany from the Holy Roman Empire and to create independent realms" (G. Volz). In the last few years of the Seven Years' War, following the death of Elector-Archbishop Clemens August (d. 6 February 1761), the vacant archdioceses of the Wittelsbach ecclesiastical secundogenitures in the northwestern part of Germany were ideal objects for administrative realignment and compensation, not only for Prussia, England-Hanover, and Hesse-Kassel, but for a number of Catholic powers as well in order to heal the wounds of the allied electorate of Saxony and by the election of Clemens Wenzeslaus to provide for the Catholic Wettin dynasty an episcopal realm in northwestern Germany. For the northwestern German *Germania Sacra* the worst was in the end averted less by the efforts of the Emperor, the Catholic princes of the diet, or France than by the emerging differences between Prussia and England-Hanover and Holland's policy regarding the prince-bishopric of Münster. A Wettin ecclesiastical secundogeniture which would have been established at the expense of the eligible nobility was prevented by the elections *ex gremio* in Cologne, Münster, Hildesheim, and Paderborn. But in Osnabrück the election of the barely six-month-old Frederick of York, whose governmental affairs were conducted by two councilors appointed by his father, George III of England, was a step toward correcting the Peace of Westphalia.

The discrepancy between the aspirations and the capabilities in the militarily powerless ecclesiastical states, dependent for better or for worse on the Empire, and between the aspirations and obligations of the imperial and also the papal policies became more and more manifest during the second third of the eighteenth century. For the states under the crosier and infula the three peaceful decades between the Peace of Hubertusburg and the outbreak of the Wars of Revolution were neither tired and stifling nor were they the halcyon days that they were called by contemporary sources and historical presentations. Indeed, the vast majority of the ecclesiastical territories were flourishing to a greater or lesser degree under a moderate enlightenment, and respectable scholarly activities developed at many Catholic universities and monastic institutions which did not have to shrink from a comparison with developments in the Protestant parts of the Empire. Yet this blossoming in the bishoprics and abbeys and the eudaemonia of the Catholic Enlightenment was frequently achieved at the expense of the basic religious-ecclesiastical ideas. At the same time, the belletrists, hostile to the Church, and the enlightened advocates of the rights of the state raised more and more probing questions regarding the justification for being of the ecclesiastical states and authority over the Church assets.

It is difficult to determine with any precision the significance of the publicity campaign of the cathedral canon Philipp Anton von Bibra of Fulda, the writings of Baron K. von Moser, Schnaubert, und Weiße for the preparation of secularization. The veritable flood of paper was certainly not quite as harmless to the existence of the ecclesiastical states as even some contemporary episcopal censors, such as Turin in Mainz, or later historians have occasionally assumed. It was actually more a signal for the attack of secularization and — inasmuch as it came from within the ecclesiastical states themselves — an expression of a growing "feeling of impending doom" (F. Schlegel). The signs of an inner readiness for secularization on the part of ecclesiastical institutions and territories increased, as shown by the transformation of abbeys and convents into secular institutions for nobles or institutes for secular priests, by the suppression of monastic establishments even by ecclesiastical princes with or without papal permission, and, lastly, by the growing severity of the amortization laws. No doubt the tendency toward secularization was also promoted by the old rivalry between the secular and the regular clergy, by comparisons between the economic backwardness of Catholic states and the prosperity of Protestant ones, as well as by strong immanent forces within the Catholic reform movement, the concepts of Muratori, the Jansenists, and Catholic advocates of Catholic enlightenment.

After the expulsion of the Society of Jesus from the Bourbon states and its suppression in 1773 its assets were claimed by the respective states and used in accordance with the enlightened doctrines of state law which held that it was within the competency of the state to dispose of the church property in a manner most useful for the commonweal. Fiscal policies and the argument of the commonweal played a decisive role in secularizations, not least in the abolition of monastic establishments for the purpose of reform or the creation of new Catholic universities (for instance Mainz and Münster). Next to fiscal policy it was for reasons of ecclesiastical reform, especially parish regulation, that the Josephinist "Klostersturm" took place in 1781, to which more than seven hundred monastic houses fell victim in Austria. Disciplinary problems or economic abuses were rarely the reason for the abolitions. The loss of cultural assets was immeasurable, the damage to learning considerable, but most serious were the negative effects on the ministry and religious life, which were certainly not made up for by the reforms actually achieved.

In connection with the Bavarian succession on the one hand and the Josephinist established church system reaching over into the Church of the Empire on the other, the ecclesiastical territories were not only confronted by "northern despotism" (Franz v. Fürstenberg) but by the Catholic power of Austria as well. In addition to the northwestern German archbishoprics, those of Fulda, Bamberg (for Saxony), and Würzburg also played a part in the exchange and compensation projects of the time; there was even talk of a secularization of Cologne in favor of Prussia and fears for the continued existence of the other two Rhenish archbishoprics were not without foundation. As the state minister of Münster, Franz von Fürstenberg, remarked bitterly in April 1778: "The most convenient thing would be to abolish a few bishoprics and justify it by saying that the property of the Church could never be put to a better use than to prevent bloodshed." Plans to realize the concept of a third, neutral Germany in addition to the great powers Prussia and Austria failed. They were to secure the continued existence of the ecclesiastical principalities within the framework of an interdenominational union to include the princes of the Imperial Diet. Efforts to unite the episcopate on the basis of the old constitution of the Church of the Empire in order to counter the territorial claims of princely proponents of their respective established Churches and their plans for secularization were also unsuccessful. These efforts met with the resistance not only of Austria, whose policy regarding the Empire rested largely on the ecclesiastical princes and — after the issue of the Bavarian succession — was predicated on the unavoidability of secularizations. They were also resisted by Prussia, which was "prone to conquest," and by Bavaria with its established Church.

The danger of members of the Imperial Diet being affected by secularization surfaced when Archduke Max Franz was elected prince-bishop of Münster, again when Joseph II made a surprise attack on the prince bishopric of Passau following the death of Bishop Leopold Ernst von Firmian (d. 11 March 1783), and when the Emperor spawned the fantastic plan to transfer the archbishopric of Salzburg to Liège, but to secularize that prince-bishopric together with the chapter of Berchtesgaden in favor of Austria. This project, originating as it did with the Emperor, the *Defensor ecclesiae,* five years before the outbreak of the French Revolution, and plans discussed in the electorate of Bavaria and executed in the form of "cold secularizations" made abundantly clear just what the situation of the ecclesiastical states would be if the decaying Empire were to fall apart because of the egotistical interests of the states or if a European conflict were to place the "conquering" states in a position where they could cut equivalents from the last remaining patches of the ecclesiastical "robe of the old Empire' (J. J. Moser).

After the warning signals of the late eighteenth century the strongest impulses for a comprehensive secularization emanated from the French Revolution. A proposal by Talleyrand was followed on 2 November by a decree nationalizing all church property. The Civil Constitution of 12 July 1790 shattered the hierarchical order of the old France. More than fifty bishoprics, all church offices without ministry, all religious orders and congregations were abolished; in 1792 papal Avignon and Venaissin and in 1798 and 1808 the Papal States were secularized.

The attitude of the ecclesiastical princes toward the French Revolution, by no means negative at first, although it was determined by totally varying motives and differing views, became noticeably more negative after the issuance of a Civil Constitution. The ecclesiastical princes of the western German border areas were involved in their first conflict with revolutionary France when the manorial and ecclesiastical rights of princes of the Empire were abolished in Alsace. The Civil Constitution eliminated the dependence of the dioceses of Metz, Toul, Verdun, Nancy, and Saint-Dié on the archbishopric of Trier, that of Strasbourg on Mainz, and revoked the jurisdiction of the bishop of Speyer in the Alsatian part of his see; in addition, it transferred the deanery of Carignan to the newly established bishopric of Sedan. The demand by the imperial bishops for the restoration of the imperial and ecclesiastical status quo in Alsace, Lorraine, and in the *Terra Gallica* belonging to the bishopric of Trier had no tangible results; neither did the call for help to Russia as a guarantor of the Peace of Westphalia nor the condemnation of the Civil Constitution by Pope Pius VI. Leopold II was unwilling to make the violation of the rights of German princes and bishops by revolutionary France the cause for an intervention. He especially warned the Rhenish elector-archbishops not to take any intemperate steps in connection with their emigration policies.

The direct confrontation with France was overshadowed by the rebellion in the Austrian Netherlands, arising from opposition of the estates and ecclesiastical circles to the policies of Joseph II and the resistance of the estates against the prince-bishop of Liège, Konstantin Franz von Hoensbroech. The electors of Cologne, Trier, and Mainz, together with the neighboring estates of the Empire had to pay with a defeat for their attempt, ordered by the supreme court of the Empire, to return the Liège prince-bishop to the fold. Only after the Liège issue had widened into a real crisis for the Empire and an agreement between the two great powers had been laboriously achieved did Austria take over the imperial execution and restore the original status in Liège by force of arms.

It was under the impact of the events on the western border of the Empire and individual cases of unrest in certain German territories that the governments started to dismantle enlightened reforms and to disavow Febronianism and the Congress of Ems. This point also marked the transition from a moderate Catholic enlightenment to an ecclesiastical restoration, from indifferentism to a more profound religiosity. Flight onto the harassed ship of Saint Peter seems to have been the only way out of "punishment by temporal potentates."

The relationship of several ecclesiastical states (Speyer, Mainz, Trier) with revolutionary France was complicated by their policy regarding the royalist-aristocratic and ecclesiastical emigrants. Worms, or Mainz, Coblenz or Schönbornslust might have appeared to the royal and aristocratic emigrants like a small foreign Versailles, a Versailles *in partibus*, with its favorites and mistresses. While these emigrants — in spite of their political and military activities — did not pose a danger to France as long as they were not supported by the European powers, unwise and provocative policies which went beyond their merely being tolerated by their host countries offered sufficient grounds to the Girondists for counter-provocations and warnings to the ecclesiastical states. Clearly distinct from the aristocratic emigrants, who were often seen as an economic burden and an offense to the religious population, were the ecclesiastical emigrants. Through their generally exemplary religious work and their ministry they enjoyed a hospitable reception by the population and the ecclesiasts.

On 20 April 1792, opposed by the group around Robespierre, the Girondists prevailed on Louis XVI to declare war against the King of Hungary and Bohemia to defend France against alleged unjust attacks, to maintain freedom, and to demonstrate the will to expand its power. The Austro-Prussian campaign, in which the ecclesiastical electors did not take part, did not, however, result in the restoration of the status of 1789 or 1782 as had been hoped within the Church of the Empire. Instead the cannonade of Valmy on 20 September 1792 led to the occupation a few days later of the episcopal residences of Speyer and Mainz, the archdiocese of Liège, the left-bank territories of the rivers Erft and Roer. The archdiocese of Basel was declared the Raurachian Republic and united with France as the Département Mont-Terrible. Church property in all the conquered territories was to be confiscated; an oath on the Civil Constitution was to effect apostasy to the schismatic national Church. After the declaration of war by the Empire (22 March 1793) the Austrian Netherlands and the left-bank ecclesiastical territories of the middle Rhine were reconquered. Yet the disunity of the allies, a general aversion to the war, and especially the political-military disinterest of Prussia prompted the proposal by the lord chancellor, the elector-archbishop of Mainz, at the Imperial Diet in Regensburg on 24 October 1794 that the Empire should attempt to make peace with France.

In the meantime new plans for secularization were discussed in Vienna and Berlin. Prussia, the "natural opponent of the ecclesiastical states" (H. von Treitschke), raised a demand for the secularization of several prince-bishoprics to satisfy its cost of the war, since this was "sufficiently justified by history" and moreover "would not create any actual disadvantage nor dissatisfaction." Reports by agents said that even Rome was not entirely against these secularizations. By virtue of the separate peace of Basel (5 April 1795) and the secret supplemental agreements (5 August 1795) Prussia received assurances for right-bank compensations (parts of the archdiocese of Münster and Recklinghausen), with the proviso for adding other stipulations should they become suitable, in exchange for the commitment of strict neutrality. The Prussian example was followed by Hesse-Kassel (28 August 1795), whose dynasty was related to the Hohenzollern, Württemberg (7 August 1796), Baden (22 August 1796), and Bavaria (7 September 1796). The fact that the principle of compensation by means of secularizations was intended even then to be considerably expanded and not limited to fiefs of the Empire is shown by the secret treaty between Prussia and France in favor of the hereditary governor of the Netherlands, a brother-in-law of the Prussian King. He was to be compensated by the prince-bishoprics of Würzburg and Bamberg in exchange for the commitment that these areas were to go to Prussia when the house of Orange became extinct.

Military successes by Austria in the southern German theater of war did not change the development presaged by these treaties since Napoleon, by advancing through northern Italy into the heart of the Austrian hereditary lands, was able to force Austria to accept the armistice of Leoben (18 April 1797) and the subsequent Peace of Campoformio (17 November 1797). The agreements of Campoformio went well beyond the contradictory ones of Leoben concerning the recognition of the constitutional borders of France and the integrity of the Empire: Francis II as King of Hungary and Bohemia promised to take an active part in the cession of the left-bank areas from Basel to the Nette-Roer line. This agreement would not have ceded the Cologne electorate and the Prussian duchies of Cleves and Gelderland to France and Prussian compensations on the right bank of the Rhine would have been prevented. All the ecclesiastical states west of the line of Basel-Andernach-Venlo went to France and were secularized (Speyer Worms, Mainz, Trier, Stablo-Malmedy, Liège, Prüm, etc.). The archdiocese of Salzburg was to compensate Austria for its loss of the Netherlands and northern Italy and in exchange for the Prussian territorial gains in Poland. While Austria had not basically been an opponent of secularization since the period of Josephinism, it did want to prevent a large-scale liquidation of ecclesiastical states. According to the stipulations of Campoformio, therefore, the ecclesiastical electors were to be assured of compensation on the right bank for their left-bank losses. Detailed arrangements were to be worked out at a congress in agreement with the French republic.

In spite of the formal announcement asserting the integrity of the Empire and contrary to the misgivings held by some of the estates (especially the Saxon electorate and Würzburg) the imperial delegates in Rastatt, yielding to pressure from France, accepted the principle of indemnification by means of secularization as the basis for peace. Thereupon "the legates of the knights of the Empire in savage greed crowded upon the plenipotentiaries of the Directorate in order to obtain by favor of the enemy of the Empire a rich piece from the territories of their ecclesiastical compatriots" (Treitschke). Partial secularization would have sufficed for compensation, but the tendency, only temporarily slowed down by the victories of the second coalition, was in the direction of total secularization. Since the Austrian withdrawal from Mainz there was a growing fear of total secularization in the ecclesiastical territories on the right bank of the Rhine not only because the appropriation of ecclesiastical property was fiscally expedient given the expenditures for the war, but also because the Pope, already on his way into French imprisonment, had helped bring about a situation in Bavaria "which could not but trigger directly the process of secularization" (L. Hammermayer).

Following the military defeats in the second war of the coalition (Marengo, Hohenlinden) the Peace of Lunéville (7 March 1801; 16 March 1801) forced the Empire to cede the left bank areas and — implying a secularization of the ecclesiastical states — to compensate the dispossessed hereditary princes "from the womb of the Empire" (*dans le sein de l'Empire*). In regard to these compensations, which were to be born by the Empire in its totality (*collectivement*), the indefinite guidelines of the Congress of Rastatt were invoked. The four ceded Rhenish *départements* were declared part of the French Republic by law of 9 March 1801; the Napoleonic concordat (15 July 1801; 8 April 1802) signaled the end of the Church of the Empire in the left-bank territories. In conjunction with the ratification bull *Ecclesia Christi* (15 August 1801) Pope Pius VII asked all the bishops of France and those in the ceded areas of the Empire to resign. In the subsequent new circumscription Mainz and Trier lost their position as metropolitanates; Cologne did not even retain its see; the *départements* of the Roer and the Rhine-Mosel were combined into a new bishopric with its residence in Aachen. Together with the newly circumscribed bishoprics of Ghent, Liège, Mainz, Namur and Tournai it formed the archdiocese of Mechelen. With some exceptions, the total secularization of the entire ecclesiastical property and the abolition of the monastic institutions were decreed (9 June 1802) in order to put the left-bank territories of the Church of the Empire on an equal footing with the rest of France. In many cases the right-bank real properties and taxed revenues of the abolished left-bank sees were immediately confiscated (for instance in Hesse-Darmstadt and Hesse-Kassel) and transferred to the respective territories even prior to ratification by the Imperial delegates' final recess.

Rome had recognized the secularization in France as well as in the ceded left-bank areas in the concordat of 1801. It had also substantially agreed in advance to the secularization in the Empire even though other promulgations designed for the German Church were to create a different impression. Severing the left-bank parts of dioceses, abolishing the left-bank bishoprics, and realigning these areas as implemented by Caprara practically brought the Church of the Empire to ruin. The papal bull *Qui Christi Domini,* which expressly excepted the remainder of the archdioceses and sees outside the French rule from recircumscription and guaranteed them the maintenance of their ecclesiastical status quo, had no effect. The fact that France sought to have the bishops of the abolished sees of Basel and Liège transferred to vacant right-bank sees in order to avoid having to pay their pensions — Franz Xaver von Neveu, bishop of Basel, personally tried for a future new Baden bishopric — puts a characteristic light on the waning days of the Church of the Empire, as does the strange reserve of Rome when Archduke Anton Viktor was elected bishop of Münster.

Since the imperial delegation was totally unable to solve the issue of compensation, the role of arbitration — implied but not expressly mentioned in the treaty of Lunéville — devolved upon France. It created the foreign policy conditions for a territorial reorganization and disintegration of the Empire by peace treaties with England (1802) and an understanding with Russia (1801), which had claimed the right of participation as a guarantor of the Westphalian peace. On 23 November 1802, the design for compensation, submitted by the arbitrating powers France and Russia, was accepted by the imperial delegation with a few changes. The imperial decree by the ratification commission (27 April 1803), brought about by a Russian threat, elevated the final recess to the status of a binding basic law of the Empire. This sealed the fate of the ecclesiastical states by shifting the burden of compensation on them and by sanctioning the secularizations. In fact, the secularization, more trenchant in its effects than the Reformation and the Peace of Westphalia, "shook the last vestiges of imperial authority, which rested on the ecclesiastical states, whose rise, after all, had given birth to the Holy Roman Empire and from whose existence it could not be separated" (D. Schäfer). Henceforth the union of crosier and sword was prevented, the interlacing of Church and Empire severed, and the constitution of the German Church shattered, or rather changed to a provisional arrangement.

There was an almost total absence of resistance to the secularization on the part both of Rome and the ecclesiastical princes, either from helplessness or political considerations, from indifference or curial antipathy against the Church of the Empire. Rome was neither able nor willing to prevent the secularization; it merely wanted to see it limited. It condemned secularization as unjust and an act of violence, but did not consider it a misfortune for the Church and at times even emphasized its beneficial effects. In many cases, even ecclesiastics did not shrink from making demands for compensation from church assets and secularization. Elector-Archbishop Clemens Wenzeslaus of Trier had designs on the prince-bishopric of Constance and the prince-abbey of Kempten; the Mainz elector Friedrich Karl von Erthal demanded the prince-bishopric of Fulda as compensation; Dalberg professed himself basically in agreement with the secularization; Wessenberg advocated a partial secularization; the Knights of Malta tried to enrich themselves by means of ecclesiastical property.

Among the stipulations of the Imperial delegates' final recess we have to distinguish between: 1. the political secularization or that of estates of the Empire, which consisted of awarding ecclesiastical compensatory territories as sovereign states to new temporal sovereigns and was based on the supreme liegedom of the Emperor, benefiting primarily the states of medium size; 2. secularization in right of one's property (paragraphs 34—36), which granted "all properties of the cathedral chapters and their dignitaries together with the episcopal domains, all properties of the endowed sees, abbeys and monastic establishments... to the free and full disposition of the respective sovereign for the benefit of expenditures for church services, educational institutions, and others of public benefit, as well as for the alleviation of their finances... with the firm proviso of certain and constant provision of the cathedral churches... and pensions for the suspended clergy."

The Imperial delegates' final recess secularized on the right bank of the Rhine all imperially immediate ecclesiastical territories (two ecclesiastical electoral states, one prince-archbishopric, nineteen prince-bishoprics, numerous abbeys of the Empire), with the exception of the territories of the Knights of Malta and those of the Knights of the Teutonic Order (abolished in 1809), as well as the state of the lord chancellor under K. T. von Dalberg, which was newly created from the remainders of ecclesiastical territories. It represented an enclave primarily in the expanded Bavarian state and was essentially incorporated in the Kingdom of Bavaria after the ratification of the Peace of Paris. The Imperial delegates' final recess transferred the Mainz archiepiscopal see to Regensburg, combining in this way the dignities of an elector, lord chancellor, metropolitan-archbishop, and primate of Germany. More than two hundred monastic institutions were secularized. In the Habsburg realm, which was in the incipient stage of an ecclesiopolitical restoration under Francis II, those monastic institutions which had avoided secularization in 1781 were not affected.

Also not affected was the old diocesan organization until "another decision is made on the basis of imperial law" (par. 62). Bishops and cathedral chapters were to be awarded pensions, the exercise of ecclesiastical office not to be obstructed, the existing exercise of religion "protected against all sorts of abolition and injury" (par. 63). Yet the denominational status quo guarantee was restricted by the proviso that the sovereign had the privilege of tolerating hitherto not admitted denominations in his land and of granting their followers "the full enjoyment of civil rights."

The compensatory transactions of secularization were, from an overall point of view, political instead of lawful ones, even though they were clad in the mantle of the basic law of the Empire by the Imperial delegates' final recess. "Few among the upheavals of state in modern history appear as ugly, as common, as low as this revolt of the princes of 1803" (Treitschke). Even such princes who had not suffered any territorial losses on the left bank of the Rhine, such as the archduke of Tuscany, the duke of Modena, and the hereditary governor of the Netherlands were awarded compensations by secularization. Secularized ecclesiastical territories and property also went to the Helvetian Federation, the imperial city of Frankfurt, and others. Frequently the loss bore no relationship to the compensation. Prussia, for example, received five times the compensation of its loss, Hesse-Darmstadt eight times, and Baden ten times.

An immediate political consequence of the secularization was that the ratio of Catholics to Protestants in the Imperial Diet shifted at the expense of the Catholics and that a decisive step was taken toward the removal of Austria from the Empire. The future political development was presaged by the territorial expansion of Prussia, Bavaria, Württemberg, Baden, and the two Hesses. Secularization placed the majority of those ecclesiastical states which were almost entirely Catholic under rulers of another denomination. The Protestant powers and the non-Catholic segment of the population were provided a numerical, political, and economic superiority and the foundation was laid for the typical diaspora situation of the Catholic population. The transition to parity was not without great tension and harsh disputes.

As a revolt of the princes and an attempt at state reform, secularization resulted in the elimination of the Church of the Empire, the end of the Empire itself, and of the German Middle Ages. The surviving temporal territories, now enlarged, strove to adapt their church organization to their state borders either by joining the secularized areas to already existing state bishoprics or by establishing their own state or "national bishoprics." According to the Imperial delegates' final recess a reorganization of the dioceses was to be undertaken by imperial law, but before the necessary foundation could be laid on the basis of law and concordats, the Empire ceased to exist as a result of Napoleon's dictum and the resignation of the imperial crown by Francis II. The reordering of the German church organization was then — if not put in doubt — at least pushed into a distant future and placed in the hands of the individual territories, whose late-absolutist, bureaucratic established church systems welcomed the fact that sees and cathedral chapters were now orphaned.

Prior to secularization the centers of the church administration had been situated in the imperially immediate, prince-episcopal areas. The established Churches of the temporal governments faced a final barrier in the sovereign independence of the imperial episcopate. At a time of vacant sees, following the secularization of the ecclesiastical states, the absolutist states were enabled to prevail in their claims vis-à-vis a powerless and disowned Church which was thoroughly shaken in its organization. The fifteen years between the Peace of Lunéville and the beginning of the vast circumscriptions were a period of more recent German church history, which had neither concordats nor bishops. By 1811 the German Church had all of nine bishops left, including those not in residence or living in exile; five of them were well into their seventies, Dalberg at the age of sixty-seven was one of the youngest. The cathedral chapters, largely deprived of their revenues, were dispersed here and there. Many capitulars had withdrawn to the quietude and obscurity of private life, demoralized and humiliated by the events. A regeneration of the chapters, whose members were all advanced in years, could not take place because the sustentation and pension obligation of the states extended only to those ecclesiastics who had been suspended from positions recognized by imperial law, but not to their successors. The German Church was threatened by anarchy. The vagaries of the times had uprooted the leadership of those nobles who were eligible for ecclesiastical office and had dispersed them in every direction. The feeling of humiliation, the distrust by Rome of advocates of Enlightenment and Febronianism, fear and the prospect of a dark future led to passivity and resignation. Those who were eager to get into the consistories and to seize the administration of the remainders of dioceses usually bowed, dumb and obsequious, to the established church system. For a considerable part of the regular clergy the transfer to collective monasteries ("Krepierinstitute") was not a good solution. The vacant sees, the negligent search, at times determined by the sovereign's desire for splendor, for one's own, if possible a "cheap" bishop — to quote the words of a minister of Nassau-Weilburg — the usurpation of episcopal rights, the expansion of the rights of sovereignty not only *circa sacra* but *in sacra* were elements, according to the mild-mannered bishop of Augsburg, Clemens Wenzeslaus, which constituted a fatal danger for the Church. It was largely due to the efforts of Prince-Primate von Dalberg that this danger was averted.

The closing of Catholic universities, schools, and orders had an extremely negative effect on the intellectual life of the Catholic population. The education of future clerics and an orderly ministry were put in doubt; the closings marked the downfall of episcopal culture in southern Germany and the beginning of the decline of Catholic education and culture. Henceforth the patronage by the ecclesiastically eligible nobility was lacking, as was the possibility for social, economic, and intellectual rise which entering the large monastic institutions and rich abbeys had offered the Catholic segment of the population. A most regrettable concomitant phenomenon was the cheap sale of works of art, libraries, manuscripts, and archives, the use for other purposes and the profanation of ecclesiastical structures. In Cologne more than fifty churches and chapels were torn down; some of the most precious library holdings in Trier were used for heating purposes; the tradition of rich artistic work, of respectable scholarly achievement among the Catholics was suddenly interrupted. The economic loss due to secularization was considerable. Redistribution of wealth — while it had been initiated before — reached a climax with the sale of church property.

In the period between secularization and its laboriously achieved legal position and relative freedom, the Church "instead of the scepter of lost sovereignty bore the cane of impotence and the crown of thorns of servitude" (J. Görres). But the loss of almost a thousand years of ballast, of feudal abuses, aristocratic exclusivity of the cathedral chapters and the episcopate, of nepotism, at times abundant, and of Frebronianism, connected with the favored position of the Church of the Empire, were beneficial to the Church. Fruitful impulses and forces from the very roots of religion and Church were freed in the bitter years following the secularization. The soil was prepared for the alliance of "Church and nation." Not only under the Napoleonic bishops, the zealous Colmar in Mainz, Mannay in Trier, Berdolet in Aachen, did new life begin to flourish in the Church, but even in the pseudo-constitutional states of the Rhenish Confederation as well. Within the powerless, impoverished Church, oppressed by the established church system, the concept of church unity and papal authority took on added strength. The new generation of clerics "had no home other than the Church" (Treitschke). The fight against episcopalism, Febronianism, established Church, and Wessenbergianism assumed a more determined character. The ecclesiastical space was tightened, as it were, and filled up from within by an atmosphere of struggle; it was quite frugal in comparison with the old Church of the Empire. "As a consequence of secularization the Church was more modern than the state which gave it lodging." In the nineteenth century it "was able to become the champion of an extraterritorial sphere of freedom, not intent on successes of the day vis-à-vis the omnipotence of the state" (W. H. Stuck).

Chapter 136

Attempts at Church Reunion

The outcome of the Thirty Years' War, which had, at least in part, been conducted as a religious war, and the stipulations of the Peace of Westphalia had all but dashed the expectation of a restoration of religious unity in the Empire. The irritant of a split Christianity had grown apace with the consolidation of denominational consciousness and denominational territories. But at the same time it had become less objectionable, since it denoted the triumph of politics in the widest sense over theology, the victory of state authority, and a beginning awareness in the German territories which indicated a shift from goals in the hereafter to the task in this world. The withdrawal from specifically religio-ecclesiastical tasks in the early absolutist territories began as a process of general secularization; in the leading segments of the population it started as a renunciation of the theological spirit of strife and disputatiousness, as indifferentism and skepticism in which rationalist and materialist ideas gained ground. Friedrich von Logau expressed the sentiments of his generation in his well-known distich: "Lutheranism, Papism, and Calvinism, these faiths, all three of them, are here; yet there is doubt where Christianity could be." The bitter words of the "Augsburg confusion" made the rounds. The different religious parties had to learn to coexist peacefully within the Empire, a laborious process full of quarrels and hatred among territories of different denominations. The political and military impotence in the face of the enemies of Christianity to the east and those of the Empire to the north and west, the *calamitas imperii,* was to some extent held to be a consequence of the denominational strife. For that reason plans for religious reunion on the one hand and reform in the Empire on the other had had some relationship with each other since the seventeenth century. This was also the case in the opposition of the Church of the Empire to Rome as well as in Pietism and Enlightenment. Motives of patriotism for the Empire, episcopalism, Pietism, and Enlightenment played concomitant and successive roles in the history of reunion projects, as did indifferentism, credulity, theological ignorance, and material and political interests.

"All dogmatic questions," admitted the philosophical wife of the bishop of Osnabrück, Sophie of the Palatinate, "touch my heart but little." To her, religion is love of God and one's neighbor, everything else is "a bunch of priestish squabbling, up to the princes to settle." Reasonable people are not bothered by it. Yet Sophie, like her religiously indifferent brother, Elector Karl Ludwig, who built the Concordia church in Mannheim and wanted to tolerate "all sorts of religions" in the Palatine electorate, discussed the possibility of conversion with her sister Louise Hollandine, the abbess of Maubuisson, and showed a massive material and political interest in reunion transactions.

Indifferentism, rationalism, and materialism on the one hand, religiosity (deepened by the dire straights of the Thirty Years' War), eschatological and pietistic currents, religio-ecclesiastical and political motives on the other are all in league with one another in the irenical efforts and those aimed at reunion. Tolerance became the political motto of state in the denominationally mixed territories and in the flourishing mercantilist thinking. The idea of the authority of the state began to surmount denominational limits and prejudice. The connection between the schism and the decline of the Empire, the question of religious reunion, reform of the Empire, and a European structure of peace were acute topics for discussion.

A bridge for reunion were those "in between things" (Latin chant, liturgical vestments, crucifixes, auricular confession, the hours), continued in the Lutheran Church and, above all, the Catholic canon law, to which the Protestant cathedral and collegiate chapters adhered "with admirable tenacity." Numerous historical relics also pointed to a reunion. These included the existence of mixed chapters in Strasbourg, Lübeck, Osnabrück; the observance of celibacy in Protestant institutions, the alternation in the archdiocese of Osnabrück and the effects of the Volmar list in the parish of Goldenstedt, where the pastor was Catholic, the sexton Protestant, and where the Protestants attended Catholic Mass in which songs from the Lutheran hymnal were sung.

After the Peace of Westphalia the different currents tending toward reunification all converged at the court of the senior ecclesiastical elector, the lord chancellor and *Primas Germaniae* in Mainz. Johann Philipp von Schönborn, the "German Solomon," his suffragan bishop Peter van Walenburch, and his minister of state Johann Christian von Boineburg, who defended the rights of the *Natio Germanica* against the Roman Curia, together with other irenicists and reunionists worked on reunion projects and promoted the reduction of denominational differences. Yet the so-called Mainz Plan for Reunion of 1660 is not likely to have originated with either the elector, Boineburg, or Leibniz; it is probably the product of Landgrave Ernst von Hessen-Rheinfels. As an intellectual broker of his time, a friend of Boineburg and the brothers Adrian and Peter van Walenburch from their Düsseldorf period, this prince was a member of the innermost circle of reunion politicians. By means of his worldwide correspondence, especially with Georg Calixt, Leibniz, Spener, Antoine Arnauld, Johannes Neercassel, the administrator of the Utrecht diocese, the reunionist dukes of the Guelfs, the nuncios in Cologne, and through numerous writings of his own he supported the efforts for reunion in his time.

In connection with his own conversion Landgrave Ernst, who had become familiar with the mediation theology of Georg Witzel in Vienna, brought together the theologians Eberhard Happel, Peter Haberkorn, Balthasar Menser, a fellow student of Boineburg's, and the famous Capuchin friar Valerian Magni for a religious discussion in December 1651 at his castle Rheinfels above Sankt Goar. In 1652 he set up a like discussion in Kassel between his confessor, the Jesuit Johannes Rosenthal, and Johannes Crocius, and a year later between Rosenthal and Haberkorn in Gießen. Although these three discussions had no tangible results other than unpleasant literary feuds for the landgrave and a campaign by the Jesuits against Valerian Magni because of his pronouncement at Rheinfels that the infallibility of the Pope as *ex solo sancto textu* could not be proved, the reunion of a split Christianity continued to be his primary and most important desire.

The connection with the Erasmian spirit and the Mainz efforts is manifest in the *Motiva Conversionis Ernesti Landgravii* by the brothers Adrian and Peter van Walenburch, and, more so, in the best-known work by the landgrave of Hesse-Rheinfels himself, the *Discrete Catholische.* According to his own testimony he wrote this work for all the Catholics and Protestants "whose hearts are sincerely touched by the grievous split in Christendom." Leibniz became familiar with the *Discrete Catholische* in his Mainz period and received important suggestions from it for his own efforts toward reunion. He thought the book contained an exhortation to the Protestants that they were obliged to seek reunification with the Catholic Church with all their strength, but also a challenge to the Catholics to smooth the path for reunion by eliminating the abuses and by bringing about a true reform.

After Mainz under the reign of Johann Philipp von Schönborn the courts of Braunschweig-Lüneburg were the most fertile and receptive soil for reunion in the last third of the seventeenth century. This had primarily political as well as denominational, personal, and ideological reasons. Duke Johann Friedrich of Hanover (d. 1679), who had converted to the Catholic Church in Rome in 1650, had close connections to the reunionist *aula laboriosa* of the Mainz elector Johann Philipp. Leibniz's entering the service of the duke of Hanover was due in some measure to the assistance of Landgrave Ernst von Hessen-Rheinfels. The latter, moreover, supported the Catholic succession in Hanover.

The expectation that negotiations in Hanover would lead to reunion proved to be unfounded when the Catholic Duke Johann Friedrich was succeeded by his denominationally indifferent brother Ernst August, who was interested solely in expanding his power. When he was still pseudo-bishop of Osnabrück and then again as duke of Hanover after 1679 he repeatedly made vaguely formulated offers for his or his sons' conversion to Catholicism in exchange for the secularization of Hildesheim and the cancellation of the alternation in the diocese of Osnabrück in favor of his house. The Hanover negotiations of 1683 played a particular role in the reunion attempted by the bishop of Tina, Christoph de Rojas y Spinola. This reunion was supported by Emperor Leopold primarily for political reasons and encouraged by Clement X and Innocent XI. While the danger posed by the Turks in the east grew to alarming proportions and more and more territories were lost by reunions in the west, discussions took place in Hanover between Spinola, Walter Molanus, the abbot of Loccum, the younger Calixt, and Theodor Mayer. But a firm programmatic draft could not be obtained. Among the concessions from the Lutheran side were: celibacy for the pastors, provided the existing marriages were recognized, infallibility of the councils, recognition of the Pope as the visible head of the Church, the presence of Christ in the Eucharist and submission to a future universal council. Additional demands raised by Molanus in 1683, the resistance of the French party in Rome, who feared that reunion would strengthen the Empire, and, lastly, the fact that the "sacred cause" was subordinated to the power politics of the Guelfs led to the failure of Spinola's efforts. As Landgrave Ernst wrote in a letter to Spener and in his memoranda to Duke Anton Ulrich von Wolfenbüttel and to Leibniz, the two parties were *"in principiis et suppositis* too far apart from each other," separated by political interests, for theological issues according to the opinion of the court of Hanover were mere insignificant details.

Attempts by Spinola to eliminate the denominational tensions in Hungary failed as well, nor did the union negotiated by his successor at Wiener Neustadt, Bishop Franz Anton von Buchheim, Leibniz and Molanus in 1686 come about. In the meantime Rome's reticence became more and more manifest. The political situation, influenced by the expulsion of the Huguenots, the religious clause in the Peace of Rijswijk (1697), and the expectation of a Hanoverian succession in England were unfavorable to a reunion.

There was no notable reaction to the *Friedreiche Gedanken über die Religionsvereinigung in Teutschland* (1679) by Johann Friedrich Ignaz Karg von Bebenburg, the future supreme chancellor of the Cologne electorate and abbot of Saint-Michel au Péril de la Mer (in the diocese of Avranches). Irenics and polemics were merged in the *Via pacis* (1686) by the Capuchin friar Dionysius of Werl. *Libertas ecclesiae Germanicae* and reunion in the faith by restoration of the "original" pre-Hildebrandian church constitution were the goals of the Protestant canonist Johannes Schilter in his seven books about the freedom of the German Church modeled on the *Declaratio Cleri Gallicani.* According to testimony by the Trier minister of state J. G. von Spangenberg, friend and collaborator of Hontheim, and by Marshal B. F. von Zurlauben, the Febronian ideas were gleaned at least in part from Schilter's work.

The sermons by the Jesuit Jean Dez in Strasbourg and his book *La réunion des Protestants de Strasbourg à l'Église Romaine,* translated into German by the convert Ulrich Obrecht, attempted to demonstrate that there was no obstacle to reunification and that the *Confessio Augustana* contained nothing un-Catholic. The suggestions for a reunion by the Königsberg professor Praetorius and especially his recognition of the papal primacy which he pronounced in the preface of his *Tuba pacis* (1685) after his conversion to the Catholic Church encountered opposition in Protestant Germany. The Helmstedt theologian Johann Fabricius, as did Praetorius, lost his chair at the university because he was made responsible for the expert opinion written in 1707 in connection with the conversion of Elisabeth Christine von Braunschweig-Wolfenbüttel and her marriage to Archduke Karl, the future Emperor. The Helmstedt theological faculty had stated: "We are convinced that the Catholics are the same as the Protestants and that the quarrels among them amount only to words. The basis of religion is also found in the Roman Catholic Church; one can be orthodox there, live right, die well and obtain salvation. Princess von Wolfenbüttel therefore can accept the Catholic religion for the purpose of promoting the intended marriage." As the "abbot of Königslutter," Fabricius continued to work for the idea of a religious reunification. In 1704 he published a *Via ad pacem ecclesiasticam* invoking Cassander, Witzel and Bossuet he presented the differences between the Catholics, Lutherans and Reformed as minor.

Bossuet's *Exposition de la doctrine chrétienne* (1671), which was to have the function of reclaiming the Huguenots, gave an impulse to controversial theology. Seven years later, in 1678, he started his correspondence with Leibniz. It was interrupted for a while and then resumed through Duchess Sophie of Hanover, her sister Louise Hollandine, abbess of Maubuisson, the latter's secretary Mme de Brinon, and the duchess' niece Benedicta Henrietta, who had withdrawn to Maubuisson following the death of her husband, Johann Friedrich, duke of Hanover. Parallel to Leibniz's exchange of ideas with Bossuet was his correspondence with the convert and court historiographer of Louis XIV, Pellison, and — through mediation by Ernst von Hessen-Rheinfels — with the great Jansenist Antoine Arnauld. Pellison's *Réflexions sur les différends en matière de religion,* Bossuet's monumental *Histoire des variations des Églises protestantes* (1688), and Arnauld's zealous unionism marked a promising point of departure for religious discussion. But the difficulties bound to be encountered were sufficiently characterized by the ambivalence in the behavior of the most important among the discussants.

Leibniz wanted religious unity as a condition for a European union based on Christianity first, and only then have the dogmatic issues solved by a lawful council, similar to Basel. Bossuet suggested the reverse way. The Council of Trent could not but enter into the center of the discussion: Leibniz considered it the most serious obstacle to a reunion, for Bossuet it was a position which he could not surrender. In vain Leibniz invoked patriotic motives, the Gallican provisos, the refusal by Catherine de Medici and Henry IV to recognize the council. He also argued that there existed a widespread tendency in the Church of the Empire, especially in the archdiocese of Mainz, either to ignore or even to reexamine and reject the Council of Trent. Leibniz's efforts failed because of resistance on the part of Bossuet, who in defending the Council of Trent was also defending the infallibility of the Church.

The traditional line of denominational power struggles apparently reemerged more strongly during the waning seventeenth and early eighteenth centuries: under William of Orange in England, with the persecution of the Huguenots in France, the Palatine religious quarrel and the "acts of revenge" by the Protestant territories in the Empire, the counterreformational actions of the Habsburgs in Silesia, and, finally, the Toggenburg tumults and the second war of Villmerg in Switzerland. By their ambivalent nature these events demonstrate in the one hand a revival of denominational differences and on the other a tendency toward pacification, tolerance, and equality. But a dismantling of denominationalism by means of enlightenment and tolerance alone could not revitalize the overall efforts, which had become noticeably weaker since the failure of the discussions between Leibniz and Bossuet.

On the Catholic side some hopes were connected with the conversion of Protestant princes, as in the case of Hontheim-Febronius and the Benedictine Karl von Piesport, who evinced great interest in the reunion with the Eastern Churches around the middle of the century and who was substantially involved in the Fulda plan for reunification.

In his anniversary bull of 5 May 1749, Pope Benedict XIV reiterated his desire for the reunification of Christendom. Cardinal Angelo Maria Quirini discussed Cardinal Reginald Pope's ideas for reunion with Johann Georg Schellhorn; with Johann Rudolf Kiesling he discussed Cardinal Contarini's doctrine of justification. When Johann Joseph von Trautson became archbishop of Vienna he took steps to bring the denominations closer together.

Attempts to overcome the "unnatural separation" of the Small Church after the Council of Utrecht in 1763 climaxed in the efforts by the acolyte Gabriel Dupac de Bellegarde (1717–89) at the courts of the German prince-bishops, the court of Vienna, and in Rome. Dupac de Bellegarde, in the canonical tradition of van Espen — he published Espen's biography in 1767 — was profoundly influenced by Antoine Arnauld. He reintroduced the transfigured concept of the *Ecclesia primitiva,* combined with a strong anti-Roman sentiment, to the episcopalists of the Church of the Empire, to the reformists and reunionists. He was able to call on the support of the most prominent Würzburg canonist, Johann Kaspar Barthel, and the Fulda Benedictine Karl von Piesport; his efforts were applauded by the reformists in Mainz, Passau, Laibach, and the Jansenists-Josephinists de Haen, Wittola and van Swieten in Vienna.

Whether or to what extent the Utrecht views had any influence on the reunification ideas of the *Febronius* can not yet be said with any degree of assurance. At any rate, the Utrecht cleric followed the Febronian disputes and the revocation affair with great interest and was persistently identified with Febronianism and its consequences by his contemporaries.

When Febronius' *De statu ecclesiae* was finally published, reunification, the exclusive, dominating concern in the original concept, was pushed into the background by the problems involving the rights of the Church of the Empire. Reunification was to be achieved by the elimination of the *gravamina* and the reduction of the papal primacy within the limits drawn by the original church constitution and newly circumscribed by the Councils of Constance and Basel and the *Concordata Nationis Germanicae.* Aside from the Utrecht influences, Hontheim's ideas for reunion can be explained from two roots: the tradition of the Church of the Empire and imperial patriotism as well as the personal impulses he received from his friend and collaborator, the convert Jakob Georg von Spangenberg. Even after his conversion to the Catholic Church Spangenberg's ideas were still largely determined by the late medieval-pietistic Christ mysticism, by Pietism and the Church of the Bohemian Brothers, whose episcopal head was his youngest brother August Gottlieb, and by his very personal form of piety. The Swabian Pietist Moser characterized him as God's very own creature from childhood on; the Viennese privy councillor Adolf von Krufft called him the only confidant of the Febronian secrets. The experience of Spangenberg's own life and his patriotism for the Empire must have made him feel very painfully the abuses of the church constitution and the *Calamitas Imperii,* prompting his desire for a reconciliation of denominational differences and yet — two decades after the appearance of the *Febronius* — reject the Fulda plan for reunion.

No doubt Febronius — as the Protestant opponents of his ideas such as Walch, Bahrdt, C. G. Hofmann, and also the Heidelberg Jesuit J. Kleiner explained to him — did not sufficiently recognize the divisive elements of the denominations and exaggerated the common ones out of anti-Roman sentiments and a confirmed patriotism for the Empire. His "Romantic" attitude, strengthened by his intensive historical studies, hoped that the problems of his own time could be solved through the contrast of a past historical epoch of idealized early Christian and medieval conditions. But even "if the Roman Church were to be given the shape which Febronius wants so laboriously to give it and in the process the Roman-Catholic doctrine and its pure source, the tradition so highly praised by Febronius, were to remain unchanged," the unification of the divided Christians would be impossible. The suggestions by Febronius were not judged quite so negatively by Abbot Jerusalem and Friedrich Karl von Moser. The latter publicized Spangenberg's credo and the reunion projects of 1614 and 1640 in his *Patriotisches Archiv* and defended Hontheim's honest desire for reunion.

Whether the plan for reunion was only of secondary importance to Febronius or whether — according to testimony by Martin Gerber — "he was convinced that everything possible had to be sacrificed to peace and Christian unity" has not yet been determined. Febronius' idea of striving for reunion on the basis of a purified canon law and a reformed church constitution was encountered at the court of the Mainz electorate in 1771, contained in the theses of the barrister Betzel, the canonist Benedikt Oberhauser from Fulda, in the writings of Ulrich Mayr from Kaisheim, and in the programmatic essay on reunion by Beda Mayr from Donauwörth. The elector of Trier, Clemens Wenzeslaus, repeatedly demonstrating his concern for the elimination of the Utrecht schism in his talks with the Cologne nuncios, nonetheless condemned Mayr's "scrittura scandalose sul pretesto della reunione coi Protestanti" in his capacity as bishop of Augsburg. Yet shortly thereafter in his famous pastoral letter of 1780, coauthored by Johann Michael Sailer, he called the return of those "separated from the faith into the one sheeps' pen of Christ" one of the most pressing concerns. But in this pastoral letter he is far from paving the way for reunion by dogmatic compromise or invoking Febronian or Jansenist ideas. "The doctrine of the Church has always been one and the same," and the Pope as Christ's deputy has always been charged with the unity of the Church and the purity of the doctrine. At the same time, the religious journals of the ex-Jesuit Hermann Goldhagen and the schoolteacher Johann Kaspar Mülle of Mainz, and also the enlightened journal of the Benedictine monks of Banz had reservations regarding reunification. Heretofore they had invariably published favorable and detailed reports about the literature of reunion, but now they joined Martin Gerbert of Sankt Blasien in the conclusion that a reunification of the Churches would be possible only by a return to the Catholic Church. All three parts were to be either Roman Catholic or eternally separated.

Among the numerous more or less successful attempts at reunion in the last third of the eighteenth century the Fulda Plan was the best known and also the strangest one. In 1768 the correspondence concerning a particular case of conversion to the Catholic Church between the Fulda Benedictine Karl von Piesport and Rudolph Wedekind, a professor in Göttingen and parish priest at the Church of Our Lady, suggested an association "to unite the warring factions of the faith." Although Piesport as an episcopalist was ready "in good conscience" to give in on the issue of papal infallibility and almost implored Wedekind to "Let us conciliate; let us compromise," the latter suggested breaking off this fruitless exchange because "Doctrine, rationality and church history have to take precedence over the Pope and the council."

But a decade later the climate for discussions had become more favorable by virtue of the general mood for tolerance and the threat of the Enlightenment, which was hostile to revealed religion. The efforts to bring about reunion were no doubt partly prompted by the ferment of a "negative" union, recognizable by the growing fear of additional schisms threatened by the abused "Protestant principle" and by growing admiration for the strength of the resistance and unity of the Catholic Church. As indicated in the introduction by a Benedictine monk from Fulda to *Aurelius Augustinus, Von der Nutzbarkeit des Glaubens* (1771), a future ideological front is discernible. A generation later Adam Müller, Carl Ludwig von Haller, and after them Ludwig von Gerlach and Carl Maria von Radowitz tried to establish this front by means of a reunion of faithful Catholics and Protestants or at least by drawing them closer together for the defense of "the most sacred properties" against revolution and radicalism.

In 1778/79 the plan for the formation of a private association emerged from the collaboration between five Benedictine monks in Fulda under the direction of Petrus Böhm and Johann Rudolph Piderit, professor at the Carolinum at Kassel. The association was to contribute to the reunion of the divided denominations. According to the statutes drawn up by Piderit, a committee of twelve members — six Catholic, three Calvinist, and three Lutheran theologians — in an atmosphere of "sincerity and Christian love" were to discuss the truths of the faith, formulate the differences, and investigate the possibilities for restoring harmony.

Reservations were soon announced by Johann Schmitt, a professor of theology at Mainz. The influential Kasimir Haeffelin in Mannheim reacted negatively. His friend, the abbot and librarian Maillot de la Treille, an opponent of Febronianism who used his good connections with the ultramontanes in Alsace to firm up the ecclesiastical defense from Strasbourg to Trier against the innovations of his time, raised the alarm with nuncio Garampi in Vienna. As a result of the negative reaction by the courts of Mannheim and Mainz, the solicitation of the association in Trier, Coblenz, Cologne, and Erfurt were unsuccessful. Even Spangenberg, who had provided the strongest impulses to Hontheim's reunion efforts, rejected the plan; the theologian Johann Gertz from Trier had growing doubts concerning the efficacy of such a heterogeneous association and terminated his participation in January 1782. It was alleged that Stephan Alexander Würdtwein, later suffragan bishop of Worms, was recruited to take the place of the Mainz theologian Schmitt. The prince-abbot of Sankt Blasien, Martin II Gerbert, refused his participation, and the enlightened Abbot Stefan Rautenstrauch from Braunau distanced himself when a negative review appeared in the Vienna *Realzeitung* and Emperor Joseph II, Kaunitz, and Cardinal Herzan did not react to the reunion project. There was hardly any need for the papal letter to Prince-Bishop Heinrich VIII of Bibra to make the efforts by the Benedictines of Fulda founder. Disregarding the instructions of their bishop, they maintained the connections with their Protestant partners. But the Lutherans and Calvinists were unable to agree on a common dogma and as a consequence news of he "Fulda Plan" stopped appearing after the fall of 1782.

In the last third of the eighteenth century a positive attitude toward reunion was furthered by the promotion of tolerance on the part of the Enlightenment and by its concept of an understanding and forgiving humanity. The differences between the denominations were to be reduced to the simple basic tenets of a natural religion with the help of an increasingly secularized education. In his *Betrachtungen über das Universum* Karl Theodor von Dalberg posed the question whether the time had not come to get closer to "the original Church," to the union of the "different religious parties." Christoph von Schmidt wanted to see the controversial sermons, which had been forbidden according to the Josephinist model, in the archdioceses of Cologne and Trier replaced by "union sermons" in order to "convince the Christian people that we are one in all the essentials of Christianity."

The interdenominational irenic efforts toward the end of the eighteenth century received strong impulses from the ex-Jesuit Benedikt Stattler. In his *Demonstratio catholica,* edited and published several times by his pupil Johann Michael Sailer, but primarily in his *Plan* (1781) he emphatically advocated reunion; not "in the heat of disputation" but only "in love" could this goal "of common longing" be achieved. Only dogma was to be obligatory, theories were to be voluntarily accepted. But Stattler did set one condition for Protestants in the case of a reunion: "humble submission under the unerring judgment of the Church in every matter of faith." Stattler's *Kanones der Union* were condemned in Rome, but the procedure and publication of the condemnation were delayed until 1796 because the bishop of Eichstätt took Stattler's part.

With Stattler's pupil Johann Michael Sailer (1751–1832) and his followers in Dillingen and Augsburg, in Switzerland and northern Germany the irenic mood reached a climax. Sailer saw the way to unify the Church in emulating Christ's comprehensive self-sacrificing love. The Romantic philosopher Franz von Baader interpreted the denominational splits as a mere transitional stage on the way to a higher unity, introducing an idea into the interdenominational discussions that was pursued by Sebastian Drey and by Joseph Görres until well into the latter's Strasbourg period. Johann Nikolaus Friedrich Bauer (d. 1813) attempted to take a step in the direction of reunion with the help of "sovereign reform authority." He established a theological faculty at the University of Heidelberg consisting of nine professors of all three denominations, but in 1807 the Catholic faculty members left to join the University of Freiburg. Enlightened and irenic concepts merged in the desire for reunion of Prince-Primate Karl Theodor von Dalberg, his vicar general from Constance, Ignaz Heinrich von Wessenberg, and their friends.

Political and nationalist motives played a role in the attempt by the archbishop of Besançon to glorify the coronation of Napoleon by a reunion of the denominations. The extent to which such motives were connected with the desire for reunification in Germany at the beginning of the nineteenth century, a desire fed by the Enlightenment and older roots, is shown not only by the passionate discussion of the writings of Claude Le Coz and Beaufort of the reception of the history of reunion attempts written by Mathieu Tabaraud (1808), but also by the contribution of the last abbot of Michelfeld, Maximilian Prechtl. "From his personal conviction that the religious upheaval of the sixteenth century was either the immediate or secondary cause of most of the political and ecclesiastical storms, including the most recent secularization," he attempted to establish "in the religious unification of Germany the best, albeit not the only means and main conditions for forceful resistance against the nascent universal Napoleonic rule." Among the irenic efforts in the conservative Prussian camp, in the Christian Germanic circles, and elsewhere the striving for denominational unity was henceforth most intimately connected with the striving for national unity. The historian and conservative politician Heinrich Leo saw the fusion of religious reunification and national unity in the nineteenth century more distinctly than Radowitz and Diepenbrock had: "Whoever wants a German state must first have a unified strong German Church again — this has been taught by six centuries of history" (H.-J. Schoeps).

CHAPTER 137

Ecclesiastical Learning in the Eighteenth Century—Theology of Enlightenment and Pietism

Catholic Theology

In the history of theology the period from the middle of the seventeenth to the middle of the eighteenth century marks the decline of Scholasticism; Grabmann speaks of an epigonal period. While the achievements of earlier generations were diligently collected and promulgated in compendia and textbooks, hardly anything new was added. And yet in a broad context this period was not without its own characteristics. Even the fact that moral theology was separated from dogmatics points toward growth. The theology of the period was strongly influenced by the requirements of practical ministry. Linked to medieval confessional handbooks and not without the influence of canonist tendencies, it constructed a case theory which was intended to facilitate the decisions in actual cases. To be sure, the realization of Christian faith is substantially depersonalized by this and one might well regret that such phenomena as laxism, the moral dispute over probabilism, and probabiliorism emerged. Yet behind all of it was a forceful attempt to cope with everyday problems. Moreover, the possibility of development in the area of ethical norms is visible. Parallel to all this was the great genesis of historical research which laid foundations especially in the field of Catholic theology. Since all the facts were important to them the historiographers of the baroque compiled an immense mass of materials, but they also devised methods in the science of history which are still alive. And, lastly, the Enlightenment stimulated new branches of theological science, such as scriptural science, religious science, pastoral theology with its subcategories, liturgics, catechetics, and homiletics. It is not hard to see a common element behind all these phenomena: theological speculation decreased, but actual church life was more decisively included in theological cognition. The entire situation, moreover, opened possibilities for theological points of departure which were no longer limited to the foundations derived from antiquity or the ideas of the Middle Ages.

Speculative theology was not, of course, totally extinguished; many a name is still deserving of mention. But none can be compared with the great theologians of the Middle Ages or the Spaniards of the late sixteenth or early seventeenth century. There was still a confrontation of the old theological schools. Thomism was represented by the Benedictines of Salzburg, among them Paul Mezger (1637–1702) and Ludwig Babenstuber (1660–1715) by Dominicans such as Cardinal Vincenzo Ludovico Gotti (1664–1742) Hyacinth Drouin (1680–1740) and Bernardo Maria de Rossi (1687–1775). Among the Jesuits we must mention especially the Spanish Cardinal Álvaro Cienfuegos (1657–1739) because of his special doctrine of the sacrifice of the Mass. From 1766 to 1777 four members of the Society of Jesus, professors of the University of Würzburg, wrote a remarkable *Theologia Wirceburgenis* with reference to positive-theological and speculative elements. Its concerns were presented almost simultaneously and in similar fashion by the Spanish Jesuit J. B. Genér (1711–81). A theology resembling Augustinianism was offered by August Reding (1625–92) of Salzburg, who later became abbot of Einsiedeln; Enrico Noris and Giovanni Laurenzio Berti (1696–1766) were the main representatives of the younger Augustinian school. The Franciscan Claude Frasien (1620–1711), as much as he based his ideas on Aristotle, was a Scotist. The Capuchin theologians generally went back to Bonaventure. Interest in Raymond Lull was also revived: Ivo Salzinger (1669–1728) suggested a new edition of his works (1721–42). The most important Lullist of the century, Antonio Raymundo Pascual y Flexas (1708–91) spent some time in Mainz before continuing on to Palma di Mallorca, where he worked for some decades. From the large field of controversial theology we should single out the *Ecclesiologia* (1677) by the convert Johannes Scheffler, who also created an immortal body of religious poetry under the name of Angelus Silesius.

There were times when a question of moral theology excited the seventeenth century: when there was serious doubt concerning the existence of a moral law, probabilism offered the possibility of a free decision if there were probable reasons for it. A stricter view demanded more probable reasons (probabiliorism, tutiorism); a milder view admitted weak reasons (laxism). The systematic foundation of probabilism goes back to Bartholomaeus de Medina (1577). His views were frequently represented by Dominicans and Jesuits. De Medina and all the variations of laxism were opposed by the Jansenists, especially by Blaise Pascal. In 1665 and 1666 Alexander VII condemned laxism, as did Innocent XI in 1679; Alexander VIII opposed tutiorism in 1690.

Practical need alone would have prompted the growth of works in the new field of moral theology; among the many authors there were some whose works were reprinted a number of times. Unfortunately, we must limit ourselves to a mere few of them. The most respected moral theologian was Alphonsus Liguori (1696–1787) whose influence endured for a century and a half. His harmonizing *Theologia moralis* (1748) was based on Busenbaum; he was an equiprobabilist, entirely fulfilled by the idea of God's mercy; his *Homo apostolicus* (1757) is constructed primarily by the casuistic method.

The great period of emotional mysticism had passed and none had an effect like Teresa of Ávila or John of the Cross. Yet this century of religiosity, moved by various baroque forms in which a comprehensive mode of Pietism crystallized among the Protestant believers, was not without examples of a profoundly religious life and ascetic discipline; John Eudes (1601–80) and Jean Jacques Olier (1608–57) *et al.*

The severe change in the intellectual life of the period which we designate as the "Enlightenment" could, of course, not remain without impact on the concepts of systematic theology. After 1740 Cartesian ideas and those of Leibniz, presented in the rationalistic form of Christian Wolff, whose philosophy predominated among the Protestant thinkers of the time until the arrival of Kant, were frequently though eclectically used among the Catholics as well and had to be confronted with traditional speculative theology. The Augustinian friar Eusebius Amort (1692–1775), a prolific author, who was also interested in natural sciences, worked in a historicocritical manner. Using the Scriptures intensively, he combined tradition with the new and applied a simplified Scholastic method to his work. As a moral theologian he was an equiprobabilist akin to Alphonsus Liguori. The writings of the Ingolstadt Jesuit Benedikt Stattler (1728–97), the teacher of

Johann Michael Sailer, are characterized by an impressive universal conception. His *Demonstratio evangelica* (1770) and *Demonstratio catholica* (1775), although stylistically ponderous, should be mentioned for their strict methodology if for no other reason. In 1788 he wrote an *Anti-Kant.* In the end he was subjected to church censorship and received little attention until recently, when he evoked renewed esteem. But there were some confirmed rationalists, such as Lorenz Isenbiehl (1744–1818; exegete and author of *Neuer Versuch über Weissagung von Emmanuel* [1778]) and Felix Anton Blau (1754–98; a dogmatist), both of them professors in Mainz, and Franz Berg (1753–1821), a confirmed skeptic in spite of his anti-Kantian position.

By combining Kant's categorical imperative and the biblical commandment of love, Sebastian Mutschelle (1749–1800) tried to establish a new speculative moral theology. After the condemnation of Jakob Danzer (1743–96) because of his *Anleitung zur christlichen Moral* (1787), the University of Salzburg was dominated once more by Scholasticism. The exegete Thaddäus Anton Dereser (1757–1827) had a broad impact with his *Erbauungsbuch für alle Christen auf alle Tage des Kirchenjahres* (1792). In 1813 the liturgist Vitus Anton Winter (1754–1814) published a *Deutsches kath. ausübendes Ritual* which manifested the rationalist spirit of the time more than any other contemporary work. But there were also some effective opponents of rationalism, among them Hermann Goldhagen (1718–94), with his *Religionsjournal* (1776–94; edited by the professors of Mainz), and Franz Oberthür (1745–1831), who was an opponent of Scholasticism but nonetheless in favor of a biblical theology. Gregor Zirkel (1762–1817), suffragan bishop of Würzburg after 1812, who was initially a Kantian, became a representative of a positive Catholicism. *Das Wichtigste für Eltern, Lehrer und Seelsorger* (1786) by Aegidius Jais (1750–1822) was the best example of sex education in the period of Enlightenment. Together with Johann Michael Sailer, Jais was instrumental in overcoming the rationalism of that period.

The departure into new fields of theological learning toward an overall consolidation of church history started at the turn of the seventeenth century. It was the Maurist congregation in France whose ranks provided the most prominent personalities in the field of historical research, foremost among them Mabillon. During the eighteenth century church history continued to flourish in France. Whereas the *Selecta historiae ecclesiasticae capita* (1676–86) by the Dominican Alexander Natalis, the first comprehensive church history of the modern era, was still written in a polemical and apologetical fashion, the frequently translated *Histoire ecclésiastique* (1691–1720) by the secular priest Claude Fleury (1640–1723) was influenced by Mabillon and Tillemont, showing close attention to the sources and a pleasant style. Although it had a broad effect, it also provoked criticism because of its Gallican tendencies. While these church histories were written, work continued on the sources. The Jesuit Philippe Labbé (1607–67) edited the *Sacrosancta Concilia* (1671–72), providing it with valuable annotations. He was followed by his fellow monk Jean Hardouin (1646–1729), whose *Conciliorum collectio regia maxima* (1714–15) represented a more reliable edition than that of Mansi. Jacques Goar (1601–53) was among the first to establish Byzantinistics, a field to which Charles Dufresne Sieur Du Cange (1610–88) also dedicated himself. An indispensable contribution to the field of church history is Du Cange's *Glos-*

sarium ad scriptores mediae et infirmae latinitatis (1678). In 1715–16 the cleric Eusèbe Renaudot (1648–1720) published his *Liturgiarum Orientalium Collectio.* Especially prominent among the Maurists were Gabriel Gerberon (1628–1711), who suggested the controversial edition of Saint Augustine; and Achery's and Mabillon's pupil Edmond Martène (1654–1739) with his *Commentar zur Regel des heiligen Benedikt* (1690) and his work in liturgics. In the field of exegesis there were Augustin Calmet's (1672–1757) *Dictionnaire historique... de la Bible* (1719) and Pierre Sabatier's (1683–1742) fundamental work on the *Vetus Latina, Bibliorum sacrorum versiones antiquae* (1743–49). In the area of patristics Pierre Coustant (1654–1721) published an edition of Hilarius (1693); Remy Ceillier (1688–1761) created a comprehensive *Histoire générale des auteurs sacrés et ecclésiastiques* (1729–63).

In the Netherlands Daniel Papebroch (1628–1714) persisted in his work on the *Acta sanctorum* of Johannes Bollandus, which differentiated between the older and newer sources. Papebroch established a methodology for hagiography and very strict rules for paleography, too strict in fact to be maintained. The Augustinian Hermit Christian Lupus (1612–81) of Louvain occupied himself with the provincial councils in his *Synodorum Generalium ac Provincialium decreta et canones* (1665). The Maurists had a profound influence on the scholarly efforts of the Benedictines in southern Germany. The first great mediator was Bernhard Pez (1683–1735) of Melk, who had the help of his brother Hieronymus (1685–1762). His fundamental works are *Bibliotheca Benedictino-Mauriana* (1716) and *Bibliotheca ascetica antiquo-nova* (1721–29). Historically more important were the efforts of the abbot of Göttweig, Gottfried Bessel (1672–1749); his prodromus on the *Chronicon Gottwicense* (1732) represents a first general German diplomatics. In collaboration with Pez and Bessel, Magnoald Ziegelbauer (1689–1750) of Zwiefalten worked on a source edition for the history of the Benedictine order. Anselm Desing (1699–1772) later the abbot of Ensdorf, worked in the spirit of the Maurists at the University of Salzburg, where Frobenius Forster (1709–1791) was one of his colleagues. As the abbot of Sankt Emmeram in Regensburg, Forster led this monastery to a high scholarly level; his edition of Alcuin (1777) won acclaim throughout Europe. Marquart Herrgott (1694–1762) visited the Maurists for personal instruction; after his *Vetus disciplina Monastica* (1726) he directed his efforts to the history of the archdynasty of Austria. Through him Sankt Blasien became a center of historical studies. Martin Gerbert (1720–93) abbot after 1764 became the most prominent of this group of Benedictines from the Black Forest through his works in liturgics and the history of music; his efforts ale indispensable even today: *Iter alemannicum* (1765) *De cantu et musica sacra* (1774) *Monumenta veteris liturgicae Alemanniae* (1777–79) and *Scriptores ecclesiastici de musica sacra* (1784). His most important undertaking was to organize the edition of a *Germania sacra.* With it he continued the effort of the Viennese Jesuit Markus Hansiz (1683–1765; *Germania sacra* [1727–58]), which had also been pursued by the Cologne Jesuit Joseph Hartzheim (1694–1762) in the field of the councils by his edition of the *Concilia Germaniae* (1759–63). The eight volumes of the Sankt Blasien *Germania sacra* appeared from 1790 to 1803; this promising endeavor was abruptly ended by secularization.

The new discipline of pastoral theology, at first also called practical theology —

pastoral theology taking over some practical fields hitherto served by moral theology — was not founded extensively on actual theological ideas. Instead it was shaped by the image of man and the world on the basis of common sense using the Bible and the Fathers "for useful remarks concerning the unselfish execution of the office of a minister." It was lacking a pneumatic concept of the Church. Sailer was the one who finally resorted to biblical foundations, seeking genuine Christocentricity. In fact, the first pastoral theologies were devoid of actual theology. Even the basic idea of a shepherd confronted by a herd he is to lead was inadequate, especially so if the minister was considered merely as a "servant of religion" and the "pastoral" as a description of the duties of his office. The weaknesses in this initial attempt were not overcome until the Tübingen school developed its more genuine concept of the Church (Anton Graf, 1841).

The individual disciplines in the pastoral field did not arrive at a truly scientific theology either. The oldest, liturgics, had been blessed with an abundance of sources since the seventeenth century, but did not evaluate them correspondingly. Catechetics, which proceeded radically against the existing method of memorization in Christology, was not provided with a theological foundation until the work of Johann Joseph Augustin Gruber (1832), in spite of the relatively good start by Johann Ignaz von Felbiger (1724–88; in 1767 he also published the first Catholic school Bible in German) and Michael Ignaz Schmidt (1736–94, *Methodus tradendi prima elementa religionis...* [1769]). In the field of homiletics the ex-Jesuit Ignaz Wurz (1727–84) became the most prominent scholar in the German language with his *Anleitung zur geistlichen Beredsamkeit* (Vienna 1775); he based his approach entirely on the great French forerunners such as Bossuet, Bourdaloue, Massillon and de la Rue. But homiletics did not become a science until the nineteenth century.

For a time the eighteenth century also promulgated the concept of pastoral medicine (M. A. Alberti, 1732 [Halle] and J. M. Matthiae, 1734 [Göttingen] among the Protestants; F. E. Cangiamilia, 1751 [Milan] among the Catholics). But toward the end of the century it was replaced by the concept of a *medicina ruralis* which provided for the training of rural clerics to help out as doctors where none was available.

Scholarship in Italy

While the great speculative minds in post-Tridentine theology were in Spain, the first steps in historical theology were taken in Italy. The challenge of the Magdeburg Centurists was answered by Baronius and continued in Italy as well by Raynald and Laderchi. The Venetian Sarpi turned his attention to the most recent events; his history of the Council of Trent is a very sober account, yet full of antipapal tendencies which Pallavicino tried to counter. The first Christian archeologist worked in Bosio; Lippomani created a prodromus of the *Acta sanctorum.* Lucas Wadding (1588–1657) an Irish Franciscan who lived in Rome for forty years, created the first scholarly history of the religions orders in his *Annales* (1627–54) and the *Scriptores Ordinis Minorum* (1650). The *Italia sacra* (1644–62) by the Cistercian Ferdinando Ughelli (1594–1670), categorized by dioceses, was the first church history of its kind and a model for the *Gallia christiana* and Gerbert's *Germania sacra*. This form of historiography is an especially impressive testimony of the importance ascribed to the history of the institutions by Catholic church historiography. Cardinal Enrico Noris, an Augustinian Hermit, (1631–1704) is considered the father of the younger Augustinian school. Not only was he a historian, but he was also very much involved in the emotional issues of his time concerning the interpretation of the Augustinian doctrine of grace. Yet his *Historica Pelagiana* (1673) is a superior achievement in the history of dogmatics. The Theatine Cardinal Joseph Maria Tomasi (1649–1714) published comprehensive collections of sources in the field of patristics and the history of liturgics: the *Codices Sacramentorum* (1680), *Responsalia et Antiphonaria* (1686), *Antiqui libri Missarum* (1691), and *Institutiones theologicae antiquorum Patrum* (1709–12). The Syrian Josef Simonius Assemani (1637–1768) provided productive access to the Christian East; he made the Vatican a reservoir of Eastern sources and unlocked these treasures in his *Bibliotheca Orientalis* (1719–28) and the *Bibliotheca juris Orientalis* (1762–66). Equally important was his edition of Ephraim (1732–46). Ludovico Antonio Muratori (1672–1750) enjoyed high esteem, and not only in the area of historiography. His publication of sources for the history of the Italian Middle Ages (*Rerum italicarum scriptores* [1723–51] and *Antiquitates italici medii aevi* [1738–43]) is as indispensable for Italy as the *Monumenta Germaniae Historica* started a hundred years later is for Germany. The brothers Pietro (1698–1769) and Girolamo (1702–81) Ballerini published the works of Leo the Great (1753–57). The learned canonist Prosper Lambertini (1675–1758) who occupied the papal throne as Benedict XIV and liked to encourage scholarly endeavors, had arrived at the themes for his two main works from his own practice: in his role as the *Promotor fidei* in the canonization procedures on *De servorum Dei beatificatione* (1734–38) and as archbishop of Bologna on *De Synodo diocesana* (1755). The versatile Scipio Maffei (1675–1755) edited the works of Hilarius. In Guiseppe Bianchini we again encounter an editor of liturgical sources: in 1735 he edited the *Sacramentarium Leonianum;* in his *Evangeliarium quadruplex* (1749) he supplemented Sabatier's work on the *Itala*. The canonist Lucius Ferraris (d. 1763) created a popular lexicon, *Prompta bibliotheca canonica* (1746). The Dominican Cardinal Guiseppe Agostino Orsi (1692–1761) presented a comprehensive history of the Church for the first six centuries in his *Istoria ecclesiastica* (1747–62). Giovanni Domenico Mansi joined the ranks of the great editors; his collection of the councils in two series (1748–52 and 1759–98) is indispensable even today. The Dominican Thomas M. Mamachi (1713–92) pioneered the investigation of Christian antiquity by his *Origines et antiquitates christianae* (1749–55) but he also initiated work on the history of the orders in his *Annales Ordinis Praedicatorum* (1756). Joseph Alois (1710–82) one of the two younger Assemanis, edited the *Codex liturgicus ecclesiae universae* (1749–66) while Stefan Evodius (1711–82) and his uncle edited the Vatican manuscript catalog (1756–59). The Jesuit Francesco Antonio Zaccaria (1714–92) also well versed in archaeology, wrote a *Storia letteraria d'Italia* (1750–59) as did his fellow religious Girolamo Tiraboschi (1731–94) twenty years later with his *Storia della letteratura italiana,* which was at the same time a cultural history. We should not leave unmentioned the patient work of the high-minded prefect of the Vatican archives, Cardinal Guiseppe Garampi, whose 124 volumes of *Schedulae* are still making the treasures of these archives available. If we add Giambattista Vico who has to be considered the greatest philosophical historian of the century, we can safely say that the achievements of Italy can hold their own next to the luminescence of France, which was so important for the development of the science of history.

Jansenism in Italy — The Synod of Pistoia, 1786

While Italy developed much initiative of its own, especially in the area of historical theology, Jansenism — although fairly widespread in Italy — received its impulses from outside, from France and Utrecht. But only small groups of the educated were open to its ideas, often with characteristic differences in the individual cities, as in Papal Rome, for instance, with its representatives of Augustinian thought expressing sharp anti-Jesuit tendencies, in Pavia (Pietro Tamburini), Genoa (Vincenzo Palmieri), Turin, Milan, Venice and Naples. Jansenism was given a special characteristic in a surprising late phase in Habsburg Tuscany, where it was combined with Gallican and regalist concepts and engaged in provocative activities. Grand Duke Peter Leopold (1765–90) the younger brother of Emperor Joseph II and his successor to the imperial throne as Leopold II (1790–1792) initiated reforms similar to those of his brother in the administration, economy, the universities, and penal law. He paid particular attention to the ecclesiastical realm, where he was assisted by the Jansenist Scipione de' Ricci. In 1780 he procured for de' Ricci the conjoined bishoprics of Prato and Pistoia so that there was now a bishop who would support the reforms vigorously. These rested on a meager theological fundament, which might have been found in Quesnel's works, disproportionately affecting the practical aspects: abolition of the Inquisition, the concentration of Mass stipends for the benefit of poor priests, the equalization of benefices, parish bankruptcy, the residence obligation for parish priests, the study in episcopal seminaries instead of monastic schools, the obligation to give sermons, education of the youth, the translation of the missal, Communion during Mass, reform of the breviary, revision of the hagiographies, a minimum age of twenty-four for profession, rejection of private Masses, of the Sacred Heart cult, indulgences, exercises, and the popular mission, but on the other hand strengthening the idea of the parish. The original Church was perceived as a model, the infallibility of the Church was to rest on the totality of the faithful and not on the papacy; the jurisdiction of the bishops was held to be derived from Jesus himself. Pertinent articles were passed on 18 September 1786 by a diocesan synod in Pistoia. The acts of the synod were edited immediately and distributed internationally. But only three additional Tuscan priests embraced these same principles, so that the overwhelming majority of the national synod convened in Florence in 1787 reacted negatively. Resistance among the population was also strong. When the grand duke left, the reforms were quickly terminated and Ricci had to resign his bishopric in 1791. In his bull *Auctorem fidei,* dated 28 August 1794, Pius VI condemned, in varying degrees, eighty-five of the theses established at the synod. Ricci submitted in 1805. In spite of the rapid victory by the papacy over this last outgrowth of Jansenism, the significance of this movement especially for Italy is today seen in a new light: in this totally Catholic country it paved the way for the

Risorgimento, in which many became accustomed — in spite of an anticurial attitude — to seriously seeking religious modes which seemed to be more Catholic than those proclaimed by the Curia.

Protestant Theology

After the Church was deprived of its educational function, Protestant theology and through it the universities gained a profound importance which can only be briefly discussed within the framework of this book (see especially the standard work by E. Hirsch). It was initially shaped by the old Protestant orthodoxy which in both of its currents, the Lutheran and Reformed, overcame Luther's move away from philosophy. Following Melanchthon's example, Aristotle again was made the basis for ideas; this made possible many lateral connections to Thomas and also Suárez. The directional disputes and the canonization of the reformers notwithstanding, the importance of the Holy Scripture was stressed if only through the consolidation of the concept of verbal inspiration in an attempt to elevate the Scripture as opposed to tradition. At the same time the analytical method applied since Gerhard (1582–1637) gave greater weight to systematic thought relative to the Scriptures. In addition, such concepts as federal theology (Coccius) or the theology of the kingdom of God directed attention from the individual word of the Scripture to the total meaning of divine revelation and divine mercy. In addition there was a growing appreciation of natural theology. The security of orthodoxy was shaken by two intellectual movements: Pietism and the Enlightenment. Basic to the latter was the philosophical development in England through which the so-called deism originated. While its most prominent representatives fought against the traditional Church and its doctrine, they adhered to the unity of rationalism and revelation. But their meaning was reduced to some basic truths. By this, Herbert of Cherbury hoped for a new foundation of the faith, which by that time he viewed from an exclusively anthropological standpoint. In his moderate theological rationalism Locke still recognized the function of Jesus as the messiah and accepted verification through miracles as proof of divine revelation. To him revelation was not irrational but suprarational, sharpening the vision. Locke especially established the right of the individual to think and to act for himself. Christianity in many ways became a matter of ethics for him. An aggressive deism was advocated by John Toland, who attacked the canon of the Scripture and saw the proof of the revelation not in miracles but rather in the rational nature of its content. In this he was followed by Anthony Collins, Thomas Woolston, and the most mature of the deists, Matthew Tindal (1730), for whom revelation was the promulgation of natural religion. The deist "storm flood" (Hirsch) triggered sharp reactions. But with the best of its representatives, Samuel Clarke and Joseph Butler, these could emanate only from the basis of a rational supranaturalism. David Hume criticized the security of deism as well. But its impact was greater in France and Germany than in its place of origin.

In Germany a transitional theology (Baumgarten, Buddeus, Mosheim, et al.), adhering to the existing foundations, began to stress their moral-practical aspects. For many the philosophy presented by Wolff became an important base. Also gaining in importance was the physicotheology first pronounced by the Englishman Robert Boyle. In it the work of God within all of creation is theologically formulated — an attempt to stop the separation of the temporal world from theological thought brought about by Copernicus. Very much under the influence of the Enlightenment were the so-called neologists (Ernesti, Spalding, et al.). Faith and religion were separated from theology (Semler), the Bible and dogma distinguished from one other. The Scripture was perceived as a human-historical testimony of the revelation, important wherever it serves the promotion of spirituality. Michaelis (d. 1791) advocated an explanation of the Bible free of dogma, paving the way for a historico-critical treatment of the Bible. Christian faith was reduced to those elements considered most essential, retaining recognition of the revelation and the miracles. Denominational polemics, hitherto undertaken zealously, began to recede.

Toward the end of the eighteenth century an extreme rationalism among some of the representatives of Protestant theology gained ground. The radical biblical critic Reimarus became especially well known through G. E. Lessing's defense of him. In his defense of natural religion Lessing himself dissolved the belief in the revelation and the miracles so that the dogmatic foundations were lost and the Fall and Redemption as facts of salvation disappeared from view. But revelation for him goes beyond nature; the Bible does not represent revelation but instead the profession of revelation, which can be perceived ever more clearly in God's work according to the *Erziehung des Menschengeschlechtes.*

Pietism, while definitely connected with the Enlightenment, was more effective in Protestant theology and spirituality by virtue of the fact that it was located overwhelmingly within the Church. It originated with P. I. Spener (1635–1705) and his main work, the *Pia Desideria* (1675). Following its publication, the orthodoxy and church administrations were subjected to increasing criticism by advocates of an individual religion on the basis of the inner self. The fact that subjectivity enhanced in Pietism did not contradict social efficacy and instead substantially furthered it was shown by Spener's pupil A. H. Francke (1663–1727), who made Halle a center of Pietism. His "endowed institutions," among them an orphanage and school, and his involvement with the Christian mission in India and the diaspora ministry characterized his life's work. The same missionary spirit inspired N. L. Zinzendorf (1700–1760), who came from the Halle group of Pietists and founded the Herrnhut Brotherhood in 1722, an independent community, yet following the Augsburg Confession. More radical than Zinzendorf's ecclesiology (the churches as "tropes") was the historical concept of the Church of G. Arnold. Eighteenth-century Pietism continued in the "revival movement." The reformed Pietism stems from seventeenth-century Puritanism and developed its own communities in the Netherlands. G. Tersteegen (1697–1769) wrote his hymns and sermons in the area of the lower Rhine.

The development of Protestant church history proceeded — while not exclusively yet most vigorously — in the German domain. It placed less emphasis on creating new methods, establishing source criticism, or providing an abundance of material than the Catholic side, concentrating instead on new points of departure for the total conception. The concept of decline as a basis of church history which had governed the Magdeburg Centurists was, of course, dominant also among the Baptists and in all of mystical spiritualism and was capable of intensification to the extent that all Churches, even the Protestant ones, resembled nothing short of the iniquitous Babel. The *Summarium* (1697) by the Old Orthodox Adam Rechenberg, too, is still characterized by the theory of decline, with the difference that it is turned into the opposite by the Reformation. The *Unpartheische Kirchen- und Ketzerhistorie* (1699) by the Pietist Gottfried Arnold achieved great importance. Carefully following the sources, this work deinstitutionalizes the history of the Church and, above all, deals with the question of Christian faith through rebirth. The shape of all givens is seen as being in constant motion. His basic ideas made it possible for the concept of history to be viewed as a history of the forming of man. In 1726 Johann Lorenz von Mosheim attempted a "pragmatic," that is an undogmatic factual presentation, of church history, taking it out of the context of theology. In accordance with enlightened concepts, Johann Salomo Semler applied the idea of progress to church history (1767–69) while the rationalistic Ludwig Spittler wrote his church history (1782) much like the history of a state, radically secularized. Highly influential works were written by the rationalist supernaturalists Johann Matthias Schöckh (1768–1812; forty-five volumes, also used extensively at Catholic universities) and Gottlieb Jakob Planck (1803–9).

The first attempts in the direction of dogmatic history led to several treatments of this topic around 1800. Other new theological disciplines owe their consolidation to the Enlightenment. Among them are the denominational studies (especially by Planck in 1796) and biblical theology, which was given an important impetus by the demand of Philipp Gabler (1787) to pay attention to the development of biblical ideas. Biblical studies overall received this earliest impulses in the field of the Old Testament (by the Oratorian Richard Simon in 1678). Regarding introductory studies we should mention Michaelis (1750). Semler's canonical history (1771–75) became one of the fundamental works in its field.

An assessment of Protestant theology in this period will have to take into consideration the fact that — platitudes aside, which exist in abundance within contemporary Catholic, conservative, and enlightened theology — an honest attempt was made to prevent Christian faith and modern rationality from being split apart.

Catholic Universities

After their auspicious start in the thirteenth century the history of the universities is usually viewed in terms of a productive revival by the spirit of humanism and a flourishing in Spain followed by a long period of sterility until another upswing occurred in the nineteenth century. The fact that in the meantime the universities underwent a development of their own is most often not taken into account. In accordance with the denominational character of the period they had been founded or revived by the princes or bishops with a clear predetermination of their purpose. Most of them were therefore caught up in the fight between the denominations, whether they were newly founded or not. This held true for the Protestant universities (the Saxon universities of Wittenberg and Leipzig, the Palatine university in Heidelberg, the one of Württemberg in Tübingen or the Swiss one in Basel, the new foundation by Philipp of Hesse in Marburg (1527), which was reformed in 1605, whereupon Hesse-Darmstadt established a Lutheran university in Gießen, and the university founded by Calvin in Geneva in 1559), as well as for the Catholic universities (the Austrian universities in Vienna and Freiburg, the Bavarian one in Ingolstadt, the Belgian university in Louvain, the episcopal ones in Trier and Mainz, and the municipal university in Cologne).

Catholic foundations and revivals were generally undertaken in such a way that the new teaching order, the Society of Jesus, (which was very effective) was not only given a large part if not all of the chairs of the theological faculty, but also those of the philosophical faculty, for it was here that the basic education of all the students took place even if they chose one of the "higher" courses of study in theology, law, or medicine. A university was often started with merely philosophy and theology and supplemented by the other two faculties only after decades or much longer. Such faculty assignments to the Jesuits had been practiced since the middle of the sixteenth century, the first in 1548 in Ingolstadt, 1551 in Vienna (initially with very few chairs and a good many more in 1623), 1561 in Trier, and the year after in Mainz. Jesuits were called to the university in Dillingen in 1563 after its establishment by the bishop of Augsburg in 1551. While Dillingen achieved an importance far beyond the borders of the bishopric, it was eventually outpaced by Ingolstadt. The university in Olmütz, founded by the bishop there in 1581, had a clear counterreformational purpose from the start, as did the Austrian university of Graz (1585), which gained significance for Carinthia and had an impact even in Belgium and Poland. From their inception both universities had Jesuit professors. For the bishop of Würzburg, Julius Echter von Mespelbrunn, who was not always in agreement with the Jesuits, there was no question as to who the professors would be when he established his university in 1582. The same choice prevailed when the universities of Paderborn (1614) and Osnabrück (1629) were founded. The latter was initially spared by the war but closed four years later when the fortunes of war turned. In 1620 the Austrian sovereign had also brought the Jesuits to the university of Freiburg in the Black Forest, granting them the philosophical faculty and half of the chairs in theology. Jesuits were installed in Prague when the sovereign power obtained jurisdiction over the university, which had been Protestant until then. Another Austrian university where the Jesuit order, aspiring to monopoly over the schools, was used as faculty opened in Innsbruck in 1669. Finally, the Jesuit school in Breslau, in existence since 1635 was given university status in 1702. In Erfurt, a university of the Mainz electorate, which had to admit Protestant faculty as well, only a single chair was reserved for the Jesuits. When the Wittelsbach Pfalz-Neuburg line took over the Palatinate in 1685, it was unable to change the Reformed denomination of the land but actively favored Catholicism. The University of Heidelberg, too, was no exception. Jesuits were represented on the faculty since 1706 and Catholic theology was taught along with the Calvinist brand. Only a few Catholic universities were without Jesuits: Cologne, which nonetheless maintained a definite conservative position, and Louvain, where the disputes involving Jansenism were especially vehement and episcopalism was represented prominently by van Espen. The episcopal university in Salzburg (1617) had a character of its own; it was given to the Benedictine order, which made its best people from the southern German monasteries available as professors for the university and, in fact, had a good many of its young monks educated there. Thomistic and canonical subjects were taught extremely well there, as was history as early as the seventeenth century. In 1734 when the abbot of Fulda founded a new university and split the faculty into equal parts between Benedictines and Jesuits, the resulting tensions showed how little the two factions had in common.

But in the meantime the intellectual climate had changed, leaving the rigid system of the Jesuits, who were still following the unchanged *ratio studiorum* of 1599, out of tune. The demand for the introduction of history, a field in whose research the Benedictine order as well as the Jesuits had excelled and which had been taught at the Protestant universities for a long time, could no longer be rejected. Since the chairs of philosophy were for the most part held by Jesuits, they had to occupy themselves with history whether they wanted to or not. Also important was the acceptance of new problems in the natural sciences and practical experimental methods. It took some time to overcome the concept that no new knowledge was possible beyond Arisrotle. But finally, around the middle of the century, sufficient strides were made especially in the Jesuit order. Jesuits even became leaders in the field of astronomy. Clinging to the Aristotelian-Thomistic philosophy — although the latter had already been modified to some degree by Suárez and subsequently by Gregory of Valencia — constituted the one great obstacle to Cartesian ideas and, more so, to dealing with the philosophy of Leibniz and Wolff. But by around 1740 it was abundantly clear that stubborn adherence to outmoded tradition was no longer feasible. The initial resort was to a sort of eclecticism until — another thirty years later — the modern ideas achieved dominance. And yet around the mid 1750s Bertold Hauser (Dillingen) attempted to obtain a world view by means of Scholastic principles, as did (although in a different fashion) Joseph Mangold (Ingolstadt). Benedikt Sattler, the teacher of Sailer, made the most significant effort to incorporate Leibniz and Wolff. The practice by the Society of Jesus of transferring their members in quick succession from one university, college, or seminary to another and in medieval fashion to consider the lecturing of philosophy as a mere transitional stage for one's own educational process long constituted the most serious obstacle to the development of significant scholars in any individual subject. The training of specialists, attempted in Würzburg in 1731, was initially possible in law and medicine only.

In the last few years prior to the great turn of events marked by the French Revolution German bishops succeeded in three cases in opening a university in their dioceses: when the Jesuit order was suppressed in 1773, the two faculties established by that order in 1648 were expanded into a university. In 1780 the extraordinary Vicar General Franz von Fürstenberg opened a university in Münster which was characterized by the open mind and profoundly religious spirit of its initiator. The endowment of an academy in Bonn (1777), the residence of the Cologne archbishop, which was elevated to the rank of a university in 1786, was clearly undertaken with the thought in mind of training capable civil servants, a deviation of purpose influenced by the Enlightenment.

The universities, including those in the episcopal territories, were turned more and more into territorial universities, obliged to serve the training of civil servants, an area in which the clergy serving the interests of a temporal state were also increasingly involved. The most telling sign of this situation was the

Theresian-Josephinist university reform which changed them completely from freely endowed into state institutions. At that point all applicants for a parish in the Austrian territories were obliged to pass a full course of theological studies, documented in detail and followed by an examination. Josephinism extended these rules to the regular clergy as well, simultaneously abolishing formal study within the monasteries. Everyone had to study at the universities, where they were installed at the newly established general seminaries. But these did not last long (1783–90). The content of theological studies was enriched considerably. Up to that point dogmatics and, beginning in the seventeenth century, the case study of morals, controversial theology, and the Holy Scripture had been taught. The Rautenstrauch curriculum of the Austrian government (1774) expanded scriptural study by introducing Oriental languages and, as new courses, church history (including patristics) and the pastoral. Canon law was of course taught only in accordance with the laws of the established Church. This curriculum with its attention to biblical, historical, and practical subjects prevailed in the entire German-speaking area and its basic structure has been retained until the present day. The method of teaching also changed. The tedious method of dictation was changed to the use of textbooks, at times even Protestant ones wherever Catholic books were not yet available. The language of instruction was generally changed from the traditional Latin to German. Here and there the strict denominationalism of the universities, which had never prevailed in Erfurt and Heidelberg, was relaxed. After 1746 there were Protestant students in Mainz (and Würzburg) and, following the Mainz university reform of 1784 by the elector Friedrich Karl von Erthal (under the curator Benzel-Sternau), there were also Protestant professors there. This was the case also in Freiburg after the toleration edict of Joseph II.

This express form of a state university was strongest in the University of Halle, founded in 1694. The University of Göttingen, opened in 1737, incorporated the spirit of the future. At that university it was possible to develop the ideal of a free pursuit of learning, unfettered by regulations and particular purposes, where learning was governed by the determination of truth and no longer tied to any tradition. Many impulses for a more or less radical "Enlightenment" emanated from Göttingen which had some impact on Catholic universities as well. A new spirit frequently manifested itself in journals such as the decidedly enlightened *Religionsjournal* (Mainz), *Der Freimütige* (Freiburg), the moderate *Journal von und für Deutschland* (Fulda), and the *Mainzer Monatsschrift.* Around 1790 Kantian philosophy was frequently advocated at universities such as Fulda, Bamberg, and Heidelberg. The terror of the Revolution provoked countermovements with measures taken against overly rationalistic professors. Best known are the Dillingen events, actions against Sailer and Zimmer; similar incidents occurred in Mainz and also in Freiburg. A highly respected form of open-minded university life succeeded in Würzburg under the dynamic promotion by Prince-Bishop Franz Ludwig von Erthal.

Academies

While the universities through their transformation into state institutions were ever more concentrated on the training of civil servants (in Germany this included the clergy), new associations, the academies, were formed to promote research. Such relatively loose associations had already existed in the Italian Renaissance, the "Academies" for literature and the arts. In an endeavor to encourage serious research in the natural sciences, history, or philosophy (though not in theology), various approaches were used. Among them were lectures before an audience of experts, the pursuit of topics by the dissemination of examinations, the review of submitted works, publication of discussions and treatises, or preparing editions of historical sources on well-defined themes. One of the first of its kind was the Roman Accademia dei Lincei (1603), whose research was exemplary. In 1635 the idea was adopted by Richelieu, who turned the academies into state institutions with a national accentuation. Colbert's foundation in 1662 Académie des Inscriptions et des Belles-Lettres) became highly significant because of its strong historical orientation and an abundance of publications, in part due to its intensive collaboration with the Maurists. This was in contrast to the provincial academies in France formed in the course of the eighteenth century; the finished works had little effective impact since they were left unprinted in their libraries. A private foundation in London (1645) which emerged in 1663 as the Royal Academy was devoted to research in the natural sciences; it published Newton's discoveries. Early on Leibniz also pursued the idea of an academy, but his goal, the establishment of the Berlin Academy, was not realized until 1700. The early examples of such state institutions were not emulated until the middle of the century: 1752 in Hanoverian Göttingen, 1753 in Erfurt, an outpost of the Mainz electorate in the middle of a Protestant environment, 1759 in Munich, the capital of electoral Bavaria where the motive force behind the academy was the Jurist Johann Georg Lori, who was familiar with the Italian models. Another was founded in 1763 in Palatine Mannheim, whose reigning dynasty was Catholic but whose population was overwhelmingly Calvinist. Its establishment was aided substantially by the most prominent Protestant historian of his time, Schöpflin from Strasbourg. In the Habsburg domains only one academy, the one in Prague, founded privately in 1770 and recognized by the state in 1784, was able to maintain itself. It was devoted primarily to topics prompted by the ever growing consolidation of Czech national consciousness, its own early history, and the Slavic language. While the pursuit of natural sciences prevailed in northern Germany, historical studies predominated in the Mannheim and Munich academies, giving them their high reputation. Mannheim, under the direction of Schöpflin's secretary and pupil, Andreas Lamey, primarily concentrated on four topics. The academy of Munich, which enjoyed substantial cooperation throughout the country, became the most efficient one after obtaining the services of the Protestant Alsatian Christian Friedrick Pfeffel (1763–68). It began the edition of the *Monumenta Boica* which, although somewhat deficient at first, achieved growing reliability in making an abundance of material available until the present day.

The historical themes were taken mostly from the Middle Ages and created a counterweight to the popular contemporary view of that period as one of darkness vis-à-vis the prevailing luminescence of the age of Enlightenment. The initially tendentious view of history caused by the general state of dependency on the sovereign was soon overcome, giving way to an impartial criticism; in this way a number of highly effective and long-enduring medieval falsifications were uncovered. Although themes in church history were not especially sought after, early sources kept in the domain of the Church were made available and thus much preliminary work on the history of church institutions was done. Most decisive were the dissemination and augmentation of the Maurist method. The universities of the eighteenth century did not teach the historical method, but the work of the academies brought about its adoption. This happened primarily in France (by the Académie des Inscriptions) and in Germany. The process of printing not only made the source material accessible but it also revealed and thereby disseminated the method applied to it. This made it possible to enlarge the principle of collaboration and the exchange of ideas beyond the immediate circle of the members of a particular academy. One may have misgivings concerning the fact that the academies did not exploit the coherent force of their collective membership for more comprehensive undertakings. Only Munich made a start in this direction. In general there was a lack of purposeful planning.

Occasional mention is made of an academy movement of the seventeenth and eighteenth century (which includes even the more loosely connected forms of scientific societies and associations of the time). Such a movement existed in Switzerland. One would also have to include the diverse forms of collaboration among the Benedictine monasteries that endeavored for a time to establish their own academy. Their inclusion is justified especially by such a comprehensive program as the Sankt Blasien *Germania sacra* by Martin Gerbert (after the model of the Maurists), which intended to compile an accurately documented history of the individual dioceses for all of Germany.

In Italy the Istituto delle Scienze in papal Bologna, founded in 1712, investigated the natural sciences on a level comparable to the Tuscan academies. The erudite Benedict XIV gave Rome its very efficient academies for church history (1741), for the history of ancient Rome (1744), and for the history of liturgics (1748). The academy of Madrid set an example for all of Spain (1735); it devoted itself exclusively to historical research. Its goal was a geographic-historical lexicon which actually started to appear in 1802. Next to that, its greatest undertaking was the *España Sagrada*, whose first few volumes were edited by the Augustinian friar Enrique Flórez. The Madrid academy was the dominant center of diverse research activities which spread far and wide.

Education

When the printing press made it possible to extend the ability to read and to write) it was used by the Reformation above all in the service of its demand for a personal encounter with the Holy Scripture. When the sexton was charged to assist the pastor in teaching the catechism, the seeds were planted for a broad-based establishment of schools. Early school regulations are left to us from Württemberg (1558) and electoral Saxony (1580). The idea of introducing schools everywhere was formulated in Frankfurt in 1612; mandatory attendance for all was planned in Strasbourg in 1598 and required in Anhalt (1607), Weimar (1619), Gotha (1642), Brunswick (1647), and Württemberg (1649). In rural areas it was difficult to conduct classes during the summer. Pietism not only helped in the understanding of the catechism, but also in the popularization of confirmation, customary in Hesse since Bucer, as an affirmation of baptism and preparation for Communion. In the beginning of the eighteenth century the practice of confirmation gradually prevailed (Württemberg, 1722; electoral Saxony, 1723; Denmark, 1736; Lübeck, 1817; and Hamburg, 1832), giving the school a concrete goal.

By establishing a number of schools the theologian Hermann Francke (1663–1727), a leader in the Pietist revival movement, broke through the social exclusivity of the educational system; he was the first to concern himself with the training of teachers. In 1774 Johann Bernhard Basedow (1724–94), a rationalist imbued with the ideas of Rousseau, founded a boarding school in Dessau (Philanthropinum) which had no church affiliation; it became an example for others.

Schools were increasingly established in the Catholic territories as well. Visitation reports of the seventeenth century reflect the efforts by the bishops to introduce them. When they wanted to have control over the employment of teachers, it was for reasons of ensuring themselves of their orthodoxy. Fénelon's *Traité de l'éducation des filles* (1687) also had a considerable impact in Germany. In the second half of the century the Catholic states also issued school regulations. This included the various prince-bishoprics and prince-abbeys, some of whom conscientiously took on the badly neglected task of teacher education (the teacher academy in Mainz, 1771; the teacher seminary of Saint Urban in Lucerne, 1777; bishopric of Fulda, 1781). A shining example was the work of the abbot J. I. von Felbiger at Sagan in Prussian Silesia in 1765 (*Plan der neuen Schuleinrichtung* [1770]), who was called to Vienna by Empress Maria Theresa in 1774. He divided the schools into three different kinds (the so-called trivial, main, and normal schools), introduced classroom instead of individual teaching, and incorporated religion as a regular subject, whereas before religious instruction had simply been done through the religious reading material (catechism) used in the general lessons. In western Germany Vicar General von Fürstenberg in Münster had Bernard Overberg appointed organizer of the Catholic elementary schools. His *Anweisung zum zweckmäßigen Schulunterricht* appeared in 1793. The great pedagogical verve of the period of Enlightenment helped create the teaching profession as such and finally brought some financial security. It also helped provide a proper education and to divorce the teacher from local authority. Still, it was natural for the school to be part of the respective denominational area, so that the teacher remained closely tied to the functions of the church service in his role as sexton and organist.

CHAPTER 138

Liturgy and Popular Piety—New Religious Orders

The Liturgy

After the Council of Trent had created the prerequisite; for bringing about a uniform liturgy cleansed of excesses for the entire Catholic Church, the subsequent five decades witnessed the development of the required tools; the *Breviarium Romanum* appeared in 1568, the *Missale Romanum* in 1570, the *Martyrologium Romanum* in 1584, the *Pontificale Romanum* in 1596, and the *Caerimoniale Episcoporum* in 1600. The final touch was the *Rituale Romanum* in 1614, which contained the rite of the administering of the sacraments and the sacramentals; it was not binding but rather intended as a model. This enabled the multifarious diocesan rites to be maintained along with them and made it possible to some extent to use the native language. But wherever there was no tradition with its own spontaneous forms, as in the missions, the unifying force of the centrally created liturgical materials had an effect.

In the history of liturgy the three centuries following 1614 until the reforms under Pius X proved to be the centuries of "liturgical stagnation" (Klauser). The scant "improvements," for instance, of the breviary under Urban VIII, were insignificant and pedantic. A reform prepared under Benedict XIV was not implemented. The powerful advance of historical research especially in the area of liturgics did bring about rich encounters with the forms of earlier periods, including the abundance of Eastern liturgies, but had no effect on the existing ways of celebrating the official Mass, which had become rigid and inflexible with the passing of time. Regarding the breviary as well as the missal, the Council of Trent had created the possibility of retaining customary forms if it could be ascertained that the tradition was more than 200 years old. But even where these conditions were met, it was not always possible to withstand the unifying forces for long; as a consequence the indigenous forms — with the exception of diocesan celebrations — were gradually abandoned. In France, however, the affirmation of traditional Gallicanism was too strong for a similar development to take place. During a time of emphatic canonical Gallicanism, in fact, the right to retain the old traditional ways were expanded to the point where they were further developed under the influence of contemporary ideas. New breviaries were created in France (Cluny, 1686; Paris, 1736 [for the secular clergy]; Saint Vanne, 1777; and, as a sort of continuation of the latter, Saint Maur, 1787). These were introduced even where the Roman liturgy had already been accepted. Their main characteristic was an intensive cultivation of Scripture reading to include especially the Fathers. They also manifested a strong tendency to moralize, which corresponded with the enlightened spirit of the period. A notable fact is that the Paris Breviary distributed the whole psalter over one week, using nine psalms for Matins, and that it restored the Sundays and ferial days to their customary place, two elements which were fully taken over by the Roman breviary reform of 1911. Western German dioceses were also quick to issue new breviaries which were not entirely closed to the ideas of the Gallican breviaries (Trier, 1748; Cologne, 1780). Martin II Gerbert immediately adopted the Saint Vanne Breviary for his diocese of Sankt Blasien. But aside from the calendar of religious holidays, which steadily increased the feasts of the saints and diminished the celebration of the liturgical year, public worship on the whole stayed the same. The intensity of liturgical life appears to have run aground on the excessively fastidious consolidation of the abundantly annotated rubrics; canonistic formalism and casuistry displaced the inner life of the liturgy.

The gap between liturgy and the believers, existing since the Middle Ages, was not overcome but deepened instead. The liturgy had become a liturgy for the clergy, touching the people only inasmuch as it could serve as a spectacle. The holy Mass was no longer a participatory event; the sermon had been removed from it and the Communion had become isolated from it as a separate devotion. The Mass merely had the ceremonious function of making the Eucharistic Lord present whose real presence in the sacrament was stressed most strongly. The most formal ceremony was the Mass in front of the exposed Host, where the Eucharistic blessing was pronounced right at the beginning and repeated after the sequence and again at the end. The altar was centered on the throne of exposition above the tabernacle — the latter had been prescribed by the ritual of 1614 to replace the shrine in the wall of the chancel — and on it was the monstrance, now shaped like a sun. In front of it the clergy and the acolytes performed what amounted to a courtly service. But this baroque period knew how to turn the Mass into a celebration through the splendor of the church, in which all the skill of architecture, painting, and sculpture combined to form an all-inclusive artistic frame of lofty and joyous ceremony, intensified by the multiplicity of vestments and ever more profuse music. No matter that the words of the liturgy and the individual acts were no longer taken in, the awareness of a great mystery and the will for devotion were still present.

Given the great discrepancy between the official church service and a religiosity that people were able to comprehend, it is not surprising that they intensively cultivated extraliturgical forms. The suitable organization for that purpose was still the fraternity. Under different names (Rosary, Sacred Heart, Happy Death, Saint Sebastian, etc.), infused with recurrent waves of piety, they gathered their members from far afield, calling them to fraternal celebrations with impressive processions and endowing altars in their name. The number of fraternities increased greatly, as did that of the Marian congregations promoted by the Jesuits. Beginning in 1751 such congregations were also established for girls and women, whereas formerly they had been reserved for boys and men. Different from those of the baroque, the fraternities were distinguished by social standing; some were for students, others for the bourgeoisie, for priests, and so forth. Often it was the fraternities that organized the great pilgrimages which reached their climax at this time. New ones originated, especially Marian pilgrimages. In addition to the famous places of pilgrimage, visited by groups of pilgrims who sometimes walked for days to get there, many small local shrines were set up for people from the immediate environs. The popularity of the Holy House in Loreto was reflected by the many Loreto chapels, most of them outside the city entrances, which sought to copy the Italian shrine. The devotion of relics was given a great, in fact, an excessive impetus. They were collected and displayed behind glass window; or pyramids, some of them augmented to form dressed skeletal figures kept in glass coffins; they were placed on the altar, under the mensa, or carried along at processions. A great role was played by the so-called saints of the catacombs, which were bones from the Roman catacombs In spite of an alleged authentication, they were of highly dubious origin, most of the time given a fictitious name, brought in ceremoniously, and often elevated to the position of co-patron of a church.

The desire for a chance to obtain indulgences had extraordinarily intensified. The contemporary mania for intoxicating themselves with large numbers led people not only to seek out as many opportunities as possible to obtain a plenary indulgence, but also partial ones for thousands and thousands of years. Membership in certain fraternities, which for their part had managed to participate in the indulgence privileges of others, provided offers of such possibilities: fastidiously compiled in calendars, they would tell the believer how many indulgences he could obtain on a given day. In addition, celebrations of indulgences were also very popular, especially at certain places of pilgrimage or monastic churches where the faithful came together in droves for the pronouncement of special indulgences, granted after receiving the sacrament of penance and Holy Communion. The intensification of the popular mission, organized at times with great baroque pomp and penitential processions which might involve the carrying of hundreds of crosses, went parallel to a sort of confessional movement which was intended to stimulate more frequent confessions. This explains the increased devotion of Saint John Nepomuk, promoted especially by the Jesuits, as a martyr to the seal of the confessional; his likeness soon adorned many streets and bridges and could be found in many churches.

There is no doubt that in many cases superstitions were mixed in with popular exercises of piety. The use of sacramentals was often falsified because of it. Many superstitions, carried over into our time, had a religious form in the period of the baroque; that age, in fact, was still given too much to such ideas. We have to remember that the madness of witchcraft was barely fading; here and there the fires of the autos-da-fé continued to burn the unfortunates accused of witchcraft, putting them to an agonizing death. Among the last burnings were those in Würzburg (1749), Endingen (1751; at the Kaiserstuhl), Kempten (1775), Glarus (1782), and Posen (1793).

The sermons of the baroque were in danger of getting lost in a welter of effects and external trappings. Their scriptural base was frequently inadequate. But not a few were imbued with religious depth, full of wisdom and popular, as those of the Capuchin friar Prokop von Templin (1609–80) in Austria; the Augustinian Hermit Abraham a' Santa Clara (1644–1709), who was active primarily at the court of Vienna displaying creativity and great imagination in the use of language, as well as a pointed wit; and, lastly, the Portuguese Jesuit Antonio Vieira (1608–97), who was a most moving preacher. In 1760 the excesses of the baroque sermons were attacked by an outstanding satirist in the person of Josef de Isla (1703–81), who used his *Gerundio* novel to uncover their weaknesses to such an extent that he contributed substantially to removing them from the pulpits.

At a time when more than just a few of the faithful were able to read, literary forms could be developed which had a broad impact. Among them were, on the Protestant side, Johann Arnd's *Vier Bücher vom wahren Christentum* (1605), on the Catholic side a *Hauspostille* (1690) by the Premonstratensian Leonhard

Goffiné (1648–1719) and the diverse writings of the Capuchin friar Martin von Cochem (1634–1712), especially his *Meßerklärung* and *Leben und Leiden Jesu Christi* (1677).

The great religious strength of the century — regardless of the extent of anthropocentrism — is manifest in its works of art. The stylistic means of the fine arts were formed in Italy. As signs of a living faith in the nearness of God's grace, especially in those lands which had remained Catholic, they were used to build perfect structures which imply in many ways an extension into the supernatural. The period manifested a cheerful, confident, generous, and affirmative spirit which was able to create a great abundance of multifarious religious programs. At times they addressed a certain ethnic group, such as the Romance or the Austrian-Bavarian people. While Calvinism continued to be hostile to art and music (their churches were without paintings and for a long time without organs), the depth of Lutheran religious emotion was characterized by hymns, which are precious both in text and melody, and by immortal religious music: the passions, chorales, and cantatas of Heinrich Schütz (1585–1672),Johann Sebastian Bach (1685–1750), and the oratorios of George Frederick Handel (1685–1759). On the Catholic side we should mention the great masses and oratorios of Franz Joseph Haydn (1732–1809) and the masses by Wolfgang Amadeus Mozart (1756–91). Bach's great Mass in B-Minor, which he composed for the Catholic court of Dresden, shows the extent to which the denominations can converge in their most profound aspects. Beethoven's religious music belongs to another period.

This exuberant and varied scope of religious life was bound at some point to encounter a limiting and reducing force. Secular governments, playing an increasing role which gradually encompassed all aspects of human life, demanded a reduction in the number of holidays for economic reasons (in 1642 they had already been limited to thirty-four by Urban VIII). Spain initiated this move; under Benedict XIII it succeeded in having seventeen saints' feast days changed into half-holidays. They were still holy days of obligation, but the work prohibition was canceled. In 1748 the same ruling was applied to the Two Sicilies and in 1753 to Austria as well. Clement XIV abolished these half-holidays completely. Similar holiday limitations were requested by some archbishoprics (Würzburg [1770], Bamberg [1770], and Mainz [1763–74]) and by such states as Bavaria, Prussia (1772), and Spain (1791). These measures were generally unpopular and could often be implemented only by force after a long period of time. Wherever such canceled holy days were shifted to either the preceding or the following Sunday, the reduction caused the purpose of Sunday as the day of the Lord to be obscured.

In the changing spirit of the time the curtailment of the excessive number of feasts was only a beginning; such abundance and variety were increasingly considered unessential and annoying distractions. The striving was for unadorned simplicity, which alone permits the sublime to come to the fore. Only "noble artlessness," a "purified, genuine principle" was still in demand. The idea was to separate the essential from the "coincidental," only to declare in the same breath the latter to be dispensable, indeed to be something that needed to be removed like an obstacle or could at least be neglected without harm. The application of such a differentiation was certainly indicated since it permitted a clearer perspective of things which had in many instances become hidden. So the fight began against the many processions, the pilgrimages to all sorts of large and small places of grace, against the many fraternities, and the benedictions often suffused with superstitious expectations. The use of exorcism especially seemed outmoded; now the bishops frequently made it dependent on the permission of the ordinaries. The constant repetition of the Eucharistic blessing was felt to be an exaggeration. In contrast to the overwhelming abundance of the most varied forms of veneration of saints, piety with Christ at its center was to be reemphasized. The late stage of these enlightened ideas also brought about a deeper occupation with the Holy Scripture.

These changes, penetrating as they were, did not happen all at once; they took place in phases with considerable chronological differences. The pastoral letter by the Viennese Prince-Archbishop Trautson of 1 January 1752, whose formulations were looked upon as guidelines far beyond his diocese, appeared when the art of the baroque had just entered its last formal, albeit playful stage of the rococo. In 1768 when the monastery of Sankt Blasien burned down, Martin Gerbert decided to have d'Ixnard rebuild it in the form of a classical round temple which was admired all the way to northern Germany because of its impression of sublime peace. The measures instituted by Joseph II (1780–90) were the climax of enlightened activities in the ecclesiastical realm. Not only were they frequently copied during his lifetime, but they also served as models for the position of the established church system in the first half of the nineteenth century. And yet the "modern" Mainz hymnal of 1787 caused bitter disputes. The attempt to write a ritual in German was first made by C. Schwarzel around the turn of the century and concluded with the ritual by Wessenberg in 1831. The work by the most prominent reform liturgist of the Enlightenment, Vitus Anton Winter, in Ingolstadt and Landshut is also part of the new century.

The Enlightenment definitely perceived the gap between the liturgy and the people and tried to bridge it on the one hand by curtailing the indigenous forms of popular piety and on the other by establishing a connection between the believers and the liturgical event. The strides made to include the sermon in the Mass again were notable, as were the attempts to connect the Communion with the Mass. It was tempting, of course, to make the liturgy generally accessible by translating it into the native language, that is by giving up the unintelligible Latin as the liturgical language. Generally this was dared only for the administration of the sacraments and the benedictions, or for new celebrations such as first Communion or the investiture of a parish priest, but only sporadically for the celebration of the Mass. It was not done at all under Wessenberg, who held back his friends when they wanted to forge ahead on this point. At first he tried to get the people to participate by means of a sort of prayer-song Mass using many different texts for the various times of the church year (Constance Hymnal, 1812). Praying something other than indicated by the context of the Mass, for instance the traditional rosary, was considered extremely improper. Masses at side altars, customarily conducted concurrently with the main Mass, were abolished. Preference was for only one altar in the church.

The basic idea of the enlightened service was eminently ministerial: The priest who knows his flock — it was improper to leave the parish for a monastery, pilgrimage, or an outside fraternity — takes care of them in the truest sense of the word. He imparts to them the word of God according to a deliberate plan and instructs them in all that they need. The service has to be organized so that it edifies and improves the participants. It should serve to make them recognize that they are all brothers of the common Father who is in heaven. This was the true brotherhood, the only one still admitted. Under Joseph II it was called the "brotherhood of the love of one's fellow man"; under Wessenberg "of God's love and the love of one's fellow man." All mechanical aspects were to disappear from prayer and the service. The ties between shepherd and flock were to be deepened so that confessions were made only to one's own priest, who knew the individual best and was therefore the only one who could instruct him properly. In accordance with Wessenberg's views, the responsibility of the minister for those entrusted to him was increased considerably. Seen from this point of view, the service in the period of Enlightenment did not only consist of teaching and dry moralizing mixed with a few pious sentimentalities, as it has often been represented. To be sure, the didacticism which filled the texts of the hymns as well was overstressed. Subjectivism, with its initial growth in the baroque, became dominant and the idea of the liturgy as a service before God receded to too great a degree. There is also no doubt that in the most profound sense the initial attempts in the Enlightenment to reform the service failed because the theocentricity of the service was overlooked and the attempt to improve its form missed the reality of the cultic mysticism. The strong desire for cult was no longer accorded enough significance. Piety emanating from the world all too often got stuck in the world. But to the extent that the responsibility for one another was emphasized, God, before whom the responsibility is discharged, was again included.

New Religious Orders

The history of the religious orders of the sixteenth and beginning of the seventeenth century is strongly imbued with the idea of the apostolate. This was true even more so for the following centuries. Certain characteristic concerns gained prominence, such as the construction of seminaries for the training of secular clerics among the Oratorians, the Sulpicians, and the *Congrégation de Jésus et Marie* of John Eudes; in its own fashion the work of Vincent de Paul ran parallel to that. Vincent and his Lazarists — as did the two Jesuits Paolo Segneri (1624–94) and Paolo the Younger (1673–1713) in Italy — built the type of popular mission which stayed alive until the twentieth century, representing a very important form of the apostolate of the orders. By founding the *Filles de la Charité* with the assistance of Louise de Marillac, Vincent de Paul approached the very concrete tasks of caring for orphans, the aged, and the sick in a more efficacious fashion than had ever been done before in the history of ecclesiastical charity. Similar organizations were the *Soeurs de Notre-Dame de charité de refuge* of John Eudes (1640), from whom the congregation of Our Lady of the Love of the Good Shepherd emerged in the nineteenth century, and the *Soeurs de Saint Charles* or Borromaeans who originated in Nancy and spread primarily in Lorraine after 1652. That same year the *Filles de la Charité* also started working in Poland and as late as the eighteenth century went to other European countries and America. This social and charitable service of nuns, which enabled women to take part in superior fashion in common tasks of Christian love, could be possible only by abolishing the cloistral regulations which had always been inflexible in regard to nuns. These regulations had just been reapplied more severely in order to eliminate increasing abuses. This explains the considerable difficulties initially encountered by the foundations. The order of the Elizabethan nuns which developed from the medieval Begines and spread into Italy, France, the Netherlands, and the east of the Empire during the seventeenth century were never able to overcome the requirement of reclusion. For that reason they were reduced to installing hospitals solely in their own houses. The order of the Hospitallers was not impeded by the cloistral regulations.

Overcoming this obstacle was even harder for those women's orders who were active in the third area of the apostolate, the schools. Thus the Salesians could teach only girls who lived in a boarding school. And yet there was an actual school movement among the women's orders: the Ursulines were founded in Liège in 1622 and from there spread to Germany; in 1639 they established a house in Canadian Quebec. In 1606 a free form, forgoing reclusion and vows, was established in Dôle in the diocese of Besançcon; eventually this order established houses in Switzerland and southern Germany (Freiburg, Villingen). The most spirited fight for new forms for which Mary Ward aspired when she adopted the constitution of the Society of Jesus was waged by the English Ladies. Their work on the basis of less stringent vows was not fully recognized until Benedict XIV. Other women's orders also turned to the teaching of girls: the Dominican nuns in the form of congregations of the Frauen vom Heiligen Grab who flourished in their dedication to this goal especially in the Netherlands. Among the schools for boys those of the Jesuits were the most important ones, not just in France but everywhere. But other orders, such as the Benedictine monks, also dedicated part of their energies to the schools. A specific school order were the School Brothers. The order of the Piarists, specializing in building primary and secondary schools, was now spreading far and wide. When the Jesuit order was suppressed, members of these orders often jumped into the breach and kept the schools from being closed.

The few orders newly founded in the one and a half centuries prior to the great change signaled by the French Revolution were also imbued with the idea of the apostolate. In 1640 Bartholomäus Holzhauser (1613–58) founded a priestly congregation in Tittmoning (in the archdiocese of Salzburg) which was dedicated to the training of clerics and to missions. After 1655 he worked in the archdiocese of Mainz consolidating his institute of the Bartholomites The Passionists founded by Paul of the Cross (1694–1775) in Orbetello (on the shores of the Ligurian Sea between Civitavecchia and Livorno), whose generalate has been located at the monastery of Giovanni e Paolo in Rome since 1773, while dedicated to contemplation, were nonetheless active in the popular mission as well. Paul also founded a women's branch of this order which lived a strictly contemplative life. Alphonsus Liguori (1696–1787) initially founded the contemplative women's order of the Redemptorists (1731); it was followed by the male order a year later in Scala near Amalfi. Their main purpose was the mission to the most neglected among the inhabitants of the mountains near Naples. This order, looked on with suspicion by the temporal government, first spread in the Kingdom of Naples and then in the Papal States. For a while political tensions led to a split of the order into a

Neapolitan and a Papal States branch. Not until 1784 were the first non-Italians permitted to join, among them Clemens Maria Hofbauer, who paved the way for the congregation's expansion into Germany.

In the course of the eighteenth century the interest in all forms of monastic life decreased. To the enlightened spirit of the century monasticism appeared to be the essence of the obscure and fanatical, forever dominated by impenetrable darkness and defending a useless life of indolence. As an outgrowth of pointed discussion of the principle of usefulness — as seen from a purely worldly point of view — a spirit of decided hostility against monasticism arose which stifled monastic vocations. There are some important data which characterize this movement: the agitation against the Jesuit order leading to its abolition; the suppression and consolidation beginning in 1766 of 386 monastic establishments which had in many cases already shrunk drastically in size; the secularization of monasteries and convents in Austria under Joseph II involving all the contemplative orders; and the facile manner in which monastic establishments were abolished in Germany even by bishops (as in Mainz or Münster) in order to use their assets for other good causes. These events did not occur everywhere or in equal fashion; thus the attack during the French Revolution, for example, on the convents involved establishments which had in no way declined and indeed, had preserved an excellent spirit. The case of the religious orders of men was different. For 250 years the newer orders had been dedicated to obvious usefulness, such as the ministry, the inner mission, teaching, or social and charitable work, soon emulated by most of the old orders. And should not dedication to scholarly work in accordance with the most modern of methods also be considered useful? And yet in France and Germany the axe of secularization was applied impartially to all kinds of monastic life.

Indeed, many a demand was justifiable, e.g., that the age for profession not be too young — Joseph II raised the minimum age to twenty-four — and that the size of the dowry be restricted. Th growing self-confidence of man demanded a greater sense of responsibility especially on the part of monastic institutions. But this total blow against all monastic forms of existence cannot be understood merely on the basis of the argument that improvements were necessarily based on the demands of the times. Antipathy to monastic life grew to the extent that its complete dissolution appeared imminent, a fact accepted with surprising equanimity by those affected.

Section Three

The Papacy under the Increasing Pressure of the Established Church

Burkhart Schneider

In the course of the eighteenth century the Catholic powers — France and Austria in the wake of Portugal and Spain — lost their position of primacy in Europe and overseas. Their place was taken by non-Catholic powers, Prussia in central Europe and England, which became the primary maritime power, establishing its Empire and seeking to preserve the balance of power between the states on the European continent by means of its policy of alliances and subsidies. The general development of countries into modern states, especially in the administrative and economic sectors, was not shared by the Papal States primarily because they were lacking dynastic continuity, an absolutely necessary prerequisite for long-range policies. In the crucial first half of the century, moreover, the Papal States had been sorely and repeatedly affected by wars because they were militarily and politically too weak to maintain their proclaimed neutrality and to protect themselves against violations. The discrepancy between the temporal rule of the Pope and that of the other contemporary states was steadily growing. The Papal States became a liability rather than fulfilling their original function of ensuring the Pope of the freedom and independence required for the guidance of the total Church. As the eighteenth century progressed the Papal States reached a condition which was deplored by the eminent Cardinal Consalvi.

In those states which were still nominally Catholic the leading personalities came under the influence of an ever more radical Enlightenment, so that they could hardly be called Catholic any more. These states developed an established Church down to the smallest details, which was distinguished from the Gallicanism of the preceding century primarily by a total absence of actual religiosity as well as by a brutal arbitrariness divorced from all tradition. The Church was considered a mere instrument of the state to be employed at the discretion of the state as a state institution without regard to its specific character and inner laws. The papacy was virtually helpless in the face of demands by this type of established Church. Confronted on the part of the Catholic powers by extortionist tactics which included the threat of schism, perhaps not always intended seriously, the papacy had to make one concession after another. The extreme helplessness of the papacy can best be seen by the example of the suppression of the Jesuit order when the Holy See had to lend itself to sanctioning and actively bringing to its conclusion the hunt against the Society of Jesus which had been started by the so-called Catholic states. Although future Popes also had to endure persecution, even expulsion from Rome and imprisonment, this case of compelled complicity in the destruction of an institution of great merit to Church and papacy whose downfall was destined to do noticeable damage to both was a singularly flagrant result of the weakness of the Holy See and its dependence on outer influences.

Also a sign of weakness and considerable indecision was that the leadership of the Church tried to delay long-overdue reforms and simply refused to heed justified desires submitted to the Holy See. Concerns reflecting the demands of the time which could have been solved without particular difficulty — issues concerning monastic law, ecclesiastical immunity, the adaptation of liturgical forms — while often coupled with other demands contradictory to the essence of the Church, were rejected out of hand as attacks on the rights of the Church. Conversely, positions were adhered to which had long been outmoded and were destined shortly to be destroyed by force. The negative attitude of the Church toward the demands of the Enlightenment continuously widened the gap between the Church and contemporary culture. By the same token, adherence to such formally valid but actually outmoded structures as the Vienna Concordat of 1448 for the German Empire or the Concordat of 1516 for France, made the Church drift farther and farther away from the real and constantly changing world round it. It was nothing short of fatal that in this period no actual initiatives were taken by the church leadership to adapt ecclesiastical forms and pastoral efforts to modern circumstances. In point of fact, the violent upheaval toward the end of the century found the Church basically unprepared.

CHAPTER 139

The Popes from Innocent XIII to Clement XII

Innocent XIII (1721–24)

During his long pontificate (1700–1721) Clement XI had appointed seventy cardinals, sixteen of whom had not survived the Pope. Within the traditional factions of the conclave beginning on 31 March 1721 the imperial cardinals could no longer rely on the support of their Spanish colleagues; the change of the dynasty now allied that group with the French faction. On the first day of the conclave, with barely half the cardinals present, the election of Paolucci, the secretary of state of Clement XI, appeared to be imminent. Since Vienna blamed him for the policies of the dead Pope, said to be friendly to the Bourbons, the imperial legate, Cardinal Althan, pronounced the formal exclusion against him. During the lengthy conclave many unsuccessful efforts were made until finally the candidacy of the French Cardinal Michel Angelo de' Conti was promoted, who raised the expectation of cooperation both with the French crown and the Emperor. On 8 May 1721, he was elected unanimously. The newly elected Pope took his name after the most famous member of his family, Innocent III, who had granted his brother the fiefdom of Poli, where Conti was born in 1655. He had been nuncio in Lisbon for ten years; in 1719 he had resigned from his diocese of Viterbo for reasons of health, so a lasting pontificate could not be expected. Although the Pope did invest the Emperor with Sicily and Naples, for which the latter had waited since the beginning of the War of the Spanish Succession, the negotiations for the already decided return of Comacchio turned out to be so prolonged that Innocent XIII did not live to see it. In the first year of his pontificate he appointed a total of three cardinals in two consistories. At the beginning of his second year his old affliction of lithiasis flared up again; several times he was not expected to live. His constant illness cast a shadow over his pontificate. He was released from his suffering on 7 March 1724. He is the only Pope in the history of the modern papacy who did not get a monument in Saint Peter's, although he was entombed there.

Benedict XIII (1724–30)

In the conclave beginning on 20 March 1724 the constellation of the factions was identical to the previous one. After several unsuccessful attempts a dark horse again was nominated in order to end the conclave which had already lasted far too long. On 29 May the Dominican Cardinal Vincenzo Maria (Pietro Francesco) Orsini was elected unanimously. But only after considerable resistance could he be persuaded to accept the election. He was the eldest son of the duke of Gravina near Bari, but had forgone his hereditary rights in order to enter the Dominican order. At the time of the election he was already seventy-five years old. Urged by his family, Clement X had appointed him cardinal at the age of twenty-three; he had been bishop of Manfredonia, Cesena, and Benevento (since 1686) in succession. His pastoral zeal and his ascetic life were praised everywhere. But he had no political experience. He chose his name in memory of the Dominican Pope Benedict XI. He was given the ordinal after some initial hesitation because Pedro de Luna, Benedict XIII at the time of the western schism and the Council of Constance, was considered an anti-Pope. In his personal life he continued to be a modest religious, refusing to move into the splendorous rooms of the Vatican. Even as Pope his main concern was the conduct of the diocese of Rome; the major part of his time was spent with consecrations of churches and altars, visits to the sick, religious instruction, and the administration of sacraments.

Given this attitude to his office, the selection of the Pope's co-workers took on extreme importance. While Benedict XIII made a fortuitous move in selecting Paolucci as secretary of state, his next appointment was to be fatal for his entire pontificate. As archbishop of Benevento, he had placed unlimited trust in Niccolò Coscia from the vicinity of Benevento. Now he gave him the kind of influential position at the papal court that in earlier times would most likely have been occupied only by a papal nephew. Greedy and unscrupulous, Coscia abused his position from the very start. In 1725, against the open disagreement of several cardinals, among them Secretary of State Paolucci, the Pope appointed him cardinal. Coscia promptly put a number of other Beneventans into influential positions. The climax was reached on 12 June 1726 after the death of Paolucci when the Pope, following a suggestion by Coscia, appointed the *Maestro di Camera,* Niccolò Maria

Lercari, the new secretary of state. Lercari was totally dependent on Coscia. In spite of all the accusations raised against Coscia and incontrovertible evidence of his avarice and mismanagement, Benedict XIII held fast to his favorite as though blinded. Coscia sold vacant positions or divided the revenues with their holders. He managed to isolate the Pope to such a degree that in the end the latter was advised by no one but the group around Coscia. If the financial affairs of the Papal States got into a state of total disorder as a result of his mismanagement, the all powerful Coscia would intervene in the field of foreign policy and have himself paid princely sums for his services by the ambassadors of foreign powers.

The house of Savoy, like that of the Emperor, knew how to exploit the situation in Rome to its advantage. Victor Amadeus II, who had assumed the royal title in 1713, managed — again with the help of Coscia, Secretary of State Lercari, and Lambertini — to obtain recognition of his royal title along with the presentation right for the bishoprics on the island of Sardinia. Although the Pope declared emphatically that he was unwilling to surrender a single right of the Church, the legate of Savoy succeeded by means of the concordat of 1727 in obtaining a solution which was most advantageous for Piedmont. The opinion of Cardinal Lambertini that nuisances had to be endured in order to prevent worse had made an impression on the Pope. The King was granted the right of episcopal appointments and the administration of the revenues during a *sedes vacans* virtually for the whole territory. All the officials of the Holy See who had had a part in the conclusion of the concordat were generously rewarded by the Turin government. This makes it obvious how the negotiations were conducted. By appointing a number of Dominicans to the sees the King assured himself of the Pope's continued benevolence in spite of the enormous concessions the Holy See had made in the concordat.

The Pope's lack of concern for the political issues confronting the Church was contrasted by his desire to do justice to his office as supreme head of the Church. He issued numerous orders for reforms and the restoration of discipline in the Church. But all too often his regulations were burdened by minutiae and were therefore without lasting effect. The jubilee of 1725, in the course of which the Spanish Stairs, under construction for four years, were consecrated, gave the Pope reason for many ceremonial Masses. The staircase, leading from the Piazza di Spagna to the church of the Trinità dei Monti was a legacy of the former French ambassador. In opposition to the cardinals he convened a Roman provincial council after Easter which he conducted in person. This claimed his attention for weeks to the point that all other affairs came to a halt. Benedict XIII also pursued the execution of the Tridentine resolutions concerning the establishment of diocesan seminaries; he even appointed a special congregation for seminaries. Given the Pope's nature, it is not surprising that the number of beatifications and canonizations during his pontificate was noticeably high. He also continued to be attached to his former diocese of Benevento, which he visited twice, in 1727 and 1729.

Of his twenty-nine appointments to the cardinalate, made in twelve consistories, the ones of Coscia and Lercari were disastrous because of their negative influence on the Pope, while the one of Lambertini (at the end of 1726) was to be significant. The Catholic powers pressured Benedict XIII more than any other Pope before him to have their favorites elevated to the purple. However, that he did not agree to appoint Nuncio Bichi in Portugal, where he was zealously promoted by that government.

Characteristic for the situation of the Church and the papacy was the negative reaction of the powers to the Pope's efforts to have the feast of Saint Pope Gregory VII and the appropriate readings from the breviary adopted by the entire Church. Actually a minor issue, it came to be viewed as a highly political matter because of Gregory's position in the controversy over the investiture and his stand against Emperor Henry IV. In France, Naples, Belgium, and Venice the printing and distribution of the new liturgical texts were made subject to heavy penalties because this act was considered a violation of the ecclesiastical sovereignty of the state.

Benedict XIII died on 21 February 1730 after a brief illness. In accordance with his wishes he was laid to rest in the Dominican church of Maria sopra Minerva.

Clement XII (1730–40)

The death of the Pope brought with it the immediate fall of the Beneventan group in the Curia. Coscia had to leave the Vatican on the very first day after the Pope's demise. Because the wrath of the population was directed especially against him, he was forced to flee Rome in the dead of night. A month after the start of the conclave he was permitted to return with reservations; again he had to make his way through Rome at night. In addition to the traditional factions among the papal electors there was now a Savoyard party among whom were those cardinals who had participated in the concordat of 1727. In the course of the conclave more than half of the cardinals present were at one time or another nominated as candidates. After four months, on 12 July 1730, the seventy-eight-year-old Florentine Lorenzo Corsini was elected. He had been nominated two months prior by the French faction, but at that time, being a Tuscan, he had been rejected by the imperial party, which anticipated complications upon the extinction of the Medici line. In the meantime there had been successful intercession in his behalf in Vienna. But when the imperial concurrence arrived on 7 July, the French faction demurred because it forced them to relinquish their candidate Banchieri, whom they had promoted in the interim. Moreover, they suspected some sort of imperial machination behind the suddenly resumed candidacy of Corsini. The newly elected Pope had pursued his career in Rome. His domicile in the Palazzo Pamfili on the Piazza Navona had been the center of intellectual and scholarly life in Rome. Highly esteemed, he had been close to election in the two previous conclaves, but had been excluded by the great powers. By now he was too old and his vision so impaired that he became totally blind in 1732. This left the conduct of business to the immediate circle around the Pope.

The new Pope, taking his name after Clement XI, who had appointed him to the cardinalate, immediately tried to repair the damage done during the preceding pontificate. Coscia and his group were put on trial. Having fled to Naples because he was hoping for support from the Emperor for his efforts on behalf of the *Monarchia Sicula,* Coscia was now faced by the threat of demotion and excommunication. In 1732 he decided to stand trial in order to defend himself. On

9 May 1733, he was condemned to ten years at the Castel Sant'Angelo, restitution of all unlawful gains, and payment of 100,000 scudi; his franchise was revoked for the duration of his incarceration. But at the subsequent conclave in 1740 Coscia was readmitted with full rights; Prospero Lambertini, elected at that conclave, who was heavily indebted to Coscia, canceled the remainder of his prison term.

Clement XII urged revision of the concordat with Piedmont because it had been concluded illegally. In 1731 he pronounced it invalid. After initial protests Piedmont was forced to give in and agree to renegotiate the concordat. This had not been concluded by the time the Pope died. Efforts to cure the chaotic fiscal situation proved to be extremely difficult. Although new sources of revenue were found the burden of debt carried by the Papal States kept increasing.

Initially Clement XII was able to resist pressure by the great powers, installing only Italian cardinals. The single exception was the Portuguese nuncio Bichi, whose appointment had been urged by Lisbon for more than a decade. The agreement to elevate him after Bichi tendered a formal apology for his disobedience was a special act of conciliation as well as a political necessity in order to reestablish normal relations with Portugal. In the second half of his pontificate Clement XII had to be more accessible to the wishes of the great powers. Since Portugal insisted on the appointment of the patriarch of Lisbon to the cardinalate, the Pope also had to take the demands of the larger states into account, which he did in a promotion at the end of 1737.

The first papal condemnation of the Freemasons took place in 1738. The lodges had formed about two decades before in England and spread across the continent, including Rome. The condemnation can be explained by an apprehension of indifferentism and hostility to revealed religion. It was based on incomplete and one-sided information and did not do adequate justice to the many different currents represented in Freemasonry at the time.

The decade brought about a new shift of power in Italy. When Duke Antonio Farnese of Parma and Piacenza died heirless on 20 January 1731, the issue of the feudal rights over these territories resurfaced. According to the peace treaty of 1720, Don Carlos, the son of Queen Elizabeth of Spain, was to receive the inheritance of the Farnese; Spain wanted his investiture by the Pope. But the Emperor claimed the feudal rights and had the territory occupied for Don Carlos. The Pope's protest was to no avail.

When the Polish King Augustus of Saxony died on 1 February 1732, the Pope initially sided with his son Friedrich August. But France, with the support of the Polish primate, promoted the candidacy of Stanislas Leszczyński, who was promptly elected. Encircled in Danzig by Russian and Saxon troops, he was reduced to waiting for help from the French. In the meantime France, Spain, and Piedmont had agreed to use the Polish War of Succession for the purpose of exploiting the difficult situation of the Empire and depriving the Emperor of his Italian possessions. By fall of 1733 Lombardy was in the hands of Piedmont. At the beginning of 1734 the Pope had to grant permission for an army under Don Carlos which was to occupy Naples to cross his territories. By the end of 1734 the entire Kingdom of Naples including Sicily was conquered by Spanish troops. Given the military helplessness of the Papal States, the Pope had no recourse when the Spaniards recruited soldiers there and passed through his territories at will. In the meantime the Peace of Vienna between the Emperor and France stipulated that Leszczyński would forego the Polish crown and in exchange receive the duchies of Bar and Lorraine, which were to go to France after his death. Duke Francis of Lorraine was to be compensated by the Grand Duchy of Tuscany after the death of the last of the Medici. Don Carlos was assured of the Kingdom of the Two Sicilies. The Emperor retained Lombardy, with the exception of a few areas which went to Piedmont, and the duchies of Parma and Piacenza. Lastly, the Pragmatic Sanction, intended to regulate the Austrian succession, was recognized by France. This shift of power in Italy was arranged without consulting the Pope and without regard to his feudal rights. Since Spain did not accept the Peace of Vienna, the war in northern Italy continued, repeatedly affecting the Papal States. In March 1736 the population of Rome revolted against the recruitment of troops by the Spanish. As a consequence several towns of the Papal States were occupied by Spanish troops. In May 1736 Spain, followed by Naples, broke diplomatic relations with the Holy See. To restore them, the Pope was forced to make large concessions in a concordat with Spain.

Notable administrative improvements in the Papal States were the promotion of trade and industry and the regulatory work in the Romagna. It was here that Cardinal Alberoni, back in favor since 1735, was active as papal legate. He established a permanent monument for himself by his generous endowment of a college in Piacenza named after him, which combined a theological boarding institution with a philosophical and theological university. But his attempt to incorporate San Marino into the Papal States failed because Clement XII decided that the annexation could not be made without the free consent of its citizens.

For the last several years of his life the blind Pope was almost constantly bedridden. He died on 6 February 1740.

CHAPTER 140

Benedict XIV

The conclave beginning on 19 February 1740 and lasting for exactly six months was the longest since the Western Schism. For the first time the Austrian and French interests coincided; they were opposed by the Spanish cardinals, supported by those of Naples and Tuscany. Also important was the opposition between the cardinals installed by the deceased Pope and the "old" ones, appointed by his predecessor and led by Cardinal Albani. One candidate after the other failed, often on the balance of a single vote. Four cardinals died in the course of the conclave. Finally, in about the middle of August, the crown cardinals united behind the sixty-five-year-old Prospero Lambertini, archbishop of Bologna since 1731. At the beginning of the conclave he had been able to attract a few votes, but the scrutinies of the last few days prior to the decisive agreement had not given him a single vote. Yet on 17 August he was elected unanimously. He assumed his name in memory of Benedict XIII, who had elevated him to the cardinalate. The new Pope had made an excellent reputation for himself as a canonist; his work on the beatifications and canonizations became a classic in the field. Active in the Curia since the beginning of the century, he had gained influence by virtue of his thoroughness and stamina. Benedict XIII consulted him on political issues several times. More often than not Lambertini favored a policy of conciliation with an opposing state; often enough the resulting solutions did no more than save the bare principles. Beyond his specialty of canon law he was interested in the learning of his time, especially in literature and history; he was considered an "enlightened" and modern ecclesiastical prince. Witty and liberal in his private conversations, he did not shrink from criticizing institutions and personalities of the Church. He was a generous and open man, yet not always a good judge of human character. His trust in the French ambassador to Rome (until 1742), Crown Cardinal de Tencin, reflected by his friendship and voluminous private correspondence, was certainly misplaced. The Pope frankly and without reservations entrusted his thoughts on all kinds of issues to his correspondent — among them matters of policy which required the strictest secrecy. Cardinal de Tencin, who was a dependent of his immoral sister, the mother of the Encyclopedist d'Alembert, had copies and translations of the Pope's letters made and sent to the French government.

The fifty-year-old Silvio Valenti Gonzaga, nuncio in Brussels and Madrid, became secretary of state. Like the Pope, he was open to the arts and sciences. His rural estate, later called the Villa Bonaparte at the Porta Pia, became a center for scholars and artists, including foreigners.

In attempting to solve pending issues with the Catholic powers Benedict XIV in his capacity as Pope was just as ready for large concessions as he had been as Cardinal Lambertini. First to be settled were the disputes with Naples. The Pope agreed to the establishment of a mixed court of law to include laymen which was to judge ecclesiastical issues and persons. In a secret article, moreover, the *Placetum regium* was implicitly granted. More favorable to the Church was the agreement with Piedmont, but here too most of the wishes of that government were granted. The most far-reaching concession was the concordat with Spain in 1753. After initial resistance the demand for an extension of the royal patronage, already in existence in Granada and Spanish America, to all of Spain, was in the end granted by Benedict XIV. It had been demanded by Madrid for a number of decades and rejected again by the late Pope Clement XII. In secret negotiations, with sole participation by the Pope and his secretary of state and without the nuncio, Benedict acquiesced in all the important points. A mere fifty-two benefices were left to the Holy See to fill, while the King obtained the right of appointment to approximately twelve thousand of them. To make up the financial loss to the Curia the Spanish government was prepared to pay a compensation. At that time it was already a well-known fact that the secretary of state had received a significant sum of money from Spain. This put an onus on the concordat, which was made public only after its conclusion.

Of all the political changes taking place in the year 1740 the death of Emperor

Charles VI on 20 October had the greatest impact. As far as the Austrian hereditary lands were concerned, female succession had been regulated by the Pragmatic Sanction. Yet Bavaria, Spain, and Prussia raised claims to parts of the inheritance. After some delay Benedict XIV recognized the hereditary right of Maria Theresa. In view of the impending imperial election, the Pope decided upon strict neutrality, to which he adhered in the face of tremendous pressure by the great powers, primarily France, which had entered into an alliance with Prussia against Austria. Only after Karl Albert von Wittelsbach had been elected Emperor Charles VII did Benedict announce his recognition of him. In the meantime Friedrich II of Prussia had occupied Silesia and Bavaria had invaded Austria with help by the French. Spain exploited the threat to Austria by attacking its possessions in Italy. In the course of their advance, Spanish and Austrian troops, unmindful of papal protests, marched through the papal territories unimpeded and even turned them into theaters of war. In May and June 1743, battles took place in the immediate environs of Rome, where the Austrian army remained until the fall of 1744. When Charles VII died on 20 January 1745, Benedict XIV assumed the same stance of neutrality as he had found years before.

In the Peace of Aachen (1748), Parma and Piacenza were again disposed of in total disregard of the Pope's feudal rights. The protest submitted by the papal legate and repeated by Benedict XIV in person was merely noted as the dissenting point of view of the Holy See.

The years of war placed a constant financial burden in the administration of the Papal States, reflected in increased debts and diminished revenues. The Peace of Aachen, which granted Italy a period of rest lasting almost half a century, initiated a time of economic recovery. The city of Rome started to regain its stature as a center of cultural life.

Interested in all areas of the sciences, the Pope supported individual scholars as well as large research projects not only in the humanities, foremost among them historical studies, but also in the natural sciences. A remarkable occurrence was his agreement for calling two women to the university of Bologna, his old diocese. He maintained close ties of friendship with the greatest contemporary Italian historian, Ludovico Muratori. Ill feelings were caused when the Pope accepted Voltaire's drama *Mahomet,* handed him by Cardinal Passionei, who had close ties to that representative of French Enlightenment, and the famous hexameters composed by Voltaire for the painting of the Pope. Voltaire himself soon let it be known that Benedict had thanked him, started a correspondence with him, and sent him two gold medals. This was injurious to the Pope's public esteem.

The revision of the Index and the procedure whereby printed matter was placed on the Index constituted true progress. Subsequent practice, to be sure, did not keep pace with the more modern procedure desired by Benedict XIV. He wanted the objectionable passages — in the case of a well-known Catholic author — made known to him; if the author was prepared to improve them, the prohibition was not to be published. The author, moreover, was to have the chance to defend and justify himself.

Benedict XIV was especially intent on augmenting the Vatican collections and enlarging the library. He acquired the largest private collection of books in Rome, the so called *Ottoboniana,* following the death of the last Ottoboni from the family of Pope Alexander VIII. He also planned to make the manuscript holdings of the Vatican generally accessible by means of a printed catalogue to consist of twenty volumes.

In regard to the appointment of cardinals Benedict XIV, as did his predecessors, often had to accede to the wishes of certain governments to elevate their candidates. A special case at the promotion of July 1747 was the elevation to the cardinalate of the last of the Stuarts, Duke Henry of York (d. 1807), who had joined the ecclesiastical estate after the Stuarts lost the battle of Culloden in 1746.

In questions of theology, especially in the doctrine of grace, Benedict XIV tended toward the Augustinian school. The indexing of the works of Cardinal Noris by the Spanish Inquisition was revoked by him: he succeeded in having them struck from the Spanish Index after ten years of negotiations. Prior to his election to the papacy he had once mentioned that Jansenism was merely a phantom and an invention of the Jesuits. But even though he publicly rejected complaints that he was a friend of the Jansenists and an opponent of the Jesuits, the fact remains that during his pontificate Rome became a major center of the Jesuits' opponents, whose esteem and influence were rising. Focal point and head of that group was Cardinal Passionei, who had built a popular rural retreat with a valuable library in Camaldoli near Frascati. Even at that time the efforts to have the Jesuit order suppressed, pursued by the general of the Augustinian order, Vázquez, the Spanish ambassador Roda, and several prelates of the Curia, were common knowledge.

The first blow against the society was struck in the mission territories. The controversy over the rites with its disastrous consequences for the Asiatic missions had already lasted the entire century. The pertinent condemnations pronounced by Benedict XIV in 1742 and 1744 represented a long-expected outcome. But during his pontificate the Jesuit missions in Latin America and especially their reductions were also placed in extreme jeopardy and finally marked for extinction. At the very beginning of his office Benedict XIV had already acceded to the claims of the established church of Portugal in order to alleviate the pastoral problems caused by the long *sede* vacancies in many of the Portuguese dioceses. Also fulfilled by the Pope were other demands by Portugal, such as the special recognition of the patriarch of Lisbon and his canonists and the awarding of a special title to the King (*rex fidelissimus,* in adaptation to the title *rex christianissimus,* to which the King of France was entitled). When Joseph de Varcalho e Melho, Marquis de Pombal after 1770, who had become familiar with the administration of modern state government as a diplomat in Vienna and London, was appointed secretary of state, the attack against the Jesuits began in earnest. In order to effect economic reforms in Portugal, Pombal wanted to incorporate the Church into the mechanism of the state. His measures were directed against the orders in general. After the death of the queen mother (1754) and the earthquake in Lisbon on 1 November 1755, which gave rise to some unwise utterances by a few priests, he dropped his initial caution. The Jesuits, especially, were accused of all sorts of violations and crimes. In 1758 Pombal demanded that Benedict XIV appoint the Portuguese Cardinal Saldanha, a relative of the all-powerful secretary of state and totally dependent on him, to the office of visitor of the Jesuit order for Portugal with all the requisite authority. When the Pope gave in to this demand, the fate of the order in Portugal and its overseas possessions was sealed.

In the Austro-Venetian quarrel over the patriarchate of Aquileia the Pope was also intent on a settlement which would meet the two powers halfway. In 1418/20 when Venice had annexed Friaul and terminated the temporal rule of the patriarch over that territory, the diocese was politically partitioned. The larger part with its cathedral church was given to Austria, whereas Friaul with its actual patriarchal residence of Udine became part of Venice. Since the fifteenth century Austria had repeatedly tried to be assigned its own bishop; in 1628 it finally forbade the patriarch to exercise his functions in the Austrian part and kept its subjects from turning to the bishop in Udine. In 1748 Maria Theresa again applied for the establishment of a separate bishopric. The initial solution, the establishment of an apostolic vicariate in Görz, was rejected by the seigniory, which broke off relations with Rome in the summer of 1750 after its protests had been to no avail. Upon the suggestion of France, which had intervened as a mediator in order to keep the conflict from spreading, the patriarchate of Aquileia was abolished and the two bishoprics of Udine and Görz were established. The old cathedral of Aquileia was declared exempt and the patriarch permitted to retain the title for his person.

The same conciliatory attitude which Benedict XIV manifested toward the Catholic powers and which at times prompted him to make excessive concessions was also applied to non-Catholic powers in order to improve the lot of the Catholic minorities in those countries. By means of its conquest of Silesia following the death of Charles VI, Prussia had significantly increased its Catholic population. Although the peace treaty of Breslau (1742) had assured the Catholic Church that the status quo would be maintained, the Catholics in fact became second-class citizens. According to the King's view the state was to exercise supreme supervisory power over the Protestant as well as the Catholic Church. The bishop of Breslau, Cardinal von Sinzendorf, was in no position effectively to counter the extreme steps of the established Church. He himself developed the plan for a vicariate for Prussia which was actually conceived as a "royal" rather than an "apostolic" vicariate. But Benedict XIV, whose concurrence was vigorously solicited by the Breslau cardinal, insisted that the future vicar general be lawfully installed, that is by the Pope. At the same time, Friedrich II prevailed in having the twenty-six-year-old Count Schaffgotsch, whom he liked but whose general conduct caused a lot of chagrin, accepted into the Breslau cathedral chapter. Without the count's participation and against the opposition of Rome the King appointed Schaffgotsch coadjutor to Cardinal von Sinzendorf. The Pope thereupon forbade the appointed coadjutor to be consecrated bishop. Upon Sinzendorf's death in 1747 Schaffgotsch, supported by Friedrich II's favor and skillfully feigning an inner rebirth, managed to have Benedict XIV appoint him as Sinzendorf's successor. It is probable that Benedict XIV saw through Schaffgotsch's insincerity. In connection with this affair the Pope for the first time implicitly recognized the Prussian royal title by mentioning in March 1748 the "royal person of Friedrich II." Up to that time the Curia had persistently used the earlier annoying title "Margrave of Brandenburg."

Even in his advanced years Benedict XIV displayed an astonishing stamina; after the serious illness of Secretary of State Valenti Gonzaga in 1751 until the latter's death in 1756 he did not appoint a successor but burdened himself with the major portion of the additional work. As a result his own health deteriorated;

after 1756 he was feared to be on the verge of death several times. He died on 3 May 1758; according to witnesses he remarked immediately before his passing that he had been betrayed by Spain in the matter of the concordat.

In his papal history Pastor makes an unqualified positive judgment regarding the pontificate of Benedict XIV and especially concerning his political efforts. Yet some serious misgivings have been raised about that position. Even Pope Pius XII in a prepared but undelivered allocution on the occasion of the two-hundredth anniversary of Benedict XIV mentions that the Pope probably manifested too much acquiescence and weakness in the concordats with Naples, Savoy, and Spain as well as in his attitude toward Friedrich II of Prussia.

CHAPTER 141

Clement XIII and Clement XIV

Clement XIII (1758–69)

In the conclave starting on 15 May 1758 there was an initial agreement by more than two thirds of the cardinals on the candidacy of Cardinal Cavalchini when the formal exclusion was pronounced against him by the French Crown Cardinal Luynes because of Cavalchini's position in the beatification of Bellarmine (this was the last formal exclusion of the eighteenth century and the only one from the French side). On 6 July the Venetian Cardinal Carlo Rezzonico was elected. He had been elevated to the cardinalate by Clement XII in 1737 and for that reason he chose the name of Clement. Bishop of Padua since 1743, he had proved himself to be an ardent and strict ecclesiastic.

The Jesuit issue became the dominant one of his pontificate. A few weeks after the election Secretary of State Archinto, reappointed by the Pope's predecessor, died. In the person of Luigi Torrigiani, Clement XIII appointed a confirmed friend of the society to that office. But Torrigiani was unable to stop the anti-Jesuit momentum. The rapidly spreading persecution of the Jesuit order was unique in the annals of church history by virtue of its extent and effect. A parallel has been drawn between this persecution and the fragmentation of Poland, for in addition to the coincidence of the events there was also the common element of a degree of cynicism which disregarded all existing rights. The attack on the order has also been viewed as an attack on the Church itself and especially on the papacy. There were also a variety of additional forces, such as theological and ecclesiastical special interests in a complex combination with political, anti-Church, and enlightened tendencies. All of this finally led to the vehement demand for basic changes in the structure of the Jesuit order and, in the end, for its suppression. Certainly there were faults and abuses within the ranks of the order and many of the complaints and accusations were not without justification. Yet an objective investigation will show that the discrepancy between ideal and reality in the Jesuit order was no more serious than in other ecclesiastical communities of the time.

The attack against the order began in Portugal, where a brief of Benedict XIV, dated 1 April 1758, had appointed Cardinal Saldanha, who was totally dependent on Pombal, to the office of apostolic visitor of the order with full authority. Without an actual investigation, the Jesuits were first accused of illegal commercial transactions; next, some time after the unsuccessful assassination attempt on the King on 3 September 1758, they were accused of participation in that conspiracy. In June 1759 all the assets of the order in Portugal and its overseas territories were confiscated. In September in spite of energetic intervention by Clement XIII the members of the order were deported first from Portugal and then gradually from the overseas possessions and sent to the Papal States. Many died during transport (about 90 to 100) or were kept in Portuguese jails, often under inhuman conditions (about 180), or left the order (about 250, constituting 15 percent of the Portuguese contingent of the order).

France was the first country to follow Portugal's example. But in contrast to Portugal and the other states from which the Jesuits were destined to be expelled in subsequent years, France had a strong and in part well-organized opposition against the Jesuits, especially in the parliament. This opposition increased around the middle of the seventeenth century, fueled by the disputes with the Jansenist movement and literarily well documented in Pascal's *Provincial Letters.* Immediately after the middle of the century some individual cases aggravated the already serious tensions. The year 1755 marked the beginning of the affair involving Lavalette, an economist and superior of the Jesuit order on the Antilles. In order to secure the economic aspects of the mission work he operated plantations and tried to sell their products in Europe. Losses due to war and the bankruptcy of his correspondent commercial house in France led to the failure of his undertakings. Initially the French courts made Lavalette personally liable for the damages, but then in 1760 the order as a whole and its assets in France in particular were declared liable. Furthermore, Mme Pompadour, rising to the position of favorite of the King in 1756 and becoming all powerful, disliked the Jesuits because they disapproved of her position at the court. After the assassination attempt on Louis XV (15 January 1757) public opinion was aroused against the Jesuits when they were accused of complicity on the basis of their doctrine regarding tyrannicide.

Desperate attempts by the French superiors of the order, extending to a formal recognition of the four Gallican articles of 1682 and, in some cases, advocating a secession from the united order by the establishment of a separate French vicariate general, were unable to avert the disaster. Although the great majority of the French episcopate had pronounced themselves in favor of the Jesuits, and in spite of several interventions by Clement XIII with the bishops and Louis XV, all assets of the order were confiscated in April 1762. The following August marked the beginning of deportation. A significant percentage, especially of the scholastics and the lay brothers among the almost three thousand French Jesuits, left the order with the agreement of their superiors. On 1 December 1764, the Society of Jesus in France was officially abolished. The previously prepared bull *Apostolicum pascendi,* which reacknowledged the order and made an unequivocal statement in favor of the Jesuits, was published on 7 January 1765 as a direct answer to the French abolition. As could be expected, this public pronouncement by Clement XIII had no practical result.

In 1759 Charles III, formerly King of Naples, ascended the Spanish throne. Dependent on his prime minister, Tanucci, he inclined toward an expansion of the established Church and a restriction of the liberties of the Church of Rome. But Tanucci was also a confirmed opponent of the Jesuit order. His influence and some skillfully manipulated changes in the first rank of government affected the heretofore friendly attitude toward the Jesuits. In a later stage of the investigation but without actual proof the "Hat Rebellion" of March 1766, caused by economic and social abuses, was blamed on the Jesuits. The death of Queen Mother Elizabeth Farnese precisely that same year caused the order to lose an influential patron. Certain ecclesiastical circles, especially the Augustine General Vázquez, urged the government to take steps against the Jesuit order. Giving no reasons, a royal decree of 27 February 1767 ordered the banishment of all Jesuits from Spanish territory and the confiscation of all Jesuit assets. The rules for the implementation of the decree were issued in the strictest secrecy. On 2 April the Spanish members of the order, numbering about twenty-eight hundred, were confined and deported. In the course of the year the approximately sixteen hundred Jesuits living in the overseas possessions met the same fate. In a show of resistance to the unilateral, forcible action by Spain, the papal government denied landing rights to the Spanish ships transporting the Jesuits to its ports. They finally found refuge on Corsica. In the following year when the island had become French they were able to travel to the territories of the Papal States. The protest by the Pope with the King of Spain had no effect whatsoever.

After the actions of Spain, the expulsion of the Jesuits from the Spanish secundogenitures of Naples (20 November 1767), Parma-Piacenza (7 February 1768), as well as from the island of Malta (22 April 1768) was no more than expected.

It is not surprising that an outgrowth of these individual actions would be a united plan for the total abolition of the Jesuit order by authority of the Pope. This plan seems to have been developed almost simultaneously in both France and Portugal with affirmation by Spain being assumed. The only difficult element which also took some time to overcome was the anticipated resistance of Maria Theresa, whose support could not be enlisted. Finally in 1770 she declared her neutrality and agreed not to undertake anything in favor of the Jesuits if the other powers could obtain from the Pope the abolition of the order; furthermore, she would not withhold her concurrence in the ultimate decision of the Holy See. A pretext for this alliance was the situation in Parma. Its prime minister, Du Tillot, had repeatedly violated the rights of the Church. In a decree of 16 January 1768 he stopped any and all cases from being submitted to foreign courts, meaning also the ecclesiastical courts in Rome. On 30 January a monitory declared those violations null and void and made their perpetrators subject to the penalties of the Church according to the Eucharistic bull *In coena Domini.* Since all the Bourbon courts felt affected by this monitory they decided to undertake a concerted action. In April 1768 the respective ambassadors demanded of Clement XIII the immediate revocation of the document under threat of reprisals. When the Pope did not give in, the papal enclaves of Benevento and Pontecorvo, Avignon and Venaissin were occupied. The stubborn refusal of the Pope did not deter the Catholic powers from making additional demands. A climax was reached in January 1769 when the ambassadors formally requested the Pope for the abolition of the Jesuit order.

The financial difficulties of the Papal States, aggravated by famine and rising prices in 1763 and 1764, continued because reforms could not be implemented against the will of the large property holders. Regarding architectural projects, only the completion of the Fontana Trevi and the Villa Albani took place in these years. In 1763, following a recommendation of Cardinal Albani, the Pope appointed Winckelmann commissioner of antiquities. Before that, the Pope, scrupulously fearful, had had a number of antique sculptures covered and the *Last Judgment* in the Sistine Chapel painted over again. Even then these measures had incurred Winckelmann's scorn, but he nonetheless accepted the Pope's offer.

Like his predecessors, Clement XIII favored Italian prelates for promotion, mostly those in the service of the Curia and a few candidates suggested by the Catholic powers. The appointment of his nephew met with general agreement since the latter kept aloof from the affairs of state. Unfortunate, although unavoidable, was the elevation of the short-term French foreign minister de Bernis, whose unedifying, totally secular way of life was well known. The most important of Clement XIII's appointments turned out to be that of Lorenzo Ganganelli, the future Pope Clement XIV, who was elevated to the purple in 1759.

Clement XIII died on 2 February 1769 of a heart attack after he celebrated Mass early in the morning and consecrated the candles of the day. His tomb in Saint Peter's, created by Canova, was not unveiled until twenty-three years after his death.

Clement XIV (1769–74)

The conclave beginning on 15 February 1769 was marked by the Jesuit issue. No election could take place until the Spanish cardinals arrived in Rome because the French, having arrived there a month earlier, had made it clear that they would use their exclusion against anyone who might be elected prior to the arrival of the Spaniards. The Catholic powers were agreed that no friend of the Jesuits should be elected, but there were noticeable differences regarding procedure. Whereas the great powers, with Spain in the lead, demanded a formal prior assurance from any serious candidate that he would abolish the Jesuit order, the crown cardinals viewed such a step as fulfilling the fact of simony and therefore rejected such a method. The favored candidate of the powers was the archbishop of Naples, Sersale, who failed because of his excessive acquiescence to the state. On the advice of the Spanish ambassador Azpuru, the candidacy of Cardinal Ganganelli was then promoted. It is certain that he did not give a promise prior to his election to abolish the order. When asked he merely explained that in his opinion a Pope could abolish the Society of Jesus just like any other order for very important reasons and with the proper observance of wisdom and justice. He was elected unanimously on 19 May 1769.

Ganganelli, born in 1705 in Sant'Arcangelo near Rimini, had joined the Franciscan Conventuals in 1723 and exchanged his baptismal name of Giovanni Vincenzo for that of his father Lorenzo. After several years of teaching in various Italian schools of his order, he became rector of the Bonaventura college in Rome and consultant of the Inquisition in 1746. He twice rejected election to the post of general of his order, probably in order to remain eligible for higher office. In 1759 Clement XIII elevated him to the cardinalate. At that time and previous to it he had been considered a friend of the Jesuits; as cardinal he gradually removed himself from them, seeking ties instead with the ambassadors of the Bourbon powers.

During his pontificate his fellow Augustinian Bontempi became his indispensable confidant. Cardinal Pallavicino, nuncio in Madrid from 1760 to 1767 and a confirmed friend of Spain, was appointed secretary of state. The first important step taken by the new Pope was to restore normal relations with Portugal, which had been broken off in 1759. Vacant dioceses could then be filled again, although only by candidates agreeable to Pombal. A nuncio was dispatched to Lisbon, but at the same time the Pope had to appoint Pombal's brother to the cardinalate and, when he died shortly after, he was forced to elevate the favorite of the all-powerful minister. The Pope was applauded by all the enlightened circles for omitting on Maundy Thursday 1770 the customary pronouncement of the bull *In coena Domini,* an action implicitly correcting his predecessor, who had expressly referred to that bull in his monitory to Parma in 1768. In 1774 the bull was formally revoked.

From the beginning of the Pope's pontificate Spain was the motive force behind the Jesuit issue. A routine brief acknowledging the customary indulgences granted to missionaries of the Jesuit order and their faithful provoked outrage. It prompted the united powers to have the French ambassador, Cardinal Bernis, formally approach Clement XIV with a demand for the abolition of the order. The Pope, unsure because of his earlier oblique assent and fearful of being poisoned by the Jesuits, finally gave in to the urging of France, which was reinforced by the threat of breaking off diplomatic relations. In a letter to Louis XIV in September 1769 he promised to abolish the order but did not set a firm date. He made the same promise in a letter to Charles III of Spain at the end of November, at the same time asking for the King's patience.

In spite of such firm assurances the next three years were marked by a noticeable wavering on the part of the Pope vis-à-vis the Jesuits. Individual harsh steps against the order, as for instance the punishment of members without a reason, discriminatory visitations of colleges, brusque treatment of the superiors, were not sufficient to pacify the united powers. Their ambassadors incessantly pressured the Pope, not without intriguing and raising suspicions among one another. The fall of Choiseul at the end of 1770, triggered by the influence of Mme Du Barry, did not make a difference in the French policy regarding the Jesuits. The actual turn of events in this matter, called "el negocio grande," was brought about with the change of Spanish ambassadors to Rome. Azpuru, who resigned at the end of 1771 for reasons of health, was followed by José Moñino, appointed count of Florida-blanca in 1773. His first audience with the Pope initiated the final phase of the fight against the Jesuit order. In answer to an attempt by the Pope to bring about a gradual attrition without the need for a formal document of abolition by forbidding the acceptance of novices in the order, the ambassador threatened the expulsion of all religious orders from Spain and, finally, the breaking off of diplomatic relations. The Spanish embassy then prepared a draft of an abolition bull which was submitted to the Pope at the beginning of 1773 and approved by him in all the essential points. The fact that Madrid was satisfied with the text need hardly be mentioned since the bull was drafted in its own embassy. The Spanish member of the Curia, Zelada, who was substantially involved in the editing of the text, was appointed cardinal soon after, on 19 April 1773 and — as were other pliable collaborators, foremost among them the Pope's confidant, Bontempi — richly rewarded by Spain. The last possible obstacle was overcome in the spring of 1773 when Maria Theresa, urged by Spain, reiterated Austria's neutrality in the Jesuit issue. In June — probably 9 June — Clement XIV signed the abolition document. For practical and stylistic reasons it was not composed as a bull as previously planned but in the form of a brief. The printing — as yet without a date — was provided by the Spanish ambassador, the better to ensure secrecy. In the middle of July the congregation of cardinals to be charged with the implementation of the abolition was appointed. But not until 22 July did Moñino receive permission to send copies of the brief, dated the day before, to the governments involved. On 16 August it was published in Rome and implemented the very same day.

A general historical preamble to the brief *Dominus ac Redemptor noster* presents the right of the Pope regarding the recognition as well as the abolition of religious orders. It then states the difficulties — although in a very one-sided selection of facts — which the Jesuit order had had with other orders and with temporal princes in the course of its history. This is followed by the actual decree of abolition. The voluminous document concludes with the rules of implementation.

The abolition of the Jesuit order was seen as a victory of rationalism and Clement XIV was widely celebrated for his decision. In the medal for the year 1774 he referred — although discreetly — to the abolition as a peace-making event. The enemies of the Jesuits expressed their triumph more directly in an imitation of the papal medal; in a reference to the expulsion of Adam and Eve from paradise the reverse side of the medal shows the expulsion of the Jesuits with the circular notation "I know ye not" and in reference to the psalm "This is the day which the Lord hath made: we will rejoice and be glad in it."

The various countries where any Jesuits were left implemented the abolition in different ways. Because of pressure and surveillance by the Bourbon powers the procedure was harshest in the Papal States. The general of the order, Lorenzo Ricci — and with him the more important members of the order — was held in strict incarceration at the Castel Sant'Angelo until his death. Moñino successfully opposed the release of Ricci, planned by Pius VI, the successor of Clement XIV, and also tried to prevent any alleviation of the conditions at the prison. In Austria and Germany the abolition was generally executed without harshness. Attention was paid that the work of former Jesuits was impaired as little as possible. Maria Theresa and other princes successfully resisted the demand intended by Clement XIV that the assets of the order, which were greatly overestimated, be placed at the disposal of the Holy See. Instead the property of the order was taken over by the respective states.

Only Friedrich II of Prussia, who in 1767 had welcomed the expulsion of the Jesuits from Spain, and Catherine II of Russia (in order to maintain the Catholic school system in Silesia or White Russia) prohibited the publication and implementation of the abolition brief. Whereas Prussia did formally abolish the order a few years later, the tsarina persisted in her policy and the competent bishop ordered the Jesuits to continue their work. The assurance by the suffragan bishop of Mogilev in 1785 that Pius VI had approved of the conduct of the White Russian ex-Jesuits in a conversation with him cannot be proved historically, but it was binding for the members of the order at that time. In 1801 Pope Pius VI formally recognized the Society of Jesus for White Russia.

The abolition of the order caused severe damage especially to the Catholic school system in Europe. The deportation from Portugal and Spain had already put a stop to the missionary work of the order. The Jesuits overwhelmingly acquiesced to the papal decision although it brought with it utter distress and persecution for many. Not a few ex-Jesuits continued to excel in the service of the Church.

In exchange for the abolition of the order the Catholic powers had promised the Pope to return the occupied enclaves of the Papal States. But Clement XIV could not prevail in his suggestion to have the territories returned prior to publicizing the abolition brief. Since Tanucci wanted to retain Benevento for Naples at any price, the restitution of the occupied areas was delayed until 1774 and was, moreover, encumbered with humiliating provisos.

In twelve promotions Clement XIV installed a total of seventeen new cardinals. At the last creation (26 April 1774) two new cardinals were installed by name, among them Braschi, the successor of Clement, and eleven *in petto*. The Pope never divulged the names of these candidates although he was put under extreme pressure to do so when he was seriously ill just before his death; according to contemporary opinion all of them were most likely from the ranks of opponents of the Jesuit order.

After the abolition of the order the Pope's fears of possible poisoning by his imagined opponents increased. The state of his health, not very stable at best, deteriorated steadily, probably aggravated by his depressions and the excitements. Death came on 21 September 1774. Rumors of poisoning immediately spread, but are generally rejected as baseless by more recent research. At the exequies of Clement XIV the customary presentation of special achievements made no mention at all of the abolition of the Society of Jesus. Clement XIV was initially put to rest in Saint Peter's; in 1802 he was transferred to the monastic church of SS. Apostoli, where the tomb created by Canova had been ready since 1787.